Mesolithic Horizons

Papers presented at the Seventh International Conference on the Mesolithic in Europe, Belfast 2005

Volume I

Edited by

Sinéad McCartan, Rick Schulting, Graeme Warren and Peter Woodman

OXBOW BOOKS
Oxford and Oakville

Published by
Oxbow Books, Oxford, UK

ISBN 978-1-84217-311-4

A CIP record of this book is available from the British Library

This book is available direct from:

Oxbow Books, Oxford, UK
(Phone: 01865-241249; Fax: 01865-794449)

and

The David Brown Book Company
PO Box 511, Oakville, CT 06779, USA
(Phone: 860-945-9329; Fax: 860-945-9468)

or from our website

www.oxbowbooks.com

Front cover: A view of the River Quoile, near Downpatrick, County Down.
© Ulster Museum.

Printed and bound in Great Britain by
Short Run Press, Exeter

Contents

VOLUME I

People in their environment

People and Places

Regional identities

Dwellings

VOLUME II

Transitions

Understanding Mesolithic technology

Flint alternatives

Current research

List of Contributors

JAVIER ALCOLEA
Departamento de Historia i y Filosofía, Universidad de Alcalá de Henares, Calle de los Colegios, 2, 28801 Alcalá de Henares (Madrid), Spain.
javieralcolea@ya.com

FRANCISCO ALMEIDA
Divisão de Estudos Patrimoniais e Arqueociências, IGESPAR Av. da Índia, 136, 1300-300 Lisboa, Portugal.
falmeida@igespar.pt

ESTEBAN ÁLVAREZ-FERNÁNDEZ
Investigaciones Prehistóricas de Cantabria, Universidad de Cantabria, Av. de los Castros s/n, E-39005 Santander, Spain.
esteban.alvarez@unican.es

NIELS H. ANDREASEN
Department of Archaeology, University of Cambridge, Cambridge CB2 3DZ, England, UK.
nha22@cam.ac.uk

ANA CRISTINA ARAÚJO
Divisão de Estudos Patrimoniais e Arqueociências, IGESPAR, Av. da Índia, 136, 1300-300 Lisboa, Portugal.
acaraujo@igespar.pt

PABLO ARIAS
Instituto Internacional de Investigaciones Prehistóricas de Cantabria, Universidad de Cantabria, Av. de los Castros s/n, E-39005 Santander, Spain.
pablo.arias@unican.es

ANGEL ARMENDARIZ
Investigaciones Prehistóricas de Cantabria, Universidad de Cantabria, Av. de los Castros s/n, E-39005 Santander, Spain.
armendaa@unican.es

ÁLVARO ARRIZABALAGA
Grupo de Investigación de Alto Rendimiento 9/UPV 155.130-14570/2002, Área de Prehistoria, Universidad del País Vasco, c/Tomás y Valiente, 01006 Vitoria-Gasteiz, Spain.
alvaro.arrizabalaga@ehu.es

LEIF INGE ÅSTVEIT
Norwegian University of Science and Technology, Trondheim, Norway.
leif.astveit@vm.ntnu.no

JEFF BABB
Department of Mathematics and Statistics, University of Winnipeg, Winnipeg, Canada.
j.babb@uwinnipeg.ca

ANDREA L. BALBO
Department of Archaeology, University of Cambridge, Cambridge CB2 3DZ, England, UK.
alb55@cam.ac.uk

DOUGLAS B. BAMFORTH
Anthropology Department, University of Colorado, 233 UCB, Boulder, Colorado 80309-0233, USA.
bamforth@colorado.edu

MICHELE BASSETTI
CORA Ricerche Archeologiche s.n.c., Spini di Gardolo 75, Gardolo, I-38014 Trento, Italy.
michele@coraricerche.com

SAMUEL BENGHIAT
Department of Archaeology, University of Cambridge, Cambridge CB2 3DZ, England, UK.
sbenghiat@hotmail.com

KNUT ANDREAS BERGSVIK
Department of Archaeology, History, Cultural Studies and Religion, University of Bergen, Øysteins Gate 1, 5007 Bergen Norway.
knut.bergsvik@ahkr.uib.no

STEVEN BIRCH
Sealladh Alainn, Upper Breakish, Breakish IV42 8PY, Scotland, UK.
SKYESUB1@aol.com

HEIN BJARTMANN BJERCK
Museum of Natural History and Archaeology, Norwegian University of Science and Technology (NTNU), N-7491 Trondheim, Norway.
hein.bjerck@vm.ntnu.no

STELLA M. BLOCKLEY
Department of Geography, Royal Holloway University of London, Egham, Surrey TW20 0EX, England, UK.
stella.blockley@googlemail.com

CLIVE JONATHON BOND
Department of Archaeology, Faculty of Social Sciences, The University of Winchester, West Hill, Winchester, Hampshire SO22 4NR, England, UK.
clivejbond@aol.com

ALEXANDRE BOURNERY
UMR 5197 (USM 303)
Archéozoologie, histoire des sociétés humaines et des peuplements animaux, CNRS-Muséum, Dpt. Ecologie et Gestion de la Biodiversité, Bâtiments d'anatomie comparée, CP 56, 55 rue Buffon, 75231 Paris cedex, France.
bournery@mnhn.fr

DANIEL G. BRADLEY
Smurfit Institute of Genetics, Trinity College, Dublin 2, Ireland.
dbradley@tcd.ie

CÉLINE BRESSY
LAMPEA, UMR 6636, CNRS
Maison Méditerranéenne des Sciences de l'Homme, 5 rue du Château-de-l'Horloge, BP 647, 13094 Aix-en-Provence Cedex 2, France.
cbressy@mmsh.univ-aix.fr

Erik Brinch Petersen
University of Copenhagen, Saxo Institute, Njalsgade 80, 2300 Copenhagen S, Denmark.
ebp@hum.ku.dk

Tom Carlsson
National Heritage Board, Roxengatan 8, 582 22 Linköping, Sweden.
tom.carlsson@raa.se

Richard Carter
CCE, Sussex Institute, University of Sussex, Falmer, Brighton BN1 9QQ, England, UK.
r.j.carter@sussex.ac.uk

António Faustino Carvalho
Universidade do Algarve, Faculdade de Ciências Humanas e Sociais, Campus de Gambelas, 8005-139 Faro, Portugal.
afcarva@ualg.pt

Claudio Casati
Saxo-Institute University of Copenhagen, Frederiksundsvej 150, 1th, 2700 Brønshøj, Denmark.
claudio@casati.dk

Fabio Cavulli
Laboratorio di Preistoria 'B. Bagolini', Dipartimento di Filosofia, Storia e Beni Culturali, Università di Trento, Via S. Croce 65, 1-38100 Trento, Italy.
fabio.cavulli@unitn.it

Louis Chaix
Département d'archéozoologie, Museum d'histoire naturelle – CP 6434, 1 route de Malagnou, CH-1211 Geneva 6, Switzerland.
louis.chaix@bluewin.ch

Hannah Cobb
Archaeology School of Arts, Histories and Cultures, Humanities,, Mansfield-Cooper Building, University of Manchester, Oxford Road, Manchester M13 9PL, England, UK.
hannah.cobb@manchester.ac.uk

Tracy Collins
ÆGIS Archaeology Ltd, 32 Nicholas Street, King's Island, Limerick, Ireland.
info@aegisarc.com

Chantal Conneller
Archaeology, School of Arts, Histories and Cultures, University of Manchester, Oxford Rd, Manchester M13 9PL, England, UK.
chantal.conneller@manchester.ac.uk

Laurent-Jacques Costa
CNRS, UMR 7055, University of Nanterre, Paris, France.
lj.costa@wanadoo.fr

Sheila Coulson
Department of Archaeology, Institute of Archaeology, Conservation and History, University of Oslo, Blindernveien 11 (Post Box 1008), 0315 Oslo, Norway.
sheila.coulson@iakh.uio.no

Maria Giovanna Cremona
Dipartimento di Biologia ed Evoluzione Università degli Studi di Ferrara, Corso Ercole I d'Este 32, I-44100 Ferrara, Italy.
crmmgv@unife.it

Philippe Crombé
Ghent University, Department of Archaeology and Ancient History of Europe, Blandijnberg 2, B-9000 Ghent, Belgium.
philippe.crombe@ugent.be

Enrique Cerrillo Cuenca
Consejo Superior de Investigaciones Científicas, Instituto de Arqueología – Mérida (CSIC-Junta de Extremadura-CCMM), Plaza de España, 15, 06800 Mérida, Spain.
ecerrillo@iam.csic.es

Anna Cusinato
Museo Tridentino di Scienze Naturali, Via Calepina 14, I-38100 Trento, Italy.
anna.cusinato@mtsn.tn.it

Giampaolo Dalmeri
Museo Tridentino di Scienze Naturali, Via Calepina 14, I-38100 Trento, Italy.
dalmeri@mtsn.tn.it

Eva David
Laboratoire de Préhistoire et Technologie, UMR 7055 du CNRS, Maison de l'Archéologie et de l'Ethnologie René Ginouvès, 21, allée de l'Université, F-92023 Nanterre cedex, France.
eva.david@mae.u-paris10.fr

Rodrigo de Balbín
Departamento de Historia I y Filosofía, Universidad de Alcalá de Henares, Calle de los Colegios, 2, 28801 Alcalá de Henares, Madrid, Spain.
babu@ya.com

Marc De Bie
Flemish Heritage Institute and Vrije Universiteit Brussel, Prehistoric Archaeology Unit, Celestijnenlaan 200 E, B-3001 Heverlee, Belgium.
marc.debie@rwo.vlaanderen.be

Lucyna Domańska
Institute of Archaeology, University of Łódź, 91-402 Łódź, ul. Pomorska 96, Poland.
lucynad@uni.lodz.pl

Labib Drak
Departamento de Zoología y Antropología Física, Facultad de Biología, Universidad Complutense de Madrid, Jose Antonio Novais 2, 28040, Madrid, Spain.
labibdrak@gmail.com

Killian Driscoll
School of Archaeology, University College Dublin, Belfield, Dublin 4, Ireland.
killiandriscoll@gmail.com

Roger Edenmo
Swedish National Heritage Board, Department for Archaeological Excavations, Instrumentvägen 19, 126 53 Hägersten, Stockholm, Sweden.
roger.edenmo@raa.se

Mark Edmonds
Dept of Archaeology, The King's Manor, York Y01 7EP, England, UK.
mre500@york.ac.uk

Ceiridwen J. Edwards
Smurfit Institute of Genetics, Trinity College, Dublin 2, Ireland.
ceiridwen.edwards@gmail.com

Kevin J. Edwards
Departments of Geography & Environment and Archaeology, University of Aberdeen, Elphinstone Road, Aberdeen AB24 3UF, Scotland, UK.
kevin.edwards@abdn.ac.uk

Lotte Eigeland
Museum of Cultural History, St. Olavs Gate 29, Box 6762, St. Olavs Plass, 0130 Oslo, Norway.
lotte@superheros.as

Ericka Engelstad
Department of Archaeology, University of Tromsø, 9037 Tromsø, Norway.
ericka.engelstad@sv.uit.no

Francisco Etxeberria
Facultad de Medicina y Odontología, Universidad del País Vasco, 20009 San Sebastián-Donostia, Spain.
paco.etxeberria@ehu.es

†Per Falkenström

Miguel Ángel Fano
Departamento de Historia, Facultad de Filosofía y Letras, Universidad de Deusto, Apartado 1, 48080 Bilbao, Spain.
mfano@fil.deusto.es

Patricia Fernández
Investigaciones Prehistóricas de Cantabria, Universidad de Cantabria, Av. de los Castros s/n, E-39005 Santander, Spain.
pattriciaes@yahoo.es

Juan Fernández-Tresguerres
Departamento de Historia, Universidad de Oviedo, Campus del Milán, C/Teniente Alfonso Martínez, 33011 Oviedo, Spain.
jafernan@uniovi.es

Erika Ferrari
Museo Archeologico Nazionale, Soprintendenza Archeologica dell'Emilia Romagna, Palazzo della Pilotta, Piazza della Pilotta, 5-43100 Parma, Italy.
Erica.f@tin.it

Nyree Finlay
Department of Archaeology, University of Glasgow, The Gregory Building, Lilybank Gardens, Glasgow G12 8QQ, Scotland, UK.
n.finlay@archaeology.gla.ac.uk

Lynn E. Fisher
Sociology/Anthropology Program, University of Illinois-Springfield, 1 University Plaza, MS UHB 3010, Springfield, IL 62703-5407, USA.
lfish@uis.edu

Elisabetta Flor
via G. Bresadola 14, I-38020 Cloz, Trento, Italy.
elisabettaflor@virgilio.it

Federica Fontana
Dipartimento di Biologia ed Evoluzione, Corso Ercole I, d'Este, 32, I-44100 Ferrara, Italy.
federica.fontana@unife.it

Christina Fredengren
Lake Settlement Project, The Discovery Programme, 63 Merrion Square, Dublin 2, Ireland.
christina@discoveryprogramme.ie

Silje Elisabeth Fretheim
Hans Hagerups gt. 3b, 7012 Trondheim, Norway.
siljefr@vm.ntnu.no

Josep M. Fullola
Department of Prehistory, Ancient History and Archaeology, Faculty of Geography and History, University of Barcelona, Montalegre St. 6, E-08001 Barcelona, Spain.
fullola@ub.edu

Pilar García-Argüelles
Department of Prehistory, Ancient History and Archaeology, Faculty of Geography and History, University of Barcelona, Montalegre St. 6, E-08001 Barcelona, Spain.
garciaarguelles@ub.edu

Cristina García-Moncó
Investigaciones Prehistóricas de Cantabria, Universidad de Cantabria, Av. de los Castros s/n, E-39005 Santander, Spain.
cristijarl@hotmail.com

Paula J. Gardiner
Department of Archaeology and Anthropology, University of Bristol, 43 Woodland Road, Bristol BS8 1UU, England, UK.
p.j.gardiner@bristol.ac.uk

María Dolores Garralda
Departamento de Zoología y Antropología Física, Facultad de Biología, Universidad Complutense de Madrid, Jose Antonio Novais, 2, 28040, Madrid, Spain.
mdgarral@bio.ucm.es

Frank Gelhausen
Römisch-Germanisches Zentralmuseum, Forschungsinstitut für Vor- und Frühgeschichte, Forschungsbereich Altsteinzeit, Museum Monrepos, D-56567 Neuwied, Germany.
gelhausen@rgzm.de

Jan Gillespie
Hampshire and Wight Trust for Maritime Archaeology, Room W1/95, National Oceanography Centre, Southampton SO14 3ZH, England, UK.
jan.gillespie@hwtma.org.uk

Antonio González
Museo Arqueológico de la Fundación Concha, C/ Antonio Concha, 25, 10300 Navalmoral de la Mata, Cáceres, Spain.
anmais@telefonica.net

Manuel R. González Morales
Investigaciones Prehistóricas de Cantabria, Universidad de Cantabria, Av. de los Castros s/n, E-39005 Santander, Spain.
moralesm@unican.es

Bryan C. Gordon
Research Division, Canadian Museum of Civilization, 100 Laurier St, P.O. Box 3100, Station B, Gatineau, Quebec J8X 4H2, Canada.
bryan.gordon@civilization.ca

Stefano Grimaldi
Laboratorio di Preistoria 'B. Bagolini', Dipartimento di Filosofia, Storia e Beni Culturali, Università di Trento, Via S. Croce 65, 1-38100 Trento, Italy.
stefano.grimaldi@unitn.it

Ole Grøn
Langelands Museum, Jens Winthersvej 12, DK-5900 Rudkøbing, Demark.
olegron_lmr@hotmail.com

Federico Guarisco
Museo Archeologico Nazionale, Soprintendenza Archeologica dell'Emilia Romagna, Palazzo della Pilotta, Piazza della Pilotta, 5-43100 Parma, Italy.
gudrum@tin.it

Antonio Guerreschi
Dipartimento delle Risorse Naturali e Culturali, Università degli Studi di Ferrara, Corso Ercole I d'Este 32, I-44100 Ferrara, Italy.
gue@unife.it

Sigrid Mannsåker Gundersen
Telemark fylkeskommune, Fylkeshuset, N-3706 Skien, Norway.
sigrid.gundersen@t-fk.no

F. Igor Gutiérrez Zugasti
Investigaciones Prehistóricas de Cantabria, Universidad de Cantabria, Av. de los Castros s/n, E-39005 Santander, Spain.
igorgutierrez.zug@gmail.com

Fredrik Hallgren
Department of Archaeology, Uppsala University, Box 626, 751 26 Uppsala, Sweden.
fredrik.hallgren@arkeologi.uu.se

Karen Hardy
Department de Prehistòria, Facultat de Filosofia i Lletres, Campus UAB, 08193 Bellaterra, Barcelona, Spain.
karen.hardy@uab.cat

Susan K. Harris
86 Napa Lane, Goleta, CA 93117, USA.
skharris@gmail.com

Dirk Heinrich
Zoological Institute, University of Kiel, Olshausenstr. 40, D-24118 Kiel, Germany.
dheinrich@zoologie.uni-kiel.de

Robert Hernek
Bohusläns Museum, Box 403, S-451 19 Uddevalla, Sweden.
robert.hernek@vgregion.se

Jenny Holm
Archaeological Excavations Department, National Heritage Board of Sweden, UV Bergslagen, Box 1406, SE-701 14 Örebro, Sweden.
jenny.holm@raa.se

María José Iriarte
Grupo de Investigación de Alto Rendimiento 9/UPV 155.130-14570/2002, Área de Prehistoria, Universidad del País Vasco, c/Tomás y Valiente, 01006 Vitoria-Gasteiz, Spain.
mariajose.iriarte@ehu.es

Mary Jackes
Department of Anthropology, University of Waterloo, Waterloo, Ontario N2L 3G1, Canada.
mkjackes@watarts.uwaterloo.ca

Ole Lass Jensen
Hørsholm Egns Museum, Sdr. Jagtvej 2, DK 2970 Hørsholm, Denmark.
ole.lass@hoersholmmuseum.dk

Michael Jochim
Department of Anthropology, University of California, Santa Barbara, Santa Barbara, CA 93117, USA.
jochim@anth.ucsb.edu

Robert Johnston
Department of Archaeology, University of Sheffield, Northgate House, West Street, Sheffield S1 4ET, England, UK.
r.johnston@sheffield.ac.uk

Jacek Kabaciński
Institute of Archaeology, Polish Academy of Science, Rubież 46, PL-61-612 Poznań, Poland.
jacek.kabacinski@iaepan.poznan.pl

Thomas Kador
UCD School of Archaeology, University College Dublin, Belfield, Dublin 4, Ireland.
thomas.kador@ucd.ie

Jarmo Kankaanpää
Isonpellonkuja 6, FI-02880 Veikkola, Finland.
jarmo.kankaanpaa@kolumbus.fi

Jan Kegler
Merowingerstrasse 6, D-50677 Kö, Germany.
jf.kegler@web.de

Torunn Klokkernes
Museum of Cultural History, University of Oslo, PO Box 6762, St. Olavs Plass, 0130 Oslo, Norway.
torunn.klokkernes@khm.uio.no

Klaus Kompatscher
Museo Tridentino di Scienze Naturali, Via Calepina 14, I-38100, Trento, Italy.
klaus@azzolini-kompatscher.it

Maria Hrozny Kompatscher
Museo Tridentino di Scienze Naturali, Via Calepina 14, I-38100, Trento, Italy.
nandi@azzolini-kompatscher.it

Darko Komšo
Archaeological Museum of Istria, Carrarina 3, 52100 Pula, Croatia.
komsodarko@gmail.com

Kjel S. Å. Knutsson
Department of Archaeology and Ancient History, Uppsala University, Box 626, 751 26 Uppsala, Sweden.
kjel.knutsson@arkeologi.uu.se

Stefan K. Kozłowski
Archaeological Institute, University of Warsaw, ul. Krakowskie Przedmiescie 26/28, Warsaw, Poland.
skkozlowski@op.pl

Aivar Kriiska
Institute of History and Archaeology, Universtity of Tartu, Ülikooli 18, EE50090 Tartu, Estonia.
aivar.kriiska@ut.ee

Emily La Trobe-Bateman
Gwynedd Archaeological Trust, Craig Beuno, Garth Road, Bangor, Gwynedd LL57 2RT, Wales, UK.
emily@heneb.co.uk

Nicolai Garhøj Larsen
Nyhavevej 15, DK-5600 Faaborg, Denmark.
nglarsen@yahoo.com

Lars Larsson
Department of Archaeology and Ancient History, Lund University, Box 117, SE-221 00 Lund, Sweden.
lars.larsson@ark.lu.se

Eva Laurie
Department of Archaeology, The Kings Manor, University of York, York YO1 7EP, England, UK.
eml500@york.ac.uk

Sonja Laus
Unterseebach 15, A-4560 Kirchdorf a. d. Krems, Austria.
sonja.laus@gmx.net

Karl-Fredrik Lindberg
National Heritage Board of Sweden, Archaeological Excavations Department, Riksantikvarieämbetet, Portalgatan 2 A, SE-754 23 Uppsala, Sweden.
karl-fredrik.lindberg@raa.se

Christina Lindgren
Department of Archaeological Excavations UV Mitt, National Board of Antiquities, Instrumentvägen 19, S-126 53 Hägersten, Sweden.
christina.lindgren@raa.se

Aimée Little
UCD School of Archaeology, University College Dublin, Belfield, Dublin 4, Ireland.
itiaimee@yahoo.co.nz

Lembi Lõugas
Institute of History, University of Tallinn, Rüütli 6, EE10130 Tallinn, Estonia.
lembi@ai.ee

Harald Lübke
Roman-Germanic Commission of the German Archaeological Institute, Palmengartenstrasse 10–12 , 60325 Frankfurt/Main, Germany.
harald.luebke@imail.de

Trond Lødøen
Bergen Museum, University of Bergen, Joachim Frielesgate 1, 5007 Bergen, Norway.
trond.lodoen@bm.uib.no

Sinéad McCartan
National Museums Northern Ireland, Ulster Museum, Cultra, Holywood, Co. Down BT18 0EU, Northern Ireland, UK.
sinead.mccartan@nmni.com

Anne M. G. McComb
Department of Agriculture and Rural Development, Down/Armagh District Forest Office, The Grange, Castlewellan Forest Park, Castlewellan BT31 9BU, Co. Down, Northern Ireland, UK.
anne_mccomb@hotmail.co.uk

T. Rowan McLaughlin
School of Geography, Archaeology and Palaeoecology, Queen's University Belfast, Belfast BT7 1NN, Northern Ireland, UK.
r.mclaughlin@qub.ac.uk

Melanie McQuade
Margaret Gowen & Co. Ltd, 27 Merrion Square, Dublin 2, Ireland.
archaeology@mglarc.com

Mikael A. Manninen
Institute for Cultural Research, Department of Archaeology, PO Box 59, 00014 University of Helsinki, Finland.
mikael.manninen@helsinki.fi

Marcello A. Mannino
Institute of Archaeology, University College London, 31–34 Gordon Square, London WC1H 0PY, England, UK.
m.mannino@ucl.ac.uk

Anja Mansrud
Department of Archaeology, Conservation and History, University of Oslo, Boks 1008 Blindern, N-0315 Oslo, Norway.
anja.mansrud@iakh.uio.no

Grégor Marchand
CNRS - UMR 6566, Université de Rennes 1, Campus de Beaulieu, 74205 CS, Laboratoire d'anthropologie – Archéométrie (bât. 24-25), 35042 Rennes Cedex, France.
gregor.marchand@univ-rennes1.fr

Celia Marcos
Departamento de Geología, Universidad de Oviedo, c/Jesús Arias de Velasco s/n, 33005 Oviedo, Spain.
cmarcos@uniovi.es

Ana Bélen Marín Arroyo
The International Institute for Prehistoric Research (CSIC Associate Unit), University of Cantabria, Santander, Spain.
ana_b_marin@hotmail.com

Christopher Meiklejohn
Department of Anthropology, University of Winnipeg, Winnipeg, Canada.
c.meiklejohn@uwinnipeg.ca

Nigel D. Melton
University of Bradford, Department of Archaeological, Geographical and Environmental Sciences, School of Life Sciences, Bradford BD7 1DP, England, UK.
n.d.melton1@bradford.ac.uk

Davide Mengoli
Soprintendenza Archeologica dell'Emilia Romagna, Via Belle Arti 52, I-40126 Bologna, Italy.
davide.mengoli@libero.it

Nicky Milner
Department of Archaeology, The Kings Manor, University of York, York YO1 7EP, England, UK.
nm507@york.ac.uk

Steve Mills
Cardiff School of History and Archaeology, Cardiff University, Humanities Building, Colum Drive, Cardiff CF10 3EU, Wales, UK.
millssf1@cf.ac.uk

Preston T. Miracle
Department of Archaeology, University of Cambridge, Cambridge CB2 3DZ, England, UK.
ptm21@cam.ac.uk

Fredrik Molin
National Heritage Board, Roxengatan 7, SE-582 73 Linköping, Sweden.
fredrik.molin@raa.se

Garry Momber
Hampshire and Wight Trust for Maritime Archaeology, Room W1/95, National Oceanography Centre, Southampton SO14 3ZH, England, UK.
garry.momber@hwtma.org.uk

Matt Mossop
Archaeological Consultancy Ltd, Goodagrane Farmhouse, Halvasso, Nr Mabe, Cornwall TR10 9BX, England, UK.
enquiries@archaeologicalconsultancy.com

Jordi Nadal
Department of Prehistory, Ancient History and Archaeology, Faculty of Geography and History, University of Barcelona, Montalegre St. 6, E-08001 Barcelona, Spain.
jnadal@ub.edu

Nina Nielsen
Schleppegrellsgade 1 st.tv., 8000, Aarhus C, Denmark.
farknn@hum.au.dk

Björn Nilsson
Malmo Heritage, Box 406, SE-201 24 Malmö, Sweden.
bjorn.x.nilsson@malmo.se

Liv Nilsson Stutz
Department of Archaeology and Ancient History, Sandgatan 1, 223 50 Lund, Sweden.
liv.nilsson_stutz@ark.lu.se

Bengt Nordqvist
RAÄ UV Väst, Kvarnbygatan 12, 431 34 Göteborg, Sweden.
bengt.nordqvist@raa.se

Astrid J. Nyland
Museum of Cultural History, University of Oslo, PO Box 6762, St. Olavs Plass, 0130 Oslo, Norway.
a.j.nyland@khm.uio.no

Tamsin O'Connell
McDonald Institute for Archaeological Research, University of Cambridge, Downing Street, Cambridge CB2 3ER, England, UK.
tco21@cam.ac.uk

Lorna O'Donnell
Margaret Gowen & Co. Ltd, 27 Merrion Square, Dublin 2, Ireland.
archaeology@mglarc.com

Asle Bruen Olsen
Bergen Museum, University of Bergen, SFYK, PO Box 7800, 5020 Bergen, Norway.
asle.olsen@bm.uib.no

Thomas Bruen Olsen
SFYK, Bergen Museum, Haakon Sheteligs plass 10, 5007 Bergen, Norway.
donthomasi@hotmail.com

Roberto Ontañón
Investigaciones Prehistóricas de Cantabria, Universidad de Cantabria, Av. de los Castros s/n, E-39005 Santander, Spain.
ontanon_r@gobcantabria.es

Clea Paine
Department of Archaeology, University of Cambridge, Downing Street, Cambridge CB2 3DZ, England, UK.
chp29@cam.ac.uk

Amelia Pannett
Cwm Cottage, Ty Mawr, Efail Isaf, Pontypridd CF38 1AT, Wales, UK.
amelia-pannett@tiscoli.co.uk

Rachel L. Parks
Department of Archaeology, The King's Manor, University of York, York YO1 7EP, England, UK.
archaeofish@gmail.com

Hans Peeters
National Service for Archaeology, Cultural Landscape and Built Heritage, PO Box 1600, 3800 BP – Amersfoort, The Netherlands.
h.peeters@racm.nl

Paolo Pellegatti
Department of Anthropology, University of California, Berkeley, 232 Kroeber Hall, Berkeley, CA 94720, USA.
paolo_pellegatti@yahoo.com

Eloy Gómez Pellón
Investigaciones Prehistóricas de Cantabria, Universidad de Cantabria, Av. de los Castros s/n, E-39005 Santander, Spain.
jose.gomez@unican.es

Yves Perdaen
Ghent University, Department of Archaeology and Ancient History of Europe, Blandijnberg 2, B-9000 Ghent, Belgium.
yves.perdaen@ugent.be

Thomas Perrin
CNRS – UMR5608 "Traces / CRPPM", 39, allées Jules Guesde, 31000 Toulouse, France.
tperrin@free.fr

Per Persson
Gråfjellprosjektet, Museum of Cultural History, University of Oslo, PO Box 6762, St. Olavs Plass, 0130 Oslo, Norway.
p.a.persson@khm.uio.no

Mattias Pettersson
Orrvägen 9, 718 91 Frövi, Sweden.
husbacken@telia.com

Steven Price
17 Scholes Street, Bury BL8 2RB, England, UK.
stevencprice@gmail.com

T. Douglas Price
Laboratory for Archaeological Chemistry, 1180 Observatory Drive, University of Wisconsin-Madison, Madison WI 53706, USA.
tdprice@wisc.edu

Morten Ramstad
Department of Archaeology, Tromsø University Museum, N-9037 Tromsø, Norway.
mortenr@tmu.uit.no

Tuija Rankama
University of Helsinki, Institute of Cultural Studies, Department of Archaeology, PO Box 59, FI-00014 University of Helsinki, Finland.
trankama@gmail.com

Michael P. Richards
Department of Human Evolution, Max Planck Institute for Evolutionary Anthropology, Deutscher Platz 6, 04103 Leipzig, Germany.
richards@eva.mpg.de

Felix Riede
AHRC Centre for the Evolution of Cultural Diversity, Institute of Archaeology, University College London, 31–34 Gordon Square, London WC1H 0PY, England, UK.
f.riede@ucl.ac.uk

Susanne Ritz Nicolaisen
Horsens Museum, Sundvej 1A, DK 8700 Horsens, Denmark.
sritznicolaisen@gmail.com

Mia Rizner
Ministry of Culture, Directorate for the Protection of Cultural Heritage, Conservation Department (Rijeka), Užarska 26, 51000 rijeka, Croatia.
riznermeister@gmail.com

John Griffith Roberts
Snowdonia National Park, National Park Office, Penrhyn Deudraeth, Gwynedd LL48 6F, Wales, UK.
john.roberts@eryri-npa.gov.uk

Julie Satchell
Hampshire and Wight Trust for Maritime Archaeology, Room W1/95, National Oceanography Centre, Southampton SO14 3ZH, England, UK.
julie.satchell@hwtma.org.uk

Alan Saville
Archaeology Department, National Museums Scotland, Chambers Street, Edinburgh EH1 1JF, Scotland, UK.
a.saville@nms.ac.uk

Rick Schulting
School of Archaeology, University of Oxford, 36 Beaumont Street, Oxford OX1 2PG, England, UK.
rick.schulting@arch.ox.ac.uk

Joris Sergant
Ghent University, Department of Archaeology and Ancient History of Europe, Blandijnberg 2, B-9000 Ghent, Belgium.
joris.sergant@ugent.be

Robert S. Shiel
School of Agriculture, Food and Rural Development, King George VI Building, Newcastle University, Newcastle upon Tyne NE1 7RU, England, UK.
r.s.shiel@ncl.ac.uk

David N. Simpson
University of Bergen, Bergen Museum, SFYK, PO Box 7800, 5020 Bergen, Norway.
david.simpson@bm.uib.no

Arne Sjöström
Department of Archaeology and Ancient History, University of Lund, Sandgatan 1, SE-223 50 Lund, Sweden.
arne.sjostrom@ark.lu.se

Maria Westrum Solem
Department of Archaeology, Conservation and Historical Studies, University of Oslo, Postboks 1019 Blindern, N-0315 Oslo, Norway.
mariaws@student.hf.uio.no

Harry Starr
1414 Brandt Road #44 , Vancouver, WA 98661, USA.
hestarr@msn.com

Farina Sternke
Department of Archaeology, University of Glasgow, Gregory Building, Lilybank Gardens, Glasgow G12 0QQ, Scotland, UK.
f.sternke@archaeology.arts.gla.ac.uk

Lasse Sørensen
St. Kannikestræde 2, 1169 København K, Denmark.
soerensenlasse@hotmail.com

Mikkel Sørensen
SILA, National Museum of Denmark, Frederiksholms Kanal 12, 1220 København K, Denmark.
mikkel.sorensen@natmus.dk

Søren A. Sørensen
Museet Færgegaarden, Færgelundsvej 1, 3630 Jægerspris, Denmark.
sasoe@frederikssund.dk

Hannu Takala
Lahti Museum, PO Box 113, 15111 Lahti, Finland.
hannu.takala@lahti.fi

Thomas Terberger
University of Greifswald, Hans-Falladastrasse 1, D-17489 Greifswald, Germany.
terberge@uni-greifswald.de

Kenneth D. Thomas
Institute of Archaeology, University College London, 31–34 Gordon Square, London WC1H 0PY, England, UK.
k.thomas@ucl.ac.uk

Peter Andreas Toft
Malmøgade 11, 2th, 2100 København Ø , Denmark.
patoft@yahoo.com

Rodrigue Tsobgou Ahoupe
UMR 6566 Civilisation Atlantiques et Archéosciences, Bat. 24, Campus de Beaulieu Université de Rennes 1, 263 Avenue du Général Leclerc, CS 74205, 35042 Rennes CEDEX, France.
tsar500@hotmail.com

Michail G. Turov
Institute of Archaeology and Ethnology, Iskutsk State University, 27, 25th October Street, 664022 Irkutsk, Russia.
turov@mion.isu.ru

Maria João Valente
Universidade do Algarve, Faculdade de Ciências Humanas e Sociais, Campus de Gambelas, 8005-139 Faro, Portugal.
mvalente@ualg.pt

Marijn Van Gils
Flemish Heritage Institute and Katholieke Universiteit Leuven, Prehistoric Archaeology Unit, Celestijnenlaan 200 E, B-3001 Heverlee, Belgium.
marijn.vangils@rwo.vlaanderen.be

Leo B. M. Verhart
National Museum of Antiquities, PO Box 11114, 2301 EC Leiden, The Netherlands.
l.verhart@limburgsmuseum.nl

Nikola Vukosavljević
Department of Archaeology, Faculty of Humanities and Social Sciences, University of Zagreb, I. Lučića 3, 10000 Zagreb, Croatia.
nvukosav@ffzg.hr

Graeme Warren
UCD School of Archaeology, Newman Building, University College Dublin, Belfield, Dublin, Ireland.
graeme.warren@ucd.ie

Marcin Wąs
Department of Archaeology, University of Gdańsk, 80–952 Gdańsk 5, ul. Wita Stwosza 55, Poland.
was.marcin@wp.pl

Stefan Wenzel
Römisch-Germanisches Zentralmuseum, Forschungsinstitut für Vor- und Frühgeschichte, Forschungsbereich Altsteinzeit, Museum Monrepos, D-56567 Neuwied, Germany.
wenzel@rgzm.de

Caroline R. Wickham-Jones
Cassie, St Ola, Orkney KW15 1TP, Scotland, UK.
c.wickham-jones@mesolithic.co.uk

Roger Wikell
Uppsala Archaological Society, Gamla Prefektbostaden, Villavägen 6g, 752 36 Uppsala, Sweden.
rodgeir@yahoo.com

Peter C. Woodman
University College Cork, Cork, Ireland.
p.woodman@arts.ucc.ie

Ilga Zagorska
Institute of Latvian History, Akademijas laukums 1, Riga, LV 1050, Latvia.
izagorska@yahoo.com

João Zilhão
Department of Archaeology and Anthropology, University of Bristol, 43 Woodland Road, Bristol BS8 1UU, England, UK.
joao.zilhao@bristol.ac.uk

Marek Zvelebil
Department of Archaeology, University of Sheffield, Northgate House, West Street, Sheffield S1 4ET, England, UK.
m.zvelebil@sheffield.ac.uk

Preface

Mesolithic Horizons marks the publication of the proceedings of the seventh five-yearly international conference on 'The Mesolithic in Europe' (Meso 2005). The numbers attending these five-yearly conferences continue to grow. More than 250 participants were present in Belfast during the week of 29 August–2 September 2005. Given that Ireland, on the western edge of Europe, was not a particularly convenient location for the Meso 2005 meeting, the 20% increase in attendance came as something of a surprise to the organisers. The increased participation is, of course, testimony to the growing interest in a period that less than 50 years ago was seen by the majority of European prehistorians as either a 'hiatus' between two more interesting periods or, for some, a poorly understood phase of little consequence.

The success in Stockholm (Meso 2000) of the bid to hold the conference in Ireland brought with it several challenges for the organisers. At that time, while a number of Irish archaeologists had occasional contact with the Mesolithic, only two of them had a strong interest in the period. Therefore the Meso 2005 meeting was in some ways more like the context of Edinburgh in 1985, i.e. in a location where there was no strong tradition of Mesolithic studies. It is hoped, however, that hosting the meeting in Belfast will have helped promote a greater appreciation of a period that, after all, represents 40% of Ireland's known human history.

Over 250 people participated in the Meso 2005 conference and nearly 20 countries were represented (as the list of delegates in this volume indicates). The five countries from which the majority of participants came were: England (43), Norway (36), Ireland (27), Sweden (26), and Denmark (19). Of particular interest is the proportion of delegates from Scandinavian countries (approximately 40%) who did not have access to direct flights to Northern Ireland. Overall the participants came from a wide geographical spread – from Russia in the north, Latvia and Croatia in the east, Spain and Italy in the south, and Canada and North America in the west.

Many of the trends in Mesolithic research, as reflected in the conferences, are documented in Lars Larsson's paper (this volume). However, there is the continuing worrying trend, which has been alluded to on numerous occasions by Stefan Kozłowski, of the relative decline in scholars attending from eastern and many parts of central Europe. An examination of the contents page of the original 1973 Warsaw conference proceedings provides a remarkable contrast, as the delegates then were primarily drawn from the Baltic region, as well as central and eastern Europe. A similar trend was apparent at the 1978 Potsdam conference – indeed the southern parts of Europe were extremely poorly represented in the early meetings. The shift away from eastern Europe has been happening gradually over the last few meetings, although this is now matched by a significant increase in the numbers of delegates from the Iberian Peninsula and Mediterranean countries: this change was particularly noticeable at the Belfast meeting. There are, of course, numerous regional meetings taking place all over Europe, but the five-yearly meetings were always seen as more inclusive. One of the main purposes of the five-yearly 'Mesolithic in Europe' events is to bring together people from across the whole of Europe – although we may need to define what we mean by 'Europe'. At present it appears that the conferences are not meeting this target.

From another perspective, however, it might appear that the five-yearly conference is becoming a victim of its own success. It has been an unwritten, but fundamental, principle that, where possible, all those who wish to contribute should be given an opportunity to speak. Over 140 papers were presented in Belfast with two, sometimes three, parallel sessions. Consequently, no time could be set aside for an explicit poster session that did not clash with lectures. There were times when the lecture room was, perhaps, not the right forum: for example workshops or round-table discussions may have been more productive options. Similarly there was, on occasion, limited time for discussion. It would be unrealistic to expand the number of days devoted to the conference, or to organise evening sessions. As with European Science Foundation conferences, the Meso meetings provide, through excursions and other social events, a chance for colleagues to mingle and to get to know each other. It would be a pity to be forced to give up this equally important part of the conference programme. The challenge, in the face of increasing numbers, is how to be inclusive in providing opportunities and a platform for all, while avoiding separation into a series of narrow, sectional interest groups, and losing the chance to learn more of other regions, varied interpretations, and viewpoints.

Mesolithic Horizons contains just over 140 papers that, in the main, have been categorised on the basis of the sessions cited during the conference. Some of the presentations assigned to the 'Current research' sessions were the results of timetabling problems – there being too many papers for other sessions. However, in this volume, most of these papers have been redistributed to the most relevant, or appropriate, section of the proceedings. Some of the posters presented at the conference have also been included. It is hoped that the topics and session titles chosen for the conference, and used in this publication, are sufficiently broad, reflecting the full range of topics currently of interest in the Mesolithic. Many of these topics were under consideration five years ago and will probably continue to be discussed in some form at future meetings. One possible exception was the inclusion of a session entitled 'Flint alternatives', under the chair of Kjel Knutsson, as it was felt that if the 'Alternatives to flint' meetings, three of which had taken place in northern Europe, were to continue it was important not to lose the momentum that had been created. Larsson, in his review of the history of the conference (this volume) has noted the gender imbalance between certain sessions, such as 'social relations and group formation' being presented by female speakers, while certain other sessions were partially, or totally, dominated by male presenters. To some extent a similar bias can be seen in Meso 2005 between the male dominated 'Transitions' session and the 'Understanding the social context' session, where female contributors dominated. However, these biases are not as strong as previously. Perhaps this is an indication of both changing interests and the demography of the communities involved in Mesolithic studies. In fact for many of the veterans of the 'Mesolithic in Europe' meetings there was a sense of a sea change and a feeling that, as in the 1960s, a new generation was now making many of the most significant contributions.

This volume differs from its predecessors in numerous ways. There was a realisation that the proceedings of the 2000 Stockholm conference (*Mesolithic on the Move*) had reached the limits of a single volume, and with the greater number of papers submitted for publication in *Mesolithic Horizons*, much stricter limits on paper length had to be introduced. Another change is the emergence of calibrated radiocarbon dates as the normal, but not universal, means of communicating radiocarbon dates, leading to confusion at different times. We are still in a period of transition, where even we, those at the centre of research in the Mesolithic, have difficulties establishing whether the dates quoted in numerous papers have used calendrical/calibrated dates or simply used the original radiocarbon age. The editors' preference would have been to use only calibrated dates but this has proved impossible. Therefore we have presumed upon the goodwill of numerous authors to seek ways of clarifying the manner in which they used their radiocarbon dates. Perhaps in five years' time this will be less of a problem, but at the moment too often one has to know the age of the specific specimen already before one can work out the manner in which a radiocarbon date has been expressed or used. The result is that researchers of the Mesolithic cannot always be described as producing user-friendly text for colleagues and students who wish to learn about their period. Indeed, perhaps we should even have the courage to join our colleagues in the natural sciences and use calibrated BP, thus allying those working in the Mesolithic with palaeoenvironmental research. This would, however, increase the divide with later periods, which, in Europe, invariably use cal BC.

Another difference is that for the first time the conference proceedings include keywords for each paper, an index, and a consolidated bibliography. It is to be hoped that these features will assist readers (particularly those who attended the conference) when looking for papers of interest, or a specific reference essential to complete a piece of research.

While the organisation of Meso 2005 started with two archaeologists, two new appointments at Irish universities strengthened the organising committee and later the editorial board for the conference proceedings. These four individuals are Sinéad McCartan – Conference Secretary (Ulster Museum), Rick Schulting (Queen's University of Belfast, now Oxford University), Graeme Warren (University College Dublin), and Peter Woodman – Conference Chair (University College Cork). However, the organising committee was supplemented by a broader group of interested colleagues who formed an informal scientific advisory panel – Jim Mallory (Queen's University Belfast), Aidan O'Sullivan (University College Dublin), Michael Ryan (Chester Beattie Library), and Brian Williams (Environment and Heritage Service), all providing support and advice.

One decision taken soon after the Stockholm meeting was that Belfast, rather than Cork, would be a more suitable location for the conference. In Belfast there were three institutions, each of which could provide their own forms of support. Belfast was also a centre from which most of the field excursions could be conducted. As in Stockholm, there were excursions before, during, and after the conference. A pre-conference two-day excursion through the north midlands of Ireland took place with two half-day excursions (to Strangford Lough and east Antrim) during the conference, and finally a three-day post-conference excursion to the Bann Valley, the Inishowen Peninsula and north Antrim.

No week-long conference can run without a large degree of assistance and goodwill. During the years of organisation, the Chester Beattie Library in Dublin and the Ulster Museum in Belfast provided venues for meetings. There is no doubt that the success of the conference was largely due to the generosity of the Ulster Museum, which provided a venue for lectures, hosted an evening reception, supported the website, and provided administrative, design and audio-visual help. The support, goodwill, and expertise of a number of Ulster Museum staff are recognised, in particular Moira Concannon, Jackie Hagan, Deirdre Hughes, Frank Kerr, Doreen Ritchie, Richard Warner, and Gerry Watters.

Belfast City Council also generously hosted a civic reception, providing a warm welcome to all Meso 2005 participants.

Financial support for the Meso 2005 Conference was provided by:

- The Heritage Council
- Dean's Fund, Faculty of Arts, University College Cork
- Belfast City Council
- The British Academy
- Environment & Heritage Service (Department of Environment for Northern Ireland)
- Department of Archaeology, Queen's University Belfast
- Department of Archaeology, University College Dublin

Financial support for the conference proceedings volume was provided by:

- The Heritage Council
- College of Arts, Celtic Studies and Social Sciences and the faculty of Arts Dean's Fund, University College Cork
- National University of Ireland
- The Index has been sponsored by Archaeological Development Services

The poster session was organised and co-ordinated by Emily Murray, who is thanked for the time and commitment she gave to the conference.

Information and registration desks were effectively staffed, as well as help being provided for speakers. As usual, these tasks were carried out by a cohort of graduate students drawn from across a number of Irish universities and volunteers. In particular, thanks are due to Sean Denham, Killian Driscoll, Thomas Kador, Tatiana Kytmannow, Aimée Little, Vincent McAllister, and Rowan McLaughlin.

We would very much like to thank the land-owners of all the sites we visited on our field-trips, and in particular the Port of Larne authorities for permitting access to Curran Point, as well as Campbell Tweed for access to the Linford earthworks. Many people helped in the organisation of the field-trips and acted as site guides, and we thank Gabriel Cooney, Malachy Conway, Sean Denham, Nyree Finlay, Christina Fredengren, Claire Foley, Barrie Hartwell, Wes Forsythe, Aimée Little, Jim Mallory, Vincent McAllister, Rosemary McConkey, Cia McConway, Paul McCooey, and Brian Williams.

The editorial committee would like to thank contributors for their understanding when requested to make changes and clarifications to texts and figures, as well as for providing extra information. We also thank the Session chairs and Alan Saville for their unstinting willingness to help overcome the problems that will always arise at such large events, as well as for their insightful introductions to each session. As with *Mesolithic on the Move*, Oxbow Books has been generous in their support; our thanks go to David Brown for being prepared to take on another gigantic project, and to Clare Litt, Val Lamb and Julie Blackmore of Oxbow for their help and encouragement over the last three years, as well as Rowan McLaughlin for compiling the index. Finally, we would like to acknowledge the very significant contribution of our copyeditor, Gerald Brisch, and thank him for all his work and advice, as well as his good-natured tolerance of a diverse group of scholars from different generations and cultural backgrounds.

The editors note with sadness the death of our colleague Per Falkenström. Per, who was about to celebrate his 36th birthday, passed away at the beginning of February 2009.

THE MESOLITHIC IN EUROPE
Previous Congresses and Proceedings

Warsaw, Poland
May 7–12, 1973 (*The Mesolithic in Europe* published 1973, editor: S. K. Kozłowski).

Potsdam, Germany
April 3–8, 1978 (*Mesolithikum in Europa* published 1981, editor: B. Gramsch).

Edinburgh, Scotland
March 31–April 6, 1985 (*The Mesolithic in Europe* published 1989, editor: C. Bonsall).

Leuven, Belgium
September 17–23, 1990 (*Contributions to the Mesolithic in Europe* published 1990, editors: P. M. Vermeersch and P. van Meer).

Grenoble, France
September 18–23, 1995 (*L'Europe des derniers chasseurs*, published 1999; Editors: A. Thévenin and P. Bintz).

Stockholm, Sweden
September 4–8, 2000 (*Mesolithic on the Move*, published 2003, editors: L. Larsson, H. Kindgren, K. Knutsson, D. Loeffler and A. Åkerlund).

(i) Mapping the European Mesolithic

S. K. Kozłowski

Introduction

Studies of the European Mesolithic have always been very much locally-oriented, hardly ever exceeding the regional overview at best. Long-term research experience has demonstrated, however, that particular taxonomic variants of the phenomenon have a supraregional aspect as well. Thus, it is of paramount importance for an understanding of the spread of the European Mesolithic to consider it from a point of view surmounting modern political boundaries, abandoning the local or regional description that has lain so heavily on studies in the past. The following are a few remarks illustrating the opportunities given by this new approach for a tentative mapping of the European Mesolithic, with all its diversification and cultural territories.

'One' Mesolithic and the vertical approach (Figures i.1 and i.2)

The palaeontological-geological paradigm about evolution's universality, applied to the Palaeolithic by 19th-century French researchers (influenced by the ideas of Charles Darwin), was later uncritically extended to the Mesolithic by various French amateurs who trusted in its universality. These enthusiasts – teachers, physicians and retired army men – used it to describe particular collections from the Paris Basin, and were quickly followed in this by a host of parish priests, pastors and schoolteachers from virtually everywhere in northern Europe, eagerly taking the easy path to serious science.

It soon became apparent that non-French 'Mesolithic' material was more or less similar to the French finds (in terms of the presence of microliths and geometrics). In effect, these finds were quickly and unquestioningly recognized as 'Azilian' and 'Tardenoisian' to everyone's complete satisfaction.

The European Mesolithic remained undifferentiated (except for separating 'bone' Maglemosian from 'flint' Tardenoisian), local researchers having neither the knowledge nor the broader perspective necessary to overturn the conviction about the uniform development of the Palaeo-Mesolithic world. [For detailed bibliographies on the research history of the Mesolithic see Kozłowski forthcoming.]

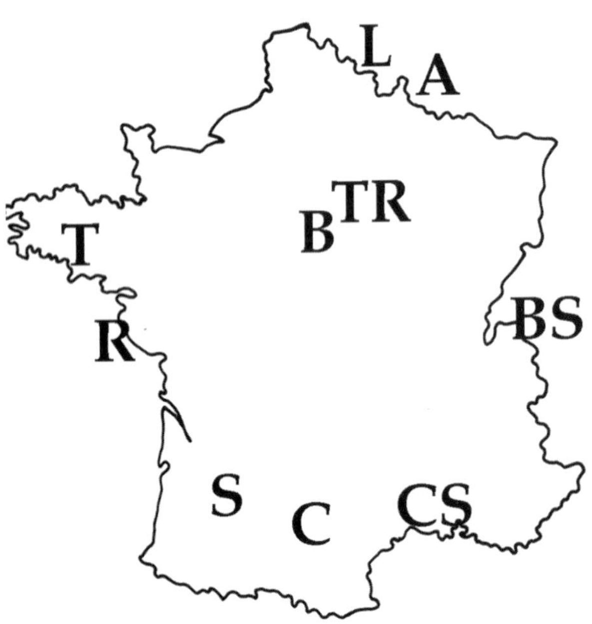

Figure i.1. The vertical approach.

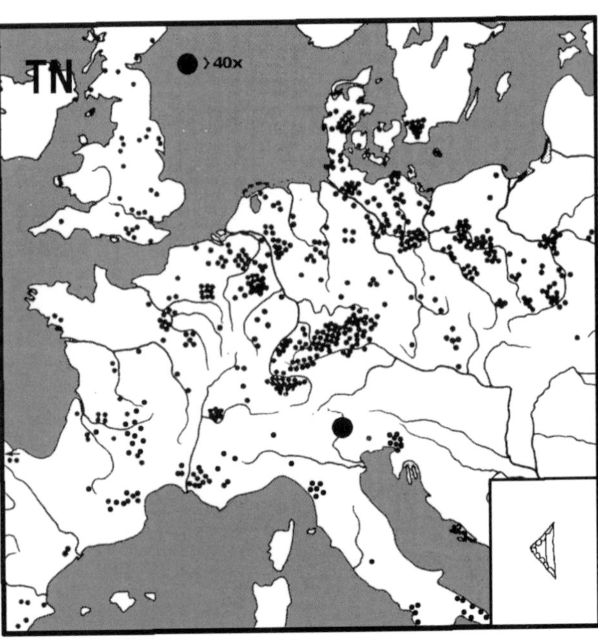

Figure i.2. 'One' Mesolithic?

Once trained professionals like Gustav Schwantes, Therkel Mathiassen, Grahame Clark, Carl J. Becker and Hermann Schwabedissen took over, they either concentrated on local studies, or took a broader look. The former (e.g. Schwantes, Mathiassen and Becker) limited themselves to specific regions, building local evolutionary sequences that often failed to compare with similar models prepared for neighbouring areas. The result was that local evolutions were well researched and known, while the supraregional perspective lagged behind. In recent decades this approach has brought some important studies: Erik Brinch-Petersen's for southern Scandinavia, Alberto Broglio's for parts of northern Italy and Jean-Georges Rozoy's for France, or, to be more precise, for a dozen plus regions ('cultures') of this country, Belgium and Switzerland.

In the 1960s these local studies, which led to the reconstruction of local evolutionary sequences, started being supplemented with regional and even supraregional surveys, coupled on occasion with tentative mapping (Grahame Clark and Roger Jacobi for Great Britain, Peter Woodman for Ireland, Raymond R. Newell, André Gob and Pierre Vermeersch for the Benelux countries, Hermann Schwabedissen, Surendra K. Arora, Bernhard Grensch and Wolfgang Taute for Germany, René Wyss for Switzerland, Alberto Broglio, Paolo Biagi, Carlo Tozzi and Fabio Martini for Italy, Jean-Georges Rozoy and André Thévenin for France, Josep Fullola I Pericot for Spain, Vasile Chivica for Romania, Georgi M. Burov, Lev V. Koltsov, Mikhail Zhylin and Svetlana V. Oshibkina for Russia, Heikki Matiskainen for Finland, Rimute Rimantiène and Thomas Ostrauskas for Lithuania, Ilge Zagorska for Latvia, Dmitryi Telegin, Volodymyr Stanko and Leonid L. Zalizniak for Ukraine, Janusz K. Kozłowski and Stefan K. Kozłowski for the Balkans, and Stefan K. Kozłowski for central Europe. Upon consideration, this appeared sufficient for undertaking a mapping of the Mesolithic in Europe.

The horizontal approach

The first large-area mapping projects date back to the turn of the 1930s. These were either regional studies (Hermann Schwabedissen for northwestern Germany in 1942), or supraregional ones (Schwabedissen in 1964 and Wolfgang Taute in 1968 for the Final Palaeolithic, referred to until recently as the 'Mesolithic', and G. Clark in 1936 for the Mesolithic/Late Palaeolithic. By the same period, a horizontal analysis of the Final Palaeolithic/Mesolithic material proved not only possible, but also successful in the supraregional scale, determining territories and borders that quite often exceeded state boundaries. From this point onward, the small-time pastors and educators were out of their depth.

The present author was one of the first to overstep modern state boundaries in his studies of the Mesolithic.

At the root of territorial differentiation

The stage on which the Mesolithic struts is of considerable size, stretching *c.* 5300km from east to west and *c.* 4000 from north to south. These distances are in themselves sufficient to indicate that no 'cultural' uniformity could have been achieved over such a large area. There was no way that small hunting and fishing communities could have communicated, and thus exchanged cultural information over such distances, separated as they were from one another by a wild 'no-man's-land' (and by huge distances) that must have figured large in scary stories told by the shamans.

This enormous territory was further differentiated morphologically (mountains, uplands and lowlands), cut across in different directions by watercourses and communicated through mountain passes, gates and river valleys. It appears, therefore, that the barriers between particular regions and their inhabitants were substantial, and that the passages between them were sometimes better, sometimes worse. Not only mountains (Alps, Pyrenees, Carpathians, Dynaric Alps, Apennines, etc.), but also seas (Baltic, Adriatic, English Channel) were onerous topographical barriers.

The third factor differentiating the region was climatic zones, which naturally determined the flora and fauna. The break-up was generally (although not always) latitudinal: from the tundra in the north to the Mediterranean flora in the south; from the reindeer (*Rangifer tarandus*) in the north through elk (*Alces alces*), roe deer (*Capreolus capreolus*) and boar (*Sus scrofa*) further south, and auroch (*Bos primigenius*) and red deer (*Cervus elaphus*) further south still.

Hydrology was yet another differentiating factor. A network of small and medium-sized rivers in some regions contrasted with wide rivers with fewer tributaries in others, or again with lakelands elsewhere.

Finally, there was the cultural factor – the Mesolithic in Europe not having developed from the same roots. In the south it originated mainly from the Epi-Gravettian, in the north from the Epi-Magdalenian, Ahrenburgian, Swiderian and Desnian, in the Pontic region from the Caucasian Palaeolithic industries, to name just the most important of the predecessors. Moreover, the same roots need not have resulted in exactly the same cultural developments, meaning that the Early Holocene culture is not an exact reflection of what preceded it in the previous period. Once these factors are considered, the strong territorial differentiation of the European Mesolithic stops being surprising. It could hardly be otherwise!

The first results

The results to start with were predictable: the Mesolithic was differentiated territorially and it was possible to distinguish areas of specific size with concrete, identifiable borders, characterized by a specific type of assemblage. The Mesolithic proved no different from other periods with cultural and territorial divisions in place. It turned out that particular characteristics could be charted and that a 'trans(political)border' description of European

Mesolithic cultures could be proposed, covering broad expanses of territory.

Europe turned out to be culturally and stylistically differentiated across the continent, with particular taxonomic units not only occupying well-defined territories (of a 'transborder' nature as a rule), but also having their own traceable external borders. It also proved possible, especially between the Atlantic and the Vistula, to isolate types characteristic of the different cultural traditions, as well as contemporaneous types of an intercultural and interregional nature, which evolved at their own pace (various triangles, trapezes). Some of these types were found to be of a supraregional character, others were no more than regional or just local.

Ultimately, a combination of homogeneous, stratified and dated assemblages, with the cartographic data coming from abundant surface collections (especially when territories or borders proved to be superimposed, and being documented by more than one type), led to the tracing of two 'cultural' maps of Mesolithic Europe, and even allowed some 'historical' events occurring in the European Mesolithic to be identified (see below).

Intraregional characteristics and interterritorial and cultural trends

A fresh look at the classification of available European Mesolithic material, meaning microliths and points, unbiased by any ideas and opinions voiced hitherto, gives a new overall division into several dozen classes or types, which can all be dated, for better or worse, and which, moreover, can be mapped.

The mapping exercise demonstrates forthwith that, contrary to the opinions of some researchers, each of the classes or types are limited territorially, meaning that the boundaries of their occurrence can be traced. It also shows that each class or type had its own shorter or longer history, which reflected either boring stabilization (range remains unchanged) or interesting dynamics (changing ranges). The former case is excellent for mapping 'cultures', in the sense of long-lasting traditions in Mesolithic Europe, and the latter illustrates the dynamics of change during the period.

This vitality is especially visible in the area between the Atlantic, Mediterranean and Baltic. The industries present here appear indivisible, all of them being characterized by a large number of similar types of armatures (backed pieces, triangles, trapezes). These triangular, crescent-like and trapezoid geometric microliths had 'always' been called 'Tardenoisian', and their interpretation had left scholars helpless. Now, we can suppose that they can be interpreted as a western and central European common *koine*, quite evidently associated with regionally differentiated specific types. The *koine* itself evolved separately from the local traditions, following its own, western-central-northern trends. This development can be described as follows:

- 10th–9th millennium cal BC: domination of broad microliths/points (backed – D; single – K and double truncations – PE; isosceles – TM and scalene – TO; TR triangles; crescents – DD, DE);
- 8th millennium cal BC: appearance and finally local or regional (?) domination of narrow scalene triangles with short base – TH, TI, TD and retouch of the third edge – TE in the second half/end of the millennium; number of broad microliths diminishes;
- 7th millennium cal BC: domination of trapezes – A, B and rhomboids – BH.

The changing trend is more or less common across a large territory (interregionally), but the application is different. For example, triangles in the south are clearly smaller than in the north, and the trapezes from the two regions are also internally differentiated. In any event, the great potful, so to speak, of 'Tardenoisian culture' now appears to contain distinctively discriminating local characteristics (e.g. Tardenois points, Sauveterrian points, *feuilles de gui*, unpolished axes, lanceolates, etc.), alongside intercultural and interregional 'trends', which extended over the entire territory from the Atlantic to the Baltic, and which evolved similarly all over the area.

The poor local pastor could not have conceived of this idea, for the phenomenon can only be understood when considered on a continental scale.

The following are a few suggested mapping reconstructions for different areas of Europe, and/or different periods of the Mesolithic, presented in illustration of my point.

The main borders

'East' versus 'West' (Figure i.3)

The first is the border located somewhere between the rivers Vistula and Bug, dividing in the 10th–8th millennia cal BC the two geographical and cultural zones of the European Mesolithic, the Maglemosian and the Kundian. The border ran from the mouth of the Vistula on the Baltic Sea, in a generally south-eastern direction to Volhynia in the Ukraine. In the material sense, the 'Maglemosian' is documented by geometrics, among other things, and especially small proximal truncations (K), isosceles (TN) and different scalene triangles (TO, TR, TH, TE), as well as some trapezes (A), along with axes and adzes. The Kunda technocomplex, on the other hand, is characterized, among others features, by a few variants of Kunda 'post-Swiderian' tanged points (L) and a few varieties of micro-retouched inserts (WA-C. There is naturally some overlapping of the western and eastern ranges, and individual types (e.g. 'Maglemosian' backed points – D) can penetrate (in this case into the east) the major cultural border described here.

On both sides of the Alps (Figure i.4)

The Alps have always been a dividing border between the Mediterranean ('Imperial') and the northern zone ('Barbaricum'). They were hardly ever easy to cross and

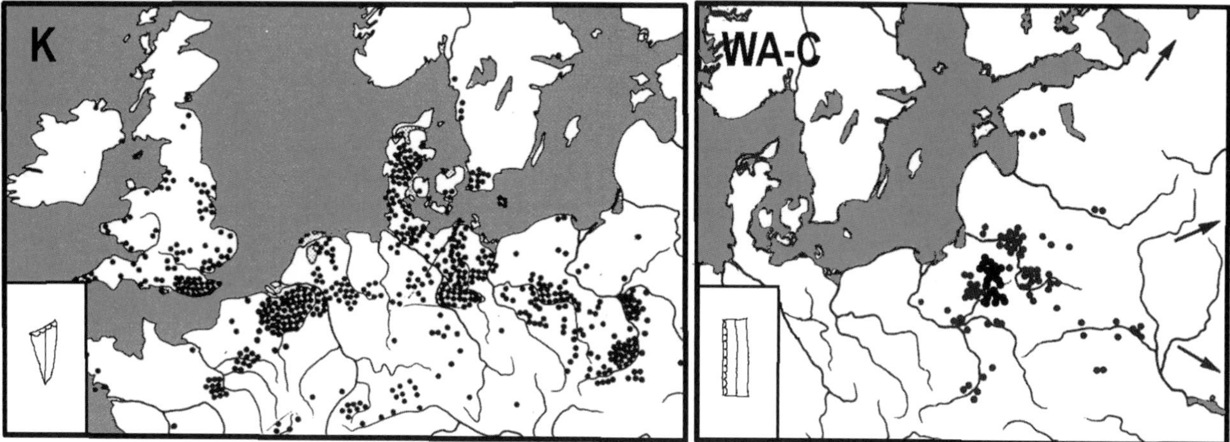

Figure i.3. 'East' versus 'West'.

the few regular transalpine roads did not help even the Holy Roman Emperors hold Italy. The same was true in the 10th–8th millennia cal BC. The uplands of Belgium, southern Germany, Switzerland, Austria, the Czech Republic, south-western Poland – but also the plains of the Paris Basin and the Netherlands – were occupied by the Beuronian unit, while the areas of France south of the Loire, westernmost Switzerland, almost all of Italy, western Slovenia and southern Slovakia all the way to the Tyrol in Austria, were the home of the Mediterranean Sauveterrian.

In the 8th millennium cal BC, the Sauveterrian influence spread towards the north (see below). This is expressed in the Beuronian C by the appearance of such elements as scalene triangles with short bases (TH, TE) and Sauveterrian points (PD). In this case, the Sauveterrian-Beuronian border north of the Loire is curious, to say the least, being determined not by any territorial barrier. On the other hand we observe the crossing of the high Alpine barrier (3500m asl) along the Italian-Austrian border in the Tyrol (i.e. Ullafelsen, a Sauveterrian site in the Austrian Tyrol).

Between the north (plain) and south (upland) (Figure i.4)

In central Europe, the north (i.e. Maglemosian), is separated from the south (i.e. Beuronian), by the 200m asl ground-contour interval, which is the arbitrary division between the lowlands and the uplands.

Ignoring typologically similar elements that constitute the *koine* in these two territories (i.e. mainly different triangles and backed pieces), we are left with some characteristic differentiating elements typical of the 10th–8th millennia cal BC. In the north, these distinctive elements include primarily slender-backed D points (also those with retouched oblique base – DF), small proximal truncations (K) and unpolished axes and adzes. In the south, there are the broad-backed points, small distal truncations, and variants of 'Tardenoisian' points (with transversal base).

The two regions are further divided by the plant cover and the fauna: deciduous forests in the uplands and pine (*Pinus*) and birch (*Betula*) in the lowlands, elk and prevailing roe deer in the north versus the predominance of red deer in the south.

Raw material borders

It is a known fact that except for Skania, the Scandinavian peninsula (with Finland, Karelia and Estonia) offers almost no flint raw material. The local Mesolithic was based therefore on material that was difficult to knap, such as quartzite, or almost impossible to knap hard rock, like quartz. It also made use of other kinds of rock (such as slate), working them with polishing techniques (axes, daggers, maceheads). Consequently, the character of the local Mesolithic culture appears to have been determined, at least in part, by the technical properties of the available raw material, which in extreme cases (like quartz) actually excludes any proper typological classification.

This factor should also be taken into account by archaeologists studying territorial borders (cf. the maps by Lars Larsson in *Mesolithic on the Move* (2003, xxii–xxxii)).

The issue of borders in the east

The Mesolithic of the 'Eastern European Lowland' causes particular trouble for two reasons, as far as cultural divisions are concerned; first because the Russian Plain is not as well researched as other regions, and second because the core of the chipped industries in this area shows considerable techno-typological similarity across the region.

Recognizing the territorial-typological aspects of the western borders of the 'Eastern Mesolithic' does not appear now to be a problem now (i.e. the Kudlaevka Culture and the Lithuanian/western variant of Kundan). What presents definitely more difficulty is the interior of Russia with its Butovo Culture on the upper Volga, and the classic Kunda Culture extending along the Baltic shores, all the way to Karelia. The lithics of the two regions are so similar that any potential division will have to be based

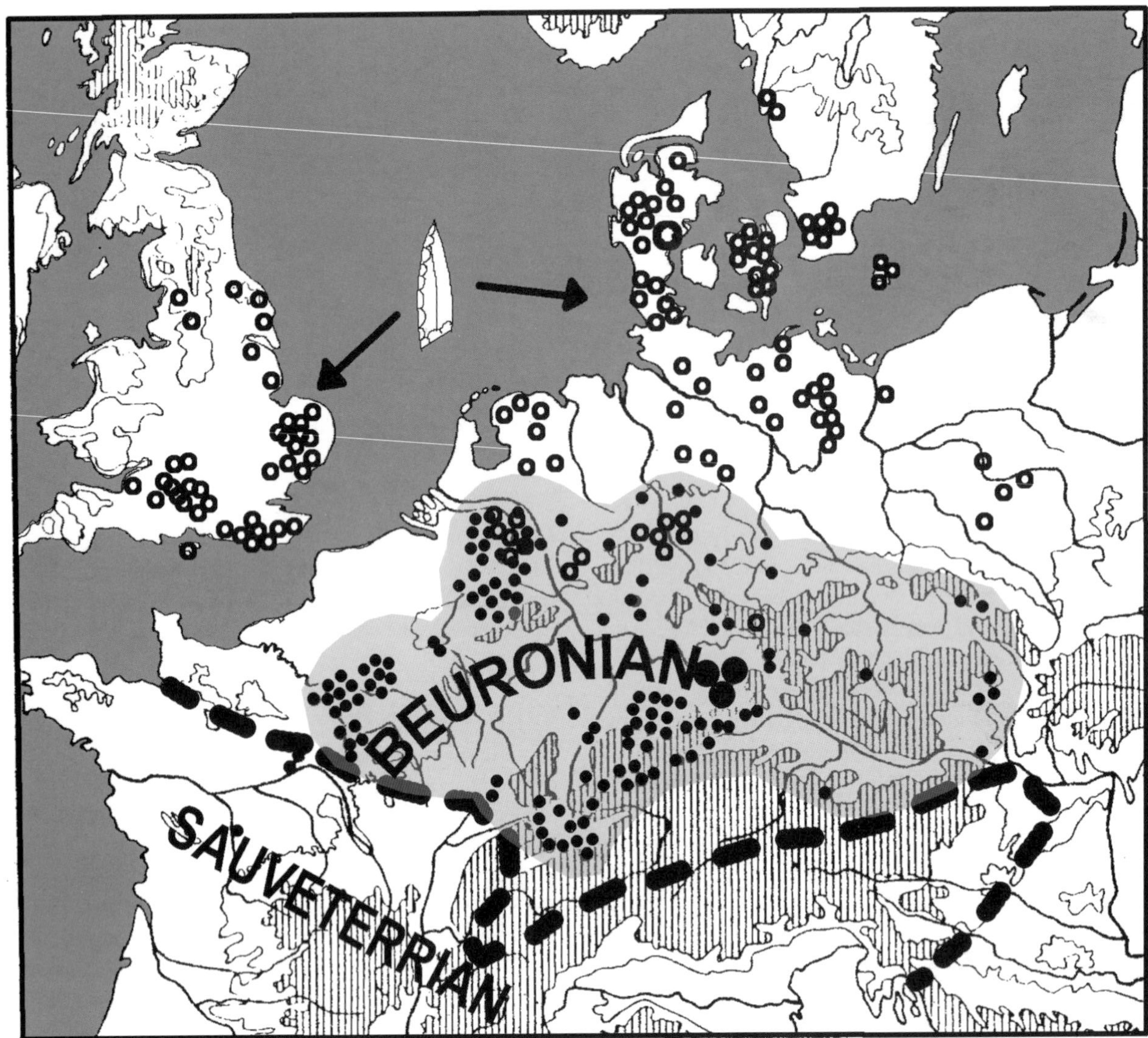

Figure i.4. On both sides of the Alps and between the north (plain) and south (upland).

on bone industries. Bone artefacts from the reaches of the Upper Volga are partly different from those found on the Baltic Sea, but since there is a dearth of bone finds from the territories in between, it is difficult to say where the actual border ran.

Contact routes

Push to the north (Figure i.5, left)

The present author has already in his time, following Graham Clark's (1955) earlier suggestion, recognized as probable an organic connection between the British Late Mesolithic (= Shippea Hill Culture or Narrow Blades Industry) and the southern European Sauveterrian. This naturally assumed a northward proliferation of Sauveterrian elements (e.g. Sauveterrian points (PD) and small scalene triangles with short base (TH), occasionally with retouching of the third edge – TE). The idea sprang from analyses of mapping and chronology, which revealed that the said elements south of the Loire were already present in the 10th–8th millennia cal BC, while north of it they did not appear until the 8th (second half) millennium cal BC and reached Britain and Ireland in the same period.

This phenomenon of the 'Sauveterrianization' of north-western Europe, as the present author called it then, concerned the Beuronian (Phase C according to Wolfgang Taute), the Boberg, but also a part of the 'Maglemosian' (appearance of the Svaerdborg industry in southern Scandinavia). In Britain, it was a younger variant of the Maglemosian, the so-called Broxbourne industry, that became 'Sauveterrianized'.

Via imperialis (Figure i.5, right and Figure i.6, left)

The route from the Mediterranean to the North Sea, via the valley of the Rhône, Saône and Rhine, turned out to be of special importance for the evolution of the early and middle 'Western' and 'Northern' Mesolithic (not only in this period, but also in Classical Antiquity and even more so in the Middle Ages). André Thevenin is of the same opinion as the present author. This trail between

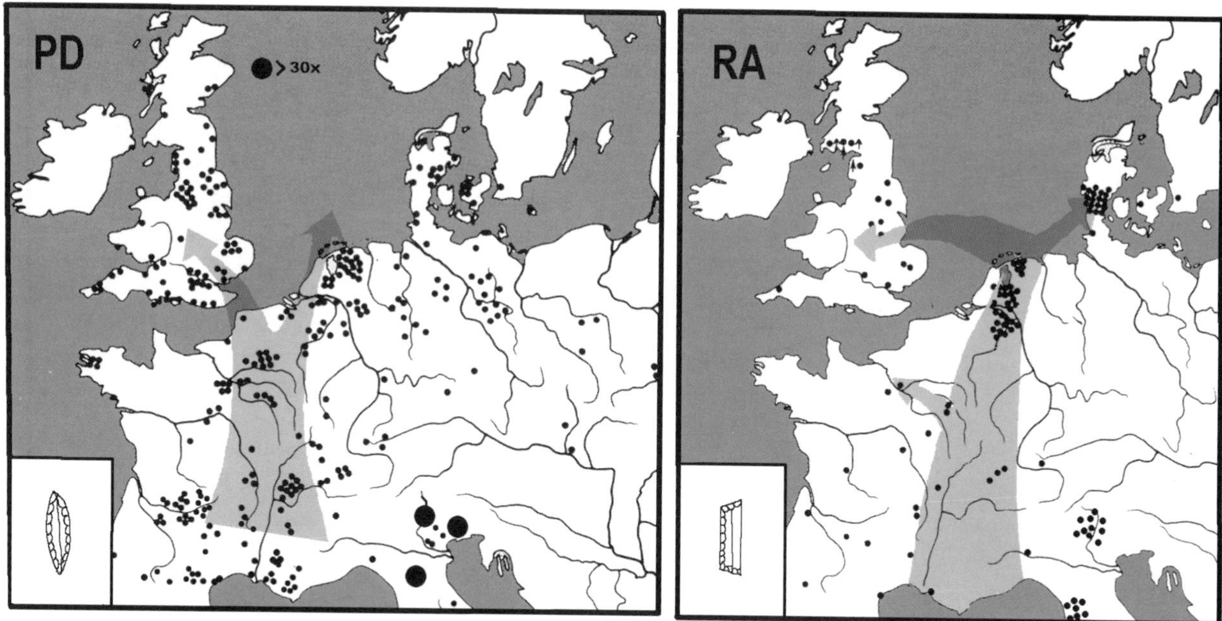

Figure i.5. Left: 'Push to the North'; right 'Via Imperialis' earlier.

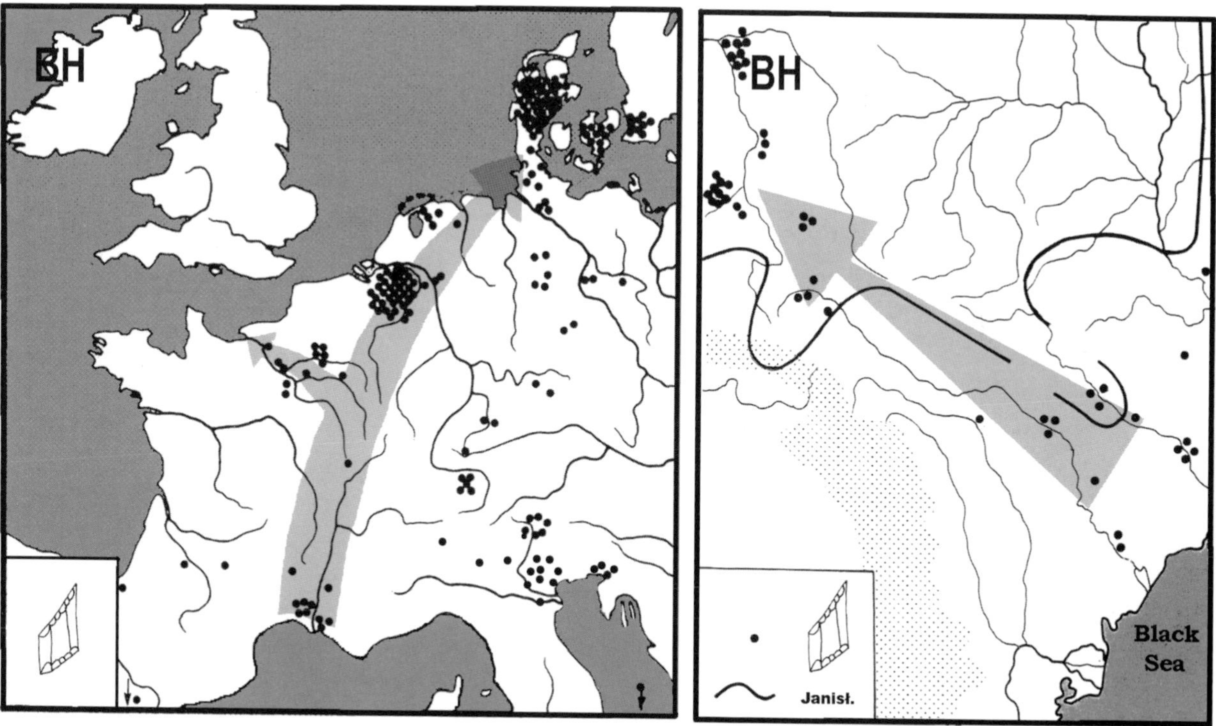

Figure i.6. Left: 'Via Imperialis' later; right: the 'Tartar route'.

the Sauveterrian and Beuronian territories appears to be marked in the 8th millennium cal BC by RA microliths occurring at least from the Rhône Valley, where it squeezes through between the Central Massif and the Alps, all the way to north-western Europe, reaching the Paris Basin and southern Scandinavia.

Sauveterrian elements most likely spread down the same route. In the 8th millennium cal BC, Sauveterrian points, for example, are found in western Beuronian C contexts, extending not only into the Netherlands, but also down the valley of the Seine, all the way to the Paris Basin and across the still non-existent Channel into Britain.

This route through the valleys of the Rhône and Rhine may have been travelled again in the 7th millennium cal BC by rhomboids of the BH type, occurring in western Europe from Provence and Trentino (Castelnovian) to the basin of the upper Rhine and Seine (Montbanian), and in southern Scandinavia (Kongemosian). Assuming all the sites mentioned here constituted links in the same chain (they differ in France and Belgium into left- and right-hand variants as far as orientation of the truncation is concerned, as Peter A. Gendel (1984) emphasizes, we would be dealing with a 'Castelnovization' of Europe that spread from the south (*c.* 7000 cal BC) and proceeded in a northerly direction (into Denmark in *c.* 6500 cal BC), down, among others, the valleys of the Rhône and Rhine.

The Tartar route (Figure i.6, right)

Mapping routes marked by BH rhomboids in the eastern part of central Europe leads to the following conclusions. The armatures form a zone 300km wide running south-east/north-west, from the Black Sea in the south to the eastern reaches of the Vistula basin in the north, east of the eastern Carpathians, along the rivers Prut, Dniestr, Boh, San, Bug and Vistula. These rhomboids appeared, contrary to western Europe, only from the second half of the 6th millennium cal BC (?). They are encountered in the south in the Grebeniki, Bug-Dniestr (ceramic culture) and early Tripolye cultures, and in the north only locally in the late Janislawician (= Polish Late Mesolithic), and perhaps also the Funnel Beaker Culture (?). Evidently the BH rhomboids were not limited to a single cultural setting and they seem to have come from the south, being obviously later in the north.

The same route from the Ponticum to the Balticum would be much travelled down the ages – by Armenian merchants from Kaffa, Crimean Tartars, Ottoman Turks, Poles and Cossacks, setting out for the Black Sea.

References

For detailed bibliographies on the research history of the Mesolithic, see S. K. Kozłowski (forthcoming), *Thinking Mesolithic*. Oxford, Oxbow Books.

(ii) The Mesolithic in Europe – some retrospective perspectives

Lars Larsson

Since 1973, altogether seven Mesolithic in Europe meetings have taken place. Every conference has resulted in a significant publication. Through a questionnaire sent before the meeting it is very difficult to get at a common opinion concerning trends in Mesolithic research. Few beliefs in general models and the environment are regarded as an important – but not always directly crucial – factor in the formation of Mesolithic societies. Several colleagues stated that research during recent years has indicated that Mesolithic societies were much more complex than previously thought. Concerning settlement analyses, scholars have intensified research on single sites or assemblages with high-resolution methods. A common thread among many respondents is the hope for a better research connection between those who are dealing with the Mesolithic and Neolithic scholars. According to the articles that appear in the different conference volumes, the female participants have increased, and there seems to be a gender division concerning the different sessions.

Keywords: Mesolithic, Europe, conferences, conference publications, questionnaire.

By way of introduction

We are gathered for the 7th Mesolithic in Europe meeting. Compared to most research areas in Prehistory, our meetings are perhaps not entirely unique, but they are rather special. I do not know of any other prehistoric European period whose long-term study has been so significantly shaped by regular meetings, defined by their definitive coverage of the ongoing scholarly activity. I do not know how long it takes to form a tradition, but 32 years should be enough. The first meeting took place in Warsaw in 1973, organised by Professor Stefan Kozlowski. I do not think he was aware of how important that initiative would become in Mesolithic research. Without his contribution, I sincerely doubt that we who work with the Mesolithic would be gathered in Belfast, or for any other regular meetings of this kind.

Just a small number of the assembled scholars were present at that first meeting, and even fewer have attended all of the meetings since then. It all started in Warsaw (1973), and then Potsdam (1978), Edinburgh (1985), Leuven (1990), Grenoble (1995), and Stockholm (2000) (Figure ii.1); one can easily get trapped in nostalgic feelings. But, of course, the most important aspect of the Mesolithic in Europe meetings is that people, some young immigrants into what a colleague has called 'the mysterious world of the Mesolithic', as well as those who are not so young any more, should come together to meet and exchange information. By so doing they come to know each other. As all of us agree, the presentations are important, but they are not as important as talking and discussing person to person. That is the most illuminating experience of these gatherings. And thanks to the meetings, I have been able to develop many friendships that I've been able to maintain in the intervening years through letters, emails, and travels.

Every conference has resulted in a significant publication. A few, for the conferences in Warsaw and Leuven, were even published before the meetings took place. Just to give a view of the increase in research intensity, I have weighed all of the volumes (Figure ii.2). The weights certainly tend to increase through time, and I just look forward to the size of the volume for this conference. If the size should continue to increase predictably, the conference volume for 2010 should weigh 4.5 kg. Even today, some people complain that one has to be a bodybuilder to work with the Mesolithic: perhaps we rather have to turn to the digital word.

A network such as the Mesolithic in Europe might create its own culture, with a self-reproducing system of rules of behaviour. However, the network could also be something constructive that its members might use in order to better understand one's own research questions, or one's own society. This is easier when one can maintain a certain distance from the special research culture. Some scholars have probably decided to position themselves intentionally outside of the network, in order to feel

Figure ii.1. The locations for the Mesolithic in Europe conferences.

free from its influence. Many archaeologists – perhaps especially researchers working on the Neolithic – consider Mesolithic studies to be too traditional. The post-processual oriented research, which has become so important in Neolithic studies, has only recently been introduced into mainstream Mesolithic research. Others have criticised Mesolithic scholars for not paying enough interest to theory developed by social anthropologists.

Present research and expectations

I sent out a questionnaire to obtain opinions about recent research in the Mesolithic and expectations for the near future (see Appendix). I received a considerable response and would like to thank all who submitted.

As expected, it is very difficult to get at a common opinion concerning trends in Mesolithic research during recent years; I would say the range of opinion mirrors scholarly views of the Mesolithic itself. Scholars no longer believe in a general model of the Mesolithic. Several researchers argue that there is now substantial evidence that Mesolithic societies displayed diversity in their constitution, structure and ways of interacting with the landscape. Most believe that Mesolithic people took an active role in the constitution and change of the society, leaving the environment as an important – but not always directly crucial – factor in the formation of Mesolithic societies. This relation between people and landscape is an aspect that several scholars are dealing with, and concerning which they are going to intensify their studies

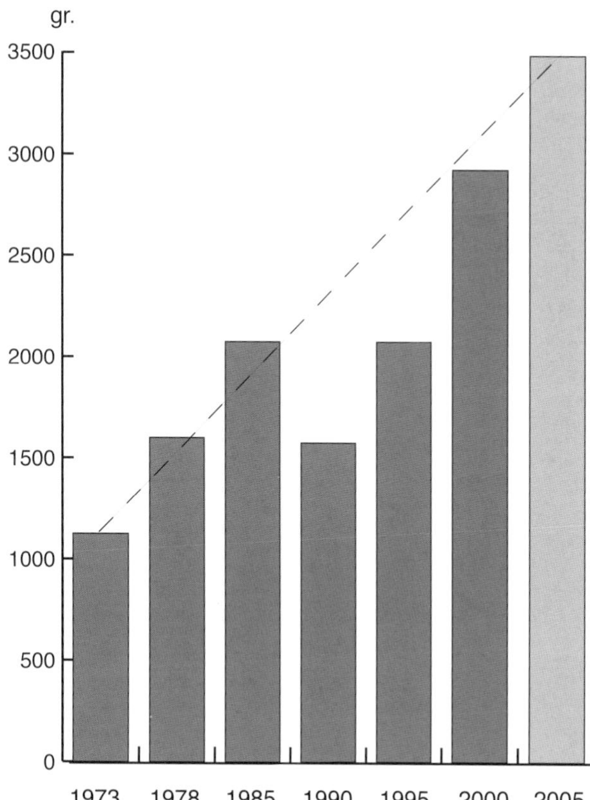

Figure ii.2. The respective weights of the Mesolithic in Europe conference publications.

in the future. Several colleagues stated that research during recent years has indicated that Mesolithic societies were much more complex than earlier thought. Respondents tend to observe great variability in behaviour. Connected to this emphasis on behavioural variation within and between societies, as well as over time, there is a major interest in stable isotope analyses of diet. Some also state their hopes for future DNA-analyses.

Concerning settlement analyses, one can discern an important shift. Some scholars have intensified research on single sites or assemblages with high-resolution methods. For instance, residue analysis on tools is one way to look at the micro-perspective. Several respondents were concerned with studying processes of deposition. Some researchers want us to neglect the traditional division of tools versus debris, and instead look at all remains as total refuse. Others are eager to find other aspects of social and ritual meaning within the finds. The *chaîne opératoire* approach is used not only as a method of looking into technology, but also as a means of studying internal social structure. Scholars are also carrying out series of new radiocarbon datings, not to get at chronological sequences as such, but instead to try to pinpoint the duration of activities that took place at sites. This is also combined with an eagerness to find features in order to trace houses and huts.

Others have realised that the most creative way to obtain new information is to open up large areas, so as to detect nearby settlements and activities – often of short duration – that took place between longer-term settlement sites. Some stated that only by this method would it be possible to get a better view of the structure of activity in space, giving us insight into what was happening in the areas between settlements, or between houses. Moreover, this could help us understand variability in social structure. However, there is a limit to how large an area can be exposed. Some colleagues have widened their scope through intensive surveys around specific sites. These might include thousands of hectares. Another point of interest is especially important when we consider that many parts of Europe exhibit poor organic preservation, or lack bone and plant remains altogether. Researchers have underscored that Mesolithic people were active, not only in the search for game, fish and plants, but also for raw material. Thus, the study of different types of raw materials has been intensified. Inland versus coastal settlement is still a potent research theme, and there seems to be an increased desire to study submerged traces of Mesolithic settlement and landscape.

Some of us are fed up with cemeteries and good preservation, and are eagerly trying to find theories and methods in order to intensify information retrieved from imperishable materials. While these researchers do not want to get so muddy, others are looking for new wetland sites. Interestingly, current investigations are not being made within the nations traditionally known for their wetland sites.

Theory and practice

I found relatively few comments involving interest theory *per se*. Those respondents emphasized the important relation between theoretical and empirical studies. Colleagues from just two Nordic countries pushed it harder, demanding research that could plant theoretical models that combine present-day societies with those of the Mesolithic. We have to realise that questions about the Mesolithic originate out of present-day society.

Some respondents stated that there rarely has been any theory in Mesolithic research. The research has been extremely empirically focused throughout the 1980s and 1990s. As one colleague indicates, this might put Mesolithic research in the spotlight in the near future; the pendulum has been swinging back towards a wider appreciation of empirical material in European archaeology.

I would say that an exceptionally small number of respondents stressed the ritual aspect of the Mesolithic. This is striking, considering its importance in sessions organized in Stockholm, and here in Belfast as well.

Judging by many of the answers, I now think that I should have put some of the questions in another way. I had expected to find a more general view concerning what colleagues find of importance for their Mesolithic research. Most answered with references to books and articles within their specific areas of interest. Of course, these are important, but I find myself agreeing with respondents who find their most interesting ideas in publications of a more

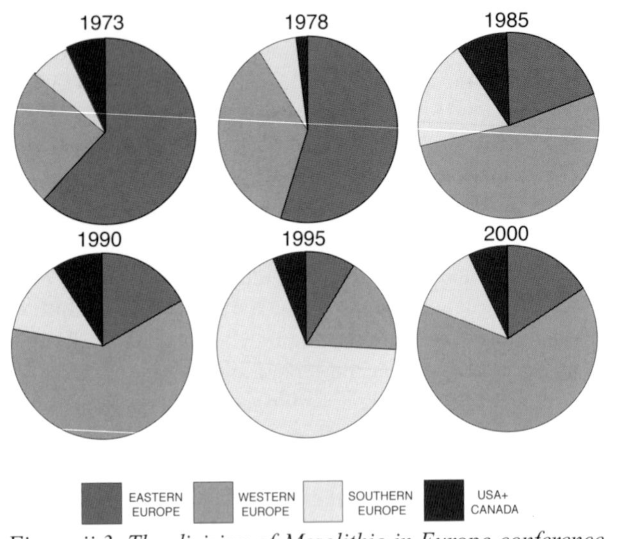

Figure ii.3. The division of Mesolithic in Europe conference participants according to geographical origins.

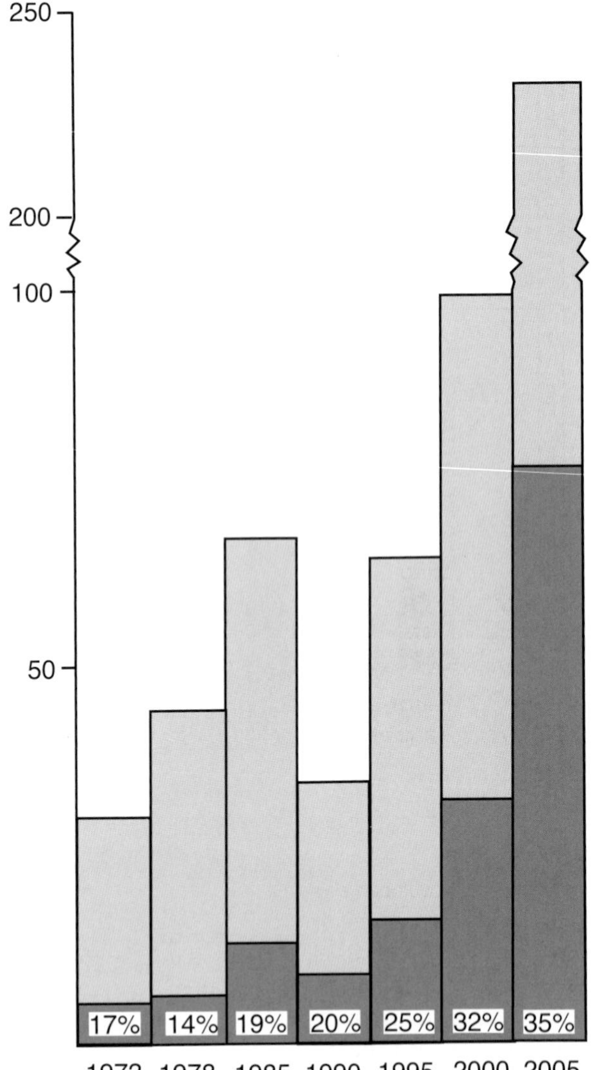

Figure ii.4. The division of Mesolithic in Europe conference participants by gender (percentages).

general nature, or in presentations that have little or nothing to do with the Mesolithic. In any event, several colleagues considered the Mesolithic in Europe conference publication of interest, but some also stated that there are other books about the Mesolithic that may be of more importance for their own particular research.

East and west, north and south

This points us towards the question of representativity! Whose research do we find in these conference publications? Several respondents identified a clear division between north and south in Europe, and some agreed that there is still a similar division between west and east. This is also evident in the four geographic divisions into which the questionnaire results have been organized: these included 'Eastern', 'Western' and 'Southern' Europe, as well as North America.

The archaeologists working with the Mesolithic sought to deal with this problem from the beginning, as the first two conferences were held in eastern Europe, to allow access to the meetings to colleagues from behind the Iron Curtain. Nevertheless, at recent meetings one could get a tangible sense of whether the conference occurred in northern or southern Europe (Figure ii.3). Thus the problem persists even if Europe has become more available for everyone. I think that the only solution is to get future conferences more spread out across Europe.

The MESO 2000 publication

And what about the survey's last question – regarding the conference publication from the Stockholm meeting? Well, most of the answers were positive, but some comments were critical, stating that the book was like peaking into an archaeological supermarket; it was overkill, or simply an eclectic publication. One comment referred to the title. Are we really moving, and if so, in what direction? Some were satisfied with the diversity of articles, while a group of equal number would have liked to see a kind of differentiation between interim reports and those articles presenting work with more theoretical and analytical depth. According to this view, the latter should have been given more space, while the former could have been reduced in number or length. Some would have liked to see some more discussion and debate, but I do not think that conference publications are the right forum for this. It is much better hold such exchanges in journals, where comments and responses might be presented, and at shorter intervals. Most would have preferred the presentation in two separate volumes.

From the comments in the survey, one gets the feeling that the number of young scholars doing research into the Mesolithic is decreasing. One might wonder if this trend is finally reversing course; in fact, this seems to be the case, looking at the number of participants in this conference.

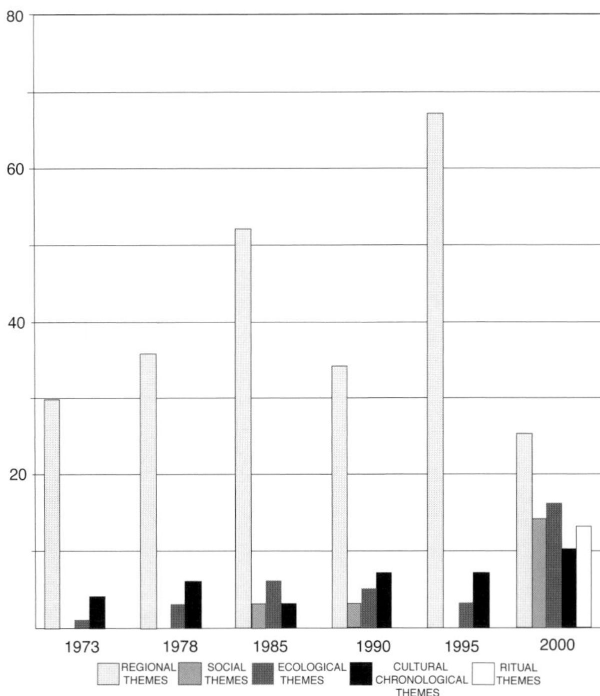

Figure ii.5. The division of Mesolithic in Europe conference participants by research themes. (After Lindgren 2004, fig. 4.4).

A common thread among many respondents is the hope for a better research connection between those scholars who are dealing with the Mesolithic and those who are researching the Neolithic. However, I did not receive any clear comments regarding interdisciplinary research. Here, I am referring especially to the role of scientific analyses in Mesolithic work.

Gender and sessions

During the editing of the Stockholm volume, we became aware of a gender division between the different sessions. Only males contributed to the session *Spatial Organisation of Sites*, while only females participated in the session *Social Relations and Group Formation*. Two other sessions, *Hunters and Gatherers in Transition* and *Colonisation Processes*, were dominated by male contributors. The division of female and male researchers according to theoretical/methodological themes is slightly different at this conference, but the split in interests within the Mesolithic still remains.

How has the gender balance looked in a retrospective view? According to the articles that appear in the different conference volumes (which do not include all of the presented papers) the percentage of women in 1973 was 17% (Figure ii.4). At subsequent conferences, the female contribution ranged between 14 and 25%, with a real step forward in MESO 2000 to 32%. According to the list of participants there is a small increase at this conference – to 35%.

It was for the second conference volume that the papers were organized into themes. Christina Lindgren has recently presented a useful classification of archaeological research themes (2004, fig. 4.4). Here, her classification has been used to look at development in Mesolithic research interests over the past few decades (Figure ii.5). In all six conferences regional themes have dominated. In addition, ecological and chronological/cultural themes have been identified as key themes in three conferences. Social themes appear at the Edinburgh conference, and in Stockholm ritual themes become important. Moreover, at the Stockholm meeting more synthetic themes became notable. While such cross-topical themes might have been a breakthrough at the Stockholm meeting, this trend is certainly continuing with the sessions here at Belfast.

References

Bonsall, C. (ed.) 1989. *The Mesolithic in Europe: Papers Presented at the Third International Symposium, Edinburgh 1985*, 29–39. Edinburgh, John Donald Publishers.

Kosłowski, S. (ed.) 1973. *The Mesolithic in Europe*. Warsaw, Warsaw University Press.

Larsson, L., Kindgren, H., Knutsson, K., Loeffler, D. and Åkerlund, A. (eds.) 2003. *Mesolithic on the Move: Papers presented at the Sixth International Conference on the Mesolithic in Europe, Stockholm 2000*. Oxford, Oxbow Books.

Lindgren, C. 2004. *Människor och kvarts: Sociala och teknologiska strategier under mesolitikum i östra Mellansverige*. Stockholm Studies in Archaeology 29. Coast to coast-book 11. Stockholm, Riksantikvarieämbetets.

Thévenin, A. (ed.) 1999. *L'Éurope des derniers chasseurs. Èpipaléolithique et Mésolithique. Peuplement et paléoenvironnement de l'Épipaléolithique et du Mésolithique*. Paris, Comité des travaux historiques et scientifiques (CTHS).

Vermeersch, P. and Van Peer, P. (eds.) 1990. *Contribution to the Mesolithic in Europe. Papers presented at the Fourth International Symposium 'The Mesolithic in Europe', Leuven 1990*. Studia Praehistorica Belgia 5. Leuven, Leuven University Press.

Gramsch, B. (ed.) 1981. *Mesolithikum in Europa. 2. internationales Symposium Potsdam, 3. bis 8. April 1978*. Veröffentlichungen des Museums für Ur- und Frühgeschichte Potsdam, Band 14/15. Berlin, Deutscher Verlag der Wissenschaften.

Appendix

Questionnaire

Dear Colleague
I have been asked to make an introductory speech at the MESO 2005 conference in Belfast. The title of my presentation is *The Mesolithic in Europe – some retrospective perspectives.* I would like to include some trends in Mesolithic research during the last, roughly, five years. Therefore I would be most grateful if you could send me comments on the following questions:

1. What are the most important results of your research into the Mesolithic during recent years?
2. What results of Mesolithic research by your colleagues do you think are the most important during recent years?
3. What kind of research in the Mesolithic do you want to prioritise in the coming years?
4. What publications have been of most importance to you in your research during recent years?
5. What do you consider the positives and negatives of the MESO 2000 conference publication *Mesolithic on the Move*?

(iii) The way forward

T. Douglas Price

The organizers of the conference and editors of this volume have asked me to conclude with some comments, based in large part on the remarks I made in a talk of the same title in Belfast. I have also had the subsequent opportunity to review the papers that appear at the beginning of this volume by Kozłowski, Larsson, and Zvelebil. My thoughts here then are a reflection of the conference itself that took place in September 2005, peppered with the remarks of the introductory speakers, and slow cooked over the last 18 months until this has been written. The title – The Way Forward – is a bold one, selected for me by others. In spite of the title, I would not pretend to know what the future holds for archaeology in general, or Mesolithic studies in particular.

Time is the most difficult dimension with which archaeologists have to contend. It's hard to enough to understand what life was like at the beginning of the 20th century A.D., much less in the Bronze Age, or Neolithic, or Mesolithic. One hundred years ago few could have believed that humans would fly, that cities would be incinerated, that a man would walk on the moon, that computers would interconnect the planet, or that a cow would be cloned. The sheer quantity of words added to our vocabulary over the last 100 years would make our conversation unintelligible to our ancestors only a few generations back. Why should it be easier to predict the future? If predicting the future was even remotely straightforward, we would not talk incessantly about the weather, economists would be rich, and political scientists would be presidents and prime ministers.

The simultaneous turn of the century and millennium in the year 2000 evoked a number of retrospectives and prospectives. In 1989 *Archaeology* magazine focused an entire issue on predictions of the future of archaeology in the year 2050; a series of articles by well-known archaeologists looked forward instead of backward. Brian Fagan anticipated the degradation of archaeological record from the expansion of human population, but remained optimistic in regarding the 21st as a global century in which archaeology would assume new and important roles in society, fostering tourism and income for distant countries and providing important symbols of our common collective human heritage. Others have also pointed to the growing importance of heritage as central in defining archaeology's role in society (e.g. Kristiansen 1998).

More recently in 1998, Fagan revised his view of the future of the discipline, describing the 'new and daunting challenges: funding shortages, destruction of the finite record of the ancient world and the need for drastic reappraisal of the basic ethics and approaches of those who study the past.' Colin Renfrew in the same year (1998) foresaw two major challenges to archaeological endeavours: '1. To give coherent account of the world's cultural, linguistic, and genetic diversity, and 2. To provide a better understanding of the development of human cognition.'

I am also supposed to attempt the impossible and suggest trends and directions in Mesolithic archaeology in the coming years. There are of course national and global trends that will impact on our lifestyles and our discipline. One of the most significant is our shrinking planet and the emergence of a global society. Communication is increasing explosively through travel and the Internet. It is an exciting period with costs and benefits. The costs will likely include a loss of innocence and the disappearance of faraway places but the benefits are great in terms of the access to and sharing of knowledge and information. Our understanding of the past will undoubtedly grow as borders and boundaries come down. This pattern suggests that Stefan Kozłowski's call for regional and supraregional studies of the Mesolithic may be heeded in the coming years.

It seems clear and predictable to me that the growing concern with global warming has reached a crescendo in the last few years. Societies around the world are beginning to focus concept and energy on dealing with this alarming issue. This concern will certainly fan the flames of emphasis on climate and environmental change in archaeological research as well. Funding agencies will no doubt stress the role of climate in studies of the past. Archaeology has a great deal to contribute to the knowledge of past climates and human response. At the same time, it is essential to avoid the explanatory determinism that is fostered by such emphasis. Climate and environment certainly condition past human behaviour, but rarely cause specific reactions.

It also seems clear that many of the major discoveries in archaeology in future years are going to come from the laboratory as well as the field. As the accuracy and resolution of archaeological tools increase, we will look more to the details of technology, of societal operation and change. New dating methods will resolve chronologies; finer and finer analyses of the physical and chemical structure of our evidence will produce many new insights. To insure the success of laboratory research, training and funding in this area will need to be emphasized. Archaeology students need to have backgrounds in the laboratory sciences – to take courses in chemistry, physics, biology, and experience laboratory and instrumental contexts. Laboratory archaeology is an expensive undertaking. Funding agencies must be informed and monies need to be directed to the creation and maintenance of laboratory science in archaeology.

Of special interest were the comments collected by Lars Larsson in his survey of Mesolithic archaeologists, which likely provides the best indicator of near future trends. Responses pointed to growing awareness of variation, of diversity, in the Mesolithic, and a lack of interest in more general models. At the same time, emphasis was on larger-scale phenomena, landscape, broad-site excavations, and regional studies. Another clear trend in the academic arena, also noted in Larsson's survey, is the growing predominance of the biological sciences. Many have predicted that this will be the century of biology. Studies of ancient DNA have already begun to rewrite our knowledge of the past. Human genetics, primate studies, evolutionary psychology will likely make powerful contributions to our view of early humans. At the same time we must guard against the dominance of biological determinism as an explanation of human culture.

The directions that archaeological investigations will take along these pathways is of interest, yet impossible to know. New theories and models will emerge to better explain our evidence. Research is a combination of merging theories and methods, and we examine possible directions in these areas below. New perspectives are emerging which may have an important influence on how archaeologists see the world. Major paradigms pass through the social sciences, and archaeology often adopts such perspectives for a period of time. One rapidly growing view of order and change in the world focuses on complex systems (e.g. Bak 1996; Waldrop 1992). Such approaches are gaining ground in a variety of disciplines involving both natural and artificial (human) systems. Such systems are characterized by complex behaviours that arise as the result of non-linear interactions in time and space among a large number of components. Examples of such natural systems include immune systems, multi-cellular organisms, insect societies, and ecological regimes. Artificial systems with such properties include computing systems, communication networks, evolutionary algorithms, economies, and cultures.

Previous hierarchical investigations of such systems have taken a top-down approach to the study of order and change, emphasizing higher-level controls and ignoring individuality and locality. Complex adaptive systems cannot be explained by the application of hierarchical models. Systems that are large and complex, but not governed by top-down rules, are said to be self-organizing. Biological complex systems employ distinctive mechanisms, such as adaptation and connectivity, to change states and evolve (Kauffman 1993). The study of self-organized complex adaptive systems involves the connections, interactions, and feedback loops among the parts of the system, known as agents.

History tends to ignore most of the people in the past, focusing on decisive events and the famous or infamous. One of the many roles of archaeology is to locate these missing persons and explore their lives and identities. Agent-based modelling attempts to specify the rules of interaction between individuals, and often uses computer simulation to discover the emergent properties of social systems (Kauffman 1993). Agent-based approaches to complexity are beginning to focus, for example, on how political actors and regions of shared culture can develop through the repeated local interactions of autonomous agents operating through socio-economic institutions (e.g. Axelrod 1997). This kind of approach was anticipated some years ago by Erik Wolf (1982, 390–1), who could not 'imagine cultures as integrated totalities . . . only cultural sets of practices and ideas, put into play by determinate human actors under determinate circumstances.' Complex adaptive system studies appeared in archaeology. Kohler and Gummerman (2000) have edited a new volume on agent-based modelling of social and spatial processes in human and primate societies. We can expect to see increasing emphasis on the individual and household as agents in past human societies in attempts to understand their operation and role in cultural change.

I would anticipate that the archaeology of the coming century will witness a stage of fluorescence unlike any we have seen to date. The ocean floor, the last major unexplored area in archaeological research, will be surveyed and no doubt yield extraordinary finds. The development of instrumental methods for obtaining extraordinary information about the past, combined with new theoretical perspectives in the social sciences will undoubtedly open our window on the past to an unimagined extent. I believe the second half of this century will see the rise of meaningful explanations to archaeological, not anthropological, questions. We know today what it is we are trying to understand, but lack an acceptable framework for explaining it. There is no question that the coming years will be an extraordinary time for the study of our human past.

In the end, however, there is a note, rather a crescendo, of urgency in that study. The archaeological record, under attack from the expansion of population and global economies, is rapidly disappearing in many areas (e.g. Knudson 1989). The growth of modern cities and transportation networks is covering the earth's surface with bricks, mortar, and pavement. The intensification of agriculture is ploughing through archaeological sites, mixing layers of soil, and lowering the groundwater table – processes extremely detrimental to the preservation of the archaeological record. Along with a concern for method and theory, it is essential that the basic archaeological information is recorded and protected before there is little left to study. That should also be a major focus of archaeology in the 21st century.

I do not believe that the history, as usually defined, of specific Mesolithic communities is a feasible goal at present. There is still so much basic information that we lack regarding the day-to-day activities, or even the existence of Mesolithic groups in many parts of Europe. Searching for the history of such groups is a bit like planning our interpretation of alien life on another planet before we encounter its inhabitants. I think that the future of Mesolithic studies lies not so much in the theories we use to orient our investigations, or even in the exciting methods emerging to investigate the past, but rather in the younger generations of students and colleagues in the discipline. If these individuals are well trained, motivated, and pointed in the right directions, the future of Mesolithic studies will be robust. In the end, the large and enthusiastic numbers of young scholars presenting exciting papers and posters at the meetings in Belfast suggest to me that the future is indeed bright. These individuals are the key to the successful study of our favourite period of prehistory.

Finally, a heartfelt thank you is due to the organizers of the Belfast meeting. There is an old Russian saying that organizing a conference is a thankless job. If something goes wrong, everyone will remember. If everything goes right, no one will notice. Well, I would like to tell Sinéad, Peter, Jim, and all the other individuals involved in the planning, organization and operation that we did not notice, but we did remember. It was a wonderful conference and we owe you our enormous appreciation, respect, and thanks for your hospitality, energy, ideas, and ability!

References

Axelrod, R. 1997. *The Complexity of Cooperation: Agent-Based Models of Competition and Collaboration*. Princeton, Princeton University Press.

Bak, P. 1996. *How Nature Works: The Science of Self-organized Criticality*. New York, Copernicus

Fagan, B. 1998. 50 years of discovery. *Archaeology* 51 (5), September/October 1998, 33–4.

Hodder, I. 1990. *The Domestication of Europe*. Oxford, Blackwell Publishing.

Kohler, T. and Gumerman, G. J. (eds.) 2000. *Dynamics in Human and Primate Societies: Agent-Based Modeling of Social and Spatial Processes*. Oxford, Oxford University Press.

Kristiansen, K. 1998. Between Rationalism and Romanticism: Archaeological Heritage Management in the 1990s. *Current Swedish Archaeology* 6, 118–22.

Renfrew, C. 1998. Re-examining prehistory. *Archaeology* 51 (5), September/October 1998, 87–8.

Waldrop, M. M. 1992. *Complexity: The Emerging Science at the Edge of Order and Chaos*. New York, Simon and Schuster,

Wolf, E. 1982. *Europe and the People without History*. Berkeley, University of California Press.

(iv) Ireland's place in the European Mesolithic: why it's ok to be different

Peter C. Woodman

This paper will show how much the distinctive differences that characterize the Irish Mesolithic are a product of human activity in Ireland's Early Holocene and how much they are a creation of Irish Archaeology. It is hoped that we can demonstrate that these differences are not anomalies that are simply based on Ireland being a moderately-sized island, but are rather a product of a complex set of interrelationships that may be relevant elsewhere.

Keywords: Irish Mesolithic, history, quaternary geology, island ecology, distribution patterns.

Introduction

One of the challenges of researching the Mesolithic of any part of Europe is to come to an understanding of how the record of the Mesolithic of that region was created. While the activities of postglacial hunter-gatherers played a major role in the creation of the Mesolithic archaeology of any region, we must ask whether this record has also been heavily moderated by other factors. These vary from the effects of geomorphological processes that could pre- and post-date phases of settlement (e.g. changing sea or lake levels or bog development), to the traditional manner in which research has been carried out, or even by the local political issues relevant to that part of Europe. Ireland, with its distinctive range of Mesolithic artefacts, particular island ecology and political history, is a perfect place for analyzing how the archaeological record is created.

Keywords for the Irish Mesolithic

If we were to establish other keywords for the Irish Mesolithic they might well be: *collectors and townlands, bogs and beaches, islands, flint.*

In understanding how research on the Irish Mesolithic developed, the first two words, *collectors and townlands* encapsulate the manner in which much of the original research into human antiquity took place. It is evident that even by the middle of the 19th century large quantities of material were being amassed by dealers and collectors (Woodman *et al.* 2006). One of the weaknesses of using collections built up by dealers is that there was a focus on the individual object and a lesser concern for locations of discovery or sites. Therefore for many collectors throughout much of the 19th, and even early 20th century, obtaining a representative selection of objects was the main priority. With a few notable exceptions, material was often recorded as stray finds that were at best located to 'townlands'. A townland is an area of land that might range from 50 to several thousand hectares in size. As will be shown below, this townland is a useful unit, but it has very definite limitations, especially as many were deliberately created to encompass a range of different type of landscapes. The result was that antiquaries were amassing collections of artefacts of unknown function, age and provenance (see Woodman *et al.* 2006 for a discussion on the development of Irish Archaeological collections).

There was also the ongoing debate about the possibility of some of the artefacts recovered belonging to the Palaeolithic. Eventually this debate concentrated on the age of the flint-rich 'raised beaches' found along the coast of north-east Ireland (Knowles 1914; Movius 1953b), although by just after 1900 a consensus was emerging that this material post-dated the last Ice Age, with the result that, in Belfast, Henry Lawlor (1928), and then C. B. Whelan (e.g. Whelan 1934), began to refocus the concept of what was beginning to be reorganized as Mesolithic. The beach-rolled material from the raised beaches was used to define the Irish Mesolithic. The several major excavations carried out in the 1930s by Hallam Movius, most notably Cushendun (1940) and Larne (1953a), where large trenches nearly 10 metres in depth were cut into raised beaches, are perfect examples of the point that one or two large, spectacular excavations can create or warp the Archaeology of any period. They helped emphasize Lawlor's ideas that during the Irish Mesolithic the areas chosen for settlement were primarily based on the search for flint, and that settlement during the Mesolithic could

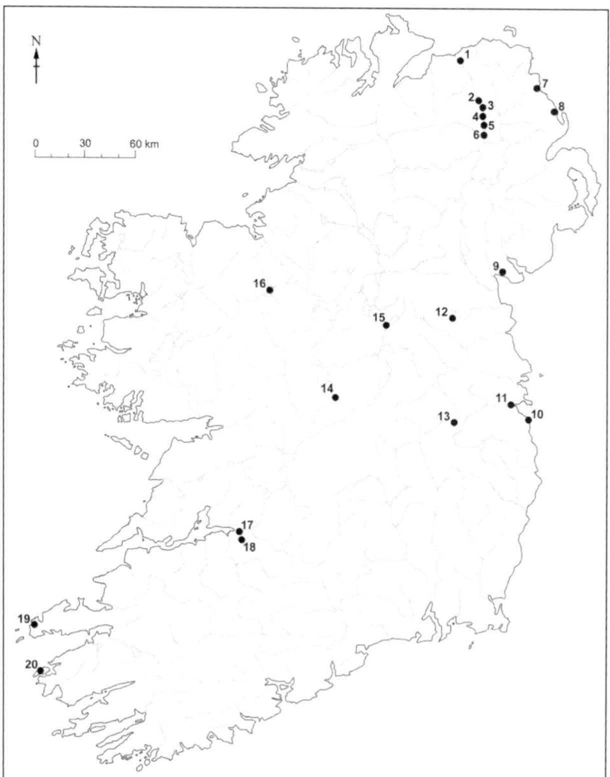

Figure iv.1. Location of sites referred to in text: 1) Mt. Sandel; 2) Kilrea; 3) Portglenone; 4) Culbane; 5) Newferry; 6) Toomebridge; 7) Bay Farm; 8) Larne; 9) Rockmarshall; 10) Dalkey Island; 11) Dublin Docks; 12) Moynagh Lough; 13) Lullymore Bog; 14) Lough Boora; 15) Lough Kinale; 16) Lough Gara; 17) Hermitage; 18) Killuragh; 19) Ferriter's Cove; 20) Clynacartan Bog, Valentia.

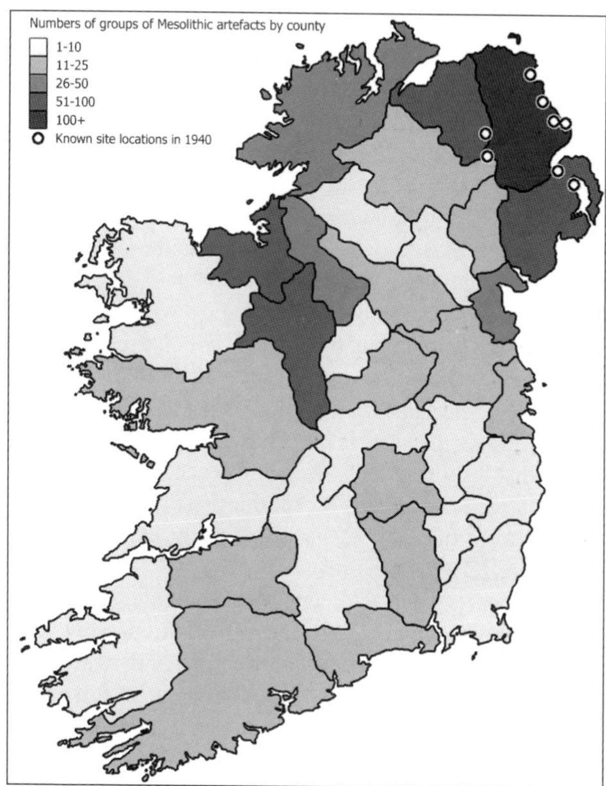

Figure iv.2. Changes in distribution of the Irish Mesolithic: a) location of the so-called Larnian (Movius 1942); b) distribution of assemblages of Mesolithic material.

not easily expand beyond the flint-rich north-east and that Ireland also had to have been settled first in the north-east, because of flint availability and the fact that here was the shortest sea route between Britain and Ireland: the 'Stranraer Larne' crossing! (Figure iv.2: a). Movius (1942) suggested that the Irish Mesolithic be called the 'Larnian' because of the apparent profusion of artefacts in the Larne excavations Movius (1953a). It was thought to consist of large blades, no real evidence of microliths, and few distinctive retouched tools.

A further, but at the time less considered aspect of the Harvard Mission was the suggestion, based on the Newferry excavations (Movius 1936), that the Bann Valley industries, characterized by what Movius described as Bann Flakes, was really part of a late or 'Secondary Neolithic'. As a result, tens of thousands of what we now recognize as Mesolithic artefacts that had been collected by the Antiquaries throughout the 19th century from the River Bann, Lough Neagh and elsewhere (Knowles 1912, Raftery 1944), were removed from the Irish Mesolithic discourse.

It is perhaps not surprising that eventually, by the 1960s, a counter interpretation emerged (Ó Riordáin 1979, 1). This carried the flint rich bias of the north-east to its logical conclusion. If accessibility to flint were the main characteristic of the 'Larnian', and because, in Ireland, there was little that resembled a 'real Mesolithic', with microliths as well as bone and antler artefacts, such as had been found at Star Carr, it was suggested that it would be better to consider the 'Larnian' as an industrial variant within the lithic technology of the Irish Neolithic. As a result, by the 1970s, even Mitchell, who had been responsible for several excavations of sites of presumed Mesolithic date further south along the east of Ireland (1970; 1971), questioned whether much of the 'Larnian' should be considered as Mesolithic. By this stage, therefore, the Irish Mesolithic was regarded as questionable.

In our case, much of the research of the last 30 years has been to escape from an archaeological enclave that assumed that the Irish Mesolithic was in numerous ways of marginal significance. In a period of just over a decade the excavations at Newferry (Woodman 1977), Mt. Sandel (Woodman 1985), Lough Boora (Ryan 1980) and Ferriter's Cove (Woodman *et al.* 1999), created a new and different view of the Irish Mesolithic. Newferry (Woodman 1977), in particular, showed that the so-called Bann Culture was of Mesolithic Age, and that a Mesolithic in the British Isles could exist without microliths, but perhaps more importantly could contain polished stone axes. Mt. Sandel (Woodman 1985) provided the evidence of a Mesolithic that was earlier than had been accepted, and put the microlithic technology in its proper chronological place at the beginning of the Mesolithic, as well as adding a fuller picture of life for Ireland's earliest colonizers. Lough

Boora (Ryan 1980) showed that even at an early date the Mesolithic was not confined to the north and that there was evidence for Mesolithic settlement in the center of Ireland. Ferriter's Cove (Woodman *et al.* 1999) showed that we could extend Mesolithic settlement across the island, and that raw material availability was not the constraint implied 50 years earlier by Lawlor.

At the moment a database of information on the Irish Mesolithic, including information on method of discovery, provenance, geographical and geological contexts, as well as ranges of implement types, etc., is being established. As a result we can document approximately 800 sets of artefacts and sites that may belong to the Mesolithic. Figure iv.2 illustrates the shift in our knowledge of the extent of the Irish Mesolithic that has taken place in just over 30 years. In particular, some Mesolithic artefacts, or traces of activity from that period, have now been found in every county in Ireland.

It is apparent that the manner in which the Mesolithic material is recovered in Ireland differs from elsewhere. The database includes material that varies from stray finds, including objects recorded only to the nearest townland, significant groups of material from shorelines, and some surface-collected assemblages; it has also resulted in a limited number of excavations. The excavations producing Mesolithic finds constitutes less than 20% of the entries in the database. Even the numbers of surface-collected assemblages are also relatively limited. It is also apparent that very large concentrations of material, nearly 50%, come from geological contexts such as bog cuttings, dredgings as well as beach deposits, and lacustrine and intertidal shorelines. In spite of the extensive commercial excavations taking place in Ireland it is remarkable how few artefacts, or sites of Mesolithic age, are turning up. (See below for a further discussion of the significance of the distribution patterns.)

One remarkable result of the survey is that little more than 10 individuals were responsible for the creation of most of the archaeological record that now forms the Irish Mesolithic. Those who contributed range from collectors, through local individuals finding sites in their own landscapes, to professional workers in archaeology and related disciplines. Given the potential political biases that resulted from independence and the division of Ireland, as well as the creation of a period by a select few, one must ask whether, along with the distinctive quaternary history of the island, the Irish Mesolithic as known today is mostly a product of human prejudice and later geomorphology, than by the behavior of communities living in Ireland during the Early Holocene.

The state of research today

At the moment, there is no evidence for a Late Glacial settlement in Ireland, nor is there any trace of Mesolithic settlement during more than the first thousand and more years of the Holocene. Ireland, and, to a great extent, Scotland and the Isle of Man, can be contrasted with much of the rest of England and Wales, as well as with coastal

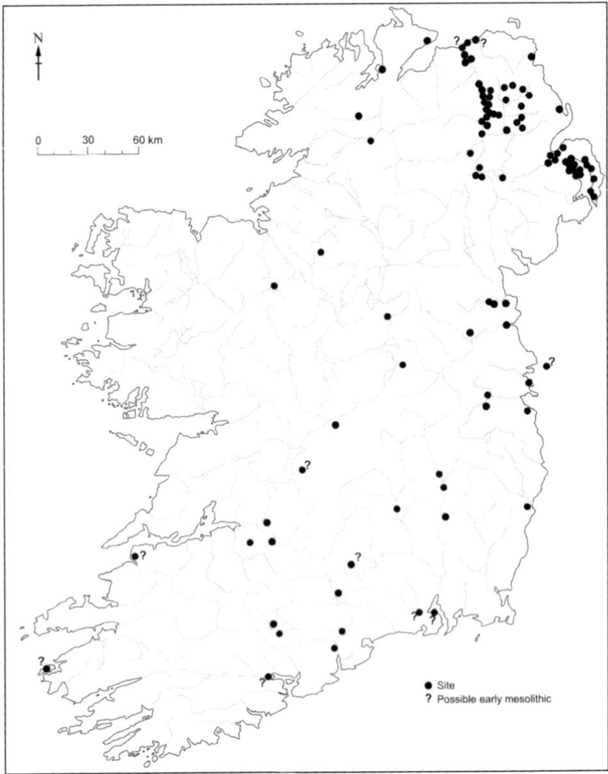

Figure iv.3. Distribution of known Early Mesolithic material.

regions of Norway, as in these latter cases initial settlement took place soon after land became available. The delay in colonization in the north and west of the British Isles remains as the most significant enigma of the Mesolithic (Woodman 2003).

Today the Irish Mesolithic appears to begin about, or more likely shortly after, 8000 cal BC. The Irish Mesolithic lasts for up to 4000 years ending about 4000 cal BC. The earliest evidence is based primarily on dates from the hut sites at Mt. Sandel (Co. Derry), where ongoing work by Bayliss and Woodman is showing that settlement may have begun by 7700 cal BC. It is of interest that this initial phase has been found throughout Ireland (Figure iv.3). Technologically, the Irish Mesolithic is characterized by two phases. There is an Early Mesolithic where microlithic forms consist of scalene triangles, rods, and needlepoints occur. These are made from blades produced through the use of hard and soft hammerstones (Costa *et al.* 2005). At one stage it was felt that they were produced using a punch. Throughout the Irish Mesolithic scrapers and burins are rare. Polished stone axes occur in the Early Mesolithic but the dominant forms are small core axes as well as a series of flake axes (Figure iv.4, and see below for a further discussion on these implements). Some of the implements recovered appear to be particular to Ireland, therefore it is probable that traces of a *slightly* older occupation (using the same general 'narrow blade' technology) have yet to be found in Ireland. The Early Mesolithic phase may extend beyond 7000 cal BC, but the date for the emergence of the Irish Later Mesolithic remains unclear.

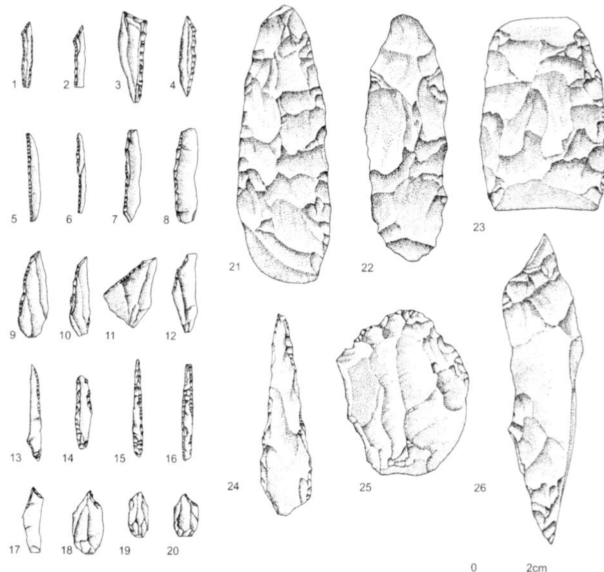

Figure iv.4. Selection of Early Mesolithic artifacts. (Drawing: R. Cronin).

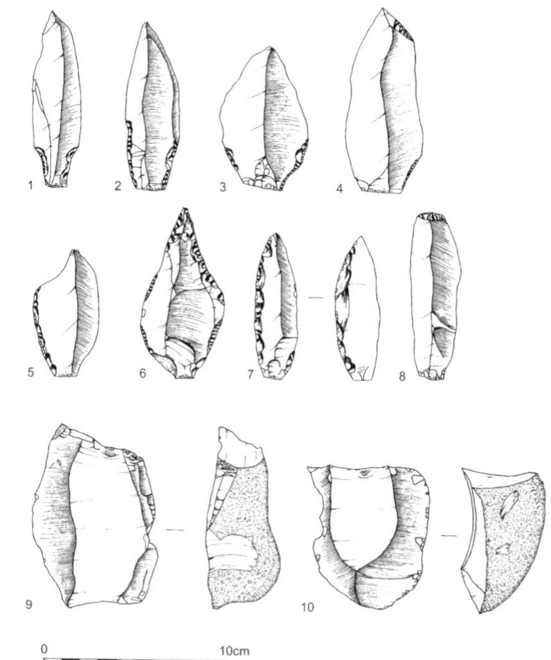

Figure iv.5. Selection of Later Mesolithic artifacts. (Drawing: R. Cronin).

The Later Mesolithic is characterized by the reliance solely on a hard hammer technology, and is associated with the production of a more macrolithic range of large blanks; these appear to be in existence by 6500 cal BC. These blanks can be trimmed into a range of hand-held tools, the more common being trimmed at the butt and often locally referred to as Bann Flakes (Figure iv.5). They occur alongside a series of robust picks and borers, as well as a series of slate tools. While flint core axes probably continue, there is a much greater emphasis on polished stone axes.

The reasons suggested for this technological shift during the Irish Mesolithic vary. They include geographical isolation, sociological factors, environmental changes, and economic considerations (Woodman 1981; Costa *et al.* 2005). It would not be too surprising if the change from the Early to Later Mesolithic began before 7000 cal BC. In Corsica, where a microlithic technology did not transfer to the island from the adjacent mainland, the Mesolithic is characterized by a series of simple, large stone tools (Costa 2001), and it might be expected that something similar would have happened in Ireland. In the Irish case, the change seems to have been somewhat slower than might have been expected. The Later Irish Mesolithic could be characterized on the whole as 'delayed adaptations to local circumstances'.

Ireland is also characterized by the development of an extensive series of quaternary deposits, which include, besides the raised beaches in the north and the loss of coastline in the south, an extensive series of raised bogs, which, in many places, have not been exploited to the point where Early Holocene levels have been exposed. Some river valleys such as the Bann River also contain extensive peat and diatomite deposits.

A further significant difference is the narrow range of fauna, both mammals and freshwater fish. The absences

Figure iv.6. Ground slate (Moynagh) points. (Photograph: National Museum of Ireland).

include many large mammals such as aurochs (*Bos primigenius*), elk (*Alces alces*), roe deer (*Capreolus capreolus*) and, apparently, red deer (*Cervus elaphus*). The latter species may only have been introduced to Ireland during the Neolithic (Woodman and McCarthy 2003). Therefore wild boar (*Sus scrofa*) is the one large mammal whose bones normally occur in some numbers at several archaeological sites. The most noticeable absences are most of the freshwater fish, including pike (Esocidae), perch (*Perca*), and bream (*Abramis brama*). Where fish remains occur they are most commonly salmon (Salmonidae) or

	Carbon 13	Nitrogen 15	Calibrated Age
Killuragh (human) (EM)	-21.13	11.12	7050–6690 cal BC
Killuragh (human) (LM)	-21.50	9.52	4680–4450 cal BC
Ferriter's Cove (human) (LM)	-13.92	16.83	4550–4350 cal BC
Dalkey Island (dog) (LM)	-13.71	15.23	5990–5770 cal BC
Rockmarshall (human) (LM)	-20.12	10.70	4780–4540 cal BC

Figure iv.7. Stable isotopes from selected bones of Mesolithic date.

eels (Anguilliformes). Many fresh water species, such as pike, were introduced at a later date.

Much of the limited surviving evidence for the economy(s) of the Irish Mesolithic suggests a coastal, lacustrine and riverine-based economy, with reliance on fish – salmon and eels – as well as some access to large mammals (such as boar) and a series of smaller ones (such as hare (*Lepus timidus*) and wildcat (*Felis silvestris*)). Stable isotope analyses (^{14}C and ^{15}N) of human remains, as well as one dog (*Canis familiaris*) jaw, suggests however that, in spite of the narrow range of resources, differences in economy exists.

The figures available are sparse and reflect the virtual absence of human remains, which usually consist of individual bones. Burials, with the notable exception of the Hermitage cremations (Collins and Coyne 2003; Collins, this volume), are not known from the Irish Mesolithic.

The low ^{13}C and high ^{15}N results from the Ferriter's Cove human, and Dalkey Island dog, suggest that in very peripheral coastal areas there is an extensive reliance on marine resources, with significant contributions from sea mammals, as is revealed from some of the Oronsay humans (Richards and Mellars 1998). In contrast, the results from Rockmarshall, which, although also on the coast, is a less peripheral site, and here a more mixed marine and land-based economy might have existed. Finally, at the inland cave of Killuragh, although it overlooks a significant salmon river, there is little to suggest that the diet was land based. None show strong indications from the ^{15}N data that, in spite of suggestions to the contrary (Maclean 1993 and McComb, this volume), there was a heavy reliance on plant foods. Perhaps in an area the size of Ireland it might have been expected that, as was suggested by the author over 30 years ago (Woodman 1978), one type of economy would have existed, however the figures above suggest a great deal more diversity within the island.

Obviously, a further question is what happens at the transition to the Neolithic. In Ireland most of those who have written about the establishment of farming have supported the invasion hypothesis. On the one hand the change in technology and material culture, as well as economy, is very radical, while similarities between Ireland and Britain in the earliest Neolithic are striking. Given the distinctive nature of the Irish Mesolithic, it should not be expected that the introduction or the transition to farming in Ireland would necessarily follow the same pattern as elsewhere. Aside from the time of invasion or acculturation, one can only note that shortly after 4000 cal BC large rectangular Neolithic houses appear, and throughout Ireland (by 3700 cal BC) burial monuments and other forms of Neolithic ritual are present.

It is of course too simple to suggest that Ireland's place in the Mesolithic, or even at the Mesolithic/Neolithic transition, is different because it is an island. Each island around Europe has its own particular dynamic of discovery and settlement. Even initial delays in settlement and suggested reasons for them, highlight the fundamental conundrum in researching the Irish Mesolithic. As noted earlier, how much of the archaeological record that we have created a product of the way we did, and still do, carry out research, or is it a product of a series of adaptations and innovations to Ireland's distinctive resources and ecology?

The challenges outlined above can be examined by exploring two issues. These focus on how distinctive tool types and settlement patterns emerged. They do not, however, purport to answer all the problems of the Irish Mesolithic

A question of axes

At one level, the occurrence of flake axes in the Irish Mesolithic is little more than an intriguing local example of difference. Core axes, whose functional edge is formed by the removal of a flake, served as chopping tools and occur in many parts of north-western Europe. We define flake axes as implements made from large flakes, where one original edge has been retained as the key functional edge (Woodman 1978, 46; 1985, 38). Besides their occurrence in the Ertebolle, flake axes mostly occur at the very beginning of the Scandinavian Mesolithic (well before 8000 cal BC), e.g. Nørregård VI in Denmark (Sørensen and Sternke 2004) and in the earliest phases of the Mesolithic of northern Scandinavia, such as western Norway (Fosna) (Bjerck 1986) and northern Norway (Komsa) (Woodman 1993; 1999). The Irish examples are obviously not contemporaneous with their Scandinavian counterparts and appear to be a local development. While many of the early Scandinavian examples could be used as butchering tools, however, based on Dumont's micro-wear analysis, the Irish examples served as woodworking adzes (Dumont 1985, 63).

Although they are relatively common, flake axes only occur in a small part of Ireland. The phenomenon is easily explained; access to reasonably good quality flint was needed for the manufacture of flake axes and so it is not surprising that they are confined to the north-east. As polished stone axes occur in Ireland's Early Mesolithic, i.e. before 7000 cal BC, and, as will be shown below, are very common in the Late Mesolithic, it is probable that polished stone axes were the preferred alternative for use elsewhere in Ireland during the Early Mesolithic, e.g. Lough Boora (Ryan 1980) or Hermitage (Collins and Coyne 2003). In the case of Irish Mesolithic examples, there is less reliance on quarried resources as occurred during the Irish Neolithic, most notably at Tievebulliagh and Brockley (Jope and Preston 1952; Cooney and Mandel 1998), or elsewhere during the Mesolithic, such as at Bomlo and Flora on the west coast of Norway (A. B. Olsen and Alsaker 1984). Irish Mesolithic 'polished' axes also differ in that many of them use appropriately shaped cobbles or blocks and are much less likely to be chipped into shape as more extensive use of grinding occur. (See Woodman *et al.* 1999 for a more detailed discussion of the potential ways of distinguishing Mesolithic forms of ground or polished axes.)

Why do these forms occur at this date in Ireland and not in Britain, and why are flake axes so localized in Ireland? In the case of flake axes, access to good flint sources may be a local contributing factor. It would appear that:

i) Flake axes would seem to be an independent stone tool development
ii) Polished stone axes became a more satisfactory alternative

Why then do polished stone axes become so common in Ireland? It is possible that the lack of suitable flint and chert sources in many parts of the island may have encouraged a search for alternatives. Perhaps the difference is that the Irish Mesolithic developed on an island where the absence of large mammals meant that bone or antler alternatives were not available (Saville 2003, 20). In Ireland, not only is there a lack of antler artefacts on archaeological sites but also no Mesolithic antler artefacts have been dredged out of the rivers or along the coast (Woodman *et al.* 1997). The oldest antler artefact from Ireland dates to well after the beginning of the Neolithic period. Antler axes exist in much of the north-eastern European Mesolithic, while bone could also be used as the raw material for heavy-duty artefacts.

The main lesson coming from these axes is that morphologically similar looking implements can develop at different dates in different parts of Europe and can be developed for different purposes. In this case the profusion of stone axes and the limited occurrence of flake axes do seem to have been the product of local resource availability and island ecology.

Going native

Even today our knowledge of the Early Mesolithic is still limited; it is primarily based on a few sites, notably Mt. Sandel and Lough Boora. In spite of some technological differences and, perhaps, the existence of a greater concentration on fishing and the lack of extensive upland settlement, much of Ireland's Early Mesolithic conforms to a European norm. Not only are microliths used, but also in many cases much of the reduction sequence in the manufacture of stone tools which took place at settlement sites are the same. However as noted earlier, by at least about 6500 cal BC, a new technology and way of using the landscape had developed. This is a change that is most evident in stone tool technology, but as Woodman pointed out (1981), these changes could only have taken place in a particular set of social contexts, perhaps driven in part by the growth to a viable, self-sufficient population.

Usually, however, the discussion of the change from Early to Later Mesolithic in Ireland is focused on the abandonment of composite tool/microlithic forms and their replacement by large blanks, which can be altered in different ways to suit particular needs. This change also seems to apply irrespective of when other raw materials besides flint are used, i.e. cherts, rhyolite, quartz, etc. What is often not appreciated is that each raw material may have its own reduction strategy by which these blanks or tools are created. Thus, while hard hammer percussion was used throughout the whole of the Later Mesolithic across Ireland, the core reduction sequence may have varied, but the end products of blanks and retouched tools are often remarkably similar irrespective of the raw materials used.

The best known is the Larnian technique. Several large blades were created from each nodule of flint by using hard hammer technologies, and where cores were abandoned when a flat knapped surface was created. This often happened, as at Bay Farm, where cores were abandoned well before they were exhausted (Woodman and Johnson 1996). In the northern part of Ireland the use of the Larnian technique was often combined with the separation of the industrial phases from the location of their use. This has been demonstrated in the very evident transfer of blanks from the East Antrim coast to the Bann Valley (Woodman and Anderson 1990). Similarly, work in the ongoing Inch Island Prehistoric Landscapes Project is documenting that blanks were transported from the north Atlantic coast to the inner parts of Lough Swilly, around Inch Island, 50km away. In other regions, where detailed reduction sequences have yet to be worked out, it would appear likely that there were patchworks of different core reduction strategies. In part, these alternative strategies may be a product of differences in raw material availabilities.

It is possible, of course, that the attention given to the production and transportation of blanks (Woodman and Anderson 1990) has diverted attention from other distinctive aspects of the Irish Later Mesolithic. One of the more common tool types of the Later Mesolithic is the ground and polished stone axe. Over 40 were found at Newferry, 5% of the retouched tools (Woodman 1977), and a similar percentage of these types of stone axes occurred at Ferriter's Cove (Woodman *et al.* 1999). At Culbane we would estimate that Knowles and others recovered an excess of 500 axes that might be Mesolithic (Woodman *et al.* 2006). Given the fact that, on occasions, the material from which these axes were made often had to be transported for up to 100km from their sources, and, based on (Hayden 1979) the manufacture (and in particular the hafting may have taken a considerable effort and time), these axes reflect a considerable portion of the time and effort associated with tool manufacture in the Irish Later Mesolithic. In addition, there are other possible Late Mesolithic forms, such as ground Moynagh points made in slates and other fine grained raw materials (Figure iv.6). These forms can exceed 200mm in length. Other, and even stranger forms

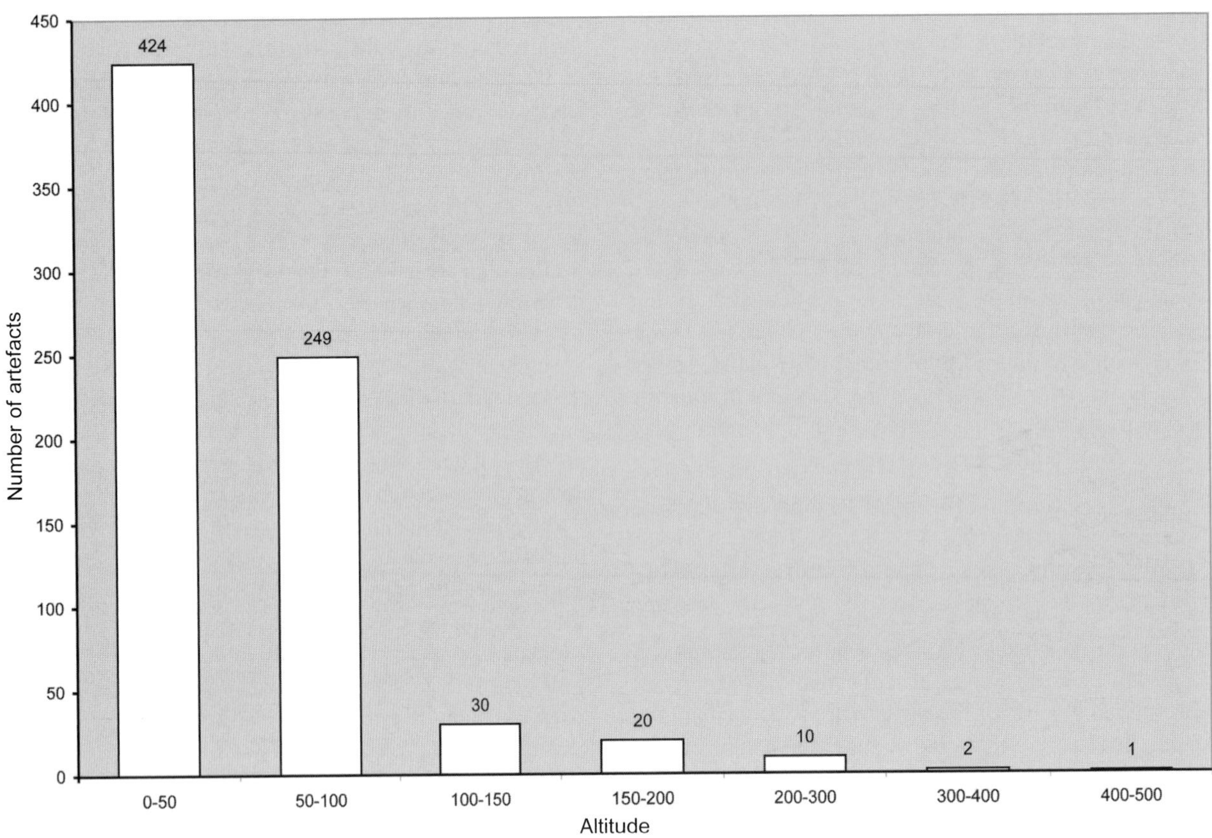

Figure iv.8. Distribution by altitude of Irish Mesolithic material.

also exist (Woodman 2005), and even the range of picks and borers occur in significant numbers and again highlight how different the Irish Later Mesolithic is.

In the context of this very distinctive equipment it is appropriate to review what we know about the Irish Later Mesolithic. In general, as can be seen from the Mesolithic Database, the Irish Mesolithic has a very lowland distribution (Figure iv.8). Although it is presented in a different format, the Irish distribution can be contrasted with the extensive use that was made of the Pennine uplands (Jacobi *et al.* 1976, fig. 1). One of the most powerful indications of this lowland distribution is from the Knowles, and other collections (Woodman *et al.* 2006, fig. 1). Even using artefacts only located to townlands across the mid-Antrim area, less than 1% of the artefacts recovered from the upper reaches of some river valleys and the overlooking hills might be Mesolithic (Figure iv.9). The rest of the stone tools found in the uplands belong to later prehistoric periods. In contrast, within the Bann Valley very large quantities have been recovered from various narrow points in the valley. At Culbane 10,000 Mesolithic tools may have been recovered, and similar numbers may have been found at Newferry and Toomebridge. Other large groups have been recovered around Portglenone and further north in the Kilrea area at Movanagher and Portna: in between these locations the river produced little. Much of the material from these regions comes from river dredgings or quaternary deposits in the floor of the valley floodplain.

Elsewhere in the midlands, notably around Lough Kinale, Lough Gara etc., similar concentrations of artefacts have been found in specific areas, particularly near river exits. The difficulty in finding and interpreting the Later Mesolithic settlement patterns in other areas appears to be twofold. Much of that area is still covered in peat bogs that are on occasions 5m or more in thickness. Peat, or diatomite cutting and drains, determine where we find Later Mesolithic objects. In fact in the case of the lowering of Loughs, such as those referred to above, there is also only a very narrow window of opportunity where artefacts could easily be collected before the newly exposed lakeshores are overgrown by reeds.

However, in the shadow of the major concentrations of artefacts, the thin scatter of Later Mesolithic material (often in the form of individual stray finds) that occurs across certain areas away from rivers and coast, such as in mid Antrim, must represent some form of activity (Woodman *et al.* 2006). There is not doubt that the whole of the landscape was used, but not to an equal extent; but these dispersed scatters of artefacts should receive more attention. Are they the tip of an archaeological pyramid of settlement and activity that we do not understand?

It is noticeable that over the last few years, monitoring of road pipelines and other developments are producing little of Later Mesolithic age, indeed any Mesolithic age. Is this due to our monitoring techniques? This is not entirely the case. The growing awareness of this issue

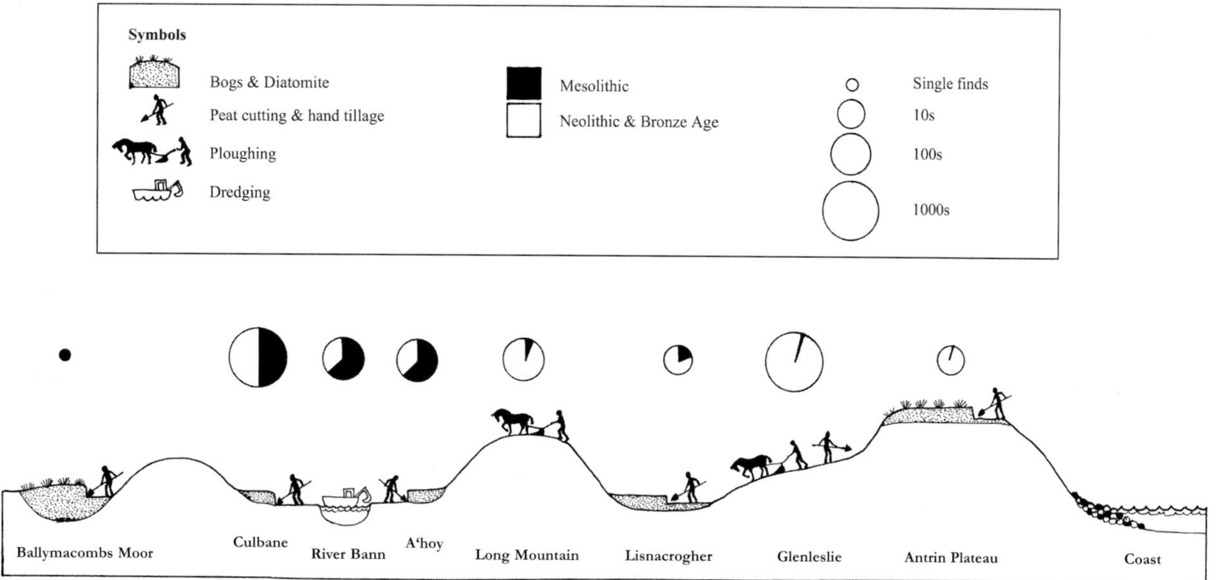

Figure iv.9. Schematic representation of distribution of Later Mesolithic material across parts of east Derry and mid Antrim (Woodman et al. 2006).

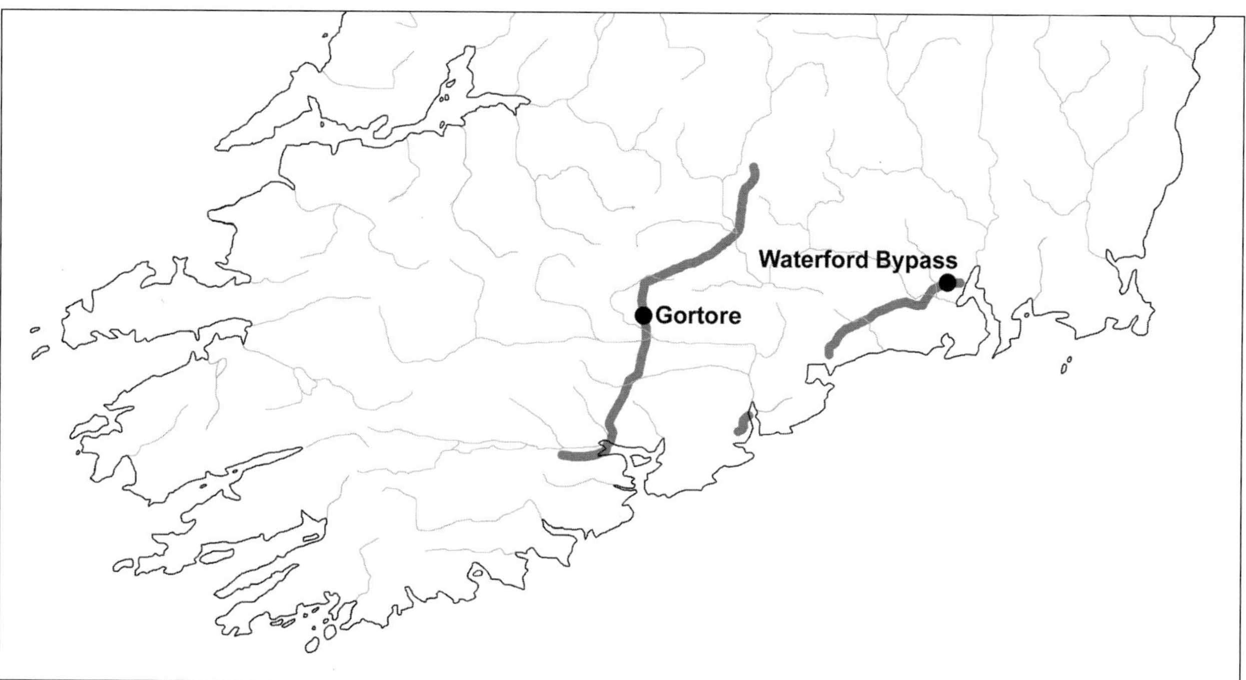

Figure iv.10. Distribution of selected NRA road building schemes and the location of Mesolithic sites.

amongst archaeologists working on National Roads Authority (NRA), and other types of development in the southern third of Ireland, has documented the discovery of a limited number of sites. The new road network is providing an important glimpse of the types of prehistoric settlement across numerous different landscapes. The areas documented in Figure iv.10 have had at least 500 excavation licenses issued, and lithic assemblages have been recovered from nearly 100 locations. While a number of Neolithic house sites, and an extensive series of Bronze Age settlement sites, have been uncovered, only a few groups of Mesolithic material have been recovered and these seem to occur particularly in the types of environments where Mesolithic sites are known to occur, e.g. on the N25 near Waterford, especially in the area of the floor of the floodplain of the Kilkenny Blackwater. Again, what appears to be a major concentration of Mesolithic artefacts has been uncovered at a key point overlooking the Funshion River in County Cork. In between, the NRA road schemes have only produced occasional Mesolithic artefacts.

Thus, the distribution patterns apparent from 19th-century collections in the north (Figure iv.9) and those in the southern third of the country, based on archaeological investigations along the new motorways, show a similar pattern. These suggest that while the patterns apparent may be somewhat biased by quaternary geology and research priorities, they do reflect a particular way the landscape was used during the Mesolithic.

Therefore, given the distinctive artefact types and the narrow range of environments in which they occur, the Irish Later Mesolithic may need to be viewed in a different manner. In particular, many of the large concentrations of material on the Bann, and perhaps elsewhere, should not be regarded as settlement sites but rather as 'persistent', and/or frequently visited locations. Where it has been possible to document the nature of the site, such as the basal layers at Newferry (Anderson 1994), refitting would suggest recurrent short-term visitations rather than a long stay campsite.

Key locations that were visited repeatedly may retain evidence of significant investments in fish weirs and other facilities. These investments in a particular location, as well as large concentrations of artefacts at key points, suggest a very organized area of the landscape, which may suggest a different perspective. Raw material may have been obtained from significant distance, but this does not imply a high degree of mobility of whole communities. The recent excavation of fish weirs and a fish trap dating to around 6000 cal BC from below several metres of estuarine deposits (McQuade, this volume), the Dublin Docks should raise the question as to whether some of the other fish weirs found along the coast, in areas such as Strangford Lough (McErlean and O'Sullivan 2002), could date to the Mesolithic period. Again, as with the polished stone axes, the attribution of a Mesolithic age to fish weir can only be considered when the evidence is incontrovertible. Of course, investment in fixed facilities for fishing would explain the large concentrations of polished stone axes and other related artefact types at these key points in the landscapes, i.e. woodworking tools. In short, the absence of large mammals, such as red deer and aurochs, may have forced a greater concentration on fishing, while their absence as a source of raw material for various implements could have increased the use of polished stone axes.

Similar investments in fixed points in the landscape are beginning to come to light around inland lakes. Fredengren's (2002) suggestions that some of the small crannogs around Lough Gara could be Mesolithic platforms were regarded with skepticism. Work at Lough Kinale as part of the Discovery Programme has shown that artificially created platforms had begun to be created in the Later Mesolithic (Fredengren, this volume). Another artificial platform is known from Bradley's excavation at Moynagh Lough (Bradley 1999). Frank Mitchell (1989) found a wooden platform at Clynacartan bog on Valentia Island, and although one extremely early date of 8347–7598 cal BC was obtained from its basal portion, a second date of 5707–5310 cal BC suggests that it is probable that the platform dates to the Late Mesolithic.

It has yet to be shown that wooden trackways extend back into the Mesolithic. In many areas the Wetland Survey has found trackways which can be shown to date from the Neolithic onwards (Raftery 1990), and it could be argued that their absence from the Mesolithic is simply because in many areas bog deposits of Mesolithic age have yet to be extensively exploited. Unfortunately no detailed records exist for one possible example: the Lullymore Bog trackway that was destroyed just after discovery (Brindley and Lanting 1998). This structure was made from pine, a material not usually used for trackways (McDermott, pers. comm.): this feature, along with the overlying bogs, been dated to 6000 cal BC. These wooden structures and other artificial platforms, irrespective of the significance of the trackways, imply more investment in parts of the landscape than would normally be recognized.

This evidence, and the large concentrations of artefacts at key points, suggests that the idea of low-density, highly-mobile Mesolithic communities that had had no impact at all on the landscape is not an appropriate model. Similarly, models based on the existence of large-scale habitation sites seem to be equally inappropriate. In spite of the fact that the later Mesolithic constitutes well over half the Irish Later Mesolithic, only one large structure of albeit questionable later Mesolithic date has so far been discovered, i.e. that from the Toome Bypass excavations (McCooey, pers. comm.). Where is the settlement evidence? This lack of the normal range of habitation evidence found elsewhere makes it difficult to fit the Irish Mesolithic into either of Binford's 'Forager' or 'Collector' models (Binford 1980): the challenge of understanding the Later Mesolithic remains. What *is* apparent is that a diverse range of landscapes was used throughout the Later Mesolithic, and that a range of different facilities, and even implements, existed. Perhaps instead of seeking a settlement site based model we should be exploring Ingold's (2000) concept of the 'Taskscape'.

Summary

In returning to our original question, how much is it our research and how much a genuine reflection of the activities of those societies? Aspects of the Irish Mesolithic would challenge much of the received wisdom. There is the development of tool types (e.g. polished/ground stone axes and flake axes) that appear to be independent responses to particular needs. It would also appear that the presence or absence of certain mammals has also strongly influenced the technology and economy of the Irish Mesolithic. It could be suggested that, while the particular research history and personalities of the Irish Mesolithic have coloured the study of the Irish Mesolithic, the actual artefacts that emerged during the Mesolithic, and the apparently distinctive use of the landscape in the Later Mesolithic in particular, left large concentrations of artefacts in quaternary deposits, or thinly scattered across the landscape; they are the products of the lifeways that developed throughout the Irish Mesolithic. Perhaps the Irish Mesolithic emphasizes that an over concentration on settlement sites can be misleading (Driscoll; Kador; Little, all this volume). Rather, in Ireland, we are moving towards a total picture of settlement, which is still difficult to identify.

References

Anderson, E. 1994. *Flint technology in the Irish Later Mesolithic.* Unpublished MA thesis, University College Cork.

Binford, L. R. 1980. Willow smoke and dogs' tails: hunter-gatherer settlement systems and archaeological site formation. *American Antiquity* 45, 4–20.

Bjerck, H. B. 1986. The Fosna-Nøstvedt problem. A consideration of archaeological units and chronozones in the south Norwegian Mesolithic period. *Norwegian Archaeological Review* 19, 103–21.

Bradley, J. 1999. Excavations at Moynagh Lough, Co. Meath, 1997–98. *Ríocht Na Midhe* 10, 1–17.

Brindley, A. J. and Lanting, J. N. 1998. Radiocarbon dates for Irish trackways. *Journal of Irish Archaeology* IX, 45–68.

Collins, T. and Coyne, F. 2003. Fire and water: Early Mesolithic cremations at Castleconnell, Co. Limerick. *Archaeology Ireland* 17 (2), 24–7.

Cooney, G. and Mandal, S. 1998. *The Irish Stone Axe Project: Monograph 1.* Dublin. Wordwell.

Costa, L.-J. 2001. *Espaces et productions lithiques en Corse (IXe–IIe millénaire cal. BC).* Unpublished Phd thesis, univ. Paris-X-Nanterre.

Costa, L.-J., Sternke, F. and Woodman, P. C. 2005. Microlith to macrolith: the reasons behind the transformation of production in the Irish Mesolithic. *Antiquity* 79 (303), 19–33.

Dumont, J. 1985. A preliminary report on the Mount Sandel micro-wear study, in P. C. Woodman (ed.), *Excavations at Mount Sandel 1973–77*, 61–70. Belfast, Her Majesty's Stationery Office (HMSO).

Fredengren, C. 2002. *Crannogs: A study of people's interactions with lakes with particular reference to Lough Gara in North West Ireland.* Dublin. Wordwell.

Hayden, B. 1979. *Palaeolithic Reflections: Lithic technology of the Western Desert Aborigines.* New Jersey, Humanities Press Inc.

Ingold, T. 2000. *The Perception of the Environment: Essays on Livelihood, Dwelling, and Skill.* London, Routledge.

Jacobi, R. M., Tallis, J. H. and Mellars, P. A. 1976. The Southern Pennine Mesolithic and the Archaeological record. *Journal of Archaeological Science* 3 (4), 307–20.

Jope, E. M. and Preston, J. 1952. Porcellanite axes from factories in North East Ireland: Tievebulliagh and Rathlin. *Ulster Journal of Archaeology* 15, 31–60.

Knowles, W. J. 1912. Prehistoric stone implements from the River Bann and Lough Neagh. *Proceedings of the Royal Irish Academy* 30C, 195–222.

Knowles, W. J. 1914. The antiquity of man in Ireland, being an account of the older series of Irish flint implements. *Journal of the Royal Anthropological Institute* 44, 83–121.

Lawlor, H. C. 1928. *The Archaeology of Ulster*. Belfast. R. Carswell and Sons.

MacClean, R. 1993. Eat your greens: an examination of the potential diet available in Ireland during the Mesolithic. *Ulster Journal of Archaeology* 56, 1–8.

McErlean, T. and O' Sullivan, A. 2002. Foreshore and tidal fish traps, in T. McErlean, R. McConkey and W. Forsythe (eds.), *Strangford Lough: An Archaeological survey of the maritime cultural landscape*, 144–85. Belfast, Blackstaff.

Mitchell, G. F. 1970. Some chronological implications of the Irish Mesolithic. *Ulster Journal of Archaeology* 33, 3–14.

Mitchell, G. F. 1971. The Larnian Culture: a minimal view. *Proceedings of the Prehistoric Society* 37 (2), 274–83.

Mitchell, G. F. 1989. *Man and environment in Valentia Island.* Dublin, Royal Irish Academy.

Movius, H. L. 1936. A Neolithic site on the River Bann. *Proceedings of the Royal Irish Academy* 43C, 17–40.

Movius, H. L. 1940. An early post-glacial archaeological site at Cushendun, Co. Antrim. *Proceedings of the Royal Irish Academy* 46C, 1–48.

Movius, H. L. 1942. *The Irish Stone Age: Its Chronology, Development and Relationships*, 339. Cambridge, Cambridge University Press.

Movius, H. L. 1953a. Curran Point, Larne, County Antrim: The Type Site of the Irish Mesolithic. *Proceedings of the Royal Irish Academy* 56C, 1–95.

Movius, H. L. 1953b. An historical account of the investigations at Larne. *Ulster Journal of Archaeology* 16, 7–23.

Olsen, A. B. and Alsaker, S. 1984. Greenstone and Diabas utilization in the Stone Age of Western Norway: technological and socio-cultural aspects of axe and adze production and distribution. *Norwegian Archaeological Review* 17 (2), 71–103.

Ó'Riordáin, S. P. 1979 (5th revised edition). *Antiquities of the Irish Countryside.* London. Methuen.

Raftery, B. 1990. *Trackways Through Time: Archaeological investigations on Irish Bog Roads 1985–1890.* Dublin, Headline Publishing.

Raftery, J. 1944. The Bann Flake outside the Bann Valley. *Journal of the Royal Society of Antiquaries of Ireland* 74, 155–9.

Richards, M. P. and Mellars, P. A. 1998. Stable isotopes and the seasonality of the Oronsay middens. *Antiquity* 72, 178–84.

Ryan, M. 1980. An Early Mesolithic site in the Irish midlands. *Antiquity* 54, 46–7.

Saville, A. 2003. A flint core-tool from Wig Sands, Kirkcolm, near Stranraer, and a consideration of the absence of core-tools in the Scottish Mesolithic. *Transactions of the Dumfriesshire and Galloway Natural History and Antiquarian Society*, 3rd Series, Volume LXXVII, 13–22.

Sørensen, M. and Sternke, F. 2004. Nørregård VI – Late Glacial hunters in transition, in T. Terberger and B. V. Eriksen (eds.), *Hunters in a changing world: Environment and Archaeology of the Pleistocene–Holocene Transition (ca 11000–9000 BC) in Northern Central Europe. Workshop of the UISPP-Commission XXXII at Greifswald in September 2002*, 85–112. Internationale Archaologie – Arbeitsgemeinschaft, Symposium, Tagung, Kongress 5. Rahden/Westphalia, Verlag Marie Leidorf.

Whelan, C. B. 1934. Studies in the significance of the Irish Stone Age: the Campignian question. *Proceedings of the Royal Irish Academy* 42C, 121–43.

Woodman, P. C. 1977. Recent excavations at Newferry, Co. Antrim. *Proceedings of the Prehistoric Society* 43, 155–99.

Woodman, P. C. 1978. *The Mesolithic in Ireland: hunter-gatherers in an insular environment.* British Archaeological Reports, British Series 58. Oxford, British Archaeological Reports.

Woodman, P. C. 1981. The Post-Glacial Colonization of Ireland: The Human Factors, in D. Ó Corráin (ed.), *Irish Antiquity: Essays and Studies Presented to Professor M. J. O'Kelly*, 93–110. Cork, Tower Books.

Woodman, P. C. 1985. *Excavations at Mount Sandel, 1973–77.* Northern Ireland Archaeological Monographs 2. Belfast, Her Majesty's Stationery Office (HMSO).

Woodman, P. C. 1993. The Komsa Culture: a re-examination of its position in the Stone Age of Finnmark. *Acta Archaeologica* 63, 57–76.

Woodman, P. C. 1999. The Early Postglacial Settlement of Arctic Europe, in E. Cziesla, T. Kersting and S. Pratsch (eds.), *Den Bogen Spannen...Festschrift für Bernhard Gramsch*, Vol. 1, 297–312. Weisbach, Beier & Beran.

Woodman, P. C. 2003. Colonising the edge of Europe: Ireland as a case study, in L. Larsson, H. Kindgren, K. Knutsson, D. Loeffler and A. Åkerlund (eds.), *Mesolithic on the Move: Papers presented at the Sixth International Conference on the Mesolithic in Europe, Stockholm 2000*, 57–64. Oxford, Oxbow Books.

Woodman, P. C. 2005. It's too light to be right, in N. Milner and P. C. Woodman (eds.), *Mesolithic Studies at the Beginning of the 21st Century*, 126–43. Oxford, Oxbow Books.

Woodman, P. C. and Anderson, E. 1990. The Irish Later Mesolithic: a partial picture, in P. M. Vermersch and P. Van Peer (eds.), *Contribution to the Mesolithic in Europe. Papers presented at the Fourth International Symposium 'The Mesolithic in Europe', Leuven 1990*, 377–87. Studia Praehistorica Belgia 5. Leuven, Leuven University Press.

Woodman, P. C., Anderson, E. and Finlay, N. 1999. *Excavations at Ferriter's Cove 1983–1995: last foragers, first farmers in the Dingle Peninsula*. Bray, Wordwell.

Woodman, P. C., Finlay, N. and Anderson, E. 2006. *The archaeology of a collection: the Keiller-Knowles collection of the National Museum of Ireland*. Bray, Wordwell.

Woodman, P. C. and Johnson, G. 1996. Excavations at Bay Farm 1, Carnlough, Co. Antrim, and the study of the 'Larnian' technology. *Proceedings of the Royal Irish Academy* 96C, 137–235.

Woodman, P. C. and Johnston, I. 1991–2. A petrological examination of some Mesolithic stone artefacts. *Ulster Journal of Archaeology* 54 (5), 134–7.

Woodman, P. C. and McCarthy, M. 2003. Contemplating some awful(ly interesting) vistas: importing cattle and red deer into Prehistoric Ireland, in I. Armit, E. Murphy, E. Nelis and D. Simpson (eds.), *Neolithic Settlement in Ireland and Western Britain*, 31–39. Oxford, Oxbow Books.

Woodman, P. C., McCarthy, M. and Monaghan, N. 1997. The Irish Quaternary Fauna Project. *Quaternary Science Reviews* 16, 129–59.

(v) The Mesolithic and the 21st century

Marek Zvelebil

My aim in this contribution is to link the archaeological cultures produced by the early Postglacial hunter-gatherers of Europe and northern Asia (the Mesolithic) with the more recent historical and ethno-historic hunter-gatherer communities of north-east Europe and Siberia into a single cultural tradition, marked by an historical continuity of development that extended for about 12,000 years into the end of the glacial epoch and the early Postglacial period. I am arguing that the early Postglacial hunter-gatherers, as represented by the cultures of the Mesolithic, do not merely represent communities that are adapting to changing environmental conditions. Instead, the Mesolithic represents an historical process involving hunter-gatherer societies in clearly defined space and time. Its historical condition is defined by a shared knowledge and a cognitive world, as well as by the dynamic changes occurring in the course of deglaciation and Postglacial changes in the environment. The historical trajectory, framed by shared cosmological structures and inter-linked by shared knowledge, provides the basis for historical continuity that marks the development of an historical tradition among northern hunter-gatherers, the early stages of which have been known as the Mesolithic. Two temporal processes characterise Mesolithic conditions of existence. One was 'deglaciation', and the reaction of hunter-gatherer communities to this process. The Mesolithic was developing in the structural conditions of deglaciation through prosecution of human agency, marked by population shifts from the south to the north within Europe, the colonisation of northern Europe, and regional resettlement. The second process was 'enculturation', whereby hunter-gatherers manipulated their environment for symbolic and cognitive purposes, as well as practical ones. This included strategic developments such as greater control over resources, including the taming of animals and tending of plants, development of contacts with farming and urban societies, and engagement in inter-regional 'world' trading systems, characterised by core-periphery relations. As a social tradition, the Mesolithic changed through such developments in terms of technological and economic innovations, and, to a lesser extent, in terms of social organisation; but it has maintained broadly the same cognitive and cosmological structures. The recent hunter-gatherer societies in Siberia and north-east Europe represent the modern outcomes of such developments within this broad social tradition.

Keywords: Mesolithic, Postglacial hunter-gatherers, Eurasia, social tradition.

Introduction

Linking the Mesolithic to the 21st century may seem a very odd thing indeed. On reflection, they do share one common quality – they both are social constructs, produced by our own modern society. Why should the 21st century be a concept in the first place? Twenty-first century of what? Indeed, other societies would call the present 58th century, or 15th century. This seems to illustrate rather neatly the arbitrary and artificial nature of our western temporal boundaries, and how socially and historically embedded the 21st century is in the western social tradition. This is where the Mesolithic and the 21st century share another quality: they are, as I shall argue, both social and historical traditions.

Yet both the Mesolithic and the 21st century remain conceptual shorthand for a whole range of ideas and thoughts that help us to situate ourselves in our modern world. At the same time, our notions about the Mesolithic, and our interpretation of it have been conditioned first by the 19th, and then by the 20th centuries. On the cusp of the 21st century, there seems to be a general move towards reflexivity in Mesolithic research (i.e. Woodman, this volume; Woodman and Milner 2005), which can help in our understanding of the Postglacial hunter-gatherer society in Europe and set the framework for research in the Mesolithic in the future.

The current debate about the nature of the Mesolithic ranges from those who regard it as a meaningless concept, which should be abandoned, to comprehension of it as a cultural adaptation to Postglacial environment, in a

Darwinian evolutionary sense. I think it is neither. Rather, I will argue that the Mesolithic is a social tradition, contingent upon the preceding cultures of the late Upper Palaeolithic, and situated historically from the end of the last glaciation within the Postglacial period.

In this sense, the Mesolithic is not a cultural evolutionary concept or a society that is merely adaptively responsive to environmental conditions. The Mesolithic represents an historical process involving hunter-gatherer communities in clearly defined space and time. Its historical condition is defined by a shared knowledge and a cognitive world.

The Mesolithic as a concept

In 1865 Sir John Lubbock defined the Palaeolithic and the Neolithic in order to distinguish the Old Stone Age and the New Stone Age. The Palaeolithic was when 'man shared the possession of Europe with the Mammoth … and other extinct animals' and stone tools were crude, flakes and unpolished. The Neolithic, on the other hand, was when man lived at least partly by cultivation and animal husbandry and was technologically advanced, using polished stone tools and pottery (Lubbock 1865, 2–3, 234–5, 247–8, 445; see also Daniel 1943; 1975; Clark 1980; Rowley-Conwy 1996).

The Mesolithic experienced a somewhat different evolution. It was Westropp who suggested the use of the term for the first time one year after the publication of *Prehistoric Times* in which Lubbock (1865) set out the definitions above. Westropp's (1866, 289) definition of the Mesolithic related to flint implements found in Ireland, England and Denmark, left by people who hunted – a period between the Palaeolithic and the polished stone using people of the Kainolithic. He retained this definition in a later volume *Pre-historic phases* (Westropp 1872) and sets his Mesolithic stage firmly within the social evolutionary paradigm (1872, figure 1).

Unlike the Palaeolithic and the Neolithic, however, the subsequent historiography of the Mesolithic was very uneven in terms of its terminological clarity and cultural significance. Rowley-Conwy (1996) argues that Westropp himself was very unclear about the meaning of the Mesolithic and that his definition could be read to include Upper and even Middle Palaeolithic remains as falling within the Mesolithic. This in turn allowed John Evans, a 'central figure in the archaeology of the day' to ignore Westropp's Mesolithic altogether in his seminal publication (1872), thereby 'casting "Mesolithic" into oblivion for a generation' (Rowley-Conwy 1996, 940).

There may be more profound reasons, however, for the non-acceptance of the Mesolithic as a period equal in status to those of the Palaeolithic and Neolithic. After all, neither Evans, Lubbock, nor other scholars were entirely consistent in the use and application of their terminology (see for example Rowley-Conwy 1996 for Lubbock and Evans; Daniel 1967 for Britain and France more broadly; Fischer and Kristiansen 2002 for Denmark). The reasons for the reluctance to accept the Mesolithic as a social 'epoch' equal to the Palaeolithic and Neolithic lay in its nonconformity with the prevailing social evolutionary views (Clark 1980). Westropp's definition was no more internally inconsistent than definitions by others; but, crucially, it was inconsistent with the notions of technological progress and social evolution. Until the more recent excavation of wetland sites both in western and eastern Europe (Clark 1954; Coles, B. 1992; Coles, J. and Lawson 1987) the Mesolithic was regarded as a period of decline, not of progress, whose diminutive stone tools – microliths – neatly symbolised the irrelevance of the period (Clark 1978, 3). As Evans put it, as recently as 1975:

> 'There is nothing of the brilliance of the upper Palaeolithic hunters living as they were in the stimulating landscape of the Ice Age, nor anything of the vital urgency with which later farming communities were to settle and cultivate the landscape of western Europe and the British Isles' (Evans 1975, 90).

When the Mesolithic was reintroduced, it emerged as a chronological period, not a social epoch; as an alternative to nothing – a hiatus which was thought to exist between the Palaeolithic and Neolithic (de Mortlillet 1883, 478–84; see Clark 1978, 2; 1980, 2–3). As such, it was introduced by Brown in 1893, to denote flint assemblages intermediate between the Palaeolithic and Neolithic, but it did not gain a measure of acceptance until the 1930s. During this period, the use of the concept remained, in fact, fairly consistent with the strictly chronological significance of the term (contra Milner and Woodman 2005, 2). While some scholars did not use the term at all, preferring to adhere either to the hiatus theory, or to the division of the Stone Age into the Palaeolithic and Neolithic (Dawkins 1894; 1894; Dechelette 1908; Childe 1927; 1935; Lyell 1873; de Mortillet 1883; Sarauw 1903), others recognised the need for a distinct chronological phase to bridge the gap between the Palaeolithic and Neolithic (Burkitt 1925; 1929; Macalister 1921; Obermaier 1924; Piette 1895; Westerby 1927), even though some of them rejected the term later because it could not show a progressive transformation (i.e. Obermaier quoted in Clark 1980, 4; for further discussion, see Clark 1978, 2–9; 1980, 1–7; Fischer and Kristiansen 2002; Milner and Woodman 2005). Such chronological understanding of the Mesolithic remained typical of the use of the term from the 1880s until the 1940s. This is implicit in the careful definition of the Mesolithic by Grahame Clark in 1932 as: 'A term of chronological significance denoting cultures that flourished between the Palaeolithic and Neolithic in point of time' (Clark 1932, xiv) and similarly in 1936:

> 'In employing this term, nothing more is implied than that the Mesolithic flourished in the main between the Palaeolithic and Neolithic civilisations in point of time; it may be emphasised that it is not intended to suggest an evolutionary stage between the two.' (1936, xiv)

Similarly, when Childe finally recognised the existence of the Mesolithic period in the second edition of *Dawn of*

European Civilisation (1947), he felt obliged to emphasise the chronological rather than socio-economic content of the period. Mesolithic assemblages were termed as such 'because in time – but only in time – they occupy a place between the latest Palaeolithic and the oldest Neolithic culture'. Later, however, Childe returned to his earlier position of dismissing the Mesolithic altogether – 'it has seemed needless in this book to complicate the picture with a Mesolithic' – he writes in the third edition of *Man Makes Himself* (1951, 44).

With the volume of research increasing, the spatio-temporal characteristics which were used to define the Mesolithic as a separate period began to dissipate. The older chronological boundary denoting the transition from Late Glacial to Postglacial conditions has emerged as a prolonged period of fluctuating climatic oscillations, lasting some 4000 years (Gamble *et al.* 2005). Coevally, the change from the Upper Palaeolithic to the Mesolithic was recognised as more gradual. Indeed it would be impossible in my view to comprehend Mesolithic societies without considering their response to the process of deglaciation (see below).

At the more recent end of the period, markers normally associated with the Neolithic have been identified among Mesolithic hunter-gatherers across a number of regions, such as polished stone tools, ceramics, cultural complexity, residential permanence, and some forms of management and taming of biologically undomesticated resources (Jordan and Zvelebil, in press; Zvelebil 1986c; 1996a; Zvelebil *et al.* 1998 and refs). More significantly, it is now recognised that hunter-gatherer communities did not come to a sudden end at the introduction of the Neolithic. In some regions co-existence with their farming neighbours lasted centuries, or even millennia, interacting in frontier and exchange zones (Zvelebil 1985; 1992; 1996b; Zvelebil *et al.* 1998), raising questions about the chronological meaning of the Mesolithic and about the transformation of the Mesolithic societies into commercially-oriented hunter-gatherers living within the context of core-periphery relations of a world system.

The spatial extent of the Mesolithic has been extended too. According to some authors, the geographical remit of the Mesolithic covers the whole of Europe and northern Asia, including the Near East (Clark 1980), China, and potentially the Jomon tradition in Japan (see Habu 2004 for further discussion).

A major element in the debate concerning the nature of the Mesolithic was the degree of cultural complexity developed by the early Postglacial hunter-gatherers. This debate mirrored developments in cultural anthropology from the mid 1960s, challenging the myth of the primitive isolate and the notion of the 'original affluent society'. Similar developments occurred in archaeology. Some workers have attempted to re-interpret the Mesolithic hunter-gatherers as more sedentary, socio-economically complex societies (Larsson 1990; Madsen 1986; Nygaard 1989; Price 1985; Rowley-Conwy 1983; Rowley-Conwy and Zvelebil 1989; Tringham 1971; Zvelebil 1986b; 1992; Zvelebil and Dolukhanov 1991), particularly within the coastal and lacustrine zones of temperate Europe. Although this reconstruction has been to some degree successful, it has generated further debate as to what is meant by complexity (Gebauer and Price 1991; Price and Brown 1985; Warren 2005; Zvelebil 1998), and a consequent reaction against seeing Mesolithic societies as normatively complex, the whole idea being too compromised by the social evolutionary paradigm (Rowley-Conwy 1999; 2001; 2004; Warren 2005). As a result, the attempts to re-define the Mesolithic as a period with social and economic content of its own, and, as a form of society broadly encompassing prehistoric hunter-gatherers with a degree of social and economic complexity, has not found a consensus (Binford 1968; Dolukhanov 1979; Kozłowski and Kozłowski 1978; 1986; Mellars 1981; Milner and Woodman 2005; Newell 1984; Price and Brown 1985; Price and Gebauer 1991; Warren 2005; Zvelebil 1986a; Zvelebil 1986b; Zvelebil and Dolukhanov 1991).

In the process, a large amount of variability became apparent among early Postglacial societies of temperate and northern parts of Eurasia, and only some of it corresponded to the view of the Mesolithic as a cultural adaptation of hunter-gatherers to the Postglacial conditions. Some Mesolithic societies were more 'Palaeolithic' in character; others exhibited 'Neolithic' features, such as polished stone tools, ceramics, or signs of domestication.

Pigeon-holing such variability proved a challenging exercise, generating a range of views. In the current situation, we can recognise four different approaches to the problem. There are those who consider the Mesolithic a redundant and misleading term, standing in the way of real innovation in the study of prehistoric hunter-gatherers in the 21st century (i.e. Dennell 1983; Gamble 1986; Gamble *et al.* 2005; see also Milner and Woodman 2005). There are those who recognize the variability in the cultural content of the Mesolithic but – perhaps for that reason – would prefer to maintain the strictly chronological definition of the concept (i.e. Kozłowski 2003; Mellars 1981). Many scholars regard the Mesolithic foremost as a process of cultural adaptation by hunter-gatherers to the new Postglacial conditions of the Holocene (e.g. Binford 1968; Clark 1962; Newell 1984). Then there are those who have been attempting to endow the Mesolithic with an historical, socio-cultural meaning (i.e. Zvelebil 1986b, 6–7).

The current state of research into the Mesolithic

There is no doubt that within the last 50 years, theoretical approaches to interpreting archaeological evidence underwent significant development. However, many European institutions continued to practise the old paradigm of culture history, predicated on the normative concept of culture that saw archaeological cultures as signatures of ethnic groups or peoples in the past – and indeed this continues today.

In Anglo-American archaeology new approaches that drew on earlier culture-evolutionary and environmental perspectives in anthropology and archaeology developed in the mid-20th century. In the United States, these perspectives fused into a culture-ecological approach in anthropology and into 'New' or processual archaeology (Binford 1962; 1968; Bettinger 1991; Schiffer 1976; Steward 1955; White 1959). Cultures were seen as adaptive responses by human communities to challenges posed by their environment (Binford 1962; White 1959). The notion of culture was seen as a system composed of several subsystems and subject to rational, systemic rules of operation.

Archaeological cultures were regarded as the end products of formation processes that included natural changes and cultural signatures of human behaviour. The notion of 'middle range theory' – a set of theoretical propositions linking the archaeological record and human behaviour in order to explain it in terms of specific human activities – was particularly applied to the Mesolithic. New or processual archaeology was therefore adaptive and evolutionary, systemic and rationalizing, behavioural and generalising in terms of human behaviour patterns.

British New Archaeology integrated environmentalist, ecological and bioarchaeological research promoted by Grahame Clark and Eric Higgs on the one hand (Clark 1972; Clarke 1979, etc.), and clearly social perspectives (for later prehistory) by David Clarke and Colin Renfrew on the other (Clarke 1968; 1972; Hodder 1978; Renfrew and Cherry 1986, etc.). This resulted in New Archaeology encompassing several traditions of research, focussed on methodology and site-formation processes, palaeoeconomy and land use, social organisation and development of social ranking.

The palaeoeconomy school, which emerged at Cambridge under the supervision of Eric Higgs, had a particular contribution to make to Mesolithic studies. This field of study included the investigation of relationships between humans, plants and animals which led to environmental management, taming and domestication; the emergence of notions of long-term resource management amongst hunter-gatherers; advances in the understanding of hunter-gatherer patterns of landscape enculturation and resource domestication; development of notions of territoriality among hunter-gatherers, which were investigated through studies of land-use patterns, the applications of catchment analyses, site/territory concepts and off-site archaeological surveys (Barker 1985; Higgs 1972; 1975; Vita Finzi and Higgs 1970; Zvelebil 1981). However, the palaeoeconomic approach did not consider notions of social, cognitive and cosmological lifeways of hunter-gatherers, and excessively emphasised subsistence strategies as central to human decision making.

In Europe, the reaction to New Archaeology ranged from reflexive hostility to active promotion. In Scandinavia the methodologically sophisticated studies of material culture meant that the normative concept of culture was never fully accepted and so the systemic and processual approach could be readily adopted (i.e. Kristiansen and Paludan-Müller 1978; Malmer 1962; Paludan-Müller 1978; Welinder 1975; 1981; 1989; 1998, etc.).

There can be no doubt that processual archaeology allowed significant advances to be made in the comprehension of archaeological cultures and the methodology of their treatment, but criticism began to emerge within the broader philosophical tenet of post-modernism and post-structuralism in the 1980s (compare, for example, Hodder 1978 and Hodder 1982). The promise of scientifically rigorous, testable conclusions about patterns of past human behaviour, made by processual archaeologists, failed to materialise; also critics found that the approach focussed on subsistence, technology and the environment at the expense of social life, cognition and cosmology. There was too much concern with behaviour rather than the motivation for human activity, and often the conclusions reached were far too general to be of real significance in terms of understanding the human condition in the past.

In post-modern archaeology, the uniting principles are focussed on the investigation of past social life in terms of cognition, worldview or cosmology and social agency – the interpretation of the past as a process of constitution and reconstitution of the past that links the people studied and ourselves (the double hermeneutic). The perception of material culture is that it is meaningfully constituted through social action and human agency, not a by-product of incidental discard or taphonomic processes. Social action is considered meaningful and pattern generating at an individual, rather than population level, with due consideration given to action and identities of individuals, to social strategies and expressions of identity of social groups (notions of personhood, routine practice, and of social agency) (see Hodder 1992; 2001; Thomas 1996; Tilley 1993).

After half a century of processual, and a quarter of a century of post-processual archaeology, archaeological cultures have ended up a far cry from the simple notion of representing peoples or ethnic groups. Theoretical developments summarised above considerably increased the complexity embedded in the archaeological record. With a degree of nostalgia, it could be said that we know much more now about the complexity and multiple meanings of the archaeological record, but much less about the human past itself. In the multi-vocality of approaches to the interpretation of the Mesolithic archaeological record, the development of Mesolithic studies reflected faithfully these more general developments in archaeology.

Mesolithic cultures as environmental adaptations

While Grahame Clark was clearly aware of the importance of social and symbolic dimensions in the constitution of Mesolithic society (Clark 1957, 175–7; 1972, 16; 1976, 4–5; 1982), and while he promoted an historically particular, rather than social evolutionary, approach to comprehension of human prehistory (Clark 1979, 1–5; 1980, 1–7; 1982, 48–62), he felt unable to characterise the Mesolithic in these terms for the lack of evidence, or to develop these themes in any great detail (i.e. Clark 1976, 5, 8, 11). Despite his interests in society and 'social and psychic needs' (i.e. Clark 1976, 70–85, 146–159, 197–200), he framed his understanding of culture change mainly in terms of economic and technological adaptations to environmental changes (Clark 1939; 1957, 174–8; 1972; 1976, 5, 8, 11).

This concentration on the functional, ecological and economic in studying the Mesolithic was partly historical. In Scandinavia, with the ready availability of organic evidence, coupled with the environmental focus of leading archaeologists from the mid-19th century almost to the present day (Fischer and Kristiansen 2002; Welinder 1975; 1989; 1998), meant that in functional terms studies of the Mesolithic were most advanced there. The study of the Mesolithic in Scandinavian archaeology influenced Britain and the Netherlands – with typology first, and then with an ecological and economic focus (Clark 1972) – while in the rest of western Europe the emphasis remained on typology and technology, reflecting the prevalence of lithics as the source of information (e.g. Rozoy 1978; Thévenin 1995, etc.). In eastern Europe, Marxist dogma – which emphasized material culture and the production of goods as benchmarks of social development – predetermined the social evolutionary focus of Mesolithic studies (the 'predatory' economy of hunter-gatherers encoded within 'original communal society' and 'primitive communism'; i.e. Gurina 1956).

Mesolithic cultures as self-aware ethnicities and the normative concept of culture

In relation to the Mesolithic, there were two other perceptions that continued to be applied, along with the culture-ecological approach. These unrelated perceptions were: the notion of hunter-gatherers as alien to our own western civilisation, and the normative concept of culture.

There was a deliberate move to invent hunter-gatherers as 'alien other', to act in categorical opposition to western civilisation. This view can be seen as something of an exaggeration, but hunter-gatherers collectively represented a continuation of the philosophical position that generated social evolutionism and earlier evolutionary perspectives. Hunter-gatherers were condemned to a fundamental binary opposition to farming societies, which, by default, represented western civilisation. The paradigmatic prejudice encapsulated in such 'agricultural thinking' (Gamble 1992; Gamble *et al.* 2005, 193, 210; Pluciennik 1998; 2002; 2004) was predicated on the perception of 'farmers as our ancestors' (Zvelebil 1996c), and generated its own research orientation and selective treatment of the evidence.

The consequences for the interrogation of the Mesolithic archaeological record were:

1. Mesolithic communities in Europe were not regarded as culturally or genetically ancestral to modern European populations and therefore they contributed little or nothing to the development of western European civilisation. As a result they were of little interest in the study of the historical record of nation states in Europe.
2. Within this nationalist perspective, and within the general confusion as to what represents the Mesolithic culturally, a major rift grew in the original concepts of the 'Mesolithic' and the 'Neolithic' – hunter-gatherers were pitted against Neolithic farming societies as two typological extremes (Zvelebil 1986c; 1996c).

The normative concept of culture was imported into Mesolithic studies from later prehistory (Childe 1925; 1929). The principle behind this approach was the belief that archaeological artefacts, by their shape and decoration, symbolise ethnic identity, and that the distribution of key artefacts identifies ethnic groups in prehistory. As a result, cultural homogeneity becomes a signature of an ethnic group; differences in material culture can be explained in terms of ethnic variation; and the replacement of one set of cultural features by another identifies migration and population replacement.

Accordingly, interpretation of the Mesolithic archaeological record focussed upon:

1. An excessive concentration on typological studies of lithic materials, with attributes seen as indicators of ethnicity.
2. Descriptive preoccupation with variations in material-culture attributes, because a covariance of attributes indicated ethnicity.
3. Characterisation of material-culture traditions, in terms of ethnic units such as the 'Beuronians', 'Maglemosians', 'Sauvetterians' and so on, resulting in a disregard for the agency and actions of individuals and smaller social groups, whose identities might have been specified by gender, age, blood ties or status.
4. The premise that replacement of one cultural tradition by another can be best explained by population movement – by one ethnic group replacing another. The result was that genetic, cultural and linguistic patterning was collapsed into a single demographic unit: an ethnically self-aware group of people.

The normative concept of culture has been discredited through processual critique (Binford 1962; 1983; Clarke 1968; 1972; Hodder 1978) and post-modernist deconstruction (e.g. Barrett 1994; Hodder 1982; 1992; etc.). Culture is represented as a social tradition in a constant state of change, and material culture is perceived as an active agent, employed by 'knowledgeable human actors' in reproducing culture as a social tradition. Material culture represents a residue of human activities and post-depositional processes – an end product of a complex taphonomic history. Artefacts do not reveal the past as it was, but are 'meaningfully constituted' by a double process of interpretation – the double hermeneutic. The first is through the agency of human actors in antiquity within the context of ideologies of the past, and the second results from the ideological codes and knowledge of contemporary investigators, including those in the 21st century.

Biosocial Mesolithic: people not cultures

Rather than the investigation of material culture alone, research into human biological remains and associated artefacts has much to offer Mesolithic studies. This approach arose in response to the increase in mortuary evidence from the Mesolithic and from the combination of biosocial investigations involving human biological sciences and the humanities (cultural anthropology and archaeology).

Although some Mesolithic cemeteries were discovered by the mid-20th century, for example Hoëdic and Téviec in Brittany (Péquart and Péquart 1954), or Olenii Ostrov in Russia (Gurina 1956), it was only with more recent discoveries in southern Scandinavia and eastern Europe (Brinch Petersen 1989; Larsson 1982; 1989; Srejovic 1969; 1971; Telegin 1987; Zagorskis 1987) that an extensive record of mortuary evidence emerged that allowed for the development of an integrated field of research into human mortuary remains and their grave goods.

The original objectives of this research were to investigate human skeletal remains for indications of Mesolithic population structure, demography, pathologies and physical appearance (Bennike 1982; Bennike and Alexandersen 2002; Larsson *et al.* 2003; Meiklejohn and Zvelebil 1991; Newell and Constandse-Westerman 1988), and assess social differentiation in Mesolithic communities through the analysis of mortuary variation. Subsequently, more post-modern concerns with ritual, cosmology, and manipulation of symbols were added to these goals on one hand (Stutz 2003), while, on the other, advances in biomolecular (bone chemistry and genetic) of prehistoric human remains began to provide information about genetic ancestry, partner exchange patterns, human mobility, as well as diet and health at an individual, household and community level (Bentley *et al.* 2002; 2003; Haak *et al.* 2005).

In the process, we have witnessed two important developments. First, a wide variety of methodological approaches, from human molecular biology (ancient DNA studies, bone chemical analyses, trace elemental analyses), physical anthropology (gross morphological traits analyses, palaeopathology, palaeodemographic analyses) and archaeology (normative mortuary variability analyses, more contextual structural and symbolic analyses, ^{14}C dating) were brought to bear upon the mortuary record, resulting in a genuinely inter-disciplinary research programme with a powerful analytical potential. Second, a new integrated theoretical approach has began to emerge, focussed on major issues of modern prehistory: human cognition and cosmology, interdependence of human biological condition and material culture, community ecology, patterns of health and disease, culture change, and genetic and cultural inheritance.

The full potential of this approach has yet to be evaluated. Unlike culture-history, and because of its methodological applications, the biosocial or bioarchaeological approach is capable of focussing on the individual as the basic unit of analysis, and on individual life histories, or life biographies, as the basic unit of reconstruction. Perhaps it will now be possible for group identity, lifestyle and community ecology to be rigorously examined through the analytical methods of biosocial archaeology. However, two major problems remain: the paucity and uneven distribution of mortuary remains in the archaeological record of the Mesolithic, and an increasing reticence by some to allow analytical examination, because of issues relating to reburial and religion.

The emotional Mesolithic: post-modern approaches

In the mistaken belief that this had never been considered before (see Milner and Woodman 2005), researchers in the 21st century began to focus more on social relations, cosmology and cognition in Mesolithic communities. Earlier studies inspired by social relations, and by cognitive concerns that would fall squarely within the remit of post-processual archaeology today, were carried out, both in continental and British Mesolithic archaeology, although not as a part of a concentrated programme (i.e. Fischer and Kristiansen 2002; Gurina 1956; Newell and Constandse-Westermann 1988; O'Shea and Zvelebil 1984; Zvelebil 1993; 1997; Young 2000, etc.). The post-processual approaches provided a more focussed initiative. Generally within a post-processual, post-modern perspective (Milner and Woodman 2005 for a review of socially-oriented research; Bevan and Moore 2003 in broader terms), these approaches can be grouped into two frameworks: deconstruction and reinterpretation.

Deconstruction aims to assess critically existing research concepts and interpretations in Mesolithic archaeology, by situating them within their own historical and philosophical research frameworks, and thereby exposing paradigmatic prejudices and political agendas, which compromise any claims to objectivity (e.g. Borić 2005; Janik 2005; Pugsley 2005; Strassbourg 2003; Warren 2005). While situating research within its historical and philosophical context is a valuable exercise, much in need of a broader application within Mesolithic studies, investigations that focussed on deconstruction often resulted in the rejection of concepts that, however flawed, were never replaced by anything of operational value (e.g. Borić 2005; Warren 2005; etc.).

Deconstructing the deconstructionists reveals other shortcomings: case studies and interpretations produced by post-modern scholars tend to be equally, if not more, flawed by dogmatic application of theoretical frameworks inappropriate for prehistoric situations and by the lack of objective assessment. The recourse to 'multivocality' used by some to get around this problem does not advance our understanding of the Mesolithic because it does not discriminate between the relative likelihood of interpretations being correct in relation to the target object of study in the Mesolithic. In the worst cases, such approach degenerates into ritual incantations of the post-modern cannon (where there is only good and evil: processual 'meta-narratives' are invariably essentialist, overly mechanistic, uniform and dichotomizing, totalizing, orientalist, teleogical and social evolutionary; whereas post-modern approaches always celebrate the complex and nuanced, fuzzy and fluid, contextualising, socially and historically embedded, multivocal bricolage of relations, permanently in a state of 'promiscuous fluidity'). It exposes the arrogance of some post-modern practitioners in advancing their studies as solely valid approaches while failing to acknowledge their own paradigmatic prejudices on the one hand, and the nihilism of those claiming that all 'confrontations with the data' are equally valid on the other.

Yet critical treatment with reconstruction and/or interpretation of evidence can offer valuable insights into Mesolithic life which processual archaeologists feel too constrained to examine. Reinterpreting specific case studies, problems or issues can have more general validity and implications, or they can result in concrete conclusions achieved through balanced evaluation (e.g. Bevan 2003; Chatterton 2003; Conneller 2003; 2005; Fewster 2001; 2005; Finlay 1997; 2003; Milner 2005; Murray 2000; Simpson 2003; Warren 2000; Young 2000).

Landscape archaeology and the Mesolithic

Landscape archaeology is a methodological approach defined by spatial scale. In the Mesolithic, landscape archaeology has been applied with different frameworks and objectives. Perhaps because of its broad cross-paradigmatic application, the landscape-oriented approach has been very productive in Mesolithic archaeology. Landscape surveys have established the widespread presence of Mesolithic activities across large parts of Europe that were previously thought to be depopulated. Landscape archaeology has complemented earlier anthropologically informed and spatially referenced approaches, and through such approaches the structure of Mesolithic landscapes could be established, developing practical and ritual aspects of human existence in the Mesolithic (e.g. Bevan and Moore 2003; Rossignol and Wandsneider 1992; Young 2000; Zvelebil 2003a; Zvelebil 2003b; Zvelebil and Jordan 1999; Zvelebil and Moore 2006).

Prehistoric hunter-gatherers in Europe: humanist, historical and anthropological approaches

The trends outlined above cover the existing research orientations in Mesolithic archaeology, among which emphasis on the cultural adaptation and techno-economic orientations remain prevalent within Europe as a whole. Landscape archaeology is gaining ground in Britain, Ireland, Netherlands and central and northern Europe, while post-modern approaches remain confined to the British Isles and Scandinavia, leaving other areas almost unaffected (see e.g. González Morales and Fano Martínez 2005 for a review of Spain; or Vencl 1992 for a review of Mesolithic archaeology in the Czech Republic).

The dominant philosophical and political discourses of the 20th century have clearly influenced, not to say prejudiced, the evaluation of Mesolithic hunter-gatherer communities and their lifeways. Just as the anthropology of hunter-gatherer societies in general, Mesolithic studies have been affected by:

(1) the normative perception of hunter-gatherers as culturally simple and egalitarian people without history;
(2) the perception of hunter-gatherers as alien to western civilisation whose roots were in the farming past, and by
(3) the ecological-adaptive imperative: as societies deprived of social agency and the capacity to change their own conditions of existence, merely reacting to changes in the environment rather than creating their own social conditions of existence: their own communal ecology.

As archaeological research practice, Mesolithic studies suffered from an additional handicap: the adherence to the normative concept of culture.

To advance research in the 21st century into Postglacial – Mesolithic – hunter-gatherers as a spatial and temporal phenomenon, we need to adopt an explicitly humanist, historical and anthropological approach, which is, at the same time, methodologically rigorous and open to rational scrutiny and scientific evaluation. Such an approach can provide an overarching framework of interpretation that can draw on existing stocks of knowledge about the Mesolithic from the disparate sources now in operation: culture-ecology and culture-history, landscape-oriented studies, human biological and biosocial investigations, and post-modern narratives. The organizing principle of this framework is a recognition that has often, sadly, been lacking – the recognition of the historicity of the Mesolithic as a collective of communities sharing broad social traditions and material culture, changing through time within structural conditions defined by their temporal situation within the course of human history. In summary, then, Mesolithic communities are, above all, products of their own history.

Such an historically-oriented paradigm is based on several key propositions:

1. The Mesolithic represents an historical process and a social tradition involving hunter-gatherer communities, clearly defined in space and time.
2. Its historical condition is defined by a shared knowledge and cognitive world.
3. Its historical condition is defined by shared practical knowledge and material culture.
4. This social tradition was predicated on shared knowledge of the world that was maintained through contact and information exchange, and evidenced through traded items.
5. New technologies of the Mesolithic have their roots in the Upper Palaeolithic, but were developed in the historical conditions of the early Postglacial period.
6. Shifts in cognition and cosmology occurred at the end of the Upper Palaeolithic and this is evident in

a shift to abstraction in symbolism, in redefinition of human/animal relationships, and in the development of the role of ritual specialists (sometimes referred to as shamanism).

7. Two temporal processes characterise Mesolithic conditions of existence. One was *deglaciation* and the reaction of hunter-gatherer communities to this process. The Mesolithic was developing in the structural conditions of deglaciation through prosecution of human agency, marked by population shifts from the south to the north within Europe, the colonisation of northern Europe, and regional resettlement.
8. The second process was *enculturation*, whereby hunter-gatherers manipulated their environment for symbolic and cognitive purposes as well as practical ones. This included greater control over resources including the taming of animals and tending of plants.
9. As a social tradition, the Mesolithic came to an end with lifestyle-changing transformations brought about by the establishment of agro-pastoral farming as the principal means of livelihood.
10. Mesolithic communities abandoned the Mesolithic as a social tradition with the rejection of symbolism marked by abstraction and reference to the animal world, reflecting a specific cosmology or worldview *ancestral* to the modern cosmologies of hunter-gatherer communities in northern Eurasia. Economic changes and cognitive transformation are not necessarily coeval, especially where the gradual transition to farming economy is concerned.

The above characterisation of the Mesolithic in calendar time and as a social tradition is admittedly very broad, and it does appear to include the more recent hunter-gatherers of later prehistory (Metal Ages technologically) and the medieval period. In the case of modern hunter-gatherers, the Mesolithic would come to an end only with the introduction of other belief systems – most clearly Christianity – into the community. Admittedly, this does call into question the use of the Mesolithic as an appropriate term, and other nominations might be more appropriate. In terms of coherence of the approach adopted here, however, such a definition does make sense. The historicity of this approach is not based upon the notion of the Mesolithic as a social-evolutionary concept, or a technological phenomenon (since stone technology was merely one, and perhaps not the most important, among the technologies used), nor as a specific process of cultural adaptation. It is predicated on the notion of a shared social tradition, reproduced and transformed from generation to generation, but nevertheless maintaining specific structural principles as a frame of reference for negotiating conditions of human existence. As such a phenomenon, the Mesolithic is comparable to classical Antiquity or to the Medieval period. As with these examples, the beginnings and ends of all such phenomena are ambiguous and gradual.

Such a description of Mesolithic hunter-gatherers is likely to provoke reaction to the effect that it is unacceptably uniform, normative, and 'totalizing' (e.g. Borić 2005; Warren 2005). Emphatically, this is not the case. Rather, the approach adopted here foregrounds the historical contingency of human existence, and emphasises the humanist approach to our past. In common with other humanist approaches, the challenge becomes one of methodological application: how best to analyse and interpret small-scale changes within a community, and a Mesolithic society more generally, unfolding at an individual or collective level and involving small groups. The analytical approach that would utilize and combine the notions of social agency, routine practice, socially embedded innovation, cross-regional transmission of knowledge and inter-generational passage of traditions can be applied to the Mesolithic at the appropriate spatial and organisational scales, and elucidate real conditions of existence of Mesolithic communities, as well as the broader nature of the Mesolithic as a social tradition.

References

Barker, G. 1985. *Prehistoric Farming in Europe*. Cambridge, Cambridge University Press.

Barrett, J. 1994. *Fragments from Antiquity*. Oxford, Blackwell.

Bennike, P. 1985. *Palaeopathology of Danish skeletons. A Comparative Study of Demography, Disease and Injury*. Kobenhavn, Akademisk Forlag.

Bennike, P. and Alexandersen, V. 2002. Population Plasticity in Stone Age Denmark, in A. Fischer and K. Kristiansen (eds.), *The Neolithisation of Denmark. 150 years of debate*, 289–301. Sheffield, J. R. Collis Publications.

Bentley, R. A., Price, T. D., Lüning, J., Gronenborn, D., Wahl, J. and Fullgar, P. D. 2002. Prehistoric migration in Europe: Strontium isotope analysis of early Neolithic skeletons. *Current Anthropology* 43, 799–804.

Bentley, R. A., Chikhli, L. and Price, T. D. 2003. The Neolithic transition in Europe: comparing broad scale genetic and local scale isotopic evidence. *Antiquity* 77 (295), 63–6.

Bettinger, R. 1991. *Hunter-gatherers: Archaeological and evolutionary theory*. New York, Plenum.

Bevan, L. 2003. Stag nights and horny men: antler symbolism and interaction with the animal world during the Mesolithic, in L. Bevan and J. Moore (eds.), *Peopling the Mesolithic in a Northern Environment*, 35–44. British Archaeological Reports, International Series S1157. Oxford, Archaeopress.

Bevan, L. and Moore, J. (eds.) 2003. *Peopling the Mesolithic in a Northern Environment*. British Archaeological Reports, International Series S1157. Oxford, Archaeopress.

Binford, L. R. 1962 (1972). Archaeology as anthropology. *American Antiquity* 28, 217–25. (Reprinted in Binford, L. R. 1972. *An Archaeological Perspective*, 20–32. New York, Seminar Press).

Binford, L. R. 1968. Post-Pleistocene adaptations, in S. Binford and L. R. Binford (eds.), *New Perspectives in Archaeology*, 313–41. Chicago, Aldine.

Binford, L. R. 1983. *In Pursuit of the Past. Decoding the Archaeological Record*. London, Thames and Hudson.

Borić, D. 2005. Fuzzy horizons of change: Orientalism and the frontier model of the Meso-Neolithic transition, in N. Milner and P. Woodman (eds.), *Mesolithic Studies at the beginning of the 21st century*, 81–105. Oxford, Oxbow Books.

Brinch Petersen, E. 1989. Vænget Nord: excavation, documentation and interpretation of a Mesolithic site at Vedbæk,

Denmark, in C. Bonsall (ed.), *The Mesolithic in Europe: Papers Presented at the Third International Symposium*, 325–330. Edinburgh, John Donald Publishers.

Brown, A. J. 1893. On the continuity of the Neolithic and Palaeolithic periods. *Journal of the Royal Anthropological Institute* XXII, 66–98.

Burkitt, M. C. 1925. The transition between Palaeolithic and Neolithic times. *Proceedings of the Prehistoric Society of East Anglia* 5, 16–33.

Burkitt, M. C. 1929. *Our Early Ancestors: An Introductory Study of Mesolithic, Neolithic and Copper Age Cultures in Europe and Adjacent Regions*. Cambridge, Cambridge University Press.

Chatterton, R. 2003. Star Carr reanalysed, in L. Bevan and J. Moore (eds.), *Peopling the Mesolithic in a Northern Environment*, 69–80. British Archaeological Reports, International Series S1157. Oxford, Archaeopress.

Childe, V. G. 1925. *The Dawn of European Civilisation*. London, Kegan Paul.

Childe, V. G. 1929. *Danube in Prehistory*. Oxford, Clarendon Press.

Childe, V. G. 1935. *The Prehistory of Scotland*. London, Kegan Paul.

Childe, V. G. 1947 (4th edition). *The Dawn of European Civilisation*. London, Kegan Paul.

Childe, V. G. 1951. *Man Makes Himself*. London, C. A. Watts.

Clark, J. G. D. 1936 (1970). *The Mesolithic Settlement of Northern Europe: a Study of the Food Gathering Peoples of Northern Europe during the Early Post-Glacial Period*. Cambridge, Cambridge University Press.

Clark, J. G. D. 1939. *Archaeology and Society*. Cambridge, Cambridge University Press.

Clark, J. G. D. 1954. *Excavations at Star Carr Mesolithic site at Seamer, near Scarborough, Yorkshire*. Cambridge, Cambridge University Press.

Clark, J. G. D. 1957. *Archaeology and society*. London, Methuen.

Clark, J. G. D. 1962. A survey of the Mesolithic phase, in *The Prehistory of Europe and South-west Asia*, Atti Vl Congresso Internazionale Scienze Preistoriche e Protostoriche. Rome, Relazione Generale.

Clark, J. G. D. 1972. *Star Carr: a Case Study in Bioarchaeology*. Modular Publications 10. Reading, MA, Addison-Wesley.

Clark, J. G. D. 1978. Neothermal orientations, in P. Mellars (ed.), *The Early Postglacial Settlement of Northern Europe*, 1–10. London, Duckworth.

Clark, J. G. D. 1979. Archaeology and Human Diversity. *Annual Review of Anthropology* 1979 (8), 1–20.

Clark, J. G. D. 1980. *Mesolithic Prelude*. Edinburgh, Edinburgh University Press.

Clark, J. G. D. 1982. *Identity of Man*. London, Methuen.

Clarke, D. L. 1968. *Analytical Archaeology*. London, Methuen.

Clarke, D. L. (ed.) 1972. *Models in Archaeology*. London, Methuen.

Clarke, D. L. 1979. *Analytical Archaeologist. Collected papers of David L. Clarke*. London, Academic Press.

Coles, B. (ed.) 1992. *The Wetland Revolution in Prehistory*. Exeter, University of Exeter Press.

Coles, J. M. and Lawson, A. J. (eds.) 1987. *European Wetlands in Prehistory*. Oxford, Clarendon Press.

Conneller, C. J. 2003. Star Carr recontextualised, in L. Bevan and J. Moore (eds.), *Peopling the Mesolithic in a Northern Environment*, 81–86. British Archaeological Reports, International Series S1157. Oxford, Archaeopress.

Conneller, C. J. 2005. Moving beyond sites: Mesolithic technology in the landscape, in N. Milner and P. Woodman (eds.), *Mesolithic Studies at the Beginning of the 21st Century*, 42–55. Oxford, Oxbow Books.

Daniel, G. E. 1943. *The Three Ages. An essay on archaeological methods*. Cambridge, Cambridge University Press.

Daniel, G. E. 1967. *The Origins and Growth of Archaeology*. Harmondsworth, Penguin.

Daniel, G. E. 1975. *A Hundred and Fifty Years of Archaeology*. London, Duckworth.

Dawkins, W. B. 1894. On the relation of the Palaeolithic to the Neolithic period. *Journal of the Anthropological Institute* 22, 242–54.

Dechelette, J. 1908. *Manuel d'archéologie préhistorique, celtique et gallo-romaine* (Vol. 1). Paris, Auguste Picard.

Dennell, R. 1983. *European Economic Prehistory*. London, Academic Press.

Dolukhanov, P. M. 1979. *Ecology and Economy in Neolithic Eastern Europe*. London, Duckworth.

Evans, J. C. 1975. *The Environment of Early Man in the British Isles*. London, Duckworth.

Fewster, K. J. 2001. Petso's field: ethnoarchaeology and agency, in K. J. Fewster and M. Zvelebil (eds.), *Ethnorachaeology and hunter-gatherers: pictures at an exhibition*, 81–90. British Archaeological Reports, International Series S995. Oxford, Archaeopress.

Fewster, K. J. 2005. Petso's field: ethnoarchaeology and agency, in N. Milner and P. Woodman (eds.), *Mesolithic studies at the beginning of the 21st century*, 106–25. Oxford, Oxbow Books.

Finlay, N. 1997. Kid Knapping: the missing children in lithic analysis, in J. Moore and E. Scott (eds.), *Invisible People and Processes. Writing Gender and Childhood into European Archaeology*, 203–12. Leicester, Leicester University Press.

Finlay, N. 2003. Cache and carry: defining moments in the Irish later Mesolithic, in L. Bevan and J. Moore (eds.), *Peopling the Mesolithic in a Northern Environment*, 87–94. British Archaeological Reports, International Series S1157. Oxford, Archaeopress,

Fischer, A. and Kristiansen, K. (eds.) 2002. *The Neolithisation of Denmark: 150 years of debate*. Sheffield Archaeological Monographs. Sheffield, J. R. Collis Publications.

Gamble, C. 1986. *The Palaeolithic settlement of Europe*. Cambridge, Cambridge University Press.

Gamble, C. 1992. Archaeology, history and the uttermost ends of the earth – Tasmania, Tierra del Fuego and the Cape. Special Section, *Antiquity* 66, 710–71.

Gamble, C., Davies, W., Pettitt, P., Hazelwood, L. and Richards, M. 2005. The archaeological and genetic foundations of the European population during the Late Glacial: implications for 'agricultural thinking'. *Cambridge Archaeological Journal* 15 (2), 193–223.

Gebauer, A. B. and Price, T. D. (eds.) 1991. *Transitions to Agriculture in Prehistory*. Madison, Prehistory Press.

González Morales, M. R. and Fano Martínez, M. Á. 2005. The Mesolithic of Cantabrian Spain: a critical review, in N. Milner and P. Woodman (eds.), *Mesolithic studies at the beginning of the 21st century*, 14–29. Oxford, Oxbow Books.

Gurina, N. N. 1956. *Oleneostrovski Mogilnik*. Materialy i Issledovaniya po Arkheologii SSSR 47. Moscow, Nauka.

Haak, W., Forster, P., Bramanti, B., Matsumura, S., Brandt, G., Tänzer, M., Villems, R., Renfrew, C., Gronenborn, D., Werner Alt, K. and Burger, J. 2005. Ancient DNA from the first European farmers in 7500-year-old Neolithic sites. *Science* 310, November 2005, 1016–18.

Habu, J. 2004. *Ancient Jomon of Japan*. Cambridge, Cambridge University Press.
Higgs, E. S. (ed.) 1972. *Papers in Economic Prehistory*. Cambridge, Cambridge University Press.
Higgs, E. S. (ed.) 1975. *Palaeoeconomy*. Cambridge, Cambridge University Press.
Hodder, I. (ed.) 1978. *The Spatial Organisation of Culture*. London, Duckworth.
Hodder, I. 1982. *The Present Past*. London, Batsford.
Hodder, I. 1992. *Theory and Practice in Archaeology*. London, Routledge.
Hodder, I. 2001. *Archaeological Theory Today*. Cambridge, Polity Press.
Janik, L. 2005. Redefining social relations – tradition, complementarity and internal tension, in N. Milner and P. Woodman (eds.), *Mesolithic Studies at the beginning of the 21st century*, 176–93. Oxford, Oxbow Books.
Jordan, P. and Zvelebil, M. (in press 2008). *Origins of ceramics and hunter-gatherers of northern Eurasia*. New York, John Allen.
Kozłowski, J. K. and Kozłowski, S. K. 1986. Foragers of Central Europe and their acculturation, in M. Zvelebil (ed.), *Hunters in Transition: Mesolithic Societies of Temperate Eurasia and their Transition to Farming*, 95–108. Cambridge, Cambridge University Press.
Kozłowski, S. K. 2003. The Mesolithic: What do we know and what do we believe? in L. Larsson, H. Kindgren, K. Knutsson, D. Loeffler and A. Åkerlund (eds.), *Mesolithic on the Move: Papers presented at the Sixth International Conference on the Mesolithic in Europe, Stockholm 2000*, xvii–xxi. Oxford, Oxbow Books.
Kozłowski, S. K. and Kozłowski, J. K. 1978. Le role du substrat mésolithique dans la néolithisation de la partie nord de l'Europe central. *Godišnjak – Centar za Balkanoloska Ispitivanja* 14.
Kristiansen, K. and Paludan-Müller, C. (eds.) 1978. *New Directions in Scandinavian Archaeology*. Copenhagen, Danish Museum.
Larsson, L. 1982. *Skateholmsprojektet. En utställing om ett fångstsamhälle för 7000 år sedan*. Report series no. 13. Lund, Institute of Archaeology.
Larsson, L. 1989. Late Mesolithic settlements and cemeteries at Skateholm, southern Sweden, in C. Bonsall (ed.), *The Mesolithic in Europe*, 367–78. Edinburgh, John Donald Publishers.
Larsson, L. 1990. The Mesolithic of Southern Scandinavia. *Journal of World Prehistory* 4, 257–309.
Larsson, L., Kindgren, H., Knutsson, K., Leoffler, D. and Åkerlund, A. (eds.) 2003. *Mesolithic on the move: Papers presented at the Sixth International Conference on the Mesolithic in Europe, Stockholm 2000*. Oxford, Oxbow Books.
Lubbock, J. 1865. *Pre-historic Times, as Illustrated by Ancient Remains, and the Manners and Customs of Modern Savages*. London, Williams and Norgate.
Lyell, C. 1873 (4th edition). *The geological evidences of the antiquity of man*. London, John Murray.
Macalister, R. A. S. 1921. *Textbook of European Archaeology*. Cambridge, Cambridge University Press.
Madsen, T. 1986. Where did all the hunters go? An assessment of an epoch-making episode in Danish prehistory. *Journal of Danish Archaeology* 5, 229–47.
Malmer, M. 1962. *Jungneolitische Studien*. Acta Archaeologica Lundensia, Series in 8°, 3. Lund, C. W. K. Gleerup.
Meiklejohn, C. and Zvelebil, M. 1991. Health status of European populations at the agricultural transition and the implications for the adoption of farming, in H. Bush and M. Zvelebil (eds.), *Health in Past Societies: Biocultural Interpretations of Human Skeletal Remains in Archaeological Contexts*, 129–45. British Archaeological Reports, International Series S567. Oxford, Tempvs Reparatvm.
Mellars, P. 1981. Towards a definition of the Mesolithic. *Mesolithic Miscellany* 2 (2), 13–16.
Milner, N. 2005. Seasonal consumption practices in the Mesolithic: economic, environmental, social or ritual?, in N. Milner and P. Woodman (eds.), *Mesolithic Studies at the beginning of the 21st century*, 56–68. Oxford, Oxbow Books.
Milner, N. and Woodman, P. (eds.) 2005. *Mesolithic Studies at the beginning of the 21st century*. Oxford, Oxbow Books.
Mortillet, de, G. 1883. *Le Préhistorique Antiquité de l'Homme*. Paris, C. Reinwald.
Murray, J. 2000. Peau noire, masques blancs: self-image in the Mesolithic-Neolithic transition in Scotland. *Antiquity* 74 (286), 779–85.
Newell, R. R. 1984. On the Mesolithic contribution to the social evolution of Western European society, in J. Bintliff (ed.), *European Social Evolution: Archaeological Perspectives*, 69–82. Bradford, Bradford University Press.
Newell, R. R. and Constandse-Westerman, T. S. 1988. The significance of Skateholm I and Skateholm II to the Mesolithic of western Europe, in L. Larsson (ed.), *The Skateholm project. I. Man and Environment*, 164–74. Acta Regiae Societatis Humaniorum Litterarum Lundensis LXXIX. Stockholm, Almquist & Wiksell International.
Nygaard, S. E. 1989. The stone age of Northern Scandinavia: a review. *Journal of World Prehistory* 3 (1), 72–116.
O'Shea, J. and Zvelebil, M. 1984. Oleneostrovskii Mogilnik: reconstructing social and economic organisation of prehistoric hunter-fishers in Northern Russia. *Journal of Anthropological Archaeology* 3 (1), 1–40.
Obermaier, H. 1924. *Fossil man in Spain*. New Haven, Yale University Press.
Paludan-Müller, C. 1978. High Atlantic food gathering in north-western Zealand, ecological conditions and spatial representation, in K. Kristiansen and C. Paludan-Müller (eds.), *New Directions in Scandinavian Archaeology*, 120–57. Copenhagen, Danish Museum.
Péquart, M. and Péquart, St.-J. 1954. *Hóedic. Deuxième Station. Nécropole due Mésolithique Cotier Armoricain*. Antwerpen, De Sikkel.
Piette, E. 1895. Hiatus et Lacune. Vestiges de la Période de Transition dans la Grotte du Mas-d'Azil. *Bulletin of the Society of Anthropology of Paris* 4 (6), 235–67.
Pluciennik, M. 1998. Deconstructing 'the Neolithic' in the Mesolithic-Neolithic transition, in M. Edmonds and C. Richards (eds.), *Understanding the Neolithic of North-Western Europe*, 61–83. Glasgow, Cruithne Press.
Pluciennik, M. 2002. The invention of hunter-gatherers in seventeenth-century Europe. *Archaeological Dialogues* 9 (2), 98–151.
Pluciennik, M. 2004. The meaning of 'hunter-gatherers' and modes of subsistence: a comparative historical perspective, in A. Barnard (ed.), *Hunter-gatherers in history, archaeology and anthropology*, 17–29. Oxford, Berg.
Price, T. D. 1985. Affluent foragers of Mesolithic southern Scandinavia, in T. D. Price and J. A. Brown (eds.), *Prehistoric Hunter-Gatherers: The Emergence of Cultural Complexity*, 341–60. Orlando, Academic Press.
Price, T. D. 1987. The Mesolithic of Western Europe. *Journal of World Prehistory* 1, 225–332.

Price, T. D. and Brown, J. A. 1985. Aspects of hunter-gatherer complexity, in T. D. Price and J. A. Brown (eds.), *Prehistoric hunter-gatherers: The Emergence of Cultural Complexity*, 3–20. Orlando, Academic Press.

Price, T. D. and Gebauer, A.-B. 1991. The final frontier: foragers to farmers in Southern Scandinavia, in A.-B. Gebauer and T. D. Price (eds.), *Transitions to Agriculture in Prehistory*, 97–115. Madison, Wisconsin, Prehistory Press.

Pugsley, L. B. 2005. Sex, gender and sexuality in the Mesolithic, in N. Milner and P. Woodman (eds.), *Mesolithic Studies at the beginning of the 21st century*, 164–75. Oxford, Oxbow Books.

Renfrew, C. and Cherry. J. F. 1986. *Peer-polity Interaction and socio-political change*. Cambridge, Cambridge University Press.

Rossignol, J. and Wandsneider, L. 1992. *Space, Time and Archaeological Landscapes*. New York, Plenum Press.

Rowley-Conwy, P. 1983. Sedentary hunters: the Ertebølle example, in G. N. Bailey (ed.), *Hunter-Gatherer Economy in Prehistory: A European Perspective*, 111–26. Cambridge, Cambridge University Press.

Rowley-Conwy, P. 1996. Why didn't Westropp's 'Mesolithic' catch on in 1872? *Antiquity* 70 (270), 940–4.

Rowley-Conwy, P. 1999. Economic Prehistory in Southern Scandinavia. *Proceedings of the British Academy* 99, 125–59.

Rowley-Conwy, P. 2001. Time, change and the archaeology of hunter-gatherers: how original is the 'Original Affluent Society'?, in C. Panter-Brick, R. H. Layton and P. Rowley-Conwy (eds.), *Hunter-gatherers. An interdisciplinary perspective*, 39–72. Cambridge, Cambridge University Press.

Rowley-Conwy, P. 2004. Complexity in the Mesolithic of the Atlantic Façade: Development or Adaptation?, in M. R. González Morales and G. A. Clark (eds.), *The Mesolithic of the Atlantic Façade*, 1–12. Anthropological Research Papers 55. Tempe, Arizona State University.

Rowley-Conwy, P. A. and Zvelebil, M. 1989. Saving it for later: storage by prehistoric hunter-gatherers in Europe, in P. Halstead and J. O'Shea (eds.), *Bad Year Economics*, 40–56. Cambridge, Cambridge University Press.

Rozoy, J.-G. 1978. *Les Derniers Chasseurs. L'Épipaléolithique en France et en Belgique*. Bulletin de la Société Archéologique Champenoise (special issue in 3 volumes). Paris, Comitée des travaux historiques et scientifiques (CTHS).

Sarauw, G. F. L. 1903. En Stenålders Boplads i Maglemose ved Mullerup, sammenholdt med beslegtede fund, in *Årbøger for Nordisk Oldkyndighed og Historie 1903*, 148–315. København, Det Kongelige Nordiske Oldskriftselskab.

Schiffer, M. 1976. *Behavioural Archaeology*. Academic Press, New York.

Simpson, B. 2003. The Humble Bead: Body Adornment and Burial Practices in the British Palaeolithic and Mesolithic, in L. Bevan and J. Moore (eds.), *Peopling the Mesolithic in the Northern Environment*, 45–52. British Archaeological Reports, International Series S1157. Oxford, Archaeopress.

Srejović, D. 1969. *Lepenski Vir – nova praistorijska kultura u Podunavlju*. Beograd, Srpska Književna Zadruga.

Srejović, D. 1971. The Roots of the Lepenski Vir culture. *Archaeologia Iugoslavica* 10, 13–22.

Steward, J. 1955. *Theory of Culture Change*. Urbana, University of Illinois Press.

Strassburg, J. 2003. Rituals at the Meso 2000 Conference and the Mesolithic-Neolithic terminological breakdown, in L. Larsson, H. Kindgren, K. Knutsson, D. Loeffler and A. Åkerlund (eds.), *Mesolithic on the Move: Papers presented at the Sixth International Conference on the Mesolithic in Europe, Stockholm 2000*, 542–6. Oxford, Oxbow Books.

Stutz, L. N. 2003. *Embodied rituals and ritualised bodies*. Acta Archaeologica Lundensia, Series in 8°, 46. Lund, Almqvist & Wiksell International.

Telegin, D. Y. 1987. Neolithic cultures of the Ukraine and adjacent areas and their chronology. *Journal of World Prehistory* 1 (3), 307–31.

Thévenin, A. 1995. Le peuplement de l'Est de la France au Tardiglaciaire et au début du Postglaciaire, in A. Thévenin (ed.), *Épipaléolithique et Mésolithique entre Seine et Rhin. Table ronde d'Ancerville 1989*, 213–73. Annales littéraires de l'Université de Besançon, série Archéologie 41. Besançon, Presses universitaires de Franche-Comté.

Thomas, J. 1996. *Time, Culture and Identity. An Interpretative Archaeology*. London, Routledge.

Tilley, C. (ed.) 1993. *Interpretative Archaeology*. Oxford, Berg.

Tringham, R. 1971. *Hunters, Fishers and Farmers of Eastern Europe 6000–3000 BC*. London, Hutchinson.

Vencl, S. 1992. Záchranný Výzkum v Praze 9 – Dolních Počernicích v roce 1982. *Archeologické rozhledy* 44, 29–65.

Vita-Finzi, C. and Higgs, E. S. 1970. Prehistoric economy in the Mount Carmel area of Palestine: site catchment analysis. *Proceedings of the Prehistoric Society* 36, 1–37.

Warren, G. M. 2000. Seascapes: boats and inhabitation in the later mesolithic of western Scotland, in R. Young (ed.) *Mesolithic Lifeways: Current Research in Britain and Ireland*, 97–104. Leicester, Leicester University Press.

Warren, G. M. 2005. Complex arguments…, in N. Milner and P. Woodman (eds.), *Mesolithic Studies at the beginning of the 21st century*, 69–80. Oxford, Oxbow Books.

Welinder, S. 1975. Agriculture, inland hunting, and sea hunting in the western and northern region of the Baltic, 6000–2000 BC, in W. Fitzhugh (ed.), *Prehistoric Maritime Adaptations of the Circumpolar Zone*, 21–39. The Hague, Mouton.

Welinder, S. 1981. The disappearance of a hunting-gathering economy, in B. Gramsch (ed.), *Mesolithikum in Europa. 2. internationales Symposium Potsdam, 3. bis 8. April 1978*, 151–63. Veröffentlichungen des Museums für Ur- und Frühgeschichte Potsdam, Band 14/15. Berlin, Deutscher Verlag der Wissenschaften.

Welinder, S. 1989. Mesolithic forest clearance in Scandinavia, in C. Bonsall (ed.), *The Mesolithic in Europe*, 362–77. Edinburgh, John Donald Publishers.

Welinder, S. 1998. Pre-Neolithic Farming in the Scandinavian Peninsula, in M. Zvelebil, R. Dennell and L. Domańska (eds.), *Harvesting the Sea, Farming the Forest. The Emergence of Neolithic Societies in the Baltic Region*, 165–74. Sheffield Archaeological Monographs 10. Sheffield, Sheffield Academic Press.

Westerby, E. 1927. *Stenålderbopladser ved Klampenborg. Nogle Bidrag til Studiet af den Mesolithiska Periode*. Copenhagen, C. A. Reitzel.

Westropp, H. 1866. On the analogous forms of implements amongst early and primitive races. *Memoirs of the Anthropological Society of London* 11, 288–93.

Westropp, H. 1872. *Prehistoric phases; or, introductory essays on prehistoric archaeology*. London, Bel and Daldy.

White, L. 1959. *The Evolution of Culture*. New York, McGraw-Hill.

Young, R. (ed.) 2000. *Mesolithic Lifeways. Current Research from Britain and Ireland*. Leicester, University of Leicester.

Zagorskis, F. 1987. *Zvejnieku Akmens Laikmeta Kapulauks*. Riga, Zinatne.

Zvelebil, M. 1981. *From Forager to Farmer in the Boreal Zone*. British Archaeological Reports, International Series S115. Oxford, British Archaeological Reports.

Zvelebil, M. 1985. Iron Age Transformations in Northern Russia and the Northeast Baltic, in G. Barker and C. Gamble (eds.), *Beyond Domestication in Prehistoric Europe: Investigations in Subsistence Archaeology and Social Complexity*, 147–80. London, Academic Press.

Zvelebil, M. (ed.) 1986a. *Hunters in Transition. Mesolithic Societies of Temperate Eurasia and their Transition to Farming*. Cambridge, Cambridge University Press.

Zvelebil, M. 1986b. Mesolithic prelude and Neolithic revolution, in M. Zvelebil (ed.), *Hunters in Transition*, 5–15. Cambridge, Cambridge University Press.

Zvelebil, M. 1986c. Mesolithic societies and the transition to farming: problems of time, scale and organisation, in M. Zvelebil (ed.), *Hunters in Transition*, 167–87. Cambridge, Cambridge University Press.

Zvelebil, M. 1993. Concepts of Time and 'Presencing' the Mesolithic. *Archaeological Review from Cambridge* 12 (2), 51–70.

Zvelebil, M. 1996a. Farmers: our ancestors and the identity of Europe, in S. Jones, C. Gamble and P. Graves (eds.), *Cultural identity and archaeology. The construction of European communities*, 145–66. London, Routledge.

Zvelebil, M. 1996b. The agricultural frontier and the transition to farming in the circum-Baltic region, in D. Harris (ed.), *The Origins and Spread of Agriculture and Pastoralism in Eurasia*, 323–45. London, University College London Press.

Zvelebil, M. 1996c. Hunting, gathering or husbandry? Management of food resources by the late Mesolithic communities of Temperate Europe, in D. V. Campana (ed.), *Before Farming: Hunter-Gatherer Society and Subsistence*. MASCA Research Papers in Science and Archaeology. Philadelphia, The University of Pennsylvania Press.

Zvelebil, M. 1998. What's in a name? The Mesolithic, the Neolithic and social change at the Mesolithic-Neolithic transition, in M. R. Edmonds and C. Richards (eds.), *Understanding the Neolithic of North-Western Europe*, 1–35. Glasgow, Cruithne Press.

Zvelebil, M. 2003a. Enculturation of Mesolithic landscapes, in L. Larsson, H. Kindgren, K. Knutsson, D. Loeffler and A. Åkerlund (eds.), *Mesolithic on the Move: Papers presented at the Sixth International Conference on the Mesolithic in Europe, Stockholm 2000*, 65–73. Oxford, Oxbow Books.

Zvelebil, M. 2003b. People behind the lithics. Social life and social conditions of Mesolithic communities in temperate Europe, in L. Bevan and J. Moore (eds.), *Peopling the Mesolithic in a Northern Environment*, 1–26. British Archaeological Reports, International Series S1157. Oxford, Archaeopress.

Zvelebil, M., Dennell, R. and Domańska, L. (eds.) 1998. *Harvesting the Sea, Farming the Forest. The Emergence of Neolithic Societies in the Baltic Region*. Sheffield Archaeological Monographs 10. Sheffield, Sheffield Academic Press.

Zvelebil, M. and Dolukhanov, P. 1991. Transition to farming in eastern and northern Europe. *Journal of World Prehistory* 5 (3), 233–78.

Zvelebil, M. and Jordan, P. D. 1999. Hunter Fisher Gatherer Ritual Landscapes: Questions of Time, Space, and Presentation, in J. Goldhahn (ed.), *Rock Art as Social Representation: papers from a session held at the European Association of Archaeologists Fourth Annual Meeting in Göteborg 1998*, 101–27. British Archaeological Reports, International Series S794. Oxford, Archaeopress.

Zvelebil, M. and Moore, J. 2006. Assessment and representation: the information value of Mesolithic landscapes, in E. Rensink and H. Peeters (eds.), *Preserving the Early past. Investigation, selection and preservation of Palaeolithic and Mesolithic sites and landscapes*, 151–66. Nederlandse Archeologische Rapporten 31. Amersfoort, National Service for Archaeological Heritage.

Session I

New Lands

1. Introduction: New lands

Peter C. Woodman

Roughly the same number of papers is included in the 'New Lands' section as were published in the 'Colonization Processes' section of *Mesolithic on the Move* (Larsson *et al.* 2003). There are some differences between the two sets of papers. The most notable is the absence of papers from the British Isles while there is a more significant contribution from regions around the Mediterranean. Most of the papers in the Stockholm session concentrated on descriptions of the evidence for early settlement in that particular region. The introduction to the Colonization processes (Woodman 2003) ended with the wish that the contributions published in *Mesolithic on the Move* would represent the beginning of a long and fruitful discussion. Indeed we did not have to wait for 5 years to see the change as several papers that related strongly to this topic were published elsewhere in the same volume, notably Åkerlund *et al.* (2003) contribution in the same volume 'Peopling a Forgotten Landscape', which is less concerned with finding the earliest sites and more on how the arrival in a new region creates choices for new colonisers. This includes new challenges created around their lithic technology. Similarly the paper by Fuglestvedt (2003), 'Enculturating the Landscape beyond Doggerland', raised issues around the perceptions and feelings of those who first attempted to explore a new landscape. These and other topics have been taken up in the following set of papers.

The papers can be divided into two sections. As in *Mesolithic on the Move* the majority of the papers in 'New Lands' are based on Scandinavian topics. They also provide, on occasions, different perspectives on the same problem. Three papers discuss in very different ways the role of reindeer (*Rangifer tarandus*) during the northern movement of peoples after the Last Glacial Maximum. Both Reide and Nordqvist provide a critical analysis of the potential of reindeer economies and both refer back to Burch's (1972) critical observations on the potential of the reindeer in economies that relied on low density and scattered populations. In Reide's paper the difficulties of successful and reliable long-term settlement in newly deglaciated areas dominated by dead ice, etc., are highlighted. Thus Late Glacial and Early Holocene communities are very exposed to the effects of the variable and rapid climatic changes. In contrast Nordqvist raises doubts about the extent to which reindeer formed the basis of the economy of these initial colonists. He notes that this model is based on a limited number of sites which may present spectacular, if partial, pictures of Late Glacial hunters. He also notes that the interpretation of the significance of the classic sites, such as Stellmoor and Meindorf, was influenced by a number of researchers who had worked with the Inuit, e.g. Troels Smith. Nordqvist would argue that the potential of other sources such as fish and birds has been underestimated, and that those who were the first colonists of Sweden and Norway in particular should be regarded as marine hunters. The theme of the role of the sea has been explored in more detail by Bjerck, who has drawn comparisons between the coast of Norway and other areas such as Patagonia. He would suggest the 'skerry/fiord seascape' was a new phenomenon that emerged at the beginning of the Holocene. This potentially rich shoreline could be contrasted with the less productive coast of Doggerland and its availability, combined with the development of a new technology associated with seal hunting, provided the springboard for a rapid expansion along the coast of Norway.

The role of archipelagos is also explored by Wikell and Pettersson. In this case it is the initial settlement of eastern central Sweden that is examined. This is a region where a change in sea level of 80m has created a whole new landscape. They would note that the Archipelagos or 'skerrygards' emerged particularly during a phase of uplift that occurred throughout the earlier half of the Mesolithic which began as the Yoldia sea was converted into the landlocked Ancylus Lake, and continued through until the waters of the Baltic poured back in. This created an environment that had, in its diversity, huge potential not only in food sources but in the availability of safe harbours. The authors also explore how early hunters would have viewed this landscape and even the extent to which stories and memories would have survived in such a rapidly changing world.

Wikell and Pettersson have difficulty identifying an area from which to derive the initial settlement of eastern central Sweden, i.e. from within Sweden or across the mountains from Norway. In contrast Takala explores the background and origins of the early settlement of southern Finland. This takes place in the context of the lithic assemblage from the multi-period site of Rissole. The shoreline displacement suggests that occupation could have been possible by, or even before, 9000 cal BC. Here, while most of the assemblage is made up of local quartz, part of the assemblage comprises imported flint that has been used to make a series of implements. These seem to suggest contacts with the Kunda/Butovo, Post Swiderian culture. It is of interest that this earliest phase is associated with imported flint rather than using the local quartz. A similar trend can be seen further north in Finnish Lapland at Sujala. This is in a paper by Kankaapää and Rankama. They describe two assemblages that were recovered from the shores of LakeVetsijärvi. Both were based on the use of a tuffaceous chert to produce a range of blades and other tools. These included a series of points that were similar to Post Swiderian examples. The site provides an interesting paradox as the raw material would appear to come from 60kms further north, on or near the Norwegian coast; but many aspects of the technology would seem to have more in common with the Post Swiderian culture to the south and east. These papers demonstrate that in some regions the initial Mesolithic settlement seems to have relied on the use of non-local materials. In the context of the issue raised by Åkerlund *et al.* (2003), do colonizers immediately adapt to local materials or rely on imported raw material as well as tried and tested technologies? It would appear that there are numerous instances where the latter strategies are used.

Similar issues are discussed in papers by Pellegatti and Andreasen. These concern the colonisation of the Istrian Peninsula on the north-eastern shores of the Adriatic. This is an area that saw settlement delayed until the Late Glacial, when sea levels in the Adriatic began to rise. It is also an area where a new group of farmers occupied the region at the beginning of the Neolithic. Pellegatti has documented that the initial Late Glacial settlers relied heavily on exogenous sources of flint, i.e. those found more than 50km from Pupićina and Nagljanska Caves, and that throughout the Mesolithic there was a shift towards sources that were closer at hand, although not the local ones – i.e. those within 5km of the site. A third site at Sebrn Abri, which was only used during the Mesolithic, relied on regional and local sources. How much is this shift through time part of the colonisation process itself, and how much is due to other factors causing changes in the manner in which this region was used? An interesting addendum to this conundrum is provided by Andreasen's analysis of the lithic assemblages associated with the Neolithic of the same region. He argues that these new farmers, who were arriving into the area as part of along distance process of colonisation, had to learn a new landscape and redevelop new procurement strategies. As a result local sources and a more *ad hoc* technology were used in the earlier part of the Neolithic, while it was only at a later date that the full range of regional and other resources were used. Thus the different groups of new arrivals in a region, each of which has a different economy, find alternative ways of developing lithic procurement strategies.

The one type of new land that has received little attention since the Grenoble meeting is the more mountainous parts of Europe. While there are papers in other sessions, only one has dealt explicitly with the issues of the colonisation of the Alpine region. Dalmeri and co-workers have documented the shift up into the mountains during the Bolling- Allerod interstadial and the subsequent retreat during the Younger Dryas. The Val Di Non project has identified several sites of Younger Dryas age in the Regole Bog area at 1200m asl, which lie well above the timberline, suggesting that in this case climatic change and temperature drop have only caused a partial retreat from the mountains and brought about a different type of use of higher altitudes.

The hope that the intervening years between Stockholm and Belfast would see an enrichment of the discussions on the process of colonisation appears to be coming to fruition. The discussions are less about dates and rather about process, choices and limitations. It is apparent that colonisation is not an automatic process, as it requires a combination of climate and environment as well as the appropriate technology. However, in many regions some of these issues are only just being identified. What brings about change in raw material procurement or the development of local implement types? Especially when dealing with what are perceived as marginal areas, how can we break away from the view that the emergence of new local implement types is the substitution of something inferior for the type of fossils found in the 'Mesolithic Heartlands'? Similarly what causes economic change when new areas are settled? Perhaps instead of simply examining how and when different regions were colonized we should pay more attention to how the process of local adaptation allows for long-term or continuous settlement.

References

Burch, E. S. 1972. The caribou/wild reindeer as a human resource. *American Antiquity* 37, 339–68.

Fuglestvedt, I. 2003. Enculturating the landscape beyond Doggerland, in L. Larsson, H. Kindgren, K. Knutsson, D. Loeffler and A. Åkerlund (eds.), *Mesolithic on the Move: Papers presented at the Sixth International Conference on the Mesolithic in Europe, Stockholm 2000*, 103–7. Oxford, Oxbow Books.

Woodman P. C. 2003. Introduction to 'Colonisation Processes' session, in L. Larsson, H. Kindgren, K. Knutsson, D. Loeffler and A. Åkerlund (eds.), *Mesolithic on the Move: Papers presented at the Sixth International Conference on the Mesolithic in Europe, Stockholm 2000*, 1–2. Oxford, Oxbow Books.

Åkerlund, A., Gustaffsson, P., Hammer, D., Lindgren, C., Olsson, E. and Wikell, R. 2003. Peopling a forgotten landscape, in L. Larsson, H. Kindgren, K. Knutsson, D. Loeffler and A. Åkerlund (eds.), *Mesolithic on the Move: Papers presented at the Sixth International Conference on the Mesolithic in Europe, Stockholm 2000*, xxxiii–xliv. Oxford, Oxbow Books.

2. Climate change, demography and social relations: an alternative view of the Late Palaeolithic pioneer colonization of southern Scandinavia

Felix Riede

This paper addresses the biological and cultural dynamics of Prehistoric pioneering societies from a demographic and ecological perspective. In discussing the archaeological signature of the Late Palaeolithic Hamburgian culture in southern Scandinavia it is suggested that forager colonizations were often demographically more structured than has hitherto been appreciated and that local extinction and re-colonisation may have played an important role in human colonisations at the end of the Pleistocene.

Keywords: pioneer colonization, demography, ecology, Hamburgian, southern Scandinavia.

Introduction

Pioneer colonizations in Prehistory have lately received considerable attention (Knutsson 2005; Rockman and Steele 2003). Living in little-known landscapes requires specific socio-economic adaptations and the lack of social relations poses particular difficulties (Åkerlund 2002; Meltzer 2002; 2003). In addition, the low population densities of forager groups in Prehistory would have also presented significant demographic and hence *biological* challenges.

Cultural-ecological theory suggests that human tool-use and landscape modifications are responsible for the remarkable glove-in-hand fit of human societies to their environment (Laland *et al.* 2000; Odling-Smee *et al.* 2003), but it also cautions (Laland and Brown 2006, 98) that 'even the most adaptable of creatures will experience limits to its tolerance space, outside of which it is unable to behave adaptively'. This paper considers the adaptive limits of the earliest Late Glacial pioneers in southern Scandinavia (see also Riede 2005a; 2005b). These were groups carrying a Hamburgian/Havelte technology (Eriksen 2002; Figure 2.1), placed chronologically into the Greenland Interstadial (GI) 1e/Bølling. The Hamburgian/Havelte tradition is characterised by a complex technology (Madsen 1992) with strong links to the Magdalenian (Schmider 1982). Some workers have suggested that the cultural changes in the Late Palaeolithic of southern Scandinavia reflect a number of migration episodes (e.g. Madsen 1996), whereas others see these developments as 'basically sequential, representing stadia in one connected sequence of cultural development' (Fischer 1993, 52). Here, an attempt is made at evaluating these opposing hypotheses in the light of archaeological information from similar case studies, radiocarbon dates, and demographic considerations. It is suggested that the extreme mobility of Hamburgian groups in the context of their adaptation as 'reindeer-followers' (Aaris-Sørensen *et al.* 2007, 291) may have made them particularly susceptible

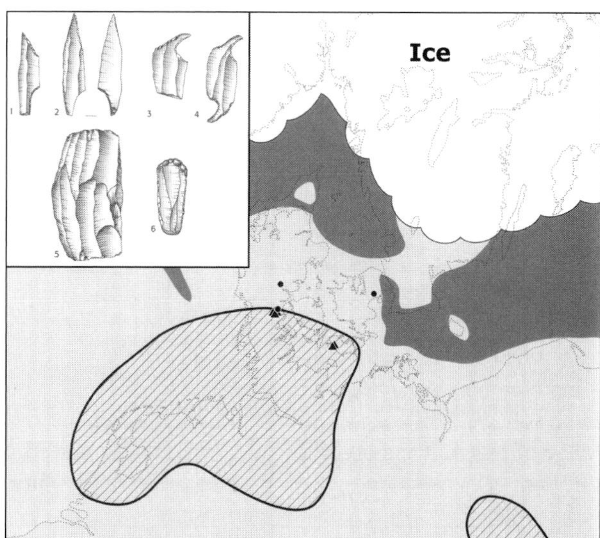

Figure 2.1. A map of the North European Plain (after Erikson 2002, 30), the occurrence of the Hamburgian/Havelte techno-complex and its diagnostic artefacts (1: classic Hamburgian point; 2: Havelte point; 3: Zinken (bec); 4: Doppelzinken; 5: blade core with opposing platforms; 6: end-scraper with fine lateral retouch). (Lithics not to scale; after Andersson and Knarrström 1999, 84).

to demographic fluctuations, which in turn influenced cultural evolution. The climatic downturn at the GI-1d/ Older Dryas may have precipitated a collapse of bio-social networks and heralded the end of the Hamburgian/Havelte tradition in southern Scandinavia.

'A Very Model' of human colonizers

Hazelwood and Steele (2003) have presented a useful summary of the work on Palaeolithic pioneer colonisations. As there are no suitable ethnographic analogues for pioneer hunter-gatherer societies (e.g. Keeley 1991; Kelly and Todd 1988), we can use such an amalgam of case studies as a baseline for comparison. Figure 2.2 presents a 'very model' (Davies 2001, 195) of how foragers cope with the challenges of pioneer colonisation, and the evidence for the Hamburgian/Havelte can be compared against this.

Sites of the Hamburgian/Havelte tradition are known from classic locales in northern Germany, but also from the Netherlands, Denmark and Scania (Andersson *et al.* 2004; Eriksen 2002; Johansen 2000). Only limited information about the organic component of Hamburgian technology is available (Lund 1993; Rust 1943) and several recent studies have cast doubt on the stratigraphic integrity and the associations of lithic and organic material in many of the classic excavations (Bratlund 1991; Tromnau 1992).

Hamburgian technology and settlement structure conform well to similar scenarios as listed in Figure 2.2. Faunal assemblages are dominated by reindeer (*Rangifer tarandus*) and are relatively small (Bokelmann 1991; Bratlund 1994). Residential as well as logistic mobility are high and linearly organised (Vang Petersen and Johansen 1993; 1994; 1996). High residential linear mobility has been suggested as a particular adaptive strategy for colonizing hunter-gatherers (Surovell 2000), but this linearity also puts high demands on the maintenance of social and biological networks (Fix 1999; Wobst 1974; 1976), particularly in unstable environments (Mandryk 1993). While reconstructions of settlement patterns during the Hamburgian/Havelte remain largely speculative, any herd-following economy would have required largely linear movements channelled along natural corridors. With regards to bio-social relationships (Wobst 1974; 1976), linear mobility is difficult to sustain adaptively, especially in pioneer colonization scenarios. The bio-social costs of low population density are well known (Fix 1999). Starvation and local extinction of hunter-gatherer groups caused by environmental change are ethnographically documented, even during the relatively moderate Holocene climate changes (Burch and Blehr 1991; Minc and Smith 1989). No doubt, the Late Glacial environment would have been a dangerous and treacherous one (Gustafsson 1998).

Although the Hamburgian divides into an earlier classic and a later Havelte phase (Clausen 1998), regional variation within these phases is low. The use of settlement locales appears short and redundant (Bokelmann 1996). Little task specialization between sites is evident, further supporting the notion of high residential mobility. There is no evidence for food storage (Bratlund 1994), and Grønnow (1984, 155; original emphasis) has argued that the exploitation patterns of the Hamburgian faunal material reflect periods of '*resource scarcity*'. Flint caches are only known from Teltwisch 1 (Tromnau 1984b). However, personal inspection of this material at the Museum Schloß Gottorf by the author during 2005 revealed that this material cannot be seen as a cache but rather as the remains of nodule preparation and waste discard. Instead, range mobility along natural linear corridors compensated for storage. This resulted in a limited stock of landscape knowledge, focussed on familiar pathways along major river valleys (Riede 2005b).

Hamburgian lithic technology also falls in line with this pattern. Using sophisticated core exploitation methods to manufacture a range of lightweight tools, it represents a 'complex technology, perfectly fitted to having scarcer and perhaps more distant and varied lithic resources'

Archaeol. Signature / Case Study	*(1) Landscape Knowledge*	*(2) Resource Focus*	*(3) Mobility Strategy*	*(4) Regional Variation*	*(5) Settlement Strategy*	*(6) Technology*	*(7) Storage*	*(8) Strat. Position*
Model	Limited local knowledge	Animal focus, periodic shortages dealt with by range relocation; smaller assemblages	High residential and logistic mobility; high range mobility	Low	Short-term, redundant use of 'known places'	A: Portable; high quality raw material; long use-life / B: simple with few tool types; small to medium-sized assemblages	Range mobility substitutes for storage; some caching	Underlying or pre-dating 'developed phase' cultures; duration 500–600 years
Hamburgian	√	√	√	√	√	**A**	**(√)**	**X**

Figure 2.2. The model of pioneer foragers: a summary of the characteristics of pioneering forager groups in the European Early Upper Palaeolithic (Davies 2001), the Late Palaeolithic (Housley et al. *1997) and the North American Late Pleistocene (Kelly and Todd 1988) juxtaposed to the evidence for the Hamburgian. Legend: √ = Matches to above case studies, X = Does not match above cases. Symbols in brackets denote limited evidence. See Hazelwood and Steele (2003) for further information.*

(Madsen 1992, 128). Flint, however, is abundant in southern Scandinavia. The lack of fit between the local resource base and Hamburgian/Havelte behaviour may be a result of cultural inertia or a lack of landscape knowledge. Neither the dog nor any other transport aids are documented for the Hamburgian. The long-standing discussion of herd-following in Prehistory (see Baales (1996) for a good summary) emphasizes that herd-following represents a high-risk economic strategy in the absence of aided means of transport.

It is worth noting that the total chronological span of the Hamburgian/Havelte is *c.* 600 years (Figure 2.3), a duration that has to be further divided if one follows Terberger's (1996) and Grimm and Weber's (2008) suggestion of separating the Hamburgian and Havelte cultures (and if these correspond to separate colonisation episodes). Hamburgian technology differs substantially from that of the following Federmesser groups (Fischer 1988; Hartz 1987). A 'developed' Hamburgian is absent and at sites where Hamburgian/Havelte points and Federmesser co-occur, they generally do so in discrete clusters not linked by refits, indicating temporally distinct occupations (e.g. Sølbjerg (Vang Petersen 2006), Jels (Holm and Rieck 1992)). Although the Hamburgian culture seems to be fine-tuned to pioneer colonization, a significant cultural and biological break between this and the following groups can be postulated.

An economy specialized in reindeer is vulnerable to the large-scale fluctuations of herds in size and migration routes (Binford 1991; David 1973; Spiess 1979; Stenton 1991). In a classic paper, Burch (1972) argued that unaided herd-following is not known ethnographically and concluded that 'people cannot follow the herds' because 'the energy expenditure would be so great, and the net production so low, as to be disastrous for people who tried it'; herd-following would 'lead to substantial overestimates of human population size and stability' (Burch 1972, 344–346).

Reindeer became abundant during the Bølling in southern Scandinavia and the presence of Hamburgian/Havelte groups shows a strong chronological association with this peak in reindeer abundance (Figure 2.3). More recent work on the Hamburgian/Havelte does consider them to be herd-followers (Aaris-Sørensen *et al.* 2007). Burch's argument then should be turned on its head: If Hamburgians were indeed herd-followers the implication is low human population size and demographic instability. In addition, forager groups specialized in reindeer rely on social relations in times of scarcity (Minc and Smith 1989). These social relations, allowing for symbiotic inter-group resource buffering, were not in place during the Bølling. The post-Pleistocene diversification of regional economies providing complementary resource bases had not developed yet and the very low population density at the fringe of the known world (Bocquet-Appel *et al.* 2005), coupled with linear mobility, indicate that Hamburgian groups were perhaps operating at the limit of human adaptive capability (Figure 2.4). This contrasts with later reindeer-hunting societies, such as the Ahrensburgian, which, despite the

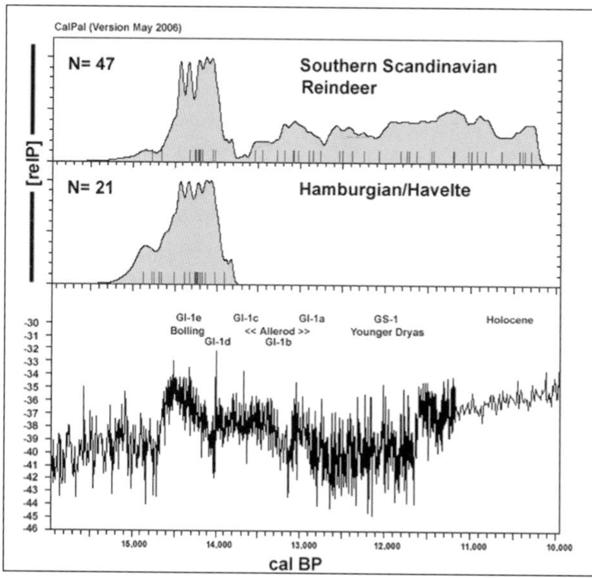

Figure 2.3. The summed probability distributions for the calibrated radiocarbon dates for the Hamburgian/Havelte and the reindeer of southern Scandinavia (see Aaris-Sørensen et al. 2007). The calibration is done using the latest version of CalPal (CalPal). The dates are juxtaposed to the high-resolution (20-year interval) $\delta^{18}O$ temperature-proxy data from the GISP2 ice-core, which shows clearly the rapid climatic down-turn at the GI-1d/Older Dryas. See also Grimm and Weber (2008) for a recent re-assessment of the radiocarbon record for the Hamburgian.

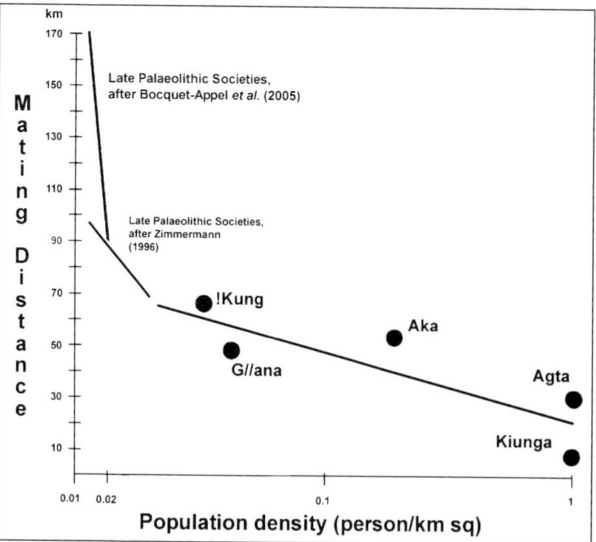

Figure 2.4. The mobility required to maintain bio-social networks amongst foragers has been investigated in ethnographic field studies (Boyce et al. *1967; Cavalli-Sforza and Hewlett 1982; Hewlett et al. 1982), and, using different estimates of Late Glacial population densities (e.g. Bocquet-Appel* et al. *2005; Zimmermann 1996), can be extrapolated in the past. For reproductive reasons alone, mobility would have been exceedingly high.*

vagaries of the GS-1/Younger Dryas cold period, thrived in a territory larger than that of the Hamburgian. However Ahrensburgian groups not only had a less specialized economy, now including a significant marine component (Bokelmann 1991; Kindgren 2002; Schmitt *et al.* 2006), but they probably also had aided means of transport (Clausen 2004; Ellmers 1980; Tromnau 1984a), as well as more efficient hunting strategies (Bratlund 1999). We observe regional diversification and the long-term development of an early Ahrensburgian into later 'developed' facies (e.g. Fischer 1978; Taute 1968). Similarly, for the reindeer hunters of Early Holocene Norway, extensive social networks are documented (Madden 1983), and it is the greater robusticity of these social networks that allow the development of societies to go from 'pioneer' to 'developed' phase, with evidence for varied landscape engagements, art, and regionalization (Bang-Andersen 2003; Forsberg and Knutsson 1997).

Terrestrial climatic records in southern Scandinavia show a 'widespread occurrence of dead ice, unstable soils, heavy in-wash of minerogenic matter' (Bennike *et al.* 2004, 465), implying ecologically fragile communities. If life during GI-1e/Bølling in southern Scandinavia was so tenuous, one might ask why forager groups moved northwards at this early date. The reason lies, perhaps, in *opportunity*. As Carlsson *et al.* (2005, 23) note, Prehistoric people were 'takers of opportunity': *If* extreme mobility is accepted as a necessary cost, herd-following does present itself as a 'walking larder' (Burch 1972, 344). The perception of risk/opportunity is culturally determined (van der Leeuw 1989), and the Hamburgian colonizers, making the choice to maintain their ancestral reindeer-hunting lifestyle and move north with the herds, were unable to foresee the consequences of their actions.

Demographic models stress the role of local extinction and re-colonisation in human dispersals (Eller 2002; Eller *et al.* 2004). Bar-Yosef and Belfer-Cohen (2001) have remarked that similar processes structured early hominin dispersals out of Africa, and Goldstein and Chikhi (2002, 132) add that 'there is no reason to suppose that our demographic history suddenly simplified'. Recent work on human genetics provides a further clue. Molecular-clock dating of genetic diversification in Europe favours successful colonization only after 13,000 BP, and is generally associated with the Ahrensburgian (Achili *et al.* 2004; Forster 2004; Loogväli *et al.* 2004; Passarino *et al.* 2002; Pereira *et al.* 2005; Torroni *et al.* 1998; Torroni *et al.* 2001). This begs the question of what happened to those colonisers who came before the Ahrensburgian. One way of reconciling the archaeological and genetic evidence is to view pre-Ahrensburgian colonisation attempts as effectively unsuccessful. Increased mortality during the GI-1d/Older Dryas, particularly amongst the young and the old, may have depressed hunting success (Gurven *et al.* 2006; Walker *et al.* 2002) and have posed difficulties for the effective maintenance of cultural traditions (Hawkes 2004; Henrich 2004).

Such processes of social isolation and increased mortality may then have precipitated a rapid collapse of group structures and coherence (Soltis *et al.* 1995). Whether individuals were eventually subsumed into other groups, or whether Hamburgian society as a whole became extinct, are moot points. Nonetheless, Prehistoric forager societies were not immune to environmental change, which was mediated through demographic and social structures.

Conclusions

Although the details of hunter-gatherer demography are not well understood (Pennington 2001), demographic fluctuations, particularly in relatively unproductive environments are known to be highly pronounced (Bernbeck 1991; Keckler 1997). These fluctuations are synchronized with similar cycles in faunal communities, which in turn relate to environmental variables (Minc and Smith 1989). Throughout the Holocene, foragers have developed a number of stable adaptations in a wide variety of environments (I. F. Collard and Foley 2002; M. Collard *et al.* 2005). The occasional lack of resources is compensated for with extensive social networks, but this option would not have been open to prehistoric colonizers, living as they did a 'life without close neighbours' (Åkerlund 2002, 43). Even historically documented colonization attempts have failed when social buffering networks were not in place (Diamond 2005; Rockman and Steele 2003). Importantly, Late Pleistocene and Early Holocene climate was highly variable (Burroughs 2005), and rapid climate change would have strongly affected faunal and hence human population densities. Environmental and social stresses can lead to cultural restructuring (Laughlin and Brady 1978; Soltis *et al.* 1995), some of which may be detectable archaeologically.

Many current models in Palaeolithic and Mesolithic archaeology assume stable populations, but this may be misleading (Boone 2002; Price 1999). Catastrophic mortality events are partly responsible for the periodic decline in forager populations (Keckler 1997). Using calibrated radiocarbon dates as proxies for population density (e.g. Gamble *et al.* 2004; 2005; Kuper and Kröpelin 2006; Shennan and Edinborough 2007), the strong correlation between environmental changes and cultural changes – either side of the Pleistocene-Holocene boundary – implies that we cannot sideline climate change in our discussions of long-term culture change. Demography acts as an intermediary mechanism that links climate change to the transmission and maintenance of cultural knowledge (Shennan 2000). Here, an alternative interpretation of the archaeological data on the pioneer Late Glacial colonisers in southern Scandinavia, the Hamburgian/Havelte culture, has been offered. While taphonomic distortions make it difficult to test alternative scenarios of population stability or discontinuity, ethnographic and theoretical considerations suggest that we: a) might have to incorporate more explicit demographic thinking into interpretations of prehistoric forager colonisations; and b) may have to take greater account of unsuccessful colonisations attempts.

References

Aaris-Sørensen, K., Mühldorff, R. and Brinch Petersen, E. 2007. The Scandinavian reindeer (*Rangifer tarandus* L.) after the last glacial maximum: time, seasonality and human exploitation. *Journal of Archaeological Science* 34, 914–23.

Achili, A., Rengo, C., Magri, C., Battaglia, V. and Olivieri, A. 2004. The Molecular Dissection of mtDNA Haplogroup H Confirms That the Franco-Cantabrian Glacial Refuge Was a Major Source for the European Gene Pool. *American Journal of Human Genetics* 75, 910–18.

Andersson, M., Karsten, P., Knarström, B. and Svensson M. 2004. *Stone Age Scania. Significant places dug and read by contract archaeology*. Riksantikvarieämbetets Skrifter 52. Malmö, Riksantikvarieämbetet.

Andersson, M. and Knarrström, B. 1999. *Senpaleolitikum I Skåne – en studie av materiell kultur och ekonomi hos Sveriges första fångstfolk*. Lund, Riksantikvarieämbetet.

Baales, M. 1996. *Umwelt und Jagdökonomie der Ahrensburger Rentierjäger im Mittelgebirge*. Bonn, Verlag Rudolf Habelt GmbH.

Bang-Andersen, S. 2003. Southwest Norway at the Pleistocene/Holocene Transition: Landscape Development, Colonization, Site Types, Settlement Patterns. *Norwegian Archaeological Review* 36 (1), 5–25.

Bar-Yosef, O. and Belfer-Cohen, A. 2001. From Africa to Eurasia – early dispersals. *Quaternary International* 75, 19–28.

Bernbeck, R. 1991. Crisis in the Foraging Mode of Production: Long-Term Cyclical Processes in Hunter-Gatherer Societies, in P. T. Miracle, L. E. Fisher and J. Brown (eds.), *Foragers in Context: Long-Term, Regional and Historical Perspectives in Hunter-Gatherer Studies*, 47–62. International Monographs in Prehistory. Ann Arbor, Department of Anthropology, University of Michigan.

Binford, L. R. 1991. When the going gets tough, the tough get going: Nunamiut local groups, camping patterns and economic organization, in C. Gamble and W. A. Boismier (eds.), *Ethnoarchaeological Approaches to Mobile Campsites*, 25–137. International Monographs in Prehistory. Ann Arbor, Department of Anthropology, University of Michigan.

Bocquet-Appel, J.-P., Demars, P.-Y., Noiret, L. and Dobrowsky, D. 2005. Estimates of Upper Palaeolithic meta-population size in Europe from archaeological data. *Journal of Archaeological Science* 32, 1656–68.

Bokelmann, K. 1991. Some new thoughts on old data on humans and reindeer in the Ahrensburg tunnel valley in Schleswig-Holstein, Germany, in N. Barton, A. J. Roberts and D. A. Roe (eds.), *The Late Glacial in North-west Europe: human adaptation and environmental change at the end of the Pleistocene*, 72–81. Council for British Archaeology (CBA) Research Report 77. London, Council for British Archaeology.

Bokelmann, K. 1996. Ahrensburg, Kr. Stormarn. Baggersondagen bei Vierbergen in Ahrensburger Tunneltal. *Offa* 53, 372.

Boone, J. L. 2002. Subsistence strategies and early human population history: an evolutionary ecological perspective. *World Archaeology* 34, 6–25.

Boyce, A. J., Küchemann, C. F. and Harrison, G. A. 1967. Neighbourhood knowledge and the distribution of marriage distances. *Annals of Human Genetics* 30, 335–8.

Bratlund, B. 1991. Die spätglazialen 'Opfertiere' von Meiendorf und Stellmoor, Kreis Stormarn. *Offa* 48, 41–73.

Bratlund, B. 1994. A survey of subsistence and settlement pattern of the Hamburgian culture in Schleswig-Holstein. *Jahrbuch des Römisch-Germanischen Zentralmuseums Mainz* 41, 59–93.

Bratlund, B. 1999. A Survey of the Ahrensburgian Faunal Assemblage of Stellmoor, in S. K. Kozłowski, J. Gurba and L. L. Zaliznyak (eds.), *Tanged Points Cultures in Europe. Read at the International Archaeological Symposium. Lublin, September, 13-16, 1993*, 47–59. Lublin, Maria Curie-Skłodowska University Press.

Burch, E. S. 1972. The Caribou/Wild Reindeer as a Human Resource. *American Antiquity* 37, 339–68.

Burch, E. S., Jr. and Blehr, O. 1991. Herd Following Reconsidered. *Current Anthropology* 32, 439–45.

Burroughs, W. J. 2005. *Climate Change in Prehistory. The End of the Reign of Chaos*. Cambridge, Cambridge University Press.

CalPal (Cologne Radiocarbon Calibration & Palaeoclimate Research Package) at: www.calpal.de (accessed 09/2007).

Carlsson, T., Gruber, G. and Molin, F. 2005. The Mesolithic in Östergötland: an introduction, in G. Gruber (ed.), *Identities in Transition: Mesolithic Strategies in the Swedish Province of Östergötland*, 8–23. Arkeologiska undersökningar, Skrifter 46. Stockholm, Riksantikvarieämbetet.

Cavalli-Sforza, L. L. and Hewlett, B. 1982. Exploration and mating range in African Pygmies. *Annals of Human Genetics* 46, 257–70.

Clausen, I. 1998. Neue Untersuchungen an späteiszeitlichen Fundplätzen der Hamburger Kultur bei Ahrenshöft, Kr. Nordfriesland. Ein Vorbericht. *Archäologische Nachrichten aus Schleswig-Holstein* 8, 8–49.

Clausen, I. 2004. The Reindeer antler axe of the Alleröd period from Klappholz LA 63, Kreis Schleswig-Flensburg/Germany. Is it a relict of the Federmesser, Bromme or Ahrensburg culture?, in T. Terberger and B. V. Eriksen (eds.), *Hunters in a changing world: Environment and Archaeology of the Pleistocene–Holocene Transition (ca 11000–9000 BC) in Northern Central Europe. Workshop of the UISPP-Commission XXXII at Greifswald in September 2002*, 141–64. Internationale Archaologie - Arbeitsgemeinschaft, Symposium, Tagung, Kongress 5. Rahden/Westphalia, Verlag Marie Leidorf.

Collard, I. F. and Foley, R. A. 2002. Latitudinal patterns and environmental determinants of recent human cultural diversity: do humans follow biogeographical rules? *Evolutionary Ecology Research* 4, 371–83.

Collard, M., Kemery, M. and Banks, S. 2005. Causes of Toolkit Variation Among Hunter-Gatherers: A Test of Four Competing Hypotheses. *Canadian Journal of Archaeology* 29, 1–19.

David, N. 1973. On upper palaeolithic society, ecology, and technological change: the Noaillian case, in C. Renfrew (ed.), *The Explanation of Culture Change. Models in Prehistory*, 277–303. London, Duckworth.

Davies, W. 2001. A Very Model of a Modern Human Industry: New Perspectives on the Origins and Spread of the Aurignacian in Europe. *Proceedings of the Prehistoric Society* 67, 195–217.

Diamond, J. M. 2005. *Collapse. How Societies Choose to Fail or Survive*. Harmondsworth, Penguin Books.

Eller, E. 2002. Population extinction and recolonization in human demographic history. *Mathematical Biosciences* 177/178, 1–10.

Eller, E., Hawks, J. and Relethford, J. H. 2004. Local extinction and recolonization, species effective population size, and modern human origins. *Human Biology* 76, 689–709.

Ellmers, D. 1980. Ein Fellboot-Fragment der Ahrensbuger Kultur aus Husum, Schleswig-Holstein? *Offa* 37, 19–24.

Eriksen, B. V. 2002. Reconsidering the geochronological framework of Lateglacial hunter-gatherer colonization of southern Scandinavia, in B. V. Eriksen and B. Bratlund (eds.), *Recent studies in the Final Palaeolithic of the European plain*, 25–42. Højbjerg, Jutland Archaeological Society.

Fischer, A. 1978. På sporet af overgangen mellem palæolitikum og mesolitikum i Sydskandinavien. *Hikuin* 4, 27–50.

Fischer, A. 1988. A Late Palaeolithic Flint Workshop at Egtved, East Jutland. *Journal of Danish Archaeology* 7, 7–23.

Fischer, A. 1993. The Late Palaeolithic, in S. Hvaas and B. Storgaard (eds.), *Digging into the Past: 25 Years of Archaeology in Denmark*, 51–7. Højbjerg, Jutland Archaeological Society.

Fix, A. 1999. *Migration and Colonization in Human Microevolution*. Cambridge, Cambridge University Press.

Forsberg, L. and Knutsson, K. 1997. Converging conclusions from different archaeological perspectives: the early settlement of Northern Sweden, in P. Bintz and A. Thévenin (eds.), *L'Europe des derniers Chasseurs. Épipaléolithique et Mésolithique. Actes du 5ième colloque international UISPP, Comission XII. Grenoble, 18-23 septembre 1995*, 313–9. Paris, Comité des travaux historiques et scientifiques (CTHS).

Forster, P. 2004. Ice Ages and the mitochondrial DNA chronology of human dispersals: a review. *Philosophical Transactions of the Royal Society of London, Series B* 359, 255–64.

Gamble, C., Davies, W., Pettitt, P. and Richards, M. 2004. Climate change and evolving human diversity in Europe during the last glacial. *Philosophical Transactions of the Royal Society of London, Series B* 359, 243–54.

Gamble, C., Davies, W., Pettitt, P., Hazelwood, L. and Richards, M. 2005. The Archaeological and Genetic Foundations of the European Population during the Late Glacial: Implications for 'Agricultural Thinking'. *Cambridge Archaeological Journal* 15, 193–223.

Goldstein, D. B. and Chikhi, L. 2002. Human Migrations and Population Structure: What We Know and Why it Matters. *Annual Review of Genomics and Human Genetics* 3, 129–52.

Gurven, M., Kaplan, H. and Gutierrez, M. 2006. How long does it take to become a proficient hunter? Implications for the evolution of extended development and long life span. *Journal of Human Evolution* 51, 454–70.

Gustafsson, P. 1998. The Earliest Stone Age Occupation of Eastern Middle Sweden. *Current Swedish Archaeology* 6, 47–62.

Grimm, S. B. and Weber, M.-J. 2008. The chronological framework of the Hamburgian in the light of old and new ^{14}C dates. *Quartär* 55, 17–40.

Grønnow, B. 1985. *Meiendorf and Stellmoor Revisited. An Analysis of Late Palaeolithic Reindeer Exploitation*, 131–66. Acta Archaeologica 56. University of Copenhagen, Department of Archaeology.

Hartz, S. 1987. Neue spätpaläolithische Fundplätze bei Ahrenshöft, Kreis Nordfriesland. *Offa* 44, 5–52.

Hawkes, K. 2004. The grandmother effect. *Nature* 482, 128–9.

Hazelwood, L. and Steele, J. 2003. Colonizing new landscapes: archaeological detectability of the first phase, in M. Rockman and J. Steele (eds.), *Colonization of Unfamiliar Landscapes: The archaeology of adaptation*, 203–21. London, Routledge.

Henrich, J. 2004. Demography and Cultural Evolution: How Adaptive Cultural Processes Can Produce Maladaptive Losses – the Tasmanian Case. *American Antiquity* 69, 197–214.

Hewlett, B., van de Koppel, J. M. H. and Cavalli-Sforza, L. L. 1982. Exploration Ranges of Aka Pygmies of the Central African Republic. *Man* (n.s.) 17, 418–30.

Holm, J. and Rieck, F. 1992. *Istidsjægere vid Jelssøerne*. Skrifter fra Museumsrådet for Sønderjyllands Amt 5. Haderslev, Haderslev Museum.

Housley, R. A., Gamble, C., Street, M. and Pettitt, P. 1997. Radiocarbon evidence for the Late Glacial human recolonization of northern Europe. *Proceedings of the Prehistoric Society* 63, 25–54.

Johansen, L. 2000. The Late Palaeolithic in Denmark, in P. Bodu, M. Christensen and B. V. Eriksen (eds.), *L'Europe centrale et septentrionale au Tardiglaciaire. Mémoires du Musée de Préhistoire d'Ile-de-France no 7, Nemours*, 19–54. Paris, Association pour la Promotion de la Recherche Archéologique en Ile-de-France (APRAIF).

Keckler, C. N. W. 1997. Catastrophic Mortality in Simulations of Forager Age-at-Death: Where Did All the Humans Go?, in R. R. Paine (ed.), *Integrating Archaeological Demography: Multidisciplinary Approaches to Prehistoric Population*, 205–28. Carbondale, IL, Center for Archaeological Investigations, Southern Illinois University.

Keeley, L. H. 1991. Ethnographic models for Late Glacial hunter-gatherers, in N. Barton, A. J. Roberts and D. A. Roe (eds.), *The Late Glacial in North-west Europe: human adaptation and environmental change at the end of the Pleistocene*, 179–90. Council for British Archaeology (CBA) Research Report 77. London, Council for British Archaeology.

Kelly, R. L. and Todd, L. C. 1988. Coming into the Country: Early Paleoindian Hunting and Mobility. *American Antiquity* 53, 231–44.

Kindgren, H. 2002. Tosskärr. Stenkyrka 94 revisited, in B. V. Eriksen and B. Bratlund (eds.), *Recent studies in the Final Palaeolithic of the European plain*, 49–60. Højbjerg, Jutland Archaeological Society.

Knutsson, H. (ed.) 2005. *Pioneer settlements and colonization processes in the Barents region*. Vuollerim Papers in Hunter-Gatherer Archaeology 1. Vuollerim, Vuollerim Museum Press.

Kuper, R. and Kröpelin, S. 2006. Climate-Controlled Holocene Occupation in the Sahara: Motor of Africa's Evolution. *Science* 313, 803–7.

Laland, K. N. and Brown, G. R. 2006. Niche Construction, Human Behavior, and the Adaptive-Lag Hypothesis. *Evolutionary Anthropology* 15, 95–104.

Laland, K. N., Odling-Smee, F. J. and Feldman, M. W. 2000. Niche construction, biological evolution, and cultural change. *Behavioural and Brain Sciences* 23, 131–75.

Laughlin, C. D. and Brady, I. A. (eds.) 1978. *Extinction and Survival in Human Populations*. New York, Columbia University Press.

Loogväli, E.-L., Roostalu, U., Malyarchuck, B. A., Derenko, M. V., Kivisild, T., Metspalu, E. and Tambets, K. 2004. Disuniting Uniformity: A Pied Cladistic Canvas of mtDNA Haplogroup H in Eurasia. *Molecular Biology and Evolution* 21, 2012–21.

Lund, M. 1993. Vorschäfte für Kerbspitzen der Hamburger Kultur. *Archäologisches Korrespondenzblatt* 23, 405–11.

Madden, M. 1983. Social Network Systems Amongst Hunter-Gatherers Considered within Southern Norway, in G. N. Bailey (ed.), *Hunter-Gatherer Economy in Prehistory: A European Perspective*, 191–200. Cambridge, Cambridge University Press.

Madsen, B. 1992. Hamburgkulturens flintteknologi i Jels (The Hamburgian Flint Technology at Jels), in J. Holm and F. Rieck (eds.), *Istidsjægere ved Jelssøerne*, 93–132. Haderslev, Skrifter fra Museumsrådet for Sønderjyllands Amt.

Madsen, B. 1996. Late Palaeolithic cultures of south Scandinavia:

tools, traditions and technology, in L. Larsson (ed.), *The Earliest Settlement of Scandinavia and Its Relationship with Neighbouring Areas*, 61–73. Acta Archaeologica Lundensia, Series in 8°, 24. Stockholm, Almqvist & Wiksell.

Mandryk, C. A. S. 1993. Hunter-Gatherer Social Costs and the Nonviability of Submarginal Environments. *Journal of Anthropological Research* 49, 39–71.

Meltzer, D. 2002. What Do You Do When No One's Been There Before? Thoughts on the Exploration and Colonization of New Lands, in N. G. Jablonski (ed.), *The First Americans: the Pleistocene colonization of the New World*, 27–58. Golden Gate Park, CA, University of California Press.

Meltzer, D. 2003. Lessons in landscape learning, in M. Rockman and J. Steele (eds.), *Colonization of Unfamiliar Landscapes: The archaeology of adaptation*, 222–41. London, Routledge.

Minc, L. D. and Smith, K. P. 1989. The spirit of survival, in P. Halstead and J. O'Shea (eds.), *Bad Year Economics: Cultural responses to risk and uncertainty*, 8–39. Cambridge, Cambridge University Press.

Odling-Smee, F. J., Laland, K. N. and Feldman, M. W. 2003. *Niche Construction. The Neglected Process in Evolution*. Princeton, Princeton University Press.

Passarino, G., Cavalleri, G. L., Lin, A. A., Cavalli-Sforza, L. L., Børresen-Dale, A.-L. and Underhill, P. A. 2002. Different genetic components in the Norwegian population revealed by the analysis of mtDNA and Y chromosome polymorphisms. *European Journal Human Genetics* 10, 521–9.

Pennington, R. 2001. Hunter-gatherer demography, in C. Panter-Brick, R. H. Layton and P. Rowley-Conwy (eds.), *Hunter-Gatherers. An Interdisciplinary Perspective*, 170–204. Cambridge, Cambridge University Press.

Pereira, L., Richards, M., Goios, A., Alonso, A., Albarran, C., Garcia, O., Behar, D. M., Golge, M., Hatina, J., Al-Gazali, L., Bradley, D. G., Macaulay, V. and Amorim, A. 2005. High-resolution mtDNA evidence for the late-glacial resettlement of Europe from an Iberian refugium. *Genome Research* 15, 19–24.

Price, T. D. 1999. Human Population in Europe during the Mesolithic, in E. Cziesla, T. Kersting and S. Pratsch (eds.), *Den Bogen spannen...Festschrift für Bernhard Gramsch*, 185–195. Weissbach, Beier & Beran.

Riede, F. 2005a. Darwin vs. Bourdieu. Celebrity Deathmatch or Postprocessual Myth? Prolegomenon for the Reconciliation of Agentive-Interpretative and Ecological-Evolutionary Archaeology, in H. Cobb, S. Price, F. Coward and L. Grimshaw (eds.), *Investigating Prehistoric Hunter-Gatherer Identities: Case Studies from Palaeolithic and Mesolithic Europe*, 45–64. British Archaeological Reports, International Series S1411. Oxford, Archaeopress.

Riede, F. 2005b. To boldly go where no (hu-)man has gone before. Some thoughts on the pioneer colonisations of pristine landscapes. *Archaeological Review from Cambridge* 20, 20–8.

Rockman, M. and Steele, J. (eds.) 2003. *Colonization of Unfamiliar Landscapes: the archaeology of adaptation*. London, Routledge.

Rust, A. 1943. *Die Alt- und Mittelsteinzeitlichen Funde von Stellmoor*. Neumünster, Karl Wachholtz Verlag.

Schmider, B. 1982. The Magdalenian Culture of the Paris River-Basin and Its Relationship with the Nordic Cultures of the Late Old Stone Age. *World Archaeology* 14, 259–69.

Schmitt, L., Larsson, S., Schrum, C., Alekseeva, I., Tomczak, M. and Svedhage, K. 2006. 'Why They Came': The Colonization of the Coast of Western Sweden and its Environmental Context at the End of the Last Glaciation. *Oxford Journal of Archaeology* 25, 1–28.

Shennan, S. J. 2000. Population, Culture History, and the Dynamics of Culture Change. *Current Anthropology* 41, 811–35.

Shennan, S. J. and Edinborough, K. S. A. 2007. Prehistoric population history: from the Late Glacial to the Late Neolithic in Central and Northern Europe. *Journal of Archaeological Science* 34 (8), 1339–45.

Soltis, J., Boyd, P. and Richerson, P. J. 1995. Can Group-functional behaviors evolve by cultural group selection? An empirical test. *Current Anthropology* 63, 473–94.

Spiess, A. E. 1979. *Reindeer and Caribou Hunters. An Archaeological Study*. New York, Academic Press.

Stenton, D. R. 1991. Caribou Population Dynamics and Thule Culture Adaptations on Southern Baffin Island, N.W.T. *Arctic Anthropology* 28, 15–43.

Surovell, T. A. 2000. Early Palaeoindian Women, Children, Mobility, and Fertility. *American Antiquity* 65, 493–508.

Taute, W. 1968. *Die Stielspitzen-Gruppen im nördlichen Mitteleuropa. Ein Beitrag zur Kenntnis der späten Altsteinzeit*. Köln, Böhlau Verlag.

Terberger, T. 1996. The early settlement of North-East Germany (Mecklenburg-Vorpommern), in L. Larsson (ed.), *The Earliest Settlement of Scandinavia and its relationship with neighbouring areas*, 111–22. Acta Archaeologica Lundensia, Series in 8°, 24. Stockholm, Almqvist & Wiksell.

Torroni, A., Bandelt, H.-J., D'Urbano, L., Lahermo, P., Moral, P., Sellitto, D., Rengo, C., Forster, P., Savontaus, M. L., Bonne-Tamir, B. and Scozzari, R. 1998. mtDNA Analysis Reveals a Major Late Paleolithic Population Expansion from Southwestern to Northeastern Europe. *American Journal of Human Genetics* 62, 1137–52.

Torroni, A., Bandelt, H. J., Macaulay, V., Richards, M., Cruciani, F., Rengo, C., Martinez-Cabrera, V., Villems, R., Kivisild, T., Metspalu, E., Parik, J., Tolk, H. V., Tambets, K., Forster, P., Karger, B., Francalacci, P., Rudan, P., Janicijevic, B., Rickards, O., Savontaus, M. L., Huoponen, K., Laitinen, V., Koivumaki, S., Sykes, B., Hickey, E., Novelletto, A., Moral, P., Sellitto, D., Coppa, A., Al-Zaheri, N., Santachiara-Benerecetti, A. S., Semino, O. and Scozzari, R. 2001. A signal, from human mtDNA, of postglacial recolonization in Europe. *American Journal of Human Genetics* 69, 844–52.

Tromnau, G. 1984a. Rentierjagd während des Spätpaläolithikums von Booten aus? *Hammaburg N.F.* 6, 29–38.

Tromnau, G. 1984b. Siedlungsmuster Hamburger Kultur. Beispiel Teltwisch 1 (Ahrensbuger Tunneltal), in H. Berke, J. Hahn and C.-J. Kind (eds.), *Jungpaläolithische Siedlungsstrukturen in Europa*, 235–39. Tübingen, Archaeologica Venatoria.

Tromnau, G. 1992. Anmerkungen zur Rengeweih-Harpune von Meiendorf, in B.-E. Krause and B. Mencke (eds.), *Ur-Geschichte im Ruhrgebiet. Festschrift Arno Heinrich*, 79–83. Gelsenkirchen, Agora.

van der Leeuw, S. 1989. Risk, perception, innovation, in S. van der Leeuw and R. Torrence (eds.), *What's New? A closer look at the process of innovation*, 301–29. London, Unwin Hyman.

Vang Petersen, P. and Johansen, L. 1993. Sølbjerg I – An Ahrensburgian Site on a Reindeer Migration Route through Eastern Denmark. *Journal of Danish Archaeology* 10, 20–37.

Vang Petersen, P. and Johansen, L. 1994. Rensdyrjægere ved Sølbjerg på Lolland. *Nationalmuseets Arbejdsmark* 1994, 80–97.

Vang Petersen, P. and Johansen, L. 1996. Tracking Late Glacial Reindeer Hunters in Eastern Denmark, in L. Larsson (ed.), *The Earliest Settlement of Scandinavia and its relationship with neighbouring areas*, 75–88. Acta Archaeologica Lundensia, Series in 8°, 24. Stockholm, Almqvist & Wiksell International.

Walker, R., Hill, K., Kaplan, H. and McMillan, G. 2002. Age-dependency in hunting ability among the Ache of Eastern Paraguay. *Journal of Human Evolution* 42, 639–57.

Wobst, M. 1974. Boundary conditions for Paleolithic social systems: a simulation approach. *American Antiquity* 39, 147–78.

Wobst, M. 1976. Locational Relationships in Paleolithic Society. *Journal of Human Evolution* 5, 49–58.

Zimmermann, A. 1996. Zur Bevölkerungsdichte in der Urgeschichte, in I. Campen, J. Hahn and M. Uerpmann (eds.), *Spuren der Jagd – Die Jagd nach Spuren. Festschrift Müller-Beck*, 49–61. Tübingen, Archaeologia Venatoria.

Åkerlund, A. 2002. Life without close neighbours. Some reflections on the first peopling of east Central Sweden, in B. V. Eriksen and B. Bratlund (eds.), *Recent studies in the Final Palaeolithic of the European Plain*, 43–8. Højbjerg, Jutland Archaeological Society.

3. Late Palaeolithic reindeer hunters – from a coastal perspective

Bengt Nordqvist

This article is a discussion of the contradiction between the archaeological and anthropological models concerning Late Palaeolithic reindeer hunters. The main issues are that reindeer is an unpredictable species and that it is very difficult to survive within only this unique ecological niche. The conventional standpoint is that groups hunting reindeer survive for the remainder of the year by exploiting mostly marine resources. During the Late Palaeolithic, the crucial means of livelihood for these groups involved seasonal movements between the main hunting reindeer grounds in northern Germany and the distant coastal areas in the archipelago of western Sweden, which provided fishing and the hunting of marine mammals. From this perspective, the majority of the Late Palaeolithic population should be seen as marine hunters who, during a month or two of every year, were hunting reindeer or elk in the interiors of the northern European mainland.

Keywords: Late Palaeolithic, reindeer, sea mammals, interior, coast, seasonal movements, scientific 'soap bubble'.

The archaeological model

The archaeological interpretation of the Ahrensburgian sites has been to view them as reindeer hunting camps. The remains if these sites have been seen as the faunal and flint debris of groups living by the seasonal hunting of reindeer (*Rangifer tarandus*) as their main means of nourishment. For the remaining part of the year these groups moved inland and hunted other terrestrial animals. The traditional archaeological model was to see these groups as the vestiges of an inland population that moved in a comparatively restricted area. The concept of the hunter was synonymous with humans hunting terrestrial mammals – predominantly reindeer; therefore they and their remains were conveniently labeled as, for example, 'Rentierkultur', or as reindeer hunters. This traditional interpretation is fully understandable, based, as it is, on faunal remains from the sites of Stellmoor-Ahrenburg. Grønnow states that, as well as at the surrounding sites with similar artefacts, all the indications are that these groups lived exclusively on reindeer (Grønnow *et al.* 1983, 159).

One explanation for this limited archaeological model is the sole use of generally accepted assemblages: this concept had no room for hypothetical models with seasonal movements that might explain how these reindeers hunters could have lived for the remainder of the year – a way of life which included the use of distant and foreign resources, located, for example, in coastal environments.

This present archaeological research suggests an interpretation for these remains as debris from limited regional groups. The objective was to focus on differences, rather than similarities, between the existing flint assemblages of that time. This was obvious when flint assemblages had already been named as coming from different 'culture groups', as at Ahrensburg, Swidry, Hensbacka, Fosna, amongst others. It could be said that the archaeological model was aligned to modern national borders. There are, however, even other problems connected with the north German finds, when these are predetermined as the remains from groups based exclusively on the hunting of reindeer.

If we look beyond today's borders we have to consider the flooded areas along the southern part of the North Sea: this landscape, 'Doggerland', has become a very interesting area in recent discussions. There is no doubt that there was a population living in this constantly shrinking landscape. Doggerland has provided a range of artefacts found in modern fishing nets (Bjerck 1994, 35; Verhart 1995, 294). The oldest item is a barbed point from the Leman and Ower banks. This object has been ^{14}C-dated to 11,700 cal BC. Although this item comes from far out in the North Sea, the actual find spot was already by that time hundreds of kilometres from the coast, in the location of the former interior. A somewhat younger site has been found at Brown Bank. From this area comes a variety of implements, such as axes, adzes, and picks. They are mainly made of bones from aurochs (*Bos primigenius*) and have been dated to Preboreal and Boreal times (Bjerck 1994, 35). To date there are no finds from Doggerland (either inshore waters or former coastal areas) that can be connected with marine activities (Bjerck 1994, 49; Verhart 1995, 294). Bjerck is of the opinion that the coastline along Doggerland was flat and with no related archipelago (Bjerck 1994, 49). This implies a monotonous coastal area, and it was, presumably, in no way a favourable marine environment. These people were living simultaneously in such a coastal landscape, probably exposed all year to extreme weather conditions while undertaking their marine activities

This coastal landscape seems to have been similar to the shoreline of the southern part of western Sweden. Here the flat landscape meets the sea directly, with no archipelago; the seabed being also relatively flat. Coastal settlements in this area are rare and the few we know are all located at sites connected with estuaries.

Presumably the coastal environment along the Doggerland had been inhabited in a similar way, with few, very concentrated settlements connected to the estuaries.

The anthropological model

Another aspect is that the traditional, archaeological concept has concerned itself in a narrow sense with its conclusions about reindeer economies in terms of other disciplines. Sturdy and Speiss point out one such conclusion originating from paleozoological interpretations based on the living conditions for reindeer hunters. According to Sturdy, all groups depending on caribou had exceptionally low population densities (1975, 77). Even for a site containing large amounts of reindeer bones, it tells us next to nothing about how the local population adapted for the remainder of the year (Speiss 1979, 133). Knowing that people hunted reindeer at one point in their seasonal cycle is a poor indicator of how they survived for the rest of the year: other sites must to be found to represent other seasonalities. Compared with groups with seasonal maritime-hunting or salmon-fishing activities (Speiss 1979, 139), the year-round reindeer-hunter groups exhibit lower population densities overall. Burch gives an example for a group who had a fairly reliable resource base, comprising mostly of fish, that had a population density nearly 20 times as great as the group who lived almost entirely on reindeer (1972, 365). His standpoint is that the greater the dependence of human population on reindeer, the lower its population density will be (1972, 366).

It is also a high-risk strategy to rely just on reindeer. The reindeer as species has a tendency suddenly to alter its routes dramatically between on year and the next; additionally the populations can vary in a decade from tens of thousands to a few hundreds (Burch 1972, 352, 365; Grønnow *et al.* 1983, 13). The current state of knowledge, therefore, is that human populations largely dependent upon caribou will faced with a major resource crises at least once every two or three generations (Burch 1972, 356).

Burch (1972, 364) brings to a head this problem when he discusses the current interpretation for those groups whose bone remains show an extremely high proportion of reindeer: '... the most important question about the people who lived on sites characterized by exceptionally high percentages of caribou/reindeer remains is *where* the lived and *what* they lived on during the rest of the year.' He also point out that groups hunting reindeer usually had other food resources to exploit over the rest of the year, and that even the Palaeolithic hunter must have had a diversified resource base – one probably including fish and/or sea mammals as important elements (Burch 1972, 351, 365).

Contradictions between the two models

Today, it is obvious that there was a major difference between the ethnographical/anthropological and archaeological interpretation of the Late Palaeolithic finds and the artefacts found in southern Scandinavia and northern Germany. Based on research results collected from Inuit groups from Greenland, Alaska and northern Canada, ethnographists/anthropologists such Troel-Smith (1963), Burch (1972) and Grønnow (1985) in the main agree on Late Palaeolithic artefacts. The conditions of these arctic living groups have been documented in historic time.

Against their model of interpretation stands the archaeological point of view. This model is represented by many archaeologists, such as Rust (1937, 116, 140; 1943, 199, 230), Taute (1968, 265 ff.), Clark (1975, 90), Tromnau (1975, 42) and Bokelmann (1979, 19 ff.). Recently, similar interpretations have been put forward by, for example, Holm and Rieck (1992, 66), Vang Petersen and Johansen (1996, 85), Eriksen (1996, 18; 2002, 36) and Bratlund (1996, 27; 2002, 106). These archaeological interpretations have been based mainly on faunal and flint debris from German, Polish and Danish sites.

Limitations of the models

The ethnographists/anthropologists saw in the Late Palaeolithic artefact assemblages a correspondence between the remains from the Inuit culture and those from northern Europe; they were looking for similarities instead of differences: an opposite approach to that which we have seen from the archaeological perspective. The ethnographical/anthropological focus was on the survival strategy needed for a population characterized by a sophisticated hunting strategy in an exposed artic environment. Their models were based on different sources from archaeology, zoology, ethnography and ethnohistory (e.g. Grønnow 1985; Burch 1972). The basis for these models, in relation to Palaeolithic sites, was that the remains of reindeer proved only one part of the economy of Palaeolithic groups. An obvious feature for these groups was the seasonal movements between the reindeer grounds in northern Germany and the distant coastal areas for fishing and hunting marine mammals, presumably at sites situated along the North Sea littoral. I believe we find the remains of these groups in the archipelago of western Sweden and south-western Norway (Burch 1972, 365; Grønnow *et al.* 1987, 159; Troel-Schmitt 1963, 51). It is commonly thought that these arctic-living people had a strategy to utilize the extreme seasonal accumulation of natural resources within the marine and terrestrial environments (Nordqvist 2000, 228). This way of life was not new: constantly during the Palaeolithic, groups travelled long distances between the sea and interior (Cleyet-Merle and Madelaine 1995, 303).

Contributions from western Sweden: another viewpoint

An outline of the Preboral period in western Sweden is as follows. When the ice started melting, about 11,000 years ago, there was also a change in the way groups of people began to utilize the resources around them. The whole archipelago was now inhabited. It was a process that continued until 10,500 years ago. In this area it is possible to observe two main concentrations of settlements. One is outside Uddevalla, the other in the Gothenburg area. In this coastal landscape there are at least 500 known settlements from the Preboreal phase. At some sites only a few tanged points have been collected, and at others at least 30–50 flake axes of Preboreal type were found. The natural question is why there are so many sites situated in western Sweden? The answer lies in the rich marine biotopes at that time. These biotopes were beyond the straits and were extremely high in nutritional values during the melting phase of the inland ice. This was the result of the melting fresh water flowing through these vast straits and meeting the very salt seawater in the archipelago of western Sweden. This environment was particularly nutrient rich during late spring and summer. These conditions were, of course, very attractive for all sea living animals. These conditions lasted until the straits were blocked (around 10,500 years ago). The evidence of this very rich marine environment can be found in the surviving, gigantic natural shell-middens of this period.

Already 50 years ago, the archaeologists of western Sweden realized that there were flint scatters that had originated from an extensive utilization of the marine environment during the late Palaeolithic (see for example Fredsjö 1953, 137 ff.). This opinion found little favour outside of western Sweden and Norway, as European colleagues had only the settlement sites from inland to go on, and they lacked the flint debris from the coastal activities. These differences in flint typology and preservation conditions brought about a common and generally accepted interpretation that the German and Danish sites were the remains of groups living in the interior and hunting reindeer and elk (*Alces alces*). The chronology of the coastal Swedish sites and their relations with other 'culture' groups were disputed. However, among the archaeologists of western Sweden it always has been common ground that these flint assemblages are the remains of groups living as marine hunters-fishers during the late Palaeolithic (e.g. Fredsjö 1953; Cullberg 1974; Andersson *et al.* 1988; Schmitt 1995; Kindgren 1995; Nordqvist 1995). In addition, there is Troels-Smith's model indicating populations adapted to coastal conditions and moving southwards on a seasonal basis from the archipelago of western Sweden (and south-western Norway) to the northern parts of Europe (Kindgren 1996, 203; Nordqvist 2000, 228; Schmitt 1995, 168; Troel-Smith 1963, 51).

Reconsidering Late Palaeolithic hunting complexes as a whole

To sum up, we have seen that the overriding and frequent archaeological interpretations of the Late Palaeolithic groups were based on regarding them as depending on a single economy. This point of view was based on people living in an arctic climate and mainly hunting terrestrial mammals such as reindeer and elk. These groups were also presumed to have a limited mobility that was restricted to the interior. They seem to be characterized by limited flexibility, in the sense that they did not have the ability to adapt to the seasonal and annual changes in the landscapes that surrounded them. This archaeological model does not describe the lifestyles of these peoples as dynamic, but rather as rigid (simple model).

The archaeological points of view described above are in contrast to the ethnographic/anthropologic concept. An opposing view is, for example, presented in the work undertaken by Grønnow and Meldgaard (Grønnow 1985; Grønnow *et al.* 1983; Meldgaard 1995, 2003). One of the most basic concepts presented is that the surrounding ecosystems and the different biotopes are constantly changing and are to be seen as unstable over time (Meldgaard 1995, 367). Groups of people living in such exposed environment must, broadly speaking, exploit all of the resources available to them at that time. Because of the unpredictable environment it was important for these groups to have flexible hunting strategies as well as placing economic emphasis on all available resources (complex model). This adaptation explains why these groups are characterized as being highly mobile, as well with developing methods for food storage (as in Greenland).

It seems that, in the traditional archaeological model, the human populations were not parts of the prevailing ecosystems. These Late Palaeolithic groups appear to have been living in a scientific 'soap bubble', in the sense that they lived unaffected to the unpredictable environment around them. This model must be seen as very simplistic; it stands in contradiction to the ethnographical/anthropological points of view, where humans lived as part of the ecological system. In reality, these groups had to pay regard to changes in nature and the surrounding biotopes. Bjerck points out various issues with the simplified archaeological perspective. He emphasized that we, the archaeologists, do not show enough respect for the complexity within the artic marine environment (Bjerck 1994, 49). It is a standpoint worthy of consideration and has its greatest relevance with the time period under discussion – the Preboreal (Nordqvist 2000, 228) – a time period is characterized by dramatic changes in the living conditions caused by major transformations in the surrounding ecosystems. These changes were dependent on extreme climate development, which affected and totally changed the fauna and flora, as well as the coastal landscape. Of course these changes must have affected the lives of humans in a dramatic way. Therefore the majority of these Late Palaeolithic hunting groups should probably be seen as marine hunters who, during a month or two of each year, would be hunting reindeer and elk in the interiors of the northern part of the European mainland.

References

Andersson, S., Wigforss, J. and Nancke-Krogh, S. 1988. *Fångstfolk för 8000 år sedan – om en grupp stenåldersboplatser i Göteborg*. Arkeologi i Västsverige 3. Göteborg, Göteborgs arkeologiska museum.

Bjerck, H. B. 1994. Nordsjøfastlandet og pionerbosetningen i Norge. *Viking* LVII, 25–58.

Bokelmann, K. 1979. Rentierjäger am Glescherrand in Schleswig-Holstein? *Offa* 36, 12–22.

Bratlund, B. 1996. Archaeozoological Comments on the Final Paleolithic Frontiers in South Scandinavia, in L. Larsson (ed.), *The Earliest Settlement of Scandinavia and its relationship with neighbouring areas*, 23–34. Acta Archaeologica Lundensia, Series in 8°, 12. Stockholm, Almqvist & Wiksell International.

Bratlund, B. 2002. The faunal remains from Wilszyse, in B. V. Eriksen and B. Bratlund (ed.), *Recent studies in the Final Paleolithic of the European plain*, 101–8. Jutland Archaeological Society Publications 39. Århus, Århus University Press.

Burch, E. S. 1972. The Caribou/Wild Reindeer as a Human Resource. *American Antiquity* 37 (3), 339–68.

Clark, G. 1975. *The Earlier Stone Age settlement of Scandinavia*. Cambridge, Cambridge University Press.

Cleyet-Merle, J.-J. and Madelaine, S. 1995. Inland evidence of human sea coast exploitation in Paleolithic France, in A. Fischer (ed.), *Man and Sea in the Mesolithic: coastal settlement above and below present sea level*, 303–8. Oxbow Monographs 53. Oxford, Oxbow Books.

Eriksen, B. V. 1996. Regional variations in Late Pleistocene subsistence strategies. Southern Scandinavian reindeer hunters in a European context, in L. Larsson (ed.), *The earliest settlement of Scandinavia and its relationship with neighbouring areas*, 7–22. Acta Archaeologica Lundensia, Series in 8°, 24. Stockholm, Almqvist & Wiksell International.

Eriksen, B. V. 2002. Reconsidering the geochronological framework of Lateglacial environments in European plain: potentials and limitations, in B. V. Eriksen and B. Bratlund (eds.), *Recent studies in the Final Paleolithic of the European plain*, 25–42. Jutland Archaeological Society Publications 39. Århus, Århus University Press.

Cullberg, C. 1974. Cullberg svarar på Welinders kritik. *Fornvännen 3*, 155–64.

Fredsjö, C. 1953. *Studier i västsveriges äldre stenålder*. Göteborg, Göteborg Archaeological Museum.

Grønnow, B. 1985. *Meiendorf and Stellmoor revisited. An Analysis of Late Palaeolithic Reindeer Exploitation*, 131–66. Acta Archaeologica 56. University of Copenhagen, Department of Archaeology.

Grønnow, B., Meldgaard, M. and Berglund Nielsen, J. 1983. *Aasivissuit – The Great Summer Camp. Archaeological, ethnographical and zoo-archaeological studies of a caribou-hunting site in West Greenland*. Meddelser om Grønland, Man and Society 5. Copenhagen, Commission for Scientific Research in Greenland.

Holm, J. and Rieck, F. 1992. *Istidsjægere vid Jelssøerne*. Skrifter fra Museumsrådet for Sønderjyllands Amt 5. Haderslev, Haderslev Museum.

Kindgren, H. 1995. Hensbacka-Hogen-Hornborgasjön: Early Mesolithic coastal and inland settlements in western Sweden, in A. Fischer (ed.), *Man and Sea in the Mesolithic – coastal settlement above and below present sea level*, 171–84. Oxbow Monographs 53. Oxford, Oxbow Books.

Kindgren, H. 1996. Reindeer or seals? Some Late Palaeolithic sites in central Bohuslän, in L. Larsson (ed.), *The Earliest Settlement of Scandinavia and its relationship with neighbouring areas*, 191–205. Acta Archaeologica Lundensia, Series in 8°, 24. Stockholm, Almqvist & Wiksell International.

Meldgaard, M. 1995. Resource pulses in a marine environment: a case study from Disco Bugt, West Greenland, in A. Fischer (ed.), *Man and Sea in the Mesolithic – coastal settlement above and below present sea level*, 361–68. Oxbow Monographs 53. Oxford, Oxbow Books.

Nordqvist, B. 1995. The Mesolithic settlements of the Swedish west coast – with special emphasis on chronology and topography of coastal settlements, in A. Fischer (ed.), *Man and Sea in the Mesolithic – coastal settlement above and below present sea level*, 185–96. Oxbow Monographs 53. Oxford, Oxbow Books.

Nordqvist, B. 2000. *Coastal Adaptations in the Mesolithic. A study of coastal sites with organic remains from the Boreal and Atlantic periods in Western Sweden*. Gotarc Series B. Göteborg Archaeological Theses 13. Göteborg, Göteborgs Universitet, Institutionen för arkeologi.

Rust, A. 1937. *Das Altsteinzeitlische Rentierjägerlager Meiendorf.* Neumünster, Karl Wachholtz Verlag.

Schmitt, L. 1995. The West Swedish Hensbacka: a maritime adaptation and a seasonal expression of the North-Central Europian Ahrensburgian?, in A. Fischer (ed.), *Man and Sea in the Mesolithic – coastal settlement above and below present sea level*, 161–70. Oxbow Monographs 53. Oxford, Oxbow Books.

Spiess, A. 1979. *Reindeer and Caribou Hunters. An Archaeological Study*. New York, Academic Press.

Sturdy, D. A. 1975. Some Reindeer economies in Prehistoric Europe, in E. Higgs (ed.), *Paleoeconomy*, 55–95. Cambridge, Cambridge University Press.

Taute, W. 1968. *Die Stielspitzen-Gruppen im nördlichen Mitteleuropa. Ein Beitrag zur Kenntnis der späten Altsteinzeit.* Fundamenta, Reihe A5. Köln/Graz, Böhlau Verlag.

Troel-Smith, J. 1963. Danmark og den Svenske vestkysts mesolitiske stenaldersbegyggelse, *FYND* 1963, 43–52.

Tromnau, G. 1975. *Die fundplätze der Hamburger kultur von Heber und Deimern, Kreis Soltau*. Materialhefte zur Ur- und Frühgeschichte Niedersachsens, hgg. i. A. der archäologischen Kommission von Klemens Wilhelmi, Heft 9. Hildesheim, Lax Verlag.

Vang Petersen, P. and Johansen L. 1996. Tracking Late Glacial Reindeer Hunters in Eastern Denmark, in L. Larsson (ed.), *The Earliest Settlement of Scandinavia and its relationship with neighbouring areas*, 75–88. Acta Archaeologica Lundensia, Series in 8°, 24. Stockholm, Almqvist & Wiksell International.

Verhart, L. B. M. 1995. Fishing for the Mesolithic. The North Sea: a submerged Mesolithic landscape, in A. Fischer (ed.), *Man and Sea in the Mesolithic - coastal settlement above and below present sea level*, 291–302. Oxbow Monographs 53. Oxford, Oxbow Books.

4. Colonizing seascapes: comparative perspectives on the development of maritime relations in the Pleistocene/Holocene transition in north-west Europe

Hein Bjartmann Bjerck

The lowering of global sea level during the Pleistocene by more than 100m constitutes a problem in terms of general research on early maritime-oriented societies. However, Postglacial isostatic rise in the glaciated regions has produced raised shorelines of Late Pleistocene/Early Holocene age, e.g. Scandinavia, Patagonia and North America. Comparative perspectives from these areas are of vital interest in this discussion. The extensive Norwegian coastline appears to have been colonized in the course of the few hundred years around 9500 cal BC. An overwhelming majority of Preboreal sites are found in the fiord/skerry coastal landscape, indicating that marine resources were vital in the subsistence pattern. The lithic tradition is clearly linked to specialized mega fauna hunters in the continental plains (Ahrensburg), but facts and dynamics of the development of the marine subsistence pattern is unclear. This paper focuses on this problem – with comparative perspectives towards the emergence of maritime foragers in Patagonia.

Keywords: colonizing seascapes, Pleistocene/Holocene transition, marine adaptation, Scandinavia, Patagonia.

Introduction. The fiord/skerry seascapes and marine foraging societies

This paper aims to highlight the archaeological record from the Scandinavian seascapes in the discussion of marine foraging societies. To my knowledge, the earliest part of the Komsa/Fosna/Hensbacka traditions (9500–9000 cal BC) are the oldest documented marine foragers in north-west Europe. The colonization of Scandinavia seemingly encompasses the emergence and development of marine subsistence strategies. Thus, this record is important to the understanding of the Pleistocene/Holocene transition, and a case of relevance to general studies of marine foraging societies.

The Scandinavian seascape is a stretch of 3000km coastal area facing a range of marine environments – the Skagerak, the North Sea, the Norwegian Sea and the Barents Sea. This is a highly productive marine habitat today, and there is no reason to believe that this was different in the Mesolithic. Judging from the abundance of archaeological material, the Scandinavian seascapes were once home to large and numerous groups of sustainable marine foragers.

Similar seascapes are found in other glaciated areas of the world, e.g. North America, Patagonia and New Zealand. Likewise, these regions inhibit substantial archaeological material and ethnographical record documenting maritime foragers. In fact, these areas are the host some of the most extreme maritime adaptations the world has seen: e.g. the Kwakiutl, Makah, Tlingit, Haida, Aleuts in North America, the Inuits of Greenland and Canada, the Chukchee in north-west Asia, the Huillche, Chonos, Kawéskar and Yámana in Patagonia, and the Maori of New Zealand.

These seascapes are bountiful and varied habitats, ideal for marine exploitation. The borderline between land and sea disintegrates into fiords, bays, channels, islands, skerries and submerged reefs, implying ample areas of sheltered seas, safe transport routes and natural harbours. With all these advantages, one would expect that these seascapes were settled immediately after deglaciation in the Late Pleistocene. It is intriguing, somewhat disappointing, and quite contrary to popular beliefs that this seems *not* to be the case. The Scandinavian seascapes were freed from ice *c.* 13,500 cal BC, but there is no hard archaeological evidence at the raised shorelines until around 9500 cal BC. Why was this bountiful habitat neglected by the surrounding hunter-gatherers for more than 100 generations?

A similar 'delayed' colonization seems to be the case in other skerry/fiord seascapes. There are reasons to highlight this, as the seascapes of the glaciated archipelagos contain the oldest preserved shores on dry land in the world. Globally, the Holocene inundation of Pleistocene coastal areas also drowned the archaeological record in these seascapes. However, in the areas with the largest ice shields, deglaciation runs parallel with a considerable crustal rebounce, creating raised beaches (see below). Consequently, the archaeological evidence from these shores is of great value in the discussion of the roots of marine adaptations.

A long list of what may be labelled as aquatic elements is documented from archaeological contexts far back in the Pleistocene (Erlandson 2001). The majority are indirect evidence of some kind of contact with marine environments and it is unclear to what degree this evidence reflects proper marine adaptations. However, one may ask – how is it possible that the optimal fiord/skerry seascapes, prime habitats for the most pronounced maritime human adaptations ever documented, are neglected? My assumption is that the delayed colonization is a cultural issue, and that the (presumed) negative evidence from the oldest shorelines is a ghost image of marginal/less elaborate marine relations of the surrounding hunter-gatherers.

Backdrop 1. Pleistocene glaciations and maritime environments

The actual record of the origins of maritime adaptations is inadequate. The most important reason is the dramatic changes in sea level (*eustacy*) during and immediately after the last ice age, resulting in a worldwide submergence of the Pleistocene coastal areas (Andersen and Borns 1997). Large portions of the water in the world's oceans were bound in the great ice caps. During the maximum extent of the Late Pleistocene ice sheets around 22,000 cal BC, the sea level was around 120m lower than today (Fairbanks 1989). Thus, the contemporaneous coastal areas are found at sea depths that are relatively inaccessible for archaeological research. Subsequently, the knowledge of human activity in coastal areas during and just after the ice age is limited. In rare cases, sites have been found as a result of strategic marine archaeological inventories, as shown, for example, by Bell and Renouff (2004), Faught (2004), and Fisher (1995). In line with the melting of the ice caps, sea level rose to today's level. Roughly speaking, sea level approached its present status 2000–5000 cal BC (Pirazzoli 1991; 1996; Lewis 2000, 527).

The weight of the ice masses led to local compressions of the earth's crust (*isostacy*) followed by a rebounce in parallel with deglaciation. The isostatic rise was in many places greater than the eustatic rise, and resulted in a series of elevated shorelines. In these areas, Late and Early Postglacial coasts are preserved, as well as possible traces of maritime activities. In Scandinavia, a considerable isostatic rebounce is documented. At most, land rise is close to 300m asl (Bothnia Bay), and in several coastal areas in Norway more than 100m asl (Andersen 2000, 159). It is also noteworthy that the shore displacement rate was very rapid in the Early Holocene (3m/100 years), and gradually slower in later periods. The glacio-isostacy of Patagonia and Pacific North America is more complex because of high tectonic activity.

Perhaps even more important are the common environmental characteristics of the seascapes in the glacially formed areas. The coastal topography is characterized by a broad belt of archipelago seascapes, often more than 100–200km wide, made up of islands, inlets, skerries, bays, points and deep fjords (Klemsdal 1982), which may be labelled the *fiord/skerry seascapes*. In fact, the Norwegian shoreline (including islands of all sizes) is the equivalent of more than twice the equatorial circumference of the Earth, and the ratio coastal length/shoreline is on average 1/30 (Bjerck 2008). Globally, this coastal landscape is exclusive to the glacial areas of North America (primarily Canada), Greenland, Svalbard, Scandinavia, Scotland, and northern parts of the Eurasian continent. The southern ice cap areas were considerably smaller, the largest located in Patagonia and New Zealand (Flint 1971, 78–9). I recommend a quick glance in a general Atlas or GoogleEarth for a better impression of these seascapes.

These areas are among the most *productive* marine biotopes in the world. One factor is the general high productivity of the cold/temperate waters surrounding the polar areas. Another is the varied topography, with changing depths and passages, combined with the tidal currents that mix water masses of different temperatures, salinity and microbiology, stimulating the biological life on both micro- and macro-levels (Rinde *et al.* 1998; Skjolddal 2004). Another factor is that these seascapes imply safer conditions for marine exploitation. In fjords and inlets, and between skerries and islets, there are large bodies of sheltered seas. The varied topography also provides ample numbers of natural harbours that make secure the connection between land and sea – between people and their subsistence base. The rich resources and lower risk factors are probably important prerequisites for human society developing a pronounced, maritime, subsistence pattern in these areas during the Holocene.

The marine environments are also subject to the pronounced climatic changes in the Late Pleistocene/Holocene. Changes in the general pattern of the ocean streams, and their influence on the position of the oceanic polar front are important to consider (e.g. Lehman and Keigwin 1992). These factors imply substantial differences in biological regimes and sea-ice conditions that are highly relevant to the details of this discussion.

Backdrop 2. Maritime adaptations and the archaeological record

The archaeological record from the submerged shorelines has been much debated (e.g. Reid 1913; Nummedal 1924; Bailey and Parkington 1988). Some researchers point to the vast productivity of marine environments, and find it hard to believe that these reserves were neglected at any time. This 'Garden of Eden' view is contrasted by the 'Gates of Hell' perspective, suggesting that the marine orientation in hunter-gatherer adaptations is a hallmark of the Holocene

(Yesner 1980; 1987; Erlandson 2001, 290). Erlandson's interesting paper *Archaeology of Aquatic Adaptations* is one of only a few globally-oriented studies, reviewing facts, belief and discussions. However, opposing views have one thing in common: they are based on a vide variety of *indications*, and next to no hard facts.

What is maritime adaptation? In my view, the debate tends to suffer from a lack of operational analytical terms. *Maritime adaptation* tends to be a question of presence or absence, a question of marine or terrestrial, and fails to include the multitude of variations and strategic complexity. Instead of *adaptations* I would like to use the term *relations*, i.e. the multitude of components, factors and circumstances that are the building blocks in 'real life' holistic and complex adaptations.

Another problem is that definitions tend to be based on criteria which are hard to identify in the archaeological record. Erlandson (2001, 299) lists definitions based on habitats, technology, and percentage of diet. I think operational definitions can be found within the framework of a variety of *aquatic relations* (and in this paper, the term *aquatic* refer to water in general, *maritime* equates to 'coastal'), in contrast to *marine* that are related to open sea, not as evolutionary stages, but rather a complexity of lifestyles within a variety of habitats encompassing all the relevant elements above. The term *relation* implies an almost unlimited array of combinations in actual adaptation strategies. A crucial point in this complexity is the matter of scale. This is illustrated by the lists of the aquatic evidence presented in Erlandson (2001, 306 ff.), starting with a possible 2.3-million-year-old exploitation of fresh water fish in the Olduvai Gorge. The long list is interesting, but is confusing without more clear-cut definitions. The cultural difference between finding a shell on the beach at the edge of the ocean and earning a livelihood in the open sea is tremendous, but difficult to grasp without considering scale and variations (see Ames 2002, 21).

I would think that very few societies have no aquatic relations. However, one may distinguish between *Lacustrine*, *Littoral* and *Marine* relations. These are broad habitat characteristics that are operational in the present discussion, as one may use general spatial distribution of sites as a basis for interpretation. In addition, these three also entail distinct differences in the resource base, foraging strategies, tools and equipment.

Lacustrine relations: A variety of relations to bodies of fresh water, rivers and lakes, encompassing resources in this habitat (e.g. fish, birds), transport routes (using boats), or utilising bodies of water to control movements of prey (e.g. reindeer), or as kill sites.

Littoral relations: Land-based maritime relations (beaches, estuaries, tidal flats), encompassing resources in this habitat (e.g. collecting of shells, eggs, seaweed, fishing by traps, scavenging, clubbing of seals on shore). As strict littoral relations do not include boats, activities on open seas are marginal. However, it is natural to include a range of relations concerning sea-ice, e.g. ice fishing and hunting seal by air holes.

Marine relations: This is a wide range of relations to open sea, fishing, hunting, travelling, transporting. Inevitably, marine relations depend on elaborate boats that are capable of facilitating and ensuring this variety of activities. Frequent occupation of islands, and frequent relations between sites and natural harbours are archaeological indications of marine relations.

The division between the latter two may be crucial in the discussion of the colonization of fiord/skerry seascapes. Elaborate marine relations, including seaworthy vessels/boats are essential to life in these areas. Strictly littoral relations would not even permit moving around in this landscape.

Additionally, more clear cut and focussed case studies at key points in time and space may facilitate more targeted research likely to produce archaeological facts of relevance to the discussion of the development of maritime relations. In this respect, the cultural development in the different fiord/skerry seascapes in Late Pleistocene/Early Holocene is worthy of closer study. In my brief review, I will focus on the seascapes in Patagonia and Scandinavia.

Backdrop 3. The Patagonian case

Chile stretches along more than half of the Pacific coast of South America, with more than 4000km of coastline between 18° and 55° S; sub-tropical in the north, the outer reaches of the Antarctic in the south. Two-thirds of the Chilean coastline is unprotected beaches facing the Pacific. The southern section is characterized by a fiord/skerry seascape similar to Scandinavia. Patagonia is the southern cone of the continent, including Chile's coastal landscape from Puerto Montt to Cape Horn, and with the southern Argentinean mainland and Tierra del Fuego. The area encompasses very different environments, from Chile's seascape, the alpine Andes, the Argentinean pampas and the unsheltered beaches/coastal cliffs facing the south Atlantic. Junius Bird, one of the pioneers in the archaeological research of the region in the 1930s, described this landscape as a mixture of Norwegian coast and North American prairie (Bird 1988, 3).

As in Scandinavia, the maximal extent of the latest ice-cover occurred in Patagonia around 22,000 cal BC, with a Late Glacial period from *c.* 14,000 cal BC, with oscillations of the ice masses up to deglaciation in the millennia after 9500 cal BC (McCulloch *et al.* 1997, 20–3). The Patagonian ice cap was around 700,000km2, i.e. *c.* 1/10 of the Baltic ice cap (Flint 1971, 78–9), and the isostatic rise was correspondingly less. Late Glacial and Early Holocene coastlines are therefore found below today's sea level. The Holocene transgression passes today's sea level at about 7000 cal BC, and culminating around 5000 cal BC at 4 to 8m asl. After this, isostatic rise resulted in successive shorelines leading up to modern sea level. However, the factor of unstable tectonics in the area implies many exceptions to this general picture (McCulloch *et al.* 1997, 26–7).

The age of the earliest human settlement in the Americas

is much debated (e.g. Borrero and McEvan 1997, 32; Dillehay 2000, 15 ff.). However, there is indisputable Late Glacial evidence of humans in Patagonia. *Mont Verde*, situated on the coastal plain near Puerto Montt, is dated to c. 12,500 cal BC (Dillehay 2000, 160 ff.). In addition, a number of sites, mainly in Pampas areas east and south of the Andes, are dated earlier than 9500 cal BC (McCulloch *et al.* 1997, 36 ff.; Dillehay 2000, 90). The finds point to a terrestrial based subsistence pattern where mega-fauna is a major factor.

The earliest evidence of clear-cut *marine relations* is dated as late as 5520–5320 cal BC (Piana 2005, 121; Mena 1997, 51). This is the date of the Tunel I site in Canal Beagle at Tierra del Fuego, where a definite marine adaptation is documented – shells, seals, fish, harpoons made of seal bones. Older cultural deposits (5980–5750 cal BC) at the same site, with a clear terrestrial subsistence pattern (no marine elements) may indicate that the maritime adaptation was developed around 5500 cal BC (Orquera and Piana 1999a, 45 ff.). The sites demonstrate subsistence strategies focussed on shellfish (numerous and large shell middens) and varied sea mammals, but also encompassing some birds, fish and terrestrial mammals (guanacos).

From about 5000 cal BC there are numerous sites documenting definite littoral and marine relations in Canal Beagle, Isla de Navarino, Estrecho de Magallanes, Seno Otway, and Seno Skyring (Legoupil 1997; Ocampo and Rivas 2000; Piana 2005). Interestingly enough, this very area is the meeting point of the vast Argentinean Pampas and the Patagonian skerry/fiord seascapes. A similar situation is documented in the Chiloe area, on the northern border of the Patagonian skerry/fiord seascape, i.e. the marine-oriented site Puente Quilo, dated to *c.* 4500 cal BC (Rivas *et al.* 1999).

The timing of the elaboration of *marine relations* is connected to the forestation of the area, which is considered essential for vital tools and equipment (harpoon handles, canoes, fuel) (Orquera and Piana 1987, 153; Piana 2005, 122). The distribution of sites paints a picture of mobile hunter groups with distinctive, shared characteristics in material culture over large areas, and a broad spectrum of resource utilization at the cutting edge of diverse resources, both marine and terrestrial. These are the roots of the historically documented, marine hunter-gatherers of Patagonia, Yámana and Kawéskar (Borrero 1997, 60 ff.; Mena 1997, 54). The extremely marine lifestyle of the 'Nomads of the sea', or 'Los Canoeros', in early historical sources are well worth a further study (e.g. Gusinde 1931; Borrero 1997; Orquera and Piana 1999b). The Yámana spend a large part of their lives in their canoes (with fireplaces on a layer of gravel), hunting, fishing, travelling – the male up front with his harpoon, always ready for his prey, women astern paddling, not for life, but for a lifetime. The result is visible to the naked eye from the skeletal evidence, i.e. the powerful muscle-attachment sites and twisted *humerii* (Aspillaga *et al.* 1999, 132).

All in all, the marine-oriented lifestyle in Patagonia is a mid-Holocene development. Interestingly, the early maritime sites are found in the interfaces between the Pampas (i.e. habitats for Late Pleistocene mega-fauna hunter groups) and the fiord/skerry seascapes. This also seems to be the case in the Puerto Montt area – the meeting point between the extensive coastal plain along the Pacific side of the Andes.

Backdrop 4. Colonization of the Scandinavian seascapes and the elaboration of marine relations

The Norwegian seascapes were ice-free throughout the entire Late Glacial period, from around 13,500 cal BC (Andersen *et al.* 1995). Prior to about 9500 cal BC the archaeological record is limited to sporadic indications – single artefacts believed to be of Late Glacial age (e.g. Rolfsen 1972, 148), and the much debated faunal remains dated to the Ålesund (*c.* 30,000 radiocarbon years BP) and Bølling interstadials (*c.* 12,000 cal BC) in the Sjong cave, and from the Bølling deposits at Blomvåg (Lie 1986; 1990; Larsen *et al.* 1987, 285; Johansen and Undås 1992). The lack of undisputable evidence contrasts sharply with the wealth of settlement sites from the period *after* 9500 cal BC. In sum, the Preboreal Fosna techno-complex constitutes the pioneer settlement of Norway (Bjerck 1995; 2008, with references). This situation is parallel to western Sweden and the Hensbacka techno-complex (e.g. Kindgren 1996; Larsson 1996; Nordqvist 1999). It seems the entire coastline from western Sweden to Varanger was settled in the course of 200–300 years prior to 9000 cal BC (Bjerck 1995, 138).

The north European Early Postglacial period is characterised by marked similarities in material culture (technology, tool tradition and choice of raw material), and points to strong affinities between Fosna, Hensbacka (Kindgren 1996; Nordqvist 1999; Schmitt 1999), Late Glacial Ahrensburg (Fischer 1996; Eriksen 2002, 34; Kutschera 1999; Fuglestvedt 2001; 2003; Waraas 2001), and Danish Preboreal finds (Fischer 1996). The Late Glacial hunters of the north European plains seem to have had a mobile settlement pattern with large fauna, particularly reindeer (*rangifer tarandus*), as an important resource base (Eriksen 1996). A common explanation for the initial settlement of Scandinavia has been that hunter groups began to follow as reindeer herds shifted towards the north in parallel with the deglaciation (e.g. Rolfsen 1972, 146; Johansen and Undås 1992, 16; Fuglestvedt 2001; 2003). Preboreal sites, most likely related to seasonal reindeer hunting, are documented in the high mountain areas of south Norway (Gustafson 1988; Bang-Andersen 2003). Still, the majority of sites are found in the outer-lying areas of the Norwegian fiord/skerry seascape. I estimate that more than 90% of the sites are in coastal areas and that two-thirds of these are situated on islands and islets. Obviously, marine resources were a significant factor in the subsistence pattern of the Fosna tradition (Bjerck 1995; Pettersen 1999; Bang-Andersen 2003). Although remains of boats are unknown, we need not doubt the existence of a well-developed boat technology, since it is impossible otherwise to travel in this landscape – or move among the Preboreal settlements. This picture is strikingly similar to the distribution of Hensbacka sites in west Sweden (Kindgren 1995; 1996; 1999, 58).

If subsistence strategies in the now submerged coastal regions along the north European plains in Late Pleistocene included elaborate marine relations (e.g. Fischer 1996, 171), why did colonization of the Norwegian seascapes occur 3000 years after the emergence of this advantageous coastal habitat? There is a definite possibility that elaborate marine relations are a Mesolithic development that occurred as an integrated part of the colonization of Scandinavian seascapes (Bjerck 1995). The circumstances of the earliest settlement of Ireland (Woodman 2003) and Scotland (Saville 2004) seem to be similar, and may also be related to this process (Tolan-Smith 2003).

Discussion: aquatic relations in the north European setting at the Pleistocene/Holocene transition

Inspired by the Patagonian case, and assuming that my interpretation of the present archaeological record is valid, one can examine a Scandinavian focal point in time, space and cultural traditions. In time: around 9500 cal BC, when a rapid and accelerating cultural process, including an intensification of marine relations occurred within the Ahrensburg/Fosna/Hensbacka traditions. In space: the interface between the continental plains and the skerry/fiord seascape in western Sweden.

In the archaeological record from the Late Glacial traditions (including Ahrensburg), a series of *lacustrine relations* are indicated. The spatial distribution of lithic traditions proves that the large rivers that cut through the European plains were frequently crossed (Eriksen 2002, 29), suggesting that some kind of boats were used. There are indications that lakes and rivers were used in subsistence strategies – to direct reindeer herds in communal drives, and, perhaps, the killing of animals in the water and also the exploitation of aquatic birds (Eriksen 1996, 121). Inherent in the *lacustrine relations* is a wide range of ontological, practical and technological challenges that are relevant to the elaboration of maritime relations. *Littoral relations* are unknown, but likely. However, it is important to bear in mind that the coastal areas of the continental plains were quite different from the Scandinavian seascapes: long stretches of unprotected beaches, few natural harbours; all in all seascapes less resourceful and more risky to approach. On the other hand, it is difficult to believe that members of Late Glacial hunter groups never roamed the borders of the sea, and that the obvious resources of these beaches were never tasted. If it ever was experienced (very likely), basking seals must have been a temptation to great to resist. However, the elaboration of *marine relations* during the Late Glacial is disputable, as indicated by the absence of sites in the Norwegian seascapes.

Seal hunting may have been a decisive factor in this process (Bjerck 1995; Schmitt 1995; Kindgren 1996), as the species constitutes a considerable resource in the interface of littoral and marine relations. Seals (Phocidae) have a series of characteristics that must have aroused the curiosity of people specialised in the hunting of large terrestrial mammals. They are warm-blooded, with skin, fat, teeth, meat, blood, intestines, sinews and bone. It may be hunted on beaches, often in large numbers. The large fat reserves must have been a useful resource as food, fuel, and in the production and maintenance of tools and equipment (e.g. Eidlitz 1969), and the easy killing on shore must have been an added inducement. Seal can also be hunted on sea-ice during winter and spring, i.e. within what I have defined as littoral relations. But if seals are included as a staple in the subsistence base, a problem quickly arises. Seals tend to avoid kill-sites and continually move to new areas. Hence, the need for more reliable supplies of seal may act as a 'pull factor' towards the elaboration of marine relations, allowing for hunting in the open sea. The rate of development of sea-going boats capable of secure voyaging and hunting in open (and very cold) water, may have been the biggest technological drawback to the emergence of an economy grounded in marine relations. In short, members of the Ahrensburg tradition may have chased seals out to the sea, found the 'Gate to Eden' in western Sweden, and eventually ended up as the early Fosna/Komsa tradition in Preboreal Norway. Here, the dominance of sites in the outer archipelagos, the abundant use of small islands and natural harbours all demonstrate *pronounced marine relations*. Seemingly, the distribution of Preboreal sites in the seascapes of Sweden and Norway is concordant with presumed rich seal biotopes that differ from the more inner-coastal distribution of Late Mesolithic sites, probably indicating a shift towards a more fish-based subsistence pattern.

Seal numbers, reliable hunting sites, and sheltered seas that make hunting at sea safer, are more favourable along the Scandinavian coastline. The Swedish Skagerak coast is a meeting point between the continental plains and the fjord/skerry coastal landscape. This may have been an important area for the development of seaworthy vessels and open-sea hunting, eventually penetrating the hitherto inaccessible Scandinavian coast. Such a development seems to tie in both with the absence of archaeological remains from the Late Glacial period, and rapid colonization in the Early Postglacial.

There is no reason to believe that Late Glacial people had less clearly defined notions about relationships between land and sea than modern people. This barrier has powerful ontological connotations and the development of hunting at sea must have been influenced by more than just the gradual overcoming of the technical and practical challenges. However, the evident *lacustrine* and presumed *littoral* relations encompass a variety of cognitive challenges, knowledge, skills, traditions and equipment relevant to a more marine orientation, *within* a lifestyle that may be labelled as 'terrestrial'. The single most important barrier may have been a fear of venturing out into bodies of open, arctic waters. This may have been a threshold that the Late Glacial hunters lacked the motivation to cross.

Conclusions

Current data indicate that the initial peopling of the Scandinavian and Patagonian seascapes is a Holocene phenomenon. In both cases, a time lag is documented between the emergence of these seascapes and their colonization. The existence of considerably older terrestrial-oriented hunter-gatherers is documented on the adjacent plains. In spite of their obvious advantages to marine exploitation, this delayed colonization seems to have counterparts in other skerry/fiord seascapes around the world, in the North Pacific-Bering sea regions (e.g. Coupland 1998; Yesner 1998, Gusev *et al.* 1999; McCartney and Veltre 1999; Fitzhugh 2002), in Arctic North America and Greenland (e.g. Møbjerg 1990; McGhee 1996; Gulløv *et al.* 2004, 39), in Atlantic Canada (e.g. Renouf 1999), in Scotland (e.g. Saville 2004), and Ireland (Woodman 2003).

The skerry/fiord seascapes presented a new environment that emerged from under the ice with deglaciation. If elaborate marine foragers inhabited the adjacent shores, or, if marine relations were elaborate in subsistence strategies of the terrestrial groups that roamed the adjacent plains, why all this time before the discovery and exploitation of this advantageous environment? In my view, the most plausible explanation is that the hunter-gatherers inhabiting the vicinity of the skerry/fiord seascapes lacked elaborate marine relations, and hence lacked the motivation, knowledge, and the technology needed to approach this seascape. Seaworthy boats are a crucial factor in this process (see Ames 2002).

I do not deny the existence of much older traditions in littoral relations in these areas, or, for that matter, much older marine oriented foragers along more distant and more temperate seashores. The main point is neither that all marine developments are Holocene, nor that these processes follow general laws of cultural development. The important issue is that the skerry/fiord seascape was a new environmental setting in the Pleistocene/Holocene transition, and a new challenge to the adjacent hunter-gatherers. And for archaeologists today, this is an opportunity to study a multitude of cultural approaches to a new setting. The archaeological record of this area is amenable to revealing a multitude of responses to the new possibilities in the marine habitat – barriers, motivation, technology, knowledge and ontology. The delayed colonization, the rate of migration, environmental pull/push factors, spatial hotspots, technological traditions and reorientation, and details in relation to the selection of resources and settlement patterns are all general issues of interest in this discussion.

However, I believe that the debate on human approaches to the marine may benefit from a clearer-cut recognition of the complexity of marine lifestyle, and the dimensions of the cultural barriers in the venture towards the marine environment. Neither 'Gates to Hell' nor 'Garden of Eden' are illustrative metaphors, as they both fail to focus the cultural challenges needed to pass the threshold to the marine.

The venture of marine lifestyles encompasses a cultural complexity similar to the emergence and development of agriculture. However, the lack of data from Pleistocene/Early Holocene coastal areas, the oversimplified view of the processes concerning marine adaptations, and the smaller impact in today's debates on the global economy are important reasons why the notion of the 'Marine revolution' is less prominent in the archaeological discourse than that of the 'Neolithic revolution'. In the list of developments that help our understanding of human responses to new challenges, I am certain that the gradual process of daring to venture further out to sea has an important place.

Acknowledgements

To help the development of comparative perspectives on these issues, I undertook a two-month study trip to Buenos Aires, Santiago, and the seascapes of Patagonia, observing sites from Monte Verde to Imiwaia in Canal Beagle. I am deeply indebted to Carlos Ocampo, Pilar Rivas, Eugenio Aspillaga, Diego Carabias (Santiago, Chile), Alfredo Prieto, Manuel San Roman, Flavia Morello (Punta Arenas, Chile), Ernesto Piana, and Louis Orquera (Tierra del Fuego, Argentina) for their generous contributions. This line of research was extended by participating in the session *ARQ-1: Perspectivas comparativas del desarrollo de adaptaciones maritimas circumpolares* (organised by Carlos Ocampo, Pilar Rivas and myself) during the 51° Congreso Internacional de Americanistas, Santiago, Chile, 2003. I would also like to thank Knut Andreas Bergsvik, Terje Brattli, Martin Callanan, Asle Bruen Olsen, Bjørnar Olsen, Kristian Pettersen, Frode Svendsen, Peter Woodman, and Leif Inge Åstveit for fruitful discussions on this subject.

References

Ames, K. M. 2002. Going by Boat. The Forager-Collector Continuum at Sea, in B. Fitzhugh and J. Habo (eds.), *Beyond Foraging and Collecting. Evolutionary Change in Hunter-Gatherer Settlement Systems*, 19–52. New York, Kluwer Academic/Plenum.

Andersen, B. G. 2000. *Istider i Norge*. Oslo, Universitets-forlaget.

Andersen, B. G. and Borns, H. 1997. *The Ice Age World.* Oslo, Scandinavian University Press.

Andersen, B. G., Mangerud, J., Sørensen, R., Reite, A., Sveian, H., Thoresen, M. and Bergstrøm, B. 1995. Younger Dryas ice marginal deposits in Norway. *Quarternary International* 28, 147–69.

Aspillaga, E., Ocampo, E. C. and Rivas H. P. 1999. *Restos oseos humanos de contextos arqueologicos del area de Isla de Navarino: Indicadores de estilos de vida en indigenas canoeros.* Annales del Instituto de la Patagonia, Serie Ciencias Humanas 27, 123–35. Punta Arenas, Universidad de Magallanes.

Bailey, G. and Parkington, J. 1988. The Archaeology of Prehistoric Coastlines: An introduction, in G. Bailey and J. Parkington (eds.), *The Archaeology of Prehistoric Coastlines*, 1–10. Cambridge, Cambridge University Press.

Bang-Andersen, S. 2003. Southwest Norway at the Pleistocene/Holocene Transition: Landscape Development, Colonization

Progress, Site Types, Settlement Patterns. *Norwegian Archaeological Review* 36 (1), 5–25.

Bell, T. and Renouf, M. A. P. 2004. Prehistoric cultures, reconstructed coasts: Maritime Archaic Indian site distribution in Newfoundland. *World Archaeology* 35 (3), 350–70.

Bird, J. B. 1988. *Travels and Archaeology in South Chile*. Iowa City, University of Iowa Press.

Bjerck, H. B. 1995. The North Sea Continent and the pioneer settlement of Norway, in A. Fischer (ed.), *Man and Sea in the Mesolithic: coastal settlement above and below present sea level*, 131–44. Oxbow Monographs 53, Oxford, Oxbow Books.

Bjerck, H. B. 2008. Norwegian Mesolithic Trends: a Review, in G. Bailey and P. Spikins (eds.), *Mesolithic Europe*. Cambridge, Cambridge University Press.

Borrero, L. A. 1997. The origins of ethnographic subsistence patterns in Fuego-Patagonia, in C. McEwan, L.A. Borrero and A. Prieto (eds.), *Patagonia. Natural history, prehistory and ethnography at the uttermost end of the earth*, 60–82. New Jersey, Princeton University Press.

Borrero, L. A. and McEwan, C. 1997. The peopling of Patagonia. The first human occupation, in C. McEwan, L. A. Borrero and A. Prieto (eds.), *Patagonia. Natural history, prehistory and ethnography at the uttermost end of the earth*, 32–46. New Jersey, Princeton University Press.

Coupland, G. 1998. Maritime Adaptation and Evolution of the Developed Northwest Coast Pattern on the Central Northwest Coast. *Arctic Anthropology* 35 (1), 36–56.

Dillehay, T. 2000. *The Settlement of the Americas*. New York, Basic Books.

Eidlitz, K. 1969. *Food and emergency food in the circumpolar area*. Studia Ethnographica Uppsaliensis 32. Uppsala, Almqvist & Wiksell International.

Eriksen, B. V. 1996. Regional variations in Late Pleistocene subsistence strategies. Southern Scandinavian reindeer hunters in a European context, in L. Larsson (ed.), *The earliest settlement of Scandinavia and its relationship with neighbouring areas*, 7–22. Acta Archaeologica Lundensia 24, Series in 8°, 24. Stockholm, Almqvist & Wiksell International.

Eriksen, B. V. 2002. Reconsidering the geochronological framework of Lateglacial hunter-gatherer colonization of southern Scandinavia, in B. V. Eriksen and B. Bratlund (eds.), *Recent studies in the Final Palaeolithic of the European plain*, 25–41. Højbjerg, Jutland Archaeological Society.

Erlandson, J. M. 2001. The archaeology of aquatic adaptations: paradigms for a new millennium. *Journal of Archaeological Research* 9 (4), 287–350.

Fairbanks, R. G. 1989. A 17,000-year glacio-eustatic sea level record: influence of glacial melting rates on the Younger Dryas event and deep-ocean circulation. *Nature* 342, 637–42.

Faught, M. K. 2004. The underwater archaeology of paleolandscapes, Apalache Bay, Florida. *American Antiquity* 69 (2), 275–90.

Fischer, A. 1995. An entrance to the Mesolithic world below the ocean, in A. Fischer (ed.), *Man and Sea in the Mesolithic: coastal settlement above and below present sea level*, 371–84. Oxbow Monographs 53. Oxford, Oxbow Books.

Fischer, A. 1996. At the border of human habitat. The late Palaeolithic and early Mesolithic in Scandinavia, in L. Larson (ed.), *The earliest settlement in Scandinavia*. Acta Archaeologica Lundensia, Series in 8°, 24. Stockholm, Almqvist & Wiksell International.

Fitzhugh, B. 2002. Residential and logistical strategies in the evolution of complex hunter-gatherers on the Kodiak archipelago, in B. Fitzhugh and J. Habo (eds.), *Beyond Foraging and Collecting. Evolutionary Change in Hunter-Gatherer Settlement Systems*, 19–52. New York, Kluwer Academic/Plenum.

Flint, R. F. 1971. *Glacial and Quaternary Geology*. New York, John Wiley & Sons.

Fuglestvedt, I. 2001. *Pionerbosetningens fenomenologi. Sørvest-Norge og Nord-Europa 12200/10000–9500 BP*. Unpublished PhD thesis, University of Bergen.

Fuglestvedt, I. 2003. Enculturating the landscape beyond Doggerland, in L. Larsson, H. Kindgren, K. Knutsson, D. Loeffler and A. Åkerlund (eds.), *Mesolithic on the Move: Papers presented at the Sixth International Conference on the Mesolithic in Europe, Stockholm 2000*, 103–7. Oxford, Oxbow Books.

Gulløv, H. C., Andreassen, C., Grønnow, B., Fog Jensen, J., Appelt, M., Arneborg, J. and Berglund, J. 2004. *Grønlands forhistorie*. København, Gyldendal.

Gusev, S. V., Zagoroulko, A. V. and Porotov, A. V. 1999. Sea mammal hunters of Chukotka, Bering Strait: recent archaeological results and problems. *World Archaeology* 30 (3), 354–69.

Gusinde, M. 1931. *Die Feuerland Indianer : Ergebnisse meiner vier Forschungsreisen in den Jahren 1918 bis 1924, unternommen im Auftrage des Ministerio de instruccion publica de Chile / herausgegeben von Martin Gusinde*. Mödling bei Wien, Verlag der Internationalen Zeitschrift 'Anthropos'.

Gustafson, L. 1988. Fjellpionerene, in S. Indrelid, S. Kaland and B. Solberg (eds.), *Festskrift til Anders Hagen*, 50–67. Arkeologiske Skrifter 4. Bergen, Historisk museum, University of Bergen.

Johansen, A. B. and Undås, I. 1992. Er Blomvågmaterialet et boplassfunn. *Viking* 55, 9–26.

Kindgren, H. 1995. Hensbacka-Horgen-Hornborgasjön: Early Mesolithic coastal and inland settlements in western Sweden, in A. Fischer (ed.), *Man and Sea in the Mesolithic – coastal settlement above and below present sea level*, 171–84. Oxbow Monographs 53, Oxford, Oxbow Books.

Kindgren, H. 1996. Reindeer or seals? Some Late Palaeolithic sites in central Bohuslän, in L. Larsson (ed.), *The Earliest Settlement of Scandinavia and its Relationship with Neighbouring Areas*, 193–203. Acta Archaeologica Lundensia. Series in 8o (24). Stockholm, Almqvist & Wiksell International.

Kindgren, H. 2002. Torskärr. Stenkyrka 94 revisited, in B. V. Eriksen and B. Bratlund (eds.), *Recent studies in the Final Palaeolithic of the European plain*, 49–60. Højbjerg, Jutland Archaeological Society.

Klemsdal, T. 1982. *Coastal classification and the coast of Norway. Norsk Geografisk Tidsskrift* 36, 129–52.

Kutschera, M. 1999. Vestnorsk tidligmesolitikum i et nordvest-europeisk perspektiv, in I. Fuglestvedt, T. Gansum and A. Opedal (eds.), *Et hus med mange rom. Vennebok til Bjørn Myhre på 60 års dagen*, 43–52. AmS Rapport 11A. Stavanger, Archaeological Museum of Stavanger.

Larsen, E., Gulliksen, S., Lauritzen, S.-E., Lie, R., Løvlie, R., Mangerud, J. 1987. Cave stratigraphy in western Norway: multiple Weichselian glaciations and interstadial vertebrate fauna. *Boreas* 16, 267–92.

Larsson, L. 1996. The Colonization of South Sweden During the Deglaciation, in L. Larsson (ed.), *The Earliest settlement of Scandinavia and its relationship with neighbouring areas*, 141–56. Acta Archaeologica Lundensia, Series in 8o, 24. Stockholm, Almqvist & Wiksell International.

Legoupil, D. 1997. *Bahía Colorada (ile d'Englafield): les*

premiers chasseurs de mammiféres marines de Patagonia australe. Paris, Editions Recherche sur les Civilisations.

Lehman, S. J. and Keigwin, L. D. 1992. Sudden changes in North Atlantic circulation during the last deglaciation. *Nature* 356, 757–62.

Lewis, R. B. 2000. Sea level rise and subsidence effects on Gulf coast archaeological site distribution. *American Antiquity* 65 (3), 525–41.

Lie, R. W. 1986. Animal bones from the Late Weichselian in Norway. *Fauna Norvegica Ser.* A7, 41–6.

Lie, R. W. 1990. Blomvågfunnet, de eldste spor etter mennesker i Norge? *Viking* 53, 7–21.

McCartney, A. P. and Veltre, D. W. 1999. Aleutian Island prehistory: living in insular extremes. *World Archaeology* 30 (3), 503–15.

McCulloch, R. D., Clapperton, C. M., Rabassa, J., Currant, A. P. 1997. The natural setting: The glacial and Post-glacial environmental history of Fuego-Patagonia, in C. McEwan, L. A. Borrero and A. Prieto (eds.), *Patagonia. Natural history, prehistory and ethnography at the uttermost end of the earth*, 12–32. New Jersey, Princeton University Press. McGhee, R. 1996. Ancient People of the Arctic. Hull, Canadian Museum of Civilisation.

Mena, F. 1997. Middle to late Holocene adaptations in Patagonia, in C. McEwan, L. A. Borrero and A. Prieto (eds.), *Patagonia. Natural history, prehistory and ethnography at the uttermost end of the earth*, 46–60. New Jersey, Princeton University Press.

Møbjerg, T. 1990. Center og pereferi i Arktis belyst udfra den palæoeskimoiske bosætning i Grønland, in B. Wik (ed.), *Sentrum – pereferi. Sentra og sentrumsdannelser gjennom forhistorisk og historisk tid. Den 18. nordiske arkeologkongress, Trondheim 28.8.–4.9.1989*, 165–78. Gunneria 64 (1). Trondheim, Vitenskapsmuseet.

Nordqvist, B. 1999. The chronology of the western Swedish Mesolithic and Late Paleolithic: old answers in spite of new methods, in J. Boaz (ed.), *The Mesolithic of Central Scandinavia*, 235–54. Universitetets Oldsaksamlings Skrifter Ny Rekke 22. Oslo, Universitetets Oldsaksamling.

Nummedal, A. 1924. Om Flintpladsene. *Norsk Geologisk Tidsskrift* 7 (1923), 89–141.

Ocampo, E. C. and Rivas, H. P 2000. *Nuevos fechados 14C de la costa norte de la Isla Navarino, costa sur del Canal Beagle, Provincia Antártica Chilena, Región de Magallanes*, 197–214. Annales del Instituto de la Patagonia, Serie Ciencias Humanas 28. Punta Arenas, Universidad de Magallanes.

Orquera, L. A. and Piana, E. L. 1987. Human littoral adaptation in the Beagle Channel region: The maximum possible age. *Quarternary of South America and Arctic Peninsula* 5, 133–62.

Orquera, L. A. and Piana, E. L. 1999a. *Arqueología de la región del canal Beagle, Tierra del Fuego, República Argentina*. Buenos Aires, Sociedad Argentina de Antropología.

Orquera, L. A. and Piana, E. L. 1999b. *La vida social y material de los Yámana*. Buenos Aires, Eudeba – Instituto Fuegino de Investigaciones Científicas.

Pettersen, K. 1999. The Mesolithic in Southern Trøndelag, in J. Boaz (ed.), *The Mesolithic of Central Scandinavia*. Universitetets Oldsaksamlings Skrifter Ny Rekke 22. Oslo, Universitetets Oldsaksamling.

Piana, E. L. 2005. Cetaceans and human beings at the Uttermost Part of the America: A lasting relationship in Tierra del Fuego, in G. G. Monks (ed.), *The Exploitation and Cultural Importance of Sea Mammals*. Oxford, Oxbow Books.

Pirazzoli, P. A. 1991. *World Atlas of Holocene Sea level Changes*. New York, Elsevier.

Pirazzoli, P. A. 1996. *Sea level Changes: The Last 20,000 Years*. Chichester, John Wiley & Sons.

Reid, C. 1913. *Submerged forests*. The Cambridge Manuals of Science and Literature. Cambridge, Cambridge University Press.

Rinde, E., Bjørge, A., Eggereide, A. and Tufteland, G. (eds.) 1998. *Kystøkologi – den ressursrike norskekysten*. Oslo, Universitetsforlaget.

Renouf, M. A. P. 1999. Prehistory of Newfoundland hunter-gatherers: extinctions or adaptations? *World Archaeology* 30 (3), 403–20.

Rivas, H. P., Ocampo, E. C. and Aspillaga, F. E. 1999. *Pobliamiento temprano de los canales Patagonicos: El nucleo ecotonal septentrional*, 221–30. Annales del Instituto de la Patagonia, Serie Ciencias Humanas (1999). Punta Arenas, Universidad de Magallanes.

Rolfsen, P. 1972. Kvartærgeologiske og botaniske betingelser for mennesker i Sør-Norge i seinglasial og tidlig postglasial tid. *Viking* XXXVI, 131–53.

Saville, A. (ed.) 2004. *Mesolithic Scotland and its neighbours: early Holocene prehistory of Scotland, its British and Irish context and some North European perspectives*. Edinburgh, Society of Antiquaries of Scotland.

Schmitt, L. 1995. The West Swedish Hensbacka: a maritime adaptation and a seasonal expression of the North-Central European Ahrensburgian?, in A. Fischer (ed.), *Man and Sea in the Mesolithic Mesolithic – coastal settlement above and below present sea level*, 161–70. Oxbow Monographs 53. Oxford, Oxbow Books.

Schmitt, L. 1999. Comparative Points and relative Thoughts: the Relationship between the Ahrensburgian and Hensbacka Assemblages. *Oxford Journal of Archaeology* 18 (4), 327–37.

Skjoldal, H. R. (ed.) 2004. *The Norwegian Sea Ecosystem*. Trondheim, Tapir Academic Press.

Tolan-Smith, C. 2003. The social context of landscape learning and the Lateglacial–Early Postglacial recolonization of the British Isles, in M. Rockman and J. Steele (eds.), *Colonization of unfamiliar landscapes*, 116–129. London, Routledge.

Waraas, T. A. 2001. *Vestlandet i tidleg Preboreal tid. Fosna, Ahrensburg eller vestnorsk tidlegmesolitikum?* Unpublished Masters thesis, University of Bergen.

Woodman, P. C. 2003. Colonising the edge of Europe: Ireland as a case study, in L. Larsson, H. Kindgren, K. Knutsson, D. Loeffler and A. Åkerlund (eds.), *Mesolithic on the Move: Papers presented at the Sixth International Conference on the Mesolithic in Europe, Stockholm 2000*, 57–64. Oxford, Oxbow Books.

Yesner, D. R. 1980. Maritime hunter-gatherers: Ecology and Prehistory. *Current Anthropology* 21 (6), 727–50.

Yesner, D. R. 1987. Life in the 'Garden of Eden': Constraints of maritime diets for human societies, in M. Harris and E. Ross (eds.), *Food and Evolution*, 285–310. Philadelphia, Temple University Press.

Yesner, D. R. 1998. Origins and developments of maritime adaptations in the Northwest Pacific region of North America. *Arctic Anthropology* 35 (1), 204–22.

5. Entering new shores. Colonization processes in early archipelagos in eastern central Sweden

Roger Wikell and Mattias Pettersson

During the Mesolithic, eastern central Sweden consisted of vast archipelagos; as a result of land upheaval, new land was constantly being formed. Recent surveys and excavations have revealed a cultural landscape made up of thousands of sites from the time span (shoreline dating) c. *8600–4000 cal BC (9400–5000 BP). Colonization processes can thus be studied in a long- term perspective. During some periods of fast, regressive shore displacements and the formation of new land, colonization must have been a part of the cultural pattern in the coastal areas of the region. How was this undertaken? Studies of Mesolithic sites in 'newborn' archipelagos within the ancient island-world of eastern central Sweden can shed light on how people claimed virgin land.*

Keywords: Ancylus Lake, shore displacement, small boats, archipelagos ('skerry-gards'), peneplain, fractal structure, round rocks, seals, colonization, stories.

Introduction

Recently, about 1000 Mesolithic sites have been found during field surveys on the Södertörn peninsula, south of Stockholm, eastern Sweden (Figure 5.1). The dominant find-material is knapped quartz. If the sites were situated close to the shoreline at the time of occupation, the highest of them, at 80m asl, can be dated somewhere between 8600 and 8200 cal BC (9400 and 9000 BP) (Figure 5.2). (Unless indicated otherwise, all radiocarbon dates in the text are as cited in the publications from which they come and are expressed in uncalibrated radiocarbon years before present (14C BP)). At this time, when the Weichselian ice still lingered around the Gulf of Bothnia, the region of eastern central Sweden was dominated by the vast gulf of the Ancylus Lake, a freshwater stage of the Baltic. In today's province of Södermanland, a narrow scatter of islands then stretched 130km to the east from the mainland. At the east end of this island chain was a somewhat larger archipelago, where the, presumably, oldest sites have been found (Figure 5.3).

The first boat-transported pioneers travelled through a seascape that featured an almost unbroken horizon, as they 'hopped' from island to island over vast stretches of open sea. It seems dramatic, but the early colonization of the archipelagos of eastern central Sweden was part of similar, and sometimes more courageous, occurrences at the end of the Weichselian and the early Holocene. On the Swedish west coast, and all along the Norwegian coast, are Ahrensburgian sites (labelled Hensbacka and Fosna cultures respectively), indicating marine subsistence and technology already as far back as 10,500/10,000 BP (Bjerck 1995, this volume; Fuglestvedt, this volume; Grydeland, this volume; Kindgren 2002; Nordqvist, this volume). In Finland the oldest sites have been shoreline-dated to 9500–9000 BP. The find of a fishing net and other items on the ancient sea floor at Antrea, dated to 9200 BP, bear witness to the technological prerequisites of a marine economy (Carpelan 1999, 161).

Rich marine resources must have been the prime reason why people voyaged 130km out in the sea. The sites at 80m asl on the Södertörn peninsula indicate a boat-based culture, with great potential for long journeys. Furthermore, they show an early use of quartz for their lithic production. Here we have a culture, or rather a group of people, within a larger cultural sphere, who were bent on the colonization of the productive environments of new archipelagos: new lands on the horizon.

But where did they come from? Geography points to the west. The presence of the Hensbacka culture along the Swedish west coast, with offshoots inland as far east as lake Hornborgasjön in the county of Västergötland, and perhaps to the north of lake Vänern, where a flake, axe-like artefact has been found, presents a good argument for a route from the west along the shores of ancient lake

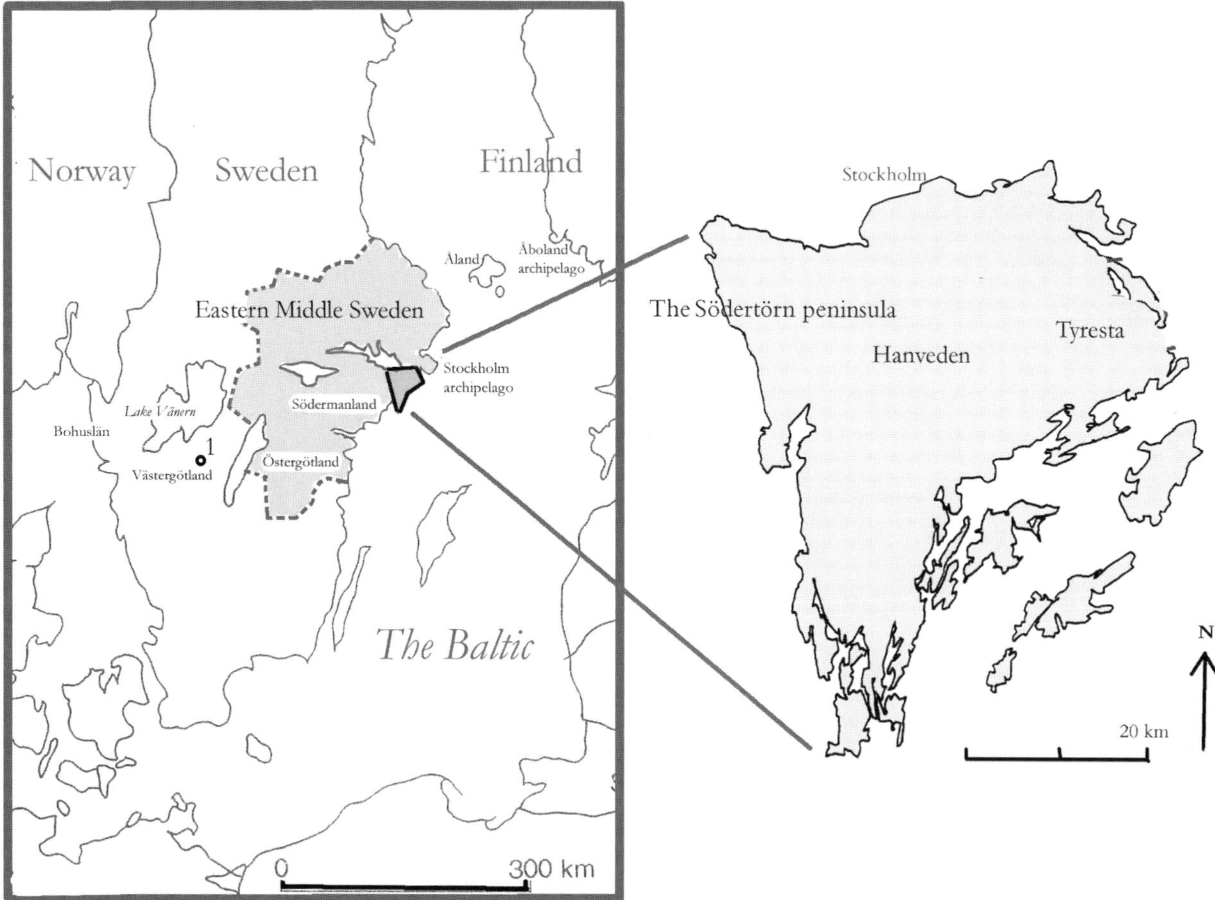

Figure 5.1. Key map showing areas mentioned in the text. 1 is Lake Hornborgasjön (after Dag Hammar).

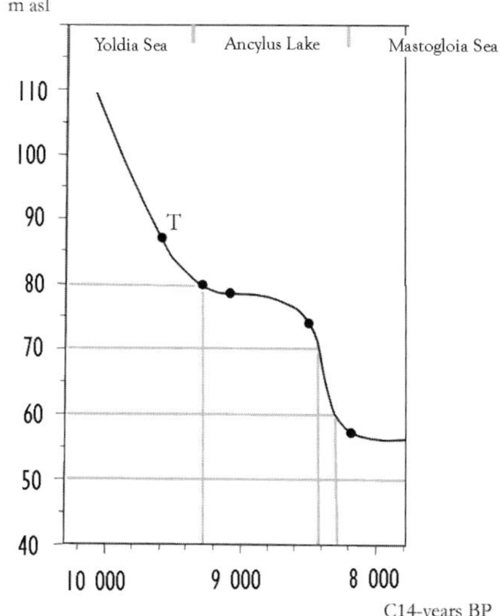

Figure 5.2. Shore-displacement curve for the Södertörn peninsula, covering the period c. *10,000–7800 BP (Risberg 2003).*

Vänern (Kindgren 2002). The first exploratory journeys could have taken place very early, during the Yoldia Sea stage of the Baltic, but they seem more likely from around 9500 BP, when the straits in Bohuslän were closed and this rich marine environment came to an end (Kindgren 2002), giving economic grounds for dispersal to new, prosperous lands. Furthermore, settlements from *c.* 9000 BP in both the counties of Västergötland and Östergötland, and a recently discovered, probably shore site in Södermanland from *c.* 8500 BP, have Cambrian flint (from western Sweden), indicating east-west contact routes as early as 9000 BP. But the presence of south Scandinavian flint on the same sites also points towards the south (Gustafsson and Nordin 2006; Molin, this volume; Patrik Gustafsson, Hans Kindgren and Fredrik Molin, pers. comm.).

Or did the Fosna people from Norway cross the Scandinavian mountains and follow the great rivers all the way to the Ancylus Lake? Did the pioneers come from Finland, where there was an early use of quartz and archipelagic settlements? At a glance, the quartz craft points towards Finland. But the oldest known sites here are interpreted as the remains of people recently arrived from areas where flint dominated the lithic production, and does not, accordingly, constitute the firmly established

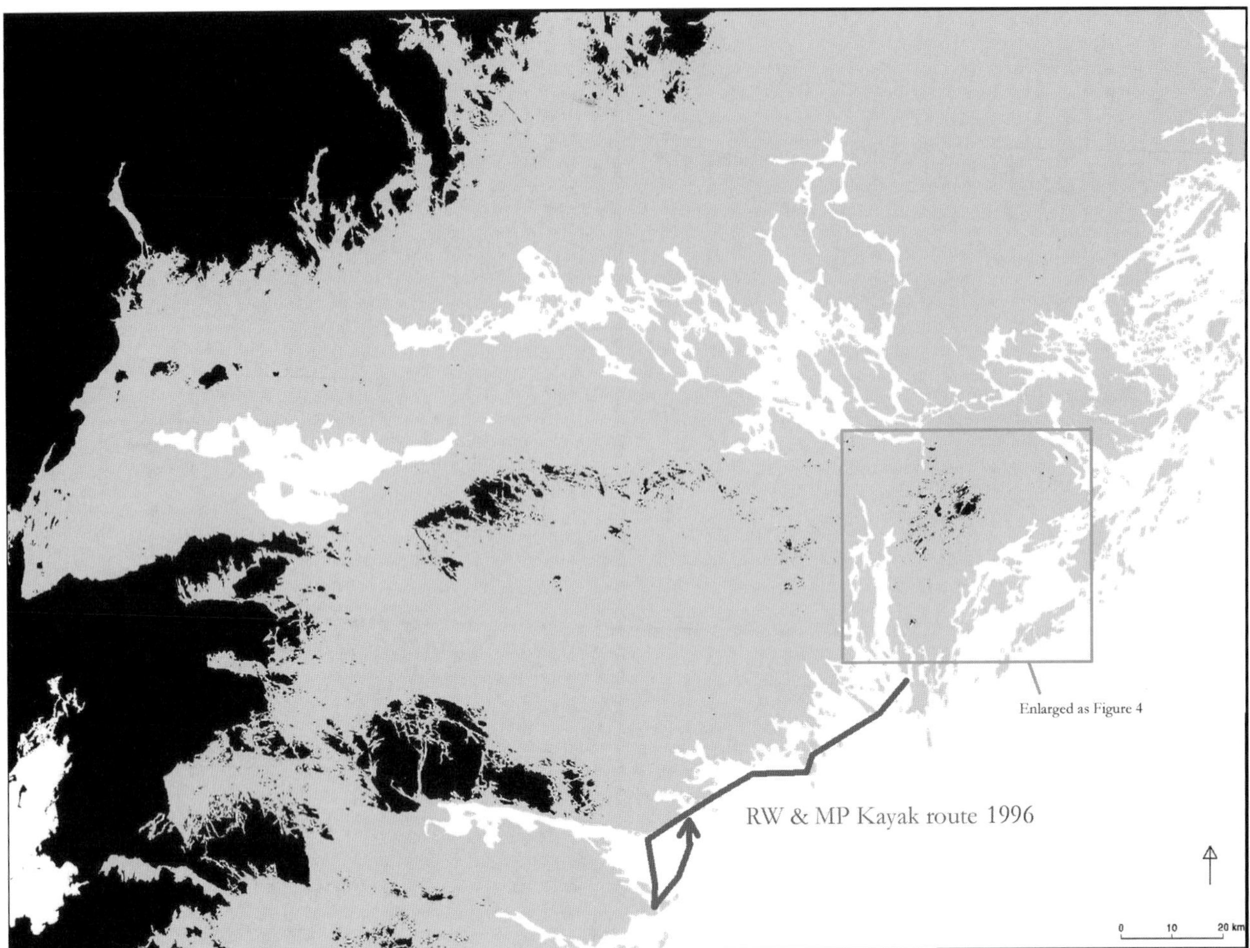

Figure 5.3. Eastern central Sweden at a sea level 75m above the present (black areas), in the south-east half of the map and roughly corresponding to 8500 BP, but with later dates in the north because of the differences in land upheaval. White is the present Baltic Sea, grey the present-day land areas. A section of the authors' kayak-tour in the summer of 1996 is indicated. This distance was comfortably paddled in three days, with numerous stopovers along the way. (Map: Dag Hammar and Roger Wikell).

quartz-culture we, in this case, look for as the source of colonization (Jussila and Matiskainen 2003, 667–8).

The archaeological picture

The Mesolithic archipelago is to be found in the higher forest areas of the Södertörn peninsula, between *c.* 80 and 40m asl. Surveys have revealed a landscape rich in sites, with knapped quartz, most of them dating to the Middle Mesolithic, *c.* 8000–6000 BP. The Eklundshov site (55–60m asl) is the oldest confirmed site on Södertörn, at *c.* 8000 BP. A general assumption that the sites were situated close to the shoreline at the time of occupation is supported by 14C dates of excavated sites, and observations concerning the altitudinal distribution of both the sites and certain find-materials (Hammar and Wikell 1994; 1996; Pettersson and Wikell 2004; 2005; Åkerlund 1996; 2002; Åkerlund *et al.* 1995). Very importantly, no sites have been found higher than 82m asl, despite the fact that there are many suitable areas for settlements above this altitude, with a good many places for camping, which, if they were at lower levels, typically would have given finds; there are only a few doubtful fragments of knapped quartz at *c.* 85m asl.

Following the general assumption that the sites were situated on the shoreline, the altitude then gives a rough chronology. In our surveyed material we see the following 'development of colonization' or 'colonization process' on the Södertörn peninsula during the Ancylus Lake phase (Åkerlund *et al.* 2003, xxiv).

The following shoreline dating is based on Risberg's shore-displacement model (2003):

Phase 0

c. 85m asl and above (older than 8600 cal BC (9400 BP)). Fast regressive shore-displacement. The Yoldia Sea is transformed into the Ancylus Lake. It is already a small archipelago with some larger islands; there are only a few sites with (possibly) knapped quartz. Sporadic visits might have occurred, but they left few or no archaeological traces. Phase of discovery?

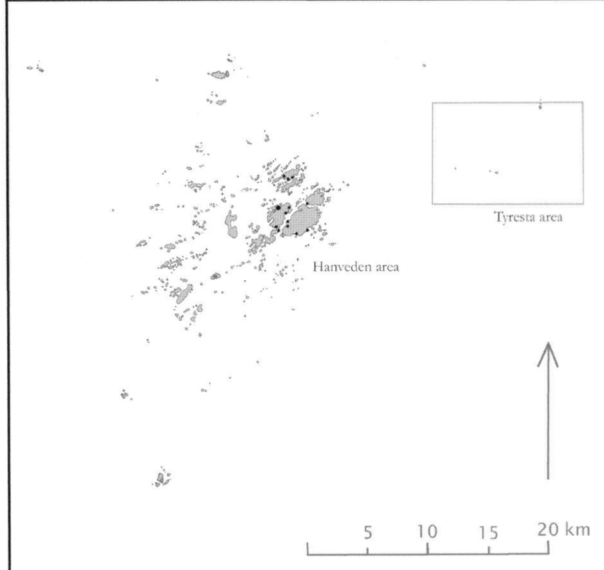

Figure 5.4. The Södertörn peninsula at 80m asl, c. *9000 BP. Black dots show find-spots for knapped quartz around 80 m asl, interpreted as shore areas at the time of occupation. Large dots are complexes with 5 sites. The rectangle indicates the Tyresta area, enlarged in Figures 5.5 and 5.6. (Map: Dag Hammar and Roger Wikell).*

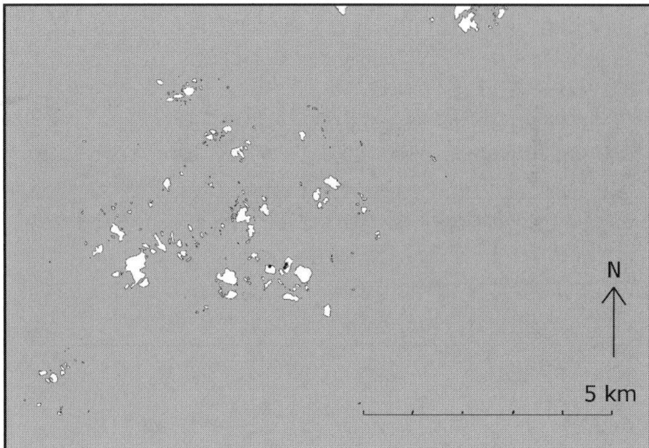

Figure 5.5. The Tyresta area at 70m asl, c. *8400 BP. Sheltered landing-places are few and the find-spots for quartz (black dots) represent accidental landings. (Map: Dag Hammar and Mattias Pettersson).*

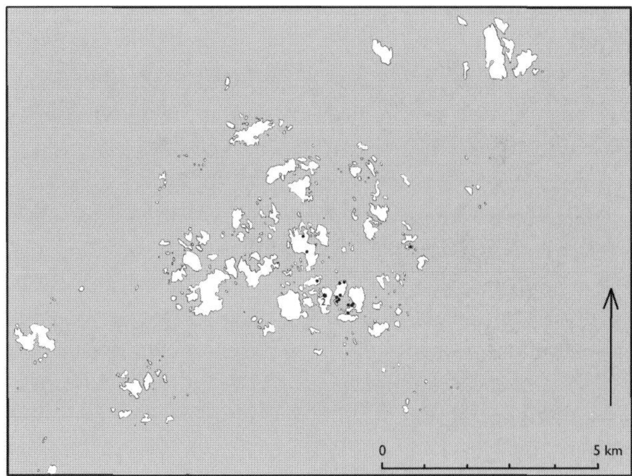

Figure 5.6. The Tyresta area at 65m asl, c. *8325 BP. Fast shore-displacement has resulted in a dramatic increase in land mass. Sheltered landing-places now occur here and there. Black dots are quartz find-spots. This level, the authors believe (see Discussion), corresponds to the first serious claim to the land. (Map: Mattias Pettersson).*

Phase 1

c. 80m asl (8600–7700 cal BC (9400–8700 BP)). Archipelago with *c.* 750 islands of different sizes (Figure 5.4). The shoreline halts during the early phase of the Ancylus Lake. There is a sudden presence of spatially small sites on very sheltered beaches and (probably) small groups utilize the outer archipelago. Seasonal movements over great distances and between the archipelago and the mainland are likely. No flint. Quartz occurs abundantly at places on the highest situated sites. The quartz is knapped with the platform method only, but the bipolar technique follows soon after – just a few metres below.

Phase 2

c. 75m asl (*c.* 7500 cal BC (8500 BP)). Onset of fast regressive shore-displacement during the terminal phase of the Ancylus Lake. There are twice as many islands (1615) as at 80m asl. There is a variation between medium-sized, very find-rich sites, and small sites. Quartz is knapped using both the bipolar and platform methods. Greenstone and other local non-quartz rocks are, as far as we know, used for the first time. Larger social groups predominate, (possibly) occasionally over-wintering. The small surrounding outer skerries are probably regularly visited, but there are still no finds here.

c. 70m asl (*c.* 7400 (8425 BP)). Continuous fast regression. An increase in the number of sites, large and small. Large groups occupy the entire central archipelago, typically on the long straits. Massive sites on some rather open sandy shores, exposed towards smaller islands, could have been true seal-butchering sites. Quartz dominates the lithic material, but there is also some quartzite and greenstone. Hammer-, anvil-, and fire-cracked stone occur. There is the first (scarce) evidence of activity on the outer skerries. Small, newborn satellite archipelagos are being 'colonized' (Figure 5.5).

c. 65m asl (*c.* 7300 cal BC (8350 BP)). Continuous fast regression. Large and small sites (and everything in between), exactly as at 70m asl. There are greenstone axes; there is quartz, greenstone and flint. The outer skerries are very much included in the settlement pattern (Figure 5.6).

Phase 3

c. 60m asl (*c.* 7200 cal BC (8275 BP)). The fast regression begins to slow down. The number of sites increases continually. A year-round human population, we believe, is now probably established in the Södermanland archipelagos.

Why did people go to this wind-blown archipelago as early as *c.* 8200 cal BC (9000 BP)? Surveys on the neighbouring mainland have given very few finds: were the archipelagos more important, in a regional perspective, than the mainland (Åkerlund *et al.* 2002)? The fact that marine resources are stable and reliable (Woodman 1985) supports this, and further indications are given from the geography itself. The large, shallow areas in the archipelagos must have been prosperous marine environments. Furthermore, the Södermanland archipelago, jutting out like an enormous pier of shallow water, must have acted as a 'trapping device' for flocks of seal migrating north-south along the east coast of Sweden (Figure 5.3) (see also Haglund, 1971, 25). We imagine an (initially) naïve fauna, unaware of the deadly threat the first small boats carried with them. This fauna must have been established during the Yoldia Sea phase of the Baltic, 10,300–9500 BP, when the Baltic was connected to the ocean (Björck 1995). Ringed seal (*Phoca hispida*), grey seal (*Halichoerus grypus*), and many species of fish immigrated through the large straits and were subsequently isolated in the Ancylus Lake, some still to be found as arctic relicts in some far inland lakes in Sweden and Finland (Fredén 1988).

In addition, the small archipelagos must have functioned as 'trapping devices' for material culture: there was plenty of sea, little land. There will be a concentration of artefacts from a regionally scarce human population.

The preference for archipelagos is not uniquely an early Mesolithic phenomenon – it continues all the way through the Mesolithic. Results from surveys on the Södertörn peninsula and other parts of the county of Södermanland indicate that the periphery of the archipelago is richer in sites than the larger landmasses and the mainland coast, especially during the Middle Mesolithic.

The archipelago or 'skerry-gard'

To understand why the archipelagos were the places of choice during the Meolithic, we must start in the landscape structure.

Today, the Stockholm archipelago, with the Åland and Åboland archipelagos (south-west Finland), constitute one of the world's heaviest concentrations of islands. Eastern central Sweden is a lowland area. It is a fissure-valley landscape, consisting of rather flat peneplains, of Precambrian age, divided by younger fissure-valleys crossing each other in a net-like pattern. Seen from above, the landscape appears almost flat, but in the immediate, human perspective it shows dramatic differences in altitude. The fissure-valley landscape experienced by the hiker is a labyrinthine terrain with intersecting fissure-valleys of different sizes, divided by rocky outcrops of the peneplain. It is a landscape with a high *fractal structure*. Now if we imagine it rising through the water surface, it will become an archipelago, characterized by many islands, bays, and straits. It also features long stretches of shoreline per km2. From an onboard view, there will be an abundance of suitable littoral campsites at many levels.

This archipelago differs fundamentally from a larger-scale landscape with large, local, altitudinal differences, such as the fiord-like coast of Höga kusten, some 500km to the north of Södertörn. In the latter case, shore-displacement is noticeable, but without the usual dramatic results characteristic of the distribution of land and sea. In eastern central Sweden's archipelagos, on the other hand, new land is formed often many kilometres out into the sea. Because of the flat character of the landscape, entire peneplains are elevated above the surface. Where once there was open (but shallow) sea, there were soon hundreds of small skerries and islands (Figures 5.5 and 5.6): a skerry-gard is forming. Because of the land elevation, the topographical sequence of the landscape, generally sloping to the east, has created new skerry-gards with innumerable islands of different size – from the Yoldia Sea stage right up to the present day.

With regard to marine fauna and flora, skerry-gards are favourable. The waters afford many ecological niches. The many shifting milieus are important, for example the hard and soft sea floors, the differences in water depth, light conditions, currents: all conditions that favour high biodiversity. The shallow-water areas are often much larger than the islands themselves. The peripheral zone, among the outermost skerries, is especially rich in fish and seal.

The archipelago, or skerry-gard, as living-space

Island connoisseur Sven Barthel (1950, 8) has captured the essence of the skerry-gard in a few lines: 'All that is needed to come from windward to lee is to turn around a point of land; the open coast has only one shore-line and it is windward.' (Our translation)

On the whole, a skerry-gard is one great harbour for small boats. Flat-bottomed boats especially give great freedom in this landscape. (Inevitably, the kayak is brought to mind.) Mesolithic vessels still wait to be unearthed, but the position in the landscape of the sites is proof itself of good boats. The sites are, as a rule, in terrain positions that ensured good harbours – suitable and strategic beaches for landing – at the time of occupation.

The critical moments when using small boats are getting in and out; a calm, and for the sake of comfort, not (too) stony beach is preferred. Injuries to the boatmen and women, and damage to the equipment must be avoided. However, depending on the activities being undertaken, the best landing places normally select themselves: micro- and macro-perspectives are taken into account. The sites are often situated strategically from a communications perspective: the more exits and entrances from the landing-beach the better. It is important to avoid being driven ashore by the winds; this explains why straits and *strait-crossings* are especially rich in sites, while open beaches are avoided. In the favourable straits there are often large continuous 'zones' of find-rich sites close to each other. Here, base-camps could have been situated. If a strait, through shore-displacement, is silted up and becomes a narrow bay, the finds and number of sites tend to diminish: the place has lost its significance.

From our own experience of over twenty years of

kayaking around the Stockholm and neighbouring archipelagos, we know how to move among typical central Swedish skerry-gards. At sea, one is busy observing the seascape, looking for geographical fixed points. The seascape appears as if viewed through a kaleidoscope, shifting constantly: closer up, what seen from distance as a massive wall of land can be broken up into many islands.

Sheltered landing places are of vital importance: literally, your life can depend on it. You could land on flat rocks, but it is to be avoided (although we have found a few quartz sites on bare rock). Beyond the landing site, an even, and (at least) fairly horizontal, place for pitching your tent is required. But many quartz sites do not have this type of terrain, being situated half way up a slope. After landing, one typically walks a little along the shoreline. If the island is not too big, one could also stroll up the island's highest hill for a 360-degree view. We can assume that the Mesolithic people mapped their islands this way.

Looking beyond the artefact concentrations on Stone Age sites, and abandoning the often-held view that the surrounding rocky terrain delimits the site, such paths around a site could hypothetically be reconstructed, especially in small-scale rocky landscapes, such as are to be found on the Södertörn peninsula. Clusters of sites on smaller islands might possibly be regarded as one large site (having many 'doors' (beaches))? In the same way, sites around a particular strait could be seen as different 'rooms' in one, all-embracing site.

At this point we are ready to look at an ancient archipelago and use our knowledge of small-boat seafaring. We chose the Södertörn archipelago, at a sea level of 80m above that of the present, corresponding to between 9400 and 9000 BP. Situated some 130km out in the Ancylus Lake, the little archipelago seems a dangerous place to be when looking at the regional map (Figure 5.3). But at a closer view, many strategic and sheltered places appear in the straits and bays of the central cluster of larger islands (Figure 5.4). The largest island is *c.* 2 × 4km, and reaches some 30m above the surface; from its most sheltered sites, the horizon cannot be seen.

By contrast, now look at the Tyresta area at 70m asl (Figure 5.5), *c.* 8400 BP. This is a true outer archipelago: only the peaks of the peneplain reach above the water. In a boat, the experience is that of sitting on the open sea, surrounded by a few low, grey skerries: round rocks, open sea, unlimited sky. There are only very few sheltered landing places and the find-spots for quartz are likewise limited.

Discussion

Only in the time-period 9400–8000 BP, we believe, was there a true colonization of the archipelago of eastern central Sweden. Colonization really takes place only once, and by a group of people making the surrounding territory 'their' land. Later, a constant process of exploration takes place on an individual level, an ever-ongoing 'colonization' if you like. The (at times) fast shore-displacement in the shallow archipelagos of eastern central Sweden offered a special scenario: the constant formation of new land. Entire peneplains were elevated from the deep. Man follows closely all the time, as is indicated by scarce finds on the very first small skerries in the Tyresta area. One can imagine how a steady change would be observed; at certain times, in fact, visible over a single generation. A grandfather can be imagined telling his grandchildren, 'Out there, where your father now hunts seal, only a few round rocks broke the waves when I was a boy!'

In the process of island formation, an important stage is reached when the first sheltered landing places are formed. Accidental landings were probably made at unsheltered places on the first tiny islets, during calm weather or when the ice lay in the winter. Deposition of artefacts might well have occurred directly on the rock, but storm-waves have since washed them away, or re-deposited them in sediments in lower levels. This was clearly observed during our field survey in the Tyresta area, where we encountered an upper, find-free zone, corresponding to the first tiny islets. Only when really safe landings could be made did the islands' significance in the 'mental' map increase. It was probably then that a particular island was really 'occupied' by a group of people (Figure 5.6).

There must have been stories and legends tied to the formation of new land and the people's relationship to the seascape. The following (written down) 'creation myth' comes from Svenska Högarna, a small skerry-gard, and, since Medieval times, an important fishing village situated 'on the horizon', 45km east of the Swedish mainland, in the Stockholm archipelago:

'One day, a fisherman from Gillöga saw the Large Island rise from the sea. Straightaway he shot a silver bullet over the island to make it stay fixed above the water. When he *entered the shore*, a large old troll stood there with his legs deep down in the rock. He promised the fisherman that if he would help him out, he would vanish forever and the fisherman could take over the island. And so he did. The troll's footprints are still there – twin potholes (Sw. *jättegryta*), one and a half metres deep.' (Wahlstedt 1999:59, our translation and parenthesis)

In a larger sense, perhaps there were stories about their origins; how their ancestors arrived at a land different from the others they had previously encountered as the pioneers made their way through the landscapes of central Sweden. In the inner parts of the region's ancient coastal area, till dominated the landscape, with only minor areas of bare rock. But at the far, east end of the archipelago, similar to the area of the present-day Södertörn peninsula, the seascape was of another character. Here, in the Land of Seals, bare, round rocks filled the view. (In fact bearing a resemblance to the Bohuslän archipelago, on the Swedish west coast, from where the first pioneers might possibly have come.) Ingrid Fuglestvedt has proposed that during the pioneer phase, there could have been an engagement between man and landscape, technology and animals (2005, 86). Her ideas can be applied to the outer archipelago phenomena: round rocks, small boats and seals. These three elements could have been woven into stories and legends. Newly risen round rocks both *look like seals* and *host seals* – and both coming from the waters below – and they recalled the land in the creation myth: the land to which the first humans came. The colonization is then repeated, over and over again, in the actions of men and women, when newly-risen skerries are claimed.

Around 8000 BP the fast regression comes to an end. The formation of new archipelagos slows down. Saltwater flows into the Baltic basin through the Danish straits. It is a new era, with new geographical prerequisites, and the memory of origin perhaps fades away, or is transformed, or woven into new stories.

Acknowledgements

Per Falkenström, Michel Guinard, Dag Hammar. Personal communications: Patrik Gustafsson, Sörmlands Museum, Hans Kindgren, Bohuslän Museum, and Fredrik Molin, UV Öst.

References

Barthel, S. 1950. *Öar i urval.* Stockholm, Bonnier.

Bjerck, H. B. 1995. The North Sea Continent and the pioneer settlement of Norway, in A. Fischer (ed.), *Man and Sea in the Mesolithic: coastal settlement above and below present sea level*, 131–44. Oxbow Monographs 53. Oxford, Oxbow Books.

Björck, S. 1995. A review of the history of the Baltic Sea, 13.0–8.0 ka BP. *Quaternary International* 27, 19–40.

Carpelan, C. 1999. On the Postglacial Colonisation of Eastern Fennoscandia, in M. Hurre (ed.), *Dig it all. Papers dedicated to Ari Siiriäinen*, 152–71. Helsinki, Finnish Antiquarian Society.

Fredén, C. 1988. *Marine life and Deglaciation Chronology of the Vänern Basin Southwestern Sweden.* Sveriges Geologiska Undersökning 71. Uppsala, Offsetcenter.

Fuglestvedt, I. 2005. Contact and communication in Northern Europe 10 200 – 9000 / 8500 BP – a phenomenological approach to the connection between technology, skill and landscape, in H. Knutsson (ed.), *Pioneer settlements and colonization processes in the Barents region*, 79–96. Vuollerim Papers on Hunter-Gatherer Archaeology 1. Vuollerim, Voullerim Museum Press.

Gustafsson, P. and Nordin, M. 2006. Ett nytt land – tidig-mesolitikum i Kolmården. *Fornvännen* 101.

Haglund, B. 1971. *Säl.* Stockholm, PAN/Norstedt.

Hammar, D. and Wikell, R. 1994. Nyupptäckta stenåldersboplatser på Södertörn, in *Arkeologi i Sverige*, 217–33. Ny följd 3. Stockholm, Riksantikvarieämbetet.

Hammar, D. and Wikell, R. 1996. 250 nyupptäckta stenåldersboplatser på Södertörn, in P. Bratt (ed.), *Stenålder i Stockholms län*, 15–21. Stockholm, Stockholms Länsmuseum.

Jussila, T. and Matiskainen, H. 2003. Mesolithic settlement during the Preboreal period in Finland in L. Larsson, H. Kindgren, K. Knutsson, D. Loeffler and A. Åkerlund (eds.), *Mesolithic on the Move: Papers presented at the Sixth International Conference on the Mesolithic in Europe, Stockholm 2000*, 664–70. Oxford, Oxbow Books.

Kindgren, H. 2002. Tosskärr. Stenkyrka 94 revisited, in B. V. Eriksen and B. Bratlund (eds.), *Recent studies in the Final Palaeolithic of the European plain*, 49–60. Höjbjerg, Jutland Archaeological Society.

Pettersson, M. and Wikell, R. 2004. The Outermost Shore: Site-location in Mesolithic Seascapes of Eastern Central Sweden. With a Case-study in a Burnt-off Forest Area in Tyresta National Park, in H. Knutsson (ed.), *Coast to Coast – Arrival. Results and Reflections*, 435–67. Coast to Coast-book 10. Uppsala, University of Uppsala.

Risberg, J. 2003. Landscape History of the Södertörn Peninsula, Eastern Sweden, in L. Larsson, H. Kindgren, K. Knutsson, D. Loeffler and A. Åkerlund (eds.), *Mesolithic on the Move: Papers presented at the Sixth International Conference on the Mesolithic in Europe, Stockholm 2000*, xlv–xlviii. Oxford, Oxbow Books.

Wahlstedt, J. 1999. *Strandhugg och upptäcktsfärder i Stockholms havsskärgård.* Stockholm, Wahlström and Widstrand.

Wikell, R. 2005. Many Mesolithic sites along the shores. Some results from surveys in Kolmården and Vikbolandet, Östergötland in eastern central Sweden, in G. Gruber (ed.), *Identities in Transition. Mesolithic Strategies in the Swedish Province of Östergötland*, 154–67. Arkeologiska undersökningar, Skrifter 64. Linköping, Riksantikvarieämbetet.

Woodman, P. 1985. Mobility in the Mesolithic of Northwestern Europe: an alternative explanation, in T. D. Price and J. A. Brown (eds.), *Prehistoric hunter-gatherers. The emergence of complexity*, 325–39. London, Academic Press.

Åkerlund, A. 1996. *Human Responses to Shore Displacement. Living by the Sea in Eastern Middle Sweden during the Stone Age.* Arkeologiska Undersökningar, Skrifter 16. Stockholm, Riksantikvarieämbetet.

Åkerlund, A. 2002. Life without close neighbours. Some reflections on the first peopling of east Central Sweden, in B. V. Eriksen and B. Bratlund (eds.), *Recent studies in the Final Palaeolithic of the European plain*, 43–7. Höjbjerg, Jutland Archaeological Society.

Åkerlund, A., Hammar, D. and Wikell, R. 1995. Pioneers in the archipelago of Eastern Middle Sweden 9000 BP, in A.-M. Robertsson, T. Hackens, S. Hicks, J. Risberg and A. Åkerlund (eds.), *Landscapes and life*, 109–120. PACT 50, Rixensart, PACT.

Åkerlund, A., Risberg, J., Hammar, D., Wikell, R., Luthander, A., Pettersson, M., Andersson, H. and Asplund, M. 2002. *Människan i det tidiga landskapet. Inventeringar i högländta skogsområden i nordvästra Södermanland, sydöstra Närke och nordöstra Östergötland.* Stockholm Archaeological Reports. Field Studies 8. Stockholm, Stockholm University.

Åkerlund, A., Gustafsson, P., Hammar, D., Lindgren, C., Olsson, E. and Wikell, R. 2003. Peopling a forgotten landscape, in L. Larsson, H. Kindgren, K. Knutsson, D. Loeffler and A. Åkerlund (eds.), *Mesolithic on the Move: Papers presented at the Sixth International Conference on the Mesolithic in Europe, Stockholm 2000*, xxxiii–xliv. Oxford, Oxbow Books.

6. The flint collection from the Ristola site in Lahti and the cultural contacts of the earliest Postglacial settlement of southern Finland

Hannu Takala

This article briefly describes Finland's oldest known Postglacial finds and the cultural contacts they indicate with neighbouring areas of Finland. The author focuses in particular on flint artefacts from the Ristola site in Lahti. The studied material shows that although the earliest Postglacial settlement in southern Finland had contacts with the so-called Kunda-Butovo cultural sphere as a whole, the strongest connections appear to have been with the Kunda culture. The oldest dwelling-site finds from south Finland are dated to the Preboreal period, c. *9000–8400 cal BC.*

Keywords: Lahti Ristola, Kunda culture, cultural contacts.

Introduction

According to latest studies, the first pioneer settlement of present-day Finland made its way around 9500–9200 BP (9000–8400 cal BC) into south Finland, from where colonization spread to the north-west and into northern Finland (Takala 2004, 148). The Mesolithic of south Finland can be divided into the Preboreal and Boreal periods, with *c.* 9000 BP (8150 cal BC) as a chronological divide (Mangerud *et al.* 1974). A division into the Ancylus period, *c.* 9500–8000 BP (9000–6900 cal BC) and Litorina period, *c.* 8000–6000 BP (6900–4900 cal BC) has also been applied (Matiskainen 1989, 389).

It is possible to date the beginning of the pioneering settlement to the transgression and culmination stages of the Ancylus Lake, *c.* 9500–9000 BP (8850–8150 cal BC), but to provide an exact time for its end is more complicated. The shore-displacement curves of southern Finland show that at the end of the Ancylus period, *c.* 8500 BP (7550 cal BC), so much new land was exposed from under water that the habitat changed dramatically from the beginning of the pioneer phase (Takala 2004, 52, figure 45). Also the Preboreal period was well under way at this time, marking a difference in flora and fauna with regard to the beginning of the pioneer settlement stage.

As late as the mid-1990s, only half a dozen finds that could be dated to the pioneer stage were known from Finland and the former Finnish parts of Karelia. Since then, active research has resulted in a multiplied number of known sites, which have provided new information on the age and extent of settlement. Briefly listed in the following are all the sites related to the pioneer settlement stage in Finland, but the presentation of the material focuses on flint artefacts or tools from Ristola and other sites. Recent studies have opened up completely new perspectives on settlement in the northernmost parts of Finland and are discussed elsewhere in this volume (Rankama and Kankaanpää). The finds from the latter contexts are only mentioned in the present article.

The information discussed in this article is presented in greater detail in the author's published doctoral dissertation (Takala 2004). All the radiocarbon datings are given as both conventional (BP) and calibrated (cal BC/AD) dates, calibration having been carried out with the INTCAL98 cal40 curve (Stuiver *et al.* 1998).

The earliest Postglacial finds from southern Finland

The oldest archaeological site known in Finland at present is the Myllykoski site at Orimattila, situated approximately 12 kilometres south of the Ristola site. The finds from the site consist of quartz and burnt bone, and the site is dated to 9480±90 BP (9070–8670 cal BC; Hela-552) (Takala 2004, 149). Of almost the same age are the north Karelian sites of Rahakangas in Eno (9405±80 BP; 8800–8550 cal BC; Hela-882) and Kirkkolahti at Jänisjärvi (9300±85 BP; 8640–8430 cal BC; Ua-24774), the material from which also consisted of quartz and other lithic artefacts and burnt bone (Forsberg 2006; Pesonen 2005). The Kuurmanpohja site at Joutseno is dated to 9350±75 BP (8710–8490 cal BC; Hela-728) (Takala 2004, 150) and excavation finds from it include flint artefacts and an item comparable to arrowheads of the Sigir type (Jussila and Matiskainen 2003, 668–70). The age of the famous Antrea net has been established as 9140±135 BP (8530–8220 cal BC; Hela-404), according to the latest dating of the fibrous inner bark of the net (Ylikoski 2004, 25). However, in the summer of 2004 a site named Suuri Kelpojärvi was excavated only a few kilometres from the location of the net find. A sample of burnt bone from this site was radiocarbon dated to 9275±120 BP (8670–8360 cal BC; Hela-931) (Takala 2004, 151–2).

In the immediate vicinity of Ristola is the Myllyoja, Lahti site, which has revealed quartz artefacts, burnt bone and lithic artefacts. The site is dated to 9265±95 BP (8610–8350 cal BC; Hela-544) (Takala 2004, 150). According to shore displacement chronology, over 20 dwelling sites dating from the turn of the Preboreal and Boreal periods are known from the environs of Myllyoja

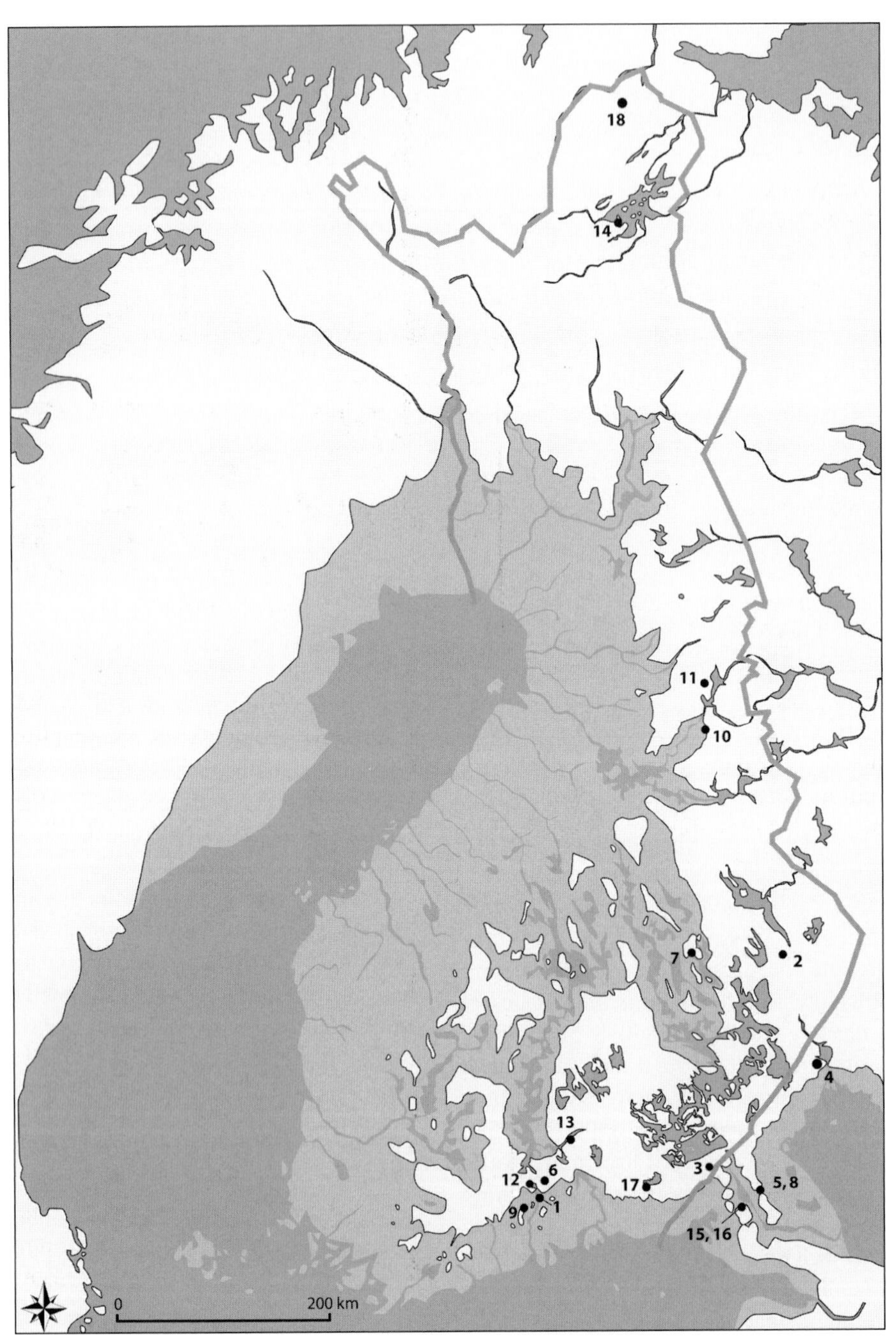

Figure 6.1. The oldest Postglacial finds in Finland according to the radiocarbon datings. The background map shows the shorelines of c. *8500 cal BC (map courtesy of Microlith Ltd.). 1: Orimattila, 2: Eno, 3: Joutseno, 4: Jänisjärvi, 5: Antrea Suuri-Kelpojärvi, 6: Lahti Myllyoja, 7: Juankoski, 8: Antrea (net find), 9: Mäntsälä, 10: Hyrynsalmi, 11: Suomussalmi, 12: Lahti Ristola, 13: Heinola (sleigh-runner find), 14: Inari, 15 and 16: Heinjoki, 17: Luumäki, 18: Sujala.*

(Takala 2004, 157–8). The Akonpohja site at Juankoski is dated to 9200±75 BP (8610–8270 cal BC; Hela-918), and it has also revealed a few finds of flint (Jussila *et al.* 2006). Of somewhat younger date is the Pukinkallio site at Mäntsälä with finds consisting of quartzes and burnt bone. This site is dated to 8960±65 BP (8230–8010 cal BC; Hela-706) (Takala 2004, 160).

Other sites of almost the same age, but investigated several years previously, are Nuoliharju at Hyrynsalmi, 8960±120 BP (8250–7910 cal BC; Hela-3924) (Korteniemi and Suominen 1998, 54), Vanha Kirkkosaari at Suomussalmi (8950±120 BP; 8240–7890 cal BC; Hela-2313) (Jungner and Sonninen 1996), the site of the Viikinäinen sledge runner find at Heinola (8840±90 BP; 8150–7800 cal BC; Su-1710) (Seger 1988, 21), and the Sámi Museum site in Inari (8760±75 BP; 7970–7690 cal BC; Ua-4296) (Carpelan 1999, 165).

In 2003 and 2004 two Preboreal sites, at a distance of some two hundred metres from each other, were excavated on the Karelian Isthmus. Heinjoki Valklampi 1 was dated to 8765±65 BP (7950–7710 cal BC; Hela-743) from a sample of burnt bone, and Valklampi 2 to 8720±70 BP (7900–7660 cal BC; Hela-744). The Tarhojenranta site was discovered in their immediate vicinity and is of the same age, according to shore displacement chronology, although no datable organic material was found. There were, however, ten tools, 13 blades, 43 flakes and one core – all made of flint. Five of the tools are retouched blades, two points, one scraper, one burin, and one knife. All the flint blades were thin and narrow. The burin was made on a broken blade. 44% of the blades and retouched blades were broken medial parts, and 80% of the flakes, blades and retouched blades, where a core can be identified, were struck from single platform cores. The only discovered core, however, was a bipolar core (Takala 2004, 154–6).

The latest site currently dated to the pioneer settlement stage in south Finland is Mustaniemi at Luumäki, which has been dated from a charcoal sample to 8580±140 BP (7870–7520 cal BC; Hela-4395) (Takala 2004, 159). The chronological difference between this site and the oldest one is almost 1000 radiocarbon years. Also the Sujala site at Utsjoki in northenmost Finland must be mentioned in this connection as the material and preliminary datings link the site to the earliest Postglacial settlement in all Finland (for further details see Rankama and Kankaanpää, this volume).

Cultural contacts indicated by the finds

It has been traditionally maintained that the Kunda and Butovo cultures were separate entities in the near vicinity of Finland at the time of the pioneer settlement. The roots of the Kunda culture, situated closest to Finland, lie in the Swiderian culture, although the origins of the culture have been regarded as partly unresolved (Jaanits 1990, 10–12; Kozlowski 1989, 426, figure 2; Schulz 1996, 28; Sulgostowska 2003, 50). The Butovo culture has also been regarded as a Post-Swiderian culture, but the latest results from excavations in the Upper Volga region show that the earliest stage of the Butovo culture may be as old as the Swiderian, and that the flint collection of the culture may derive partially from the local Palaeolithic (Zhilin 1998; Zhilin 1996a, 278–82; Zhilin 2003, 688; Zhilin 2004; Zhilin and Matiskainen 2003, 697).

According to Zhilin, there is a significant similarity among the flint assemblages from various sites over a zone extending from the east Baltic to southern Finland, and in the east as far as the Upper Volga (Zhilin 2003, 691; Jaanits 1990, 9–10). The similarities of the Butovo and Kunda cultures are evident not only in the flint material but also in the bone artefacts (Zhilin 2003, 691–2). In Finland bones are almost completely absent, which is explained by the fact that bone material does not survive in the country's acidic soils (e.g. Ukkonen 1996, 66–7). It can be said that a uniform Kunda-Butovo cultural sphere emerged in north-east Europe during the turn of the Preboreal and Boreal periods.

Ristola, Lahti

Excavations at the Stone Age site of Ristola in Lahti in 1970 and 1971, and between 1995 and 1999, have brought to light over 60,000 finds. Of these items, 140 were of burnt bone and 315 of flint; over 57,000 were quartz artefacts and flakes, and there were over 500 other lithic objects. Ristola is a multi-period site, as indicated by finds of almost 1,600 sherds of Corded Ware pottery. A piece of burnt bone was radiocarbon dated to 8880±75 BP (8170–7880 cal BC; Hela-727) (Takala 2004, 50). Ten other radiocarbon dates have been obtained from the site, ranging from the end of the Stone Age to as late as historically documented times.

According to shore displacement, the Mesolithic settlement of Ristola can be dated, at the latest, to the culmination stage of the Ancylus Lake, *c.* 9200–9000 BP (8400–8150 cal BC). It is also possible that the site was already occupied around 9500 BP (8850 cal BC). The greatest point of interest in the finds from Ristola is the flint material, because it can be dated more precisely than the quartzes and lithic artefacts: flints can also outline cultural contacts.

With regard to the types and age of the flint, the Ristola material falls into two groups: 1) cretaceous flint (14.3% of the flint finds), and 2) carboniferous flint (85.7% of the finds). The carboniferous flints include partly burnt pieces and 'chert-like' finds of rough texture, and are mostly of various hues of brown and opaque. The cretaceous flints are black or dark grey, transparent or semi-transparent.

The occurrence of cretaceous flint is clearly a phenomenon belonging to the Kunda culture, although this type of flint is also known outside its region (e.g. Kriiska 2001, 24–5; Zhilin 2003). Of all the flint tools found at Ristola, 32% were made of cretaceous flint, while the number is less than 1% within the sites of the Butovo culture (Zhilin 2003, 690). 68% of the tools at Ristola were made of carboniferous flint, which was used less within the Kunda culture but played a major role in western Russia, the area of origin of this type of flint (Zhilin 2003, 691). The origin of the carboniferous flint found at Ristola remains obscure, but it is possible that this flint came to Ristola through the same contacts as the cretaceous flint. It is also possible that at some stage there may have been direct links between south Finland and west Russia, but sites indicating such contacts are lacking in areas east of Finland (e.g. Matiskainen 1996, 260; Schulz 1996, 29).

Five arrowheads were found in the excavations (Figure 6.2). These objects belong to the class of Post-Swiderian arrowheads and even to the group of Pulli-type arrowheads, which is marked by flat ventral retouch. The base fragment is most likely the fragment of a Pulli-type point, but it can just as well be classified as a Post-Swiderian point. Arrowheads of the Pulli type, or their fragments, are known from 37 dwelling sites and 43 stray find locations in northeast Europe and western Russia, in addition to Ristola (Koltsov and Zhilin 1999a, 58–61; Ostrauskas 2000, 170–2).

Two backed pieces and one small truncation-like microblade were classified as inserts and the collection has also one point or perforator. One artefact is classified as a borer as the retouch is suitable for boring instead of using the tool as a mere point or a perforator (Figure 6.3).

Inserts shaped with steep retouch are a Preboreal artefact type in the Kunda and Butovo cultures, although individual items of this type are also known from the Boreal period in the Butovo culture (Koltsov and Zhilin 1999a, 60; Koltsov and Zhilin 1999b, 349; Ostrauskas 2000, 172). Inserts with semi-steep retouch have been found in Preboreal and Boreal contexts in the Kunda culture, the region of the Volga and the Oka, and in the territory of the Veretje culture east of Lake Onega (Jaanits and Ilomets 1988, 58; Koltsov and Zhilin 1999b, 349, 356–7; Kriiska *et al.* 2002, 33; Kriiska *et al.* 2003, 35–6; Oshibkina 1989; Oshibkina 1999). Chronological or culture-bound properties are not seen in the manufacturing technology or typology of borers and points (e.g. Sulgostowska 1999, 87, figure 1, 89–90; Zhilin 1996a, 275–83).

The knives from Ristola are all very small fragments, the largest only 17mm long. The eight multi-purpose tools from Ristola are all combinations of knives: either scraper-knives or burin-knives. Of the scrapers from Ristola, 50% are end scrapers, 37.5% are double scrapers, and 12.5% are side scrapers. The side burins from Ristola (86% of the burins) have one, two or even three working edges. The remainder are so-called convergent burins. 36% of the burins from Ristola were made on flakes and 64% were made on blades. Moreover, 57% of all the burins were made on broken blades (Figure 6.4).

Flint knives are a typical artefact form in western Russian cultures (e.g. Koltsov and Zhilin 1999a, 58–61; Oshibkina 1989, 404, 411), but are almost completely absent in the Kunda culture (e.g. Kriiska *et al.* 2002, 30; Kriiska *et al.* 2003, 30, 36; Ostrauskas 2000, 172). With regard to the sites of the Kunda culture, this may depend on a different manner of classification or on the actual rarity of the type in the area of the culture. Predominating among the flints of the Kunda culture are scrapers of various types, while in the Mesolithic cultures of western Russian, burins are the largest category of finds, although at some sites, especially later ones, scrapers prevail. Throughout the Butovo, Veretje and other cultures of western Russia, end scrapers are the most common type of scraper (Koltsov and Zhilin 1999a, 58, 59; Koltsov and Zhilin 1999b, 348, 354; Oshibkina 1989, 404, 411; Sorokin 1999, 312–14). A chronological change can be seen in the Kunda culture:

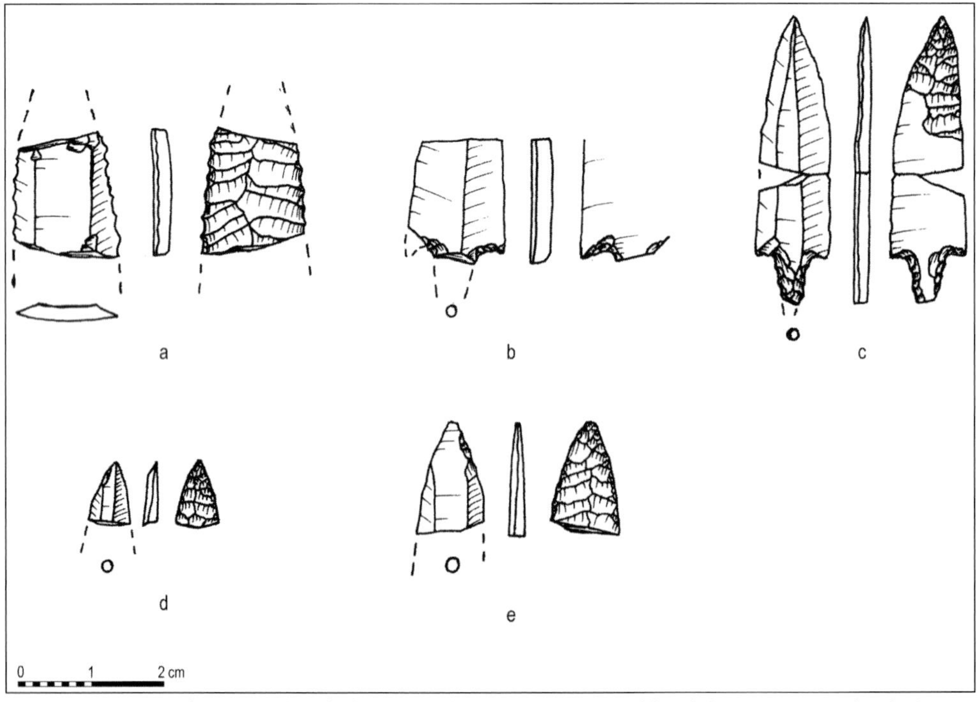

Figure 6.2. Flint arrowheads from Ristola. (Drawings: Mickle Zhilin, Museum of Lahti).

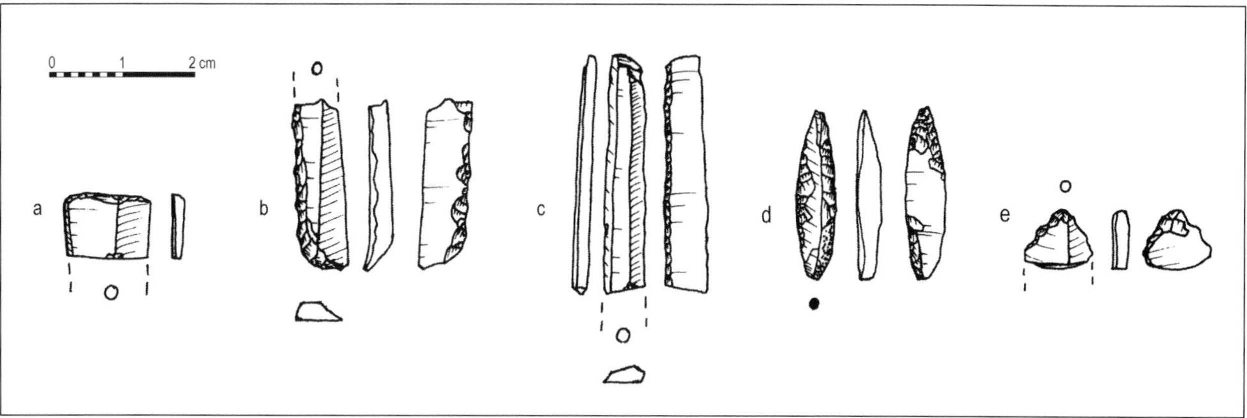

Figure 6.3. Inserts (a–c), point (d) and borer (e) from Ristola. (Drawings: Mickle Zhilin, Museum of Lahti).

during the Preboreal period most of the scrapers are end-scrapers, while at the Boreal period sites side scrapers predominate (Jaanits and Ilomets 1988, 58; Kriiska *et al.* 2003, 33–5). It is thus possible to say that in typological terms, the Ristola scrapers are closest to the finds from the early stage of the Kunda culture.

The fact that clearly over half of all the burins from Ristola were made on blades is a feature corresponding to the sites of the early stage of the Kunda culture. Most of the burins were made on flakes in the later stage of the Kunda culture (Jaanits and Ilomets 1988, 58; Kriiska *et al.* 2003, 35). The predomination of burins made on broken blades at Ristola is a feature generally associated with the Kunda culture (Ostrauskas 2000, 172; Sulgostowska 1999, 90, 91).

60% of the flint blades from Ristola are broken medial parts. Ever since its initial stages, the Kunda culture included the deliberate breaking of blades as raw material for inserts (Sulgostowska 1999, 89), and it is possible that the medial parts of the Ristola blades were the result of such deliberate breaking for later use.

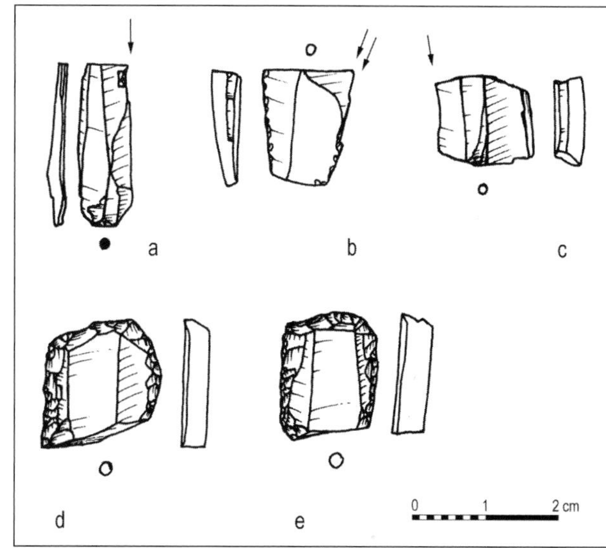

Figure 6.4. Some flint burins (a–c) and scrapers (d, e) from Ristola. (Drawings: Mickle Zhilin, Museum of Lahti).

Other finds

Typologically and technologically, the flint material from the Tarhojenranta site on the Karelian Isthmus can be linked to the Kunda culture and the whole Post-Swiderian cultural sphere, although some undatable finds from the site may belong to the younger phase of the site. The thin and narrow medial parts of blades, retouched blades, the burin on a broken blade, the predominance of single platform cores in producing blades and flakes, and, finally, the use of pressure technique in blade production are all typical of this period and the related cultural spheres. The typological dating of the flint artefacts covers a long time span at the turn of the Preboreal and Boreal periods, but the finds and their elevations suggest a tentative dating to the culmination stage of the Ancylus Lake, *c.* 9200–9000 BP (8400–8150 cal BC). Of the flint material found at Tarhojenranta, there was 10% of black cretaceous flint and 90% of carboniferous flint.

The flint assemblage from Joutseno is much smaller than the Ristola material, but the artefacts have the same features as those of the Ristola site and the Kunda and Butovo cultures – the flint insert in particular being a typical find of these cultures (Jussila and Matiskainen 2003, 688, figure 83.7, 669). In addition, a bone point fragment that can be compared to the Sigir-type arrowheads is similar to artefacts known from among all the Post-Swiderian cultures (Jussila 2001, 5; Jussila and Matiskainen 2003, 669–70; Zhilin 2001, 65, figure 7, 67–8, figures 8, 9). The type is dated to *c.* 9650–6000 BP (*c.* 9000–4900 cal BC) (Zhilin 1996b). The flint finds from the Mesolithic site at Juankoski are not yet published and they cannot be used in the study of cultural contacts.

Conclusions

The flint finds indicate that the Ristola site had contacts with sites of the Post-Swiderian Kunda culture. At the same time, the flint inventory from Ristola has also similarities with the flint of Butovo and other cultures of western

Russian cultures, but these analogies are partially based on the general typological and technological characters of flint at the turn of the Preboreal and Boreal periods. It must also be noted that the Butovo culture influenced its neighbouring cultures.

The similarities of the flint and osteological assemblages in the regional cultures also permit the use of the term Kunda–Butovo cultural sphere, extending from northern Poland via the Baltics, southern Finland and east Karelia to the Volga and Oka rivers. The flint material indicates that the Ristola site belonged to this cultural sphere while it was also part of the Kunda culture. The flint finds from Tarhojenranta and Kuurmanpohja support this view in addition to the information we have from the Antrea net and Heinola sleigh-runner.

As Ristola is dated as one of the first Postglacial dwelling sites in southern Finland, and for the time being is the only one from which large amounts of imported material, i.e. flint, have been found, it can be assumed that direct contacts were involved here, at least in the initial stage. The people who moved to the site had brought with them raw material for artefacts, such as flint cores and half-finished blades, and possibly also complete flint artefacts. At a later stage, the import of artefacts, or raw material based on exchange or trade, could have become established, but it must also be noted that local materials, rather than flint, came into use before long.

References

Carpelan, C. 1999. On the Postglacial Colonisation of Eastern Fennoscandia, in M. Huurre (ed.), *Dig it all. Papers dedicated to Ari Siiriäinen*, 151–71. Helsinki, Finnish Antiquarian Society.

Forsberg, O. 2006. Jänisjoen reitin Varhaisin asutus – inventointituloksia Laatokan pohjoispuolelta. *Muinaistutkija* 1/2006, 2–16.

Jaanits, K. 1990. The origin and development of the Kunda culture, in *Finno-ugric studies in Archaeology, Anthropology and Ethnography. Estonian Papers Presented at the Sixth International Finno-Ugric Congress 1985*, 7–15. Tallinn, Department of Archaeology, University of Tallinn.

Jaanits, K. and Ilomets, M. 1988. *Umbusi mesoliitilise asula vanusest ja kohast Eesti keskmise kiviaja kronoloogias*. Tallinn, Department of Archaeology, University of Tallinn.

Jungner, H. and Sonninen, E. 1996. *Radiocarbon dates IV*. University of Helsinki. Radiocarbon Dating Laboratory Report 4. Helsinki, University of Helsinki.

Jussila, T. 2001. *Joutsenon Kuurmanpohjan kivikautisten asuinpaikkojen koekaivaus v. 2000*. Unpublished excavation report.

Jussila, T. and Matiskainen, H. 2003. Mesolithic settlement during the Preboreal period in Finland in L. Larsson, H. Kindgren, K. Knutsson, D. Loeffler and A. Åkerlund (eds.), *Mesolithic on the Move: Papers presented at the Sixth International Conference on the Mesolithic in Europe, Stockholm 2000*, 664–70. Oxford. Oxbow Books.

Jussila, T., Kriiska, A. and Rostedt, T. 2006. Varhaismesoliittisesta asutuksesta Koillis-Savossa – alustavia tuloksia Juankosken Akonpohjan Helvetinhaudanpuron asuinpaikan kiviaineistosta, in P. Pesonen and T. Mökkönen (eds.), *Arkeologiapäivät 2005*, 50–61. Helsinki, Suomen Arkeologinen Seura.

Koltsov, L. V. and Zhilin, M. G. 1999a. *Mezolit Volgo-Okskogo Mezhdurechia. Pamiatniki Butovskoi Kultury*. Moscow, Nauka.

Koltsov, L. V. and Zhilin, M. G. 1999b. Tanged points cultures in the upper Volga basin, in S. K. Kozłowski, J. Gurba and L. L. Zaliznyak (eds.), *Tanged points cultures in Europe*, 346–60. Lublin, Maria Curie-Skłodowska University Press.

Korteniemi, M. and Suominen, E. 1998. Nuoliharju W – Suomen vanhin pyyntikuoppa? *Studia Historica Septentrionalia* 34 (Rajamailla IV 1997), 51–67. Rovaniemi, Societas Historica Finlandiae Septentrionalis.

Kozłowski, S. K. 1989. A Survey of Early Holocene Cultures of the Western Part of the Russian Plain, in C. Bonsall (ed.), *The Mesolithic in Europe: Papers presented at the Third International Symposium Edinburgh 1985*, 424–41. Edinburgh, John Donald Publishers.

Kriiska, A. 2001. *Stone Age Settlement and Economic Processes in the Estonian Coastal Area and Islands*. Academic Dissertation. Helsinki, University of Helsinki.

Kriiska, A., Johanson, K., Saluäär, U. and Lõugas, L. 2003b. The results of research of Estonian Stone Age, in U. Tamla (ed.), *Archaeological field works in Estonia 2000*, 25–41. Tallinn, Historic Preservation Department.

Kriiska, A., Saluäär, U., Lõugas, L., Johanson, K. and Hanni, H. 2002. Archaeological excavations in Sindi-Lodja, in U. Tamla (ed.), *Archaeological field works in Estonia 2001*, 27–40. Tallinn, Historic Preservation Department.

Mangerud, J., Andersen, S. T., Berglund, B. and Donner, J. 1974. Quaternary stratigraphy of Norden, proposal for terminology and classification. *Boreas* 3, 109–28.

Matiskainen, H. 1989. The Chronology of the Finnish Mesolithic, in C. Bonsall (ed.), *The Mesolithic in Europe. Papers presented at the Third International Symposium Edinburgh 1985*, 379–90. Edinburgh, John Donald Publishers.

Matiskainen, H. 1996. Discrepancies in deglaciation chronology and the appearance of man in Finland, in L. Larsson (ed.), *The Earliest Settlement of Scandinavia and its neighbouring areas*, 251–62. Acta Archaeologica Lundensia, Series in 8°, 24. Stockholm, Almqvist & Wiksell International.

Oshibkina, S. V. 1989. The Material Culture of the Veretye-type Sites in the Region to the East of Lake Onega, in C. Bonsall (ed.), *The Mesolithic in Europe. Papers presented at the Third International Symposium Edinburgh 1985*, 402–13. Edinburgh, John Donald Publishers.

Oshibkina, S. V. 1999. Tanged points industries in the north-west of Russia, in S. K. Kozłowski, J. Gurba and L. L. Zaliznyak (eds.), *Tanged points cultures in Europe*, 325–32. Lublin, Maria Curie-Skłodowska University Press.

Ostrauskas, T. 2000. Mesolithic Kunda Culture: A Glimpse from Lithuania, in *De temporibus antiquissimis ad honorem Lembit Jaanits*, 167–80. Muinasaja teadus 8. Tallinn, University of Tallinn.

Pesonen, P. 2005. Sarvingin salaisuus – Enon Rahakankaan varhaismesoliittinen ajoitus. *Muinaistutkija* 2/2005, 2–13.

Schulz, H.-P. 1996. Pioneerit pohjoisessa. Suomen varhaismesoliittinen asutus arkeologisen aineiston valossa. *Suomen Museo* 1996, 5–45. Helsinki, The Finnish Antiquarian Society.

Seger, T. 1988. Heinolan esihistoria, in J. Wilmi (ed.) *Heinolan pitäjän historia*, 17–73. Jyväskylä, Gummerus.

Sorokin, A. N. 1999. Neighbours of the Butovo culture on the upper Volga and Oka rivers, in S. K. Kozłowski, J. Gurba and L. L. Zaliznyak (eds.), *Tanged points cultures in Europe*, 311–17. Lublin, Maria Curie-Skłodowska University Press.

Stuiver M., Reimer, P. J., Bard, E., Beck, J. W., Burr, G. S., Hughen, K. A., Kromer, B., McCormac, G., van der Plicht, J. and Spurk, M. 1998. INTCAL98 Radiocarbon Age Calibration, 24000-0 cal BP. *Radiocarbon* 40 (3), 1041–83.

Sulgostowska, Z. 1999. Final Palaeolithic Masovian Cycle and Mesolithic Kunda Culture Relations, in S. K. Kozłowski, J. Gurba and L. L. Zaliznyak (eds.), *Tanged points cultures in Europe*, 85–92. Lublin, Maria Curie-Skłodowska University Press.

Sulgostowska, Z. 2003. Mesolithic Colonisation of South-Eastern Subbalticum, in L. Larsson, H. Kindgren, K. Knutsson, D. Loeffler and A. Åkerlund (eds.), *Mesolithic on the Move: Papers presented at the Sixth International Conference on the Mesolithic in Europe, Stockholm 2000*, 47–51. Oxford, Oxbow Books.

Takala, H. 2004. *The Ristola Site in Lahti and the Earliest Post-glacial Settlement of South Finland.* Jyväskylä, Gummerus.

Ukkonen, P. 1996. Osteological analysis of the refuse fauna in the Lake Saimaa area. Environmental studies in eastern Finland. *Helsinki Papers in Archaeology* 8, 63–147.

Ylikoski, K. 2004. *Antrean kivikautisen verkkolöydön iänmääritys*. Unpublished M.A. thesis. Department of Geology, University of Helsinki.

Zhilin, M. G. 1996b. Arrowheads of the 'Shigir' type in the Mesolithic and Early Neolithic of Eastern Europe (English summary). *Tverskoy arheologicheski Sbornik* 2, 50–6. Tver, University of Tver.

Zhilin, M. G. 1996a. The western part of Russia in the Late Palaeolithic–Early Mesolithic, in L. Larsson (ed.), *The Earliest Settlement of Scandinavia and its relationship with neighbouring areas*, 273–84. Acta Archaeologica Lundensia, Series in 8°, 24. Stockholm, Almqvist & Wiksell International.

Zhilin, M. G. 1998. Adaptation of Mesolithic Cultures of the Upper Volga to Lithic Raw Materials (English summary). *Tverskoy arheologicheski Sbornik* 3, 25–30. Tver, University of Tver.

Zhilin, M. G. 2001. *Kostyanaya industriya mezolita lesnoj zoni Vostochnoj Evropi* (Mesolithic bone industry of the eastern European forest zone). Moscow, URSS Publishing.

Zhilin, M. G. 2003. Early Mesolithic communication networks in the East European forest zone, in L. Larsson, H. Kindgren, K. Knutsson, D. Loeffler and A. Åkerlund (eds.), *Mesolithic on the Move: Papers presented at the Sixth International Conference on the Mesolithic in Europe, Stockholm 2000*, 688–93. Oxford, Oxbow Books.

Zhilin, M. G. 2004. Some results of the research of the Volga-Oka Mesolithic during last years, in H. A. Amirkhanov (ed.), *Problems of the Stone Age of the Russian Plain*, 92–139. Moscow, Nauchnyi Mir.

Zhilin, M. and Matiskainen, H. 2003. Deep in Russia, deep in the bog. Excavations at the Mesolithic sites Stanovoje 4 and Sakhtys 14, Upper Volga region, in L. Larsson, H. Kindgren, K. Knutsson, D. Loeffler and A. Åkerlund (eds.), *Mesolithic on the Move: Papers presented at the Sixth International Conference on the Mesolithic in Europe, Stockholm 2000*, 694–702. Oxford, Oxbow Books.

7. The Sujala site in Utsjoki: Post-Swiderian in northern Lapland?

Jarmo Kankaanpää and Tuija Rankama

The Sujala site consists of two small clusters of finds located by Lake Vetsijärvi in the borough of Utsjoki, northernmost Finnish Lapland. The finds consist primarily of artefacts and debitage produced by a macroblade industry utilizing tuffaceous chert. This lithic material is not native to the area and probably derives from the Varanger Peninsula in Norway, roughly 100km north of the site. The raw material may suggest a connection with the Preboreal Komsa Phase of the North Norwegian Finnmark Mesolithic, which is also characterized by a macroblade technology. However, the typological features of the Sujala arrowheads and certain characteristics of the blade technology suggest an origin in the Post-Swiderian cultures of north-eastern Europe. Post-Swiderian sites are not previously known from Lapland. Radiocarbon dates place the site near the Preboreal/Boreal boundary.

Keywords: Lapland, Post-Swiderian, blade technology, tanged points.

The location

The Sujala site lies on a gravel ridge overlooking Lake Vetsijärvi, a large tundra lake located on a fell plateau in Utsjoki, Finland's northernmost borough (Figure 7.1). The ridge forms a peninsula that protrudes into the lake from the south. The peninsula is also the terminus of a rough track that connects the lake with the main road, some 20km distant. That the site was discovered at all is largely due to the track, which, running the length of the ridge, has destroyed the ground vegetation in its path, leaving surface finds in full view.

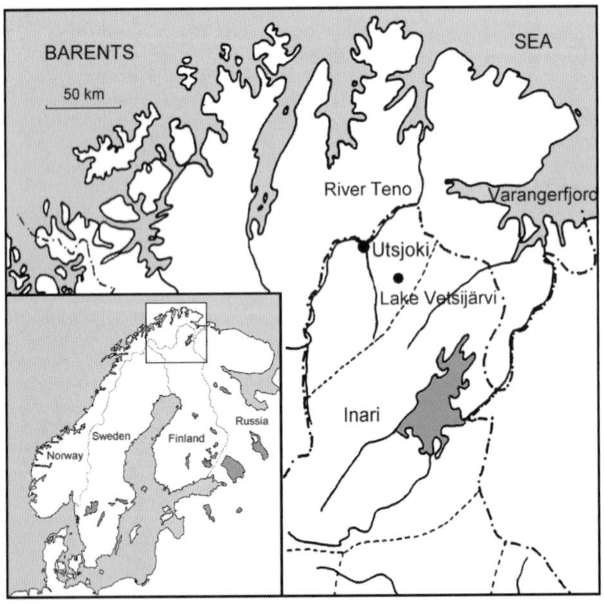

Figure 7.1. Location of the Sujala site.

The survey

The site was discovered by the authors in 2002 during an archaeological survey of what was then an archaeologically uncharted area (Rankama and Kankaanpää 2003; Rankama 2005). The survey was mounted in order to test Tuija Rankama's hypothesis that the inland tundra lakes of Utsjoki were already playing a role in the local economy in the Mesolithic (Rankama 1996, 528–31, 557). Searching the lakeshores by kayak, and the track on foot, turned up one *Sámi* campsite, one undated pitfall, and ten Stone Age sites, nine of which produced a quartz inventory typical of Finnish prehistoric sites from the Boreal to the Bronze Age. The tenth site, however, produced fragments of large blades made from a weathered chert-like material quite alien to Finnish archaeology. This site was dubbed 'Sujala' after Eero Sujala, whose fishing cabin stood nearby.

Large blade technology is very rare in Finland, which has no native sources of flint or chert. The material of the Sujala finds is a microcrystalline stone that was originally reported from coastal sites in Norwegian Finnmark (Lapland), and erroneously called 'dolomite' because in its weathered form the stone turns whitish and rather light and soft (e.g. Simonsen 1961, 14). Recently, however, the material has been redefined as 'tuffaceous chert' by Bryan Hood (1992,

91–3). In its unweathered form, it is dark, greenish grey or nearly black, and much more dense and hard than the weathered variety. No quarries or outcrops of the stone have been reported so far, but Finnish geologists who have seen the Sujala material have stated that it cannot originate in the Fennoscandian Shield. The nearest likely source is the Varanger Peninsula, in Norwegian Finnmark, some 100km due north of the Sujala site (Jukka Välimaa, Tuomo Manninen and Reino Kesola, pers. comm., 2005).

The first potential 'parent' coming to mind for the Sujala finds was the earliest occupation of Norwegian Finnmark, a Preboreal phase referred to as Mesolithic Period I, or the Komsa phase, and dated to 10,000–9000 BP (*c.* 9500–8250 cal BC) (Olsen 1994, 30–1; Woodman 1993, 74). Like the Sujala assemblage, the Komsa phase is characterized by both large blades and tuffaceous chert. All previously known sites of this phase, however, are located on the coast. This currently lies some sixty kilometres north of Lake Vetsijärvi, but fiords reaching up the Teno River and Lake Pulmankijärvi valleys would have shortened the distance to thirty kilometres during the Preboreal Period with its higher sea levels. Were its roots to be found in this direction, the Sujala site promised to be not only the first inland Komsa-phase site, but also the first Komsa site in Finnish Lapland (Kankaanpää and Rankama 2005, 150–3).

The excavations

A test excavation was carried out at the Sujala site in 2004. Surface collecting resulted in the pinpointing of two scatters of tuffaceous chert artefacts, located roughly 200m apart. Test pitting showed that the scatters were some 10–15m in diameter and fairly dense. The northern scatter (Area 1) produced 177 artefacts of tuffaceous chert and 8 of quartz, while the southern scatter (Area 2) produced 161 and 4 respectively. A small, sparse scatter of 21 artefacts made from various lithic materials (quartz, quartzite, flint, and white chert), discovered some 25 metres south of Area 1, probably represents a later event. The most remarkable finds were two blade cores and a tanged arrowhead, all from Area 2. Blades and blade fragments – many of them retouched – were numerous, accounting for a good 35% of all tuffaceous chert artefacts.

Excavations continued in Area 2 in 2005. The choice fell on this area because it had produced not only the blade cores and arrowhead but also a more varied selection of other lithic artefact types. The 33 square metres that were excavated during a two-week field season covered an estimated 3/5 of the scatter (Figure 7.2). The removal of a thin layer of sod and mixed soil revealed an untouched, leached podsol surface that was first excavated down in one 5cm spit, followed by two 2.5cm spits, and a final emptying out of two small pit-like features no deeper than another 5cm. The find layer was quite thin and included the mixed top layer; the lowest finds lay no deeper than 15cm below the surface. The most notable feature was a sizeable dark stain that contained wood charcoal and burnt bone, in addition to a concentration of lithic finds. The stain, which was some 2m in diameter, probably represented the remains of a campfire and the floor of a light shelter, since particularly the eastern edge was very clearly demarcated, not only by the colour but by the finds as well. No evidence of a stone hearth was noted. In terms of finds, the excavation was very productive: 42 charcoal samples were collected for dating, the dark stain produced 606g of burnt bone, and lithic finds numbered 4808, of which 4781 (99.4%) were tuffaceous chert.

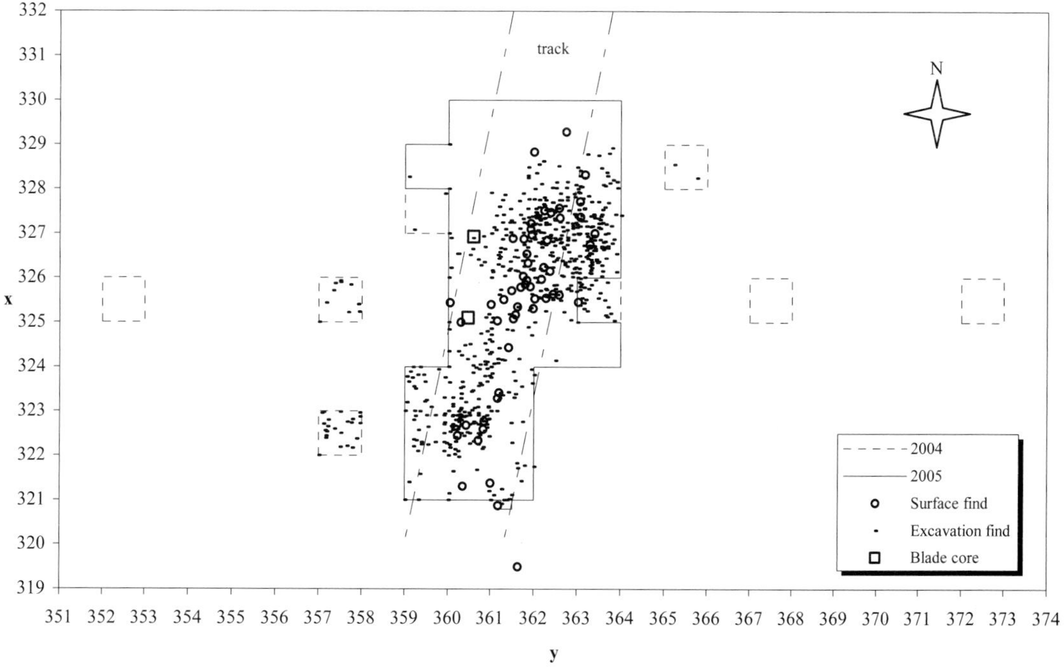

Figure 7.2. The distribution of finds in Area 2 (grid in m).

The dates

Three samples were sent to the University of Helsinki Dating Laboratory for radiocarbon dating. One sample was charcoal, the two others burnt bone. The bone samples gave AMS dates of 8940±80 BP (8290–7820 cal BC; Hela-1103) and 8930±85 BP (8290–7790 cal BC; Hela-1104), while the charcoal sample was dated to 9265±65 BP (8640–8300 cal BC; Hela-1102) (calibrations by OxCal 3.10, Bronk Ramsey 2005). The bone dates were considered more reliable, since old wood (specifically pine (*Pinus*)) has proven to be a problem in some Lapland sites (e.g. Carpelan 2003, 34) and the species of the charcoal sample was not identified. However, two other charcoal samples from nearly the same location were subsequently analysed by Tuuli Timonen and Pirkko Harju of the Finnish Museum of Natural History and found to be birch (*Betula*) (T. Timonen, pers. comm., 2006). With birch, the potential old wood error would be shortened to less than 100 years, since birches do not live very long (as compared to conifers) and rot quickly once dead. Birch would also fit the botanical succession better, as the local arboreal vegetation during the Preboreal would have been mainly birch (Hyvärinen 1975; Seppä 1996). There is thus the possibility that the charcoal date is valid.

The lithic finds

A table of the lithic finds from the 2004 and 2005 Sujala excavations is presented in Figure 7.3. The columns with question marks indicate uncertain identifications. The cherts include five artefacts of cherty materials differing somewhat from the 'normal' tuffaceous chert, while the 'other' category consists of quartz, quartzite, and a slate-like material. The 'fragment' category consists of artefacts that cannot be assigned to any of the other categories because of the absence of diagnostic features. Most of the fragments appear to be very small blade fragments.

Formal tools include whole and fragmentary examples of side and end scrapers, burins, and tanged arrowheads on blades, as well as a possible borer/reamer. In addition, there are a large number of retouched blades and fragments of various kinds. The 30 arrowhead finds include one whole point, 16 tip fragments, four base fragments (three with the tang intact), seven tang fragments, and two fragments that are either tips or tangs. One artefact was identified as an arrowhead preform and two as preform fragments.

All of the unambiguous cores from Sujala derive from blade production. The assemblage includes two complete cores. One of them (Figure 7.4: 1) is almost conical in shape. It has a flat base and regular blades have been detached from three of its sides. The platform has been formed by radial flake detachments. One of them has overshot and destroyed part of the core edge; nevertheless, some further core tablets were removed after that. The length of the core is 51.3mm, and the width of the last detached blades is 5–10mm.

The other core (Figure 7.4: 2) has, in its present state, two opposing platforms and acute platform angles. One of the platforms has only been used to detach two short and wide blades. The detachments from the other direction are narrow and regular. The platform at this end has been completely removed. Therefore it is impossible to say what the platform angle has originally been. When this core was found in 2004 it was missing a part of the platform as a result of a frost fracture. The missing part was, however, recovered during the 2005 excavation (Figure 7.4: 3). The length of the core is 59.7mm and its latest blade scars are 8–9mm wide.

The other discovered cores are all fragmentary. Three of the fragments are small bases of conical cores (Figure 7.5: 41–3). They have been deliberately struck off, apparently in an effort to make the bottom of the core flatter, perhaps to sit better on an anvil during reduction. One larger core end (Figure 7.5: 37) is from a wedge-shaped core and has blade scars on one broad side only.

At least 298 core tablets have been discovered (Figure 7.5: 38–40), ranging in size from 65mm in the largest dimension to thumbnail size and smaller. Only one (Figure 7.5: 40) has removed the whole striking platform. A common feature among the rest is hinge termination. This may be due to the normal behaviour of flake detachments from a flat surface (cf. Cotterell and Kamminga 1987, 701).

Artefact type	Cherts	?	Other	?
Tanged arrowhead/fragment	30			
Tanged arrowhead roughout/fragm.	3			
Scraper on blade	14			
Scraper on flake		1		
Borer/reamer		1		
Burin on blade, incl. fragmentary	12	7		
Burin spall implement	1			
Burin spall/spall fragment	19	3		
Unspecified tool on blade	6	1		
Retouched blade/blade fragment	307			
Retouched flake/flake fragment	6			
Retouched core tablet	5			
Retouched core-edge trimming flk.	1			
Retouched fragment	14			
Blade/blade fragment	1309		7	1
Blade-like flake	3			
Core or tool	1			
Blade core	2		1	
Blade core fragment	8	1	1	
Other core			1	
Core tablet	298	15		
Core rejuvenation flake	6			
Core-edge trimming flake	1131			
Flake	113		15	5
Fragment	1806		2	
Raw material chunk				1
total	**5095**	**29**	**27**	**7**

Figure 7.3. Table of finds from the Sujala excavations in 2004 and 2005.

It may also be a deliberate way of avoiding overshot flakes that can destroy the core edge on the opposite side.

Only four of the core tablets show signs of having been used as tools (e.g. Figure 7.5: 38). The rest are waste and qualify as evidence that the core reduction has taken place at Sujala. The number of small trimming flakes that exceeds 1100 also indicates *in situ* core reduction.

The sizes of some of the core tablets attest to the large original format of the cores reduced at Sujala. The width of the largest blades provides additional evidence: the maximum width is 42.6mm and blades exceeding 20mm in width are not rare. Among the retouched blades from the 2005 excavations only, there are fifty such blade fragments (Figure 7.5: 5, 10, 24, 25, 29, 30), and with many the measured width represents a minimum, since one or both edges are retouched.

The assemblage, however, also includes quite a number of small bladelets (Figure 7.5: 21). In the 2004 assemblage the width category 3–10mm formed *c.* 30% of the whole. The size distribution did not show any evidence of a separate microblade component, however (Kankaanpää and Rankama 2006, 125).

The Sujala blades are characterized by their strict regularity. The sides are usually almost exactly parallel and the dorsal ridges follow the same alignment. The profile of the blades is very straight. In the 2004 material, only one of the proximal ends showed no trimming, while more than half of the proximal ends had been both trimmed and abraded (Kankaanpää and Rankama 2006, 126). The 2005 material has not yet been analysed.

Retouch along the blade edges is typical of the Sujala material. This can take the form of very small retouch only discernible through a microscope (Figure 7.5: 29), or, more often, larger detachments that occasionally show coarse use wear (e.g. Figure 7.5: 25, 26). Quite often the whole length of the blade edge is retouched. It is also common to find ordinary retouch along one edge and inverse retouch along the other. Short blade segments with retouch along one or both edges are typical. They often have retouched notches on the edges where the blade has broken (Figure 7.5: 20, 22). The occurrence of notches is so common that it might be considered a method of snapping the blades. The snapping has almost invariably occurred perpendicular to the long axis of the blade. Thus, we are not dealing with a microburin technique, and microliths are absent from the assemblage: with the exception of scraper-like tools, retouch along the snapped surfaces is unknown.

The function of the retouched blades is unknown. Most of them seem too thick and large to have worked as insets for bone implements. Some have doubtless been used as knives, but in others the angle of the retouch seems too obtuse for that. A use as side scrapers does not seem very probable, at least for such long retouched blade fragments as in Figure 7.5: 24 or 31. Very wide scraper edges do not work on pliable material and hafting would be very difficult. Coarse wear, nevertheless, occurs on some of the retouched blade edges. A few shorter blade segments with very worn undercut edge retouch have been defined as side scrapers (Figure 7.5: 18, 19).

End scrapers are also included in the 2005 assemblage (Figure 7.5: 15–17). They are not common, and in some cases the scraper retouch is rather coarse – or possibly so worn that the original shape has been lost.

Blade burins are also present. The two largest specimens,

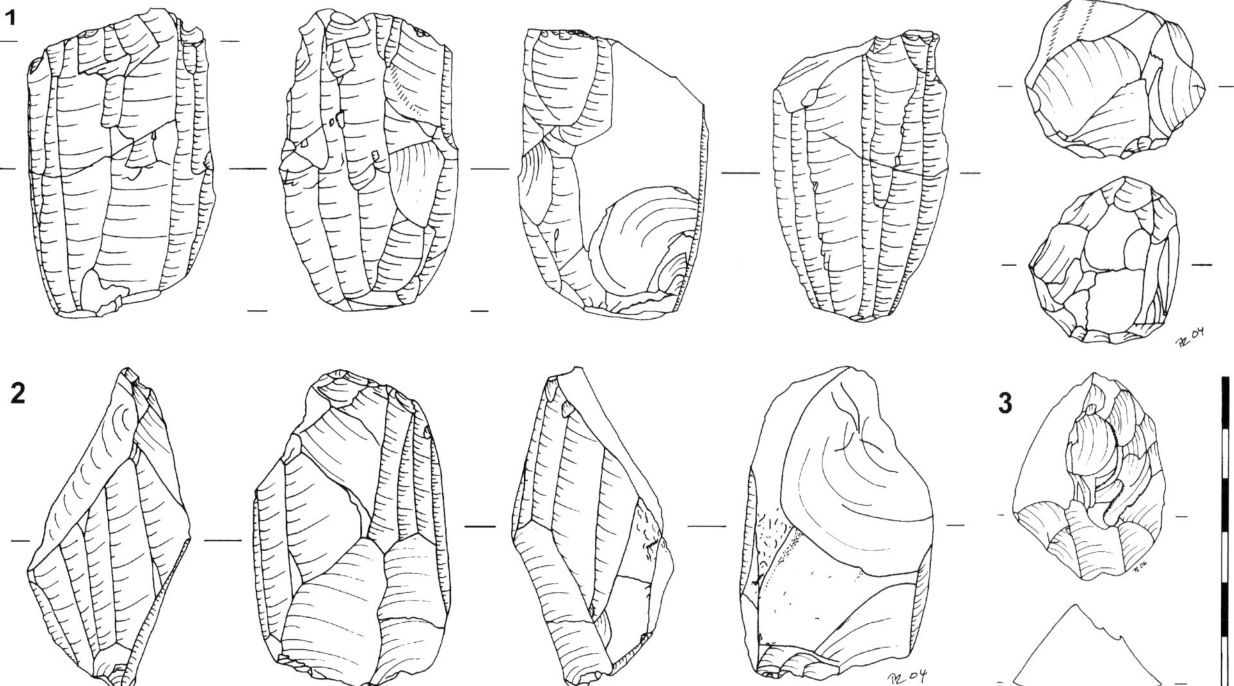

Figure 7.4. Blade cores from the Sujala site: 1) conical core, to the right the striking platform and core base; 2) bi-directional core; 3) frost fragment of bi-directional core. (Drawings: T. Rankama; scale in cm).

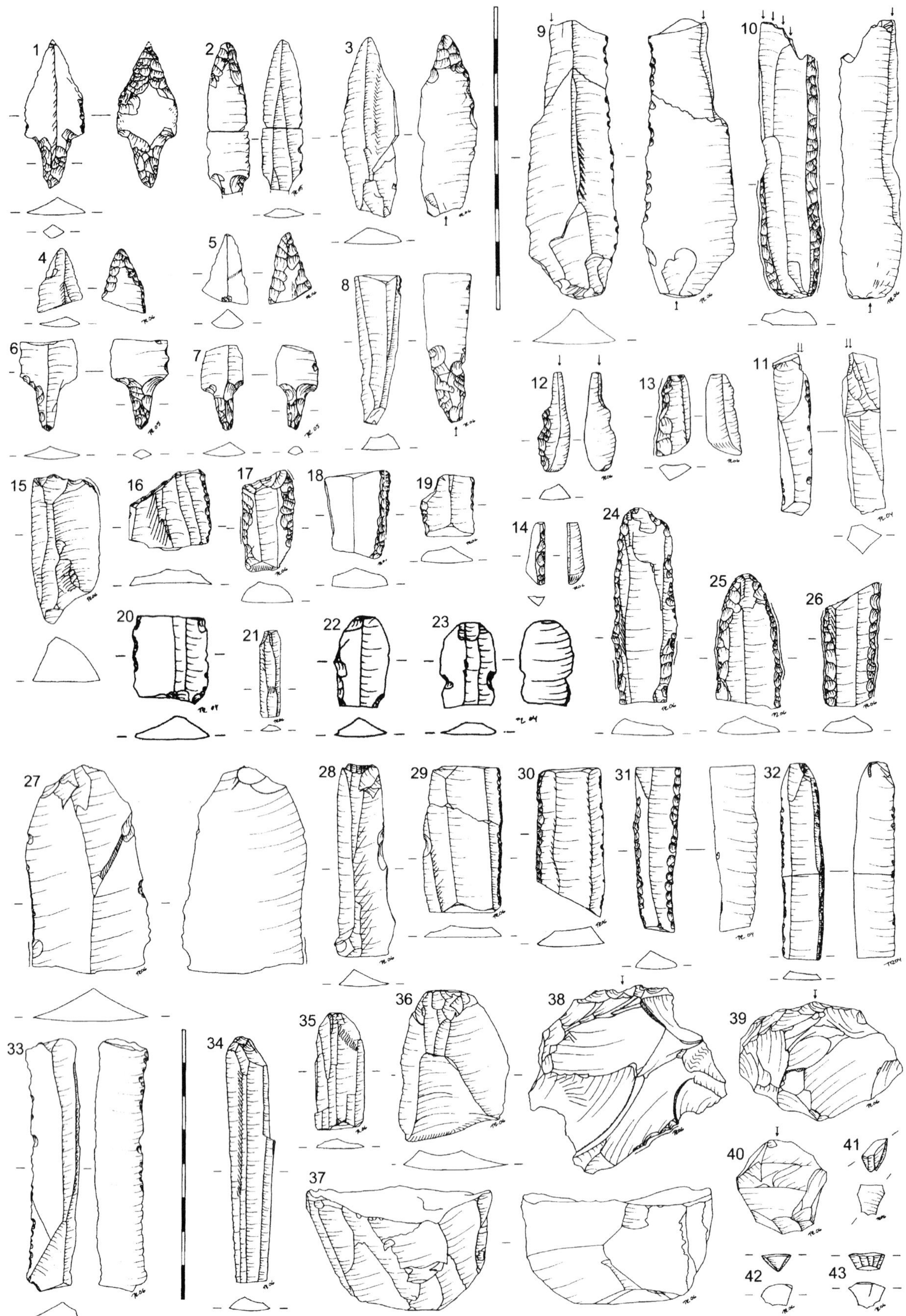

Figure 7.5. A selection of artefacts from the Sujala site: 1) tanged arrowhead; 2, 4–7) arrowhead fragments; 3) arrowhead preform; 8) perforator/reamer?; 9–11) burins; 12–14, burin spalls; 15–17) end scrapers; 18–19) side scrapers; 20, 22–23) notched blade fragments; 21) microblade; 24–27, 29–36) retouched and unretouched blade fragments; 37, 41–43) core bases; 38–40) core tablets. (Drawings: T. Rankama; scale in cm).

and a smaller one, are depicted as Figure 7.5, 9–11; the rest are smaller. The burin blows have always been struck on a snapped surface. The retouched edges in Figure 7.5: 10 seem to be typical: although only one edge-retouched burin has been found so far, several of the 19 burin spalls have been struck from similarly retouched blade edges (Figure 7.5: 12–14). The retouched edges in Figure 7.5: 10 are coarsely worn. It is possible, therefore, that the modification as a burin represents a secondary function. Hinge termination seems to be a typical feature of the burin spalls.

The Sujala assemblage also includes one whole blade arrowhead and 29 arrowhead fragments (Figure 7.5: 1, 2, 4–7). Two of the fragments can be refitted to form an almost complete point, with only part of the tang missing. All of the arrowheads are of the same type: tanged but not barbed, with the tang retouched on both edges and sometimes bifacially. The alignment of the points is along the central axis of the blades. The ventral side of the tip has invasive retouch from both edges meeting in the middle. The tip of the point is at the distal end of the original blade. The complete arrowhead is 42mm long and 17.9mm wide, while the almost complete specimen is 45mm long and 13mm wide. The fragments are within a similar size range. Three arrowhead roughouts have also been found (Figure 7.5: 3). In addition, one artefact with invasive ventral retouch (Figure 7.5: 8) has been tentatively classified as a perforator or reamer.

The Sujala assemblage, thus, is characterised by a well-developed, carefully executed blade technology, producing extremely regular blades. No evidence of flake core reduction has been found. The absence of cortex indicates that the blade cores have been brought to the site ready-shaped. The size of the largest core tablets and the width of the largest blades speak of a very large initial core size. In the light of the number of blades, blade fragments, core tablets, and other artefacts it can be safely said that a considerable amount of core reduction took place at this site.

The secondary modification of the blades usually took the form of retouch along the blade edges, as well as snapping the blades into segments, perhaps with the aid of notches retouched on the edges. Some of the blades with edge retouch may have been used as scrapers, others as knives, but the functions of the rest are not yet known. In addition, burins and end scrapers were manufactured but their numbers are still fairly low. The most obviously diagnostic implement types are the arrowheads, especially since they are very uniform in shape and manner of production.

Discussion

The Sujala assemblage is exceptional in Finnish archaeology. Only one other site, Lahti Ristola, has produced evidence of Early Mesolithic blade production (Takala 2004, 106–47); the few other flint blades from Mesolithic sites appear to have been imported ready-made. Parallels for the Sujala material are therefore best sought outside the Finnish borders.

The large blades and raw material that characterize the Sujala finds appeared originally to suggest affinities with the Komsa culture of the northern Norwegian coast. However, the arrowheads clearly differ from the mostly irregular and asymmetric Ahrensburg-derived tanged points of the Norwegian Early Mesolithic (e.g. Prøsch-Danielsen and Høgestøl 1995, figure 4; Woodman 1993, figure 2: 1–8), and exhibit, instead, features typical of the Post-Swiderian points of the Baltic countries and northern Russia: the symmetry of the point and its alignment along the axis of the blade, the forming of the tang, and, most importantly, the invasive ventral retouch of the tip (e.g. Sorokin 1984, figure 3: 11; Takala 2004, figure 143; Volokitin 2005, figures 2 and 3; Zhilin 1996, figure 4).

Other similarities with Post-Swiderian assemblages include the regularity of the blades, suggesting the use of the pressure technique in manufacture (cf. Sulgostowska 1999, 89–90). This differs from the early Komsa technology, which is characterized by hard hammer or punch percussion blade technology (Woodman 1993, 70). The total absence of flake core reduction at Sujala is another feature that distinguishes it from Komsa assemblages, where, for example, discoidal or globular cores are common (e.g. Bøe and Nummedal 1936, figures 181–3).

Additional similarities between Sujala and Post-Swiderian assemblages can be found in the retouch along the edges of the blades (e.g. Sorokin 1984, figures 2–4), the burins on a snapped blade with retouch along the edges (e.g. Sulgostowska 1999, 89), and the snapping of blades by first retouching notches on one or both sides (Koltsov 1989, figure 4; Ostrauskas 2000, figure 3: 30). The latter feature is common in Russian materials, but opinions differ as to its intentionality (A. Volokitin, pers. comm., 2005; cf. Ostrauskas 2000, 175).

Three possible interpretations, then, arise: the Sujala material represents either true inland Komsa with anomalous, fortuitously Post-Swiderian-like features, inland Komsa with actual Post-Swiderian influence, or true Post-Swiderian.

Although the distance to the Norwegian coast is short and the raw material points in that direction, no Komsa sites have previously been discovered on the inland. The Sujala tanged points and blade technology clearly differ from typical Komsa finds. Together with the apparent inland adaptation, they place the Sujala finds closer to the Post-Swiderian cultures. This conclusion is also supported by the other similarities with Post-Swiderian assemblages. No Preboreal Post-Swiderian sites are previously known from Lapland, however; the nearest known ones lie 1000 kilometres away in southern Finland. Evidence of Post-Swiderian penetration into northern Lapland, therefore, has consequences not only for the early settlement of Lapland itself, but also for the Early Postglacial prehistory of eastern Finland and Karelia, which formed the most likely route. Its consequences for the subsequent development of the Mesolithic occupation of northern Fennoscandia remain to be studied.

Acknowledgements

In addition to the much-appreciated work of our volunteer excavation teams, research at Sujala has been made possible by grants from the Finnish Cultural Foundation, the Niilo Helander Foundation, and the Oskar Öflund Foundation. The analyses and understanding of the material have benefited from the comments of geologists Tuomo Manninen, Jukka Välimaa, and Reino Kesola, and a large number of archaeologists both home and abroad, including Charlotte Damm, Sheila Coulson, Ericka Engelstad, Ingrid Fuglestvedt, Sven Erik Grydeland, Esa Hertell, Kjel Knutsson, Aivar Kriiska, Mikael A. Manninen, Morten Ramstad, Aleksei Sorokin, Mikkel Sørensen, Miikka Tallavaara, Aleksandr Volokitin, Peter Woodman, and Mikhail G. Zhilin.

References

Bøe, J. and Nummedal, A. 1936. *Le Finnmarkien. Les origines de la civilization dans l'extrême-nord de l'Europe*. Oslo, Instituttet for sammenlignende kulturforskning.

Bronk Ramsey, C. 2005. OxCal 3.10. WWW program and documentation available at http://www.rlaha.ox.ac.uk/oxcal/oxcal.htm (accessed 10/2007).

Carpelan, C. 2003. Arkeologiset vaiheet, in V.-P. Lehtola (ed.), *Inari – Aanar. Inarin historia jääkaudesta nykypäivään*, 30–95. Oulu, Inarin kunta.

Cotterell, B. and Kamminga, J. 1987. The Formation of Flakes. *American Antiquity* 52 (4), 675–708.

Hood, B. 1992. *Prehistoric Foragers of the North Atlantic: Perspectives on Lithic Procurement and Social Complexity in the North Norwegian Stone Age and the Labrador Maritime Archaic*. Unpublished PhD thesis, University of Massachusetts.

Hyvärinen, H. 1975. Absolute and relative pollen diagrams from northernmost Fennoscandia. *Fennia* 142.

Kankaanpää, J. and Rankama, T. 2005. Early Mesolithic Pioneers in Northern Finnish Lapland, in H. Knutsson (ed.), *Pioneer settlements and colonization processes in the Barents region*, 109–61. Vuollerim Papers on Hunter-Gatherer Archaeology, Vol. 1. Vuollerim, Vuollerim Museum Press.

Kankaanpää, J. and Rankama, T. 2006. Säleitä ja säletekniikkaa Utsjoen Vetsijärveltä, in P. Pesonen and T. Mökkönen (eds.), *Arkeologia ja kulttuuri. Uutta kivikauden tutkimuksessa. Arkeologipäivät 2005*, 118–31. Hamina, The Archaeological Society of Finland.

Kankaanpää, J. and Rankama, T. (in press). Säleitä ja säletekniikkaa Utsjoen Vetsijärveltä. *Arkeologipäivät* 2005.

Koltsov, L. V. (ed.) 1989. *Mezolit SSSR*. Arkheologiya SSSR. Moscow, Nauka.

Olsen, B. 1994. *Bosetning og samfunn i Finnmarks forhistorie*. Oslo, Universitetsforlaget.

Ostrauskas, T. 2000. Mesolithic Kunda Culture. A Glimpse from Lithuania, in *De temporibus antiquissimis ad honorem Lembit Jaanits*, 167–80. Muinasaja teadus 8. Tallinn, University of Tallinn.

Prøsch-Danielsen, L. and Høgestøl, M. 1995. A coastal Ahrensburgian site found in Galta, Rennesøy, Southwest Norway, in A. Fischer (ed.), *Man & Sea in the Mesolithic – coastal settlement above and below present sea level*, 123–30. Oxbow Monographs 53. Oxford, Oxbow Books.

Rankama, T. 1996. *Prehistoric Riverine Adaptations in Subarctic Finnish Lapland: The Teno River Drainage*. PhD dissertation, Brown University Department of Anthropology. Ann Arbor, UMI Dissertation Services.

Rankama, T. 2005. Kajakki-inventointia Vetsijärvellä. *Kentältä poimittua 6, Museoviraston arkeologian osaston julkaisuja* 11, 31–44.

Rankama, T. and Kankaanpää, J. 2003. *Utsjoki Vetsijärvi. Arkeologinen inventointi 18–23.7.2002*. Unpublished survey report, archives of the Finnish National Board of Antiquities.

Seppä, H. 1996. Post-glacial dynamics of vegetation and tree-lines in the far north of Fennoscandia. *Fennia* 174 (1).

Simonsen, P. 1961. *Varanger-Funnene II. Fund og udgravninger på fjordens sydkyst*. Tromsø Museums Skrifter VII (2). Tromsø, Tromsø Museum.

Sorokin, A. N. 1984. Mezolit Velikikh Meshtsherskikh Ozer. *Sovetskaya Arkheologiya* 1984/1, 46–65.

Sulgostowska, Z. 1999. Final Palaeolithic Masovian Cycle and Mesolithic Kunda Culture Relations, in *Tanged Points Cultures in Europe*, 85–92. Lublin, Maria Curie-Skłodowska University Press.

Takala, H. 2004. *The Ristola Site in Lahti and the Earliest Postglacial Settlement of South Finland*. Jyväskylä, Gummerus.

Volokitin, A. 2005. Some peculiarities of colonization of the European north-east in Mesolithic, in H. Knutsson (ed.), *Pioneer settlements and colonization processes in the Barents region*, 11–18. Vuollerim Papers on Hunter-Gatherer Archaeology 1. Vuollerim, Vuollerim Museum Press.

Woodman, P. C. 1993. The Komsa Culture. A Re-examination of its Position in the Stone Age of Finnmark. *Acta Archaeologica* 63, 57–76.

Zhilin, M. G. 1996. The western part of Russia in the Late Paleolithic - Early Mesolithic, in L. Larsson (ed.), *The Earliest Settlement of Scandinavia and its relationship with neighbouring areas*. Acta Archaeologica Lundensia Series in 8o (24), 273–84. Stockholm, Almqvist & Wiksell International.

8. Hunter-gatherers of the Istrian peninsula: the value of lithic raw material analysis to study small-scale colonization processes

Paolo Pellegatti

The study of the human colonization of previously inaccessible or 'empty' landscapes is a popular topic in hunter-gatherer archaeology. These studies are often developed on a continental, and sub-continental scale, and over long periods of time. In this paper I present the preliminary results of an on-going project that aims to study hunter-gatherer adaptation processes, such as landscape learning, on a smaller, regional scale, between the late Upper Palaeolithic and the Mesolithic, through the analysis of lithic raw material at three sites on the Istrian peninsula (Croatia). The analysis showed that as the colonization of the Ćićarija uplands proceeded, changes in raw material procurement and use occurred throughout the settlement network. Flint from distant sources decreased in importance, while Mesolithic hunter-gatherers started to exploit more local raw materials for their lithic assemblages.

Keywords: late Upper Palaeolithic, Mesolithic, flint sources, lithic technology, regional studies, small-scale colonization.

Introduction

The study of the processes that led to the colonization of previously 'empty' regions has recently become popular in archaeological research (Larsson *et al.* 2003; Rockman and Steele 2003). What most of these studies have in common is the attention they pay to human adaptation to new landscapes from an explicit ecological perspective. Moreover, most of them address the issue on a large scale, either continental, as in the case of the peopling of the Americas, or Australia (Beaton 1991; Kelly and Todd 1988), or the 'neolithization' of Europe (Ammerman and Cavalli-Sforza 1984; Whittle 1996), or sub-continental, as regards the re-colonization of northern Europe in the Late Glacial (Gamble 1991; Housley *et al.* 1997).

Landscape learning is recognized as an important aspect in the successful adaptation of to unknown landscapes (Hegmon and Fisher 1991). Because they are fixed features of the landscape, raw material sources can be used as proxy measures to assess the pace and sequence of the acquisition of natural resource information by hunter-gatherers. Based on the assumption that 'raw material procurement is embedded in basic subsistence schedule' (Binford 1979; Butzer 1982, 259), and that the relationship between sites and raw material sources appear to be the 'archaeological correlates of past strategies of mobility' (Rensik *et al.* 1991, 145), lithic raw material studies have been successful in tackling issues related to hunter-gatherer mobility, group migration, and colonization. There is some skepticism that landscape learning processes could leave visible traces in the archaeological record (Kelly 2003, 55), but this could be due to the large scale on which these processes are often examined. As Crumley and Marquardt (1990, 73) have noted, 'when we choose a particular scale during one moment of our analysis, we do so because at that effective scale we can comprehend patterns: functional centers and the connection between them'. I propose that this particular scale should be regional rather than continental or sub-continental. In a regional study, 'the region is a unit that we recognize at a certain scale in its distinctiveness from and interrelations with other such units, both spatially and temporally' (Crumley and Marquardt 1990, 74).

The Pupićina Peć Project has been active on the Istrian peninsula since 1996 (Miracle 1997). A dozen sites in the north-west portion of the peninsula have been excavated, and the database that the project has been compiling over the last decade is sufficiently rich and detailed, in terms of temporal and spatial resolution, to provide an opportunity to address some of the same issues outlined above, only on a much smaller spatial and temporal scale, such as the Ćićarija region across the Pleistocene-Holocene transition.

We previously indicated (Pellegatti *et al.* 2004) that the two-phase model developed by Housley *et al.* (1997) is a useful starting point to understand regional adaptations and the strategies hunter-gatherers used to colonize the landscape. The 'Pioneer' phase is marked by ephemeral sites with relatively small inventories, few site features, and a single season of use. It would be expected that the initial 'pioneers' would be equipped with more tools related to hunting activities. These were prepared in advance and transported to the location. Additionally, these 'pioneers' would have transported blanks that could be modified when needed. Assuming that these 'pioneers' had little or no knowledge of raw material resources in the new landscape, their tools should be made of raw materials that were available closer to their place of origin, or collected as they were on the move. This process is also known as 'provisioning places' (Kuhn 1995).

The 'Residential' phase is characterized by a shift to longer-term occupation of sites. These sites are larger and with a more structured use of living space. There is greater differentiation within the region, in seasonality of occupation, site type, and feature content. Residential sites contained more diverse and larger assemblages that reflect a greater variety of task carried out at the location. The residential phase features a wider range of tools, indicating a wider range of activities linked to more permanent settlements, with a heavier reliance on locally available raw material, thus demonstrating landscape learning processes at work (Mandryk 2003; Rockman and Steele 2003).

Here I present the preliminary results of the analysis of three lithic assemblages from the Istrian peninsula (Figures 8.1 and 8.2).

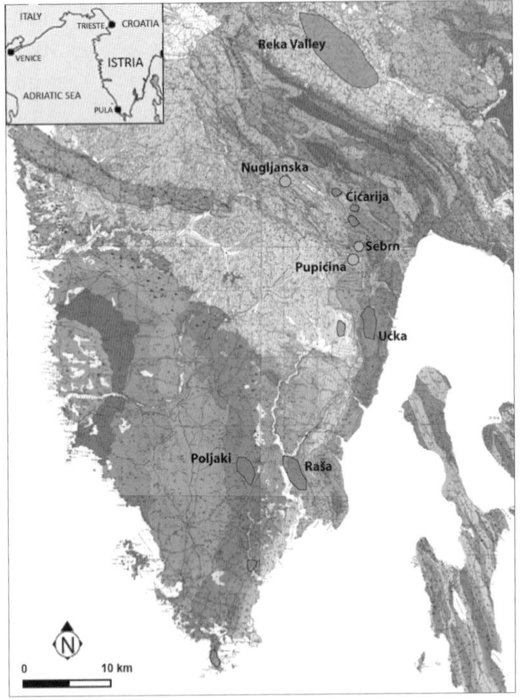

Figure 8.1. Map of the Istrian peninsula with the sites and the flint sources located by the survey.

Archaeological background

Istria is the largest peninsula in the Adriatic, covering about 3500km^2. Geographically, the peninsula was created by sea-level increase at the end of the last glaciation phase (Shackleton and van Andel 1985; Shackleton *et al.* 1984). The archaeological record of this period shows a very sparse human presence in the greater Adriatic region. According to Mussi (2001), there are only 50 sites in Italy that date between 25,000 and 16,000 BP (uncalibrated). Between 18,000 and 14,000 BP (uncalibrated), humans almost disappear from the Adriatic area. (Unless indicated otherwise, all radiocarbon dates in the text are as cited in the publications from which they come and are expressed in uncalibrated radiocarbon years before present (^{14}C BP).)

It was during the Late Glacial and Early Holocene, when the great Adriatic plain was almost completely flooded, that more and more sites were established across the region. Late Upper Palaeolithic (of Epigravettian tradition) and Early Mesolithic sites (Sauveterrian) are numerous throughout

Sites	Period or Horizon	Levels	^{14}C Dates	Cal BC
Pupićina	Upper Midden Mesolithic	24, 202, 203	8710±170	8200–7550
			9200±170	8690–8240
	Lower Midden Mesolithic	25-27/203A, 206	9590±180	9220–8740
	Early Mesolithic	28-29/207–208	10,000±270	10,200–9200
			9840±60	9310–9225
	Late Upper Paleolithic	30–38	10,020±180	10,150–9300
			10,150±60	10,050–9450
Nugljanska	Early Mesolithic	4	8150±70	7335–7040
	Late Upper Paleolithic	8	11,520±90	11,605–11,365
Šebrn	Upper Mesolithic	3C	9070±90	7695–8240
		3B	8810±80	7610–8230
	Basal Mesolithic	6	9280±40	8160–8400

Figure 8.2. Radiocarbon and absolute dates for the three caves analysed in this study.

north-eastern Italy (Veneto and Friuli Venezia-Giulia), in the regions of Trieste and the Slovenian Karst.

The archaeological record of the Istrian peninsula is extremely similar to that of its neighboring regions. Until recently (Balbo *et al.* 2006), human presence in Istria between the Aurignacian and Early Gravettian periods (*sensu* Broglio 1994), was represented solely at Šandalja II, a cave site located at the southern tip of the peninsula, which was occupied roughly between 21,000 and 10,500 BP (Mihovilic 1994; Miracle 1996).

The current archaeological record of north-eastern Istria indicates that early exploitation of the area started in the Late Glacial period, as testified by absolute dates at three locations, the caves at Vešanska (11,530–11,300 BC), Nugljanska (11,605–11,365 BC), and Pupićina (10,050–9450 BC) (Miracle and Forenbaher 2000). Notwithstanding the Late Glacial date at Nugljanska, it appears that the uplands of Ćićarija and Ućka are devoid of Palaeolithic sites, although it is likely that Palaeolithic hunter-gatherers visited the areas for hunting purposes (Miracle 2002).

In the early Holocene, hunter-gatherers equipped with Mesolithic assemblages begin to exploit and establish sites in the uplands (Komšo 2006; Miracle *et al.* 2000). Mesolithic sequences at Šebrn, Klanjčeva, Ovcja, and Sklepova indicate the beginning of a process of colonization that continues in the Late Mesolithic with the open-air site at Lokve. For the purpose of this study, I analyzed lithic samples from three of those locations: Pupićina and Nugljanska caves, and the rock shelter at Šebrn.

Methodology

Survey of flint sources

Between 2000 and 2003, a non-systematic survey located about a dozen flint sources within the Istrian peninsula. Flint samples were collected at each outcrop in order to form the core of a comparative collection to match the archaeological finds.

After the sources were mapped, they were classified according to their distance from the three caves. There is no clear consensus in the literature on how to classify flint sources based on relative distance, as many analysts account for their specific regional situation (Feblot-Agustins 1993; Geneste 1989; Hahn 2002). Thus, we developed our own classification system as follows: *local*: if the source is found within what is commonly referred to as the hunter-gatherer median foraging radius, about 5km (Binford 1978); *regional*: if the source is found within a radius of 5–50km; and *exogenous*: when the source is further than 50km.

Six local sources were located. All outcrops on the Ćićarija and Ućka uplands fell within this category. They include flint in both primary and secondary deposition. Flint in primary deposition was found in very thin layers. It is generally of low quality, as it is normally very coarse, quite soft (the edges dull very quickly), and brittle. Colours range from dark green to light grey, to dark grey and black. Cortex colours and morphology are different between outcrops. Flint in secondary deposition was found at Trebisca, along a profile cut by the nearby stream. Nodules were normally between 15 and 25cm in diameter, with smooth white cortex. The flint is light grey with abundant black inclusions between one and two millimetres in size. The quality appeared poor, exhibiting a tendency to split along numerous internal fractures, although at least one large un-worked block was imported to Šebrn in the Early Mesolithic levels.

Three regional flint sources were located within this distance. Large quantities of flint nodules in secondary deposition were found in the ploughed fields along the Reka Valley in Slovenia (about 40km north-west). Their average sizes range between 3 and 8cm, making them easy to collect and transport. The overall good quality of this material, however, is hampered by the fact that many of these nodules are internally flawed; at least 35–40% of the nodules we tested could not be worked beyond removing primary flakes. This flint is otherwise very fine grained, translucent, and easy to work, especially with a bipolar percussion technique. Colours range from uniform light to dark grey, sometimes with red and green shades closer to the cortex. The cortices are normally very smooth and polished, and, with few exceptions, dark grey. Another source of raw material was traced to central Istria, where nodules were found embedded in the limestone bedrock and in the soil around the town of Poliaki. A few kilometres north, a thin layer of good quality, fine-grained flint was exposed in the low hills around the village of Luktici. A third source was located near the south-east coast of the peninsula, at the mouth of the Rasa Valley. This flint was among the easiest to recognize in the archaeological record because of its white, flat cortex and the numerous white spots within the dark grey flint.

One exogenous outcrop was located on the Premantura peninsula on the southern tip of Istria. This particular flint does not appear in the archaeological record of the caves under analysis. Flint nodules were also located on the beach at Uvala Kale, along the eastern coast of the peninsula. To visit or locate exogenous sources outside of the Istrian peninsula was beyond the scope of our survey. The most important flint sources in the greater Adriatic region are well known and their characteristics often recur in the literature (Benedetti *et al.* 1994; Clark 2000), for example the outcrops in the Trentino and Veneto regions in Italy.

As this study is concerned with chronological changes in raw material procurement and use, samples that would represent the entire occupational sequence at each site were selected. One columnar sample was taken from each cave.

Lithic technology

All the lithics recovered from excavation and from flotation were analysed and classified into simple morphological classes (Figure 8.3). Pieces lacking a bulb of percussion or a clear platform were classified as debris. The remaining pieces were classified as flakes, small flakes, blades,

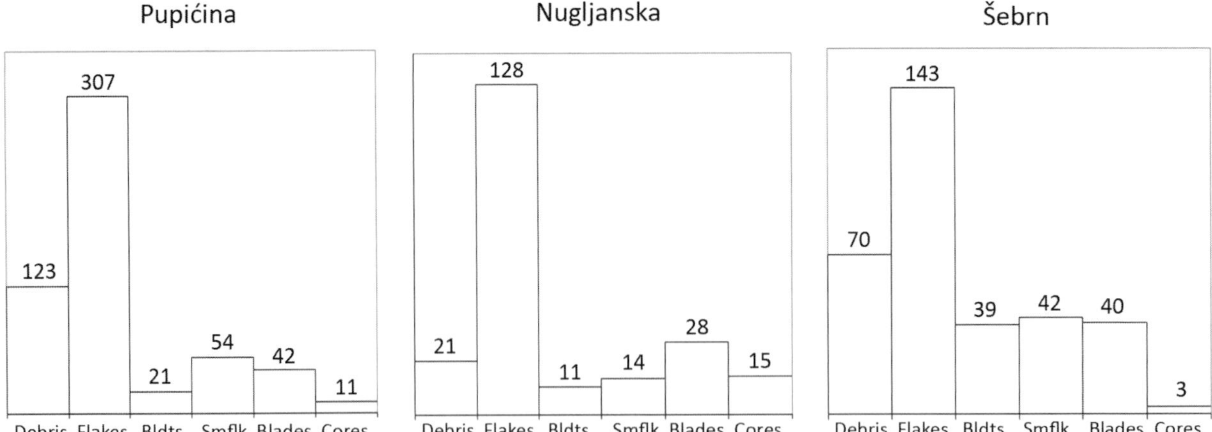

Figure 8.3. Morphological composition of the lithic assemblages.

bladelets, and cores. Further observations indicate if the pieces were related to tool production (i.e., microburins, crested) or were retouched into tools. Tools were further divided into typological classes (i.e. endscrapers). Pieces with cortex were classified as cortical. When the cortices extended to more than 50% of the dorsal surface, they were further classified as decortification (opening flakes). All pieces were measured by their three dimensions and each of them weighed. The data indicate that there is a high degree of technological similarity between the three different sites, thus suggesting that all of them could be part of the same settlement network (Figure 8.3).

Lithic raw material

All lithics were observed by their macroscopic features, such as colour, grain size, texture, cortex, and the size and frequency of visible inclusions. The analyses were carried out mostly by simple visual inspection with the aid of a magnifying lens and (infrequently) the use of a low-power binocular microscope. Despite the advances in laboratory techniques (such as trace-element analysis, etc.), inexpensive macroscopic examination in respect to sourcing is still widespread among lithic analysts (Eriksen and Fisher 2002). In this specific case, visual inspection was further aided by the characteristics of the samples collected at the sources around the peninsula. Raw material variability between different outcrops was very marked. Most sources exhibited clearly distinguishable characteristics in terms of colour, cortex shape and colour, presence of distinguishable inclusions, or grain size. There were few exceptions to this. Some of the flint collected near the summit of the Ućka Mountain was very similar in colour and grain size to the flint from the Kriznjica outcrop, which is located in the lowlands at the base of the Ućka foothills. An attempt to distinguish them by the use of an ultra-violet lamp (Adams 1998) was not successful. This was not however perceived as a major problem, as both sources, although in different general directions, fell within the local zone of 5km.

All the pieces were analysed in an attempt to recognize the raw material and match it against our collections. Few exceptions were made. Pieces that were smaller than five by five millimetres were set aside after their technological classification, and raw material identification was not attempted. The same procedure was undertaken for the few implements that showed evidence of patina, and for pieces with features typical of burning, or extreme heat exposure, that can alter their visual characteristics (Patterson 1995).

The sites

Pupićina Cave

Pupićina Cave is a fairly large, funnel shaped, limestone cave located inside the Vranja Canyon, which runs at the bottom of the western slope of the Učka Mountain (Miracle 1997). The cave was excavated between 1995 and 2002. Over 60m^2 of deposits were removed, with bedrock reached at a depth of about 7m below the surface. The sample from Pupićina consisted, in total, of 558 pieces and with a total weight of 584.8 grams. Throughout the entire sequence, the assemblage is dominated by flakes and simple debris. The low percentage of bladelets may indicate an overall low importance in 'gearing up' hunting equipment. 25 pieces (4.5%) were classified as technical pieces. Of the entire sample, 206 (36.9%) were cortical pieces and 117 (31%) were decortification. 173 pieces (16.9%) were burned (Figure 8.4).

For the purpose of this study, the occupation sequence of the cave across the Pleistocene-Holocene transition was divided into three main horizons: the Pleniglacial, the late Upper Palaeolithic, and the Mesolithic horizon (which includes the Early Mesolithic levels and the lower and upper midden deposits). The Pleniglacial sequence features very shallow layers between periodical flooding episodes of the nearby stream, when small groups left sparse faunal remains and a small lithic assemblage. Our analysis indicates that Pupićina was provisioned with flint

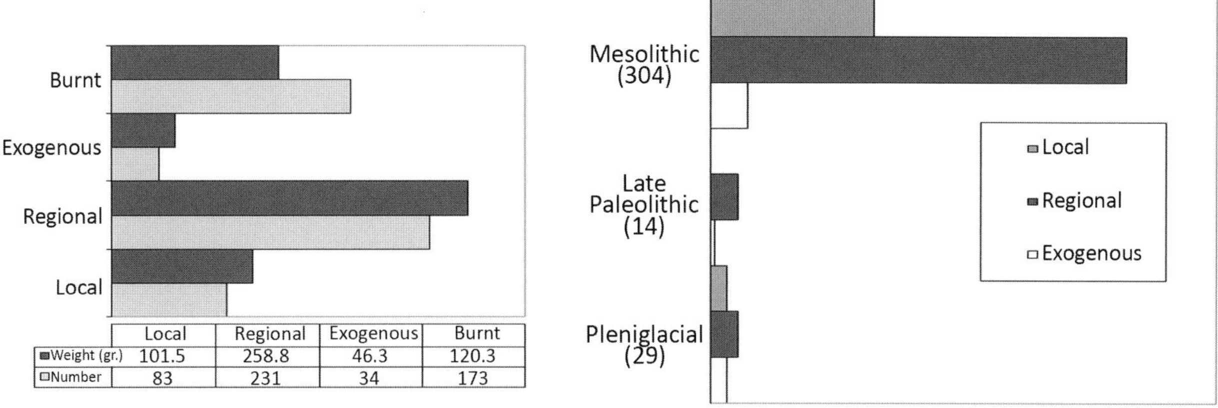

Figure 8.4. Raw material types and distribution at the Pupićina Cave.

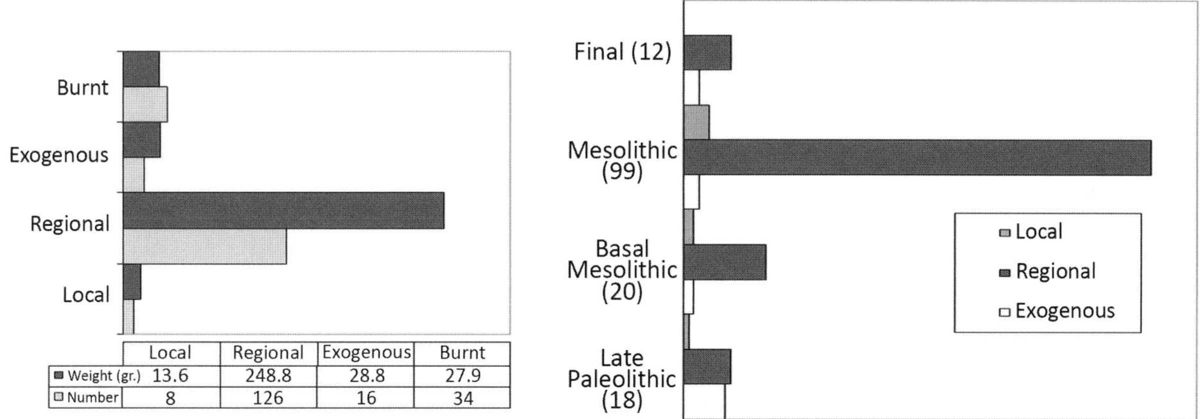

Figure 8.5. Raw material types and distribution at the Nugljanska Cave.

from exogenous sources (red flint from the Italian Alps) and regional (from the Reka Valley in Slovenia) for 70% of the total assemblage. While there is some use of local material, it is limited to sources on the Ućka Mountain where chamoix/ibex were likely hunted (Miracle 2002). The faunal data clearly indicate that the intensity of occupation greatly increased around 11,500 years ago (Pellegatti *et al.* 2004), although this is not well reflected in the lithic data. In fact, the overall number of pieces is lower and the overall weight is about 50% less than the earlier level, possibly indicating a need to conserve raw material. The analysis showed that, in the following phase – the late Upper Palaeolithic – there was a sharp decrease in the frequency of exogenous flint, and local flint almost completely disappears from the record. The small assemblage consists almost entirely of flint from the Reka Valley, a regional source.

Occupation intensity increases dramatically in the Holocene, as is testified by the amount of faunal refuse (Miracle 2002) and the overall number of lithics. With the beginning of the Mesolithic occupation, lithics become visibly smaller (the average weight is 0.9 grams, as opposed to 2.6 and 2.0 for the earlier horizons). Through the Mesolithic sequence, the use of local flint – still mainly from the Učka Mountain area – increases to 27%; Slovenian flint (with the addition of a few pieces from central Istria) remains the most common material (68%), while exogenous material is limited to 5%.

Nugljanska Cave

The cave at Nugljanska opens at the very edge of the Ćićarija chain overlooking the modern town of Buzet, at an altitude of 550m asl. The sample from Nugljanska consisted of 218 pieces, with a total weight of 377 grams (Figure 8.5). The ratio between different morphological classes shows some similarity to Pupićina, except for the higher core percentages, which, in addition to a high percentage of decortification flakes, indicate that flint was imported to Nugljanska in a less pre-worked form. However, a lower incidence of debris in our sample could possibly indicate that flint knapping activities were carried out in a different area of the cave.

The occupation of the cave is framed by two radiometric dates (Figure 8.2). The earliest date indicates a late Upper Palaeolithic occupation, while the other is Mesolithic. However, a group of hunter-gatherers briefly visited the cave earlier than indicated by the radiometric date, possibly

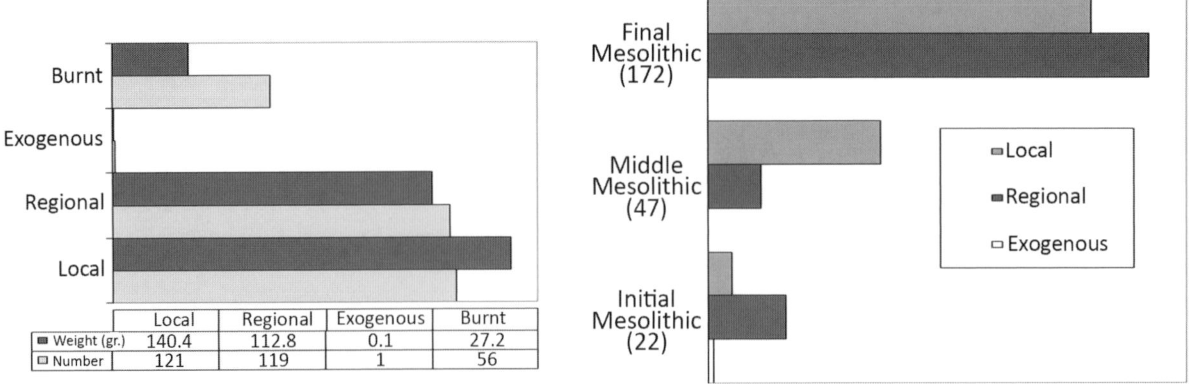

	Local	Regional	Exogenous	Burnt
Weight (gr.)	140.4	112.8	0.1	27.2
Number	121	119	1	56

Figure 8.6. Raw material types and distribution at Šebrn Abri.

during the interstadial, and it should be pointed out that the 1997 excavation did not reach bedrock. In the sample, this visit is represented by a single, almost complete, fire-cracked flint nodule that was collected in the Reka Valley in Slovenia. The rest of the later Palaeolithic assemblage is represented by 23 pieces. The assemblage is rather heavy (the average weight is 3.6 grams – excluding the exploded nodule). Similar to Pupićina, it is dominated by regional and exogenous flint, respectively 50% and 44%. There are important differences, however. While at Pupićina these materials were almost exclusively of Slovenian and Italian origin, at Nugljanska, there is more variety in exogenous material of unknown provenance, including one piece of red jasper. We also recorded a larger number of pieces made of flint from the Rasa Bay in central Istria.

Following a trend similar to that in Pupićina, the overall number of pieces increases dramatically during the Mesolithic sequence – 61% of the entire assemblage comes from levels 3 and 5. Pieces become smaller between the three Mesolithic horizons, namely the basal, middle, and final (2.1, 1.5, and 0.9 grams respectively). What differentiates the Mesolithic levels at Nugljanska from those at Pupićina is the dependence on regional flints that come from a variety of sources, including the Učka Mountain, central Istria (Poliaki and Sv. Magdalena) and Slovenia, while only odd pieces are local or exogenous. Raw material data seem to point to the fact that, since the end of the Pleistocene, hunter-gatherers using Nugljanska Cave maintained a clear connection with the central part of the eastern coast of Istria, despite the fact that the cave is located further inland, and at a higher altitude than Pupićina.

Šebrn Abri

Šebrn Abri lies at the base of a massive overhang, along one of the many routes that connect the lowlands of Istria and the Ćićarija uplands (Miracle *et al.* 2000). The lithic sample from Šebrn Abri consisted of 337 pieces with a total weight of 303.7 grams (Figure 8.6). A very small percentage of them were classified as technical pieces (5, 1.5%). 114 pieces (33.8%) had traces of cortex, out of which 54 (16.2%) were decortification. Given the nature of the site, it is not surprising that the lithic assemblage features larger percentages of bladelets and blades. The former reflect a higher percentage of hunting-related tools, such as backed bladelets and points, while blades could be carried as blanks to be modified into tools at the location.

Data on lithic technology and typology indicate that the site contains a single, Early Mesolithic component that spans about 800 calendar years. In contrast to the Mesolithic levels at both Pupićina and Nugljanska, the lithic assemblage is dominated by hunting gear, and, differently from Pupićina, seasonality indicators point to a spring and summer occupation. The first use of Šebrn, at about 8400 BC, was as a temporary shelter, where small groups of hunter-gatherers stopped for very short periods – possibly only a few days – but shortly thereafter people came to stay for extended periods – possibly for weeks – while targeting more specific resources that were locally consumed, as opposed to being transported elsewhere. Occupation length, and perhaps frequency, decreased again in the final levels just before the rock shelter was abandoned. Raw material data provide further support to this interpretation. In fact, at the beginning, people supplied the site with regional flint (72%), mostly from Slovenian sources, while in the second phase local flint from the slopes of Učka, and the nearby Ćićarija outcrops, rises from 22% to 77% of the assemblage, with few larger, un-worked blocks brought to the site. Pieces become bigger as the average weight increases from 0.5 grams during the basal Mesolithic, to 1.1 grams in the upper Mesolithic levels. In addition, hunting gear and blades are now preferentially made of local flint, perhaps indicating that the ready availability of material was more important than its quality. The final phase is characterized by a balance between regional and local flint (53% and 47% respectively), with a noticeable increase in the frequency of material from central Istria.

Discussion

A number of interesting patterns emerge from the

data obtained through the analysis of these three lithic assemblages. As the uplands of Ćićarija and Učka become populated, and sites, such as Šebrn Abri and Klanjceva are established, synchronic changes in raw material procurement also occur at Pupićina and Nugljanska, thus signalling that the dynamics at work during the initial exploration and settling phases in the new area occur throughout the entire settlement network, not just at the sites that are only apparently 'closer to the action'. At the beginning of the pioneering phase in the upland, the frequency of exogenous raw materials – primarily from sources in the Italian Alps – decreases, and almost disappears in Pupićina and Nugljanska: it is completely absent at Šebrn Abri.

Through time, the hunter-gatherers who lived at Nugljanska and Pupićina manufactured their tools mostly with regional flint from Slovenia and central Istria, while more local outcrops were clearly less important in these now residential camps. Flint from the slopes of Učka, and, in lesser amounts, from Ćićarija, were seldom tested and rarely used for manufacturing tools. With regard to the beginning of the upland colonization, the model predicted that early visitors at Šebrn would import flint to the site, sometimes in the shape of small, un-worked nodules. The model also predicted that for periods marked by longer staying occupations, hunter-gatherers would rely on local material to maintain their supplies. This differential provisioning of raw material is well reflected in the fact that, through time, while at Šebrn the size of tools and debris increases, at Pupićina and Nugljanska the opposite trend was apparent. These data indicate that, as the colonization of the Istria peninsula uplands proceeded with the establishment of numerous sites, some of the behavioural features that were characteristic of Late Pleistocene hunter-gatherers, such as a high degree of mobility and large areas of exploitation, cease to be implemented, while Mesolithic groups turned their attention to a more geographically-restricted area and took advantage of its resources to the maximum extent possible.

Conclusions

For a number of reasons, the results presented in this paper are preliminary. I could only present some of the general results of our project, because at the time this paper was written I was in the process of expanding the sample for Pupićina, so as to include more of late Upper Palaeolithic assemblage. In addition, I could not include detailed analysis and data on the retouched tools from Pupićina and Šebrn, because of early difficulties in obtaining permission to export them from the museum in Pula. Those data will be presented in future publications. What is important, however, is the fact that our results indicate that it is possible to explore dimensions of Mesolithic hunter-gatherer adaptation, such as landscape learning and colonization, on a smaller, regional scale. To understand the dynamics at play within small regional realities it is important to resolve satisfactorily certain larger issues, such as dietary diversification, social territories, and cultural identities, which form part of the future research agenda for the project.

References

Adams, B. 1998. *The Middle to Upper Paleolithic Transition in Central Europe. The record from the Bükk Mountain region.* British Archaeological Reports, International Series S693. Oxford, Archaeopress.

Ammerman, A. J., Cavalli-Sforza, L. L. 1984. *The Neolithic Transition and the Genetics of Population in Europe.* Princeton, Princeton University Press.

Balbo, A. L., Komšo, D., Miracle, P. T. 2006. Prehistory of the Open Karst, Further Discoveries from the Geoarchaeological Survey of Polje Cepic, Croatia. *Istria Archaeologica* 34, 3–12.

Beaton, J. M. 1991. Colonizing Continents: Some Problems from Australia and the Americas, in T. D. Dillehay and D. J. Meltzer (eds.), *The First Americans: Search and Research*, 209–30. Boca Raton, Fl, CRC Press.

Benedetti, R., Campana, R., D'Amico, C., Nannetti, M. C. 1994. Petroarchaeometry of Epigravettian and Mesolithic Flint in the Val Cismon-Lagorari (NE Italy): The Flint Supply Question. *Preistoria Alpina* 28 (1), 33–49.

Binford, L. R. 1978. *Nunamiut Ethnoarchaeology*, xiii, 509. New York, Academic Press.

Binford, L. R. 1979. Organization and Formation Processes: Looking at Curated Technologies. *Journal of Anthropological Research* 35, 255–72.

Broglio, A. 1994. Il Paleolitico Superiore Del Friuli-Venezia Giulia, in *Atti Della Xxix Riunione Scientifica. Preistoria E Protostoria Del Friuli Venezia-Giulia E Dell'istria. 28–30 Settembre 1990*, 37–56. Firenze, Istituto Italiano di Preistoria e Protostoria.

Butzer, K. W. 1982. *Archaeology as Human Ecology. Method and Theory for a Contextual Approach.* Cambridge, Cambridge University Press.

Clark, R. 2000. *The Mesolithic Hunters of the Trentino. A Case Study in Hunter-Gatherer Settlement and Subsistence from Northern Italy.* British Archaeological Reports, International Series S832. Oxford, John and Erica Hedges.

Crumley, C. L. and Marquardt, W. H. 1990. Landscape: A Unifying Concept in Regional Analysis, in K. M. S. Allen, S. W. Green and E. B. W. Zubrow (eds.), *Interpreting Space. Gis and Archaeology*, 73–80. London, Taylor & Francis.

Eriksen, B. V., Fisher, L. E. 2002. Lithic Raw Material Economies in the Late Glacial and Early Postglacial Western Europe: Introduction, in L. E. Fisher and B. V. Eriksen (eds.), *Lithic Raw Material Economies in the Late Glacial and Early Postglacial Europe*, 1–7. British Archaeological Reports, International Series S1093. Oxford, Archaeopress.

Feblot-Agustins, J. 1993. Mobility Strategies in the Late Middle Palaeolithic of Central Europe and Western Europe: Elements of Stability and Variability. *Journal of Anthropological Archaeology* 12 (3), 211–65.

Gamble, C. S. 1991. The Social Context for European Palaeolithic Art. *Proceedings of the Prehistoric Society* 57, 3–15.

Geneste, J.-M. 1989. Economie des ressources lithiques dans le Moustérian du sud-ouest de la France, in L. Freeman and M. Patou (eds.), *L'homme de Neandertal, Tome 6: La Subsistance*, 75–97. Liège, Université de Liège.

Hahn, J. 2002. Mobility and Lithic Economy at the Buttental Site: A Case Study, in B. V. Eriksen and L. E. Fisher (eds.),

Lithic Raw Material Economies in the Late Glacial and Early Postglacial Europe, 19–26. British Archaeological Reports, International Series S1093. Oxford, Archaeopress.

Hegmon, M. and Fisher, L. E. 1991. Information Strategies in Hunter-Gatherer Societies, in P. T. Miracle, L. E. Fisher and J. Brown (eds.), *Foragers in Context: Long-Term, Regional and Historical Perspectives in Hunter-Gatherer Studies*, 127–45. International Monographs in Prehistory. Ann Arbor, MI., Department of Anthropology, University of Michigan.

Housley, R. A., Gamble, C. S., Street, M. and Pettitt, P. 1997. Radiocarbon evidence for the Late Glacial human recolonization of northern Europe. *Proceedings of the Prehistoric Society* 63, 25–54.

Kelly, R. L. 2003. Colonization of New Land by Hunter-Gatherers: Expectations and Implications Based on Ethnographic Data, in M. Rockman and J. Steele (eds.), *Colonization of Unfamiliar Landscapes. The Archaeology of Adaptation*, 44–59. London, Routledge.

Kelly, R. L. and Todd, L. C. 1988. Coming into the Country: Early Paleoindian Hunting and Mobility. *American Antiquity* 53, 231–44.

Kuhn, S. L. 1995. *Mousterian Lithic Technology: An Ecological Perspective*. Princeton, Princeton University Press.

Larsson, L., Kindgren, H., Knutsson, K., Leoffler, D. and Åkerlund, A. (eds.) 2003. *Mesolithic on the Move: Papers presented at the Sixth International Conference on the Mesolithic in Europe, Stockholm 2000*. Oxford, Oxbow Books.

Mandryk, C. A. S. 2003. Foreword, in M. Rockman and J. Steele (eds.), *Colonization of Unfamiliar Landscapes*, xiii–xv. London, Routledge.

Mihovilic, K. 1994. Preistoria Dell'istria Dal Paleolitico All'eta' Del Ferro, in *Atti Della XXIX Riunione Scientifica. 'Preistoria e Protostoria del Friuli-Venezia Giulia e dell'Istria'. (Trieste, Istria, 28-30 Settembre 1990)*, 101–18. Firenze, Istituto Italiano di Preistoria e Protostoria.

Miracle, P. T. 1996. Diversification in Epipaleolithic subsistence strategy along the eastern Adriatic coast: a simulation approach applied to zooarcheological assemblages. *Atti della Società per la Preistoria e Protostoria della Regione Friuli- Venezia Giulia* IX, 33–62.

Miracle, P. T. 1997. Early Holocene foragers in the karst of Northern Istria. *Poročilo o raziskovanju paleolita, neolita in eneolita v Sloveniji* XXIV, 43–61.

Miracle, P. T. 2002. Mesolithic meals from Mesolithic middens, in P. T. Miracle and N. Milner (eds.), *Consuming Passions and Patterns of Consumption*, 65–88. Cambridge, McDonald Institute for Archeological Research.

Miracle, P. T. and Forenbaher, S. 2000. Pupićina Cave Project: Brief Summary of the 1998 Season. *Histria Archaeologica* 29, 27–48.

Miracle, P. T., Galanidou, N. and Forenbaher, S. 2000. Pioneers in the Hills: Early Mesolithic Foragers at Šebrn Abri (Istria, Croatia). *European Journal of Archaeology* 3 (3), 293–329.

Mussi, M. 2001. *Earliest Italy. An Overview of the Italian Palaeolithic and Mesolithic*. New York, Kluwer Academic/ Plenum Press.

Patterson, L. W. 1995. Thermal Damage of Chert. *Lithic Technology* 20 (1), 72–80.

Pellegatti, P., Miracle, P. and Galanidou, N. 2004. Adaptation in the balance. Scales of action across the Pleistocene-Holocene Boundary in Istria, Croatia. Paper presented at the 69th Annual Meeting for the Society for American Archaeology, Montreal, March 30–31, 2004.

Rensik, E., Kolen, J. and Spieksma, A. 1991. Patterns of Raw Material Distribution in the Upper Pleistocene of Northwestern and Central Europe, in A. Montet-White and S. R. Holen (eds.), *Raw Material Economies among Prehistoric Hunter-Gatherers*, 141–59. Lawrence, KS, University of Kansas.

Rockman, M. and Steele, J. (eds.) 2003. *Colonization of Unfamiliar Landscapes: the archaeology of adaptation*. London, Routledge.

Shackleton, J. C. and van Andel, T. H. 1985. Late Palaeolithic and Mesolithic Coastlines of the Western Mediterranean. *Cahiers ligures de préhistoire et de protohistoire* 2, 7–19.

Shackleton, J. C., van Andel, T. H. and Runnels, C. N. 1984. Coastal Paleogeography of the Central and Western Mediterranean during the last 125,000 years and its archaeological implications. *Journal of Field Archaeology* 11, 307–14.

Whittle, A. 1996. *Europe in the Neolithic: The Creation of New Worlds*, xv, 443. Cambridge, Cambridge University Press.

9. Early farmers on the coast: lithic procurement strategies of colonists in the eastern Adriatic

Niels H. Andreasen

This paper theorises the implications of the implementation of a landscape learning approach to the coastal phenomenon of the initial Early Neolithic colonisation of the east Adriatic. By recognising that structured behaviour characterises migration, it is suggested that lithic procurement and production may hold evidence of social and technical adjustments associated with exploitation of non-organic resources in new lands. Observations on lithic assemblages from a group of Early Neolithic Impressed Ware sites in southern Istria are used for constructing a model that incorporates expectations related to patterns of procurement and production. While the behavioural issues that operate the model are of general significance, it is also stressed that a model-based approach must consider regional variables, such as topography and distribution of resources, as well as indications of contact with indigenous hunter-gatherers. These variables affect the learning process and potentially exert a strong influence on the patterning of lithic assemblages.

Keywords: landscape learning, adaptation, colonisation, maritime landscapes, lithics, early farmers, eastern Adriatic.

Introduction

Interdisciplinary research in archaeology, crop and livestock studies, genetics, and historical linguistics has been directly involved in revitalising explanations of migration and colonisation to describe episodes of extensive cultural change. Archaeological and bio-archaeological evidence suggest that the establishment of agricultural communities of the Early Neolithic Impressed and Cardial Ware complexes between *c.* 7000 and 5400 cal BC in the Mediterranean fertile lowland basins was largely the result of colonisation through population dispersal (Bass 1998; Forenbaher and Miracle 2005; Runnels and van Andel 1988; Tringham 2000; Zilhão 2001). For the most part, the impact of relocation on farming communities is downplayed or ignored altogether in the literature because the archaeological evidence for initial colonisation events appears rather elusive. Consequently, little attention is given to the significance of knowledge and to behavioural concerns in relation to colonisation processes. This is particularly frustrating when considering that the settlement of new lands was very much a knowledge-based process, in which the major challenge would have been the identification of appropriate locations with the best soils, landforms, raw materials, etc. While it can be hard to identify evidence of actual colonisation events, it is an intriguing notion that migration reveals regular patterns and can be formulated as structured behaviour, and that learning itself takes place in stages (Anthony 1997; Rockman 2003, 12).

New research and regional-scale models for the spread of farming in the eastern Adriatic (Bass 1998; Chapman and Müller 1990; Forenbaher and Miracle 2005) have drawn attention to this poorly understood region. The long stretch of coast from Greece to North Italy is an important zone for the emergence of early farming in Europe, which allows for the examination of spatial and temporal patterns of dispersal processes in the context of a varied and unique coastal landscape. In this paper, I will briefly address one particular aspect of human migration and outline a model related to lithic procurement strategies as a means of getting closer to the role of knowledge in colonisation among early farmers.

Transmission and acquisition of information about resources in maritime environments

The coastal distribution of Early Neolithic sites and their existence on islands in both the Aegean and the eastern Adriatic (Bass 1998; Forenbaher 1999) underlines the fact that maritime communication and boat technology were major shaping factors in both local and long-distance movements, and that access to information and known maritime travelling routes played an important role in settlement choice. The scarcity of sailable rivers in the area most probably had an initial discouraging effect on inland voyages along much of this coast. This was amplified by the wall-like massifs of the Dinaric chain from the Kvarner Bay to the Bojana River, with several peaks of over 1700m stretching in a parallel line with the coastline, in many parts descending abruptly into the sea. From the coast, initial farmers could maintain the vital, coastal-based lines of communication with other Neolithic groups and exploit the pockets of low, sloping coastal strips of productive land characteristic of much of the eastern Adriatic. Furthermore, resource mapping was done most effectively from the sea. The distinction between mainland and islands is often far from clear-cut, as much of the Croatian part of the coast is quasi-insular in its configuration. Long, narrow islands running along the coast allowed seafarers to navigate with the help of fixed points on either side of the boat and greatly facilitated exploration. These straits would therefore have made important corridors of movement.

It is reasonable to believe that boats navigating the Mediterranean were not merely makeshift crafts constructed for the purpose of colonisation. Boats that could safely carry livestock and facilitate regular visits to islands in deep water locations (e.g. Melos in the Aegean) would have had to be well-built and reliable vessels. This type of sea-craft construction most likely had its roots in a long tradition of seafaring that reached deep into the Mesolithic period. Indirect evidence of more advanced vessels suggests the existence of specialised knowledge related to boat-technology, such as, perhaps, rigid hulls. The ability to navigate vessels successfully would have been a prestigious type of knowledge in any coastal Neolithic community and suggests the possibility that a degree of inequality in the Early Neolithic allowed certain individuals to develop and maintain knowledge regarding boat building and navigation. Another, and in some instances related specialisation, could have been the procurement of key local resources, as suggested for Melian obsidian in the Aegean (Perlès and Vitelli 1999, 97) and the Pre-Pottery Neolithic B (PPNB) (8600–7500 cal BC) Kaletepe workshops in Anatolia (Binder and Balkan-Atli 2001; Briois *et al.* 1997). The boat-builders were likely the same prominent individuals responsible for the transfer of colonisers and livestock; they must have played a central or dominant role both in the initiative to move, and in the continued decision-making process in the new lands. There is no reason to believe that these leading mariners or 'aggrandisers' were not well informed about their destination. Exploration would have preceded colonisation that was purposive and aimed at specific tracts of land along the coast. It is possible that scouting farmers in many cases would have maintained a relationship with local hunter-gatherers and acquired a 'Mesolithic teacher package', a fitting term that denotes the varied types of information potentially transferred from hunter-gatherers to farmers as distinguished from information brought back by scouts or acquired from neighbouring farming communities. The information was probably not always transferred as rational guidelines but would have been imbedded in stories, legends and beliefs (perhaps transferred by partner exchange). Although such stories and beliefs would have been different in character and content from the pioneering farmer's own cultural heritage, they would have functioned as a framework for learning about the new environment. It is very likely that the colonizing farmers adopted elements of the hunter-gatherer belief system/myths in modified form as part of this enculturation process, or even took on some of the characteristics of the indigenous subsistence pattern (e.g. Reitz 1985).

Landscape learning and procurement of lithic raw materials

Landscape learning is a neologism that refers to a new theoretical arena in archaeology (Rockman and Steele 2003). The concept is central to archaeological research relating to people who colonised new lands in the past, and a useful analytical tool in modelling how pioneer communities developed knowledge and engaged with a new landscape. Landscape learning is part of a cultural adaptation process in which it plays the vital role of mapping variety and constraints of a new or changing environment into a community's organisation as structure and/or information (Buckley 1968). It has its most distinct expression in colonizing communities characterised by a low degree of initial 'adaptedness'. Through learning and interaction processes, such communities are likely to undergo continual morphogenic change until they achieve a state of 'adaptedness' (Kirch 1980, 109).

Raw material procurement is one of several culturally transmitted behaviours with which a population interacts with its natural and social environment. Colonisation entails re-negotiation of a given procurement strategy, and the construction of a successful new scheme of acquisition is influenced by the community's ability and motivation to obtain knowledge about the new landscape that they are moving into. An adaptive trajectory for a procurement strategy is shown in Figure 9.1. It illustrates how a strategy is expected to go through an initially abrupt and later gradual transformation process before it can be used to respond effectively to the adaptive challenges posed by the new environment. In other words, it is anticipated that 'pioneer' procurement strategies differ from strategies employed by the same group at a later stage.

It is widely accepted that the availability of lithic raw materials is an important variable conditioning stone-tool production technology (Andrefsky 1994). As it is necessary to *locate* non-organic natural resources in order to access and assess it, *knowledge* is a precondition for availability. Rockman, in fact, suggests that procurement of lithic raw material requires colonisers to acquire substantial knowledge about the locations, usefulness and reliability of resources and shape this knowledge into a 'working environment' (2003, 19). She argues that information related to non-organic resources may be the

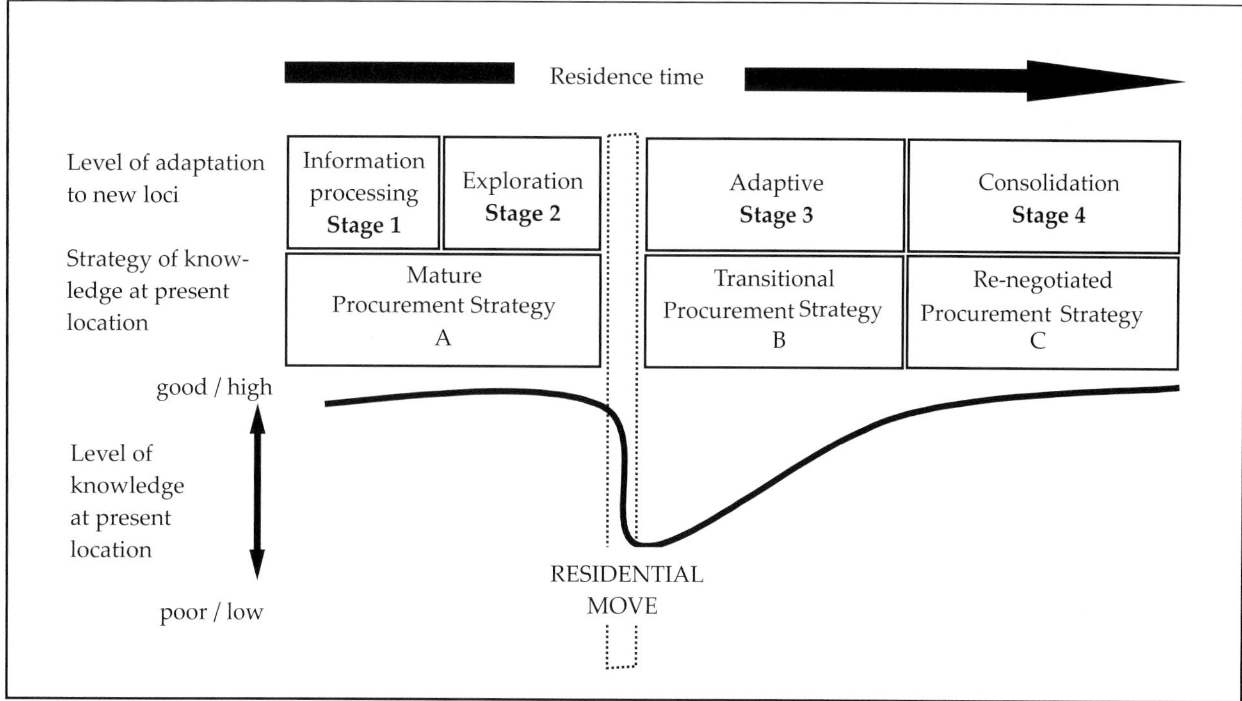

Figure 9.1. A model for the adaptive process associated with the re-negotiation of procurement strategies under the influence of landscape learning (see text for discussion).

least transferable across long distances, and that substantial social adjustments may be necessary to establish new non-organic resource access patterns or maintain access to previously used sources. Lithic materials may arguably be the best evidence of landscape learning that we have on hand, but, as several other causal factors influence the variability in lithic assemblages, it is relevant, at a methodological level, to demonstrate the potential relevance of landscape learning to observational data.

Integrating lithic data into models of changing procurement strategies

Variations between lithic industries are the result of the interaction of many variables, which are typological, conceptual, technical and economic. This variability arose during the production process, of which the first stage was raw material procurement. Procedures for recovery and transport would have been further assessed in terms of variables, such as time, materials, technical or social advantages, etc. These variables took on different values depending on how constraining they were in a particular context (Perlès 1992, 225). Generally, values changed only gradually and within relatively large timescales, e.g. as a result of resource depletion, technical developments, or changes in group traditions. Therefore, as long as it was viable, a raw material procurement strategy was elaborated, implemented, and integrated within group behaviour/organisation (Perlès 1992, 225). Crucial information relating to the strategy may have been transmitted across several generations and changed only when new circumstances and constraints made the adoption of a new strategy appropriate.

In a colonisation scenario, most variables in the group's procurement strategy, if not all, would simultaneously have taken on different values within a very short time span – possibly from day to day. Each variable would have been re-evaluated/re-negotiated within the group in order to determine its new value in the context of the new setting. The frequency of disadvantageous procurement behaviour would have dropped sharply as knowledge increased, although this may initially have required time and resources and involved surveying for raw materials, learning about the character of the new materials, and possibly the establishment of contacts with resident hunter-gatherers. It was of obvious importance to the group to identify and 'map' new circumstances and constraints accurately and within a short period of time in order to form an effective new raw material strategy. Although the community solved many logistical problems during the pioneer phase, the impact of the shift would have reverberated for some time and continued to do so until a level of 'adaptedness' had been reached (Figure 9.1). It may therefore be possible to identify transitional procurement strategies and formulate specific expectations to these (Figure 9.2).

Anthony pointed out that there are structural differences between short- and long-distance migrations and their effect on material culture (1990, 901). Although distance itself was not a significant obstacle for Early Neolithic colonisation in the Adriatic (Bass 1998, 180) and the rest of the Mediterranean, one would expect a correlation between distance and an increasing need to re-negotiate procurement strategies. This would have been amplified in the Adriatic, where the configuration of potential raw material sources tends to be localised. In connection to *short-distance moves*, initial adaptedness was considerable

Aspect	Expectations
Overall exploitation pattern	Under-utilisation/sporadic use of local micro- and macro-environments in terms of resources.
Procurement strategy	*Poorly structured*; as in a colonisation situation there is typically little knowledge of the distribution and character of surrounding resources, lithic strategies would tend to be less structured; tactical and particularistic choices are made regularly to compensate for the absence of a coherent procurement strategy.
Local raw material use	*Opportunistic use* of local 'first-encounter' sources, exploited by direct procurement, regardless of quality. Generally, the mode of acquisition (and distribution) is not yet structured enough to generate a strong and visible activity close to the sources. Possible evidence of experimentation/innovation.
Non-local raw material use	*Limited*; import of higher quality materials to the settlements from distant sources was limited due to a lack of established, dependable exchange or trade networks. Some curated tools may have been brought along from the area of departure.
Reduction strategy	*Varying*; employment of different (non-standardised) reduction strategies to compensate for different raw material qualities. Highly flexible conceptual scheme.
Tool production	*Local raw materials*; strong connection between the tool materials dominant in each site and the local geological background. Lithic production conforms to the boundaries imposed by local quality chert, and expedient flake-based tools were produced when systematic blade-production was not possible. Exceptions may be blade tools that were brought along by the colonisers from somewhere else.

Figure 9.2. Archaeological signatures related to lithic procurement and technology in colonizing farming communities. The right-hand column lists expectations related to lithic procurement and technology in circumstances of poor knowledge and low adaptedness, following a residential move ('Transitional Procurement Strategy B').

since communities continued to exploit known raw material sources and maintained existing exchange ties. New elements were integrated, however, and smaller adjustments probably occurred in the new setting, but the move did not significantly disrupt the existing procurement strategy. Migration models consistent with this type of movement are 'Individual Frontier Mobility' (Zvelebil and Lillie 2000, 62) and 'Wave of Advance' (Ammerman and Cavalli-Sforza 1973). With *longer-distance moves* (actual colonisation, perhaps as 'leap-frogging'), it was no longer practical, cost efficient or viable to exploit old raw material sources systematically. The result was a serious disruption in procurement strategy, requiring re-negotiation and leading to a high-level adjustment of variables. A low degree of initial adaptedness would probably have characterised these communities.

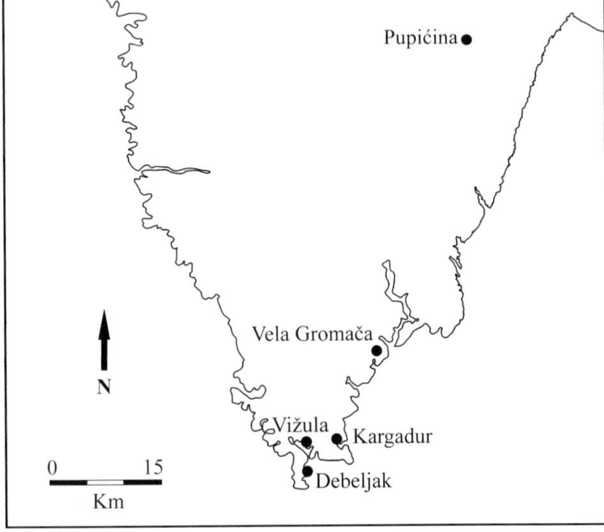

Figure 9.3. Istrian sites mentioned in the text.

Procurement and production at Early Neolithic sites in Istria

A number of Early Neolithic open-air sites are found on the lowland tip of the Istrian Peninsula (Figure 9.3). These are characterised by the presence of Impressed Ware pottery and sporadic remains of domestic animals (goat/sheep) and plants. Three sites, Vižula (Baćić 1969; Müller 1994; Codacci 2002; Spataro 2002), Kargadur (Komšo 2006), and Debeljak lie directly on the present coast, while Vela Gromača (Baćić 1973) is located on hilly inland terrain, overlooking the Budava Bay to the south and the Kvarner Bay to the east. A radiocarbon date of 6850±180; 6100–5450 cal BC; HD-12093 (Bronk Ramsey 2005) is available from the Impressed Ware site of Vižula (Chapman and Müller 1990), while additional radiocarbon dates from Kargadur have not yet been published.

The south Istrian lithic assemblages are characterised by a wasteful and almost exclusive use of two types of directly procured local cherts. Both sources are easily located, very visible outcrops. *Vižula* chert is a light grey to pale yellow, silicified limestone, which was extracted from beach cliffs or exposures along beaches. The raw material is easy to remove as nodules are continuously being eroded out from a secondary position within a soil that rests on the limestone bedrock. The overall less commonly used *Marlera* chert was collected from the surface of the Marlera Peninsula, south-east Istria, where it can still today be found as cobbles and small boulders in cultivated fields. Unsystematic knapping experiments show that local outcrops of Vižula-chert permit the production of any type of desired blanks, such as blades, bladelets and larger laminar flakes. However, the raw material is only suitable for the manufacture of a limited range of larger tools, as thin blanks from this material generally are too brittle for regular use. The largest assemblage from Vižula (over 1700 lithic products) contains a few prismatic blades, a number of regular bladelets and some bladelet cores. These products demonstrate that the physical qualities of the rock varied and occasionally allowed knappers to produce more delicate debitage. Other characteristics of the assemblages are production of tools mainly from flakes, an absence of composite tools, very little investment in retouch, and a rough, technological execution which produced significant amounts of angular debris or chunks (Andreasen, in preparation). The Vižula settlement can be viewed as a 'primary lithic reduction centre' where nearby quarry activity was continued at the site (Codacci 2002). Implements of non-local material (such as a sickle-insert of unknown provenience at Vižula) so far appear to be very few, and obsidian, common on the Italian side of the Adriatic, is found alongside local materials only in Middle Neolithic contexts (e.g. at Kargadur), and then mostly in the form of very small flake fragments (Komšo 2006).

The Mesolithic assemblage from Pupićina Cave in the north-east corner of the peninsula (Miracle and Forenbaher 2006) reveals some evidence of raw material circulation. The source of the non-local lithics has not yet been identified, but some fine-grained, orange and red nuances resemble Cretaceous flint from the Biancone and Scaglia formations on Monte Avena in north Italy. However, procurement was mostly practiced in proximity of the cave in a home range, direct access strategy, using also poorer quality raw materials. The morphologies and dimensions of procured pebble-flints did not allow for easy exploitation by means of blade debitage, and lithic production was mainly geared towards making small flakes and short bladelets.

For the Istrian sites, it is difficult to test expectations of early farmers in relation to lithic procurement and technology against those of hunter-gatherers, as they are separated in time and space and each reflect different technological needs and use of different environments. The only common features seem to be a reliance on mainly local raw materials, direct procurement, and expedient production technologies. In contrast to the early farmers, the indigenous Mesolithic populations supposedly had excellent knowledge of resources and were highly adapted to the local environment. From a lithic perspective, this is reflected by the exploited raw materials at Pupićina, which show a fuller utilisation of a range of sources and a procurement strategy consistent with occasional 'gathering'. It is perhaps more useful to look at the evidence from the first post-Mesolithic occupation at Pupićina Cave, which took place during the Middle Neolithic, some 200–300 years later than the Early Neolithic sites on the tip of the peninsula. The lithic assemblage is small (n=86) but the data suggests that the occupants relied on locally available chert, of which tools were made by employing simple *ad hoc* flaking strategies (Forenbaher 2006). Prismatic blade technology was rare. The employment of different lithic reduction methods may have been a tactical response to different raw material qualities and expedient, flake-based tools seem to be associated with poorer raw materials. This pattern changes in the following sub-phase of the Middle Neolithic. By this stage most artefacts are made of non-local cherts and blade technology is more common (Forenbaher 2006). While such a shift can be related to the widely observed increased interaction between regional groups, it is also indicative of a re-negotiated procurement strategy and a changing relationship vis-à-vis local resources.

The south Istrian case illustrates how an Early Neolithic community adapted its technical goals to the constraints of relatively poor local materials. At the same time, there was no system in place there, or at other Early Neolithic sites in south Istria, that was based on the acquisition of distant, higher-quality (and perhaps costly) raw materials from sources outside the immediate site catchment area. Did they not have access to such sources or did they lack either direct or indirect knowledge of their existence? Both alternatives can be seen as indications of a community which is new to the area and has not yet established its position in a system of regional interaction. In contrast, the two locally utilised raw materials were easily accessible and their detection was not dependent upon information required from local hunter-gatherers.

While the profiles of the lithic industries from both the Middle Neolithic Pupićina Cave and the open-air Early Neolithic sites in south Istria run counter to traditional expectations of Neolithic lithic production (Miracle and Forenbaher 2005, 265), they are essentially compatible with predicted expressions of landscape learning in colonizing agro-pastoral communities as briefly outlined above. A raw material strategy focusing on poor and local materials reflects a lack of access to better alternatives or to information about these. For colonizing farmers this may be interpreted as evidence of limited familiarity with the surrounding environment and perhaps a low degree of interaction with indigenous hunter-gatherers. But the less stringent raw material requirements and a non-reliance on a blade-based toolkit also express an *ad hoc* flexibility towards locally encountered raw materials, which, it can be argued, is characteristic of initial colonisation processes. Colonisation has been described as a variety-generating process on both the regional and settlement level (Kirch 1980, 117). Permanent or semi-permanent settlements of small, self-contained colonizing groups would have responded to adaptive pressures by increasing experimentation/innovation (Fitzhugh 2001). Variants of behaviour were probably already available in the repertoire of the community to act as pre-adaptations for new forms, scales, and patterning of organisation. As knowledge and access to better alternatives improved with time, the range of behavioural variation would have decreased, since variety-limiting selection would have impacted upon the earlier range of experimental behaviour. This is because long-term viability of colonizing communities required a degree of adaptedness to the environment, but also called for the participation in, and compliance with, regional systems of interaction.

In spite of their strategic, coastal locations, a slightly marginal position of the south Istrian sites could have prolonged the landscape learning/enculturation process if this pioneer community, for some reason, was precluded from regular participation in information- and commodity-sharing regional networks (involving both hunter-gatherers and other Neolithic communities). Some degree of mobility between local resource patches could have contributed to keeping flexibility at a maximum and minimize resource stress. Only at a later stage, perhaps as late as in the late Early Neolithic or Middle Neolithic, did they return to a more settled or 'normal' mode of life and started partaking more actively in circulation of raw materials and other goods. Although this needs to be confirmed archaeologically, the introduction of modest amounts of obsidian at Kargadur no earlier than the Middle Neolithic could be an indication in this direction.

Conclusions

Even when colonisation is accepted as an important process involved in the transition to farming, it is not sufficiently recognised that the Early Neolithic in much of the Mediterranean developed in the structural conditions of colonisation. Incoming farmers manipulated their environment for symbolic and cognitive purposes, as well as for practical ones, and this led to greater control over resources. The capacity to do this was structured or conditioned by the existing level of knowledge about the new landscape. An important statement formulated by landscape learning is that communities approach landscapes in different ways, according to their knowledge of natural resources in a region. An employment of landscape learning in archaeology must be used in terms of empirical variables and I argue that, with other proponents of landscape learning, the process of enculturating new landscapes has a technological response that is visible in the archaeological record.

I have outlined some of the potential implications of agro-pastoral migration on lithic procurement strategies and argued that long-distance colonisation entails an extensive reorganisation of a community's procurement system. The main reasons are a lack of detailed knowledge about the configuration of potential raw materials sources in the new lands and a disengagement from old interaction networks. Movement would have required a suite of alternative strategies, which could mitigate the liable stresses of migration. In this context, technological flexibility and diversity in approaches towards raw material use, shaped by local factors, may be interpreted as a strategy inherently suited for settlement systems involving migrating groups of farming communities.

Acknowledgements

The present work derives from part of my doctoral dissertation. My supervisor, Preston Miracle, has supported me with helpful comments and criticism, and the paper has further benefited from the critical comments of Darko Komšo, Stašo Forenbaher, and Kevin Lane. To the latter, I owe the term 'Mesolithic Teacher Package'.

References

Ammerman, A. J. and Cavalli-Sforza, L. L. 1973. A population model for the diffusion of early farming in Europe, in C. Renfrew (ed.), *The Explanation of Culture Change: Models in Prehistory*, 335–58. London, Duckworth.

Andreasen, N. H. (in preparation). *Landscape learning and changes in mobility and land use patterns during the Mesolithic and Neolithic periods in the East Adriatic – A study based on evidence of acquisition, use and exchange of lithic material.* Unpublished PhD thesis, University of Cambridge.

Andrefsky, W. 1994. Raw-material availability and the organization of technology. *American Antiquity* 59 (1), 21–34.

Anthony, D. W. 1990. Migration in archaeology: the baby and the bathwater. *American Anthropologist* 92 (4), 895–914.

Anthony, D. W. 1997. Prehistoric migration as social process, in J. Chapman and H. Hamerow (eds.), *Migrations and invasions in archaeological explanation*, 21–32. British Archaeological Reports, International Series S664. Oxford, Archaeopress.

Bass, B. 1998. Early Neolithic offshore accounts: remote islands, maritime exploitations, and the trans-Adriatic cultural network. *Journal of Mediterranean Archaeology* 11 (2), 165–90.

Baćić, B. 1969. Medulin, Ižula, Istra – neolitsko naselje. *Arheološki pregled* 11, 23–4.

Baćić, B. 1973. Vela Gromača kod Kavrana. *Histria Archaeologica* 4 (1), 7–29.

Binder, D. and Balkan-Atli, N. 2001. Obsidian exploitation and blade technology at Kömürcü-Kaletepe, Central Anatolia, in I. Caneva, C. Lemorini, D. Zampetti and P. Biagi (eds.), *Beyond tools. Redefining PPN lithic assemblages of the Levant*, 1–16. Berlin, Ex Oriente.

Briois, F., Gratuze, B. and Guilaine, J. 1997. Obsidiennes du site néolithique précéramique de Shillourokambos. *Paléorient* 23, 95–112.

Bronk Ramsey, C. 2005. OxCal 3.10. WWW program and documentation available at http://www.rlaha.ox.ac.uk/oxcal/oxcal.htm (accessed 10/2007).

Buckley, W. 1968. Society as a complex adaptive system, in W. Buckley (ed.), *Modern systems research for the behavioural scientist*, 490–513. Chicago, Aldine.

Chapman, J. and Müller, J. 1990. Early farmers in the Mediterranean Basin: the Dalmatian evidence. *Antiquity* 64, 127–34.

Codacci, G. 2002. Il sito neolitico di Vižula; analisa tiplogica dell'industria litica. *Histria archaeologica* 33, 143–93.

Fitzhugh, B. 2001. Risk and invention in human technological evolution. *Journal of Anthropological Archaeology* 20, 125–67.

Forenbaher, S. 1999. The earliest islanders of the Eastern Adriatic. *Collegium Antropologicum* 23, 521–30.

Forenbaher, S. 2006. Flaked stone artefacts, in P. T. Miracle and S. Forenbaher (eds.), *Prehistoric Herders in Istria (Croatia): The Archaeology of Pupićina Cave, Volume 1*, 225–57. Pula, Archaeological Museum of Istria.

Forenbaher, S. and Miracle, P. T. 2005. The spread of farming in the Eastern Adriatic. *Antiquity* 79 (305), 514–28.

Kirch, P. V. 1980. The archaeological study of adaptation: Theoretical and methodological issues, in M. B. Schiffer (ed.), *Advances in Archaeological Method and Theory*, 101–56. New York, Academic Press.

Komšo, D. 2006. Kargadur – Eine Siedlung aus dem frühen- und mittleren Neolithikum Istriens. *Mitteilungen der Berliner Gesellschaft für Anthropologie, Ethnologie und Urgeschichte* 27, 111–18.

Miracle, P. T. and Forenbaher, S. 2005. Neolithic and Bronze-Age herders of Pupićina Cave, Croatia. *Journal of Field Archaeology* 30, 255–81.

Miracle, P. T. and Forenbaher, S. (eds.) 2006. *Prehistoric Herders in Istria (Croatia): The Archaeology of Pupićina Cave, Volume 1*. Pula, Archaeological Museum of Istria.

Müller, J. 1994. Das ostadriatische Frühneolithikum. *Prähistorische Archäologie in Südosteuropa* 9.

Perlès, C. 1992. In search of lithic strategies. A cognitive approach to prehistoric chipped stone assemblages, in J.-C. Gardin and C. S. Peebles (eds.), *Representations in Archaeology*, 223–47. Bloomington and Indianapolis, Indiana University Press.

Perlès, C. and Vitelli, D. 1999. Craft specialization in the Neolithic of Greece, in P. Halstead (ed.), *Neolithic society in Greece*, 96–107. Sheffield Studies in Aegean Archaeology 2. Sheffield, Sheffield University Press.

Reitz, E. J. 1985. Comparison of Spanish and Aboriginal subsistence on the Atlantic coastal plain. *Southeastern Archaeology* 4, 41–50.

Rockman, M. 2003. Knowledge and learning in the archaeology of colonization, in M. Rockman and J. Steele (eds.), *Colonization of Unfamiliar Landscapes: The Archaeology of Adaptation*, 3–24. London, Routledge.

Rockman, M. and Steele, J. (eds.) 2003. *Colonization of Unfamiliar Landscapes: the archaeology of adaptation*, 3–24. London, Routledge.

Runnels, C. and van Andel, T. H. 1988. Trade and the origins of agriculture in the Eastern Mediterranean. *Journal of Mediterranean Archaeology* 1 (1), 83–109.

Spataro, M. 2002. *The first farming communities of the Adriatic: Pottery production and circulation in the Early and Middle Neolithic*. Trieste, Societa per la Preistoria della regione Friuli-Venezia Giulia.

Tringham, R. 2000. Southeastern Europe in the transition to agriculture in Europe: bridge, buffer, or mosaic, in T. D. Price (ed.), *Europe's First Farmers*, 19–56. Cambridge, Cambridge University Press.

Zilhão, J. 2001. Radiocarbon evidence for maritime pioneer colonization at the origins of farming in Western Mediterranean Europe. *Proceedings of the National Academy of Sciences USA* 98 (24), 14180–5.

Zvelebil, M. and Lillie, M. 2000. Transition to agriculture in Eastern Europe, in T. D. Price (ed.), *Europe's First Farmers*, 57–92. Cambridge, Cambridge University Press.

10. The colonisation of eastern alpine territories: the Val di Non case study and the 'Regole' field camps (Trento, Italy)

Giampaolo Dalmeri, Klaus Kompatscher, Maria Hrozny Kompatscher, Anna Cusinato and Michele Bassetti

Since the 1980s, the process of colonisation of the Alps during the Late Glacial and the Early Holocene has primarily been studied on the basis of the technical and typological characteristics of lithic industries. For the Late Glacial, a pattern for landscape use has been proposed which suggests seasonal movements of human groups between the valley floor and mid-mountain altitudes. New data, such as those gathered from the Riparo Dalmeri site, now allow us to postulate a more detailed mobility pattern. Moreover, a recent project of systematic survey in the Val di Non, in the Western Trentino area, has let us identify a large number of sites attributed to the Late Palaeolithic and the Mesolithic, situated at different altitudes and characterised by different topographical conditions. The first case investigated was the Regole peat bog, at an altitude of 1200 metres above sea level, where three sites were excavated and analysed. These settlements were selected in consideration of their well-preserved archaeological records. Intra-site analysis conducted through refitting has allowed us to interpret these sites as field camps.

Keywords: Late Glacial, Early Holocene, eastern Alps, hunter-gatherers, Regole peat bog, lithic industry, refitting, intra-site analysis, landscape use.

Objectives of the research

The chronological and palaeo-environmental background

Since the 1970s, the process of human colonisation of the Alps has primarily been studied by comparing the technical and typological characteristics of the lithic industries found and the palaeo-environmental data gathered from numerous sites excavated in north-eastern Italy. Research has allowed us to reconstruct the stages of human colonisation during the Late Glacial and the Early Holocene in this region. The most important spread of human groups towards the Alpine environment has been identified as occurring during the Late Glacial (Bølling-Allerød) Interstadial. From the valley floor sites, such as Riparo Soman (Battaglia *et al.* 1994), between 100 and 150m in altitude, groups of Epigravettian hunter-gatherers moved on towards the mid-mountain environment. During the Bølling, the timberline reached *c.* 1500m in altitude, or even higher in the inner Italian Alps (Kofler 1994; Schneider 1985). At the end of Bølling the paleobotanical data from the Palughetto basin on the Cansiglio plateau shows that the tree line was well over 1050m asl (Avigliano *et al.* 2000). This stage, in which groups frequented the Alpine plateaux, is documented by many open-air sites and a number of rockshelters. Since the 1980s, a pattern for landscape use has been proposed which suggests a seasonal migration of human groups between the valley floor – where large rockshelters existed that were occupied repeatedly during the year – and mid-mountain altitudes, frequented from the spring to autumn (Broglio and Lanzinger 1990). Altitudes above 1500m were frequented only sporadically, as documented by rare open-air sites (Figure 10.1).

Data recently gathered from the mountain settlement of Riparo Dalmeri, radiocarbon dated to the Late Glacial Interstadial, indicate a strategy of using resources from different natural environments. Hunting the ibex (*Capra ibex*), which populated the Alpine prairies, was supplemented by the exploitation of other ungulates that inhabited the conifer forests, and by fishing (Bassetti *et al.* 2000; Cassoli *et al.* 1999; Castelletti and Maspero 1994; Fiore and Tagliacozzo 2005). On this same site, the micro-wear analysis of lithic artefacts has revealed the importance of leatherworking and, in particular, tanning activities (Lemorini *et al.* 2006). The data gathered at Riparo Dalmeri are consistent with the proposed pattern for landscape use, but suggest a more complex scenario, with frequent movement between the Alpine plain and the valley floor during a single season. This latter hypothesis is corroborated by the discovery, at Riparo Dalmeri, of fish remains from species that are attributed to fishing activities undertaken in the (then) valley floor of the River

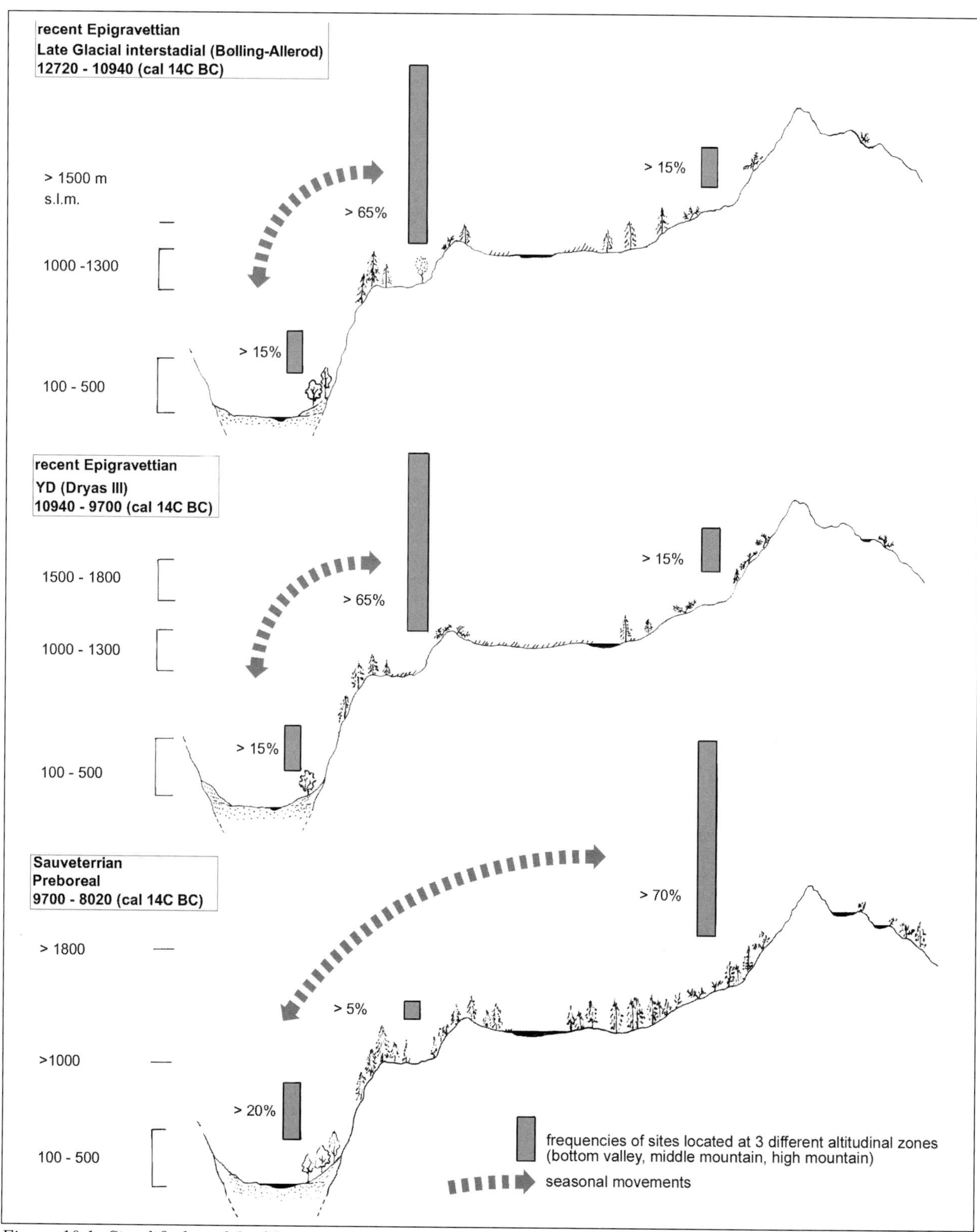

Figure 10.1. Simplified model of human penetration of the mountainous zone of the Adige and Brenta catchment areas, covering a sequence from Late Glacial Interstadial to Preboreal. For the Late Glacial Interstadial, 18 sites have been taken into consideration, for the YD 12 sites and for the Preboreal 51 sites. Modified from Bagolini and Pedrotti 1992, and Dalmeri and Pedrotti 1994.

Brenta, and now at an altitude of 200m asl (Fiore and Tagliacozzo 2005).

The cold and arid climate of the Younger Dryas (YD), interrupted by brief temperate periods, led to the retreat of the timberline (300–500m) (Schneider and Tobolski 1983; Wick 1996), and, probably, to the abandonment of sites frequented during the Allerød Interstadial. Nonetheless, recent radiocarbon dating carried out at Riparo Cogola (Bassetti *et al.* 2005), and at the Bus de la Lum site (Peresani *et al.* 2000), indicate, along with other sites dated exclusively by analysing lithic typology, that the mountain areas continued to be frequented between the Younger Dryas (YD).

During the Early Holocene, when the climate stabilised around current values and the timberline reached altitudes of around 2200–2300m (Seiwald 1980; Oeggl and Wahlmüller 1994; Speranza *et al.* 1996), Mesolithic human groups primarily frequented the rockshelters of the valley floor and at high altitude, penetrating the innermost areas of the Alpine chain. In certain rockshelters of the Val dell'Adige, such as Romagnano III (Broglio and Kozlowski 1983) and Pradestel (Bagolini *et al.* 1973), evidence has been found of continuous occupation throughout the interval from the Preboreal to the Atlantic. The occupation of rockshelters, which opened up along the rocky slopes, was favoured by the greater stability of the valley floor and the presence of small lakes, which enabled humans to intensify the exploitation of the economic resources offered by fishing and the gathering of molluscs. The majority of Mesolithic mountain Sauveterrian sites are distributed at altitudes between 1800 and 2300m (Dalmeri and Pedrotti 1994; Broglio and Lanzinger 1996) and are primarily related to the exploitation of two different natural environments, namely the mountain prairies and the woodlands, as demonstrated by the Mondeval de Sora site (Fontana and Guerreschi 1998). Many of these are situated on the shores of small lake basins (Figure 10.1). Recent archaeological research has also revealed rare Mesolithic sites at intermediate altitudes, such as Casera Lissandri on the Altopiano del Cansiglio (Peresani *et al.* 1998), which have been interpreted as intermediate stations along the ascent routes.

The recent mobility pattern (Kompatscher 1996), developed to reconstruct the main routes of Mesolithic human groups along the Alpine prairies, reveals how the morphology of the terrain strongly influences the location of a camp. During the Mesolithic, the most suitable mountain environments for hunting were located exclusively at high altitude, where the hunting grounds were scarce, and were split up and marked by abrupt variations in altitude. Relative to the recent Epigravettian, the reduction in available terrain led to two principal consequences: a greater mobility at high altitude to find new hunting grounds to the north, and a reduction in the size of residential camps, around which many more lookout posts, or hunting bivouacs, sprang up. The idea of contact between the southern and northern slopes of the Alps, as a consequence of progressively deeper penetration northwards, is supported by artefacts found at Ullafelsen (Tyrol, Austria), deriving from raw material that is southern Alpine in origin (Schäfer 1998).

The specific purpose of the project

Against this background, the research project under way in the upper Val di Non is targeted at two principal objectives: to gather new data concerning the western Trentino territory, which has been barely explored archaeologically, and to draw the focus of research towards the Upper Palaeolithic-Mesolithic transition period, which is positioned between the end of the YD and the start of the Preboreal. This particular phase was selected for study in an attempt to explore a period of change in both knapping techniques and in settlement patterns. While the majority of authors concur on the fact that the Mesolithic was a period when the Alpine region began to see the appearance of new technologies (Broglio 1973; Guerreschi 1984), which originated in the Upper Palaeolithic, studies on changes in settlement patterns and landscape use have only been made very recently and are not exhaustive (Angelucci 1996). The Val di Non territory has preserved potentially interesting archaeological records that could contribute to this issue. The territory surveyed extends from the Valle dell'Adige valley floor, the mid mountain, where the Epigravettian sites of Laghetto delle Regole were found, and the high mountain, where Mesolithic sites have been identified (between 1800 and 2350m asl).

To date, three sites have been investigated on the shores of the Regole lake basin at 1200m asl, which have been radiocarbon dated between the start of the YD and the start of the Preboreal. These are situated on the shores of an ancient lake basin, whose deposits may serve as a valuable archive for the reconstruction of the environment in this area of the Alps during the transition period between the Pleistocene and the Holocene.

Methods

The study of archaeological material from the Regole lakeshore site has been based on technological and spatial studies, conducted through refitting, to reconstruct the anthropic or natural processes that have led to the formation of the record, and to identify material concentrations and significant associations or relationships between different material categories.

The Laghetto delle Regole basin

In the upper Val di Non (Trentino) around the area of Laghetto delle Regole at 1240m asl, peat has been extracted for agricultural purposes. These activities have led to the identification of three archaeological sites frequented during the final stage of the recent Epigravettian (Dalmeri *et al.* 2002; Dalmeri *et al.* 2005; Cattani and Gosetti 2005). These excavations were conducted by the Museo Tridentino di Scienze Naturali in collaboration with the Soprintendenza per i Beni Archeologici of the municipality

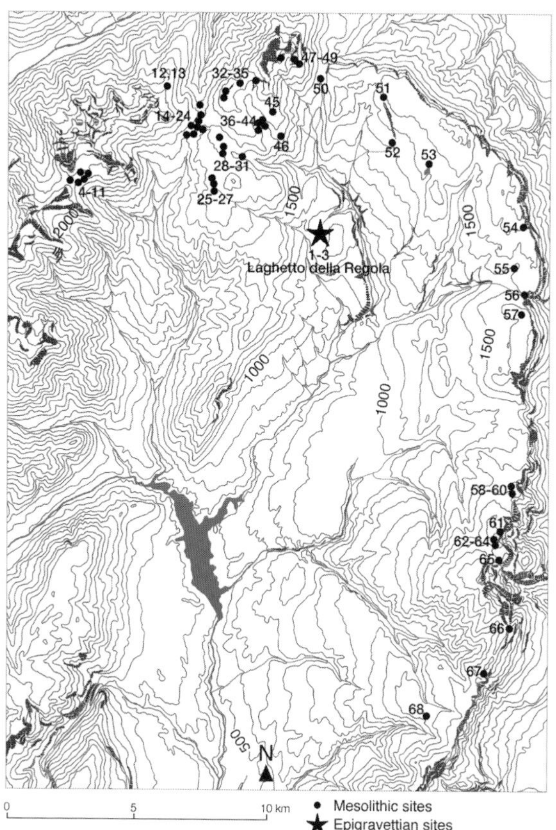

Figure 10.2. Val di Non valley location map, showing the distribution of the Mesolithic open-air sites and of the Epigravettian sites of the Laghetto delle Regole. (Graphic: K. Kompatscher and M. Hrozny Kompatscher).

Figure 10.3. The peat lake of Laghetto delle Regole (Trento) and the location of the Epigravettian sites. (Photograph: K. Kompatscher and M. Hrozny Kompatscher).

of Trento (Figure 10.2). The basin fill documents a sequence that starts with moraine deposits from the Last Glacial Maximum (LGM) and ends with the formation of peaty deposits, reaching a maximum thickness of approximately 2 metres. Human occupation, dated to the YD (site LR1: 10,445±32 BP; 10,650–10,410 cal BC; KIA-14195 and site LR2: 10,373±32 BP; 10,380 cal BC; KIA-14196) and the start of the Preboreal (site LR3: 9737±42 BP; 9220 cal BC; KIA-20343) is concurrent with the regressive phase of the ancient lake (Figure 10.3). During the Preboreal and up to the Atlantic, the ancient shore deposit developed into podzol forest soil. At site LR1, the dating of roots (6280±27 BP; 5316–5148 cal BC; KIA-14194) that were found in their original positions when alive provides a *terminus ante quem* for the development of the forest. Peat formation began in the Mid-Atlantic, thus providing an *ante quem* date (5121±24 BP; 3975–3805 cal BC; KIA-14193) relative to ligneous remains found at the base of the peat.

This work is primarily concerned with the results of the study of sites LR2 and LR3, whereas it will only make references to site LR1, where the distribution of stone artefacts has been altered by root system disturbances during the period of colonisation by a forest of Scots pine (*Pinus silvestris*). At both LR2 and LR3 sites, the archaeological material found consists exclusively of flint artefacts in undisturbed deposits and carbonaceous particles. The analysis of stone material and the characteristics of the soil stratigraphy observed allow us to consider the lithic assemblage of each site as a uniform whole attributable to a single episode of occupation. The formation of peat after the abandonment of the site may have favoured conservation and minimised post-depositional disturbance.

At site LR2, located on the northern shore of the lake basin, an area of 6m² was excavated, yielding 210 stone artefacts that were almost exclusively obtained from flint of the Scaglia Variegata Cretaceous formation, with the majority originating from the same nodule. 34 elements were refitted from 95 artefacts each measuring over 0.5cm. The examination of refitted elements proves the detachment of lamellar flakes and reveals that at least one unshaped nodule was transported to the site, where it has been knapped to obtain standardized supports and a number of retouched tools. Large portions of cortex on the dorsal surface of a number of lamellar flakes indicate that the production of supports was carried out immediately after a rough core preparation process. The microliths (segmented backed bladelets, lunate and triangle) were made from lamellar flakes by backing retouch without the use of microburin techniques. In spite of the scarcity of material, the knapping methods and the production process of microliths found at the site are compatible with the final stage of the recent Epigravettian. From a spatial point of view, the archaeological record is concentrated in two areas separated by a distance of approximately 1 metre. The first of these consists of debitage products and microliths, whereas the second consists of cortical discard flakes. The material found at these two concentrations may be interpreted as the product of a single knapping episode, during which useable tools were selected and separated from waste flakes (Figure 10.4).

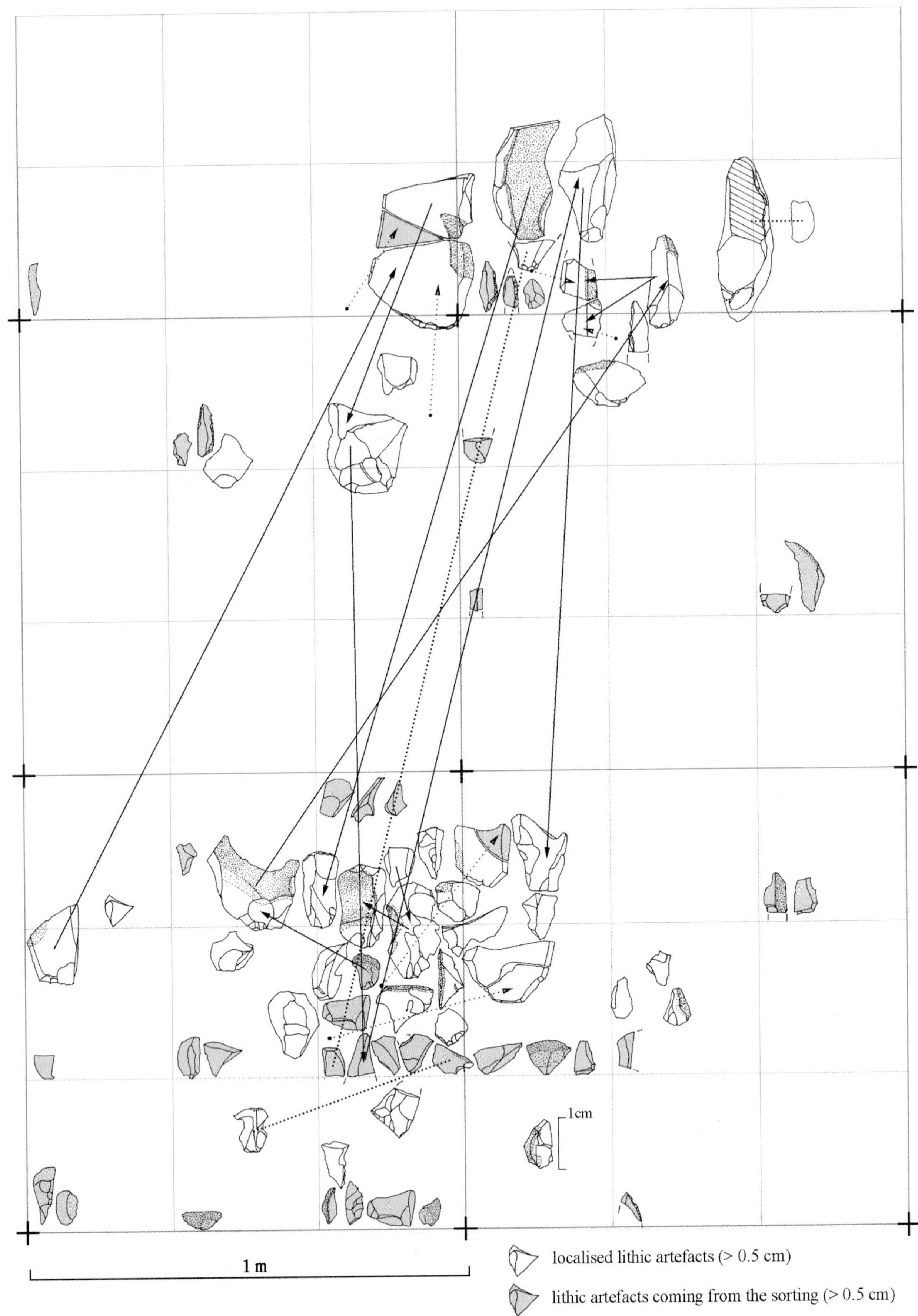

Figure 10.4. Laghetto delle Regole. Map of site 2, showing the refitting spatial distribution. (Graphic: K. Kompatscher and M. Hrozny Kompatscher).

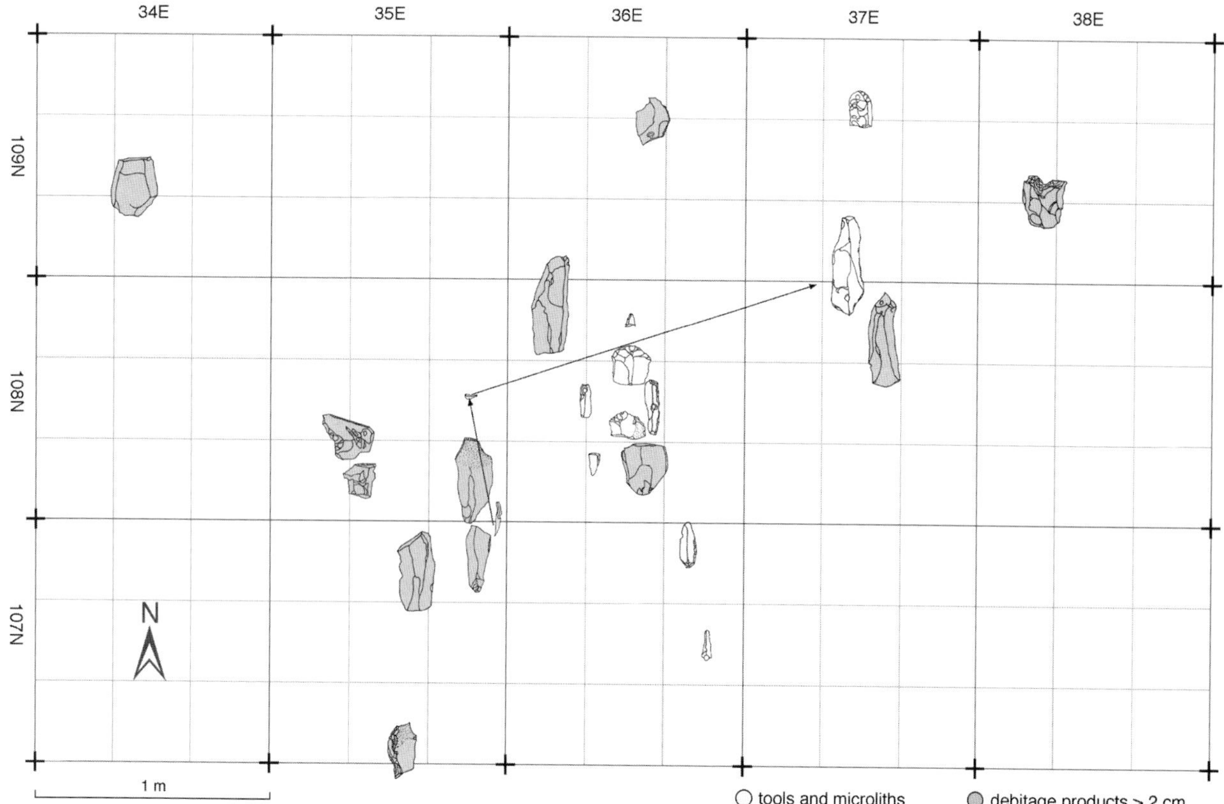

Figure 10.5. Laghetto delle Regole. Site 3. Spatial distribution of the artefacts measuring more than 2cm. (Graphic: K. Kompatscher and M. Hrozny Kompatscher).

Site LR3, situated on the southern shore of the lake basin, yielded 1147 artefacts. The majority of the tools are made from Cretaceous Scaglia Variegata and Scaglia Rossa raw materials, which outcrop locally. The debitage products found consist in blades, bladelets and flakes (Figure 10.5). The lithic artefacts, which fit neatly into the final stage of the recent Epigravettian, are relatively varied: one burin, three end scrapers, one truncation, a retouched blade and retouched flakes. Among microliths, backed points, backed bladelets and one segmented backed bladelet were identified. 135 refits were made in total from the assemblage (135 out of 380, or 35.5%). Two causes for the separation of the elements were identified: knapping and intentional retouching (28%); fracture (22%) and thermal action (50%) (Figure 10.6). This latter factor was interpreted as a natural post-depositional phenomenon, affecting 88% of the artefacts. As with site LR2, the high percentage of refits allowed us to reconstruct the behavioural components underlying the site formation. After a brief occupation by a number of hunter-gatherers, the following activities were conducted at the site: knapping (Figure 10.6.3), manufacture of microliths (Figure 10.6.2) and the manufacture of a burin (Figure 10.6.1). A difference in the spatial distribution of activities can be noted. The microliths, situated at the centre, could indicate re-hafting or retooling activities, whereas the tools, the blades and the large flakes, dispersed over the entire area of the site, are an indication that certain subsistence activities were carried out there (Figure 10.5). The area organisation of site LR3, and in particular the position of the microliths and tools, is substantially consistent with spatial distribution patterns formulated from the 1980s on for the Late Palaeolithic and the Early Mesolithic (Cziesla 1990; Bassetti *et al.* 2000).

Conclusions

The territory exploited by Epigravettian groups of humans extended from the valley floor to large Alpine plateaux at altitudes between 1000 and 1500m. We have been able to identify two types of mountain site, i.e. seasonal residential camps and field camps. Sites LR2 and LR3 may be ascribed to this latter category, as these were briefly occupied sites on the shores of a small lake basin. At other sites found on the large plains at mid-mountain altitudes, previously interpreted as field camps, the study of stone tools, based primarily on the types of retouched tools, has not allowed us to postulate how different activities carried out at the site were organised in space or time. Conversely, the archaeological record of sites LR2 and LR3 has offered the chance to carry out a thorough *intra-site* spatial analysis, enabling us to reconstruct some of the behavioural dynamics of the Epigravettian human groups. Site LR2 has preserved the traces of a single knapping episode with the concurrent selection of useable tools, whereas site LR 3 provides evidence of a brief occupation by some hunter-gatherers who carried out a series of spatially organised activities, setting aside a limited area for the manufacture of a number of microliths, probably destined for a hafting system.

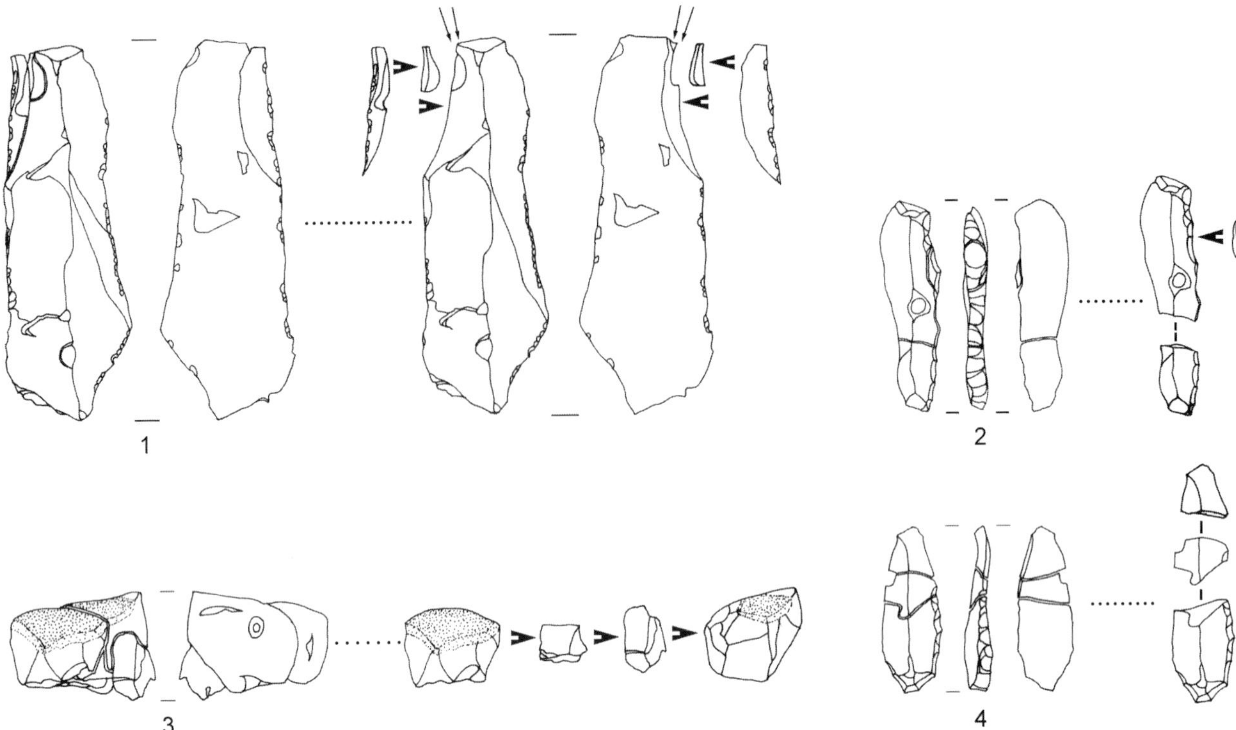

Figure 10.6. Laghetto delle Regole. Site 3. Examples of refitting sequences. (Drawing: K. Kompatscher and M. Hrozny Kompatscher; scale 1:1).

Based on radiocarbon dating, the sequence of dates identified at the Regole sites has confirmed that human groups were present in the mountain environment during the YD, providing new data to place chronologically the final Epigravettian cultural stage, during which changes began to arise in the techno-typological features of lithic industries which were to develop fully in the Mesolithic. The Val di Non project intends to extend its research to sites located at high-mountain altitudes, to ascertain their chronology and to investigate possible relations with the sites at the Regole peat bog.

References

Angelucci, D. 1996. *Adattamenti tardi e post-glaciali. Gli ultimi cacciatori-raccoglitori del versante meridionale delle Alpi orientali.* Unpublished PhD thesis, Università di Ferrara-Bologna-Parma.

Avigliano, R., Di Anastasio, G., Peresani, M. and Ravazzi C. 2000. A new Late Glacial-Early Holocene Palaeobotanical and Archaeological Record in the Eastern Pre-Alps: the Palughetto basin (Cansiglio Plateau, Italy). *Journal of Quaternary Science* 15, 789–803.

Bagolini, B., Barbacovi, F., Bergamo, G., Bertoldi, L., Mezzena, G. and Postal, L. 1973. Pradestel (Trento). *Preistoria Alpina* 9, 243–4.

Bassetti, M., Cusinato, A., Dalmeri, G., Kompatscher, K. and Hrozny Kompatscher, M. 2000. Riparo Dalmeri (Trento. L'industria litica negli spazi d'abitato epigravettiani. *Preistoria Alpina* 31 (1995), 23–36.

Bassetti, M., Dalmeri, G. and Peresani, M. 2005. Riparo Cogola. Note preliminari sulla successione stratigrafica. *Preistoria Alpina* 40, 91–9.

Battaglia, L., Broglio, A., Castelletti, L., Lanzinger, M. and Maspero, A. 1994. Abri Soman, Excursions dans les sites paléolithiques et mésolithiques du bassin de l'Adige, des Dolomites et du Plateau d'Asiago. *Preistoria Alpina* 28/2 (1992), 291–8.

Broglio, A. 1973. L'Epipaléolithique de la Vallée de l'Adige. *L'Anthropologie* 77, 5–34.

Broglio, A. and Kozłowski, S. K. 1983. Tipologia ed evoluzione delle industrie mesolitiche di Romagnano III. *Preistoria Alpina* 19, 93–148.

Broglio, A. and Lanzinger, M. 1990. Considerazioni sulla distribuzione dei siti tra la fine del Paleolitico superiore e l'inizio del Neolitico nell'Italia nord-orientale, in P. Biagi (ed.), *The Neolithisation of the Alpine Region. International Round Table 'The Neolithisation of the Alpine Region', Brescia, 29 April - 1 May 1988*, 53–69. Monografie di Natura Bresciana 13. Brescia, Museo civico di scienze naturali di Brescia.

Broglio, A. and Lanzinger, M. 1996. The human population of the Southern slopes of the Eastern Alps in the Würm Late Glacial and early Postglacial. *Italian Journal of Quaternary Sciences* 9 (2), 499–508.

Cassoli, P. F., Dalmeri, G., Fiore, I. and Tagliacozzo, A. 1999. La chasse dans un gisement épigravettien de montagne : Riparo Dalmeri (Trento, Italie), in A. Thévenin and P. Bintz (eds.), *L'Europe des derniers Chasseurs. Épipaléolithique et Mésolithique. Actes du 5ième colloque international UISPP, Comission XII. Grenoble, 18-23 septembre 1995*, 459–64. Paris, Comité des travaux historiques et scientifiques (CHTS).

Castelletti, G. and Maspero, A. 1994. Dati antracologici relativi all'ultima glaciazione nelle Alpi Orientali italiane. *Preistoria Alpina* 28, 105–14.

Cattani, L. and Gosetti, C. 2005. Laghetto delle Regole di Castelfondo: risultati delle analisi polliniche. *Preistoria Alpina* 40 (2004), 27–35.

Cziesla, E. 1990. Siedlungsdynamik auf steinzeitlichen Fundplätzen: methodische Aspekte zur Analyse latenter Strukturen. *Studies in Modern Archaeology* 2, 172–8.

Dalmeri, G. and Pedrotti, A. 1994. Distribuzione topografica dei siti del Paleolitico superiore finale e del Mesolitico in Trentino Alto-Adige e nelle Dolomiti venete (Italia). *Preistoria Alpina* 28/2 (1992), 247–67.

Dalmeri, G., Bassetti, M., Cusinato, A., Kompatscher, K. and Hrozny Kompatscher, M. 2002. Laghetto della Regola di Castelfondo (Trento). Primi risultati delle ricerche paletnologiche e paleoambientali. *Preistoria Alpina* 38, 35–65.

Dalmeri, G., Kompatscher, K., Hrozny Kompatscher, M., Bassetti, M., Cusinato, A. and Piazzi, O. 2005. Le dinamiche comportamentali degli ultimi cacciatori raccoglitori in area alpina. Il caso di studio del sito LR3 del Laghetto delle Regole (Castelfondo, Trento), *Preistoria Alpina* 40 (2004), 5–27.

Fiore, I. and Tagliacozzo, A. 2005. L'analisi dei resti faunistici: il contesto paleocologico e l'economia del sito, in A. Broglio and G. Dalmeri (eds.), *Pitture paleolitiche nelle Prealpi. Venete Grotta di Fumane e Riparo Dalmeri*, 116–21, Verona, Cierre Edizioni.

Fontana, F. and Guerreschi, A. 1998. The Mesolithic mountain camp-site of Mondeval de Sora (Italian Dolomites), in *Atti del XIII Congresso Internazionale di Scienze Preistoriche e Protostoriche, Forlì, 8–14 settembre 1996*, Vol. 3, 55–62. Arcola (La Spezia), ABACO Edizioni.

Guerreschi, A. 1984. Tendenze evolutive in senso mesolitico dell' Epigravettiano italico recente dell'Italia nord-orientale. *Preistoria Alpina*, 209–12.

Kofler, W. 1994. Die Vegetationsentwicklung im Spätpaläolithikum und Mesolithikum im Raume Trient. *Preistoria Alpina* 28/1 (1992), 83–103.

Kompatscher K. 1996. Zum räumlichen Verhalten mittelsteinzeitlicher Jäger. *Der Schlern Heft* 1, 70.

Lemorini, C., Rossetti, P., Dalmeri G., Cusinato, A., Hrozny Kompatscher, M. and Kompatscher, K. 2006. L'analisi delle tracce d'uso e l'elaborazione spaziale: il riconoscimento di un'area specializzata nel sito epigravettiano di Riparo Dalmeri, livelli 26b e 26c (Trento). *Preistoria Alpina* 41 (2005), 171–97.

Oeggl, K. and Wahlmüller, N. 1994. Vegetation and climate history of a high alpine Mesolithic campsite in the Eastern Alps. *Preistoria Alpina* 28/1 (1992), 71–82.

Peresani, M., Bertola, S. and Di Anastasio, G. 2000. Epigravettien récent et Mésolithique ancien en contexte préalpin: les données du haut plateau du Cansiglio (Italie du Nord). *Cahiers d'archéologie romande* 81, 267–76.

Peresani, M., De Stefani, M., Di Anastasio, G. and Masin, I. 1998. Studi preliminari sul sito epigravettiano di Bus de la Lum nell'Altopiano del Cansiglio. *Bollettino della Società naturalisti 'Silvia Zenari'* 22, 7–34.

Schäfer, D. 1998. Zum Untersuchungsstand auf dem altmesolithischen Fundplatz vom Ullafelsen im Fotschertal (Stubaier Alpen, Tirol). *Germania* 76, 439–96.

Schneider, R. 1985. Palynologic research in the Southern and Southeastern Alps between Torino and Trieste. *Dissertationes Botanicae* 87, 83–103.

Schneider, R. and Toboloski, K. 1983. Palynologische und stratigraphische Untersuchungen im Lago di Ganna (Varese, Italien). *Botanicae Helveticae* 93, 115–22.

Seiwald, A. 1980. Beiträge zur Vegetationsgeschichte Tirols IV: Natzer Plateau – Villanderer Alm. *Berichte des naturwissenschaftlich – medizinischen Vereins* 67, 31–72.

Speranza, A., Ravazzi, C., Baroni, C., Carton, A., Van Geel, B. and Mommersteeg, H. 1996. Holocene vegetation development and human impact in the Central Alps: the 'Pian Venezia' paleobotanical records (Trento, Italy). *Italian Journal of Quaternary Sciences* 9 (2), 737–44.

Wick, L. 1996. Late-Glacial and Early-Holocene palaeoenvironments in Brianza, Northern Italy. *Italian Journal of Quaternary Sciences* 9 (2), 653–9.

Session II

Mobility

11. Introduction: Mobility

C. R. Wickham-Jones

The concept of mobility is central to most interpretations of the Mesolithic in Europe. There are two problems with this. First it is clear from a general scan of the literature that there is no uniform definition of mobility; and second, how best to recognize and study mobility? This session set out to discuss these issues and certainly sparked some lively debate.

With regard to the definition of mobility, previous *Mesolithic in Europe* publications have highlighted the different perceptions of various workers. Some (Zhilin 2003) consider journeys of up to 1000km, while others (Hardy and Wickham-Jones 2003) consider distances around 70km. Perhaps the question is even more fundamental: Brody has queried the very assumption that hunter-gatherer societies be seen as mobile (2001).

The session papers vary in topic and in scale. None attempt to introduce a universal definition of mobility, although most consider their own use of the concept. Useful discussions of previous definitions in Europe as well as North America are provided by Kador and Bamforth, both of whom recognize the essential dichotomy between deterministic views of mobility as a human standard and variable views of mobility as a changeable element of society, best viewed by looking at the evidence.

Interestingly, all the authors take it for granted that hunter-gather (Mesolithic) communities are essentially mobile. Bamforth is perhaps the most archaeologically introspective in his discussion of what this might mean, and the attraction for the archaeological community of previous models of behaviour such as Binford's work in 1979. Both Bamforth and Kador argue coherently that assumptions of a generalized uniformity in behaviour between human groups should be dropped. They are in agreement that a more appropriate way forward is to be found by working from the evidence on the ground and interpreting upwards towards the varied behavioural explanations for the material remains.

This concept, of bottom up analysis and the variety that we might expect, is illustrated nicely by the session as a whole, as each paper provides a coherent and distinct case study. Bamforth himself offers a wide-ranging review of work in North America that emphasizes the variety, not only of the material evidence, but also of the behaviour that we are trying to reach. In contrast, the discursive arguments in Kador's paper are followed with a consideration of his own approach and its application to a specific region and type of evidence, namely the Barrow Valley in Ireland and the lithic material to be found there. Kador picks up on Finlay's point that we tend to ignore the constructs of mobility and look instead at its effects (2004) and he suggests that one way around this is to consider pathways as a central element of mobility. He uses the patterning of lithic finds across the landscape as an indicator of connections between sites; the patterning is then refined with the application of topographical and geological information in order to reconstruct movement and journeys.

The theme of pathways and the actual movement that mobility implies is relatively new for Mesolithic studies (but see Warren 2003) and it is also considered by Starr and Harris, who approach mobility through the analysis of movement and navigation in their study which involves the application of GIS and topographical information. While other archaeologists have long studied routeways, Mesolithic consideration is different in that it does not (to date) concern monumental or even necessarily overtly human constructs. Starr and Harris provide a useful review of previous definitions and distinctions between path types; they remind us of the importance of natural features, and perhaps most importantly they remind us that pathways are integrally linked with cultural knowledge. One way forward that they suggest is to examine traditional literature for information relating to movement and orientation within the landscape. The application of their method is set around the Federsee in south-west Germany and it provides a pointer for some new directions.

One factor that unites many of the regional studies presented in this section is the use of information relating to the natural landscape at a broad level to refine the archaeological interpretation of material remains. This is perhaps most explicit in Cavulli and Grimaldi's study, which makes use of archaeological material within distinct altitudinal niches in the mountainous Trentino region of northern Italy in order to look at the use of the landscape. By adding information relating to the raw material sources exploited at different periods they have begun to approach issues relating to the constraints on movement within the landscape and how they varied through time.

Regional studies are also provided by the two papers of Manninen and Harris and her colleagues, and perhaps not surprisingly lithic artefacts feature in many of these papers. Not only do stone tools provide one of the most enduring and visible markers for ancient human activity, but they are also linked inextricably to human movement through the identification of geological sources, which differ in many cases from the archaeological locations where artefacts are recovered today. Where natural forces, such as glacial transport, can be ruled out the obvious implication is that lithics were moved by their human users. Manninen's study of lithic artefacts, raw material sources and the landscape in the Lake Inari region of northern Fennoscandia, provides an application of the data which both supports and adds to the existing interpretation of the Mesolithic settlement of the area, as well as providing its own definitions of long distance mobility.

Harris and colleagues also use lithics to provide baseline archaeological information in their work to extend traditional studies of Mesolithic settlement around the Federsee in northern Germany. Their work is regional in basis and integrates surface survey and topographical analysis with the archaeological material in order to approach the human cost of journeys. The study is further refined by a consideration of two different scales of mobility: daily mobility which might operate out of a single camp; and re-locational mobility which might mean the movement of the camp itself.

Finally the session moved from regional studies to work at a smaller scale. In his analysis of the season of death of wild boar (*Sus scrofa*) from the three Danish sites of Holmegaard, Mullerup and Ertebølle, Carter has extended the likely season of activity at the sites and provided another useful tool to play into wider interpretations of human movement. Gordon, meanwhile, looks at mobility within an individual site in the Canadian Barrenlands. His paper provides a way to make sense of those archaeological palimpsests with which we are all too familiar. Gordon's work concentrates on the detailed analysis of lithic remains, but in other circumstances could be adapted to include other materials.

So, what have we learnt? A few constants stand out. For me perhaps most telling is the reminder that archaeology cannot exist in isolation. It may seem obvious that in order to study movement we have to include the characteristics of the world through which that movement takes place, but this has not always been so. It is also worth noting that we cannot assume that the world as we see it today parallels the world in which our ancestors lived. Changes in sea level, erosion, deposition and human constructs such as the large scale drainage schemes that have accompanied farming in the last few centuries all mean that related skills, such as geomorphology, have to be drafted in if we are to understand the landscape properly. It is also interesting how many of the studies made use of the lithic remains – some with detailed analysis and others with more general work. Once again relevant related skills include the incorporation of geological knowledge of source sites and potential mechanisms of movement both natural and human. Other studies bought in information from ethnography and local oral history; this is a field which has only just begun to reach its potential with regard to archaeology.

Curiously none of the papers address another important aspect of mobility – that of the restrictions that help to define movement. What of territoriality? What bounds exist? Why was movement restricted to specific areas? How was movement organised and how did the rounds of separate groups relate to one another? Aspects such as this have been addressed elsewhere (e.g. Mendoza 2003) and it would be good to see them extended to European material. Sometimes it is important to examine what is not in order to fully understand that which is.

Mobility studies have moved forward. We need to be wider in our approaches. We need to define the stand from which we view mobility and we need to be explicit about our methods and assumptions. This collection of papers shows clearly that to seek for a universal truth is a false goal. Not only did different groups practise distinct types of mobility, but individual archaeologists each seek out that which is useful to them – at their own different scale. Whether we are dealing with transcontinental movement, journeys around a lake or coast and into the hinterland, or the use of different parts of a site, there is no constant against which to set our own interpretations. We can, however, learn from each other.

References

Binford, L. 1979. Organization and formation processes: looking at curated technologies. *Journal of Anthropological Research* 35 (iii), 255–73.

Brody, H. 2001. *The Other Side of Eden*. London, Faber and Faber.

Finlay, N. 2004. E-scapes and E-motion: other ways of writing the Mesolithic. *Before Farming* 2004 (1), 1–9.

Hardy, K. and Wickham-Jones, C. R. 2003. Scotland's First Settlers: an Investigation into Settlement, Territoriality and Mobility During the Mesolithic in the Inner Sound, Scotland, First Results, in L. Larsson, H. Kindgren, K. Knutsson, D. Loeffler and A. Åkerlund (eds.), *Mesolithic on the Move: Papers presented at the Sixth International Conference on the Mesolithic in Europe, Stockholm 2000*, 369–81. Oxford, Oxbow Books.

Mendoza, M. 2003. Range area and seasonal campsites of Toba bands in western Chaco, Argentina. *Before Farming* 2003 (2), 203–15.

Warren, G. 2003. Life in the Trees: Mesolithic people and the woods of Ireland. *Archaeology Ireland* 17 (3), 20–3.

Zhilin, M. 2003. Early Mesolithic communication networks in the East European forest zone, in L. Larsson, H. Kindgren, K. Knutsson, D. Loeffler and A. Åkerlund (eds.), *Mesolithic on the Move: Papers presented at the Sixth International Conference on the Mesolithic in Europe, Stockholm 2000*, 688–93. Oxford, Oxbow Books.

12. Moving perceptions: movement, mobility and the material dimension

Thomas Kador

In this paper I will argue that human movement presents an excellent medium to understand Mesolithic lives and that the concept of mobility can form the basis for a research strategy engaging with the evidence on a direct and intimate level. However, this is clouded by an implicit yet seemingly highly standardised view of what the concept stands for. With most accounts emphasising a bird's-eye perspective of an abstract disembodied mobility, I will demonstrate that, in contrast to such typical 'top-down' approaches to the Mesolithic in general, and Mesolithic mobility in particular, a more intimate engagement with the material has the potential of providing us with new insights and a much richer picture of the lives of Mesolithic people. After outlining some practical steps how this can be achieved, I will present a case study from my own research in south-central Ireland. In this contribution I consciously avoid capitalisation of periods, like 'the Mesolithic', to stress that these are modern constructs rather than real entities that existed in the past (Zvelebil 1998, 23-26). As de-capitalised adjectives, the terms are simply employed to delimit chronological episodes rather than objectifiable and distinct entities, as would be suggested by proper nouns.

Keywords: movement, mobility, bottom-up perspective, Ireland, river fords, social practice.

Introduction

> 'It is important that we learn to recognise the various forms of mobility archaeologically, because the ways people move exert strong influences on their culture and society.' (Kelly 1992, 43)

Despite a widespread acceptance of the archaeological importance of people's movements there appear to be two central problems impeding our understanding of mobility in mesolithic Europe. Firstly, the lack of a clear and common definition of what we mean when we discuss mobility in a mesolithic context and secondly, a difficulty in moving beyond 'speculative interpretation' and towards providing 'hard evidence' for people's mobile lifestyles (Wickham-Jones 2005, 30). I will aim to deal with these two issues in turn through briefly reflecting on how we could or should define mesolithic mobility on one hand, followed by a practical case study of how we can utilise a body of evidence made up entirely of lithics to discuss people's past movements. In fact I would like to go one step further and not only utilise the lithic evidence to discuss people's movements but employ the concept of mobility as a basis for a research strategy to explore mesolithic daily and social lives more generally.

Many mesolithics – many mobilities

> 'We measure movement not by considering the processes involved: the following of tracks and trails, the paths and routeways, but like the wind, by its effects on other things.' (Finlay 2004, 3)

Mobility has been a central consideration in hunter-gatherer and mesolithic studies at least since the 'Man the Hunter' conference in 1965 (Lee and DeVore 1968). However, actual definitions of what we mean by mobility are hard to come by. The problem that 'everyone works to their own (often not clearly articulated) ideas of what mobility involves' has been identified by Caroline Wickham-Jones in the abstract for the conference session at which this paper was first presented. This has led to 'gross inconsistencies [...] in the interpretation of the word "mobile" by those working on mesolithic material in different places' (Wickham-Jones 2005, 31). Therefore, if our aim is to revive the debate about mesolithic mobility it would seem sensible to first of all make explicit and define what we understand by it.

A common way of defining mobility in archaeology is to oppose it with sedentism; hence mobile groups are groups that are not sedentary. The difficulty with this is that we would have to first specify who qualifies as either sedentary or non-sedentary. Moreover, if we concur with Kelly (Kelly 1992, 60) that in fact '[n]o society is sedentary, not even our own industrial one – people simply move in different ways', we must question the helpfulness of such a black and white dichotomy (Varien 1999, 194; Eder 1984). Attempting to delineate archaeological concepts by what they are not, echoes previous generations of prehistorians who defined mesolithic as being neither palaeolithic nor neolithic (e.g. Macalister 1928, 8; Clark 1932; Rowley-Conwy 1996, 944), and it took several decades thereafter until scholars across Europe could agree even on a working definition. Therefore, if we consider mobility a useful concept, we would probably be better advised to be more concrete and imaginative and aim to define this concept in its own right.

Another common way of discussing mobility in early prehistory is to consider it as a function of people's subsistence practices. We correlate economic activities, which people are deemed to have engaged in – so as to most efficiently exploit their 'resource base' – with 'mobility patterns'. Based on perceived mobility patterns we describe groups as foragers or collectors who engaged in direct, logistical or embedded procurement strategies (e.g. Binford 1980). This approach to mobility confines itself to rather clinical and abstract grand narratives and large-scale models steering well clear of the messy, intimate and intricate detail of how and why people moved and what their journeys were like. Instead of the paths and tracks people travelled along, the tedious and seemingly endless trek or the easy stroll, we think of lines and arrows across maps. Yet all too often when discussing people adhering to one or another mobility template we tend to forget to consider what this actually means with regard to their movements. In short, such 'top-down' models have little potential to enhance our understanding of people's actual movements through the land. They abstract them from real, experienced and lived practices into two-dimensional representations on paper, with little regard for the physical and social activities underlying them. 'Geometries of abstract space will not help us to understand the ways that people move around, perceive and engage with their surroundings' (Hind 2004, 39). Just as the above models distort the complexity of people's movements spatially, concepts such as the 'seasonal round' confuse 'different temporal scales, conflating a number of diachronic episodes into an overarching, cyclical long-term temporality' (Conneller 2005, 53). Despite most of us regularly employing these concepts and abstractions, a review of the literature on hunter-gather and early prehistoric mobility – frequently asking 'how far, in what direction, how often and even why' – would suggest that it is in fact people's actual movements we are interested in (Close 2000, 50).

If this is the case it is somewhat curious that our discussions of the topic have predominantly remained abstract and have failed to engage directly with the physical processes involved when people move through the land. Given the 'baggage' attached to the term 'mobility', and the difficulty in finding an agreed definition (Wickham-Jones 2005, 31; see also above), it may be useful to replace it with the, perhaps, less laden and more clear-cut 'human movement'. Movement forces us to confront the very issues that mobility has, for the largest part, enabled us to ignore – the paths people take and the physical, emotional and social implication of travel. By refocusing the archaeological lens in this way the seasonal round becomes a sequence of journeys and sojourns. Every journey turns into a collection of movements along paths, tracks and trails, undertaken and experienced by real people. Every 'path reappears close up as an array of minor paths, so that movement along them seems more capillary than arterial' (Ingold 1986, 153).

Having cleared the path to do so I will now begin with reflecting on the potential that such a direct engagement, in the form of an intimate 'bottom-up' perspective of human movement, holds for mesolithic research. Moreover, I will argue that as a basis for a research strategy movement can actually enable us to study the often quite limited, low-key evidence for mesolithic activities in novel and exciting ways. A mobile perspective may therefore help us address some of the most common difficulties in our work and turn perceived shortcomings in our available dataset into hard evidence.

Movement as a research strategy

> 'Routines are the stuff of life: innumerable, repeated actions, which time after time keep the world in existence.' [...] 'They may be both generated by and in their turn help to generate culturally specific principles and worldviews.' (Whittle 2003, 22)

Movement certainly qualifies as one such routine, in fact it could be described as one of the most common and habitual human practices. If in turn routine activities are closely linked not only to economic pursuits but also to people's worldviews, achieving an understanding of people's movements in the past should grant us insight into some of the very core aspects of their everyday lives, comprising the whole spectrum of their social, economic and spiritual activities. But how can we study people's movements in mesolithic times given an oftentimes very limited data set? In many cases, as here in Ireland, the available evidence comprises almost exclusively pieces of worked stone. Judging by the narrow focus of interpretation manifest in the literature, heavily biased towards the functional domain, it would seem that this limited and inconspicuous body of evidence equally restricts the potential for variety in our interpretations. However, this need not be the case. Lithics – which we have seen form the main source of our evidence – could be described as being generally highly mobile by their very nature. Their size, shape and life history often suggest that people designed them to be moved around and to carry them along on their journeys. Thus we could view lithics in the archaeological record as indicators for people's movements in the past. This view is admittedly somewhat simplistic as there is equally evidence for lithics not being moved. Nonetheless, the essential point is that there clearly exists a relationship between the movements of lithic artefacts and those of people. The study of these movements can thus form the basis for a research strategy allowing us, on one hand, to accommodate the rather limited and low-key body of data available to us, and, on the other, to interpret this material in a novel and imaginative way. We shall now briefly explore how this could work in practice.

Making lithics move – from small stones to a methodology

In mesolithic archaeology we often find most attention being focused on well-studied 'sites', generally in the form of extensive area excavations. These are then further categorised according to site types such as 'stone working areas', 'kill sites' or 'butchery camps'. Such a treatment of the evidence conveys the image of the landscape as being made up of a patchwork of more or less discrete and isolated clusters 'enclosed and demarcated by artefacts [...] and human activity within it thus becomes conceptualised as a mosaic of disjointed, functionally specific, artificially bounded segments' (Conneller 2000, 145). But if we think about people moving through the land as they make, obtain, otherwise use and dispose of lithics – as part of their day-to-day routine activities – it becomes obvious that not every location at which such artefacts are found can qualify as a 'site', showing evidence for intensive or prolonged activity. This insight corresponds rather well with the record for mesolithic activity in many areas. That is, large numbers of locations producing single object finds and low-density scatters, compared to only a small proportion which could be described as elaborate sites. It is important not to dismiss the lower density finds as 'background scatter' but to recognise that they are equally significant and have the potential to reveal much about people's engagements, and movements within the land. Consequently we must ask how we can study such finds in a meaningful manner.

The key to answering this question lies in a successful combination of the lithic and spatial dimension of the material. Put differently our study of the artefacts is made meaningful through repositioning them in the landscape within the context of the social activities and collective rhythms that brought them into being (Bourdieu 1977, 162–3). Practically this is achieved by way of bringing together the results of lithic analysis, on one hand, and landscape surveys on the other, through 'exploding artefacts back out to their relationships across the landscape' (Warren 2006, 20). This approach enables us to integrate and consider evidence from several intersecting spatial scales, but, critically, commencing from the smallest – the individual artefact and its find location. Starting out from this intimate scale, investigation can work up towards a bigger picture of people's movements and activities within the landscape. Such a 'bottom-up' approach to the data set contrasts markedly with the more typical 'top-down' approaches to early prehistoric mobility, such as those that we considered above. Others (Bamforth, this volume) advocate an alternative, although complementary, viewpoint of a 'bottom-up' approach to mesolithic mobility, focusing on an Americanist perspective. Having sketched out the theoretical and methodological considerations of the approach suggested here we can now move towards examining the steps outlined in practice, based on a study of early prehistoric remains in the middle Barrow Valley of south-central Ireland.

Movement in the middle Barrow Valley – a case study

The River Barrow with a total length of about 195km – from its source in the Slieve Bloom Mountains, County Laois, to its estuary at Waterford harbour – is Ireland's second longest river, after the Shannon, and drains a catchment of over 3000km^2 (Lucey 1998, 102). Throughout history and until quite recently the river has served as one of the main north-south communication routes for the southern half of Ireland, linking the midlands to the sea (Lucey 1998, 100; Fewer 1997, 1; O'Sullivan 2001). Archaeological evidence would lead us to suggest that this may also have been the case for large parts of prehistory (O'Donovan 1994). The study area focuses on the middle reaches of the Barrow, from just north of Monasterevin, County Kildare, to the Burrin Valley south of Carlow town. This area of approximately 675km^2 comprises parts of counties Kildare,

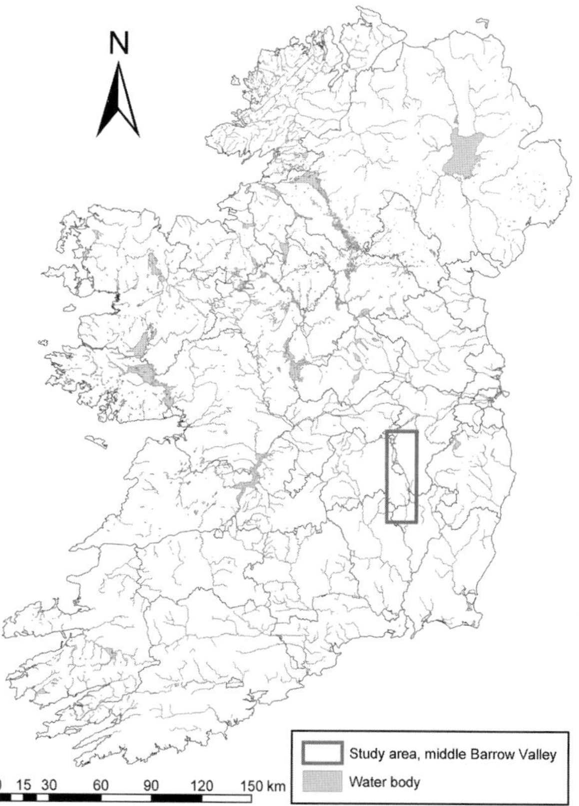

Figure 12.1. Location of the study area in the middle Barrow Valley.

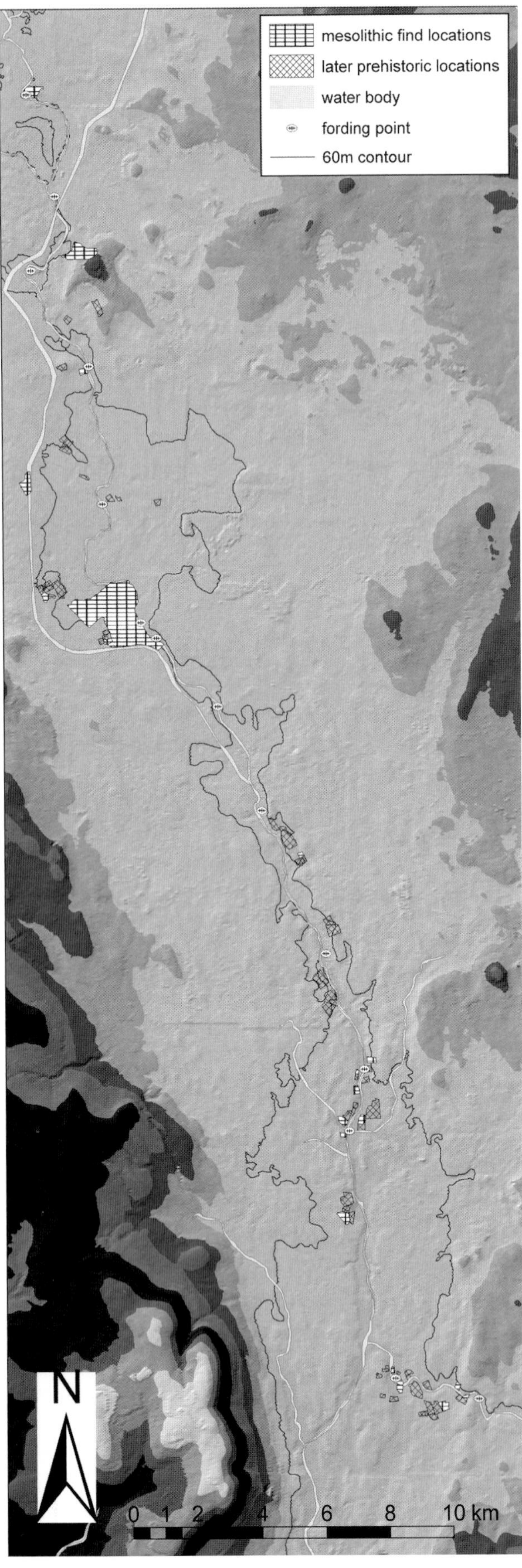

Figure 12.2. Study area showing mesolithic and later prehistoric find locations and fording points in the River Barrow.

Laois and Carlow (Figures 12.1 and 12.2). Although the chipped stone assemblage from the area is rather small, with only 803 known objects, it represents the greatest concentration of early prehistoric artefacts in Ireland's south-central region. This fact can be largely attributed to a programme of systematic field surveys carried out in the area between 1990 and 1992 by the Ballylough Archaeological Project (BLAP), under the direction of Marek Zvelebil and Peter Ramsden (Ramsden *et al.* 1995; Zvelebil *et al.* 1996). Thirty-nine of the 803 artefacts could be identified as diagnostic mesolithc pieces with six dating to the early (*c.* 8000–7000 BC), and 33 to the later parts of the period (*c.* 7000–4000 BC). A recent discussion on the dating of Irish mesolithic material can be found in Costa *et al.* (2005).

The 39 mesolithic objects can be further divided into 28 chert (26 later and two early), 10 flint objects (six later and four early), and one later mesolithic rhyolite flake. Chert, which forms not only the majority of mesolithic artefacts but also the largest component of the Barrow assemblage overall (i.e. 51.4%), can be found naturally cropping out of the Carboniferous limestone west of the study area, as well as in glacial drift deposited throughout the valley (Feehan 1983, 26–7, 95). The quality of this material varies strongly and this is reflected in the varying character of chert artefacts in the assemblage. Flint also occurs in the form of small riverine and glacial drift pebbles throughout the Barrow Valley, albeit rather infrequently. Most of the 186 flint objects within the Barrow assemblage (representing 23.2%) could well have been derived from such local pebbles. However, as I will explain in greater detail below, not all the flint objects within the collection appear to be from this source. There are smaller amounts of several other stone types in the assemblage, such as mudstone, shale, quartzite and sandstone, all of which could have theoretically been derived from sources nearby. The only other material which does not appear to be of local origin is the later mesolithic rhyolite flake, which was found at Clogheen, Co. Kildare (Rynne 1983/1984). I have discussed the significance of this object in relation to people's movements in greater detail elsewhere (Kador 2007, 37–40).

In short, the mesolithic assemblage from the middle Barrow Valley, as well as the Barrow assemblage generally, is dominated by materials that probably could have been obtained within a day's walk from any of the find locations in the area. This is certainly the case for the cherts and most of the other stones. While most of the flint objects within the overall assemblage would equally seem to have been knapped on locally available pebbles, a small proportion of flints, and in particular the diagnostic later mesolithic ones, appear to be of a different character, in terms of size and appearance, and thus stem perhaps from a different source (Figure 12.3). This has already been identified by Zvelebil *et al.* (1996, 23), who suggested that 'the larger tools, usually made from a flint of better quality, were imports form outside the region'. This difference is best borne out by a comparison of the size of the objects. The average

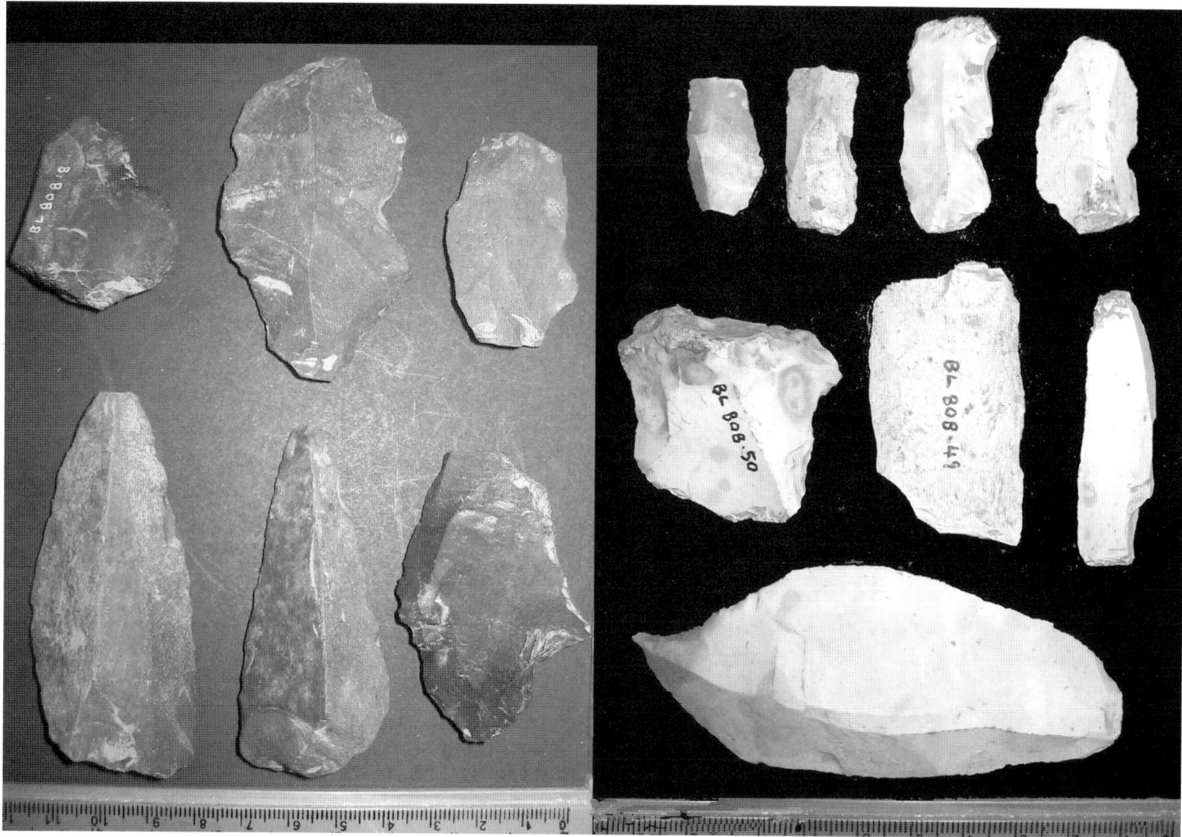

Figure 12.3. Different character of materials within the Barrow assemblage: chert objects (left), flint objects (right), and Later Mesolithic, butt-trimmed, flint blade (bottom right).

length of flints across the entire assemblage is 34.2mm, whereas the diagnostic later mesolithic flint flakes and blades are on average 66.7mm long. The latter would thus seem to be too large, as well as too superior in quality, to have been made from the local riverine and drift pebbles – which rarely exceed 50mm in length – and may have reached the Barrow Valley from much greater distance. In fact the nearest conceivable place of origin for nodular flint of an adequate size and quality would seem to be along the north Leinster, or even the east Ulster coast – that is at a distance of between 100 and 200km north-east.

If we are interested in people's movements then we must wonder how the objects travelled this distance, what type of journeys were involved, and who the people were who embarked on them. I am not suggesting, however, that these objects were brought into the region from the north-east as part of a deliberate effort to do so. While this is one possibility, there are several others that are equally valid, yet, critically, each of them would have involved some degree of human movement, even though at different scales.

If we now turn to the locations within the middle Barrow region where the mesolithic objects were found we will immediately observe a correlation between the positions of these finds and a number of outcropping rock banks within the river bed. These locations would have served as natural crossing points or fords and some of them were visible as banks and islands jutting out of the river until its drainage in the 1930s (Figure 12.2). This relationship between the distribution of mesolithic material, the river in general and fording points in particular, serves as a reminder of the significance of river systems to people's movements during early prehistory. It emphasises not only movements up and down the river, be they on the water or along its banks (Spikins 1996, 88), but also highlights the importance of suitable crossing points. What is particularly interesting is the fact that the large later mesolithic flint flakes and blades, alluded to above, have only been encountered in two areas within the Valley. In both these cases the artefacts have been found in fields located in close proximity to multiple crossing points, as well as junctions between the Barrow and some its most important tributaries within the area.

If the association of mesolithic object finds with fording points of the river makes reference to people's movements then the connection between mesolithic activity and people's movements is doubly emphasised at these locations where fords coincide with major confluences. Such locations clearly indicate the importance of movements along the Barrow and its tributaries, as well as across them. In an area such as the middle Barrow Valley, with relatively few striking natural landmarks, where in many places 'the horizon is free of hills or any charismatic landscape features' (Clements 2005, 251), such locations could have represented welcome focal points. They would have been easily named and identified and could have served as ideal locales for meetings and gatherings, perhaps bringing together people from areas quite far apart. The large later mesolithic flint objects exclusively found at these locations, emphasising both movement and congregation, could perhaps have epitomised tokens for contacts and connectedness with people and places elsewhere, in particular places and communities in those areas along the east coast, where the flints had originated. These associations gave the objects special meaning and value. In turn this high regard for them may have found expression in their being left or deposited at locations that referenced these contacts.

'Each place is part of a network that connects places together in a chain, and the links on either side depend for their connection on the one in the middle' (Morphy 1995, 186). These are places right in the centre of one of Ireland's largest river systems, draining an enormous catchment and connecting the southern, the northern parts of the country and the midlands (Lucey 1998, 99). They are ideal locations to bring people from different areas together. Such places could have represented locales where social ties were forged and renewed, where people came together and exchanged not only materials and objects, but also news, gossip, and possibly partners.

Although the stone artefacts and their relation to the surrounding landscape are the only direct archaeological evidence we have to support this interpretation, ethnographic examples may help us further to substantiate them. For example, '[t]he junction of the Liard and Mackenzie Rivers has always been important in the spiritual life of the Dene [of British Columbia]. This meeting place became a focus for the fur trade in the Deh Cho region. [...] Prior to European contact, people would gather here to renew friendships after the long winter months apart' (Legislative Assembly of the Northwest Territories). The eighteenth-century explorer Samuel Hearne reports of such gatherings: 'By the end of July, as more Dene arrived in the area, Hearne found himself encamped among seventy tents and six hundred people. Such regional gatherings occurred annually at fixed locations, usually beside a lake or a river [...]. They offered the men a chance to mingle, gamble and, above all, to take wives from among the women of other bands' (McGoogan 2003, 114). Equally, the seasonal and annual movements of the Easern Khanty of western Siberia are closely aligned to the Maly Iugan River System. Traditionally their base camps, or *yurts*, were invariably situated at culturally defined positions along the river (Jordan 2003, 40–6, 71–5). 'As summer approached households moved away from this yurt [at the river's edge] to smaller fishing camps, some of which were located on smaller tributary rivers.' Once a year families gathered at annual trade fairs. There they paid the yearly fur tax (*yasak*) but these gatherings were 'also an opportunity to trade furs for flour, salt, ammunition, etc.' (Zvelebil and Jordan 1999, 106).

These examples illustrate how the movements and social interactions of traditional small-scale communities can often be structured around locales of special significance situated at the banks of a river, and how river junctions served as nodes for meetings and gatherings as well as points of departure for movement along tributaries. Furthermore, ethnographic observations such as these allow us to enliven our lifeless archaeological data sets with colourful impressions of people's day-to-day interactions, and may thus inspire us equally to liven up our often monotonous interpretations.

Conclusions

In the course of this paper I hope to have demonstrated a way of studying human movement in early prehistory, even in cases where our evidence constitutes little other than lithic artefacts largely without stratigraphic association. Moreover, we can actually employ mobility as a means to bring us closer to people's everyday activities and relationships. I have argued that to achieve this it may be helpful to substitute our abstract conception of mesolithic mobility – represented in top-down generic models – with a more intimate understanding of people's movements, as they are performed and experienced on a human level. Based on such a perspective we can translate our direct engagements with the evidence, both material and landscape, into inferences about people's most intimate life spheres, and starting from there gradually build our narratives, quite literally, from the ground up. On the one hand mesolithic archaeologists have always been ambitious – hoping to answer questions about past 'macroeconomics' and social organisation, the adoption of new technologies and the arrival of new ideas – yet on the other, we have displayed an intrinsic pessimism when it comes to our ability to make concrete statements about people's social lives, beyond the strictly functional. In contrast to this, I would contend that 'starting small', from a personal and direct engagement with the small-scale remains, reflecting the rhythms and processes that structured the minutiae of people's daily lives, will gradually allow us to recognise wider social and economic changes and developments as they impacted upon people on the ground.

Acknowledgements

I would like to express my thanks to the Irish Research Council for the Humanities and Social Sciences (IRCHSS) and the UCD Humanities Institute of Ireland (HII) for supporting my research. Furthermore I am also grateful to Professor Marek Zvelebil for his helpfulness and assistance in relation to the material from the Ballylough Archaeological Project, Professor Peter Woodman for comments in relations to some of the points I make in this contribution, and Graeme Warren for his general support and encouragement. Thanks must also go to Mel Giles and Dan Hind for their support of my work with the Ballylough collections in Sheffield, and, finally, to Sinéad McCartan for her work in organising the MESO 2005 conference and Caroline Wickam-Jones for chairing the mobility session.

References

Binford, L. R. 1980. Willow smoke and dogs' tails: hunter-gatherer settlement systems and archaeological site formation. *American Antiquity* 45, 4–20.

Bourdieu, P. 1977. *An Outline of a Theory of Practice*. Cambridge, Cambridge University Press.

Clark, J. G. D. 1932. *The Mesolithic Age in Britain*. Cambridge, Cambridge University Press.

Clements, P. 2005. *The Height of Nonsense: a ramble around the highest places in 'Oulde' Ireland*. Dublin, Collins Press.

Close, A. E. 2000. Reconstructing Movement in Prehistory. *Journal of Archaeological Method and Theory* 7, 49–77.

Conneller, C. 2000. Fragmented Space? Hunter-gatherer landscapes of the Vale of Pickering. *Archaeological Review from Cambridge* 17, 139–50.

Conneller, C. 2005. Moving beyond sites: Mesolithic technology in the landscape, in N. Milner and P. C. Woodman (eds.), *Mesolithic Studies at the Beginning of the 21st Century*, 42–55. Oxford, Oxbow Books.

Costa, L.-J., Sternke, F. and Woodman, P. C. 2005. Microlith to macrolith: the reasons behind the transformation of production in the Irish Mesolithic. *Antiquity* 79, 19–33.

Eder, J. F. 1984. The impact of subsistence change on mobility and settlement pattern in a tropical forest foraging economy: some implications for archaeology. *American Anthropologist* 86, 837–53.

Feehan, J. 1983. *Laois: an environmental history*. Stradbally, Co. Laois, Ballykilcavan Press.

Fewer, M. 1997. *Irish Waterside Walks*. Dublin, Gill and MacMillan.

Finlay, N. 2004. E-scapes and E-motion: other ways of writing the Mesolithic. *Before Farming* 2004 (1), 1–9.

Hind, D. 2004. Where many paths meet: towards and integrated theory of landscape and technology, in A. M. Chadwick (ed.), *Stories from the Landscape: archaeologies of inhabitation*, 35–51. British Archaeological Reports, International Series S1238. Oxford, Archaeopress.

Ingold, T. 1986. *The Appropriation of Nature: essays on human ecology and social relations*. Manchester, Manchester University Press.

Jordan, P. D. 2003. *Material Culture and Sacred Landscape: the anthropology of the Siberian Khanty*. Lanham, MA, AltaMira Press.

Kador, T. 2007. Stone Age motion pictures: an object's perspective from early prehistoric Ireland, in R. Johnston and V. Cummings (eds.), *Prehistoric Journeys*, 33–44. Oxford, Oxbow Books.

Kelly, R. L. 1992. Mobility/Sedentism: Concepts, Archaeological measures and effects. *Annual review of Anthropology* 21, 43–66.

Lee, R. B. and DeVore, I. (eds.) 1968. *Man The Hunter*. Chicago, Aldine.

Legislative Assembly of the Northwest Territories. http://www.assembly.gov.nt.ca/ (accessed: 01/10/2005).

Lucey, J. 1998. The Barrow, the Nore and the Suir, in C. Moriarty (ed.), *Studies of Irish Rivers and Lakes*, 99–117. Dublin, Marine Institute.

Macalister, R. A. S. 1928. *The Archaeology of Ireland*. London, Methuen.

McGoogan, K. 2003. *Ancient Mariner: The Amazing Adventures of Samuel Hearne the Sailor Who Walked to the Arctic Ocean*. Toronto, Harper Flamingo.

Morphy, H. 1995. Landscape and Reproduction of the Ancestral Past, in E. Hirsch and M. O'Hanlon (eds.), *The Anthropology of Landscape: Perspectives on Place and Space*, 185–209. Oxford, Clarendon Press.

O'Donovan, E. 1994. *The finds from the river Barrow and its tributaries*. Unpublished MA thesis, Department of Archaeology, University College Dublin.

O'Sullivan, T. F. 2001. *Goodly Barrow: a voyage on an Irish river*. Dublin, Townhouse.

Ramsden, P., Zvelebil, M., Macklin, M. G. and Passmore, D. G. 1995. Stone Age Settlement in Southeastern Ireland. *Current Anthropology* 36, 330–2.

Rowley-Conwy, P. A. 1996. Why didn't Westropp's 'Mesolithic' catch on in 1872? *Antiquity* 70, 940–4.

Rynne, E. 1983/4. An Antrim Bann flake from near Monasterevin. *Journal of the Kildare Archaeological Society* 16, 328–30.

Spikins, P. 1996. Rivers, Boundaries and Change: a hypothesis of challenging settlement patterns in the Mesolithic of Northern England, in T. Pollard and A. Morrison (eds.), *The early prehistory of Scotland*, 89–107. Edinburgh, University of Edinburgh Press.

Varien, M. D. 1999. *Sedentism and mobility in a social landscape: mesa Verde and beyond*. Tucson, University of Arizona Press.

Warren, G. M. 2006. Technology, in C. J. Conneller and G. M. Warren (eds.), *Mesolithic Britain and Ireland*, 13–34. Stroud, Tempus.

Wickham-Jones, C. R. 2005. Summer Walkers? Mobility and the Mesolithic, in N. Milner and P. C. Woodman (eds.), *Mesolithic Studies at the Beginning of the 21st Century*, 30–41. Oxford, Oxbow Books.

Whittle, A. 2003. *The Archaeology of People: Dimensions of Neolithic Life*. London, Routledge.

Zvelebil, M. 1998. What's in a name? The Mesolithic, the Neolithic and social change at the Mesolithic-Neolithic transition, in M. R. Edmonds and C. Richards (eds.), *Understanding the Neolithic of North-Western Europe*, 1–35. Glasgow, Cruithne Press.

Zvelebil, M. and Jordan, P. D. 1999. Hunter Fisher Gatherer Ritual Landscapes: Questions of Time, Space, and Presentation, in J. Goldhahn (ed.), *Rock Art as Social Representation: papers from a session held at the European Association of Archaeologists Fourth Annual Meeting in Göteborg 1998*, 101–27. British Archaeological Reports, International Series S794. Oxford, Archaeopress.

Zvelebil, M., Macklin, M. G., Passmore, D. G. and Ramsden, P. 1996. Alluvial archaeology in the Barrow Valley, Southeast Ireland: The 'River Ford' Culture re-visited. *Journal of Irish Archaeology* 7, 13–40.

13. Top-down or bottom-up?: Americanist approaches to the study of hunter-gatherer mobility

Douglas B. Bamforth

American archaeologists have made the concept of mobility central to our understanding of hunter-gatherers at least since the mid-twentieth century. However, they have approached mobility from at least two distinct perspectives. The first of these – a 'holistic' perspective – tends to view hunter-gatherer lifeways as tightly bundled packets of characteristics. This has fostered a 'top-down' approach to the archaeological record, in which models of the organization of these bundles are taken as a basis for understanding the past: in essence, this perspective argues that seeing one component of the bundle implies the presence of the other components. In contrast, a second perspective views hunter-gatherer lifeways on a 'variable-by-variable' basis, asserting that we do not know enough to predict how the many components of those lifeways are related to one another in specific cases. This fosters a 'bottom-up' approach to archaeology, which attempts to define specific aspects of past human lifeways and to link these to specific aspects of the archaeological record, in order to build up a view of the past. This paper argues that the latter perspective better reflects what we know about hunters and gatherers, and illustrates this approach with a North American case.

Keywords: hunters and gatherers, lifeways, mobility, Paleoindian.

Introduction

Americanist archaeological research on hunters and gatherers has focused extensively – one might almost say obsessively – on mobility strategies since the 1970s. This research has yet to provide a complete guide to understanding these strategies, but it does provide important lessons about how mobility patterns vary and about how to consider and study them. Mobility research is diverse, but I argue here that there are two relatively distinct streams of thought within this diversity, streams that have important implications for conceptualizing and explaining hunter-gatherer mobility and for examining such mobility in the archaeological record. On one hand, a perspective with a relatively long history in the field tends to view mobility patterns as tightly and more or less deterministically linked to many, and perhaps most, of the other components of hunter-gatherer ways of life. On the other, a perspective that has its roots in this work and that has more recently merged with the formal models of behavioral ecology views these patterns as composed of sets of quasi-independent variables whose interrelations are complex, poorly known, and in need of both theoretical and empirical evaluation.

I will refer to the first of these perspectives as a 'holistic' view that sees mobility patterns essentially as packages that vary along a limited number of dimensions. This view, in turn, has driven a 'top-down' approach to archaeological research, in which identifying any part of a package makes it possible to infer the other parts more or less automatically. I will refer to the second of these perspectives as a 'variable-by-variable' view that, in contrast, sees mobility patterns as varying along many potentially uncorrelated dimensions. I will argue that this view leads to a 'bottom-up' approach, in which archaeologists attempt to link specific aspects of the archaeological record with specific behavioral variables without assuming *a priori* the relations among those variables. I will suggest that this second approach offers a better fit for the complexity of the real world than does the alternative.

Holistic views of hunter-gatherers

One of the core efforts of American anthropology during the mid-twentieth century was the explicit development of organized ways of thinking about the range of variation in human lifeways on a global basis. Among the major outcomes of this development were stage classifications of cultures, particularly Service's (1971) band-tribe-chiefdom-state classification. Service defined each of these stages on the basis of different sets of interrelated characteristics, placing hunter-gatherers into his 'band' level of organization. In Service's view, bands are mobile, have small residence groups with flexible membership, low overall population densities, a social order based on egalitarian relations woven together by kinship, simple technology, an economy based on generalized reciprocity, and a largely vegetarian diet (Service 1966). By the late 1960's, Lee's work with the Kalahari Bushmen (Lee 1968) had highlighted this general kind of lifeway and its close links to the natural environment and Sahlins (1968) had idealized it as 'the original affluent society'. Kelly (1995, 15) refers to the Service/Lee/Sahlins view of hunters and gatherers as the 'generalized foraging model'. Periodic movement from place to place – that is, mobility – lies at the heart of both Service's view of band societies and the generalized foraging model, and such movement is clearly a critical part of the ways of life of the desert and arctic groups who structured anthropological views of hunter-gatherer societies for most of the twentieth century.

These views dominated archaeological understanding of hunters and gatherers until Binford's (1980) publication of the 'forager-collector' continuum provided a more general theoretical account of variation in hunter-gatherer mobility that included something like a universally applicable set of concepts and archaeological implications. Although Binford explicitly argued that mobility patterns varied on a continuum, the bulk of his discussion, and virtually all applications of his ideas, focused on a dichotomy between the two ends of this continuum (a dichotomy that Binford himself continues to refer to today; Binford 2001). At one end, *forager* societies move entire social groups from resource locale to resource locale (a pattern referred to as 'residential mobility'). In contrast, at the other end, *collector* societies use special task groups to move relatively distant resources to a larger social group (a pattern referred to as 'logistical mobility').

The forager-collector continuum almost instantly became the central organizing concept of Americanist hunter-gatherer archaeology, at least partly because of the elegance and breathtaking scope of Binford's arguments. Binford grounded the forager/collector distinction in ethnographic data on modern hunter-gatherers, and explained this distinction in terms of the distribution of resources within a local environment. He then arrayed additional ethnographic information to argue for at least some of the proposed correlates of the continuum, and pointed out (in part on the basis of his own ethnoarchaeological observations) that residentially and logistically mobile ways of life produce distinct and archaeologically visible signatures on the landscape. His argument thus ranged in a coherent, integrated way from explanatory human ecology to relatively concrete archaeological expectation.

The forager-collector continuum fairly clearly reflects the general intellectual tradition exemplified by Service's stage approach, both in its emphasis, intended or not, on categories of mobility strategies and in the assertions by Binford and others that identifying a group as foragers or collectors made it possible to predict many other aspects of that group's way of life. Collectors have been said to store food while foragers did not, and collectors relied on 'curated' technology, foragers on 'expedient' technology. Large-scale communal hunting has been taken as a hallmark of collectors, while foragers are seen as relying on small-scale encounter hunting. Collectors have been asserted to move less often and over shorter distances, to live in larger social groups, and even, in an unpublished paper, to experience the flow of time in a qualitatively different way than foragers (Amick 1984; Binford 1980; 2001; Kelly and Todd 1988; Torrence, no date).

In my terms, this is a classically holistic view, and it fostered what I refer to here as a top-down approach to hunter-gatherer archaeology. Most prominently, for example, many studies have asserted that identifying 'curated' technological strategies made it possible to infer many important aspects of hunter-gatherer ways of life (i.e. Binford 1979): if we know how they made and used stone tools, we know how they moved across the landscape. As popular and important as the forager-collector continuum has been, though, it illustrates the significant problems with both holistic views of human variation and top-down approaches to archaeological studies of that variation.

The most important of these is the near total absence of evidence supporting the supposed linkages between Binford's continuum of mobility and any of the other things hunter-gatherers do. Cross-cultural data indicate that groups who can be clearly identified as relying primarily on residential mobility (foragers) or logistical mobility (collectors) do not differ predictably on most of the proposed correlates of the continuum, including reliance on food storage and on large-scale communal hunting, frequency of residential movement, and others (Bamforth (1997) discusses this in detail). Furthermore, Binford's arguments linking technology and mobility are self-contradictory: he simultaneously asserts that curated technological strategies, said to characterize collectors but not foragers, are responses to high mobility, which he claims characterizes foragers but not collectors (compare Binford 1979; 1980; also see Parry and Kelly 1987). Similar problems arise in other work linked to this stream of thought; for example, Torrence (1983) and Shott (1986) analyzed much the same set of data on ethnographic hunter-gatherer technology – derived largely from Oswalt (1976). However, where Torrence notes correctly that complex tools in this dataset are highly specialized, generally to ensure successful hunting of marine mammals, Shott claims that such tools are designed to be general-purpose tools in response to highly mobile ways of life. Arguments like these also tend to ignore the many forces that interact to structure any specific technological stance, and are directly contradicted by information on the technology of some of the groups that Binford himself discusses (Bamforth 1986; 1991; Bamforth and Bleed 1997).

Closely examining the definition of the forager-collector continuum highlights an additional problem. Binford defines this continuum in terms of what he describes as a single axis of variation from logistically organized groups who store food, to residentially mobile groups who do not. However, ethnographic data indicate that food storage is not inextricably linked to logistical organization (Bamforth

1997); these are separate dimensions of variation in hunter-gatherer lifeways. Similarly, virtually all hunter-gatherer societies rely to some extent on *both* residential and logistical mobility (see, for example, Kelly's data (1983; 1995)), indicating that these are best treated as potentially independent dimensions as well. The forager-collector continuum is thus not one continuum, but at least three, and knowing where a given society falls on one of these does not necessarily tell us where it falls on the other two.

There is no doubt that the holistic/top-down approach to mobility that dominated Americanist hunter-gatherer archaeology for much of the late twentieth century opened our eyes to important aspects of ancient lifeways. However, there is also no doubt that the details of this approach are incapable of coping both with known patterns of variation in hunter-gatherer use of the landscape and with the problem of studying these patterns using archaeological data. In particular, it is clear that the many variables that have either been used to define the continuum or linked to it do not vary together in the ways they have been asserted to vary together. The world of hunters and gatherers is (and was) more complex, and more complexly determined, than much of the research from the 1980s and early 1990s that was grounded in the forager-collector continuum would have it be. However, a second approach to mobility studies that began to develop in the 1970s and 1980s builds on and integrates many of the important insights of Binford's work and helps to evade these problems.

Variable-by-variable views of hunter-gatherers

The observation that there appear to be no simple deterministic relations among the many aspects of hunter-gatherer lifeways that we would like to understand suggests that, instead of bundling these aspects together, we might do well to consider them individually. I refer to work that does this as grounded in a 'variable-by-variable' perspective, and I argue that such a perspective leads to a 'bottom-up' approach to archaeological analysis. Two papers from the 1980s – Kelly's (1983) almost universally cited analysis of ethnographic data on several aspects of hunter-gatherer mobility and Chatters' (1987) almost universally ignored discussion of the archaeology of mobility – lay the basis for this second perspective.

Rather than focusing on Binford's continuum, Kelly (1983) defined five specific aspects of hunter-gatherer movements and winnowed data on them from the ethnographic literature. These variables include number of residential moves per year, average distance traveled per move, total distance moved per year, the size of the area covered over the course of a year, and average distance of logistical movements. He then considered the linkages between these variables and very general measures of diet and of environmental characteristics. In a more recent reexamination of these data, Kelly (1995, 111–60) discusses these linkages in the context of the optimization perspective of behavioral ecology (cf. Smith and Winterhalder 1992; Winterhalder and Smith 1981). Binford's (2001) recent *magnum opus* takes a similar approach.

Kelly's data document many of the ways in which subsistence patterns and environmental characteristics affect mobility, although they show few or no simple or deterministic effects. However, he does not extend his discussion to consider possible relations among the various aspects of mobility that he considers, and his analyses (like Binford's (2001) more recent study) focus on how single environmental variables correlate with single components of mobility strategies. In addition, while he dissects the concept of mobility into many of its important components, Kelly does not explicitly address the ways in which these components interact to produce the range of known mobility patterns, or for the specific ways in which such patterns can be studied archaeologically. Chatters (1987) outlines a way of approaching these issues.

Chatters (1987, 337–8) specifically argues that hunter-gatherer mobility strategies vary along multiple dimensions and that these dimensions are at least potentially independent of one another. Rather than thinking of mobility patterns as scaled along a single continuum, then, he suggests that we should think of them as 'N-dimensional space(s), or hypervolume(s), with individual cases identifiable as the intersections of the many dimensions' (Chatters 1987, 338). In this view, the many aspects of mobility can combine in many different ways to produce a potentially dizzying array of different ways to move human populations across a landscape. Chatters also identifies six specific components of an overall mobility pattern along which societies can vary: mobility type (residential or logistical), mobility frequency, stability (or repetitiveness) of a mobility pattern, demography (or group size), scheduling (seasonality), and range size. It is worth noting that these overlap with, but do not exactly reproduce, Kelly's variables, a point I return to shortly.

Like Binford, Chatters also argued for specific and archaeologically visible signatures of his variables. Unlike Binford, though, Chatters advocated linkages between specific aspects of mobility and relatively specific lines of archaeological evidence. Thus, in his view, if we want to infer how long a group occupied a particular locality, we need to look at aspects of the archaeological record that measure duration of site occupation, and, if we want to understand how repetitive a particular pattern of land use was, we need to search for evidence on patterns of site reoccupation.

Figure 13.1 presents Chatters' six components of a mobility strategy and his descriptions of the lines of archaeological evidence he links to them. Some of these lines of evidence (for example, site size and house floor area) can be read fairly directly from the archaeological record. Others (for example, technological organization) are complex inferences that are themselves potentially open to variable-by-variable approaches; Chatters' discussion does not offer us a simple recipe that we can take to specific archaeological analyses. However, Chatters' discussion provides an important step towards isolating specific aspects of mobility patterns and lines of archaeological evidence that are clearly and specifically relevant to them, and exemplifies a bottom-up approach to the study of

Variable	Definition	Archaeological measures
Mobility type	residential or logistical	'Assemblage diversity, tendency to cluster as site Types, between-type similarity, anatomic part frequencies, bone fragment size'
Mobility frequency	number of moves/duration of	'Occupancy duration measured through seasonal indicators, refuse amounts and distributions, feature discreteness, FCR [fire-cracked rock] sizes, technological organization'
Settlement pattern	stability or repetitiveness	'Permanance of structures, cemeteries, redundancy of site function'
Demography (group size)	group size and composition	'Site size, floor areas'
Scheduling	seasonality of movements	'Seasonality and demography'
Range	size of area used	'Lithic source distribution'

Figure 13.1. Components of hunter-gatherer mobility strategies and archaeological measures of them. (After Chatters 1987, 339).

mobility, in which we attempt to build an understanding of past ways of life piece by piece. Done systematically, this kind of work can help us to construct an understanding of the ways in which past humans used the landscape that is not constrained either by our knowledge of the range of land use patterns among modern hunters and gatherers or by the limitations on our ability to imagine possible uses of the landscape. In addition, by forcing us to attend specifically and in detail to the links between evidence and inference, a bottom-up approach helps to clarify both what we know and what we do not know.

This approach also highlights the difficulties of studying ancient mobility patterns, difficulties that arise in at least two areas. First, as the differences between Kelly's and Chatter's sets of variables illustrate, it is possible to debate exactly how many variables go into defining a single 'mobility strategy'. For example, neither Kelly's nor Chatters' variable sets focuses on the size of logistical groups moving across the landscape, and neither specifically considers the age or gender composition of these groups. In addition, following Kelly, Chatters' 'mobility type' should probably be broken down into multiple variables pertaining to residential and logistical movements, both of which can vary in frequency, distance, duration, group size, etc.

Second, archaeological indicators of many of these variables are also not always as straightforward as we might like them to be. To take only one example, hunter-gatherer archaeologists often infer range or territory size from the distribution of the sources of stone represented in a tool assemblage. However, Ingbar's (1994) elegant model demonstrates that mobile groups occupying the same territory and exploiting the same set of raw material sources in the same proportions can produce radically different raw material frequencies in a given set of sites by varying the rate at which they expend the material and the rate at which they move from place to place. Ethnoarchaeological studies and other research have given us powerful measures of such variables as duration of site occupation, but variables like the age and gender composition of the groups that produced a particular archaeological assemblage are notoriously resistant to rigorous analysis. Problems like these are difficult to solve, but a bottom-up perspective makes it clear just how important they are.

An example: Paleoindian land use on the North American Great Plains

A brief example illustrates the potential value of a bottom-up approach. Research on the Paleoindian period (11,500 to 6900 cal BC) in North America in general and the North American Great Plains in particular has for decades been intimately linked to archaeological approaches to hunters and gatherers in general, and has been dominated by holistic/top-down conceptual frameworks, including both the generalized forager model and more Binfordian views.

Paleoindian research relying to one degree or another on the first of these was particularly prominent in the late 1960s and 1970s, and is clearest in Hester and Grady's (1977) synthesis of data on the Paleoindian occupation of the Southern High Plains of west Texas and eastern New Mexico (but note that Renfrew and Bahn (2004, 179) explicitly retain much of this perspective). This synthesis begins by presenting the generalized foraging model as a basis for deriving an overall analogy that describes hunters and gatherers world-wide (Hester and Grady 1977, 78–9). It then relies on several lines of evidence to assess whether or not this analogy fits the Southern Plains Paleoindian case. Hester and Grady (1977, 94–5) conclude:

Model component	Archaeological evidence
Low population density (30% of carrying capacity)	none
diet 35% hunted/65% gathered (low work effort)	none
20% species in diet provide 90% of food	none
food shared/little storage	none
hunters male/gatherers female	none
seasonal aggregation and dispersal	style(s) of points in kills
band size 25	number/style of points in kills
dialectical tribe 500	none
territories several hundred to 1000 square miles	regional site distributions; distance to raw material sources
political leadership by prominent hunter	number of knappers suggested by variation in points
exogamous marriage pattern	none
patrilineal/patrilocal bands	none
sex ratio 150 males: 100 females	none

Figure 13.2. Components of the generalized foraging model specified by Hester and Grady (1977, 78–9), and archaeological evidence considered to examine them.

> 'All evidence, while fragmentary and scientifically unverifiable in many instances, supports the general analogy we outlined at the beginning. Band territory is estimated at a radius of 90 to 120 miles. . . . Band size is estimated at six families totaling approximately 25 members of whom 5 to 10 served as hunters. Band leadership was vested in a headman who may have functioned as the tribal armorer or shaman. During large hunts where several hundred bison were killed, two or possibly more bands probably joined forces.'

However, Hester and Grady explicitly argue that Paleoindian society should have had many more attributes of the generalized foraging model than the ones just noted. Figure 13.2 summarizes the full range of the attributes they discuss and the lines of evidence used to examine each, illustrating fairly clearly how few of them were actually considered empirically. In effect, what this argument does is document a limited number of patterns, often anecdotally, that are roughly consistent with some components of the generalized foraging model, and then simply maps the rest of that model onto the past.

Since the late 1980s, however, reconstructions of Paleoindian ways of life on the Plains have drawn more on Binford than on Lee and Sahlins. These reconstructions more or less take Kelly and Todd's (1988) arguments essentially as their unchallenged starting point. These arguments (summarized below) build directly on the holistic/top-down perspective that societies that can be placed on the extremes of the forager-collector continuum show the complexes of deterministically related characteristics that Binford described – for example, foragers move residential sites very often, collectors rely on complex and highly 'curated' technology, etc. Kelly and Todd (1988) go beyond Binford's stereotypes in arguing that Paleoindian archaeology suggests a mix of forager-like and collector-like characteristics, but they do not extend this observation to critique the stereotypes themselves.

Kelly and Todd label Paleoindians as 'high-tech foragers', suggesting most fundamentally that early occupants of North America combined high frequencies of residential moves and limited (or perhaps no) flux in the composition of residential groups with a technically sophisticated and carefully designed flaked stone technology. In Binford's terms, the first of these characteristics would make them foragers and the second would make them collectors. In addition, Kelly and Todd follow Witthoft (1952), MacDonald (1968), and Goodyear (1979, reprinted 1989) in arguing that evidence for long-distance transport of at least some raw material implies that Paleoindian groups moved within much larger territories than more recent groups. They suggest further that the absence of evidence for reuse of large-mammal kill sites on the Plains and incomplete carcass processing at these sites indicate an unpredictable and non-repetitive pattern of movement within these territories, and infer that the technological patterns they see reflect the need to economize raw material, in large part by extending tool use lives, in order to cope with unpredictable access to raw material sources.

There are a number of objections to this perspective, based primarily on significant discrepancies between patterns in the archaeological record. For example, although large bison kills appear to have been carried out at many times of the year, there is a clear concentration of such kills in the cold season, particularly on the north-western Plains of Wyoming, and large and small kills on the Southern Plains show seasonal differences as well as differences in butchery practices (Bement 1999; Frison 1982; McCartney 1990). Patterns of raw material use are far from uniform – many Paleoindian sites show almost no long-distance transport of raw material – and the technological inferences on which the 'high-tech' arguments rest are incompatible with most aspects of what we now know about patterns of Paleoindian stone tool production and use (Bamforth 2002a; 2003; Bamforth and Becker 2000). It is true that the sites used for large bison kills were virtually always used only once, but sites used for other activities (for example, campsites and localities used for small-scale hunting) were often used redundantly for millennia (Bamforth *et al.* 2005).

These conflicts between evidence and inference suggest that archaeological views of Paleoindian use of the Great Plains landscape are ripe for revision. I consider the evidence from one Paleoindian site – the Allen site, a Paleoindian camp in south-western Nebraska that was occupied intermittently from 10,000 to 7000 cal BC – from a bottom-up perspective to illustrate how this might be done. The full analyses of the Allen site material are available elsewhere (Bamforth 2002b; 2003; 2007; Bamforth *et al.* 2005); I simply summarize the results of these studies here. To illustrate how a bottom-up approach might be taken to these data, and also to illustrate how such an approach illuminates both the past that we hope to understand and the limits on that understanding, I focus on four aspects of the mobility pattern represented at the site: the geographic scale of group movement, the frequency of site reuse, the duration of site occupation, and the composition of the groups occupying the site. As my previous discussion indicates, these do not exhaust the topics that matter to the study of mobility strategies, and I choose them because they vary significantly in what we can say about them.

Archaeologists focus on long-distance transport of raw material as evidence that Paleoindian groups moved within extraordinarily large territories. However, well over 99 percent of the Allen site collection (a total of nearly 300 retouched pieces and some 13,000 unmodified flakes) is made from a single variety of stone – Smoky Hill jasper – that outcrops within a kilometre or two of the site, and is otherwise found only within a relatively small region around the site in south-western Nebraska and north-western Kansas. Non-local stone is present in the assemblage (in the form of three projectile points and roughly two dozen flakes), and some of this material comes from sources from 250 to 500 kilometers away; in addition, most of the 11 fragments of grinding stones in the collection also come from fairly distant sources, roughly 200 kilometers distant. However, it is not difficult to account for these exotics by small-scale exchange of high quality (unusually visually attractive) or locally rare but technologically important raw material, or perhaps by the movements of individuals rather than social groups. Furthermore, the frequency of local raw material is as overwhelmingly high in those components of the collection that are most likely to have been carried from place to place across the landscape (hafted tools, tiny bipolar cores, etc.) as it is in the components of the collection that are likely to have been procured and discarded locally. The overwhelming weight of the Allen site data implies that the site's occupants moved within a small area of the Plains.

How did they move within this area? Detailed analysis of the spatial structure of the site (Bamforth *et al.* 2005) indicates that, despite the accumulation of roughly a meter of sediment, trash was deposited in almost the exactly the same areas throughout the 3000 years over which the site was occupied. This suggests strongly that the site was reoccupied at intervals short enough that trash-heaps produced by previous occupations were still visible on the ground surface, and were used by subsequent visitors. The excavated area of the site may not have been occupied every single year, but it was certainly reused very, very frequently for a very long time. Combined with the absence of long-distance raw material transport, this strongly suggests a regular and fairly repetitive pattern of land use in the region around the site that persisted for millennia.

We can examine the duration of individual site occupations from two perspectives. First, a variety of indicators suggests that later groups occupied the site for shorter periods of time than earlier groups: for example, later hearths are less heavily burned than earlier hearths, and later assemblages of flaked stone include more production waste and fewer discarded finished tools than earlier assemblages. This shift in the *relative* duration of site occupation over time, though, does not tell us how long people lived there in *absolute* terms. Comparison of patterns in the faunal assemblage with ethnoarchaeological data on recent hunter-gatherer camps (Hudson 2007) suggests that occupations likely ranged from a week or two to a month or two in length. However, this comparison is very general: at present, we have no rigorous quantitative yardstick for transforming bone counts and condition into time. Data from the lithic assemblage leave us in a similar situation. Although the assemblage of worked stone contains few cores and many bifaces, refitting of the collection indicates that cores were reduced more often than bifaces (Bamforth and Becker 2000). This pattern implies that more cores were flaked at the site than were discarded there, implying in turn that occupations of the site were shorter than the useful life of a core. However, we also have no rigorous yardstick for transforming rates of core reduction into time, although we can suggest tentatively that people did not stay at the site very long.

Finally, it would be useful to know what kinds of people lived at the Allen site. Was it occupied by family groups or single-sex procurement groups? Did children play at the site, or were only adults present? And, did any of this change over time? Certainly, the diversity of material at the site (with many bone and stone perforating tools – including needles, grinding stones, hide scrapers, and a variety of enigmatic pieces that probably served unknown domestic purposes) could be taken as evidence that general family groups were present. However, we cannot confirm this inference given what we know at present unless we are willing to assume the kind of stereotypic gendered division of labor that is clearly untenable. The range of knapping ability indicated by the flaked stone assemblage implies that both skilled and unskilled knappers were present (Bamforth and Hicks 2008). The latter were likely older children or early adolescents, and a single child's deciduous tooth in the collection certainly implies that a child was probably once present at the site. But saying more than this is largely speculation – a good story, perhaps, but a story that is minimally supported by evidence.

It is thus reasonable to argue that the Allen site data tell us fairly strongly that the Paleoindian groups who occupied the site moved within relatively small territories and did so regularly and repetitively, a conclusion that is at odds with most views of Paleoindian mobility. However, it is fairly clear that the argument that people stayed at the site for relatively short periods of time is plausible but not as strongly supported as these inferences, and that reconstructing the age and gender composition of the groups who stayed at the site verges on the construction of a just-so story. That is, we can make a strong case that we understand some important aspects of the mobility strategy followed by the occupants of the Allen site, but we have to admit that there are other equally important aspects of this strategy that we can assess empirically only tentatively, if at all. Admitting this, in turn, focuses on specific issues for future work. Can we find faunal or lithic yardsticks to quantify more precisely duration of occupation? Are there reliable ways to assess the ages and genders of ancient hunters and gatherers by examining material culture?

Conclusions

Anthropologists and archaeologists have recognized for decades that patterns of movement across the landscape are central to hunter-gatherer ways of life. As we have focused on this topic, we have also come to recognize the great diversity of such patterns. I suggest here that the overall approach to mobility studies that dominated Americanist archaeology during the late 20th century makes it difficult to address this variability, and that a less prominent approach is better-suited to this. The general conceptual underpinnings of a variable-by-variable approach to mobility are particularly compatible with the intellectual framework of behavioral ecology, and it is telling that Kelly (1995) has recently analyzed mobility within this framework.

The bottom-up or variable-by-variable approach that I advocate here is, at least implicitly, not new in our field. For example, many approaches to the study of technological organization advocate isolating specific aspects of technology – in effect, independent variables – for focused analysis (i.e. Bamforth 1986; Nelson 1991). Some 20 years ago, McGuire (1983) pointed out that social 'complexity' is comprised of at least two distinct and not necessarily mutually deterministic components, which he referred to as inequality (differential access to wealth and power) and heterogeneity (the number of different social positions within a community); he showed that each of these has distinct archaeological signatures. Clark (2002) has similarly attempted to specify the myriad of different components of craft specialization. The approach I have advocated here also has clear ties to Wylie's (2002) more general discussion of the ways in which relational analogies can strengthen archaeological inference; in Wylie's (2002, 153) terms, I have advocated an approach to inference that relies on the construction of '"multiply connected" paramorphic model(s)'. Indeed, in most cases, analogies derived from ethnoarchaeological or other actualistic research provide the strongest bridges between specific aspects of hunter-gatherer mobility patterns and specific lines of archaeological evidence. It seems reasonable to argue that archaeology's overall increasing emphasis on defining our research goals more precisely and increasing the rigor of the arguments on which our assertions about the past rely may inherently lead us towards a variable-by-variable/bottom-up approach to our work.

Whether this is so or not, however, it is important to acknowledge that shifting from a top-down to a bottom-up approach makes it more difficult to tell grand stories about the hunter-gatherer past, stories like the ones we have told about North American Paleoindian adaptations. However, such a shift makes it easier to tell stories that are more likely to stand the test of time and evidence, as many of our Paleoindian stories have not. I hope it is clear that the approach I advocate here is in its infancy and that it will take a substantial amount of work to achieve its potential. However, admitting clearly what we do and do not know about the past has the potential to focus this work clearly and productively in ways that will enrich our field in the long-term.

References

Amick, D. S. 1984. Designing and testing a model of raw material variability for the central Duck River Basin, Tennessee, in B. Butler and E. May (eds.), *Prehistoric chert exploitation: studies from the mid-continent*, 167–84. Occasional Paper 2. Carbondale, IL, Southern Illinois University, Center for Archaeological Investigations.

Bamforth, D. B. 1986. Technological efficiency and tool curation. *American Antiquity* 51, 38–50.

Bamforth, D. B. 1991. Technological organization and hunter/gatherer mobility: A California example. *American Antiquity* 56, 216–34.

Bamforth, D. B. 1997. Adaptive change on the Great Plains at the Paleoindian/Archaic transition, in M. Larson and J. Francis (eds.), *Changing Perspectives on the Archaic of the Northwest Plains and Rocky Mountains*, 14–54. Vermillion, SD, University of South Dakota Press.

Bamforth, D. B. 2002a. High-tech foragers? Folsom and later Paleoindian technology on the Great Plains. *Journal of World Prehistory* 16, 55–98.

Bamforth, D. B. 2002b. The Paleoindian occupation of the Medicine Creek drainage, southwestern Nebraska, in D. Roper (ed.), *Medicine Creek: 70 Years of Archaeological Investigations*, 54–83. Tuscaloosa, AL, University of Alabama Press.

Bamforth, D. B. 2003. Rethinking the role of bifacial technology in Paleoindian adaptations on the Great Plains, in M. Soressi and H. Dibble (eds.), *Multiple Approaches to the Study of Bifacial Technologies*, 209–28. Philadelphia, PA, University of Pennsylvania Press.

Bamforth, D. B. (ed.) 2007. *The Allen Site: A Paleoindian Camp in Southwestern Nebraska*. Albuquerque, University of New Mexico Press.

Bamforth, D. B. and Becker, M. 2000. Core/biface ratios, mobility, refitting, and artifact use-lives: A Paleoindian example. *Plains Anthropologist* 45, 273–90.

Bamforth, D. B., Becker, M. and Hudson, J. 2005. Intrasite spatial analysis, ethnoarchaeology, and Paleoindian land-use on the Great Plains: the Allen Site. *American Antiquity* 70, 561–80.

Bamforth, D. B. and Bleed, P. 1997. Technology, flaked stone technology, and risk, in G. Clark and M. Barton (eds.), *Rediscovering Darwin: Evolutionary Theory and Archaeological Explanation*. Archaeological Papers of the American Anthropological Association no. 7, 109–41. Arlington, VA, American Anthropological Association.

Bamforth, D. B. and Hicks, K. 2008. Production skill and Paleoindian work group organization in the Medicine Creek drainage, southwestern Nebraska. *Journal of Archaeological Method and Theory* 15, 132–53.

Bement, L. 1999. *Bison Hunting at the Cooper Site*. Norman, OK, University of Oklahoma Press.

Binford. L. 1979. Organization and formation processes: looking at curated technologies. *Journal of Anthropological Research* 35, 255–73.

Binford, L. 1980. Willow smoke and dogs' tails: hunter-gatherer settlement systems and archaeological site formation. *American Antiquity* 45, 4–20.

Binford, L. 2001. *Constructing Frames of Reference*. Berkeley, University of California Press.

Chatters, J. 1987. Hunter-gatherer adaptations and assemblage structure. *Journal of Anthropological Archaeology* 6, 336–75.

Clark, J. 2002. Craftsmanship and craft specialization, in K. Hirth (ed.), *Mesoamerican Lithic Technology: Experimentation and Interpretation*, 220–33. Salt Lake City, University of Utah Press.

Frison, G. 1982. Paleoindian winter subsistence strategies on the High Plains, in D. Ubelaker and D. Stanford (eds.), *Plains Indian Studies: Papers in Honor of John C. Ewers*, 193–201. Smithsonian Contributions to Anthropology 30. Washington, DC, Smithsonian Institution Press.

Goodyear, A. 1989. A hypothesis for the use of cryptocrystalline raw materials among Paleoindian groups of North America, in C. Ellis and J. Lothrop (eds.), *Eastern Paleoindian Lithic Resource Use*, 1–9. Boulder, CO, Westview Press.

Hester, J. and J. Grady. 1977. Paleoindian social patterns on the Llano Estacodo, in E. Johnson (ed.), *Paleoindian Lifeways*, 78–96. Lubbock, TX, The Museum Association.

Hudson, J. 2007. Faunal evidence for subsistence and settlement patterns at the Allen site, in D. B. Bamforth (ed.), *The Allen Site: A Paleoindian Camp in Southwestern Nebraska*. Albuquerque, NM, University of New Mexico Press.

Ingbar, E. 1994. Lithic raw material selection and technological organization, in P. J. Carr (ed.), *The organization of North American Prehistoric Chipped Stone Technologies*, 9–34. International Monographs in Prehistory, Archaeological Series 7. Ann Arbor, Department of Anthropology, University of Michigan.

Kelly, R. L. 1983. Hunter-gatherer mobility strategies. *Journal of Anthropological Research* 39, 277–306.

Kelly, R. L. 1995. *The Foraging Spectrum: Diversity in Hunter-Gatherer Lifeways*. Washington, DC, Smithsonian Institution Press.

Kelly, R. L. and Todd, L. 1988. Coming into the country: early Paleoindian hunting and mobility. *American Antiquity* 53, 231–44.

Lee, R. B. 1968. What hunters do for a living, or, how to make out on scarce resources, in R. Lee and I. Devore (eds.), *Man the Hunter*, 30–48. Chicago, Aldine.

McCartney, P. 1990. Alternative hunting strategies in Plains Paleoindian adaptations, in L. Davis and B. Reeves (eds.), *Hunters of the Recent Past*, 111–29. London, Unwin-Hyman.

MacDonald, G. 1968. *Debert: A Paleo-Indian site in Central Nova Scotia*. Buffalo, NY, Persimmon Press.

McGuire, R. 1983. Breaking down cultural complexity: inequality and heterogeneity. *Advances in Archaeological Method and Theory* 6, 91–142.

Nelson, M. 1991. The study of technological organization, in M. B. Schiffer (ed.), *Archaeological Method and Theory* 3, 57–100. Tuscon, University of Arizona Press.

Oswalt, W. 1976. *An Anthropological Analysis of Food-Getting Technology*. New York, Wiley and Sons.

Parry, W. and Kelly, R. 1987. Expedient core technology and sedentism, in J. Johnson and C. Morrow (eds.), *The Organization of Core Technology*, 285–308. Boulder, CO, Westview Press.

Renfrew, C. and P. Bahn. 2004. *Archaeology: Theories, Methods, and Practice* (4th ed.). New York, Thames and Hudson.

Sahlins, M. 1968. Notes on the original affluent society, in R. Lee and I. Devore (eds.), *Man the Hunter*, 85–9. Chicago, Aldine.

Service, E. 1966. *The Hunters*. Englewood Cliffs, NJ, Prentice-Hall.

Service, E. 1971. *Primitive Social Organization: An Evolutionary Perspective* (2nd ed.). New York, Random House.

Shott, M. 1986. Technological organization and settlement mobility: an ethnographic examination. *Journal of Anthropological Research* 42, 15–51.

Smith, E. and Winterhalder, B. 1992. *Evolutionary Ecology and Human Behavior*. Hawthorne, NJ, Aldine de Gruyter.

Torrence, R. 1983. Time budgeting and hunter-gatherer technology, in G. Bailey (ed.), *Pleistocene Hunter-Gatherers in Europe*, 11–22. New York, Cambridge University Press.

Torrence, R. (no date). *Procurement*. Manuscript in author's possession.

Winterhalder, B. and Smith, E. 1981. *Hunter-Gatherer Foraging Strategies*. Chicago, University of Chicago Press.

Witthoft, J. 1952. A Paleoindian site in eastern Pennsylvania, an early hunting culture. *Proceedings of the American Philosophical Society* 96, 464–95.

Wylie, A. 2002. The reaction against analogy, in A. Wylie (ed.), *Thinking From Things*, 136–53. Berkeley, University of California Press.

14. Are we there yet? Using GIS to investigate paths and landmarks in the Mesolithic of south-west Germany

Harry Starr and Susan Harris

The dense temperate forest that covered much of central Europe during the Mesolithic likely presented a significant barrier to mobility. Archaeologists might assume that the best way to move between two places was with the most direct route available. However, ethnographic examples suggest that the most efficient path was frequently not selected for travel. Familiar landmarks and paths would have been required for successful navigation in areas with few recognizable features. What kinds of topographic features served as landmarks in the past and what relationship did such landmarks have to routes of travel? Geographic information systems can be used to identify potential routes and investigate the spatial relationships between these routes and landmarks that could have been used during prehistory.

Keywords: Mesolithic, southern Germany, geographic information systems, least-cost paths.

Introduction

The research presented in this paper will address the organization of hunter-gatherer mobility in the region around the Federsee in south-west Germany using data recorded by the 'Southwest Germany Regional Archaeological Survey Project' (SWGRASP). The incorporation of the SWGRASP data into a geographical information system (GIS) database makes it possible to evaluate the use of GIS methods, including least-cost path analysis, for understanding the organization of mobility during the Mesolithic in southern Germany.

Archaeologists have given attention to movement within and between sites since the beginnings of the discipline, and mobility is a central theme in Mesolithic research. However, our understanding of the process of movement is usually implicit. We speak of exchange, or more broadly interaction, between places without specifying how this interaction takes place. Obviously, exchange or interaction requires movement. This might include movement of people, things, or ideas. In the particular context of the Mesolithic of southern Germany, one question that we might ask is how did people find their way through the forest?

Archaeological approaches to landmarks and paths

We do not have good records for estimating how often native hunter-gatherers got lost in the woods. There must have been strategies for avoiding this experience, even if it was rare, and there must have been rules for how to deal with becoming lost. Two tools for dealing with the general problem of navigation are landmarks and defined routes of travel in the form of paths or roads. The analysis in this paper begins to address how we might recognize landmarks and paths in the Mesolithic of southern Germany.

If we look at the historic and ethnographic record, we can see that a wide range of natural and built features are used as landmarks. Natural topographic features including mountain peaks, river valleys, waterfalls, lakes, or caves are used as landmarks by native peoples. But many smaller features were used as well, including large rocks and boulders or particular stands of trees. Many of these natural features were described in vivid detail in the myths and creation stories of peoples around the world. People also modified their landscapes to create recognizable features such as marked trees, cairns, alignments of rocks, and other monuments. Many of these modifications are unlikely to survive in the archaeological record. Therefore, some archaeologists have focused on identifying natural features of the landscape that might have been used by prehistoric people (Bradley 2000).

Southern Germany does not have many large spectacular features, but a few natural landmarks do exist that might have been used by Mesolithic people. The Swabian Alb is a limestone plateau with many steep cliffs and deep cut river valleys. The Danube River valley cuts from west to east along the southern edge of the Alb. The lakeshore of the Federsee would have had identifiable points or bays and it also contained a large island that would have been clearly visible from nearly any part of the lake. The Bussen, a large solitary hill, is clearly visible from the Federsee and could easily have been a local landmark between the lake and the Danube valley. There are also unique topographical features such as the Blautopf, a deep pool in the Alb with a striking blue/green colour.

Any of these locations might have been incorporated into the local knowledge of Mesolithic people. They may have been the centrepieces of elaborate myths, or they may simply have been useful because they were readily recognizable and visible from particular parts of the landscape. However, identifying potential landmarks only places a new kind of dot on our maps. We still need to address how people actually move through the landscape.

It is likely that prehistoric travel frequently took the form of walking along paths. Defined routes of travel such as paths and roads are unique, multifunctional structures that provide physical evidence of repeated economic and political interaction, and that also provide a model of order for society (Tilley 1994). Once a path has been etched into the ground, there is literally a 'right way to go' and anyone who moves though that space faces the choice of following the culturally approved route or forging something new.

The vast majority of archaeological studies of prehistoric routes have focused on the relationships between roads and monumental architecture. There are many well-known road networks in prehistory including the Inka Highways and the Chaco road system. Such roads were used to link regions into a system of tribute with important economic centres ruled by powerful political leaders.

Hyslop (1985) defined a typology of paths and roads that described paths as informal, irregular, redundant, avoiding obstacles that would require large-scale construction, and growing to meet the needs of individual travelers. Roads are described as formal, carefully planned, less redundant, overcoming obstacles, and requiring organized labor for construction. It should be recognized that a wide variety of routes exist between these ideal types. Paths may be upgraded into roads, and roads may decay into paths.

Earle (1991) provided a typology of paths and roads based on several important characteristics including: the volume of transport as measured by the width and wear of routes, the types of facilities constructed, including steps, ramps, bridges, or causeways, and the amount of labour invested in improvements. For hunter-gatherers, we should imagine a regional web of relationships that is not centrally organized, but that includes frequent interaction, perhaps in the form of group ceremonies.

Landscape studies in the Neolithic of Britain have frequently focused on the connections between routes and monuments. For example, the West Kennet Avenue connects the Late Neolithic monument of Avebury to a construction on a hill to the south-east known as the Sanctuary. Several authors have suggested that this route served as a ritual procession way that defined how one should move between and experience these monuments. Thomas (1993) linked the views of Avebury to social classes that had differential access to ritual knowledge. Perhaps some individuals were not allowed to enter the great monument and could only view it from the pathway.

Economic, political, and religious interactions were no less significant for hunter-gatherers, but there has been little attention given to networks of paths. Perhaps this is for the obvious reason that paths are unlikely to preserve in the archaeological record. However, it seems that if we want to understand the connection between mobility and regional interaction, we should try to understand paths.

One of the rare examples of research focused on hunter-gatherer paths is the work of Davis (1961) on trade routes and economic exchange among the Native Americans of California. This work included a map showing a network of trails running throughout the state of California linking all of the major tribal groups. Most of the manuscript was devoted to a table that detailed the items that were exchanged between different tribal groups. The map and the table were based on ethnographic sources and travellers' accounts from the late 1800s through to the 1950s. He suggests that investigators acquired little information about routes because it would not be volunteered by informants. Native American informants might reasonably assume that anyone would know how to get to a place that was talked about from a given starting point.

An earlier work by Sample (1950, 1) stated that, 'Myriads of Indian trails crisscrossed each other in the valleys of California. Early travellers were often confused by the multitude of choices; they needed and used Indian guides to show the correct paths...the trails in the sierra regions followed natural passes. Many trails were wide and worn a couple of feet deep from long use.' From such accounts it is easy to imagine a network of paths that matches Hyslop's descriptions. We also need to imagine the cultural knowledge that went along with these routes: stories that connected supernatural events and locations on the landscape.

The social context of mobility in the Mesolithic is obviously difficult to recover. However, it may be possible to begin to explore the use of paths in the past using GIS. Archaeologists have used least cost path analysis to recreate the most efficient travel routes through the landscape and have then compared these paths to known site distributions (for example, see Whitley and Hicks 2003). The attempt to transform environmental variables into paths begins a process of using the existing environment to understand how prehistoric people perceived the world in which they lived.

The dataset

The Early Mesolithic in southern Germany lasts for about 2500 years, from 10,300 BP (*c.* 10,390–9880 cal BC; approximate calibration by present authors) to 7800 BP (*c.* 6690–6530 cal BC; approximate calibration by present authors) (Stuiver *et al.* 2005; Reimer *et al.* 2004; Stuiver and Reimer 1993). The Early Mesolithic was selected for this analysis because sites dating to this time period are easily identified through the presence of characteristic microliths. Early Mesolithic sites have been found in a wide variety of locations including caves, rockshelters, hilltops, lakeshores, and river valleys. Figure 14.1 shows the Early Mesolithic site locations included in this analysis. The 25 locations are examples of well-known Early Mesolithic sites described by Jochim (1998) that show evidence of interaction through artefact style and raw material types. In some cases, a single location represents the general location of several recorded sites. The locations selected for this analysis include: 18 surface sites recorded in the Rhine lowlands near Baden-Baden, one cave and 15 surface sites recorded in the Rhine valley, many sites in the Neckar valley including Rottenburg-Siebenlinden and 200+ sites south of Stuttgart, 9 surface sites recorded in the Nagold River valley on the eastern side of the Black Forest, numerous cave and rockshelter locations on the Swabian Alb, a variety of sites recorded on the rolling plains of Oberschwaben, including those near the lakeshore of the Federsee and Pfrunger Ried and several sites in the Aitrach valley, and numerous sites recorded on the western shore of Lake Constance. Also included in this analysis are three raw material locations in Bavaria that produce a characteristic banded chert that is found in sites throughout the study area.

It should not be assumed that all of these sites were occupied at the same time or even that there was necessarily interaction between all of these locations. The purpose of this paper is to explore how these locations might have been connected through mobility during the Early Mesolithic. It is clear that if archaeologists ignore movement, the patterned activity of people in space and time, we are left with a static picture of the geography of past lives. Our pictures of the past will be confined to dots on maps, like those seen in Figure 14.1. How were those dots connected?

Analysis

The ethnographic record illustrates the tremendous amount of cultural knowledge associated with environmental features by hunter-gatherers. In the absence of contem-

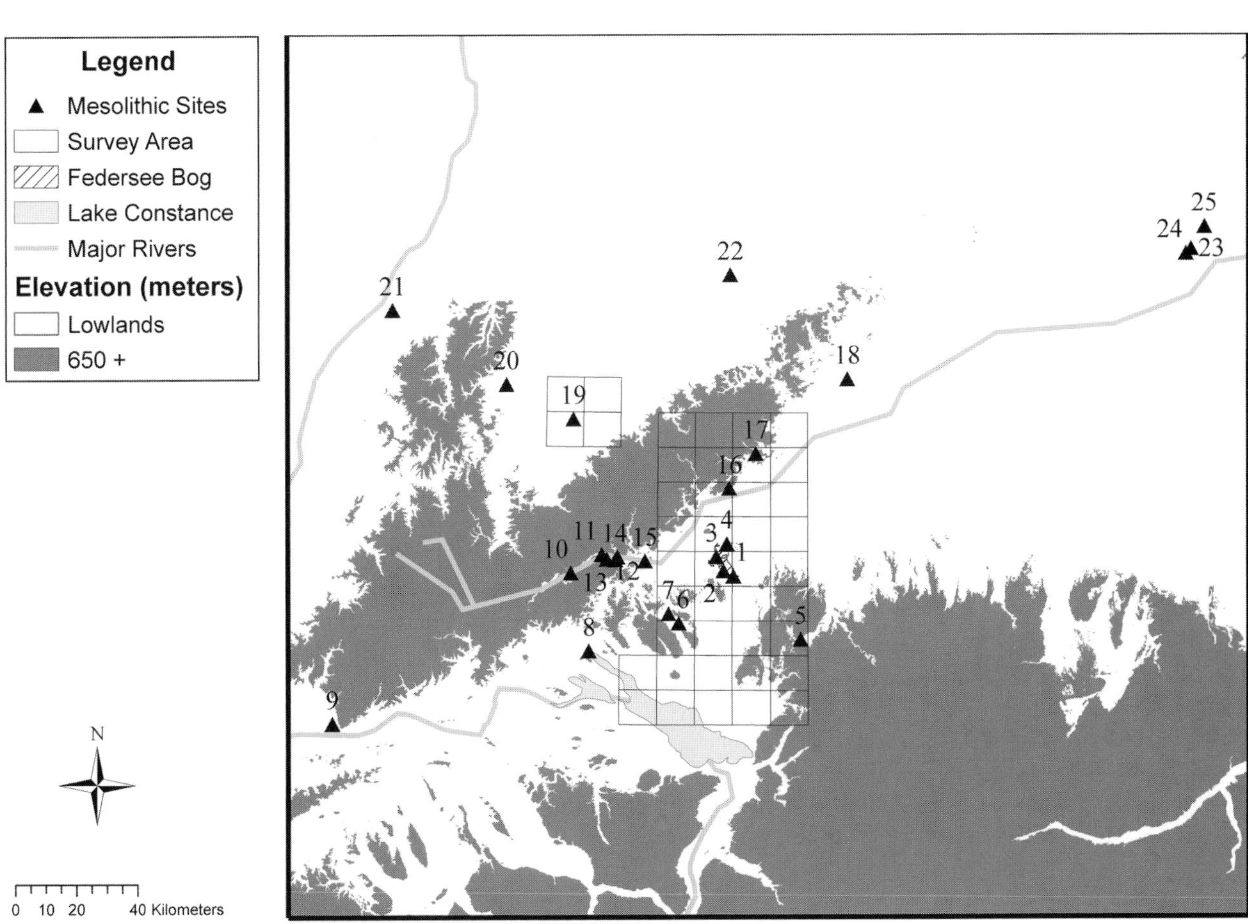

Figure 14.1. The location of Early Mesolithic sites included in the study. Sites include: 1) Aichbuhl; 2) Henauhof; 3) Moosburg; 4) Ödenahlen; 5) Aitrach Valley; 6) Pfrunger Ried South; 7) Pfrunger Ried North; 8) Western Lake Constance; 9) Rhine Valley; 10) Jaegerhaus-hoehle; 11) Falkensteing Hohle; 12) Burghohle Dietfurt; 13) Inzigkofen; 14) Ziguenerfels; 15) Lautereck; 16) Felsstaelle; 17) Helga Abri; 18) Malerfels; 19) Rottenburg-Siebenlinden; 20) Nagold; 21) Baden-Baden; 22) Stuttgart-Neckar; 23) Baiersdorf; 24) Emmerthal; 25) Hamberg. (DEM source: CIAT and CGIAR 2004).

porary accounts or other measurable criteria in prehistoric contexts, archaeologists might benefit from a terrain-based approach to analysis using modern environmental data. GIS can be used to explore how Mesolithic people might have moved across the landscape of southern Germany. Tobler's hiking algorithm can be applied to a DEM (CIAT and CGIAR-CSI 2004) to generate an anisotropic cost surface (for details of this process, see Harris *et al.*, this volume). The anisotropic surface is directionally based. The cost of moving across any grid square depends on the direction in which it is traversed. Using this cost surface, optimal least-cost paths can be generated between two or more known points. This basic model only takes into account the cost of moving across the landscape generated by changes in slope. Other landscape factors that might affect travel, such as crossing rivers or moving through thick vegetation, are not included. This simple example is intended as a starting point for understanding Mesolithic mobility.

Figure 14.2 shows the cost surface generated for one site location on the southern end of the Federsee. This map demonstrates that all of the sites included in the analysis are within a 60-hour walk. Most of the locations are within a 20-hour walk. The cost surface reveals the importance of very broad regional surveys for understanding the mobility patterns of hunter-gatherers. In southern Germany, Mesolithic foragers used large areas of land, and the scale of mobility would be impossible to capture with a project that examined a small area. Ethnographically, it is rare for hunter-gatherers to walk more than 8 hours in a day (Kelly 1995). This means that it would be almost a two-week round trip for someone to walk from the Federsee to obtain the banded chert material available at the locations in Bavaria to the north-east; such a trip at least seems possible, if unlikely. Infrequent trips of this type might account for the small amount of this material found in sites in the Federsee area.

Figure 14.3 shows the least-cost paths generated from one site on the southern end of the Federsee to all of the other site locations. The paths represent the routes requiring the lowest effort to move across the landscape from the origin point to each of the destination points. According to the available ethnographic information, we might expect least-cost paths to match natural routes through the landscapes. For example, we might expect a path to travel along a river valley rather than to cross over the ridges bounding the valley. In this way, the least-cost paths presented here reflect a very simple model of what Mesolithic paths might have been like.

In general, south-west to north-east movement follows the Danube valley. Schlichtherle (1990) suggests that this is a natural corridor that was used during the Neolithic and was likely used by other prehistoric peoples. The top

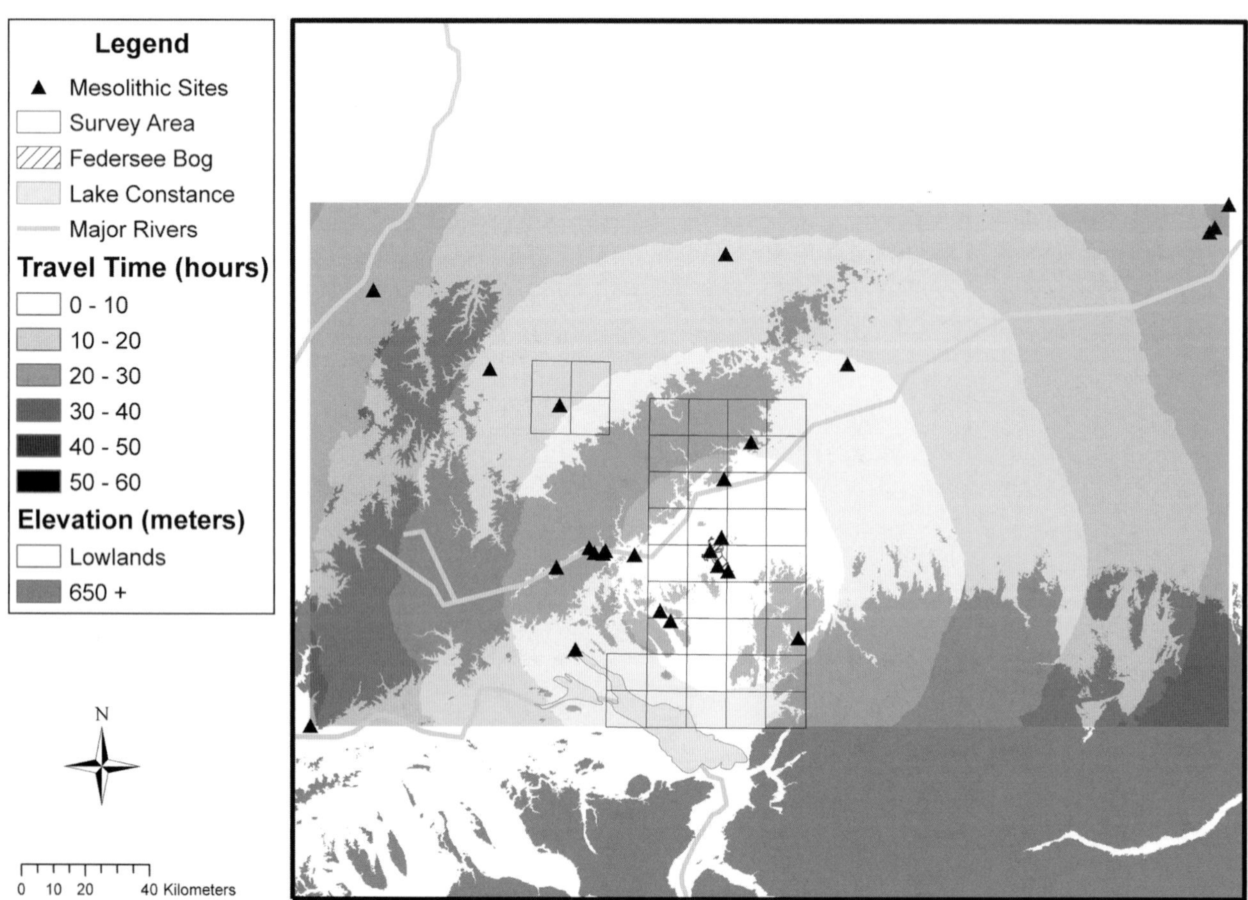

Figure 14.2. A cost surface generated with site 1 (Aichbuhl) as the origin illustrating the cost of travel across the study region. (DEM source: CIAT and CGIAR 2004).

of the Alb plateau is relatively flat, and from the south the slope is gradual, but from the north the steep grade to the plateau might prove decisive in path selection. However, paths that cross the Swabian Alb do not take advantage of natural passes. It seems that with the algorithm selected for this analysis, the slopes involved do not present a serious barrier to foot traffic.

It would be useful to examine the patterns of paths generated from different starting points. The analysis is sensitive to the direction of travel, and multiple paths might be used to define general travel corridors rather than the narrow paths represented here. There is much more work to be done to improve this analysis, but based on this example we can begin to asses the potential of GIS for asking questions about Mesolithic mobility and find new aspects to include in future models.

There are several ways to critique this approach. For example, this simple least-cost paths model does not take into account obstacles that would be difficult to cross on foot such as large streams or heavy brush, or areas that would be impossible to cross by foot such as the Federsee. There are a number of important variables in mobility. Transport technology is just one variable that has not been considered in this analysis. If Mesolithic peoples had access to small watercraft, then the paths across the lake might not be so unrealistic. The use of watercraft during this time may be inferred from the presence of sites on islands in the lakes. The use of boats on the Danube might considerably lower the costs of east-west movement. It would be useful to consider how transport technology and other variables, such as differences in paths between residential camps and to and from logistical camps, might be modelled within the GIS.

It is also important to recognize that there might be many reasons to deviate from the most efficient path through an area. The paths in this analysis might be interpreted as major routes of travel between Mesolithic locations. Many other types of paths would be necessary to achieve goals other than efficient travel. The distribution of particular resources, such as hazelnuts or stone for making tools, might not be available along the most convenient paths. If security was a concern, campsites near easily travelled paths might be avoided. Future work might attempt to model ecological goals or social variables in order to understand deviations from the least-cost paths presented here.

It would clearly be difficult to test the existence of such paths in the past using available archaeological data. However, the SWGRASP survey data can be used to identify Mesolithic sites near the least-cost paths. How many of the fields can be found close to the least-cost paths? A distance of one hundred meters was selected arbitrarily as an initial measure for this analysis. The distances that

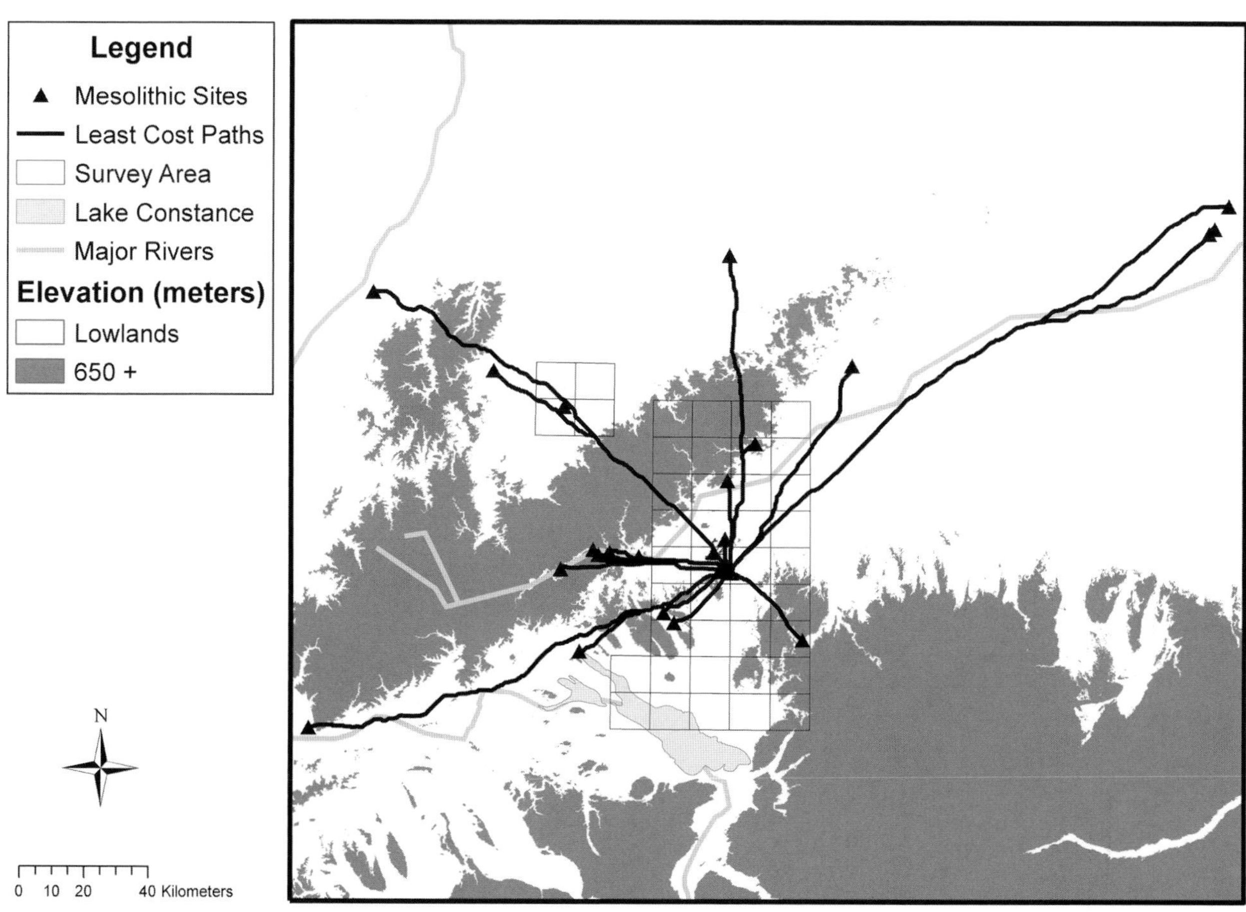

Figure 14.3. The least-cost paths generated from site 1 (Aichbuhl) to the other site locations. (DEM source: CIAT and CGIAR 2004).

people walk from camps to major paths are a topic for further investigation. Figure 14.4 shows the least cost paths and the 98 fields from the SWGRASP survey that contain diagnostic Early Mesolithic artefacts or a number of heat-treated artefacts. Of the 3278 fields surveyed, 116 are within one hundred meters of the least-cost paths and fourteen of these fields have a Mesolithic component. Therefore, 3.5% of all of the surveyed fields are within one hundred meters of the least-cost paths and 14.3% of the fields with a Mesolithic component are within the same distance. This does not demonstrate a strong pattern of association, but it is a question worth pursuing. One question that might be addressed in the future is whether lithic scatters of different density can be associated with the paths. For example, one might expect to see large dense scatters at intervals along the paths representing locations where people stopped to camp while travelling. The least-cost paths generated for this analysis do not represent the entire network of travel routes that was used during the Mesolithic. Many Mesolithic sites are not preserved in the archaeological record and others remain to be discovered. The sites do cluster in natural corridors such as the Danube valley and they can be found in the directions indicated by the least-cost paths. It might be useful to consider the paths individually and look for patterns in the types of sites that are nearby.

The value of this approach is not in the objective result. We are not trying to demonstrate that Mesolithic people walked across the landscape along these least-cost paths. GIS provides a powerful spatial analysis tool that can be used as a heuristic for thinking about what prehistoric paths might have been like. The SWGRASP survey data might be used to strengthen such models by identifying the places on the landscape that were the most likely starting and ending points for paths. Models like this also help to interpret the survey data. For example, common travel corridors might explain the low density finds between the northern end of the Federsee and the Danube Valley.

Conclusions

The answer to the question, 'Are we there yet?', suggested in the title of this paper, must be no. Powerful tools for spatial analysis are becoming more readily available and easier to use, but we lack good models for understanding the basic mechanics of hunter-gatherer mobility. This is especially true for forested environments that characterize much of the Mesolithic in Europe. We have tried to answer a basic question connected to mobility: how did people find their way through their environments?

This is not a new question in archaeology. Considerable

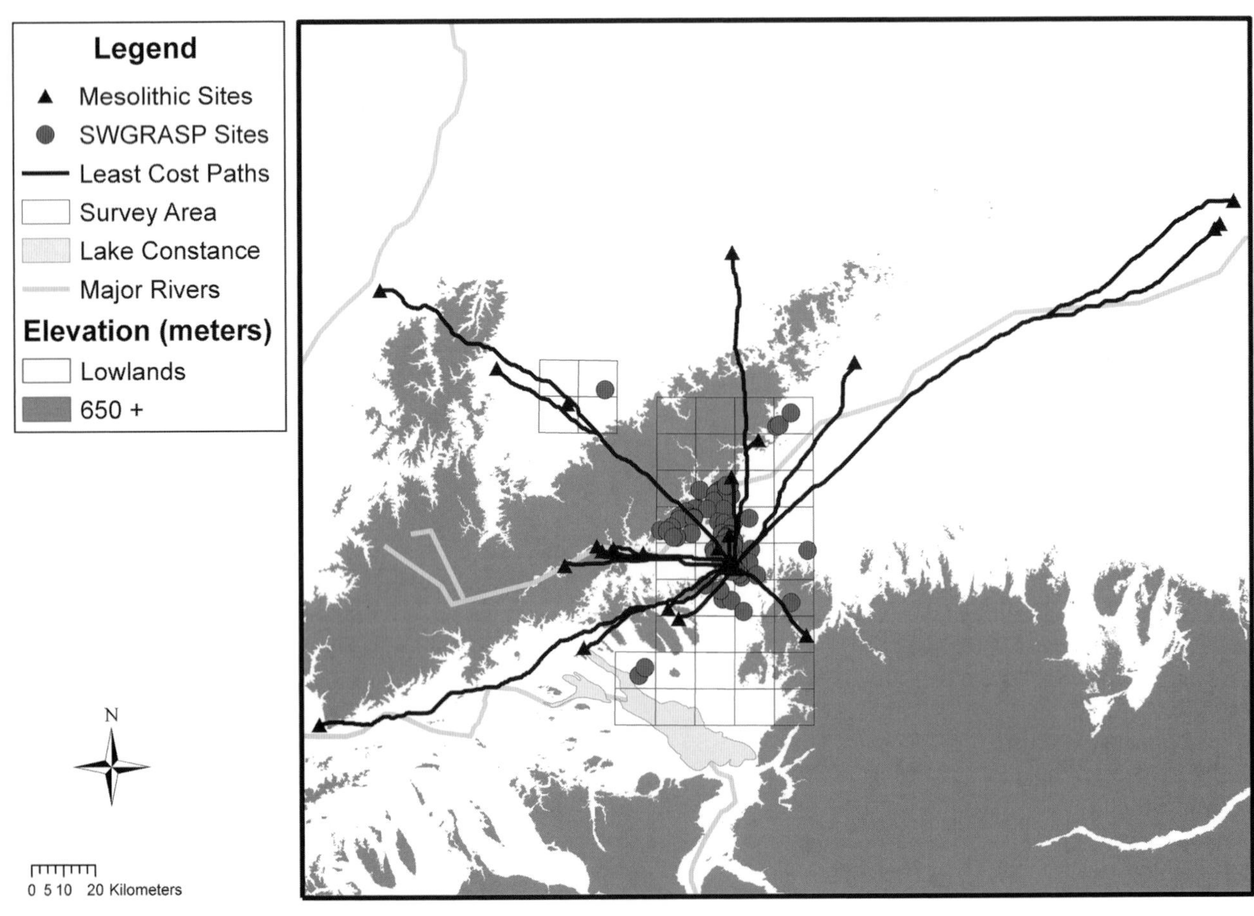

Figure 14.4. A comparison of the locations of the least-cost paths with the Mesolithic site locations recorded by SWGRASP. (DEM source: CIAT and CGIAR 2004).

attention has been given to the connection between political and economic interaction and the creation of road networks in societies ranging from Neolithic Britain to Inka Peru. Questions regarding these issues are no less important to hunter-gatherer societies like those of the Mesolithic, but they have rarely been pursued.

GIS provides a tool that can be used to generate hypotheses about prehistoric mobility by hunter-gatherer groups. Unfortunately, because paths are unlikely to preserve in the archaeological record, any models that are generated are difficult to test.

Information that is useful for survival is often encoded in stories and myths. For example, in the western United States there are stories about what one should do when threatened with starvation. We might look in the ethnographic literature specifically for clues about how hunting and gathering peoples solved the problem of getting lost. Ethnographic examples from Australia and other parts of the world suggest that group identity is closely tied to knowledge of spatial environment. In order to better model hunter-gatherer mobility, we need to understand how spatial information is transmitted in hunter-gatherer societies.

The presence of known landmarks and paths marks the boundary between the familiar and the unfamiliar. Different individuals in society will have access to different sets of spatial knowledge. For example we might expect different kinds of mobility for men and women based on a division of labour by sex. Representing this kind of cultural knowledge within a GIS presents a particular challenge to current technology. Many authors have suggested viewshed analysis as one way to try to model cultural knowledge of the spatial environment (e.g. Wheatley 1995; van Leusen 1999; Tschan *et al.* 2000). The ability to determine whether a line-of-sight exists between two points on the landscape might make it possible to test GIS models of paths by examining the relationship between views from the paths and potential landmarks. If we pursue the questions raised by this paper, we will be able to improve our understanding of mobility in prehistoric cultural landscapes.

References

Bradley, R. 2000. *An Archaeology of Natural Places*. London, Routledge.

CIAT and CGIAR-CSI 2004. Void-filled seamless SRTM data V1, 2004, International Centre for Tropical Agriculture (CIAT), available from the CGIAR-CSI SRTM 90m Database: http://srtm.csi.cgiar.org (accessed 10/2007).

Davis, J. 1961. *Trade Routes and Economic Exchange Among the Indians of California*. Berkeley, The University of California Archaeological Survey.

Earle, T. 1991. Paths and Roads in Evolutionary Perspective, in C. Trombold (ed.), *Ancient Road Networks and Settlement Hierarchies in the New World*, 10–16. Cambridge, Cambridge University Press.

Hyslop, J. 1985. *The Inka Road System*. Orlando, Academic Press.

Jochim, M. A. 1998. *A Hunter-Gatherer Landscape: Southwest Germany in the Late Paleolithic and Mesolithic*. New York, Plenum.

Kelly, R. L. 1995. *The Foraging Spectrum: Diversity in Hunter-Gatherer Lifeways*. Washington, DC, Smithsonian Institution Press.

Reimer, P. J., Baillie, M. G. L., Bard, E., Bayliss, A., Beck, J. W., Bertrand, C. J. H., Blackwell, P. G., Buck, C. E., Burr, G. S., Cutler, K. B., Damon, P. E., Edwards, R. L., Fairbanks, R. G., Friedrich, M., Guilderson, T. P., Hogg, A. G., Hughen, K. A., Kromer, B., McCormac, F. G., Manning, S. W., Bronk Ramsey, C. B., Reimer, R. W., Remmele, S., Southon, J. R., Stuiver, M., Talamo, S., Taylor, F. W., van der Plicht, J. and Weyhenmeyer, C. E. 2004. IntCal04 Terrestrial radiocarbon age calibration, 26–0 ka BP. *Radiocarbon* 46, 1029–58.

Sample, L. 1950. *Trade and Trails in Aboriginal California*. Berkeley, The University of California Archaeological Survey.

Schlichtherle, H. 1990. Aspekte der Siedlungsarchäologischen Erforschung von Neolithikum und Bronzezeit im Südwestdeutschen Alpenvorland. *SiedlungsarchäologischeUntersuchungen im Alpenvorland*, 208–44. Mainz, Bericht des Römisch-Germanischen Kommissions.

Stuiver, M., Reimer, P. J. and Reimer, R. W. 2005. CALIB 5.0. WWW program and documentation, at http://calib.qub.ac.uk/calib/calib.html (accessed 01/2008).

Stuiver, M. and Reimer, P. J. 1993. Extended 14C database and revised CALIB radiocarbon calibration program. *Radiocarbon* 35, 215–30.

Thomas, J. 1993. The Politics of Vision and the Archaeologies of Landscape, in B. Bender (ed.), *Landscape: Politics and Perspectives*, 19–48. Oxford, Berg.

Tilley, C. 1994. *A Phenomenology of Landscape: Places, Paths, and Monuments*. Oxford, Berg.

Tschan, A., Wlodzimierz, R. and Latałowa, M. 2000. Perception and viewsheds: are they mutually inclusive?, in G. Lock (ed.), *Beyond the Map: Archaeology and Spatial Technologies*, 28–48. Amsterdam, IOS Press.

van Leusen, M. 1999. Viewshed and Cost Surface Analysis Using GIS (Cartographic Modelling in a Cell-Based GIS II), in J. A. Barcelo, I. Briz and A. Vila (eds.), *New Techniques for Old Times CAA 98: Computer Applications and Quantitative Methods in Archaeology. Proceedings of the 26th Conference, Barcelona, March 1998*, 215–23. British Archaeological Reports, International Series S757. Oxford, Archaeopress.

Wheatley, D. 1995. Cumulative viewshed analysis: a GIS-based method for investigating intervisibility and its archaeological application, in G. Lock and Z. Stančić (eds.), *GIS and Archaeology: a European Perspective*, 171–86. London, Taylor & Francis.

Whitley, T. and Hicks, L. 2003. A Geographical Information Systems Approach to Understanding Potential Prehistoric and Historic Travel Corridors. *Southeastern Archaeology* 22, 77–91.

15. Raw material and settlement strategies at the Pleistocene/Holocene boundary in Trentino (north-eastern Italian Alps)

Fabio Cavulli and Stefano Grimaldi

The insertion of archaeological as well as environmental data on the Trentino region (north-eastern Italian Alps) in a GIS project highlighted two main themes that will be key subjects for future research: differential use of areas of varying altitude in Alpine territory, and the different exploitation of flint sources among the Upper Palaeolithic and Mesolithic human groups who inhabited this region. While the different use of altitude may be partly or entirely due to several natural constraints which remain still unknown in their detail, differences in raw material procurement strategies should be mainly interpreted as a remarkable variation in human behavior.

Keywords: GIS, raw material, settlement, Alps, Italy, Upper Palaeolithic, Mesolithic.

Introduction

Today, north-eastern Italy (Figure 15.1) represents one of the most archaeologically rich areas in the Alps. Several hundred archaeological sites (i.e., excavations in well-stratified deposits, as well as surface finds), attributed to the late Upper Palaeolithic/Early Mesolithic, are known. Field data have been gathered over several decades and, accordingly, literary sources are abundant (see main references in, amongst others, Broglio and Improta 1994/1995; Dalmeri *et al.* 2001). The main goal of this paper is to show, using a Geographical Information System (GIS) approach, the relation between human settlements and raw material distribution during the Pleistocene/Holocene transition. We limited our research to the 172 archaeological sites located in Trentino Province (see list in Dalmeri and Pedrotti 1995, recently updated by the authors).

Geological background

Trentino and the surrounding areas are characterised by a great variety of environmental, geological, and geomorphological features. Particularly, they are rich in geological formations containing flint. These raw materials, characterized by a geographically differentiated distribution, show a high variety of colours, mineral characteristics and qualities. The most significant geological flint formations are those of the Jurassic and Cretaceous. The *Scaglia Rossa*, the most important Upper Cretaceous geological formation, is a 'rock formation whose colour varies from whitish-pink to brick red, consisting of micritic limestone rich in planktonic foraminifers. Always represented in this, sometimes in great quantities, are flint layers in beds and nodules with colours that vary from brownish-red to bluish-red' (Avanzini *et al.* 2002, 83). The *Biancone* formation (Lower-Middle Cretaceous) is characterized by white or light-greyish carbonatic layers. This formation has a thickness ranging from 20m in the Adige valley, to more than 300m towards the east. Flint is very abundant and varies in colour: 'in general, at the base of the formation, the flint is a typical yellowish colour and has pinkish tones in the areas where the thickness of the formation increases and the passage from the underlying *Rosso Ammonitico* is very gradual. In the intermediate part a greyish tone predominates, from tones in yellow in the low parts, progressively darker towards the top, in correspondence with the passage from the *Scaglia Variegata*' (Avanzini *et al.* 2002, 83–4). Other flint formations are *Rosso Ammonitico* and *Scaglia Variegata*. *Rosso Ammonitico* is characterized by a 'sequence of tightly stratified red and pinkish limestone in which the violaceous red to greenish flint is present in beds and nodules. This stratigraphical layer is well represented in the eastern sector of the Veneto-Trentino area and it gradually gets thinner towards the Adige Valley where in some cases it is not even present' (Avanzini *et al.* 2002, 84). *Scaglia Variegata* 'is represented by greyish marly limestone marked with bioturbation and organised in decametre wide layers which alternate with blackish-grey marl. The transition from the underlying formation

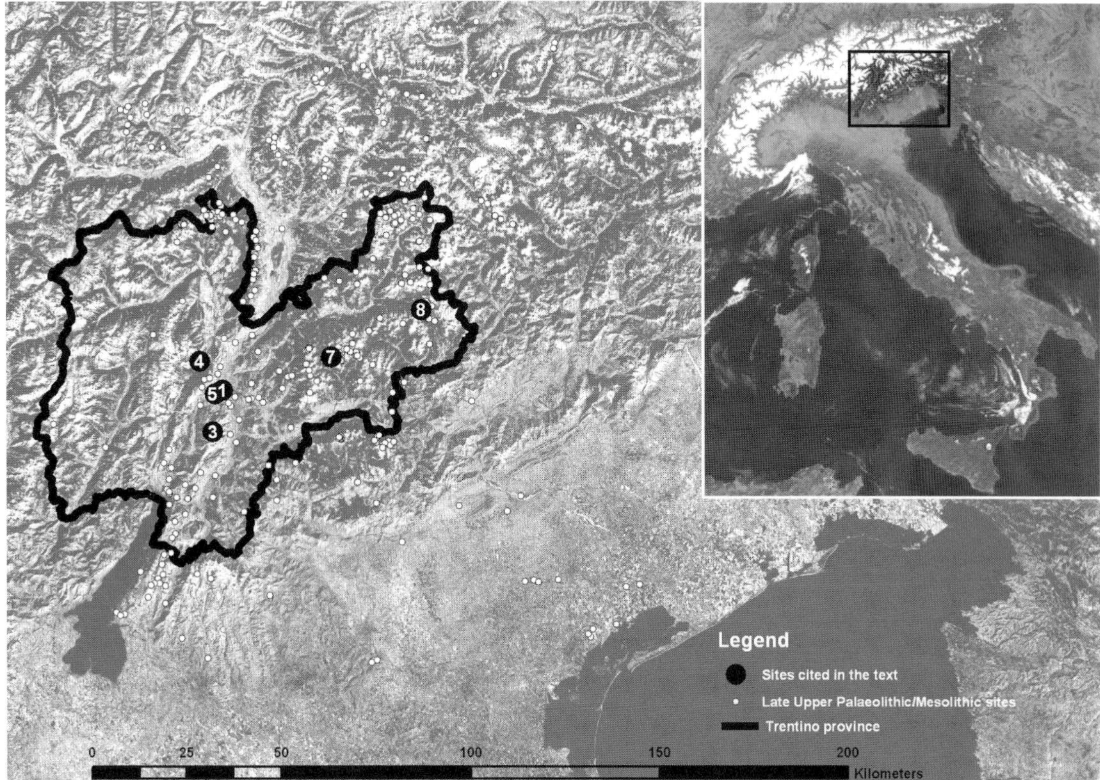

Figure 15.1. The Trentino region in the north-eastern Italian Alps. Epigravettian sites mentioned in the text: 3) Andalo; 4) Terlago; 5) Viotte. Sauveterrian sites mentioned in the text: 1) Pradestel rockshelter; 7) Lago delle Buse; 8) Colbricon.

is progressive and sometimes difficult to determine and is characterised by a progressive increase of the organic fraction of the sediment. The flint is typically dark, grey with blackish streaks or more commonly tending toward black, often with differently coloured flecks' (Avanzini *et al.* 2002, 84). A relatively characteristic sequence of yellowish flint layers, due to their limited vertical geological distribution, is present at the proximity of the transition between the *Scaglia Variegata* and *Scaglia Rossa* formations. Other flint formations are located in north-eastern Trentino and the surrounding areas. *Livinallongo*, *Marne del Puez*, and other formations provide the so-called 'Dolomitic flint', which, often 'opaque, has a granular appearance, colour between black and blackish-brown, greenish or greenish-brown' (Avanzini *et al.* 2002, 84). Finally, rock crystal is geologically found in the northernmost areas, outside the current Trentino region, between the Pusteria valleys and the Alpine watershed (Broglio and Lunz 1984).

Methodology

A database was created using *Access* software. It is divided into nine tables: 1) Sites; 2) ^{14}C dates; 3) Artefacts; 4) Typology; 5) Microburin; 6) Blade Technology; 7) Flake Technology; 8) Retouch; 9) Core. The tables are linked together by ID codes. Each table consists of several records that are helpful in providing a detailed description of the related item. The creation of the GIS project in *ArcInfo 9* required the insertion of a raster cartography and themes in a vectorial format, which facilitated this research. In this work we used: a) topographic maps (1:10,000 scale); b) themes regarding physical data and modern 'anthropization', such as hydrography, soil use, hydrographic basins, footpaths, mountain refuges, road networks, population centres, toponymy; c) 1:100,000-scale map of the main geological formations; d) coloured and black and white rectified orthophotographs; e) elevation contours. We must emphasise that the greatest obstacle to our research was the lack of geomorphological maps of the area under examination.

The three-dimensional models were created, using contour lines with 10 metre steps and elevation points, to create two Triangulated Irregular Networks with differing accuracies. The data was processed in *Surfer 7*, as it provides the possibility of choosing the most suitable interpolation algorithm for the data available. Using simple overlay operations they were superimposed according to the requirements of the vectorial, cartographic, or other themes. The database with the 172 sites was then inserted into the GIS project. The sites were geo-referenced on the topographic maps.

The late Upper Paleolithic

After the Last Glacial Maximum, the first presence of human groups in Trentino is dated to 11,260±100 BP (11,354–10,998 cal BC; Ki2-3634) from the Dalmeri rockshelter, Bassetti *et al.* 2002; see also Broglio and

Improta 1994/1995), and is attributable to the Epigravettian. This chronology is strengthened by a new ^{14}C date obtained from a charcoal sample coming from the Epigravettian site of Viotte, near Trento (Grimaldi, unpublished).

It has been suggested that the entry of human groups into the mountain area took place in the south as a response to the climatic change brought about by the Late Glacial period (Bagolini and Broglio 1985). This climatic improvement caused a movement towards the northern alpine pastures, the characteristic habitat of gregarious ungulates. In particular, ibex was presumably the main focus of subsistence of prehistoric groups, as witnessed by the faunal remains from several sites such as, for instance, Riparo Dalmeri (Fiore *et al.* 2002).

Epigravettian rockshelters are mainly situated in the pre-Alps, while most of the Epigravettian open-air sites located in mountain environments are situated in wetlands, or close to small lakes. Moreover, the distribution of Epigravettian sites is characterized by low-elevation sites (up to about 500m asl) in the pre-Alps, such as the Lessini Mountains (Veneto region) and middle-elevation sites (up to about 1600m asl) in the inner mountainous region, such as Trentino (i.e. Dalmeri and Pedrotti 1995).

As already suggested by previous authors, Epigravettian lithic industries are mainly knapped from local flint (Broglio *et al.* 1995) which, eventually, might be hoarded and stored on-site (Peresani 2003); an off-site utilisation of the products made from local flint is also evident (Broglio and Improta 1994/1995).

To highlight this technical behaviour, a sample of lithic items from three different Epigravettian open-air sites located in Trentino, very close to the city of Trento, have been analysed. The sample consisted of 1115 items from Andalo (Cremaschi and Lanzinger 1984; Guerreschi 1986), 773 items from Terlago (Bagolini and Dalmeri 1982), and 820 items from Viotte (Bagolini and Guerreschi 1980). According to the published data, sampling procedures consisted of gathering all the items found in Sector 4 (levels D, E, F, and G) in Andalo; in all the layers of the central part of the excavation in Terlago; in several square metres of the two main excavated areas in Viotte.

According to their colour, the lithic items were classified in five main groups: Brown, Grey, Yellow, Red, and Black. Groups show a greater or lesser inner variety in chromatic variability, as well as in other macroscopic features (such as inclusions, striations, and so on). Therefore, this must be considered as a very coarse-grained approach.

A strikingly homogeneous flint distribution among the three sites is observed (Figure 15.2). All the sites are characterized by local brown flint, even if local grey flint is present. More interestingly, when the inner variability of the brown and grey flint is shown, a clear pattern is observed. Brown flint is always characterised by high percentages of the strictly local reddish-brown variety at all the three sites; other brown flint types are scarce. On the contrary, several types of grey flint occur in the three sites with highly varied proportions.

On the basis of what has been stated earlier about flint

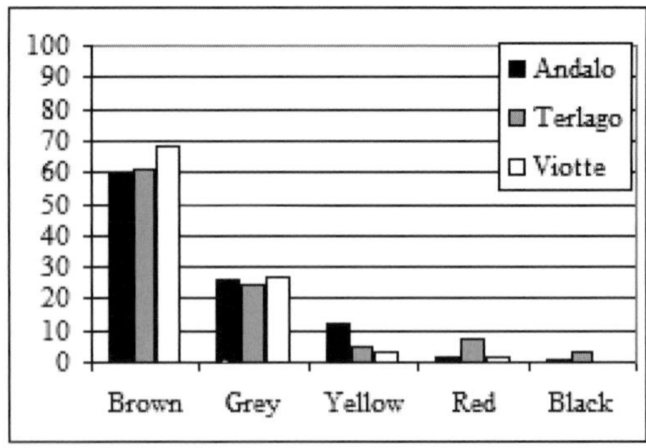

A

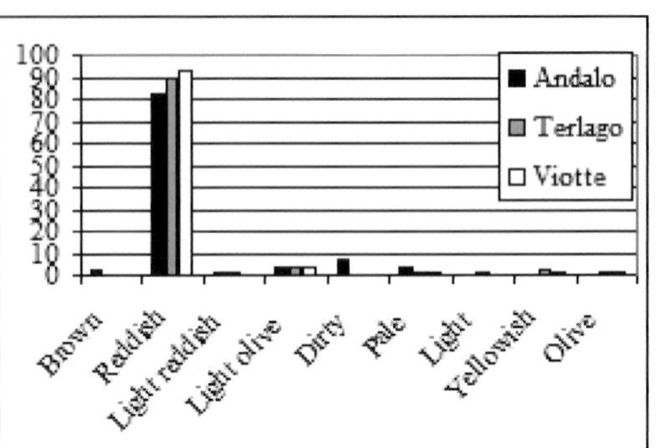

B

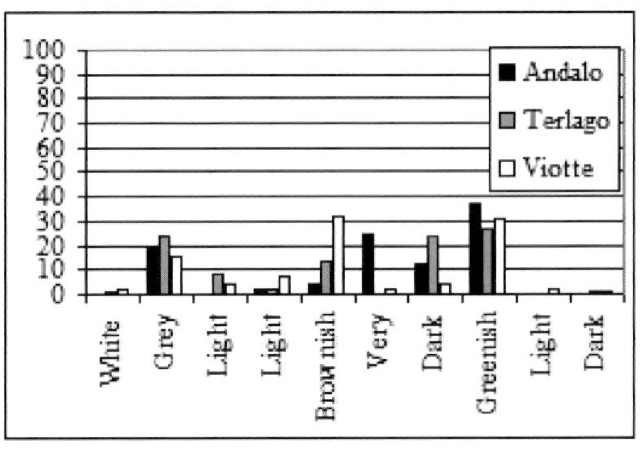

C

Figure 15.2. Raw material percentage distribution in Epigravettian sites: a) general flint colours; b) colour variation in Red flint; c) colour variation in Grey flint.

formations, it is possible to suggest that the Epigravettian human groups that inhabited the Andalo, Viotte, and Terlago sites, mainly exploited the strictly local raw material. The presence at the three sites of several types of non-local grey flint should be linked to a transportation of this flint from elsewhere. Following the 'most parsimonious' hypothesis, the nearest locations where grey flint may be found are a few tens of kilometres far in the south (presumably the Monte Baldo or Monti Lessini areas).

Accordingly, we may suggest, as a working hypothesis, that the Epigravettian human groups based their mobility strategies on the presence/absence of flint procurement areas; these areas may have acted as main 'colonizing' routes into the new mountain environment. This scenario seems to be clearly visible in Figure 15.3. Epigravettian sites are all located in, or very close to, areas characterized by

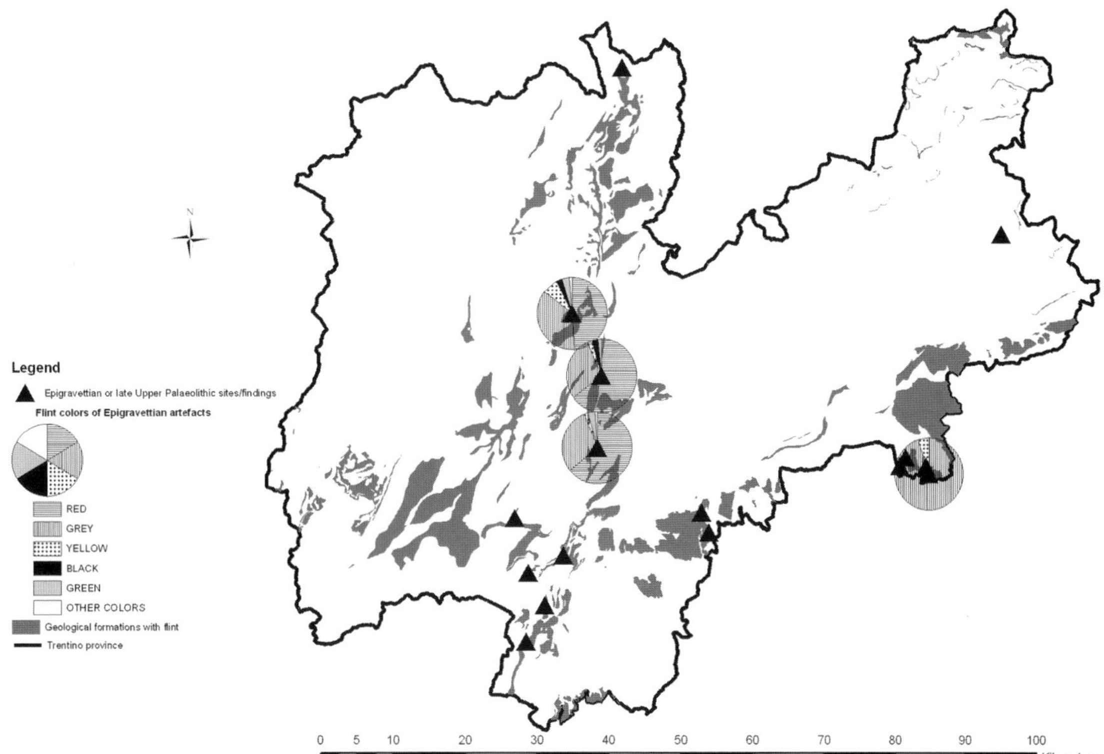

Figure 15.3. Distribution of potential flint formations vs. Epigravettian sites (the pie-charts refer to analysed sites).

the presence of geological formations that may potentially provide flint (no more than 2.5km).

The Early Mesolithic

Sauveterrian (or Early Mesolithic) human groups peopled the alpine environment from the beginning of the Preboreal to the end of the Boreal periods; now the territory seems to have been occupied overall. The distribution of the sites seems more intense than those of the preceding Palaeolithic groups. In Trentino, the altimetric distribution of Early Mesolithic archaeological evidence – taking into account the excavated sites and the surface finds of lithic artefacts – is characterised by the presence of sites on the valley floor (all the sites are located on the plain of the river Adige), and by many high-altitude sites, situated at *c.* 2000m (a review in Bagolini 1980; Dalmeri and Pedrotti 1995; Dalmeri *et al.* 2001). While the former are mainly rockshelters, all characterized by thick deposits and frequently showing complete Mesolithic stratigraphic sequences, the latter are characterized by small concentrations of lithic artefacts, with rare (if any) clear evidence of settlement features. Furthermore, faunal remains are rarely preserved at high-altitude sites.

Following the same coarse-grained methodology shown before, we sampled lithic items from several Sauveterrian sites located in Trentino: 4911 items from Layer H, L1, and L7–8 of the Pradestel rockshelter, the Adige valley (Bagolini and Broglio 1975; Bagolini *et al.* 1973), 997 items from Layer 4–5 (Site 1), Layer 6 (Site 2), and Layer 3–4 (Site 3) of the high-altitude open-air site of Lago delle Buse, central Trentino (Dalmeri and Lanzinger 1995), and 1453 items from Site 6 (entire assemblage), and from Sites 8, 8A, and 9 (several square metres showing the highest concentration of artefacts) of the high-altitude, open-air site of Colbricon, eastern Trentino (Bagolini 1972; Bagolini and Dalmeri 1988; 1995).

In contrast to the Epigravettian sites, Early Mesolithic sites do not seem to be characterized by a strikingly geographically-differentiated utilisation of raw materials. Therefore, the presence of flint of different origins is quite evident at all the sites (Figure 15.4). Variability seems to be more linked to the quantity of lithic material than to flint types. At Pradestel, where the local red flint is dominant, Grey flint occurs in the same percentages in all stratigraphic levels. At Lago delle Buse, located on the western edge of the Lagorai Mountains – an area where flint formations are completely absent – we notice a striking contrast between Site 1 and 3, where red flint is dominant, and Site 2, where Grey flint is dominant. Finally, at Colbricon, located on the eastern edge of the Lagorai Mountains, Grey flint is more abundant than the red variety. When the three localities are considered together, the average percentages of raw materials show a decreasing trend for red flint from west (Pradestel) to east (Colbricon); accordingly, the opposite trend characterizes grey flint. Lago delle Buse seems to play an intermediate role, probably the result of its geographic position between the valley of the River Adige and the eastern Lagorai Mountains.

As suggested by other authors (see, for instance, Broglio 1995), Sauveterrian human groups seem to fit a highly-mobile pattern, leading them to exploit all natural

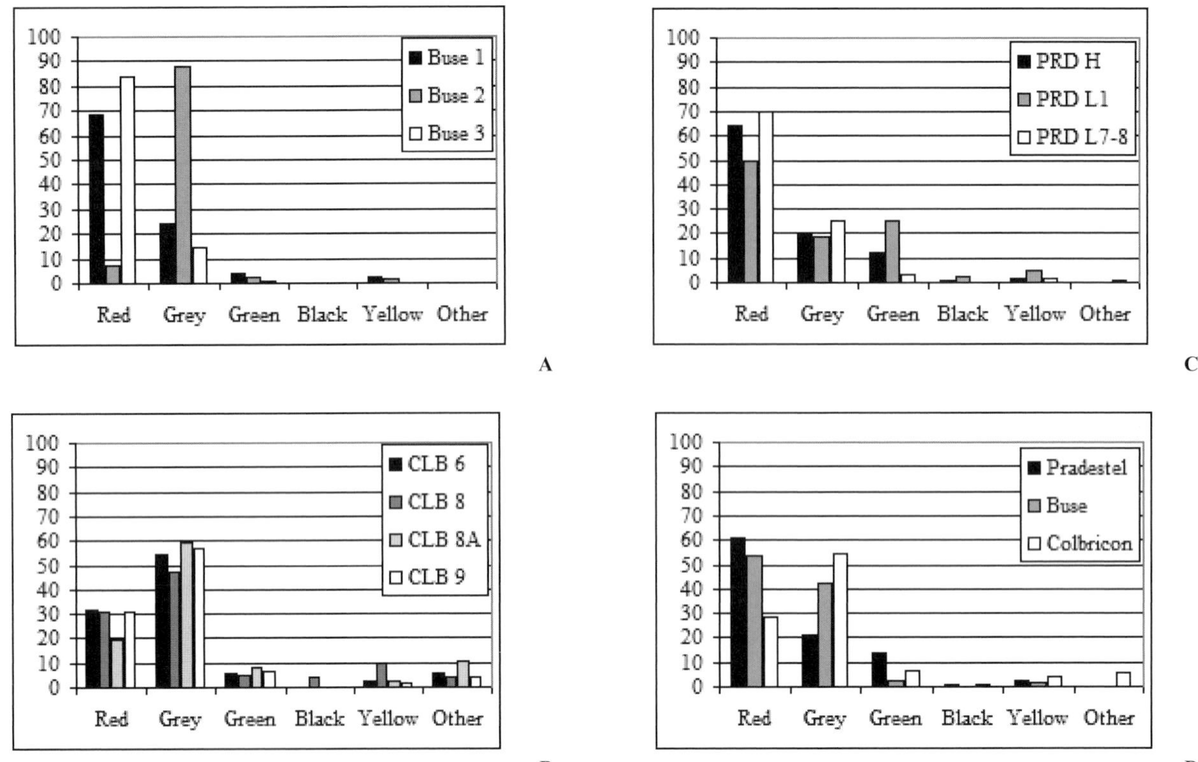

Figure 15.4. Raw material percentage distribution in Early Mesolithic sites: a) Lago delle Buse; b) Colbricon; c) Pradestel; d) mean percentage among the three Early Mesolithic sites.

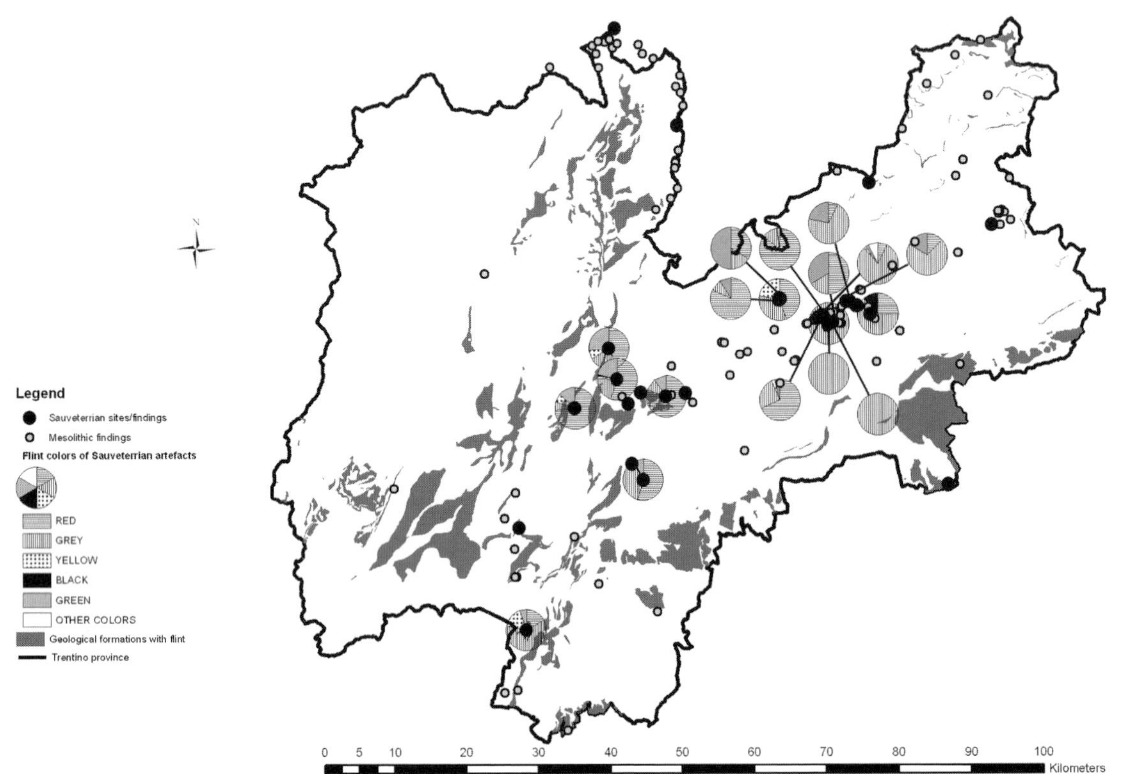

Figure 5. Distribution of potential flint formations vs. Sauveterrian sites (the pie-charts refer to analysed sites).

resources of the Alpine environment with little, if any, concern for those locations where flint formations may have been found. This is clearly visible in Figure 15.5: Sauveterrian sites are located even in areas with no flint formations. Several of them are more than 40km distant from the nearest potential flint supply.

Conclusions

The conclusions that can be drawn do not differ significantly from those already noted by previous scholars, but thanks to the use of GIS it is possible to study the variety of hypotheses formulated in more detail, and to develop new research models. The geographical relationship between the distribution of sites and the localization of flint crops suggest a mountain resource exploitation model employed by human groups from Late Pleistocene to the Early Holocene in north-eastern Italy which is much more dynamic and complex then previously described.

Settlement strategies employed by human groups in mountainous areas would seem to have gradually transformed from the abandoning of the previous Upper Palaeolithic 'opportunistic' model to a more specialised one, characterised by the intense use of high altitudes and valley floors.

In general, late Upper Palaeolithic human groups seem to show a progressive and continuous adaptation to the new mountain environment. Following the retreat of the glacier, the 'colonisation' process of this region may be seen as a consequence of the quest for natural resources available in the new exploitable mountain areas (such as flint, game, etc.). On the contrary, the climatic variations that took place from the Younger Dryas to the Boreal could have stimulated new relationships between the existing faunal and vegetal associations in the mountain areas. Mesolithic settlement dynamics, therefore, seem to be relatively independent from the distribution of flint resources and characterised by the intense use of the whole mountain environment.

Acknowledgements

Our research was financially supported by the Fondo Progetti di Ricerca Post-Doc, Provincia Autonoma di Trento. The authors are grateful to Dr Marco Avanzini (Museo Tridentino Scienze Naturali) and Dr Diego Angelucci (Trento University), who provided the basic information on the geological characteristics of the Trentino flint formations. The Geological Service of Trentino Province very kindly supplied most of the cartographic material. Il contributo degli autori è da considerarsi equivalente.

References

Avanzini, M., Broglio, A., De Stefani, M., Lanzinger, M., Lemorini, C. and Rossetti, P. 2002. The Cionstoan rockshelter at Alpe di Siusi. *Preistoria Alpina* 34 (1998), 81–98.

Bagolini, B. 1972. Primi risultati delle ricerche sugli insediamenti epipaleolitici del Colbricon (Dolomiti). *Preistoria Alpina* 8, 107–49.

Bagolini, B. 1980. *Il Trentino nella preistoria del mondo alpino*. Temi, Trento.

Bagolini, B., Barbacovi, F., Bergamo, G., Bertoldi, L., Mezzana, G. and Postal, L. 1973. Pradestel (Trento). *Preistoria Alpina* 9, 243–4.

Bagolini, B. and Broglio, A. 1975. Pradestel (Trento). *Preistoria Alpina* 11, 331.

Bagolini, B. and Broglio, A. 1985, Il ruolo delle alpi nei tempi preistorici (dal Paleolitico al Calcolitico). *Studi di Paletnologia in onore di S.M. Puglisi*, 671–76. Roma, Università 'La Sapienza'.

Bagolini, B. and Dalmeri, G. 1982. Lago di Terlago. *Preistoria alpina* 16, 101–3.

Bagolini, B. and Dalmeri, G. 1988. I siti mesolitici di Colbricon (Trentino): analisi spaziale e fruizione del territorio. *Preistoria Alpina* 23, 7–188.

Bagolini, B. and Dalmeri, G. 1995. Colbricon: a venti anni dalla scoperta. *Preistoria Alpina* 28, 285–92.

Bagolini, B. and Guerreschi, A. 1980. Notizie preliminari sulle ricerche 1977–1978 nell'insediamento paleolitico delle Viotte di Monte Bondone. *Preistoria Alpina* 14, 7–31.

Bassetti, M., Dalmeri, G., Kompatscher, K., Hrozny Kompatscher, M. and Lanzinger, M. 2002. Research on the Epigravettien site of riparo Dalmeri on the Sette Comuni plateau (Trento). *Preistoria Alpina* 34 (1998), 139–54.

Broglio, A. 1995. Mountain sites in the context of the north-east Italian Upper Paleolithic and Mesolithic. *Preistoria Alpina* 28, 293–310.

Broglio, A. and Improta, S. 1994–1995. Nuovi dati di cronologia assoluta del Paleolitico superiore e del Mesolitico del Veneto, del Trentino e del Friuli. *Atti dell'Istituto Veneto di Scienze, Lettere ed Arti* 153, 1–45.

Broglio, A. and Lunz, R. 1984. Osservazioni preliminari sull'utilizzazione del cristallo di rocca nelle industrie mesolitiche del bacino dell'Adige. *Preistoria Alpina* 19, 201–8.

Broglio, A., Castelletti, L., Frigo, G., Martello, G. V., Maspero, A. and Peresani, M. 1995. Val Lastari. *Preistoria Alpina* 28, 207–25.

Cremaschi, M. and Lanzinger, M. 1994. La successione stratigrafica e le fasi pedogenetiche del sito epigravettiano di Andalo. *Preistoria Alpina* 19, 179–88.

Dalmeri, G. and Lanzinger, M. 1995. Risultati preliminari delle ricerche nei siti mesolitici del Lago delle Buse nel Lagorai (Trentino). *Preistoria Alpina* 28, 317–49.

Dalmeri, G. and Pedrotti, A. 1994. Distribuzione topografica dei siti del Paleolitico superiore finale e del Mesolitico in Trentino Alto-Adige e nelle Dolomiti venete (Italia). *Preistoria Alpina* 28/2 (1992), 247–67.

Dalmeri, G., Grimaldi, S. and Lanzinger, M. 2001. Il Paleolitico e il Mesolitico, in M. Lanzinger, F. Marzatico and A. Pedrotti (eds.), *La preistoria e protostoria – Storia del Trentino* I, 15–118. Trento, Istituto Trentino di Cultura.

Fiore, I., Tagliacozzo, A. and Cassoli, P. F. 2002. Ibex exploitation at Dalmeri rockshelter and 'specialized hunting' in the sites of the eastern Alps during the Tardiglacial and the early Holocene. *Preistoria Alpina* 34 (1998), 173–84.

Guerreschi, A. 1986. Il sito epigravettiano di Andalo ed alcune considerazioni sull'Epigravettiano finale nel nord Italia. *Preistoria Alpina* 20, 15–38.

Peresani, M. 2003. *12000 anni fa al Bus de la Lum*. Pordenone, Società Naturalisti Silvia Zenari.

16. Evidence of mobility between the coast and the inland region in the Mesolithic of northern Fennoscandia

Mikael A. Manninen

Excavations conducted in 2004 at the Mesolithic Mávdnaávži 2 site in northern Finnish Lapland revealed an assemblage consisting mainly of chert deriving from the Barents Sea coast, although artefacts of local raw material were also found. Several details in the technological organization suggest that the site represents a location where a small number of foragers coming from the coast camped before moving on. The finds also provoke a new interpretation of a small number of finds of coastal raw materials found in assemblages dominated by local quartz further in the inland area. In the paper this data is used to devise a model of Late Mesolithic coast-inland mobility in northern Fennoscandia.

Keywords: technological organization, mobility, Finnmark, Lapland, Finland, lithic technology, oblique point, Late Mesolithic, chert.

Introduction

According to current knowledge, the pioneer habitation of the coast of Finnmark dates to *c.* 10,000–9500 BP (*c.* 9500–8800 cal BC; Thommessen 1996). Views on the pioneer settlement of the inland area of Finnmark and northern Finnish Lapland (earliest date *c.* 7830 cal BC, e.g. Carpelan 2004, 21–6) differ among researchers with the discussion centring on the question of whether the first settlers in the inland area arrived from the south (more southerly Finland), the north (Barents Sea coast), or possibly the east (Russia).

Without going any deeper into the discussion on pioneer settlement, it is important to note that there are clear typological and technological differences in many of the assemblages dated to the second phase (roughly 8000–6000 cal BC) of the Mesolithic in the area (*c.* 9000–7500/7000 BP, according to Olsen's (1994) chronology). This suggests that more or less separate populations used the inland area and the coastal area at the end of this phase (e.g. Kankaanpää and Rankama 2005, 101) and possibly also later, during the third Mesolithic phase (*c.* 6000–4400 cal BC or 7500/7000–5600 BP) (e.g. Olsen 1994, 36–42; but see Rankama 2003). However, the amount of interaction between the two populations and the possible use of both the coast and the inland by a single population, have not been sufficiently studied and the questions remain open.

Mesolithic mobility in the study area has mainly been touched upon in studies about the direction of inland settlement on the basis of raw material selection and environmental history, and the amount of sedentism vs. mobility indicated by investment in house constructions, raw material use, or artefact diversity (e.g. Bølviken *et al.* 1982, 48–51; Engelstad 1989, 335–36; Grydeland 2000; 2005; Halinen 2005, 89–90, 102, 108–9; Havas 1999; K. Helskog 1974; Odner 1964; Olsen 1994, 40–4; Rankama, 2003; Schanche 1988, 148–9). Hood (1992, 171–220) has conducted the most comprehensive research on Mesolithic mobility in the area, but in his study, as well as in other studies completed before the three-phase division of the Mesolithic in the area was developed, the Mesolithic material has been studied as a more or less monolithic entity.

In this paper I discuss the Late Mesolithic, i.e. the third Mesolithic phase of Finnmark, northern Finnish Lapland, and adjacent areas, with a special emphasis on sites around and north of Lake Inari (Figure 16.1). I then use this new evidence to devise a model of Late Mesolithic mobility between the Barents Sea coast and the inland region using the concept of technological organization (Nelson 1991; Tallavaara 2005). This framework is defined by Nelson (1991, 57) as: 'the study of the selection and integration of strategies for making, using, transporting, and discarding tools and the materials needed for their manufacture and maintenance. Studies of the organization of technology consider economic and social variables that influence those strategies.'

The geological basis for the model

The area under discussion is divided by a geological boundary. The dividing line between the Fennoscandian shield and younger sedimentary rocks of the Caledonian mountains runs roughly along the border between Finland and Norway (Lehtinen *et al.* 1998, 95). This border affects the division of lithic raw material sources: known sources of different kinds of light and dark grey fine-grained cherts are present only in the area north of the borderline between the Fennoscandian shield and the Caledonian mountains.

Hood (1992) has studied the distribution of lithic raw materials in north Norway and, according to him, sources of two types of grey chert are known from the Barents Sea coast, namely Kvenvik chert and Porsanger chert. Besides these sources, a previously unknown quarry of grey chert has been located by Halinen (2005, 27–8; 2006) in Guonjarvárri, in the northernmost part of the borough of Enontekiö, Finland (Figure 16.1). In addition, secondary rolled pebbles of several kinds of cherts can be found in the Precambrian tillites of Varangerfjord (Hood, pers. comm.). There are also sources of oolithic chert and probable, but thus far unknown, sources of tuffaceous chert in the area (Hood 1992), but these raw materials cannot be mistaken for the grey cherts.

In the area of present-day Finland the sole locally available lithic raw materials are macrocrystalline quartz and, to some degree, also different kinds of quartzites. Quartzites and macrocrystalline quartz are also available at the coast. The one-sidedness of the location of chert raw material sources opens concrete possibilities to study the flow of coastal raw materials into the inland area and to make inferences about mobility patterns, especially when combined with analyses of technological organization.

Types and dates of the Late Mesolithic

The typo-chronological definition for Late Mesolithic (*c.* 6000–4400 cal BC) in Finnmark presented by Olsen (1994, 33–5) is used in this paper for the whole study area, including northern Finnish Lapland and the county of Tromsø east of Malangenfjord. Halinen, however, has suggested a slightly different date (*c.* 6150–4850 cal BC) for the end of the third phase of the Mesolithic, since the oldest sites with Säräisniemi 1 pottery have been dated to

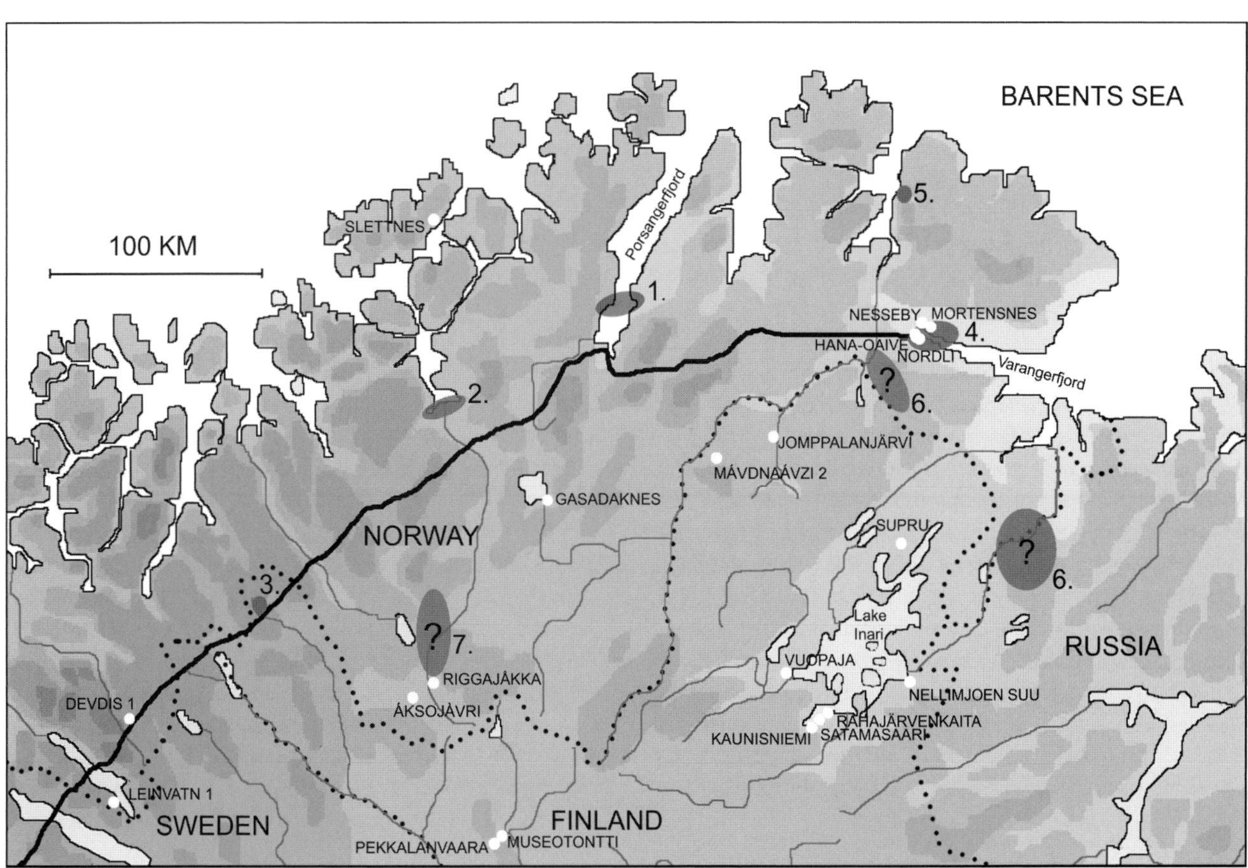

Figure 16.1. Map showing the study area and adjacent areas in Finland, Norway, Russia and Sweden. The black line indicates the border between the Fennoscandian shield and the Caledonian mountains. Known chert sources in the area are marked with numbers from 1 to 5: Porsanger chert (1); Kvenvik chert (2); Guonjarvárri quarries (3); Varanger tillites (4); Oolithic chert (5). Numbers 6 and 7 indicate possible source areas for tuffaceous chert (6) and metachert/quartzite (7) (data from Hood 1992; Halinen, pers. comm.). Sites that have yielded oblique points in excavations and surveys are marked with white dots. Data from Arponen 1990; Gjessing 1942; Halinen 2005; E. Helskog 1978; K. Helskog 1980; Hesjedal et al. 1996; Hood 1988; Manninen 2005; Nummedal 1938; Odner 1966; Kankaanpää and Rankama 2005; Schanche 1988; Simonsen 1961.

Site	Lab. No.	Date BP	cal BC 2σ	Type
Supru, Suprunoja	Hel-2117	6650±120	5780-5360	OP (a)
Devdis 1	T-1343	6575±150	5800-5200	OP (a)
Nordli	TUa-3028	6570±60	5630-5460	OP, Sär1(c)
	TUa-3021	6330±50	5390-5210	
Mávdnaávži 2	Hela-963	6455±45	5490-5320	OP (b)
Slettnes VA	Beta-49052	6390±80	5510-5210	OP (a)
	Beta-49056	6170±170	5500-4700	
	Beta-49053	5930±110	5100-4500	
	Beta-49054	5470±120	4550-3950	
Nellimjoen suu S	Hel-2678	6000±120	5250-4600	OP, Sär1 (a)
Rönkönraivio	Hela-38	5830±85	4900-4660	Sär 1 (c)
Mortensnes 8R12	T-6416	5770±190	5250-4200	OP (a)

Figure 16.2. Dates from charcoal (a), burnt bone (b), and food crust on pottery (c) associated with oblique points (OP) and Säräisniemi 1 Ware (Sär1) in the study area. Data from Carpelan 2004; Helskog 1980; Hesjedal et al. 1996; Kankaanpää and Rankama 2005; Schanche 1988; Sohlström 1992; Skandfer 2003. (Atmospheric data from Reimer et al. 2004; Bronk Ramsey 2005).

circa 4900 cal BC in northern Finnish Lapland (Carpelan 2004, 26–9; Halinen 2005, 32, 34; Torvinen 2000).

According to the typo-chronology (based on Woodman 1993), the characteristic type of lithic artefact used during the third phase of the Mesolithic, is the oblique arrowhead (e.g. K. Helskog 1980, figures 16–18; Manninen 2005, figure 7; Olsen 1994, figure 16; Schanche 1988, figure 28). I will henceforth call it the oblique point, although the edge angle varies and some points could be called single edged or even transverse (Helskog 1980, 73; Manninen 2005, 37). Points of this type have been found also on some sites that are usually considered Early Neolithic on account of a presence of Säräisniemi 1 sherds (Engelstad 1989, 336; Gjessing 1942, 174–7; Nummedal 1938, 2–7; Simonsen 1961, 104–5; Sohlström 1992).

Whether the occurrence, typologically, of both Late Mesolithic and Early Neolithic artefacts at the same sites is a consequence of pottery being adopted by the Late Mesolithic population in the area, or the spread of a new pottery-making population re-occupying old sites, is a question outside the scope of this paper. However, it is interesting to note that the earliest dates of Säräisniemi 1 pottery and the latest dates of contexts with oblique points clearly overlap in the study area (Figure 16.2). In this paper I have therefore chosen to group together all sites with oblique points and to ignore the traditional idea that sites should be divided into Late Mesolithic vs. Early Neolithic, according to the presence or non-presence of Säräisniemi 1 pottery.

In the map (Figure 16.1) the sites that have yielded oblique points in northern Finnish Lapland (Arponen 1990; Halinen 2005; Kankaanpää and Rankama 2005; Manninen 2005) are presented alongside the published sites from north Norway (E. Helskog 1978; K. Helskog 1980; Hood 1988; Nummedal 1938; Simonsen 1961; Odner 1966; Schanche 1988). Most of the sites are concentrated around the biggest lake in the area, Lake Inari, and on the shores of Varangerfjord, but the picture is probably biased since most of the archaeological research in Finnmark and northern Finnish Lapland has been conducted in these areas.

Many of the sites around, and north of Lake Inari have yielded oblique points of grey chert as well as points of tuffaceous chert, black chert, quartz and quartzite. It is once more worth emphasizing that no chert sources are known from this area and consequently, especially the fine-grained grey cherts found on some of the sites, must have been imported from the coast. Raw materials, as well as ready-made tools, could obviously have been transported to the inland area through many different mechanisms. A key site in this sense is the Mávdnaávži 2 site, situated around 50km as the crow flies from the nearest point of the Barents Sea coast. The assemblage from the site strongly suggests direct movement of people between the coast and the inland region.

The Mávdnaávži 2 site

The Mávdnaávži 2 site is situated on a small moraine ridge on the bank of a small stream in the Báišduottar – Paistunturi wilderness area. The site was found in a survey conducted in 1999 (Valtonen 1999). An excavation led by the author was conducted at the site in June 2004. Scarce vegetation and wind erosion enabled reliable surface observations of find distribution, making it possible to place the excavation accordingly. The limits of an area covering 52 square meters were marked and excavated. The area was kept as small as possible to avoid further erosion of the riverbank.

The structure of the site is clear. Activity at the site was situated parallel to the riverbank. The floor of a dwelling with, roughly, a three-metre diameter had been cleared out of stones at the north-east end of the otherwise stony camp area. Approximately 6m south-west of the hut there was an outdoor activity area. Both inside the hut and in the centre of the outdoor activity area there were traces of a fireplace. Stones had not been used in constructing the hearths, but burnt sand, and in the fireplace inside the dwelling burnt bone, small fire-cracked stones and charcoal indicated the place where the hearth had once been. Both hearths were surrounded by clearly defined lithic scatters. The only clear post-depositional disturbance in the horizontal stratigraphy was the movement of some artefacts on the surface along reindeer tracks. Vertically, all artefacts were situated in a tight, mostly four- to five-centimetre-thick layer right below the surface.

The scatter in the outdoor activity area consisted of retouch flakes, flake blanks and scrapers of quartz and quartzite, and a flake of black chert. The activity area inside the hut consisted of debitage, retouched flakes, backed pieces, and intact and broken oblique points of grey chert. An accelerator mass spectrometry (AMS) dating obtained from burnt bone (from a small pit associated with the hearth inside the hut) gives the site a Late Mesolithic date (Figure 16.2). Although a single date, the result is in accordance with the typologically Late Mesolithic find material and is therefore considered reliable.

Nodule	No of art.	Weight g	Tools	Tool types
GyC	726	**137.1**	47	Points, retouched pieces
BC	1	**0.9**	0	
GQz	8	**29.5**	4	Scrapers
LGyQz	6	**12.1**	1	Scraper
BQz	7	**9**	1	Scraper
GyQz	4	**10.1**	1	Scraper
WQz	4	**6.6**	0	
P	1	**4.9**	1	Abrader
Q	187	**277.2**	13	Scrapers

Figure 16.3. Analytical nodules in the Mávdnaávži 2 assemblage. Tool-counts include all tool fragments. GyC = grey chert, BC = black chert, GQz = green quartzite, LGyQz = Light-grey fine-grained quartzite, BQz = Greyish-brown banded quartzite, GyQz = Grey fine-grained quartzite, WQz = coarse-grained white quartzite, P = pumice, Q = quartz.

Duration of the site's use – analyses and considerations

Although the Mávdnaávži 2 site is quite obviously a campsite with a short life span, it is impossible to infer solely by reconstructing the general site structure and by classifying the finds, what kind of mobility strategy the site was a part of. With this is mind, analyses suitable for the study of future activity planning (Larson 1994) and the relative length of occupation were conducted.

The survey finds collected when the site was found in 1999 include eight artefacts of grey chert, three of quartz, and one of quartzite. The excavation yielded altogether 932 lithic artefacts. Of these 718 are of grey chert, 184 of quartz, and 28 of different kinds of quartzite. In addition, one flake of black chert and a piece of pumice were found. All the lithic artefacts were divided into analytical nodules (*sensu* e.g. Larson 1994). According to this division the assemblage consists of nine analytical nodules, i.e. the piece of pumice, five kinds of quartzite, two kinds of chert and the artefacts of white quartz (Figure 16.3). Although the raw material of the quartz artefacts varies from white to transparent, they were all classified as one analytical nodule. The reason for this is the fact that in the local quartz both transparent and milky quartz are often encountered in the same piece.

The only raw materials available locally are quartz and coarse-grained white quartzite. Of these, quartz has been frequently encountered in surveys but the coarse-grained quartzite only occasionally (Manninen 2005, 32–3). All the other raw materials used at the Mávdnaávži 2 site are exotic to the area. The nearest known sources for grey chert are located on the shores of Porsangerfjord and Varangerfjord (Figure 16.1) and it is quite safe to say that the grey chert at the site has a coastal origin. The same applies to the piece of pumice and probably also for the black chert. The fine-grained quartzites are not local, but with current knowledge it is not possible to define a source area for them.

At the site grey chert was used for oblique points and other kinds of backed pieces and retouched flakes (Figure 16.3). All the points and point fragments found in the excavation were located within the hut area, mostly in and around the hearth. It is probable that some of the point fragments have been left at the spot as a consequence of repairing broken arrows. The relatively large amount of point fragments that do not refit with other fragments supports this view. There are, however, three base fragments and three distal parts of points that do refit. At least two of these have broken during manufacture by fractures initiating from retouch scars. An interesting detail is that two of the six fragments are burnt and were obviously dropped into the fire. This has resulted in refits between burnt basal parts of points and un-burnt tips.

The overall picture of the chert material suggests that points at the site were manufactured mainly from irregular flakes/blade-flakes, but it is unclear whether the flakes were brought to the site as ready-made blanks or as a core that was not left there. It seems also likely that at least part of the retouched chert flakes are actually rejected point preforms.

Quartz and quartzite were used for scrapers. The quartz and quartzite flakes, as well as the sixteen scrapers of these raw materials found in the excavation, were located next to the presumed hearth in the middle of the outside activity area. Five of the six quartzite scrapers found at the site are made of different kinds of fine-grained quartzite. Besides these, the quartzite assemblage consists of retouch flakes of the same raw materials and three larger pieces of quartzite, of which two fit together and form a complete flake.

The quartz assemblage is more difficult to tackle because of the homogeneity of the material and difficulties related

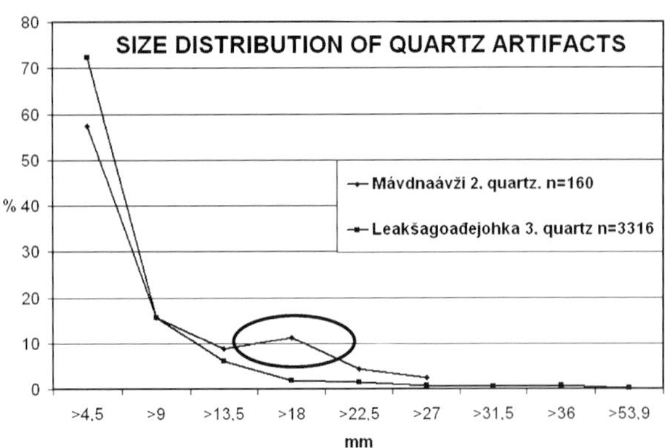

Figure 16.4. Size distribution of quartz artefacts. Leakšagoađejohka 3 (see Manninen 2002).

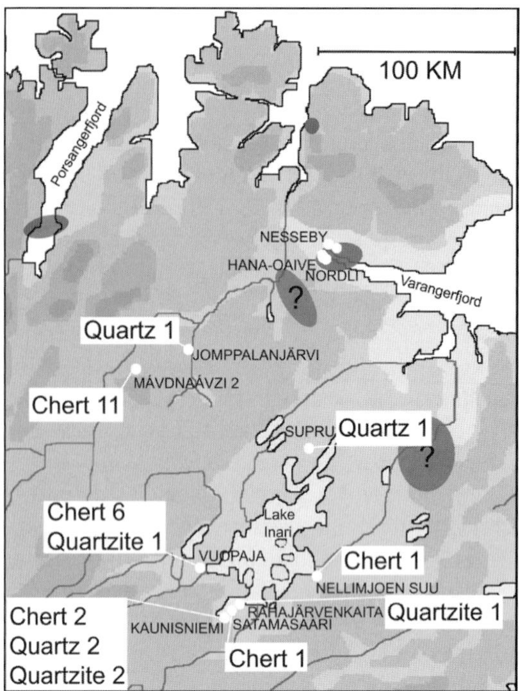

Figure 16.5. The amount of oblique points of different raw materials at sites around and north of Lake Inari. Grey chert: Utsjoki Mávdnaávži 2, 11 points; Inari Vuopaja, 4 points; Inari Kaunisniemi 3, 1 point. The other chert points are of tuffaceous chert and black chert.

to the study of quartz (Rankama *et al.* 2006). In addition to the twelve scrapers in the quartz assemblage there are several clear retouch flakes, one bipolar core, and a fair amount of flakes and fragments of different sizes. The size distribution of the quartz assemblage, however, did not seem to be a result of a complete reduction sequence. To find out if this is true, the size distribution of the assemblage was compared to the size distribution of a quartz-knapping floor situated circa 15km south-east of the Mávdnaávži 2 site (Manninen 2002) (Figure 16.4).

The comparisons revealed that there is an over-representation of quartz artefacts with a minimum dimension of *c.* 20mm in the assemblage and a relatively small amount of small flake fragments and chips. This corresponds with the picture given by the quartzite artefacts of a situation where ready-made scrapers and scraper blanks were brought along to the site and retouched to make new scrapers and to rejuvenate used edges.

In summary, the results of the analyses suggest that the site was a single-occupation hunting camp used by a group of foragers coming from the coast. All the lithic material was brought to the site as ready-made tools, flake blanks, and possibly also as a core of grey chert. Although tools of coastal raw material were carried along to the site, local quartz was used for re-tooling. The technology was not specialized in a way that moving away from the sources of coastal fine-grained raw materials would have affected it. In fact, the manufacturing of scrapers from blanks of local quartz indicates that quartz blanks were also collected for further use; and the discarding of blanks of fine-grained quartzite and chert reveal that these raw materials were not overly valued. This, combined with the fact that several different kinds of exotic raw materials were used at the site, is clear evidence of a highly mobile group, who had a technology suitable for all the raw materials encountered while changing places both in the coastal area and in the inland region.

The Model based on the Lake Inari region

The traces of a mobile group at Mávdnaávži 2 unrestricted by the locations of sources for fine-grained lithic raw-materials, encourages one to evaluate whether some of the other known Late Mesolithic assemblages indicate a similar pattern. The data presented here covers only the sites with reported oblique points or points that I have observed while analysing 'older' assemblages. It is probable that the amount of sites with oblique points will increase with further analysis, and it should be noted that there are more sites with Late Mesolithic dates in the area than the ones discussed here (see Kankaanpää and Rankama 2005). Therefore the model presented in this paper should be considered provisional until further analysis has been conducted.

In the area around and north of Lake Inari, excavations have been conducted at, at least, three other sites with oblique points: Inari Supru Suprunoja (Nieminen 1984), Inari Vuopaja (Seppälä 1993; 1994), and Inari Nellimjoen suu S (Sohlström 1992). The Mávdnaávži 2 site, however, is the only clear single-occupation site. Besides the excavated sites, there are at least five sites that have yielded oblique points in surveys: Inari Satamasaari, Inari Rahajärvenkaita, Inari Kaunisniemi 2, Inari Kaunisniemi 3 (Arponen 1990), and Utsjoki Jomppalanjärvi W (Rankama and Kankaanpää 1997).

Oblique points of grey chert (five points), black chert (two points), tuffaceous chert (three points), quartz (four points) and different kinds of quartzite (three points) have been found at these sites (Figure 16.5). At the Utsjoki Jomppalanjärvi W site, an implement of grey chert has also been found alongside an oblique point of quartz (Rankama and Kankaanpää 1997). The material from

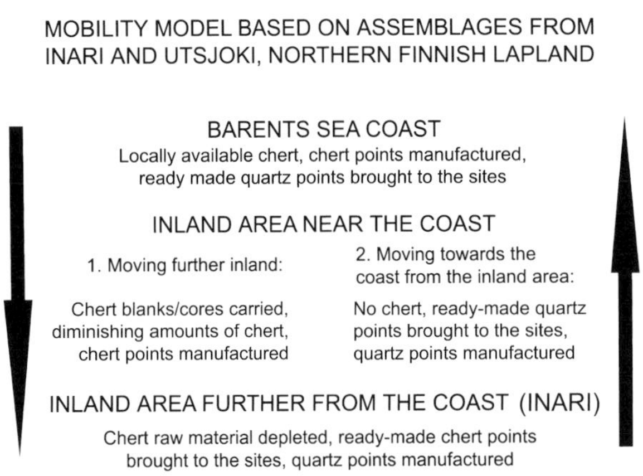

Figure 16.6. Schematic mobility model based on the assemblages discussed in the text. The model predicts what kind of Late Mesolithic assemblages should be found in and between the Barents Sea coast and the inland region.

these sites is too limited to make any definite conclusions, but it should be noted that the Mávdnaávži 2 site is the only site with evidence of chert point manufacture. For instance, the extensively excavated multi-period Inari Vuopaja-Saamenmuseo site complex on the western shore of Lake Inari has yielded two points of black chert, and four points and three flakes/bladeflakes of grey chert in two separate concentrations, but no debitage from chert point manufacture.

Although restricted, the available material allows the making of a schematic mobility model for the area (Figure 16.6). The starting point in the model is the area with the chert sources, i.e. the Barents Sea coast. The amount of grey chert, as well as other coastal raw materials, decreases towards the Lake Inari region. This should be seen in the archaeological material as a succession from sites with chert point manufacturing debitage and chert points, to sites where only quartz points and debitage is found. This would also result in sites with only quartz points and debitage and sites with only chert points and chert point manufacturing debitage in the same area, i.e. in the 'transitional zone' between the coast and the Lake Inari region. The model also predicts that oblique quartz points should be found at Late Mesolithic coastal sites, an artefact category thus far not reported in the literature concerning the coastal sites. In support of the model, however, Grydeland (2000, 44–5) has noted that quartz artefacts are very common at many Late Mesolithic sites, for instance on the shores of Varangerfjord.

To conclude, the fact that the same forager groups used both the coastal region and the inland region in the Late Mesolithic of northern Fennoscandia, as has been suggested in some of the earlier research, seems to be, if not verified, at least highly probable in light of the new data. The model presented in this paper, derived from a combination of previous research and the new data, still needs further developing and testing. It is clear, however, that long distance mobility existed in the area during the Late Mesolithic, at least to some degree. The nature of, and the reasons for this mobility, however, still need further research.

Acknowledgements

The excavations at the Mávdnaávži 2 site and the lithic analyses were financed by the Finnish Cultural Foundation, and the writing of this paper by the Emil Aaltonen foundation. I thank Petri Halinen, Esa Hertell, Bryan Hood, Eeva-Kristiina Lahti, Tuija Rankama, Hanna Suisto, Miikka Tallavaara, Riikka Tevali, Taarna Valtonen and Meri Varonen for their aid and comments, and the organizers of MESO 2005 for the opportunity to present this paper.

References

Arponen, A. 1990. *Inari. Rahajärven arkeologinen inventointi 1990*. Archived survey report. Helsinki, National Board of Antiquities, Department of Archaeology.

Bronk Ramsey, C. 2005. OxCal 3.10. WWW program and documentation available at http://www.rlaha.ox.ac.uk/oxcal/oxcal.htm (accessed 10/2007).

Bølviken, E., Helskog, E., Helskog, K., Holm-Olsen, I. M., Solheim, L. and Bertelsen, R. 1982. Correspondence analysis: an alternative to principal components. *World Archaeology* 14 (1), 41–60.

Carpelan, C. 2004. Environment, Archaeology and Radiocarbon Dates. Notes from the Inari Region, Northern Finnish Lapland, in M. Lavento (ed.), *Early in the North, 5*, 17–45. Iskos 13. Helsinki, The Finnish Antiquarian Society.

Engelstad, E. 1989. Mesolithic House Sites in Arctic Norway, in Bonsall, C. (ed.) *The Mesolithic in Europe. Papers presented at the Third International Symposium, Edinburgh 1985*, 331–7. Edinburgh, John Donald Publishers.

Gjessing, G. 1942. *Yngre steinalder i Nord-Norge*. Serie B, Skrifter 39. Oslo, Instututtet for sammenlignende kulturforskning.

Grydeland, S.-E. 2000. Nye perspektiver på eldre steinalder i Finnmark – En studie fra indre Varanger. *Viking* LXIII, 10–50.

Grydeland, S.-E. 2005. The Pioneers of Finnmark – from the earliest coastal settlements to the encounter with the inland people of Northern Finland, in H. Knutsson (ed.), *Pioneer settlements and colonization processes in the Barents region*, 43–77. Vuollerim Papers on Hunter-Gatherer Archaeology 1. Vuollerim, Vuollerim Museum Press.

Halinen, P. 2005. *Prehistoric Hunters of Northernmost Lapland. Settlement patterns and subsistence strategies*. Iskos 14. Helsinki, The Finnish Antiquarian Society.

Havas, H. 1999. *Innland uten landgrenser. Bosetningsmodeller i det nordligeste Finland og Norge i perioden 9000-6000 BP*. MA thesis, University of Tromsø.

Helskog, E. 1978. Finnmarksviddas kulturhistorie, in *Finnmarksvidda – nature – kultur*, 135–44. Norges offentlige utredninger (NOU) 1978, 18A. Oslo, Universitets-forlaget.

Helskog, K. 1974. Stone Age Settlement Patterns in Interior North Norway. *Arctic Anthropology* XI (Supplement), 266–71.

Helskog, K. 1980. *Subsistence-Economic Adaptations to the Alpine Regions of Interior North Norway*. PhD thesis. University of Wisconsin-Madison. Ann Arbor, University Microfilms.

Hesjedal, A., Damm, C., Olsen, B. and Storli, I., 1996. *Arkeologi på Slettnes. Dokumentasjon av 11. 000 års bosetning*. Tromsø Museums Skrifter 26, Tromsø, University of Tromsø.

Hood, B. C. 1988. Undersøkelse av en steinalderboplass ved Aksujavri, Kautokeino kommune, Finnmark, in E. Engelstad and M. Holm-Olsen (eds.), *Arkeologisk feltarbeid i Nord-Norge og på Svalbard 1986*, 23–31. Tromura, Kulturhistorie 14. Tromsø, Universitetet i Tromsø.

Hood, B. C. 1992. *Prehistoric Foragers of the North Atlantic: Perspectives on Lithic Procurement and Social Complexity in the North Norwegian Stone Age and the Labrador Maritime Archaic*. Unpublished PhD thesis, University of Massachusetts.

Kankaanpää, J. and Rankama, T. 2005. Early Mesolithic pioneers in Northern Finnish Lapland, in H. Knutsson (ed.), *Pioneer settlements and colonization processes in the Barents region*, 109–61. Vuollerim Papers on Hunter-Gatherer Archaeology 1. Vuollerim, Vuollerim Museum Press.

Larson, M. L. 1994. Toward a Holistic Analysis of Chipped Stone Assemblages, in P. J. Carr (ed.), *The Organization of North American Prehistoric Chipped Stone Tool Technologies*, 57–69. International Monographs in Prehistory, Archaeological Series 7. Ann Arbor, Department of Anthropology, University of Michigan.

Lehtinen, M., Nurmi, P. and Rämö, T. 1998. *Suomen Kallioperä 3000 vuosimiljoonaa*. Jyväskylä, Suomen Geologinen Seura.

Manninen, M. A. 2002. *Utsjoki Leakšagoađejohka 3. Esihistoriallisen kvartsikeskittymän kaivaus*. Archived excavation report. Helsinki, National Board of Antiquities, Department of Archaeology.

Manninen, M. A. 2005. Problems in Dating Inland Sites – Lithics and the Mesolithic in Paistunturi, Northern Finnish Lapland, in H. Knutsson (ed.), *Pioneer settlements and colonization processes in the Barents region*, 29–41. Vuollerim Papers on Hunter-Gatherer Archaeology 1. Vuollerim, Vuollerim Museum Press.

Nelson, M. C. 1991. The Study of Technological Organization, in M. B. Schiffer (ed.), *Archaeological Method and Theory* 3, 57–100. Tuscon, University of Arizona Press.

Nieminen, E.-L. 1984. *Inari 331 Supru, Suprunoja. Kertomus kivikautisen asuinpaikan kaivauksesta 1984*. Archived excavation report. Helsinki, National Board of Antiquities, Department of Archaeology.

Nummedal, A. 1938. Yngre stenaldersfunn fra Nyelven og Karlebotn I Østfinnmark II. *Universitetets oldsaksamling årbok* 1937, 1–26.

Odner, K. 1964. Erharv og bosetning i Komsakulturen. *Viking* XXVIII, 117–28.

Odner, K. 1966. *Komsakulturen i Nesseby og Sør-Varanger*. Skrifter XII. Tromsø, Tromsø Museums.

Olsen, B. 1994. *Bosetning og samfunn i Finnmarks forhistorie*. Oslo, Universitetsforlaget.

Rankama, T. 2003. The colonisation of northernmost Finnish Lapland and the inland areas of Finnmark, in L. Larsson, H. Kindgren, K. Knutsson, D. Loeffler and A. Åkerlund (eds.), *Mesolithic on the Move: Papers presented at the Sixth International Conference on the Mesolithic in Europe, Stockholm 2000*, 684–7. Oxford, Oxbow Books.

Rankama, T. and Kankaanpää, J. 1997. *Utsjoki 209 Jomppalanjärvi W. Arkeologisen kohteen tarkistus*. Archived inspection report. Helsinki, National Board of Antiquities, Department of Archaeology.

Rankama, T., Manninen, M. A., Hertell, E. and Tallavaara, M. 2006. Simple Production and Social Strategies – Do They Meet? Social Dimensions in Eastern Fennoscandian Quartz Technologies, in J. Apel and K. Knutsson (eds.), *Skilled Production and Social Reproduction: Aspects of Traditional Stone-Tool Technologies*, 1245–61. Societas Archaeologica Upsaliensis (SAU) Stone Studies 2. Uppsala, Societas Archaeologica Upsaliensis.

Reimer P. J., Baillie, M. G. L., Bard, E., Bayliss, A., Beck, J. W., Bertrand, C., Blackwell, P. G., Buck, C. E., Burr, G., Cutler, K. B., Damon, P. E., Edwards, R. L., Fairbanks, R. G., Friedrich, M., Guilderson, T. P., Hughen, K. A., Kromer, B., McCormac, F. G., Manning, S., Bronk Ramsey, C., Reimer, R. C., Remmele, S., Southon, J. R., Stuiver, M., Talamo, S., Taylor, F. W., van der Plicht, J., and Weyhenmeyer, C. E. 2004. IntCal04 terrestrial radiocarbon age calibration, 0-26 cal kyr BP. *Radiocarbon* 46 (3), 1029–58.

Schanche, K. 1988. *Mortensnes - en boplass i Varanger. En studie av samfunn og materiell kultur gjennom 10.000 år*. MA thesis, University of Tromsø.

Seppälä, S.-L. 1993. *Inari 13 Vuopaja. Kivi- ja varhaismetallikautisen asuinpaikan kaivaus* (13–27 July 1993). Archived excavation report. Helsinki, National Board of Antiquities, Department of Archaeology.

Seppälä, S.-L. 1994. *Inari 13 Vuopaja. Kivi- ja varhaismetallikautisen asuinpaikan kaivaus* (13 June–18 July 1994). Archived excavation report. Helsinki, National Board of Antiquities, Department of Archaeology.

Simonsen, P. 1961. *Varanger-Funnene II. Fund og udgravninger på fjordens sydkyst*. Tromsø Museums Skrifter VII (2). Tromsø, Tromsø Museum.

Skandfer, M. 2003. *Tidlig, nordlig kamkeramikk. Typologi-kronologi-kultur*. Unpublished PhD thesis. University of Tromsø.

Sohlström, B. 1992. En stenåldershydda – en bosättningsanalys. *Kentältä poimittua. Museovirasto, esihistorian toimisto, julkaisu* 2, 27–38.

Tallavaara, M. 2005. Arkeologisen kiviaineiston nodulianalyysi. Sovellusesimerkki Rääkkylän Vihin kampakeraamisen ajan asuinpaikan piikivimateriaaliin. *Muinaistutkija* 2/2005, 14–23.

Thommessen, T. 1996. The Early Settlement of Northern Norway, in L. Larsson, L. (ed.), *The Earliest Settlement of Scandinavia and its relationship with neighbouring areas*, 235–40. Acta Archaeologica Lundensia, Series in 8°, 24. Stockholm, Almquist & Wiksell International.

Torvinen, M. 2000. Säräisniemi 1 ware. *Fennoscandia Archaeologica* XVI, 3–35.

Valtonen, T. 1999. *Utsjoen Paistunturien inventointi* (6–28 June and 9–26 August 1999). Archived survey report. Helsinki, National Board of Antiquities, Department of Archaeology.

Woodman, P. C. 1993. The Komsa Culture: a re-examination of its position in the Stone Age of Finnmark. *Acta Archaeologica* 63/1992, 57–76.

17. Walking around the Federsee: analyzing mobility and settlement through regional surface survey in south-west Germany

Susan K. Harris, Harry Starr, Lynn E. Fisher and Michael Jochim

Archeologists have assumed that the Mesolithic of Oberschwaben in south-western Germany has been primarily a lakeside phenomenon. Since 1992 the 'Southwest Germany Regional Archaeological Survey Project' (SWGRASP) has been testing the assumption by documenting numerous prehistoric sites on and away from the shores of the Federsee Lake. The results raise questions about the influence of wetlands on Mesolithic mobility. How strongly did lakes and rivers influence prehistoric decisions about settlement patterns? Did large tracts of land away from the Federsee Lake stand unoccupied? Is surface survey an appropriate method for addressing these issues? A geographic information systems (GIS) model of travel times and lithic scatter densities is employed to begin investigating these questions.

Keywords: Mesolithic, southern Germany, geographic information systems, regional survey, hunter-gatherer mobility.

Introduction

The Mesolithic of southwest Germany has a long and thorough history of research, focused in particular upon the caves of the Swabian Alb, and upon lakeshore sites in the rolling hills of Oberschwaben (Eriksen 1991; Jochim 1998). This strong background of research makes southwest Germany an ideal location for investigations of the mobility patterns of prehistoric hunter-gatherers. The multi-year Southwest Germany Regional Archaeological Survey Project concentrated within the region from Lake Constance to the edge of the Swabian Alb (Fisher and Knipper 2003; Jochim *et al.* 1998). Based on GIS analysis of survey results using a hiking function to put site distribution in behavioral perspective, we address long-standing questions about hunter-gatherer land use in the region and begin to investigate new questions about different scales of Mesolithic hunter-gatherer mobility.

'Southwest Germany Regional Archaeology Survey Project'

The excellent preservation conditions at the Federsee Lake have led archaeologists to excavate many lakeshore sites from all phases of prehistory. However, to place the lakeshore finds into a regional context, research on areas away from the lakeshore is necessary. Previous work between the Swabian Alb and Lake Constance has identified sites from all Stone Age time periods (Figure 17.1). In addition to the sites around the Federsee, the previous work has identified other concentrations of Mesolithic sites to the north in the caves of the Swabian Alb, to the south on Lake Constance, and around the Pfrunger Ried, a small bog to the southwest of the Federsee. However, the previous work has not attempted to investigate systematically the lands away from these concentrations. Since the previous archaeological finds have clustered around lakeshores and in caves, archaeologists have generally assumed that the Federsee Lake represented an important and unique regional resource. Certainly the high density of lake sites supports this view, but it is likely that Stone Age peoples also occupied and utilized regions away from the Federsee Lake. Contextual data from the surrounding areas will be crucial to a valid assessment of the actual importance of the lake itself or of its place within regional settlement patterns.

Consideration of the high density of finds around the Federsee Lake led to the creation of SWGRASP to investigate the regional context and significance of sites on the Federsee. The empirical question behind this research is: is the pattern of high find density on the lake shore the result

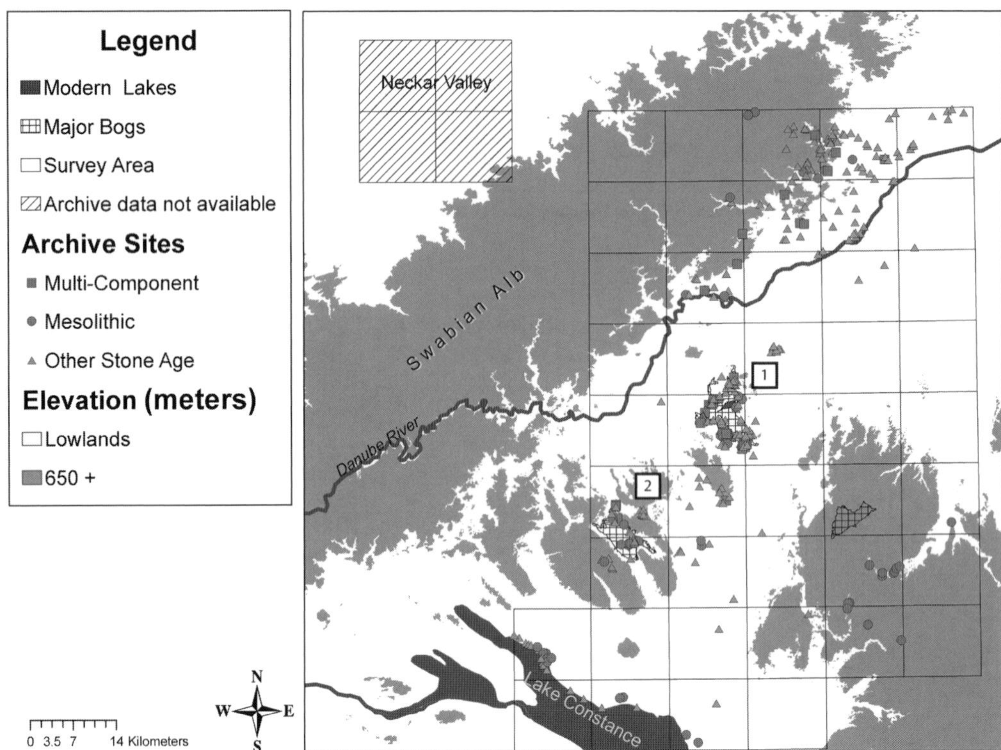

Figure 17.1. The archive database includes all known Stone Age sites for the study area, and is based on a review of published literature as well as generous access to records of the State Office of Historic Preservation. The database is not yet completed for the extended survey region in the Neckar Valley to the north-west. 1) Modern Federsee Lake and surrounding bog; 2) Pfrunger-Ried bog. (DEM source: CIAT and CGIAR 2004).

of a long history of research in that location, or was the Federsee really more intensively used during the Mesolithic than neighbouring regions. From the very beginnings of the project it was decided that only a surface survey could ensure the broad coverage of the areas surrounding the lake required to explore the currently known site distribution and determine whether or not it was representative of prehistoric land use patterns.

The survey results pose several research questions about the mobility of Mesolithic hunter-gatherers on and around the Federsee Lake. Defining mobility is a challenge for archaeologists because the deceptively simple term embraces several potential independent behavioural dimensions. Among them are the frequency of group movement, the distance that groups move, and who in the groups was involved in the moves. People also move for several reasons besides the primary pursuit of resources. They move to visit family and friends, to avoid conflicts with neighbours, or to participate in ritual activities.

In analysis of the survey data, we focus on two different scales of mobility. The first scale deals with the amount of area that might be used in the course of daily activities from a residential camp on the Federsee. Although we cannot at this time confirm that any of the surface sites from the Federsee and Pfrunger Ried are indeed residential camps, the high density and diversity of finds suggests that they are good candidates. Follow-up excavation at locations with intact buried deposits will be necessary to make this final assessment. Sites from the Alb caves have been excavated, and several have been confirmed as likely residential camp locations (Kind 1996).

The second scale of mobility concerns the distance to which residential camps might be relocated, or where logistical trips longer than one day would be necessary to take advantage of the available resources. For example, would the areas surrounding the Federsee, Pfrunger Ried, and the Alb belong to the same daily foraging radius, or would they be exploited from different residential camps?

Further consideration needs to be given to how large an area should be included in a survey if one of the project goals is to understand the mobility patterns of prehistoric hunter-gatherers. Although it is very difficult to identify the size of such areas, a small sample of data on the annual range of mobility among ethnographically documented hunting and gathering groups from Kelly 1995 provides some guidelines for the minimum and maximum extents that might be expected for people living in temperate or boreal forests (Figure 17.2).

The minimum value for such areas, from the Wiyot, is less than the size of the Federsee itself. The maximum value, from the Crow, includes much of southern Germany, Switzerland, and parts of Austria. These cases represent two major factors that tend to affect territory size: degree of reliance on terrestrial game, and modes of transportation. The Wiyot of coastal northern California relied heavily on fishing resources that allowed them to lead a more sedentary life. In the case of the historic Crow living on the Great Plains, reliance on horses for transportation likely

Group	Annual Residential Moves	Average Distance (km)	Total Distance (km)	Total Area (km^2)
Crow	38	19.2	640	61880
Montagnais	50	64		2700
Mistassini Cree	10		510	3385
Klamath	11	7.5	84	1058
Gulf Salish	3	34.9	77	631
Straits Salish	4–5		75–110	58
Ainu	2	4.3	8.6	171
Wiyot	0-2			32
Yurok	0-2			35
Twana	4		48–70	211
Makah	2	7.3	15	190
S. Tlingit	3			1953
Tolowa	2?			91
S. Kwakiutl	3, >4	13.6	35, 252–276	727
Nuuchahnulth	>3	10	30	370.5

Figure 17.2. Selected examples of forest-dwelling hunter-gatherer groups and their annual range of mobility. (Source: Kelly 1995).

accounts for the very large size of their territory. The next largest territory from the ethnographic list is the Cree from North Dakota and Montana. These areas, as well as the average taken from all the groups listed, provide better ethnographic representations of the amount of territory used by Mesolithic forest-dwelling hunter-gatherers. These areas compare favourably in size with the selected study area (Figure 17.3). Based on these comparisons, we suggest that the SWGRASP study area is large enough to offer good potential for detecting patterns in both shorter- and longer-term hunter-gatherer mobility.

The survey area also includes a variety of environmental settings. It is centred on the Federsee and is a transect from the Danube valley along the edge of the Swabian Alb to the north, through the rolling hills of Oberschwaben with its many wetlands and river valleys, to the shore of Lake Constance in the south. In 2000 the survey added an area north of the Alb in the Neckar valley, and in 2002 and 2004 it added an area on top of the limestone Alb. Analysis of the survey in the Neckar valley is still in progress. To date 23 quads within the study area have been sampled, 9 only partially due to lack of ground visibility.

Survey Results

Ground visibility in southwest Germany is severely limited, and ploughed fields in agricultural areas offer the only opportunity to assess distribution of Stone Age sites over broad areas. Groups of three to nine people spaced at ten-metre intervals walked the ploughed fields and collected all artefacts for further analysis. Surveyors also recorded information on the field and weather conditions to determine potential biases in finding artefacts. Fields were mapped on 1:25,000-scale topographic maps for entry into a GIS database. During the survey, efforts were made to select fields from all potential environmental situations to ensure that the sample was as evenly distributed as possible. Comparisons of the actual survey against random samples from the surrounding environment showed that our survey was a reasonable sample of the different environmental zones present in terms of several variables including distance to water, geologic formation, slope, and elevation (Harris 1997).

Figure 17.4 shows the locations of the fields walked during the course of the survey. A total of 3278 fields were walked covering an area of 50.5km^2, representing approximately 1.6% of the total 3146.4km^2 in the surveyed quads. Of the surveyed fields, 486 contained Stone Age finds for a total of 14.8% fields with finds.

It is difficult to assign our surface scatters, most of which are low-density, to specific time periods. However, analysis of the artefacts completed at this point does indicate that many of these scatters contain a Mesolithic component. We assigned a probable age to individual diagnostic artefacts such as microliths. Lithic scatters containing at least one Mesolithic diagnostic are identified as Mesolithic site locations in Figure 17.4. While most of these diagnostic artefacts come from relatively dense scatters on lakes or wetlands, a high frequency of heat-treated artefacts (a trait most common in the Early Mesolithic) in the sample as a whole suggests that Mesolithic activities were not restricted to these lakeshore locations (Fisher 2006). To illustrate this broad distribution, lithic scatters lacking diagnostics but containing tempered pieces are tentatively identified as locations with a 'probable Mesolithic' component.

The survey indicates that the previously established pattern of site concentrations in the Alb and around the wetlands of Oberschwaben remains strong. Clearly the Federsee and other wetland areas such as the Pfrunger Ried were frequently used and were key locations in south-western German prehistory. Indeed these regions are the most likely candidates for residential camps. But, a significant new survey project result is the discovery of Stone Age finds in regions between the previously known site concentrations. The survey results pose an important research question regarding the relationship between the previously identified sites near the former lakes and the smaller lithic scatters discovered by the

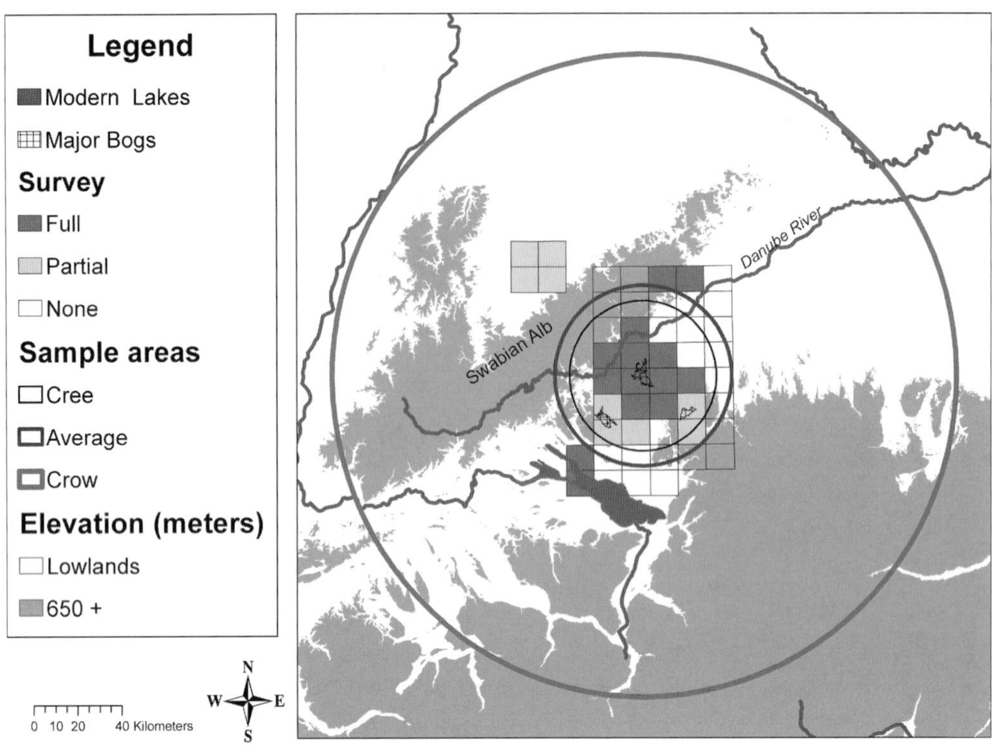

Figure 17.3. Map of SWGRASP survey area showing quads fully, partially, and not surveyed. Circles represent amount of area covered by forest-dwelling ethnographic examples such as the Crow and Cree, as well as an average range calculated from a selection of groups from Kelly 1995, listed in Figure 17.2. (DEM source: CIAT and CGIAR 2004).

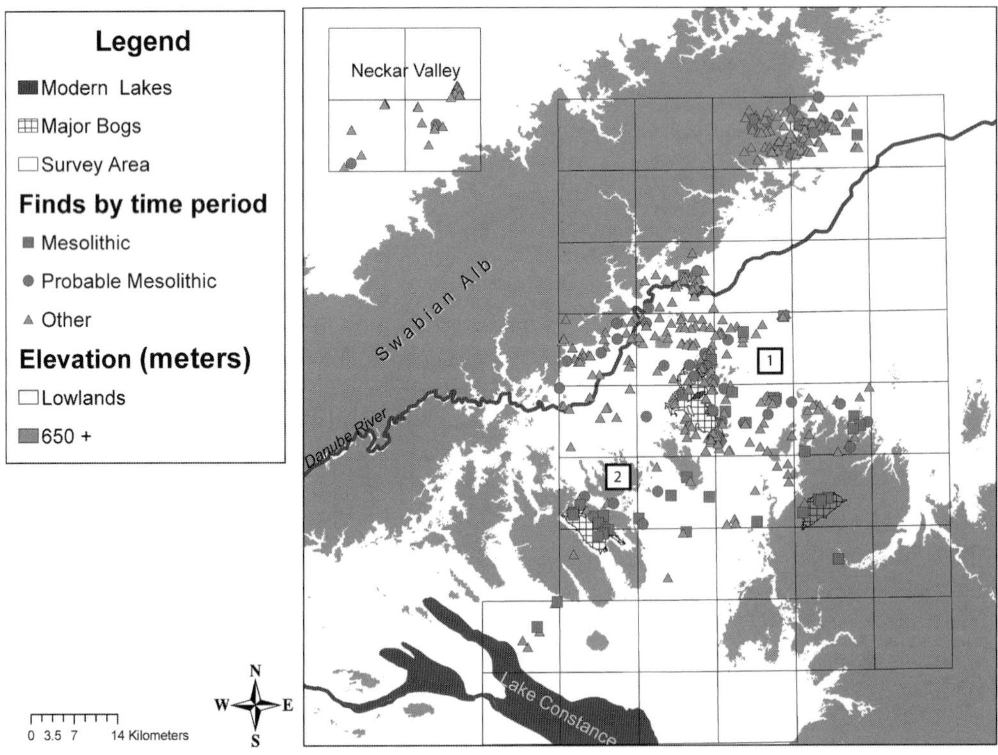

Figure 17.4. Map showing location of lithic scatters located during the SWGRASP survey from 1992–2004. Mesolithic sites identified by diagnostic microliths. Scatters with tempered artefacts are shown as 'probable Mesolithic'. 1) Modern Federsee Lake and surrounding bog; 2) Pfrunger-Ried bog. (DEM source: CIAT and CGIAR 2004).

survey in the surrounding regions. How far were people willing to walk in one day to gather resources? Based on the ethnographic literature, 'A 20–30 kilometer round trip appears to be the maximum distance hunter-gatherers will walk comfortably in a day in a variety of habitats' (Kelly 1995, 133). However, it is often not the distance travelled

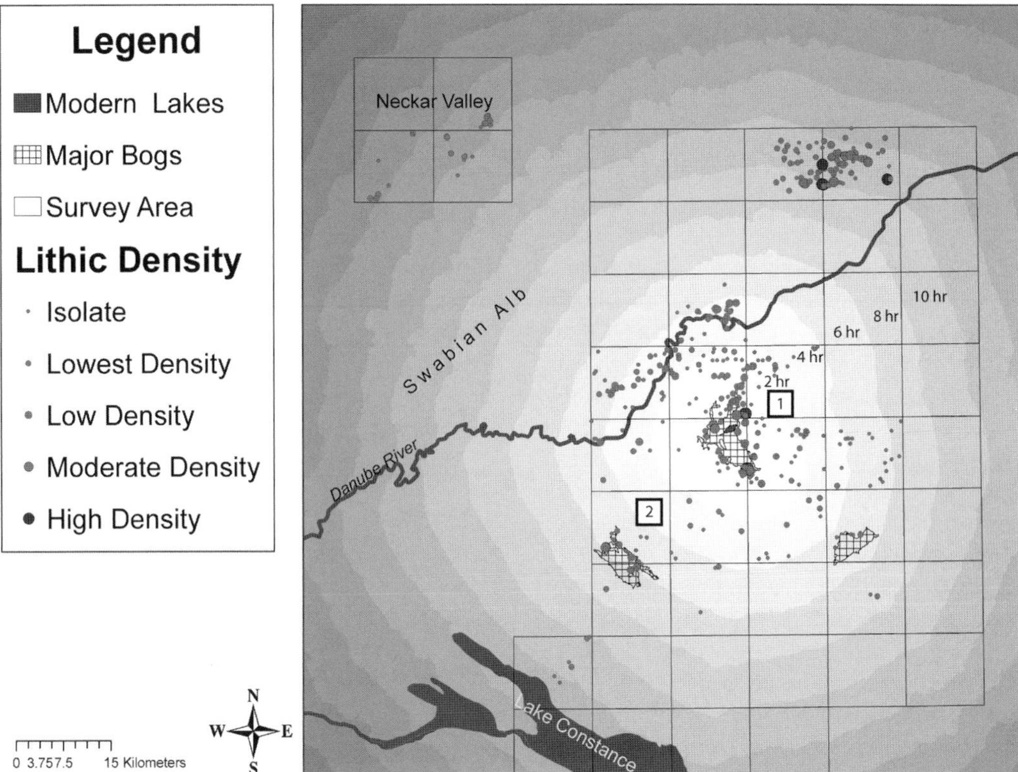

Figure 17.5. Map showing bands representing 2-hour one-way walks based on Tobler's hiking function. Lithic scatters from the survey are represented in four density classes based upon natural breaks in the density data for all but 2 scatters from the survey. One outlier was an extremely dense, small field located on the southern end of the Federsee. The other outlier was a similarly dense Neolithic site on the Swabian Alb. Both locations are shown here as belonging to the highest density class. Isolates make up the fifth class of scatters. 1) Modern Federsee Lake and surrounding bog; 2) Pfrunger-Ried bog. (DEM source: CIAT and CGIAR 2004).

that was most important but rather the time or cost of the travel. The costs of walking across country can be variable because of obstacles such as streams, vegetation, or the slope of the terrain. In order to estimate these costs, we used a 'hiking function' developed by Waldo Tobler at University of California, Santa Barbara's Department of Geography (Tobler 1993).

$$W = 6 \exp(-3.5*\text{abs}(S+0.05))$$

In this equation W, the dependent variable on the Y axis, shows the walking velocity in kilometres per hour. S, the independent variable, is the slope of the terrain. The equation is anisotropic, meaning that it takes into account the fact that it is somewhat easier to walk on a slight downhill slope, but more difficult to walk uphill. Therefore, the travel time calculated is sensitive to the direction of the slope. On flat terrain, this equation gives a walking velocity of 5 km/hr. The travel time is calculated using the inverse of this equation and multiplying by the distance travelled.

In Figure 17.5, we see the results of using Tobler's equation to estimate travel time from the Federsee. Each of the concentric circular bands represents an interval of two hours in a one-way walk from the shore of the Federsee. When the surveyed fields are categorized based on the density of finds, by far the highest density locations are found right on the shores of the Federsee and the Pfrunger Ried, with a light scattering of isolates and low density finds in between, and a few moderately dense scatters along the Danube corridor. The majority of finds are recorded within two hours of the Federsee. However, it is important to remember that the bulk of the surveyed area lies within six hours of the Federsee, so that there are no finds beyond that time range. If we assume that the highest density locations represent shorter- or longer-term residential camps, then it seems likely that the lower-density locations between the wetland areas represent the activities of daily foraging.

If a forager is unlikely to walk more than eight hours in a single round trip, we would expect in the future to find higher density locations in favourable environments beyond a four-hour walk from the Federsee. Such locations might represent areas where residential camps were relocated or where longer logistical trips were required to take advantage of available resources. At this point, the samples of artefacts from the survey are not large enough to distinguish between residential and logistical camps. The density and diversity of finds, however, do speak to the duration of occupation at the different find spots.

Conclusions

In conclusion, the pattern of dense sites in wetlands and

rockshelters remains strong, but the survey recorded many new finds in the areas between these concentrations. Although the survey confirms the pattern of concentration of finds on the Federsee and other wetlands such as the Pfrunger Reid, it also shows a rather continual background of isolate and low-density finds throughout the study area. Furthermore, areas within 3–4 hours of a residential camp were likely used for daily foraging needs. The distance between find concentrations closely matches the distance that ethnographic foragers indicated they were willing to walk during a day's activities. Areas more than 4 hours from a residential camp would be too far to use in daily foraging. To take advantage of those resources would require relocation of the residential camp or a logistical trip. Ideally, foragers would move to a new patch that minimized overlap with the previous foraging area. The sites on the Pfrunger Ried and the Alb are at a distance that may well reflect mobility that involved camp relocation.

In general, we are satisfied that a broad regional survey such as ours was necessary to address crucial questions of mobility and settlement patterns. Excavation alone cannot provide the regional coverage required to examine such issues. Only studies such as this one, incorporating large regions, can allow archaeologists to compare different scales of mobility and settlement patterns. GIS analysis using a hiking function allows us to put survey results in behavioural context and make new interpretations about hunter-gatherer mobility.

Future Directions

Four general areas show potential for continued research. Additional survey within our study area will fill in more regions further from the Federsee. To date, the survey has concentrated on the area immediately surrounding the Federsee bog. Survey of areas to the north and south will provide a greater variety of environmental regions and include other potential residential areas away from the lake such as the Danube Valley at the edge of the Swabian Alb.

Comparable surveys in neighbouring regions would allow us to see if similar patterns appear outside of our study area. Our study area falls within the larger region of the Beuron-Coincy culture, and it would be useful to know whether the patterns we see extend throughout this larger area. We note that our study area is bounded on the east by the border of Bavaria, which prehistorically had no meaning. But since modern state governments vary in how they administer archaeological materials, researchers should be alert for potential governmental influence upon variable information and interpretation on opposite sides of the boundary.

More excavation is necessary to understand the role of particular locations within the regional context. Although survey is useful for understanding broader regional patterns, excavation is necessary to understand particular locations. Some excavation has been conducted at the Federsee and Pfrunger Ried, but more is necessary to complement the results of the survey project.

Further exploration of the lithic database for behavioural variation is needed. We have, at this time, only begun to look at issues such as raw material use and the distribution of subsistence and maintenance activities.

More models of foraging and settlement can be developed with the GIS database to understand how prehistoric people used and viewed their landscape. We can improve our use of the GIS database and take our analyses further. For example Tobler's model of hiking times is overly simplistic and might be modified to reflect more accurately movement within our particular environment. We might consider the effects of walking in dense forest or using watercraft to navigate the rivers and lakes of Oberschwaben.

References

CIAT and CGIAR 2004. Void-filled seamless SRTM data V1, 2004, International Centre for Tropical Agriculture (CIAT), available from the CGIAR-CSI SRTM 90m Database: http://srtm.csi.cgiar.org (accessed 09/2007).

Eriksen, B. V. 1991. Change and Continuity in a Prehistoric Hunter-Gatherer Society: A Study of Cultural Adaptation in Late Glacial – Early Postglacial Southwestern Germany. *Archaeologica Venatoria* 12. Tübingen, Archaeologica Venatoria.

Fisher, L. E. 2006. Mobility, Land Use, and Food-Getting Tools in the Early Mesolithic: Understanding Site Distributions in the Upper Danube, in C.-J. Kind (ed.), *After the Ice Age. Settlements, Subsistence, and Social Development in the Mesolithic of Central Europe*, 155–62. Materialhefte zur Archäologie 78. Stuttgart, Konrad Theiss.

Fisher, L. E. and C. Knipper. 2003. Zur Untersuchung steinzeitlicher Landschaften – Die Besiedlung und Nutzung der Blaubeurer und Ulmer Alb im Paläolithikum, Mesolithikum und Neolithikum. *Mitteilungen der Gesellschaft für Urgeschichte* 12, 121–48.

Harris, S. K. 1997. *The use of GIS to test for bias in non-random surveys: A southwest German example*. Unpublished MA Thesis, University of California, Santa Barbara.

Jochim, M. A. 1998. *A Hunter-Gatherer Landscape: Southwest Germany in the Late Paleolithic and Mesolithic*. New York, Plenum.

Jochim, M. A., Glass, M., McCartney, P. and Fisher, L. 1998. Mapping the Stone Age: An interim report on the South German Survey Project, in N. Conard and C.-J. Kind (eds.), *Aktuelle Forschungen zum Mesolithikum, Current Mesolithic Research*. Urgeschichtliche Materialhefte 12, 121–32. Tübingen, Mo Vince Verlag.

Kelly, R. 1995. *The Foraging Spectrum: Diversity in Hunter-Gatherer Lifeways*. Washington, Smithsonian Institution Press.

Kind, C.-J. 1996. Bemerkungen zur Diversität des südwestdeutschen Frühmesolithikums, in I. Campen, J. Hahn and M. Uerpmann (eds.), *Spuren der Jagd – Die Jagd nach Spuren. Festschrift für Hansjürgen Müller-Beck*, 325–30. Tübingen, Mo Vince Verlag.

Tobler, W. 1993. Non-isotropic Geographic Modeling, in *Three Presentations on Geographic Analysis and Modeling*, 2–5. National Center for Geographic Information and Analysis, University of California Technical Report, 93/1. http://www.ncgia.ucsb.edu/Publications/Tech_Reports/93/93-1.PDF (accessed 01/2007). Santa Barbara, University of California.

18. One pig does not a winter make. New seasonal evidence at the Early Mesolithic sites of Holmegaard and Mullerup and the Late Mesolithic site of Ertebølle in Denmark

Richard Carter

Important new seasonal evidence has been derived from three Mesolithic sites based upon tooth development stages in dentally immature wild boar. Radiographs of the developing molars and premolars have been used to provide an accurate indication of age at death by comparing them with modern known-age specimens. These new results from the early Mesolithic sites of Holmegaard and Mullerup and the late Mesolithic site of Ertebølle have been combined with other seasonal indicators based on the developing dentition of red deer and roe deer. Knowledge of their age when killed indicates at what time of the year humans were present at the sites. Determining whether a site was occupied seasonally or year round is critical to subsequent interpretations of human economic and social activity. Based on this new line of enquiry there is evidence that wild boar at Holmegaard were killed during the spring and autumn. At Mullerup wild boar were killed from late summer to early winter, whilst at Ertebølle they were killed during the autumn and winter months. The significance of these new results for understanding human presence at these sites has been assessed.

Keywords: tooth development, Mesolithic, wild boar, red deer, roe deer, seasonality.

Introduction

In this paper I will summarise some new results from work done over a number of years looking at site seasonality during the Mesolithic era. Tooth development has been used to estimate the ages at death of wild boar (*Sus scrofa*) at three Danish Mesolithic sites. The scheme used has been adapted from a technique developed by Brown and Chapman, (1991a; 1991b), which estimate the ages at death of fallow deer (*Dama dama*) and red deer (*Cervus elaphus)* from radiographs of developing dentition. The new scheme is fully described in Carter and Magnell 2007 and will not be discussed in detail here. Estimating the ages at death of animals from tooth development provides information about when during the year they were killed. When applied to archaeological specimens of red deer and roe deer (*Capreolus capreolus)* it has been possible to obtain important evidence of seasonal human presence at Mesolithic sites (Carter 1997; 1998; 2001b; 2004; 2006). For the first time I will combine the red deer, roe deer and wild boar results at the three aforementioned Mesolithic sites and discuss how they might contribute to existing models of early and late Mesolithic settlement.

It is acknowledged that any analysis is reliant on evidence derived from sites whose main criterion for selection was the availability of mandibular bone and teeth from three species of animal. Nevertheless it is felt that the ubiquity of red, roe deer and wild pig throughout Mesolithic north-west Europe, and their appearance at most sites, provides an indication of their importance to Mesolithic communities. It should be pointed out that this paper does not comprehensively re-assess other seasonal evidence recovered from these sites, or propose definitive seasonal assessments at each site.

Site backgrounds

Holmegaard

A complex of Maglemose sites was excavated at the inland bog of Holmegaards Mose during the first part of this century. Occupation ranges from approximately 7540 to 7585 cal BC and the complex is contemporary with Mullerup Syd (*c.* 7650–7410 cal BC) and the Sværdborg complex (*c.* 7540–6670 cal BC) (Bille Henriksen 1976). Holmegaard is a classic Maglemosian bog site with cultural layers enclosed by swamp vegetation – mainly sedges (*Cladium*) and reeds (*Phragmites*). The site is traditionally thought to be a temporary seasonal hunting camp, but with an uncertain season of occupation (Grøn 1987; Rowley-Conwy 1993). At Holmegaard I, the excavator Broholm states that of the 4584 animal bones recovered, 3666 could be identified to species by the osteologists Jessen and Winge (in Broholm 1924). He goes on to comment on how similar in composition they are to the contemporary sites at Mullerup and Sværdborg I. There is a comment that the 1922 excavations produced assemblages that were dominated by the bones of red deer and wild boar, followed by roe deer. Aurochs (*Bos primigenius*) and elk (*Alces alces*) were also well represented (Bille Henriksen 1976). There are many barbed bone points and one made of antler; other antler artefacts included hammers and pressure tools and a shoulder blade wedge from an aurochs was recovered from Holmegaard I (Bille Henriksen 1976).

Twelve red deer and four roe deer jaws were radiographed from the sites of Holmegaard I (1922 and 1923), IV and V permitting reasonable assessments of seasonality to be made (Carter 2001). These estimations are that Holmegaard I and IV were occupied mainly in the summer months, at Holmegaard V there is a single roe deer killed in early autumn (Figures 18.1 and 18.2). However it has been possible to update these assessments from the examination of 17 wild boar jaws.

Mullerup

The site is sometimes referred to as Maglemose and was the first bog site to be excavated in southern Scandinavia. It has become the type-site for an entire material culture spanning north-west Europe. It is 15km from the coast at Maglemose, close to Mullerup in Sjaelland, and is a classic Early Mesolithic bog settlement, comprising Mullerup Syd (South) and Nord (North). All the material examined in this study comes from the former site excavated in November 1900 by Sarauw (1903) and on a smaller scale in 1915 by Koch and Mathiassen (unpublished). They uncovered a small concentration of bones, flints, birch bark, charcoal and hazelnut, approximately 120m north of the original excavation. This was unpublished and is only evidenced from a report in the Danish National Museum (Grøn 1995).

Little is known about the site because of its incomplete documentation and minimal research since excavation. It was occupied between approximately 7650–7410 cal BC based on hazelnut and charcoal radiocarbon dates (Brinch Petersen 1973). There is evidence for the hunting of red deer, roe deer, wild boar, aurochs and elk, and of pike (*Esox lucius*) fishing. Altogether 32 species have been identified at the site including swan (*Cygnus cygnus*), crane (*Grus grus*), cormorant (*Phalacrocorax carbo*), and pond tortoise (*Emys orbicularis*). The site is traditionally thought to have been a temporary seasonal hunting camp with occupation either in the winter (Grøn 1987) or summer (Rowley-Conwy 1993, Blankholm 1996). The winter evidence is inferred by the presence of a juvenile beaver (*Castor fiber*) jaw, in contrast hazelnut shells may indicate summer occupation. Recent examination of ten roe deer jaws (Carter 2001a and 2001b) supported human presence at the site during the warmer parts of the year (Figure 18.3).

Ertebølle

During the Atlantic period the late Mesolithic site of Ertebølle was located on the coast near the Limfjord in north-western Jutland, Denmark, but today lies slightly inland. It was first excavated between 1893 and 1897 (Madsen *et al.* 1900), becoming famous for its large shell midden (*Køkkenmødding*) and in 1919 became the type-site for the 'Ertebølle culture'. Occupation extended from approximately 4615 to 3890 cal BC and is contemporary with many smaller coastal sites nearby, and the large midden site of Bjørnsholm, 8km further north (Andersen 2000). It appears that the site was repeatedly occupied for several hundred years prior to the accumulation of the shell midden, which took *c.* 700 years (Andersen and Johansen 1986). Despite its fame as a classic *Køkkenmødding* site it is not just a midden but also has evidence of activity areas. There are no definable traces of houses on or around the midden, but well-built stone fireplaces and cultural remains have been found on the subsoil beneath it. Originally dwellings may have been sited adjacent to the midden and became covered as it advanced from north to south along the coast (Andersen 2000).

The shell midden is dominated by oysters (*Ostrea* sp.), followed by cockles (*Cerastoderma* sp.), mussels (*Mytilus* sp.) and periwinkles (*Littorina littorea*). Large numbers of eel bones (*Anguilla anguilla*) are present throughout the midden and were clearly important to the occupants for a considerable period of time. Other aquatic species caught include grey seal (*Halichoerus grypus*), cod (*Gadus morhua*) and garfish (*Belone belone*). The main terrestrial species hunted at Ertebølle were red deer, roe deer and wild pig, but relatively few aurochs and elk. Animals hunted for their pelts rather than meat include pine martin (*Martes martes*), wild cat (*Felis silvestris*), lynx (*Lynx lynx*), fox (*Vulpes vulpes*), otter (*Lutra lutra*), and wolf (*Canis lupus*).

There are a few seasonal indicators which, when drawn together, indicate human presence in all seasons at this site. The only possible exception is springtime, although, according to Andersen and Johansen (1986), juvenile red deer and wild pig could have been killed in either spring or summer. The gathering of cockles and catching of garfish and eels most likely occurred in the summer and a single charred hazelnut shell provides the only autumnal evidence. Enghoff (1995) concluded that late summer to autumn was the principal fishing season at Ertebølle and Bjørnsholm. She used growth-ring analyses of fish otoliths from cod and saithe (*Pollachius virens*) from both sites to support this assertion. The marine molluscs from the Ertebølle midden were probably collected during the spring and summer (March–July) according to Andersen (2000). Indirect evidence for winter presence relies on assumptions that fur bearing animals were probably exploited during the colder months of the year (Andersen and Johansen 1986). More direct winter indicators include the presence of attached red deer antlers, ducks and swan bones. Examination of four red deer and two roe deer jaws indicate that the most concentrated period within which all the deer could have been killed is between April and August (Carter 2001b, Figure 18.4). Overall the longevity and size of the site, combined with the clear demarcation of activity areas, points to a stable settlement system at the site with the potential for year round settlement.

Results

A March birth date has been used to calculate the ages at death of the archaeological specimens of wild boar. The birth date of wild boar may vary (Lauwerier 1983), but studies in Sweden and Germany have shown that 65% and 90%, respectively, are born between March and May and the median months are March and April, respectively (Briedermann 1990; Lemel 1999). It is likely that spring births during the Mesolithic era would also have ensured the highest survival rates of piglets. The estimated age of each specimen has been calculated, and, based on a March birthing period, the season of death is shown in a series of charts for each site (Figures 18.1–18.6).

The wild boar results for Holmegaard have been combined with the red and roe deer results (Carter 2001b) and are shown in Figures 18.1 and 18.2.

It can be seen that the new wild boar ages add considerably to the seasonal evidence at this complex. This is particularly evident for animals less than a year old where ageing resolution is highest (Figure 18.1). Here there appears to be a concentration of wild boar deaths during the autumn months. For red and roe deer, killing occurs earlier in the year during summer and early autumn (Figure 18.2). For older red deer the ageing resolution is reduced and these animals may have been killed at almost any time of the year.

At Mullerup (Figure 18.3) the pattern of killing is similar to Holmegaard. It is interesting that both sites also have a similar faunal composition and for a time were contemporary. However, this time roe deer rather than red deer yearlings were killed during the warmer months, and there is now evidence for the killing of wild boars in the colder months.

For the Late Mesolithic site of Ertebølle very young wild pigs were killed sometime between October and April. Red deer fawns were killed in late spring/early summer. An older roe deer was killed slightly later during late summer/early autumn. The ageing resolution of these young animals is high.

Discussion

In an attempt to increase the seasonal resolution at each site I have selected specimens whose age estimations are two years and under and have an age range estimation of four months or less (five months for Mullerup). I have then shown the percentages of red and roe deer and wild boar that may have been killed for each month of the year. There are some clear differences and similarities between the killing profiles at the sites.

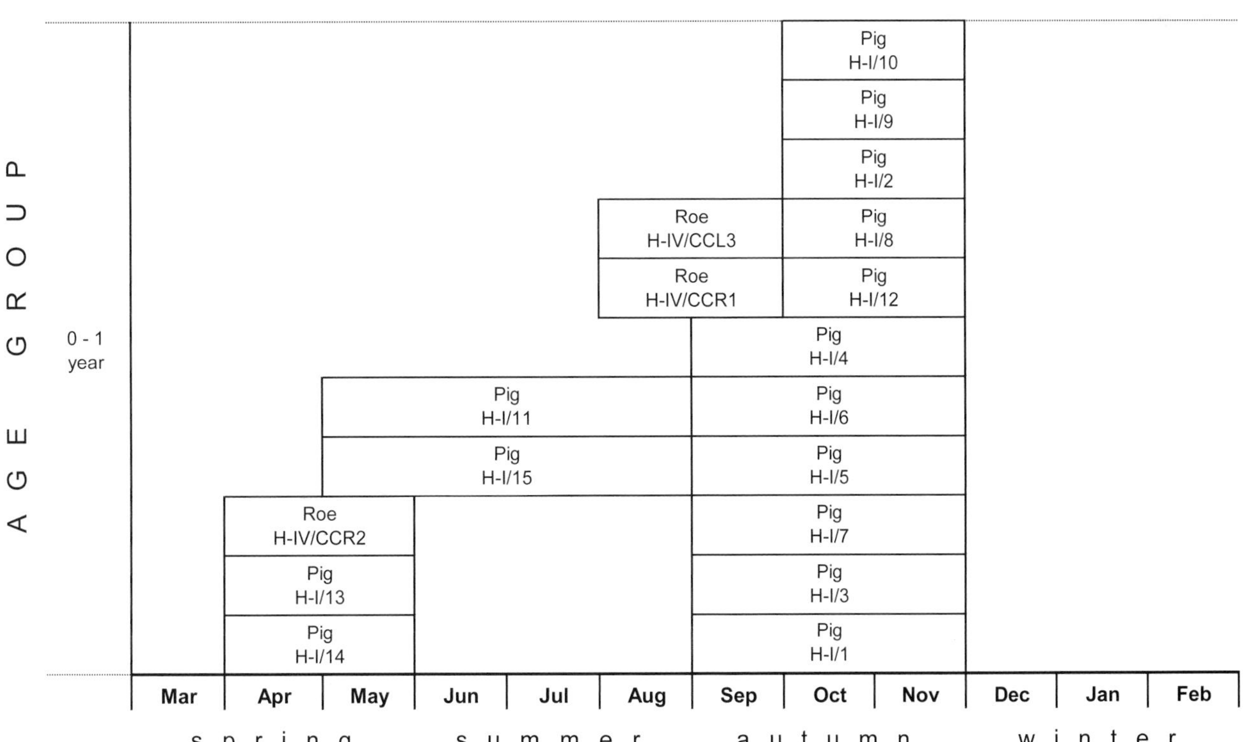

Figure 18.1. Season of death of dentally immature wild boar and roe deer aged 0–1 year from Holmegaard (boar: n = 15; roe: n = 3).

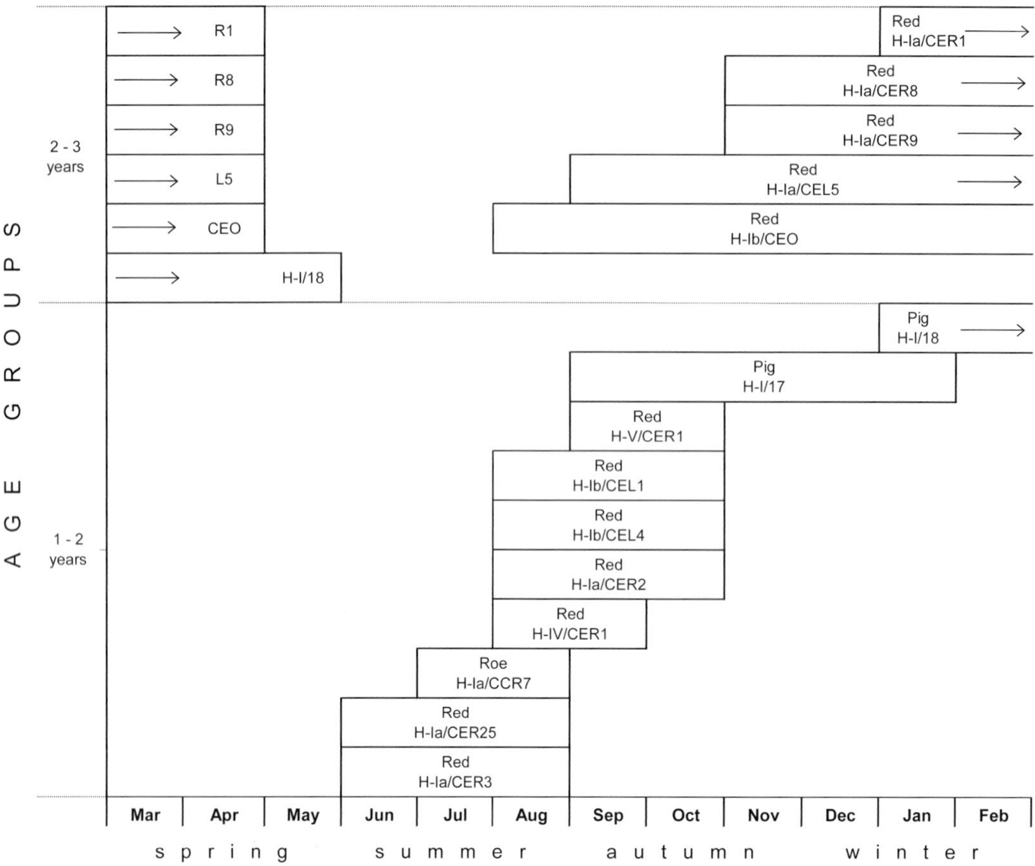

Figure 18.2. Season of death of dentally immature wild boar, red deer and roe deer aged 1–3 years from Holmegaard (boar: n = 2; red: n = 11; roe: n = 1).

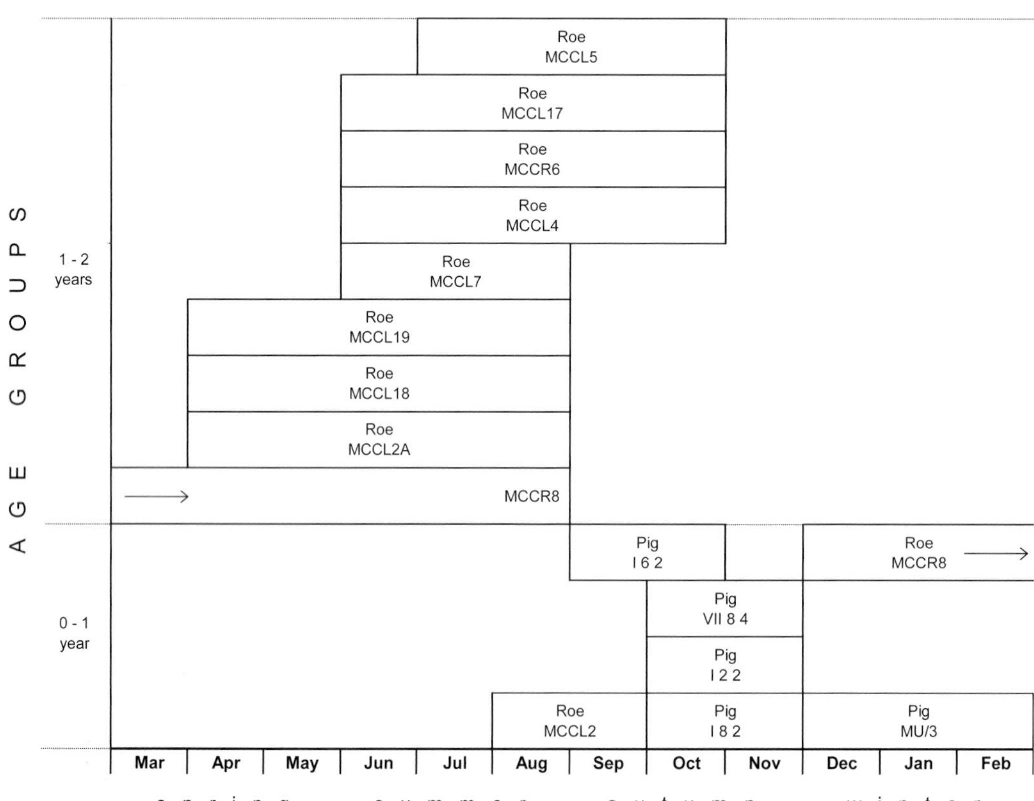

Figure 18.3. Season of death of dentally immature wild boar and roe deer aged 0–2 years from Mullerup (boar: n = 5; roe: n = 10).

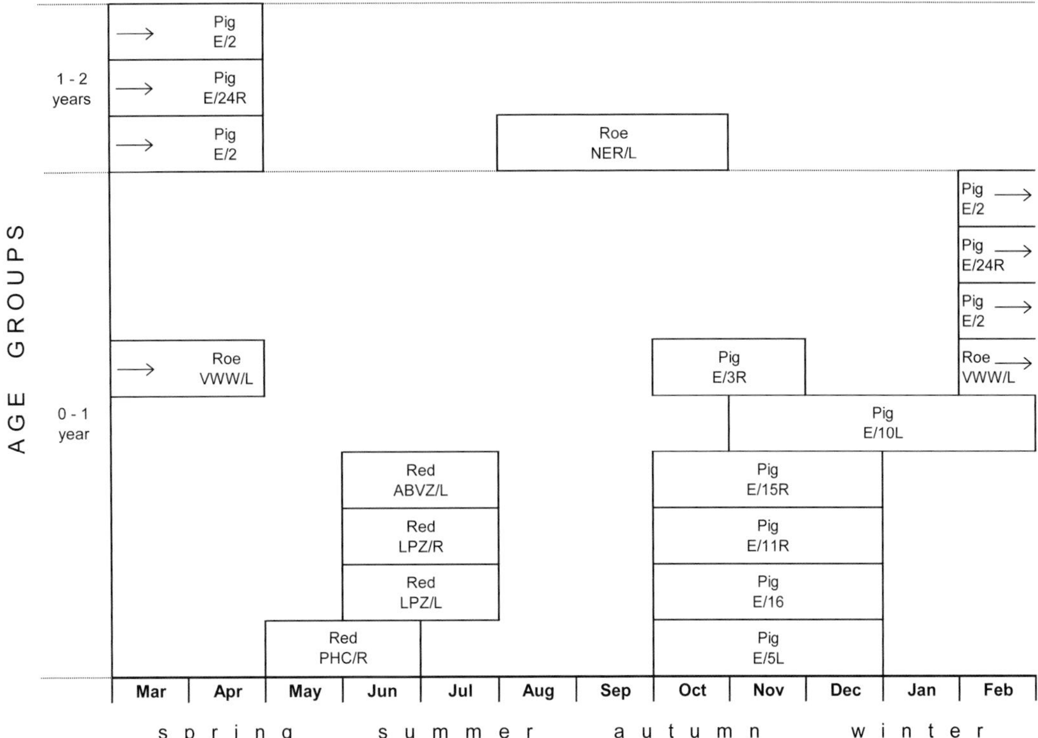

Figure 18.4. Season of death of dentally immature wild boar, red deer and roe deer aged 0–2 years from Ertebølle (boar: n = 9; red: n = 4; roe: n = 2).

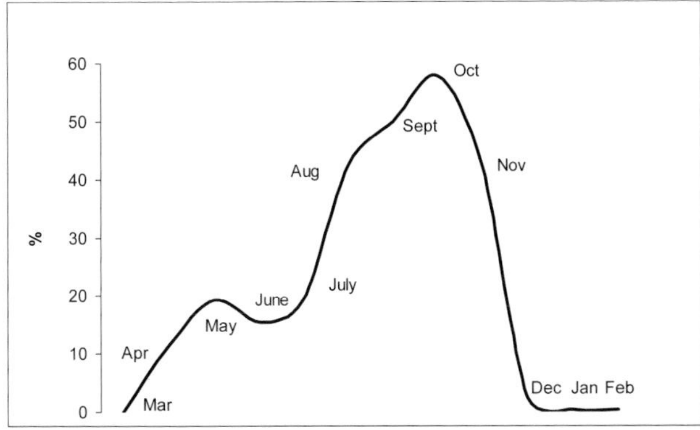

Figure 18.5. Percentages of wild boar, red deer and roe deer at Holmegaard (n = 26) possibly killed for each month of the year that have age-range estimations of 4 months or less and are under 24 months old.

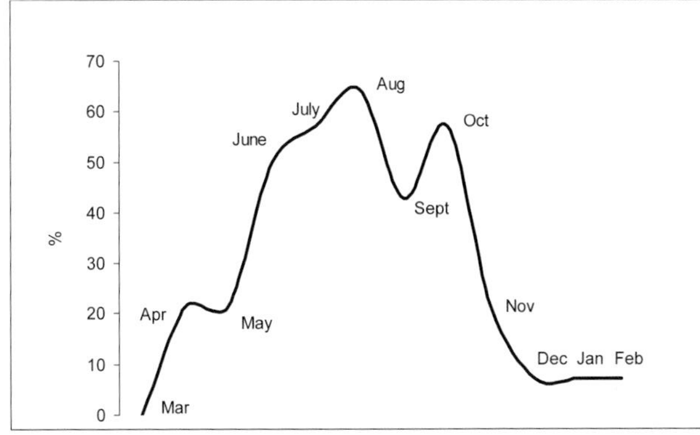

Figure 18.6. Percentages of wild boar and roe deer at Mullerup (n = 14) possibly killed for each month of the year that have age-range estimations of 5 months or less and are under 24 months old.

Holmegaard and Mullerup

At both sites the red and roe deer evidence supports the traditional interpretation of a summer hunting complex (Blankholm 1996; Carter 2001b), but the new pig evidence extends human presence into the cooler months of the year. The high proportion of animals killed during late summer/ early autumn seems to indicate a seasonal intensification of hunting. This is at a time of the year when wild boars were in prime condition and hunters able to optimise yields (Magnell 2005).

Local conditions may have restricted occupation to the drier months of the year. But it may be that sites within the Holmegaard complex could have been occupied at different times of the year, dependant on water levels, resulting in a pro-active rather than passive response to seasonal change with the inhabitants remaining in one prime location for most if not all the year. Similar seasonal movements may have occurred at the Ulkestrup complex of sites in Denmark (7445–6950 cal BC) (Richter 1982). A study of prevailing summer and winter wind directions by Grøn (1995) at this complex showed that sites were orientated so as to be protected from seasonal winds. Protection from winter winds is evident at Star Carr (Cloutman and Smith 1988), and examination of the Holmegaard complex may reveal similar site orientations.

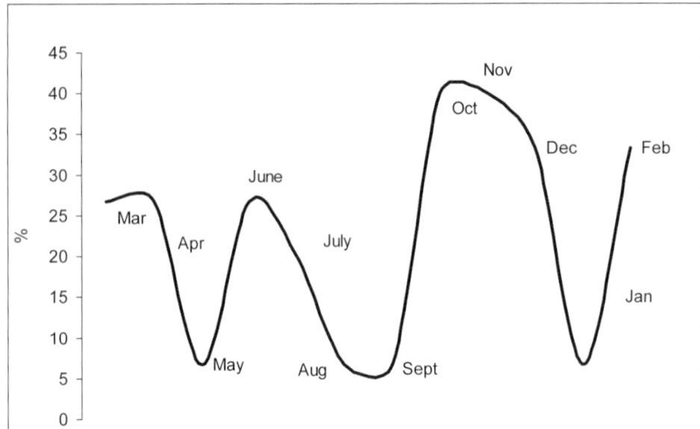

Figure 18.7. Percentages of wild boar, red deer and roe deer at Ertebølle (n = 15) possibly killed for each month of the year that have age-range estimations of 4 months or less and are under 24 months old.

Ertebølle

Previously there appeared to be a lack of direct winter evidence at Ertebølle (Carter 2001b). Now the killing of deer and pig appears to be taking place throughout the year, supporting the view of year-round human presence at the site. Clearly this is only a snapshot of activity from a site with tremendous longevity. The excavators Andersen and Johansen (1986) have proposed a stable settlement system over a long period of time at the site and year-round presence is probably more likely than abandonment during the winter. Should the domestic areas ever be located these may yield further seasonal evidence upon which to base a more accurate seasonal assessment. The low assemblage numbers may reflect the exploitation status of terrestrial mammals. The large shell midden indicates the importance of marine resources, but the local hinterland would also have provided an ideal habitat for ungulates, and, like Holmegaard and Mullerup, there seems to be a similar seasonal intensification of wild boar hunting during the autumn. Nevertheless it may be that the occupants relied more on aquatic than terrestrial fauna to meet their subsistence needs.

Acknowledgements

I would like to thank the following people and organisations for their support: Professor Kim Aaris-Sørensen and Knud Rosenlund, Zoological Museum, University of Copenhagen; Dr Ola Magnell, University of Lund; Dr Elvira Szuma and staff at the Mammal Research Institute, Bialowieza, Poland; Professor Ken Thomas, University College, London; Copenhagen Biosystematics Centre (COBICE) funding; Staff Research Fund, University of Sussex.

References

Andersen, S. H. 2000. 'Køkkenmøddinger' (Shell Middens) in Denmark: a Survey. *Proceedings of the Prehistoric Society* 66, 361–84.

Andersen, S. H. and Johansen, E. 1986. Ertebølle Revisited. *Journal of Danish Archaeology* 5, 31–61.

Bille Henriksen, B. 1976. *Sværdborg I, Excavations 1943–44: A Settlement of the Maglemose Culture*. Arkæologiske Studier III. Odense, Akademisk Forlag.

Blankholm, H. P. 1996. *On the track of a prehistoric economy: Maglemosian subsistence in early postglacial South Scandinavia*. Aarhus, Aarhus University Press.

Briedermann, L. 1990. *Schwarzwild*. Berlin, VEB Deutscher Landwirtschartverlag.

Brinch Petersen, E. 1973. A survey of the late Palaeolithic and Mesolithic of Denmark, in S. K. Kozłowski (ed.), *The Mesolithic in Europe*, 77–127. Warsaw, Warsaw University Press.

Broholm, H. C. 1924. Nye fund fra den ældste Stenalder – Holmegaard og Sværdborgfundene, in *Aarbøger for Nordisk Oldkyndighed og Historie 1924*, 1–144. København, Det Kongelige Nordiske Oldskriftselskab.

Brown, W. A. B. and Chapman, N. G. 1991a. Age assessment of fallow deer (*Dama dama*): from a scoring scheme based on radiographs of developing permanent molariform teeth. *Journal of Zoology* 224, 367–79.

Brown, W. A. B. and Chapman, N. G. 1991b. Age assessment of red deer (*Cervus elaphus*): from a scoring scheme based on radiographs of developing permanent molariform teeth. *Journal of Zoology* 225, 85–97.

Carter, R. J. 1997. Age estimation of roe deer (*Capreolus capreolus*) mandibles from Mesolithic site of Star Carr, Yorkshire, based on radiographs of mandibular tooth development. *Journal of Zoology* 241, 495–502.

Carter, R. J. 1998. Reassessment of Seasonality at the Early Mesolithic Site of Star Carr, Yorkshire Based on Radiographs of Mandibular Tooth Development in Red Deer (*Cervus elaphus*). *Journal of Archaeological Science* 25, 851–6.

Carter, R. J. 2001a. *Human Subsistence and Seasonality in Mesolithic Northwest Europe Based on Studies of Mandibular Bone and Dentition in Red Deer (*Cervus elaphus*) and Roe Deer (*Capreolus capreolus*)*. Unpublished PhD thesis, University of London.

Carter, R. J. 2001b. Dental indicators of seasonal human presence at the Danish Boreal sites of Holmegaard I, IV and V and Mullerup and the Atlantic sites of Tybrind Vig and Ringkloster. *The Holocene* 11, 359–65.

Carter, R. J. 2004. Seasonal Human Presence at the Late Mesolithic sites of Tågerup, Segebro, Skateholm I, Bökeberg III and Ageröd V from the Developing Mandibular Dentition of Red Deer (*Cervus elaphus*) and Roe Deer (*Capreolus capreolus*). *Lund Archaeological Review* 10.

Carter, R. J. 2006. A Method to Estimate the Ages at Death of Red Deer (*Cervus elaphus*) and Roe Deer (*Capreolus capreolus*) from Developing Mandibular Dentition and it's Application to Mesolithic NW Europe, in D. Ruscillo (ed.), *Recent Advances in Ageing and Sexing Animal Bones. Proceedings of the 9th Conference of the International Council of Archaeozoology, Durham, August 2002*, 40–61. Oxford, Oxbow Books.

Carter, R. J. and Magnell, O. 2007. Age estimation of wild boar based on molariform mandibular tooth development and its application to seasonality at the Mesolithic site of Ringkloster, Denmark, in U. Albarella, K. Dobney, A. Ervynck and P. Rowley-Conwy (eds.), *Pigs and Humans: 10,000 Years of Interaction*, 197–217. Oxford, Oxford University Press.

Carter, R. J. and Magnell, O. (in press). A new method of age estimation in wild boar (*Sus scrofa*) based on molariform mandibular tooth development and its application to Mesolithic N.W. Europe, in U. Albarella, K. Dobney, A. Ervynck and P. Rowley-Conwy (eds.), *Pigs and Humans: 10,000 Years of Interaction*. Oxford, Oxford University Press.

Cloutman, E. W. and Smith, A. G. 1988. Palaeoenvironments in the Vale of Pickering. Part 3: environmental history at Star Carr. *Proceedings of the Prehistoric Society* 54, 21–36.

Enghoff, I. B. 1995. Fishing in Denmark during the Mesolithic Period, in A. Fischer (ed.). *Man and Sea in the Mesolithic: coastal settlements above and below present sea level*, 67–74. Oxbow Monographs 53. Oxford, Oxbow Books.

Grøn, O. 1987. Seasonal variation in Maglemosian group size and structure. A new model. *Current Anthropology* 28, 3.

Grøn, O. 1995. *The Maglemose Culture: the reconstruction of the social organisation of a Mesolithic culture in Northern Europe*. British Archaeological Reports, International Series S616. Oxford, Tempvs Reparatvm.

Lauwerier, R. C. G. M. 1983. Pigs, piglets and determining the season of slaughtering. *Journal of Archaeological Science* 10, 483–8.

Lemel, J. 1999. *Populationstillväxt, dynamik och spridning hos vildsvinet, Sus scrofa, i mellersta Sverige. Slutrapport.* Uppsala, Forskningsavdelningen, Svenska jägareförbundet.

Madsen, A. P., Müller, S., Neergaard, C., J. Petersen, C. G., Rostrup, E., Steenstrup, K. J. V. and Winge, H. 1900. *Affaldsdynger fra Stenalderen I Danmark: undersøgte for Nationalmuseet*. Copenhagen, C. A. Reitzel.

Magnell, O. 2005. Harvesting Wild Boar – a study of prey choice by hunters during the Mesolithic in South Scandinavia by analysis of age and sex structures in faunal remains. *Archaeofauna* 14, 27-41

Richter, J. 1982. Adult and juvenile aurochs, *Bos primigenius*, from the Maglemosian site of Ulkestrup Lyng Øst, Denmark. *Journal of Archaeological Science* 9, 247–59.

Rowley-Conwy, P. 1993. Season and reason: the case for a regional interpretation of mesolithic settlement patterns, in G. L. Peterkin, H. Bricker and P. Mellars (eds.), *Hunting and Animal Exploitation in the Later Palaeolithic and Mesolithic of Eurasia*, 179–88. Archaeological Papers of the American Anthropological Association 4. Berkeley, University of California Press.

Sarauw, G. F. L. 1903. En Stenalders Boplads i Maglemose ved Mullerup, sammenholdt med beslegtede fund, in *Aarboger for Nordisk Oldkyndighed og Historie* 1903, 148–315. Copenhagen, Nordiske Oldskrift-selskab.

19. Deciphering archaeological palimpsests: an example from a Canadian Barrenland caribou hunting camp

Bryan C. Gordon

Archaeological site KjNb-7 is a Thelon River water-crossing in the Beverly caribou migratory range (Rangifer tarandus groenlandicus) of Canada's Northwest Territories. Its use by ancestral Chipewyan Indian hunters is confirmed in three buried radiocarbon-dated artefact and bone levels spanning the last three millennia. These levels represent three Taltheilei archaeological phases, the central or Middle phase level having the densest palimpsest. Like the Early phase palimpsest below, it was in turn buried by windblown sand, then occupied by Late phase people who formed the upper palimpsest. Sterile sand separates each palimpsest, allowing independent placement of tasks and showing that the task areas remain consistent. The KjNb-7 palimpsest is analyzed into specific tasks by colour separation using databases, and gender, aided by ethnohistoric accounts. Colour involves the separation of more than 200 hues of quartzite, the stone of choice in producing cores and their fragments, flakes and broken unused tools, which are of identical hue in a specific knapping station. We present a technique for recognizing, dissecting and interpreting these components. My project customized a free web-based program (Xamplite) *to separate gender-based tools into activity areas by type, material, colour and traits.*

Keywords: Palimpsest, spatial analysis, gendered tasks, Barrenlands, Beverly caribou, butchering, Chipewyan, Dene, hide preparation, knapping, marrow (grease) extraction.

Introduction

An archaeological palimpsest is a seemingly random, dense and confusing accumulation of living debris scattered over a surface or buried floor over time. Palimpsests created from accumulated constant use or repeated seasonal use of an archaeological site are often ignored because of the difficulty separating their components. We present a technique for recognizing, dissecting and interpreting these components. (For further details of our technique see (June 2007) *http://http-server.carleton.ca/~bgordon/Spatial/xyproject_main.htm*) Members of my project customized a free web-based programme to separate gender-based tools in activity areas in caribou (*Rangifer tarandus groenlandicus*) hunting sites by type, material, colour and traits. A second method using an algorithmic crawler function authenticated our first method.

Mobility was central in Canadian Barrenland prehistory, where summer sites were occupied for only a few weeks and winter sites, at most, several months. I address this paper to those of you with palimpsest problems, not just seasonal sites but also permanent camps, and begin by locating my study area in northern Canada. Here, four 600–1000km-long Barrenland caribou ranges of southern forest and northern tundra overlap four hunting territories (Figure 19.1). The central territory, or Beverly Range, extends from north Saskatchewan to its calving ground at Beverly Lake. Its 1002 hunting camps of all four Barrenland traditions span the past 8000 years, based on 100 radiocarbon dates, with 20 dates on the Middle Taltheilei phase (Gordon 1996, 86, 247). The human yearly cycle closely interlinks with the migration of the caribou, as they move to and from remote, high, dry and windy calving grounds in the northeast. Both hunter and herd were simultaneously either on the summer tundra, at the autumn tree line or in the winter forest. For a week or two in summer both were present at water crossings. Of the four ranges the Beverly Range has the largest number and widest distribution of sites in its Middle Talthelei phase, because it had the greatest range exploitation of all people under a warm stable climate.

Gender attribution of tasks remains controversial in the archaeological community, but is clearer among northern hunting families, particularly ethnohistoric Inuit and Dene Athapascan, where women did a great deal of work. Our gender attribution was taken from explorer Samuel Hearne's 1770–1772 diary of his crossing of the Canadian Barrenlands with the Chipewyan Dene (Hearne 1795, 55). His great Chipewyan guide Matonnabbee was crucial in helping Hearne reach the Coppermine River. Matonnabbee attributed Hearne's earlier failures to not taking women, adding, 'when all the men are heavy laden, they can neither hunt nor travel (but that women) ... were made for labour; one can carry as much as two men. They also pitch our tents, make and mend our clothing, keep us warm at night... are maintained at a trifling expense; for as they cook, the very licking of their fingers is sufficient for their subsistence... and it is likely they help themselves when the men are not present'. Besides cooking, women prepared skins, embroidered and mended clothing, made rope and nets, pitched tents and carried heavy loads (Hearne 1795, 205). On April 8, 1771, Hearne (1795, 88) explained the qualities that the Chipewyan liked best in their women, mainly strength and size. I suspect men also valued the beauty of youth, but in terms of the persistence and strength needed for the palimpsest tasks studied in this paper, women were ideally suited, although most of their results, as represented by their discarded tools, are hidden by thick stone knapping debris left by the men. The maxim that a wife, sister or mother's work is never finished and seldom visible, certainly applies here. Hearne's diary and ethnohistory say men made tools and hunted; women prepared meat, hides and food, and both sexes gutted and butchered carcasses. I think gender lines were sometimes crossed, but the overall gender division for the Chipewyan is quite clear.

The KjNb-7 Middle Taltheilei palimpsest

Archaeological site KjNb-7 is a tundra water-crossing camp on the south side of the Thelon River, on the shore opposite a huge V-shaped sand blowout (Figure 19.1, inset top right, circled). Satellite sites, used in those summers when the herd did not cross directly to KjNb-7, are scattered east along the arc-like series of sand blowouts. The distances of the sites from the river mandated skinning, gutting and quartering of each carcass along its bank. The river also protected KjNb-7 and other camps, somewhat, from grizzly bears (*Ursus horribilis*) and other predators, as unwanted guts and hooves, and sometimes the hide, could be thrown into the river and carried away.

KjNb-7 was found in 1970 and excavated in 1971 and 1976 (Gordon 1975, 133–35; 2007). During its excavation my crew viewed a small sub-herd that had just crossed the river, a harbinger of the thousands of caribou moving over the next few days (Figure 19.2). This, plus plentiful caribou bone in all levels, is dramatic proof that KjNb-7 was used seasonally from the time of its lowest level dating, 6120 years ago. Continuous use of this site resulted in the forming

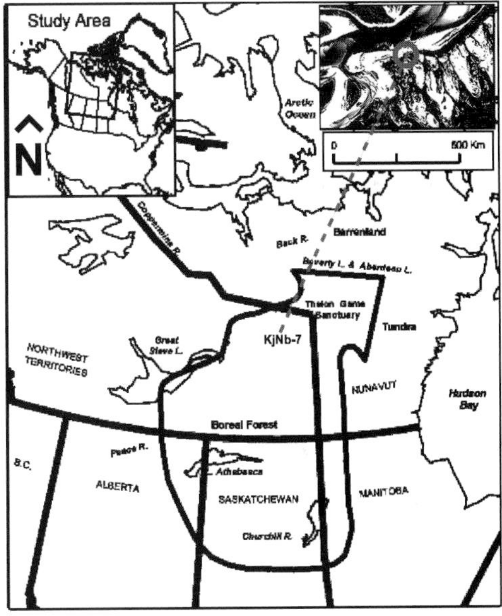

Figure 19.1. Study area in north-central mainland Canada.

Figure 19.2. Confirmation KjNb-7 was used seasonally for 6000 years.

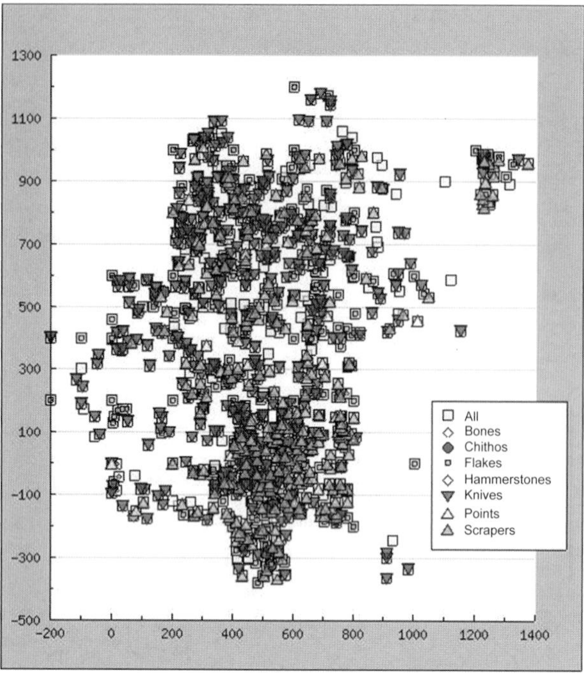

Figure 19.3. KjNb-7 Middle Taltheilei phase palimpsest.

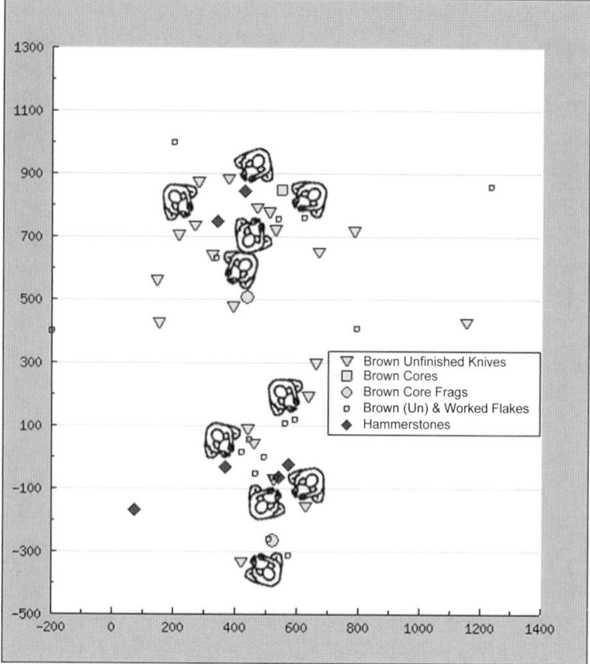

Figure 19.5. Brown quartzite knapping stations.

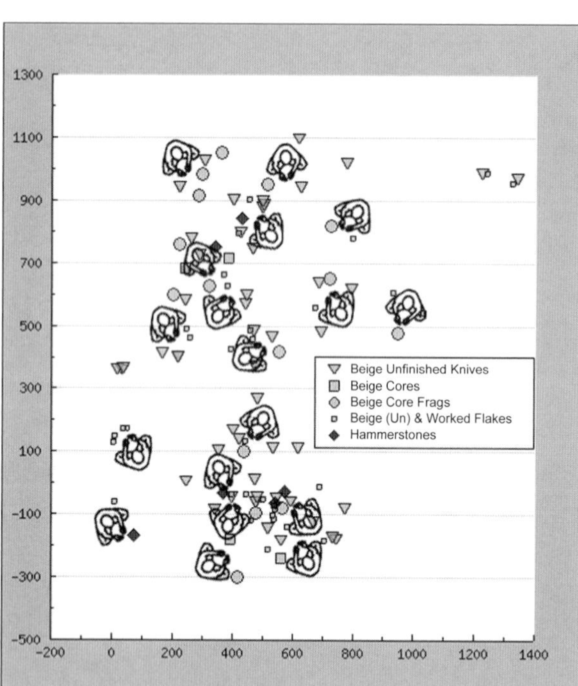

Figure 19.4. Beige quartzite knapping stations.

of palimpsests on all cultural levels; its heaviest occurring in the Middle phase, dating 1400 to 1800 years ago (Gordon 1996, 86, 238). Even after removing dozens of kilograms of flakes, cobbles, charcoal and soil samples and bone and teeth (not depicted in Figure 19.3), the Middle phase distribution remains a veritable cloud of artefacts. What can we do with this maze? Must we label it a puzzle of skin scrapers, butchering knives and knapping debris? Can we penetrate its depths? Can we sequence its activities?

Finding activity areas in palimpsest

Other than fishing in the river for immediate sustenance, the preparing of dozens of knives for butchering caribou was the first major activity while awaiting herd arrival. Assuming some artefact clustering remained after 400 years of use, we first plotted the knapping activity (Figure 19.4). With many colours and hues represented, all clustered unworked flakes, broken knives and core fragments of the same material and hue were interpreted as coming from the same knapping station, via one core and a hammerstone of unrelated hue and material (hammerstones appear in other activities). Finished knives would have been removed for use elsewhere, while broken unused scrapers were absent. First, we grouped flakes, broken knives and core fragments in relation to their hue, removing beige artefacts from the palimpsest, then brown (Figure 19.5), grey (Figure 19.6) and orange (Figure 19.7). Pink, beige and pink, beige and grey, white, beige and green, and beige and orange-banded artefacts were also plotted but not depicted due to publishing constraints. Other colours were too rare to consider. For clarity, human icons were added to graphs based on the activity represented. Shoulder widths of men (45cm) and women (35cm) are to scale. Icon orientation was based on artefact distribution, the space needed for the activity, and handedness (8–15% left-handed as in modern populations, with more men than women being so) (Hardyck and Petrinovich 1977).

This technique may seem inapplicable to Palaeolithic, Mesolithic and Neolithic archaeologists analysing flint blades, blade-like knives and scrapers, and points and cores of the same colour, but do not despair – it is only one of seven techniques we used, colour being unimportant in the remaining six.

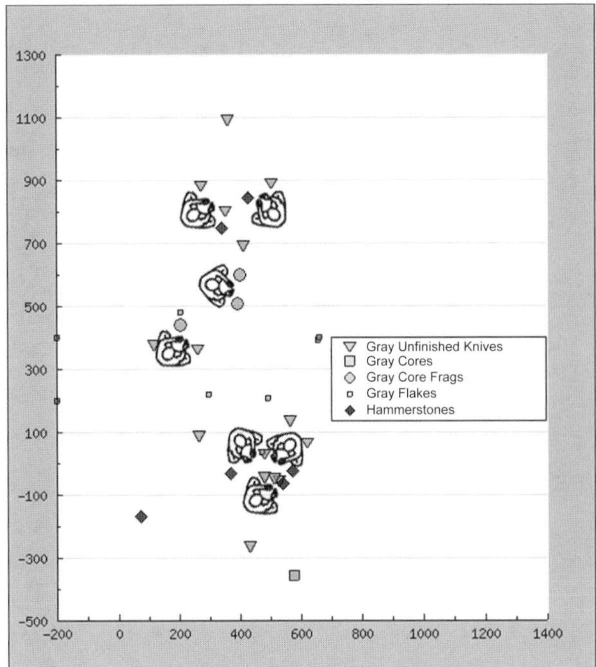

Figure 19.6. Grey quartzite knapping stations.

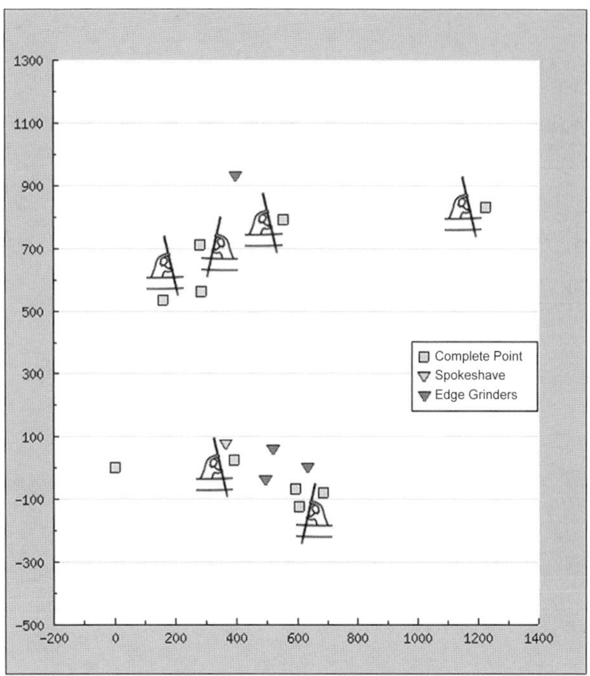

Figure 19.8. Middle phase lance production stations.

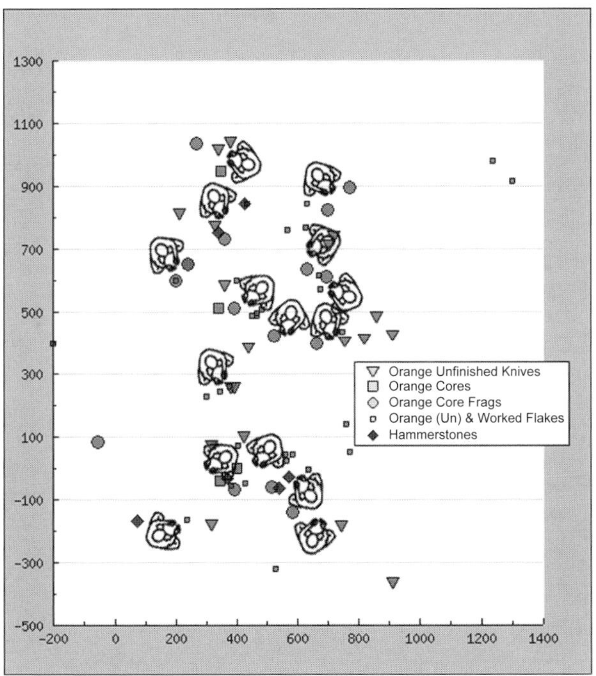

Figure 19.7. Orange quartzite knapping stations.

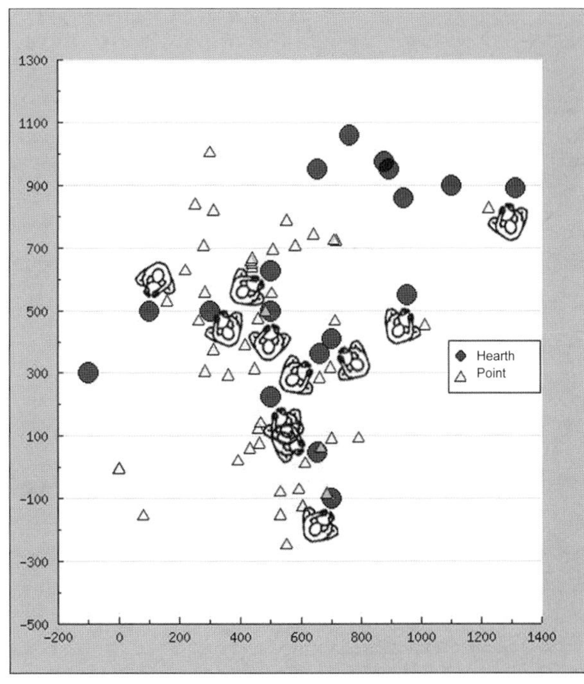

Figure 19.9. Middle phase lance repair stations.

The second major activity was lancing caribou crossing the river (Figure 19.8). Although wood is unpreserved, a quartzite spokeshave may have been used to round lance shafts. Three edge grinders were used to dull lance or point bases to protect the hafting sinew from being cut (Gordon 1996, 96, 111). Ten complete lance heads with ground bases were ready for hafting. A subsequent, more intense, activity was lance head or point repair (Figure 19.9). Loosening broken lance heads from their shafts involved water and heat to liquefy the blood glue from the sinew binding. That is why we found 49 lance head bases in, or near hearths. The six hearths to the north (top) were confined to grease extraction and roasting meat (to follow).

For the third activity (Figure 19.10) we plotted butchering stations, involving the use of worn knives, where women cut meat from each carcass quarter for thin slicing and wind-drying, setting aside long bones for later fragmenting. Hearne's (1795, 73) diary of January 22,

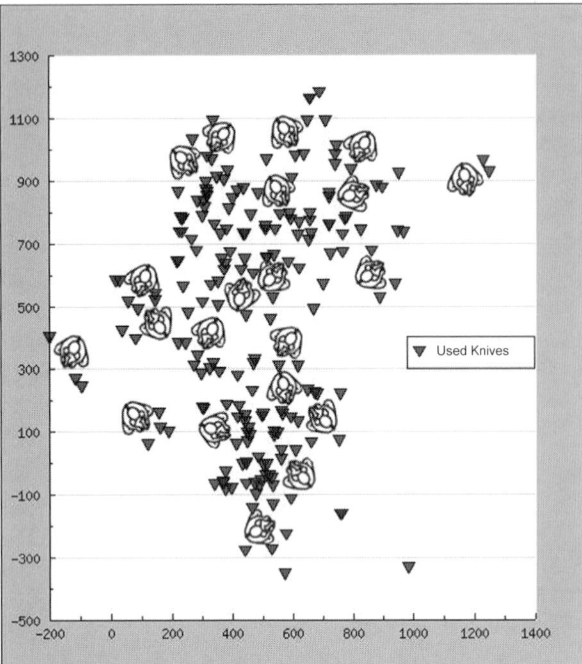

Figure 19.10. Middle phase butchering stations.

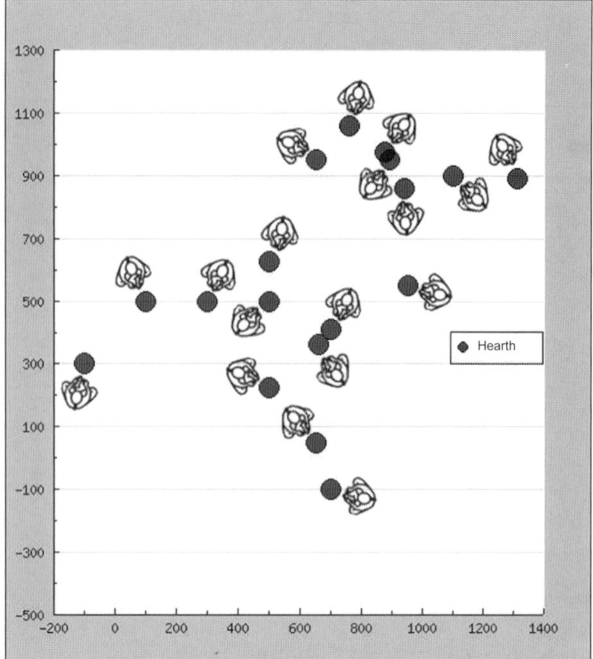

Figure 19.11. Middle phase meat roasting stations.

1771, said women cut the meat from long bones, then sliced and dried it; 21 icons of women were oriented according to clustered worn knives. They likely cut and piled the strips on a partial or full hide, perhaps a metre or so in diameter, so that others, perhaps their daughters, could wind-dry it on willows or suspended rawhide rope (see tundra example in Morriset 1998–1999). Each icon required a minimum of several knives in an arc of 60–120º from the centre of the hide and many more could be added in both dense central areas.

The fourth activity (Figure 19.11) is hearth-centred and involved the roasting of non-marrow bones to cook adhering meat and brain for immediate consumption. Here, nine hearths contained non-marrow, calcined cranial, rib, vertebral, and distal leg and ankle bones.

In the fifth activity the residual long bones from butchering were smashed with a hammerstone, exposing marrow for later grease extraction using boiling water flotation (Figure 19.12). This involved a hammerstone, hearth, fire-cracked rock, uncalcined long bone fragments and space for a birch-bark boiling vessel or a rawhide-lined ground depression filled with water. Here, 17 women with forked sticks for relaying hot rocks from hearth to water for boiling were placed according to handedness, probably 8–15% being left-handed, as with modern populations. Right-handed women extracting grease would have the fire on their left and transfer rocks and broken long bones to a pool on their right. Left-handed women were placed on the assumption that the fire would be to their right and rocks and broken long bones would therefore be transferred to a pool on their left. By adding rocks until the water boiled, they skimmed the floating grease off its surface to a skin or bark container. It was later mixed with dried meat powder, as pemmican, and stored. When the pool

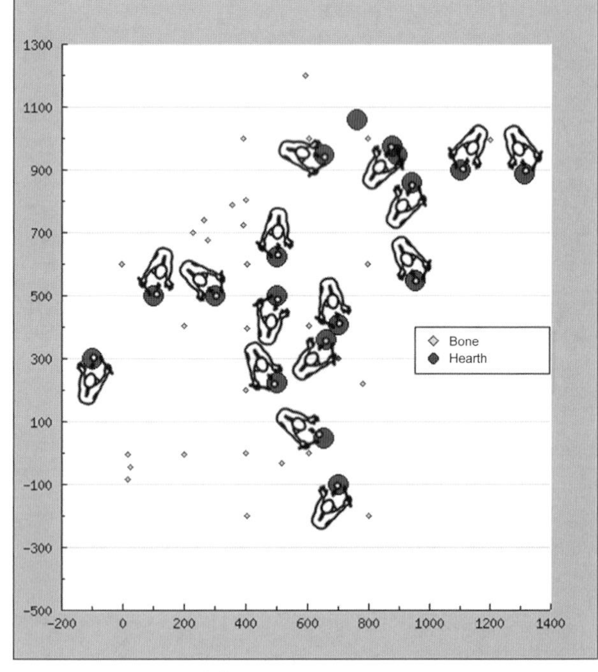

Figure 19.12. Middle phase marrow extraction stations.

filled with extracted bone and fire-cracked rock, both were thrown further right, or left, according to handedness, and where we excavated them. The boiling water was rarely east of the hearth because the dominant west wind (from the left) would cover it with ash and cinders. Nearby hammerstones for smashing bone may have been used earlier for knapping.

For the sixth activity (Figure 19.13), or hide preparation, we plotted used scrapers and *chithos*, the latter being thin

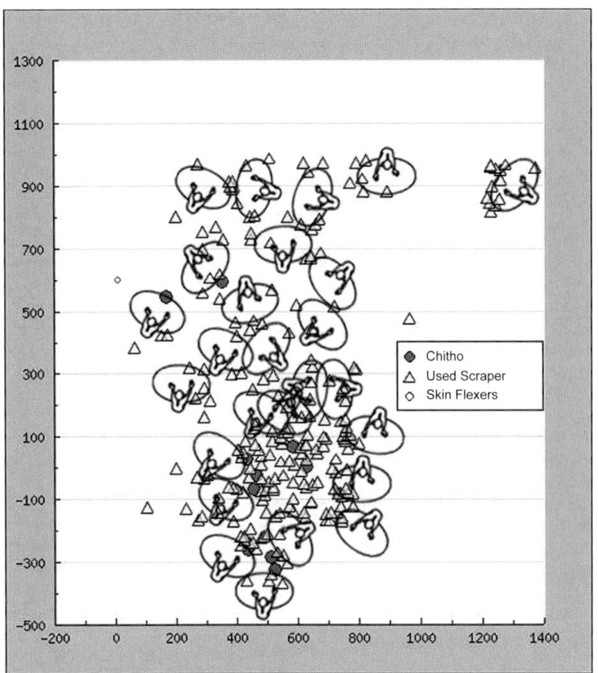

Figure 19.13. Middle phase hide preparation stations by query.

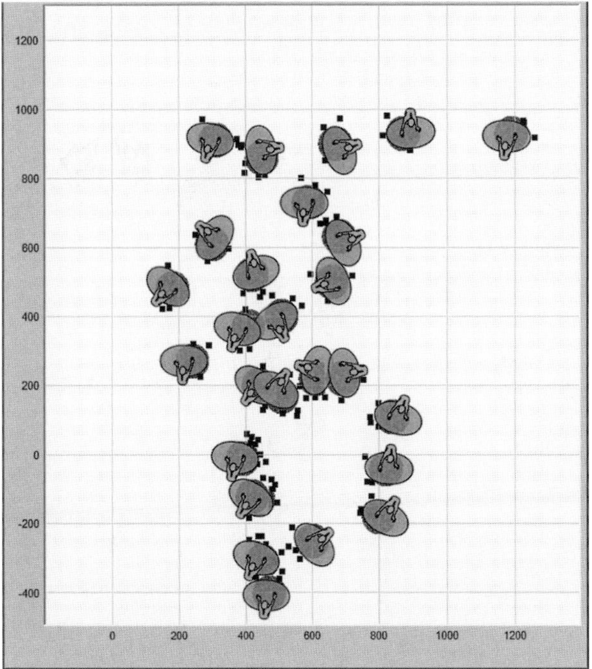

Figure 19.14. Middle phase hide preparation stations by algorithm.

rough sandstone discs pulled scraper-like at a steep angle out from the centre of a pegged hide to stretch and soften it. Assuming these tools were not completely dispersed over the years this floor was used, their distribution would form a partial arc of a hypothetical 60–90cm oval hide. To reduce subjectivity, Ricardo Santiago of our group designed algorithmic crawler software to penetrate the palimpsest to look for 60–120° arcs of scrapers and *chithos* along hide borders, also finding 26 stations (Figure 19.14).

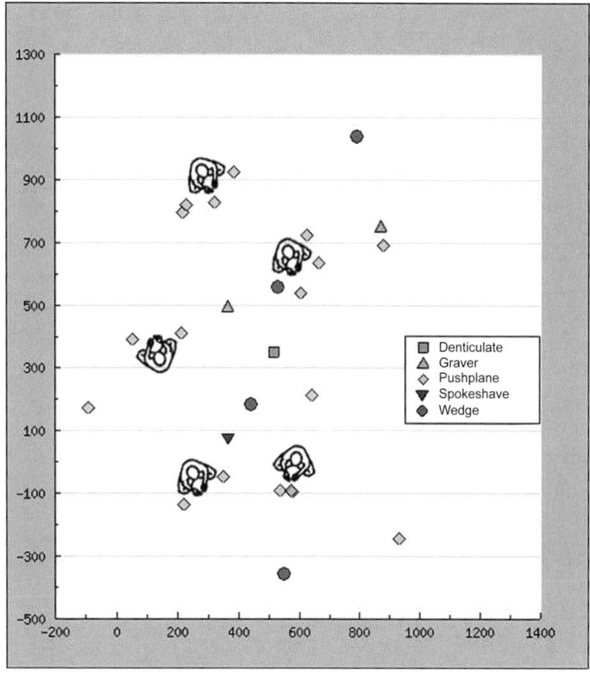

Figure 19.15. Middle phase woodworking stations.

Our seventh and final activity is woodworking (Figure 19.15). On April 8, 1771, Hearne (1795, 87–88) mentions men gathering and trimming birch trees for tent poles and the frames of canoes and snowshoes. Tool handles were split from spruce poles with a wedge, sawn to length with a denticulate, shaped with a push-plane and rounded with a spokeshave. We inserted five icons of men, but more are obviously needed.

Removing artefacts of all seven activities from our palimpsest resulted in an empty hearth (warmth, insect repelling or hide tanning), a tent weight cobble, uncalcined jaws and teeth not in hearths, charcoal and soil samples and a chopper (Figure 19.16), all present in Figure 19.3 but absent in its legend due to space. It may be possible to use dated artefacts of identical hue in nearby sites to arrange chronologically the knapping sequence of KjNb-7 over its 400-year occupation.

In sum, palimpsest spatial analyses reflect the conservative nature of hunters and their families to use the same areas of a campsite for the same sequence of activities and allow delineation of gender-based activity areas. Our techniques are beneficial if you have repeated site usage in any time period. The techniques demonstrated here can be applied elsewhere to sites where similar conditions exist.

Acknowledgements

I thank my XY Spatial Analysis Group for its input. Results were possible due largely to software programmers Raymond Cheng (main customized programme) and Ricardo Santiago (algorithmic crawler method). The final figures for publication were prepared by Elizabeth Creary (also text editing) and Alanna Caples (figure arrangement and graphic art), with overhead human icons by Sylvie

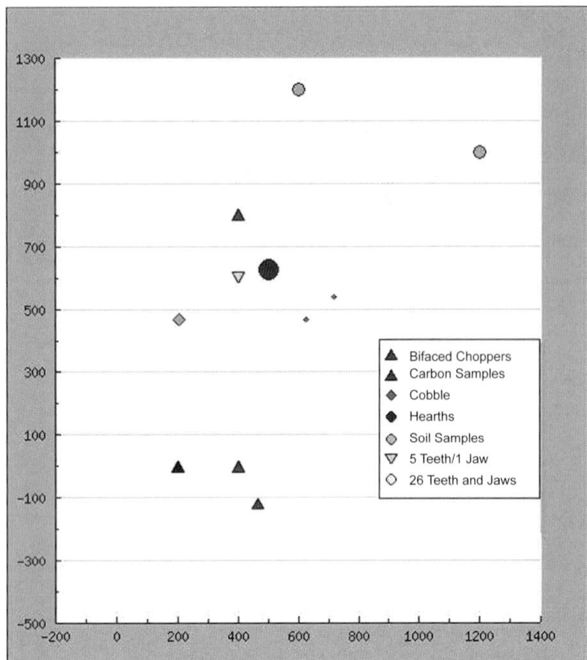

Figure 19.16. Middle phase palimpsest leftovers.

Pelletier. For testing palimpsest decipherment, many figures were first generated by Katherine Herbert and Lori Howey. I thank them all for lively discussions on icon orientation and symbol selection. There was general agreement once the activity parameters were established.

References

Gordon, B. C. 1975 *Of Men and Herds in Barrenland Prehistory*. Mercury Series 28, Archaeological Survey of Canada. Ottawa, National Museum of Man.

Gordon, B. C. 1996. *People of Sunlight; People of Starlight: Barrenland Archaeology in the Northwest Territories of Canada*. Mercury Series 154, Archaeological Survey of Canada. Gatineau, Canadian Museum of Civilization.

Gordon, B. C. 2007. *Deciphering Archaeological Palimpsests as a Key to Showing Centuries of Repeated Rangifer Processing Tasks in Identical Locations by Men and Women in Northern Hunting Families*. Submitted for publication to Rangifer Journal, Norway.

Gordon, B. C. *Archaeological Gender-Based Spatial Analysis* at http://http-server.carleton.ca/~bgordon/ Spatial/xyproject_main.htm (accessed 06/2007).

Hardyck, C. and Petrinovich, L. F. 1977. Left-handedness. *Psychological Bulletin* 84, 385–404.

Hearne, S. 1795. *A Journey from Prince of Wales's Fort, in Hudson's Bay, to the Northern Ocean: Undertaken by Order of the Hudson's Bay Company for the Discovery of Copper Mines, a North West Passage, and c. in the Years 1769, 1770, 1771 and 1772*. London, A. Strahan and T. Cadell Publishers.

Morriset, J. 1998–99. Cover photograph of *Recherches amérindiennes au Québec* XXVIII (3).

Session III

People in their Environment

20. Introduction: People in their environment

Rick Schulting

The papers in this session cover a range of topics relating to aspects of the environment. Although there are a few exceptions, the 'environment' in the contributions by and large refers to subsistence resources, and in particular animal resources. The 'people' are present to varying degrees, sometimes more implicitly than explicitly, in part no doubt because of the format of the volume, and the space limitations it imposes. But there is probably also an element of research specialisation involved here, so that those primarily interested in (for example) zooarchaeological analyses, itself a complex field, may not have the same interest in writing a more explicitly social archaeology. This is in itself neither necessarily a good thing nor a bad thing – it depends on what uses are made of the information, and, most crucially, that it is used. The inescapable fact of modern archaeological inquiry is that it often necessitates a high degree of specialisation in one area or another. Some sense of this comes through in the papers here, which range from 'traditional' zooarchaeological analyses, to biochemical approaches.

Seasonality analysis of shellfish features prominently in Milner's paper and in both contributions by Mannino and Thomas. Milner begins by introducing the debate over the continued use of marine resources in the Neolithic of Denmark, before moving to a detailed case study of the Norsminde shellmidden, noting both continuities but also differences in how shellfish were exploited across the Mesolithic-Neolithic transition. In one of their two contributions, Mannino and Thomas are able to use stable oxygen isotope analysis to document changing patterns of shellfish exploitation in northwest Sicily, from almost exclusively winter collection in the Final Epigravettian and Early Mesolithic, to collection at all times of the year in the Later Mesolithic. They relate this to increasing concerns over controlling access to resources patches in an environment that is not particularly rich. The fact that the Mediterranean is comparatively impoverished in terms of the world's seas is a useful point to make to those more familiar with Mesolithic archaeology along the Atlantic coast of Europe, anticipating the degree of variability to be expected in the use of marine resources at this time. In their other contribution, Mannino and Thomas demonstrate a focus on winter collection of rocky shore molluscs at a Late Mesolithic site on the Isle of Portland in southern England. Most intriguingly, all three of the above papers document a decrease in the size of the shellfish taken over time, and raise the possibility that human overexploitation played a part in bringing the resource under pressure (an hypothesis also proposed by C. Dupont (2006) for the French Atlantic coast), although other factors, and in particular sea-level and climate changes, are also acknowledged. Sorting out these different contributing factors presents an important interpretive challenge, and an especially relevant one in light of the renewed emphasis on the interplay between climate change and human response.

Seasonality studies of shellfish are becoming an increasingly standard application, and provide an important tool in understanding how (mainly) coastal sites were used, and how they fit into larger settlement systems. But it will be crucial to sample more widely across single sites, horizontally as well as vertically, in order to be confident of the patterns observed. What is perhaps most striking about these seasonality studies is that they work at all, alluding to the highly structured and repetitive ways in which people moved around and utilised their environments, often over periods that must have lasted centuries if not longer. This evokes the notion of 'persistent places' (Barton *et al.* 1995), and must surely put to rest any surviving traces of the idea (more popular than academic) that hunter-fisher-gatherers wandered rather aimlessly across the landscape, eking out an existence.

The exploitation of shellfish is often seen in the context of expanding diet breadth at the end of the Pleistocene. Small game also features here, and Bournery discusses the increasing use of small vertebrates from the start of the Holocene at the Abeurador Cave in the Languedoc region of southern France. This site provides one of the most comprehensive stratigraphic sequences in the north-west Mediterranean, especially for the Preboreal period, which is more developed here than at any other location. In particular, Bournery focuses on the evidence for the systematic exploitation of rabbits, game birds and tortoises, showing how taken together these comprise over two-thirds of the NISP in the Mesolithic levels. While this is consistent with the common characterisation of Mesolithic economies as participating in a 'broad spectrum revolution', Bournery notes that the proportion of small game was also significant (up to 45%) in Late Palaeolithic levels. A key area being explored in further work is the complex interplay between changing capture technologies, prey availability, and human decision making.

Not surprisingly, relative sea-level change plays a central role in explaining at least some aspects of changing economic evidence. Gutiérrez Zugasti summarises the shellfish species found at two sites with Azilian and Mesolithic deposits on the Cantabrian coast of northern Spain. In line with increasing evidence from other sites and regions in the Late Pleistocene and Early Holocene (e.g. Lubell 2004; Mussi *et al.* 1995; Rizner *et al.* this volume), the Azilian levels at La Fragua have large numbers of land snails rather than marine molluscs, although the same levels at nearby la Peña del Perro show the opposite, showing that more is involved than proximity to the sea, although this was a factor in the changing proportions of species. Kriiska and Lõugas explore the complex environmental history and its effect on human settlement and economy in Estonia, on the eastern Baltic. Simpson makes a different kind of contribution, presenting details of his efforts to develop automatically generated sea-level displacement curves for a region of western Norway. Mesolithic settlements here are closely bound to their contemporary shorelines, making this model an indispensable tool, both for surveying and understanding aspects of site location.

Changing sea levels play another role altogether in Melton's contribution, coastal erosion being the agent responsible for the exposure of a shellmidden at West Voe on Shetland. The lower part of this midden has been dated to *c.* 4200–3600 cal BC, placing it at the very end of the Mesolithic or the beginning of the 'Neolithic', however that is to be defined this far north (although only a few centuries later a Neolithic farming presence is well attested at Scord of Brouster (Whittle 1986). Only wild species have so far been identified in the limited fauna. The intriguing question is whether a Mesolithic or Early Neolithic population was already resident on the island group at this early date – as seems to be implied by the presence of multi-season indicators in the lower midden – or whether it was visited only sporadically, implying considerable sea voyages over open water. Or was it perhaps a failed colonisation attempt, which may have been a more common occurrence in prehistory than is realised?

Chaix reports on the fauna from the important Mesolithic site of Zamostje 2, north of Moscow, with its excellent organic preservation. A wide range of fauna is represented, including birds and abundant freshwater fish as well as both small and large mammals. The main emphasis in the paper is on the elk (*Alces alces*) remains, and, linking subsistence and ideological aspects, Chaix is able to draw upon the well-known corpus of elk imagery in the form of portable carvings and perforated elk incisors from sites across Russia and further west as well. The importance of elk antler as a raw material is seen as a possible reason for the emphasis on male animals at Zamostje 2.

Mansrud, in the context of eastern Norway, explores the links between animals and ideology more explicitly, and in fact she focuses on the same two animals – elk and beaver (*Castor fiber*) – that dominate Zamostje 2, showing the widespread importance of these species across northern Europe. Reminiscent in general of the practices of many northern hunter-gatherers known ethnographically, in Mesolithic eastern Norway the remains of elk and beaver appear to be treated differently, with elk dominating the rare unburnt bone assemblages, and beaver dominating the burnt assemblages. While suggestive, this is difficult material with which to work, with taphonomic factors featuring prominently, as Mansrud acknowledges. Equally challenging is the attempt to account for absences from faunal assemblages, in this case of the bear (Ursidae), a rich source of meat and fat that was and is widely hunted by many arctic and subarctic groups in recent times, and is found depicted in rock art in other parts of Norway. Was the bear really not hunted in eastern Norway, or does their absence reflect different disposal practices relating to the 'proper' way to treat a certain animal's remains to ensure future hunting success?

In their paper on small-scale variability among the Evenk hunters and herders of Siberia, Grøn *et al.* make the most explicit connection between the environment and culture (*cultural ecology* in its fullest sense), here primarily taking the form of the creation of group identity. But they are able to do so in an ethnoarchaeolgical context, and the challenge is how to apply these ideas in the absence of the rich detail that both direct observation and living informants can provide, and for human groups whose culture may have no modern parallel. Their discussion of the role of traditional keepers of knowledge is particularly interesting given the pivotal role these individuals might be expected to play in cultural transmission, an area of research that has received considerable attention of late (Aldenderfer 1993; Shennan 2000).

A different approach to investigating diet is taken by Paine *et al.*, who employ stable isotopes on human and faunal remains at the Early Mesolithic site of Pupićina Cave, Croatia. Although based on a very small dataset, their results suggest that only very limited use was made of marine resources, despite the sea being only some 20km from the site, well within the distances hunter-gatherers are expected to move. Occasional forays to the coast are seen in the presence of mussel shells and fish remains.

Edwards and Bradley discuss the results of recent DNA research into the origins of a number of Irish mammals, noting how this provides support for the time-depth of the Lusitanian phylogeography, i.e. a link between the fauna of Ireland and the Iberian Peninsula. This is remarkable research, given the difficulties of extracting and amplifying non-contaminated ancient DNA, and probably one of the very first attempts to use this demanding technique for reconstructing the biogeographical history of a well-delimited area. As with the now famous Orkney vole (*Microtus arvalis orcadensis*) or Mediterranean island mammals, Edwards and Bradley raise the possibility that many Irish mammals were introduced to the island by humans from the Neolithic onwards, whether intentionally or accidentally.

In the only paper in this session to deal explicitly with the exploitation of plants by Mesolithic communities, McComb summarises her research into some of the practicalities involved in harvesting and storing that quintessential contribution to north-western European Mesolithic cuisine, the hazelnut (*Corylus*). She finds that the window of opportunity for collecting nuts in the autumn is a very narrow one, as a result of direct competition from woodland creatures, in this case the red squirrels (*Sciurus vulgaris*) that were in large part to blame for a paltry human take of 15 ripe nuts from an initially promising harvest. This has clear implications for the exploitation of the resource, which becomes time-stressed in a way that probably applies to a number of wild plant foods (and to domestic cereals in the Neolithic): the impact of non-human competitors is often not fully appreciated (although if Edwards and Bailey are correct that the red squirrel is a much later arrival, then this situation would change for Ireland at least). Some simple storage experiments also provide some interesting results, and these – at the risk of proving Richard Bradley's oft-quoted dictum true ('Successful farmers have social relations with one another, while hunter-gatherers have ecological relations with hazelnuts' (1984, 11)) – could profitably be expanded to cover longer periods and different conditions, and include roasting at different stages (cf. Score and Mithen 2000).

Various themes emerge from the papers. While many of the questions are not dissimilar to those that have been the focus of research for many years, the methodologies being brought to bear are more sophisticated. Continuing developments in analytical methods and techniques are providing increasingly detailed information, in turn offering the opportunity for more nuanced accounts of people-environment interactions in the past, as well as for revisiting what we think we know. A number of contributions, for example, while agreeing with the principle, raise questions over the formulation of the 'broad spectrum revolution' and how it applies to the Mesolithic. Another notable trend is the domination of site-based studies in the session; these allow for different scales of investigation, and also form the building blocks for a greater consideration of regional variation, and for finer-grained chronological resolution. At the same time, it is important not to lose sight of the larger picture, as it is this that provides a context, a backdrop against which smaller-scale events and processes stand out. People and environments usually operate at very different time-scales (cf. Bailey 1983). A clear example of this is the idea, raised in a number of papers, that people may have adversely affected at least local resources through overexploitation to a greater extent than is usually acknowledged. Such unintended consequences would have occurred slowly over a long period, and probably not be recognised by the communities themselves. At this scale, it is difficult to speak of agency. Yet in other cases, and at other scales, human agency takes on much more immediate relevance. Seasonality studies, analysis of human hunting and gathering decisions, butchery and disposal practices, all combine to inform our accounts of how people moved around and utilised their environment, a crucial underpinning whether one is interested in foraging theory or in people's engagements with, and phenomenological understanding of, their landscapes.

References

Aldenderfer, M. 1993. Ritual, hierarchy and change in foraging societies. *Journal of Anthropological Archaeology* 12, 1–40.

Bailey, G. N. 1983. Concepts of time in Quaternary prehistory. *Annual Review of Anthropology* 12, 165–92.

Barton, R. N. E., Berridge, P. J., Walker, M. J. C. and Bevins, R. E. 1995. Persistent places in the Mesolithic landscape: an example from the Black Mountain uplands of south Wales. *Proceedings of the Prehistoric Society* 61, 81–116.

Bradley, R. 1984. *The Social Foundations of Prehistoric Britain. Themes and variation in the archaeology of power*. Longman Archaeology Series. Harlow, Longman.

Dupont, C. 2006. *La malacofaune de sites mésolithiques et néolithiques de la façade atlantique de la France. Contribution à l'économie et à l'identité culturelle des groupes concernés. British Archaeological Reports, International Series S1571. Oxford, Archaeopress.*

Lubell, D. 2004. Are land snails a signature for the Mesolithic-Neolithic transition? *Documenta Praehistorica* 31, 1–24.

Mussi, M., Lubell, D., Arnoldus-Huyzendveld, A., Agostini, S. and Coubray, S. 1995. Holocene land snail exploitation in the highlands of Central Italy and Eastern Algeria: a comparison. *Préhistoire Européenne* 7, 169–89.

Score, D. and Mithen, S. 2000. The experimental roasting of hazelnuts, in S. Mithen (ed.), *Hunter-Gatherer Landscape Archaeology: The Southern Hebrides Mesolithic Project 1988-98. Vol. 2*, 507–12. McDonald Institute Monographs. Cambridge, McDonald Institute for Archaeological Research.

Shennan, S. 2000. Population, culture history, and the dynamics of culture change. *Current Anthropology* 41, 811–35.

Whittle, A. 1986. *Scord of Brouster: An Early Agricultural Settlement on Shetland, Excavations 1977–79*. Oxford University Committee for Archaeology Monograph 9. Oxford, Oxford University Committee for Archaeology.

21. Coastal perspectives on the Mesolithic-Neolithic transition

Nicky Milner and Eva Laurie

There is some debate as to the role of marine resources around the Mesolithic-Neolithic transition and into the Early Neolithic. Stable isotopes suggest a dramatic shift from marine to terrestrial resources at this time, but in southern Scandinavia there is much evidence, particularly from shell middens, that marine foods were exploited into the Early Neolithic. This paper will examine this evidence at a different scale and focus in on a case study of a shell midden at Norsminde. Both oysters and cockles from this site have been examined for evidence of seasonal exploitation and the intensity of exploitation for a period spanning the Late Mesolithic and Early Neolithic. The results show that there is some continuity but also subtle changes in the consumption of these species, which may be related to a variety of social, economic and environmental factors. Trying to reconcile this data with the broader picture of economic change at this time brings up a host of new questions that also need to be addressed.

Keywords: shell midden, oyster, cockle, Mesolithic, Neolithic, Norsminde, seasonality, exploitation, incremental growth.

Introduction

The idea that marine and coastal resources were heavily used in many parts of Europe in the Mesolithic period is well established, particularly due to extensive work on shell middens (e.g. see Andersen 2000) and also recent stable isotope work on human bone (e.g. Richards and Hedges 1999; Richards *et al.* 2003; Schulting and Richards 2001; 2002a; 2002b). It is more debatable as to the scale and extent of marine exploitation in the Early Neolithic period, particularly in southern Scandinavia (Eriksson 2004; Lidén *et al.* 2004; Milner *et al.* 2004). Many of the shell middens continued to accumulate in the Early Neolithic period and yet the stable isotope analyses on human bone suggest a shift towards the exploitation of terrestrial foodstuffs rather than marine.

This debate focuses on the larger-scale issues of diet and economy and covers a long time span and a large geographical area. However, it is also important to consider consumption practices at other scales in order to identify in what ways different resources were used, what food was consumed, and how practices changed, particularly the consumption of marine foods at the end of the Mesolithic and in the Early Neolithic.

Shell middens provide a range of stratified data which can offer a fairly sensitive measure of change. In this paper we wish to focus down and present work that considers a category of marine resources which is often considered to be of minor significance in the overall diet, and yet which dominates the archaeological record: this is of course the marine molluscs found in their millions within the middens. By considering the seasonal shellfish gathering strategies and the intensity of exploitation we can begin to build up a picture of how people may have used these resources and how this relates to both social practice and the environment.

In this paper we will firstly outline the methods we have developed for the incremental growth analysis of oysters and cockles in order to investigate both seasonality of gathering and the intensity of exploitation. A case study from the site of Norsminde, Denmark, will then be presented. Finally the use of marine molluscs will be considered within the wider context of coastal exploitation for the Mesolithic-Neolithic transition.

Incremental growth analysis

Shellfish grow incrementally like trees. Growth varies seasonally and so, like trees, growth breaks or lines form in the colder parts of the year. These can sometimes be observed macroscopically on the exterior of the shell as with cockles, and for oysters they are more visible on the hinge of the shells. However, in order to get more detailed information on seasonal growth it is necessary to section the shells and inspect the structure microscopically.

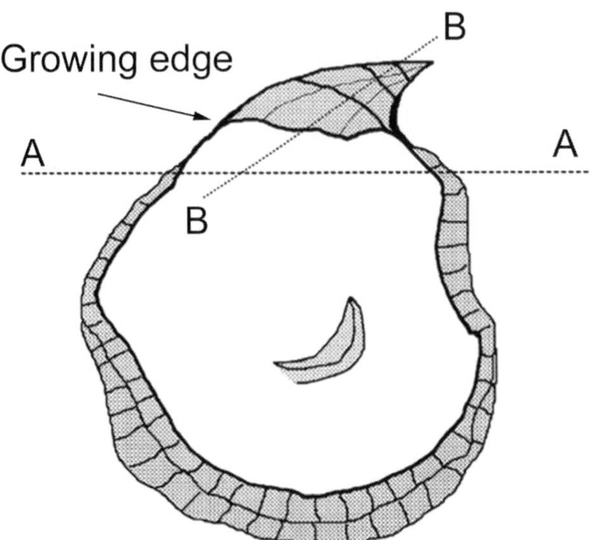

Figure 21.1. Sectioning the flat valve of the oyster: the hinge is cut off (A–A), the hinge is then sectioned (B–B) at right angles to the growing edge.

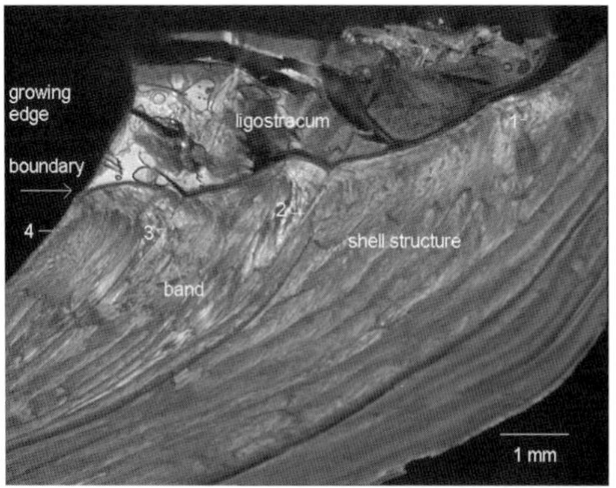

Figure 21.2. A picture of a thin section of an oyster from the modern control sample, collected in May. Four annual lines have been identified, with number 4 having just formed on the edge.

In order to understand how the growth varies through the year it is also important to use modern control samples, collected at regular intervals throughout the year, preferably for several consecutive years (Claassen 1998). For this study, oysters (*Ostrea edulis*) were collected monthly from three different locations around the British coast over a period of almost two years, and 484 oysters were studied in order to examine the incremental growth (Milner 2001). Thin sections were made of the hinges of the flat oyster shells and examined under the microscope (Figure 21.1). From the analysis of the modern controls, it was found that the annual growth lines occur in the spring, round about March and April, at the end of the cold season and as growth begins again due to warming waters and an explosion of plankton (Milner 2002). Blind testing was carried out to test the results and it was found that seasonal estimates can be made within the error of ±1 month, which means that evaluations are accurate to within a season (Milner 2002).

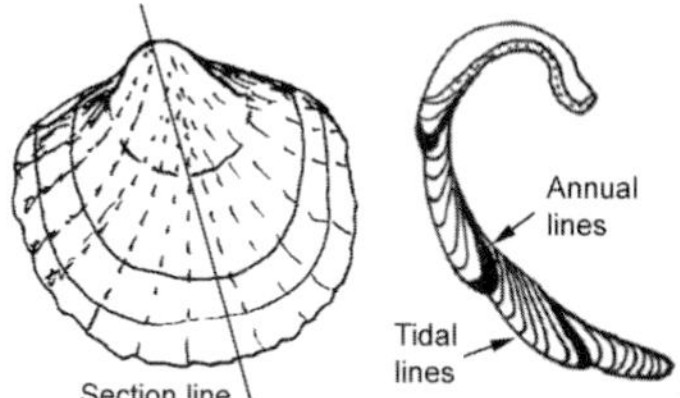

Figure 21.3. Sectioning a cockle: the cockle is sectioned through the shell from the hinge to the growing edge. Annual lines can be seen macroscopically and under the microscope tidal lines can be observed.

Figure 21.4. Microstructure of a cockle at 40x magnification, clearly showing tidal micro-lines, which are formed twice a day in the warmer months of the year.

Figure 21.2 shows an example of a thin section of a modern shell collected in May. The growth breaks are clearly visible, with one having formed right on the growing edge. If there were more growth between the last line and the edge the oyster would have been collected later in the year.

Collections of modern cockles (*Cerastoderma edule*) have also been made from four different locations around the British coast. The cockles are sectioned from hinge to growing edge (Figure 21.3), the surfaces are polished and etched and acetate peels are made. Cockles grow differently to oysters in that they form tidal lines which can be identified microscopically, see Figure 21.4. As growth slows in the colder months of the year the tidal lines stop forming and an annual line can be observed macroscopically on the exterior of the shell. It has been found that there is also some variation in when cockles begin to grow again in the spring, which has an impact on evaluating season of death. Consequently, as with oysters, it is not possible to identify the month of death but seasonal interpretations can be made.

Norsminde shell midden

Studies have been conducted on a number of archaeological shell middens in Denmark, but here we wish to focus on the site of Norsminde as a case study. Norsminde is located on Jutland, to the south of Aarhus, and in the Mesolithic period would have been at the mouth of an estuary (Andersen 1991). It was discovered in 1972 and was excavated by Søren H. Andersen from 1972–89. The midden was roughly oval, about 30m long, between 5 and 12m wide and up to 1.5m thick. The deposit appears to have built up from west to east and then vertically at the east end. There are Mesolithic and Neolithic layers in the midden, the Neolithic layers overlaying the Mesolithic layers, and on the whole the shellfish are smaller in the Neolithic layers (Bailey and Milner, in press). The Mesolithic layers contain Ertebølle cultural artefacts and the Early Neolithic layers contain cultural artefacts associated with the Funnel Beaker Culture.

Seasonality

In the 1970s a cubic metre from the central part of the midden was excavated in 10 arbitrary spits (*c.* 10cm thick and referred to here as layers) and brought to Cambridge for analysis (Bailey and Milner, in press). Layers 10–7 are dated to the Mesolithic, and are largely composed of oysters and cockles, while layers 6–1 are dated to the Neolithic and are largely composed of cockles, fire-cracked stone and burnt material (Figure 21.5). Oysters and cockles have been sampled through the 10 layers in order to examine seasonality. It is assumed from the dates taken from the 10 layers of this column sample, and elsewhere through the midden, that the Mesolithic layers cover roughly 200 years; the transition occurs at about 3950 cal BC and the Neolithic layers again span roughly 200 years (Andersen, pers. comm.). Although it is acknowledged that the analysis on this column will not provide evidence for seasonal gathering of shellfish for elsewhere in the midden, it should provide some indication of patterns and changes in seasonal consumption over this time period.

The results of the oyster and cockle seasonal exploitation are presented in Figures 21.6 and 21.7. The thin sections of the oysters showed particularly clear annual breaks in growth (Milner 2002). The results have been grouped according to season and presented by layer. It can be seen that in the Mesolithic part of the midden the oysters have consistently been gathered in the spring. Because there is some margin of error in making seasonality assessments it may be that the oysters categorised as summer or winter may in fact have been gathered in the spring, but equally those categorised as late spring may in fact have been gathered in the summer. In the Neolithic layers there is some continuation in spring gathering, but certainly by layer 4 the pattern appears to change with more gathering in the summer months as well as continued gathering in the spring months. Again there is some flexibility in interpretation but it can be argued that there is a fairly clear shift within the Neolithic layers.

The cockle data show a slightly different pattern. The

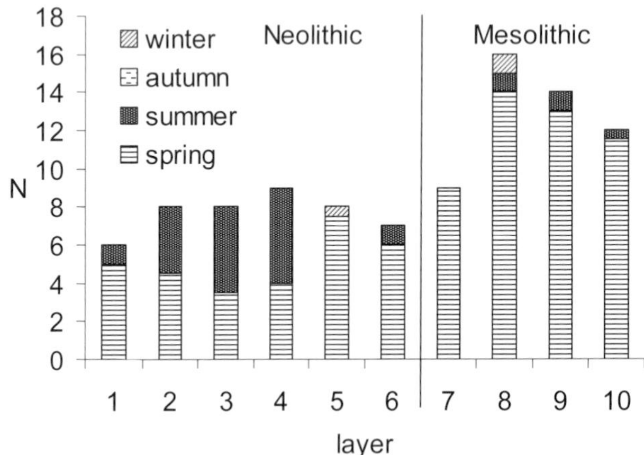

Figure 21.6. Bar chart showing the seasonality of oyster gathering for each layer of the Norsminde midden. Assessments of seasonality were made by month (see Milner 2002) and the numbers of oysters have been tallied for each season. Key: spring (March, April, May); summer (June, July, August); autumn (September, October, November); winter (January, February, March).

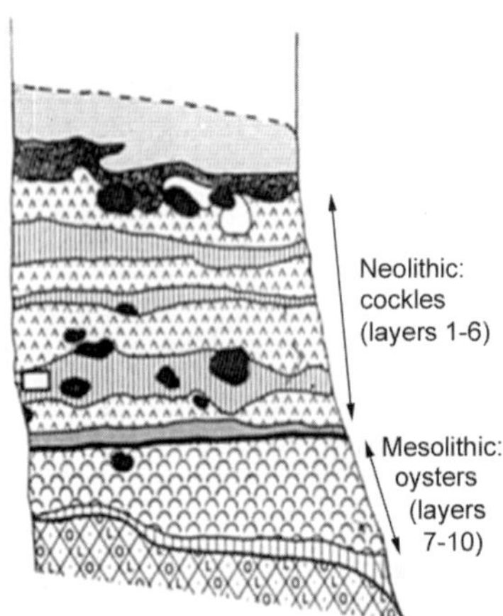

Figure 21.5. Section through the Norsminde midden. Layer 10 is at the base of the midden and layer 1 at the very top (adapted from Andersen 1989, 18, Figure 21.6).

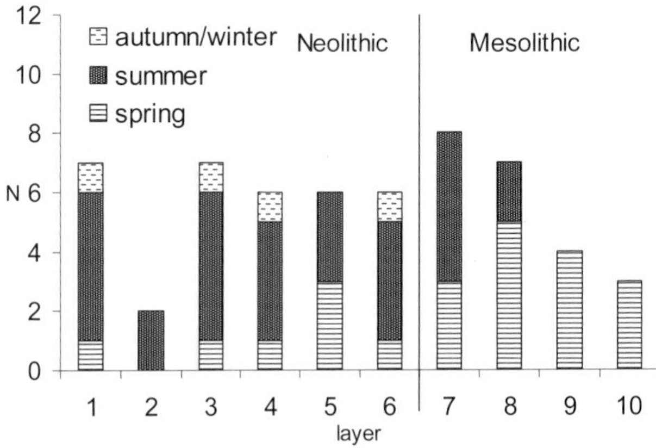

Figure 21.7. Bar chart showing the seasonality of cockle gathering for each layer of the Norsminde midden. Assessments of seasonality have been made by counting tidal lines and grouping counts into seasons (Laurie unpublished data). Because there is little to no growth in autumn and winter these seasons have been combined.

cockles in the Mesolithic layers 9 and 10, at the base of the midden, appear to have been collected in the spring, but there appears to have been some summer gathering in layers 7 and 8 as well. This continues in layers 5 and 6 but in the uppermost part of the midden, layers 4 to 1, summer appears to be the dominant season of gathering. Some of the Neolithic cockles also appear to have been gathered in the autumn/winter. As with the oyster data there is some margin of error, but by looking at the general spread of results we can identify some shifts in seasonal exploitation.

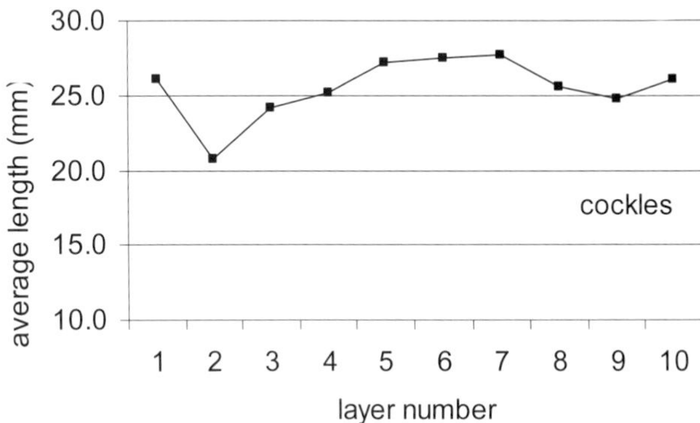

Figure 21.8. The mean length of cockles per layer, from a sample of 981 shells.

Intensity of exploitation

We can also investigate how intensively the shellfish were being gathered. Changes in midden composition are often observed in shell middens around the world and changes in shell size, particularly shells getting smaller in size through time, are often argued to be a result of intensive exploitation. Claassen (1998, 45) has listed a number of ways in which scholars have identified over-exploitation including: 1) mean shell length will decrease from the bottom of a deposit sample to the top; 2) the modal size of the archaeologically derived population of a species, when examined against figures for an unexploited population of a species, will be significantly smaller; and 3) less easily procured individuals or species will increase in number from bottom to top of the deposit.

In the case of Norsminde, it has been observed that both oysters and cockles on the whole become smaller through the midden and that there is a change in dominant species from oysters and cockles in the Mesolithic midden to cockles in the Neolithic midden. Claassen (1998, 45), however, strongly argues that it would have been very difficult for humans to over-exploit a natural population of shellfish. This is hotly debated (see Mannino and Thomas 2002) but one way of strengthening an argument for intensive exploitation is to look at the age structure of the shells against the size. Simply put, if the size is decreasing but so is the average age, it would tend to indicate that the age structure of the natural population is being depressed through gathering. If the average size of the shells is decreasing but the average age remains constant it is more likely that some sort of environmental change, such as change in temperature or salinity, may be to blame for the size change.

Again we can test this in the archaeological middens. On the whole, the shellfish are larger in the Mesolithic layers of Norsminde than in the Neolithic layers. Figures 21.8 and 21.9 present the mean sizes of the cockles and oysters by layer: it can be seen that for both species, the shells in layer 10 are large and for the oysters are particularly suggestive of an unexploited population; they then drop in size in the Mesolithic layers before getting larger again in layers 6 and 7; there is a steady drop off in the Neolithic layers until layer 2, in which both species are very small; and this is then followed by a final increase in size in layer 1. In order to test whether this pattern was due to the intensity of exploitation or some sort of environmental change the ages of the shellfish have been calculated by counting the annual bands identified on the thin-sectioned shells.

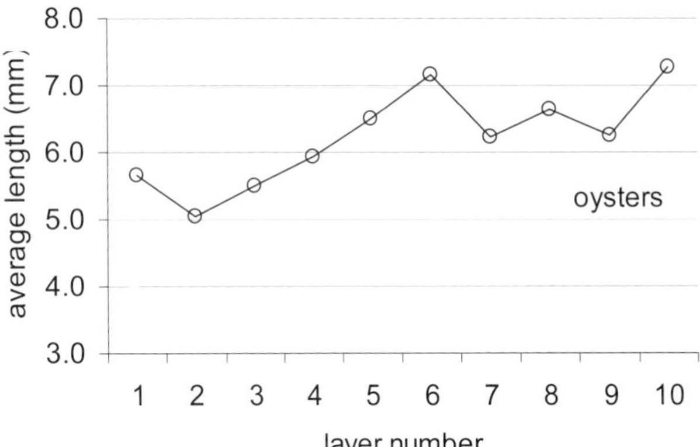

Figure 21.9. The mean length of oyster hinge per layer, from a sample of 668 shells.

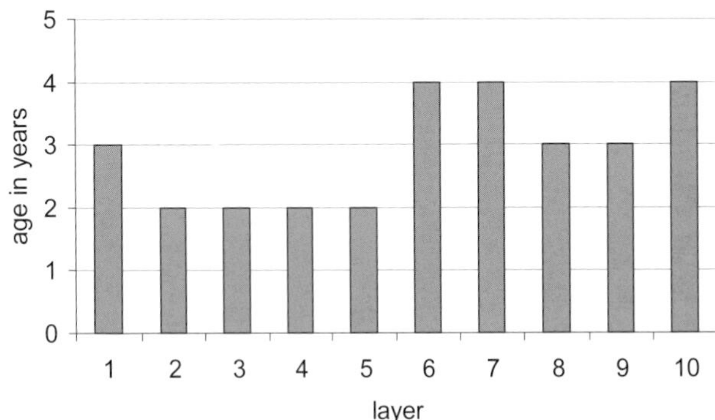

Figure 21.10. Average age of oyster shells for each layer, calculated by counting the annual lines of the oysters thin sectioned for seasonality. It should be noted that larger shells from the Mesolithic layers were not sectioned because they are difficult to analyse for seasonality, so in fact the oysters in the Mesolithic layers are probably on average even older.

If these sizes are compared with the average age per layer it can be seen that the oysters in the Mesolithic layers tend to be older compared to those in the Neolithic layers, see Figure 21.10. Again the same has been seen so far for the cockles. We believe this pattern suggests that the age structure of the natural shellfish populations was decreasing, and this may have been due to some degree of intensity of gathering in the Neolithic. However, the picture is probably not that simple: environmental factors may also have had a part to play. There appears to have been rapid silting in the Early Neolithic due to changes in the tidal amplitude (Petersen 1993). It is possible that, at least for the oysters, this silting may have clogged up some of the oyster beds, thus reducing the size of the natural population available for harvesting, and consequently a continuation of gathering particularly over a longer season may have resulted in some degree of negative impact on these smaller beds.

Peter Rowley-Conwy (1984) has also argued for a lowering of salinity as part of an argument that oysters were essential in plugging a gap in the Mesolithic yearly round, and that the decline of oysters may have triggered the adoption of farming in Denmark. Although there is some evidence that salinity may have dropped to some degree it is not clear at the present time whether this would have affected the oysters so drastically. Certainly this effect would have varied regionally and in some areas such as Jutland, and particularly around the Limfjord, oysters persist in the Early Neolithic middens, such as at Visborg and Krabbesholm II (Andersen 2005). In addition, a drop in salinity would not have affected the cockles to the same degree, as they can tolerate lower salinities than oysters, and yet the pattern in size and age is similar to the pattern observed for the oysters.

Discussion

As discussed at the beginning of this paper, there is clearly evidence in Denmark which shows that people were still exploiting marine resources in the Early Neolithic period (see also Milner *et al.* 2004). If the shell midden material is examined at a finer resolution it can be seen that, in fact, the situation is more complex than a simple shift in exploitation from oysters to cockles in the Early Neolithic middens. In the case of the Norsminde midden there is some degree of continuity in that shellfish are consumed through the lifespan of the midden, and yet there are changes, with shifts in seasonal shellfish gathering, a change in the species being gathered, and changes in shell size. However, not all these changes happen at the same time, or indeed are coincident with the change in material culture from Mesolithic to Neolithic within the shell midden.

The cockles are being gathered in large numbers through both the Mesolithic and Neolithic periods, but a change from spring to spring and summer gathering may well occur within the Mesolithic layers. The oyster gathering, however, appears to be focused in the spring in the Mesolithic and Early Neolithic, and shifts into spring and summer gathering in the top part of the Early Neolithic midden, not at the point when oysters become much less abundant in the midden sequence. It is very difficult to know how representative this picture is because, of course, we are dealing with small sample sizes and time-averaged layers. However, one thing is certain and that is that seasonal gathering does not appear to be consistent through time, and this highlights the benefits of sampling from different parts of the midden sequence. It is also difficult to interpret why there may be these changes, because seasonal gathering practices may be related to a number of different economic, environmental, social and ritual practices (Milner 2005a). The size and age measurements demonstrate similar patterns of exploitation for both oysters and cockles. It appears that they become smaller in size at roughly the same time and this may be partly due to a changing environment, but also the continued intensity of gathering, which continues over a longer season (spring and summer) in the Early Neolithic and may also have contributed to the observed impact on the natural populations.

It does seem difficult to reconcile this picture with the overview from the stable isotope data that there is a pronounced shift from marine to terrestrial resources in the Early Neolithic, but we must remember that these are very different scales of analyses and both sets of data are subject to a number of biases (Milner *et al.* 2004; Milner *et al.* 2006; Richards and Schulting 2006). There are many questions that need to be addressed in order to understand more about why there are these differences. For instance we should be asking whether the people consuming this marine food are represented in the stable isotope data. Is it possible that the marine food is being eaten more sporadically so it contributes less to individuals' overall diets, or could it be that there are different groups with different diets, as has been suggested for the Baltic (Eriksson 2004)? Or, could it be that the overall size of the human population was larger in the Neolithic, resulting in a situation where the proportion of marine food in the diet was lower than before?

This work also needs to be connected to the broader picture of what was happening in terms of settlement and economy over this time period. Can these readings of seasonal shell gathering practices fit into interpretations of changing settlement patterns in the Early Neolithic, with people moving away from the coast and the introduction of domesticated animals and grain, albeit on probably a small scale at the beginning? The fact that the shellfish appear to be intensively exploited during the spring and summer through the Early Neolithic at Norsminde certainly suggests that, for this site at least, marine resources are still a much used resource. But in order to investigate these types of questions, the seasonality of shellfish gathering needs to be related to other investigations of seasonal resource procurement, at similar scales of analysis, although unfortunately this is rarely done and palimpsests such as these are often reduced to a representation of a typical yearly round (see Milner 2005b).

In sum, it is important to consider regional variation when investigating the Mesolithic-Neolithic transition, and to attempt different scales of analysis. By performing fine-grained analyses on sites like shell middens, with clear stratigraphy and long life spans, it may be possible to get more subtle understandings of the continuity and changes in the economy and food consumption across the Mesolithic-Neolithic transition.

Acknowledgements

We would like to thank Professor Søren H. Andersen for access to the material from Norsminde and for his continued collaboration. We should also like to thank Professor Geoff Bailey for many discussions on this material.

References

Andersen, S. H. 1991. Norsminde. A 'Kjøkkendmødding' with late Mesolithic and early Neolithic occupation. *Journal of Danish Archaeology* 8, 13–40.

Andersen, S. H. 2000. 'Køkkenmøddinger' (Shell Middens) in Denmark: a Survey. *Proceedings of the Prehistoric Society* 66, 361–84.

Andersen, S. H. 2005. Køkkenmøddingerne ved Krabbesholm. Ny forskning i stenalderens kystbopladser. *Nationalmuseets Arbejdsmark* 2005, 151–71.

Bailey, G. N. and Milner, N. (in press). The marine molluscs from the Norsminde shell midden, in S. H. Andersen (ed.), *Stone Age Settlement of the Norsminde Fjord, Jutland, Denmark.*

Claassen, C. 1998. *Shells.* Cambridge, Cambridge University Press.

Eriksson, G. 2004. Part-time farmers or hard-core sealers? Västerbjers studied by means of stable isotope analysis. *Journal of Anthropological Archaeology* 23 (2), 135–62.

Lidén, K., Eriksson, G., Nordqvist, B., Götherström, A. and Bendixen, E. 2004. 'The wet and the wild followed by the dry and the tame' – or did they occur at the same time? Diet in Mesolithic-Neolithic southern Sweden. *Antiquity* 78 (299), 23–33.

Mannino, M. A. and Thomas, K. D. 2002. Depletion of a resource? The impact of prehistoric human foraging on intertidal mollusc communities and its significance for human settlement, mobility and dispersal. *World Archaeology* **33,** 452–74.

Milner, N. 2001. At the cutting edge: using thin sectioning to determine season of death of the European Oyster, *Ostrea edulis*. *Journal of Archaeological Science* 28, 861–75.

Milner, N. 2002. *Incremental growth of the European Oyster, Ostrea edulis: seasonality information from Danish kitchenmiddens.* British Archaeological Reports, International Series S1057. Oxford, Archaeopress.

Milner, N. 2005a. Seasonal consumption practices in the Mesolithic: Economic, Environmental, Social or Ritual?, in N. Milner and P. C. Woodman (eds.), *Mesolithic Studies at the Beginning of the 21st Century*, 56–67. Oxford, Oxbow Books.

Milner, N. 2005b. Can seasonality studies be used to identify sedentism in the past?, in D. Bailey, V. Cummings and A. Whittle (eds.), *(Un)settling the Neolithic*. Oxford, Oxbow Books.

Milner, N., Craig, O. E., Bailey, G. N. and Andersen, S. H. 2006. A response to Richards and Schulting. *Antiquity* 80 (308), 456.

Milner, N., Craig, O. E., Bailey, G. N., Pedersen, K. and Andersen, S. H. 2004. Something fishy in the Neolithic? A re-evaluation of stable isotope analysis of Mesolithic and Neolithic coastal populations, *Antiquity* 78 (299), 9–22.

Petersen, K. S. 1993. Environmental changes recorded in the Holocene molluscan faunas from Djursland, Denmark, *Scripta Geology Special Issue* 2, 359–69.

Richards, M. P. and Hedges, R. E. M. 1999. Stable isotope evidence for similarities in the types of marine foods used by Late Mesolithic humans on the Atlantic coast of Europe. *Journal of Archaeological Science* 26, 717–22.

Richards, M. P. and Schulting, R. J. 2006. Against the grain? A response to Milner *et al.* (2004). *Antiquity* 80 (308), 444–56.

Richards, M. P., Schulting, R. J. and Hedges, R. E. M. 2003. Sharp shift in diet at onset of Neolithic. *Nature* 425, 366.

Rowley-Conwy, P. 1984. The laziness of the short-distance hunter: the origins of agriculture in Denmark. *Journal of Anthropological Archaeology* 3, 300–24.

Schulting, R. J. and Richards, M. P. 2001. Dating women becoming farmers: new paleodietary and AMS dating evidence from the Breton Mesolithic cemeteries of Téviec and Hoëdic. *Journal of Anthropological Archaeology* 20, 314–44.

Schulting, R. and Richards, M. P. 2002a. The wet, the wild and the domesticated: the Mesolithic-Neolithic transition on the West Coast of Scotland. *Journal of European Archaeology* 5, 147–89.

Schulting, R. J. and Richards, M. P. 2002b. Finding the coastal Mesolithic in southwest Britain: AMS dates and stable isotope results on human remains from Caldey Island, Pembrokeshire, South Wales. *Antiquity* 76, 1011–25.

22. Current research on prehistoric human coastal ecology: Late Pleistocene and Early Holocene hunter-gatherer transitions in north-west Sicily

Marcello A. Mannino and Kenneth D. Thomas

The numerous caves of north-west Sicily often have Upper Palaeolithic and Mesolithic occupation, along with food remains, especially substantial accumulations of marine shells. These shellfish assemblages are being used to investigate prehistoric human ecology and subsistence in this Mediterranean coastal region, from the Upper Palaeolithic, through the Mesolithic and into the Neolithic. Shells are also being used to obtain AMS radiocarbon dates for critical levels at important sites. This paper presents preliminary results on the seasonality of shellfish collection, based on oxygen isotope analysis of the marine gastropod Monodonta turbinata, *which are interpreted in relation to environmental, palaeoeconomic and cultural transitions from the Late Pleistocene to the mid-Holocene.*

Keywords: north-west Sicily, Upper Palaeolithic, Mesolithic, coastal ecology, shellfish exploitation, seasonality, Addaura caves, Grotta di Cala dei Genovesi, Grotta dell'Uzzo, *Patella ferruginea*, *Monodonta turbinata*.

Introduction

North-western Sicily is characterised by coastal limestone hills, rich in caves and rockshelters that were occupied in prehistory (Figure 22.1). Numerous caves have yielded surface scatters or stratified finds, including assemblages of lithics, animal bones and marine shells. A few also contain human burials. On the basis of lithic typologies, the initial occupation of many of these sites has been attributed to the final stages of the Upper Palaeolithic (which in Italy is termed the Epigravettian). The few absolute dates available (Skeates 1994), confirm the estimation of the initial occupation of these caves to the Upper Palaeolithic. There is relatively less evidence for the Mesolithic, because the cave deposits have been subject to substantial disturbance, usually arising from pastoral activities or to the recent use of these shelters for human habitation. Many caves were used until recently for keeping sheep (some are still being used in this way) and periodically the dung accumulations within them had to be dug out, with the uppermost archaeological deposits also being removed or severely disrupted. Over time, this has caused the destruction of progressively older deposits. Another reason for the *apparent* scarcity of Mesolithic deposits is that the early Holocene lithic industries of Sicily closely resemble those of the Final Epigravettian. Artefact types such as geometric microliths occur in both Epigravettian and early Mesolithic assemblages (e.g. Segre and Vigliardi 1983; Lo Vetro and Martini 2000) and Martini (1997) has grouped Sicilian 'Mesolithic' assemblages into the category *Epigravettiano indifferenziato*. In consequence, it has proved difficult to identify early 'Mesolithic' occupation at sites from lithic assemblages, and it is likely that the number of sites of this period has been underestimated (Tusa 1999). In this paper we will refer to Early Holocene occupation horizons as 'Mesolithic'. Deposits of Mesolithic age have been identified by radiocarbon dating at the Grotta dell'Uzzo, Grotta di Cala dei Genovesi and Grotta Molara (Tusa 1999).

Various important transitions in the environment, caused by changes operating at the global scale and influencing climate, vegetation, faunas, etc., must have occurred during the periods when the caves of north-west Sicily were occupied, but there is currently little local evidence for these. Sea levels rose as a consequence of global warming, leading to the progressive submergence of coastal areas such as, for example, the stretch of land attaching the Egadi Islands (Levanzo and Favignana) to the mainland (Antonioli 1997). The only pollen sequence available for Sicily is from Lake Pergusa in the centre of the island (Sadori and Narcisi 2001). It shows that tree cover extended significantly in the Postglacial and, by the Late Mesolithic, had probably reached the coastal hills in which most of the cave sites are located. A recent study of a speleothem from the Grotta di Carburangeli, near Carini, showed evidence

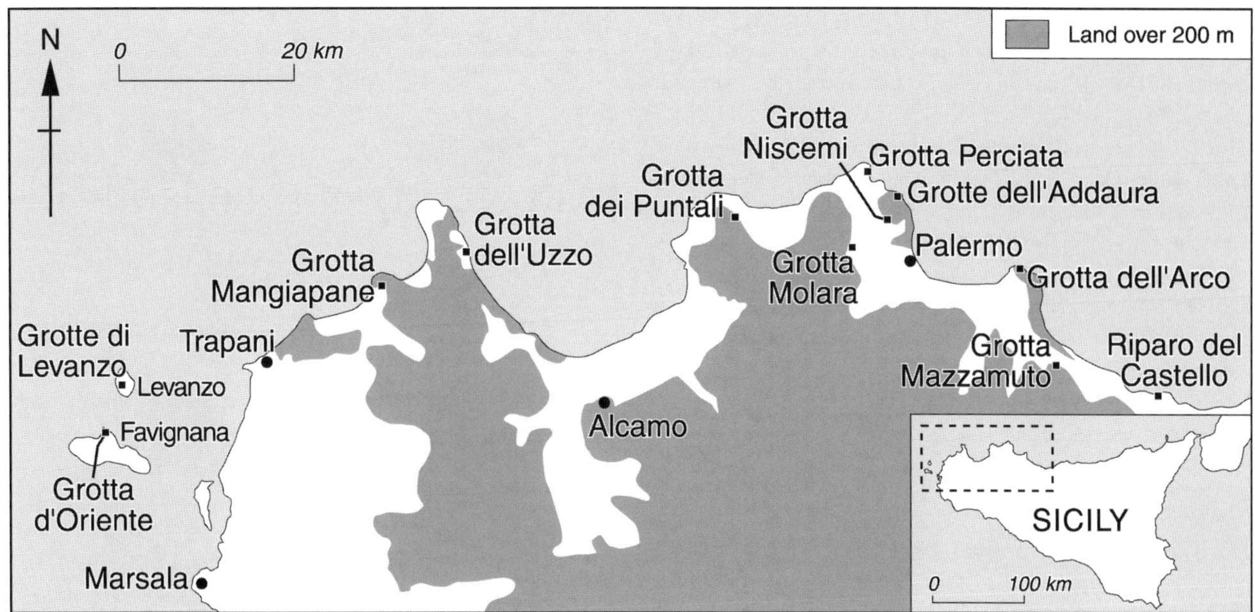

Figure 22.1. Map of north-west Sicily showing the location of some of the prehistoric coastal sites, including those mentioned in the text. The Grotta di Cala dei Genovesi is one of a cluster of sites identified as 'Grotte di Levanzo', on the west coast of the island of Levanzo.

of climatic instability during the Holocene (Madonia *et al.* 2005), with an early Holocene humid phase being followed by a prolonged phase of greater aridity from around 6000 BP. In this paper, we consider whether human subsistence behaviour changed as a result of the environmental changes that occurred between the end of the Pleistocene and the early to mid-Holocene, even though there do not appear to have been significant differences in the lithic assemblages over this period.

Epigravettian and Mesolithic deposits

Our research is specifically concerned with shellfish exploitation, based mainly on the study of materials from sites that have been excavated in the last sixty years, now stored in the Archaeological Museum in Palermo. The first step was to select those sites that had been excavated to acceptable standards, among which are the Addaura cave complex, the Grotta di Cala dei Genovesi and the better-known Grotta dell'Uzzo. *Monodonta turbinata* (topshells) have been selected from these sites for accelerator mass spectrometry (AMS) radiocarbon dating, to provide an absolute chronology for the sites and for the phases of shellfish exploitation. For the Grotta dell'Uzzo, the dates on shells of *M. turbinata* selected from the sequences of Trench A and Trench F are (after correction for the marine reservoir effect and calibration) fully consistent with the absolute chronology previously obtained from combined charcoal samples for the Mesolithic and Neolithic layers. This is discussed in more detail by Mannino *et al.* (2006; 2007a), who conclude that the shell-based AMS dates are reliable. The dates from the Addaura caves and from Grotta di Cala dei Genovesi will be discussed below, in relation to each site, although a more detailed account of these sites has been published elsewhere (Mannino and Thomas 2007).

The Addaura caves

The Addaura caves are located on the north-eastern slopes of Monte Pellegrino (Figure 22.1). Three caves are of particular interest for their prehistoric deposits: the Grotta Addaura Caprara, the Grotta dei Bovidi and the Grotta delle Incisioni. This last cave is famous for the rock art scene depicting a number of human figures 'dancing' around two central figures. In 1946–7 Jole Bovio Marconi, in collaboration with Luigi Bernabò Brea, excavated four trenches within these caves or just outside them (Bovio Marconi 1946). Trench III, excavated in the talus of the Grotta delle Incisioni, is the most interesting one in terms of the shellfish remains. The deposit was mixed down to about a metre, but was deemed by the excavators to be *in situ* from around 1.40m. The finds from these levels confirmed the probable integrity of the deposits. Shells of *M. turbinata* were selected to date three consecutive spits (Spit 13, Spit Bis 1 and Spit Bis 2). The calibrated dates (2-σ range) are, respectively, 11,780–11,410 cal BC, 11,880–11,530 cal BC and 12,070–11,780 cal BC, confirming the assemblages as Final Epigravettian. Trench IV, at Grotta Addaura Caprara, contained Mesolithic materials, although the deposit was partly mixed. A shell from the second lowermost spit (Spit 25) of this trench has been dated to 9130–8620 cal BC, making it Early Mesolithic.

Grotta di Cala dei Genovesi

The Grotta di Cala dei Genovesi is situated on the island of Levanzo in the Egadi archipelago off the north-western tip of Sicily (Figure 22.1). The materials examined in this project are those from Bovio Marconi's excavation of Trench I (Bovio Marconi 1952). This trench was opened in an area in which Graziosi later excavated, and from which he recovered Upper Palaeolithic and Mesolithic lithic assemblages (Vigliardi 1982) and animal bones (Cassoli and Tagliacozzo 1982), as detailed by Mannino *et al.* (2007b). The materials from Bovio Marconi's and Graziosi's trenches are similar, which is not surprising given the contiguity of the two trenches. Shells of *M. turbinata* from three spits (Spits 6, 10 and 12), distributed through the stratigraphic sequence, have produced dates of 6800–6450 cal BC, 10,380–9790 cal BC and 10,910–10,710 cal BC, spanning the Mesolithic and Final Epigravettian.

Prehistoric marine mollusc exploitation

The shell-based AMS dates have shown that shellfish collection in the region dates at least from the Final Epigravettian (at the Addaura caves, Grotta di Cala dei Genovesi and also other caves, such as Grotta Niscemi). Ongoing studies on the mollusc assemblages from the Addaura caves, Grotta di Cala dei Genovesi and Grotta dell'Uzzo indicate that shellfish were relatively important resources, both at the end of the Upper Palaeolithic and at the beginning of the Mesolithic. The shellfish exploited for food were almost invariably rocky shore inter-tidal mollusc species and the main taxa collected were species of limpet (*Patella* spp) and *M. turbinata*. The most noticeable difference in the assemblages between the Upper Palaeolithic deposits of the Addaura cave (Mannino and Thomas, in press) and the Mesolithic deposits of the Grotta dell'Uzzo (Compagnoni 1991) is a drop in the numbers of *Patella ferruginea*, the largest and probably the most desirable inter-tidal mollusc to be found on the rocky shores of the Mediterranean. A reduction in abundance of this species has also been observed at other sites (e.g. Durante and Settepassi 1972) and could be due to the impact of human exploitation. Preliminary data also show a reduction in the mean size *M. turbinata* from the Upper Palaeolithic (Addaura caves) to the Mesolithic (Uzzo cave); this is currently being studied in more detail. Another important issue being investigated is if there were any differences in the patterns of shellfish exploitation between the Epigravettian and the Mesolithic. For example, was exploitation all year round or seasonal, and in which seasons?

Stable oxygen isotope analyses on *M. turbinata* from a number of sites, including the three discussed in this paper, have been undertaken. The methods employed for the isotope analyses and interpretation of season of collection are explained in detail elsewhere (Mannino *et al.* 2007a). The results of the oxygen isotope analyses on shells from Final Epigravettian deposits at the Grotta delle Incisioni (Addaura) and the Grotta di Cala dei Genovesi (Figure 22.2) clearly demonstrate that the collection of *M. turbinata* and, by inference, of the other inter-tidal species present, occurred during restricted 'seasons' of the year. At the Grotta delle Incisioni, collections were mainly in the winter, with some in the autumn (Figure 22.2). At the Grotta di Cala dei Genovesi winter, followed by autumn, are the main collecting seasons, with some collection in summer. The evidence for the 'Early' Mesolithic at the Addaura and Uzzo caves shows that winter was still the main season of

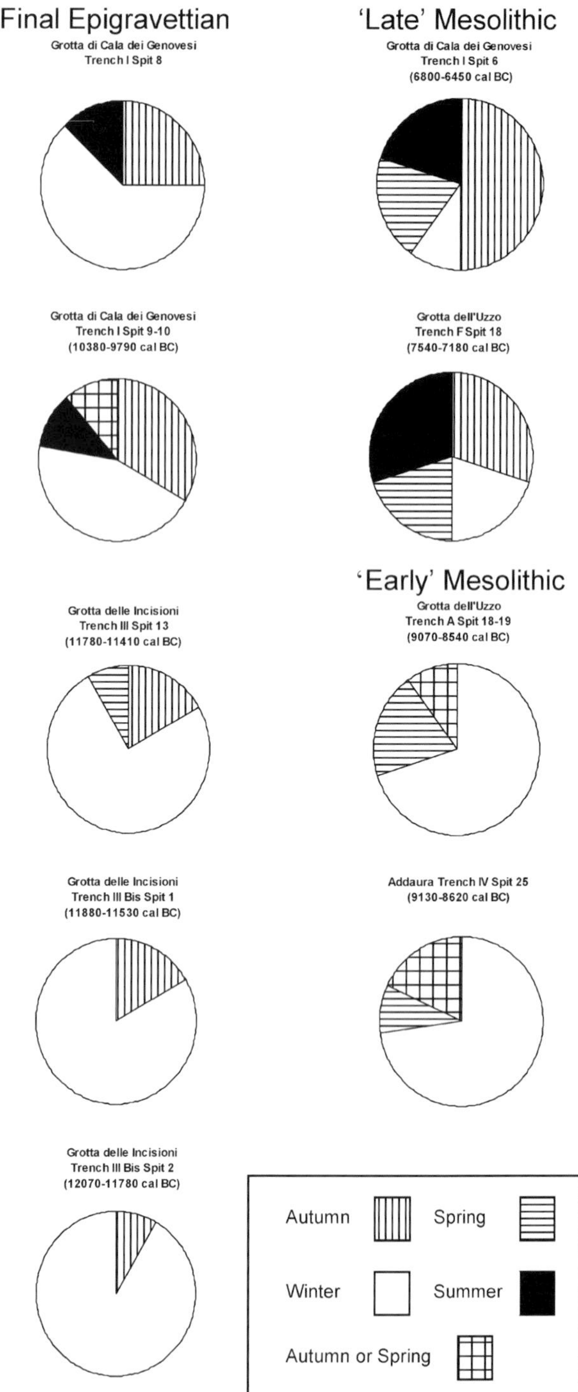

Figure 22.2. Pie charts showing patterns of inferred seasonal exploitation of inter-tidal shellfish (Monodonta turbinata) *during the Final Epigravettian (at the Grotta di Cala dei Genovesi and the Grotta delle Incisioni), the 'Early' Mesolithic (at the Grotta Addaura and the Grotta dell'Uzzo) and the 'Late' Mesolithic (at the Grotta di Cala dei Genovesi and the Grotta dell'Uzzo). Seasonal attributions made on shell-edge oxygen isotope values, as detailed by Mannino et al. 2007a.*

collection, with some exploitation in the spring. In marked contrast, the evidence from both the Grotta dell'Uzzo and from the Grotta di Cala dei Genovesi suggests that shellfish collection in the 'Late' Mesolithic occurred in all seasons. In the case of the former site, collection was evenly distributed through the year, while for the latter autumn was the dominant season of collection.

The results of the seasonality studies from these sites indicate that at the time of the most significant environmental change (between the end of the Pleistocene and the Early Holocene) there was no significant change in the seasonal pattern of shellfish collection (between the Final Epigravettian and the 'Early' Mesolithic). Within the Holocene, however, a significant change occurred, with shellfish becoming exploited in all seasons. It appears that marine molluscs were being exploited in more restricted seasons when they were probably more abundant, but later, when less abundant, they were being exploited in all seasons. Or, putting it the other way round: early on, highly seasonal exploitation of shellfish had no detectable impact on the abundance of this resource, while later, increased exploitation through the year caused a significant decline in inter-tidal shellfish populations. This interesting association is still being investigated, alongside the evidence for other components of the subsistence economies (Mannino and Thomas, in preparation).

'Transitions' in subsistence strategies through the Mesolithic

The evidence for Mesolithic food economy in the region comes from the Grotta dell'Uzzo (Tagliacozzo 1993), the Grotta di Cala dei Genovesi (Cassoli and Tagliacozzo 1982) and the Grotta d'Oriente (Mannino 2004; Mannino and Thomas 2004). Only limited data are available for the latter two sites, but the abundant animal remains from the Grotta dell'Uzzo show that the later part of the Mesolithic was characterised by a wide array of food species, including small animals, fish, and birds, with the addition of marine mammals rather later on. Increase in human population is a frequently invoked 'explanation' for a broadening of the spectrum of resources exploited. Is there any evidence for this in this region? As noted above, Mesolithic sites are likely to be underrepresented in north-west Sicily, but there is no reason to suppose that they ever exceeded in number the Final Epigravettian ones. There is, therefore, no basis for hypothesizing a demographic increase. From the limited evidence available, it appears that changing environmental conditions linked to the impact of human predation pressure might have had an effect on resource diversity and abundance. The widening in the seasonality of exploitation of resources seen at some sites (discussed above) could indicate reduced food security and therefore a need to exploit different types of resources and habitats with increased frequency, rather than focussing on a restricted range of seasonally dependable resources and habitats (as appears to have happened in the Final Epigravettian and 'Early' Mesolithic).

The shift towards a broader spectrum of resources at the Grotta dell'Uzzo has been interpreted as indicating increased sedentism (Piperno 1997; Tusa 1999) and as a sign of increased food availability. The seasonal data presented here, indicating exploitation of resources in all seasons of the year, could be taken as supporting this view. The adoption of a broad-spectrum diet could, however, be the result of a range of complex ecological and social processes, some of which we note in the previous paragraph. Important factors to consider are: the ecological potential of Mediterranean environments, the fact that Sicily is an island and the potential effects of prolonged human pressure on the main food resources. Mediterranean environments have high levels of biodiversity but low primary productivity (Allen 2001, 145). Much of the terrestrial vegetation is woody and sclerophyllous (Blondel and Aronson 1999) and difficult for browsing animals to digest. Therefore, the establishment of a typically Mediterranean climate, with its marked seasonality of production and leading to the development of the typical Mediterranean-type woodland and *macchia* vegetation, could have posed problems for hunter-gatherers. Moreover, although Sicily is a large island close to the mainland, its isolation had filtered the species of mammals which could reach it at the height of the last glaciation, producing an impoverished mammalian faunal complex compared with continental Italy (Burgio 1997).

Because of poor preservation and recovery, little can be said about the importance of plant foods. From an analysis of a bladder stone from one of the burials at the Grotta dell'Uzzo, D'Alessio *et al.* (2005) suggested that plant foods might have been important in the diet of that individual. Based on the animal bones present at most sites, the main sources of protein were probably terrestrial mammals and in particular large herbivores. However, as Tagliacozzo (1993) has noted for the territory around the Grotta dell'Uzzo, by the very end of the Mesolithic wild equids and bovids were becoming rare, and cervids appear to have become depleted by prolonged human exploitation.

Shellfish resources, although abundant in Mesolithic deposits in the region, do not have high population numbers or densities on the local shores when compared with, for example, shores along the Atlantic façade. This is because the biological productivity of the Mediterranean Sea is among the lowest in the world (e.g. Estrada *et al.* 1985) and also because tidal amplitude in the Mediterranean is extremely narrow, a factor which restricts the space available to inter-tidal mollusc species, making them highly susceptible to local over-exploitation. The long-term and intensive exploitation of both limpets and *M. turbinata*, as indicated by assemblages in caves all along the coast from Termini Imerese to the Egadi Islands (Figure 22.1), could have had an effect on the availability of such animals.

Other inter-tidal animals and shallow water animals, such as sea urchins (Echinoidea) and crabs, probably constituted minor sources of food. There is little evidence that marine fish were exploited to any significant degree until the Late Mesolithic, while at the Uzzo cave these resources became progressively more important from the end of the Mesolithic. Marine mammals are very rare in these sites. Seals (Phocidae) were occasionally hunted and cetaceans found stranded, and were not necessarily consumed. Species of large edible land molluscs might have been favoured by the more humid conditions of the Late Pleistocene and Early Holocene (Preboreal), judging by the increase in their exploitation throughout the Mediterranean at that time (Lubell 2004). With the increased aridity of the Boreal, possibly coupled with the effects of local over-exploitation, they were being collected less abundantly by the later Mesolithic, at least at the Uzzo cave (Compagnoni 1991).

Developing territoriality?

In general, when compared to large game animals, lower-ranked resources are found at higher population densities in more restricted habitat patches, and their exploitation requires frequent movements within defined areas or territories. The trends observed in the seasonality data from the Addaura caves, Grotta di Cala dei Genovesi and Grotta dell'Uzzo are compatible with these needs and with the necessity to secure specific resource patches through social mechanisms (as discussed by Mannino and Thomas, ch. 23, this volume). This scenario would suggest the existence of well-defined, customary territories within which Mesolithic hunter-gatherers moved to exploit predictable and localised resources.

A 'new' territorial division, or the development of recognised territorial rights of access to specific resource patches, would have affected many aspects of hunter-gather ways of life, not only subsistence. The perception of the environment probably changed, and space (comprising combined resource patches) might itself have become directly perceived as a 'resource', not only because extensive coastal areas were being submerged by rapidly rising sea levels (Antonioli 1997), making resource spaces smaller or more restricted, but also because increased arboreal cover on the hills would have made internal areas less readily accessible and less productive.

Other spheres of hunter-gatherer culture also changed in the Mesolithic of the region. Rock art changed from the naturalistic style of the late Upper Palaeolithic to the more schematic and abstract forms of the Mesolithic. There was an increase in portable art objects (Pluciennik 1994), which might also reflect increased mobility. The use of caves appears to have changed during the Mesolithic, from having probably been inhabited in the Epigravettian, to being increasingly used as burial places towards the later stages of the Mesolithic, as seen at the Grotta dell'Uzzo, Grotta Molara and Grotta d'Oriente (Mannino 2004; Mannino and Thomas 2004).

Conclusions

Our research is showing that, as for other areas of the Mediterranean such as Spain, southern Italy and Greece (Bailey 2004), the exploitation of marine molluscs in Sicily dates at least from the final stages of the Late Pleistocene. Shellfish exploitation continued into the Mesolithic, generally in much the same way as in the Final Epigravettian. From our investigations of the mollusc faunas and our review of other sources of evidence, the most significant transitions in the hunter-gatherer way of life did not occur in the transition to the Holocene, but during the Holocene itself, specifically from the later stages of the Mesolithic onwards. In the light of our argument that resources were not abundant in the Late Mesolithic, looking ahead to the next major cultural and economic transition in the region, we suggest that the arrival of herding and farming was unlikely to have been resisted.

Acknowledgements

We are grateful to the Leverhulme Trust for Research Grant No. F/07196/B; KDT thanks the Natural Environment Research Council for Grant No. IP/780/0503 for stable isotope analyses (at NIGL – the NERC Isotope Geosciences Laboratory, Keyworth), and Grant No. 2003/1/10 for AMS radiocarbon dates (at ORADS – the Oxford Radiocarbon Accelerator Dating Service). We are indebted to Dr Melanie Leng and Ms Hilary Sloane of NIGL; Dr Tom Higham of ORADS; Prof. Marcello Piperno, Prof. Sebastiano Tusa, Mr Giovanni Mannino, Dott.ssa Valentina Colella and Ms Mirella Lo Cascio; Dott.ssa R. Camerata Scovazzo (Director), Dott.ssa Agata Villa and Dott.ssa Rosaria Di Salvo, of the Museo Archeologico Regionale 'A. Salinas' (Palermo); Dott.ssa Maria Antonietta Fugazzola, Director of the Museo Nazionale Preistorico Etnografico 'L. Pigorini' (Rome) and Dott. Antonio Tagliacozzo of that Museum.

References

Allen, H. D. 2001. *Mediterranean Ecogeography*. London, Prentice Hall.

Antonioli, F. 1997. Problematiche relative alle variazioni recenti del livello del mare e sue interazioni con le comunità preistoriche in Sicilia, in S. Tusa (ed.), *Prima Sicilia. Alle Origini della Società Siciliana*, 147–55. Palermo, Ediprint.

Bailey, G. N. 2004. The wider significance of submerged archaeological sites and their relevance to world prehistory, in N. C. Flemming (ed.), *Submarine prehistoric archaeology of the North Sea. Research priorities and collaboration with industry*, 3–10. Council for British Archaeology Report 141. York, Council for British Archaeology.

Blondel, J. and Aronson, J. 1999. *Biology and Wildlife of the Mediterranean Region*. Oxford, Oxford University Press.

Bovio Marconi, J. 1946. Relazione preliminare sugli scavi nelle grotte dell'Addaura. *Notizie degli Scavi di Antichità* 5–6, 160–7.

Bovio Marconi, J. 1952. Esplorazioni archeologiche a Levanzo e Favignana. *Notizie degli Scavi di Antichità* 12, 185–99.

Burgio, E. 1997. Le attuali conoscenze sui mammiferi terrestri quaternari della Sicilia, in S. Tusa (ed.), *Prima Sicilia. Alle Origini della Società Siciliana*, 54–71. Palermo, Ediprint.

Cassoli, P. F. and Tagliacozzo, A. 1982. La fauna della Grotta di

Cala dei Genovesi a Levanzo. *Rivista di Scienze Preistoriche* 37, 48–58.

Compagnoni, B. 1991. La malacofauna del sito meso-neolitico della Grotta dell'Uzzo (Trapani). *Rivista di Scienze Preistoriche* 43, 49–72.

D'Alessio, A., Bramanti, E., Piperno, M., Naccaroto, G., Vergamini, P. and Fornaciari, G. 2005. An 8500-year-old bladder stone from Uzzo Cave (Trapani): Fourier transform-infrared spectroscopy analysis. *Archaeometry* 47, 127–36.

Durante, S. and Settepassi, F. 1972. I molluschi del giacimento quaternario della grotta della Madonna a Praia a Mare (Calabria). *Quaternaria* 16, 255–69.

Estrada, M., Vives, F. and Alcaraz, M. 1985. Life and the productivity of the open sea, in R. Margalef (ed.), *Western Mediterranean*, 148–97. Oxford, Pergamon Press.

Lo Vetro, D. and Martini, F. 2000. L'Epigravettiano finale siciliano: dinamiche strutturali e trasformazioni tecnotipologiche degli strumenti a dorso e dei geometrici. *Rivista di Scienze Preistoriche* 50, 39–102.

Lubell, D. 2004. Prehistoric edible land snails in the circum-Mediterranean: the archaeological evidence, in J. P. Brugal and J. Desse (eds.), *Petits animaux et sociétés humaines. Du complément alimentaire aux resources utilitaires*, 77–98. Antibes, Éditions APDCA.

Madonia, G., Frisia, S., Borsato, A., Macaluso, T., Mangini, A., Paladini, M., Piccini, L., Miorandi, R., Spötl, C., Sauro, U., Agnesi, V., Di Pietro, R., Palmeri, A. and Vattano, M. 2005. La Grotta di Carburangeli – ricostruzione climatica dell'Olocene per la piana costiera della Sicilia nord-occidentale. *Studi Trentini di Scienze Naturali, Acta Geologica* 80, 153–67.

Mannino, G. 2004. La Grotta d'Oriente a Favignana (Egadi, Sicilia). Risultati di un sondaggio esplorativo. *Quaderni del Museo Archeologico Regionale 'Antonino Salinas'* 8, 9–22.

Mannino, M. A., Colella, V. and Thomas, K. D. 2007b. Studio preliminare su collezioni dei siti paleolitici e mesolitici della Sicilia occidentale: nuove indagini e datazioni rediometriche. *Quaderni del Museo Archeologico Regionale 'Antonino Salinas'* 9, 29–44.

Mannino, M. A. and Thomas, K. D. 2004. Studio archeozoologico dei reperti faunistici dalla Grotta d'Oriente a Favignana (Trapani). *Quaderni del Museo Archeologico Regionale 'Antonino Salinas'* 8, 23–54.

Mannino, M. A. and Thomas, K. D. 2007. New radiocarbon dates for hunter-gatherers and early farmers in Sicily. *Accordia Research Papers* 10, 13–33.

Mannino, M. A. and Thomas, K. D. (in press). Studi archeozoologici ed archeometrici sui reperti di malacofauna della Grotta dell'Uzzo (TP). *Atti della XLI Riunione Scientifica dell'Istituto Italiano di Preistoria e Protostoria.*

Mannino, M. A., Thomas, K. D., Leng, M. J., Piperno, M., Tusa, S. and Tagliacozzo, A. 2007a. Marine resources in the Mesolithic and Neolithic at the Grotta dell'Uzzo (Sicily): evidence from isotope analyses of marine shells. *Archaeometry* 49, 117–33.

Mannino, M. A., Thomas, K. D., Piperno, M., Tusa, S. and Tagliacozzo, A. 2006. Fine-tuning the radiocarbon chronology of the Grotta dell'Uzzo (Trapani). *Atti della Società per la Preistoria e Protostoria della Regione Friuli-Venezia Giulia* 15, 17–31.

Martini, F. 1997. Il Paleolitico superiore in Sicilia, in S. Tusa (ed.), *Prima Sicilia. Alle Origini della Società Siciliana*, 111–24. Palermo, Ediprint.

Piperno, M. 1997. La Sicilia all'inizio dell'Olocene. Aspetti del popolamento Mesolitico, in S. Tusa (ed.), *Prima Sicilia. Alle Origini della Società Siciliana*, 134–45. Palermo, Ediprint.

Pluciennik, M. 1994. Space, time and caves: art in the Palaeolithic, Mesolithic and Neolithic of southern Italy. *Accordia Research Papers* 5, 39–71.

Sadori, L. and Narcisi, B. 2001. The Postglacial record of environmental history from Lago di Pergusa, Sicily. *The Holocene* 11, 655–71.

Segre, A. and Vigliardi, A. 1983. L'Epigravettien évolué et final en Sicile. *Rivista di Scienze Preistoriche* 36, 351–69.

Skeates, R. 1994. A radiocarbon date-list for prehistoric Italy (c. 46400 BP – 2450 BP/400 cal. BC), in R. Skeates and R. Whitehouse (eds.), *Radiocarbon Dating and Italian Prehistory*, 147–288. Archaeological Monograph of the British School at Rome 8, Accordia Specialist Studies on Italy 3. London, Accordia Research Centre and The British School at Rome.

Tagliacozzo, A. 1993. Archeozoologia della Grotta dell'Uzzo, Sicilia. Da un'economia di caccia ad un'economia di pesca ed allevamento. *Supplemento del Bullettino di Paletnologia Italiana* 84. Roma, Poligrafico e Zecca dello Stato.

Tusa, S. 1999. *La Sicilia nella preistoria.* Sellerio Editore, Palermo.

Vigliardi, A. 1982. Gli strati paleo-mesolitici della Grotta di Levanzo. *Rivista di Scienze Preistoriche* 37, 79–134.

23. The tragedy of the shoreline? Social ecology of Mesolithic coastal subsistence, with reference to the site of Culverwell, Isle of Portland (southern England)

Marcello A. Mannino and Kenneth D. Thomas

Analysis of assemblages of rocky shore molluscs through the Mesolithic midden of Culverwell, Isle of Portland, shows an increase in the intensity of exploitation of these resources. The site was occupied in the autumn and winter periods and people returned each year to the site, which was within their broader customary resource territory. A combination of over exploitation and environmental change appears to have led to a permanent decline in populations of shellfish on Portland.

Keywords: Mesolithic, social ecology, coastal resources, shellfish exploitation, seasonality, resource depletion, shellmidden, Culverwell, *Monodonta lineata*.

Introduction

It is apparent from studies of recent small-scale societies, whether hunters, gatherers, foragers, fishers or farmers (or combinations of these categories), that many social interactions are mediated through environmental and subsistence/resource factors. The complex inter-play between the spatial and temporal distribution of resources, the resilience of those resources in the face of exploitation, and the knowledge-based exploitation strategies of the social groups dependent on them, comprise the research arena for human social ecology.

Hardin's celebrated 'Tragedy of the Commons' is, perhaps, a suitable starting point for our discussion. Hardin (1968) reasoned that free access to exploit a resource would eventually have negative consequences for everyone exploiting it. Each exploiter would attempt to maximise their share of the resource, because others would also be seeking to do so. From the perspective of each individual exploiter, the negative consequences of acting selfishly are not borne by the individual alone but are shared between all the exploiters of the resource. The advantages that arise from acting selfishly therefore outweigh those of not doing so, and, because it is in the individual interests of all exploiters to act in this way, the resource will ultimately be destroyed.

Is it inevitable? Can the 'tragedy' be avoided, or at least postponed? Probably not, if the resource is both freely open to exploitation and the exploiters are ignorant, or unmindful, of the likely consequences of their actions. But is this realistic? Fundamental to any modelling of the social ecology of past hunter-foragers is an acceptance that, as a consequence of living in the world, they were environmentally aware and able to make sophisticated decisions based on their acquired and transmitted traditional ecological knowledge. Such acquisition of environmental knowledge and skills has been discussed perceptively and in depth by Ingold (2000). Moreover, some social ecologists take the view that the resilience of social systems themselves may be closely linked to the resilience of the ecological systems on which they depend (Adger 2000; Handmer and Dovers 1996). This is most clearly shown by social systems that are dependent on a single ecosystem or a single resource, when migration often represents a resilience-enhancing strategy for resource-dependent communities (Locke *et al.* 2000). Other social means, such as inter-group recognition of customary territorial rights of access to a range of resource patches, can also enhance long-term stability. As noted by Adger (2003, 195): '*subsistence fishing communities* (among other communities listed by Adger) *often have sophisticated community-based rules for access to the scarce resources on which they depend.*'

If, following Hardin, we accept that human resource use has the potential to deplete a resource, then resource security (in terms of supply and access), as well as sustainability, become vitally important to social groups. In this paper we are mainly concerned with issues of food security linked to the sustainable exploitation of biological resources.

Food security requires:

- Ecological knowledge of where various categories of food resources can be found, when they are available and how they respond to exploitation;
- Security of access through social mechanisms which ensure that a range of location-specific resource patches are available to the social group, involving either restricted access or sharing with other groups – the conditions for which are discussed by Winterhalder (2001, 23);
- Security of supply, involving management strategies to ensure the long-term sustainability of resources.

There is evidence from the archaeological record that human foraging can deplete spatially restricted resources, and that foragers can adapt to resource depression in various ways (e.g. Nagaoka 2002). Reviews by Mannino and Thomas (2001; 2002) have shown that coastal resources, in particular populations of inter-tidal shellfish, can become significantly depleted by prehistoric human foragers. Coastal shell midden sites are especially suitable for investigating such issues because:

1. Various ethnographic studies (e.g. Bird and Bliege Bird 1997; Meehan 1982) have shown that shellfish are not usually transported over large distances between the place of acquisition and where they are consumed. Therefore the relationships between the site and the specific shores from which the resources were acquired can be inferred, with long-term accumulations of shells at a site indicating long-term exploitation of mollusc populations living on those shores.
2. Inter-tidal shellfish resources are highly predictable in terms of availability. Most species are essentially stenotopic, not moving around on spatial scales relevant to human foragers. They represent a 'fixed resource' that can be exploited with ease at any time. It should therefore be possible to infer the strategic and ecologically informed choices made by human foragers from detailed analyses of the remains of the shellfish that were exploited.

In this paper we consider the evidence for resource exploitation at the Mesolithic shellmidden site of Culverwell, on the south coast of England (Figure 23.1), and develop a model for the social ecology of the people once associated with the site.

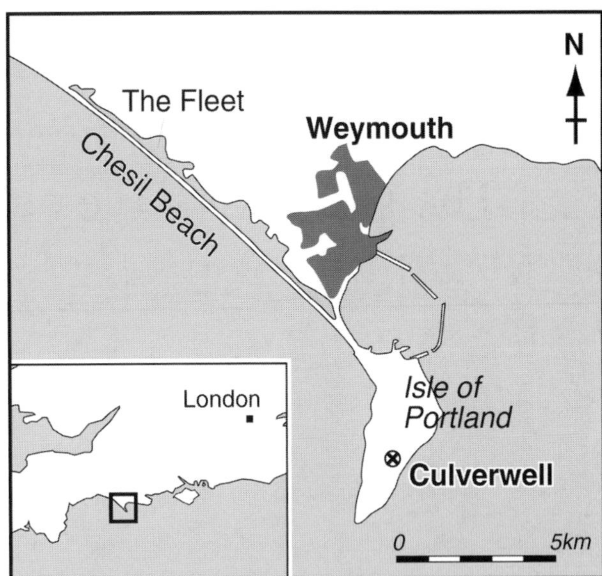

Figure 23.1. Location map of the site of Culverwell.

Culverwell

The site is located in the southern part of the Isle of Portland (Figure 23.1) at 30m above sea level and some 200m from the present-day cliff line.

The Mesolithic deposits at Culverwell are on the lower part of a steep slope, the profile of which has been modified by a series of Medieval strip lynchets. Most of the excavated trenches lie to the south-east of the lowest lynchet, where the Mesolithic deposits are close to the surface. It is likely that the Mesolithic deposits have been truncated or disturbed by Medieval and later agricultural activity, and that some of the deposits containing marine shell, and artefacts have been colluviated from upslope. Palmer (1999) has described the features excavated at the site, including the postholes of supposed structures, an extensive 'floor' of flat limestone slabs, a number of 'hearths', a pit cut into the limestone bedrock, and an extensive shellmidden. These features led Palmer (1990; 1999) to suggest that the site was occupied all-year-round. The midden deposit contains abundant shells of marine molluscs, mixed with struck stone (mainly of locally available Purbeck chert), non-struck stone artefacts, huge quantities of fragmented chert and limestone, and small quantities of sandstone (Stewart 1999).

During cleaning-up operations at the site, a well-stratified midden deposit was found under what had been supposed to be natural deposits. In 1995 English Heritage gave permission for the authors to excavate a trench to investigate this new feature and to collect samples from the midden for analysis. It became clear that the midden had accumulated in a gully in the limestone bedrock: for details see Thomas and Mannino (1999) and Mannino and Thomas (2001). The stratigraphy of the midden deposits is shown in Figure 23.2. The radiocarbon determinations on marine shells from the layers of the midden are in reasonable accord with the stratigraphic sequence (Thomas and Mannino 2001). The 2-σ calibrated ranges are: Layer 12: 5960–5660 cal BC (7285±60 BP, AA-28217); Layer 9: 5810–5530 cal BC (7145±70 BP, AA-28216); Layer 8: 5450–5200 cal BC (6730±55 BP, AA-28214) and 5100–4780 cal BC (6410±55 BP, AA-28215), based on the CHRONO Marine Reservoir Database and the Marine04 calibration (Hughen *et al.* 2004).

The biological resources recovered from the midden were, in terms of relative abundance:

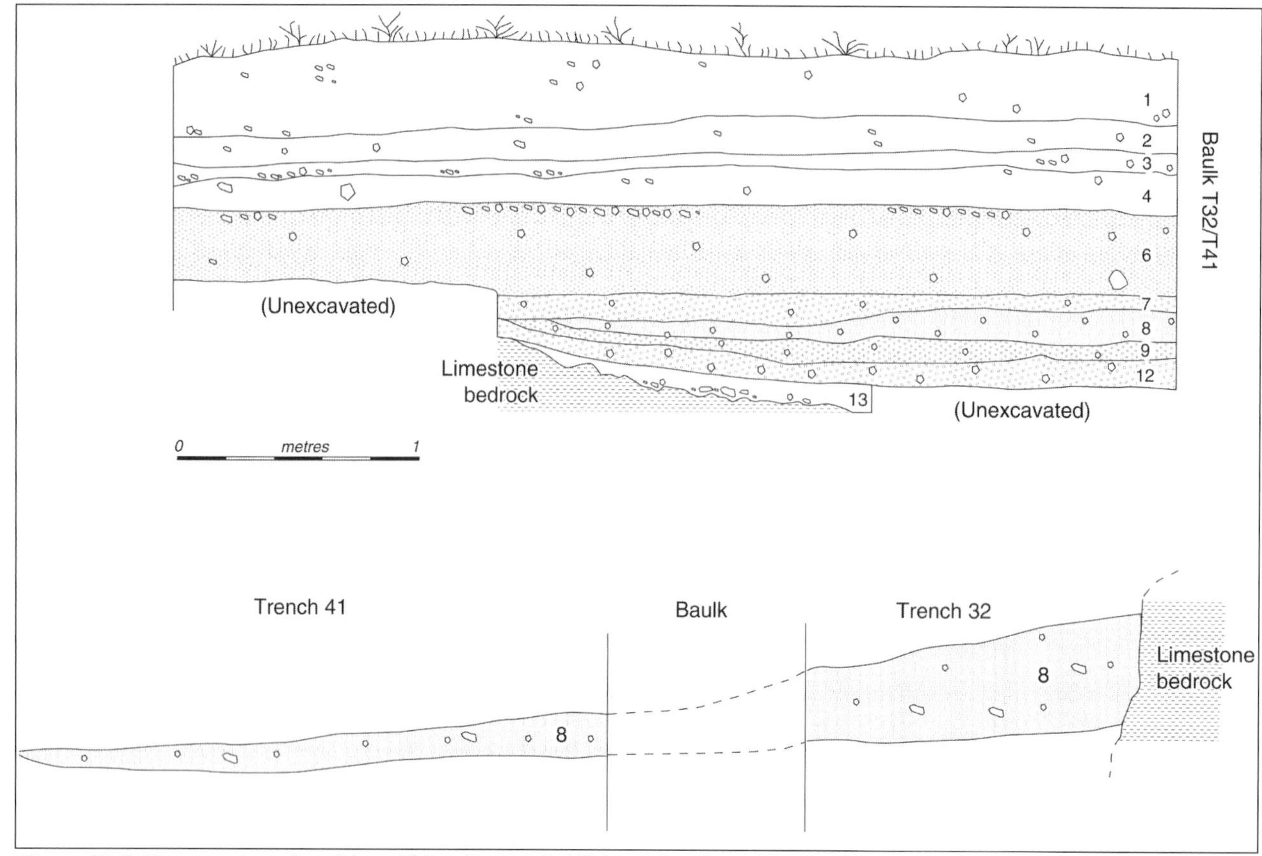

Figure 23.2. Top: stratigraphy of the midden (Layers 8–12) buried under colluvium (Layers 1–7), north-west face of trench 41, Culverwell. Bottom: Layer 8 thinning out away from the north-eastern edge of the limestone gully. (Reprinted from Mannino and Thomas (2001), figure 4, with permission).

Species	**L8**	**L9**	**L12**
Littorina littorea	191	160	50
Patella species	89	151	62
Monodonta lineata	110	132	46
Total MNI	397	447	159

Species	**L8, upp**	**L8, mid**	**L8, low**
Littorina littorea	67	102	224
Patella species	32	25	72
Monodonta lineata	25	34	97
Total MNI	126	167	401

Figure 23.3. Abundance (MNI per 2000cm^3 of deposit) of marine molluscs in Layers 8–12 of the Culverwell midden and between successive cuts in the dense midden in Layer 8.

Highly abundant: limpets (*Patella* species), edible periwinkle (*Littorina littorea*) and topshell (*Monodonta lineata*);

Frequent: dog whelk (*Nucella lapillus*) and flat topshell (*Gibbula umbilicalis*);

Infrequent: various other gastropods, bivalves and edible crab (*Cancer pagurus*);

Very rare: fish, wild pig (*Sus scrofa*), hazel nuts (*Corylus avellana*).

The abundance (minimum numbers of individuals per standard volume of deposit) of the main mollusc taxa through the midden is shown in Figure 23.3. There is an overall increase in abundance between Layers 12 and 9, with a fall off in Layer 8. Within Layer 8, there is a progressive reduction in abundance from the lowest cut, up through to the top of this deposit.

Mannino and Thomas (2001) argued that changes in human predation pressure, rather than factors such as environmental change or changes in human food preferences, were responsible for the fluctuations in abundance of these species.

In support of this, age-structured assemblages of *Monodonta turbinata* were found to change from older age distributions (with larger mean shell sizes) to younger ones (with smaller mean shell sizes) through the midden (Figures 23.4 and 23.5). Overall, and as expected, all the age-structured assemblages are biased away from the youngest age classes (i.e. shells too small to collect and having low meat yields). There is an overall reduction in mean age through the sequence (Figure 23.4), as seen in shifts in the modal age classes. Within Layer 8 (Figure 23.5) there is a shift towards younger age classes and a marked reduction in the 5–8 varix classes. Our studies of 24 modern populations across the range of the species show that age classes with 6–8, and often more, varices are consistently represented, so the age-structured assemblages from Layer 8 are markedly different from the age structures of any modern populations known to us.

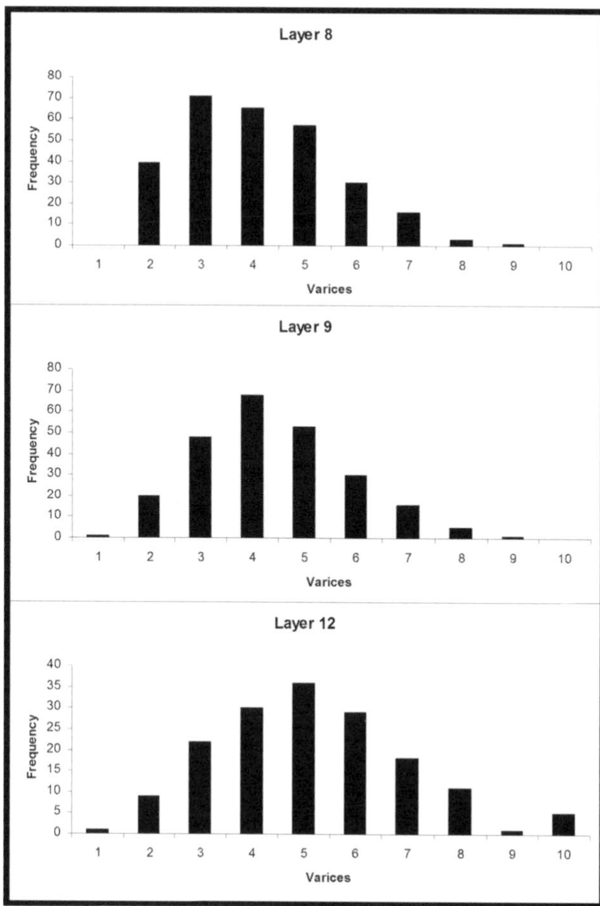

Figure 23.4. Variation in age profiles, based on annual varix (growth line) counts, of assemblages of Monodonta lineata *through the midden.*

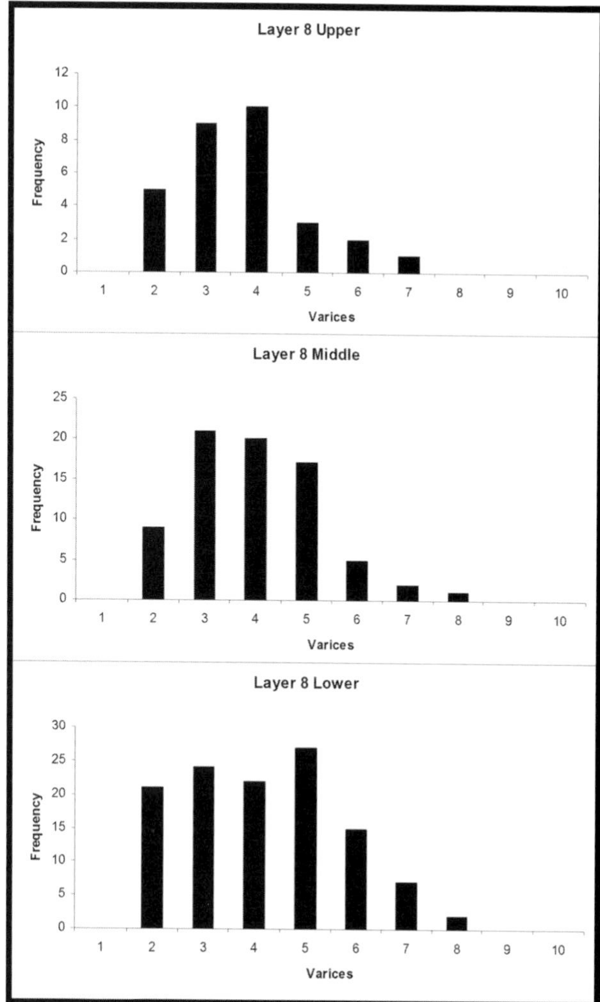

Figure 23.5. Variation in age profiles of assemblages of Monodonta lineata *through Layer 8 of the Culverwell midden.*

Overall, the mollusc data are interpreted as showing an intensification of the exploitation of inter-tidal mollusc resources through the midden. This is reflected by changes in the abundance of shellfish through the midden (Figure 23.3), as well as by changes in age structures (Figures 23.4 and 23.5). In Layer 8, the fall off in abundance, coupled with shifts in the age structure of assemblages, coincides with an increase in the abundance of artefacts, burnt stones and charcoal fragments, indicative of a more intensive phase of occupation.

Because the assemblages are time-averaged samples, the reduction of varix (age) classes 6–8, or more (Figure 23.5), probably indicates that human predation became sufficiently heavy and frequent, possibly even annual, so as to have prevented animals in the shore populations from growing on into these older age classes. If people were returning annually, this suggests that the locality and associated foreshores could have been part of a group's customary territory.For how long and at what times in each year might people have been at the site?

Seasonality of biotic resource exploitation: Oxygen isotope ($\delta^{18}O$) analyses of aperture-edge samples of shell carbonates of *Monodonta lineata* from each layer in the midden show that they were collected in the autumn and winter periods of the year (Mannino *et al.* 2003). There is little other evidence from the site for seasonality, although the ages of juvenile wild boar are compatible with a winter kill; the charred fragments of shells of hazel nuts indicate early autumn gathering, although they could have been stored for later consumption; and (rather negative evidence) the virtual absence of fish accords with a general lack of evidence for summer season resources.

Non-biotic resources: Large quantities of worked Portland limestone and Portland chert occur in the midden, and the cliffs around Portland provide easy access to these resources. There are few tools but many cores and waste flakes, suggesting that semi-finished lithic artefacts were being taken elsewhere from the site. Artefacts in these materials have been found at various localities across south-west England (Palmer 1970), suggesting either the existence of exchange networks or that the people who acquired these resources at their geological source were moving over these distances. We think it unlikely that territories would have been on a regional scale and prefer the idea that exchange networks existed between groups having adjacent customary territories.

Site function or functions: In terms of the abundance of material evidence, the gathering and consumption of shellfish and the acquisition and processing of lithic resources appear to have been particularly important activities. Was the main purpose of the occupation the acquisition and preliminary processing of lithic resources, with the shellfish being the food that kept people going? This scenario is unlikely because lithic resources around Portland would have been available at any time of year, while the biological evidence points strongly to an autumn-winter presence at the site. This suggests that biotic resources were the main determinants of the seasonal patterning of human presence at the site.

However, the shellfish would also have been available at any time of year, yet were exploited only in the autumn-winter period. This strongly suggests that the seasonality was being 'driven' by factors operating elsewhere. Autumn-winter resource shortages at other localities within the group's territory could have caused them to move to the Culverwell locality during this period. The evidence suggests that during the accumulation of the midden, such seasonal visits became increasingly frequent (possibly annual) events and that this had an impact on inter-tidal populations of shellfish, as shown by changes in the abundance and age-structure of the assemblages.

A social ecology of Culverwell?

The evidence presented here suggests that Mesolithic people migrated regularly to Portland in the autumn and winter seasons to exploit both lithic and inter-tidal shellfish resources. Rather than wandering around the landscape living in a hand-to-mouth manner, we suggest that people moved strategically between different resource localities (or patches) within customary territories, which were defined by recognized rights of access. A prime factor influencing these movements could have been seasonal resource shortages in various parts of these territories.

Such movements could have been important elements of ecologically-informed resource management strategies, adopted to ensure long term sustainability of resources in various resource patches. Alternatively, they could have been the consequence of optimal foraging decisions taken in the face of declining yields, as has been discussed by Aswani (1998) for shellfish exploitation strategies in the Solomon Islands. In the case of Culverwell, intensified predation pressure on inter-tidal shellfish resources, associated with an increased frequency of return to the site (possibly annually), appears to have significantly depleted shellfish populations on the local shores. The reasons for this change in the pattern of mobility are not clear. Changes in regional demography, changes in inter-group social interactions (possibly involving increased competition for space and/or specific resources), or longer-term resource depletion in other places, could all be invoked as possible factors, but we have no direct evidence for any of them.

This is not, of course, the full story ...

The midden at Culverwell is far more extensive than the part which has been studied by us. We believe that most of it is no longer in its original depositional state, having been significantly disturbed and redistributed by centuries of agricultural activity. We cannot be sure that the resource depletion scenario developed here was the cause of the end of Mesolithic occupation at the site. While there is evidence that shellfish resources were depleted by human predation, it is unlikely that this would have led to the complete elimination of these species from the shores of Portland, because they all recruit from the plankton. Possibly the site was abandoned when the local shores failed to produce sustainable yields, although if exploitation pressure was reduced or suspended for a decade or so, the shellfish populations should have recovered their 'natural' densities and age structures.

The species discussed here were very abundant on the shores of Portland during the occupation at Culverwell, but today they (especially *Monodonta lineata*) are infrequent. Recruitment from the plankton is reduced by the strong water currents that now exist off Portland, notably the 'Portland race'. These currents are associated with shallow sand-banks, such as the Shambles and Portland Banks (Bastos *et al.* 2002). When sea levels were lower, these banks would not have existed in their current locations, so planktonic mollusc larvae would not have been prevented by sea currents from reaching the rocky shores of Portland. Sea levels reached their present level, some time before 4000 BP (Brunsden and Goudie 1997). At, or even before, this time the supply of larval recruits could have been cut off by the newly-developed sea currents and mollusc populations on the shores of Portland would have declined.

Possibly mollusc populations were becoming 'squeezed' at both ends of the age spectrum by human predation on the adults and by reduced rates of recruitment of juveniles from the plankton. It is the recruitment, or 'supply side', that would ultimately have led to the decline in the species that we see today on Portland, where infrequent recruitment leads to populations with very low densities and which lack age-stable structures. Had this started to occur in the later Mesolithic, for human foragers it would have reduced the significance of Portland as a valued seasonal locality for shellfish resources. Even without this effect, the 'top-down' impact on populations of frequent and heavy exploitation of shellfish would have caused a significant decline in the yield of shellfish from foraging excursions, as we hope to have demonstrated in this brief discussion.

Acknowledgements

We thank English Heritage for permitting us to excavate in the 'deep midden' at Culverwell. Susann Palmer, Myfanwy Stewart, Chris Stevens, and Daniel Clark for advice and valuable assistance. The Natural Environment Research Council (Grant No. IP/499/1096), Dr Baruch Spiro and Hilary Sloane for analyses at the NERC Isotope Geosciences Laboratory. NERC (Radiocarbon Dating Allocation No. 677/1296), Dr Charlotte Bryant and Dr Margaret Currie for AMS dates at the Radiocarbon

Laboratory, East Kilbride. Grants from the Institute of Archaeology (University College London), the Graduate School (UCL), and the University of London Central Research Fund. MAM acknowledges a research studentship from the NERC.

References

Adger, W. N. 2000. Social and ecological resilience: are they related? *Progress in Human Geography* 24, 347–64.

Adger, W. N. 2003. Governing natural resources: institutional adaptation and resilience, in F. Berkhout, M. Leach and I. Scoones (eds.), *Negotiating Environmental Change: New Perspectives from Social Science*, 193–208. Cheltenham, Edward Elgar.

Aswani, S. 1998. Patterns of marine harvest effort in southwestern New Georgia, Solomon Islands: resource management or optimal foraging? *Ocean and Coastal Management* 40, 207–35.

Bastos, A. C., Kenyon, N. H. and Collins, M. 2002. Sedimentary processes, bedforms and facies, associated with a coastal headland: Portland Bill, southern UK. *Marine Geology* 187, 235–58.

Bird, D. W. and Bliege Bird, R. L. 1997. Contemporary shellfish gathering strategies among the Meriam of the Torres Strait islands, Australia: testing predictions of a central place foraging model. *Journal of Archaeological Science* 24, 39–63.

Brunsden, D. and Goudie, A. 1997. *Classic Landforms of the West Dorset Coast*. Sheffield, The Geographical Association.

CHRONO Marine Reservoir Database: http://calib.qub.ac.uk/marine/ (accessed 10/2007).

Handmer, J. W. and Dovers, S. R. 1996. A typology of resilience: rethinking institutions for sustainable development. *Industrial and Environmental Crisis Quarterly* 9, 482–511.

Hardin, G. 1968. The tragedy of the commons. *Science* 162, 1243–8.

Hughen, K. A., Baillie, M. G. L., Bard, E., Bayliss, A., Beck, J. W., Bertrand, C., Blackwell, P. G., Buck, C. E., Burr, G., Cutler, K. B., Damon, P. E., Edwards, R. L., Fairbanks, R. G., Friedrich, M., Guilderson, T. P., Kromer, B., McCormac, F. G., Manning, S., Bronk Ramsey, C., Reimer, P. J., Reimer, R. W., Remmele, S., Southon, J. R., Stuiver, M., Talamo, S., Taylor, F. W., van der Plicht, J. and Weyhenmeyer, C. E. 2004. Marine04 marine radiocarbon age calibration, 0-26 Cal Kyr BP. *Radiocarbon* 46, 1059–86.

Ingold, T. 2000. *The perception of the environment. Essays in livelihood, dwelling and skill*. London, Routledge.

Locke, C., Adger, W. N. and Kelly, P. M. 2000. Changing places: migration's social and environmental consequences. *Environment* 42, 24–35.

Mannino, M. A., Spiro, B. F. and Thomas, K. D. 2003. Sampling shells for seasonality: oxygen isotope analysis on shell carbonates of the inter-tidal gastropod *Monodonta lineata* (da Costa) from populations across its modern geographical range and from a Mesolithic site in southern Britain. *Journal of Archaeological Science* 30, 667–79.

Mannino, M. A. and Thomas, K. D. 2001. Intensive Mesolithic exploitation of coastal resources? Evidence from a shell deposit on the Isle of Portland (Southern England) for the impact of human foraging on populations of inter-tidal rocky shore molluscs. *Journal of Archaeological Science* 28, 1101–14.

Mannino, M. A. and Thomas, K. D. 2002. Depletion of a resource? The impact of prehistoric human foraging on intertidal mollusc communities and its significance for human settlement, mobility and dispersal. *World Archaeology* 33, 452–74.

Meehan, B. 1982. *Shell Bed to Shell Midden*. Canberra, Australian National University.

Nagaoka, L. 2002. The effects of resource depression on foraging efficiency, diet breadth and patch use in southern New Zealand. *Journal of Anthropological Archaeology* 21, 419–42.

Palmer, S. 1970. The stone age industries of the Isle of Portland, Dorset, and the utilization of Portland chert as artefact material in southern England. *Proceedings of the Prehistoric Society* 36, 82–115.

Palmer, S. 1990. Culverwell – unique opportunities for studying the intra-site structure of a Mesolithic habitation site in Dorset, England, in P. M. Vermeersch and P. van Peer (eds.), *Contributions to the Mesolithic in Europe. Papers presented at the Fourth International Symposium on the Mesolithic in Europe*, 87–91. Leuven, Leuven University Press.

Palmer, S. 1999. *Culverwell Mesolithic Habitation Site, Isle of Portland, Dorset. Excavation report and research studies*. British Archaeological Reports, British Series 287. Oxford, Archaeopress.

Stewart, M. 1999. The use of non-knapped stone at Culverwell, in S. Palmer, *Culverwell Mesolithic Habitation Site, Isle of Portland, Dorset. Excavation report and research studies*, 67–84. British Archaeological Reports, British Series 287. Oxford, Archaeopress.

Thomas, K. D. and Mannino, M. 1999. The bioarchaeology of the Culverwell shell midden, in S. Palmer, *Culverwell Mesolithic Habitation Site, Isle of Portland, Dorset. Excavation report and research studies*, 94–114. British Archaeological Reports, British Series 287. Oxford, Archaeopress.

Winterhalder, B. 2001. The behavioural ecology of hunter-gatherers, in C. Panter-Brick, R. H. Layton and P. Rowley-Conwy (eds.), *Hunter-Gatherers: An interdisciplinary perspective*, 12–38. Cambridge, Cambridge University Press.

24. Small game exploitation through the Mediterranean Pleistocene-Holocene transition in southern France: a key resource augmenting the dietary range

Alexandre Bournery

Pleistocene faunal assemblages, which previously concentrated on a limited range of large, high-return mammal species, have shown a marked increase in the number of small vertebrates in Mediterranean regions during the Holocene. As in many other parts of the world, this development began in the Upper Palaeolithic, demonstrating evidence of a subsistence intensification that can be seen within Epipalaeolithic-Mesolithic deposits from southern France. Here we present three zooarchaeological assemblages from a current PhD research project that centres on the faunal remains from a reference locality for the western Mesolithic, the Abeurador cave from Languedoc (Hérault, France). Among the variety of small animals hunted, the range of prey includes rabbits, game birds (such as choughs and partridges), and tortoises; there is a distinct lack of larger game remains. Two additional sites are also examined so as to provide a broader, regional representation of Epipalaeolithic-Mesolithic subsistence in southern France. These preliminary results outline a relative abundance of a wide variety of prey types when investigating site-use intensity (i.e. establishing the function of prey species) and regional hunting pressure. Of particular interest in this research are factors such as the fundamental interaction between those lower-ranked, faster-reproducing species and hunter-gatherer societies, and how the availability of prey influences the subsequent hunting decisions of humans.

Keywords: small game, Mesolithic, diet breadth, rabbits, partridges, tortoises, Boreal.

Introduction

The Pleistocene-Holocene transition in the Mediterranean area is of anthropological interest because it precedes the adoption of the first agricultural economy. Although there is as yet no consensus on the causes of the adoption of agricultural (Davis 2005), archaeologists consistently return to a few ecological themes to explain the transition of the Upper/Epi-Palaeolithic-Mesolithic adaptation, and of subsequent agricultural economies (Klein and Scott 1986; Stiner 1994; Stiner and Tchernov 1998).

The theoretical expectations of the 'broad-spectrum revolution' (Flannery 1969) first supposed that the widespread exploitation of small game was caused by an unprecedented demographic crowding, resulting in increased pressure on the environment. Binford (1968) and Flannery (1969) described the notion of diversification at the end of the Palaeolithic, both assuming a common origin brought about by demographic crowding, and of which the inclusion of small game and the grains of wild grasses in the diet was thought to be the ultimate manifestation. The focus on small game was later documented by Tchernov (1993a; 1993b; 1994) and Davis *et al.* (1994) in the southern Levant. Until recently, evidence and studies of extensive small animal exploitation by people has been hampered by theoretical biases. Most of the early investigators rejected the anthropogenic origin of these bones, attributing their presence instead to non-human predators; consequently most interest has been on palaeo-environmental information, rather than on the role of small game in human subsistence.

However, throughout the world, small animals have been important to many human societies for food, clothing, and, more recently, companionship (Guilaine and Vigne 2004; Vigne, Guilaine *et al.* 2004). Within the archaeological record, small game species appear to be frequent components of Late Pleistocene and early- to mid-Holocene sites all over the circum-Mediterranean region. In addition, they have often been associated with evidence for a general decrease in the sizes of a range of species (Davis 1981; 1982; Davis *et al.* 1994).

Nevertheless, the likelihood of human over-population (Stiner *et al.* 1999; 2000; Stiner and Munro 2002; Munro 2001; 2003) is disputable (see comments in *Current Anthropology* 41, 59–66 and 45, 22–27). It is a real phenomenon, but it is expressed by a change in the types of animals captured by humans on the Pleistocene-Holocene boundary, rather than by their diversity. Stephens (Stephens 1990; Stephens and Krebs 1986, chapter 4) suggests that the existence of types (recognizable classes of resource items or patches) assumes a repetitive cycle of search/encounter for resource items (types). The range of prey types hunted (birds, lagomorphs, tortoises) increases at the close of certain Palaeolithic sequences for the southern Levant (Davis *et al.* 1994; Munro 1999). In Mediterranean Spain, remains of small game are consistently important components, dominating archeofaunal assemblages from the Magdalenian through to the Mesolithic (Villaverde, Aura and Barton 1998; Aura *et al.* 2002; Pérez Ripoll 2002), and a similar pattern is witnessed also in Italy (Tagliacozzo and Fiore 1998; Fiore, Pino Uria and Tagliacozzo 2004), and Portugal (Bicho 1994; Haws 2003).

In the Mediterranean islands (Blondel and Vigne 1993; Masseti 1998; Vigne 1999), observations of the Pleistocene/Holocene transition provide particularly relevant evidence of human pressure, and some 'complete turnovers' of mammal faunas are attested (e.g. in Corsica, Mesolithic humans depended mainly on a single lagomorph, *Prolagus sardus*, which represented 70–80 % of the diet: Vigne 1999; 2004; Vigne and Marinval-Vigne 1983).

Archaeological evidence from three case studies

Even though a detailed taphonomic investigation is beyond the scope of this paper, research on the potential agents of deposition (Bournery *et al.* 2004) confirms that the most likely depositional agent of small animals at these sites was human.

Our preliminary conclusions are based on an archaeozoological analysis (Bournery, current PhD) of three faunal assemblages: Abeurador, Sorgues-Seve, and Fontbregoua.

The western Mesolithic of Languedoc (Abeurador Cave: Early Magdalenian – 14,000 BP; later Sauveterrian – <8700 BP: Vaquer et al. 1986) (c. 14,700 to 7600 BC)

The Abeurador cave is the centrepiece of a wide-ranging study exploring human occupation in the Languedoc from the Upper Pleistocene onwards. The site lies on the southern margin of the Massif Central, between the Minervois plain and the summit of the Montagne Noire (1231m; Figure 24.1), 50km from the present-day Mediterranean coastline. Its stratigraphic sequence contains 11 distinct levels, which can be placed into eight major subdivisions, covering the Late Palaeolithic to the Mid-Neolithic (Vaquer and Barbaza 1987), and constitutes the best sequence in western Languedoc for the study of Epipalaeolithic adaptations to the Postglacial. Numerous studies were conducted as a result of the significant quantities of charcoal and other botanical remains found (Heinz 1991; Heinz and Thiébault 1998; Heinz, Ruas and Vaquer 1992). They constituted a reference collection for Late Glacial/Holocene environmental understanding in that area. As numerous carbonized macrobotanic remains were observed, all the sediment excavated was water-sieved in very fine-mesh sieves (0.1–1mm), limiting biases in the skeletal representations of small animals.

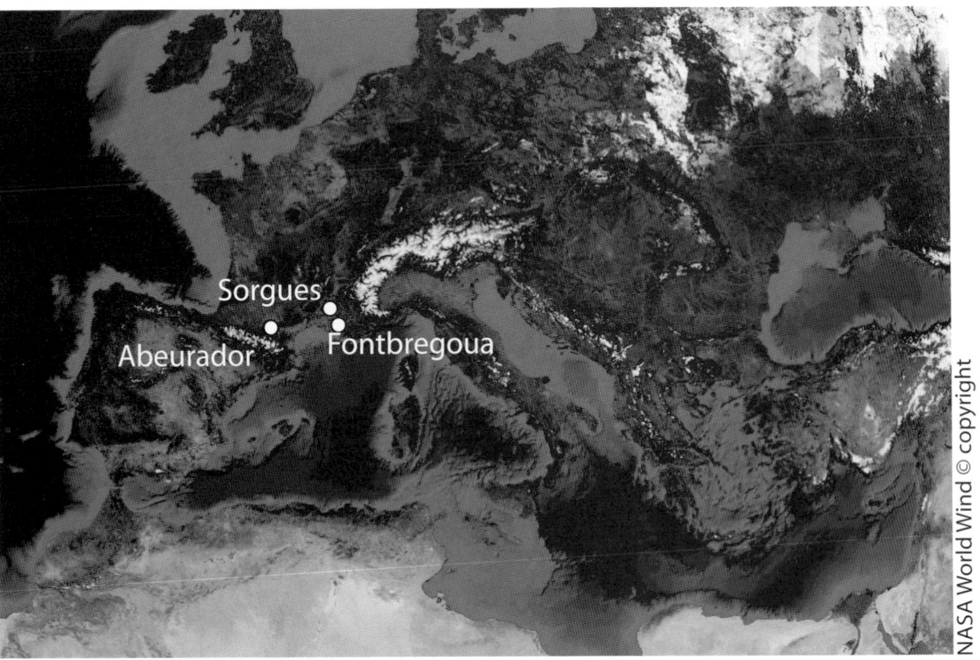

Figure 24.1. Geographic location of the three southern faunal series mentioned from France (Abeurador, Sorgues, Fontbregoua).

Final Mesolithic to Early Neolithic assemblages

Two additional sites were also examined so as to provide a broader regional representation of Epipalaeolithic-Mesolithic subsistence in southern France.

Sorgues-Seve rockshelter (Castelnovian: 8400 BP–6400 BP (c. 7500–5400 BC) Binder 1994)

The materials analysed came from the *sector interior*, with deposits spanning the final Mesolithic (i.e. ancient Castelnovian: Binder 1994), through to the final Neolithic and Iron Age (the latter attributed to colluvium). The excavated layers were grouped into four units for analysis: C_{inf}, which includes Sauveterrian (i.e. Early Mesolithic) horizons; and C_{sup}, the Castelnovian level, radiocarbon dated between 7730±60 BP (6655–6455 cal BC), 7640±65 BP (6630–6395 cal BC), and 7415±60 BP (6425–6105 cal BC).

Fontbregoua (Upper Palaeolithic to Early Neolithic Chasséen–5000 BP/3850 BC: Courtin 1975)

Although diverse references to the fauna from this rockshelter exist (Villa *et al.* 1985; 1986; Vilette 1983; Helmer 1979, unpublished), most zooarchaeological data from the site remain unpublished. The collection analysed here derives from two units (central and southern areas), dated from 11,200±150 BP (11,380–10,920 cal BC) to 5050±120 BP (4230–3540 cal BC; GsY-2753) (Courtin and Degaugue 1986; Courtin 1975). Analysed collections consist of a detailed taphonomic survey of birds (Vilette 1983) and tortoises (*Emys orbicularis*: Cheylan and Courtin 1976).

Patterns of small game exploitation

Although the economic use of small game may have differed from that of larger ungulates, their bones have been shown to yield important information about subsistence practices, mobility patterns, and demographic trends. These taphonomic perspectives rely on the following criteria applied here to the remains of lagomorphs, birds and reptiles:

- Counting and analysis of cut mark distribution on the bones (and frequency of other anthropogenic features, e.g. breakage patterns)
- Presence of burning marks (roasting) concentrated on limb epiphyses rather than on diaphyses (Vigne and Marinval-Vigne 1983)
- Analysis of bone surface (intensity of digestion)
- Skeletal representation; comparing relative bone frequencies (e.g. relative frequencies of hind limb and forelimb bones) and the relative survival of the skeletal parts
- Spatial analysis
- Age of death (for reptiles and lagomorphs: number/ratio of fused bones, epiphyses detached from the diaphyses; birds: presence of medullary bone (gives indication of laying, also as sex attribution)

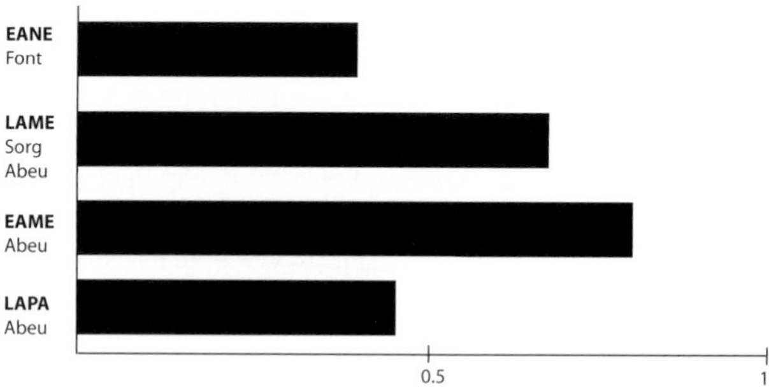

Figure 24.2. Relative abundance of small game (birds, lagomorphs and tortoises) at Mesolithic and Early Neolithic sites in southern France. Site names and time period abbreviations are as follows: ABEU = Abeurador, SORG = Sorgues, Font = Fontbregoua; LAPA = Late Palaeolithic, EAME = Early Mesolithic, LAME = Late Mesolithic, EANE = Early Neolithic.

- Abundance of long bone cylinders (by breaking or snapping the ends of long bones in order to extract marrow; mainly for lagomorphs: Drews and Schmitt 1986; Hockett 1991; 1994; Hockett and Bicho 2000; Pérez Ripoll 1992; 1993; Schmitt 1990; Villa *et al.* 1985)

Results

Figure 24.2 represents the relative proportions of small and large game, based on NISP (number of identified specimens) counts in terms of the abundance of small game in relation to ungulate taxa. In the Late Palaeolithic, the small game component is substantial (up to 45%) compared to ungulates (mostly fragmented caprinae); its importance becomes even larger in the Mesolithic (<80–68% for the Late Mesolithic levels).

1. The European pond turtle (case study: Fontbregoua)

We analysed approximately 2100 limb, carapace, and plastron fragments from the Fontbregoua rockshelter, including the tortoise remains recovered by the 1970–1972 excavations (Courtin 1975; Cheylan and Courtin, 1976; NISP=267). Data recording from turtle shells (*Emys orbicularis*) on isolated plates was easily done (Schleich 1984). The unique configurations of isolated plates, their morphological characters, such as the intersections between bony plates, epidermal scutes or the interneural plates sutures (e.g. combinations of groove sulci of epidermal scutes, sutures between bony plates) allowed three related MNI estimations to be established, and also permitted a small number of refittings. Figure 24.3 presents the three different MNI sets according to skeletal location: one MNI relates to the upper carapace (left on the x-axis), another to the plastron refittings (1.9% of the carapace bones; central on the x-axis), and the third to the limb bones (right on the x-axis).

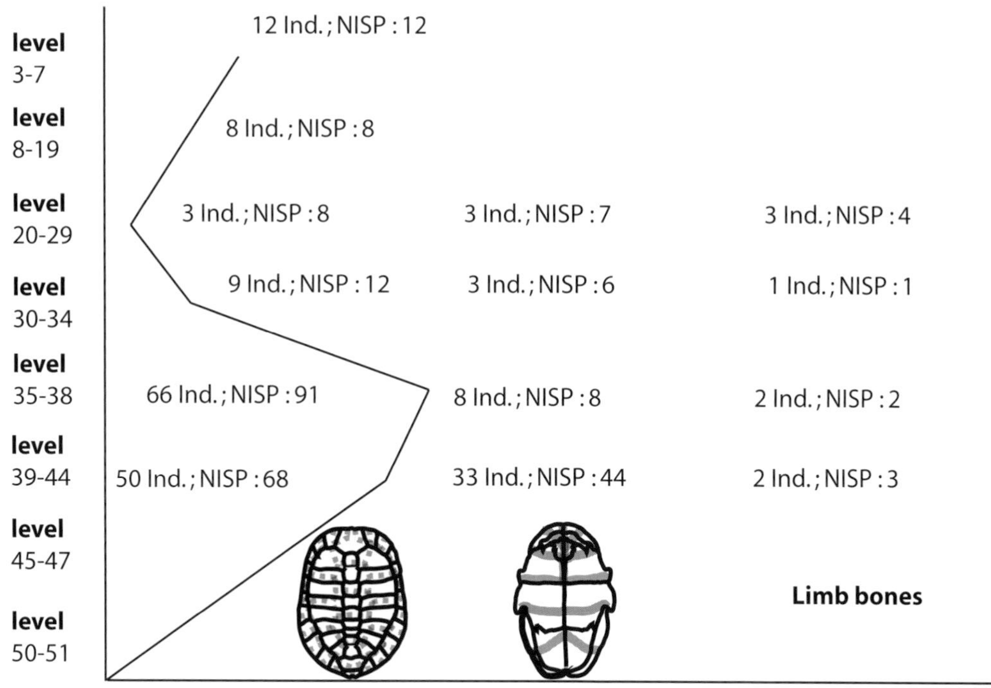

Figure 24.3. Relative MNI estimations (from carcasses and limb bones) of the European pond turtle. Cultural attributions are as follows: 3–19: Late Chassean; 20–29: Early Chassean; 30–38: Middle Neolithic; 39–44: Cardial; 45–51: Mesolithic to Early Cardial.

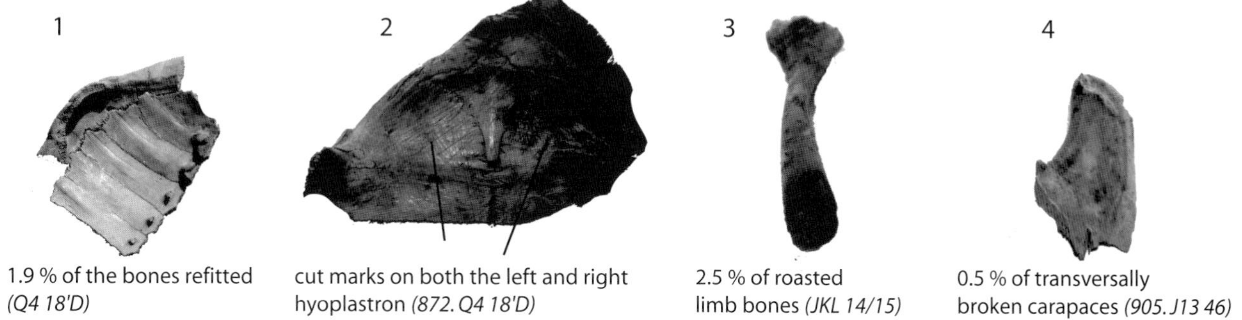

Figure 24.4. Pattern of small game exploitation: the European pond turtle. Examples (left to right) of 1: bone refitting; 2: cut mark distribution; 3: evidence of roasting; 4: fractured carapaces.

Of the tortoises bones studied, only the peripheral bones of the carapace have not been coded (NISP=354), leaving an estimated 1739, mostly carapace and plastron, fragments. A total of 1486 bones (70.9%), clearly most abundant during the Mesolithic to Early Neolithic levels, and 607 (29%) from the Chasséen (Late Neolithic) levels. Carapace fragments make up approximately 57.7% (1003) of the coded sample. Of the remainder, about 39.9% are plastron fragments (695), and 2.3% are limbs and other post-cranial elements (41).

All of the tortoise remains that can be identified with reasonable confidence appear to derive from a single taxon, the European pond turtle, although there may be some confusion with the Mediterranean turtle (*Mauremys leprosa*) (Cheylan 1981; Holman 1995).

Evidence of predator damage (i.e. punctures, gnawing) is rare on the carapace and plastron remains, and none of the bones show signs of having passed through the gut of a predator. Only 6.7% of the Mesolithic to Early Neolithic tortoise remains are burned (Figure 24.4), compared to 3.9% from the Chasséen (Late Neolithic) levels. The distribution of signs of burning on the various parts of the tortoise skeleton is also very informative; burning is most common on fragments of the carapace (61.2%), compared to 36.2% of the plastron fragments, and only 2.5% of limb bones.

A curious butchery pattern was observed on both a left and right hyoplastron (Figure 24.4) from the Late Mesolithic level. A series of numerous cut-marks, of equal depth, was noticed, probably attributable to a particular use of the carapace (J. Frazier, pers. comm.), and associated in the same levels with 0.5% of transversally broken

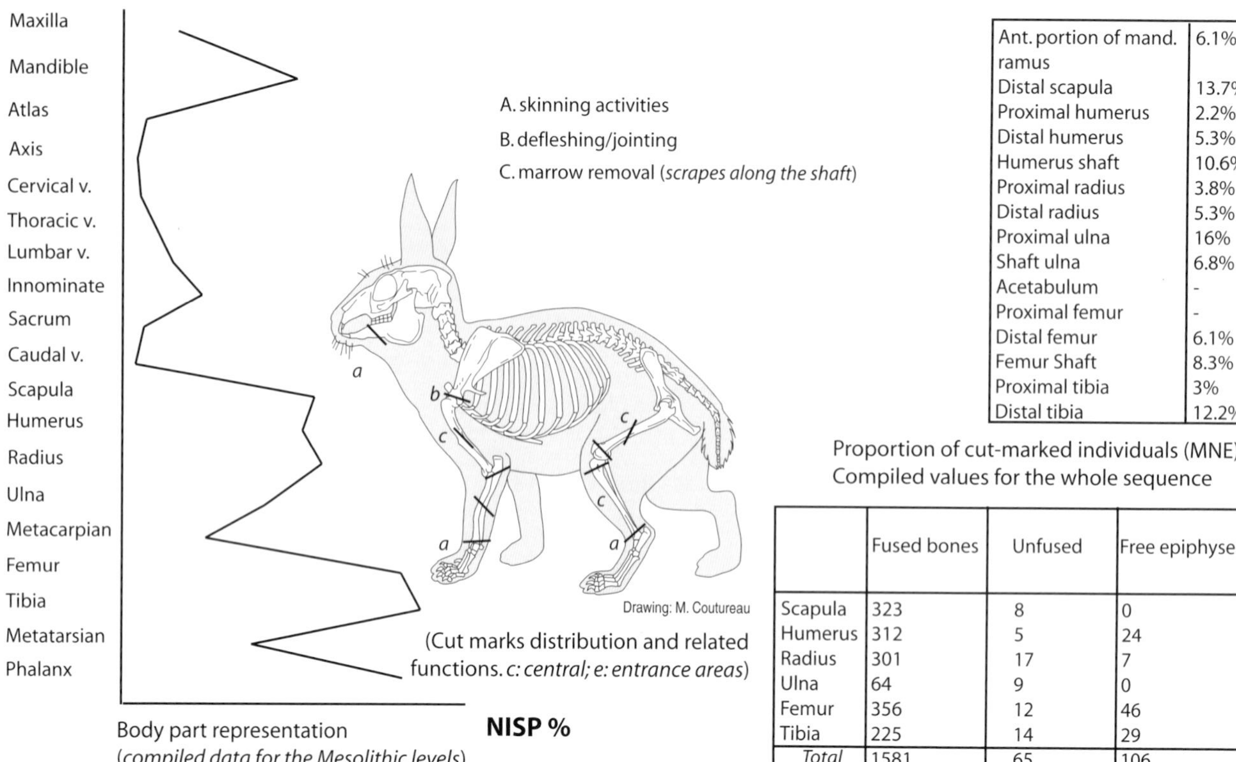

Ant. portion of mand. ramus	6.1%
Distal scapula	13.7%
Proximal humerus	2.2%
Distal humerus	5.3%
Humerus shaft	10.6%
Proximal radius	3.8%
Distal radius	5.3%
Proximal ulna	16%
Shaft ulna	6.8%
Acetabulum	-
Proximal femur	-
Distal femur	6.1%
Femur Shaft	8.3%
Proximal tibia	3%
Distal tibia	12.2%

	Fused bones	Unfused	Free epiphyses
Scapula	323	8	0
Humerus	312	5	24
Radius	301	17	7
Ulna	64	9	0
Femur	356	12	46
Tibia	225	14	29
Total	1581	65	106

Figure 24.5. Data for Mesolithic rabbit accumulation from Abeurador. Averaged profile of skeletal parts, cut mark distribution/quantification and juveniles to adult proportions.

carcasses, considered as an anthropogenic breakage pattern (compression fractures).

2. *The European rabbit (case study: Abeurador)*

Taken together, entrance and inner Mesolithic deposits of rabbits comprise a total of 15,862 remains at Abeurador. The deposits from these locations do not support relevant changes in proportion (not presented here, with the exception of the Azilian level; mainly a natural deposit). The proportion of skeletal elements of rabbits (*Oryctolagus cuniculus*) varies (Figure 24.5) from one level to another, depending on either taphonomic agents or the nature of human exploitation.

All the bones of the skeleton are in evidence (Figure 24.5), while the unequal presence in high frequencies of mandibles (and others related cranial elements) and hind limbs (mainly tibia cylinders) bias the skeletal representation (48 and 83% respectively). This closely matches the characteristic observations suggestive of anthropogenic accumulations (Hockett 1991; 1994; Hockett and Bicho 2000; Pérez Ripoll 1992; 1993; Figure 24.6: 1) and the process of marrow extraction. No clear evidence of butchering methods can be deduced from the relative frequencies of hind limb and forelimb bones: the distal and proximal parts of the long bones (tibiae, femora and humerii) are missing, leaving the parts with the highest meat content. The general scarcity of juveniles (92.4–95.5% of the extremities are fused; Figure 24.5) could be interpreted both in terms of seasonality and/or the use of hunting/gathering techniques, which resulted in the selection of adult individuals.

As shown in Figure 24.5, the presence of all the bones indicates that butchering and disposal of rabbit carcasses took place within the cave.

The rabbit remains show clear evidence of processing activity by humans, with 6.6% of the assemblage providing definite signs of modification, including cut marks and traces of burning (Figure 24.6: 2, 3). Stone tool cut marks are located on limb bones (Figure 24.5) and the processing pattern indicates skinning, removal of the meat from the bone, disarticulation, and supports the further breaking of the long bones (Bournery, current PhD).

The cut marks created during the meat removal are more numerous (Figure 24.5) than those created during disarticulation. Their morphology is varied, appearing as longitudinal cuts of unequal depths, or as scrapes, mainly located on the diaphyses of the long bones (Figure 24.5). The humerii generally exhibit the greatest number of these cut marks.

3. *The Birds (case study: Abeurador)*

Figure 24.7 summarizes the frequency of Mesolithic bird bone remains from the Abeurador rockshelter. The avifauna comprise more than 11 bird species, represented by 10,432

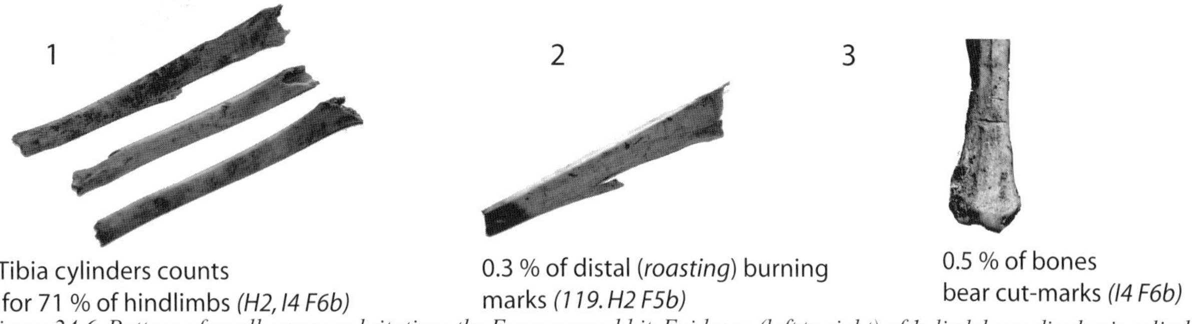

Figure 24.6. Pattern of small game exploitation: the European rabbit. Evidence (left to right) of 1: limb bone diaphysis cylinders; 2: roasting; 3: bone cut marks (radius).

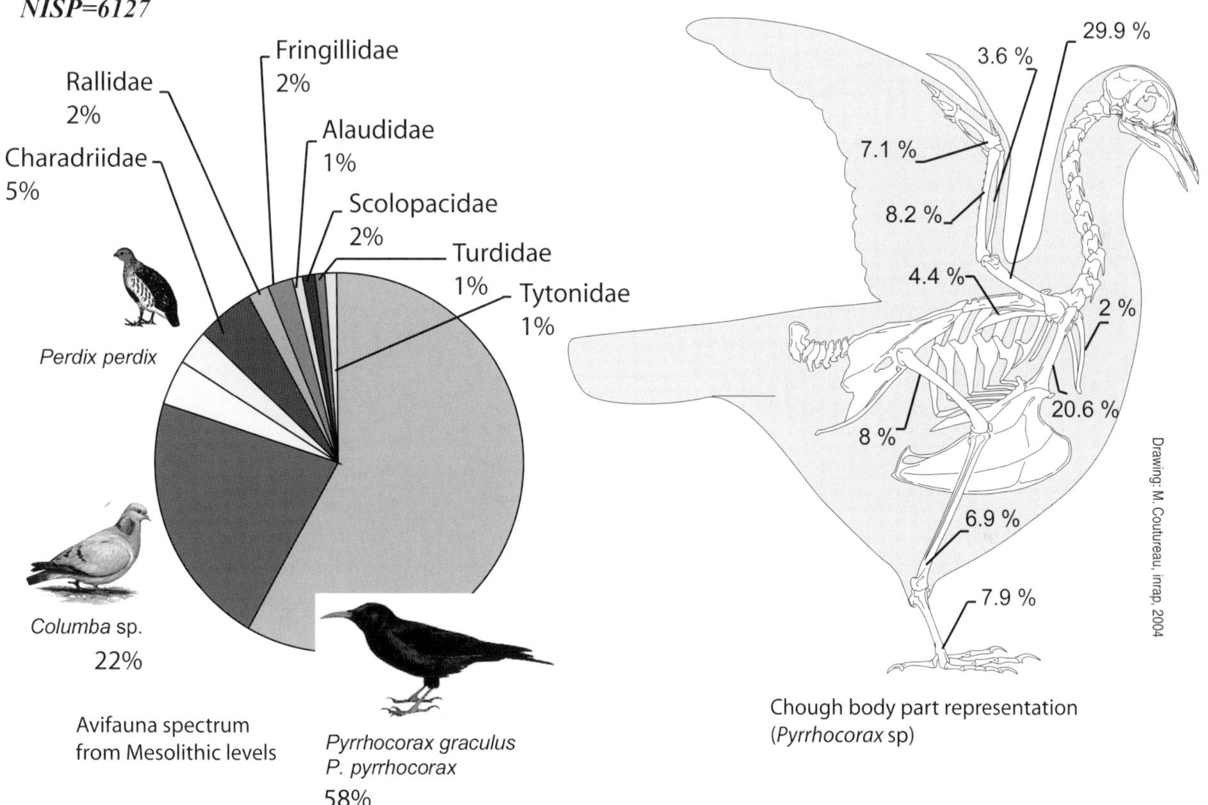

Quantitative summary of Characteristic Taphonomic traces left on choughs bones	
Cut-marked bones	5.1 %
Burnt bones (i.e. roasting)	3.1 %
Evidence of disarticulation (perforation of the distal humerus, see figure 8; 3)	8.3 % (of the total number of humerus)

Figure 24.7. Data for Mesolithic avifauna from Abeurador.

bone remains. Birds outnumber other small game (in terms of the numbers of individuals) in the three archaeological contexts presented here. Thus far we have analysed more than 6100 (6127) bird bones.

As mentioned earlier, the recovery of so many fragments was primarily the result of systematic wet- and dry-sieving (especially at Abeurador).

The importance of choughs

By far, the most numerous bird bone remains (58%, Figure 24.7) were those of corvids (*Pyrrhocorax* sp.). Most of the bones identified can be classified as choughs, of which 57% are attributed to the Red-billed variant (*Pyrrhocorax pyrrhocorax*) and 78% to the Alpine chough (*Pyrrhocorax graculus*). The two species are similar to each other,

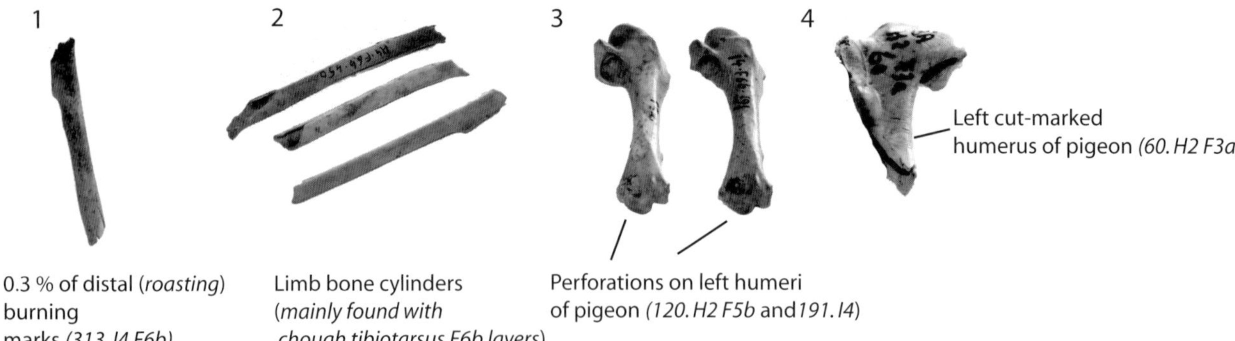

Figure 24.8. Pattern of small game exploitation: birds. Examples (left to right) of 1: roasting; 2: limb bone cylinders; 3: perforations caused by disarticulation; 4: cut marks.

although they differ in size (Tomek and Bochenski 2000) and the Red-billed chough is somewhat more robust than the Alpine. We were able to take measurements when the archaeological material was not fragmented (i.e. total length, minimal diameter of the shaft). Elements belonging to all skeletal parts indicate that whole birds were brought into the rockshelter.

Cut marks (5.1%) are slightly more abundant on chough bones than for any other small game category (pigeons, partridges), but they still constitute less than 200 occurrences. The removal of feathers, or meat, from a bird carcass can be performed neatly with minimal damage to the skeleton. Cut marks are well distributed (with the exception of the carpometacarpus), particularly on the humerus – the most abundant skeletal element (Figure 24.7). In a very few cases, the distal tibiotarsis has been cut just above the distal condylus, apparently to take advantage of the natural foramen in the articular end.

Evidence of wing dislocation comes from the recorded number of cut marks on the proximal end of the humerus (and also from the distal end of the humerus and proximal ends of radius and ulna). This processing is much more evident (Laroulandie 2000) with some particular perforations (Figure 24.8) of the olecranon, through to the olecranon fossa (while dismembering the elbow joint). Defleshing or the removal of meat from the skeleton involves cutting muscles insertions and other direct attachment occurring at these muscle attachments, such as on the shafts of long bones.

Discussion

These preliminary indicators are suggestive, and further work with big game is needed to investigate whether or not the small game exploitation pattern offers a signature for the 'broad-spectrum revolution'. Small game can represent some long-term shifts in the range of different *types* of small game available through the Pleistocene/Holocene transition.

Whether they were being caught by hand, in nets, or in traps, small game provides as much in the way of nutritional benefits as larger terrestrial mammals (see Hockett and Bicho 2000 for the lagomorphs).

These results, in turn, drive other issues related to technological innovations (Oswalt 1976), techniques, and technology- and taxon-focused approaches (Speck and Schaeffer 1950). Bar-El and Tchernov (2000) noted the possible role of new technologies in the late Upper Palaeolithic, such as traps and snares, which may have increased the effectiveness of capturing small game.

The latter is particularly interesting as its strategy ('catchability') depends strongly on the behaviour and ecology of a particular prey type – by taking advantage of the specific attributes of small game (e.g. annual migrations).

Grahame Clark's seminal volume *Prehistoric Europe: the economic basis* (1952) first drew to prominence the potential contribution of small game animals for Palaeolithic and Mesolithic communities. The three sites mentioned above are illustrative of the complex processes of cultural and economic development in train during the Early Holocene, at a time of significant adaptation by Epipalaeolithic groups to Postglacial climatic and environmental conditions.

Small game reliance could be interpreted both in terms of the general hunting system in use (i.e. trapping), combined with the nature of the environmental conditions: The Lateglacial created optimal environmental conditions for small animals to reproduce easily, suggesting that local factors involving their densities and environmental conditions likely influenced the nature and timing of small game acquisition during the Epipalaeolithic-Mesolithic transition. The next step is now to integrate these results, including taphonomy, subsistence and demographic trends, mobility patterns, as well as regional comparisons of faunal remains (Bournery, current PhD research).

Acknowledgements

I am grateful to Sinéad McCartan for hosting the 7th International Conference on the Mesolithic in Europe, in Belfast, and to Jean Denis Vigne for providing valuable comments and suggestions on this paper beforehand. I am also grateful to colleagues who have provided collections and helpful comments: in alphabetical order, Didier Binder, Marc Cheylan, Jean Courtin, Anne Delestrade, Daniel Helmer, Véronique Laroulandie, and Jean Vaquer.

References

Aura Tortosa, J. E., Villaverde Bonilla, V., Pérez Ripoll, M., Martinez Valle, R. and Guillem Calatayud, P. 2002. Big game and small prey: Paleolithic and Epipaleolithic economy from Valencia (Spain). *Journal of Archaeological Method and Theory* 9, 215–68.

Bar-El, T. and Tchernov, E. 2000. Lagomorph remains at prehistoric sites in Israel and Southern Sinai. *Paléorient* 26, 93–109.

Bicho, N. F. 1994. The end of the Paleolithic and the Mesolithic in Portugal. *Current Anthropology* 35, 664–74.

Binford, L. R. 1968. Post-Pleistocene Adaptations, in S. R. Binford and L. R. Binford (eds.), *New Perspectives in Archaeology*, 313–41. Chicago, Aldine.

Binder, D. 1994. Néolithisation et fonctionnement des réseaux néolithiques en Vaucluse. *BSR SRA-PACA*, 268–70.

Blondel, J. and Vigne J.-D. 1993. Space, Time and Man as determinants of Diversity of Birds and Mammals in the Mediterranean Region, in E. Ricklefs and D. Schluter (eds.), *Species Diversity in Ecological Communities. Ecological and Geographical perspectives*, 135–46. Chicago, Chicago University Press.

Bournery, A., Vigne, J. D. and Vaquer, J. 2004. Origine des accumulations mésolithiques des lagomorphes du secteur entrée de la Balma de l'Abeurador (Félines Minervois, Hérault), in J.-P. Brugal and J. Desse (eds.), *Petits animaux et sociétés humaines. Du complément alimentaire aux ressources utilitaires. XXIV rencontres internationales d'archéologie et d'histoire d'Antibes*, Antibes, 257–72. Éditions APDCA.

Cheylan, M. 1981. *Biologie et écologie de la tortue d'Hermann Testudo Hermanni Gelin, 1789. Contribution de l'espèce à la connaissance des climats quaternaires de la France.* Unpublished PhD thesis, University of Montpellier.

Cheylan, M. and Courtin, J. 1976. La consommation de la tortue Cistude *Emys orbicularis* (L.) au post-glaciaire dans la grotte de Fontbrégoua (Salernes-Var). *Bulletin du Muséum d'Histoire Naturelle, Marseille* 36, 41–6.

Clark, G. 1952. *Prehistoric Europe: the economic basis*. London, Methuen.

Courtin, J. 1975. Le Mésolithique de la Baume Fontbrégoua à Salernes (Var). *Cahiers ligures de Préhistoire et d'Archéologie* 24, 110–18.

Courtin, J. and Degaugue, F. 1986. Tufs et travertins Holocènes du Var, in *Edifices travertineux et Histoire de l'environnement dans le midi de la France. Edifices travertineux et histoire de l'environnement dans le Midi de la France. Livret-guide d'excursion en Basse-Provence effectuée par les chercheurs de l'A.T.P.-PIREN*. Aix-en-provence, Institut de Géographie.

Davis, S. J. 1981. The effects of temperature change and domestication on the body size of Late Pleistocene to Holocene mammals in Israel. *Paleobiology* 7, 101–14.

Davis, S. J. 1982. Climatic change and the advent of domestication: The succession of ruminant artiodactyles in the Late Pleistocene-Holocene region in the Israel region. *Paléorient* 8, 5–14.

Davis, S. J. 2005. Why domesticate food animals? Some zoo-archaeological evidence from the Levant. *Journal of Archaeological Science* 32, 1408–16.

Davis, S. J., Lernau, O. and Pichon, J. 1994. Chapitre VII: The animal remains: new lights on the origin of animals husbandry, in M. Lechevallier and A. Ronen (eds.), *Le site de Hatoula en Judée occidentale, Israël*, 333–50. Monographs in History. Paris, Association Paleorient.

Drews, M. P. and Schmitt, D. N. 1986. Other prehistoric artefacts, in C. Zeier and R. Elston (eds.), *The archaeology of the vista site*, 283–310. Carson City, Nevada Department of Transportation.

Fiore, I., Pino Uria, B. and Tagliacozzo, A. 2004. L'exploitation des petits animaux du Paléolithique supérieur–Mésolithique en Italie : l'exemple de la Grotta del Santuario della Madonna de Praia a Mare (Cosenza, Italie), in J.-P. Brugal and J Desse (eds.), *Petits animaux et sociétés humaines. Du complément alimentaire aux ressources utilitaires. XXIV rencontres internationales d'archéologie et d'histoire d'Antibes*. Antibes, Éditions APDCA.

Flannery, K. V. 1969. Origins and ecological effects of early domestication in Iran and the Near East, in P. J. Ucks and T. W. Dimbleby (eds.), *The domestication of plants and animals*, 73–100. London, Duckworth.

Guilaine, J. and Vigne, J.-D. 2004. Le chat, l'homme et la souris. *La Recherche* 378, 54–6.

Haws, J. A. 2003. *An investigation of Late Upper Paleolithic and Epipaleolithic hunter-gatherer subsistence and settlement patterns in Central Portugal*. Unpublished PhD thesis, University of Wisconsin-Madison.

Heinz, C. 1991. Upper Pleistocene and Holocene vegetation in the south of France and Andorra. Adaptations and first ruptures: new charcoal analysis data. *Review of Paleobotany and Palynology* 69, 299–324.

Heinz, C., Ruas M.-P. and Vaquer, J. 1992. La grotte de l'Abeurador (Félines-Minervois, Hérault): paléo-écologie d'après l'anthracologie et la carpologie. Les Charbons de bois, les anciens écosystèmes et le rôle de l'Homme, Colloque de Montpellier 1991. *Bulletin de la Société Botanique de France* (T. 139, 1992–4), 465–82.

Heinz, C. and Thiébault S. 1998. Characterization and Palaeo-ecological significance of archaeological charcoal assemblages during Late and Post-Glacial phases in Southern France. *Quaternary Research* 50, 56–68.

Helmer, D. 1979. *Recherches sur l'économie alimentaire et l'origine des animaux domestiques d'après l'étude des mammifères post-paléolithiques (du Mésolithique à l'Age du Bronze) en Provence*. Unpublished PhD thesis, University of Languedoc.

Hockett, B. S. 1991. Toward distinguishing human and raptor patterning on leporid bones. *American Antiquity* 56, 667–79.

Hockett, B. S. 1994. A descriptive reanalysis of the leporid bones from Hogup cave, Utah. *Journal of California and Great Basin Anthropology* 16, 106–17.

Hockett, B. S. and Bicho, N. F. 2000. The rabbits of Picareiro cave: small mammal hunting during the Late Upper Paleolithic in the Portuguese Estramadura. *Journal of Archaeological Science* 27, 1408–16.

Holman, J. A. 1995. On the identification of Emydid (*Reptilia: Testudines*) shell bones in the Pleistocene of Britain. *British Herpetological Society Bulletin* 53, 37–40.

Klein, R. G. and Scott, K. 1986. Re-analysis of faunal assemblages from the Haua Fteah and others Late Quaternary archaeological sites in Cyrenaican Lybia. *Journal of Archaeological Science* 13, 515–42.

Laroulandie, V. 2000. *Taphonomie et Archéozoologie des oiseaux en grotte: Applications aux sites Paléolithiques du Bois-Ragot (Vienne), de Combe Saunière (Dordogne) et de la Vache (Ariège)*. Unpublished PhD thesis, University of Bordeaux I.

Masseti, M. 1998. Holocene endemic and anthropogenous wild animals of the Mediterranean islands. *Anthropozoologica* 28, 3–20.

Munro, N. D. 1999. Small game as indicators of sedentization during the natufian period at Hayonim cave in Israel, in J. C. Driver (ed.), *Zooarchaeology of the Pleistocene/Holocene boundary. Proceedings of a Symposium held at the 8th*

Congress of the International Council for Archaeozoology (ICAZ), Victoria, British Columbia, Canada, August 1998, 37–45. British Archaeological Reports, International Series S800. Oxford, John and Erica Hedges.

Munro, N. D. 2001. A prelude to agriculture: game use and occupation intensity during the natufian period in the Southern Levant. Unpublished PhD thesis, University of Arizona.

Munro, N. D. 2003. Small game, the younger dryas, and the transition to agriculture in the southern levant. *Mitteilungen der Gesellschaft für Urgeschichte* 12, 47–64.

Oswalt, W. H. 1976. *An anthropological analysis of food-getting technology*. New York, Wiley.

Pérez Ripoll, M. 1992. *Marcas de carcarniceria, fracturas intencionadas y mordeduras de carnivoros en huesos prehistoricos del mediterraneo espanol*. Coleccion patrimonio 15. Alicante, Instituto de Cultura Juan Gil Albert.

Pérez Ripoll, M. 1993. Las marcas tafonomicas en huesos de lagoformos. *Estudios Sobre Cuaternario*, 227–31.

Pérez Ripoll, M. 2002. The importance of taphonomic studies of rabbit bones from archaeological sites, in M. de Renzi (ed.), *Current Topics on Taphonomy and Fossilization. Proceedings of the International Conference Taphos 2002, Valencia, Spain*, 499–508. Valencia, Ayuntamiento de Valencia.

Schleich, H.-H. 1984. Data recording on turtle shells. *Studia Geologica Salmanticensia, Volumen Especial 1 (Stvdia Palaeocheloniologica I)*, 239–48.

Schmitt, D. N. 1990. Bone artifacts and human remains, in E. E Buddy and R. G. Elston (eds.), *The archaeology of James Creek Shelter*, 117–27. Salt Lake City, University of Utah Press.

Speck, F. G. and Schaeffer, C. E. 1950. The deer and rabbit hunting drive in Virginia and the Southeast. *Southern Indian Studies* 2, 3–20.

Stephens, D. W. 1990. Risk and incomplete information in Behavioral ecology, in E. Cashdan (ed.), *Risk and uncertainty in tribal and peasant economies*, 19–46. Boulder, CO. Westview Press.

Stephens, D. W. and Krebs, J. R. 1986. *Foraging theory*. Princeton, Princeton University Press.

Stiner, M. C. (ed.) 1994. *Honor among thieves. A zooarchaeological study of neandertal ecology*. Princeton, Princeton University Press.

Stiner, M. C. and Munro, N. D. 2002. Approaches to prehistoric diet breadth, demography, and prey ranking systems in time and space. *Journal of Archaeological Method and Theory* 9, 181–214.

Stiner, M. C., Munro, N. D. and Surovell, T. A. 2000. The tortoise and the hare. Small game use, the broad spectrum revolution and paleolithic demography. *Current Anthropology* 41, 39–59.

Stiner, M. C., Munro, N. D., Surovell, T. A., Tchernov, E. and Bar-Yosef, O. 1999. Paleolithic population growth pulses evidenced by small animal exploitation. *Science* 283, 190–4.

Stiner, M. C. and Tchernov, E. 1998. Pleistocene species trends at Hayonim cave: Changes in climate versus human behaviour, in T. Akazawa, K. Aoki and O. Bar-Yosef (eds.), *Neanderthals and modern humans in West Asia*. New York, Plenum.

Tagliacozzo, A. and Fiore, I. 1998. Butchering of small mammals in the Epigravettian levels of the Romanelli Cave (Apulia, Italy), in J.-P Brugal, L. Meignen and M. Patou-Mathis (eds.), *Economie Préhistorique: les comportements de subsistance au Paléolithique. XVIII Rencontres Internationales d'Archéologie et d'Histoire d'Antibes, Octobre 1997*, 313–23. Antibes, Association pour la promotion et la diffusion des connaissances archéologiques (APDCA).

Tchernov, E. 1993a. The effects of sedentism on the exploitation of the environment in the Southern Levant, in *Exploitation des animaux sauvages a travers le temps, XIIIe Rencontres Internationales d'Archéologie et d'Histoire d'Antibes, IVe Colloque international de l'Homme et l'Animal*, 137–159. Société de Recherche Interdisciplinaire. Antibes, Association pour la promotion et la diffusion des connaissances archéologiques (APDCA).

Tchernov, E. 1993b. Exploitation of birds during the Natufian and Early Neolithic of the Southern Levant. *Archaeofauna* 2, 121–43.

Tchernov, E. 1994. New comments on the biostratigraphy of the middle and Upper Pleistocene of the southern Levant, in O. Bar-Yosef and R. S. Kra (eds.), *Late quaternary chronology and paleoclimates of the eastern Mediterranean*, 333–50. International Monographs in History. Paris, Association Paleorient.

Tomek, T. and Bochenski, Z. M. 2000. *The comparative osteology of European corvids* (Aves: Corvidae), *with a key to the identification of their skeletal elements*. Krakow, Polska Akademia.

Vaquer, J. and Barbaza M. 1987. Cueillette ou horticulture Mésolithique : La Balma de l'Abeurador, in *Premières communautés paysannes de la Méditerranée occidentale. Actes du colloque de Montpellier 1983*, 231–42. Paris, Editions du CNRS.

Vaquer, J., Geddes, D., Barbaza, M. and Erroux, J. 1986. Mesolithic plant exploitation at the Balma Abeurador (France). *Oxford Journal of Archaeology* 5 (1), 1–18.

Vigne, J.-D. 1999. L'abri du Monte Leone (Bonifacio, Corse du Sud): vaste site pré-néolithique en contexte insulaire, in P. Bintz and A. Thévenin (eds.), *L'Europe des derniers Chasseurs. Épipaléolithique et Mésolithique. Actes du 5ième colloque international UISPP, Comission XII. Grenoble, 18–23 septembre 1995*, 645–50. Paris, Comité des travaux historiques et scientifiques.

Vigne, J.-D. 2004. Accumulations de lagomorphes et de rongeurs dans les sites mésolithiques corso-sardes: origines taphonomiques, implications anthropologiques, in J.-P. Brugal and J. Desse (eds.), *Petits animaux et sociétés humaines. Du complément alimentaire aux ressources Utilitaires. XXIV rencontres internationales d'archéologie et d'histoire d'Antibes*, 285–305. Antibes, Association pour la promotion et la diffusion des connaissances archéologiques (APDCA).

Vigne, J.-D., Guilaine, J., Debue, K., Haye, L. and Gérard, P. 2004. Early Taming of the Cat in Cyprus. *Science* 304, 259.

Vigne, J.-D. and Marinval-Vigne, M.-C. 1983. Méthode pour la mise en évidence de la consommation du petit gibier, in J. Clutton-Brock and C. Grigson (eds.), *Animals and Archaeology, 1. Hunters and their Prey*, 239–42. British Archaeological Reports, International Series S163. Oxford, British Archaeological Reports.

Vilette P. 1983. *Avifaunes du Pléistocène final et de l'Holocène dans le sud de la France et en Catalogne*. Atacina No. 11. Carcassonne, Laboratoire de Préhistoire et de Palethnologie.

Villa, P., Bouville, C., Courtin, J., Helmer, D., Mahieu, E., Shipman, P., Belluomini, G. and Branca, M. 1986. Cannibalism in the Neolithic. *Science* 233, 431–7.

Villa, P., Helmer, D. and Courtin, J. 1985. Restes osseux et structures d'habitat en grotte : l'apport des remontages dans la Baume de Fontbrégoua. *Bulletin de la Société Préhistorique Française, Etudes et travaux*, Vol. 2, 10–12, 389–421.

Villaverde, V., Aura, J. E. and Barton C. M. 1998. The Upper Paleolithic in Mediterranean Spain: a review of current evidence. *Journal of World Prehistory* 12, 121–98.

25. An examination of Mesolithic shellfish gathering activities in the lower Asón river basin (Cantabria, España)

F. Igor Gutiérrez Zugasti

This paper will present the results of the shellfish analysis and interpretation of shellfish gathering activities practised by the Mesolithic populations who occupied the La Fragua cave site and la Peña del Perro rockshelter in the lower Asón River basin (Cantabria, Spain). Traditionally, it has been thought that the rise in Holocene sea levels initiated a change in Mesolithic hunter-gatherer subsistence strategies that resulted in the increased collection of shellfish. Through the analysis of Azilian and Mesolithic shellfish gathering activities it is possible to address such specific issues as collection techniques, catchment areas, and seasonality, as well as other general aspects of economic organization. Methodological aspects of shellfish analysis and the changes associated with the contemporaneous climate and environment will also be examined.

Keywords: Mesolithic, archaeomalacology, shellfish gathering, Asón, Cantabria, Azilian, molluscs.

Geographic Context

The lower Asón river basin is located in the north of the Iberian Peninsula, more specifically in the autonomous administrative region of Cantabria (Spain) (Figure 25.1). The location of the sites analysed in this investigation (La Fragua cave and Peña del Perro rockshelter) are situated on Mount Buciero, in Santoña.

During the Mesolithic, sea levels fluctuated from lower than present day levels at the beginning (*c.* 9500 years BP; *c.* 8800) to similar levels to today at the end (*c.* 5500 years BP; *c.* 4350 cal BC). These fluctuations are believed to have directly influenced the functional and subsistence-related advantages associated with the occupation and abandonment of numerous Mesolithic settlements along the coast of northern Spain, for example, the Peña del Perro rockshelter.

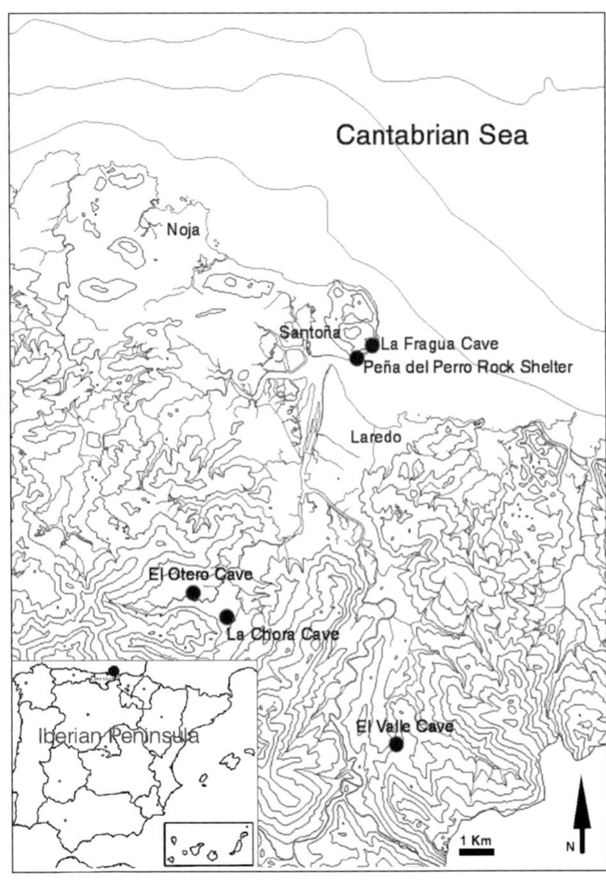

Figure 25.1. Location of the sites mentioned in the text.

Material and Methods

To evaluate the importance of molluscan exploitation in the lower Ason Basin at the beginning of the Holocene, a modern and original methodological analysis, developed by Moreno (1994) and completed by the author (Gutiérrez Zugasti 2005), has been conducted on the molluscan faunas from the before-mentioned sites.

The analysis began with the anatomical and taxonomic identification of the different mollusc remains recovered from each site. The anatomical identification criteria included taking into account the morphological particularities of each kind of mollusc (bivalves and gastropods) and echinoids. For this work, we used different field guides (Hayward *et al.* 1998; Kerney and Cameron 1979 and 1999; Lindner 1983; Palacios and Vega de la Torre 1997; Poppe and Gotto 1993a and b; Rolán 1984; Rolán *et al.* 1990) and reference collections.

The taphonomic analysis was designed to identify if there were any taphonomic processes associated with the physical alteration of each specimen, both in individual shells (bioerosion, carbonification, abrasion, etc.) and in the complete shellmidden (cementation, displacements, etc.), to identify the taphonomic agents which provoked the alterations (biologicals, chemicals, physicals or humans), and to identify the taphonomic groups based on its functionality (feeding, modification, intrusives and/or unknown functionality).

Afterwards, all fragments were divided into fragmentation categories based on the typological breakages associated with the different classes of molluscs and echinoids. These fragmentation categories were created for bivalves, gastropods and sea urchins. For bivalves, the categories are Complete Valve (COMV), Fragmented Valve (FRAV), Fragment with Complete Hinge (FCH), Anterior/Posterior Hinge Fragments (AHF/PHF), and Fragments (FTS). For gastropods the categories are Complete Individual (COMI), Fragmented Individual (FRAI), Apical-Umbilical Fragment (AUF), Apical Fragment (APIF), Stoma Fragment (STOF), Umbilical Fragment (UMBF), and Fragments (FTS). Finally, the categories for echinoids are Complete Semipyramid (COMSP), Semipyramid Apical Fragment (SPAF), Semipyramid Basal Fragment (SPBF), Complete Rotule (COMR), Complete Compass (COMC), Complete Tooth (COMT), Tooth Apical Fragment of Tooth (TAF), Tooth Basal Fragment of Tooth (TBF), Buccal and Shell Fragments (BSF), and Spines Fragments (SF).

These categories permit us, starting from the corresponding formulae, to obtain a more reliable quantification of the materials present within each examined site. From this study, we have obtained the number of identified specimens (NISP) and the minimum number of individuals (MNI) of the different taxons in each archaeological level, which has allowed us to make important interpretations regarding the subsistence and functional roles that each malacological taxon has played within the lives of Azilian and Mesolithic hunter-gatherers in the lower Ason basin over time. The formulas used for each kind of molluscs were as follows:

Bivalves: COMV+FRAV+FCH+ (AHF or PHF, the larger). Separate into right and left valves. Taking the largest value

Gastropods: COMI+FRAI+AUF+[APIF or (STOF+ UMBF), the larger]

Gastropods without whorl: COMI+FRAI+APIF

Echinoids: Four calculations depending on the type of remains:

Semipyramids: COMSP+(SPAF or SPBF, the larger)/5

Rotules: COMR/5

Compasses: COMC/5

Teeth: COMT+(TAF or TBF, the larger)/5

Archaeomalacological Analysis

I shall now summarize the results of the archeomalacological analysis associated with the Azilian and Mesolithic levels in the La Fragua cave (Gutiérrez Zugasti 2006) and the Peña del Perro rockshelter.

La Fragua cave is a small cave site with a temporal sequence covering the Upper Magdalenian, Azilian and Mesolithic time periods (González Morales 1999, 27; 2000, 178; Gutiérrez Zugasti 2005, 98) (Figure 25.2). Just to note, the Azilian date presents some doubt to its cultural attribution because it is on the limit between the Azilian and Mesolithic and the lithic tool kit is not totally diagnostic. But since the intention is to reflect the changes in molluscan exploitation and utilization over the full course of the Holocene, the (supposedly) Azilian data will be included in this research.

As can be seen in Figure 25.3, the Azilian level of the La Fragua cave presents a complete predominance of *Cepaea nemoralis* (brown-lipped banded snails), while the taxons of marine origin present marginal quantities. However, the Mesolithic level is dominated by the presence of limpets (*Patella* sp.), and, in smaller quantities, by other marine taxons such as mussels (*Mytilus galloprovincialis*), periwinkles (*Littorina littorea*), and oysters (*Ostrea edulis*).

Site	Level	Lab nº	Date BP	SD	2σ cal BP	2σ cal BC	Material	Method
La Fragua	1	GrN-20963	6650	120	7730–7310	5780–5360	Charcoal	C14 Conventional
La Fragua	1	GrN-20964	6860	60	7830–7580	5880–5630	Charcoal	C14 Conventional
La Fragua	1	GrN-20665	7530	70	8450–8180	6500–6230	Charcoal	C14 Conventional
El Perro	1	GrN-18116	9260	110	10720–10220	8770–8270	Charcoal	C14 Conventional
La Fragua	3	GrN-20966	9600	140	11250–10500	9300–8550	Charcoal	C14 Conventional
El Perro	2	GrN-18115	10160	110	12350–11250	10400–9300	Charcoal	C14 Conventional
El Perro	3	GrN-20962	12140	180	14850–13550	12900–11600	Charcoal	C14 Conventional
La Fragua	4	GrN-29440	12960	50	15650–15000	13700–13050	Bone	C14 AMS

Figure 25.2. Chronology of the analysed sites. Calibration programme: OxCal 3.10 (Bronk Ramsey 2005); Calibration curve: IntCal04 (Bronk Ramsey 1995; 2001).

Site	**El Perro**				**La Fragua**			
Level	**2**		**1**		**3**		**1**	
Bivalves	**MNI**	**%MNI**	**MNI**	**%MNI**	**MNI**	**%MNI**	**MNI**	**%MNI**
Acanthocardia sp.					1	0.009		
Anomia ephippium	1	0.007					1	0.008
Cardiidae	7	0.048						
Cerastoderma sp.	5	0.034	4	0.026	1	0.009		
Chlamys varia					1	0.009	1	0.008
Hiatella spp.			3	0.019				
Irus irus			2	0.013				
Mytilus galloprovincialis	573	3.941	7274	46.978	29	0.268	1028	8.329
Ostreidae	73	0.502	770	4.973	1	0.009	58	0.469
Petricola lithophaga	1	0.007	3	0.019				
Pholadidae			1	0.006			4	0.032
Pododesmus sp.							6	0.048
Scrobicularia plana			1	0.006				
Solen marginatus					1	0.009	47	0.38
Striarca lactea			1	0.006				
Tapes/Veneridae	14	0.096	71	0.459	1	0.009	38	0.307
Tellinidae	1	0.007						
Gastropods								
Calliostoma sp.	1	0.007						
Cantharus pictus			4	0.026				
Capulidae	1	0.007						
Charonia lampas			1	0.006				
Gibbula sp.	57	0.392	95	0.614	1	0.009	10	0.08
Haliotis tuberculata			2	0.013				
Hexaples trunculus			5	0.032				
Littorina littorea	7683	52.837	55	0.355	21	0.194		
Littorina neritoides			1	0.006				
Littorina obtusata	148	1.018	28	0.181	52	0.481	4	0.032
Littorina saxatilis	192	1.32	31	0.2	92	0.851		
Melampidae			1	0.006				
Osilinus lineatus	114	0.784	1907	12.316	1	0.009	541	4.383
Nassaridae	4	0.028	38	0.245			1	0.008
Naticidae			1	0.006				
Nucella lapillus	164	1.128	9	0.058			1	0.008
Ocenebra erinaceus			1	0.006				
Patella sp.	5186	35.665	4931	31.846	123	1.138	10361	83.955
Theodoxus sp.	2	0.014						
Tricolia pullus			1	0.006				
Trivia sp.	2	0.014	1	0.006				
Scaphopods								
Dentalium sp.	1	0.007						
Land Snails								
Cepaea nemoralis					10144	93.891	214	1.734
Cochlostoma sp.	1	0.007	3	0.019	41	0.379	5	0.04
Elona quimperiana					4	0.037	1	0.008
Helicella itala					213	1.971	1	0.008
Helicidae	309	2.125	238	1.537				
Oestophorella buvinieri					28	0.259		
Pomatias elegans	1	0.007	1	0.006	1	0.009	17	0.137
Pyrenaearia cantabrica					9	0.083		
Echinoids								
Paracentrotus lividus					4	0.037	1	0.008

Figure 25.3. Molluscan absolute and relative frequencies by levels (El Perro data taken from Moreno 1994).

On the other hand, the Peña del Perro rockshelter is a site that, in spite of its small present size, a result of the erosion of the hillside, would have originally been much larger during its occupation. This site was frequently occupied, as reflected by the remains of a brecciated shellmidden nearly two metres from the present ground surface. This site has the same Upper Magdalenian, Azilian and Mesolithic cultural sequences as La Fragua (González Morales 1990; 1999, 27; Gutiérrez Zugasti 2005, 142; Moreno 1994, 232).

The Azilian level contains a predominance of marine species, among the most numerous being periwinkles and limpets. The rest of the taxons are present in very small quantities. The predominance of periwinkles is probably related to the rather severe climate at the beginning of the Holocene.

The Mesolithic level shows a slight change, with mussels being the most predominant taxon, followed by limpets, *Osilinus lineatus* (thick topshells) and oysters. Therefore marine taxons are the most numerous, but with slight differences in quantities in terms of the Azilian level. We must also emphasize the change in species of marine snail, with the presence of *Osilinus lineatus* in Mesolithic levels (while quantities of periwinkles are insignificant), which is related to the improvement of climatic conditions connected with the advance of the Holocene.

Apart from these sites, we proceeded to review the mollusc collections from some other sites located in the interior of the Ason basin. These are the cave sites of La Chora, El Otero and El Valle (Gutiérrez Zugasti 2005, 153; Yudego 1995). Unfortunately, because these sites were excavated without using modern methods, the information from these sites can only be used generally. But it is worth mentioning that at La Chora (González Echegaray *et al.* 1963; Madariaga 1963) and El Otero (González Echegaray *et al.* 1966; Madariaga 1966), a rather intense harvesting of estuary products did occur, with the predominance of species such as oysters and the presence of species characteristically found in sandy and muddy areas. These types of species are more appropriate to the sites in interior locations that favour the exploitation of estuary-type resources. At the same time, at El Valle (García Gelabert and Talavera 2004; Obermaier 1925), land snails were exploited to a similar degree as within the Azilian level at La Fragua.

Discussion

First of all it should be explained how the exploitation of molluscs has changed through time. If we focus on the species' temporary evolution in the lower Asón River basin during the Azilian, periwinkles and limpets are the predominant species, but they are selected less at the end of this period. This decline coincides with the increase in *Cepaea nemoralis*. During the first part of the Mesolithic, mussels and limpets are the most selected species. However, while limpets continue to increase throughout the Mesolithic, mussels decline quite considerably. The presence of *Cepaea nemoralis* at this time is hardly noticeable compared to its abundance during the Azilian.

It is important to emphasize the decline of periwinkles at the beginning of the Mesolithic, which contrasts with the increase of *Osilinus lineatus* at that same time. The harvesting of marine snails does not decrease through time. On the other hand, oysters are present throughout the sequence, but in limited quantities, although there is an increase in their frequency at the beginning of the Mesolithic, with an eventual slight decrease later on.

Based on this research, we can see a temporal evolution in the preference for the exploitation of rocky molluscs, especially gastropods, among them limpets, as the most selected species throughout this time period. The importance of other rocky gastropods, for example spirals such as periwinkles at the beginning of the temporary sequence, and *Osilinus lineatus* at its end, must also be taken into consideration. But at the end of the sequence, the tendency points to a decrease in all the percentages of the species, with the exception of limpets, as mentioned earlier.

Therefore, it can be observed that there was very similar mollusc exploitation during both the Azilian and Mesolithic periods, with slight changes introduced by the more temperate climate conditions during the later period, which promoted increased harvesting in the estuary areas and other inter-tidal regions. So, in general, we can state that there are no big qualitative changes in the exploitation of marine molluscs over time in the Asón basin. In particular it should be emphasized that the exploitation of land snails during the Azilian level at La Fragua cave contrasts with the harvesting strategies identified in the other levels and sites analysed. It is also important to emphasize the different exploitation strategies regarding the predominant species used during the Mesolithic. These changes were probably related to increases in those mollusc populations that preferred more temperate climates, or to the way that particular species were being harvested.

During the Azilian, the increase in land snail exploitation may have been because of their abundance within the vicinity of the site (La Fragua), while later in the same period exploitation may have centred on marine taxons (El Perro). When we take into account the study of the rest of the materials from these sites we see that during the Azilian there was a diversification in the collection of resources. In addition to the exploitation of molluscs, small and large mammals were also hunted, and wild plants must have been gathered.

During the Azilian the harvesting of malacological resources was generally focused on areas around the settlement (land snails), and around rocky areas near the sea (marine taxons). More specifically, they probably targeted open zones such as beaches or rocky areas, whereas collecting around estuary areas would have been scarce.

During the Mesolithic, however, the exploitation of molluscs was based primarily on marine taxons, principally limpets and mussels, but also including *Osilinus lineatus* and oysters. This focus was probably the result of increased accessibility to these resources, from higher population counts brought about by improved weather conditions, and the close proximity of the coastline. As with the Azilian, there was also a similar overall diversification in the exploitation of molluscs, mammals, and vegetables resources during the Mesolithic. In contrast to the Azilian, the Mesolithic catchment areas were concentrated mainly around the more exposed inter-tidal areas, such as beaches and rocky zones. However, the exploitation of estuary zones was also incorporated into the general subsistence pattern.

Finally, I would like to say that the collection techniques and use of instruments for gathering molluscs were also very similar between the Azilian and Mesolithic cultures. 1) With a complete knowledge of the tidal system, they could collect molluscs over an optimal amount of time; 2) With the probable use of stone cobble tools they could prize the tightly-fixed species off wet rocks (although based on worked bone recovered from La Fragua, bone tools may also have been used; 3) They could gather those species that commonly lived in sandy/muddy areas by using instruments such as the digging stick, 4) or even use their hands to pick up those marine species that were not strongly fixed to the substrate, or the more easily-gathered of land snail species.

Conclusions

Several conclusions appear from this data. First, there are some noticeable differences between the sites in terms of their use. On one hand, El Perro was a large site during the Azilian and Mesolithic, able to give shelter to large human populations. For this reason, the occupation was probably more extensive and for longer durations, and the activities carried out in it more varied. However, on the other hand, La Fragua is a very small cave, unable to shelter sizable populations; it was, therefore, probably a seasonal settlement, sheltering smaller numbers of people. These arguments are supported by the mammalian fauna exploitation patterns (Marín Arroyo 2004; Morales and Moreno 1998).

We can also state, as mentioned earlier, that there are no large differences in mollusc exploitation between the Azilian and Mesolithic levels, and, therefore, the exploitation pattern is very consistent over time, with only slight changes in the species collected, resulting from climatic amelioration and subtle increases in the exploitation of more exposed rocky shores and estuary areas during the Mesolithic. The collection of land snails during certain phases of the Azilian period is the only distinct change in the exploitation pattern, but it should be noted that land snail collection was a common practice during both the Azilian and Mesolithic periods throughout the Cantabrian region (Ruiz Cobo *et al.* 1999).

Acknowledgements

I would like to thank to Professor M. R. González Morales (University of Cantabria) for his help in this research, the University of Cantabria for its financial support, and Merche Angulo, John Rissetto and Matt Dawson (University of New Mexico), and Eva Laurie (University of York) for help with the translation.

References

Bronk Ramsey, C. 1995. Radiocarbon calibration and Analysis of Stratigraphy: The Oxcal Program. *Radiocarbon* 37 (2), 425–30.

Bronk Ramsey, C. 2001. Development of the Radiocarbon Program Oxcal. *Radiocarbon* 43 (2A), 355–63.

Bronk Ramsey, C. 2005. OxCal 3.10. WWW program and documentation available at http://www.rlaha.ox.ac.uk/oxcal/oxcal.htm (accessed 10/2007).

García-Gelabert, M. P. and Talavera, J. 2004. *La cueva del Valle, Rasines, Cantabria, España*. British Archaeological Reports, International Series S1252. Oxford, John and Erica Hedges.

González Echegaray, J., García Guinea, M. A. and Bejines, A. 1963. *Cueva de La Chora*. Excavaciones Arqueológicas en España 26. Madrid, Dirección General de Bellas Artes.

González Echegaray, J., García Guinea, M. A. and Bejines, A. 1966. *Cueva del Otero*. Excavaciones Arqueológicas en España 53. Madrid, Dirección General de Bellas Artes.

González Morales, M. R. 1990. La Prehistoria de las Marismas: excavaciones en el Abrigo de la Peña del Perro (Santoña, Cantabria). Campañas 1985–1988. *Cuadernos de Trasmiera* 2, 13–28.

González Morales, M. R. 1999. La Prehistoria de Santoña. *Monte Buciero* 2, 17–28.

González Morales, M. R. 2000. La Prehistoria de las Marismas: Excavaciones en la Cueva de La Fragua (Santoña). Campañas de 1990, 1991, 1993, 1994 y 1996, in R. Ontañón (ed.), *Actuaciones arqueológicas en Cantabria, 1984–1999*, 177–9. Santander, Gobierno de Cantabria.

Gutiérrez Zugasti, F. I. 2005. *La explotación de moluscos en la cuenca baja del río Asón (Cantabria, España) a inicios del Holoceno (10000–5000 BP) y su importancia en las comunidades humanas del Aziliense y del Mesolítico*. Unpublished PhD research, University of Cantabria.

Gutiérrez Zugasti, F. I. 2006. Análisis Arqueomalacológico de la Cueva de La Fragua (Santoña, Cantabria, España), in N. F. Bicho (ed.), *Animais na Pré-história e Arqueología da Península Ibérica. Actas do IV Congresso de Arqueologia Peninsular*, 197–210. Promontoria monográfica 3. Faro, Universidade do Algarve

Hayward, P., Nelson-Smith, T. and Shields, C. 1998. *Flora y Fauna de las costas de España y de Europa*. Barcelona, Ediciones Omega.

Kerney, M. P. and Cameron, R. A. D. 1979. *A Field Guide to the Land Snails of Britain and North-West Europe*, London, Collins.

Kerney, M. P. and Cameron, R. A. D. 1999. *Guide des Escargots et limaces d'Europe*. Lausanne-Paris, Delachaux & Niestlé.

Lindner, G. 1983. *Moluscos y caracoles de los mares del mundo*. Barcelona, Ediciones Omega.

Madariaga, B. 1963. Análisis Paleontológico de la fauna terrestre y marina de la Cueva de La Chora, in J. González Echegaray, M. A. Garcia Guinea and A. Begines (eds.), *Cueva de La Chora*, 51–74. Excavaciones Arqueológicas en España 26. Madrid, Dirección General de Bellas Artes.

Madariaga, B. 1966. Análisis Paleontológico de la fauna terrestre y marina de la Cueva del Otero, in J. González Echegaray and P. Janssens (eds.), *La Cueva del Otero*, 61–80. Excavaciones

Arqueológicas en España 53. Madrid, Dirección General de Bellas Artes.

Marín Arroyo, A. B. 2004. *Análisis arqueozoológico, tafonómico y de distribución espacial de la fauna de mamíferos de la Cueva de La Fragua (Santoña, Cantabria)*. Santander, Ediciones TGD.

Morales, A. and Moreno, R. 1998. *El Abrigo de la Peña del Perro. Estudio óseo*. Unpublished Report, Universidad Autónoma de Madrid.

Moreno, R. 1994. *Análisis arqueomalacológicos en la Península Ibérica. Contribución metodológica y biocultural*. Unpublished PhD thesis, Universidad Autónoma de Madrid.

Obermaier, H. 1925. *El Hombre Fósil* (2ª edición). Memoria 9. Madrid, Comisión de Investigaciones Prehistóricas y Paleontológicas.

Palacios, N. and Vega de la Torre, J. J. (eds.) 1997. *Guía de conchas de las playas y rías de Cantabria*. Ceceñas (Cantabria), N. Palacios Egüen.

Poppe, G. T. and Gotto, Y. 1993. *European Seashells, Volumes I (Polyplacophora, Caudofoveata, Solenogastra, Gastropoda) and II (Scaphopoda, Bivalvia, Cephalopoda)*. Wiesbaden, Verlag Christa Hemmen.

Rolán, E. 1984. Moluscos de la Ría de Vigo I: Gasterópodos. *Thalassas* 1 (1).

Rolán, E., Otero-Schmitt, J. and Rolán Álvarez, E. 1990. Moluscos de la Ría de Vigo II: Policlopóforos, Bivalvos, Escafópodos y Cefalópodos. *Thalassas* 7 (2).

Ruiz Cobo, J., Muñoz Fernández, E. and Smith, P. 1999. Los concheros de caracoles (Cepaea) en el sector oriental de Cantabria. *Altamira* LV, 7–27.

Yudego, C. 1995. *Estudio arqueológico de las ocupaciones post-magdalenienses de los yacimientos de la cuenca baja del Asón y valle de Aras (Cuevas de La Chora, El Otero, El Valle y Cobrante)*. Unpublished PhD research, University of Cantabria.

26. Stone Age settlement sites on an environmentally sensitive coastal area along the lower reaches of the River Pärnu (south-western Estonia), as indicators of changing settlement patterns, technologies and economies

Aivar Kriiska and Lembi Lõugas

Environmental conditions, including sea-level changes, have undoubtedly influenced human settlement on the coastal areas of the Baltic Sea throughout history. In south-western Estonia, where the Postglacial isostatic uplift is relatively slow, influences on the Baltic Sea were especially severe. There, on an environmentally sensitive coastal area, two transgressions and three regressions have occurred over the last 11,500 years. As a result of sea-level changes, human settlement in south-western Estonia has also been cyclical. A shift is visible, too, in the economic conditions; in addition to terrestrial animals, sea mammals also began to be hunted during the Late Mesolithic. The majority of Early Mesolithic flint originates as much as 500km away to the south; local flint dominates during the Late Mesolithic, whereas during the Early Neolithic a large percentage of the raw material derives from just over 500km away eastwards. Two important factors are evident in relation to the flint industry – the decreasing importance of blade technology over time and the introduction of bifacial retouch at the beginning of the Neolithic.

Keywords: Mesolithic, Estonia, settlement, economy, lithics, environment.

Introduction

Changes in Stone Age subsistence economies and settlement patterns have been of great interest to researchers in the eastern Baltic region over the last decade. The current view of the Stone Age, as a comparatively heterogeneous period until the introduction of farming, has been modified mainly on the basis of new data from the Estonian coastal areas and west Estonian archipelago.

Studies during the second half of the 1990s made it possible to discern the marine-orientated settlements and subsistence strategies of the Late Mesolithic. The main platform of this research was provided by investigations made on the islands of the Baltic Sea, whereas settlements along the mainland coast have seen only minimal investigation. The chance to rectify this state of affairs presented itself through a series of newly discovered settlement sites discovered in south-western Estonia after 2000.

The natural conditions, including changes to the Baltic Sea basin and local water systems, undoubtedly influenced coastal human settlement. In south-western Estonia, where Postglacial isostatic uplift has been relatively slow, the various marine regressions and transgressions brought about especially drastic results. The low coastal area in south-western Estonia reacts drastically to any fluctuation in sea level; sea level and storms can easily change this shoreline. The environmentally sensitive coastal area in this region, approximately 10–30km wide, has been influenced by three regressions and two transgressions over the last 11,500 years. As a consequence, human habitation in the region has also been cyclical. This trend is especially noticeable along the lower reaches of the River Pärnu, which became famous for numerous discoveries of Stone Age bone and antler stray finds at the beginning of the 20th century; several Stone Age settlement sites (Figure 26.1) have since been found there.

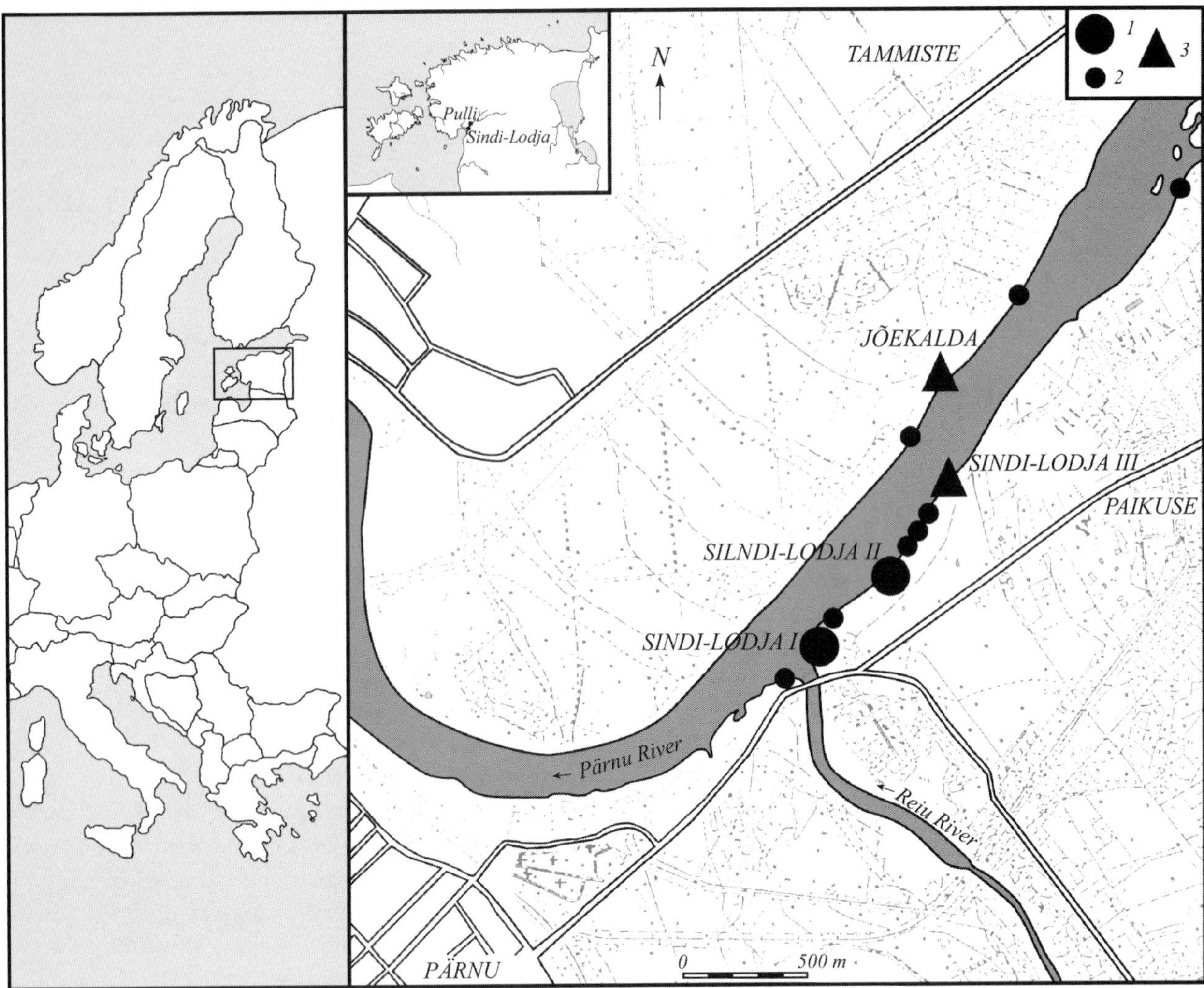

Figure 26.1. Mesolithic (1) and Neolithic sites (3) of Sindi-Lodja and Jõekalda; also areas with high concentration of finds within the riverbank sediments (2).

Stone age settlement sites along the lower reaches of the River Pärnu

Pulli

The site of Pulli is located on the right bank of the Pärnu, approximately 15km from the present seashore (Figure 26.2): the settlement site was discovered in 1967. Extensive archaeological excavations were carried out there under the direction of Lembit Jaanits between 1968 and 1973, and in the season of 1975/76; an area of 1159m² was investigated (Jaanits and Jaanits 1975; 1978). Several radiocarbon dates were made from the organic material obtained from the cultural layer. Results proved that the settlement site at Pulli dates to the Early Mesolithic, *c.* 9300–8200 cal BC (Figure 26.3).

Sindi-Lodja I

Sindi-Lodja I is at the mouth of the River Reiu, on the left bank of the Pärnu (Figure 26.1): the settlement site was discovered in 2000 (Kriiska 2001a, 21), and excavations took place there between 2001 and 2003 (Kriiska *et al.* 2002; Kriiska *et al.* 2003); an area of 115m² was excavated. Relatively few archaeological finds were recovered, indicating that we might be dealing with the marginal area of a settlement site. The charcoal collected from this part of the settlement layer was dated *c.* 7050–6700 cal BC (Figure 26.3), i.e. from the Late Mesolithic.

Sindi-Lodja II

The site of Sindi-Lodja II is located on the left bank of the Pärnu, approximately 400m upstream from the mouth of the Reiu (Figure 26.1): the settlement site was discovered in 2000 (Kriiska 2001a, 27), and small-scale excavations took place there in 2001 (Kriiska *et al.* 2002). The cultural level, alternating with layers of sand, is located on the steep river-bank, about six metres lower than today's ground level (Figure 26.2). The find material obtained from the small area excavated was relatively rich. The radiocarbon dates obtained from the wood gathered from the cultural layer gave a result of *c.* 7200–6650 cal BC (Figure 26.3), i.e. the Late Mesolithic.

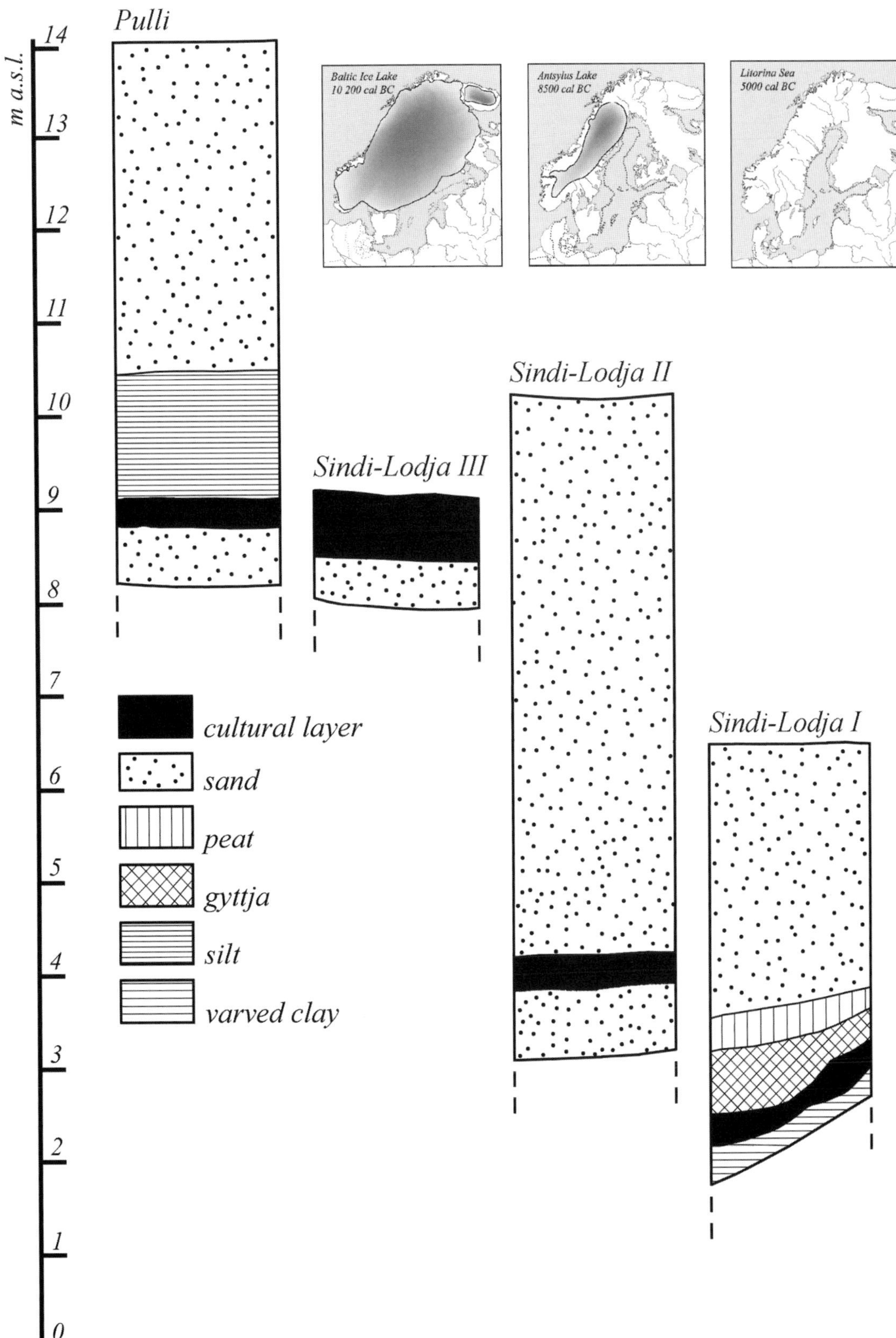

Figure 26.2. Profiles of sites (Pulli after Raukas et al. *1999, 22), and Baltic Sea phases (after Nils-Olaf Svensson, in Burenhult 1999).*

Sindi-Lodja III

Sindi-Lodja III is situated on the left bank of the Pärnu, 300m north-east of the Sindi-Lodja II settlement (Figure 26.1). A settlement site was discovered in 2001 (Kriiska *et al.* 2002, 31), and excavations took place between 2001 and 2004; an area of around 75m² has been opened so far. The cultural layer was rich in finds, coming from different Neolithic periods. Among the pottery there are extensive

Site	^{14}C (BP)	Calibrated date 2σ (cal BC)	Calibrated date 1σ (cal BC)	Lab no.	Sample material
Pulli	9620±120	9300–8650	9230–8830	Hel-2206A	Soil
Pulli	9600±120	9300–8650	9230–8830	TA-245	Cultural layer
Pulli	9575±115	9300–8600	9160–8790	TA-176	Cultural layer
Pulli	9385±105	9150–8300	8810–8470	Ua-13351	Charcoal
Pulli	9350±60	8790–8440	8720–8540	Ta-949	Charcoal
Pulli	9290±120	9150–8250	8700–8680	Hel-2206B	Soil
Pulli	9095±90	8600–7950	8450–8230	Ua-13352	Elk bone
Sindi-Lodja I	8070±70	7300–6700	7180–6820	Ua-17013	Charcoal
Sindi-Lodja I	7780±100	7050–6400	6750–6470	Ta-2826	Wood
Sindi-Lodja II	8035±80	7200–6550	7080–6810	Ta-2769	Wood

Figure 26.3. Table of reliable radiocarbon dates from Stone Age settlement sites along the lower reaches of the River Pärnu. Calibrations: Atmospheric data from Reimer et al. 2004; OxCal 3.10 Bronk Ramsey 2005; cub r: 5 sd: 12 prob. usp. (chron). (After Jaanits and Jaanits 1975, 65; Kriiska 2001a, 21; Kriiska et al. 2002, 30; Veski et al. 2005, table 2).

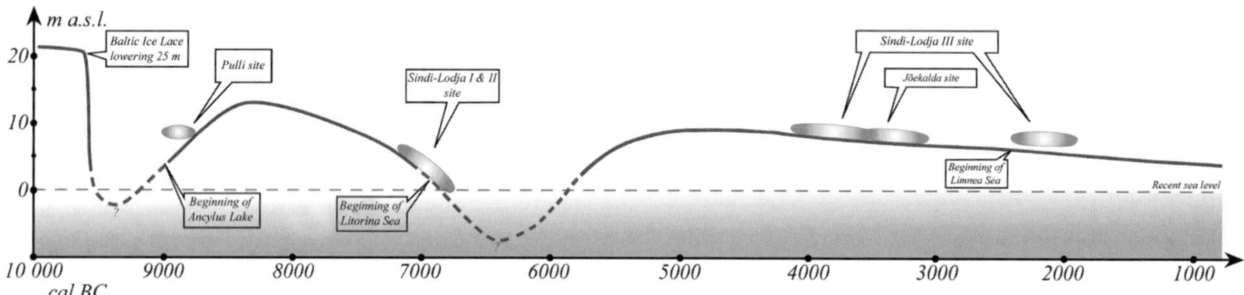

Figure 26.4. Shoreline displacement curves for the lower reaches of the Pärnu River and Stone Age settlement sites.

examples of typical and late 'comb ware', although Narva-type pottery and Corded Ware are also present. According to the shore displacement chronology, the settlement site can be dated to between 3980 and 3230 cal BC (Jussila and Kriiska 2004, 13), i.e. to the Early Neolithic. However, signs of Late Neolithic human habitation have also been found.

Jõeääre

Jõeääre is situated on the right bank of the Pärnu, *c.* 500m north of the settlement of Sindi-Lodja III (Figure 26.1): the settlement site was discovered in 2002, however no excavations have been taken place so far. According to the shore displacement chronology, the settlement site can be dated to between 3980 and 3230 cal BC (Jussila and Kriiska 2004, 13), i.e. the Early Neolithic.

Natural environment

The area of the lower reaches of the River Pärnu was cleared of the continental glacier relatively late. A few kilometres north of the area under discussion there is a zone of marginal eskers – the glacial marginal formation that developed just before 11,000 cal BC (Veski 1998, 71; Kriiska and Tvauri 2002, 19). Several large ice lakes were formed in lower south-western Estonia during this period, later becoming parts of the Baltic Ice Lake in the Baltic Sea basin (Raukas 1997, 268 ff.).

The area joined the mainland for the first time approximately 9600 cal BC, when the Baltic Ice Lake opened into the Atlantic (Andrén *et al.* 1999, 369). A new developmental stage of the Baltic was begun, the so-called Yoldia Sea, which is characterised by a lowering of the water level by 25 metres (Veski *et al.* 2005, 82). The ancient River Pärnu broke through, gaining an access to the sea roughly above the present riverbed. A new area of land was gradually covered by vegetation typical to the Preboreal chronozone, dominated by forests of birch (*Betula*) and pine (*Pinus*) (Veski *et al.* 2005, 80).

After the interruption of the connection between the Baltic and Atlantic about 9000 cal BC, the water level started to rise again, leading to a new phase, the so-called Ancylus Lake. The shoreline of the area under discussion, at the time of maximum transgression, was around 14–15m higher than the present sea level (Veski *et al.* 2005, figure 1) (Figure 26.4).

This stage was followed by a new regression, and the water could well have fallen below its present-day sea level (Veski *et al.* 2005, 83). During the contemporary Boreal chronozone, the sandy soils around the lower reaches of the River Pärnu were mainly covered by pine forests, although alder (*Alnus*) was also present (Veski *et al.* 2005, 80).

Water levels rose again at the beginning of the Litorina

Sea phase, thus inundating once more extensive areas of south-western Estonia. However the sea did not reach as far inland now as it had during the previous overwhelming transgression phase, remaining some 8–10m higher than present-day sea level at *c.* 4500 cal BC (Jussila and Kriiska 2004, 13, 23) (Figure 26.4). This was the final extensive, long-term inundation, and since then the sea has, in the main, only retreated. Broad-leaved trees dominated in the contemporaneous Atlantic chronozone, and dense forests, rich in species, were formed; at the same time, the new, sandy landscape, recently drained of seawater, was most probably covered by pine (Rõuk 1992; Veski 1998).

Settlement

As with most Stone Age settlement sites discovered in the eastern Baltic, the sites of south-western Estonia are also located on the shores of ancient water-bodies. The Early Mesolithic dwelling site at Pulli was situated on the ancient Pärnu River, a few kilometres upstream from the Ancylus Lake. The lower part of the cultural layer was a typical molli-eutric gley soil, suggesting that the site of the settlement may have had a seasonally increased risk of inundation. From the relatively scanty find material (cultural artefacts and fish bones) and the general character of the soil, it can be assumed that Pulli was a seasonal hunting and fishing camp. It was likely to have been inhabited repeatedly in summers (Raukas *et al.* 1995, 121–2), but the animal remains also testify to hunting in winter and spring (Lõugas 2008).

In the case of Sindi-Lodja I and II, dwelling sites were situated on the shore of the ancient River Pärnu, relatively close to the estuary that flows into the Litorina Sea. Judging from the animal bones, one may assume that the sites were inhabited, at least, in spring – the best time for taking ringed seal (*Phoca hispida*) and pike-perch (*Sander lucioperca*) – although the choice of location and general Late Mesolithic contexts might even justify the assumption of year-round base camps.

For the spans of their main inhabitation periods, the Sindi-Lodja III settlement was probably situated on the peninsular, and Jõekalda on the island that separated a small lagoon from the Litorina Sea. Numerous bone finds from ringed seals demonstrate that the locations were inhabited at least during the early spring, when the species breeds on the ice, or in late summer/autumn, when it makes feeding forays in the bays and rivers. The intensive cultural layers, rich in finds, as well as the diversity of artefacts and size and location of the dwelling sites, could also be evidence for year-round base camps.

Lithic raw materials

Flint is the prevalent rock at all the Mesolithic settlement sites along the lower reaches of the Pärnu. At the Pulli settlement site the majority of the flint is of high quality, often (brownish) black, more seldom grey in colour (Jaanits 1989, 32). There are no clear indications of the rock's origin, or concentration areas. It is considered mostly to originate from southern Lithuania, Belorussia, or the Ukraine (Jaanits *et al.* 1982, 32; Koltsov and Žilin 1999, 62; Lisitsyn 2003, 45), but similar material was also widely distributed in Poland (Sulgastowska 1989, 237), southern Scandinavia (Herforth and Albers 1999, figure 1), and the upper reaches of the Volga in Russia (Zhilin 1997, 331). Despite the plethora of possibilities, the most likely sources of the flint are Lithuania and Belorussia.

This type of flint is comparatively widely distributed throughout Early Mesolithic Post-Swidrian cultural groups. The most northerly finds have been collected in Finland (Takala 2004, 107 ff.; Jussila *et al.* 2006, 53). In the east, this material is only known from central Russia (Koltsov and Žilin 1999, 62). In the eastern Baltic, the flint occurs most commonly in Lithuania, however only single finds are known from Early Mesolithic Latvian settlement sites and from Estonian Mesolithic settlement locations (Jaanits 1989, 13, 32; Kriiska 2001a, 24–5).

Regarding settlement dates from Latvia, Estonia and Finland, one may assume that the greater quantities of flint there reached these territories over a relatively short period in Early Mesolithic times. However, the present data suggests that there were exceptions at the settlement sites of Sindi-Lodja, where flint was more frequently used during the second half of the Mesolithic. At present it remains unclear whether the flint was imported simultaneously from its source, or whether we are dealing with secondary usage. In the latter case, the rock derives from some Early Mesolithic cultural layers from the lower reaches of the Pärnu.

A percentage of the reddish flint found at Pulli might originate from the upper Volga, in Russia. During the Mesolithic, some flint from this region found its way into certain areas of the Baltic Sea. Single finds are known from Mesolithic settlement sites in Estonia (Kriiska *et al.* 2004, 44), as well as the Carelian Isthmus and Finland.

A relatively important flint assemblage from the settlement sites of the lower reaches of the Pärnu is comprised of local Estonian flint. This was formed during the Paleozoic, particularly in the Silurian limestones (Jürgenson 1958; 1974). The quality of the local flint is not high, and the nodules are small. People used pebbles as a matter of routine, but flint was already also being extracted from Estonian limestone during the Mesolithic. From Estonian Late Mesolithic settlement sites only a few examples (1–20, less than 1%) of 'southern' (non-local) flint artefacts have been found. Sindi-Lodja I and II have revealed only a few more.

By the time typical 'comb ware' was in use, the whole area was dependent on imported Russian flint, although local flint was also used in the Pärnu area to some extent.

Flint industry

During the Stone Age, several changes occurred in flint-working practices. The first major difference is in the ratio of flake and blade technique. In the oldest site, Pulli, the percentages of blades, blade fragments, artefacts made of blades and their fragments, as well as blade cores, are more than double those of the younger settlement sites (Figure 26.5). The blades were detached by both soft and hard stone percussion, but pressure flaking and even indirect percussion techniques were also used.

The bipolar flaking technique dominated in the Neolithic: in the assemblages from Sindi-Lodja III, the majority of cores, as well as flakes and microblades (in as much as the technological features are identifiable), are all made by the process of bipolar flaking. There are scarce examples of platform flaking, and both hard and soft percussion techniques were used.

Significant differences appear in the artefacts produced from secondary processing. Quantities of these at Pulli are more than double those seen in the settlements of Sindi-Lodja (Figure 26.6). This probably results from the practice of manufacturing most of the artefacts elsewhere and importing them to Pulli, where they were used and discarded; working of local stone was probably rather restricted. Stones were worked continuously at the settlements of Sindi-Lodja, and perhaps over a longer period.

Irrespective of the age of the settlement sites, a common feature is the abundance of scrapers (Figure 26.7). In the Early Neolithic, scrapers dominate the formally worked tools, while in the Mesolithic, retouched flakes and blades are also numerous. The latter includes many microblades or blade fragments that are totally absent from Sindi-Lodja III. An important trend presents itself in the percentages of burins: the highest quantities are found in the earliest settlement site, but they are not found at all in the latest. Arrowheads, or fragments of them, appear only in Early Mesolithic and Neolithic settlement sites. The Neolithic arrowheads were finished by bifacial retouching, but at Pulli only the tang, and to some extent the blade from one side of the face, were retouched.

Settlement site / Primary flaking technique	Pulli	Sindi-Lodja II	Sindi-Lodja III
Flake technique	59.9%	85.9%	83.9%
Blade technique	40.1%	14.4%	16.1%

Figure 26.5. Table showing relative distribution of flake and blade technique at settlement sites along the lower reaches of the River Pärnu within more representative flint material.

Animal bones and hunter-fisher-gatherer economy

The bone material from Pulli is well preserved. The composition of animal species is typical of the hunter-fisher-gatherer economy (Figure 26.8). The dominance of elk (*Alces alces*) and beaver (*Castor fiber*) remains is characteristic for faunal assemblages from the European forest zone during the Preboreal period. However, bones of wild boar (*Sus scrofa*) and roe deer (*Capreolus capreolus*) are also present, indicating already the arrival of early Boreal climatic conditions at that time. In addition, a somewhat warmer climate may be presupposed as pike-perch remains are represented at Pulli. Of the bird bones, divers (*Gavia* sp.) predominate but black grouse (*Tetrao tetrix*) and long-tailed duck (*Clangula hyemalis*) have also been identified (Lõugas 2008).

The bone material from Sindi-Lodja I differs to some extent from the Pulli finds. Significantly, quantities of beaver bones are very small, and also the volumes of elk and wild boar remains are low, or they were so fragmentary that it was impossible to identify them. At the same time, ringed seal is well represented in terms of bone finds, indicating the growing importance of seal hunting in coastal areas. Pike-perch bones were in evidence – an important fish species for Pärnu Bay dwellers throughout the millennia. In addition, both perch (Perca) and pike (*Esox lucius*) remains have been recovered.

The bone material from the settlement site at Sindi-Lodja III contained only small fragments of animal bones, and these were burnt and broken. As was the case with the bones

Settlement site / Artefacts with secondary processing	Pulli		Sindi-Lodja II		Find material from Sindi-Lodja III (2004)	
Artefacts with secondary processing among flint finds	12.3%	273	5.9%	18	4.6%	19
Retouched blades and flakes among flint artefacts	38.1%	104	44.4%	8	15.8%	3
Scrapers among flint artifacts	30.8%	84	44.4%	8	78.9	15
Burins among flint artifacts	20.9%	57	5.6%	1	0%	0
Arrowheads among flint artefacts	6.6%	18	0%	0	5.3%	1

Figure 26.6. Table showing relative distribution of artefacts with secondary processing at settlement sites along the lower reaches of the River Pärnu within more representative flint material.

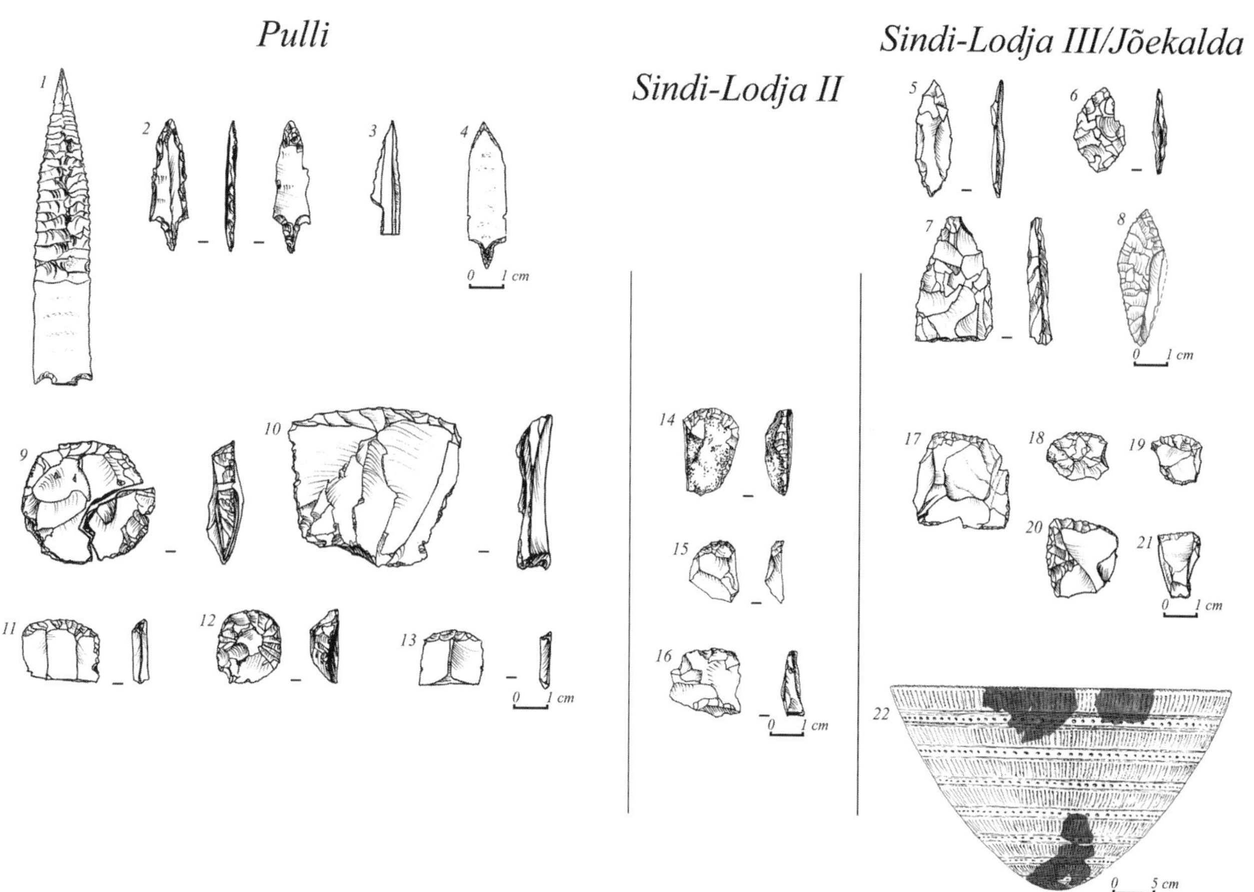

Figure 26.7. Typical artefacts from Stone Age sites along the lower reaches of the River Pärnu River: 1–8) Flint arrowheads (AI 4476: 355, 199, 432, 110, PäMu A 2561: 784, 1493, 1565, PäMu A 2565: 1); 9–21) Flint scrapers (AI 4476: 696/699, 100, 1159, 890, 784, PäMu A 2554: 129, 28, 144, PäMu A 2561: 639, 1565, 346, 65); 22) Reconstruction of typical 'comb ware' (PäMu A 2561: 5, 416, 495, etc.). (Drawings: Kristel Külljastinen).

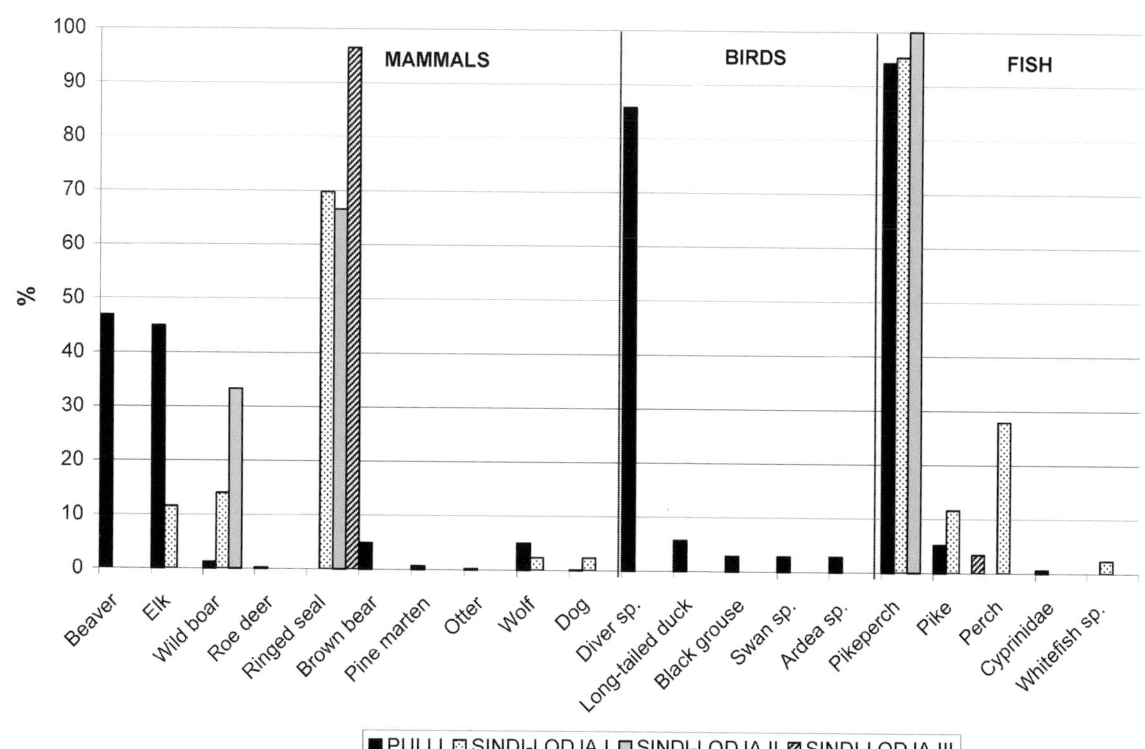

Figure 26.8. Animal remains (relative percentages of NISP) from Pulli, Sindi-Lodja I, Sindi-Lodja II and Sindi-Lodja III.

from Sindi-Lodja I, the finds from Sindi-Lodja III mainly consist of seal material. Even though the exact species of seal have not always been identified because of the poor preservation conditions (in the sandy soil), it is clear that most, if not all, come from ringed seal.

Early Mesolithic hunting seems to have been limited to game species of terrestrial or semi-aquatic origin, while Late Mesolithic and Early Neolithic communities were orientated towards seal hunting. Although ringed seal may be trapped in coastal zones, and even in rivers and lakes at certain times of the year, we cannot exclude the possibility of winter-hunting, on ice, far from the shore. This is evident when analysing the habitation remains on those islands that are quite some distance from the mainland (i.e. Saaremaa and Hiiumaa) (Lõugas 1997a; 1997b; Kriiska 2001b). However, at sites such as Sindi-Lodja, the hunting of ringed seal could have taken place close to the river estuary. (There is no Stone Age evidence of island rookeries, only human habitation remains (seal hunters' camps), where seal bones have been preserved.)

Fishing during the Mesolithic and Early Neolithic was centred on the exploitation of local waters: for millennia pike perch were fished in the estuary and bay of the Pärnu River.

The ecotonal zone of the shorelines provided a variety of resources, a suitable environment, and the opportunity to continue moving along forest borders and bodies of water, and was actively utilized by Mesolithic and Early Neolithic people when selecting habitation sites. Game, aquatic animals, birds, and fresh water were obtained from these places. Gradually the coastline and offshore islands were settled, and local dependence on terrestrial game often diminished.

Conclusions

In south-western Estonia, where Postglacial isostatic uplift was relatively slow, and the relief flat, the Baltic's periodic regressions (three) and transgressions (two) have had an especially strong effect over the last 11,500 years. As a result of theses fluctuations, Stone Age human habitation in the area under discussion has also been cyclical. This is especially vividly expressed in the lower reaches of the River Pärnu.

In the Early Mesolithic, a seasonal dwelling site was probably situated on the bank of the river, several kilometres from the Ancylus Lake in the Baltic Sea Basin; later settlements were placed closer to the coast. The movement towards an increased dependence on the sea is also apparent in the economy – in the Late Mesolithic, in addition to terrestrial species, marine mammals were also hunted. The contact areas of several habitat types were exploited, wherever favourable living conditions produced a richer, more varied biota than could be found in the surrounding areas. Salinity in the Baltic during the Litorina Sea stage increased, which also augmented the marine biomass, and hence seal populations at the upper end of food chain. These new conditions were exploited by inhabitants of the coastal areas during the Late Mesolithic and Neolithic. As for local resources, these locations were suitable for the establishment of year-round base camps, of which the settlement sites at Sindi-Lodja are probably examples.

The majority of the flint used during the Early Mesolithic originated 500km to the south; local flint predominated during the Late Mesolithic, and during the Early Neolithic a significant percentage of the raw material was obtained from less than 500km to the east. A decrease in blade technique over time, the prevalence of bipolar flaking in the Early Neolithic, as well as the use of bifacial retouch for arrowheads during the Early Neolithic, represent significant changes in the flint industry.

Acknowledgements

The archaeological fieldwork in south-western Estonia (grant numbers 3332, 4558 and 5328) and the analyses of animal bones (grants 5098 and 6899), have been supported by the Estonian Science Foundation. Tartu University's science project, 'Interdisciplinary archaeology: the past interactions of culture and history', and the science-funding project of the Institute of History, University of Tallinn (number 0042476s03), also contributed towards the research reported in this paper.

References

Andrén, T., Björck, J. and Johnsen, S. 1999. Correlation of Swedish glacial curves with the Greenland (GRIP) oxygen isotope record. *Journal of Quaternary Science* 14 (4), 361–71.

Bronk Ramsey, C. 2005. OxCal 3.10. WWW program and documentation available at http://www.rlaha.ox.ac.uk/oxcal/oxcal.htm (accessed 10/2007).

Burenhult, G. (ed.) 1999. *Arkeologi i Norden* 1. Stockholm, Natur och kultur.

Herforth, A. and Albers, H. J. 1999 (1980). Geologische Grundlagen des Feuersteinbergbaus in Europa, in G. Weisgerber, R. Slotta and J. Weiner (eds.), *5000 Jahre Feuersteinbergbau. Die Suche nach dem Stahl der Steinzeit* (= *Veröffentlichungen aus dem Deutschen Bergbau-Museum Bochum* 77, 14–20). First edition, Bochum, Deutsches Bergbau-Museum.

Jaanits, K. 1989. *Кремневый инвентарь стоянок кундаской культуры* (Kremnevyi inventar' stoyanok kundaskoi kul'tury). Диссертация на соискание ученой степени кандидата исторических наук kundaskoi kul'tury (Dissertatsiya na soiskanie uchenoi stepeni kandidata istoricheskih nauk). Unpublished dissertation in the archives of the Institute of History, Tallinn.

Jaanits, L. and Jaanits, K. 1975. Frühmesolithische Siedlung in Pulli. *Eesti NSV Teaduste Akadeemia Toimetised. Ühiskonnateadused* 24 (1), 64–70.

Jaanits, L. and Jaanits, K. 1978. Ausgrabungen der frühmesolithischen Siedlung von Pulli. *Eesti NSV Teaduste Akadeemia Toimetised. Ühiskonnateadused* 27 (1), 56–63.

Jaanits, L., Laul, S., Lõugas, V. and Tõnisson, E. 1982. *Eesti esiajalugu*. Tallinn, Eesti Raamat.

Jussila, T., Kriiska, A. and Rostedt, T. 2006. Varhaismesoliittisesta asutuksesta Koillis-Savossa – alustavia tuloksia Juankosken Akonpohjan Helvetinhaudanpuron asuinpaikan kiviaineistosta, in P. Pesonen and T. Mökkönen (eds.), *Arkeologiapäivät 2005*, 50–61. Helsinki, Suomen Arkeologinen Seura.

Jürgenson, E. 1958. О кремневых образованиях в ордовикских и силурийских карбонатных породах Эстонской ССР (O kremnevyh obrazovaniyah v ordovikskih I siluriiskih karbonatnyh porodah Estonskoi SSR). *Eesti NSV Teaduste Akadeemia Geoloogia Instituudi uurimused* II, 87–93.

Jürgenson, E. 1974. Распределение аутиенного кремнезема в силурийских отложениях Прибалтики. (Raspredelenie autennogo kremnezema v siluriiskih otlizheniyah Pribaltiki). *Eesti NSV Teaduste Akadeemia Toimetised*. Keemia. Geoloogia 23 (4), 322–31.

Jussila, T. and Kriiska, A. 2004. Shore displacement chronology of the Estonian Stone Age. *Estonian Journal of Archaeology* 8 (1), 3–32.

Koltsov, L. V. and Žilin, M. G. 1999. *Мезолит Волго-Окского междуречья. Памятники бутовской культуры* (*Mezolit Volgo-okskogo mezhdurech'ya. Pamyatniki butovskoi kul'tury*). Moscow, Nauka.

Kriiska, A. 2001a. Archaeological field work on Stone Age settlement site of SW Estonia, in Ü. Tamla (ed.), *Archaeological field works in Estonia 2000*, 19–33. Tallinn, Historic Preservation Department.

Kriiska, A. 2001b. *Stone Age Settlement and Economic Processes in the Estonian Coastal Area and Islands*. Academic Dissertation, University of Helsinki.

Kriiska, A., Haak, A., Johanson, K., Lõhmus, M., Vindi, A. 2004. Uued kiviaja asulakohad ajaloolisel Viljandimaal. *Viljandi Muuseumi aastaraamat*, 35–51.

Kriiska, A., Johanson, K., Saluäär, U. and Lõugas, L. 2003. The results of research of Estonian Stone Age, in Ü. Tamla (ed.), *Archaeological field works in Estonia 2000*, 25–41. Tallinn, Historic Preservation Department.

Kriiska, A., Saluäär, U., Lõugas, L., Johanson, K. and Hanni, H. 2002. Archaeological excavations in Sindi-Lodja, in Ü. Tamla (ed.), *Archaeological field works in Estonia 2001*, 27–40. Tallinn, Historic Preservation Department.

Kriiska, A. and Tvauri, A. 2002. *Eesti muinasaeg*. Tallinn, Avita.

Lisitsyn, S. N. 2003. *Проблемы разделения смешанных комплексов финального палеолита и мезолита Двинско-Ловатского междуречья. Древности Подвинья: исторический аспект. По материалам груглого стола, посвященного памяти А. М. Микляева (6-8 октября 1999)* (*Problemy razdeleniya smeshannyh kompleksov final'nogo paleolita i mezolita Dvinsko-Lovatskogo mezhdurech'ya. Drevnosti Podvin'ya: istoricheskii aspect. Po materialam gruglogo stola, posvjashchennogo pamyati A. M. Miklyaeva (6-8 oktyabrya 1999)*), 40–7. Saint Petersburg, Izdatel'stvo Gosudarstvenogo Ermitazha.

Lõugas, L. 1997a. Subfossil seal finds from archaeological coastal sites in Estonia, east part of the Baltic Sea. *Anthropozoologica* 25/26, 699–706.

Lõugas, L. 1997b. *Postglacial development of vertebrate fauna in Estonian water bodies: a palaeozoological study*. Dissertationes Biologicae Universitatis Tartuensis 32. Tartu, Tartu University Press.

Lõugas, L. 2008. Mõnedest mesoliitilistest faunakompleksidest Läänemere idakaldalt. *Muinasaja teadus* 17, 253–62. Tallinn, University of Tallinn.

Raukas, A. 1997. Evolution of the Baltic Sea, in A. Raukas and A. Teedumäe (eds.), *Geology and mineral resources of Estonia*, 268–74. Tallinn, Academy of Estonia.

Raukas, A., Moora, T. and Karukäpp, R. 1995. Läänemere arengust ja inimasustusest Pärnu ümbruses, in L. Ainsaar and K. Kirsimäe (eds.), *Liivimaa geoloogia*, 119–23. Tartu, Tartu Ülikool.

Raukas, A., Moora, T. and Karukäpp, R. 1999. The Development of the Baltic Sea and Stone Age Settlement in the Pärnu Area of Southwestern Estonia, in U. Miller, T. Hackens, V. Lang, A. Raukas and S. Hicks (eds.), *Environmental and Cultural History of the Eastern Baltic Region*, 15–34. PACT 57. Rixensart, PACT.

Reimer, P. J., Baillie, M. G. L., Bard, E., Bayliss, A., Beck, J. W., Bertrand, C. J. H., Blackwell, P. G., Buck, C. E., Burr, G. S., Cutler, K. B., Damon, P. E., Edwards, R. L., Fairbanks, R. G., Friedrich, M., Guilderson, T. P., Hogg, A. G., Hughen, K. A., Kromer, B., McCormac, G., Manning, S., Bronk Ramsey, C., Reimer, R. W., Remmele, S., Southon, J. R., Stuiver, M., Talamo, S., Taylor, F. W., van der Plicht, J. and Weyhenmeyer, C. E. 2004. IntCal04 terrestrial radiocarbon age calibration, 0–26 cal kyr BP. *Radiocarbon* 46 (3), 1029–58.

Rõuk, A.-M. 1992. Looduslikud olud hilisjääajast tänapäevani. *Eesti talurahva ajalugu* 1, 16–41.

Sulgostowska, Z. 1989. *Prahistoria międzyrzecza Wisły, Niemna I Dniestru u schyłku plejstocenu*. Warsaw, Institute of Archaeology and Ethnology.

Takala, H. 2004. *The Ristola Site in Lahti and the Earliest Postglacial Settlement of South Finland*. Jyväskylä, Gummerus.

Veski, S. 1998. Vegetation history, human impact and palaeogeography of West Estonia. Pollen analytical studies of lake and bog sediments. *Striae* 38.

Veski, S., Heinsalu, A., Klassen, V., Kriiska, A., Lõugas, L., Poska, A. and Saluäär, U. 2005. Early Holocene coastal settlements and palaeoenvironment on the shore of the Baltic Sea at Parnu, southwestern Estonia. *Quaternary International* 130 (1), 75–85.

Zhilin, M. G. 1997. Flint raw material from the Upper Volga basin and its use in the Final Palaeolithic-Neolithic, in R. Schild and Z. Sulgostowska (eds.), *Man and Flint. Proceedings of the VIIth International Flint Symposium. Warszawa – Ostrowiec Świętokrzyski, September 1995*. Warsaw, Institute of Archaeology and Ethnology.

27. Automating the extrapolation of sea-level displacement curves: implications for Mesolithic research in western Norway

David N. Simpson

The focus of this contribution is the presentation of a spreadsheet that simplifies the process of extrapolating sea-level displacement curves for a region in western Norway. This is an implementation of research conducted by geologists at the University of Bergen, and has been used with regard to archaeological survey and excavation projects. The spreadsheet also facilitates prehistoric landscape reconstructions, with significant implications for locating Mesolithic sites, including transgressed and currently submerged sites.

Keywords: shorelines, sea-level curves, postglacial, Mesolithic archaeology, western Norway.

Introduction

In areas affected by postglacial sea-level fluctuations the ability to extrapolate sea-level displacement curves for any given place within a region can be of great value with regard to locating shore-bound archaeological sites. This is particularly so in the case of western Norway, where experience suggests that the majority of Mesolithic sites in the vicinity of the coast are shore-bound. Beyond this, extrapolated sea-level curves also facilitate prehistoric shoreline and landscape reconstructions, which can serve archaeological research in a variety of ways.

As early as the 1980s, two studies dealing with the sea-level history of western Norway were presented. These described sets of empirically derived sea-level curves, as well as separate methods for extrapolating local sea-level curves for any location across the regions involved. The first of these studies (Kaland 1984) described how to extrapolate sea-level curves along a 75km section of the coast near Bergen in the county of Hordaland (Figure 27.1). The second study (Svendsen and Mangerud 1987; cf. Bondevik, Svendsen and Mangerud 1998) addressed a larger region further north in the counties of Sunnmøre, Nordmøre and Sør-Trondelag, an area that stretches along more than 200km of the coast and extends some 170km inland from the outer coast (Figures 27.1 and 27.2). Extensive references have been made in the archaeological literature of western Norway to the empirically derived sea-level curves presented in these works. Unfortunately, however, archaeologists working in western Norway have, to a large degree, overlooked the fact that these works also describe how to extrapolate sea-level curves for any location in the regions involved.

In an attempt to rectify this situation the author prepared a set of spreadsheets (Simpson 2001; 2003a; 2003b) based on the methods and data presented in the noted works, which, in conjunction with a set of maps, allow

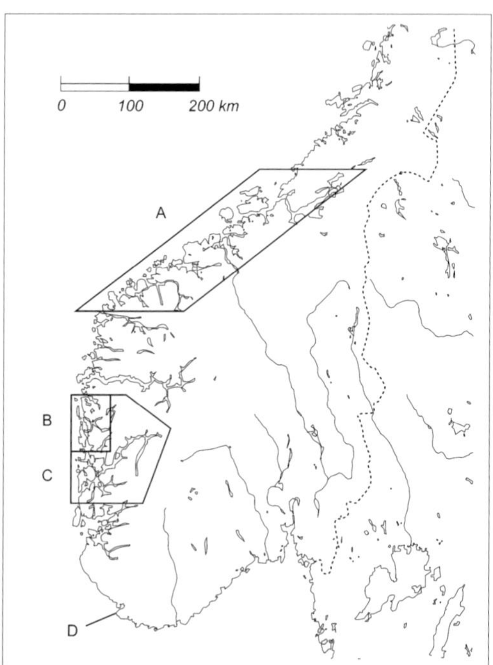

Figure 27.1. Southern Norway showing (A) the Sunnmøre, Nordmøre, Sør-Trondelag region, (B) the Bergen district, (C) the Bergen-Hardangerfjord region in the county of Hordaland, and (D) and Lista. (Map: Arkikon ANS, used with permission).

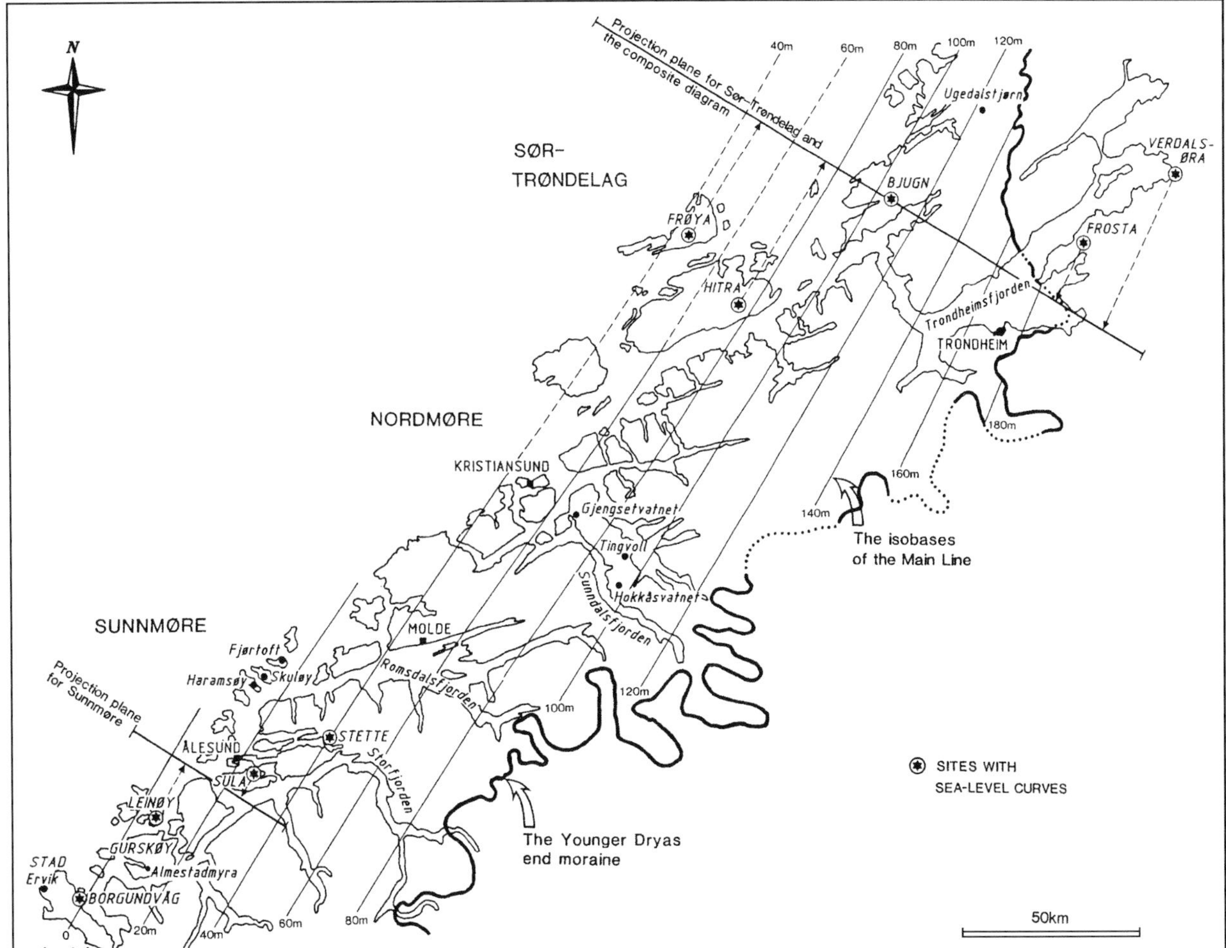

Figure 27.2. Younger Dryas isobases and locations with empirically derived sea curves in the Sunnmøre, Nordmøre, Sør-Trondelag region of western Norway. (Adapted from Svendsen and Mangerud 1987, 115).

one quickly and efficiently to derive sea-level curves for any location in these regions. In the case of the Hordaland study, a recent empirically derived sea-level curve from the region (Lohne, pers. comm.) suggests that the data and/or methodology used in this region should be re-examined before the spreadsheet is distributed for use. However, the spreadsheet for the northern area was distributed for use in 2001, and a revised version (which corrected an error in some of the resulting sea-level curves) was presented in 2003 (see discussion below). This latest spreadsheet has been successfully employed for a variety of purposes by archaeologists working in that region. This paper presents a brief background with regard to the methods and data on which the spreadsheet is based, provides examples and certain implications of its use, and addresses some of the perspectives being evaluated with regard to its future development.

Postglacial sea-level fluctuations: a brief background

Postglacial sea-level fluctuations are the result of a combination of factors, those most commonly addressed being isostatic rebound and eustatic sea-level rise. Isostatic rebound is the vertical movement of the earth's crust, resulting from decreased weight on the crust due to melting of the glacial ice. Eustatic sea-level rise is a rise in sea-level resulting from an increase in the volume of water in the ocean due to melting of glacial ice. Thus, as glacial ice melts, the underlying landmass rises, as does the level of the ocean as it fills with more water. However, these two processes do not proceed in perfect synchronization. In some periods isostatic rebound proceeds at a greater rate than eustatic sea- level rise, thus resulting in a lowering of the relative sea-level. In other periods eustatic sea-level rise is greater than isostatic rebound, resulting in a rise in the relative sea-level. Note that the sea-level fluctuations referred to in this paper are thus actually *relative* sea-level changes. The combination of these factors can lead to complex sea-level histories, which, as will be demonstrated below, can vary significantly across relatively short distances.

Extrapolating sea-level curves, data and methods

The background data and principles involved in extra-polating sea-level curves in the Sunnmøre, Nordmøre, Sør-Trøndelag region of western Norway will be described here.

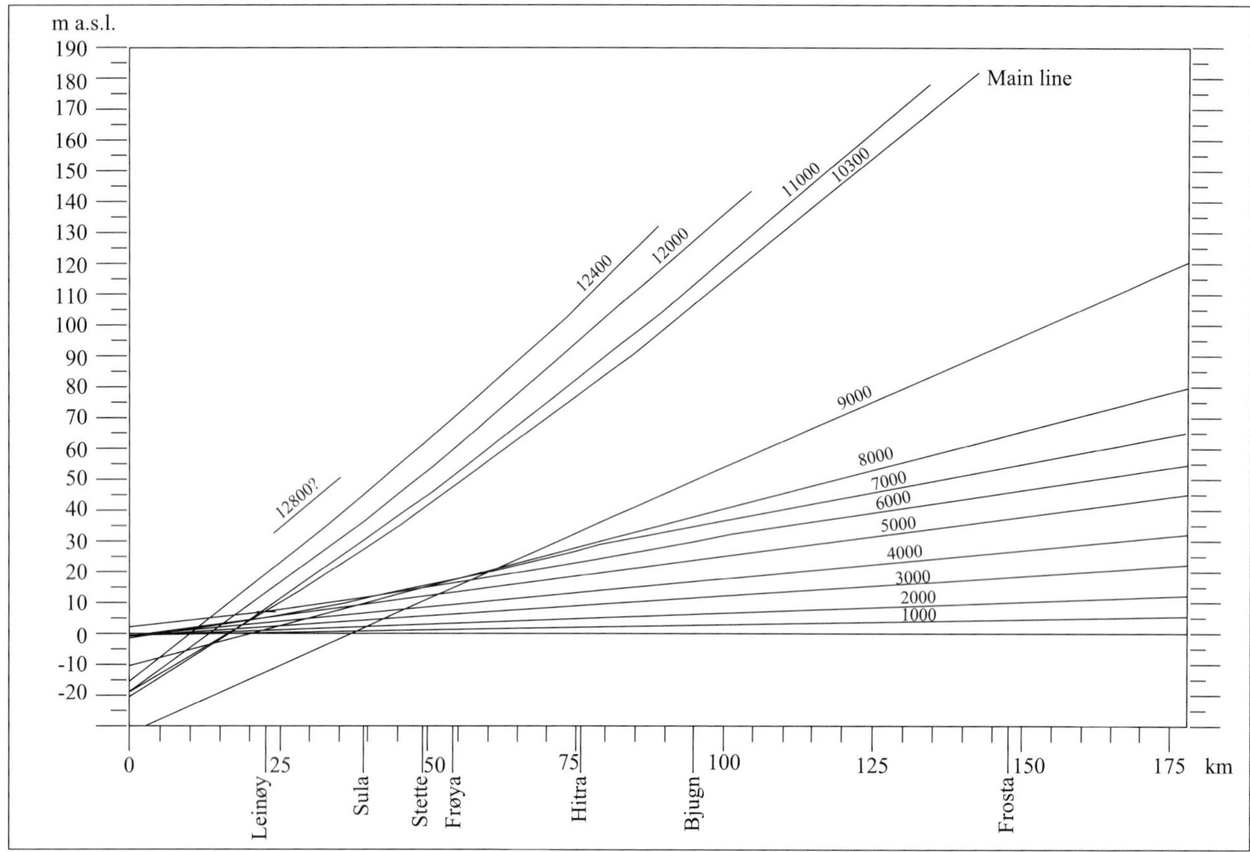

Figure 27.3. Shoreline diagram for Sunnmøre, Nordmøre and Sør-Trondelag. (Adapted from Svendsen and Mangerud (1987, 123) and modified on the basis of Bondevik et al. 1998).

This description draws upon the original study; however, inasmuch as space limitations require that the description be brief and somewhat over-simplified, the reader is referred to Svendsen and Mangerud's (1987) original study for a more thorough discussion. The extrapolations are based on a set of seven empirically derived sea-level curves (Leinøy, Sula, Stette Frøya, Hitra, Bjugn, and Frosta), as well as a set of isobases along which the sea-level changes are interpreted to be identical (Figure 27.2). The empirically derived sea-level curves rely for the most part on data previously published by other authors, although Svendsen and Mangerud (1987) did contribute some original data from the southern area of the region.

Each empirically derived sea-level curve was constructed according to the classical Scandinavian method, which involves stratigraphic analysis of a series of stepped basins (basins with thresholds at different elevations) that are located within a restricted area. The principle behind the method is that, in the late glacial period, a given basin was submerged in the ocean, and the sediments being deposited in it at that time were of a marine character. As the sea-level receded to the level of the basin's lowest threshold, the water in the basin became brackish, and this in turn was reflected in the sediments being deposited in the basin. As the sea-level receded further, the basin was flushed with fresh water, and this again was reflected in the sediments. If the sea-level later rose to the level of the basin's threshold then a new brackish sediment would have been deposited, and if the sea-level rose *above* the threshold a new marine sediment would have been deposited. Cores are extracted from the basin's sediment, thus allowing the identification of these stratigraphic transitions employing pollen and diatom analysis. By radiocarbon dating these transitions it is possible to track when the sea-level fell below, or rose above, the level of the basin's threshold. This type of analysis is then repeated at several nearby basins, basins that have thresholds at different elevations. The (threshold) elevation and age of each of the dated sea-levels are then plotted on an age-elevation diagram and a curve is drawn through the points. This curve thus describes the local sea-level history of that restricted area. In the case of the Sunnmøre, Nordmøre, Sør-Trøndelag study, this whole procedure was repeated at seven distinct 'localities' (restricted areas), yielding the set of seven empirically derived sea-level curves noted above.

The isobases referred to earlier were derived by an analysis of prehistoric beach ridges. Of the three well developed prehistoric shorelines along the west coast of Norway that are believed to have been deposited within relatively short time frames, only the Younger Dryas beach, which is dated to 10,300 BP and referred to as the Main Line, had been documented throughout the region (all dates are presented as uncalibrated radiocarbon years BP). Furthermore, this shoreline in particular was also

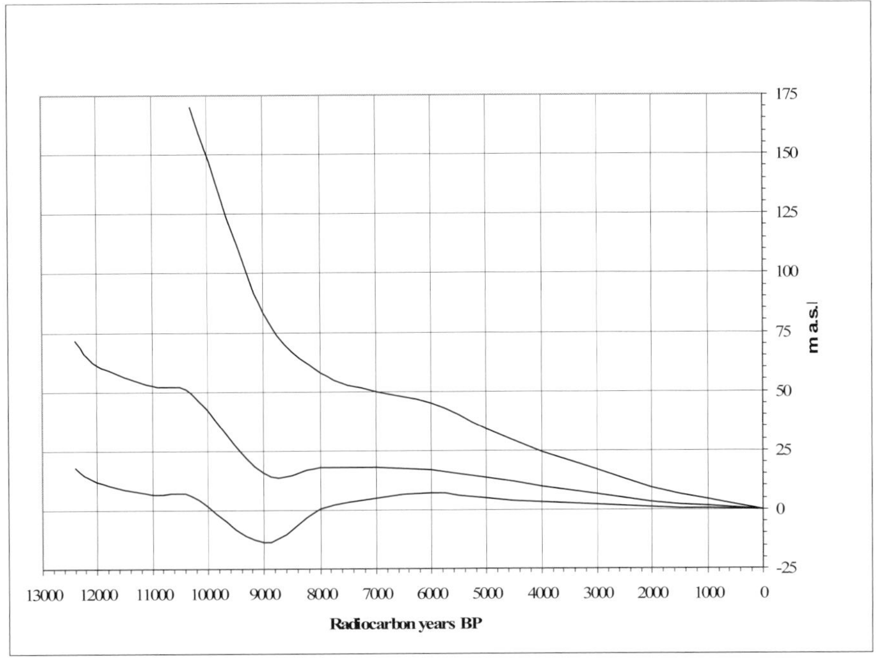

Figure 27.4. Sea-level curves for Trondheim (above), Molde (middle) and Leinøy (below).

understood to have been formed 'as a nearly synchronous shoreline' (Svendsen and Mangerud 1987, 116). By undertaking a surface-trend analysis of terraces along the Younger Dryas beach an isobase map (Figure 27.2) was constructed.

In order to employ these data (empirically derived sea-level curves and isobase map) to extrapolate sea-level curves, it is first necessary to condense key elements of the sea-level curves into a single shoreline diagram (Figure 27.3). In a shoreline diagram, data from the empirically derived sea-level curves is projected onto a distance-elevation plot, where the horizontal axis (distance) runs perpendicular to the isobases, and roughly depicts an axis from the outer coast to the inner fjord zone. The elevation axis represents sea-level displacement relative to the present sea-level. The elevation of the sea-level at selected time intervals is extracted from each of the sea-level curves, and these are plotted as a set of 'age lines' on the shoreline diagram. Each line thus depicts the amount of displacement from the outer coast to the inner fjords at a given point in time. It is noted that the description of the construction of the shoreline diagram under discussion here is somewhat over-simplified. The authors have in fact constructed one shoreline diagram for the southern part of the region (Sunnmøre) and combined it with data from the northern part of the region (Sør-Trondelag) in order to construct a composite shoreline diagram. The reader is referred to Svendsen and Mangerud (1987) for a more fully developed discussion.

Using the Shoreline Diagram

Given the shoreline diagram (Figure 27.3) and the isobase map (Figure 27.2) it is possible to extrapolate sea-level curves for any location in the region. The first step is to determine the 'elevation' of a given location with reference to the Younger Dryas (10,300 BP Main Line) isobases in Figure 27.2. As an example, the value for Trondheim can be estimated to be 170m. On the shoreline diagram, Figure 27.3, this elevation is located on the left axis, and a horizontal line is drawn across to where it meets the 10,300 BP Main Line. A vertical line is then drawn through this intersection. The elevations of the intersections of this vertical line with each of the 'age lines' then constitute the basis of the extrapolated sea-level curve for this location. The ages and elevations of these intersections are plotted on an age-elevation diagram, thus yielding the extrapolated sea-level curve for that location. Using the example of Trondheim, the value for 10,300 BP is 170m, the value for 9000 BP is 84m, the value for 8000 BP is 58m, and so on. The extrapolated sea-level curve for Trondheim is presented in Figure 27.5 (uppermost curve).

Using the Spreadsheet

After having extrapolated numerous sea-level curves in the manner described above, this author was struck by the fact that it would be a relatively simple matter to have a computer calculate the intersections described above and construct the sea-level curve automatically. To that end, the shoreline diagram was digitized, the formulas for each of the 'age lines' were calculated, and an Excel (© Microsoft) spreadsheet was prepared that would calculate the intersections, read off the critical age-elevation values, and automatically construct a sea-level curve (Simpson 2001; 2003a). Thus, by simply determining the Younger Dryas isobase elevation value of a location on the isobase map, and entering that value in the spreadsheet, a publication

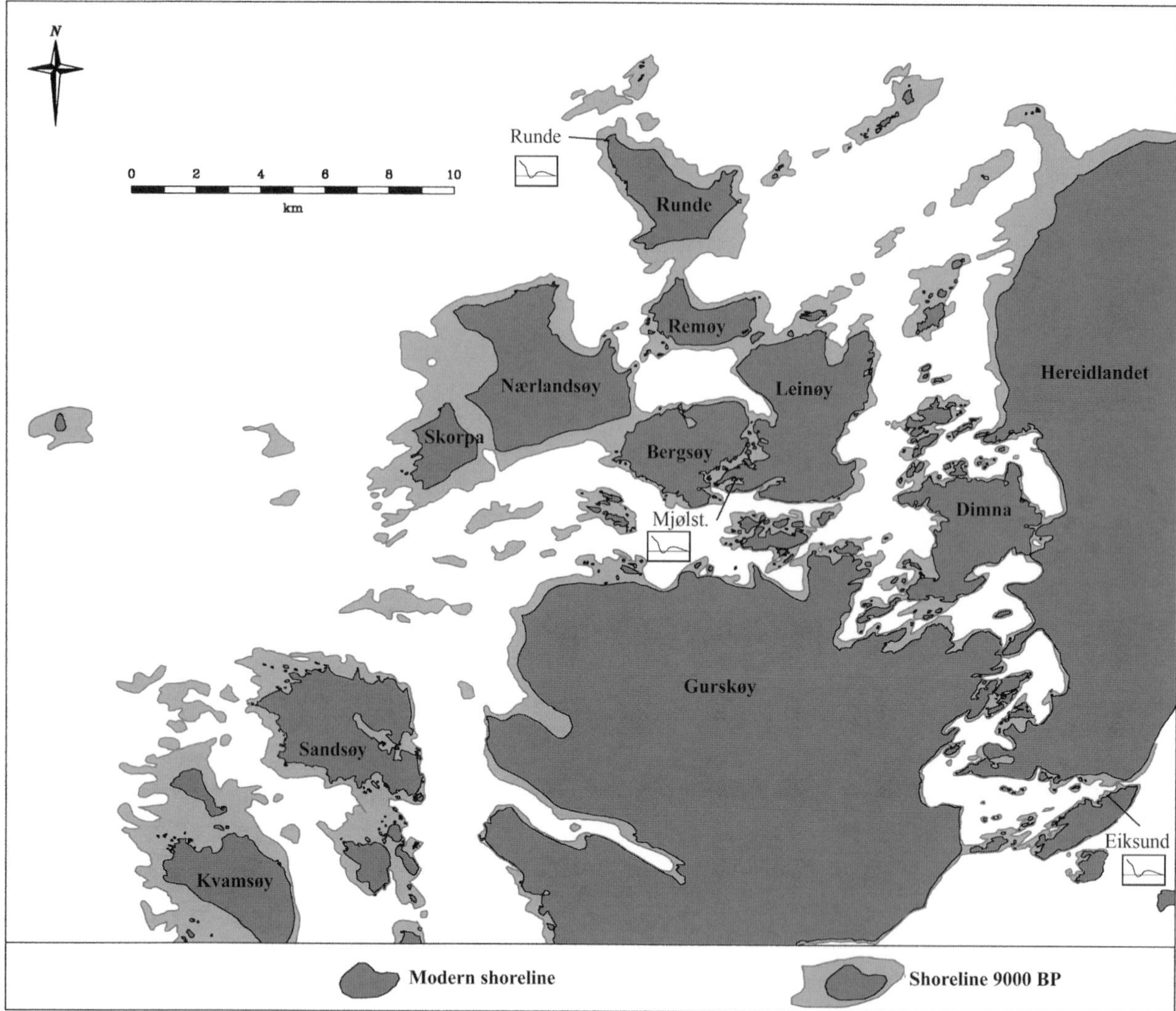

Figure 27.5. A portion of the outer island zone in Sunnmøre, showing a reconstruction of the 9000 BP shoreline. (Adapted from Series Q Small Craft Charts, 2002–3. Reproduced with permission from the Norwegian Hydrographic Service, permission no. 555/07).

quality sea-level curve for that location can be constructed in a matter of minutes. The use of a digitized version of the isobase map has simplified the process even further.

Examples of use and implications for Mesolithic archaeology

Given the observation that most of the Mesolithic sites in the vicinity of the coast in western Norway appear to be shore-bound (generally no more than perhaps 7 to 10m above the sea-level at the time of occupation), this spreadsheet and isobase map constitute invaluable tools for locating these sites. Should one, for example, wish to locate sites from approximately 9000 BP, one might be best served by surveying with regard to the elevation/location of the 9000 BP shoreline. Inspection of Figure 27.4 reveals that at Trondheim, in the inner fjord zone, the sea-level at that time was 84m above the present level, while at Molde it lies at 15m asl, and at Leinøy, in the outer island zone, that prehistoric shoreline is currently 13m *below* the current level. Without this information surveyors could conceivably waste significant amounts of time looking for these sites at locations/elevations where they either do not exist (below the indicated elevation), or where they are unlikely to exist (well above the indicated elevation).

These tools also facilitate landscape reconstructions, for given points in time, that can contribute to a better understanding of site location factors, or they may provide an explanation for the absence of sites of a certain age in a given area. In the case of one island group in the outer island zone of Sunnmøre, western Norway (Figure 27.5), extrapolated sea-level curves from the south-east of the area (Eiksund) indicate that sites from 9000 BP might be situated one to two meters below the present sea-level, whereas in the north-west of the area (Runde) sites from this period may currently be submerged by as much as 24m. The 9000 BP shoreline for this area has been reconstructed, and is presented in Figure 27.5. Inspection of the figure reveals that in certain locations this prehistoric shoreline lies, at present, as much as three kilometres offshore. Furthermore,

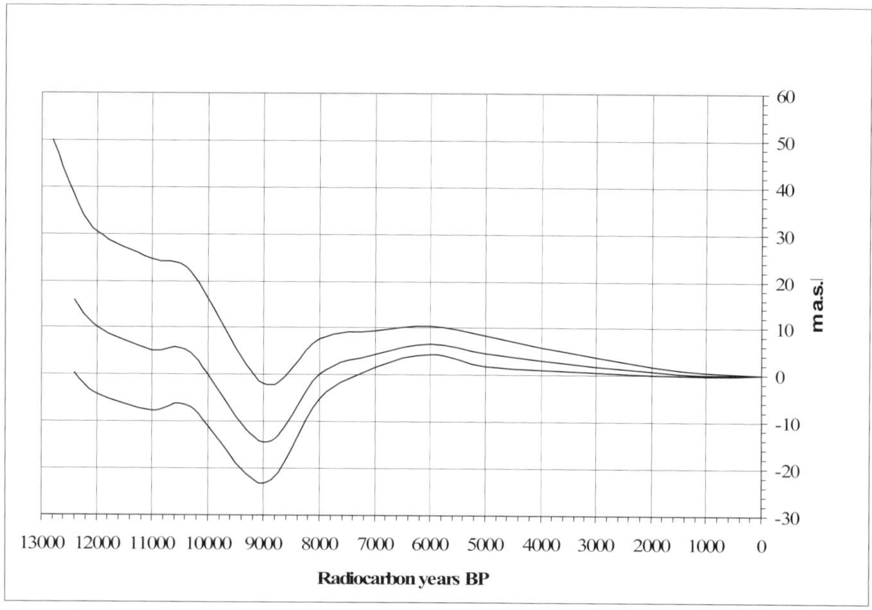

Figure 27.6. Sea-level curves for Runde (below), Mjølstadneset (middle) and Eiksund (above).

it is revealed that the group of islands consisting of Skorpa, Nærlandsøy, Bergsøy, Leinøy, Remøy, and Runde once constituted a single landmass that encompassed a large lagoon. That is to say, the geographic configuration of the landscape here has changed considerably, and the implications of this with regard to locating prehistoric sites, and to understanding why they might be situated where they are, are significant.

In order to illustrate how dramatically sea-level curves can differ over short distances, three sea-level curves from this outer island area are presented in Figure 27.6. The figure reveals not only the previously noted differences with regard to the 9000 BP regression minimum, but also that the level of the Tapes transgression maximum (6000 to 7000 BP) also varied significantly. Given the relative stability of the sea-level at each location during this transgression maximum, archaeologists in western Norway traditionally expect to find more sites than usual at, or about, the Tapes level. In the case of this island group, in the south-east of the area (Eiksund) this 'Tapes site concentration' can be expected at, or slightly above, 10m asl, while in the north-west (Runde) the Tapes level is approximately 5m asl. Note also that at this part of Runde, shore-bound sites that are younger than the Tapes maximum level are likely to be found in the active beach zone, and *all* shore-bound sites older than roughly 7500 BP are currently submerged. It is important to observe that the maximum distance involved in the preceding discussion of these sea-level curve differences in this island group is only 24km.

A final implication that will be addressed with regard to locating Mesolithic sites along the western Norwegian coast is the case of transgressed sites. As a result of the Tapes transgression many shore-bound sites have been submerged and damaged. This has left archaeologists in the region with a disturbing gap in their data for the period from approximately 9500 BP to the transgression maximum at 6000 to 7000 BP. However, not all of the sites from this period were damaged or destroyed by the rising level of the ocean. Some were sealed under Tapes-maximum beach ridges, and were preserved in virtually perfect condition. Given that these beach ridges lay at different elevations at different locations, and considering that they have, in many cases, been ploughed and damaged in connection with recent agriculture, these beaches and terraces are often difficult to locate. Compounded by the fact that the Tapes-maximum beach ridges themselves can be several metres thick, locating preserved sites beneath them can be notoriously difficult. In order to address this bias in the data of coastal Norway the only alternative this author can see is to employ tools such as those presented in this paper that allow one to locate and identify these prehistoric beaches, and to radically alter survey methods to include deep trenching through the beach deposits. Progress has been made in this regard in several areas of western Norway, but there is still a great deal of room for improvement.

Assumptions and Cautions

As with any body of research, there are a number of assumptions, problems and cautions which need to be addressed when extrapolating sea-level curves in this region. First and foremost, it should be stated that the reliability of the sea-level curves is difficult, if not impossible, to quantify. However, based on observations to date in connection with archaeological investigations in the southern area of the region (Sunnmøre), this author is satisfied that the Sunnmøre sea-level curves probably have a margin of error of no more than one, or perhaps two metres.

The reliability of the extrapolated sea-level curves is clearly dependent on the amount and quality of the data available at the time of the original analysis, as well as the correct interpretation of that data. As an example, after the original study was published it became apparent that an error had been made in the interpretation of certain basin sediments. What was initially interpreted to be a deposit related to the Tapes transgression maximum was later shown to be the result of an earlier tsunami. As a result, the extrapolated sea-level curves yielded a level for the Tapes transgression maximum that was two metres too high. A modified shoreline diagram for the area involved was published (Bondevik, Svendsen and Mangerud 1998) and these results have been incorporated in a revised version of this author's spreadsheet (Simpson 2003a). It is evident that future research may require additional modifications of the shoreline diagram and the spreadsheet.

With regard to the use of the shoreline diagrams and isobase maps generally, it should be stated that the method described assumes that the orientation of the isobases has remained stable through time. In the case of the study at hand, Svendsen and Mangerud (1987, 117) regard the isobases as having been 'approximately parallel' through time, however they consider it unlikely that they would have remained perfectly 'parallel in detail', over such a large region, through more than 12,000 years. It remains to be seen what impact such deviations might have on the extrapolated sea-level curves. In other areas where significant changes in the orientation of the isobases through time are understood to exist, it will be necessary to construct 3D shoreline diagrams (distance-elevation-time), in order reliably to extrapolate shoreline curves (Svendsen, pers. comm.).

An important factor regarding the sea-level curves extrapolated using this stepped-basin method is that the curves indicate average high-water levels, not average sea-level. This is because, during a regression, sediment transition dates from the basins, in combination with the basin threshold elevations, reflect roughly the last time seawater entered the basin. That is to say, as a result of wave action and tides, the last time seawater flowed into a basin during a regression was when the true average sea-level was actually slightly below the level of the basin's threshold. In a similar manner, during a transgression, the first time seawater entered a basin, the average sea-level was slightly below the elevation of the basin's threshold. One inconsistency in the extrapolated sea-level curves presented here, therefore, is that the curves are drawn down to 0 for the present date, when they should properly be drawn to a given location's average high-water level. This inconsistency has not been corrected because of the difficulties in determining the present-day average high-water levels for all locations across the region. This author has decided to accept this inconsistency for the purposes of convenience, but has notified users of the spreadsheet of the anomaly.

A final problem to be addressed, particularly with regard to the use of extrapolated sea-level curves during archaeological survey, is to what degree the Mesolithic sites along the coastal areas of western Norway were shore-bound – as has already been referred to earlier (and, incidentally, the observation is also of relevance for Early and Middle Neolithic sites). However, a recent study from Lista (southern Norway) questions the validity of this observation (Berg-Hansen 2001). This study presents the results of an intensive coastal region survey where numerous Stone Age sites were found that were *not* shore-bound. The inconsistencies between Berg-Hansen's (2001) results and those of archaeologists operating in western Norway remain unsatisfactorily explained at present. It is possible that site location factors at Lista were different from those in western Norway. Alternatively, it may be that there are many new sites waiting to be discovered in the near-shore zone in western Norway. A third option relates to the fact that in Berg-Hansen's (2001) survey area, the local sea-level curve indicates that all sites which once may have been shore-bound are currently submerged, or have been eroded. Therefore this study's near-shore data has no local shore-bound component to compare it with. In other words, there may be many more undocumented (now submerged) shore-bound sites at Lista than there are near-shore sites. If this is so, the results of this study do not necessarily conflict with the observation in western Norway that the *majority* of Mesolithic sites (as well as Early and Middle Neolithic ones) in the vicinity of the coast are shore-bound. In any event, this study raises issues that should be addressed by future research.

Future Directions

The most immediate action planned with regard to extrapolating sea-level curves in Sunnmøre, Nordmøre and Sør-Trøndelag is the development of online versions of the isobase map and shore-line diagram, so that it will be possible for a wider public to generate, automatically, sea-level curves for this region. An online solution will also simplify the process of updating the program package for all users, in the light of any new data which might require modifications of the shoreline diagram. Beyond this, geologists at the University of Bergen are currently collecting and analysing data that will soon enable reliable extrapolation of sea-level curves in the Bergen – Hardangerfjord region, in the county of Hordaland, western Norway (Figure 27.1). A resent study (Romundset 2005) provides the data necessary to extrapolate preliminary sea-level curves for Hardangerfjord. It is hoped that it will also be possible to develop an online computer application to extrapolate sea-level curves for this region in the near future. Finally, it is important to note the potential role that modern GIS systems can offer with regard to generating dynamic 3D landscape models of sea-level fluctuations through time; although real progress is being made in this area by several groups in Bergen, the full potential of GIS in terms of this application remains to be exploited.

Acknowledgements

I would like to thank John Inge Svendsen, Jan Mangerud, and Øystein Lohne of the ICEHUS group (Ice Age

Development and Human Settlement in Northern Eurasia) at the Department of Earth Science, University of Bergen, for their personal communications and many fruitful discussions. The ICEHUS group has graciously offered to finance the development of the online computer tools referred to in this paper.

References

Berg-Hansen, I. M. 2001. *Registrering som erfaring: En undersøkelse av metoden for steinalderregistrering i Norge med eksempel fra Lisa i Vest-Agder*. Unpublished Magister thesis, University of Oslo.

Bondevik, S., Svendsen, J. I. and Mangerud, J. 1998. Distinction between the Storegga Tsunami and the Holocene Marine Transgression in Coastal Basin Deposits of Western Norway. *Journal of Quaternary Science* 13 (6), 529–37.

Kaland, P. E. 1984. Holocene Shore Displacement and Shorelines in Hordaland, Western Norway. *Boreas* 13, 202–42.

Romundset, A. 2005. *Strandforskyvning og isavsmelting i midtre Hardanger*. Unpublished MA thesis, University of Bergen.

Simpson, D. N. 2001. *SeaLevelCurvesSunm-STrondelag_v.1.xls*. Spreadsheet for extrapolating sea-level curves in Sunnmøre, Nordmøre and Sør Trøndelag, Western Norway. (Available from the author).

Simpson, D. N. 2003a. *SeaLevelCurvesSunm-STrond_v2.xls*. Spreadsheet for extrapolating sea-level curves in Sunnmøre, Nordmøre and Sør Trøndelag, Western Norway. (Available from the author).

Simpson, D. N. 2003b. *SeaLevelCurvesHordaland_beta.xls*. Spreadsheet for extrapolating sea-level curves in a portion of Hordaland, Western Norway. (Available from the author).

Svendsen, J. I. and Mangerud, J. 1987. Late Weichselian and Holocene Sea-level History for a Cross-section of Western Norway. *Journal of Quaternary Science* 2, 113–32.

28. Shells, seals and ceramics: an evaluation of a midden at West Voe, Sumburgh, Shetland, 2004–5

Nigel D. Melton

Work carried out in 2004–5 on Late Mesolithic and Early Neolithic middens exposed by coastal erosion at West Voe, Sumburgh, Shetland, has provided the first evidence for coastal hunter-gatherers and for the Mesolithic-Neolithic transition in the Northern Isles of Scotland. Two middens were present, the earlier was dated to c. 4200–3600 cal BC and provided evidence of a sequence of targeted shellfish species, namely: oysters; limpets; mussels, as well as for the hunting of seal and seabirds. Quartz lithics and a small number of potsherds were recovered from this midden. The upper midden, which was deposited after a change in the coastal environment that was represented by a 0.5m-thick layer of sand, was dated to c. 3500–3300 cal BC. This midden butted a structure and was composed entirely of cockles, the majority of which were fragmented.

Keywords: Mesolithic, Mesolithic-Neolithic transition, Shetland, midden, oysters, seal, cockles.

Introduction - Background to the 2004–5 investigations at West Voe

In his account of his tour of Orkney and Shetland in 1774, the Reverend George Low describes a 'stratum' of large oyster shells that was to be found in the seabank at Sumburgh (Low 1978, 186–7). Low writes of spending a day digging in this layer and finding not only intact oysters (*Ostrea edulis*), some of which contained pearls, but also limpets (*Patella vulgata*) and cockles (*Cerastoderma edule*). He described the oysters as 'entirely fossil', commenting that no other living examples occurred within twenty miles of Sumburgh and considered them as representing an ancient oyster bed rather than midden material.

Despite Low's opinion that the layer represented an ancient oyster bed, it was decided to follow up this eighteenth-century reference. If the site proved to be a midden, then it was likely to be early in date as oysters were not recorded in the Bronze Age middens excavated at the Jarlshof site on the opposite side of West Voe (Hamilton 1956), and it seemed unlikely that such a rich local resource would have been ignored.

The Shetland Sites and Monuments Record (SSMR) contains an entry (No. 5625) that is described as a shell midden, apparently prehistoric in character, containing oysters, cockles and bones, but no artefacts, that was eroding out of the sand cliffs at West Voe, Sumburgh at grid reference HU 39181012. The SSMR entry described the midden as *c.* 0.75m thick and as extending about ten metres north-south. This entry had obvious similarities to Low's account, and, with this in mind, the site was visited in 2002 and some preliminary cleaning and sampling was carried out. This work revealed that there were actually two shell middens present. The lower of these overlay a thin, apparently natural, greasy black layer that in turn sealed glacial till and sandstone bedrock. Separated from this earlier midden by an approximately 0.5m-thick layer of sand was an upper midden that butted a dry-stone wall. A thick deposit of sterile dune sands sealed the archaeological layers and features.

Samples obtained from the lower midden revealed that it contained a range of marine molluscs (mainly oysters, but with smaller numbers of limpets, cockles and razor shells (*Ensis* spp.), and seal, seabird and cetacean bones (Melton and Nicholson 2004). A small sample obtained from the upper midden was found to be composed entirely of complete and fragmented cockles.

No pottery, lithics or other dating evidence was recovered from either midden, but the fact that the lower midden was located almost immediately above glacial deposits reinforced the earlier impression that it had the potential to be early in date, and scientific dating of the site was considered essential. An OSL (optically stimulated luminescence) date was obtained from the sand layer separating the two middens, together with radiocarbon dates from a shell from each of the middens (Melton and Nicholson 2004). The dates obtained, 4830±430 BC (OSL: X1461) from the sands, 4320–4030 cal BC (GU-11218) from the lower midden, and 3750–3520 cal BC (GU-11219) from the upper midden, indicated that the lower, oyster, midden was Late Mesolithic in date and, perhaps more unexpectedly, that the upper, cockle, midden dated to the Early Neolithic.

The site, therefore, was of considerable importance, both as the first of Mesolithic date to be found on the Northern Isles, and also as providing evidence of the Mesolithic–Neolithic transition in the region (Melton 2005). Prior to its discovery, the evidence for a Mesolithic presence in the Northern Isles had been restricted to finds of Mesolithic-type flints on Orkney and Fair Isle (Mithen 2000, 15; Saville 2000, 94), and to interpretations of pollen core evidence of vegetation changes on Shetland in the period 7500–5400 BP as being the result of the human introduction of grazing animals (Bennett *et al.* 1992, 241, 267; Bennett and Sharp 1993a, 18; Bennett and Sharp 1993b, 77; Edwards 1996, 29, 34). Furthermore, it had generally been assumed that any trace of Mesolithic coastal settlement that might have been present on the Shetland archipelago would have been lost to the rise in sea levels that has occurred over the past 6000 years. At Lerwick, radiocarbon dating of submerged peats has indicated a sea level rise of at least nine metres since *c.* 5500 BP (Mykura 1976, 110–11). (Unless indicated otherwise, cited radiocarbon dates in the text are as cited in the publications from which they come and are expressed in uncalibrated radiocarbon years before present (^{14}C BP).)

The 2004 investigations

Following confirmation of the midden dates, further work was carried out on the site in the summers of 2004 and 2005 (Figure 28.1). In 2004 a 7.5m section of the lower part of the cliff section, located to the north of, and partially incorporating, the section of the midden that had been examined in 2002, was cut back to expose a narrow strip of the lower midden. The 2004 section was positioned to permit examination of both the upper and lower middens, the wall that the former butted, any archaeology present to the north of the wall (Figure 28.2), and the apparent northern limit of the lower midden.

The strip of the lower midden exposed was divided into 0.5m sample blocks (Figure 28.3). These blocks were excavated in stratigraphic units, with 100% sampling of each context. The upper midden was column sampled, and a second column was cut for recording and sampling the lower two metres of the sequence of dune sands that sealed archaeological deposits.

A more complex and continuous archaeological sequence was revealed than had been recognised in 2002. It could now be seen that the lower midden had an internal stratification, particularly towards its northern edge. Lateral changes were also apparent in this midden. At the southern end of the section the midden consisted of a basal layer of oyster shells that had been pressed into the underlying black greasy layer and which was sealed by a mixed midden layer that contained a jumble of oysters, limpets and seal and seabird bones that was, in turn, sealed by a greasy black layer containing oysters and seal and seabird bones. This sequence extended as far as sample blocks 6 and 7, where the midden thinned considerably, the thinning coinciding with a change in natural from sandstone to glacial till. At the junction of the two types of natural there was an apparent 'cut feature' with vertical sides and a flat base that contained saturated coarse, angular gravel (Figure 28.2). There was no evidence for human activity in this gravel and it is possible that this feature is geological rather than archaeological in origin.

To the north of the 'cut feature' the midden thickened, achieving a maximum thickness of *c.* 0.3m in sample blocks 11–14. The sequence present in this part of the midden comprised: the basal oysters, again pressed into the underlying black greasy layer; a mixed layer containing limpets and seal and seabird bones, often occurring in groups or pockets and with occasional evidence for articulation (especially the bird bones); a thin activity surface of trampled and concreted mussels (*Mytilus edulis*); a greasy layer containing shells and bones.

The 2004 fieldwork season also revealed a number of linear features and pits cut into the sands that lay between the two middens (Figure 28.2). One pit that had cut through the lower midden in sample blocks 11 and 12 contained large stones and a thin deposit of cockles in its base. The other features present were two intersecting ditches (or possibly a ditch that had been recut) and a shallow pit. The ditches, each of which contained sandy fills with lenses of organic sand, were difficult to interpret, as they ran at acute angles to the line of the section. The shallow pit that formed the last in this series of features contained numerous cockles in the upper part of its fill and was sealed by the wall, the south face of which was butted by the cockle midden. The wall survived to a height of 0.6m, and, although its precise function remains uncertain, a second structural feature was noted, a vertical 0.1m-diameter stake hole, located 1.0m to the south of the wall. To the north of the wall there was a ground surface contemporary with the cockle midden. In the sands that butted the wall and sealed this ground surface was a layer of shells and fragmented shells (Figure 28.2), from which a cow tooth and a fragment of sheep skull were recovered. This latter layer represented the final evidence for human activity on the site and was sealed by more than six metres of sand.

The lateral extent of the middens was determined by taking column samples at points along the cliff section to the north and south of the main section and auger samples to the rear of it. The lower midden was found to extend approximately twenty metres north-south, its northern edge occurring in sample block 15 at the end of the section. It was not found in the auger samples and it appears that the coastal erosion is now exposing the last remnants of this midden. The upper midden was proved to extend more than four metres to the south of the wall and was located in an auger sample approximately five metres to the rear of the cliff face.

The 2005 investigations

On arrival on site in 2005 it was found that the severe storms of January 2005 had resulted in significant coastal

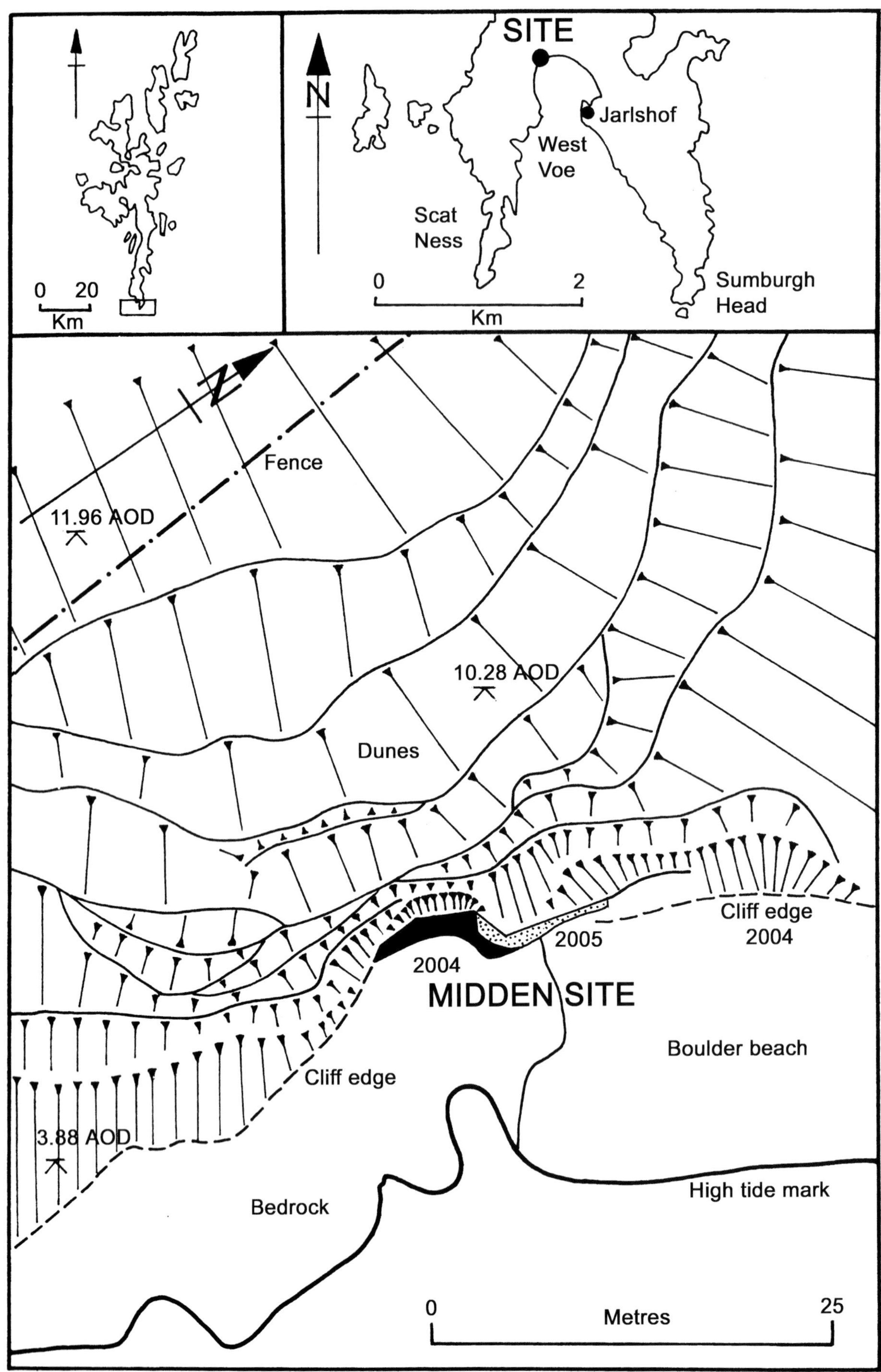

Figure 28.1. Location of the 2004–5 investigations at West Voe.

erosion. At the northern end of the 2004 section, where the midden sequence was thickest, up to 0.7m of erosion had occurred. Fortunately, although some midden deposits were lost (Figure 28.3), the bulk of the erosion was of the 'step' of natural left after removal of the midden and overlying deposits the previous summer.

In 2005 the fieldwork concentrated on the earlier midden. The aims were to look in more detail at the trampled activity surface and the northern edge of the midden, and to look for evidence of off-midden activity. A section that overlapped with, and extended to the north of, that investigated in 2004 was cut back to expose a further narrow strip of the midden and the ground surface to the north of it. Excavation methodology was the same as the previous year, with 0.5m sample blocks being excavated in stratigraphic units (Figure 28.3).

It was confirmed that the oyster and limpet/seal layers had a coincident northern edge in sample block 20, to the rear of the 2004 block 15. A small lens of uncrushed mussels in sample blocks 17 and 18 represented a final phase of midden use not seen in 2004. A sequence of thin organic lenses, containing mussels and occasional quartz debitage provided evidence of a northwards migration of human activity in the final phase of midden use. These lenses extended as far as sample block 25, at which point there was a band of trampled shells overlain by a small deposit of mussels.

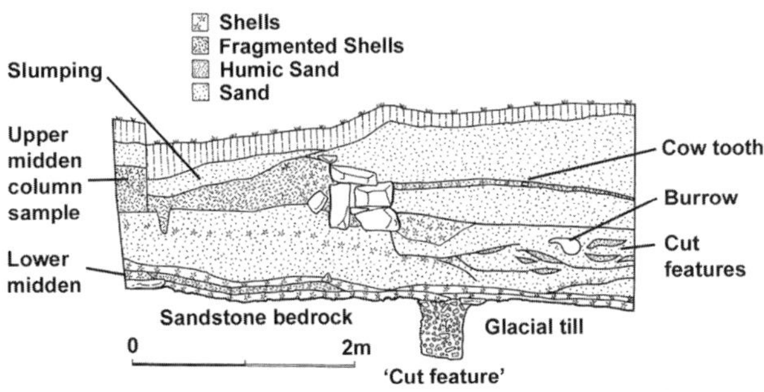

Figure 28.2. Elevation of the southern end of the 2004 section.

The economic evidence

Preliminary analyses of material recovered in 2004 (Nicholson 2005a; 2005b; Worley 2005) have shown that the lower, Late Mesolithic, midden contains a sequence of targeted species. Initially procurement was of large specimens of oysters; these were then superseded by limpet, seal (both common/harbour (*Phoca vitulina*) and grey (*Halichoeus grypus*) and including immature individuals) and marine birds (dominated by shag (*Phalacrocorax aristotalis*) but including eider duck (*Somateria mollissima*), mallard (*Anas platyrhynchos*), gannet (*Sula bassana*), large gull (probably greater black-backed (*Larus marinus*)) and puffin (*Fratercula artica*)). Mussel was the dominant species present in the final phase of midden use. In addition to the marine mammals, two rib fragments from large ungulates were recovered from the upper section of the lower midden.

The upper midden was composed entirely of cockles. These were generally fragmented, although there was a pocket of complete shells where the midden butted the wall. Many of the shells in this midden were discoloured, possibly the result of heating. Further evidence for the use of heat in processing the cockles was the discovery of minute fragments of hearth bottom slag in the dark matrix containing the shells (Blockley *et al.* 2005).

A range of seasonality evidence was obtained for the lower midden. The seal remains indicate that culling was occurring in summer (harbour seal pups) and late autumn (grey seal pups), whilst the marine birds present indicate spring-autumn collection (Nicholson, pers. comm.). Microanalysis of oyster shells (Milner 2005) indicates that those from blocks 13 and 14 were collected in the spring and early summer, whilst examples from blocks 1 and 2 were collected in the winter and spring. This latter evidence appears to corroborate the archaeological interpretation of different depositional conditions either side of the thinning of the midden in sample blocks 6 and 7.

Stable isotope analyses of limpets and cockles from the West Voe middens (Leng 2005) has indicated that cockles from the upper midden were collected in winter/spring and that there was a slight cooling (<0.5°C) in sea temperature between the deposition of the lower and upper middens.

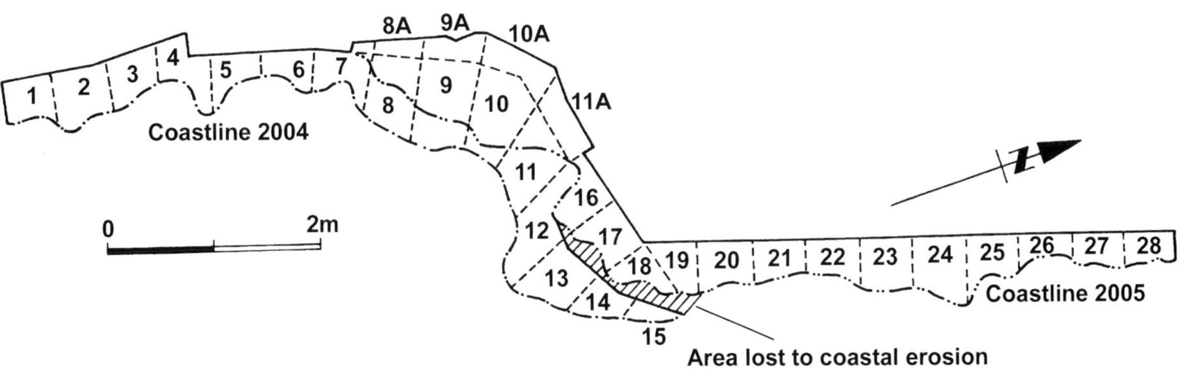

Figure 28.3. The 2004–5 midden sample blocks.

The finds

The programme of 100% sampling and processing, using a siraf-style flotation tank, of all excavated contexts at West Voe led to the recovery of a significant assemblage of 289 lithic artefacts (Ballin 2006). Whilst larger specimens were hand-collected as small finds, the vast majority of the finds were tiny chips and flakes of quartz debitage that were recovered from the 1–4mm fraction of the sieved samples. The assemblage comprises 263 quartz, 23 quartzite, 2 sandstone and 1 rock crystal fragments, only three tools were present: two hammerstones and one quartz flake with edge retouch. Flint was not represented in the assemblage.

One of the two hammerstones found at West Voe is a small sandstone beach cobble, the other comprises a section of vein quartz, which possibly represents a secondary use of material that had been brought to the site for processing artefacts, as the few quartz chips and flakes that retained any cortication suggest that their source was the quartz veins that occur at a number of localities within a few kilometres of the site. The quartzite lithics, a core and 22 chips and flakes, were all a light-pink colour, suggesting that derivations from a single source pebble is possible.

The West Voe lithics were overwhelmingly from the early midden. Analysis of the material from the individual midden blocks shows that the density of the lithics found corresponds, in general, with the area of trampled mussels, and also north of the main midden where the final phase of use was present. A number of 'hot spots' within the general spread of debitage may represent knapping locations.

Of particular interest were four small potsherds that were recovered in 2004. All were found within the lower midden; two from sample block 5 were in a coarse fabric with quartz inclusions. Both of these sherds had soot deposits on their outer surfaces and were probably from the same vessel. The other two sherds were found in sample blocks 4 and 13, and had finer grained fabrics. The sherd from sample block 13 was concreted to the crushed mussel surface. All of the sherds were from the walls of vessels and, although it is difficult to assess the precise vessel sizes represented, all probably had diameters within the range of 14 to 20cm.

The date of the middens

An integrated programme of radiocarbon and optically stimulated luminescence (OSL) dating was undertaken in 2004. Shells from both middens and charcoal from the lower midden were submitted for radiocarbon dating. OSL samples were obtained from the sands sealing the upper midden, together with further samples from the sands separating the two middens.

The radiocarbon dating samples were mainly from the lower midden, with marine shells being submitted from the main oyster, limpet and mussel layers, together with charcoal from the crushed mussel activity surface. Cockles were submitted from the upper midden and from the pit sealed by the wall. The dates obtained for both middens were slightly later than those indicated by the 2002 samples. Dates from the lower midden cluster in the period *c.* 4000–3600 cal BC, with samples from the oyster and the mixed limpet and seal and seabird layers dated to *c.* 4200–3600 cal BC (OxA-14146, 14179, 14213, 14214, 14215), and the mussel layer and activity surface to *c.* 3700–3600 cal BC (OxA-14242). A cockle from the upper midden provided a date of *c.* 3500–3300 cal BC (Oxa-14161), and one from the pit sealed by the wall was dated at *c.* 3500–3100 cal BC (OxA-14180).

The column of OSL dates indicated that the sands sealing the site were Neolithic in date as far as a band of humic sand situated approximately one metre above the ground surface associated with the cockle midden. The humic sand was dated to the Bronze Age, whilst the sands above it were dated to the seventeenth to nineteenth centuries AD.

Conclusions

The middens exposed by coastal erosion at West Voe provide a highly significant addition to understanding the colonization of, and early settlement in, the Shetland Isles. Although the extent of the investigations at West Voe was limited by the thick sequence of unstable sands that sealed the archaeological deposits, the methodology adopted, that of total sampling and the use of a range of environment and scientific analyses, has permitted unique insights into the procurement strategies of coastal hunter-gatherers and the Mesolithic-Neolithic transition in this, the most northerly island group in the British Isles.

It is interesting to note that the relationship of the dominant molluscan species in the two middens, namely oysters in the Late Mesolithic midden and cockles in the Early Neolithic midden, reflects changes in the Danish coastal middens such as Norsminde (Milner 2002, 70). At West Voe this change is clearly linked to a changing coastal environment when the 0.5m of sand that separates the two middens was deposited. The 2004 radiocarbon dates indicate that this occurred *c.* 3600–3500 BC. The lower midden oysters, the initially targeted resource, are all large specimens and appear to represent the primary exploitation of the oyster bed, whilst the large number of seal bones recovered emphasises the importance of seal hunting to the early settlers.

The potsherds found in 2004 provide another point of similarity to the Danish Ertebølle middens. The sherds raise the question of where the Mesolithic–Neolithic transition occurs within the West Voe sequence – in the latest phases present in the lower midden or in the separate midden depositions either side of a relatively brief, but significant, period of change in the coastal environment? Whichever of these is correct, and it is hoped that additional radiocarbon dates from samples taken in 2005 (from the final phase of use of the lower midden) will help clarify this point, it is clear that the cockle midden represents the continuing importance of coastal resources into the Neolithic. The evidence from West Voe that the transition to agriculture took place within the early part of the fourth millennium BC is entirely consistent with that obtained from the Early Neolithic site at Scord of Brouster (Whittle *et al.* 1986).

Acknowledgements

This project has been funded by research grants from Historic Scotland, NERC (NER/B/S/2003/00779), and The Prehistoric Society. The midden site lies within the boundary of Sumburgh Airport and I am particularly grateful to Scotair Properties for permission to carry out the investigations and to Mr N. Flaws, Airport Manager, for providing indoor space for finds processing and storage. Dr Becky Nicholson (Oxford Archaeology) coordinated and supervised the programme of environmental sampling and analyses in 2004. Thanks are also due to Dr Ed. Rhodes, University of Oxford, for providing the initial OSL dates in 2002, to Dr C. Christiansen, Shetland Amenity Trust, for provision of GPS co-ordinates of the site survey stations, and to Malakov Ltd, Lerwick, for providing soil sampling equipment.

References

Ballin, T. B. 2006. *West Voe, Sumburgh, Shetland: the lithic assemblage*. Unpublished report.

Bennett, K. D., Boreham, S., Sharp, M. J. and Switsur, V. R. 1992. Holocene history of environment, vegetation and human settlement on Catta Ness, Lunasting, Shetland. *Journal of Ecology* 80, 241–73.

Bennett, K. D. and Sharp, M. J. 1993a. Holocene vegetation and environment, in J. Birnie, J. Gordon, K. Bennett and A. Hall (eds.), *The Quaternary of Shetland*, 18–22. Cambridge, Quaternary Research Association.

Bennett, K. D. and Sharp, M. J. 1993b. Holocene environmental history at Dallican Water, Northeast Mainland, Shetland, in J. Birnie, J. Gordon, K. Bennett and A. Hall (eds.), *The Quaternary of Shetland*, 77–82. Cambridge, Quaternary Research Association.

Blockley, S. M., Lane, C., Hatton, G. and Watson, J. 2005. Tephrochronological analyses, in N. D. Melton, *A Late Mesolithic midden at West Voe, Sumburgh, Shetland: archaeological evaluation 2004*, 19–22. University of Bradford, unpublished Data Structure Report.

Edwards, K. 1996. A Mesolithic of the Western and Northern Isles of Scotland? Evidence from pollen and charcoal, in T. Pollard and A. Morrison (eds.), *The Early Prehistory of Scotland*, 23–38. Edinburgh, Edinburgh University Press.

Hamilton, J. R. C. 1956. *Excavations at Jarlshof, Shetland*. Edinburgh, Her Majesty's Stationery Office.

Leng, M. 2005. *Stable isotope data from modern and midden shells from Shetland (and Orkney) – interim report*. Unpublished report.

Low, G. 1879 (1978). *A Tour through Orkney and Schetland 1774*. Facsimile edition of original 1879 publication. Inverness, Melven Press.

Melton, N. D. 2005. *A Late Mesolithic midden at West Voe, Sumburgh, Shetland: archaeological evaluation 2004*. University of Bradford, unpublished Data Structure Report.

Melton, N. D. and Nicholson, R. A. 2004. The Mesolithic in the Northern Isles: the preliminary evaluation of an oyster midden at West Voe, Sumburgh, Shetland, UK. *Antiquity* 78 (299). Project Gallery: http://antiquity.ac.uk/ProjGall/nicholson/index.html (accessed 10/2007).

Milner, N. 2002. *Incremental growth of the European Oyster, Ostrea edulis: seasonality information from Danish kitchenmiddens*, British Archaeological Reports, International Series S1057. Oxford, Archaeopress.

Milner, N. 2005. *Seasonality of oysters from West Voe*. Unpublished report.

Mithen, S. 2000. The Scottish Mesolithic: Problems, prospects and the rationale of the Southern Hebrides Mesolithic Project, in S. Mithen (ed.), *Hunter-gatherer Landscape Archaeology: The Southern Hebrides Mesolithic Project 1988–98*, 9–37. McDonald Institute Monographs. Cambridge, McDonald Institute for Archaeological Research.

Mykura, W. 1976. *British Regional Geology: Orkney and Shetland*. Edinburgh, Her Majesty's Stationery Office.

Nicholson, R. A. 2005a. The Shells, in N. D. Melton (ed.), *A Late Mesolithic midden at West Voe, Sumburgh, Shetland: archaeological evaluation 2004*, 23. University of Bradford, unpublished Data Structure Report.

Nicholson, R. A. 2005b. Bird bone, in N. D. Melton, *A Late Mesolithic midden at West Voe, Sumburgh, Shetland: archaeological evaluation 2004*, 24. University of Bradford, unpublished Data Structure Report.

Saville, A. 2000. Orkney and Scotland before the Neolithic Period, in A. Ritchie (ed.), *Neolithic Orkney in its European context*, 91–100. McDonald Institute Monographs. Cambridge, McDonald Institute for Archaeological Research.

Whittle, A., Keith-Lucas, M., Milles, A., Noddle, B., Rees, S. and Romans, J. C. C. 1986. *Scord of Brouster an early agricultural settlement on Shetland*. Oxford Committee for Archaeology, Monograph 9. Oxford, Oxford Committee for Archaeology.

Worley, F. 2005. Mammal bone, in N. D. Melton, *A Late Mesolithic midden at West Voe, Sumburgh, Shetland: archaeological evaluation 2004*, 25–7. University of Bradford, unpublished Data Structure Report.

29. Mesolithic elk (*Alces alces* L.) from Zamostje 2 (Russia)

Louis Chaix

Mesolithic elk from the Russian site of Zamostje 2 are briefly presented: these animals are the main providers of meat and raw materials for the inhabitants of this lakeside dwelling. Elk from Zamostje were tall and robust animals and males clearly predominated. This can be explained by the important use of antlers to make various objects. All the animals were exploited on the site itself, as indicated by the presence of all the skeletal elements. Elk were hunted mainly during summer, autumn and winter. Antlers and bones were used to make various implements, such as different forms of projectile points, spearheads, hooks, axes, and adzes. The importance of elk for the Mesolithic cultures of the Great Russian Plain is attested by many sculptures representing this large cervid.

Keywords: Europe, Russia, Mesolithic, elk, exploitation, hunting, osteometry, archaeozoology.

Introduction

The prehistoric site of Zamostje 2 is situated in the northern area of Sergiev-Posad, around 110km north of Moscow. It lies on the left bank of the River Dubna, a tributary of the Volga (Figure 29.1). The settlement is located on a large alluvial plain, close to the marginal formations of the Moscow ice-sheet. The ancient lacustrine sediments are covered by layers of peat bogs. Remains of Mesolithic and Neolithic occupations were discovered along a drainage-channel. During the Mesolithic, the lake was surrounded by large forests, comprised of pine and birch, with many aquatic plants growing on the shores (Lozovski 1996; 1997).

Around 200m² were excavated, displaying an important stratigraphy to a depth of 3.5m. Zamostje 2 was occupied during the Late Mesolithic. There were two principal levels; the lowest is dated from 7450±100 BP (6470–6090 cal BC; GIN-6565), and the upper layer from 7380±60 BP (6390–6090 cal BC; GIN-6201). Above were found intermediate layers dated between 7400 and 7300 BP. Finally, on the surface, Early Neolithic occupations are attested towards 6680±100 BP (5775–5468 cal BC; GIN-6198) (Figure 29.2).

The Mesolithic layers contain well-preserved organic materials, with a good number of wood chips and wooden objects such as bowls, paddles, spoons, and fish traps. The animal bones and bone tools are also very well preserved. We therefore have a good opportunity to give a precise vision of animal exploitation during the 7th millennium BC.

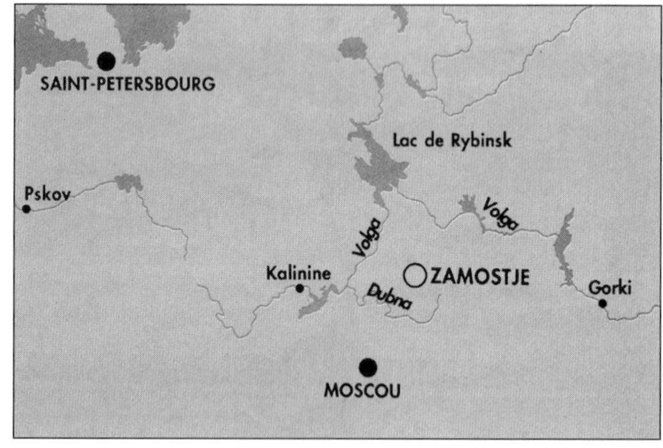

Figure 29.1. Geographical position of Zamostje 2.

The Mesolithic fauna

As mentioned above, the bones were in an exceptional state of conservation with a low fragmentation rate. This good level of preservation is illustrated by the numerous examples of fish bones – from small and fragile skeletons. The bones are dark brown in colour, as a result of their long stay in the peat. The surfaces reveal various anthropogenic and natural marks. The two Mesolithic levels revealed a wide variety of taxa. The complete study of the species found has not yet been completed, but we can note the presence of elk (*Alces alces*), reindeer (*Rangifer tarandus*), wild boar (*Sus scrofa*), and many carnivores: (brown bear (*Ursus arctos*), red fox (*Vulpes vulpes*), badger (*Meles meles*), otter (*Lutra lutra*), and pine marten (*Martes martes*). The list of mammals is

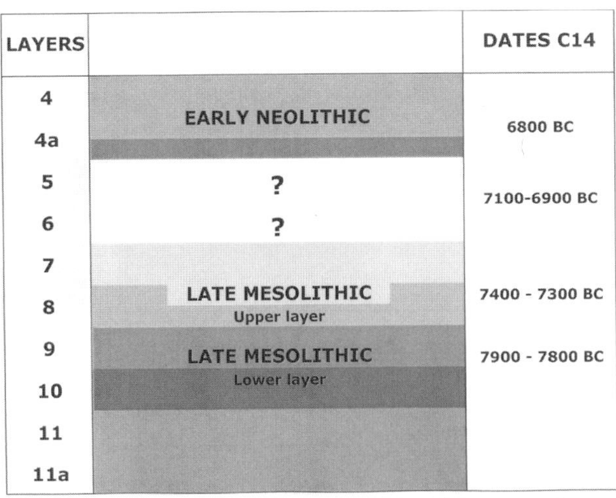

Figure 29.2. Schematic stratigraphy of Zamostje 2.

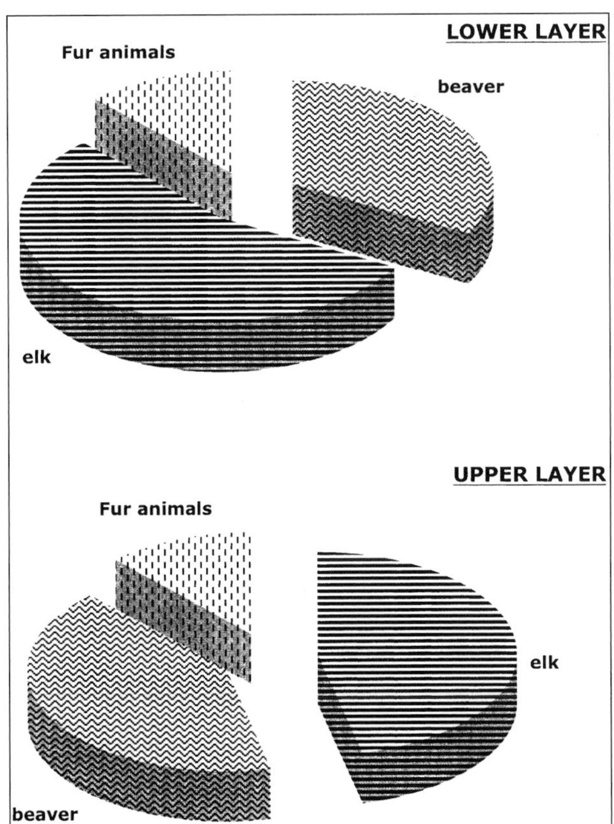

Figure 29.3. Distribution of the main mammal groups across the two Mesolithic layers.

completed by numerous beaver (*Castor fiber*) and hedgehog (*Erinaceus europaeus*). Birds are well represented: many different ducks, other aquatic birds, and the remains of white-tailed eagle (*Haliaëtus albicilla*) (Chaix 1996). Fish bones are abundant (mainly from small pike and cyprinids, and it is also particularly interesting to note the presence of domestic dogs (*Canis familiaris*). (These robust animals, very similar to those of north-eastern Europe (Benecke 1993), were eaten.) The distribution of the main groups of mammals is illustrated in Figure 29.3.

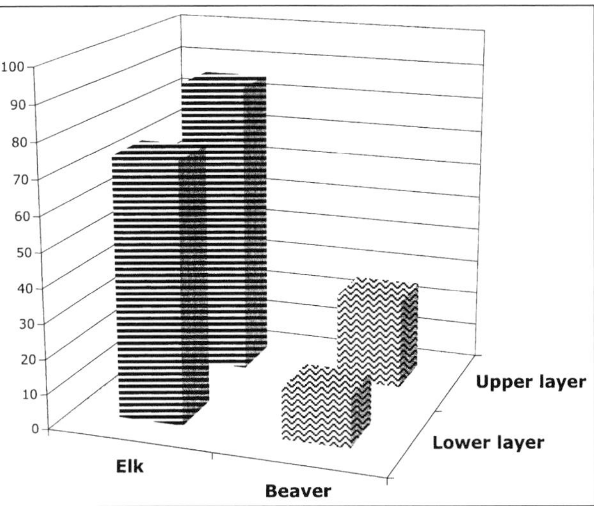

Figure 29.4. Meat-producing comparisons between elk and beaver.

In the two Mesolithic levels there is a clear dominance of elk and beaver, in terms of the number of identified specimens. In the lower level, elk represents 46.3% and beaver 41.6%. In the upper level beaver are more abundant (55%), with elk 33.1%. If we consider meat production, elk are clearly dominant in the two phases (Chaix 2004). The results of this estimation, based on parameters used by different scholars (Vigne 1988), are presented in Figure 29.4.

Elk

The lower Mesolithic level revealed 20 individuals, the upper 15. If we consider the morphology and the stature of these cervids, many measurements may be used to provide accurate descriptions. Three elements were selected: the lower third molar, and the first and second phalanx. The metrical data from Zamostje is compared to Holocene elk (mainly from Neolithic lake dwellings in Switzerland) and to modern elk from various collections (Chaix and Desse 1981).

The results are presented in the Figure 29.5. As we can see, the elk from Zamostje 2 are large, robust individuals, in the upper part of the variation range of Holocene and modern animals. This position may be linked with the sex of the animal, as we will see next.

For discrimination between the sexes, different parameters can be useful. First, the presence of antlers is a male characteristic: numerous fragments were found, but they were mostly the remains of tool making and cannot be linked to a specific number of individuals, nevertheless, some skulls exhibit pedicels of males. We considered the shape of the pelvic symphysis, and, in addition, measurements of various leg bones were also analysed (Figure 29.6).

Using a combination of these different indicators, we have obtained for the lower layer a sex ratio of eleven males to four females. The upper layer shows a sex ratio of ten

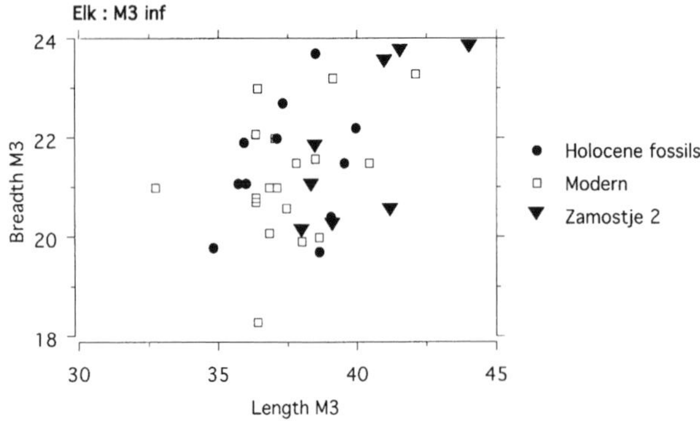

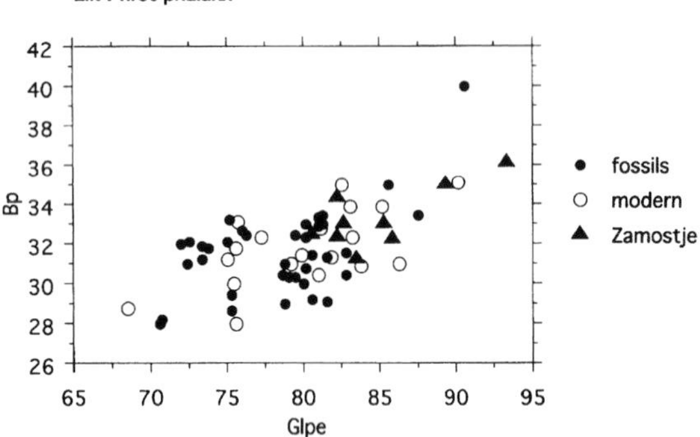

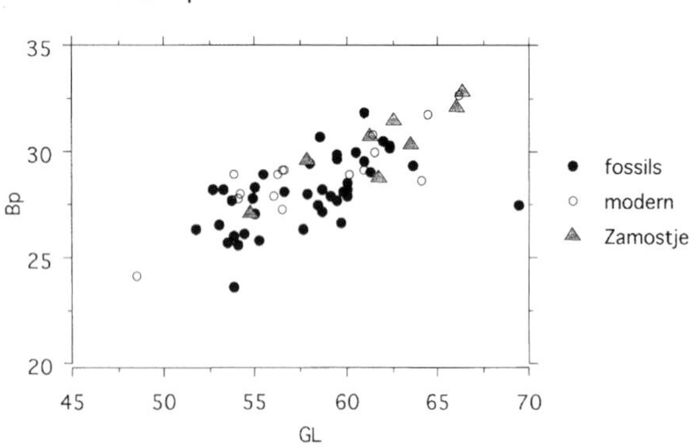

Figure 29.5. Mesolithic elk from Zamostje 2: metrical comparisons.

males to three females. These two values are very different from the normal distribution of sexes, which is around 1:1 (Heptner and Nasimovitsch 1974). This indicates hunting activities that were clearly focused on male elks and this can be explained by the use of antlers to make a considerable number of tools, weapons, and other objects (Lozovski 1996; David 2001).

The individual ages of the Zamostje-2 elk were established using tooth eruption, tooth-wear, and fusion of long bone epiphyses (Quimby and Gaab 1957; Knight 1966; Iregren 1975): the age distribution is presented in Figure 29.7. It is interesting to note that in the lower part of the Mesolithic layers, the majority of animals were killed between the ages of two and three. Contrary to this, hunting preferences in the upper part seems to favour young individuals less than a year old, and adults aged between three and four. As we have considered the different strata together in two groups, seasonality cannot explain theses differences. It is possible that during the recent phase the inhabitants of Zamostje 2 were more interested in catching younger individuals for their more tender meat.

The ages of the Zamostje elk show that they were killed mainly during summer, autumn, and winter; very few animals were caught during spring. It seems that the best period to use the antlers for raw material extended from September to January – when the horn is completely ossified and resistant enough to be worked (Bubenik 1966; Nygrén 1986).

The archaeology

Turning now to more archaeological aspects, we must consider the preservation and distribution of skeletal elements. Figure 29.8 shows the representation of the various bones in the two chronological groups. Firstly, we must note that almost all the skeletal elements are present on the site. This demonstrates a clear indication of the local preparation of elk; some skulls (with their pedicels) are also present. Looking to a more schematic representation of the skeletal parts, we have categorized the bones into five groups: head, forelimb, rachis, hind limb, and extremities. We have compared this distribution with a theoretical model based on the analysis of a single skeleton; therefore it is possible to observe any over-representation, or deficit, for the different parts selected. The results are presented in Figure 29.9.

The lower layer is characterised by the presence of portions rich in meat, such as fore and hind limbs. Clear deficits in head elements and extremities are observable: these parts are not considered as a good source of edible meat. In the upper layer the picture is rather different. Head fragments are well attested, whereas rachis bones are manifestly under-represented. Fore and hind limbs are significantly present.

The differences between the two levels can be explained either by the different distribution of activities in the two groups, or by different carcass use. We do not yet have a convenient explanation for this.

As mentioned above, elk are the most important game animals at Zamostje 2. The fragmentation of bones and the various anthropic marks are indicators of a significant dependence on these animals. Figure 29.10 summarizes the different skeletal marks, and we do not observe clear differences between the two chronological levels. Antlers were exploited to make tools, weapons, and other objects. This material is presented in detail elsewhere (Lozovski 1996, 1999; David 2001). Among the items we noted axes, adzes, spearheads, conical projectile points, and spoons.

Traces of skinning are rare, but some transversal marks on phalanxes may be linked to this activity. Signs of butchering include disarticulation (DIS) – visible near the limbs joints: between scapula and humerus, humerus and radius, and/or femur and tibia. Traces of cutting are visible

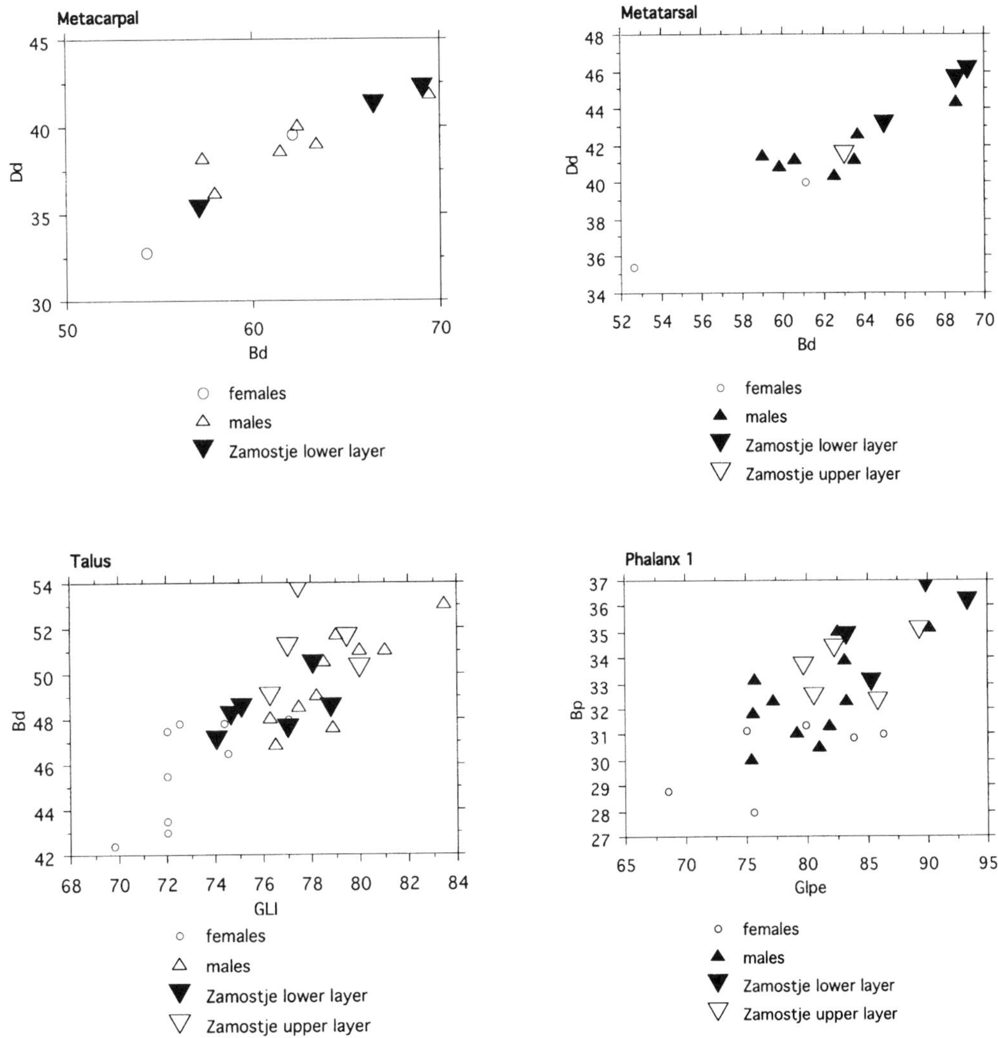

Figure 29.6. Osteometrical sexual discriminations.

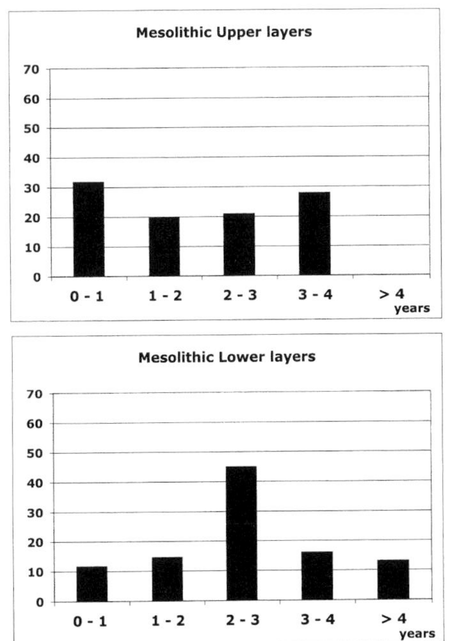

Figure 29.7. Age distribution of elk across the two Mesolithic layers.

on the vertical branch of the mandible, corresponding to the separation of the jaw from the skull, to have access to the tongue: marks on the hyoids indicate the consumption of this muscle. Defleshing (DF) is well indicated by marks on the maxillary, the flat parts of the scapula, and on the diaphysis of the long bones. Extraction of grease and marrow is shown by the systematic splitting of the first and second phalanxes (Figure 29.11). We have also noted some enigmatic perforations on the external part of the calcaneum (Figure 29.12), perhaps indicating that the carcass was hung before dismembering, or alternatively some process to do with marrow extraction?

Many skeletal elements were used for technological purposes (Lozovski 1999). As well as antlers, the base of the horizontal branch of the mandible was cut to obtain a long stick. Scapula spines were also systematically cut for the same purpose (Figure 29.13). Many metapodials were worked and the *chaîne opératoire*, studied by Eva David (2004), suggests that various objects, such chisels, points, hooks, etc., were manufactured. Ribs were worked as tools for fish preparation – scaling and filleting (Clemente *et al.* 2002).

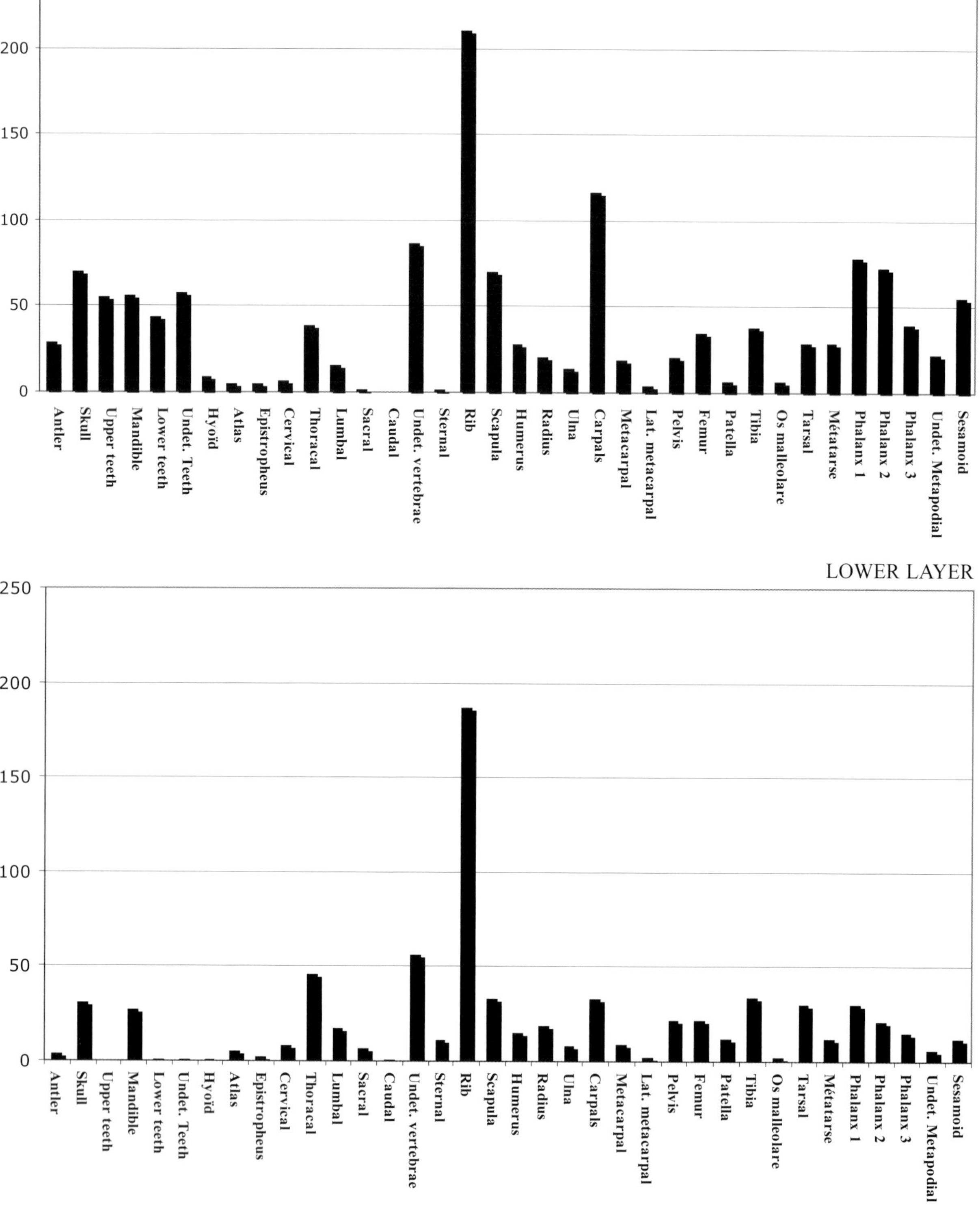

Figure 29.8. Detailed distribution of skeletal elements.

Finally, elk antlers and bones were used to make objects associated with art and the spirit-life. Many pendants and ornaments were processed from incisors. These adornments are frequently found in the Mesolithic and Neolithic graves of this region (Lozovski 1996), as well as in other areas (Chaix 2005). In addition to these objects of individual property, many other artefacts (always made of elk bone and antler) were found. Some sculptures and carved pieces represent birds, but most depict elk heads. A small profile of an elk carved into an elk rib is very characteristic (Chaix

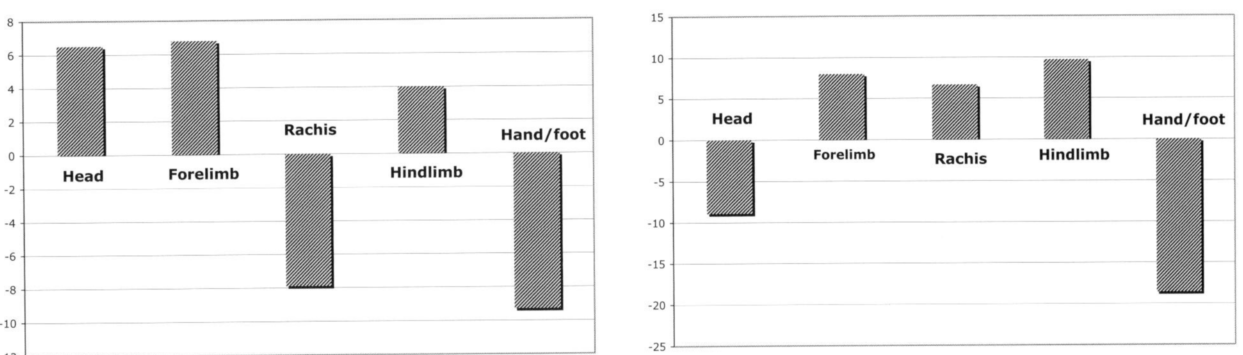

Figure 29.9. Comparisons between the distribution of skeletal parts across the two Mesolithic layers.

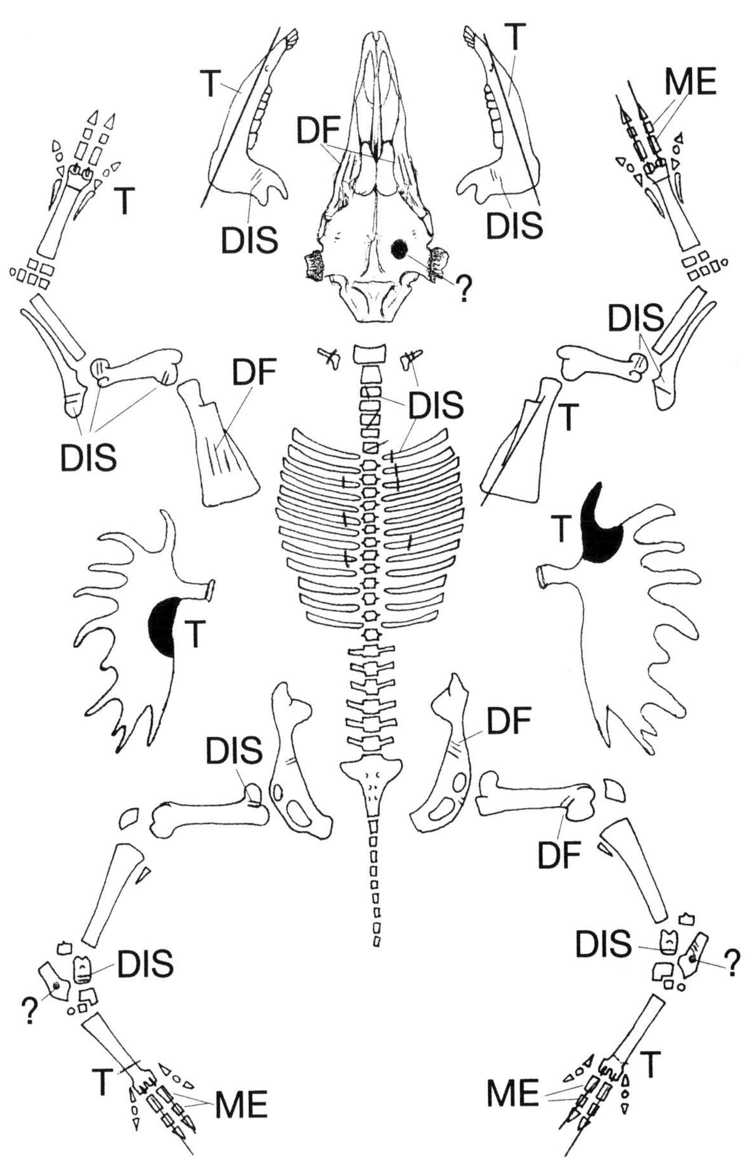

Figure 29.10. Schematic distribution of the various anthropic marks (DIS: disarticulating, DF: defleshing, M: marrow and grease extraction; T: technical operations). (After Helmer 1987, figure 3).

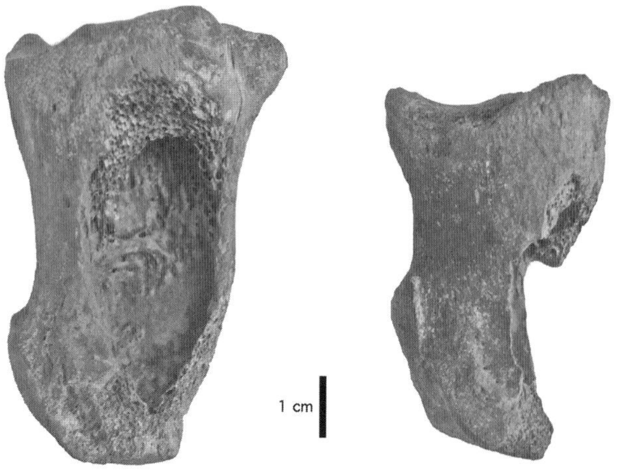

Figure 29.11. Exploitation of the second phalanxes.

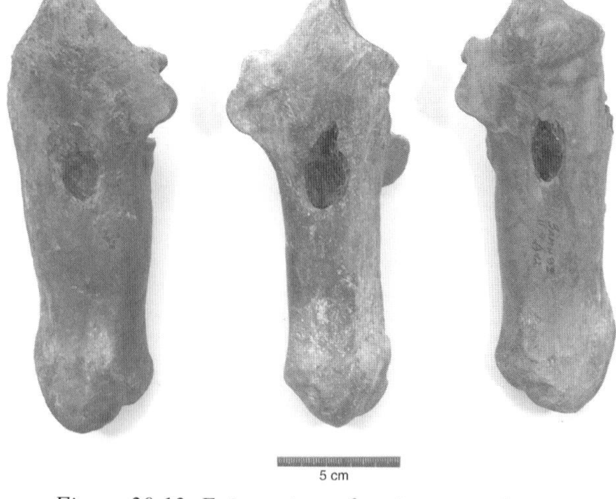

Figure 29.12. Enigmatic perforations on calcanei.

Figure 29.13. Scapula showing cut spine.

2003). Two heads were sculpted and made of antler: they are perforated to enable them to be fixed to sticks (Figure 29.14).

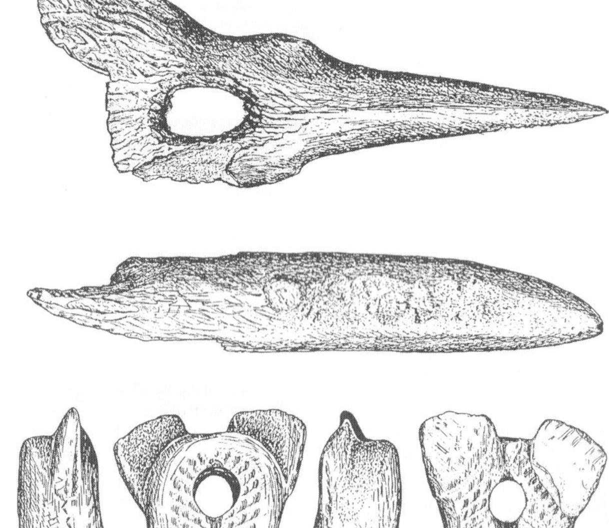

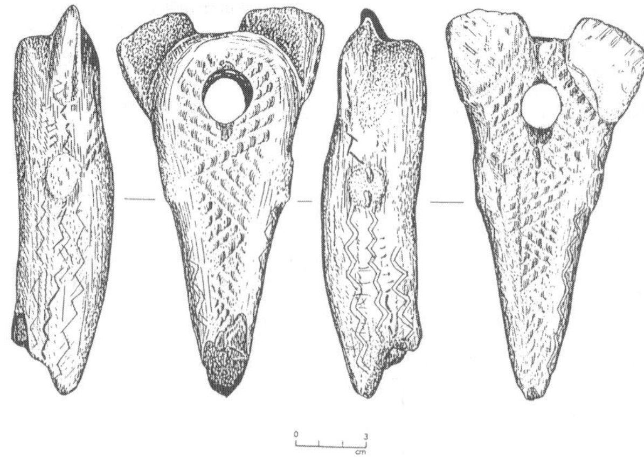

Figure 29.14. Elk-head representations from elk antler. (After Lozovski 1996, 77).

Conclusions

During the Mesolithic of northern Europe (and particularly in the Great Russian Plain), elk played a dominant role in everyday life – not only dietary, but in the art and beliefs of the hunting and fishing population. The site of Zamostje 2 provides a fine opportunity to study this important animal in the Mesolithic levels. This large and impressive cervid was, at this site, the principal source of meat, grease and marrow. Antlers and bones from elk were also a useful source of raw materials (Lozovski 1999). In addition to these alimentary and technological roles, various other factors endorse its importance in the art and beliefs of the hunting and fishing populations, not only in that part of Russia, but over a wider area stretching from Denmark to southern Siberia.

Acknowledgements

The detailed study of the extensive faunal collection of Zamostje 2 was made possible thanks to the generosity of the Museum of Sergiev-Posad, and to Vladimir and Olga Lozovski.

References

Benecke, N. 1993. Zur Kenntnis der mesolithischen Hunden des südlichen Ostseegebiet. *Zeitschrift für Archäologie* 27, 39–65.

Bubenik, A. B. 1966. *Das Geweih*. Hamburg/Berlin, Paul Parey.

Chaix, L. 1996. The fauna of Zamostje, in V. M. Lozovski, *Les derniers chasseurs-pêcheurs préhistoriques de la plaine russe*, 85–95. Guides archéologiques du « Malgré-Tout ». Treignes, Centre d'études et de documentation archéologique de Treignes (CEDARC).

Chaix, L. 2003. A short note on the Mesolithic fauna from Zamostje 2 (Russia), in L. Larsson, H. Kindgren, K. Knutsson, D. Loeffler and A. Åkerlund (eds.), *Mesolithic on the Move: Papers presented at the Sixth International Conference on the Mesolithic in Europe, Stockholm 2000*, 645–8. Oxford, Oxbow Books.

Chaix, L. 2004. Le castor, un animal providentiel pour les Mésolithiques et les Néolithiques de Zamostje (Russie), in J. P. Brugal and J. Desse (eds.), *Petits animaux et sociétés humaines. Du complément alimentaire aux ressources utilitaires. XXIVe Rencontres internationales d'archéologie et d'histoire d'Antibes*, 325–36. Antibes, Éditions APDCA.

Chaix, L. 2005. Héteroclite et éclectique : la faune épipaléolithique de l'Aven des Iboussières (Drôme, France). *Munibe* 57 (I), 411–20.

Chaix, L., Chenal-Velarde, I. and Velarde, L. 2001. Archaeozoology of the Mesolithic at Zamostje 2: preliminary results (in Russian), in V. Lozovski (ed.), *« Zamostje 97 », Conference on the Stone Age of the European plains: objects of organic material and settlement structure as reflections of human culture, Serguiev-Posad (Russia), 30 June – 6 July, 1997*, 255–61. Moscow, Podkova.

Chaix, L. and Desse, J. 1981. Contribution à la connaissance de l'élan (*Alces alces* L.) postglaciaire du Jura et du Plateau suisse – Corpus de mesures. *Quartär* 31/32, 139–90.

Clemente, I., Gyria, E. Y., Lozovska, O. V. and Lozovski, V. M. 2002. Análisis de instrumentos en costilla de alce, mandibulas de castor y en caparazón de tortuga de Zamostje 2 (Russia), in I. Clemente, R. Risch and J. F. Gibaja (eds.), *Análisis funcional. Su aplicació al estudio de sociedades prehistóricas*, 187–96. British Archaeological Reports, International Series S1073. Oxford, Archaeopress.

David, E. 2001. The bone and antler artefacts from the Late Mesolithic level of Zamostje II – 1991 (Russia): the technological point of view, in V. Lozovski (ed.), *« Zamostje 97 », Conference on the Stone Age of the European plains: objects of organic material and settlement structure as reflections of human culture, Serguiev-Posad (Russia), 30 June – 6 July, 1997*, 292–303. Moscow, Podkova.

David, E. 2004. Fiche transformation des matières d'origine animale dans le Mésolithique ancien d'Europe du Nord. *Matières et techniques, Industrie de l'os préhistorique* (Cahier XI, Fiche no. 9), 113–49. Paris, Société Préhistorique Française.

Helmer, D. 1987. Fiches descriptives pour les relevés d'ensembles osseux animaux, in J. Desse and N. Desse (eds.), *Fiches d'ostéologie animale pour l'archéologie, Serie B: Mammifères, No. 1*, Figure 3. Antibes, Éditions APDCA.

Heptner, W. G. and Nasimovitch A. A. 1974. *Der Elch* (Alces alces). Wittenberg Lutherstadt, Die Neue Brehm-Bücherei.

Iregren, E. 1975. Age dependant changes in the lower extremities of the elk (*Alces alces*) in central Sweden, in A. T Clason (ed.), *Archaeozoological Studies*, 367–80. Amsterdam, North Holland Publishing Co.

Knight, R. R. 1966. Bone characteristics associated with ageing elk. *Journal of Wildlife Management* 30, 2, 369–74.

Lozovski, V. M. 1996. *Zamostje 2. Les derniers chasseurs-pêcheurs préhistoriques de la plaine russe*. Guides archéologiques du « Malgré-Tout ». Treignes, Centre d'études et de documentation archéologique de Treignes (CEDARC).

Lozovski, V. M. 1997. Mesolithic and Early Neolithic art of the Volga-Oka region (according to the materials of Zamostje 2 site), in V. Lozovski (ed.), *« Zamostje 97 », Conference on the Stone Age of the European plains: objects of organic material and settlement structure as reflections of human culture, Serguiev-Posad (Russia), 30 June – 6 July, 1997*, 33–51. Moscow, Podkova.

Lozovski, V. M. 1999. The Late Mesolithic bone industry in Central Russia, in A. Thévenin (ed.), *L'Europe des derniers chasseurs. Epipaléolithique et Mésolithique. Actes du 5e Congrès International UISPP, Commission XII*, 417–24. Paris, Éditions du Comité des travaux historiques et scientifiques (CTHS).

Nygrén, K. 1986. *Alces alces* (Linnaeus, 1758) – Elch, in J. Niethammer and F. Krapp (eds.), *Handbuch der Säugetiere Europas*, 173–97. Wiesbaden, Aula Verlag.

Quimby, D. C. and Gaab, J. E. 1957. Mandibular dentition as an age indicator in Rocky Mountain elk. *Journal of Wildlife Management* 21, 4, 369–74.

Vigne, J.-D. 1988. *Les mammifères post-glaciaires de Corse. Etude archéozoologique*. XXVIe supplément à *Gallia Préhistoire*. Paris, Éditions du Centre national de la recherche scientifique (CNRS).

30. Animal bone studies and the perception of animals in Mesolithic society

Anja Mansrud

This paper will focus upon the relationship between humans and animals in Mesolithic hunter-gatherer societies, using animal bones from settlement sites in eastern Norway. Despite obvious source-critical constraints, osteological material can give valuable information about the Mesolithic environment and the fauna that were exploited. However, deposits of animal bones at a site are not only indicative of available resources. The relations that humans have with their immediate environments and animals is strongly culturally dependent. Bone deposits may also reveal information regarding food preferences, rather than available edible species. In addition, ideas about the regeneration of prey through hunting occur in many hunter-gatherer cosmologies, and these concepts are often reflected in the handling of animal remains. Combined with studies of visual representations of animals, and the use animals in burial practices, animal bone studies might give insights into Mesolithic perceptions of animals.

Keywords: zooarchaeology, animal exploitation, rock carvings, elk, beaver, belief-systems.

Animal bones and rock art – approaches to understanding animals in the Mesolithic society of eastern Norway

Faunal remains have always played an important part in studies of prehistoric hunter-gatherer societies. The identified animal species from settlement sites can give valuable information about ecology and climate, while the bone material has been used to interpret cultural aspects concerning subsistence, settlement patterns and seasonality. Zooarchaeological research relating to the Mesolithic has mainly been directed towards the economic exploitation of different species. But human interaction with animals is not solely economic; animals also play important symbolic and ritual roles (Ingold 2000; Shanklin 1985; Willis 1994). This paper will focus on questions concerning the social and ideological aspects of human-animal relations in Mesolithic hunter-gatherer societies, using animal bones from settlement sites as a point of departure. The occurrence of the combination of beaver (*Castor fiber*) and elk (*Alces alces*) as dominant game animals is common at Mesolithic sites in northern Europe (Andersen *et al.* 1990; Chaix 2003; Ekman and Iregren 1984; Lindquist 1999; Lõugas 1996; Zhilin 1997). In this short paper I will focus mainly on these two species. My aim is to apply a contextual approach, combining different categories which deal with animals (i.e. Holt 1996). I will argue that a comparison of zooarchaeological finds and rock art depicting animals, together with a careful use of ethnographic analogy, might be a fruitful way of studying the relationship between animals and humans. This paper is a preliminary presentation of a recently instituted research project concerning animal bone material from hunter-gatherer sites in the eastern part of Norway.

The bone material from eastern Norway

The discipline of zooarchaeology, defined as *the study of animals in archaeological context* (O'Day *et al.* 2004), is a field of research that is practically non-existent in Norway. The bone material has mainly been studied by zoologists, with little connection to the archaeological context. The material in this study comes from open-air sites, where soil conditions do not favour preservation of organic materials. A large number of bones are fragments of burned bones, which better resist decomposition. The poor condition of the material complicates the anatomical identification of bone elements and prevents many zooarchaeological analyses, such as assessing the number of individuals and sexing and ageing the animals. For the same reason, other quantitative studies, aimed at helping us understand the economic importance of different species, will not give reliable results (Amorosi *et al.* 1996, 138). Despite these obvious source-critical constraints, small, low intensity sites with small amounts of bone residue may still offer potential, depending on the questions being asked. Studies that look at the presence/absence of species, in a regional perspective

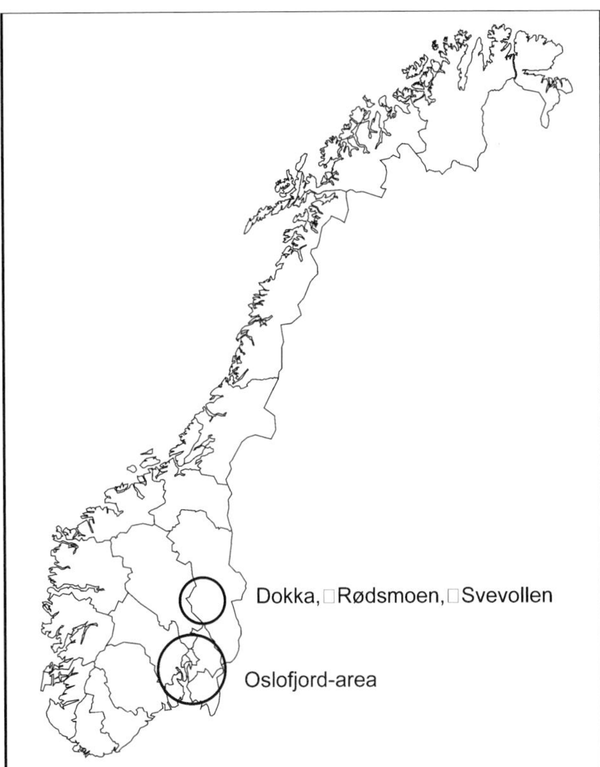

Figure 30.1. Location of sites from the interior and coastal areas of eastern Norway.

may be employed successfully. By investigating a large number of sites from the same area it is possible to obtain some proxy indicators that may reveal a general pattern, which is more important than exact numbers (Amorosi *et al.* 1996, 134). In applying a contextual approach, other sources should also be included, both the archaeological context, and comparison with areas with similar fauna that have better preserved bone material.

In eastern Norway, both coastal and inland sites have been investigated (Figure 30.1). The bone assemblages show a predominance of two game species: elk and beaver (Fuglestvedt 1995; Hufthammer 1989; 1990; 1993; Hufthammer and Hodgetts 1997; Jaksland 2001b; Mikkelsen 1989; Mikkelsen *et al.* 1999). Other species are poorly represented, but the remains of birds, sea mammals, deer (*Cervus elaphus*), roe deer (*Capreoleus capreoleus*), wild boar (*Sus scrofa*), and fur-bearing animals such as otter (*Lutra lutra*), fox (*Vulpes vulpes*) and pine marten (*Martes martes*) are present. Although investigated sites are few, it is surprising that the percentage of sea mammals at coastal sites is so low. The location of these sites, close to ancient seashores, should indicate marine adaptation; yet the remains of terrestrial mammals dominate. Only at two sites are sea mammals well represented (Hufthammer 1993; Mikkelsen 1975). In addition fish bones are surprisingly few. This is probably due to a combination of bad preservation and lack of sieving at the older excavations (cf. Amorosi *et al.* 1996, 130; Chaix 2003, 646); this is highlighted by the abundance of fish bones at newly excavated sites with middens (Jaksland 2001b, 4–22).

Taphonomic processes and human activity

Working with organic matter like bones, causes major methodological problems because of the transitory nature of the material. Any discussion concerning bones must take taphonomic problems into consideration. An osteological assemblage is formed partly through processes of natural decomposition and partly through cultural formation which result from different social practices (O'Connor 1996). Bones left on the surface of a camp will have only a slight chance of survival. Human activity, such as deposition in a shell midden, or in water, enhances the possibilities of preservation. Determining the nature of taphonomic variability is very important, as otherwise it is easy to assume that observed species or element distributions entirely reflect human activity (Amorosi *et al.* 1996, 30). Human hunters also function as important taphonomic agents, and social factors, such as hunting strategies, seasonal mobility, and exchange of animal products, may affect the composition of the faunal assemblage (Noe-Nygaard 1987). It is also reasonable to assume that carcasses were not always transported complete to the sites, but were sometimes killed and butchered elsewhere. Such behaviour may have greatly influenced the number of identified species at a site (Binford 1978). Native cosmologies represent another important factor in the treatment of animal remains (Ingold 2000). Hunters are constantly dealing with the deaths of the game animals they hunt, and the hunt itself is often strongly ritualized. As hunting inevitably involves the dismemberment of dead animals, rituals involving slaughtering, to a great extent involve the preservation of bones and other inedible parts. The rituals are often concerned with securing the regeneration of prey animals (Woodburn 1987).

From site-catchment to an interpretive zooarchaeology

Within zooarchaeological research, prehistoric animal exploitation has traditionally been investigated using optimization theories, for example *site-catchment analysis*. Site-catchment analysis is based on ecological and economic models which aim to reconstruct past environments and predict available resources (Styles 1985). These studies treat the bone material quantitatively, analysing variables such as prey size, meat weight and fat content, to explain why certain species were preferred (Bettinger 1982; Jochim 1976; Styles 1985). This approach has also been widely used within Norwegian Mesolithic research (Lindblom 1984; Mikkelsen 1975, Mikkelsen *et al.* 1999). Past diets within this framework are regarded as ways of adapting to the environment, and the majority of zooarchaeological works are explicitly functionalist and empirical, as explicitly stated by Rowley-Conwy (2000, x).

However, ethnographic studies clearly show that animals play an important part in prehistoric hunter-gatherer belief-systems, as well as in their economy. What people eat is therefore not exclusively determined by what is available, but is also strongly dependent on the perception of animals in their belief-system (Lévi-Strauss 1986; Bourdieu 1995). The appreciation of what is or is not edible represents one of the most fundamental distinctions between different human groups (Falk 1991), and these distinctions are based on taxonomy, or systems of classification. While optimization theories might be useful in explaining why certain animals were chosen for exploitation, they are less successful in explaining why others were not (Holt 1996, 91). The elk is a large animal with a high content of meat and fat, and is thereby ideal for economic utilization. However, so are other large marine mammals that were equally available, and the apparent preference for terrestrial mammals may result either from cultural choice, or taphonomic factors. Investigations of bones from burned and unburned collections in central Sweden show that elk dominates the unburned sample, whereas the beaver is more frequent among the burned fragments. This may point to different treatment of the waste products from these two species (Lindquist 1999, 88). Waste, especially animal remains, may be treated in specific ways, according to cultural rules and regulations. For example, the Siberian Evenks, as reported by Grøn and Kuznetzov (2003), employ different methods for treating different types of animal waste. The cadavers of bears are placed on a platform close to the site, and should not be mixed with bones of other animals. Likewise, the remains of the elk are placed in water, because the beast, with its habit of eating water plants, is classified as a water-animal. Such practices will leave very few animal bones in a context that could be preserved and studied by the archaeologist.

The elk was perhaps a more important meat resource than the beaver, but bone fragments of beavers are common at all sites, both interior and coastal. The large percentages of beaver bones may result from the fact that these bones are very robust. They also have a very characteristic anatomy, and are thereby easy to identify. Because of this the amount of beaver tends to increase when bones are burned and fragmented. The dominance of beaver may therefore not reflect a true prehistoric situation, but rather a consequence of taphonomic processes favouring these bones. Bone collections with well-preserved unburned skeletal remains also reveal the importance of the animal skeleton itself, which was used as raw material for tools. One of the reasons for the exploitation of the beaver may be explained in this way – as its front teeth are frequently used as chisels (Chaix 2003, 646). Bones and antler have also been used for decoration and making sculptures and carvings (Chaix 2003, 647; Plonka 2003). Animal bones are often encountered in settings which indicate a non-rational or 'ritual' significance (O'Connor 1996, 12). In a Mesolithic context, the most obvious example is the deposition of animal remains and teeth in burials (Albrethsen and Brinch Petersen 1977; Larsson 1990). This practice suggests that animals, or parts of animals, were perceived as more than just food.

In eastern Norway, no Mesolithic burials have yet been found, and art objects made from wood and bone are uncommon. There are also very few artefacts of Mesolithic origin that can be interpreted as 'ritual' material, but at Neolithic hunter-gatherer sites, where slate was a favoured raw material, carvings, figurines and decorated tools are found made of it: the elk head is the most common motif (Lindquist 1978). This area is also rich in rock art. Ingold (2000, 131) points out that the depictions made by hunter and gatherers, regardless of whether their belief-system was animistic or totemic, are not representational; its purpose is 'not to represent, but to reveal, to penetrate beneath the surface of things so as to reach deeper levels of knowledge and understanding'. Studying depictions may therefore reveal significant information of prehistoric attitudes towards animals.

Rock art and perceptions of animals

Rock carvings are dated by shoreline displacement in the Mesolithic to approximately 6000–7000 cal BC (Mandt and Lødøen 2005, 276–7). When the bone finds from settlement sites are compared to the rock art in the area, an interesting pattern emerges. The elk is the dominating motif in the rock art, both in eastern Norway (Mandt and Lødøen 2005; Mikkelsen 1977, 1981), and in adjacent areas on the Swedish side of the border (Lindquist 1999) (Figure 30.2). Perhaps this particular species is emblematic of social relations between people in this region. One site contains a beautiful picture of a whale, but apart from this other animals have not been identified with certainty. This points to different symbolic perceptions of animals. The beaver seems to have been heavily exploited as a game animal, but it does not appear in contexts that are traditionally understood as 'symbolic' or 'ritualistic', whereas the elk occurs in both. The presence of rock carvings is commonly explained as 'hunting magic', a ritual that secures the regeneration of prey. But if the purpose of the carvings was to make animals regenerate, it seems strange that other regularly consumed animals, such as the beaver, are not depicted. A parallel to this phenomenon has been observed at Late Palaeolithic sites in France. The faunal remains from the Lascaux cave

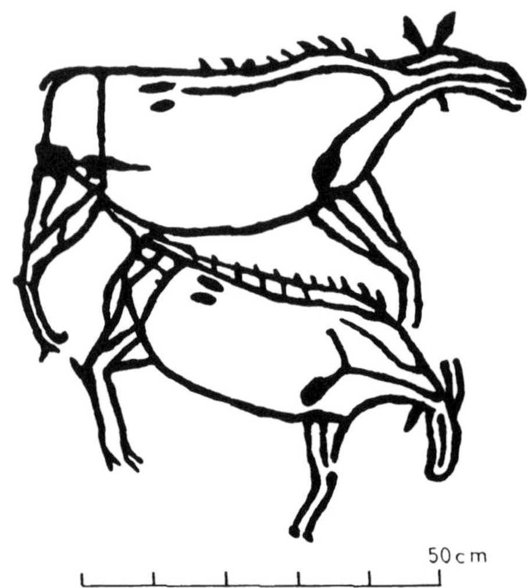

Figure 30.2. Rock art carving of elk from Kløftefoss, Drammen (after Mikkelsen 1981, 38).

reveal that reindeer (*Rangifer tarandus*) constitute 90% of the identified species from the bone assemblages. On the other hand, reindeer represent less than 1% of the motifs in the cave paintings, which are dominated by horses (Bahn 1997, 177). The 'hunting magic' explanation, therefore, seems very unlikely, and other explanations will eventually be sought as the project develops.

In ethnographic research, traditional hunter-gatherer belief-systems have been described as variations of animism, totemism, and shamanism. These concepts are analytical instruments, generally operating in different geographical areas, and should not be regarded as doctrinal systems (Ingold 2000, 112), but may be employed as models that are 'good to think' in approaching these matters. Some very simplified definitions, taken from the *Macmillan Dictionary of Anthropology*, state that *animism* may be defined as the belief that natural phenomena are endowed with life or spirit, and the tendency to attribute supernatural characteristics to plant, animals and landscapes. Game animals are accorded important ritual significance as manifestations of supernatural power. *Totemism* is a range of customs in which human groups are associated with animal species, among them the belief that the animal is the mythological ancestor of the clan, and the associated ritual procedures, or avoidance, of eating the animal concerned. Animals are exceedingly important and function in different roles as human guides, rescuers, ancestors, and sacrificial victims; but whereas the totemic ontology is *essential*, focusing on the landscape and its immanent ancestral powers, the animic cosmology is *dialogical*, forging a dialogue between humans and non-human habitants, seeking to regenerate their common life-world (Ingold 2000). Connected to both cosmologies is the s*haman*, who acts in different animal disguises and mediates between different levels of the world (Ingold 2000). The concept of shamanism has become an increasingly popular dimension in which to interpret both Mesolithic and Palaeolithic cosmology (i.e. Clottes and Lewis-Williams 1998; Strassburg 2001).

An animal that might be expected to appear within the faunal range of eastern Norway in the Mesolithic is the brown bear (*Ursus arctos*); but this species is almost absent. There does not seem to be a taphonomic explanation for the lack of bear bones. Being equally robust, these bones should be as easily detectible as the elk or beaver. The bear is commonly depicted on rock art sites in other areas of Norway (Mandt and Lødøen 2005), but it is non-existent at the localities in eastern Norway. One has to be cautious of making assumptions from negative evidence, but considering the prevalent position of the bear (and the bear hunt) among most arctic and sub-arctic foragers, it would be natural to assume that the bear was indeed hunted. The ritual hunting and subsequent reburial of its body has been practised by indigenous groups in the circumpolar area up to recent times (Ingold 2000) – among them the Saami people of Norway. In the Saami religion, the bear skeleton is considered to be animated, and the correct treatment of the remains was a premise for the resurrection of the animal (Schanche 2000). Killing therefore became a sacrificial act, opening up the possibility of cosmological renewal and regeneration (Ingold 2000). May similar rituals have existed in the past, and is this the reason why bear bones are missing from the sites? The only bear item found to date was a claw deposited in a pit, which also contained two complete and polished stone axes (Jaksland 2001a). This specific context may be interpreted as ritualistic: perhaps an offering. Another possibility is that the bear was a totemic animal and not eaten at all.

In this presentation I have tried to put the animal bones from settlement sites into a wider archaeological context, and point out some alternative explanations for why some animals have been found and others not. The suggestions made here are superficial ones, and must be regarded as tentative, as this project is still at a preliminary stage. At the moment there seem to be more questions than answers, but even at this early stage the investigations reveal a systematic pattern which has to be explained by the cultural agency of prehistoric hunters.

References

Albrethsen, S.-E. and Brinch Petersen, E. 1977. Excavation of a Mesolithic cemetery at Vedbæk, Denmark. *Acta Archaeologica* 47, 1–28.

Amorosi, T., Woolett, J., Peridikaris, S. and MacGovern, T. 1996. Zooarchaeology and landscape change, problems and potentials of inter-site comparisons of archaeofaunas, in K. D. Thomas (ed.), *Zooarchaeology: New Approaches and Theory. World Archaeology* 28 (1), 126–57.

Andersen, S. H., Bietti, A., Bonsall, C., Broadbent, N. D., Clark, G. A., Gramsch, B., Jacobi, R. M., Larsson, L., Morrison, A., Newell, R. R., Rozoy, J. G., Straus, L. G. and Woodman, P. C. 1990. Making cultural ecology relevant to Mesolithic research: I. A. database of 413 Mesolithic fauna assemblages, in P. M. Vermeersch and P. van Peer (eds.), *Contributions to the Mesolithic in Europe. Papers presented at the Fourth International Symposium on the Mesolithic in Europe*, 23–51. Leuven, Leuven University Press.

Bahn, P. 1997. *Journey Through the Ice Age*. Berkeley and Los Angeles, University of California Press.

Bettinger, R. L. 1982. Predictive/explanatory models of hunter-gatherer adaptation, in M. B. Schiffer (ed.), *Advances in Archaeological Method and Theory, Vol. 3*, 189–255. New York, Academic Press.

Binford, L. 1978. *Nunamiut Ethnoarchaeology*. New York, Academic Press.

Bourdieu, P. 1995. *Distinksjonen. En sosiologisk kritikk av dømmekraften. Oversatt av Annick Prieur*. Oslo, Pax forlag.

Chaix, L. 2003. A short note on the Mesolithic fauna from Zamostje 2 (Russia), in L. Larsson, H. Kindgren, K. Knutsson, D. Loeffler and A. Åkerlund (eds.), *Mesolithic on the Move: Papers presented at the Sixth International Conference on the Mesolithic in Europe, Stockholm 2000*, 645–8. Oxford, Oxbow Books.

Clottes, J. and Lewis-Williams, D. 1998. *The Shamans of Prehistory: Trance and Magic in the Painted Caves*. New York, Harry N. Abrams.

Ekman, J. and Iregren, E. 1984. *Archaeo-zoological investigations in Northern Sweden. Early Norrland 8*. Stockholm, Kungliga Vitterhets Historie och Antikvitets Akademien.

Falk, P. 1991. The Sweetness of Forbidden Fruit: towards an anthropology of taste, in E. L. Fürst, R. Prättälä, M. Ekstrom, L. Holm and U. Kjærnes (eds.), *Palatable Worlds. Sociocultural Food Studies*. Oslo, Solum Forlag.

Fuglestvedt, I. 1995. Svevollen – spor av senmesolittisk bosetning i lavlandets indre skogssone, in K. A. Bergsvik, S. Nygård and A. J. Nærøy (eds.), *Arkeologiske Skrifter 8. Steinalderkonferansen i Bergen 1993*, 95–110. Bergen, Arkeologisk Institutt, Bergen Museum.

Grøn, O. and Kuznetzov, O. 2003. Ethno-archaeology among Evenkian forest hunters. Preliminary results and a different approach to reality!, in L. Larsson, H. Kindgren, K. Knutsson, D. Loeffler and A. Åkerlund (eds.), *Mesolithic on the Move: Papers presented at the Sixth International Conference on the Mesolithic in Europe, Stockholm 2000*, 216–21. Oxford, Oxbow Books.

Holt, J. Z. 1996. Beyond optimization, alternative ways of examining animal exploitation, in K. D. Thomas (ed.), *Zooarchaeology: New Approaches and Theory. World Archaeology* 28 (1), 5–19.

Hufthammer, A. K. 1989. *Det osteologiske materialet fra steinalderundersøkelsene ved Dokkfløyvatn*. Unpublished report. Zoologisk Museum, University of Bergen.

Hufthammer, A. K. 1990. *Det osteologiske materialet fra 5 steinalderboplasser ved Saugbruks i Halden. Arkeologiske utgravninger, Saugbruks. Haldenprosjektet*. Unpublished report IAKN, University of Oslo.

Hufthammer, A. K., Østmo, E., Hulthen, B., Isaksson, S., Sørensen, R., Bakkevig, S. and Skovhus Thomsen, M. 1993. *Auve II. Tekniske og Naturvidenskaplige Undersögelser*. Norske Oldfunn XVII. Oslo, Universitetets Oldsaksamling.

Hufthammer, A. K. and Hodgetts, L. 1997. Faunal material from the Stone Age excavations at Rødsmo. Appendix 1, in J. Boaz (ed.), *Steinalderundersøkelsene på Rødsmoen*, 149–58. Varia 41. Oslo, Universitetets Oldsaksamlings/Kulturhistorisk Museum.

Ingold, T. 2000. *The Perception of the Environment. Essays in livelihood, dwelling and skill*. London, Routledge.

Jaksland, L. 2001a. *Vinterbrolokalitetene – en kronologisk sekvens fra mellom- og senmesolitikum i Ås, Akershus*. Varia 52. Oslo, Universitetets Oldsaksamlings/Kulturhistorisk Museum.

Jaksland, L. 2001b. Kjøkkenmøddingen på Skoklefald – Endelig funn av velbevarte kulturlag fra eldre steinalder i Oslofjordregionen. *Nicolay Arkeologisk Tidsskrift* 84, 4–22.

Jochim, M. A. 1976. *Hunter-Gatherer Subsistence and Settlement. A Predictive Model*. New York, Academic Press.

Larsson, L. 1990. Dogs in fraction – symbols in action, in P. M. Vermeersch and P. van Peer (eds.), *Contributions to the Mesolithic in Europe: papers presented at the 4th International Symposium on the Mesolithic in Europe*, 153–60. Leuven, Leuven University Press.

Lévi-Strauss, C. 1986. *The Raw and the Cooked. Introduction to a Science of Mythology*. Harmondsworth, Penguin Books.

Lindblom, I. 1984. Former for økologisk tilpasning i mesolitikum, Østfold. *Universitetets Oldsakssamlings Årbok* 1982/1983, 43–86.

Lindquist, C. 1978. *Älghuvudmotivet i nordfennoskandisk plastikk och hällkonst; det nordeuropeiska jägarsamhället under sten och bronsålder*. Stockholm, Institutionen för arkeologi, särskilt nordeuropeisk, Stockholm Universitet.

Lindquist, C. 1999. Nämforsenristningarna – en återspegling av jägarnas liv och världsbild. *Tidsspår* 99 (1997), 105–35.

Lõugas, L. 1996. Analyses of animal remains from the excavations at the Lammasmägi site, Kunda, North-east Estonia, in T. Hackens, S. Hicks, V. Lang, U. Miller and L. Saarse (eds.), *Coastal Estonia: Recent Advances in Environmental and Cultural History*, 273–91. PACT 51. Rixensart, PACT.

Mandt, G. and Lødøen, T. 2005. *Bergkunst. Helleristningar i Noreg*. Bergen Museum, University of Bergen.

Mikkelsen, E. 1975. *Frebergsvik. Et mesolittisk boplassområde ved Oslofjorden*. Universitetets Oldsaksamlings Skrifter, Ny rekke 1. Oslo, Universitetets Oldsaksamlings.

Mikkelsen. E. 1977. Østnorske veideristninger – kronologi og økokulturelt miljø. *Viking* XL, 147–201.

Mikkelsen, E. 1981. Veideristninger ved Geithus, Modum, Buskerud, in *Universitetets Oldsaksamlings Årbok 1980/81*, 35–53. Oslo, Universitetets Oldsaksamlings.

Mikkelsen, E. 1989. En 6000 år gammel steinhytte i Heradsbygd. Vinterkvarter for elg- og beverfangst, in *Alfarheim Årbok for Elverum 4*, 39–54. Oslo, Elverum.

Mikkelsen, E., Ballin, T. B. and Hufthammer, A. K. 1999. Tørkop. A boreal settlement in South-Eastern Norway. *Acta Archaeologica* 70.

Noe-Nygaard, N. 1987. Taphonomy in archaeology, with special emphasis on man as a biasing factor. *Journal of Danish Archaeology* 6, 7–52.

O'Connor, T. 1996. A critical review of archaeological animal bone studies, in K. D. Thomas (ed.), *Zooarchaeology: New Approaches and Theory. World Archaeology* 28 (1), 5–17.

O'Connor, T. 2000. *The Archaeology of Animal Bones*. Stroud, Sutton Publishing.

O'Day, S. J., Van Neer, W. and Ervynck, A. 2004. Behaviour Behind Bones. The Zooarchaeology of ritual, religion, status and identity, in S. J. O'Day, W. Van Neer and A. Ervynck (eds.), *Proceedings of the 9th ICAZ Conference, Durham 2002*, xi–xv. Oxford, Oxbow Books.

Plonka, T. 2003. *The Portable Art of Mesolithic Europe*. Wroclaw, Wydawnictwo Univwersytetu Wroclawskiego.

Rowley-Conwy, P. 2000. *Animal Bones, Human Societies*. Oxford, Oxbow Books.

Schanche, A. 2000. *Graver i ur og berg. Samisk gravskikk og religion fra forhistorisk og nyere tid*. Karasjok, Davvi Girji.

Seymour-Smith, C. 1986. *Macmillan Dictionary of Anthropology*. London, Macmillan.

Shanklin, E. 1985. Sustenance and symbol, Anthropological studies of domesticated animals. *Annual Review of Anthropology* 14, 375–403.

Strassburg, J. 2000. *Shamanic Shadows. One Hundred Generations of Undead Subversion in Southern Scandinavia 7000–4000 BC*. Stockholm Studies in Archaeology 20. Stockholm, Arkeologiska institutionen, Stockholms universitet.

Styles, B. W. 1985. Reconstruction of availability and utilization of food recourses, in R. I. Gilbert and J. H. Mielke (eds.), *The Analysis of Prehistoric Diets*. New York, Academic Press.

Willis, R. 1994. Preface, in R. Willis (ed.), *Signifying animals. Human meaning in the natural world*. Our World Archaeology 16. London, Routledge.

Woodburn, J. 1987. Social dimensions of death in four African hunting and gathering societies, in M. Bloch and J. Perry (eds.), *Death and the Regeneration of Life*, 197–210. Cambridge, Cambridge University Press.

Zhilin, M. G. 1997. Artifacts Made of Animals' Teeth and Jaws in the Mesolithic of Eastern Europe, in M. Pearce and M. Tosi (eds.), *Papers from the EAA Third Annual Meeting at Ravenna 1977. Volume I: Pre- and Protohistory*, 26–30. British Archaeological Reports, International Series S717, Oxford, Archaeopress.

31. Cultural small-scale variations in a hunter-gatherer society: or 'everybody wants to be a little bit different!' An ethnoarchaeological study from Siberia

Ole Grøn, Torunn Klokkernes and Michail G. Turov

Where archaeology tends to focus on large-scale cultural uniformity with a low degree of dynamics in its approach to prehistoric hunter-gatherers, ethnographic and ethnoarchaeological observations indicate that significant and highly dynamic small-scale variations in material culture, economy, spiritual culture and language must be accepted as general features in such societies. An understanding of the mechanisms behind this variability and its dynamics is seen as important for archaeology's ability to interpret the Mesolithic materials better than is the case today. On the basis of the spatio-temporal dynamics that appear to be a central trait in hunter-gatherer societies, the question seems to be one of how stable and uniform traditions could persist for long periods in prehistory rather than why, and how, they changed. The paper focuses on cultural small-scale variation related to environmental factors (topography, microclimates, etc.) and the maintenance of group identity, as well as to group wealth and status.

Keywords: ethnoarchaeology, small-scale variability, exploitation strategy, eco-determinism, cultural dynamics, micro-climates, topography, status, stratified society.

Introduction

Where archaeology tends to focus on large-scale cultural uniformity in its approach to prehistoric hunter-gatherers, ethnographic and ethnoarchaeological observations point to the existence of a significant and highly dynamic small-scale variation in material culture, economy, spiritual culture, and/or language as general features in such societies (Grøn *et al.* 2003; Shirokogoroff 1935, 12–39). It is obvious that environmental small-scale variations related to topography and microclimates can cause variation in cultural expression at the small-scale level (Bennett 1944; Best 2003, 158–71; Klokkernes 2007; Ohnuki-Tierney 1976; Steward 1955). This paper's main focus, however, is on cultural small-scale variation related to group identity features at the clan level (Barth 1987, 55–64; Best 2003, 158–71; Donner 1915, 75; Grøn and Kuznetsov 2003, Grøn *et al.* 2003; Vang Petersen 1984; Shirokogoroff 1935, 12–39; Wiessner 1983; 1984) and on variation in exploitation strategies related to differences in the clan's status and wealth.

Cultural variation related to environmental variation is, in principle, well described and accepted in the anthropological theoretical literature (Bennett 1944; Steward 1955; Ohnuki-Tierney 1976). However, this acceptance seems not to apply to the small-scale level in archaeology, where an underlying concept of resources that are evenly distributed on isotropic surfaces seems to underpin theoretical constructs such as the site-catchment model (Jarman *et al.* 1972). Even at such a small scale this is very far from reality. Many animals have strong preferences for strictly confined zones in an area, depending on availability of the resources they rely on, topography, their possibilities for moving on the surface (quality/thickness of snow, sand…), etc. A detailed knowledge of animal behaviour under given environmental circumstances will often be important for understanding how the hunting resources in a specific area behaved spatially. The spatiality of the plant resources is no less complex. We shall present some illustrative examples of complexity in the following sections.

The relation between social and ideological features related to group identity and cultural aspects, such as material culture, ritual, cosmology, language, resource strategy, etc., is well established in social anthropology as a central theme in the later development of the cultural ecology, but has, so far, only begun to win acceptance in ethnoarchaeology and archaeology (Barth 1987, 55–64; Best 2003, 158–71; Ellen 1982; Grøn *et al.* 2003; Shirokogoroff 1935, 12–39; Wiessner 1984). Where small-scale variations appear in the typological picture from prehistoric hunter-gatherers they are often conceived of as local variations with little relation to ideological and identity features in the society that produced them. At times they are seen as reflecting the existence of isolated cultural sub-groups (Vang Petersen 1984). Taking into account the prehistoric small-scale cultures' mobility, as it is documented by long-distance exchange of objects (Klassen 2004, 100–8), as well as in the mobility of recent hunter-gatherer cultures, ideas of isolation appear to be most unlikely. As indicated by the ethnographic documentation of small-scale group identity-features it seems much more likely that typological small-scale variations in many cases reflect group identity features at the same scale level.

The Evenk

Apart from *Orochen* and *Tungus*, a large number of other names have been applied to groups with a closer or more distant relation to the Evenk culture (Shirokogoroff 1929). Evenk groups still subsisting on hunting often use 15–30 domesticated reindeer (*Rangifer tarandus*) for transportation – riding them or using them to pull their sledges. The domesticated reindeer of the Evenk can be compared to the dogs of the Greenland Inuit. The hunting groups subsist on the meat of wild reindeer, elk (*Alces alces*), red deer (*Cervus elaphus*), musk deer (*Moschus moschiferus*) and mountain sheep (*Ovis musimon*), as well as birds and fish from the lakes and rivers (Anderson 1991; Grøn 2005; Shirokogoroff 1929).

Evenk groups are found throughout central and eastern Siberia, where they exploit a wide variety of biotopes and resources mainly in the taiga zone. The basis of this study is data collected from three zones in the central Evenk area. One is the Kalar Region, with taiga up to the tree limit at a level of approximately 2000m, and with mountains going up to 3000m in the northern part of Chita County, where the Evenk traditionally subsist mainly on hunting non-migratory wild reindeer that find the variation they need over the year locally in the mountain areas (Grøn and Kuznetsov 2003). The second is the undulating Olenok Region in the Sacha Republic/Yakutia, with taiga vegetation and mountains up to around 600m, where the Evenk mainly subsist on migrating reindeer (Grøn 2005). The third is the Katanga Region in the northernmost part of Irkutsk County, which is undulating with low mountains like the Olenok Region, but where the Evenk traditionally subsist on elk, because the migrating wild reindeer, on account of natural barriers, are diverted from this region, which is in fact ideal for reindeer (Grøn and Turov, in press).

The average temperature varies from -40°C to -60°C in the winters, to +20°C to +40°C in the summers. The snow cover in these regions is normally relatively restricted,

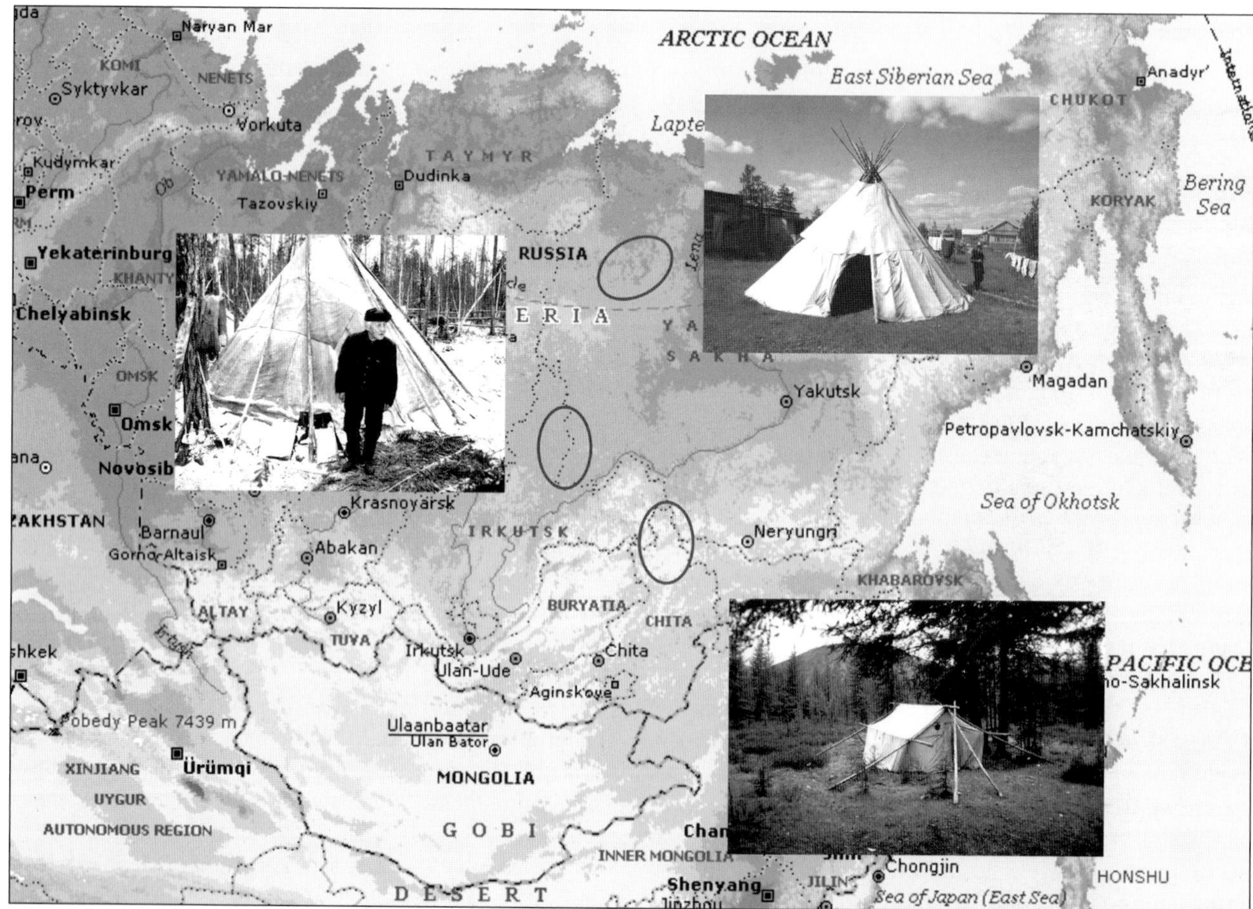

Figure 31.1. The use of traditional Evenk 'djus' (tents) in the plains, but a fast change to tents of Russian type in the mountain zone west of Lake Baikal.

due to a low precipitation that maintains the permafrost condition (Baulin *et al.* 1984; Ivanenkov and Fraicheva 1997; Wright and Barnovsky 1984).

The territorial unit in the Evenk society is the clan ('rod') (Shirokogoroff 1929, 195), which consists of from three to around 10 families. The smaller clans are often organized in strong alliances, so that they in fact function as one of the larger clans with about 10 families. The larger clans are often subdivided into two or three sub-clans. The single households' hunting territories within their clan territories can vary from year to year.

Small-scale variation due to environmental factors

This section presents some examples of small-scale variation due to environmental factors.

Differences in material culture

In the Katanga and Olenok Regions, which are relatively flat, the traditional 'tepee' type of tent is still used 'because it is the most comfortable' (Figure 31.1). In the mountainous Kalar Region, however, it was many years ago replaced by an Evenk version of the Russian ridge-tent, because this, on account of its smaller weight, is easier to transport on reindeer, or on sledges in the mountains.

Weight reduction can also be observed in artefacts other than tents in the Kalar Region. The Evenk here cut all unnecessary wood off their rifles, use small steel axes with smaller handles than in other areas, and generally try to reduce weight in any way they can to make it easier to move in the mountains. In practice this causes, at the moment, a significant difference in the material culture of groups belonging to the same culture.

Differences in settlement patterns related to topography and micro-climates

Especially in the Kalar Region, with its steep mountains, it is obvious that the topography has an effect on the settlement pattern. Some valleys serve (depending on their steepness, narrowness and location in relation to other valleys) as cold traps (Figure 31.2). The temperatures in winter, at their top levels, can be 10–15°C above their lowest locally. This means that the game will choose a higher position, if there are food resources, and this can be combined with snow conditions that allow proper mobility. As a consequence the Evenk, in some locations, will place their camps at quite high positions in the winter, which is the main hunting season (Grøn 2005). Access to the water bodies of rivers and lakes is not a problem at this time of year when water is normally obtained by melting snow. Some Evenk state that this water tastes better and that they therefore would prefer melted snow, even though they had access to water from the water bodies. One of the authors, Ole Grøn, has not stayed in such winter camps in the Kalar Region, but has observed that the winter houses in the

Figure 31.2. Naled-area (= 'ice area') in Chinaskaya Naled, Kalar region, June.

Katanga Region, where this effect is much less pronounced, can be located at least up to 5 kilometres from rivers or lakes. In other valleys in the Kalar Region, which do not serve as cold traps, the winter settlement can often be at the bottom of the valleys. As a consequence, clans with neighbouring territories can, as a result of the topography, have very different settlement patterns.

An important type of microclimate zones in the mountain areas are the so-called 'naled areas'. Due to permafrost and shadow from the mountains, some lakes and rivers will remain frozen solid until August-September. Even though the temperatures around the naled areas are normal for the season during summer, the air above the ice is so cold that mosquitoes drop dead immediately if they enter it. Because the mosquitoes are a pestilence that can drive the reindeer mad, the wild and domesticated reindeer will concentrate around the naled areas in the summer. For this reason the Evenk with domesticated reindeer will also camp near naled areas. This results in a highly concentrated distribution of the game, that far from conjoins with the distribution of the grazing-resources of the season.

Deep lakes serve as climate buffers. Around Lake Nitchatka, in the northern part of the Kalar Region, the winter-climate is 10–20°C warmer than in the area in general, because of the water from the deep lake. Because this attracts the game, the small group living there can maintain a quite permanent base camp that only moves a little up and down the Sen River, which drains the lake when the settled area starts 'stinking' and needs to regenerate for a period. Extensive naled areas nearby provide summer grazing for the clan's *c.* 40 domestic reindeer.

In periods when hunting is a central part of the Evenk's activities, they tend to place their camps where two rivers merge. This is because such positions give access to 'more meat'. Such a statement reflects that the rivers/river valleys generally function as transport corridors for boats, sledges, and people mounted on reindeer, as well as walking – and that a position where two rivers join is the meeting point of three corridors. Hunting is, to a high degree, carried out along the rivers. If the game killed is transported to the camp by boat, such a location provides two corridors where it can be transported downstream.

Small-scale variations related to group identity features

The Evenk are often not too happy about entering into discussion on the differences between their clans' traditions. This is mainly because, from a strategic point of view, they tend to think it can weaken their appearance as a unified group politically if they appear as small separate entities. However, once they have engaged in the discussion, they will list numerous such differences: different pronunciations used by the neighbours, making them difficult to understand; different styles of ornamentation of reindeer harness, etc. are discussed with enthusiasm. They generally avoid touching upon differences related to ritual. They seem to have a problem giving such comparative information because 1) it is very impolite to give this type of information about other clans, and 2) this type of information should be disseminated only by the elder responsible for, and who 'keeps', this type of knowledge in the clan.

The right to use territory is traditionally maintained through continued ritual negotiations with the spirits of the land, and is therefore a mainly ritual phenomenon. In some cases it has been observed how some hunters present in a discussion could draw the surrounding territories, so that they showed the exact outline of a territory whose occupier was not present. At the same time, they would make it clear that they did not know the border of this latter territory. The suggestion that it might follow the border of its neighbouring territories could only obtain a 'maybe, but we don't know'. It is obvious that one can only give information about ritual features from one's own clan. In cases where informants are under pressure to reveal the ritual customs of other clans, they will typically try to avoid further discussion by saying 'it is the same as here'. This phenomenon is probably responsible for many of the similarities in the anthropological literature.

Old people, because of the enormous experience they have gained, are regarded as wiser than younger community members (Figure 31.3). Old hunters who, because of their experience, are able to predict the movements of the animals are, for instance, said to 'become small shamans' because of this ability. The status as 'keepers of central parts of the group's' 'knowledge' is important for the old, as a kind of life insurance. It provides them with an important function in the group at an age when their physical ability is reduced. Old Lasar Petrovich Cichogir, who recently reached 80, expressed, in an interview about tent organization, deep concern about how the 'young' (who were then 50–60 and living in separate households) in his clan should manage to put up their tents when he was no longer there. He likes to demonstrate his superiority in this field of expertise. Once, when the expedition arrived at his camp, Ole Grøn noted when entering his tent that male and female sides had switched since his last visit. When Lasar was asked why, he burst out laughing. It was a joke, and he had been excited to see if it would be noticed. He then explained that it was, in fact, the normal organization,

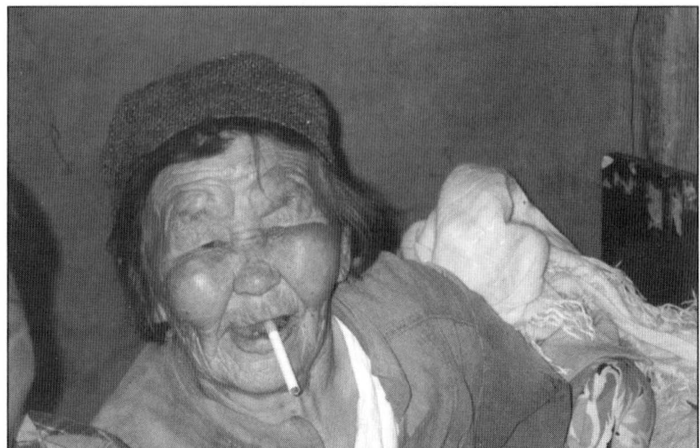

Figure 31.3. Elders play an important role as keepers of knowledge. (Photograph: Ole Grøn).

but that the entrance had just been placed in the back and not in the front. This is, in practice, an easy operation, because the lower section of the tent-cover consists of two parts. In general he was eager to demonstrate his capability in tent organization, at the same time making irritated remarks about his legs, which were no good for hunting any more. Lasar would never discuss cosmology or shamanism. All questions in that direction he would answer by saying that he knew nothing about such things, whereby he probably meant that this was not his sphere of knowledge. This knowledge belonged to his brother-in-law, the famous shaman, Vasili Dimitrievich Kaplin, who lived his active life as a hunter in Lasar's clan's territory until he withdrew to the nearby village of Erbogachen, about 150km from its hunting territory, and finally died in 2003. Vasili Dimitrievich had no problems answering questions about cosmology and shamanism – his field of expertise.

Many members of a clan will know what the 'keeper' of a specialized part of the clan's knowledge knows. But only the keeper has the right to disseminate it after his/her preference. Therefore the interviewer often meets the reply: 'That, you will have ask this or that old person'. When a keeper of knowledge faces death, he or she will transfer the knowledge, and the right to keep it, to another member of the clan. A similar organization of knowledge keeping can be observed in many other small-scale societies. The saying, 'When an elder dies, a library burns', which appears to be widely known, and possibly originated in other places, reflects this (Native Science 2006, African National Congress 2006).

The dynamics of the tradition of the single clan are closely related to the keeper concept. A keeper of the knowledge within an area of expertise is obliged to update the knowledge. This will generally mean modifying or changing an aspect of the cultural tradition. A person who is married into a clan with a different tradition, and who at the time of arrival is mature, will tend to maintain the tradition of the clan he/she was brought up in. If such a person becomes the 'old person', keeping a certain aspect of the new clan's knowledge – which may well happen – this can cause an abrupt change in the local tradition within this field of knowledge.

Practical knowledge is generally not passed on through explanation but through demonstration. Not only purely practical skills, but also practical knowledge about how rituals should be carried out, or how ritual structures should be constructed, etc., are generally 'demonstrated' to the learners. More abstract knowledge is often explained in relation to demonstrations of the more practical aspects of the themes in focus. The Sami use the expression 'čalbme' for this type of native knowledge which is communicated through practical actions and body language; a type of knowledge transfer that is central in hunter-gatherer societies (Barth 2002; Dunfjeld 2001, 28; Fors 2004, 6; Hamilton 1980; Native Science 2006; Sillitoe 1998).

The maintenance of knowledge of cultural features that do not occur frequently can be difficult when observation plays such an important a role, as with boys' initiation rites in New Guinea (Barth 1987, 55–64). The killing of bears is generally avoided in the Evenk society unless it is necessary in self-defence. If young hunters from one clan have their only early experience in how the bear-ritual is carried out with adult hunters from another clan, they may adapt to the neighbours' tradition with regard to this ritual. Thus in regions with bear problems the differences between the clan's bear-rituals should be clear and well defined, whereas in areas with only a few bears a certain blurring should be expected. In Terteia in the Katanga Region, Irkutsk County, such a blurring in the tradition was observed, because, as one of the hunters with a differing tradition expressed it: 'it is so seldom you see it carried out that you must use what you have seen'.

It is seen as essential to gain a better understanding of the mechanisms and the dynamics behind small-scale variation in material culture, language, ideology, ritual, cosmology, etc., of hunter-gatherer societies, because these small-scale strains seem to form the basis of the changes that can be observed at larger-scale levels (Barth 1987, 55–64; Best 2003, 158–71; Donner 1915, 75; Grøn 2003; Grøn and Kuznetsov 2003; Grøn *et al.* 2003; Shirokogoroff 1935, 12–39; Wiessner 1983; 1984).

That cultural, small-scale variations are important as a basis for the creation and maintenance of group identity in hunter-gatherer societies is obvious. In a discussion of these aspects one of the Evenks, shaking his head because of our questions about something so obvious, said: 'Of course! Everybody wants to be a little bit different!'

Small-scale variations in exploitation strategy

Evenk society is clearly stratified. The economic stratification is mainly observable between the clans within which redistribution is an active factor. The consciousness of one's own status in relation to that of other Evenk clans is clearly expressed in relation to discussions of problems concerning the finding of suitable marriage partners. Roughly four groups can be distinguished: a) hunter-gatherer clans with no domestic reindeer for transportation, b) well-off hunter-gatherer clans with a reasonable number of reindeer for transportation (15–30 per family), c) rich hunter-gatherer clans with a surplus of domestic reindeer (up to 80–100), and d) groups with more reindeer per family – normally by the Evenk not regarded as hunter-gatherers, but as pastoralists.

During a stay with the 'wealthy' Cichigor clan in the Katanga Region, where there are no wild reindeer to hunt and the hunt therefore is focussed on elk, it became obvious that the traditional focus on elk for subsistence, and on reindeer for transportation and 'wealth investment', revealed a significant small-scale variation in resource strategy in relation to the 'poor' clans that hunt on foot.

The elk population remains concentrated all year round in the vicinity of larger rivers, where it mainly grazes on aquatic vegetation in the summer and willow in the winter. Reindeer prefer to graze grass and a number of other plants on the larger rivers in the summer, but must go to the dry areas with lichen, far from the larger rivers, in winter. The winter is also the main hunting season (Grøn 2005). Apparently the Evenk with domestic reindeer should have the problem that their main game, the elk, stays on the larger rivers in the winter, when they have to leave these to follow their domestic reindeer to the dry lichen areas. It seems the old solution to this problem was to create a significant over-population of elk on the rivers by systematically killing the wolves there. This strategy created pressure on the elk populations, squeezing out the young and inexperienced individuals into the peripheral elk-areas: the lichen areas. The Evenk grazing their reindeer in these areas during the winter would therefore, in this season, be provided with young, inexperienced wild elks that were easy to kill (an especially important factor in relation to hunting with bows and arrows). Interestingly enough, the traditional winter clothing in this area is made of wolf skin, which can be replaced with dog skin when necessary, whereas the customary and predominating picture is that reindeer skin is used. This system has broken down in recent years because of over-hunting of elk by commercial Russian hunters.

The poor Evenk hunters who hunt on foot use a different strategy. As they have no domestic reindeer that need grazing, they simply follow the elk population and stay on the larger rivers during the winters. This means that neighbouring Evenk clans can have 'complementary' resource utilization strategies and settlement patterns.

A third exploitation pattern from the Katanga Region is known from the Kaplin clan living on the Terteia River in the 19th century. According to our information, they had so many domestic reindeer that they were pastoralists. They were not happy with all the mobility that necessarily followed having large reindeer herds which they had to provide grazing for. They therefore organized other Evenks to take care of their reindeer within the Kaplin territory, whereas they themselves lived a kind of sedentary hunter-gatherer life in a base-camp with eight tents on the Terteia River.

Conclusions

An archaeological focus on distinction of small-scale variations in the material culture, which can represent social groups at the clan-level in prehistoric hunter-gatherer societies, in combination with a continued ethnoarchaeological effort to understand the physical/economic and spiritual/ideological organization of hunter-gatherer territories, is seen as an approach that has the potential to significantly improve archaeological methodology.

One pre-condition is that the archaeological focus on distinction of large typologically homogeneous cultural units is replaced by a more fine-grained approach. Another is that the distinction of the general features that seem to play a central role in living hunter-gatherer societies is given more status in itself – as a research theme – and in the interpretation of the prehistoric materials.

An important issue is to what degree hunter-gatherers actually managed the resources in their environment. Does the material from some prehistoric 'hunter-gatherer' cultures actually represent a variation of economic strategies, of which some can be described as resource management with features in common with agricultural strategies?

It is surprising to see how Shirokogoroff's study (in English), in 1935, of the dynamics and small-scale variation of hunter-gatherer societies, which were already described for the Evenk, has never had the impact it should have had on later archaeological research (Shirokogoroff 1935, 12–39).

References

African National Congress 2006. www.anc.org.za/ancdocs/pubs/umrabulo/umrabulo18/fought.html (accessed 01/2006).

Anderson, D. 1991. Turning hunters into herders: A critical examination of Soviet development policy among the Evenki of Southeastern Siberia. *Arctic* 44 (1), 12–22.

Barth, F. 1987. *Cosmologies in the Making. A Generative Approach to Cultural Variation in Inner New Guinea.* Cambridge, Cambridge University Press.

Barth, F. 2002. An Anthropology of Knowledge. *Current Anthropology* 43 (1), 1–18.

Baulin, V. V., Belopukhova, Y. B. and Danilova, N. S. 1984. Holocene permafrost in the USSR, in A. A. Velichko, H. E. Wright Jnr. and C. W. Barnosky (eds.), *Late Quaternary Environments of the Soviet Union*, 87–91. Minneapolis, University of Minnesota Press.

Bennett, J. W. 1944. The Interaction of Culture and Environment in the Smaller Societies. *American Anthropologist*, (New Series) 46 (4), 461–78.

Best, A. 2003. *Regional Variation in the Material Culture of Hunter Gatherers. Social and Ecological Approaches to Ethnographic Objects from Queensland, Australia.* British Archaeological Reports, International Series S1149. Oxford, Archaeopress.

Donner, K. 1915. *Bland Samojeder i Sibirien åren 1911–1913, 1914.* Helsingfors, Söderström & Co.

Dunfjeld, M. 2001. *Tjaalehtjimmie. Form og innhold I sørsamisk ornamentikk.* PhD thesis, University of Tromsø.

Ellen, R. 1982. *Environment, Subsistence and System. The Ecology of Small-Scale Social Formations.* Cambridge, Cambridge University Press.

Fors, G. 2004. *Selskinn som en mulig ressurs. Bruk av sel i Finnmark, Grønland og Island.* Master's thesis, Høgskolen i Finnmark, Norway.

Grøn, O. 2003. Mesolithic dwelling places in south Scandinavia: their definitions and social interpretation. *Antiquity* 77, (298), 685–708.

Grøn, O. 2005. A Siberian perspective on the north European Hamburgian Culture: a study in applied hunter-gatherer ethnoarchaeology. *Before Farming* (online version) 2005/1, article 3. http://www.waspress.co.uk/journals/beforefarming/ (accessed 10/2007).

Grøn, O. and Kuznetsov, O. 2003. Ethno-archaeology among Evenkian forest hunters. Preliminary results and a different approach to reality!, in L. Larsson, H. Kindgren, K. Knutsson, D. Loeffler and A. Åkerlund (eds.), *Mesolithic on the Move: Papers presented at the Sixth International Conference on the Mesolithic in Europe, Stockholm 2000*, 216–21, Oxford, Oxbow Books.

Grøn, O., Kuznetsov, O. and Turov, M. G. 2003. Cultural micromosaics – a problem for the archaeological culture concept?, in J. Bergstøl (ed.), *Scandinavian Archaeological Practice – in Theory. Proceedings from the 6th Nordic TAG, Oslo 2001*, 342–50. Oslo Archaeological Series (1). Oslo, University of Oslo.

Grøn, O. and Turov, M. G. (in press). Resource 'pooling' in hunter-gatherer resource-management strategies. An ethnoarchaeological study of the Evenki in Katanga County, Siberia.

Hamilton, A. 1980. *Nature and Nurture.* Canberra, Australian Institute of Aboriginal Studies.

Ivanenkov, P. M. and Fraicheva, L. B. (eds.) 1997. *Altas Chitinskoi oblasti I Aginskogo Buriatskogo aytonomiog okruga. Federalnayar Cluhva Geodesii I kartografii Rossii.* Moscow, Federalnayar Slushba Geodesii i Kartografii Rossii.

Jarman, M. R., Vita-Finzi, C. and Higgs, E. S. 1972. Site catchment analysis in archaeology, in P. Ucko and R. Tringham (eds.), *Man, settlement and urbanism*, 61–6. London, Duckworth.

Klassen, L. 2004. *Jade und Kupfer. Untersuchungen zum Neolithisierungsprozess im westlichen Ostseeraum unter besonderer Berücksichtigung der Kulturentwicklung Europas 5500–3500 BC.* Jutland Archaeological Society Publications 47. Århus, Jutland Archaeological Society.

Klokkernes, T. 2007. *Skin Processing Technology in Eurasian Reindeer Cultures. A Comparative Study in Material Science of Sàmi and Evenk Methods – Perspectives on Deterioration and Preservation of Museum Artefacts.* Rudkøbing, LMR-PRESS free digital publication: http://www.langelandsmuseum.dk/LMR-PRESS.htm (accessed 01/2008).

Native Science 2006. www.nativescience.org/html/traditional_knowledge.html (accessed 01/2006).

Ohnuki-Tierney, E. 1976. Regional variations in Ainu Culture. *American Ethnologist* 3 (2), 297–329.

Shirokogoroff, S. M. 1929. *Social Organization of the Northern Tungus.* Shanghai. Shanghai Commercial Press.

Shirokogoroff, S. M. 1935. *Psychomental Complex of the Tungus.* London, Kegan, Paul, Trench.

Sillitoe, P. 1998. The Development of Indigenous Knowledge. A New Applied Anthropology. *Current Anthropology* 39 (2), 224–52.

Steward, J. 1955. The Concept and Method of Cultural Ecology, in J. Steward (ed.), *Theory of Culture Change. The Methodology of Multilinear Evolution*, 30–42. Urbana, IL, University of Illinois.

Vang Petersen, P. 1984. Chronological and Regional Variation in the Late Mesolithic of Eastern Denmark. *Journal of Danish Archaeology* 3, 7–18.

Wiessner, P. 1983. Style and social information in Kalahari San projectile points. *American Antiquity* 48 (2), 253–76.

Wiessner, P. 1984. Reconsidering the Behavioral Basis for Style: A Case Study among the Kalahari San. *Journal of Anthropological Archaeology* 3, 190–234

Wright, H. E. and Barnosky, C. W. 1984. Introduction to the English Edition, in A. A. Velichko, H. E. Wright Jnr. and C. W. Barnosky (eds.), *Late Quaternary Environments of the Soviet Union*, xiii–xxii. Minneapolis, University of Minnesota Press.

32. Stable isotopic reconstruction of Early Mesolithic diet at Pupićina Cave

Clea Paine, Tamsin O'Connell and Preston T. Miracle

Palaeodietary analysis of stable isotopes of carbon and nitrogen was performed on human and animal bones from the Mesolithic Midden levels at Pupićina Cave, located on the peninsula of Istria, in northern Croatia. Results of isotopic analysis indicate that humans at the site derived most of their dietary protein from terrestrial herbivores, and a model of subsistence is proposed for Istria in which people focused their foraging efforts on the abundant resources provided by hinterland contexts, with coastal and riparian ecosystems making minimal contributions to diet. The varied topography of the karstic terrain around Pupićina Cave creates diverse microclimates; Mesolithic visitors to the site took advantage of predictable concentrations of plant and animal resources to minimize effort in food procurement. The study is the first of its kind in the eastern Adriatic.

Keywords: carbon, nitrogen, Croatia, collagen, diversification, Adriatic.

Introduction

A broad base for human subsistence has been observed at Mesolithic sites throughout Europe; increases in the consumption of small game, birds, and fish have long been cited as defining characteristics of the period (Binford 1968). Stable isotopic palaeodietary research conducted so far at northwest European Mesolithic sites indicates heavy reliance on marine and freshwater foods, particularly in the later Mesolithic. The inclusion in human diet of resources held by foraging theorists to be nutritionally, energetically, or otherwise undesirable has been the main support for inferences of resource scarcity during the European Mesolithic; the questions of seasonal mobility, resource scheduling, foraging strategy, and human interaction with the landscape during the period have therefore taken on broader significance as attributes which may account for the agricultural adaptation which defines its close.

The Mesolithic at Pupićina Cave

Pupićina cave, located on the peninsula of Istria, in north-western Croatia, provides an ideal opportunity to explore Mesolithic subsistence strategies at the northern end of the Adriatic basin, an area in which such studies have not previously been conducted. Pupićina is one of many caves located in the karstic terrain of the peninsula (Komšo 2003) (Figure 32.1). The role of Pupićina Cave and its neighbours in Mesolithic subsistence and mobility strategies have until now been examined primarily through faunal analysis (Miracle 1997; 2001; 2002; Miracle *et al.* 2000). Although the shortest distance between Pupićina and the coast is approximately 9km, a range of mountains, including 1,400m Učka peak, lies between the site and the ocean, making the likeliest route for coastal access by prehistoric visitors to the cave a walk of 20km to the south-east. The cave can therefore be considered within a hinterland rather than a coastal foraging context.

Faunal evidence suggests that people came to Pupićina during the autumn and winter to exploit red deer, boar, and roe deer, but, as with many Mesolithic sites, the question of group movement and subsistence strategy throughout the rest of the year has not yet been answered (Miracle 1997). This question is particularly pertinent at Pupićina, as its location in a hinterland context sets it apart from many of the European Mesolithic sites selected for palaeodietary research so far. Previous analysis at Pupićina has focused on the interaction of coastal and hinterland sites, and the role of hinterland contexts in the subsistence strategies and mobility patterns of hunter-gatherers (Miracle and Forenbaher 2000). This palaeodietary study seeks to elucidate aspects of group movement in other seasons, including the possibility of group movement to the coast for some portion of the year, and to infer overall foraging emphasis.

Several distinct phases of occupation, extending from the late Pleistocene through the Holocene, can be observed in the stratigraphy of the cave. Thin lenses of anthropogenic debris, including several hearths, occur in the otherwise clean late glacial deposits at the cave and are AMS dated to 10,150±60 BP (10,110–9460 cal BC, Beta-131626, Miracle and Forenbaher 1998), contemporary with the end of the Younger Dryas. (Radiocarbon dates were calibrated using OxCal 4.0 on IntCal04 (Bronk Ramsey 1995; 2001; Reimer *et al.* 2004).) Deposits from the early Mesolithic see an intensification of occupation, with a higher frequency of charcoal and animal bone. In the overlying Mesolithic deposits, a large midden, divided into two layers, can be identified. The 'Lower Midden' (Horizon N) is tentatively dated to 9590±180 BP (9450–8350 cal BC; z-2572; Miracle 1997), while the 'Upper Midden' (Horizons M1–M4) has associated dates of 9200±170 BP (9120–7960 cal BC; z-2634; Horizon M1, Miracle 1997) and 8710±170 BP (8270–7510 cal BC; z-2635; Horizon M2, Miracle 1997); the different layers of the midden can be distinguished by their contents, with the Lower Midden containing a large number of animal bones, and the Upper Midden containing abundant large edible snail shells (*Helix* spp.) (Miracle 1997; 2001; 2002) (Figure 32.2).

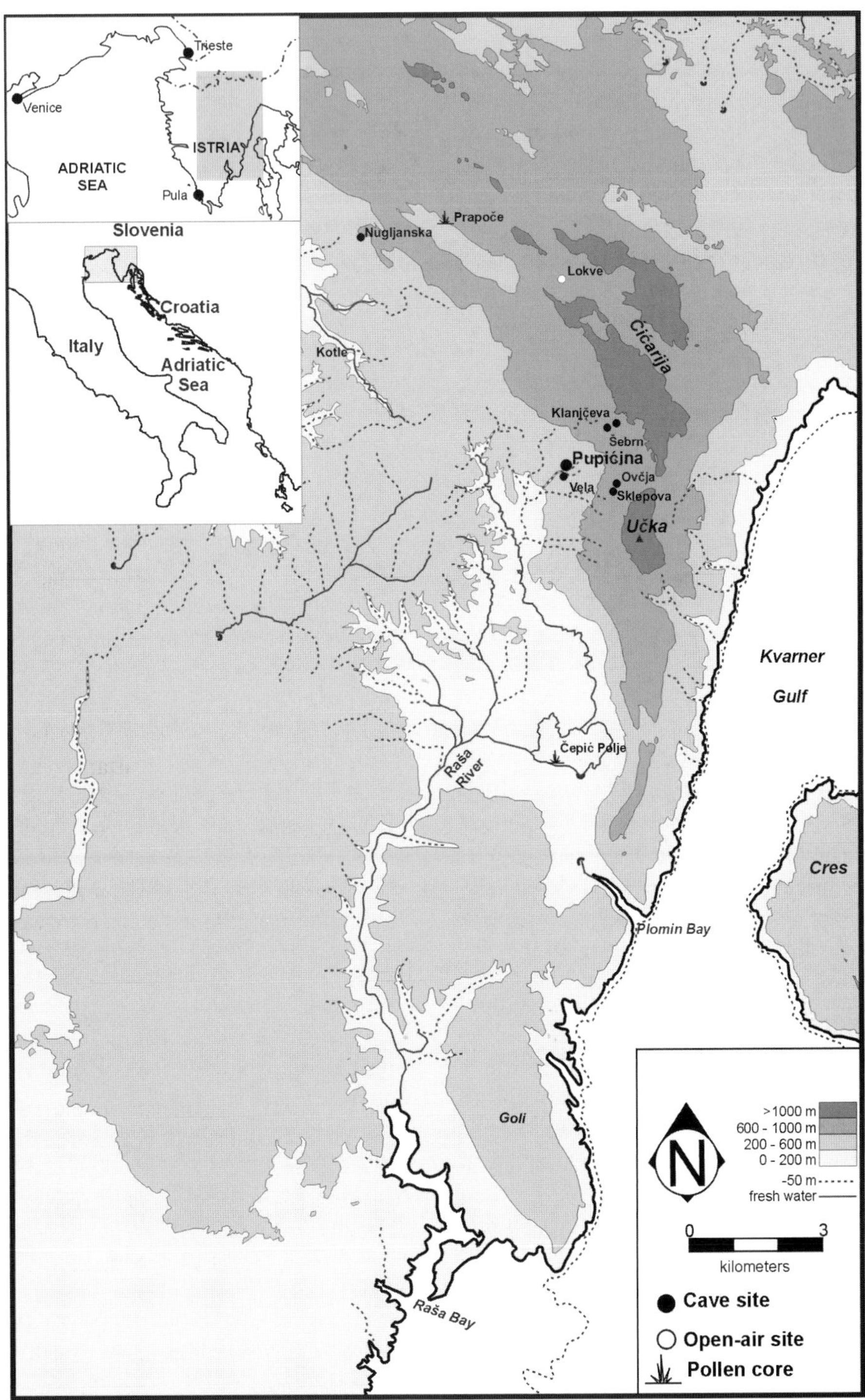

Figure 32.1. Location of Pupićina Cave and other Mesolithic sites in the region.

Figure 32.2. Stratigraphy of Pupićina Cave – North Section (squares L–N/1). (Photograph: P. T. Miracle).

A wide range of faunal remains occurs in the Mesolithic levels at the site, consistent with a broad-spectrum diet. Red deer (*Cervus elaphus*) dominate the mammal assemblage represented in the two midden levels, followed by roe deer (*Capreolus capreolus*) or wild pig (*Sus scrofa*), with chamois and small mammals, such as badger (*Meles meles*) and hare, occurring more rarely. Occupants also appear to have exploited small carnivores and omnivores such as marten (*Martes martes*), wild cat (*Felis silvestris*), and fox (*Vulpes vulpes*), for meat as well as pelts (Miracle 1997; 2001; 2002). The midden levels contain a number of fish bones from a euryhaline species (gilthead bream (*Sparus aurata*)), as well as marine mussel (*Mytilus* spp.) shells, which must have been transported from the coast. Mussels are adapted to intertidal zones and can live out of water for extended periods of time; despite the effective distance of 20km lying between the site and the coast, mussels could have been transported to the site either through trade or by site occupants making a move inland from the coast, and would have remained viable for consumption for several days (Miracle 1997).

Evidence of a broadening diet, along with the extensive fracturing of marrow and grease-bearing bones from Mesolithic levels, may indicate resource stress (Miracle 1997; 2001). Changes in intensity of carcass use and the emphasis on edible snails as an apparent food source are also consistent with a change in the function of the site, or the kinds of people using it, between the Early Mesolithic and Lower and Upper Middens (Miracle 1997). As an alternative to inferences of resource stress, Miracle (2002) uses evidence of provisioning of ungulate meat to the site in the midden phases to suggest a scenario in which Pupićina would have been central to a regional resource exploitation strategy that took advantage of the diverse animal and plant resources supported by the Istrian karst, hosting periodic aggregations of people.

Animal bones excavated throughout the Mesolithic layers, and human bones from the Upper and Lower Middens and Upper silts are examined in this study. Animal and human remains are therefore assumed to date between approximately 9500–7500 cal BC, a period during which autumn exploitation of red deer took place at the site with a secondary focus changing from roe deer to pig, and with tertiary and somewhat enigmatic exploitation of a variety of other food sources including small game, fish, and edible snails. The human bones are assumed to be roughly contemporary with one another and with the faunal remains.

Materials and methods

Bones representing a wide variety of taxa were selected for analysis from the Mesolithic levels of the cave, both in order to paint an isotopic picture of the ecosystem around Pupićina cave during the Mesolithic, and in order to reconstruct human diet as accurately as possible. 10 taxa from the Upper and Lower Midden layers were selected for analysis, and samples were taken from between four and six individuals per taxon. Terrestrial herbivores analysed were red deer, roe deer, hare (*Lepus europaeus*), and chamois (*Rupicapra rupicapra*). Terrestrial omnivores analysed were fox, badger, marten, and (wild) pig. Wild cat, a carnivore, was also analysed, as were the jaws of five freshwater and estuarine fish identified as gilthead bream. Identifications of terrestrial mammals were made by Preston Miracle. Identifications of the fish were made by the late Maja Paunović; we are very grateful for her help. Where possible, all samples from a given taxon were taken from the same skeletal element, but in most cases at least one sample is from a different element. Elements from juvenile individuals (based on epiphyseal fusion or bone texture) were excluded, and mammalian samples therefore come from weaned individuals, in most cases clearly adult.

The minimum number of individuals (MNI) represented by the human bones available for analysis is 1. Four rib fragments and one long bone fragment recovered from the Mesolithic layers were selected for the study. PUP 52, 53, and 54 were collected from the Lower Midden, PUP 55 from the Upper Silts, and PUP 56, the long bone fragment, from the Upper Midden. Identifications of the human remains were made by Preston Miracle and Jay Stock. Sample PUP56 was identified as 'human?'.

Most bones used in the study were fragmentary, but fragments were fairly large, and were identifiable to species and body part. Burnt bone was not used. There was no visible evidence of diagenesis or of any post depositional alteration which might have affected bone chemistry. Bones were structurally competent in most cases. Samples were prepared using the modified Longin method (Longin 1971; Ambrose 1990).

Isotopic results are measured as the ratio of the heavier isotope to the lighter isotope relative to an internationally defined scale, VPDB for carbon, and AIR for nitrogen (Mariotti 1983; Gonfiantini 1990). Isotopic results are reported as δ values ($\delta^{13}C$ and $\delta^{15}N$) in parts per 1000 or 'permil' (‰), where, for example, $\delta^{15}N_{AIR} = [(^{15/14}N_{sample} / ^{15/14}N_{AIR}) - 1] \times 1000$. Based on repeat analysis of international and in-house standards, the analytical error is less than ±0.2‰ for $\delta^{13}C$ and $\delta^{15}N$. Calculation of the atomic carbon:nitrogen ratio for the samples processed

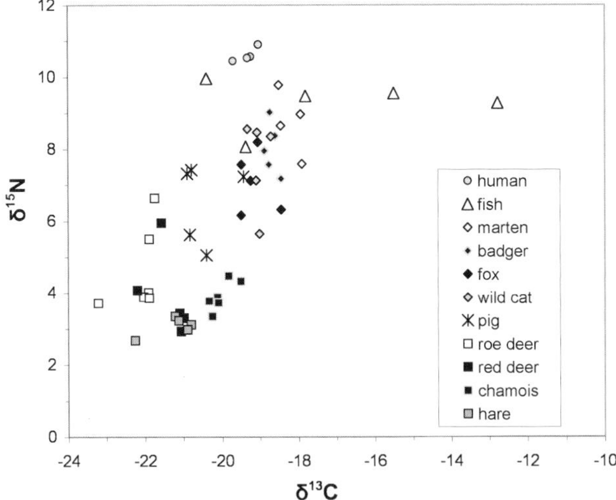

Figure 32.3. Results of stable isotopic analysis of human and animal remains from the Mesolithic levels of Pupićina Cave, plotted by species. Each data point represents the average value for an individual sample, calculated from values measured for the three replicates analysed. Measurement errors are less than 0.2‰ for both carbon and nitrogen.

confirms that the majority of collagen was well preserved (2.9 to 3.4‰) (DeNiro 1985). The C:N values for one replicate of a sample for each of two samples fell outside of the acceptable range and were excluded from averages; several others were marginal, falling between 3.4 and 3.6, but were deemed usable. The mass percent collagen yields calculated for the bone samples analysed in this paper fall within the range of acceptable values (2 to 20%: Ambrose 1990). Reprecipitated alkaline materials, present in some samples after the demineralization process, inhibited complete collagen extraction, generating artificially low collagen yields. One sample, PUP 51, yielded only 0.99 % collagen, but C:N ratios for the sample were acceptable, and all data for the sample are therefore included.

Results of Isotopic Analysis

$\delta^{13}C$ values for all species analysed are broadly similar, and removal of outlying points belonging to fish, whose $\delta^{13}C$ values meet expectations in being wider-ranging and averaging higher than terrestrial species, shows all $\delta^{13}C$ values to be clustered between -17.9‰ and -23.2‰, consistent with expected values for C_3-based terrestrial ecosystems (Chisholm *et al.* 1982; Schoeninger and DeNiro 1984). $\delta^{15}N$ values fall between 2.7‰ (hare) and 10.9‰ (human), and are vertically stratified according to the trophic level of the animals analysed. $\delta^{13}C$ values are consistent within individual consumer groups, with distinctive clusters for herbivores and carnivores.

Results for terrestrial mammals are consistent with animals belonging to a single ecosystem. The average $\delta^{15}N$ value for herbivores is 3.9‰, while carnivores and omnivores excluding pig average 7.8‰, showing a +3 to +4‰ stepwise increase in $\delta^{15}N$ with trophic level. A scatter plot of average $\delta^{15}N$ and $\delta^{13}C$ values by species divides the results of the isotopic analysis into four clusters relating to diet and trophic level (Figure 32.3).

Terrestrial mammals

$\delta^{15}N$ and $\delta^{13}C$ results for the herbivores analysed are consistent with expected values (Chisholm *et al.* 1982; Schoeninger and DeNiro 1984), and show minor variation likely associated with different ranges and diets of individual species and individual animals. Variability in red deer and roe deer $\delta^{15}N$ values is noteworthy, but consistent with studies of isotopic composition of modern adult red deer populations (Stevens 2006); causes may include dietary variability, for example the consumption of bone, antler, and marine plants (Stevens 2006), and temporal variation between samples. The nursing effect is unlikely to be the source of the variability, as samples were taken from weaned individuals, which in most cases were clearly adult. Chamois results are also noteworthy; no overlap occurs between chamois and other herbivores on the $\delta^{13}C$ axis despite their relative proximity to one another on the graph, possibly a consequence of the particular foraging preferences and range of that species. Miracle and Sturdy (1991) propose that chamois in Herzegovina were able to exploit late glacial 'angry karst' in low altitude environments; the same may be true at Pupićina Cave, which is located in karstic terrain well away from alpine areas. Isotopic analysis indicates that chamois and deer came from distinct, probably spatially proximal, microenvironments.

Terrestrial Carnivores and Omnivores

Badger, marten, wild cat, and fox collagen $\delta^{15}N$ values plot in a cluster consistent with expected values for terrestrial carnivores (Schoeninger and DeNiro 1984). Pig although an artiodactyl, is considered separately because of its omnivorous diet. It takes up a position intermediary between herbivores and carnivores in $\delta^{15}N$ isotopic composition, but clusters closer to herbivores in terms of $\delta^{13}C$ values.

Fox is reported to consume small mammals, insects, and fruit (Nowak 1999), and this may have an effect on variable $\delta^{15}N$ composition for the species. Wild cat $\delta^{15}N$ values, however, are perplexingly low, and marten and badger values are perplexingly high. Both badger and marten are slightly enriched in $\delta^{13}C$ and $\delta^{15}N$ relative to all other terrestrial mammals, supporting the consumption of some aquatic ecosystem foods, such as freshwater fish, turtles, or birds, and implying marten and badger procurement in stream valleys.

Fish

Gilthead bream have a large possible range of habitats including fresh, brackish, and salt waters of the Mediterranean region. $\delta^{13}C$ and $\delta^{15}N$ values are intermediate between terrestrial and marine values, consistent with expectations for freshwater fish (Schoeninger and DeNiro 1984). $\delta^{15}N$ values are fairly consistent within the group analysed, falling between 8.07‰ and 9.95‰, but $\delta^{13}C$ values are the widest-ranging of any animal analysed, from -20.40‰ to -12.78‰. Multiple sources of carbon used by primary producers in freshwater ecosystems, the bedrock geology, and the effects of turbulence on phytoplankton ^{13}C uptake lead to a large degree of variation in $\delta^{13}C$ values between bodies of water, and therefore within fish species collected from different bodies of water (France 1995; Dufour *et al.* 1999), and the story told by the gilthead bream is complicated by its euryhaline tolerances. Fishing may therefore have taken place in more than one location in the region of Pupićina Cave.

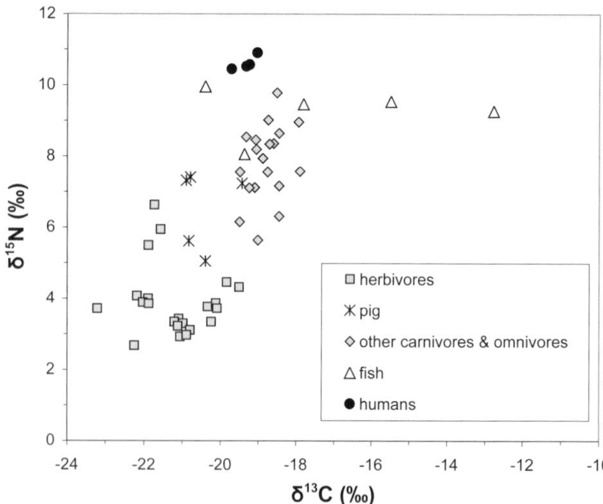

Figure 32.4. Results of stable isotopic analysis of human and animal remains from the Mesolithic levels of Pupićina Cave, plotted by diet. $\delta^{13}C$ and $\delta^{15}N$ values for human samples indicate that the majority of dietary protein was supplied by pig, red deer, and roe deer, with limited input from other herbivores, fish, carnivores, or marine resources.

Humans

One individual, PUP 56, a long bone fragment osteologically identified as probably human, was indicated by isotopic analysis to be a terrestrial herbivore, yielding a $\delta^{15}N$ value of 3.3‰, and was therefore omitted from further interpretation. Single replicates belonging to two individuals (PUP 53 and PUP 54) were excluded on the basis of unacceptably high C/N ratios. Data plots in Figures 32.3 and 32.4 include only the results deemed valid.

The mean human $\delta^{13}C$ value was -19.33‰ (ranging between -19.04 and -19.71‰) and the mean human $\delta^{15}N$ value was 10.62‰ (ranging between 10.45 and 10.91‰). Data points cluster tightly, with the least intragroup variability in $\delta^{15}N$ values of all species analysed and comparably low variability in $\delta^{13}C$. Sex and age data were not available for human rib fragments, but diet is fairly uniform among the samples analysed. The minimum number of individuals (MNI) analysed is 1, and there is a high likelihood that two data points, PUP 52 and PUP 54, are from the same individual, as they are very close in isotopic composition and were excavated from the same stratigraphic context. The range of variability among samples is consistent either with one or multiple individuals.

The sample size is small, which limits the interpretations possible from the data, but despite this, we can draw some valid conclusions. Carbon and nitrogen isotope ratios are fairly unequivocal in indicating a predominantly terrestrial diet for humans at Pupićina Cave. Humans have the highest $\delta^{15}N$ of all species analysed, indicating that they consume foods of higher trophic level than other species, including carnivores. These elevated $\delta^{15}N$ values relative to carnivores and fish could indicate some utilization of resources with higher $\delta^{15}N$ values, such as aquatic resources, carnivores or pig. Relatively low $\delta^{13}C$ values rule out marine shellfish as major contributors of dietary protein to humans occupying the site, and combined $\delta^{13}C$ and $\delta^{15}N$ values indicate a minimal input of marine fish to human diet. The small body size of carnivores and omnivores analysed means that humans at Pupićina would have had to consume a large number of individuals in order to affect their bone collagen isotopic composition; it can safely be concluded that humans did not rely on fox, wild cat, badger, or marten for more than 30% of their dietary protein. Although we conclude that pig and freshwater fish are therefore most likely to be responsible for human ^{15}N enrichment relative to other carnivores, the wide range of $\delta^{13}C$ values for freshwater ecosystems and for the individual fish analysed renders impossible a quantitative estimate of the contribution of fish to the dietary protein intake of humans at Pupićina Cave.

The relationship of human collagen $\delta^{13}C$ to values for potential prey, grouped according to diet, is shown in Figure 32.4; the plot can be used to explore the relative contributions of small game and economic species to human dietary protein. Although all terrestrial mammals form part of the same ecosystem, and were probably procured in relative geographic proximity to one another, two component 'food chains' can be inferred from the bimodal distribution of $\delta^{13}C$ values, one linking hare with small predators, and one linking red deer (and other economic species) with humans. Human collagen is enriched by more than 2‰ above the average value for red deer, which slightly exceeds the trophic level effect in carbon predicted by van der Merwe (1989). The enrichment in human collagen $\delta^{13}C$ and $\delta^{15}N$ is most suggestive of a combination of extensive red deer and pig exploitation (consistent with the faunal remains at the site). Hare and small game, meanwhile, are unlikely to have made a large contribution to subsistence. Chamois cluster with small game in their $\delta^{13}C$ composition. This supports a relatively minor contribution to human diet for the species.

Conclusions

The isotopic results indicate that people at Pupićina Cave

relied primarily on ungulates, particularly red deer and pig, for their dietary protein. The broad resource base mobilized by cave occupants is manifest in the archaeofaunal assemblage from the site, and isotopic analysis of human and animal bones supports Miracle's (1997) interpretation that humans probably ate some small game, such as badger and marten. In comparison with ungulates, however, small game and fish appear to make a limited contribution to diet. In spite of the easy access to the coast from the region of the site, and in apparent contrast with the evidence provided by marine mussels from Mesolithic layers of the cave, marine resources appear to have played a negligible role in the diet of cave occupants, and visits to the coast by members of the group, if they occurred at all, must have been brief. Freshwater or estuarine resources, available to site occupants from several rivers within a few kilometres of the cave, made a similarly minor contribution to group subsistence. Limited utilization of coastal resources is therefore likely by choice, since nutritionally comparable resources available locally are also used only in limited quantities.

Pupićina Cave was a centre for the autumn exploitation of large and medium-sized ungulates at the beginning of the Holocene, with tertiary contributions to diet from a variety of prey animals probably culled in the wooded bottom of the Vela Draga. The dietary emphasis on terrestrial ungulates among humans at Pupićina Cave suggests that the hinterland was the principal zone in which hunting and foraging took place, not just in the particular season during which Pupićina Cave was occupied, but throughout the year. If people made forays to the coast, they continued to rely on terrestrial game. Pupićina Cave was likely an important stop in annual population movement, possibly seeing the congregation of a large group for some part of the year (Miracle 2001; 2002).

Our evidence for a mostly terrestrial source of protein in the human diet during the Early Mesolithic occupation at Pupićina Cave fits a pattern noted by Richards and Schulting (2003) for the Early Mesolithic in Britain. These authors noted a 'focus ... towards inland, terrestrial food resources', and remarked on the 'lack of marine foods in the diet of the human at the coastal Breakwater Quarry' (Richards and Schulting 2003). Two other studies of Mesolithic human populations have also yielded isotopic data indicating a similar reliance on terrestrial resources: one in Sweden (Liden *et al.* 2004), and one in Ukraine (Lillie and Richards 2000), although both sites are later than Pupićina by several thousand years.

In contrast, stable isotope palaeodietary analyses carried out on later Mesolithic human remains from coastal sites throughout Europe support the idea that the people there relied heavily on marine resources for a considerable portion of their diet. There is evidence that between 50 and 90% of the protein intake of Mesolithic populations on the Atlantic coast of Europe came from marine foods (Richards and Hedges 1999). Similarly high numbers (with notable variation between sites and individuals) have been generated by studies in Brittany (Schulting and Richards 2001), Denmark (Tauber 1981), and Portugal (Lubell *et al.* 1994).

Palaeodietary studies at inland sites with access to freshwater ecosystems show a similar reliance on aquatic protein. Aquatic food sources supply the majority of protein to Mesolithic populations at three sites in the Iron Gates region (Bonsall *et al.* 1997). Studies of Neolithic sites with a hunter-gatherer subsistence mode in the region of Lake Baikal show heavy reliance on aquatic protein in individuals buried near the lake, with a more balanced intake of aquatic and terrestrial proteins at sites more than 100km away (Katzenberg and Weber 1999). Two palaeodietary studies of archaeological populations from the Eurasian Steppe show that freshwater fish contributed a surprisingly large percentage of dietary protein during the Mesolithic, and particularly during the Bronze and Iron Ages (O'Connell *et al.* 2000; Privat 2004).

Diet at Pupićina Cave presents a marked contrast to these examples. The diet breadth evidenced in faunal remains at the site is real; red deer and pig provide for the bulk of human protein needs, with consumption of other protein resources providing variety and balance. Diverse diet at Pupićina Cave is made possible by locally abundant game, and takes place in a context not of resource stress, but of resource sufficiency.

The stable isotopic paleodietary research conducted at Pupićina Cave is the first of its kind in the region of the Adriatic, and one of the first studies on Mesolithic human remains from the Mediterranean region. As such, our admittedly limited data add considerably to knowledge of subsistence and mobility in the region. Stable isotope results from Pupićina suggest that people made relatively little use of aquatic protein sources, despite the close proximity of the coast and freshwater habitats like Lake Čepić (Balbo *et al.*, this volume). Either early Mesolithic people at Pupićina did not travel regularly to the coast, perhaps using only a hinterland territory, or they did not use marine resources when they were at the coast. Although we currently lack evidence to distinguish between these alternative scenarios, both are unexpected and at odds with commonly held assumptions about Mesolithic subsistence and mobility strategies. Our results indicate that broad-spectrum diet existed at the site, albeit in a different form than has been suggested for other Mesolithic sites on the basis of faunal remains. Isotopic evidence from Pupićina is therefore unusual for its time, and adds to the growing body of literature documenting a variety of subsistence strategies during the Mesolithic.

References

Ambrose, S. H. 1990. Preparation and characterization of bone and tooth collagen for isotopic analysis. *Journal of Archaeological Science* 17, 431–51.

Binford, L. 1968. Post Pleistocene Adaptations, in S. R. Binford and L. R. Binford (eds.), *New Perspectives in Archaeology*, 313–41. Chicago, Aldine.

Bonsall, C., Lennon, R., McSweeney, K., Stewart, C., Harkness, D., Boroneant, V., Bartosiewicz, L., Payton, R. and Chapman,

J. 1997. Mesolithic and Early Neolithic in the Iron Gates: a Palaeodietary Perspective. *European Journal of Archaeology* 5, 50–92.

Bronk Ramsey, C. 1995. Radiocarbon calibration and analysis of stratigraphy: The OxCal program. *Radiocarbon* 37 (2), 425–30.

Bronk Ramsey, C. 2001. Development of the Radiocarbon Calibration Program OxCal. *Radiocarbon* 43 (2A), 355–63.

Chisholm, B. S., Nelson, D. E. and Schwarcz, H. P. 1982. Stable-Carbon Isotope Ratios as a Measure of Marine versus Terrestrial Protein in Ancient Diets. *Science* 216, 1131–2.

DeNiro, M. J. 1985. Postmortem preservation and alteration of in vivo bone collagen Isotope Ratios in Relation to Palaeodietary Reconstruction. *Nature* 317, 806–9.

Dufour, E., Bocherens, H. and Mariotti, A. 1999. Palaeodietary Implications of Isotopic Variability in Eurasian Lacustrine Fish. *Journal of Archaeological Science* 26, 617–27.

France, R. C. 1995. Carbon-13 Enrichment in Benthic Compared to Planktonic Algae: Foodweb Implications. *Marine Ecology Progress Series* 124, 307–12.

Gonfiantini, R., Rozanski, K. and Stichler, W. 1990. Intercalibration of environmental isotope measurements: the program of the International Atomic Energy Agency. *Radiocarbon* 32, 369–74.

Katzenberg, M. A. and Weber, A. 1999. Stable Isotope Ecology and Palaeodiet in the Lake Baikal Region of Siberia. *Journal of Archaeological Science* 26, 651–9.

Komšo, D. 2003. Pećine Istre – mjesta življenja od prapovijesti do srednjega vijeka. *Histria Antiqua* 11, 41–54.

Lidén, K, Eriksson, G., Nordqvist, B., Gotherstrom, A., and Bendixen, E. 2004. 'The wet and the wild followed by the dry and the tame' – or did they occur at the same time? Diet in Mesolithic-Neolithic southern Sweden. *Antiquity* 78, 23–33.

Lillie, M. and Richards, M. 2000. Stable Isotope Analysis and Dental Evidence of Diet at the Mesolithic-Neolithic Transition in Ukraine. *Journal of Archaeological Science* 27, 965–72.

Longin, R. 1971. A New Method of Collagen Extraction for Radiocarbon Dating. *Nature* 230, 241–2.

Lubell, D., Jackes, K., Schwarcz, H., Knyf, M. and Meiklejohn, C. 1994. The Mesolithic-Neolithic Transition in Portugal: Isotopic and Dental Evidence of Diet. *Journal of Archaeological Science* 21, 201–16.

Mariotti, A. 1983. Atmospheric nitrogen is a reliable standard for natural ^{15}N measurements. *Nature*, 303, 685–7.

Miracle, P. T. 1997. Early Holocene Foragers in the Karst of Northern Istria. *Poročilo o raziskovanju paleolitika, neolitika in eneolitika v Sloveniji* XXIV, 43–61.

Miracle, P. T. 2001. Feast or Famine? Epipalaeolithic subsistence in the northern Adriatic Basin. *Documenta Praehistorica* XXVIII, 177–97.

Miracle, P. T. 2002. Mesolithic meals from Mesolithic middens, in P. T. Miracle and N. Milner (eds.), *Consuming Passions and Patterns of Consumption*, 65–88. McDonald Institute Monographs. Cambridge, McDonald Institute for Archaeological Research.

Miracle, P. T. and Forenbaher, S. 1998. Pupićina Cave Project: Brief summary of the 1998 season. *Histria Archaeologica*, 29, 27–48.

Miracle, P. T., Galanidou, N. and Forenbaher, S. 2000. Pioneers in the hills: Early Mesolithic foragers at Šebrn Abri (Istria, Croatia). *European Journal of Archaeology* 3 (3), 293–329.

Miracle, P. T. and Sturdy, D. 1991. Chamois and the Karst of Herzegovina. *Journal of Archaeological Science* 18, 89–108.

Nowak, R. M. 1999. *Walker's Mammals of the World, v. I and II.* Baltimore, Johns Hopkins University.

O'Connell, T. C., Levine, M. and Hedges, R. E. M. 2000. The Importance of Fish in the Diet of Central Eurasian Peoples from the Mesolithic to the Early Iron Age, in M. Levine, K. Boyle and C. Renfrew (eds.), *Prehistoric Steppe Adaptation and the Horse*, 253–68. McDonald Institute Monographs. Cambridge, McDonald Institute for Archaeological Research.

Privat, K. L. 2004. *Palaeoeconomy of the Eurasian Steppe: Biomolecular Studies*. Unpublished DPhil Thesis, Department of Archaeology, University of Oxford.

Reimer, P. J., Baillie, M. G. L., Bard, E., Bayliss, A., Beck, J. W., Bertrand, C. J. H., Blackwell, P. G., Buck, C. E., Burr, G. S., Cutler, K. B., Damon, P. E., Edwards, R. L., Fairbanks, R. G., Friedrich, M., Guilderson, T. P., Hogg, A. G., Hughen, K. A., Kromer, B., McCormac, G., Manning, S., Bronk Ramsey, C., Reimer, R. W., Remmele, S., Southon, J. R., Stuiver, M., Talamo, S., Taylor, F. W., van der Plicht, J. and Weyhenmeyer, C. E. 2004. IntCal04 terrestrial radiocarbon age calibration, 0-26 cal kyr BP. *Radiocarbon* 46 (3), 1029–58.

Richards, M. P. and Hedges, R. E. M. 1999. Stable isotope evidence for similarities in the types of marine foods used by late Mesolithic humans at sites along the Atlantic coast of Europe. *Journal of Archaeological Science* 26, 717–22.

Richards, M. P. and Schulting, R. J. 2003. Characterising Subsistence in Mesolithic Britain Using Stable Isotope Analysis, in L. Bevan and J. Moore (eds.), *Peopling the Mesolithic in a Northern Environment*, 119–28. British Archaeological Reports, Interntional Series S1157. Oxford, Archaeopress.

Schoeninger, M. J. and DeNiro, M. J. 1984. Nitrogen and Carbon Isotopic Composition of Bone Collagen from Marine and Terrestrial Animals. *Geochimica et Cosmochimica Acta* 48, 625–39.

Schulting, R. J. and Richards, M. P. 2001. Dating women becoming farmers: new paleodietary and AMS dating evidence from the Breton Mesolithic cemeteries of Téviec and Hoëdic. *Journal of Anthropological Archaeology* 20, 314–44.

Stevens, R. E., Lister, A. M. and Hedges, R. E. M. 2006. Predicting diet, trophic level and palaeoecology from bone stable isotope analysis: A comparative study of five red deer populations. *Oecologia* 149, 12–21.

Tauber, H. 1981. ^{13}C Evidence for Dietary Habits of Prehistoric Man in Denmark. *Nature* 292, 332–3.

Van der Merwe, N. J. 1989. Natural Variation in ^{13}C Concentration and its Effect on Environmental Reconstruction using ^{13}C/^{12}C Ratios in Animal Bones, in T. D. Price (ed.), *The Chemistry of Prehistoric Human Bone*, 105–25. Cambridge, Cambridge University Press.

33. Human colonisation routes and the origins of Irish mammals

Ceiridwen J. Edwards and Daniel G. Bradley

Ireland's fauna is unusual due to particular combinations of natural circumstances and human intervention that has led to their introduction or extinction. Some animals may have survived the last glacial maximum within a refugium in the south-west (e.g. hare). Others may have entered naturally by sea (e.g. otter), whilst many were introduced/released by man, either deliberately (e.g. domesticates, red deer) or accidentally (e.g. woodmouse). Although current distribution data cannot distinguish between these differing hypotheses, genetic data from the same species in Ireland and elsewhere in Europe can be compared to infer original population sources. Whilst modern samples of several species of both wild and domesticated animals have been analysed, ancient DNA techniques are also necessary to describe Irish phylogeography, as many populations have been replaced by more recent introductions. Extensive analyses of phylogenetic affinities of Ireland's mammals should enable valuations of faunal origins and may point to human migration and trade routes.

Keywords: Ireland, landbridge, faunal colonisation, mammals, human introduction, Lusitanian phylogeography, mitochondrial DNA.

Introduction

Ireland has 22 terrestrial mammals (Figure 33.1), a limited subset of those found in Great Britain and mainland Europe. The origins of the mammals of Ireland are controversial. There are three plausible modes of colonisation by terrestrial animals of Ireland:

1. Some animals may have survived the last glacial maximum (20,000 years ago) within an unglaciated area in the south-west of the island. However, given the severity and length of the glacial period, it remains unlikely that the majority of Irish fauna are a legacy of a refugium within the island.
2. Terrestrial migration via a landbridge, which may have persisted between Ireland and Britain after the retreat of the glacial ice, but which was subsequently submerged by rising water levels in the Holocene. Such a link certainly existed between Britain and the continental mainland, and is postulated as the major source of biota there. However, no such certainty surrounds the existence of such overland links within the British Isles or their availability to migrating animals. Geologists differ on this point (Cooper *et al.* 2002; Devoy 1985; 1995) and some data, such as the relative paucity of animal species in Ireland relative to Britain, suggest that there was no major corridor. Importantly, this scenario implies a specific phylogeographic pattern within species: the genetic diversity observed within Irish samples should be a subset, or derivative, of that observed in Britain.
3. Alternately, there was no contribution from a landbridge and those animals that did not swim or fly to the island are the result of passive or intentional human transport. The first human settlers in Ireland were Mesolithic and probably arrived by boat around 8000 cal BC with the arrival of the first (Neolithic) agriculturists *c.* 4000 cal BC. Animals may have been introduced accidentally, or else intentionally for a purpose, such as future hunting or, as in the case of domesticates, farming. This scenario does not imply the same strong phylogeographic affinity within species between Ireland and Britain. Whereas many seaborne introductions may have been from Britain, there are some grounds to expect that prevailing trade routes, cultural links and even human migrations may give links directly with the continent, particularly south-western Europe. A phylogeography linking Irish animal diversity to these latter regions rather than Britain can be interpreted as a signature of human introduction and an indication, by proxy, of direct early human contact between Ireland and southern continental Europe.

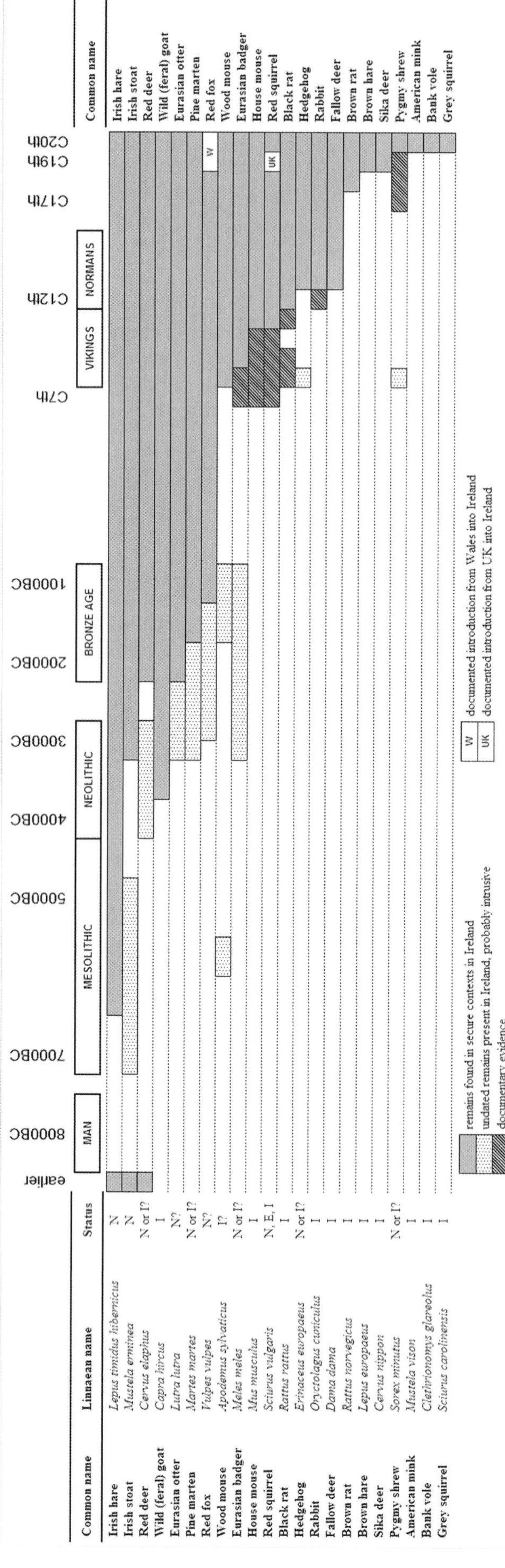

Figure 33.1. Graphic representation showing the approximate times of introduction for the 22 extant terrestrial mammals present in Ireland (information taken from McCormick, 1999; Hayden and Harrington, 2001; Sommer and Benecke, 2004). Common and Latin names noted, and probable status indicated: N, native; I, introduced; E, extinct; ?, native status uncertain (modified from Woodman et al. 1983). The sequence N, E, I indicates a native form, becoming extinct and then reintroduced.

Lusitanian phylogeography

Looking solely at distribution patterns of species, the northern hemisphere has many cases where wide gaps can be seen to occur in a species' range, so called disjunct distributions or climatic relicts. There are a group of 12 species of Irish flora that exhibit this distribution pattern, being found mainly in Spain and Portugal, but with isolated outposts in south-western Ireland (i.e. along the western shoreline of Europe but not in the mainland interior, even though in several cases the species are not coastal dwelling). This is in contrast to the usual plant and animal species distribution in Europe, where more species occur towards the centre and less towards the margins. The distribution of these former species, known as Hiberno-Lusitanian, is controversial and some (sometimes it is argued all) are likely to have been introduced by man over the last few hundred years. Two representatives of this Lusitanian flora are the strawberry tree (*Arbutus unedo*) and Saint Patrick's cabbage (*Saxifraga spathularis*), being found mainly in Spain and Portugal but with isolated outposts in southwest Ireland. An example of a faunal species is the Kerry spotted slug (*Geomalacus maculosus*).

Whilst the natural history and archaeology of Irish mammals has been discussed in depth (e.g. Browne 2005; Hayden and Harrington 2001; McCormick 1999), Irish faunal phylogeography has been incompletely studied. Nevertheless, a few species have been sampled with some rigour using mitochondrial (mt) DNA sequencing, and have been found to also show a Lusitanian pattern. Pygmy shrews (*Sorex minutus*), for example, show two major clades within Europe – northern and southern. Interestingly, the samples from Ireland cluster with those from Spain (nearest variants being found in the Pyrenees), unlike those from Britain, which cluster securely with northern European haplotypes (Mascheretti *et al.* 2003). The authors interpret this as a clear indication of an Atlantean introduction. Pine martens (*Martes martes*) have also been analysed, although with a smaller sample distribution, and they too show an Irish-Spanish affinity (Davison *et al.* 2001). A recent study of mitochondrial fragmentation patterns from Irish crayfish (*Austropotamobius pallipes*) echoed this pattern (Gouin *et al.* 2003).

Lusitanian phylogeographies may be interpreted as the result of prevailing human communications between the western regions of the British Isles and the western Atlantic seaboard of continental Europe. Interestingly the phylogeography of human genetic systems show concordance.

Origins of Irish people

The origins of the people of Ireland are interesting. The island's position on the edge of Europe suggests that genetic patterns of its people may be essentially Western Atlantic European, relatively unperturbed by the many known and unknown migrations that the continental mainland has experienced over the millennia. Indeed, several data treatments suggest genetic affinity with Basque populations from northern Spain (Hill *et al.* 2000; McEvoy *et al.* 2004; Figure 33.2). Other populations from the British Isles (namely Scotland, Wales and Cornwall) show a similar affinity, pointing to a shared western Atlantic genetic heritage that may be very ancient. Interestingly, there is also evidence of a separate ancestral influence within these islands; English samples of Y-chromosome haplotypes from East Anglia and the British Midlands show sharply different haplotype frequencies from those in Wales and Ireland (Weale *et al.* 2002), and those from eastern Ireland differ from those in the west (Hill *et al.* 2000). These two discernible strands of ancestry are often termed Celtic and Anglo-Saxon, but this is not the only possible interpretation for the surprising east-west dichotomy in gene frequencies within such a narrow geographical range. A plausible, but far from accepted, hypothesis is that the two strata within the British Isles are due to substantial migrations alternately from southern France/Spain and north-central Europe. Faunal Lusitanian phylogeographical patterns could, in some part, owe to such a major population introduction from southern Europe. Alternately, the patterns in humans and other species could owe themselves to separate events along prevailing trade routes.

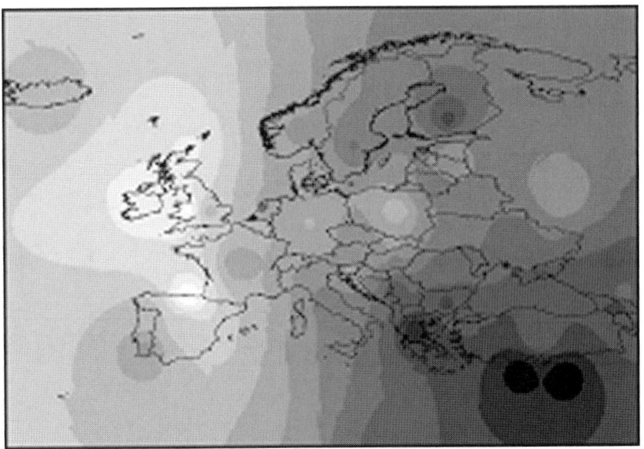

Figure 33.2. A synthetic map of the first dimension of Y-chromosome variation in Europe, taken from McEvoy et al. *(2004). This was constructed using pairwise FST values derived from the human Y-chromosome haplotype data from Rosser* et al. *(2000). FST is a common measure of differentiation among populations. A clear Lusitanian pattern is observed in Atlantean Europe, with the western regions of the British Isles displaying affinity to north-western Spain and south-western France. This pattern is also seen in treatments of mtDNA and classical gene frequency data (McEvoy* et al. *2004).*

Research questions

1. Is the Lusitanian pattern (phylogenetic affinity with southwest Europe) the prevailing theme in the phylogeography of Irish mammals, or are the few results to date just chance departures from a more normal affinity with British populations?
2. Does the Lusitanian theme extend to agricultural species?

Common name	Ireland	England	Scotland	Wales	Great Britain	Iberia	Rest of Europe	Non-European	Region of mtDNA	Reference
Pygmy shrew	14	5	2	2	x	5	41	5	1110bp cyt*b*	Mascheretti *et al.* (2003)
Pine marten	9	6	52	1	x	1	70	x	325bp CR	Davison *et al.* (2001)
Hedgehog	8	x	x	x	33	15	174	x	383bp cytb + 452bp CR	Seddon *et al.* (2002)
Goat	4	x	x	x	6	40	121	171	481bp CR	Luikart *et al.* (2001), Mannen *et al.* (2001)
Mountain hare	3	x	5	x	x	x	14	2	294bp CR	Thulin *et al.* (1997), Pierpaoli *et al.* (1999), Waltari *et al.* (2004)
Badger	2	x	x	x	10	12	52	39	512bp CR	Marmi *et al.* (2006)
Red squirrel	x	134	30	10	x	x	45	x	536bp CR	Barratt *et al.* (1999)
Otter	x	x	18	x	x	x	110	1	300bp CR	Cassens *et al.* (2000)
Rabbit	x	x	x	x	1	95	52	18	233bp cyt*b*	Hardy *et al.* (1995)
Red deer	x	x	1	x	x	2	7	33	1140bp cyt*b*	Ludt *et al.* (2004)
Wood mouse	x	x	x	x	x	12	91	9	965bp cyt*b*	Michaux *et al.* (2003)
Red fox	x	x	x	x	x	8	30	3	375bp cyt*b*	Frati *et al.* (1997)

Figure 33.3. Summary of published mtDNA sequence population data in eleven species sampled in European populations. Number of sampled haplotypes are given, with references for data, with cytb = cytochrome b gene and CR = control region. Note that Irish samples have been analysed for six species.

3. Have prevailing Irish phylogeographic affinities altered over time because of overlaid introductions of species?

Mitochondrial population genetics

There are numerous reasons why mtDNA diversity has become the central focus of phylogeographic research. These include its maternal, clonal inheritance and high variability. Because of almost 20 years of extensive research, a substantial body of analytical theory and accompanying software has evolved to enable inference of ancient demographic events. MtDNA has an added advantage in the effort to study ancient trends because its phylogeography in mammals appears to be more resistant to secondary introductions; i.e. introgressing genomes advance more rapidly through male insemination (which does not affect mtDNA) than through maternal transmission.

Figure 33.3 summarises published mtDNA sequence population data in Irish species sampled in European populations. As can be seen, modern Irish populations have been sampled and published in six of these.

1. Pygmy shrew

Work carried out by Mascheretti *et al.* (2003) uncovered three main genetic lineages in pygmy shrew, with Ireland grouping with Andorra and also, to some extent, Italy (Figure 33.4). This fits well with historical records that first document the presence of pygmy shrew in Ireland in the 17th century AD, possibly associated with wine trade links between Ireland and Italy around this time. France is not well covered in this survey and more regions in northern Spain could be targeted to fully determine the source population. Work is currently underway at University College Dublin (UCD) to further investigate the genetic diversity of Irish pygmy shrew populations.

2. European pine marten

Pine marten sequences (Davison *et al.* 2001) can be grouped into three main genetic lineages (I, II and III). Although it is thought that two of these are the result of introgression with closely related species of marten, the third (group I) could be further split into two subgroups, Ia and Ib. Although these latter subgroups do not show a definitive distribution split across Europe, all Irish pine martens share their sole subgroup (Ib) with Spain, whilst Britain only has representatives from group Ia alone (Figure 33.4). The sample numbers are too small to be able to draw any strong conclusions, but further studies underway at Trinity College Dublin (TCD) may shed light onto whether the pine marten is indeed part of the Lusitanian fauna.

3. Western European hedgehog

It is generally believed that hedgehogs (*Erinaceus europaeus*) were introduced to Ireland by the Normans in the 13th century AD, possibly as a food source. From the 230 hedgehogs surveyed across Europe (Seddon *et al.* 2002), three genetic lineages were found and could reasonably be linked to recolonisation of Europe out of the three refugia of Iberia, Italy and the Balkans. The similarity seen between French and Irish individuals is to be expected given a Norman influence (Figure 33.4), however, as the genetic signature shared between Ireland and France is seen all along the Atlantic façade, it is, as yet, unclear where exactly the original hedgehog source population originated.

4. Domestic goat

Domestic goat (*Capra hircus*) have been extensively studied for mtDNA diversity across the Old World, with phylogenetic distributions suggesting at least three geographically disparate captures of wild female progenitors during the formation of early domestic herds (Luikart *et*

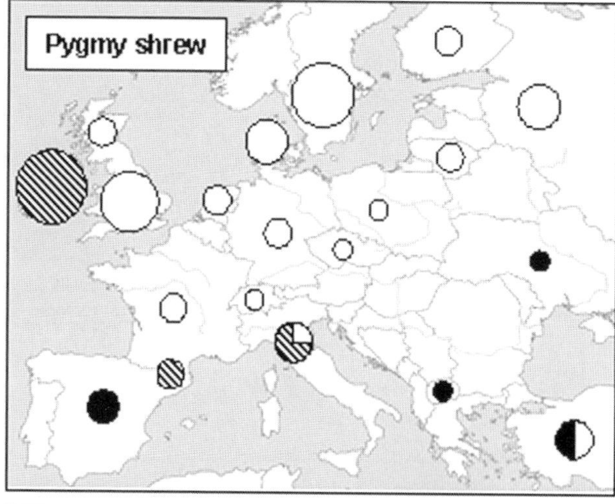

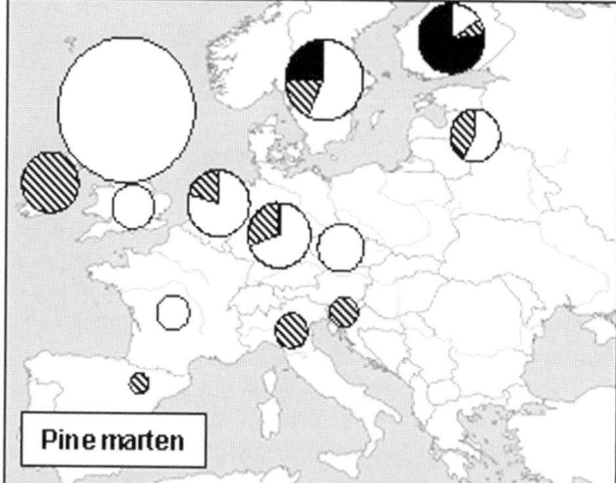

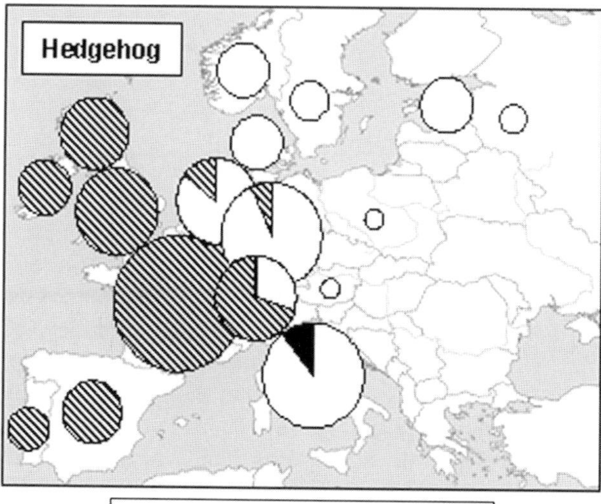

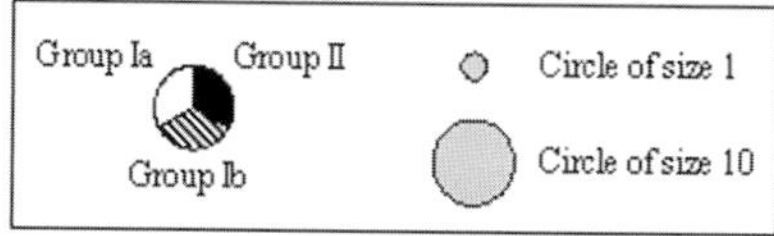

Figure 33.4. Map summarising published data from pygmy shrew, pine marten and hedgehog (see Figure 33.3 for references). Circles sizes are proportional to the number of animals surveyed from that country, with the key showing sample sizes for 1 individual and 10 individuals. The shadings in the pie-charts are explained in the key, with groups determined from analysis of the raw data. Each species shows some degree of Lusitanian phylogeography.

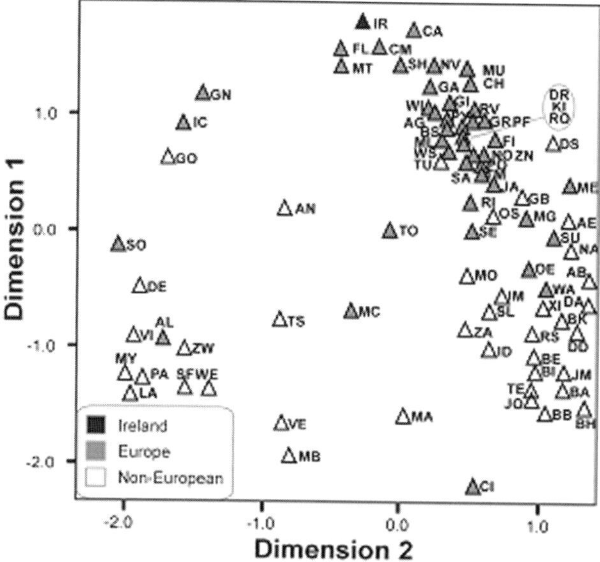

Figure 33.5. Multidimensional scaling analysis (MDS) of pairwise FST values (mtDNA) among goat breed samples (data from Luikart et al. *2001 and Mannen et al. 2001; analysis by Bradley and Freeman 2003). MDS here assigns each sample a location in a two-dimensional space, such that the differences between each observation match the dissimilarities as closely as possible. Furthermore, each axis may demonstrate a discrete trend in the data. In this case, the first dimension divides breeds from Europe from breeds sampled in other continents. The Irish sample (feral Connemara goat, IR) shows closest affinity with breeds from southern Europe (Portugal (CA), Spain (FL) and Italy (CM)).*

al. 2001). Although modern mitochondrial data has been collated from over 340 goat sequences, 171 of these from Europe, the western Atlantic phylogeography has never been examined in detail. However, a preliminary analysis of published goat sequences (Bradley and Freeman 2003) does show some tentative suggestion of Lusitanian phylogeography (Figure 33.5), with the Irish sample (feral Connemara goat, IR) showing closest affinity with breeds from southern Europe (Portugal (CA), Spain (FL) and Italy (CM)).

5. *Mountain hare*

Only three Irish hare (*Lepus timidus*) samples have been analysed to date (Thulin *et al.* 1997), but, in conjunction with two other studies (Pierpaoli *et al.* 1999; Waltari *et al.* 2004), a total of 22 samples from the vestiges of mountain hare populations in Europe can be considered (Figure 33.6). The main conclusion is that the Irish hare samples do not group with those from Scotland, as might be expected. Of course, as Irish hare are a temperate species, it is highly possible that this species survived in a refugium in Ireland during the last glaciation, and similar refuges may have also been present in Scotland and Scandinavia, arguing for a splitting of these three populations from mainland groups around the time of the last glaciation, 12,000 years ago.

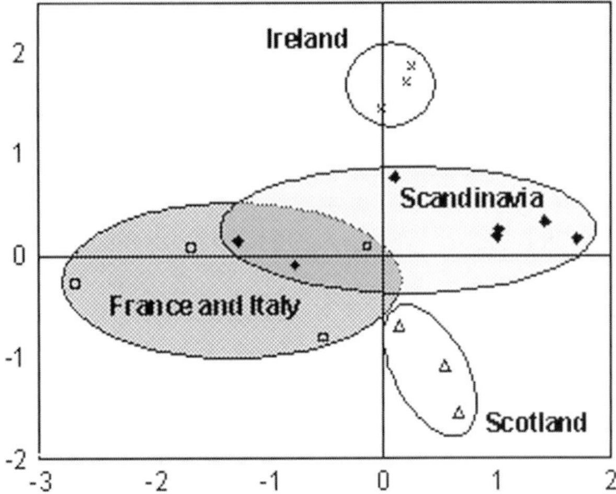

Figure 33.6. MDS of pairwise FST values among mountain hare samples (data from Thulin et al. 1997; Pierpaoli et al. 1999; Waltari et al. 2004). Note that the Irish hare samples do not group with those from Scotland, as might be expected.

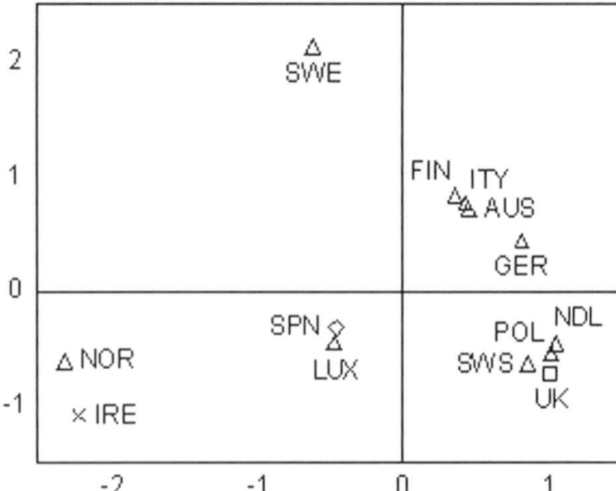

Figure 33.7. MDS of pairwise FST values among European badger samples (data from Marmi et al. 2006). The key is as follows: AUS, Austria; FIN, Finland; GER, Germany; IRE, Ireland; ITY, Italy; LUX, Luxembourg; NDL, The Netherlands; NOR, Norway; POL, Poland; SPN, Spain; SWE, Sweden; SWS, Switzerland; UK, United Kingdom. The small Irish population (n = 2) groups with individuals from Norway.

As no Irish hares survive in Iberia, neither this hypothesis nor a possible Lusitanian link can be tested.

6. Eurasian badger

Marmi *et al.* (2006) included two Irish badger (*Meles meles*) samples in their examination of global badger populations. This small Irish population exhibited a novel type unseen in the other 74 badger from Europe, and it groups with individuals from Norway (Figure 33.7). To understand fully the positioning of Irish badger in a European context, we are currently studying an additional 145 Irish and 36 British badger samples at TCD, as part of collaboration with the Waterford Institute of Technology and UCD.

The remaining 16 Irish mammals

From the remaining list of 16 terrestrial mammals (Figure 33.1), the house mouse (*Mus musculus*), black and brown rats (*Rattus rattus*, *Rattus norvegicus*), fallow and sika deer (*Dama dama*, *Cervus nippon*), brown hare (*Lepus europaeus*), American mink (*Mustela vison*), bank vole (*Myodes glareolus*) and grey squirrel (*Sciurus carolinensis*) are all well-documented recent historical introductions, dating from 1000 years ago to the 20th century AD. Of the other seven species, several studies are underway to look at Irish specimens and fill in the gaps seen in Figure 33.3.

a) Irish stoat (Mustela erminea) and Eurasian river otter (Lutra lutra)

A comprehensive study of Irish stoat has recently been completed at the University of York, by the same team that published the pygmy shrew paper in 2003. Although this has yet to be published in the public domain, it seems to point towards the survival of stoat in an Irish refugium during the last glaciation (Jeremy Searle, pers. comm.). Similarly, a major survey of mtDNA diversity in otter from across Europe is currently being spearheaded at the Istituto Nazionale per la Fauna Selvatica, Italy. Results so far show that the control region is not divergent enough between individual otters to be of much analytical use, but more variation has been located in other areas of the mitochondrial genome.

b) Red fox (Vulpes vulpes) and Eurasian red squirrel (Sciurus vulgaris)

Work is ongoing at TCD on both red fox and red squirrel. In an unpublished study undertaken in 1999, 17 Irish and 18 Swiss red fox samples were combined with previously published data from populations in Spain, Italy, Austria, Bulgaria and Israel (Frati *et al.* 1997). In this preliminary study, the Irish samples formed a distinctive population but, to get a more detailed picture of the biogeography of the red fox, we are in the process of analysing a further 180 Irish specimens, plus over 260 new tissue samples from individuals across Great Britain and Europe. It is widely thought that red squirrel was introduced into Ireland from Britain in the 1800s. Populations from across Ireland are being investigated to determine if the two populations (indigenous and introduced) are still present, but additional sampling from across Europe will also be required fully to analyse affinities between these animals and populations in Britain and the mainland continent.

c) Red deer (Cervus elaphus), woodmouse (Apodemus sylvaticus) and European rabbit (Oryctolagus cuniculus)

In contrast to the four species mentioned above, it is not known if any studies are currently underway or planned to look at red deer, woodmouse or rabbit. Published mtDNA research into red deer appears to be concerned chiefly with understanding the origin, phylogeny, and phylogeography of the various subspecies of red deer (e.g. Ludt *et al.* 2004), but a concerted approach to look at this species in Ireland could tackle the controversy surrounding the method and timing of its introduction (Woodman *et al.* 1997); i.e. is it truly a native animal that arrived in Ireland under its own steam, or rather was it introduced by man during the Neolithic? In 2003, Michaux *et al.* sequenced woodmice from 40 locations across Europe, with results pointing toward the recolonisation of Europe from two refugial populations in Iberia and France. QUB have collected Irish samples in order to analyse mating systems and relatedness in natural populations using nuclear genetic markers, and perhaps mtDNA could also be analysed in this study.

Rabbits are now widely distributed throughout the world as a result of transportation by man. The original populations, however, were confined to southern France and Spain. In order to investigate the role of human intervention in determining the genetic diversity of rabbit populations through time, Hardy *et al.* (1995) extracted DNA from rabbit bones found in archaeological sites, from England, France, Italy, Spain and Portugal, dated to between the Mesolithic and recent times. In comparison to modern-day individuals, the ancient populations of wild rabbit exhibited remarkable stability over time until the Middle Ages, at which time a novel lineage abruptly appeared into wild French populations, corresponding to that present in extant domestic rabbit breeds. The swift appearance of a new type into the gene pool occurred around the same time as the documented establishment of warrens after the 10th century AD in Europe. The study of rabbit diversity in Ireland, in comparison with the data of Hardy *et al.*, could throw light upon the extent that certain practices of animal husbandry reached this island.

Ancient DNA

The retrieval of mtDNA sequences from archaeological specimens (which is much more feasible than from other regions of the nuclear genome) would add a temporal dimension to the analysis of Irish phylogeography. However, the field of biomolecular archaeology (ancient DNA or aDNA) remains hampered by the lack of retrievable DNA in many targeted specimens and the constant danger of contamination. Feasibility of aDNA analyses in Ireland is enhanced by several factors: (1) the age horizons of specimens that would be under consideration fall within that which is considered feasible; (2) animal aDNA is many times less prone to contamination than human remains; (3) preservation conditions in colder countries, such as Ireland, are more suitable for aDNA retrieval (as shown by analysis of Dublin Wood Quay cattle remains; Edwards *et al.* 2003; MacHugh *et al.* 1999). Ancient DNA analysis of mammalian bones, when placed in an informative context, has the potential to add much-needed time depth to Lusitanian patterns and may, in concert with historical knowledge, allow attribution of certain genetic patterns to particular introductions with known time depth (e.g. in the case of the red squirrel, where individuals were introduced in the 19th century AD). In addition, aDNA techniques may be necessary to describe Irish phylogeography in some species where populations may have been replaced by introductions within recent centuries. For example, red fox are known to have been imported from France during the 19th century AD to improve hunting yield. It will also be useful in cases where possible source populations are now extinct, such as is the case with the mountain hare, where relic populations survive only in Ireland, Scotland, Italy/France and Scandinavia.

Conclusions

Ireland has a much more reduced range of faunal species than either its near neighbour Great Britain, or the mainland continent. Until recently, many people favoured a landbridge model to explain the introduction of mammals to Ireland, but it is just as likely that the majority of species were human-mediated introductions, whether accidental or deliberate. When this is taken into consideration, it is quite easy to hypothesise that these introductions could have been directly from southern Europe, and not via Great Britain, and this can be tested through the use of mitochondrial genetic studies on both modern and archaeological specimens.

Acknowledgements

We thank Brian McEvoy and Ruth Freeman for access to electronic versions of Figures 33.2 and 33.5 respectively, as well as for helpful comments on the script. Ceiridwen J. Edwards is supported by the Irish Research Council for Science, Engineering and Technology Basic Research Grant Scheme (project number SC/2002/510).

References

Barratt, E. M., Gurnell, J., Malarky, G., Deaville, R. and Bruford, M. W. 1999. Genetic structure of fragmented populations of red squirrel (*Sciurus vulgaris*) in the UK. *Molecular Ecology* 8 (12 Supplement 1), S55–63.

Bradley, D. G. and Freeman, A. R. 2003. *Livestock Phylogenetics and Geography: The Clarification of Disease Spread from South Asia to the Mediterranean Basin, Including the Arabian Peninsular*. Food and Agriculture Organization of the United Nations (FAO) Report. Geneva, United Nations.

Browne, J. 2005. *Ireland's Mammals*. Kildare, Browne Books.

Cassens, I., Tiedemann, R., Suchentrunk, F. and Hartl, G. B. 2000. Mitochondrial DNA variation in the European otter (*Lutra lutra*) and the use of spatial autocorrelation analysis in conservation. *Journal of Heredity* 91, 31–5.

Cooper, J. A. G., Kelley, J. T., Belknap, D. F., Quinn, R. and McKenna, J. 2002. Inner shelf seismic stratigraphy off the north coast of Northern Ireland: new data on the depth of the Holocene lowstand. *Marine Geology* 186, 369–87.

Davison, A., Birks, J. D., Brookes, R. C., Messenger, J. E. and Griffiths, H. I. 2001. Mitochondrial phylogeography and population history of pine martens *Martes martes* compared with polecats *Mustela putorius*. *Molecular Ecology* 10,

2479–88.

Devoy, R. J. N. 1985. Problem of a late Quaternary landbridge between Britain and Ireland. *Quaternary Science Reviews* 4, 43–58.

Devoy, R. J. N. 1995. Deglaciation, earth crustal behaviour and sea level change in the determination of insularity: a perspective from Ireland, in R. C. Preece (ed.), *Island Britain: A Quaternary Perspective*, 181–208. Geological Society Special Publication 96. London, Geological Society.

Edwards, C. J., Connellan, J., Wallace, P. F., Park, S. D., McCormick, F. M., Olsaker, I., Eythórsdóttir, E., MacHugh, D. E., Bailey, J. F. and Bradley, D. G. 2003. Feasibility and utility of microsatellite markers in archaeological cattle remains from a Viking Age settlement in Dublin. *Animal Genetics* 34, 410–16.

Frati, F., Hartl, G. B., Lovari, S., Delibes, M. and Markov, G. 1997. Quaternary radiation and genetic structure of the red fox (*Vulpes vulpes*) in the Mediterranean Basin, as revealed by allozymes and mitochondrial DNA. *Journal of Zoology* 245, 43–51.

Gouin, N., Grandjean, F., Pain, S., Souty-Grosset, C. and Reynolds, J. 2003. Origin and colonization history of the white-clawed crayfish, *Austropotamobius pallipes*, in Ireland. *Heredity* 91, 70–7.

Hardy, C., Callou, C., Vigne, J.-D., Casane, D., Dennebouy, N., Mounolou, J. C. and Monnerot, M. 1995. Rabbit mitochondrial DNA diversity from prehistoric to modern times. *Journal of Molecular Evolution* 40, 227–37.

Hayden, T. and Harrington, R. 2001. *Exploring Irish Mammals*. Dublin, Town House & Country House Ltd.

Hill, E. W., Jobling, M. A. and Bradley, D. G. 2000. Y chromosome variation and Irish origins. *Nature* 404, 351–2.

Ludt, C. J., Schroeder, W., Rottmann, O. and Kuehn, R. 2004. Mitochondrial DNA phylogeography of red deer (*Cervus elaphus*). *Molecular Phylogenetics and Evolution* 31, 1064–83.

Luikart, G., Gielly, L., Excoffier, L., Vigne, J.-D., Bouvet, J. and Taberlet, P. 2001. Multiple maternal origins and weak phylogeographic structure in domestic goats. *Proceedings of the National Academy of Sciences of the United States of America* 98, 5927–32.

MacHugh, D. E., Troy, C. S., McCormick, F., Olsaker, I., Eythórsdóttir, E. and Bradley, D. G. 1999. Early medieval cattle remains from a Scandinavian settlement in Dublin: genetic analysis and comparison with extant breeds. *Philosophical Transactions of the Royal Society of London Series B* 354, 99–109.

McCormick, F. 1999. Early evidence for wild animals in Ireland, in N. Benecke (ed.), *The Holocene History of the European Vertebrate Fauna: Modern Aspects of Research: Workshop, 6th–9th April 1998, Berlin*, 355–72. Archäologie in Eurasien, Bd. 6. Rahden/Westphalia, Verlag Marie Leidorf.

McEvoy, B., Richards, M., Forster, P. and Bradley, D. G. 2004. The Longue Duree of genetic ancestry: multiple genetic marker systems and Celtic origins on the Atlantic facade of Europe. *American Journal of Human Genetics* 75, 693–702.

Mannen, H., Nagata, Y. and Tsuji, S. 2001. Mitochondrial DNA reveal that domestic goat (*Capra hircus*) are genetically affected by two subspecies of bezoar (*Capra aegagurus*). *Biochemical Genetics* 39, 145–54.

Marmi, J., Lopez-Giraldez, F., Macdonald, D. W., Calafell, F., Zholnerovskaya, E. and Domingo-Roura, X. 2006. Mitochondrial DNA reveals a strong phylogeographic structure in the badger across Eurasia. *Molecular Ecology* 15, 1007–20.

Mascheretti, S., Rogatcheva, M. B., Gunduz, I., Fredga, K. and Searle, J. B. 2003. How did pygmy shrews colonize Ireland? Clues from a phylogenetic analysis of mitochondrial cytochrome *b* sequences. *Proceedings of the Royal Society of London Series B Biological Sciences* 270, 1593–9.

Michaux, J. R., Magnanou, E., Paradis, E., Nieberding, C. and Libois, R. 2003. Mitochondrial phylogeography of the Woodmouse (*Apodemus sylvaticus*) in the Western Palearctic region. *Molecular Ecology* 12, 685–97.

Pierpaoli, M., Riga, F., Trocchi, V. and Randi, E. 1999. Species distinction and evolutionary relationships of the Italian hare (*Lepus corsicanus*) as described by mitochondrial DNA sequencing. *Molecular Ecology* 8, 1805–17.

Rosser, Z. H., Zerjal, T., Hurles, M. E., Adojaan, M., Alavantic, D., Amorim, A., Amos, W., Armenteros, M., Arroyo, E., Barbujani, G., Beckman, L., Bertranpetit, J., Bosch, E., Bradley, D. G., Brede, G., Cooper, G., Corte-Real, H. B., de Knijff, P., Decorte, R., Dubrova, Y. E., Evgrafov, O., Gilissen, A., Glisic, S., Golge, M., Hill, E. W., Jeziorowska, A., Kalaydjieva, L., Kayser, M., Kivisild, T., Kravchenko, S. A., Krumina, A., Kucinskas, V., Lavinha, J., Livshits, L. A., Malaspina, P., Maria, S., McElreavey, K., Meitinger, T. A., Mikelsaar, A. V., Mitchell, R. J., Nafa, K., Nicholson, J., Norby, S., Pandya, A., Parik, J., Patsalis, P. C., Pereira, L., Peterlin, B., Pielberg, G., Prata, M. J., Previdere, C., Roewer, L., Rootsi, S., Rubinsztein, D. C., Saillard, J., Santos, F. R., Stefanescu, G., Sykes, B. C., Tolun, A., Villems, R., Tyler-Smith, C. and Jobling, M. A. 2000. Y-chromosomal diversity in Europe is clinal and influenced primarily by geography, rather than by language. *American Journal of Human Genetics* 67, 1526–43.

Seddon, J. M., Santucci, F., Reeve, N. J. and Hewitt, G. M. 2002. DNA footprints of European hedgehogs, *Erinaceus europaeus* and *E. concolor*: Pleistocene refugia, postglacial expansion and colonization routes. *Molecular Ecology* 10, 2187–98.

Sommer, R. and Benecke, N. 2004. Late- and Post-Glacial history of the Mustelidae in Europe. *Mammalian Review* 34, 249–84.

Thulin, C. G., Isaksson, M. and Tegelström, H. 1997. The origin of Scandinavian mountain hares (*Lepus timidus*). *Gibier Faune Sauvage/Game and Wildlife* 14, 463–75.

Waltari, E., Demboski, J. R., Klein, D. R. and Cook, J. A. 2004. A molecular perspective on the historical biogeography of the northern high latitudes. *Journal of Mammalogy* 85, 591–600.

Weale, M. E., Weiss, D. A., Jager, R. F., Bradman, N. and Thomas, M. G. 2002. Y chromosome evidence for Anglo-Saxon mass migration. *Molecular Biology and Evolution* 19, 1008–21.

Woodman, P. C., Devoy, R. J. N. and Sleeman, D. P. 1983. Introduction, in P. C. Woodman, R. J. N. Devoy and D. P. Sleeman (eds.), *Proceedings of The Postglacial Colonization Conference*, 1–7. Occasional Publication of the Irish Biogeographical Society 1. Dublin, Irish Biogeographical Society.

Woodman, P., McCarthy, M. and Monaghan, N. 1997. The Irish Quaternary Fauna Project. *Quaternary Science Reviews* 16, 129–59.

34. The ecology of hazel (*Corylus avellana*) nuts in Mesolithic Ireland

Anne M. G. McComb

Interpretation of the pollen records suggests that the hazel shrub may have been one of the dominant plants in the forests of Ireland during the Mesolithic period. Evidence from excavated Mesolithic sites in Ireland indicates that hazelnuts were harvested and that they may have been stored in pits. Experiments demonstrated the conditions necessary for the carbonisation of hazelnut shells to take place and the randomness of these conditions occurring. A practical methodology illustrated the complexities of ensuring a successful harvest of hazelnuts. Presumed Mesolithic-appropriate hazelnut storage methods were tested which allowed insight into the feasibility and duration of storage and its possible implications. These studies illustrated how the processes involved with the utilisation of hazelnuts might have impacted on the lives and technologies of the Mesolithic peoples.

Keywords: hazelnuts, pollen, Mesolithic, pits, carbonisation, harvesting, storage.

Introduction

Carbonised, fragmented hazelnut (*Corylus avellana*) shells are probably the most commonly found botanical remains on excavated Mesolithic sites. The nuts' dense cellular structure and the fact that they have become carbonised preserves them in an easily recognisable form as the cell structure of the hazelnut is virtually unchanged by charring (Dimbleby 1978, 128). Both carbonised hazelnut shell fragments and preserved whole hazelnuts have been recovered from Mesolithic sites in Ireland. The presence of the hazelnut remains has often led the excavator or other commentator to remark that the site was likely to have been occupied during the autumn and/or hazelnuts were an important part of the Mesolithic diet. This concept is explored in an essentially Irish situation, which may also be appropriate to Britain and Continental Europe.

Postglacial colonisation of the hazel bush

By approximately 9500 BP (9300–8300 cal BC; Stuiver *et al.* 2005) the pollen of hazel had begun to appear in Irish pollen counts. Hazel must have found conditions in Ireland at that time very favourable for it expanded rapidly (Mitchell 1994, 32). That may have been because of its ability to better tolerate the climate during this period of mainly hot dry summers and cold winters and its superior power of recovery after forest fires.

Hazel must have been at its peak around 6900 cal BC, as indicated by the high pollen values of *corylus*-type pollen which was over 50% of the total tree/shrub pollen over most of Ireland at this time (Huntley and Birks 1983, 373). Around 7500 cal BC woodland trees such as the oak (*Quercus*) and elm (*Ulmus*) had arrived and were beginning to over-shade the hazel (Mitchell and Ryan 1998, 117) and gradually reduce it to an undershrub, as well as easing it to the forest margins. In the almost vegetative state of an undershrub or marginal plant, hazel could not have produced the high pollen rates that have been found. It is therefore likely that the forests of the Mesolithic period in Ireland were predominately patchworks of different tree and shrub species growing separately (Rackham 1980, 99), which allowed the relatively high abundance of hazel to continue for several millennia.

Mesolithic hazel nuts

The early Mesolithic site of Lough Boora near Birr, Co. Offaly, dated to approximately 7650 cal BC, was found on the gravel ridge of a fossil lakeshore (Ryan 1980, 46). Dr Michael Ryan excavated this site and both preserved (uncarbonised) whole and fragmented hazelnuts and carbonized hazelnut shell fragments were recovered. The uncarbonised hazelnut remains had been preserved through waterlogging and the action of anaerobic conditions (Godwin 1956, 198; Girling 1978, 257). The majority of the hazelnut remains were found within or adjacent to the charcoal and artefact scatters of the Lough Boora site (Ryan, pers. comm.). Some time after occupation the site at Lough Boora had been swallowed up as bog vegetation developed (Mitchell 1986, 79).

An unusual find at Lough Boora was what Dr. Ryan called a 'cache' of whole hazelnuts preserved through the conditions of water logging. These were found in a circular depression of approximately 30cm diameter in an area where fish, meat, etc. had been eaten. No other preserved organic matter was found among the 487 hazelnuts of this cache. These hazelnuts may have been part of the diet of the people who had inhabited the Lough Boora site. Animals that hoard foodstuffs, and that may have been present in Mesolithic Ireland, are unlikely to have been responsible for the Lough Boora cache. Red squirrels are inclined to scatter-hoard their food in many small caches of one to four items over a wide area (Rice-Oxley 1993, 93). Other hoarders may have been the badger and the wood mouse, but their caches were unlikely to be of a comparable size. A further 143 preserved whole hazel nuts were found scattered through out the Lough Boora site.

At Aghnadarragh, Co, Antrim, on the east shore of Lough Neagh, some ancient sand horizons believed to be older than 46,850 BP (McCabe *et al.* 1987, 11) were examined. They were found to contain seams of washed-in vegetable debris, which included preserved whole hazelnuts similar to those found at Lough Boora. Hazelnuts preserved in this manner are likely to be part of mixed vegetable debris washed up on an ancient shore. The absence of other preserved organic matter in the Lough Boora hazelnut cache indicates that it was unlikely to have been the result of wash-in. Louise Van Wijngaarden-Bakker (1989, 131) presumed that storage had not been carried out on any scale at Lough Boora because the conditions of resource abundance and mass harvest were not present. According to pollen samples taken from Littleton Bog, Co. Tipperary (see above), 52km south of Lough Boora, hazel would have been widespread at the time the Lough Boora site was occupied. It is highly probably that hazelnuts could have been collected in the immediate surroundings of Lough Boora.

The Lough Boora cache may be the remnants of an unrecovered store of hazelnuts, which had been harvested and placed in a pit. The pit containing the cache may have been truncated by encroaching lake-water, causing a portion of its contents to be scattered over the site surface before being covered and sealed in by the advancing bog vegetation.

Another early site of human occupation was discovered at Mount Sandel, south of Coleraine, Co. Londonderry, and was dated to approximately 7800 cal BC (Mitchell 1986, 79). Scattered over the site and in the postholes, hearths and pits were found large quantities of carbonised hazelnut shell fragments. A number of the pits excavated were straight-sided, 40–50cm deep and about 1.0m in diameter. Professor P.C. Woodman who excavated Mount Sandel in the 1970s commented that he found what might be evidence that hazelnuts had been kept in storage and used during the winter months. Large quantities of foetal pig bones, which could only have come from animals caught and killed at the end of winter, together with carbonized hazelnut shell fragments, which may have been eaten at the same time, were present in two of the pits (F27 and F31/0) (Woodman 1985, 176). Hazelnuts may have been stored in these pits, but little is known of their precise function, and their contents on excavation may not be related to their primary use.

The large quantities of carbonised hazelnut shells found indicate that hazelnuts must have been freely available in the neighbouring woods around the Mount Sandel site (Mitchell 1986, 79; Van Winjgaarden-Bakker 1989, 131), and also undoubtedly indicate their dietary importance in the Mesolithic economy practiced at Mount Sandel. This dominance is not however particular to Mount Sandel since many other Mesolithic sites in both Britain and Ireland have produced numerous hazelnut remains (Monk and Pals 1985, 80).

Evidence from the Irish Mesolithic sites indicates that hazelnuts were plentiful in the woodland and that they were an important part of the diet of the people. In Britain it has been suggested that Mesolithic pits were sometimes used to store nuts (Clarke 1976, 449). In Ireland the evidence from the sites at Lough Boora and Mount Sandel indicate that hazelnuts may have been stored and that storage may have been in pits.

At the Mount Sandel site the average size of the larger circular pits was 100cm diameter by 40cm deep. The cubic capacity of 340 fresh ripe native hazelnuts of various sizes and shapes was found to be 770cc (McComb 1998, 43). If storage in pits had taken place at Mount Sandel, an average large circular pit could have held approximately 147,000 hazelnuts, which would have weighed over 205kg. A hazelnut is approximately 64% waste (the shell) this means the average large circular pit at Mount Sandel could have held approximately 74kg of nutmeat. The edible carcass of an adult wild boar (*Sus scrofa*) is believed to have been approximately 53.4kg. Therefore this average large pit could have held hazelnut meat equivalent to almost 1.4 wild boars. This calculation demonstrates the approximate food storage capacity of these pits.

Carbonisation

The majority of hazelnut remains found on Mesolithic sites are carbonised hazelnut shell fragments. Carbonisation is the destructive distillation of organic substances out of contact with air, accompanied by the formation of carbon in addition to liquid and gaseous products (Collocott and Dobson 1974, 184). We have no knowledge of the circumstances that may have allowed carbonisation to take place on a Mesolithic site. Stephen Mithen (1994, 35) found dense quantities of burnt hazelnut shells at the Mesolithic site of Staosnaig on the east coast of Colonsay in the southern Herbrides of Scotland. He believes that they may be the remains of a procedure by which hazelnuts were roasted (Score and Mithen 2000, 507).

Unless hazelnut shells became carbonised through the process of roasting the hazelnuts prior to eating them or to prepare them for storage, the carbonisation of the hazelnut shell fragments was likely to have been related to their disposal. It has generally been assumed that after hazelnuts had been cracked open and the kernels extracted to be eaten or processed, the shell was waste and likely to be discarded into the fire (Legge 1989, 218). At the Mesolithic campsite, it is likely that many activities including the preparation and eating of food centred round the campfire, especially in the colder seasons of the year. The ground area in the vicinity of a campfire may have been swept clear of debris, which would likely have included hazelnut shells, which was then put into the fire. When thrown into a fire hazelnut shells usually quickly burn up and disappear: so how did those recovered from archaeological sites become carbonised?

Under Mesolithic campfire conditions hazelnut shells excluded from the air by being buried in ash or soil may, in the appropriate temperatures and over a particular period of time, have become carbonised.

Using the stone shattered shells of five groups of 100 hazelnuts and one group of 100 whole hazelnuts, a grid of six squares, each square holding a different experiment testing depths and conditions of burial in soil and wood ash, was implemented. Hot wood embers and firewood were placed on the top right hand corner of the grid and the fire burned vigorously for almost two hours.

The hazelnut shell fragments of squares 2 and 6 became carbonised and were similar in appearance to those found on Mesolithic sites. On square 4 the remaining 70 whole hazelnuts had become carbonised. When struck with a pebble they fragmented into curved, angular fragments. The contents of these squares (2, 4 and 6) had been buried under 8–10cm of wood ash. The hazelnut shell fragments of squares 1, 3 and 5 had become shiny, dark brown, thinned, hardened and reduced in size. They had not become carbonised, perhaps due to their burial in compacted soil and/or the temperatures they were exposed to.

These experiments revealed that the carbonisation of hazelnut shells happens when they become buried in wood ash in the proximity of a hearth fire and experienced periods of high temperature (McComb 1996, 36). Knowledge of the circumstances necessary for carbonisation to occur creates an appreciation of how unique the carbonised hazelnut shell fragments recovered from the Mesolithic sites are, and how those recovered may represent only a small percentage of the total number of hazelnuts utilised on site.

But before hazelnuts can be eaten, stored or carbonised they first have to be harvested.

Harvesting

There has been considerable controversy concerning the amount of hazelnuts a hazel bush is capable of producing, and how many hazelnuts would be available for humans to harvest. While there have been a number of studies undertaken in America (Gregg 1988, 174), mostly of cultivated hazelnuts, there does not appear to have been any productive studies carried out on the hazel bushes of north-western Europe.

The hazel coppices of Moneyscalp and Clonacullion are located in the foothills of the eastern Mourne Mountains in Co. Down, Northern Ireland. Years of neglect mean that the majority of the hazel bushes of both coppices are between 6–9m tall, with their nut-bearing branches on the bush tops, where they compete with other top branches of hazel bushes reaching for the light. Most of the hazel bushes have no side branches but come together as one bush, and as a result only those hazel bushes at the edges of the coppices have nut-bearing branches that are reachable for nut counting and harvesting. Both of the coppices are located on rocky, wet ground that is grazed by sheep and cattle and fallen hazelnuts are inclined to disappear into the churned up ground.

A nut-bearing hazel bush, standing approximately 7m away from the edge of the Moneyscalp coppice, was selected as suitable for a productivity study. This sample hazel bush was 3–4m tall and 1.37m in circumference at the stool base. It stood on a piece of unbroken ground which was covered in grass (*Gramineae*) and bracken (*Pteridium*), and all of its nut-bearing branches were easily reached. This hazel bush was evenly covered in hazelnuts on all sides down to the browse line that was 1.3m above ground level. During the last week of August the green hazelnuts were large enough to be counted. A total of 950 hazelnuts were on the bush and 20 unopened, wind-blown nuts on the ground.

The sample hazel bush was visited every week to ten days to record the progress of the hazelnuts towards ripening and harvesting. All fallen nuts were counted and taken away on each visit.

Harvesting study results

- 8th September: seven wind-blown hazelnuts were recovered from the ground beneath the hazel bush.
- 16th September: 27 fallen hazelnuts were collected from beneath the hazel bush.
- 26th September: 39 hazelnuts were gathered from beneath the hazel bush.
- 6th October: the hazel bush had been visited and plundered by red squirrels. There were 580 hazelnuts, either in half shells or unopened, collected from the ground beneath the bush. The unopened hazelnuts later proved to be blind, which means they had no kernel.
- 13th October: the red squirrels had visited again; 140 discarded hazelnut remains were on the ground. The hazelnuts on the bush were beginning to ripen.
- 22nd October was the last visit as the hazelnuts were now ripe and coming free of their husks. The remains of 18 hazelnuts were gathered from the ground and 15 hazelnuts were harvested from the bush.

124 hazelnuts were unaccounted for. These were probably hazelnuts, containing kernels, which had been carried off by woodland creatures to be eaten or stored; it is unlikely empty, blind nuts would have been taken away.

The sample hazel bush had produced 15 ripe hazelnuts for human harvest out of the total of 970 green hazelnuts recorded in August.

The principal challenge for ownership of the hazelnuts in this harvesting study came from the red squirrels. To date there is no evidence that red squirrels were present in Mesolithic Ireland. However bones of the goshawk (*Accipiter gentilis*) (Van Wijngaarden-Bakker 1989, 128) were recovered from the Mount Sandel excavation and from the late Mesolithic site of Dalkey Island, Co. Dublin (Cabot 1999, 22). The principal prey species of the goshawk is the red squirrel (Halliwell 1997, 39), so it is likely that the red squirrel was present in Ireland during the Mesolithic period.

The harvesting study also demonstrated that there might only be a narrow window of opportunity for the successful human harvesting of hazelnuts. Zenk (pers. comm.) tells of the Indian people of Oregon who gathered hazelnuts in July and early August. They picked them green and took them to temporary camps where they were spread on the ground to lie in the sun for 3–4 days to ripen. The nuts were then beaten with clubs to remove the husks, put into sacks and taken to the village where they were stored in sacks and pits. They likely picked the hazelnuts green in order to maximize their harvest in the face of competition from the nut-eating creatures of the woods.

The harvesting study illustrated the importance of devising a more efficient method of harvesting than that demonstrated by this study. Harvesting would need to be planned to tie in with important aspects in the life cycle of the hazelnuts, such as their maturing, and the feeding of the mammals and birds. It would probably be expedient to harvest the hazelnuts when the kernels were fully developed within their shells, and still unripe and in their husks, and before the woodland creatures began to feed on them.

In Mesolithic Ireland hazelnut gathering may have been one of those tasks of autumn that tradition has designated to women, children and the elderly (Woodman 1985, 163), but autumn is probably too general a term to describe the gathering period. It is more likely to have been condensed into an intense period of communal gathering, preparation and storage (Clark 1976, 449), planned with deliberation based on observation of the forest ecosystem.

The Mesolithic people, acutely aware of the ecosystem in which they lived, would probably have harvested their hazel nuts when the kernel was fully grown in the shell and the nut still green, and placed to dry and ripen in the sun. If the hazelnut crop was important, they may have camped in the hazel coppices and guarded the bushes from predators for a period before harvest time. This may also have presented a hunting opportunity, as birds, wild boars, etc., would be drawn to the hazel woods by the ripening nuts.

A plentiful harvest of hazelnuts may have instigated storage taking place as a buffer against food shortages. But could hazelnuts be stored until winter and early spring when they may have been needed?

Storage

One of the main problems for Mesolithic people living in the area of the temporal forest will have been that of over-wintering in an ecology which effectively shuts down for several months each year (Clarke 1979, 250). The temporal forests of north-western Europe provide little food during the winter and early spring of the year. Few plants grow at this time and many of the mammals, fish and birds may be either hibernating or have migrated, and those that remain local and active are likely to become hungry and lean. There is reason to believe that there may have been a food procurement crisis in the second half of the winter and therefore food storage would have been essential (Woodman 1985, 128). The obvious reaction of human populations faced with seasonal fluctuations in food supplies is to build up a surplus of resources during the seasons of abundance and to preserve these in some way for consumption during periods of scarcity (Mellars 1976, 381). The necessity for food storage is easily recognised in the conditions that may have prevailed in Mesolithic Ireland.

There may not have been a wide range of foods available in Mesolithic Ireland that could have been easily stored, because of factors such as availability, suitability and climatic conditions. Green, leafy foods, seeds and fruits would have been difficult to preserve and keep in dry conditions in order to prevent mould and decay. It is possible that fish, mammal or bird flesh could have been preserved by being smoked, salted or dried, although there has been little evidence found of these types of activities having taken place.

Hazelnut kernels seem to be an exception, coming as they do with their own storage package or shell, which means they require minimum processing prior to storage. The shell is comparatively resistant to decay as it contains lignin, a tough, woody substance which serves to protect it from damp, moulds, and some predators; it is also smooth and rounded which may allow little or no purchase for moulds and fungi (Game, pers. comm.). Hazelnuts appear to fulfil the four conditions described as determining the practice of storage: the resource is (a) abundant, (b) seasonal, and they can effectively be (c) harvested and (d) stored (Testart 1982, 527).

Hazelnuts may be likely candidates for storage, but we have no positive evidence of what methods of storage may have been used in Mesolithic Ireland. Being aware of their forest environment, the people may have practised the storage of hazelnuts, perhaps by mimicking the red squirrel (Clarke 1979, 250) or other creatures that store caches of hazelnuts in holes they have dug in the ground.

Storing hazelnuts in pits has many advantages; the buried nuts are being kept at cool, even temperatures, which may inhibit disease and mould from affecting the kernels, also the damp of the pit may prevent the kernels drying out. At the same time the buried nuts are likely to be protected from frost and pests and their presence is not visible to human or animal thieves. There are, however, some disadvantages to pit-storage for hazelnuts: burrowing animals may locate and steal the nuts; poor choice of pit site may cause the nuts to become infested, and poor drainage in the area of the pit may result in the nuts becoming wet and being attacked by mould or fungi and rot. Stored above ground the hazelnuts may be vulnerable to thieves and may dry out, but they would be away from the damp of the pit (and possible decay).

Evidence from the Mesolithic sites of Mount Sandel and Lough Boora suggest that hazelnut storage may have taken place and that storage may have been in pits (see above).

To test the possibility and practicalities of storage, four assumed Mesolithic appropriate methods were devised – an above-ground rush bag, and three different pit-storage methods: directly into the earth; within a basket; layered with river sand. For the storage experiment, local wild hazelnuts were gathered and spread out to dry off in the sun. The drying hazelnuts were turned daily and any diseased, unripe and blind hazelnuts were removed. When completely dried there were 16kg of hazelnuts available for the storage experiments.

On a dry day in mid-November three pits were dug in a wooded hillside at the eastern edge of the Mourne Mountains near to the hazel coppices. The pits were 35cm diameter by 50cm deep, meaning that they had approximately half the capacity of the average large pits excavated at Mount Sandal (see above). A willow (*Salix*) basket was made and a rush bag was woven.

Storage Experiments

- Hazelnuts weighing 7kg were poured into Pit 1 and covered by 30cm of soil.
- 2.5kg of hazel nuts were put into the willow basket and placed into Pit 2, which was then filled in with soil.
- The bottom and sides of Pit 3 it were lined with dry river sand. Hazelnuts weighing 4kg were buried, layered with sand and the pit was filled in.
- The rush bag was filled with 0.5kg of hazelnuts, sewn shut, and hung in a woodshed.

The pits were located on a well-drained site, and a downhill tilting cap-stone was placed on top of the hazelnut contents of each pit to assist in surface water drainage and to inhibit animals from digging up the nuts.

Results of Storage Experiments

- At the end of January, after 10 weeks, Pit 1 was opened: a random selection of 300 hazelnuts was made, and 46% were edible and had a rich, pleasant flavour.
- By mid-February, after 13 weeks, Pit 2 was opened: 70% of the random selection of 300 hazelnuts were fit to eat and tasted good.
- At the end of February, after 14 weeks, the rush bag was opened: 35% percent of the random selection of 60 hazelnuts were fit to eat, but they were shrivelled, chewy, and not a pleasant flavour.
- At the beginning of April, after eighteen weeks, Pit 3 was opened: 47% of the random selection of 300 hazelnuts were fit to eat, but the majority of these were shrunken, bitter, and not pleasant to eat.

The four storage experiments demonstrate that it is possible to store hazelnuts to be retrieved in an edible condition, from harvest time through winter to mid-spring. The method of storage used in Pit 2 was the most successful, with 70% of the hazelnuts that had been stored in a willow basket still good enough to eat after 13 weeks. The hazelnuts in Pits 1 and 2 were beginning to shoot and may not have remained edible for many more weeks. The edible, but unpleasant tasting, kernels from the rush bag and Pit 3 may have been revived and their unpleasant flavour removed by soaking in water, roasting, or some other method of processing.

One of the factors in the difference in taste between the two groups may have been the degree of moisture present in the storage methods. The contents of Pits 1 and 2 were stored in a damp environment while those in the rush bag and Pit 3 were stored in a drier situation. Another factor was time; the better tasting hazelnut kernels had been stored for a shorter period of time than the less pleasantly flavoured ones.

The different storage methods tested illustrated that some were more successful than others over different periods of time. What may be judged as successful storage would likely depend upon whether what is required is a comparatively small percentage of pleasantly flavoured and textured hazelnut kernels, or a larger percentage of edible, though tasteless to bitter and chewy, hazelnut kernels. The acceptable end-condition of the stored hazelnuts would likely depend or whether hazelnuts were stored as a luxury food item or as an important staple in the diet of the people, or something in between. The Mesolithic people would likely have evolved more efficient and successful means of storing hazelnuts to suit their needs.

The experiments demonstrated that hazelnuts can be successfully stored, thus making them a food resource, which, if required, could be consumed over six months of the year.

Conclusions

Evidence from the pollen records suggests that hazelnuts may have been abundant in Mesolithic Ireland. The majority of preserved hazelnut remains found on archaeological sites are carbonised hazelnut shell fragments. Experiments in carbonising hazelnut shells demonstrated that a precise menu of events, whose occurrence was probably random, were necessary for carbonisation to happen. The carbonisation experiments also indicated that it was highly probable that large amounts of hazelnut shells were discarded into a hearth fire, before a relatively small percentage of them became carbonised. This suggests that hazelnuts may have been extensively used on Mesolithic sites in Ireland.

A hazelnut harvesting study demonstrated that the successful harvesting of hazelnuts would have involved awareness and observation of the ecosystem and careful planning and management. An interpretation of the finds and features of the Mesolithic sites of Mount Sandel and Lough Boora suggest that hazelnuts were part of the diet of the people, that they may have been stored, and that storage may have been in pits. Experimentation showed that it was possible to store hazelnuts in pits, and above ground, from harvest time until mid-spring. The storage experiments, it is hoped, will put to rest the old chestnut that hazelnuts found on archaeological sites were signs of autumn occupation. Hazelnuts may certainly be indicative of autumn occupation, but taking the high probability of storage into account, would suggest that the remains of hazelnuts on a Mesolithic site may also tell of winter, spring, and perhaps even early summer occupation (McComb and Simpson 1999, 15).

Impact on the lives and technologies of the Mesolithic people would probably have evolved around processes concerned with maximizing the hazelnut harvest and the successful storage of this resource. This may have involved planning and organisation associated with coppicing, preparation for harvesting, the gathering and care of the harvest, and the storage of the hazelnuts. These processes may have also involved the collection, preparation, and creation of equipment such as baskets, tools, etc., for harvesting and storage. The implementation of harvesting, storage, and the eventual redistribution of the stored hazelnuts would likely have involved a programme of decision making and planned procedures, which may have instigated elements of leadership and control.

It is perhaps possible to overestimate the importance of the hazelnut to the Mesolithic people because it is the most common archaeologically recovered foodstuff. The remains of most other foods which may have been eaten at this time, such as fruits, green, leafy vegetation, roots, fungi, etc., do not often survive. However, it is the ability of the hazelnut to be successfully stored which makes them a food, which, if required, could have been consumed over approximately six months of the year. This maximizes their likely usage when compared to other foodstuffs whose consumption may only have been in their season.

Dependence on the hazelnut during the Mesolithic period may have been conditional, as yield can vary from year to year. Although the hazelnuts were likely an important part of the diet, they were probably not regarded as a staple when meat and fish were plentiful, but when these were scarce or absent, hazelnuts may have been a main element of the diet for part of the year.

Acknowledgements

For personal communications: M. Game, Chairperson, Kentish Cobnut Association, Kent, England; M. Ryan, Director, The Chester Beatty Library and Gallery, Dublin, Ireland; H. Zenk, Anthropologist, Portland, Oregon, U.S.A. Thanks are also due to Professor J. Pilcher of Queens University Belfast for his help with the calibration of the radiocarbon dates.

References

Cabot, D. 1999. *Ireland, A Natural History*. London, Harper Collins.

Clarke, D. 1976. Mesolithic Europe: The Economic Basis, in G. de G. Sieveking, I. H. Longworth and K. E. Wilson, (eds.), *Problems in Economic and Social Archaeology*, 449–81. London, Duckworth.

Clarke, D. L. 1979. Mesolithic Europe: The Economic Basis, in *Analytical Archaeologist: Collected Papers of D. L. Clarke* (edited by his colleagues), 207–62. London, Academic Press.

Collocott, T. C. and Dobson, A. B. (eds.) 1974. *Chambers Dictionary of Science & Technology* (revised). Edinburgh, W. and R. Chambers.

Dimbleby, G. 1978. *Plants and Archaeology*. London, John Baker.

Girling, D. A. (ed.) 1978. *Everymans' Encyclopaedia*, 6th Edition, Vol. II. London, Dent and Sons.

Godwin, H. 1956. *The History of the British Flora*. Cambridge, Cambridge University Press.

Gregg, S. A. 1988. *Foragers and farmers*. Chicago, University of Chicago Press.

Halliwell, E. 1997. Red Squirrel Predation by Pine Martens in Scotland, in J. Gurnell and P. Lurz (eds.), *The Conservation of Red Squirrels*, 39–48. London, The People's Trust.

Huntley, B. and Birks, H. 1983. *Atlas of past and present pollen maps for Europe 0–13,000 years*. Cambridge, Cambridge University Press.

Legge, A. J. 1989. Milking the Evidence: A Reply to Entwistle and Grant, in A. Milles, D. Williams and N. Gardner (eds.), *The Beginnings of Agriculture*, 218–36. Oxford, British Archaeological Reports, International Series S496. Oxford, Tempvs Reparatvm.

McCabe, A. M., Coope, C. R., Gennerd, D. E. and Doughty, P. 1987. Freshwater organic deposits and stratified sediments between Early and Late Midlandian (Devensian) till sheets at Aghnadarragh, Co. Antrim, N. Ireland. *Journal of Quaternary Science* 2 (1), 11–33.

McComb, A. M. G. 1996. *The Ecology of Hazelnuts in Prehistoric Ireland*. Unpublished BSc thesis, The Queens' University, Belfast.

McComb, A. M. G. 1998. The Carbonised Hazelnut Shell Fragments from Feature No. 283 at Haughey's Fort, Co. Armagh. *Emania* 17. Belfast, Navan Research Group.

McComb, A. M. G. and Simpson, D. 1999. The Wild Bunch: Exploitation of the Hazel in Prehistoric Ireland. *Ulster Journal of Archaeology*, 3rd Series, Vol. 58. Belfast, Ulster Archaeological Society.

Mellars, P. 1976. Settlement Patterns and Industrial Variability in the British Mesolithic, in G. De G. Sieveking, I. H. Longworth and K. E. Wilson (eds.), *Problems in Economic and Social Archaeology*, 375–99. London, Duckworth.

Mitchell, F. 1986. *The Shell Guide to Reading the Irish Landscape*. Dublin, Wild Ireland Library.

Mitchell, F. 1994. *Where has Ireland come from?* Dublin, Country House.

Mitchell, F. and Ryan, M. 1998. *Reading the Irish Landscape*. Dublin, Town House & Country House.

Mithen, S. (ed.) 1994. *The Southern Hebrides Mesolithic project, (7th) Interim Report*. University of Reading, Department of Archaeology.

Monk, M. A. and Pals, J. P. 1985. Charred Plant Remains, in P. C. Woodman, *Excavations at Mount Sandel, 1973–1977*, 79–81. Belfast, Her Majesty's Stationery Office.

Rackham, O. 1980. *Ancient Woodland*. London, Edward Arnold.

Rice-Oxley, S. B. 1993. Caching Behaviour of Red Squirrels under Conditions of High Food Availability. *Mammal Review* 23 (2), 93–100.

Ryan, M. 1980. An Early Mesolithic site in the Irish midlands. *Antiquity* 54, 46–7.

Score, D. and Mithen, J. S. 2000. The experimental roasting of hazelnuts, in J. S. Mithen (ed.), *Hunter-gatherer Landscape Archaeology: The Southern Hebrides Mesolithic Project 1988–1998*, Vol. 2, 507–12. McDonald Institute Monographs. Cambridge, McDonald Institute for Archaeological Research.

Stuiver, M., Reimer, P. J. and Reimer, R. W. 2005. CALIB 5.0. WWW program and documentation, available at http://calib.qub.ac.uk/calib/calib.html (accessed 01/2008).

Testart, A. 1982. The Significance of Food Storage among Hunter-Gatherers. *Current Archaeology* 23, 523–37.

Van Wijngaarden-Bakker, L. H. 1989. Faunal Remains and the Irish Mesolithic, in C. Bonsall (ed.), *The Mesolithic in Europe: Papers Presented at the Third International Symposium*, 125–33. Edinburgh, John Donald Publishers.

Woodman, P. C. 1985. *Excavations at Mount Sandel, 1973–77.* Northern Ireland Archaeological Monographs 2. Belfast, Her Majesty's Stationery Office.

Session IV

People and Places

35. People and Places: Introduction

Sinéad B. McCartan

Introduction

This session focussed on the connections between people and place. Across Europe, Britain and Ireland different places or landscapes, and their respective range of environments and resources, presented different challenges to early Holocene hunter-gatherers. Some places indicate intense human activity and, or settlement; other areas indicate sparse activity and certain places appear to be devoid of any human presence. Hunter-gatherers ability to adapt to and exploit a landscape or a range of landscapes provides important insights to their relationship with, and perceptions of their living world. Initially, ten papers were presented in this session, all of which are included in this chapter. An additional four papers have been moved from two other sessions – Current Research (Domańska and Wąs; Momber *et al.* and Persson) and Regional Identities (Sergant *et al.*).

Three papers from Scandinavia present evidence for Mesolithic activity in a variety of landscapes. Gundersen explores the issue of perception of landscape based on the contrasting evidence for settlement on the coastline and the fjords during the Late Mesolithic in western Norway. Virtually all sites, those indicating both short and long-term settlement, are located on the coast or outer fjord areas which contrasts with the paucity of sites in the fjords which are represented by single stray finds. Gundersen suggests that these single finds are 'ritual expressions' and indicate that the fjords were part of a ritual landscape while the coastal zone was exploited for practical purposes.

Persson reviews Boaz's model for inland settlement in southern Norway and highlights concerns about the reliability of the model which does not appear to be substantiated by the radiocarbon evidence. Persson proposes with the Rena Project to explore the use of different dating techniques, the results of which will either confirm or challenge Boaz's model, and provide new independent evidence for the use of the inlands during the Mesolithic.

In the final paper from Scandinavia, Casati and Sørensen present the results of two survey projects which have shed light on how the geological and environmental changes impacted on settlement patterns, and consequently social and cultural contacts within the Maglemose culture on Bornholm, Denmark.

Moving to the Baltic region, Zagorska provides an overview of the Zvejnieki archaeological complex and the use of the landscape for both settlement and burial in the Lake Burtnieks region of northern Latvia. At Dąbrowa Diskupia 71 in the Kuiavian region of Poland, Domańska and Wąs have been investigating a specialised hunting camp which appears to have been a satellite site within the broader settlement pattern of the Maglemose Culture.

The Netherlands and Belgium are covered by three presentations. Using the site of Hoge Vaart-A27 in the Flevoland region of the Netherlands, Peeters presents an account of the interplay between a changing dynamic environment and forager land-use over a period of several thousand years. Peeters argues that the persistent use of specific places in the landscape is not simply determined by available economic resources and that the ritual, ideological and cosmological perspectives by forager of the landscape were also critical.

Sergant *et al.* present the results of extensive field survey in the Sandy Flanders area of north-west Belgium which indicates three major changes from the Early/Middle Mesolithic to the Late Mesolithic – a dramatic reduction in the number of sites, a shift in the location of sites and the use and distribution of raw materials. It is argued that while the first two changes could be explained by changes in subsistence patterns, the third change must be the result of social expression.

Another perspective of landuse is offered by De Bie and Van Gils through their systematic large-scale and intensive fieldwork programme in the Campine region in Belgium. Survey results indicate that sites are all very large, on dry sandy ridges and usually on the northern bank of rivers or fens. It is argued that rather than interpreting these extensive site complexes as 'gathering' areas or special places in the landscape for Mesolithic groups, it is more likely they can be explained as a result of an economic subsistence pattern indicating preferential utilisation of specific ecological habitats.

The Croatian evidence indicates Mesolithic use of a range of environments and of different settlement types. Firstly, the utilisation of uplands is explored by Komšo whose work in northern Istria, Croatia builds upon previous fieldwork that revealed a once 'empty' landscape was in fact heavily utilised during the Palaeolithic and Mesolithic.

Komšo's paper concentrates on three upland sites noting that while each was involved with subsistence-based activities, variation amongst sites also existed indicating the complexity associated with economic activities. Secondly, Balbo *et al.*'s paper illustrates how dedicated fieldwork orientated to ask specific questions can shed light on a new dimension to Mesolithic activity. Previously, several authors have noted the paucity of Mesolithic sites in south-eastern Europe with existing evidence dominated by cave sites with only a few open-air sites. Balbo *et al.*'s survey of Polje Čepić (Istria, Croatia) where a shallow lake once existed prior to its drainage in more recent times, resulted in the discovery of new sites including five open-air Mesolithic sites. The site at Kostadini, in particular, provides new insights to the utilisation of a wetland environment and the relationship between people and place.

A perspective from southern Europe is summarised in three papers commencing with Fontana *et al.* who discuss the variation amongst five Early Mesolithic sites on the central Po Plain in Italy. These sites which were found buried under alluvial deposits, afford a new perspective and evaluation of landuse activities in the region. Preliminary assessment of raw material procurement strategies, variation in the lithic technologies and structural evidence indicate intra-site variation.

The use of inland or interior areas is presented by Arias *et al.*, commencing with an interesting short discussion on the definition of 'interior' which is often coloured by modern perceptions and current political boundaries. Following a thorough overview of the archaeological evidence, Arias *et al.* conclude that while it is partial, the evidence clearly indicates that there was Mesolithic activity in the interior regions of the Iberian Peninsula and this activity was of a permanent nature, although less dense compared to coastal areas.

Valente and Carvalho present a summary of the evidence for Mesolithic sites in the western Algarve, Portugal, which appears to suggest that Mesolithic activity in this coastal area was restricted to the temporary or seasonal exploitation of marine resources, and sometimes flint, resulting in the development of shell middens. The outstanding issue, however, is the location of the 'base camps', possibly sited within the interior of the Algarve, although further investigations are required in order to make this determination.

In the final paper in this section, Momber *et al.* illustrate the possibilities offered by the investigation of submerged landscapes highlighted by their work around the Solent, a waterway that separates the Isle of Wight and mainland Britain. The preservation of remains, both archaeological and palaeo-environmental, within the drowned landscape has presented an opportunity to examination the changing relationship between people and an evolving, fluctuating environment over some 8000 years.

The interplay between people and place was approached in different ways by the authors. Some authors concentrated on the evidence from one site, while others took a wider or even regional perspective. Whatever the approach, the papers indicate that while landscape and place had a vital subsistence perspective for hunter-gatherers, there was also a crucially important social and cultural dimension.

36. Settlement patterns, landscape and society in western Norway during the Late Mesolithic

Sigrid Mannsåker Gundersen

Researchers of the Stone Age in western Norway have long been aware that the settlement sites dating to the Late Mesolithic (6300–4000 cal BC) are situated mainly along the coastline. Findings from the fjords consist almost exclusively of stray finds of axes/adzes. In the mountains further inland there are sites connected to hunting and quarrying. With few exceptions, researchers have interpreted this pattern to be the result of seasonal movements and logistical activities by Mesolithic communities. The lack of settlement sites along the fjords has traditionally been explained by limited inland surveys. However, a new study indicates that this pattern has less to do with modern research/activities, or Mesolithic economy, than with ideas and understanding of landscape and ideology among the Late Mesolithic population. In this paper it is argued that the everyday world of these people only encompassed the coastal zone. The fjords were considered wild areas, fitted for ritual activity. Emphasis is laid on how people experienced their surrounding landscapes, and on how sedentism and ideology were connected to these experiences.

Keywords: landscape, Late Mesolithic, ritual activity, sedentism, settlement patterns, single finds.

Introduction

In this paper, archaeological material from the Late Mesolithic of western Norway is presented and discussed. The area of study is shown in Figure 36.1. In this region, the Late Mesolithic corresponds to *c.* 6300–4000 cal BC (Bergsvik 2001a). The aim is to discuss Late Mesolithic peoples' use and perception of the landscape that surrounded them, by studying the patterns formed by known sites from the period.

For a couple of decades, researchers have discussed whether the archaeological data from the Late Mesolithic are the remains of sedentary or mobile communities (e.g. Nygård 1987; Olsen 1992; Bergsvik 2001a; 2002a). This is not only a question of interpretations, but also one of definitions. Leaning on Rafferty (1985, 115), Kent (1989, 2) and Bergsvik (2001a, 2), and picking from all of them, I find the following to be a reasonable definition of 'sedentism': *A situation in which at least part of the group spends over six months a year at one location, and the same group later returns to this location.* Following this, it seems fair to call the Late Mesolithic communities sedentary – at least by the second half of the period. Both settlement sites with thick cultural layers, and osteological evidence, support the theory that people were now spending far more time at certain sites than their predecessors (Olsen 1992; Bergsvik 2001a).

However, this understanding of sedentism obviously allows for quite a lot of mobility. The archaeological material consists of sites of varying sizes and characteristics, showing that the full group of people, or just a part, certainly moved to other areas for shorter periods. This could be connected for instance to hunting, raw material procuring, or social activities such as trading or raiding (Bergsvik 2002b).

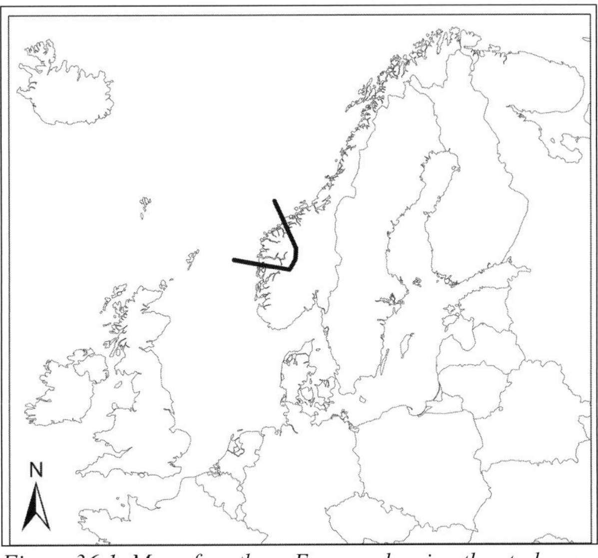

Figure 36.1. Map of northern Europe, showing the study area in the north-western Norway.

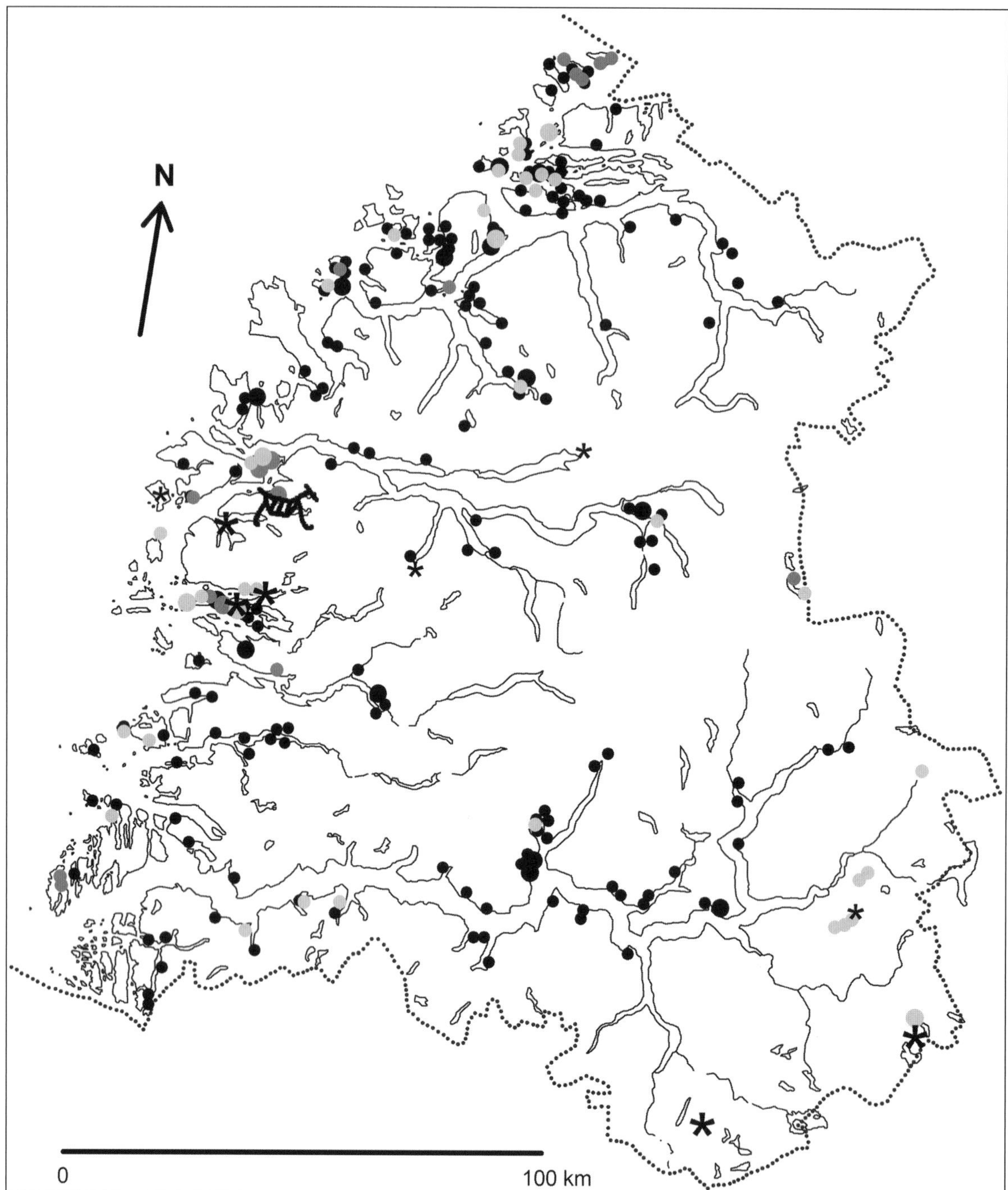

Figure 36.2. Map showing the distribution of archaeological sites within the study area. Star = quarry or area of origin for lithic raw material. Animal drawing = the rock-carving site at Vingen. Black dot = single find. Dark grey dot = long-term settlement. Light grey dot = short-term settlement. Small symbols represent one site; larger symbols represent 2–7 sites (Gundersen 2004).

These sedentary, yet mobile, communities might have left some kind of recognizable pattern in the archaeological record. If one could identify such patterns this could illuminate several aspects of Late Mesolithic society. To achieve a more solid basis for further discussions, some kind of complete overview of known sites from the period is necessary. I have tried to create this (Gundersen 2004). The basis for the data used is the published catalogues from Bergen Museum, along with all the published archaeological reports from the University of Bergen. Further, the artefacts in three museums have been studied (Bergen, Sunnmøre, and Ålesund museums). As exploring the material and documentation available proved time-consuming, the study was limited to a part of western Norway (Figures 36.1 and 36.2). The area comprises the county of Sogn and Fjordane, and the Sunnmøre region within Møre and Romsdal county. This geographical unit includes several fjord systems, a continuous coastline with islands and skerries, and mountain areas both between and beyond the fjords.

The pattern of known sites

The distribution of known sites is shown in Figure 36.2. These are sites that, according to the present level of knowledge, must be considered Late Mesolithic. They are dated either through radiocarbon, or by the presence of artefacts known to belong to the period. An important exception to these criteria is the axes (in this paper, the term 'axe' refers to a variety of axes and adzes). Currently, there are no means of distinguishing between Middle and Late Mesolithic axes. Still, leaving them out of the study for this reason is not a constructive alternative, as they constitute a large and important body of material. However, the reader should be aware that some of the sites could date from the Middle Mesolithic. Hopefully, the inaccuracies related to this problem are evenly spread across the study area, and will make little difference to the patterns presented and discussed.

Considering the map (Figure 36.2), an important trait to notice is that practically all settlement sites, whether they show signs of long-term or short-term occupation, are situated along the coastline, or in the outer fjord areas. Other types of sites include a few quarries, along with the assumed sources of certain favoured lithic raw materials. Only one of the region's three known sites of rock art was, for certain, in use in the Late Mesolithic.

The most dominant feature of the distribution map is the abundant amount of single finds. They mostly consist of stray finds of axes. A few mace-heads are also included.

Studying this distribution, it seems clear that the Late Mesolithic population spent most of its time on the coast, and that this was their preferred environment for all kinds of settlement. This is not hard to understand from an ecological point of view, as living on the coast would give access to the widest variety of resources. The coastal zone was ideal for fishing, hunting and gathering. Flint and different kinds of lithic raw materials were also found on the coast, as were materials for boats and dwellings (Lillehammer 1994, 32–44). In short, there seems to have been no *material* need to leave the coast.

But even if people did not *have* to leave the coast, they obviously did. The single finds, and also the sites in the mountains, can be seen as signs of mobile activity directed away from the coast. They might be understood as the remains from task groups. If so, the challenge must be to identify what kinds of tasks these sites represent.

Some traditional explanations and their difficulties

Many researchers reckon that the coastal population spent some time every summer, or autumn, going reindeer-hunting in the mountains (Johansen 1970; 1978; Randers 1986; Olsen 1992; Bergsvik 2002a). As the most obvious route from the coast to the mountains further east is through the fjords, it is believed that the sites in the fjords represent transit camps between these two areas (Olsen 1992).

There are at least two problems with this model. First, there is no clear evidence of a connection between the coast and the mountain areas east of the Sognefjord. In these mountains, which constitute the south-eastern part of the region under discussion (Figure 36.2), almost all the known mountain sites in the study are concentrated. Although it is natural today to include these mountains in what is perceived as 'western Norway', this might not have been the case in the Mesolithic. The most convincing arguments state that these quarries and settlements should be interpreted as parts of settlement systems and societies that had their basis further east (Lødøen 1995). Consequently these sites and areas can be omitted from further discussions concerning the coastal population.

Secondly, the single finds consist of tools only – mainly axes. Information is mostly lacking, but where records of the find context exist, the sites do not resemble any kind of camp. It seems strange if people kept leaving an axe – and only that – each time they went camping in the fjords.

Some archaeologists express the belief that there are in fact many camps – or short-term settlement sites – in the fjords (e.g. Olsen 1981; Bergsvik 2002a, 308); we simply have not found them yet. The idea seems to be that the single finds are the only items recognized as man-made by the local inhabitants who found them, and that the rest of the sites would be found if more surveys were conducted (Olsen 1981, 187).

This could, of course, be the case. But ten years ago, surveys *were* conducted along the Sognefjord (the southernmost fjord in Figure 36.2) (Lødøen 1995). This is the longest fjord not only in the study area, but in all of Norway. After searching through the most suitable areas, paying attention to changes in the sea level and the landscape, and specifically looking in and near places where axes were known to have been found, settlement sites are still limited. The project concluded that the single finds from the fjords should instead be interpreted as evidence of ritual activities (Lødøen 1995, 113).

The single finds as ritual expressions

Among colleagues, it is often joked that if something in the archaeological material is difficult to explain, the easiest way out is to claim that it is 'probably ritual'. In this particular case, however, there was more to the argument than the mere lack of economic explanations. Although the records of find contexts in most instances are insufficient, there are still enough documented examples to recognise some kind of pattern: several of the axes from the Sognefjord were found in contexts typically associated with sacrifice (Mandt 1991); such as close to large boulders, near, or even in water, and often in places not suitable for putting up a camp – for instance in screes (Lødøen 1995).

Similar contexts have been reported from the rest of the region under study – from both the coastal areas and the fjords (Figure 36.3). Some axes and mace-heads seem to have been thrown into the fjord or sea, or left in ponds or marshes. A prime example consists of two axes found together underneath a large boulder in the middle of a stream (Gundersen 2004, 82).

Area (kommune)	Catalogue no	Artefact type	Landscape type	Context
Askvoll	B11274	axe	coast	In a bog.
Askvoll	B12188	axe	coast	By a large boulder, *c.* 30cm deep in the ground on coarse, compact soil.
Balestrand	B7584	axe	fjord	In a hill/scree.
Balestrand	B7616 B8362 B10471	4 axes, together with blade, microblade, retouched flake and more.	fjord	Next to boulder, underneath a large flagstone. The items were placed on coarse, compact soil, underneath *c.* 250mm of soil.
Balestrand	B7901	2 axes	fjord	Underneath 1m of soil, next to boulder.
Balestrand	B8217	axe	fjord	On a smooth, ice-shaped rock.
Balestrand	B9168	axe	fjord	In a scree.
Balestrand	B10514	axe	fjord	About 1m underneath the surface, on clayish soil.
Balestrand	B13056	2 axes	fjord	Together, on a headland.
Bremanger	B13432	axe	coast	In the foreshore.
Eid	B6374	axe, miniature	fjord	Close to the beach, and 30cm north of a huge boulder. A lot of charcoal found on the spot; a 25cm-thick layer *c.* 1 m beneath the surface.
Eid	B9600	cross-shaped mace-head	fjord	In the sea.
Fjaler	B10574	axe	coast	On the riverside.
Gloppen	B10197	cross-shaped mace-head	fjord	By a boulder.
Gulen	B7402	3 axes (2 are lost)	coast	In a scree.
Gulen	B8224	axe	coast	Underneath a small flagstone, in a scree by the beach.
Haram	B6531a	axes	coast	Several Mesolithic and Neolithic axes found in a place where there is a 'corner' in the rock outcrop.
Hareid	B9146	axe	coast	In the foreshore 2m below the high-water mark.
Luster	B7974	axe	fjord	In a bog.
Luster	B8444	3 axes	fjord	Together, on a terrace.
Luster	B11791	2 axes	fjord	Together, by a large boulder.
Sande	B9549	axe	coast	In the foreshore.
Stryn	B9053a–b	2 axes	fjord	Found together underneath a boulder in the middle of a river.
Ulstein	B9457	axe	coast	By the waterfront, just north of the point where the river meets the sea.
Vik	B8236	axe	fjord	About 0.5m deep in the soil, in an old riverbed.
Volda	B10653	axe	fjord	In a bog.
Vågsøy	B12352	axe	coast	By the waterfront.
Ørsta	B10642	2 axes	fjord	In a bog, 50m from the fjord.
Ålesund	B8477	axe	coast	In the foreshore.
Ålesund	B9351	axe	coast	In a bog, *c.* 0.6m deep.

Figure 36.3. Finds from the study area interpreted as sacrifices, according to their contexts (Lødøen 1995; Gundersen 2004).

Considering all the above, it seems reasonable to view the single finds as probable sacrifices.

The perception of the landscape

Studying Figure 36.2, there are at least two important traits to notice. First, there are single finds both at the coast and along the fjords. Second, in the fjords there are practically *only* single finds.

If one agrees to the argument that the single finds mainly represent sacrifices, this distribution should be taken to mean that Late Mesolithic people found suitable places for making sacrifices both close to their homes and in remote parts of the fjords. Deducing from this, it is probable that all landscape areas, or at least places within all kinds of landscapes, were considered to possess abilities or characteristics that made them suitable for ritual activities. It is not possible to claim that the coast was a purely practical landscape. On the other hand, the fjord areas seem to have been found suitable for ritual activities *alone*. As such, they might be said to have constituted a *purely ritual landscape*. If this is the case, it would be of interest to understand what properties the fjords contained to give them this particular position in the Late Mesolithic world.

Trying to imagine how people of the Stone Age experienced the landscape is difficult. Their perceptions must have been rooted in a multitude of factors that we know very little about, such as what they considered valuable in economic, aesthetic, religious, or other senses, or what they knew of a place from their own experiences or those of others. Ethnographic examples suggest that specific places in the landscape might have played parts in myths and be considered to possess a spirit or will of their own (e.g. Taçon 1999).

What we do know, however, is that people spent most of their time at the coast (Figure 36.4). This is where they lived and where all their physical and social needs could be met. They were familiar with all its sounds and smells; they knew how to get from place to place, and what to expect beyond the next bend. Furthermore, the coastline would show many signs of human presence, like dwellings, boats, smoke from fireplaces, rock art and quarries (Bergsvik 2001b, 28). The distribution of artefacts and different raw materials show that communications north and south along the coast were important (e.g. Olsen and Alsaker 1984; Bergsvik 2003). This must have been the highway for those who travelled and whatever they carried with them: thoughts and attitudes as well as possessions.

Figure 36.4. Typical inner coast landscape in western Norway.

Figure 36.6. Middle/Late Mesolithic axe made of diabase from the quarries at Stakaneset. (Photograph: Svein Skare, Bergen Museum, University of Bergen).

Figure 36.5. Typical fjord landscape in western Norway.

Moving eastwards into the fjords must have made a huge contrast (Figure 36.5). The views, the vegetation, and the smells and sounds would be different. There would be few, if any, signs of human presence. Maybe it was exactly this aspect of the fjords that was most significant to people of the Late Mesolithic: the absence of other people.

The fjords must have presented a somehow different world. Their exotic, perhaps even unsafe, mystic aura might in itself have made the fjords ideal for creating and maintaining contact with forces beyond the human world (Lødøen 1995).

What kind of rituals?

It is one thing to claim that rituals were conducted in specific areas – it is quite another matter to make good suggestions on what kind of rituals they were, and why they were performed. The way I have described the fjords, as landscapes outside human society, makes it tempting to think in terms of rites of passage: the fjords sound like ideal places for spending the liminal phase (cf. Turner 1967; Lødøen 1995, 109). The single finds could be interpreted as the results of ritual quests, where individuals had to face the unknown before returning back home to the coast, to once again be incorporated into society.

Another, and less obvious suggestion, is that these offerings are connected to ideological negotiations within the sedentary communities. Sedentism is often assumed to favour social stratification, as some individuals may find it easier to gain control over other people when a population keeps living together at the same place (Sundström 2003). Sedentism eases the accumulation of material wealth for the lucky or the clever. When the only accepted way of living is staying together as a group, in one place, it is difficult to escape influential individuals.

However, from what has survived of material culture from the Late Mesolithic, there is very little that points to social stratification in this part of western Norway. Picks and mace-heads, some of them with elaborate patterns, are known from the period and often interpreted as symbols of wealth and personal prestige (Glørstad 1999; Skår 2003). But, while such artefacts have been found in abundance both north and south of the study area, as well as in eastern Norway, they do not seem to have become popular in this part of western Norway. Only five picks and ten mace-heads are known from the area under study – compared to 516 axes from within the same area (Gundersen 2004, 69).

This may not be a coincidence. The Mesolithic population of the region might have been careful to maintain an egalitarian society. Through focusing on material culture that expressed unity and egalitarianism, they might have tried to counteract the mechanisms of social stratification often believed to be part of sedentism. Instead of sacrificing status symbols like mace-heads, they preferred the axe as an important ritual object (Figure 36.6). The axes from the period come in many forms, and of many raw materials. Some are beautifully polished, and others quite crudely shaped. But in contrast to the mace-heads, the axe was a useful tool, and something that very many, if not everybody, could get their hands on (Olsen and Alsaker 1984).

The axes must have had several meanings and values locked into them. They were both useful tools, and suitable objects for sacrifice. More than 50 percent of the single finds of axes, which is a significant amount, are made of rock from one particular place: Stakaneset near the modern city of Florø (Olsen 1981, Gundersen 2004) (Figure 36.7).

Like the axes, Stakaneset with its quarries probably had several meanings to the Late Mesolithic population. The fact that its raw material was so favoured over others, and that it was spread throughout the region (Olsen and Alsaker 1984), shows that the rock from this quarry was of greater value than geology alone can explain. Through the generations, this particular place most likely played a part both in mythology and in the regional identity. It has been argued that people from all over the region must have had free access to the quarry, at least in the sense that no local group or chief controlled the place (Olsen and Alsaker 1984). This can be considered an egalitarian practice.

Both making, using, and sacrificing these axes can be seen as ways to maintain and revitalize all the meanings connected to the quarry – including the egalitarian ideology. The sacrifices might have been considered especially

Figure 36.7. Stakaneset, location of diabase quarries.

powerful when they were made in what people perceived as purely ritual landscapes.

Conclusions

The relationship between the coast and the fjords in the Late Mesolithic was not a passive one. The lack of settlements in the fjord areas was a side effect of peoples' strong attachment to the coast. However, it was also something else and something more: as areas empty of humans, they became powerful contrasts to the everyday world. Sticking to their choices for settlement, and using the fjords ritually, meant that people maintained and reinforced this contrast. Hence, coastal, sedentary societies would increasingly be considered the only right way to live, while the fjords continued to represent the strange and unfamiliar. By maintaining this contrast, they added meaning to their own, coast-bound existence, at the same time as they kept the fjords as an undisturbed ritual arena. In this manner, everyday life, ideology, and mythological notions could reinforce each other.

It can be added that in spite of new tool forms, and increasing variation in the use of raw materials, the hunter-gatherer societies of western Norway appear to have changed very little through the millennia, judging from the settlement patterns and the practice of axe sacrificing. It seems as if the perception and use of the landscape mainly stayed the same, all the way from the Middle Mesolithic through the first half of the Middle Neolithic (Lødøen 1995). This implies that the choices made to stabilize the egalitarian society, however consciously they were made, were very successful – that is until a more Neolithic way of thinking became established. At this point in prehistory, the quarry at Stakaneset was also abandoned (Olsen 1981), and peoples' perception of the landscape must have developed into quite another than the world-view as seen in the Late Mesolithic.

References

Bergsvik, K. A. 2001a. Sedentary and Mobile Hunter-Fishers in Stone Age Western Norway. *Arctic Anthropology* 38 (1), 2–26.

Bergsvik, K. A. 2001b. Strømmer og steder i vestnorsk steinalder. *Viking* 2001, 11–34.

Bergsvik K. A. 2002a. *Arkeologiske undersøkelser ved Skatestraumen.* Bind I. Arkeologiske avhandlinger og rapporter 7. Bergen, University of Bergen.

Bergsvik, K. A. 2002b. Task groups and social inequality. *Norwegian Archaeological Review* 35 (1), 1–28.

Bergsvik, K. A. 2003. *Ethnic boundaries in Neolithic Norway.* Unpublished PhD thesis, University of Bergen.

Glørstad, H. 1999. Lokaliteten Botne II – et nøkkelhull til det sosiale livet i mesolitikum i Sør-Norge. *Viking* 62, 31–68.

Gundersen, S. M. 2004. *Landskap og samfunn i seinmesolitikum. Distribusjon og diskusjon av lokaliteter og gjenstander i Sogn og Fjordane og på Sunnmøre.* Unpublished Cand. Philol. thesis, University of Bergen.

Johansen, A. B. 1970. *Høyfjellsfunn ved Lærdalsvassdraget. Den teoretiske bakgrunn og det første analyseforsøk.* Bergen/Oslo/Tromsø, Universitetsforlaget.

Johansen, A. B. 1978. *Høyfjellsfunn ved Lærdalsvassdraget II. Naturbruk og tradisjonssammenheng i et sørnorsk villreinområde i steinalder.* Bergen/Oslo/Tromsø, Universitetsforlaget.

Kent, S. 1989. Cross-cultural perceptions of farmers as hunters and the value of meat, in S. Kent (ed.), *Farmers as hunters: the implications of sedentism*, 1–17. Cambridge, Cambridge University Press.

Lillehammer, A. 1994. Fra jeger til bonde – inntil 800 e.Kr. *Aschehougs Norgeshistorie* (bind 1). Oslo, Aschehoug & Co.

Lødøen, T. K. 1995. *Landskapet som rituell sfære i steinalder.* Unpublished Cand. Philol. thesis, University of Bergen.

Mandt, G. 1991. *Vestnorske ristninger i tid og rom. Kronologiske, korrologiske og kontekstuelle studier* (bind 2). Unpublished PhD thesis, University of Bergen.

Nygård, S. 1987. Socio-economic Developments Along the Southwestern Coast of Norway Between 10,000 and 4,000 BC, in P. Rowley-Conwy, M. Zvelebil and H. P. Blankholm (eds.), *Mesolithic Northwest Europe: Recent trends.* Sheffield, Department of Archaeology and Prehistory, University of Sheffield.

Olsen, A. B. 1981. *Bruk av diabas i vestnorsk steinalder.* Unpublished Mag. Art. thesis, University of Bergen.

Olsen, A. B. 1992. *Kotedalen - en boplass gjennom 5000 år. Bind 1: Fangstbosetning og tidlig jordbruk i vestnorsk steinalder: Nye funn og nye perspektiver.* Bergen, Historical Museum, University of Bergen.

Olsen, A. B. and Alsaker, S. 1984. Greenstone and Diabase Utilization in the Stone Age of Western Norway: Technological and Socio-Cultural Aspects of Axe and Adze Production and Distribution. *Norwegian Archaeological Review* 17 (2), 71–103.

Rafferty, J. 1985. The archaeological record on sedentism: Recognition, development and implications. *Advances in Archaeological Method and Theory* 8, 113–56.

Randers, K. 1986. *Breheimenundersøkelsene 1982–1984. I: Høyfjellet.* Arkeologiske rapporter 10. Historisk museum, Universitetet i Bergen.

Skår, Ø. 2003. *Rituell kommunikasjon i seinmesolitikum.* Unpublished Cand. Philol. thesis, University of Bergen.

Sundström, L. 2003. *Det hotade kollektivet.* Uppsala. Department of Archaeology and Ancient History, University of Uppsala.

Taçon, P. S. C. 1999. Identifying Ancient Sacred Landscapes in Australia: From Physical to Social, in W. Ashmore and A. B. Knapp (eds.), *Archaeologies of Landscape. Contemporary Perspectives*, 31–57. Oxford, Blackwell Publishing.

Turner, V. 1967. *The Forest of Symbols. Aspects of Ndembu Ritual.* Ithaca, Cornell University Press.

37. Mesolithic inland settlement in southern Norway

Per Persson

Joel Boaz has proposed a model for two periods of intense inland settlement during the Stone Age in Norway. The Boaz model is, however, contradicted by radiocarbon dates from the inland sites. In connection with an ongoing rescue archaeological project on the River Rena, the question will be investigated by alternative dating methods, such as radiocarbon dating of the burnt bones, luminescence dating on thermally altered stones, and dating of human impact in the sediment.

Keywords: inland settlement, Mesolithic, Stone Age, dating methods, Norway.

The River Rena sites

The background for this paper is an archaeological project along the River Rena in south-eastern Norway: the excavations are rescue excavations in advance of a new military training area. The Norwegian military is heavily concentrated in the area, and, since the end of the cold war, Norwegian defence policy has shifted its focus from northern Norway to more central areas. The Rødsmoen project, which ended 10 years ago and adjoins the Rena project, was also in advance of military activity. Both Mesolithic and Neolithic sites were excavated on the Rødsmoen plain, several kilometres from the Rena and along the Yggla – a small stream (Boaz 1997). The Rødsmoen sites became widely known due to the fact that similar structures to the house pits found in the interior of northern Sweden (Lundberg 1997) and Finland (Pesonen 2002) were identified and excavated. The current area along the Rena has been intensively surveyed and 26 sites have been identified within the project area. Four of these were excavated in 2004 and the remaining sites will be excavated in 2006 and 2007 (Figure 37.6).

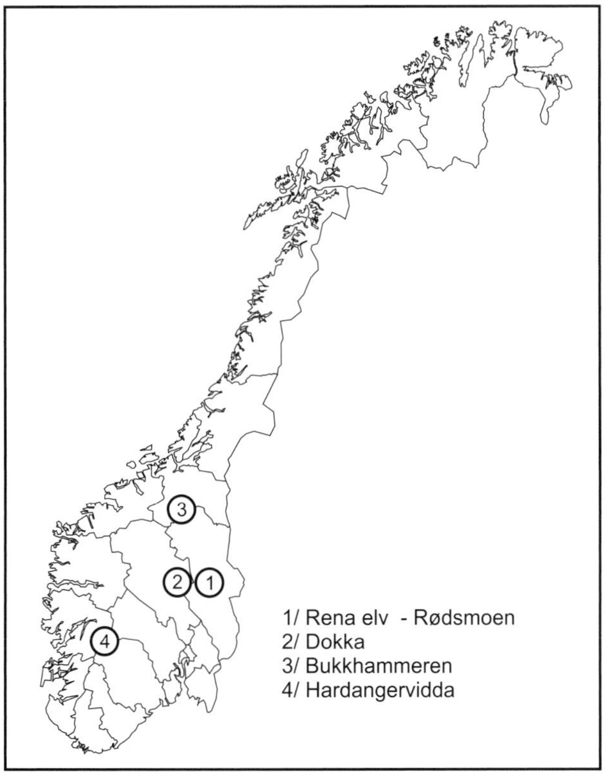

1/ Rena elv - Rødsmoen
2/ Dokka
3/ Bukkhammeren
4/ Hardangervidda

Figure 37.1. Map of Norway showing sites mentioned in the text.

The Rena was dammed in the 1970s, just a few kilometres downstream from the project area, but despite this today's topography is the same as shown on maps from the last century. The Rena is a tributary of the River Glomma – one of the longest rivers is Scandinavia. The Rena runs into the River Glomma 20km downstream from the project area and reaches the sea some 220km further south. The river is 236m asl in the investigation area. The immediate landscape to the west of the river is rather flat, with moraine formations, while the east bank is stepped with mountain peaks over 1000m asl.

The Boaz model

Joel Boaz's model is known from the excavations undertaken the middle of the 1990s, and from numerous test pits along the river, that produced both Mesolithic and Neolithic finds (Boaz 1999). One of the goals of the forthcoming excavations on the Rena is to investigate the dating of the sites in relation to Boaz's model of inland Mesolithic settlements, see Figure 37.2 (Boaz 1999, Fig. 11). According to Boaz, the inland was utilised mainly in

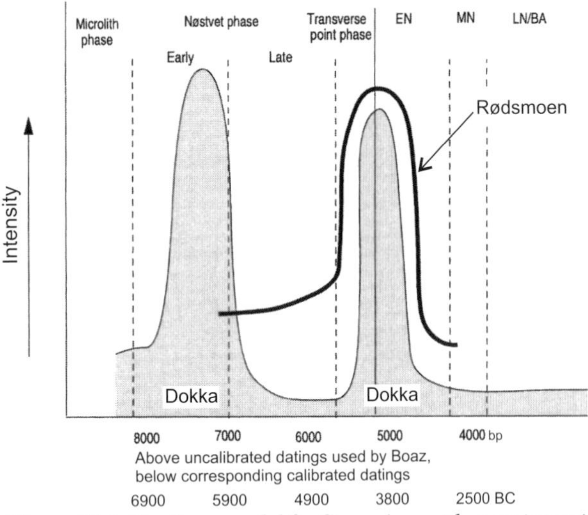

Figure 37.2. The Boaz model for Stone Age settlement intensity in inland southern Norway. (After Boaz 1999, figure 11; calibrated dates added).

two phases of the Stone Age – around 6000 and 4000 cal BC. The period with low intensity of inland settlements falls in between, at 5000 cal BC, and Boaz explains this by the intense utilization of coastal areas at the time.

In Boaz's diagram the Y-axis represents 'intensity'. The term is rather vague and can be criticised for meaning different things in different periods. For instance if the inland was utilized by many small groups over a short season each year, how should this be accounted for in terms of 'intensity', and how should this 'intensity' be compared with the situation when a few large groups lived in the inland all year round? However this criticism is unfair, as although today's knowledge is vague in terms of seasonality, group size, etc., for the Stone Age it can be no more than pure speculation. At the moment we must be content with a vague measurement of intensity that should correlate with 'sites used per year'.

Despite the high degree of uncertainty when using the term 'intensity', it could be argued that the similarities in variation over time between the Rødsmoen area and the Dokka area as shown by Boaz act to strengthen his argument. This, however, depends on whether the interpretations and dates of the sites are viewed as independent and reliable. The Boaz dating method is a combination of artefact and ^{14}C dating. For instance the early Nøstvet phase in the Dokka area consists of two phases of occupation dated by ^{14}C (DR-178, 107), three that are dated by ^{14}C and artefacts (DR-174, 85, 89), and three that are dated only by artefacts (DR-291, 22, 94).

There are few diagnostic artefacts on the inland sites, and those that appear have a very wide date range. For instance, one of the three sites dated by Boaz to the Early Nøstvet phase at Dokka, had both a conical core and a handle core, together with microblades, while the other sites contained conical cores and microblades. None of these artefacts can be dated more accurately than within a span of thousands of years. Microblades do appear at least from 7000 to

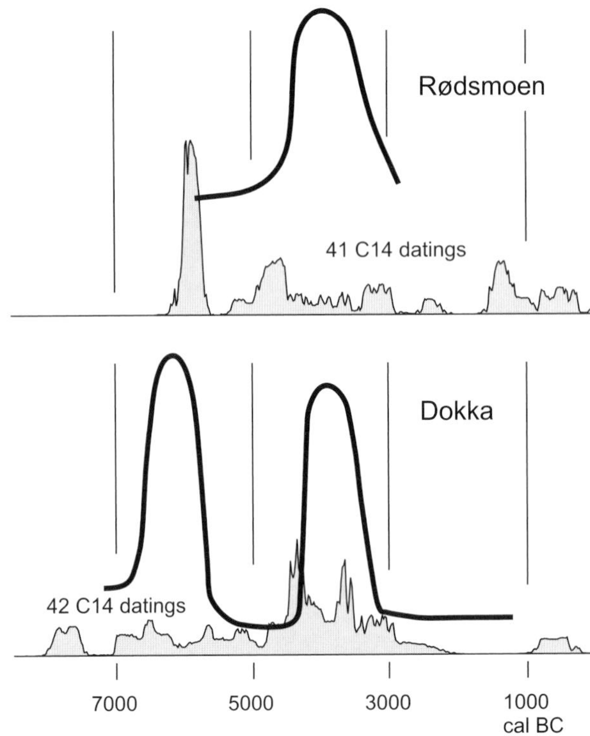

Figure 37.3. The Boaz intensity curves compared with the accumulated probability curve for calibrated radiocarbon dates from Stone Age sites in two inland areas in southern Norway.

4000 cal BC. The only way that artefact dating can be of any chronological value in this context is to assume that all artefacts found at one site are all from the same period; the combination of types can then be used to clarify the dating. This is the method used by Boas. At inland sites where all the finds originated from a shallow soil layer and there is no chronologically useful stratigraphy, the assumption of contemporaneousness between the finds is highly doubtful.

This use of artefact dating results in a low degree of correlation between the Boaz model and the accumulated radiocarbon dates (Figure 37.3). The pattern for settlement intensity proposed for the Dokka area does not correlate with the ^{14}C dates from the sites in that area, as there are no ^{14}C dates from the supposed period of intense settlement around 6000 cal BC. The opposite is the case in the Rødsmoen area. Here there are many dates from around 6000 cal BC, while the supposed period of intensity around 4000 cal BC is supported by only a few. Such problems relating to dating are even more apparent inland than along the coast. Here a shoreline displacement curve has to be used: in many coastal areas the same spot was suitable for settlement only for a shorter period of time. The topography around the inland sites has in many cases remained unchanged for 10,000 years cal BC, and sites at attractive locations may have been in use over long periods. In addition, the interior sites contain very shallow layers (a few centimetres) and lack a chronologically useful stratigraphy.

Problems with the use of radiocarbon dating

The problems that exist with dating southern Norwegian sites can be shown in one particular location – Bukkhammeren (Gustafson 1990). The settlement remains accumulated along a narrow strip under an overhang, producing a cultural layer 10m long, 1m wide and about 1m deep. 15 ^{14}C dates from charcoal broadly relate to what was observed in the stratigraphy and give an even spread over about 8000 years cal BC. As well as burnt stones and burnt bones, 290 stone artefacts were recovered from the site, including both tools and waste. Without the stratigraphy, which in this case was preserved under the overhang, the small number of artefacts from the Bukkhammeren site would have been interpreted as meaning that the location was only occupied for a short period.

Standard deviation and calibration factors introduce an element of uncertainty into the radiocarbon dates. However that is only a minor problem and ^{14}C dates are always better than artefact dating, at least for the type of sites considered here. But there are greater problems with the use of radiocarbon dates and these are well illustrated by the R39 site at Rødsmoen (Boaz 1997, 57 ff.). R39 is one of the pits that was interpreted as hut remains and 13 radiocarbon dates were taken from it. One of these was from carbonised wood from the construction and it produced a Middle Neolithic date, however, another, on a hazelnut, gave an Early Neolithic date. These two dates seem to be in accordance with most of the artefacts from the site, as there are, for instance, many fragments of polished flint axes and slate implements. No Mesolithic artefacts are mentioned in the report, however 11 of the 13 radiocarbon results show a dating from around 6000 cal BC. The 11 dates are from carbonised hazelnut shells, which were selected to be representative and were from different depths within the fill of the pit, as well as from different spots outside the pit. The 'R_Combine' function in the OxCal program (v. 3.10) includes a χ^2-test for internal consistency and these 11 dates passed this test without a warning for low consistency. According to this it is very likely that all 11 dates originate from a very short period: a period where there were no artefacts found, or, at least, not mentioned in the excavation report.

The above illustrates the main problems with the use of radiocarbon dates from charcoal. First, it is unlikely that human settlements will produce a fixed volume of charcoals every year, and therefore there is no direct correlation between radiocarbon dating and settlement. Second, charcoal is not only created by human agency but also by natural processes. The idea of using hazelnuts for dates, as with the R39 finds, is to try to avoid the latter problem. This method was introduced by Stig Welinder in the 1980s at those central Swedish sites with shallow layers of topsoil, and where other charcoals tended to give radiocarbon dates that appeared at variance with results from artefacts (Persson 1999, 95). Dating hazelnuts worked much better simply because they are more likely to originate from human settlement, although, of course, this is not guaranteed.

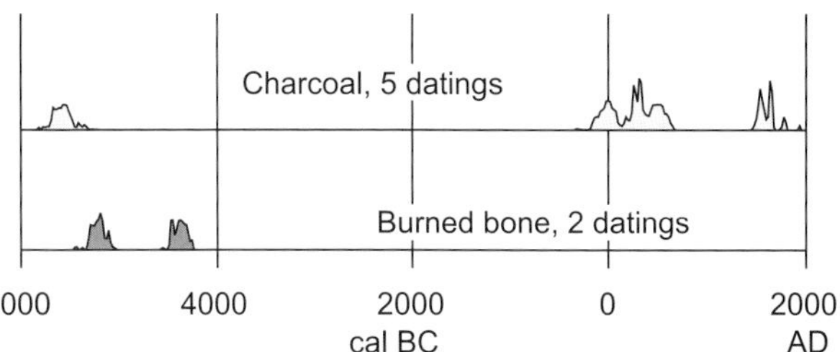

Figure 37.4. Accumulated probability curves for calibrated radiocarbon dates from the Stræten Terrasse site on the River Rena.

A further problem with radiocarbon dating, and in particular for dates obtained prior to the general acceptance of the accelerator method for measurement, is that an erroneous date can result if more than one piece of charcoal is used. If these pieces are of different age, then a date will appear somewhere in between the ages of the individual charcoal pieces, and this could be from a period without actual human settlement on the spot. Field-archaeological interpretation of charcoal pieces being of one and the same age has often proved to be totally wrong in cases where more than one ^{14}C date is obtained from the same context.

Other dating methods

Neither radiocarbon dates from charcoal, nor artefact dating, will prove or disprove Boaz's model. To take the discussion further the range of dating methods needs to be increased. In the Rena project we will try to do this by applying three new ways to date human activity – radiocarbon dates from burnt bones, luminescence dating from thermally altered stones, and the dating of human impact within geological layers.

Lanting has made recent use of radiocarbon dating from burnt bones (Lanting, Aerts-Bijma and van der Plicht 2001). The method has the advantage that burnt bone can be more safely connected with human activity than can charcoal. Burnt bones can also be better preserved, and are much more common at inland sites in Norway than unburnt bones. This may give us a higher degree of correlation with human occupation than charcoal. An example of this can be shown from two dates taken from burnt bones originating from one of the sites along the river Rena (Figure 37.4). The dated bones are both from the Mesolithic and correlate to a greater extent with the archaeological interpretation than dates provided by charcoal from the same site. Only one of the five radiocarbon dates gained from charcoal gave a Mesolithic date. Despite this, however, there are nearly 1000 years between the two bone dates which do not correlate with the archaeological interpretation that the site was a short-stay one. The reason might be that the method for dating burnt bones is still new and that there may be some unknown sources of error connected with the method. But as far as it is possible to judge today, it is more likely that the archaeological interpretation is wrong.

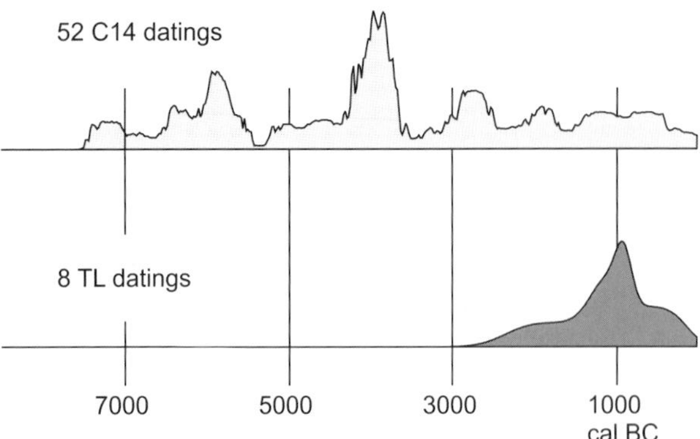

Figure 37.5. Accumulated probability curves for calibrated radiocarbon dates from Stone Age sites in the Hardangervidda area of southern Norway (above), and for thermoluminescence dates in the same area (below). (Data from Indrelid 1994, tables 87 and 88).

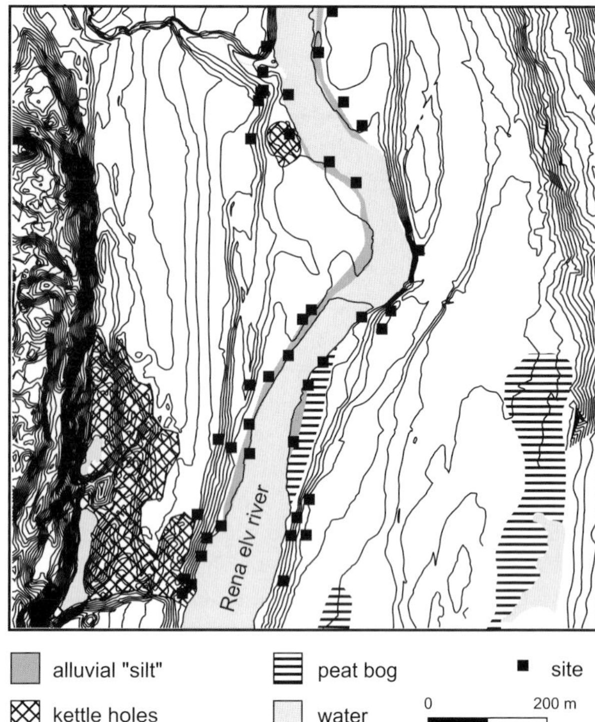

Figure 37.6. The investigation area on the River Rena. Postglacial sediments and 5m contour lines are indicated.

Dating thermally altered stones by an optical stimulated, or thermoluminescence based method (OSL/TL) has been available now for some time, although neither has been widely applied to Stone Age research. A probable reason is that luminescence dates give rather uncertain results: ±250 years cal BC, or more. This may at first glance seem too inaccurate, but it nevertheless represents an improvement on artefact dating. Burnt stones are artefacts produced by humans. Rocks without soil cover can be burned by forest fires, but this must be an infrequent phenomena compared with the huge accumulation of thermally altered stones found at some locations. At the above-mentioned R39 site, the total volume of thermally altered stones is some 15,000kg (Narmo 2000, 39). TL dating has been used on material from inland Stone Age sites in southern Norway, particularly from the Hardangervidda area at the beginning of the 1980s (Indrelid 1994, 168–9). The results are presented in Figure 37.5, and are compared to radiocarbon dates obtained from sites in the area. There is a high level of discrepancy between the two dating methods. This might be the result of cultural differences: the use of stones for boiling might have first started in the Bronze Age. It could be, therefore, that the thermally altered stones recovered from the sites are younger than the artefacts and the radiocarbon dates obtained from charcoal. On the other hand, the method has not yet been widely applied to open Stone Age sites, and there may well be an erroneous factor giving too low an age for them. In the Rena project we intend to make a new series of luminescence dates in order to evaluate the method.

Dating human impact within geological layers

At the inland settlement sites there are only shallow layers of soil, and no chronologically useful stratigraphy can be expected. The above-mentioned Bukkhammeren overhang was preserved by chance, and even if there were more sites of this type to be discovered they are likely to remain very rare. At the same time, these inland areas have a good deal of natural stratigraphy. In the relatively small Rena project area the greater part of the geology consists of postglacial sediments in river deposits, peat bogs, and sediments in glacial kettle holes (Figure 37.6). The sediments provide a tremendous stratigraphic record going back to Late Glacial times. In some cases the resolution can even narrow down to a single year, as evidenced by laminated sediments in certain small lakes and kettle holes (Olofsson and Widell 1986). In many cases sediments can be dated directly by radiocarbon. In later periods, and for areas where agriculture is prevalent, pollen analysis can be of fundamental importance when discussing the level of settlement activity over different periods. This can apply even if the level of influence human settlement had upon the pollen record, in relation to the level of human occupation, is disputed: during the Neolithic in central agricultural districts, human impact on vegetation is always one of several factors taken into consideration when discussing settlement activity. For periods and areas with little or no agriculture, pollen analysis has not been of great importance. Near Mesolithic sites it has been possible to trace human activity as a factor influencing pollen records; settlements tend to favour plants demanding greater light, nitrogen, etc. However these influences are difficult to interpret as they are of a very local character, with no direct connection to the settlement layer. Most attention has been given to the possibility that humans cleared forests to produce better conditions for wildlife, and, perhaps, also to promote the growth of hazel. Such clearances are then supposed to be viewed as horizons of charcoal appearing within lake or riparian sediments (Bos and Urz 2003). The problem here is that it is hard to distinguish between human-produced clearances and natural forest fires.

Chemical alterations in sediments are used to indicate human presence, but these are either linked to fires (and therefore indistinguishable from forest fires), or to agriculture: in one case, phosphate accumulation in the sediments has been used to localize settlement sites in peat bogs. This is the well-known Mesolithic/Neolithic transition-phase site at Hüde in Niederschasen (Deichmüller 1963). In Scandinavian archaeology there is a long tradition in the use of phosphate mapping as a method for finding sites on dry ground, and to distinguish different types of activity areas within sites. Phosphate accumulates at locations where large volumes of organic waste occur, and human activity is one of the main indicators of such accumulations. In caves the amount of phosphate in different layers has been used to suggest whether or not the layers originated from periods with human occupation (Marwick 2005).

Conclusions

The Boaz model for changes in the intensity of Mesolithic inland settlement in southern Norway is of great interest. It may well prove that the model is a correct one, but for the moment this it still not possible to determine. The dating methods used so far – radiocarbon dating of charcoal and artefact typology – are still too inaccurate. During the ongoing Rena project, one research emphasis will be to try to find new ways to date the settlements and thereby gain new insights into the question of the use of inland areas during the Mesolithic. The proposed methods for this project are radiocarbon dating of burnt bones, luminescence dating of the thermally altered stones, and dates indicated by the traces of human influences in the sediments.

References

Boaz, J. 1997. *Steinalderundersøkelsene på Rødsmoen*. Varia 41. Oslo, Universitetets Oldsaksamling.

Boaz, J. 1999. Pioneers in the Mesolithic: The Initial Occupation of the Interior of Eastern Norway, in J. Boaz (ed.), *The Mesolithic of Central Scandinavia*, 125–52. Universitetets Oldsaksamlings Skrifter, ny rekke 22. Oslo, Universitetets Oldsaksamling.

Bos, J. A. A. and Urz, R. 2003. Late Glacial and early Holocene environment in the middle Lahn river valley (Hessen, central-west Germany) and the local impact of early Mesolithic people: pollen and macrofossil evidence. *Vegetation History and Archaeobotany* 12, 19–36.

Deichmüller, J. 1963. Neue Untersuchungen am Dümmer, Kreis Grafschaft Diepholz, im Jahre 1961. *Neue Ausgrabungen und Forschungen in Niedersachsen* 1, 75–88.

Gustafson, L. 1990. Bukkhammeren, en beverfangstplass i Innerdalen, Kvikne. *Viking* LIII, 21–49.

Indrelid, S. 1994. *Fangstfolk og bønder i fjellet. Bidrag til Hardangerviddas førhistorie 8500–2500 år för nåtid.*

Universitetets Oldsaksamlings Skrifter, ny rekke 17. Oslo, Universitetets Oldsaksamling.

Lanting, J. N., Aerts-Bijma, A. T. and van der Plicht, J. 2001. Dating of cremated bones. *Radiocarbon* 43, 249–54.

Lundberg, Å. 1997. *Vinterbyar: ett bandsamhälles territorier i Norrlands inland 4500–2500 f. Kr*. Studia Archaeological Universitatis Umensis 8. Umeå, Arkeologiska institutionen Umeå Universitet.

Marwick, B. 2005. Element concentrations and magnetic susceptibility of anthrosols: indicators of prehistoric human occupation in the inland Pilbara, Western Australia. *Journal of Archaeological Science* 32, 1357–68.

Narmo, L. E. 2000. *Oldtid ved Åmøtet. Østerdalens tidlige historie belyst av arkeologiske utgravinger på Rødsmoen i Åmot. Ved Åmøtet*. Gjøvik, Åmot Historielag.

Olofsson, E.-B. and Widell, A. 1986. *Varviga sjösediment. Klimat och vegetation under förhistorien i Vilhemina*, 33–6. Acta Bothniensia Occidentalis. Skrifter i västerbottnisk kulturhistoria 8. Umeå, University of Umeå.

Persson, P. 1999. *Neolitikums början. Undersökningar kring jordbrukets introduktion i Nordeuropa*. Coast to coast-books 1. Göteborg, Universtiy of Göteborg.

Pesonen, P. 2002. Semisubterranean houses in Finland – a review, in H. Ranta (ed.), *Huts and Houses. Stone age and early metal age buildings in Finland*, 9–41. Helsinki, National Board of Antiquities.

38. The settlement patterns of the Maglemose culture on Bornholm, Denmark. Some preliminary results and hypotheses

Claudio Casati and Lasse Sørensen

The current research on Bornholm is based on two survey projects that analyse the possibilities of mapping the Mesolithic landscape by using old geographical maps and GIS-based computer programmes. This method has made it possible to create some settlement models that have been used to search for Maglemose settlements located on various topographical positions. The alternate types of settlements, such as coastal sites, inland settlements near larger lakes, observation sites on the higher grounds, and short-term transitory, hunting and fishing camps lying near the different creeks give us a unique chance to study a settlement pattern which integrates many varied topographical characteristics. The different types of sites are all registered in the Early and Middle phases of the Maglemose culture, when Bornholm was more or less connected to modern Germany-Poland. During the late Maglemose culture, Bornholm became an island and the settlement pattern changed. The site distribution declined and was concentrated near the coastal areas. These facts illustrate how geographic developments challenge a hunter-gatherer group to the limit and prove their ability to adapt to these incidents during the Maglemose culture in the Baltic region.

Keywords: Bornholm, Early Mesolithic, Maglemose culture, Ancylus Lake, survey projects, settlement patterns, site distribution, diversity, adaptation.

Introduction

During early prehistory the Baltic Sea underwent some drastic changes that had a major impact on the geographical situation on Bornholm. These changes had a serious influence on the living conditions for both animals and the hunter-gatherers, who lived on the island during the Maglemose culture (9500–6400 cal BC). Recent research results from two survey projects are described and the interpretations regarding the geographical and faunal changes are presented, together with the proposed development of the settlement patterns.

Geographical changes on Bornholm

The geographical development in the Baltic region can be divided into three main stages: the Baltic Ice Lake stage, 12,000–9300 cal BC; the Yoldia Sea stage, 9300–8500 cal BC; and the Ancylus Lake stage, 8500–7000 cal BC. During these stages, the only brackish phase occurred at 9000–8900 cal BC. From the Baltic Ice Lake stage until the beginning of the Ancylus Lake stage (*c.* 8200 cal BC), the island was either the northern part of a peninsula, which covered an area from Germany and Poland to Bornholm, or an island with a substantial land bridge towards Vorpommeren. In the following phases, from 8200–7200 cal BC, the sea level of the Ancylus Lake was low, which, together with the continued transgressions, flooded the land bridge gradually and created several smaller islands between Vorpommeren, Rügen and Bornholm, at Adlers Grund and the banks of the Oder and Rønne. The size and geographical distribution of these smaller islands is still heavily debated, but it is clear that Bornholm became an island sometime during the Boreal period (Figure 38.1) (Jensen *et al.* 2002, 7).

Faunal changes and isolation

The faunal picture from the Preboreal, containing reindeer (*Rangifer Tarandus*), elk (*Alces alces*) and beaver (*Castor fiber*), proves that Bornholm had a complete range of migrating animals during this period, and that the animals managed to establish themselves on the peninsula. The finds from the Preboreal are especially dominated by reindeer, where the youngest has been ^{14}C dated to the Early Preboreal (K-7070, 9660±85 BP, 9280–8800 cal BC). Elk were also present in the Preboreal. Seven have been ^{14}C dated, and the youngest date to the transition between

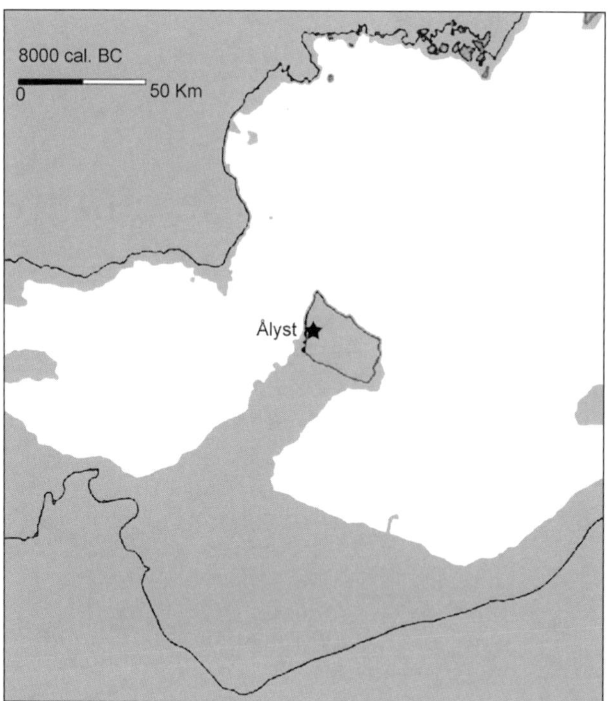

Figure 38.1. The geographical situation in southern Scandinavia, c. 8000 cal BC, when Bornholm was part of a peninsula in the Ancylus Lake (after Jensen et al. *2002, 7).*

Late Preboreal and Early Boreal (K-4402; 9020±130 BP, 8550–7750 cal BC). This particular date indicates that some time after the isolation of the island elk became extinct. However, when the land-bridge towards the south gradually disappeared it did not have any effect on other larger mammals, such as red deer (*Cervus elaphus*), roe deer (*Capreolus capreolus*) and wild boar (*Sus scrofa*), who migrated to Bornholm during the Late Preboreal and Early Boreal. This is proven by ^{14}C dates of red deer (K-4879, 9270±130 BP, 8850–8200 cal BC) and wild boar (K-4637, 9120±120 BP, 8650–7950 cal BC). These animals had a high ability to reproduce and adapt to both a warmer climate and denser forest conditions during the Boreal and Atlantic periods, when Bornholm became an island (Aaris-Sørensen 1998, 127; Kim Aaris-Sørensen, pers. comm.). These faunal changes had an impact on the hunter-gatherers who lived on Bornholm during the Preboreal.

Raw material studies on Bornholm

The Preboreal migration of hunter-gatherers provides an example of humans entering an area following a climatic amelioration. Limited finds from the Preboreal phase have been recorded on Bornholm. From Lundebro a few microliths and blanks were found, showing similarities with regard to the Early Mesolithic Barmose phase (Casati *et al.* 2004, 123). The size and quality of the tools indicate that this assemblage probably derives from a Senon source in Rügen, which could have been imported to Bornholm as finished tools. The pieces are on average up to three times broader than the typical blades from the Middle and Later

Typological Diagram					
Phase	Bornholm		Phase	Denmark	
1	Lundebro		1	Klosterlund	
2	Melsted		2	Sdr. Hadsund	
			3	Bøllund	
3	Kobbebro		4	Early Sværdborg	
4	Frennegård		5	Late Sværdborg	

Figure 38.2. Microlithic typology and chronological development on Bornholm and in Denmark (after Casati and Sørensen 2006).

Maglemose phases on Bornholm. This proves that the later habitants on Bornholm were forced to adapt and adjust to a totally different raw material situation, which gave the lithic industry an extremely small and microlithic appearance.

The raw materials from Bornholm are located in secondary deposits and were brought to the island with the glaciers from the quaternary period. The most common flint type is Kugleflint, which is a Senon type, often of good quality and not larger than four to six cm. The second most common material is the Kristianstad flint, which is a Danien type. It is dark grey and quite coarse and often up to 10–15cm in size. The third flint type is a bright Danien type, which is coarse- to fine-grained and tends to vary in size from four to six cm to around 10–15cm in size. The fourth flint type is the grey Danien type, which has the same morphological characteristics and size as the bright Danien (Becker 1952, 172; 1990, 13). Compared to all other prehistoric cultures on Bornholm, the Maglemose period seems to be the only phase where the local raw materials were the prefered materials used for flint knapping (Nielsen 2001, 87). The local raw materials were also exploited in the other Mesolithic and Neolithic cultures on Bornholm. However, these later assemblages are easy to separate from the Maglemose assemblages because of the different tool morphology and flint knapping techniques. This provides us with an ideal opportunity to find Maglemose settlements.

Current survey projects

The apparent topographical position of the different types of settlements on Bornholm gives us a unique opportunity to study a settlement pattern which integrates many settlement types and topographical characteristics. This gives us a unique chance to observe a settlement pattern which integrates many types of settlements and topographical characteristics. Future research may yield new results when focusing on some tentatively predictive models as a backdrop.

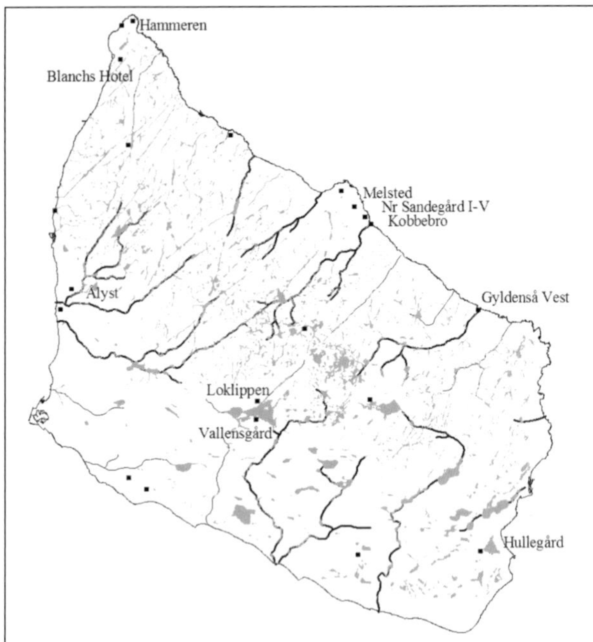

Figure 38.3. Site distribution from the Early Mesolithic during the Lundebro and Melsted phases. Note the clear differentiation of the former inland lakes and selected creeks, which contained a substantial amount of trout. This reconstruction of the Mesolithic landscape has been used in two survey projects that have concentrated on locating Maglemose settlements near different types of water resources (partly after Nielsen 2001, 92) (scale = 1:400,000).

Figure 38.4. Site distribution from the Middle Mesolithic during the Kobbebro phase (partly after Nielsen 2001, 95) (scale = 1:400,000).

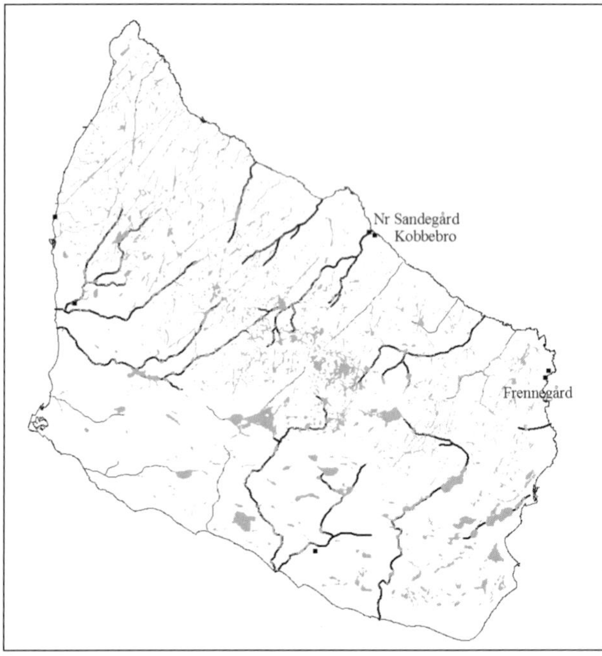

Figure 38.5. Site distribution from the Late Mesolithic during the Frennegård phase (partly after Nielsen 2001, 97) (scale = 1:400,000).

The first survey project focused on sites from inland areas, situated unusually far from any water resources. Information retrieved from old maps revealed all the old bogs and lakes that had been drained over the last 100 years, and, therefore, do not exist today. By raising the ground water level on modern maps using GIS, it was possible to recreate the size of the former inland lakes and thereby reconstruct the former landscape and lake. The majority of Maglemose sites were located exactly on the edge of these former lakes. The locations of springs have also proven to be useful guides to discovering new sites. These methods make it possible highlight future survey areas for amateur archaeologists (Figures 38.3, 38.4 and 38.5).

The second survey project involves sites lying near the different creeks and springs. These sites were repeatedly visited during all phases of the Maglemose culture. What caused the habitants to return to a certain area over a 1000-year period? One of the reasons could be the access to migrating salmon and trout (Salmonidae), which return to the same creek to spawn every year. This makes the trout (*Salmo trutta*) an important, stable, and regular resource during the Maglemose culture. Old statistics from the Bornholm region prove that, from 1909 until 1929, an average angler could fish 700kg of trout every year from the larger creeks (Jespersen 2004). Today trout are not used for consumption as they swim up creek to spawn; they are not considered worth eating, although their roe, on the other hand, is regarded as a delicacy. Recent biological reference on the trout population indicates that, in the larger creeks, a large number of migrating trout still swim up these creeks; this could determine some of the Maglemose hotspots (Figures 38.3, 38.4 and 38.5). This 'creek model' can be used in future surveys for other Maglemose hotspots in other creek systems, and this should give us a more updated image of Maglemose settlement distribution on the island.

Settlement types identified on Bornholm

In the following paragraphs, a general overview of excavated Maglemose settlements is used to describe the different types of sites and their topographical characteristics.

Excavated coastal settlements

Two distinct types of coastal site have been observed on Bornholm. The preliminary intra-site analysis, however, proves a major difference in the accumulation, use and exploitation of the settlement area. Kobbebro is located 60m from the current beach and has a 70cm-thick stratigraphic layer that could be divided into three major layers, and where some chronological variances were observed (Figure 38.2) (Thorsen 2000, 21). The site has been settled on exactly the same spot over most of the Maglemose period. An area of 30m^2 was excavated, but it is presumed that the actual site is much larger, covering an area of 100 × 100m. The three registered layers show one of the largest lithic assemblages in Denmark, with approximately 13 core axes, 900 microliths, 500 cores, 5300 blades and 75,000 flakes, totalling some 2000–2500 flint artefacts per square metre (Høier 1995; Thorsen 2000, 20). The uppermost layer belonged to the Frennegård phase, which had a depth of 15–30cm, and was filled with fire-cracked stones, lithics, charcoal, and burned hazelnut shells. It has been interpreted as a large layer of continuous hearths with burned stones. It is at present unclear if the hearths are synchronic, or if they were connected to different events. Some larger pits were excavated in the underlying layers dated to the Kobbebro and Melsted phases (Høier 1995).

Less than 500m from Kobbebro, towards the other side of the Kobbe Å (creek), the sites of Melsted and Nørre Sandegård have been excavated (Becker 1952). At these locations a different picture of a coastal-site type emerges, with clear and defined flint concentrations found in a 30cm-thick cultural layer that covers a larger area than at Kobbebro. Both sites are dominated by microliths, indicating that hunting must have played an important role. The concentrations are of various sizes, between five to ten metres in diameter. The excavations at Melsted covered 42m^2, with a 40cm-thick cultural layer. The site yielded 22,000 fragments of flake, 632 blades, 354 cores, 174 microburins, 537 micoliths, 45 splintered pieces, 44 scrapers, 31 knives, 16 burins, one core axe, and three hammer stones. Nørre Sandegård I also had a vast amount of material – 23,700 flakes, 743 blades, and 514 cores. The tool assemblage contained 727 microliths, 126 microburins, 43 splintered pieces, 35 scrapers, 22 burins, 15 knives and two core axes. The whole tool assemblage is also represented at Nørre Sandegård III and Melsted. However, the core axes, scrapers, splintered pieces, knives and burins are very rare, or nearly entirely absent from the tool assemblages of Nørre Sandegård II, IV and V. This implies that different activities were connected to each concentration. Some evident structures such as postholes, hearths and pits were also observed at both Melsted and Nørre Sandegård I–V (Becker 1952; 1990).

These coastal sites were located 100 to 200 metres from the Ancylus Lake, which played an important economic role indicated by their repeated habitation. Furthermore, some fish bones were recovered from Kobbebro, proving the exploitation of these resources, although the importance of this remains unresolved. A more detailed picture is revealed at the Late Ertebølle coastal settlement of Grisby. Some organic material was preserved here, indicating a variety of fishing methods in both deep (large cod (*Gadus*)) and shallow (flatfish) waters. The hunting of sea mammals was the main occupation at Grisby; 68% of the identified mammal bones are of ringed (*Phoca hispida*) and Greenland (*Phoca groenlandica*) seals (Vang Petersen 2001, 170). Seal hunting in the Ancylus Lake could have taken place during the Maglemose culture; ringed seals migrated into the Bothnic Bay during the Late Glacial period, when there was an ocean connection through the centre of Sweden during the Yoldia Sea and Baltic Ice Sea transition (Aaris-Sørensen 1998, 94).

Inland settlements

All inland settlements are located on higher ground near a lake, creek, or a forced passage; they are only known from surface finds. At one of the sites in Vallensgård Mose (peat bog), a dozen core axes were found. However the possibility of interpreting the lithics at these sites, and their seasonal indicators, are very limited. The potential for finding sites around the larger inland lakes, such as Vallensgård Mose, using the described survey method is very promising. In Vallensgård, six harpoons were found and two have now been ^{14}C dated (AAR 9404, 9585±55 BP, 9200–8780 cal BC, and AAR 9280, 9280±65 BP, 8650–8310 cal BC. Peter Vang Petersen, pers. comm.), which implies that fishing and hunting occurred at Vallensgård during the Early and Late Preboreal. In some of the lakes it should be possible to find organic material, as the sites were located right on the edge of the former lakes.

Observation sites

Preliminary information was recently retrieved from two new sites, revealing both a larger (Loklippen) and smaller (Smedegade) type of observation site (Sørensen 2001; Finn Ole Nielsen, pers. comm.). Loklippen is located on elevated ground approximately 115m asl, with a wide outlook over the Vallensgård Mose; it is located near a forced passage, where hunters are still active today. The site covered an area of at least 50m^2, with a vast amount of material and much thicker stratigraphical layers than have been found at other observation sites. Unfortunately it was a small excavation, covering a sample of only one square metre, with a 40cm cultural layer. The square contained 1000 flakes, 80 blades, five cores, 50 microliths and microburins, one burin, one scraper, and one knife from the Early and Middle Maglemose phases (Figures 38.3 and 38.4). This proves that the site was used as a hunting camp through most of the Maglemose culture. The intensive blade production needed to produce the microliths indicates that the site was used as a preparation settlement before the actual hunt. The few tools and large amounts of burned flint indicate that some normal settlement activities also took place at the site. A smaller type of observation site was excavated at Smedegade in Klemensker, which was located on a high ground near a spring and with a panoramic view of the nearest lake (Figure 38.3). This site had a more typical appearance compared to other observation sites and covered an area of four to eight square metres. The site had a limited lithic assemblage, with around 70 flakes, 30 blades, one core, one hammerstone, three microliths, three fragments of microliths, and some burnt hazelnut shells. Smedegade has been interpreted as a short-term hunting station which would not have been resettled at the same location. However, the situation at Loklippen proves the fact that some observation sites were more popular and more frequently used.

Transitory hunting and fishing camps

Transit camps were located on a sandy ridge near a spring or steam, where the conditions for water transportation, fishing, and hunting and gathering were favourable. Ålyst and Hullegård are two such sites that were visited repeatedly during the Maglemose culture; they contain a complex of smaller or larger settlements (Casati and Sørensen, this volume). The majority of the concentrations vary in size from 3 × 3m and 3 × 7m. They are often isolated and only a few of them overlap. Almost no scrapers, knives, burins, core axes or hammerstones have been found in most of the concentrations, except from Ålyst, where two concentrations were connected to some hut structures. Normally there are around 1000–2500 pieces of debitage in the concentrations. The main lithic production was blades, for the preparation of microliths. The Ålyst microliths can typologically be dated from the beginning (8000 cal BC) to the end of the Boreal (7000 cal BC) (Casati *et al.* 2004). This has been confirmed by some new ^{14}C analysis which dates Hut I to (AAR-9876, 8925±65 BP, 8280–7910 cal BC) and Hut II (AAR-9881, 8870±65 BP, 8240–7780 cal BC) (Casati and Sørensen 2006). An important reason for the many incidents at these creek sites could be trout fishing, from October until December; this corresponds with the many finds of burnt hazelnut shells from all the flint concentrations at Ålyst.

The settlement pattern during the Early and Middle Maglemose culture

The settlement pattern from Bornholm integrates both coastal, inland, and transit camps during the Early to Middle Boreal, suggesting that the inhabitants lived on the peninsula all the year round (Figures 38.1, 38.3 and 38.4). However it is difficult to determine the seasonal aspects because of the poor preservation of the organic materials (Nielsen 2001, 87). The sites are located in areas where it was possible to exploit many resources connected to fishing, hunting and gathering. However it is still difficult to observe a diverse picture in the tool assemblage, which is connected to small raw nodules. The raw material situation makes lithic tool production limited to certain tool types, such as blades and microlithics, whereas scrapers, burins, knives, and especially core axes, are few. Fortunately analyses of the lithic material and evident structures indicate some differences in size and duration between the coastal and observation sites. Furthermore the intra-site comparison at Nørre Sandegård and Ålyst proves some variances in the activities and duration, which could be connected to each concentration. The majority of excavated sites show a higher density of occupation, indicating a repeated settlement pattern, closely connected to the larger creeks. This particular aspect provided ideal transportation possibilities, connecting movements from coastal areas to inland lakes (Figure 38.3).

Coastal and inland commuting

The settlement pattern on Bornholm was influenced by a regional mobility strategy linked to the special geographical conditions to be found on the peninsula. These observations also illustrate the regional differences between the Maglemose societies and their ability to change mobility pattern and adapt to local situations. However it could also prove to be a particular picture of a typical mobility pattern connected to the regions around the Ancylus Lake, which opens up discussions regarding coastal versus inland problems in southern Scandinavia. Opinions are strongly divided but all are based upon the same ^{13}C values from human and dog bones from other excavated sites concentrated on Zealand (Fischer 2003, 406; Schilling 2003, 356).

One opinion is that there may have been two distinct and divided bands – one living in the inland area and one along the coastal shore. These two bands could then have had sporadic contacts (Schilling 2003). Others are of the opinion that one band oscillated between the coastal settlements in winter and the inland settlements during the summer (Fischer 2003), a seasonal rotation, as it were. Finally, some also tend to favour the possibility that Maglemose hunter-gatherers wandered through the landscape over a whole lifecycle, implying that they chose to stay in a region for a certain amount of time and then migrated to another region (Ewald Jensen 2001).

The hypotheses could all be correct, although it is important to acknowledge that the coastal versus inland discussion from a ^{13}C perspective is fixed on a small regional area in western and southern Zealand. The discussion must consider the geographical differences, which could lead to alternative mobility strategies in each region of the Maglemose culture. In particular, during the Maglemose culture the sites from Holmegård, Sværdborg and Lundby were located closer to the Ancylus Lake than to the marine coast to the north. This location could lead to a commuting strategy between the inland lakes and the Ancylus Lake, with sporadic contacts to the marine areas, as indicated by several objects of marine origin (Schilling 2003, 357). This hypothesis is supported by the ^{13}C values from Zealand, showing some low terrestrial values that could indicate a mobility strategy orientated towards the Ancylus Lake rather than the marine coast (Schilling 2003, 356; Fischer 2003, 406). A similar observation has been made in north-eastern Sweden from the ^{13}C analysis of the Barums Kvinnen, the well-known female skeleton, dated to the Late Maglemose culture (Ua-10667, 7895±75 BP, 7010-6540 cal BC), which was located approximately 10km from the Ancylus coastline. She had a value of -20.9‰, indicating a diet of mainly terrestrial fauna (Sten *et al.* 2000, 73 ff.). All the areas surrounding the Ancylus Lake, including Bornholm, probably had a similar mobility and settlement pattern, orientated towards the Ancylus Lake and the minor inland lakes (Figures 38.3 and 38.4). However the settlement pattern around the inland lakes changed drastically in the Late Maglemose period, after Bornholm had become an island.

The settlement pattern during the Late Maglemose culture

The main difference compared to the settlement pattern of the earlier periods is the almost deliberate rejection of using the interior as a habitation zone, and concentration of settlements on the coastal zone (Figure 38.5). A possible explanation for this major change could be the fact that some important resources were lost when the larger inland lakes became overgrown and filled with sediments. This reaction made it impossible for hunter-gatherers to exploit the freshwater resources in the lakes. A similar pattern and decline of site distribution has been observed around some of the flat-bottomed lakes on Zealand, such as Barmose, Lundby, Værdborg, and Holmegård (Schilling 2003, 353). It is very likely that the island, during this late phase of the Maglemose culture, was sporadic inhabited, with settlements concentrated on the coastal area zone.

Territorial borders

Part of the repeated settlement pattern proves that some of the creeks were used over more than 1000 years through the Maglemose culture; this may have been related to both historical and ecological factors. It seems that Maglemose societies integrated the use of regular inland lakes, springs, water systems, elevated ground, paths, areas of cleared vegetation, abandoned camp-sites, and religious or ceremonial landmarks in their settlement pattern. This repeated use of landscape with special features could indicate territorial borders that were determined by creeks: individual family groups could exploit particular creeks. Unfortunately it is impossible, at present, to locate these territorial borders, because of the incomplete picture of site distribution and seasonal features.

Unknown aspects of the site distribution and settlement pattern

The settlement patterns presented in this paper must be regarded as preliminary and subject to later modification, mainly because the sites have been dated by their microlithic component. On Bornholm, a preliminary regional microlithic typology with four phases has been suggested (Figure 38.2) (Nielsen 2001, 89 ff.; Thorsen 2000, 21). However we face serious problems in fine-tuning the typo-chronology of the Maglemose culture, especially the Melsted phase, which is highly problematic as it covers most of the Boreal and thus contains many types of microliths. If the phase could be split into minor groups, the site distribution would be much sparser compared to the current picture of the site distribution (Figure 38.3). This hypothesis will be challenged by further analysis of the microlithic typology, detailed raw material studies, technological analysis, and future ^{14}C dates from selected sites, although it is clear that during the Late Maglemose a decrease in inland site distribution is witnessed.

Out of sight - out of mind?

The repeated settlement pattern and the fact that the typological and functional expressions are unchanged during the Maglemose culture indicate that the societies on Bornholm had continuous social and cultural contacts with other groups, tribes, or bands within the Maglemose culture. These aspects indicate that the hunter-gatherers on Bornholm had the seamanship skills necessary to sail towards Scania or Vorpommeren. At the end of the Maglemose culture habitation was sporadic, and the opportunities to contact other cultural groups became limited and difficult – because Bornholm was then an island. However, the regression created several smaller islands between VorPommeren and Bornholm. These would have made potential contacts easier, because the distances between these islands were reduced. The size and geographical development of these islands is still uncertain, although it is important to keep in mind that Bornholm was never totally isolated and had continuous social and cultural contact with the later Kongemose and Ertebølle cultures. This hypothesis is currently supported by the fact that the first Kongemose site (Sandemandsgård) has been identified at Bornholm. In addition a submerged site was located on southern Bornholm, at Boderne, at a depth of four to five metres, indicating a submerged landscape around Bornholm, which was settled in the Mesolithic (Finn Ole Nielsen, pers. comm.). Several submerged sites from the Late Ertebølle culture, documented at Lübeck, Wismar Bay, and Rügen (Lübke 2004, 85) also add weight to the theory. The use of this submerged landscape, and the impact on settlement patterns, are currently under debate. Another argument for continuous contact between Bornholm, Germany and Scania is the fact that the distance between Bornholm and the landmasses towards Vorpommeren was probably shorter than expected. These factors show that Bornholm was never out of sight, or out of mind, of local hunter-gatherers. The results presented in this paper illustrate how geographical changes challenge hunter-gatherer groups to the limit, and also their ability to adapt to these incidents during the Maglemose culture in the Baltic region.

References

Aaris-Sørensen, K. 1998. *Danmarks Forhistoriske Dyreverden.* Copenhagen, Gyldendal.

Becker, C. J. 1952. Maglemosekultur på Bornholm, in *Aarbøger for nordisk Oldkyndighed og Historie 1951*, 96–177. København, Det Kongelige Nordiske Oldskriftselskab.

Becker, C. J. 1990. *Nørre Sandegård. Arkæologiske undersøgelser på Bornholm 1948-1952.* Historisk-filosofiske Skrifter 13. Copenhagen, Munksgaard.

Casati, C., Sørensen, L. and Vennersdorf, M. 2004. Current research of the Early Mesolithic on Bornholm, Denmark, in T. Terberger and B. V. Eriksen (eds.), *Hunters in a changing world*, 113–32. Rahden/Westphalia, Verlag Marie Leidorf.

Casati, C. and Sørensen, L. 2006. Ålyst – et boplads kompleks fra Maglemosekulturen på Bornholm. Foreløbige resultater baseret på ukonventionelle udgravningsmetoder, in B. V. Eriksen (ed.), *Stenalderstudier*, 241–75, Århus, Århus University Press.

Ewald Jensen, L. 2001. *Maglemosekulturens Bebygelsesmønster.* Unpublished Master's Thesis. Århus University.

Fischer, A. 2003. Trapping up the rivers and trading across the sea – steps towards the neolithisation of Denmark, in L. Larsson, H. Kindgren, K. Knutsson, D. Loeffler and A. Åkerlund (eds.), *Mesolithic on the Move: Papers presented at the Sixth International Conference on the Mesolithic in Europe, Stockholm 2000*, 405–13. Oxford. Oxbow Books.

Høier, H. 1995. *Unpublished excavation report from Kobbebro, journal no. 2217.* Rønne, Bornholms Museum.

Jensen, J. B., Kuipers, A., Bennike, O. and Lemke, W. 2002. BALKAT. Østersøen uden grænser. *Geologi. Nyt fra GEUS* 4, December 2002, 2–19.

Jespersen, H. 2004. *Ørreder i de bornholmske vandløb.* Bornholms Regionskommune. Allinge, Natur and Miljø.

Lübke, H. 2004. Spät- und endmesolithische Küstensiedlungsplätze in der Wismarbucht – Neue Grabungsergebnisse zur Chronologie und Siedlungsweise. *Bodendenmalpflege in Mecklenburg-Vorpommern* 52, 83–110.

Nielsen, F. O. S. 2001. Nyt om Maglemosekultur på Bornholm, in O. Lass Jensen, S. A. Sørensen and K. Møller Hansen (eds.), *Danmarks Jægerstenalder – status og perspektiver*, 85–99. Hørsholm, Hørsholm Egns Museum.

Schilling, H. 2003. Early Mesolithic settlement patterns in Holmegård Bog on South Zealand, Denmark, in L. Larsson, H. Kindgren, K. Knutsson, D. Loeffler and A. Åkerlund (eds.), *Mesolithic on the Move: Papers presented at the Sixth International Conference on the Mesolithic in Europe, Stockholm 2000*, 351–58. Oxford, Oxbow Books.

Sten, S., Ahlström, T., Alexandersen, V. A., Borrman, H., Christensen, E., Ekenman, I., Kloboucek, J., Königsson, L.-K., Possnert, G. and Ragnesten, U. 2000. Barumkvinnan. Nya forskningsrön. *Fornvännen* 95, 73–87.

Sørensen, M. 2001. Unpublished excavation report from Loklippen. Rønne, Bornholms Museum.

Thorsen, M. 2000. Kobbebro. Nyt om Bornholms Maglemosekultur, in S. Hvass and Det Arkæologiske Nævn (eds.), *Vor skjulte kulturarv*. Copenhagen, Det Kongelige Nordiske Oldskriftselskab and Jysk Arkæologisk Selskab.

Vang Petersen, P. 2001. Grisby – en fangstboplads fra Ertebølletid på Bornholm, in O. Lass Jensen, S. A. Sørensen and K. Møller Hansen (eds.), *Danmarks Jægerstenalder – status og perspektiver*, 161–74. Hørsholm, Hørsholm Egns Museum.

39. People and places in the Latvian Mesolithic: a case study from the Zvejnieki archaeological complex

Ilga Zagorska

The eastern Baltic region was inhabited at the end of the Palaeolithic by tribes of mobile reindeer hunters. During the Mesolithic the expansion of human habitation of the land, strategies of resource use, development of procurement economy and human interaction with the environment in a practical way, as well as in a ritual and symbolic sense, are illustrated by the evidence from the investigations of the Zvejnieki archaeological complex, north-eastern Latvia.

Keywords: Latvia, Mesolithic, environment, game hunting, fishing, palaeodiet, sacred places, rituals.

Introduction

The eastern Baltic is an area where hunter-fisher-gatherer traditions were strong and persistent, maintaining their influence and significance from the time of the earliest occupation to the end of the Stone Age. It was a time when the landscape and the human and animal worlds were united on equal terms. Tim Ingold frequently emphasizes that 'people who hunt and gather for a subsistence generally have an extremely close and intimate knowledge of the landscape and its plant and animal inhabitants, on whose continuity and regeneration their life depends (Ingold 2000, 111) The Palaeolithic and Mesolithic landscape with its inhabitants – humans and animals – are characterized on the basis of the material from the Zvejnieki archaeological complex in the Lake Burtnieks region, northern Latvia.

Late Palaeolithic

On the eastern shore of the Baltic basin the ice sheet retreated some 14,000–12,000 years ago, when tundra vegetation was established and reindeer (*Rangifer tarandus*) species appeared on the land. Following them, at the very end of the Late Palaeolithic, the first people arrived, in the extensive and newly opened territories. They came from the region between the River Oder and the River Dnieper, the Carpathian basin in the south, and the River Nemuna in the north. Finds of Swiderian flint artefacts are concentrated in the valleys of the two largest rivers – the Daugava and Lielupe – indicating the main routes of human Postglacial re-colonisation. The richest collection of flint finds came from the site of Salaspils Laukskola, where six undisturbed concentrations were uncovered, each marking the outline of a tent. As Latvian sandy sites provide no dating opportunities, the finds were dated typologically to the Polish Masovian flint industry, i.e. 10,500–9700 BP (uncalibrated) (Schild 1989, 89–98).

At the end of the Late Glacial, reindeer was the main game species hunted by mobile hunter groups. Reindeer may also have been perceived as a totemic animal, playing an important part in the spiritual lives of hunters (Fuglestvedt 2003, 106). Recently, seven radiocarbon dates have placed the appearance of reindeer in the region to between 11,500 and 10,000 years BP (uncalibrated). It would appear that humans occupied Latvian territories even earlier than initially considered (Zagorska *et al.* 2005, 110).

Mesolithic

At the beginning of the Mesolithic, in approximately the second half of the Preboreal period, the climate became slightly warmer and wetter. Continuous forest cover began to form, consisting of birch forest with pine. Elk (*Alces alces*), beaver (*Castor fiber*) and wild boar (*Sus scrofa*) thrived in these forested areas, and pike was the main species in the inland lakes (Zagorska 1993, 114–15). Human settlement gradually shifted from the major river valleys to the inland lake regions (Figure 39.1). As conditions improved, a number of settlements became established. The main settlement concentrations in the Boreal period developed across Latvia, mainly in the shallow, inland basins around Lake Lubans, Lake Usmas, and Lake Burtnieks. In the Late Mesolithic – the first half of the Atlantic period – climatic amelioration occurred (the so-called 'climatic

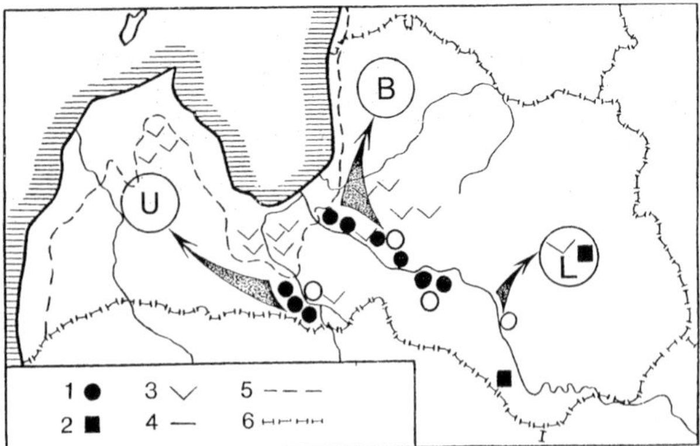

Figure 39.1. The territory of present-day Latvia at the beginning of the Mesolithic, before 10,600 BP (uncalibrated): 1) Late Palaeolithic sites with flint inventory; 2) Late Palaeolithic bone and antler stray finds; 3) Reindeer antler stray finds; 4) The Baltic Sea shore-line; 5) The Baltic Ice Lake shore-line; 6) The borders of the present-day Latvian states.

L = Lake Lubans; U = Lake Usmas; B = Lake Burtnieks. The arrows indicate the movements of humans towards the inland lakes.

optimum'), and east-Baltic fauna and flora were enriched with new species. Human habitation became more intensive and the number of settlements increased, with long-term, uninterrupted occupation at these sites with cemeteries nearby. The hunter-fisher-gatherer lifestyle is evidenced by the rich arrays of animal and fish remains, diverse hunting and fishing equipment, and representations of art. One of the main regions in which to observe the Mesolithic environment and the way of life of ancient people, over several thousand years, is the Lake Burtnieki basin and the Zvejnieki archaeological complex within it.

The Lake Burtnieks basin, northern Latvia

Lake Burtnieks, a lake of glacial origin, is located in north Latvia in the depression within the drumlin field that was left by the retreating ice (Figure 39.2). The upper sections of the drumlins surrounding the lake became ice free before 13,500–13,300 BP (uncalibrated), as evidenced by 10Be analyses of the two major stone surfaces in Davini and Bauni (Rinterknecht *et al.* 2003).

Lake Burtnieks in prehistoric times was much larger than today. The body of water in its former extent, with its sinuous shoreline, many shallow bays, peninsulas, islands, and river deltas, was a very convenient area for Stone Age inhabitants (Eberhards *et al.* 2003, 27–40). The lake, about 20km long, can be divided into two different parts: the southern (with the deepest lake bed), and the northern (shallower and with separate deep, local depressions). These depressions developed into two separate bodies of water reservoirs and gradually became overgrown. Small islands (2–4m high) of mineralground appeared in these lakes. Such places, probably, could have been used as settlement sites during the Stone Age (Figure 39.2: 4). Around Lake Burtnieks, on the highest drumlins, coarse gravel sand with pebbles and poor quality flint nodules were deposited after the ice retreat (Figure 39.2: 8). These pieces could have been used as raw material for the Stone Age flint inventory. Coloured earth or ochre layers can be found in a many boggy places and wet meadows around the lake. These deposits are formed when iron-rich subterranean waters emerged at the surface, phenomena that still occur today. Deposits of red-brown ochre are known from Rinnuklans, the Milisi farmstead and from Bauni on the opposite side of the lake at the River Seda delta, not far from the Zvejnieki site (Figure 39.2: 7). Red ochre was especially prepared for use in mortuary rites. Quartz, clay, and dolomite were added to the iron ochre and fired at a temperature of 300°–500° C (Zagorskis 2004, 87).

Archaeologists following the old shorelines of the lake to collect surface finds and undertake corings have discovered new Mesolithic and Neolithic settlement sites, as well as pottery and stray flint and stone artefacts belonging to the Stone Age (Figure 39.2: 3–5). Old and newly discovered sites indicate quite intense utilization of the landscape with dense human population in the Lake Burtnieks region during the Stone Age. Among the sites investigated previously, the archaeological complex at Zvejnieki still has much to offer researchers (Figure 39.2: 6).

The Zvejnieki archaeological complex

The Zvejnieki site located on a gravel ridge comprises two sites and an associated burial area. During the Boreal period, the Ancylus Lake stage, this ridge appeared as an island in the wide waters of the lake, not so far from the coast. Today this ancient island is about 1600m long, 2–3m high in elevation and overgrown by bushes from the previous lake plain. The island was separated from the mainland by a 100m-wide strait and existed as a true lake-island for an undetermined period. The settlement site is located on a gravel ridge at the south-eastern end of this island, at the northern leeward slope of the drumlin and the graves were arranged on the highest spot along this gravel ridge (Eberhards *et al.* 2003, 30).

Chronological interpretation

Absolute dates (^{14}C) for the chronological interpretation of the burials and settlement sites are extremely important. At present we have about 50 radiocarbon dates: four from the Zvejnieki II Mesolithic site and 45 from the burial ground, spanning four thousand years of prehistory during the Preboreal, Boreal, and Atlantic periods. The Zvejnieki II settlement site was occupied in all of these stages. Approximately two thirds of the dated graves are of Mesolithic/Early Neolithic date. The earliest graves belong to the Middle Mesolithic. During the Late Mesolithic/ Early Neolithic, the cemetery at Zvejnieki was extended, enclosing the slopes of the drumlin as well. In the western European context, all this period is considered as Late Mesolithic.

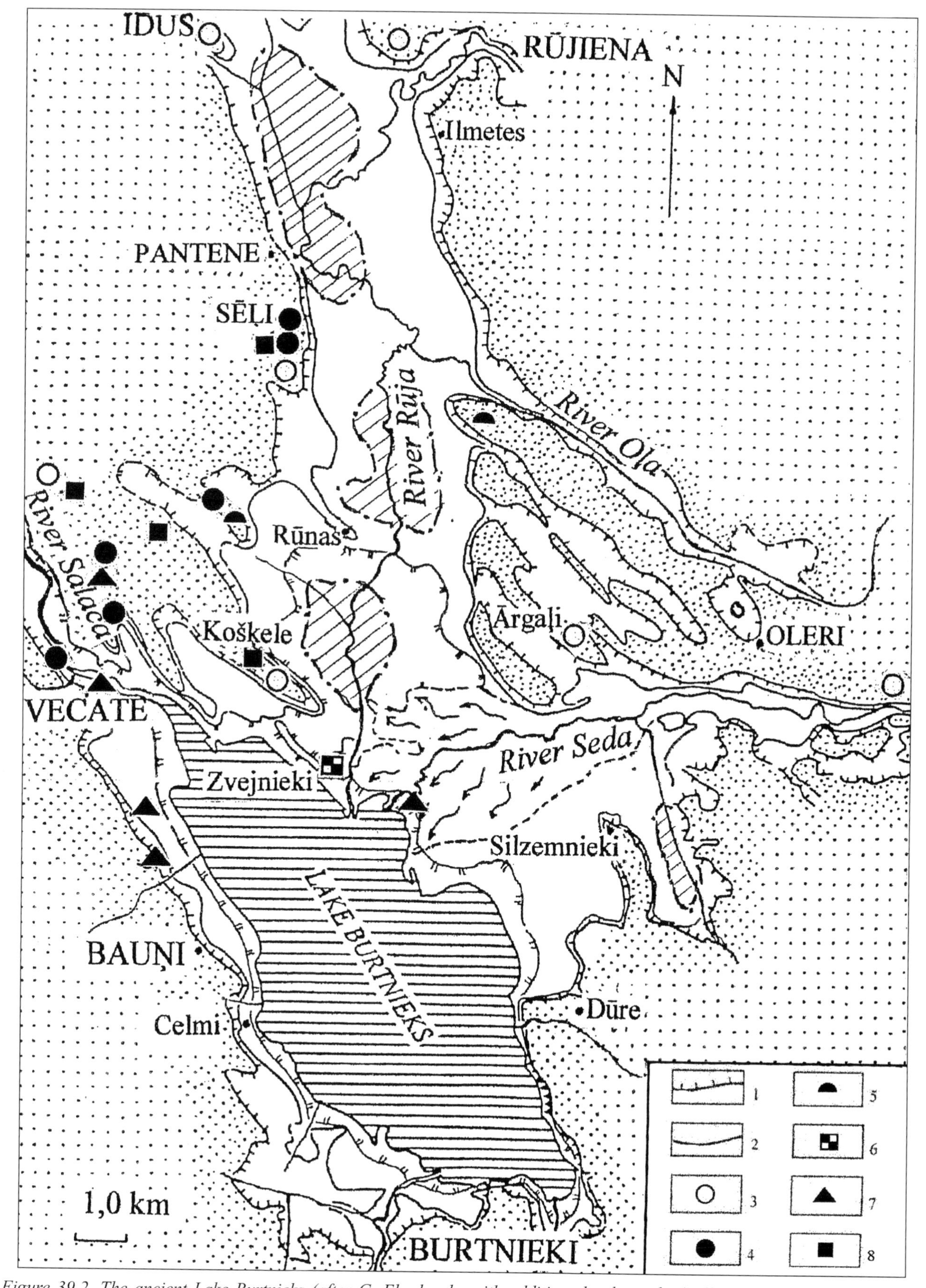

Figure 39.2. The ancient Lake Burtnieks (after G. Eberhards, with additions by the author): 1) Ancient shore-line of Lake Burtnieks; 2) The present-day shore-line of Lake Burtnieks; 3) Stray Stone Age finds in the Lake Burtnieks area; 4) Stone Age settlements in the Lake Burtnieks area; 5) Stone Age burial places sites; 6) The Zvejnieki archaeological complex; 7) Places with ochre finds; 8) Surface finds of low-quality flint nodules.

Radiocarbon dates from the settlement site have been obtained from the earliest stage of inhabitation, covering a time span from 9415±80 BP (8800–8560 cal BC; Ua-18201) to 8500±460 BP (8300–7000 cal BC; Tln-296). The earliest Middle Mesolithic graves belong to the period from 8240±70 BP (7450–7140 cal BC; Ua-3634) to 7730±70 BP (6640–6480 cal BC; Ua-3644) BP. Late Mesolithic/Early Neolithic graves cover a period from 6900±65 BP (5870–5710 cal BC; Ua-3638) to 5635±65 BP (4540–4370 cal BC; Ua-19805) (Zagorska and Larsson 1994; Zagorska 1997; Zagorska and Lougas 2000; Eriksson *et al.* 2003, 50–1). (Calibration after Reimer et al (2004); OxCal v3.10 Bronk Ramsey (2005); cub r:5, sd:12 pprob usp (chron). Calibration Sigma 1.)

Environment

The Mesolithic environment in Latvia, as well as in the Burtnieks area, was characterized by a more continental climate with dense forest cover. During the Preboreal stage birch (*Betula*) was more numerous, but later pine (*Pinus*) dominated. The second half of the Mesolithic there was some increase in birch, alder (*Alnus*) and hazel (*Corylus*). Increases in pollen from broad-leaf species, particularly elm (*Ulmus*), can be seen at the beginning of the Atlantic. Ruderal plants, and charcoal in the pollen spectra spectrum, from Zvejnieki II indicate human activity in the area (Eberhards *et al.* 2003, 35). A great variety of game has been observed in the palaeozoological material from the site and also the graves at Burtnieks. In the Preboreal period the finds of elk bones dominated; later, forest ungulates such as red deer (*Cervus elaphus*), aurochs (*Bos primigenius*) and wild boar were also hunted. Beaver was also a very important resource. At the beginning of the Atlantic period the variety of animal species hunted reached its maximum. Wild horse (*Equus ferus*), badger (*Meles meles*), dog (*Canis familiaris*), pine marten (*Martes martes*) and even seal (*Phoca*) bones appear among the faunal remains. Fish remains recovered from the site include pike (*Esox lucius*), perch (*Perca fluviatilis*), bream (*Abramis brama*), tench (*Tinca tinca*) and chub (*Leuciscus cephalus*), all caught in Lake Burtnieki. The importance of fish catches is also confirmed by the evidence for fishing equipment from the site. This evidence includes mainly the long, finely-barbed fish spears of the Kunda type. Storage pits filled with fish remains were discovered at the lowest level of the site. Surprisingly small numbers of certain types of fish species were found in the graves – pike, sturgeon (*Acipenser sturio*), and whitefish (*Coregonus* sp.) (Lõugas, in press). Small amounts of bird bones were found at the actual site of Zvejnieki II, but the burial area contained many more – as grave goods and in grave fills. Several species of duck (Anatidae) are represented – mallard (*Anas platyrhynchos*), goosander (*Mergus merganser*), merganser *(Mergus serrator*) and diving ducks (*Aythya* sp.) (Mannermaa 2006).

Stable isotope analyses

Human bones and teeth from Zvejnieki burials were subjected to stable carbon and nitrogen isotope analyses, illustrating the protein intake of individuals. The analyses were undertaken by G. Eriksson in Stockholm. The faunal remains of herbivores and carnivores, deriving from marine, terrestrial and freshwater environments, were also included in the analyses. The stable isotope values for Zvejnieki humans showed considerable variability: for one group, freshwater protein intake was revealed. The pike, a highly carnivorous fish, is thought to be an important food source. Another group appeared to include in their diet a mix of freshwater fish and hunted game, consumed in different proportions. So far only one male adult (grave 165) was found to have eaten marine creatures, perhaps seal. The average data for Mesolithic human diets are: carbon (13 C) -22.0 to -23.0 per mil, but for nitrogen (15 N) about 11.9 per mil (Eriksson *et al.* 2003, 54–5). Therefore, the analyses demonstrate considerable isotopic variability, with the emphasis on terrestrial/freshwater protein from a high level in the food chain. It is not possible to establish any gender differences in the diet (Eriksson *et al.* 2003, 54–60).

Studies of the fauna and human material from the Zvejnieki archaeological complex reveal a typical hunter-fisher-gatherer society, subsisting on an inland, freshwater ecosystem. Only during the Late Mesolithic/Early Neolithic periods did the first evidence of coastal contact appear. Possible exotic items should also be mentioned at this point, including seal-tooth pendants and the so-called 'marine dogs' (pendants made of dog teeth showing traces of marine proteins) from the Zvejnieki burial ground (Eriksson *et al.* 2003, 63).

Hunting and fishing equipment

Finds from the Zvejnieki archaeological complex, mainly settlement sites, testify to the dependence placed on hunting and fishing equipment in the lives of Stone Age inhabitants. In the Early Mesolithic assemblages some harpoons of archaic appearance, with widely-spaced barbs, needle-shaped points, and slotted points with flint inserts have all been found. In finds from the Middle Mesolithic, fish spears of the Kunda type (Clark's type 6) dominated, followed by slotted points and arrowheads with a conical tip, spears and harpoons, and daggers. In the Late Mesolithic this tool kit was enriched by spearheads with two symmetrical barbs, smoothed spearheads and different arrowheads. During this final phase of the Mesolithic the hunting and fishing assemblages were very rich and diverse. The burial area contained a similar range of offerings (graves 16, 41, 45, 57). The richest and most widespread grave goods were animal tooth pendants, predominantly from elk species. Elk also dominated in art representations (Figure 39.3); elk heads were depicted on some bone pendants (graves 100 and 162), but the most important item was a bone, elk-head staff found in the grave of an elderly female (grave 57). These art pieces reveal the hunters' keen observation and perfect knowledge of their subjects, producing true-to-life representations. To some degree these images are also linked to hunt magic and the death cult.

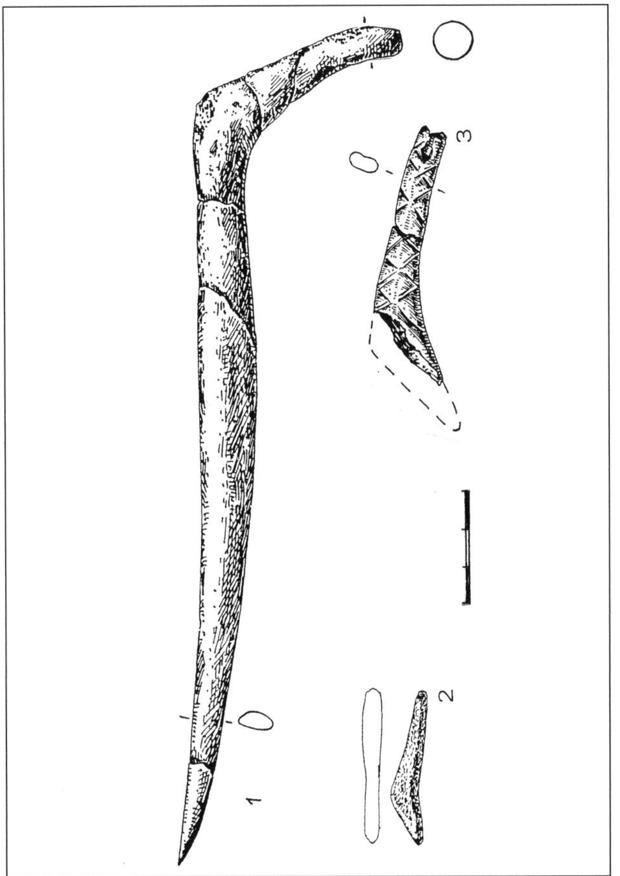

Figure 39.3. Elk representations from the Zvejnieki burial ground: 1) Bone staff with elk-head handle (grave 57); 2) Elk-head (?) bone figurine (grave 162, 3). Ornamented elk-head bone pendant (grave 100). (Drawings after Zagorskis 2004).

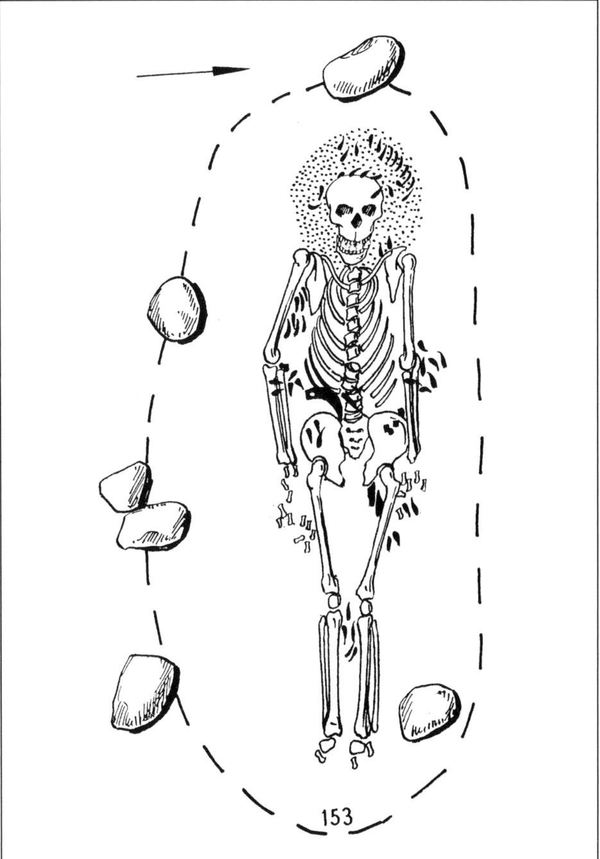

Figure 39.4. Zvejnieki burial ground: Grave 153, young male burial dated to 5745±65 BP (4690–4530 cal BC, OxA-5968); Bird offering remains close to both elbows of the interred, and special headgear consisting of 91 animal-tooth pendants (elk, dog, badger, martin), located close to the head. (After F. Zagorskis 2004).

In comparing material from the settlement site with the data from the graves, similarities as well as differences become evident. In the settlement material and graves, elk prevails as the major big-game animal. At the same time, the grave goods include hardly any, or no fishing equipment or fish (just three graves out of 315 burials) – finds that are so much in evidence at the site itself. Bird remains, however, are scarce in the settlement, but richly reflected in the grave goods – for example tubular bird-bone pendants (grave 190), a bird figurine made from a wild bore tusk (grave 74), and waterfowl offerings in other graves. Next to the elbows of one male burial (grave 153) were found a large number of duck bones which could have come from at least two individual birds (Figure 39.4) (Mannermaa 2006). It is clear that the site material reflects the everyday lives of the settlers, whereas the burials give an insight into the symbolic world of the inhabitants: a world where elk and water birds played significant roles.

Conclusions

In the layout of the Zvejnieki archaeological complex we see a typical fisher-hunter-gatherer settlement. The gravel hill rose above the lake level, giving a wide and beautiful panorama of the surroundings; even the choice of site was important – on an island in a lake. The settlement site itself reveals an intensively used location, with its thick cultural level, hearth places, storage pits, and rich array of artefacts; the site was perhaps already permanently inhabited and used all year round. On the highest part of the gravel ridge, alongside the settlement, the burial area for deceased community members was arranged. It seems that the island was not only a favoured area for subsistence strategy, but also a sacred, celestial place of great ritual and spiritual meaning. The relationship between the practical and ritual use of the landscape is a complex one (Zvelebil 2003a; 2003b). The Stone Age materials from the Lake Burtnieks region characterize a typical hunter-fisher community with strong ritual activities and traditions that were preserved over millennia.

Acknowledgements

I would like to thank all the specialists from Latvia, Estonia, Finland, and Sweden, who participated in the interdisciplinary research of the archaeological, palaeozoological, geological, and other materials from the Zvejnieki complex over the last ten years, and especially Professor L. Larsson for initiating and facilitating the project.

References

Bronk Ramsey, C. 2005. OxCal (computer program). Version 3.10. Manual available at http://www.rlaha.ox.ac.uk/oxcal/oxcal.htm (accessed 10/2007).

Eberhards, G., Kalnina, L. and Zagorska, I. 2003. Senais Burtnieku ezers un akmens laikmetā apdzīvotās vietas (Ancient Lake Burtnieks and Stone Age inhabitation). *Arheoloģija un etnogrāfija* XXI, 27–40.

Eriksson, G., Lõugas, L. and Zagorska, I. 2003. Stone age hunter-fisher-gatherers at Zvejnieki, northern Latvia: radiocarbon, stable isotope and archaeozoology data. *Before Farming* 1 (2), 1–25.

Fuglestved, I. 2003. Enculturating the Landscape beyond the Doggerland, in L. Larsson, H. Kindgren, K. Knutsson, D. Loeffler and A. Åkerlund (eds.), *Mesolithic on the Move: Papers presented at the Sixth International Conference on the Mesolithic in Europe, Stockholm 2000*, 103–7 Oxford, Oxbow Books.

Ingold, T. 2000. *The Perception of the Environment. Essays in livelihood, dwelling and skill.* London, Routledge.

Lõugas, L. 2006. Animals as subsistence and bones as raw material for settlers of prehistoric Zvejnieki, in L. Larsson and I. Zagorska (eds.), *Back to the origin. New research in the Mesolithic-Neolithic Zvejnieki cemetery and environment, northern Latvia.* Acta Archaeologica Lundensia, Series in 8°, 52. Stockholm, Almqvist & Wiksell International.

Mannermaa, K. 2006. Bird remains in the human burials at Zvejnieki, Latvia. Introduction to bird finds and a proposal for interpretation, in L. Larsson and I. Zagorska (eds.), *Back to the origin. New research in the Mesolithic-Neolithic Zvejnieki cemetery and environment, northern Latvia*, 289–330. Acta Archaeologica Lundensia, Series in 8°, 52. Stockholm, Almqvist & Wiksell International.

Reimer, P. J., Baillie, M. G. L., Bard, E., Bayliss, A., Beck, J. W., Bertrand, C. J. H., Blackwell, P. G., Buck, C. E., Burr, G. S., Cutler, K. B., Damon, P. E., Edwards, R. L., Fairbanks, R. G., Friedrich, M., Guilderson, T. P., Hogg, A. G., Hughen, K. A., Kromer, B., McCormac, G., Manning, S., Bronk Ramsey, C., Reimer, R. W., Remmele, S., Southon, J. R., Stuiver, M., Talamo, S., Taylor, F. W., van der Plicht, J. and Weyhenmeyer, C. E. 2004. IntCal04 terrestrial radiocarbon age calibration, 0–26 cal kyr BP. *Radiocarbon* 46 (3), 1029–58.

Rinterknecht, V. R., Clark, P. U., Zelcs, V. and Bitinas, A. 2003. Pēdējā apledojuma izzušanas gaitas datējumi ar 10 BE metodi. Pašreizējie rezultāti Latvijā un Lietuvā (Datings of the last ice-sheet retreat using the 10 BE method. The latest results from Latvia and Lithuania). *Ģeogrāfija, ģeoloģija, vides zinātne*, 174–6.

Schild, R. 1989. The Formation of the Homogeneous Occupation Units (Kshemenitsas) in Open Air Sandy Sites and its significance fir the Interpretation of Mesolithic Flint Assemblages, in C. Bonsall (ed.), *The Mesolithic in Europe: Papers Presented at the Third International Symposium*, 89–98. Edinburgh, John Donald Publishers.

Zagorska, I. 1993. The Mesolithic in Latvia. *Acta Archaeologica* 63, 1992, 97–117.

Zagorska, I. 1997. The first radiocarbon datings from the Zvejnieki Stone Age burial ground, Latvia, in T. Edgren (ed.), *Proceedings of the VII Nordic Conference on the Application of Scientific Methods in Archaeology, Savonlinna, Finland, 7-11 September 1996*, 42–7. Iskos 11. Helsinki, The Finnish Antiquarian Society.

Zagorska, I. and Larsson, L. 1994. New data on the chronology of the Zvejnieki Stone Age cemetery. *Mesolithic Miscellany* 15 (2), 3–10.

Zagorska, I. and Lõugas, L. 2000. The tooth-pendant head-dresses from the Zvejnieki cemetery, in *De temporibus antiquissimis ad honorem Lembit Jaanits*, 223–44. Muinasaja teadus 8. Tallinn, University of Tallinn.

Zagorska, I., Lukševiča, L., Lukševičs, E. and Jungner, H. 2005. Senie ziemeļbrieži (*Rangifer tarandus*) un to mednieki Latvijā (Ancient reindeer (*Rangifer tarandus*) and their hunters in Latvia). *Arheoloģija un etnogrāfija* XXII, 99–112.

Zagorskis, F. 2004. *Zvejnieki, Northern Latvia – Stone Age Cemetery.* British Archaeological Reports, International Series S1292. Oxford, Archaeopress.

Zvelebil, M. 2003a. People behind the lithics. Social life and social conditions of Mesolithic communities in temperate Europe, in L. Bevan and J. Moore (eds.), *Peopling the Mesolithic in a Northern Environment*, 1–26. British Archaeological Reports, International Series S1157. Oxford, Archaeopress.

Zvelebil, M. 2003b. Enculturation of Mesolithic landscapes, in L. Larsson, H. Kindgren, K. Knutsson, D. Loeffler and A. Åkerlund (eds.), *Mesolithic on the Move: Papers presented at the Sixth International Conference on the Mesolithic in Europe, Stockholm 2000*, 65–73. Oxford, Oxbow Books.

40. Dąbrowa Biskupia 71: a specialized camp from the Maglemose culture

Lucyna Domańska and Marcin Wąs

The aim of this paper is to discuss several new discoveries made in the Kuiavian region of Poland. Investigations at the site of Dąbrowa Biskupia 71 have shed new light on the issue of specialized camps from the Maglemose culture in the Polish lowlands. The site (187m²) was investigated between 2001 and 2003, and 482 flint artefacts were discovered, of which microliths represent the most characteristic and numerous finds.

Keywords: Poland, Maglemose culture, specialized camp.

Introduction

In the following paper we want to present the results of the excavations carried out on site 71 at Dąbrowa Biskupia. The site is located in the north-eastern part of Kuiavian region of Poland (Figure 40.1). The site was discovered as a result of a surface survey and represents one of many sites located in the area where single Mesolithic artefacts – mainly microliths – have been found. Dąbrowa Biskupia 71 was the only site amongst the many discovered that yielded exclusively Mesolithic flints and offered the possibility of examining the remains of a Mesolithic settlement that had not been badly destroyed in later periods. Late Mesolithic sites dominate in this area (Domańska 2004, 588–9) and only a few sites may be referred to as Early Mesolithic. Among them Dąbrowa Biskupia is the only site of Maglemose culture, the others represent the Duvensee-Komornica complex

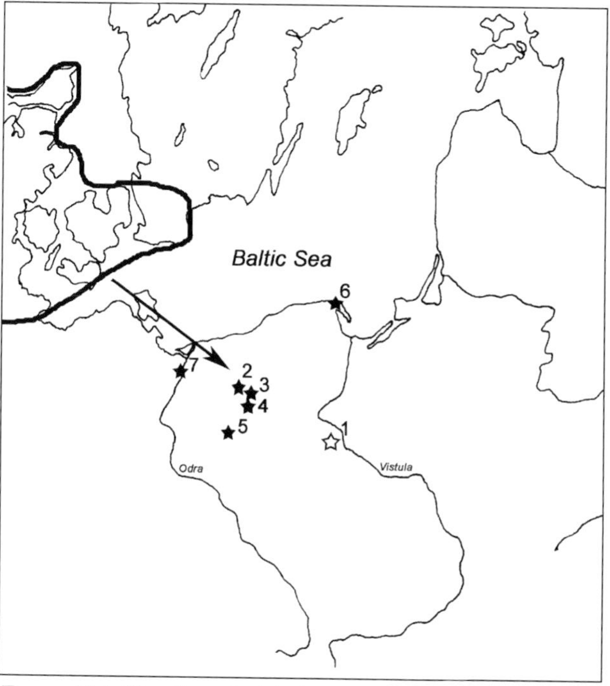

Figure 40.1. Sites from the Maglemose culture in north-western Poland. 1: Dąbrowa Biskupia 71; 2: Gudowo 3; 3: Wierzchowo 6; 4: Kalisz Pomorski 3; 5: Trzebicz Młyn 1; 6: Jastrzębia Góra 4; 7: Dobra 53. The spread of Maglemose culture in Scandinavia is marked with a thick line.

The site of Dąbrowa Biskupia 71 is located at the base of the sandy valley that joins the Toruń-Eberswalde pre-valley with the Kuiavian upland. In the neighbourhood of the find several other sites have also been recorded, at which isolated Mesolithic microliths have also been discovered. The remains of Neolithic settlements have also been found at most of these sites: only Dąbrowa Biskupia 71 has yielded exclusively Mesolithic flints. In our article we shall present the flint material from this site and attempt to define their functions.

In 2001, sondage excavations were conducted by opening four trenches in the area of the Dąbrowa Biskupia site. Each trench yielded isolated Mesolithic artefacts – exclusively microliths and bladelets. During the following two seasons (2002 and 2003), broader excavations were carried out with the aim of fully defining the site and the character of the spatial distribution of artefacts (Figure 40.2).

Characteristics of flint inventory

In the course of the excavations, 482 flint artefacts were discovered (Figure 40.3). The quantitative specification of the flint material reveals almost exclusively Mesolithic artefacts, which were made entirely of local flint.

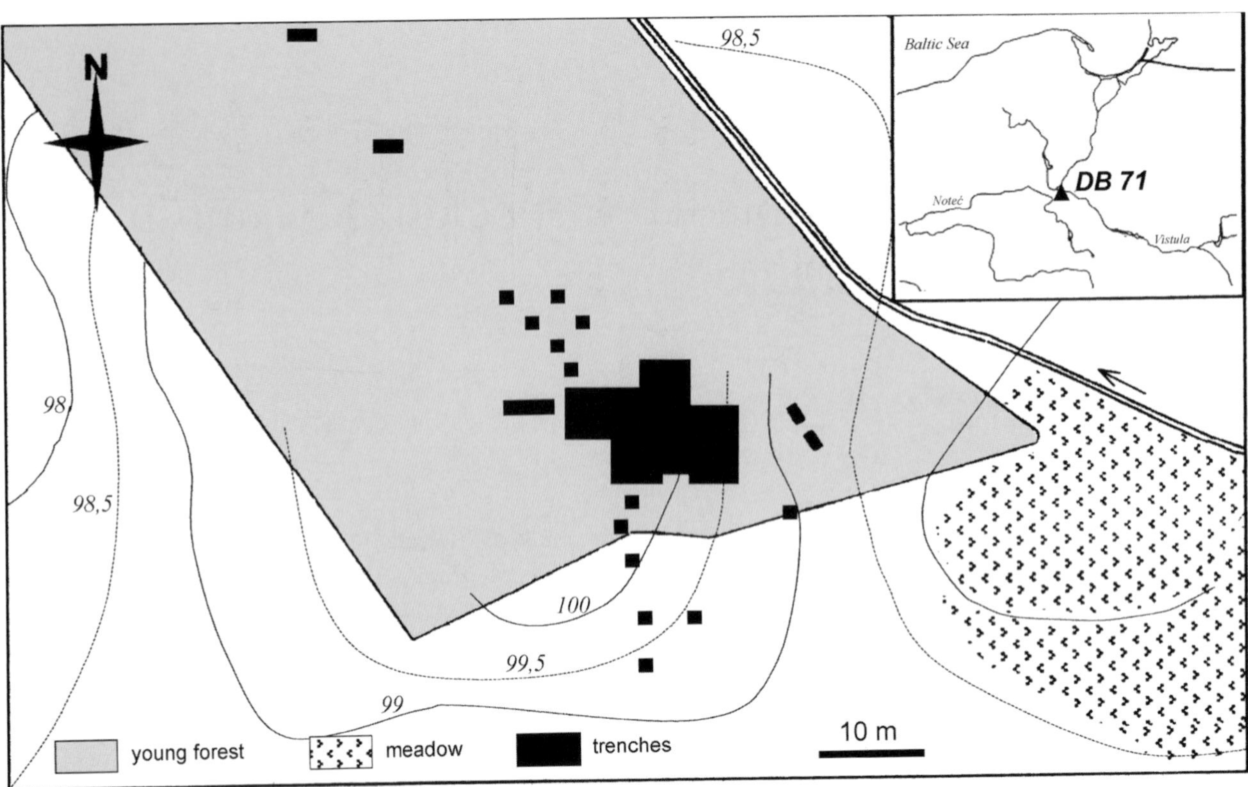

Figure 40.2. Dąbrowa Biskupia 71: location of the trenches.

The most characteristic and numerous group of artefacts (189 specimens) from Dąbrowa Biskupia 71 is the microliths. They comprise almost half of the total assemblage (40%), and nearly 100% of the tool group (Figure 40.3). Microliths of the Nowy Młyn-type predominate (52 specimens) (Figure 40.4: 1–12). Among the latter some specimens have claw-shaped tops formed by retouching both edges (Figure 40.4: 22). The second most common microlith type is the scalene triangle (50 specimens) (Figure 40.4: 14–20), sometimes similar to the rectangular examples (Figure 40.4: 13). Similarly with the latter group, evidence of retouch of the two top edges can be seen (Figure 40.4: 21). In addition to the above-mentioned larger triangles, nine smaller ones have been distinguished (Figure 40.4: 31–3) and among these the finds with preserved butt are the most numerous. Microliths with a retouched base (26 specimens) are the most morphologically differentiated (Figure 40.4: 25–6).

The remainder of the recognisable types are: 3 lancet-backed blades (Figure 40.4: 28–30), one equilateral triangle (Figure 40.4: 27), and 48 microlith fragments that very probably can be classified as fragments of the Nowy Młyn-type, or scalene triangles.

The group of finds discussed is notable for its considerable stylistic similarity. All the specimens of the Nowy Młyn-type microliths, scalene triangles, and microliths with retouched base are made of slender regular bladelets. Their shape was limited to retouch of slightly oblique base, and, with the Nowy Młyn microliths and scalene triangles one of the edges was also retouched. The range of retouch was probably dependent on the size of the raw material and may have determined the final form of the microlith. Some possible confirmation of this standardization is the relatively similar parameters of all the microliths, especially their thickness (1–3mm) and width (3–8mm). The lengths of the microliths, in spite of being dependent on the parameters of the raw material, also reveal a certain standardization.

TYPES			N1	N2	N3
Blades					154
Flakes					68
Blade-Flakes					2
Tools					192
	Microliths			189	
		Microliths of the Nowy Młyn type	52		
		Scalene triangles	50		
		Small scalene triangles	9		
		Microliths with retouched base	26		
		Lancet backed blades	3		
		Other	1		
		Unidentified	48		
	Retouched blade			1	
	Retouched flakes			2	
Microburins					20
	Basic			11	
	Middle			1	
	Top			8	
Splintered flakes					10
Chips					26
Chunks					8
Technical wates					2
	Core tablets			2	
Total					482

Figure 40.3. Dąbrowa Biskupia 71: qualitative and quantitative statements of the flint material.

Blades are the second most frequent artefact type in the inventory under consideration (154 specimens, or 32%). All

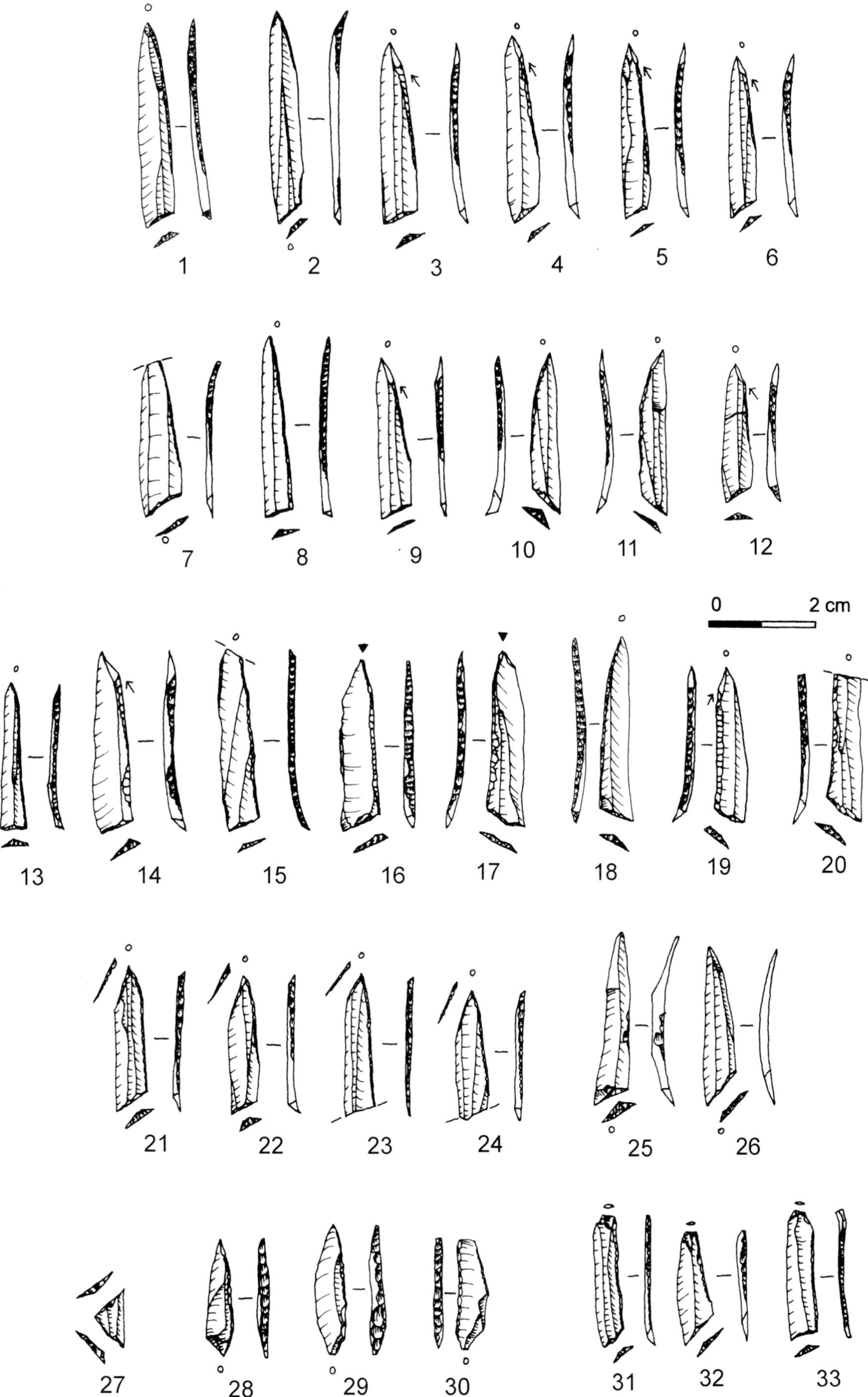

Figure 40.4. Dąbrowa Biskupia 71: microliths. (Drawings: Domańska and Wąs).

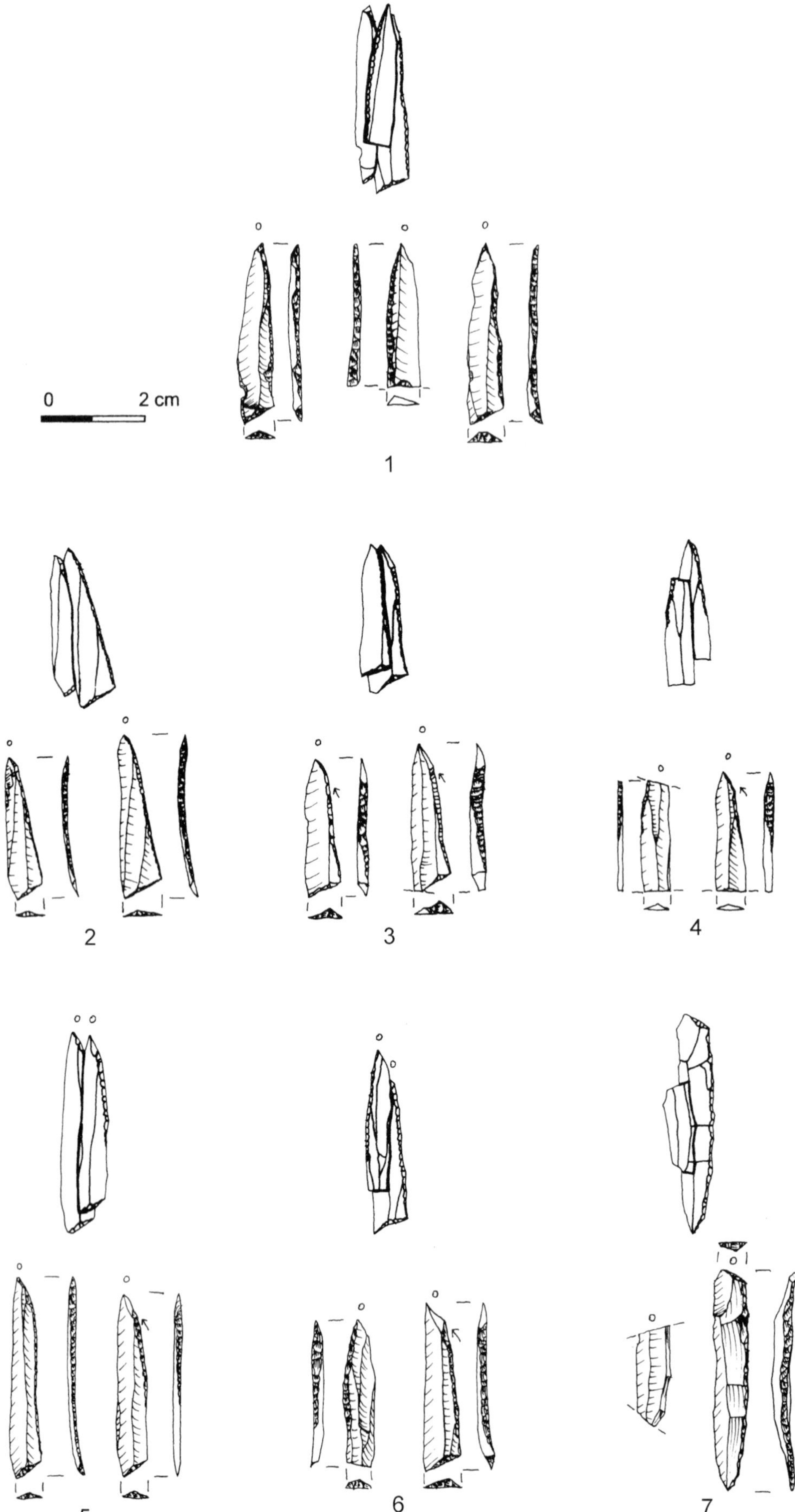

Figure 40.5. Dąbrowa Biskupia 71: refit groups of microliths. (Drawings: Domańska and Wąs).

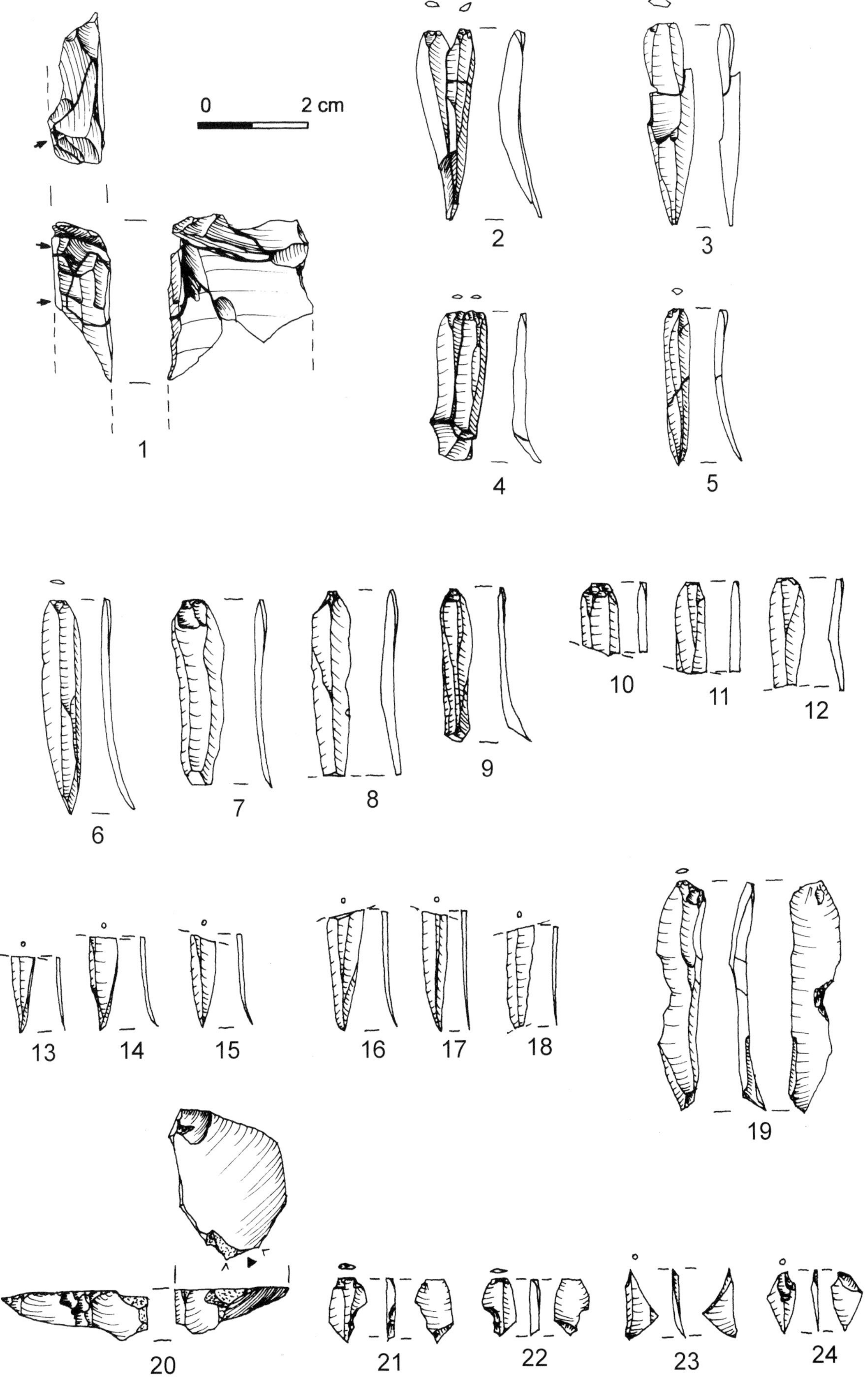

Figure 40.6. Dąbrowa Biskupia 71: refit groups (1–5), blades (6–18), notched blade (19), core tablet (20), microburins (21–24). (Drawings: Domańska and Wąs).

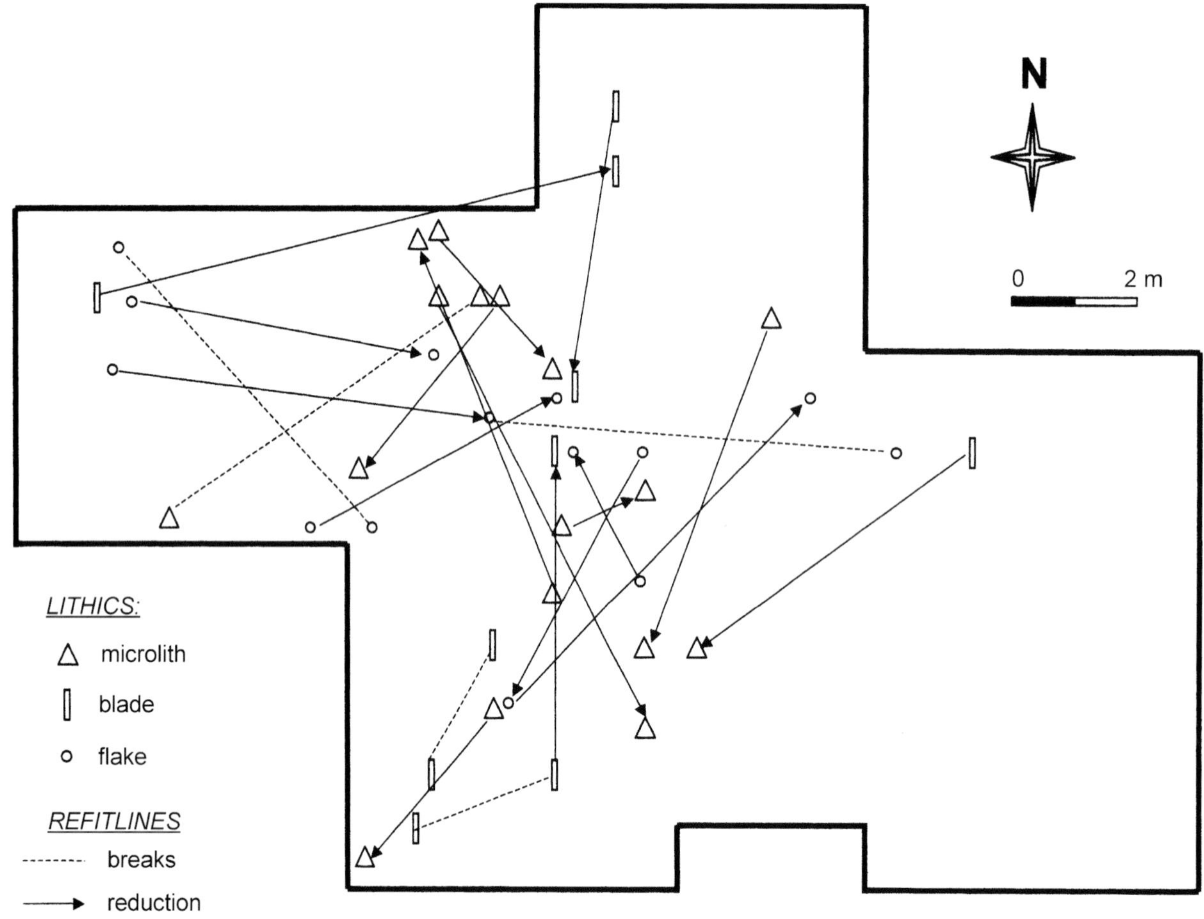

Figure 40.7. Dąbrowa Biskupia 71: map showing all refitting lines (all levels).

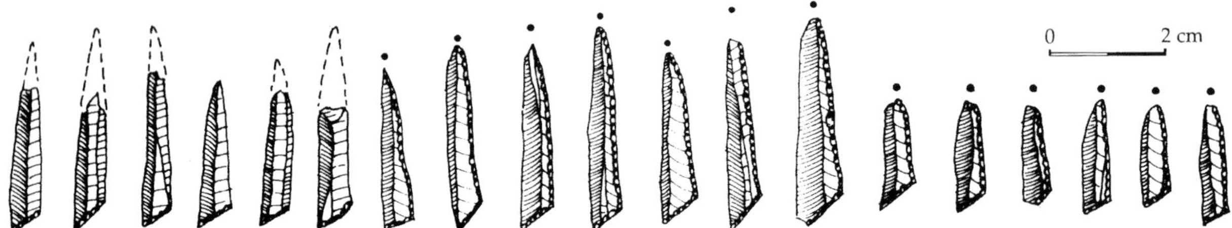

Figure 40.8. Wierzchowo 6: microliths. (After Bagniewski 1997).

the blades, regardless of their state of completeness (Figure 40.6: 2–18), show similar morphological features, making it possible to treat them as a technologically homogeneous assemblage. Among the specimens, both complete and proximal pieces (82 specimens), the frequency of flat butts and abrasion is almost the same as among the microburins and microliths (99%). However, there are more blades with defects (30%) and, at the same time, fewer blades with lips (75%). This indicates that microliths were slightly more delicate than the unmodified blades discovered here, although the differences are slight.

The whole assemblage was analyzed using a conjoining or refitting method. 41 items were grouped together, equating to 8.5% of the total. Among the conjoined material, 31 specimens were connected to the reduction sequence (core exploitation) and ten resulted from mechanical and thermal breaks. The most interesting result of the conjoining analysis is that two microliths could be conjoined, while in one instance there were three conjoined microliths and a fragment of bladelet.

As well as the conjoining of the microliths, three pairs of overlapping bladelets (Figure 40.6: 2–4) and the conjoining of broken bladelet fragments (Figure 40.6: 5) were achieved. The conjoining of a bladelet fragment with an unsuccessful blade-flake with hinged distal part (Figure 40.6: 3) indicates that they are relics of site processing of a blade core. The possibility of bringing these finished products to the site in order to use them as tools is rather doubtful. A conjoining of two blades removed from the edge part of a flaked surface can be interpreted similarly (Figure 40.6: 2).

A subsequent exercise of conjoining other flakes

enabled, among other things, the reconstruction of a fragment of a microlithic blade core (Figure 40.6: 1). It is probably a relic of a 'tablet' core with flat, unprepared sides. It had a narrow flaked surface and platform (10mm), which was rejuvenated by one-way removal from the left side. The core was exploited – at least in the final stage – using direct percussion. Numerous hinged negatives, situated stepwise on the upper part of the flaking surface, are the results of this percussion technique. Originally, it was probably a blade core exploited by the use of punch or pressure technique. The latter is most probably the case, as indirectly suggested by the morphology of most blades and microliths (Dmochowski 2002; Inizan *et al.* 1992). The final phase of the blade production took place on site, evidenced by the conjoining of blade flakes with hinged-shaped tips. The core was then fully exploited for flake production. Two further conjoined flakes originate from this stage, however they cannot be connected with the conjoining of the core fragment. Such an activity may have been economically determined by the relatively scarce supply of flint raw material (Cyrek 1981, 5–108).

In addition to the conjoining discussed above, a further nine finds were also conjoined; two probably came from another modified blade core of a very similar morphology to the above-mentioned fragment.

The distribution of conjoined and unconjoined specimens is identical; conjoined specimens are not found in any concentration on the site (Figure 40.7).

Function of the site

The microlith assemblage is the feature that arouses most interest since they represent about 40% of all finds and almost 100% of tools. Blades constitute the next largest group of artefacts at 32%. Use-wear analysis of the material discussed was undertaken by M. Winiarska-Kabacińska (2007). The research included more than 80% of all finds, and from among the specimens analyzed, 76 showed changes caused by use, enabling them to be classified as used specimens. Among the used specimens, microliths prevailed. Traces of use were registered, among other things, on microliths that were components of conjoining (for instance in a conjoining that consisted of three microliths, each of the three microliths had traces of usage on unretouched edges. Figure 40.5: 1). M. Winiarska-Kabacińska also noted that the majority of artefacts showing traces of use on their edges had been used as elements of hunting equipment or as weapon elements (2007).

Sondage research and excavations at the site showed that we are dealing with the remains of a small Mesolithic 'site'. The technological structure of the inventory, as well as the results of use-wear analysis, indicate that the site functioned as a hunting camp.

Within the context of recognized Mesolithic settlement-types in north-eastern Kuiavia (Domańska 1995, 93–118), the site of Dąbrowa Biskupia 71 can be viewed as a satellite of the large settlement concentrations in the region of the Toruń-Eberswalde valley, connected with the end of the Pleistocene. Analogous sites from other parts of Europe show that their genesis is closely connected with the specialized function of such places in Mesolithic hunter-gatherer societies (Fuglestvedt 1999, 347–53).

Taxonomical affiliation

The site of Dąbrowa Biskupia 71 not only provides interesting material from a technological and typological viewpoint, but it also presents an intriguing case in terms of the cultural taxonomy of the Mesolithic. Taking into account the special, selective character of the Dąbrowa Biskupia 71 assemblage, although it lacks representative tool forms it may be taken as indicating many convergences with Maglemose inventories. The typological content of the homogeneous group of microliths (scalene triangles of slender, short shape, microliths with retouched base and truncated blades) points to such a classification. These are, of course, not all the forms that are most typical of Svaerdborg-type assemblages, since there are no Maglemose truncated blades, or core tools (Brinch Petersen 1966, 77–185; Kozłowski 1989, 138–48). However, as previously mentioned, typological content can be functionally conditioned.

Close analogies to the discoveries at Dąbrowa Biskupia 71 have been found at some other sites in north-western Poland (Bagniewski 1997, 35–74), especially at Wierzchowo 6 (Figure 40.1: 3). Here, making no mention of the frequency of the artefacts, a typologically homogeneous group of microliths with prevailing scalene triangles and microliths with retouched base (Bagniewski 1996, 96) has been found. As at Dąbrowa Biskupia, Wierzchowo 6 also revealed numerous examples with preserved butts, typical particularly of small scalene triangles. However, Wierzchowo 6 differs from Dąbrowa Biskupia in its lack of Nowy Młyn-type microliths. Despite the great typological differentiation of other inventories from the area, some other sites are typologically close, including Kalisz Pomorski 3 and Gudowo 3 (Bagniewski 1992, 25–36; 1996, 19–53) (Figure 40.1: 2, 4). Sites that yielded similar types of microliths to those from Dąbrowa Biskupia 71 were also discovered (Figure 40.1: 7) at the estuary of the River Oder (Dobre 53) and in the western part of the Toruń-Eberswalde valley, connected with the end of the Pleistocene (Trzebicz Młyn 1) (Bagniewski 2002, 35–74).

Indirect evidence of the presence of groups of the Maglemose culture, or tradition, in north-western Poland is the larger number of sites (especially Atlantic ones) included in the so-called post-Maglemose complex (Kozłowski 1989, 138–48). In most cases they resulted from local cultural transformations in the coastal area of the south Baltic (Domańska 1985, 447–50), the best example being the site of Jastrzębia Góra 4.

Sites representing the Maglemose culture in Poland are relatively rare, so far they have only been discovered at three sites in the Polish lowlands: at the estuary of the River Oder (Figure 40.1: 7), in the area of Lake Drawsko (Figure 40.1: 2–5), and in north-eastern Kuiavia (Figure

40.1: 1). Each of these, as shown above, have their closest analogies in Danish Svaerdborg-type assemblages.

Among these sites, Dąbrowa Biskupia 71 is of special importance. The site is the easternmost of the Maglemose-culture sites (Figure 40.1: 1). In the light of the types of artefacts recovered, it may be identified as a hunting camp. It differs from other Polish sites of the same culture with high percentages of Nowy Młyn-type microliths (Figure 40.4: 1–12). The microliths are also known from certain assemblages included in the so-called post-Maglemose complex, which is dated to the Atlantic period (Kozłowski 1989, 138–48). An example of such a site (Figure 40.1: 6) is Jastrzêbia Góra 4 (Domańska 1985, 447–50). These similarities between the Boreal site of Dąbrowa Biskupia and the Atlantic site of Jastrzêbia Góra indicate a local transformation of Svadborg-type assemblages of the so-called post-Maglemose complex.

References

Bagniewski, Z. 1992. Nowe stanowisko kultury Svaerdborg na Pojezierzu Drawskim. Wyniki badań stanowiska Gudowo 3. *Śląskie Sprawozdania Archeologiczne* 33, 25–36.

Bagniewski, Z. 1996. *Mezolit Pojezierza i Równiny Drawskiej*. Studia Archeologiczne 28, Wrocław, The University of Wrocław.

Bagniewski, Z. 1997. Contacts between the Populations of Mesolithic Pomerania and the Maglemosian Traditions, in D. Król (ed.), *The Built Environment of Coast Areas during the Stone Age*, 36–49. Gdańsk, The University of Gdańsk.

Bagniewski, Z. 2002. O paleolicie schyłkowym i mezolicie zachodniej części Pradoliny Toruńsko-Eberswaldzkiej. *Archaeologia Silesiae* 1, 35–74.

Cyrek, K. 1981. Uzyskiwanie i użytkowanie surowców krzemiennych w mezolicie dorzeczy Wisły i górnej Warty. *Prace i Materiały MAiE, Seria Archeologiczna* 28, 5–108.

Domańska, L. 1985. Elements of a food-producing economy in the Late Mesolithic of the Polish Lowland, in C. Bonsall (ed.), *The Mesolithic in Europe: Papers Presented at the Third International Symposium*, 447–55. Edinburgh, John Donald Publishers.

Domańska, L. 1995. *Geneza krzemieniarstwa kultury pucharów lejkowatych na Kujawach*. Łódź, University of Łódź.

Domańska, L. 2003. Interactions between the Late Mesolithic hunter-gatherers and farming communities in Northern Poland, in L. Larsson, H. Kindgren, K. Knutsson, D. Loeffler and A. Åkerlund (eds.), *Mesolithic on the Move: Papers presented at the Sixth International Conference on the Mesolithic in Europe, Stockholm 2000*, 588–91. Oxford, Obow Books.

Dmochowski, P. 2002. *Metody wiórowe w mezolicie północno-wschodniej Wielkopolski*. Unpublished PhD thesis, University of A. Mickiewicz, Poznań.

Fuglestvedt, I. 1999. Late Mesolithic Svevollen of interior eastern Norway: normative action and consumptional control, in A. Thévenin (ed.), *L'Europe des derniers chasseurs. Épipaléolithique et Mésolithique: actes du 5e colloque international UISPP, commission XII, Grenoble, 18–23 septembre 1995*, 347–53. Paris, Comité des travaux historiques et scientifiques (CTHS).

Inizan. M. L., Roche, H., and Tixier, J. 1992. *Technology of Knapped Stone*. Meudon, Cercle de Recherches et d'Etudes Préhistoriques (CREP).

Kozłowski, S. K. 1989. *Mesolithic in Poland. A new approach*. Warsaw, University of Warsaw.

Winiarska-Kabacińska, M. 2007. Dąbrowa Biskupia 71: Mesolithic hunters' camp?, in M. Masojć, T. Płonka, B. Ginter and S. K. Kozłowski (eds.), *Contributions to the Central European Stone Age. Papers presented to the late Professor Zbigniew Bagniewski*, 153–60. Wrocław, University of Wrocław, Institute of Archaeology.

41. Early Holocene landscape dynamics and forager land use diversity: the example of Hoge Vaart-A27 (Almere, The Netherlands)

Hans Peeters

Departing from the results of large-scale excavations at the Mesolithic/Early Neolithic site of Hoge Vaart-A27 (Almere, the Netherlands), this paper discusses several aspects of forager land use diversity in the context of landscape dynamics. It is shown how structural changes in the landscape due to sea-level rise and climatic events can be related to the particular way places and landscapes have been used in the course of the Early Holocene. Evidence from the Dutch Flevoland polders also shows that forager land use was not dictated by subsistence related considerations. Instead, landscapes appear to have had a profound ideological/cosmological meaning. The persistent use of places in these changing landscapes points to the role of such locales as 'time nodes' in a spatial setting which permitted maintenance of ideological/cosmological relationships over generations.

Keywords: Early Holocene, foragers, hearth pits, Hoge Vaart-A27, land use diversity, landscape dynamics, persistent places, ritual depositions.

Introduction

Climatic events at the end of the last glacial period triggered dramatic and rapid changes in hunter-gatherer landscapes, both in terms of landscape structure as well as composition. At the start of the Holocene, especially, changes occurred very rapidly with water levels rising some 150–200cm a century (Beets and Van der Spek 2000). Places used by individuals literally drowned within their own lifetimes. With the gradual decrease of inundation rates in the course of the Early Holocene it is likely that changes in the landscape were perceived less directly. Nevertheless, the landscape continued to be highly dynamic and the coastal and back-barrier tidal zones, in particular, were subject to continuous reshaping. It is within this dynamic setting that Postglacial foragers created their own landscape according to their specific sets of beliefs and rules; landscapes with specific space-time relationships, where places had been given meaning within the various dimensions of land use.

This paper discusses some aspects of what may be called the 'landscape-places' model, departing from the results of large scale excavations at the Mesolithic to Early Neolithic site of Hoge Vaart-A27 (the region of Flevoland, the Netherlands) (Figure 41.1). The excavations covered *c.* 8600m^2 and delivered a rich body of archaeological

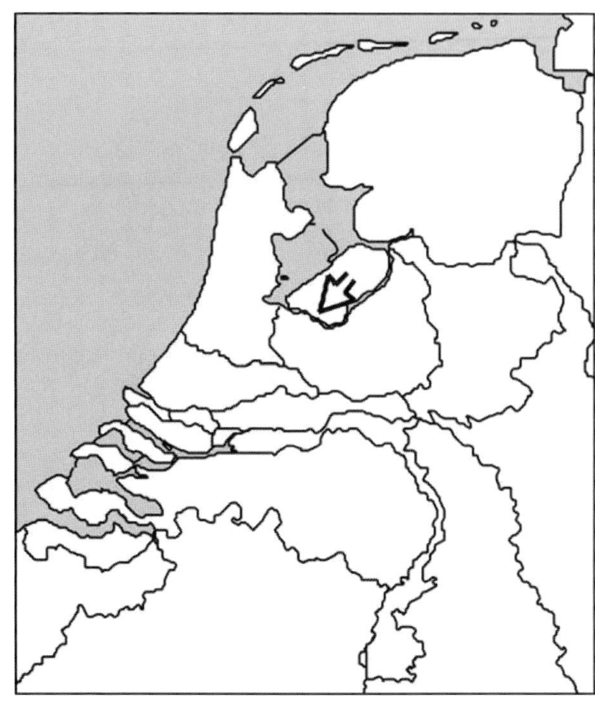

Figure 41.1. Geographical location of Hoge Vaart-A27 in the Netherlands.

and palaeo-environmental data, which have been studied and published in great detail (Hogestijn and Peeters 2001; Peeters 2004). In order to evaluate the excavation results from a broader spatio-temporal perspective, data from other localities in Flevoland and other areas is used.

The site of Hoge Vaart-A27

The Hoge Vaart-A27 locality is situated on a north-south oriented coversand ridge, flanked by a low lying area intersected by riverine and tidal gullies in the east. Westward, the coversand ridge slopes towards an undulating plain. The coversand landscape in this part of the Flevoland region was intersected by precursors of the River Eem and some smaller tributaries (Figure 41.2). Further to the north, the landscape was dominated by precursors of the Rivers IJssel and Vecht, and probably saw better drainage conditions. Here, formation of river dunes along the relatively wide floodplain characterized the Late Glacial/Holocene transition.

Detailed interdisciplinary analysis of the rich body of data has permitted us to establish an occupation sequence in relation to landscape conditions for the first half of the Holocene (Preboreal through Late Atlantic) (Hogestijn and Peeters 2001; Peeters 2004). Two Mesolithic and two Early Neolithic activity phases have been distinguished (Figure 41.3). However, information on the character of activities during the different phases is extremely variable in quality. Landscape dynamics at the Mesolithic/Neolithic frontier (in this paper the terms are used in a purely chronological sense) caused erosion of the Mesolithic land surface. Mesolithic phase 1 and phase 2 evidence is restricted to deep hearth pits and a limited amount of lithics.

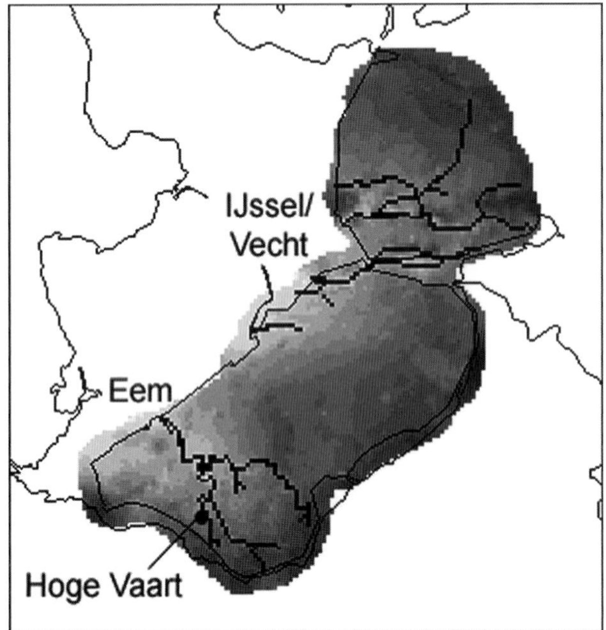

Figure 41.2. Digital elevation model of the Pleistocene surface in the Flevoland polders. The hight ranges from c. 0 (dark tone) to 13 (light tone) metres below Dutch Ordnance Level.

However, the restricted possibilities for the study of the Mesolithic at this locale are compensated by the opportunities for the study of the Neolithic (which could just as well be defined as 'ceramic Mesolithic'). Early Neolithic (Swifterbant culture) occupation remains were deposited on a 'cleared' surface that was subsequently built up through sedimentation in a wetland environment. Detailed analysis of the composition of material remains, structural features and spatial patterns combined with a large number of radiocarbon dates, provided evidence for a behavioural context that was repeated over some 350 radiocarbon years (6000–5650 BP) during phase 3. (Unless indicated otherwise, all radiocarbon dates in the text are expressed in uncalibrated radiocarbon years (^{14}C BP) before present.) Typically, the composition of a small, discrete distribution of materials in association with a surface hearth appeared to be more or less identical to that of the main accumulation zone found on top of the ridge (Peeters 2004). Quantitative analysis of the spatial properties of clusters of various materials indicates linear relationships between cluster size and contents, suggesting the presence of scaling factors in the process of palimpsest formation (Peeters, in press). Interestingly, unburned and burned materials appeared to expose structurally different properties, suggesting differential accumulation mechanisms (for instance clearing of hearths). Despite the fact that remains of many (probably between 80 and 120) activity episodes have accumulated on the surface, it would appear that structural information on different modes of behaviour can still be discerned for phase 3. Phase 4 involved no deposition of materials on top of the sand ridge, which had already disappeared in a peat swamp, and only concerns activity remains in a tidal gully.

In view of these results it is possible to look in greater detail at the way Mesolithic/Early Neolithic foragers made use of this particular locale in the context of a changing landscape. The use of data from other localities in the Flevoland area and other regions further allows us to shift from 'local/short-term' and 'local/long-term' perspectives on land use variability towards 'regional/short-term' and 'regional/long-term' perspectives (cf. Nicholas 1998).

Preboreal and Boreal landscapes and forager 'absence' (10,000–8000 BP)

Evidence for Preboreal and Boreal occupation has not been found at Hoge Vaart-A27, and indeed is rare in the entire region with few radiocarbon dates falling between 10,000–8000 BP. The earliest dates all come from the Hoge Vaart-A27 surroundings. The question arises whether or not this virtual 'absence of evidence' actually reflects limited forager activity.

In Preboreal and Boreal times, the region was still at a considerable distance from the coastline. However, occupation remains occur frequently on coversand ridges and river dunes along the IJssel and Vecht river systems, even further inland (Groenwoudt *et al.* 2001; Verlinde and Newell 2006). Widespread evidence for Preboreal-Boreal activity in the 'hinterland' is also known from other regions in the Netherlands, such as the Groningen peat reclamation district (Groenendijk 2004) and the coversand area in the southern Netherlands (Arts 1988; Verhart 2000). Near coastal evidence for Early Mesolithic activity is know in the form of hundreds of antler and bone barbed points found along the present Dutch coast, and might point at specialized exploitation of the coastal zone (Verhart 1995). Also at a relatively short distance from the Early Mesolithic coast is the site of Verrebroek-Dok in Belgium (Crombé 2005).

It cannot be excluded that the 'lack' of dates in Flevoland reflects a research bias. However, none of the potentially attractive river dune localities in the Flevoland IJssel/Vecht

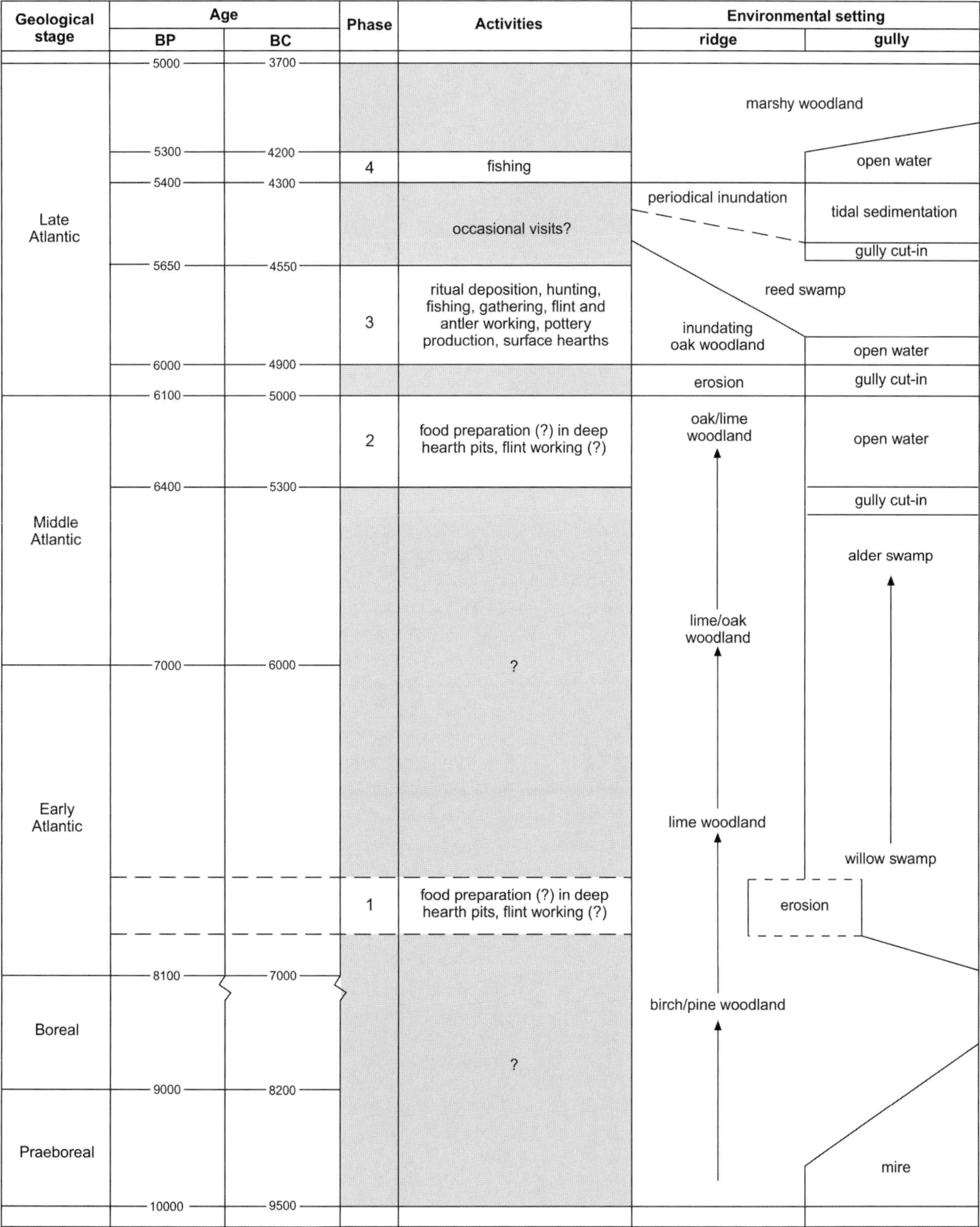

Figure 41.3. Temporal and environmental setting of the activity phases distinguished at Hoge Vaart-A27.

area has delivered any evidence for Preboreal-Boreal activity. Therefore other considerations have to be taken into account, such as the influence of hydrological conditions on the possibilities of land use. As has become clear from recent studies on Early Holocene sea-level change (Beets and Van der Spek 2000; Kiden *et al.* 2002), inundation rates may have differed significantly at a (sub)regional and local level. In view of the widespread occurrence of peat and other organic underwater sediments (e.g. gyttja), bad drainage conditions and low hydrodynamics appear to have dominated the Preboreal and early Boreal in the Flevoland area (Peeters 2007). Extensive swamps, water surfaces and low flow drainages were probably important elements in the environment (e.g. bog forests and *muskeg*-like environments), hence making it largely uninhabitable or at least not easily accessible. The nature of the activities that developed in such environments may have left little (traceable) archaeological evidence.

Figure 41.4. Section through a deep hearth pit, showing large amounts of charcoal at the base.

Early/Mid Atlantic landscape change and hearth pit firing (8000–6100 BP)

The earliest indications of forager activity at Hoge Vaart-A27 can be dated to the Early Atlantic (*c.* 7800 BP) and involved firing of deep hearth pits (Figure 41.4). The second occupation phase distinguished falls within the second half of the Mid Atlantic (6400–6100 BP) and also involved the firing of deep hearth pits. In total, some 100 of these features were uncovered. Intersections of these pits do not occur despite the repeated use of the same locality over a long time. The pits exclusively contain charcoal and have an average diameter and depth of *c.* 60cm. Localized slope erosion of the sand ridge (Figure 41.5) may have been caused by the disturbance of the

Figure 41.5. Section through the gully zone. 1: Late Glacial coversand; 2: Preboreal peat; 3: eroded coversand; 4: Mid Atlantic gyttja; 5: Late Atlantic clay; 6: gyttja-peat sequence.

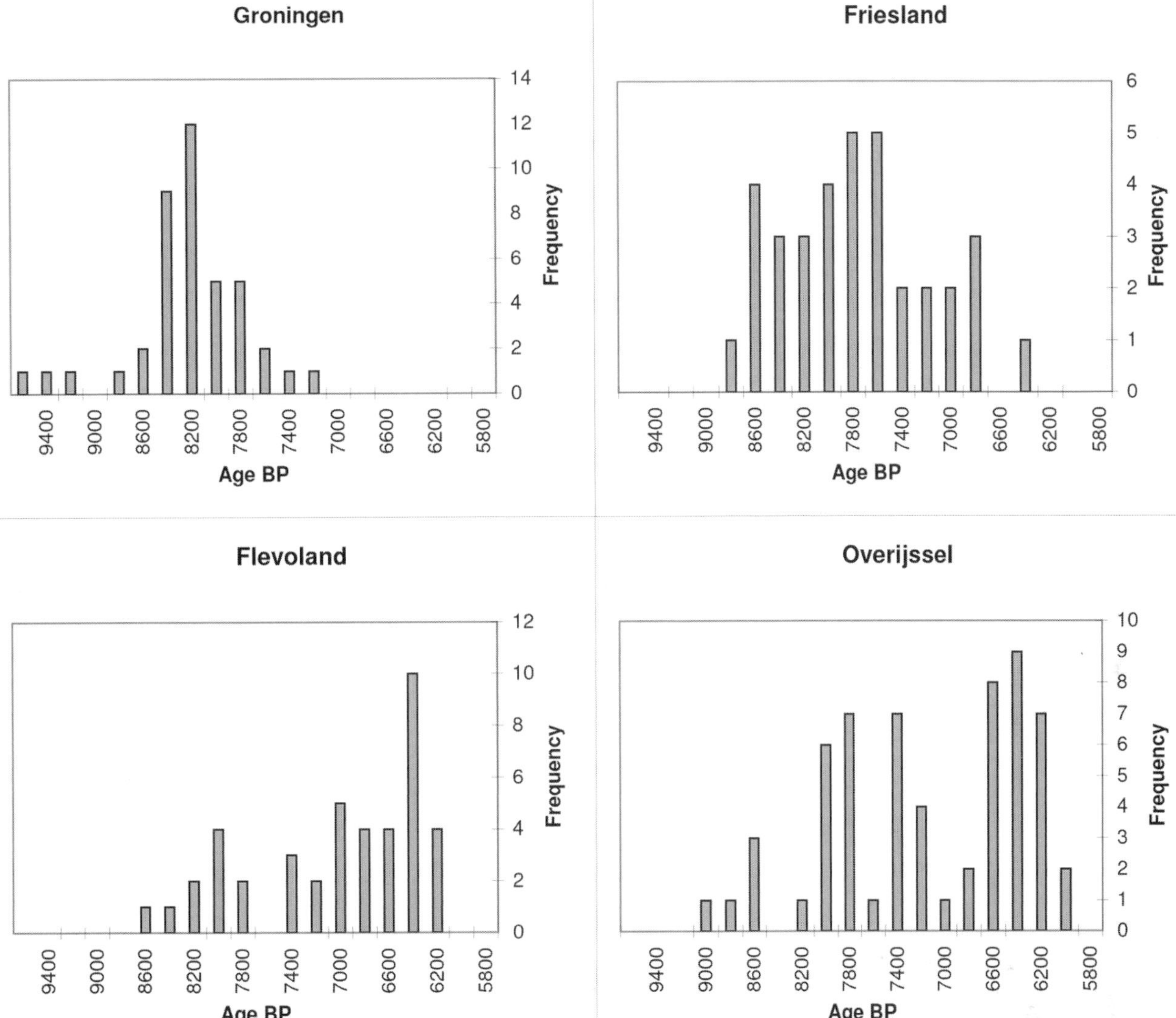

Figure 41.6. Frequency of radiocarbon dates (charcoal samples from deep hearth pits) for the regions of Groningen Friesland, Flevoland and Overijssel. (Dates in uncalibrated radiocarbon years (^{14}C BP) before present; after Peeters and Niekus 2005).

vegetation deck as a result of trampling by humans or animals. A precise date for this event cannot be given, but dates of underlaying peat and overlaying gyttja provide *post* and *ante quem* limits of 9600 and 6400 BP (Preboreal and Mid Atlantic). Micromorphological evidence for oxidation, bioturbation and intrusion of sand grains in the top of the underlaying peat layer points to dryer conditions by the end of the Preboreal. Since the overlaying gyttja was deposited underwater and slope erosion occurred under dry conditions, a Boreal or Early Atlantic date seems to be most likely.

The occurrence in the Flevoland region of more radiocarbon dates (Figure 41.6) falling in the Early Atlantic period, seems to point at a more structural – not necessarily more intense – use of the landscape. This trend seems to continue in the course of the Atlantic. The Mid Atlantic especially seems to have involved more systematic uses of the landscape, where firing of deep hearth pits formed an integral aspect of land use. Occupation remains have been found both on coversand surfaces in the Eem area and on river dunes in the IJssel/Vecht area. Radiocarbon dates from other localities elsewhere in the Netherlands, where clusters of hundreds (400 to 500) of such hearths have been found (Groenendijk 2004; Verlinde and Newell 2006), also suggest repeated use of these places for specific purposes. Time-depths generally involve between 300 and 1500 radiocarbon years. Even though a common phenomenon at many Mesolithic localities in the northern half of the Netherlands, much remains unclear as to the specific function of these pits (Groenendijk 1986; Groenendijk and Smit 1990).

The Early/Mid Atlantic period also seems to mark a turning point in the evolution of the landscape itself. For the first time, one can notice the direct influence of the nearing shoreline. With structurally rising water levels and higher mean temperatures, the geography and landscape composition altered significantly. In general terms, one can see the shift from dry woodland towards a mosaic wetlands dominated region. Gradually the vegetation deck exhibited a more open structure, which will have triggered increasing diversity of landscape zones and biotopes.

It is interesting to note that areas which saw Preboreal-Boreal occupation show a decrease of dates in the Atlantic, in contrast to an increase of dates in the Flevoland region (Figure 41.6). When looking at the frequency of radiocarbon dates from the northern Netherlands, there is a clear dip between 7600–7400 BP (Peeters and Niekus 2005; see also Niekus 2006). Interestingly, this dip coincides with the 8.2 Ka Event (8200 cal BP), which saw massive freshwater influx, causing cooling and drought of the northern hemisphere over several centuries, as a result of changes in the oceanic thermohaline circulation (Renssen *et al.* 2002). Not much is known yet about its impact on climatic and hydrological regimes on the northwestern European continent, but it cannot be excluded that the spatio-temporal patterns in the frequencies of radiocarbon dates somehow relate to this event. However, the regional differences in frequencies of radiocarbon dates do not necessarily indicate population movement related to the development of dense woodland, as suggested earlier by Waterbolk (1999). As most dates are from charcoal samples from deep hearth pits, it is likely that we are primarily 'time plotting' aspects of forager behaviour related to firing of deep hearth pits (Peeters 2007).

Inundating Late Mid/Late Atlantic landscapes and the change of land use modes (6100–5600 BP)

The end of the second occupation phase at Hoge Vaart-A27 is marked by an erosive event that largely 'swept clean' the Mesolithic surface at the Mid/Late Atlantic transition. The increase of tidal activity severely altered the hydrological regime in the area. Woodlands opened to a further extent and dry land elements were replaced by wetland components. However this period of relatively high dynamics appears to have been of short duration (Figure 41.3).

After this short period of increased dynamics, the Hoge Vaart-A27 locality was again used, at the start of the Neolithic, over a period of some 350 radiocarbon years (6000–5650 BP). In contrast to the previous Mesolithic phases, activities no longer involved the firing of deep hearth pits. Instead, activities systematically involved firing of surface hearths (in total 120), maintenance of hunting gear (e.g. production of flint trapeze points, replacement of damaged points and production/maintenance of arrow shafts), primary processing of game (e.g. production and maintenance of scrapers, scraping of fresh hides), and pottery production. Furthermore production, use and discard of antler mattocks and other bone implements (e.g. adzes and some other tools of unknown function) occurred. Consumption of food formed an integral aspect of the behavioural context and resulted in the discard of large amounts of charred bone and edible plant remains (e.g. hazelnut (*Corylus*), seeds of the yellow water lily (*Nuphar lutea*), wild apple (*Malus sylvestris*)). Even though hundreds of stake holes were recognized, no dwelling structures could be identified.

Concluding from the narrow range of tool types and tool uses, as well as the spatial structure of the already mentioned discrete distribution at some distance from the palimpsest zone, visits were probably of relatively short duration, e.g. in the order of days or weeks (Peeters 2004). Among the large amounts of charred and heavily fragmented bone, a wide variety of mammals, fowl and fish has been recognized. The species composition reflects the exploitation of a fresh, to brackish tidal environment with dryland and wetland components. No sound conclusions with regard to seasonality and/or age composition can be drawn.

Among the charred bone fragments some human material has also been found, e.g. fragments of a mandible (juvenile), cranium, axis, pelvis, and a phalanx (adult). Formal burials are absent. Most human remains have been found fairly concentrated within the large palimpsest zone on top of the sand ridge. Remains of smaller fur animals have mainly been found in the same zone, as well as some red ochre. It is tempting to consider a behavioural relationship between these elements; meaningful spatial clustering of specific animal species and human remains has also been identified at other sites, for instance at the Swedish site of Bökeberg (Karsten 2001).

Other manifestations of ritual behaviour at Hoge Vaart-A27 involve three depositions of flint objects in the peat swamp surrounding the gradually disappearing sand ridge. These consist of a hoard of tested nodules, a hoard of exhausted cores and large flakes (Figure 41.7), and a hoard of 100 flakes deposited in a small pit that had been dug into the peat. On the eastern flank of the ridge, three aurochs skulls (*Bos primigenius*), with their horns, may be associated with the remains of heavy posts that were driven into the subsoil. These are likely to bear ritual significance.

In fact, the phase 3 uses of the Hoge Vaart-A27 locality correspond to a time period which is still little understood at a more regional scale. Despite relatively many observations – especially in the IJssel/Vecht area – no secure dates exist

Figure 41.7. A deposition of exhausted cores and large (conjoining) flakes in peat deposits, with an age of c. 5800 BP.

falling between 6000 and 5600 BP; only some dates that originate from several locales downstream of the IJssel system are known (Groenewoudt *et al.* 2001).

Between landscape and seascape (5600–5300 BP)

At the end of the phase 3 activities at the Hoge Vaart-A27 locality, the coversand ridge had completely disappeared in the peat swamp around 5600 BP, where local water levels seem to have been relatively high. Shortly after, however, tidal dynamics increased and a fresh gully was cut into the eastern marsh zone, somewhere between 5600 and 5500 BP, thus partly clearing earlier sediments (Figure 41.6). The impact of brackish tidal flux appears to have been quite limited and clay was rapidly deposited in a freshwater tidal system.

This change in the local environment triggered renewed use of the Hoge Vaart-A27 locality. Three fish weirs and associated traps (with dates around 5350 BP) have been discovered in the tidal gully. However, the advantageous tidal regime for fishing seems to have been of short duration, taking into account the deposition of organic underwater sediments (e.g. gyttja-like deposits) and subsequent peat formation, indicating the decrease of hydrodynamics. Possibly the gully became cut off, but at the same time one should consider the possibility that the fish weirs played a significant role in water stagnation, thus accelerating the expansion of peat forming vegetations; the fish weirs were abandoned and peat growth led to paludification of the gully.

As far as is known from the archaeological evidence, this meant the end of Mesolithic/Early Neolithic forager activity at this specific locale, and possibly in this part of the region generally. Water dynamics in the Eem area stagnated and resulted in the extension of peat marshes, a situation that might have redefined the possibilities of land use. Evidence for activity after 5400/5300 BP is extremely sparse in the Eem area. In contrast, the IJssel/Vecht area exhibits extensive evidence for the use of a wide variety of landscape zones (dryer coversand ridges and plains, river dunes, natural levees, tidal inlets) by people of the Swifterbant culture, where activities involved dwelling, burial, resource extraction, small-scale crop cultivation, and stock herding. Despite the integration of small-scale farming practices in their subsistence economy there seems to be no evidence for fundamental changes in their forager-based life-way.

Spatio-temporal dimensions of land use and the persistence of places

The high resolution of the Hoge Vaart-A27 dataset in relation to data from other locales and regions brings forward some fascinating aspects of forager land use. What we have seen is an enormous time-depth: a place used in different behavioural contexts over many generations in variable landscape settings. Hoge Vaart-A27 is certainly not the only locale that exhibits such a long-term record of forager activity. The question is, therefore, how is one to understand such long-term use?

I would suggest that the persistent use of a site such as Hoge Vaart-A27 is not simply the result of economic attractiveness. Of course, one can argue that the availability of certain resources must have played a role, and – to an extent – that will, without doubt, have been the case. Despite changes in the landscape, certain locales are situated in gradient zones with a relatively important resource diversity, thus providing a 'secure' environment for subsistence. However, from such a perspective, the landscape is only perceived as some kind of 'supermarket' and foragers are classified as passive 'Man-the-whole-time-food-gatherer' (cf. Zvelebil and Moore 2005). Yet the Flevoland evidence suggests these landscapes to have had a profound ritual meaning, where burials and cultic depositions of material objects, and also human skeletal elements, served as a means to express the identity of particular places in the system. Despite fundamental changes in the environmental setting, it would seem that these persistent places were 'marking points' in the dynamic landscape. Even though the archaeological contents of these points may have changed over time, their position in the structure of land use was maintained. As such, they represent 'time nodes' in a spatial setting that permitted the maintenance of ideological and cosmological relationships over generations.

References

Arts, N. 1988. Archaeology, environment and the social evolution of later band societies in a lowland area, in C. Bonsall (ed.), *The Mesolithic in Europe: Papers Presented at the Third International Symposium*, 291–312. Edinburgh, John Donald Publishers.

Beets, D. J. and Van der Spek, A. J. F. 2000. The Holocene evolution of the barrier and the back-barrier basins of Belgium and the Netherlands as a function of late Weichselian morphology, relative sea-level rise and sediment supply. *Netherlands Journal of Geosciences/Geologie en Mijnbouw* 79, 3–16.

Crombé, P. (ed.) 2005. *The last hunter-gatherer-fishermen in sandy Flanders (NW Belgium). The Verrebroek and Doel excavation projects, Part 1: palaeo-environment, chronology and features*. Ghent University Archaeological Reports 3. Ghent, Academia Press.

Groenendijk, H. A. 1986. Mesolithic hearth-pits in the Veenkoloniën (prov. Groningen, the Netherlands). Defining a specific use of fire in the Mesolithic. *Palaeohistoria* 29, 85–102.

Groenendijk, H. A., 2004. Middle Mesolithic occupation on the extensive site NP3 in the peat reclamation district of Groningen, the Netherlands, in *The Mesolithic: Acts of the XIVth UISPP Congress, University of Liège, Belgium, 2-8 September 2001*, 19–26. British Archaeological Reports, International Series S1302. Oxford, Archaeopress.

Groenendijk, H. A. and Smit, J. L. 1990. Mesolithischen Herdstellen: Erfahrungen eines Brennversuchs. *Archäologische Informationen* 13, 213–20.

Groenewoudt, B. J., Deeben, J., Van Geel, B. and Lauwerier, R. C. G. M. 2001. An Early Mesolithic assemblage with faunal remains in a stream valley near Zutphen, the Netherlands. *Archäologisches Korrespondenzblatt* 31, 329–48.

Hogestijn, J. W. H. and Peeters, J. H. M. (eds.) 2001. *De Mesolithische en Vroeg-Neolithische vindplaats Hoge Vaart-A27 (Flevoland)*. Rapportage Archeologische Monumentenzorg 79. Amersfoort, State Service for Archaeological Investigations in the Netherlands (ROB).

Karsten, P. 2001. *Dansarna på Bökeberg. Om jakt, ritualer och inlandsbosättningar vid jägarstenålderns slut*. Riksantikvarieämbetet Arkeologiska undersökningar, Skrifter 37. Malmö. University of Malmö.

Kiden, P., Denys, L. and Johnston, P. 2002. Late Quaternary sea-level change and isostatic and tectonic land movements along the Belgian-Dutch coast: geological data and model results. *Journal of Quaternary Science* 17, 535–46.

Nicholas, G. P. 1998. Wetlands and hunter-gatherers: a global perspective. *Current Anthropology* 39, 720–31.

Niekus, M. J. L. T. 2006. A geographically referenced ^{14}C-database for the Mesolithic and earliest Neolithic in the northern Netherlands and some remarks on the spatio-temporal distribution of these dates. *Palaeohistoria* 47/48.

Peeters, H. 2004. The Mesolithic to Early Neolithic occupation at the Hoge Vaart (Almere, the Netherlands): forager land-use dynamics in the context of a drowning landscape, in *The Mesolithic: Acts of the XIVth UISPP Congress, University of Liège, Belgium, 2–8 September 2001*, 27–37. British Archaeological Reports, International Series S1302. Oxford, Archaeopress.

Peeters, J. H. M. 2007. *Hoge Vaart-A27 in context: towards a model of Mesolithic-Neolithic land use dynamics as a framework for archaeological heritage management*. Amersfoort, Rijksdienst voor Archeologie, Cultuurlandschap en Monumenten.

Peeters, H. (in press). Breaking down an Early Neolithic palimpsest site: some notes on the concept of percolation theory and the understanding of spatial pattern formation, in F. Niccolucci (ed.), *Beyond the artefact - Proceedings of CAA2004 – Prato 13–17 April 2004*. British Archaeological Reports, International Series. Oxford, Archaeopress.

Peeters, H. and Niekus, M. J. L. T. 2005. Het Mesolithicum in Noord-Nederland, in J. Deeben, E. Drenth, M.-F. van Oorsouw and L. Verhart (eds.), *De steentijd van Nederland*, 201–234. Archeologie 11/12. Zutphen, Archeologie Gemeente Zutphen.

Renssen, H., Goosse, H. and Fichefet, T. 2002. Modeling the effect of freshwater pulses on the early Holocene climate: the influence of high-frequency climate variability. *Paleoceanography* 17.

Verhart, L. 1995. Fishing for the Mesolithic. The North Sea: a submerged Mesolithic landscape, in A. Fischer (ed.), *Man and sea in the Mesolithic, coastal settlement above and below present sea level*, 291–302. Oxford, Oxbow Books.

Verhart, L. 2000. *Times fade away. The neolithization of the southern Netherlands in an anthropological and geographical perspective*. Leiden University Archaeological Studies 6. Leiden, Leiden University.

Verlinde, A. D. and Newell, R. R. 2006. A multi-component complex of Mesolithic settlements with late Mesolithic grave pits at Marienberg in Overijssel, in B. J. Groenewoudt, R. M. van Heeringen and G. H. Scheepstra (eds.), *Het zandeilandenrijk van Overijssel*, 83–270. Nederlandse Archeologische Rapporten 22. Amersfoort, Rijksdienst voor het Oudheidkundig Bodemonderzoek.

Waterbolk, H. T. 1999. De mens in het preboreale, boreale en atlantische bos. *Paleo-Aktueel* 10, 68–73.

Zvelebil, M. and Moore, J. 2006. Assessment and representation: the information value of Mesolithic landscapes, in E. Rensink and H. Peeters (eds.), *Preserving the Early past. Investigation, selection and preservation of Palaeolithic and Mesolithic sites and landscapes*, 151–66. Nederlandse Archeologische Rapporten 31. Amersfoort, National Service for Archaeological Heritage.

42. Mesolithic territories and land-use systems in north-western Belgium

Joris Sergant, Philippe Crombé and Yves Perdaen

Over the last decade, 'Sandy Flanders' (north-west Belgium) has been the subject of intensive Mesolithic research and has revealed much new information at both intra- and inter-site levels. Analysis of the distribution of Stone Age sites and different raw materials (local and exotic) is used to reconstruct land-use systems during different stages of the Final Palaeolithic and the Mesolithic. Preliminary results indicate not only a clear shift in site location and site density but also in the distribution of exotic raw materials (quartzites) around the middle of the Boreal (c. 7600/7500 cal BC). The first shifts might point to changing settlement systems due to environmental changes, while the latter rather seems to reflect changing social or cultural conditions.

Keywords: Belgium, exotic quartzites, land-use systems, social/cultural territories.

Introduction

Sandy Flanders is situated in north-western Belgium between the North Sea coast and the lower Scheldt River. It is a typical low-lying area (between 3 and 15m asl), lying under, mainly, coversand deposits which are only in the most eastern and northerly parts, sealed by peat and/or clay (Crombé 2005). Since 1986 this area, which covers a surface of approximately 3000km², has been surveyed mainly by students and amateur archaeologists (Van der Haegen *et al.* 1999; Van Vlaenderen *et al.* 2006). This has led to the discovery of numerous surface sites, mainly dating to the Final Palaeolithic and the Mesolithic. In some parts of the study area (i.e. Meetjesland, the Moervaart depression, and Waasland), the extensive surveys were carried out very systematically.

Our research project, which started in 2004, focuses on these three core areas. Starting with a detailed inventory of data related to the Stone Age sites, additional surveys by field walking and manual drilling were undertaken to check and/or complete the database. Once the database has been completed, an analysis using a geographical information system (GIS) will be done to attempt a reconstruction of land-use systems from the Final Palaeolithic (mainly Federmesser) until the start of the Bronze Age. At present the data of two core areas, the Meetjesland and the Moervaart depression, have already been entered into the database and a first, preliminary, spatial analysis has been carried out.

One of the major problems with surface sites is the difficulty of dating them. As absolute dates are usually missing, dating can only be obtained using typological and technological criteria. However, this implies that a considerable number of artefacts, or type fossils, are present on each individual site. Sites which are small, as a result of too limited research, have deep stratigraphical positions or short occupation histories, will be particularly difficult to date. On the other hand, large sites may yield mixed assemblages from different occupation events (palimpsests). In view of these problems we have tried to classify the sites in relatively broad chronological stages, i.e. Final Palaeolithic (Federmesser), Early Mesolithic (Preboreal – first half Boreal), Middle Mesolithic (second half Boreal), Late/Final Mesolithic (first half Atlantic), and Neolithic.

Results and discussion

The chronological distribution of the sites (minimum 50 artefacts) analysed thus far shows a variability in the number of sites per phase. If we look at the raw data expressed in number of sites per phase (Figure 42.1), there is a marked dominance of sites belonging to the Early Mesolithic (37 sites), followed by those of the Late Mesolithic (22 sites). Middle (7 sites) and Final Mesolithic sites (4 sites) are, on the other hand, hardly in evidence.

However, if the difference in the duration of each phase is taken into account another pattern emerges. As a matter of fact, the Late Mesolithic lasted approximately twice as long as the Final Palaeolithic, the Early and Final Mesolithic, and even four times longer than the Middle Mesolithic. If each chronological stage is theoretically reduced to 500 uncalibrated BP years and the number of

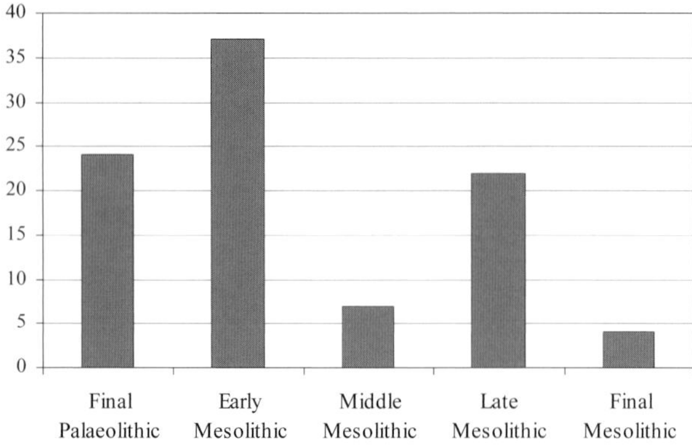

Figure 42.1. Number of sites per chronological phase.

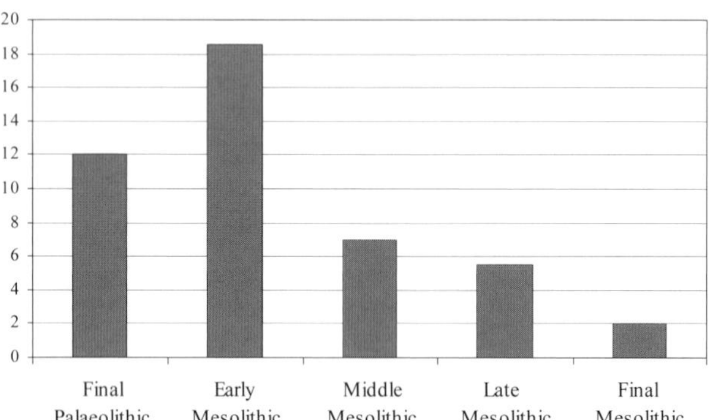

Figure 42.2. In order to avoid distortion caused by the differences in duration of the chronological phases (Middle Mesolithic: c. *500 years uncal. BP; Final Palaeolithic, Early Mesolithic and Final Mesolithic: c. 1000 years uncal. BP; Late Mesolithic:* c. *2000 years uncal. BP), each phase is reduced to 500 years uncal. BP and the number of sites is recalculated in accordance.*

sites is recalculated in accordance (e.g. by dividing the number of sites by two or more, dependent on whether the stage is reduced twice or more) (Figure 42.2), a marked and gradual decrease of sites can be noticed from the Middle Mesolithic until the Final Mesolithic. The limited number of sites belonging to the Final Mesolithic might, in part, be due to taphonomic factors. Until now sites from this stage have only been found in alluvial contexts, and through which are difficult to detect by field walking. The decline of Middle and Late Mesolithic sites, on the other hand, is much more difficult to explain: taphonomic reasons or a lesser visibility cannot be invoked here.

A similar tendency can be seen in the distribution of the radiocarbon dates obtained from salvage excavations in Sandy Flanders. At present 102 dates from different materials, coming from ten sites, are available (Crombé *et al.* 2008). The distribution of these dates shows a strong concentration between 8700 and 7000 cal BC (which corresponds to the Early Mesolithic and the first part of the Middle Mesolithic). From 7000 cal BC onwards there is a drastic decrease in the number of dates. If all charcoal dates are excluded (because these are not secure anthropogenic indicators) the tendency is even stronger: most dates cluster between 8700 and 7400 cal BC, or the Early Mesolithic.

Generally, a dramatic decline in the number of sites is interpreted as an indication of a reduced population density (Crombé *et al.* 2008). However there are other factors which might have influenced the numbers, for example changes in mobility or land-use systems in the course of the Mesolithic. There are two possibilities: either during the Late Mesolithic the same exploitation system was used as in the Early Mesolithic, but with reduced mobility, or there was a change in exploitation system, for example from a collecting to a foraging system (Binford 1980). From ethnographical studies it is known that a collecting system leads to a high number of logistical or non-residential sites, such as hunting stands, field camps, caches, etc. In an opposite sense, a foraging system creates many more residential camps than would a collecting system, because of a higher residential mobility.

However the difference between residential and non-residential camps is archaeologically hard to distinguish. When dealing with surface evidence only, it is almost impossible to assess whether there have been major changes in the mobility system throughout the Mesolithic in the study area. It is even difficult to make a distinction based on evidence retrieved from excavations such as, for example, the Early Mesolithic site of Verrebroek 'Dok I' (Crombé *et al.* 2003).

This excavation, which yielded at least 55 independent artefact concentrations, is the largest in the area so far. The largest excavated units are probably palimpsests of three or more occupation events, while the smallest ones seem to be the result of single and short-term visits. Hierarchical cluster analysis of these units indicates important intra-site variability in the tool compositions. Two major types of assemblages seem to exist. Type one is characterised by a dominance of microliths combined with a significant number of common tools: type two only consists of microliths.

Tool variability such as this is generally, or traditionally, interpreted as reflecting functional differences (Jacobi 1978; Simmons 1979; Verhart 2003). In most studies, assemblages with numerous common tools (comparable to our type 1) are interpreted as residential camps, whereas assemblages dominated by microliths (our type 2) are usually considered as non-residential camps, hunting, or field camps.

However recent microwear analysis has shown clearly that such correlations are too simplified. Three artefact concentrations from Verrebroek 'Dok I', all belonging to type 1, have been analysed so far (Beugnier and Crombé 2005). The results indicate a rather restricted number of domestic activities, with an emphasis on hide working and plant processing. Plant processing includes the scraping and splitting of non-woody plants, most likely reed or fresh hazelnut sticks. Hide working is represented only by its initial stages, namely stripping of the hides, smoothing the hides, and the treatment of hides with abrasives. What is surprising, however, is the almost total absence of other domestic activities that normally produce wear traces rather rapidly, such as wood-, bone-, and leatherworking. The activity spectrum of these three concentrations is not very consistent with what is normally expected for a residential or base camp. This spectrum might be representative of a non-residential camp type, for example a hunting field camp, where a limited set of basic domestic activities would have been performed. The only way to gain more insight into this problem is to expand the microwear analysis to other assemblage types as much as possible, on intra-site and inter-site levels.

Thus, for the time being, it is not possible to make a clear distinction between residential and non-residential sites within our study area. Hence it cannot be verified whether the decrease in sites is a result of a change from a collecting to a foraging mobility. However, besides a reduction in site numbers, a clear shift in the distribution pattern of sites between the Early and Late Mesolithic seems also to indicate a change in the settlement system.

Firstly, Early Mesolithic sites often seem to cluster in specific landscape features, for example, in the eastern part of the study area. Here Early Mesolithic sites cluster along the southern slope of a large sand ridge over a distance of more than 7km. Such extensive clusters are not known from the Late Mesolithic. Second, there seems to be a marked discontinuity in the settlement location between the Early and Late Mesolithic (Figures 42.3, 42.4 and 42.5). Final Palaeolithic sites were very often re-occupied during the Early and Middle Mesolithic (Crombé and Verbruggen 2002). However these sites are only a small percentage of the Early and Middle Mesolithic sites: most sites are situated in new locations. On the other hand the Final Palaeolithic sites were nearly all not re-occupied in the Late Mesolithic, and only 38% of the Late Mesolithic occupations were established on the same location as Early and Middle Mesolithic sites. Most of these re-used sites seem to be located close to open water systems.

Similar trends have been observed in other study areas of north-west Europe (e.g. Waterbolk 1983–4; Groenendijk 1993; Spikins 1999), and have been explained as resulting from major environmental changes, more precisely the change from a rather open coniferous forest in the Preboreal and Boreal, characterised by evenly distributed resources, to a dense and dark broad-leaf forest with clustered resources.

Another major change obviously occurred in the use and distribution of exotic raw materials. During the Mesolithic two different types of quartzites were imported in Sandy Flanders – from Tienen and Wommersom. Both raw materials originate from the Tienen region in central Belgium, more than 80km away from the research area (Caspar 1984; Crombé 1998). On Early Mesolithic sites in Sandy Flanders Tienen quartzite clearly predominates over Wommersom quartzite (Crombé *et al.* 2008) (Figure 42.6). It is remarkable that in the area to the east of Sandy Flanders, in the Campine region, Wommersom quartzite is the only exogenous raw material attested. From the Middle Mesolithic, and definitely from the Late Mesolithic onwards,

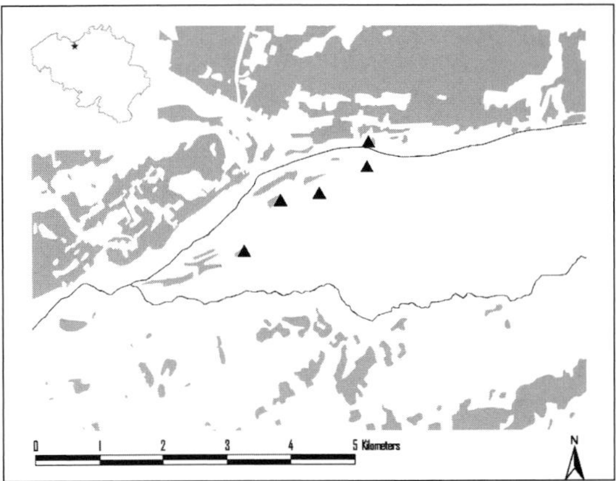

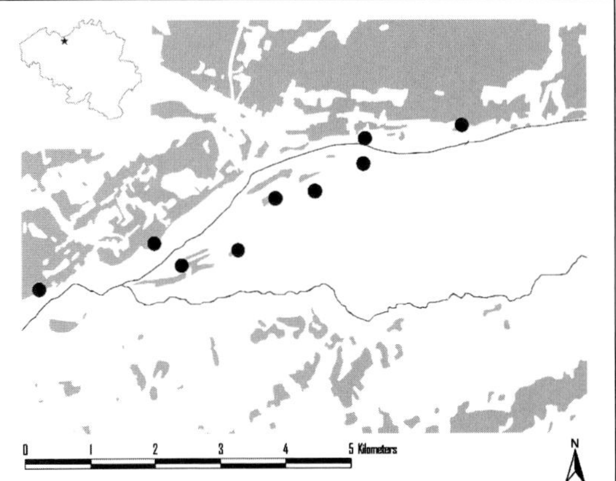

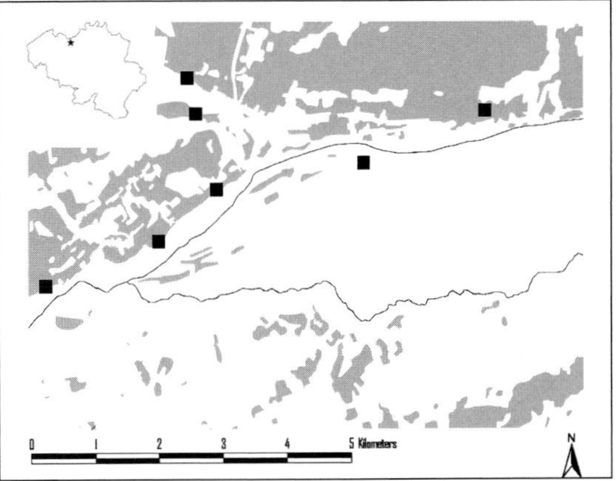

Figures 42.3, 42.4, 42.5. Distribution of Final Palaeolithic (above), Early Mesolithic (centre), and Late Mesolithic sites (below) in the western part of the Moervaart depression (grey: sand substratum).

the situation in Sandy Flanders changes completely: just as in the Campine region, Wommersom quartzite now becomes the most important, and, most of the time, the only exogenous raw material (Figure 42.7).

It is clear that environmental arguments cannot be held responsible for these changes. Rather, we should look in the direction of social and/or cultural changes. It is not unlikely that these exotic materials, originating from the same outcrop area, were used as social markers by different groups in order to visualise and defend their social territories.

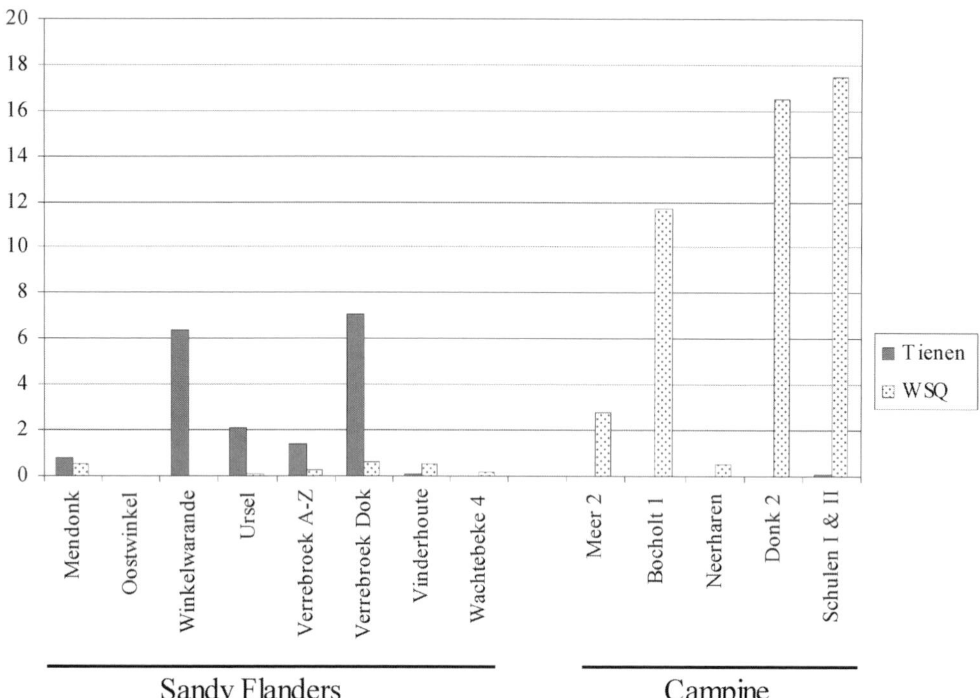

Figure 42.6. Percentages of Tienen and Wommersom quartzite from Early Mesolithic sites in Sandy Flanders and the Campine.

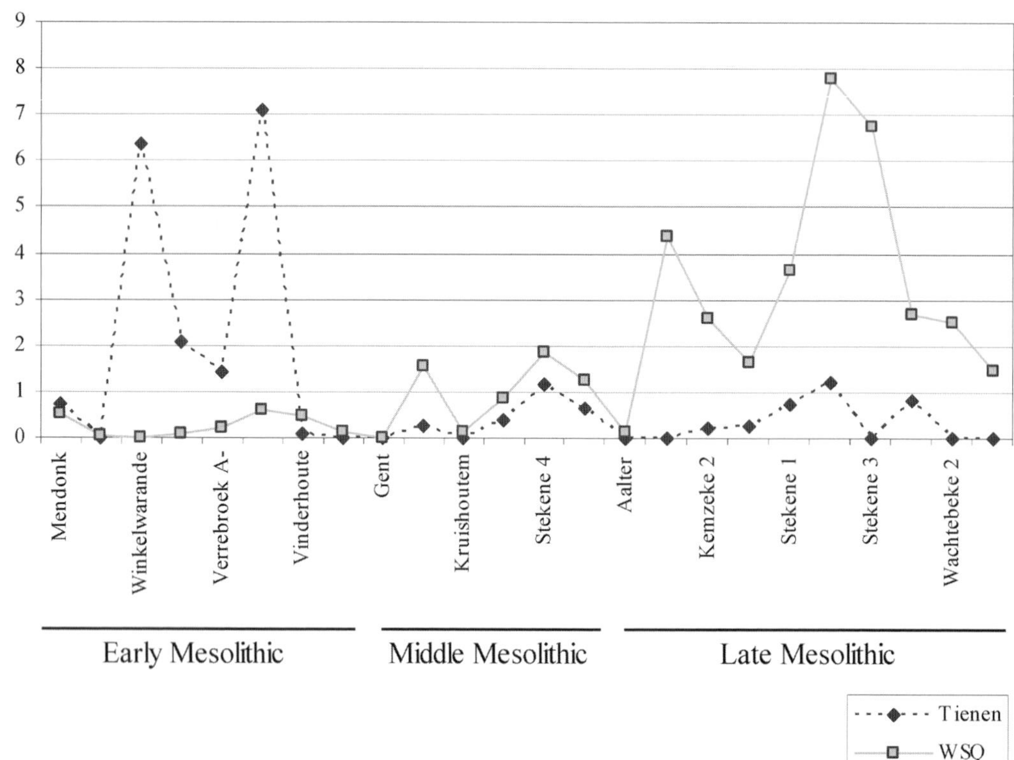

Figure 42.7. Percentages of Tienen and Wommersom quartzite from Early, Middle, and Late Mesolithic sites in Sandy Flanders.

If this were the case, then the Scheldt River in the Early Mesolithic might have been the limit between two different groups, one to the west of the Scheldt using Tienen quartzite, another to the east using Wommersom quartzite. In the Later Mesolithic the Scheldt ceased to signify a limit, or the need to visualise the borders of group territories disappeared or decreased considerably. Whether this points to a change from a period of social stress in the

Early Mesolithic to a period of more stabilisation in the Late Mesolithic remains to be further investigated.

Conclusions

The first results of our research project, although still very preliminary, indicate at least three major changes at the transition from the Early/Middle Mesolithic to the Late Mesolithic in Sandy Flanders. Changes occur in the site density with a marked reduction in site number, in the site location with a stronger emphasis on locations along open water systems, and in the use and distribution of exotic raw materials.

The first two changes might be related to changes in the landscape, forcing local hunter-gatherers to change their way of exploiting the area. The third might be an expression of changing social conditions, for example an increasing territoriality.

Acknowledgements

Our thanks are due to the Fund for Scientific Research (Flanders) for the financial assistance of our project ('Man and landscape. Study of prehistoric land-use systems in three core regions of Sandy Flanders between *c.* 12,000 and 2000 BC').

References

Beugnier, V. and Crombé, P. 2005. Etude fonctionelle du matériel en silex du site mésolithique ancien de Verrebroek (Flandres, Belgique): premiers résultats. *Bulletin de la Société préhistorique française* 102 (3), 527–38.

Binford, L. R. 1980. Willow smoke and dogs' tails: hunter-gatherer settlement systems and archaeological site information. *American Antiquity* 45, 4–20.

Caspar, J.-P. 1984. Matériaux lithiques de la préhistoire, in P. Haesaerts and D. Cahen (eds.), *Peuples chasseurs de la Belgique préhistorique dans leur cadre naturel*, 107–14, Bruxelles, Institut royal des sciences naturelles de Belgique.

Crombé, P. 1998. *The Mesolithic in Northwestern Belgium. Recent excavations and surveys*. British Archaeological Reports, International Series S716. Oxford, John and Erica Hedges.

Crombé, P. (ed.) 2005. *The last hunter-gatherer-fishermen in sandy Flanders (NW Belgium). The Verrebroek and Doel excavation projects, Part 1: palaeo-environment, chronology and features*. Ghent University Archaeological Reports 3. Ghent, Academia Press.

Crombé, P., Perdaen, Y. and Sergant, J. 2003. The site of Verrebroek 'Dok' (Flanders, Belgium): spatial organisation of an extensive Early Mesolithic settlement, in L. Larsson, H. Kindgren, K. Knutsson, D. Loeffler and A. Åkerlund (eds.), *Mesolithic on the Move: Papers presented at the Sixth International Conference on the Mesolithic in Europe, Stockholm 2000*, 205–15, Oxford, Oxbow Books.

Crombé, P., Perdaen, Y. and Sergant, J. 2008. Le Mésolithique ancien dans l'ouest de la Belgique : Quelques réflexions concernant l'occupation du territoire, in T. Ducrocq, J.-P. Fagnart, B. Souffi and A. Thévenin (eds.), *Actes de la table ronde – Le Mésolithique ancien et moyen de la France septentrionale et des pays limitrophes, Amiens 9–10/10/2004*. Mémoires de la Société Préhistorique Française. Paris, Société Préhistorique Française.

Crombé, P. and Verbruggen, C. 2002. The Lateglacial and early Postglacial occupation of northern Belgium: the evidence from Sandy Flanders, in B. V. Eriksen and B. Bratlund (eds.), *Recent studies in the Final Palaeolithic of the European plain. Proceedings of a U.I.S.P.P. Symposium, Stockholm, 14–17 October 1999*, 165–80, Jutland Archaeological Society.

Groenendijk, H. A. 1993. *Landschapsontwikkeling en bewoning in het Herinrichtingsgebied Oost-Groningen (8000 BC – 1000 AD)*. PhD thesis, University of Groningen.

Jacobi, R. M. 1978. Northern England in the eighth millennium BC: an essay, in P. Mellars (ed.), *The Early Postglacial Settlement of Northern Europe*, 295–332. London, Duckworth.

Simmons, I. G. 1979. Late Mesolithic societies and the environment of the uplands of England and Wales. *University of London, Institute of Archaeology, Bulletin* 16, 111–29.

Spikins, P. 1999. *Mesolithic Northern England. Environment, population and settlement*. British Archaeological Reports, British Series 283. Oxford, Archaeopress.

Van der Haegen, G., Crombé, P. and Semey, J. 1999. *Steentijdvondsten in het Meetjesland*. Buitengewone reeks 6. Ghent, Archeologische Inventaris Vlaanderen.

Van Vlaenderen, L., Sergant, J., De Bock, H. and De Meireleir, M. 2006. *Steentijdvondsten in de Moervaart*. Buitengewone reeks 9. Ghent, Archeologische Inventaris Vlaanderen.

Verhart, L. 2003. Mesolithic Economic and Social Changes in the Southern Netherlands, in L. Larsson, H. Kindgren, K. Knutsson, D. Loeffler and A. Åkerlund (eds.), *Mesolithic on the Move: Papers presented at the Sixth International Conference on the Mesolithic in Europe, Stockholm 2000*, 442–50, Oxford, Oxbow Books.

Waterbolk, H. T. 1983–4. The Mesolithic and Early Neolithic settlement of the Northern Netherlands in the light of radiocarbon evidence. *Jahrbuch des Bernischen Historischen Museum* 63/64, 273–81.

43. Mesolithic settlement and land use in the Campine region (Belgium)

Marc De Bie and Marijn Van Gils

Mesolithic occupation of the belgian campine region (kempen) has long been known only from surface collections and small excavations. Large-scale fieldwork of the last few years provided a better insight into the location, distribution, wealth, preservation, and nature of early postglacial site complexes as well as new opportunities to study the settlement and mobility patterns of the mesolithic societies. Sites were shown to be very extensive, situated in specific topographical contexts, and rich in artefact quantities. The vast and very rich contexts seem to be the norm, which makes it impossible to claim certain places in the landscape to have had a special meaning in the cultural hunter-gatherer tradition. The authors argue that this pattern may primarily be explained as the result of an economic, subsistence-based land use system.

Keywords: Mesolithic, Belgium, land use, mobility, Campine region, survey, settlement.

Introduction

In northern Belgium and the southern Netherlands, Mesolithic societies heavily exploited the sandy landscape presently referred to as the Campine region. Until recently, this occupation was only known from surface collections or small-scale excavations. In order to sharpen the picture, we developed new and large-scale fieldwork revealing numerous well-preserved alternative sites. Thorough assessment and excavations subsequently showed these to be rich in artefact quantities, often spread over several kilometres, and always situated in specific topographical contexts on dry soils along (former) open water (rivers or fens). In this paper we develop a strong view on Mesolithic settlement and land use patterning, providing insights on the location, preservation, wealth, distribution, and nature of Mesolithic site-complexes. The discussion focuses on the question whether this pattern should be explained either as the result of a pure economic, subsistence-based land use system, where people (like other species) were simply using preferential biotopes that were exploited in an encounter strategy, or rather as places in the landscape with a special meaning in the cultural tradition (likely also with a name), where Mesolithic groups intentionally gathered, perhaps at specific times of the year, to celebrate, exchange partners, or perform other cultural activities.

Geographical context

The Belgian region known as 'Kempen' is a sandy area, mostly consisting of Pleistocene coversands, in the southern part of the NW European Plain. Covering almost 4000km^2, this area is generally perceived as a 'flat' landscape, lacking major landmarks; it is bordered by the Scheldt and Meuse rivers, but major streams in the Campine region itself are lacking. In natural conditions (Figure 43.1), the landscape is rather attractive, with heather (*Calluna*) and wooded areas, currently mainly pine (*Pinus*) forests. However, various processes of human impact – mainly construction work and agriculture – continually threaten this picture. Throughout the 20th century, many Mesolithic sites were discovered in this region. Unfortunately, the Mesolithic occupation was only known from stray finds collected on ploughed fields or from small-scale excavations.

Figure 43.1. Example of a typical Campine landscape at Ravels Witgoor: a humid depression, currently grassland, is bordered by a dry sandy ridge, forested with pine trees.

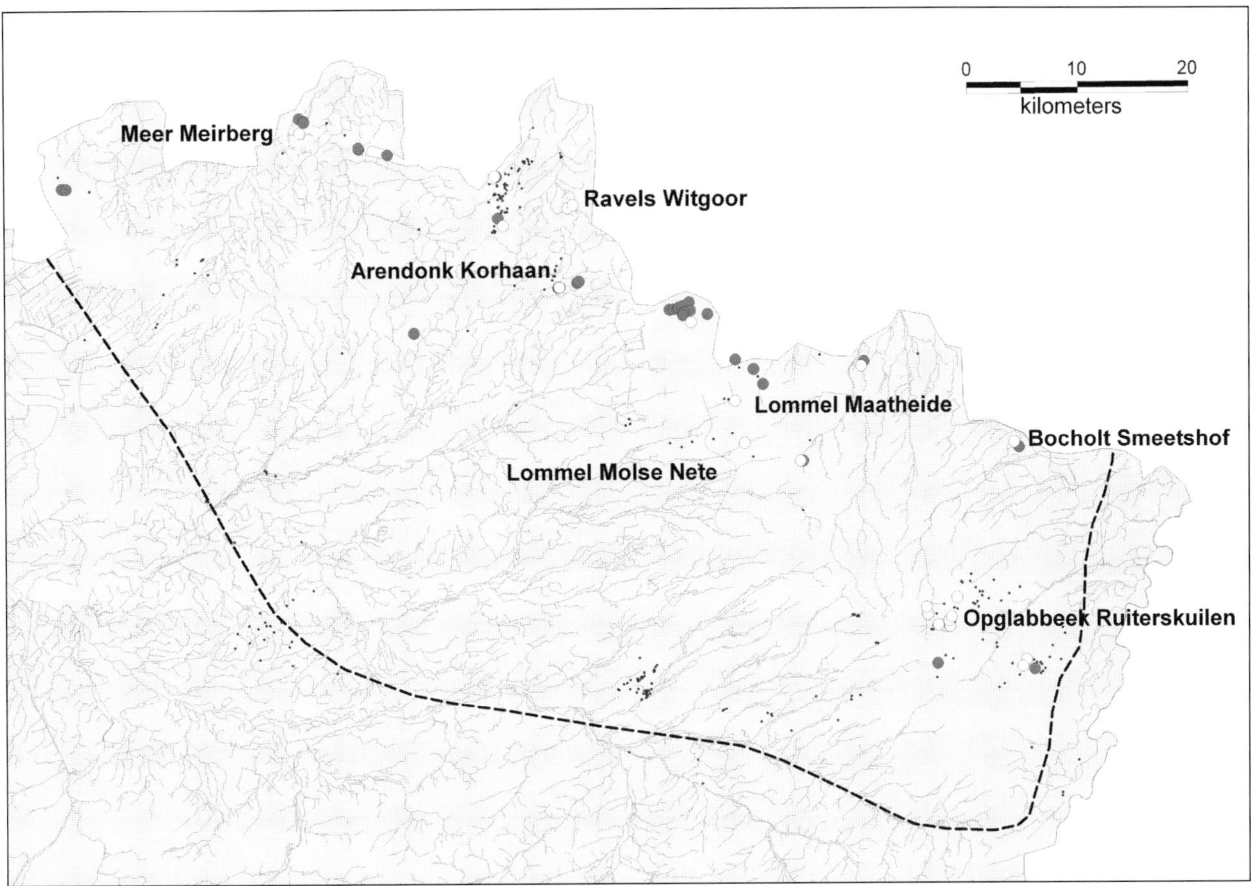

Figure 43.2. Results of the survey campaign in the Belgian Campine region. The dark dots indicate the location of the drillings, selected on the basis of topographical features and soil preservation. Light dots are new sites. Small black dots are all the Final Palaeolithic and Mesolithic sites known in the region.

Outline and methodology

In order to cope with these limitations and to be able to evaluate the older results in this region, a systematic survey project was conducted. In a first phase, many locations in the Belgian Campine region were surveyed, revealing numerous well-preserved new sites and relocating several known ones (Figure 43.2). About three quarters of the visited locations, selected for their favourable topographical context, appeared to host Mesolithic sites – a surprisingly high predictability.

Next, a number of these sites were selected for more detailed assessment. On each of these sites, numerous so-called mega-drillings were executed in a regular grid system. Sieving of the sediment cores frequently yielded flint artefacts, thus indicating the location of the artefact concentrations, and providing a good idea of the extension and wealth of the sites (Figure 43.3). The drill holes (*c.* 20cm wide and 1m deep) also allowed the soil profile to be examined, informing to some degree on the preservation of the former natural landscape(s).

Finally, excavations on some of these sites helped to clarify the picture further and to assess the survey data. The details of these new fieldwork results can be found elsewhere (De Bie 1999; 2000a; 2000b; De Bie *et al.* 2003; De Bie and Van Gils 2004; Van Gils and De Bie 2001; 2002a; 2002b; 2003a; 2003b; 2004; 2005; 2006a; 2006b). In this paper we only intend to discuss some of the major results.

Results

The distribution of sites in the landscape reveals some recurrent patterning (Figure 43.4). First, with regard to the topographical position, two major trends are observed:

1) The sites are always situated on dry sandy ridges near (former) open water, either isolated fens (small lakes), river source areas or small incipient rivers. This observation is hardly new: such contexts are well known as excellent locations for hunter-gatherer groups relying on the water itself, but also taking advantage of the rich biodiversity in vegetation and fauna (including birds, molluscs, drinking game, etc.) (David and Kramer 2001; Grøn and Kusnetzov 2004; Perdaen *et al.* 2004; Vanacker *et al.* 2001).
2) The orientation of the sites is also recurrent: they are almost systematically placed on the northern bank of the rivers or fens, looking south over the water, i.e. on the 'sunny side' of the valley.

Secondly, with regard to shape and size of the Mesolithic sites, it may be noted that they are all very large and

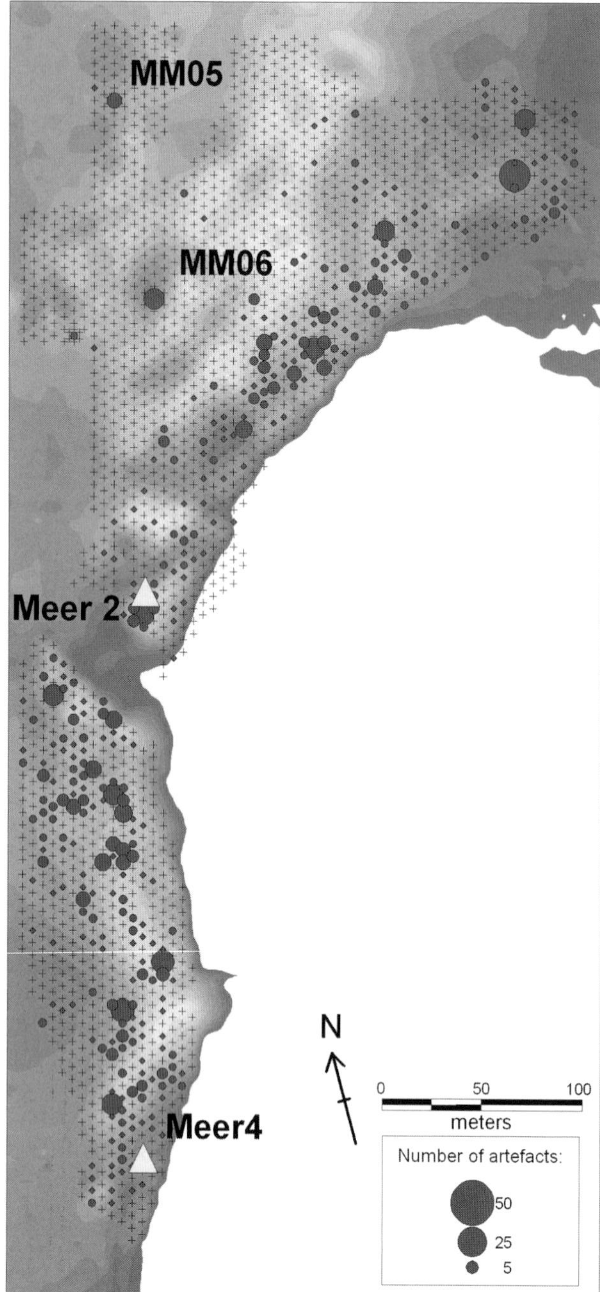

Figure 43.3. Map of the evaluation campaign at Meer Meirberg. The crosses indicate drilling locations, and the dimensions of the dots correspond to the number of artefacts retrieved in the sieve. Former excavations Meer 2 and Meer 4 are indicated by the triangles.

elongated site complexes, flanking the water. In general, they do not extend much further away than 100m from the wet areas. In length, however, they extend over many hundreds of metres, up to several kilometres. There, the edges seem to be primarily determined by the extent of the sand ridges on which the sites occur.

Discussion

By no means can these sites be interpreted as isolated artefact clusters. Once they are surveyed properly, both newly discovered sites and sites previously known from small excavations, all appear to be very large and rich site complexes. One major advantage of systematic drilling is that it allows a very accurate estimation of total artefact quantities at these places (Figure 43.5). The calculations show that the sites contain, at least, several hundreds of thousands, if not millions of artefacts.

Can these sites be so-called 'aggregation' sites where hunter-gatherers specifically gathered in large numbers to celebrate, exchange partners, or perform other cultural activities? For this function, we would expect to see a few extremely rich sites, clearly standing out from the norm. Since rich contexts seem instead to be the normal, typical situations, occurring at all the sites we studied, it is difficult to subscribe to such an interpretation.

Instead, we believe that the assemblages accumulated during repeated visits of small hunter-gatherer groups, perhaps in the course of millennia. In this way, overlapping artefact scatters were abandoned during a multitude of different occupations on the same dune. Even though a tradition might have formed around these spots, perhaps making them the favoured place to return to year after year, and probably also providing them with a name, the economic attractiveness of these locations was the first reason for their selection as habitation areas.

Can such a long-term repeated occupation be demonstrated by the actual data? Unfortunately, a major disadvantage of sampling sites, in this case by means of drillings, is the low amount of artefacts retrieved. This makes it difficult to assess the chronology of the settlement. Actually, even with detailed excavations, it is not possible to readily distinguish the different occupation episodes in these contexts. Since the topography of the natural landscape remained largely the same throughout the Mesolithic, and often even into the Final Palaeolithic, artefacts from every occupation have been abandoned on the same surface again and again. After intense bioturbation in the sandy soil, we now find them dispersed through the eluviaton and illuviation horizons of the podzol, making it very hard to understand the occupation history in detail. All we can say for now is that at several sites the formation of the archaeological record was clearly diachronic, generally starting in the Final Palaeolithic – as shown by *Federmesser* presence on many sites – and continuing into at least the first half of the Mesolithic.

However, looking more closely at the quantitative data and estimations of artefact numbers, some variation seems to occur (Figures 43.6 and 43.7). Two sites in particular, Ravels-Witgoor and Opglabbeek-Ruiterskuilen, although sampled extensively, clearly yield a lower amount of artefacts, both in total numbers and in artefact densities.

How can this relative 'poverty' be explained? Most likely, the total accumulated duration of occupation was not always the same; the few 'poor' sites being visited less frequently than the others. Can a reason for this variation in re-occupation history be found in the landscape features? With regard to the topographical context, only one major

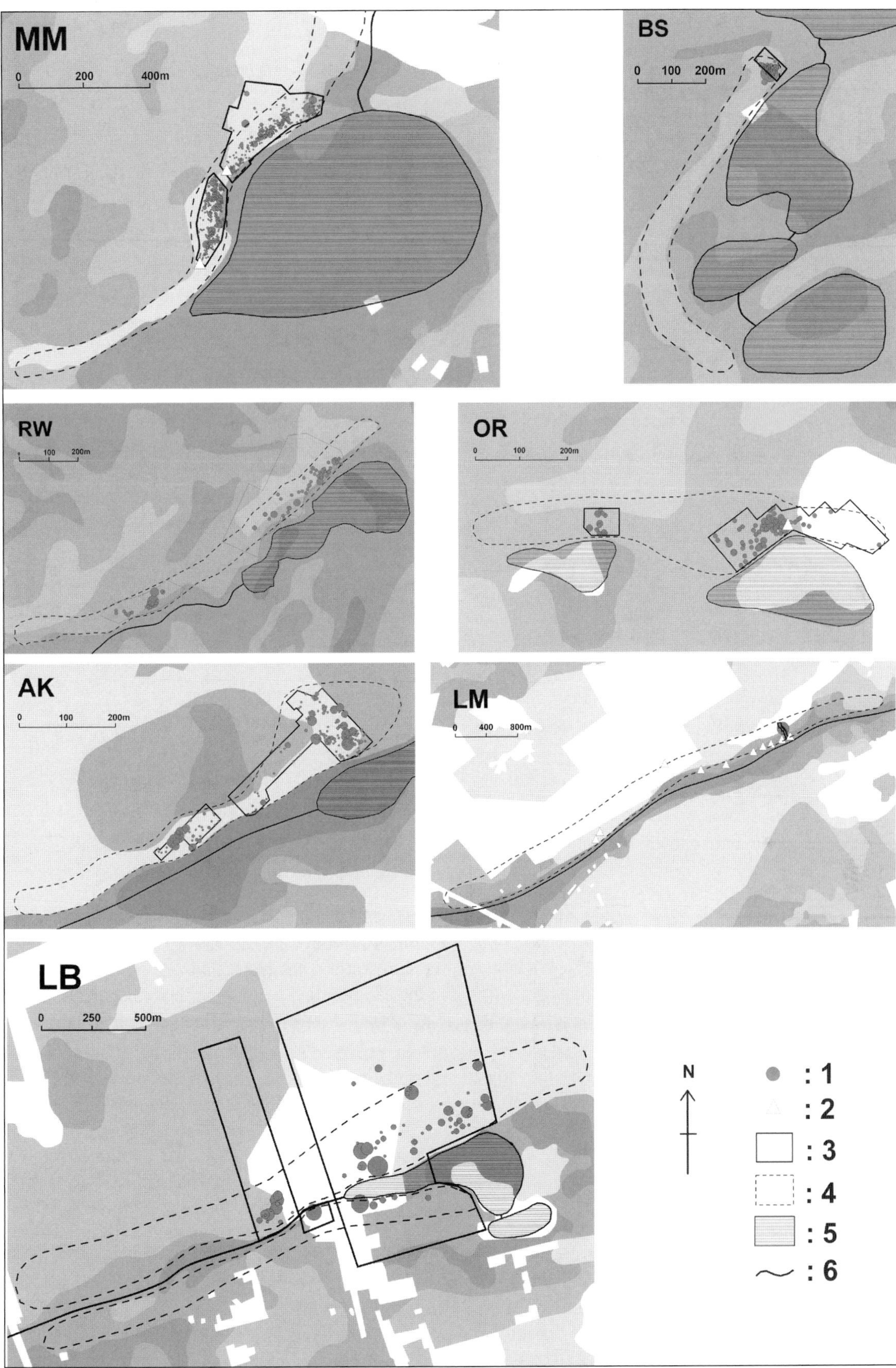

Figure 43.4. Various maps of investigated sites. Darker zones are humid areas, lighter zones are dry areas. White zones are disturbed sectors, recent dune-formations or water. RW: Ravels Witgoor; AK: Arendonk Korhaan; LM: Lommel Molse Nete; LB: Lommel Maatheide; MM: Meer Meirberg; OR: Opglabbeek Ruiterskuilen; BS: Bocholt Smeetshof. 1: Location of positive drillings. The dimensions correspond with artefact numbers (max = 30); 2: Finds from surveys or excavations; 3: Evaluated zone; 4: Site edges (estimation); 5: Estimates of the water extension during occupation; 6: Small river.

Site	Estimate of inhabited surface area (ha)	Surveyed surface area (ha)	Number of drillings	Number of positive samples	Number of uncovered artefacts	Estimate of total artefact numbers	Density (N art./ha)
Ravels Witgoor	9.5	8.10	1462	65	115	210,000	22,105
Opglabbeek Ruiterskuilen	11.5	4.20	1156	66	101	280,000	24,348
Arendonk Korhaan	8.0	3.10	806	166	434	1,120,000	140,000
Meer Meirberg	18.0	6.30	2045	360	859	2,450,000	136,111
Bocholt Smeetshof	6.0	0.25	154	59	156	3,740,000	623,333
Lommel Molse Nete	145.0	0.65	188	46	120	26,770,000	184,621
Lommel Maatheide	95.0	96.50	N/A	N/A	N/A	N/A	N/A

Figure 43.5. Surfaces, drillings, numbers and densities of artefacts per site.

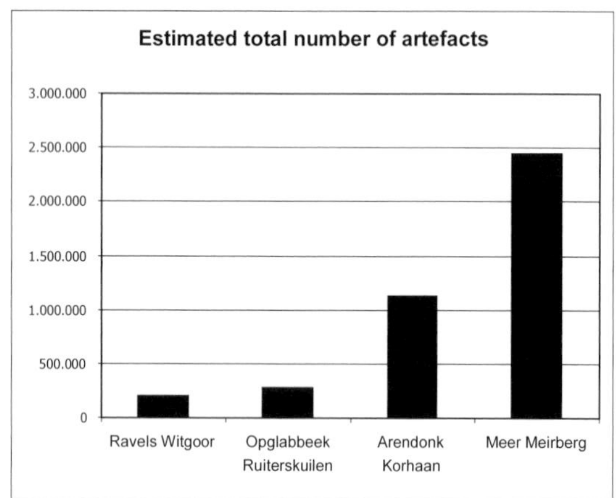

Figure 43.6. Estimates of the total number of artefacts abandoned at the sites.

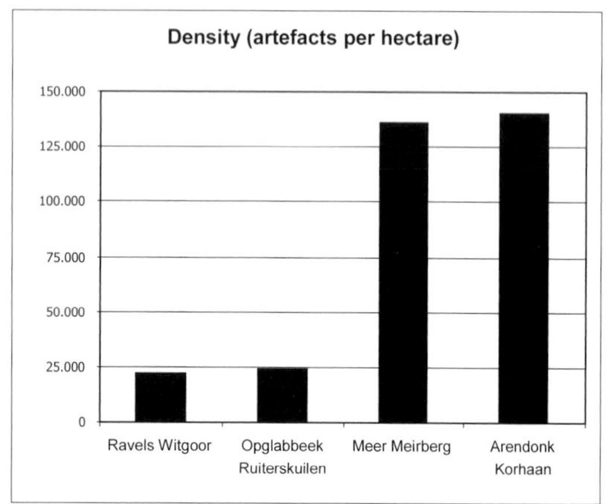

Figure 43.7. Artefact densities per site.

difference appears in comparison with the 'rich' sites: both 'poor' sites are situated along fens that are not drained by a river. Could this mean that they were less easily accessible? The question deserves some further consideration.

The Early Holocene landscape in the Campine region was relatively flat, lacking major landmarks such as hills, and with the horizon hidden from view by the expanding forests. Wet areas were the only open spaces, and travelling Mesolithic groups presumably relied heavily on the river network within their mobility system. Doing so, they must have repeatedly arrived in the river source areas where they found rich biotopes, perfectly suited for their subsistence strategies. The isolated fens were equally suited, but were only occasionally encountered, either by small task groups during foraging or other activities, or when the whole group occasionally chose to cross the interfluvia in search of a 'new' river network.

Finally, the recurrent orientation of the sites on the north-west side of the water also needs further consideration. This could also easily be explained by the traditional preferences of residing hunter-gatherers. Perhaps they were attracted by the direct sunlight they received on the northern banks of the rivers. The forests, on the other hand, at this position, could protect them from cold north-west winds. However, before hazarding such conclusions, further geomorphological work is needed to examine whether both the northern and southern sides of the open water were indeed equally available at the time of occupation.

Conclusions

A new approach of large-scale surveying, combining geographical analysis with intensive drilling and sieving in the field, and with test excavations for detection and assessment, provided new evidence for the location, distribution, wealth, preservation, and nature of early Postglacial site complexes in the Belgian Campine region.

Although it cannot be excluded that some of these locations were sometimes used as places where larger groups gathered at specific times of the year – to feast or to celebrate, to find partners or perform ritual practices – the Mesolithic settlement pattern in the Campine region can also be understood as being the result of a primarily economically or ecologically driven subsistence-based land use system where people – like other animals – were using preferential biotopes which they recurrently encountered in a mobility system heavily reliant on the river network.

References

David, N. and Kramer, C. 2001. *Ethnoarchaelogy in action*. Cambridge, Cambridge University Press.

De Bie, M. 1999. Extensieve prospectie op de Meirberg te Meer and Opgraving van Meer 5 en Meer 6 (Oud-Mesolithicum). *Notae Praehistoricae* 19, 69–70.

De Bie, M. 2000. *Het Steentijdmonument te Meer-Meirberg (Hoogstraten). Archeologisch waarderingsonderzoek, campagne 1999*. Zellik, Instituut voor het Archeologisch Patrimonium.

De Bie, M. 2000b. *Archeologische waardering in het Natuurinrichtingsgebied 'Het Smeetshof' te Bocholt. Prospectie en diagnose van een vroeg-mesolithisch site, campagne 2000*. Zellik, Instituut voor het Archeologisch Patrimonium.

De Bie, M., Gullentops, F. and Van Gils, M. 2003. Een laatpaleolithische concentratie in een Usselo-bodem op de Maatheide te Lommel. *Notae Praehistoricae* 23, 33–7.

De Bie, M. and Van Gils, M. 2004. *Steentijdsites op de Maatheide te Lommel. Archeologisch waarderingsonderzoek 2003*. Brussels, Vlaams Instituut voor het Onroerend Erfgoed.

Grøn, O. and Kuznetsov, O. 2004. What is a Hunter-Gatherer Settlement? An Ethno-Archaeological and Interdisciplinary Approach, in *Acts of the XIVth UISPP Congress, University of Liège, Belgium, 2-8 Septembe 2001, Section 7 : Le Mésolithique*, 47–53. British Archaeological Reports, International Series S1302. Oxford, Archaeopress.

Perdaen, Y., Sergeant, J. and Crombé, P. 2004. Early Mesolithic Landscape-Use and Site-Use in Northwestern Belgium: The Evidence from Verrebroek «Dok», in *Acts of the XIVth UISPP Congress, University of Liège, Belgium, 2-8 Septembe 2001, Section 7 : Le Mésolithique*, 11–18. British Archaeological Reports, International Series S1302. Oxford, Archaeopress.

Van Gils, M. and De Bie, M. 2001. Prospectie en kartering van laat-glaciale en vroeg-holocene sites in de Kempen: resultaten van de boorcampagne 2001. *Notae Praehistoricae* 21, 77–8.

Van Gils, M. and De Bie, M. 2002a. *Prospectie en kartering van laat-glaciale en vroeg-holocene sites in de Kempen. Boorcampagne 2001*. Zellik, Instituut voor het Archeologisch Patrimonium.

Van Gils, M. and De Bie, M. 2002b. Ravels-Witgoor: intensieve boorcampagne op een uitgestrekt vroegholoceen site-complex in de Kempen. *Notae Praehistoricae* 22, 83–5.

Van Gils, M. and De Bie, M. 2003a. Kartering en waardering van een Mesolithisch site-complex te Arendonk 'Korhaan'. *Notae Praehistoricae* 23, 67–9.

Van Gils, M. and De Bie, M. 2003b. Een uitgestrekt Laat-Mesolithisch site-complex langs de Molse Nete in Lommel. *Notae Praehistoricae* 23, 71–3.

Van Gils, M. and De Bie, M. 2004. Federmessersites te Lommel-Maatheide (Limburg). Opgravingscampagne 2004. *Notae Praehistoricae* 24, 89–94.

Van Gils, M. and De Bie, M. 2005. *Steentijdsites op de Maatheide te Lommel. Archeologische opgravingen 2004*. Brussels, Vlaams Instituut voor het Onroerend Erfgoed.

Van Gils, M. and De Bie, M. 2006a. Steentijd in de Kempen. Prospectie, kartering en waardering van het laat-paleolithisch en mesolithisch erfgoed, in K. Cousserier, E. Meylemans and I. In't Ven (eds.), *Centrale Archeologische Inventaris II. Thematisch inventarisisatie- en evaluatieonderzoek. VIOE-Rapporten* 2, 7–16. Brussels, Vlaams Instituut voor het Onroerend Erfgoed.

Van Gils, M. and De Bie, M. 2006b. Uitgestrekte Mesolithische site-complexen in de Kempen. Ravels Witgoor en Opglabbeek Ruiterskuilen-Turfven (boorcampagne 2002). *Relicta, Archeologie, Monumenten- en Landschapsonderzoek in Vlaanderen* 1, 11–28.

Vanacker, V., Govers, G., Van Peer, P., Verbeek, C., Desmet, J. and Reyniers, J. 2001. Using Monte Carlo simulation for the environmental analysis of small archaeological datasets, with the Mesolithic in north-east Belgium as a case study. *Journal of Archaeological Science* 28, 661–9.

44. Upland colonization: patterns of settling and habitation in northern Istria, Croatia

Darko Komšo

Over a dozen Mesolithic cave and open-air sites have been recently excavated in Istria, Croatia, as part of the project entitled 'Palaeolithic and Mesolithic Settlements in the Northern Adriatic'. Late Upper Palaeolithic cave sites are found only on the edge of upland karstic areas; regular upland settlement starts in the Early Mesolithic period. Mesolithic upland sites are located in particular environments, such as natural passages into highland territories, canyons and close to water-sources, and vary in size and density of occupational refuse. Lithic assemblages and habitation evidence from several Mesolithic caves and open air sites are analysed and compared in order to establish the chronological framework and variability in site type and function. From these data we infer strategies and patterns of upland colonisation and use in relation to lowland sites and regional settlement systems.

Keywords: upland, open-air, cave, settlement, site function.

Introduction

If one were to look at the distribution map of Mesolithic sites in Istria as known ten years ago, only a few sites were registered. Moreover; in addition these lacked absolute datings or detailed analysis, and no open-air sites were represented. This situation is now changing rapidly. In just a small part of north-eastern Istria, 20 square kilometres in size, there are up to 18 cave and open-air sites that can be dated to the Early Holocene (Balbo *et al.* 2004; Balbo *et al.*, in press ; Balbo *et al.*, this volume; Boschian 2003; Komšo 2003; Komšo 2005; Komšo and Miracle 2005; Miracle 1996; Miracle 2001; Miracle 2005; Miracle and Forenbaher 1998; Miracle *et al.* 2000; Pellegatti, this volume). Almost all these sites were found during one single ongoing project – 'Palaeolithic and Mesolithic Settlement in the Northern Adriatic', suggesting that detailed surveys and excavations can transform what is thought to be 'empty land' into a 'heavily used area' with a significant archaeological record (Figure 44.1).

The whole of Istria yields only sparse evidence of the presence of Late Upper Palaeolithic groups (Boschian 2003; Komšo 2003; Komšo 2005; Miracle 1995; Miracle 2005; Miracle and Forenbaher 1998). It was during the Early Holocene that the number of sites, especially in north-east Istria and the Trieste Karst region, increases significantly (Balbo *et al.* 2004; Balbo *et al.* 2006; Balbo *et al.*, this volume; Benghiat *et al.*, this volume; Boschian 2003; Komšo 2003; Komšo 2005; Komšo and Miracle 2005; Miracle 2005; Miracle and Forenbaher 1998; Miracle *et al.* 2000; Pellegatti, this volume). Regular upland settlements start in the early Mesolithic period, with hunter-gatherer groups beginning to use the uplands more frequently, staying there for longer periods. At present, we know of the existence of seven upland Mesolithic sites located in three different settings: A) along the natural passages into highland territories, B) inside canyons and C) on flat terraces.

In this paper we compare lithic assemblages, site size, and positions of three upland sites located in the mountains of Ćićarija and Učka in north-eastern Istria (Ovčja Cave, Abri Šebrn, and Lokve), in order to detect the variation in function and type of hunter-gatherer upland sites; this will help us to propose a settlement system and to understand the evolution of the settlement network as hunter-gatherers colonized neighbouring areas.

As groups of hunter-gatherers moved across the landscape, they may have established sites in different environments and used them for different purposes. Different activities leave different archaeological signatures (Adams 1998). Interpretation of site function based only on the analysis of a single lithic tool function is problematic because of its possible multifunctional character, discard, and deposition, as well as the complex problems posed by retouched artefacts. However, assemblage diversity is an important characteristic related to various aspects of site function, and therefore we analysed the frequencies of the whole range of tools (Andrefsky 1998, 189), and complete reduction sequence.

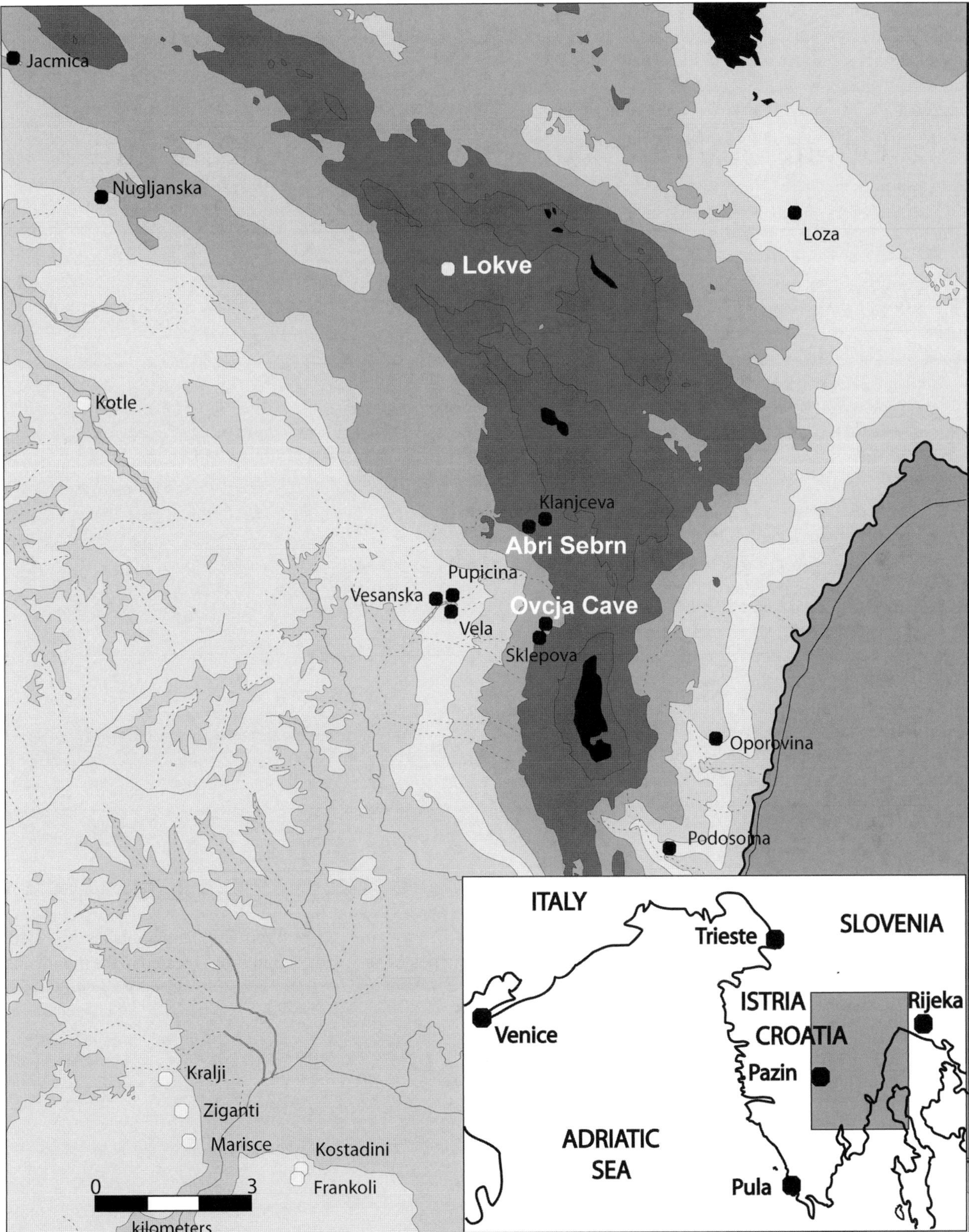

Figure 44.1. Map of north-east Istria showing the positions of Mesolithic sites. Black circles indicate cave sites, white ones the open-air sites. (Map: Preston Miracle).

We will divide the activities into two main categories: food gathering, characterized by armatures, and maintenance activities, characterized by a variety of tools. Although is difficult to make generalizations about the functions of stone tools, it is safe to assume that microlithic and non-microlithic tools form groups with contrasting functions. The non-microlithic group of tools can be characterized as being generally larger, with stable, modified edges that could stand up to relatively long wear. They have a wide range of functions such as processing hide, wood, bone or other materials (maintenance activities), and many were not directly involved with food acquisition activities. Microliths are, on the other hand, better for food-getting activities, such as hunting, fishing and fowling. Because of the many possible ways of hafting and use the tools are likely to have been multifunctional, but at least some of the backed points, backed bladelets, and geometrics were used as projectile armatures (Fisher 2002a, 61; Fisher 2002b, 172–3).

We will use Binford's 'forager'/'collector' model, as a framework for testing the archaeological record from our sites; following his model, different organizations of mobility and settlement systems would create different site types. Therefore, we expect that variations in inter-site assemblages, site position and size will be larger in 'collector' systems, and correspondingly smaller in 'forager' systems (Adams 1998; Binford 1980; Binford 1983; Habu 2002).

Ovčja Cave

The Ovčja Cave is located at an altitude of 750m asl, in the Molinarska draga, a small limestone canyon on the western slope of the Učka mountain, *c.* 4km from the present coast and 3km east of Pupićina Cave (Komšo and Miracle 2005). It is a west-facing, tunnel-shaped cave, *c.* 35m deep, 6m wide at the entrance, with approximately 140m^2 extending within the 'drip line'.

During excavations in 2002 and 2003, three small lenses separated by thin layers of red sterile clay were found, and they were interpreted as chronologically distinct occupational episodes. Only wild fauna, land snails and seashells, including perforated *Columbella rustica*, were collected, all typical of the Early Holocene in the region, confirming the Mesolithic age of the deposit.

Both the technological and typological characteristics suggest that the lithic assemblage from Ovčja Cave share a number of characteristics with other lithic assemblages from the Early Holocene in the northern Adriatic area. The assemblage from Ovčja contains a small number of artefacts and has a low density per excavated square metre. The small number of cores, decortification flakes, knapping debris, technical pieces related to core production, blanks, and technical pieces related to tool production, on the one hand, and the high number of pieces smaller than 1cm on the other, suggest that blanks were mostly prepared elsewhere and carried to the site for further transformation into tools. There are only a few tools. Tool categories and frequencies suggest specialized activities related mainly to hunting (Figure 44.2).

Previously collected data suggest that within the regional settlement system, which included residential bases (such as the Pupićina Cave), Ovčja Cave was frequently occupied by small groups as an overnight, transitory camp, and its nature did not change over time.

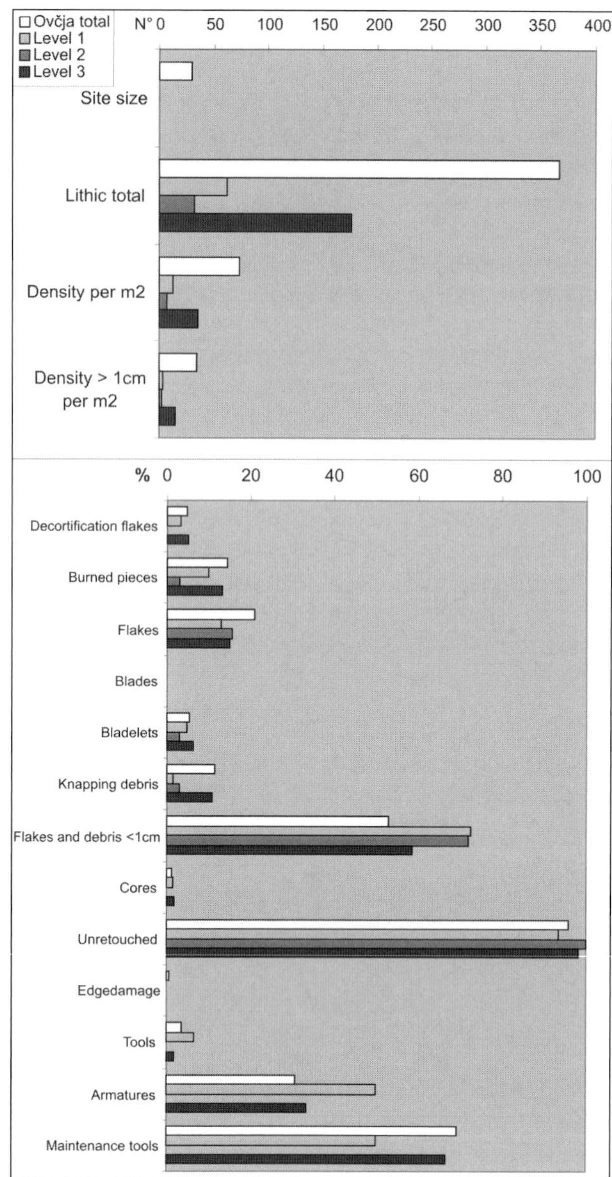

Figure 44.2. The Ovčja Cave: lithic assemblage frequencies.

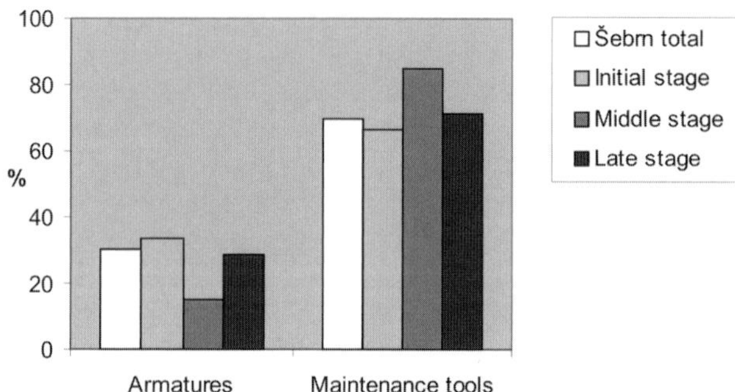

Figure 44.3. Abri Šebrn: armatures and maintenance tool frequencies.

Šebrn Abri

Šebrn Abri is located at an altitude of 750m asl, 5km from the present coast, and only 3km from Pupićina Cave, at a natural passageway into the uplands. It is a relatively small

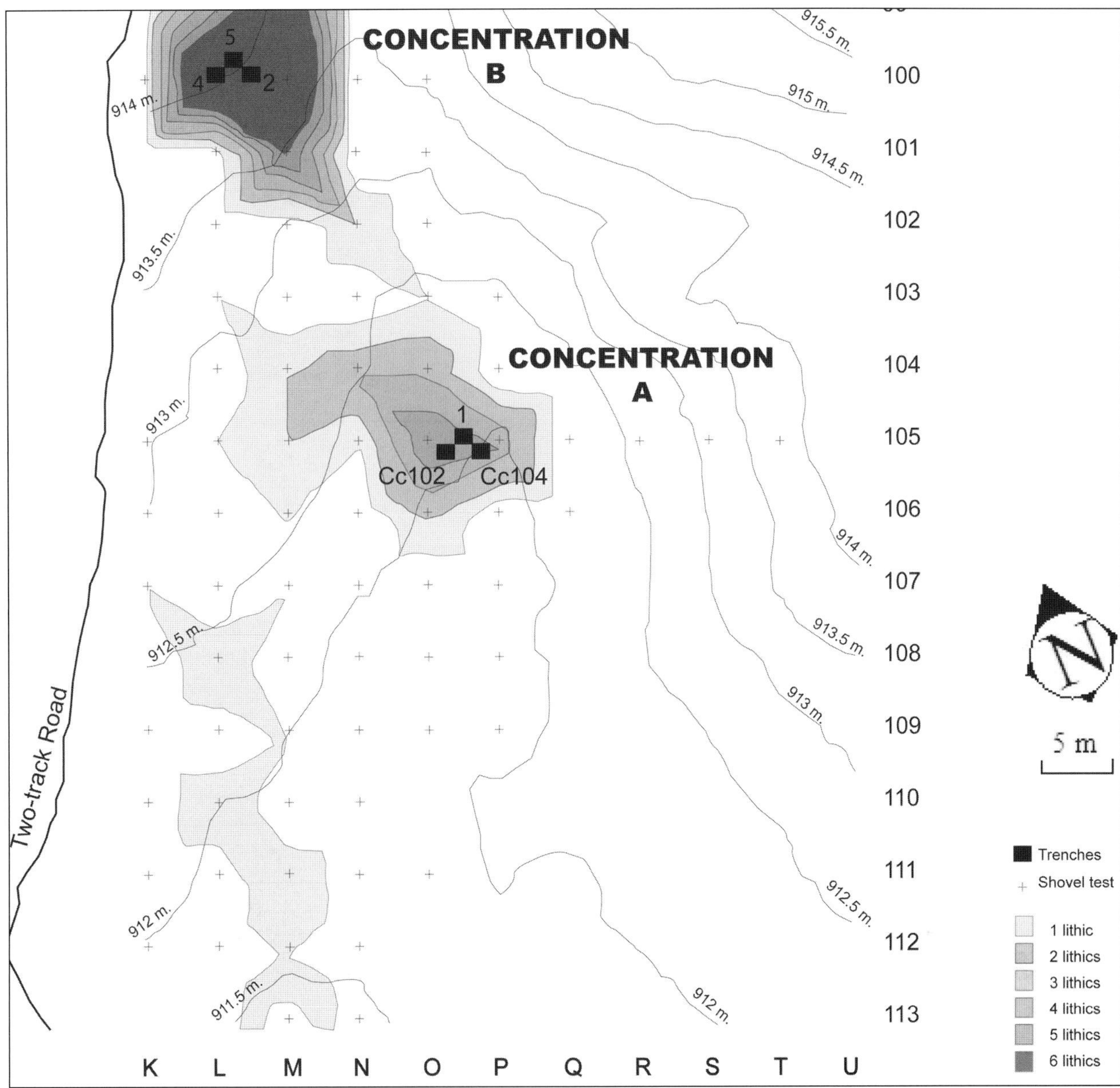

Figure 44.4. Lokve: map of site with tested and excavated areas, and showing lithic concentrations. (Graphic: Paolo Pellegatti and Darko Komšo).

and open rock-shelter, only 6m deep, while its entrance is 13m wide and some 7m high. The area inside the 'drip line' covers approximately 40m^2 (Miracle *et al.* 2000). Its strategic location would have allowed its occupants to monitor the movement of animals and people up and down the mountain.

Three radiocarbon dates (8810±80 BP, 7610–8230 cal BC, Beta-127707; 9070±90 BP, 7965–8240 cal BC, Beta-120271; 9280±40 BP, 8160–8400 cal BC, Beta-120272) suggest human use of the site within the early Holocene (Miracle *et al.* 2000). Rich faunal and lithic assemblages from the Early Mesolithic period were collected, as well as land snails and many pierced *Columbella rustica* (Benghiat *et al.*, this volume).

General technological and typological characteristics of the lithic assemblage suggest high similarities with other assemblages of the Early Holocene recovered in the northern Adriatic area. While many armatures among tools suggest the high importance of hunting activities, the presence of tools used for transformational activities, as well as technological evidence of complete lithic reduction sequences, point to activities beyond simply 'gearing up' – Šebrn was certainly more than just an upland hunting camp. However, the variation of armature frequency through the stratigraphic sequence suggests how the relative importance of different activities also varied through time, with hunting playing a greater role both early and late in the sequence (Figure 44.3). The densities of lithics and bones suggest that during the initial stage of the occupation visits were very short, followed by longer occupations of the site during the middle stage, and ending with somewhat shorter occupations in the late stages. It is interesting that

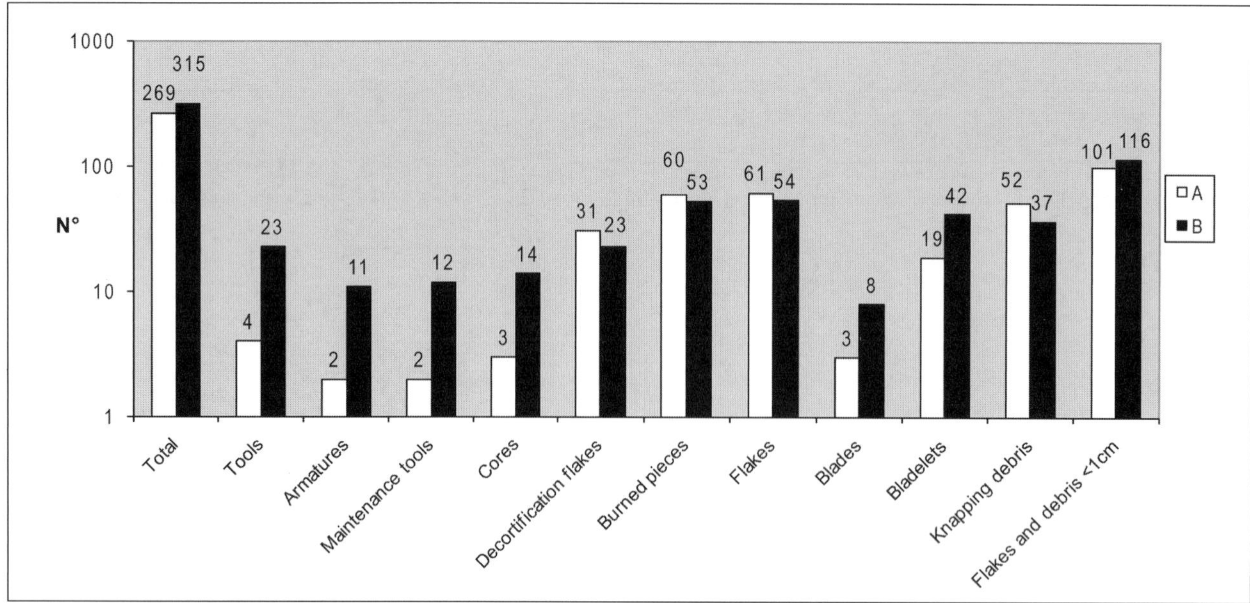

Figure 44.5. Lokve: lithic assemblage frequencies in concentrations A and B.

overall lithic artefact density per excavated square metre is the highest not only for the upland sites, but for *all* Mesolithic sites in north-eastern Istria. Overall, Šebrn was initially occupied as transitory location or as monitoring station, where people stopped, re-tooled their weapons, and monitored the area; later, people started using the site more regularly and for longer periods of time as a field camp.

Lokve

Lokve is an open-air site at an altitude of 915m asl, located on a terrace about 135m long and 35m wide, above a small, seasonal water pond that lies in the Ćićarija highland, in a zone of flysch-limestone contact. Its position may have afforded people a view of activity around the water without scaring game away.

Surveys executed in 1999 and 2002 produced a small lithic assemblage; owing to the large size of the terrace (*c.* 2600m^2) and poor ground visibility; during 2002 and 2003 the terrace was sampled with shovel-tests in order to assess the archaeological potential of the site and to estimate site size and spatial distribution. Out of 85 shovel-tests, only 30 contained archaeological material (entirely lithic artefacts). There appear to be two main concentrations of lithics and two additional concentrations with smaller densities (Figure 44.4). The approximate size of the two main concentrations is 700m^2. Further excavations confirmed the shovel-test results, without finding intact archaeological horizons.

The main concentrations are located at a distance of 20m from each other. Higher frequencies of exhausted cores, discarded tools, bladelets and small flakes in concentration B suggest activities associated with more flint knapping in general, especially blank preparation, retooling, resharpening and hafting. Lower frequencies of cores, tools, bladelets and small flakes, as well as high frequencies of knapping debris in concentration A, with average remains from all technological phases of lithic production (primary, intermediate and final), suggest different, more general sets of activities compared to concentration B (Figure 44.5). These concentrations could reflect different activity areas associated with a single occupation, or discrete occupational episodes.

From a typological viewpoint, it is important to underline the presence of trapezes made with a microburin technique at Lokve (Figure 44.6: 25, 26). Trapezes are very clear indicators of Late Mesolithic Castelnovian tradition, since they are almost unknown in the Early Mesolithic Sauveterrian, as witnessed at numerous sites in Italy and elsewhere (Broglio and Kozlowski 1983; Turk 2004). All stages of lithic reduction are present, although variously represented in the assemblage. The lithic artefact density per excavated square metre is relatively low compared with other sites in the region, mostly caves; however, we should distinguish the difference between open-air sites and caves, because the latter are space restricted. The almost equal proportion of armatures and tools for transformational activities suggests specialized activities related to hunting, but with some maintenance tasks.

All the collected data demonstrate that Lokve is a fairly large and important open-air Mesolithic site, used as a field-camp for purpose related mainly to hunting, and to a lesser degree for maintenance tasks.

Comparisons between the sites

The analyses of our three upland sites suggest a high degree of variation between them in size, function, and duration of occupation (Figure 44.7). It is obvious that sites are not scattered randomly over the area; their position was chosen based on the importance of landscape utilization. We could distinguish small overnight transitory locations located along the frequently travelled routes, as well as

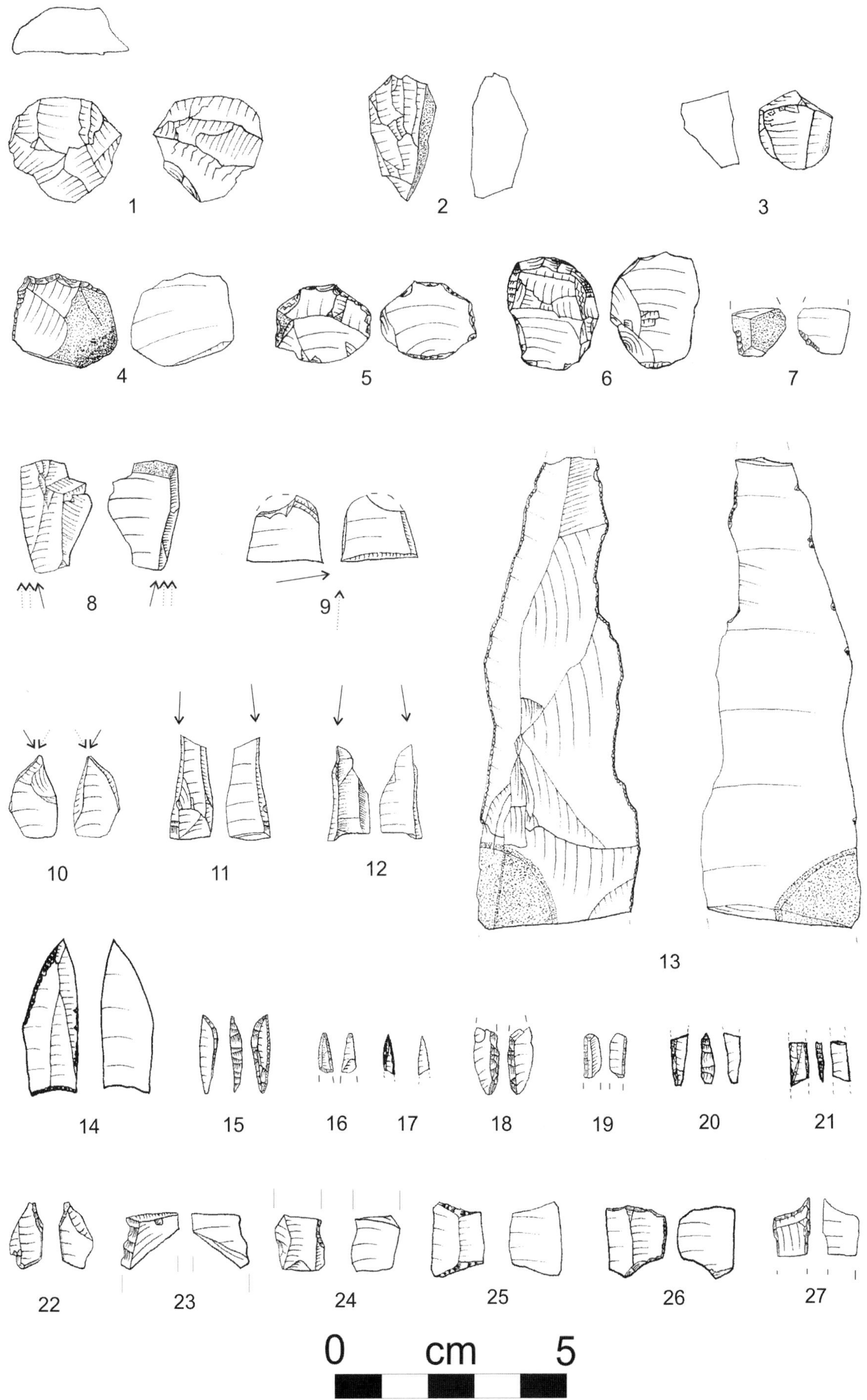

Figure 44.6. Lokve: drawings of the lithic assemblage. (Drawings: Darko Komšo).

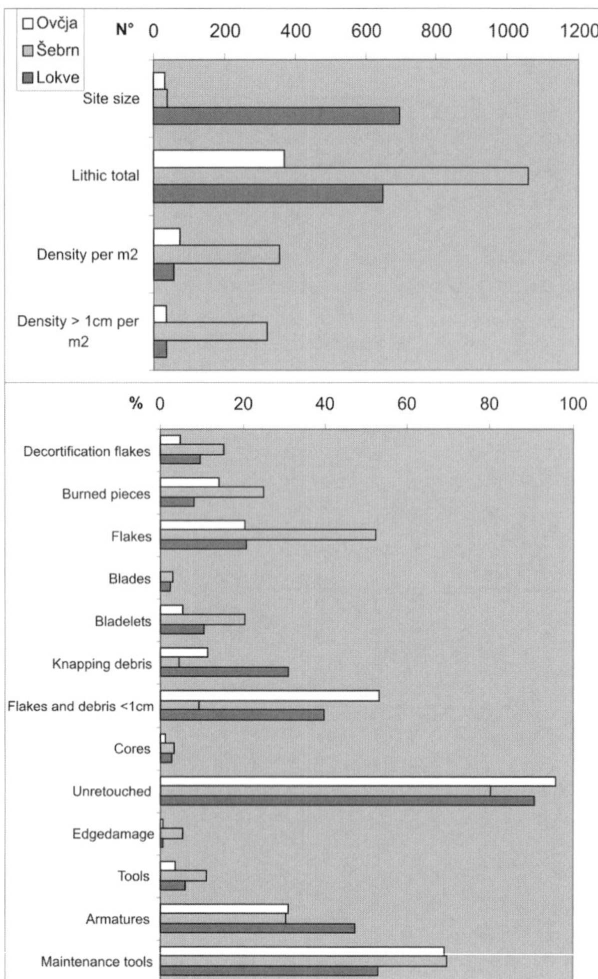

Figure 44.7. The Ovčja Cave, Abri Šebrn, and Lokve: comparisons of lithic assemblage frequencies.

monitoring stations located along the strategic positions, and field camps located along the strategic passages and close to water sources. The existence of a larger, residential base has not, so far, been recorded in the highland region. It is interesting that on Abri Šebrn both importance and function changed over time, while at the Ovčja Cave the same pattern was used throughout the whole sequence. At Lokve, on the other hand, we can assume different activity areas, however we cannot be sure if they belong to a single occupation or represent discrete occupational episodes. The most important activities at all the studied sites were related to food-gathering activities, with some maintenance activities. At field camps we have complete reduction sequences deposited, probably resulting from the existence of lithic raw material outcrops locally available on the upland. The situation was different at transitory camps and monitoring stations, where only parts of the sequence, mostly related to re-tooling and re-hafting, were preserved.

Conclusions

While the Ćićarija and Učka highlands were empty lands during the end of the Pleistocene, abrupt changes occurred during the Early Holocene, when groups of hunter-gatherers frequently settled the uplands, showing the ability of Mesolithic hunter-gatherers to adapt rapidly to different ecological areas. Initially, small groups of logistically organized 'pioneers' established a few temporary sites on neighbouring uplands to gather information on resources and conditions generally. They were followed by larger groups of hunter-gatherers, now with a sounder knowledge and control over the landscape and its resources. This phase is marked by the presence of larger, more diverse assemblages, indicating a shift from short-term use of sites to a more permanent occupation; this is reflected in the creation of a more structured settlement system with various types of sites. Based on this preliminary analysis, we can propose that during the Early Holocene these upland sites become part of a dynamic network, frequently used by special task groups; small, special purpose sites, in close connection with field camps, were used as temporary operational centres, located in strategic locations and logistically related to lowland residential bases, and most likely with coastal sites.

We conclude that there were significant variations in site function and type on the uplands, suggesting a more structured settlement system. Finally, frequent use of previously marginal landscapes suggests long-term changes in regional mobility and subsistence settlement systems during the Pleistocene/Holocene transition.

References

Adams, B. 1998. *The Middle to Upper Paleolithic Transition in Central Europe. The record from the Bükk Mountain region.* British Archaeological Reports, International Series S693. Oxford, Archaeopress.

Andrefsky, W. 1998. *Lithics: Macroscopic Approaches to Analysis.* Cambridge Manuals in Archaeology. Cambridge, Cambridge University Press.

Balbo, A. L., Komšo, D. and Miracle, P. T. 2004. Geoarchaeological Survey of Polje Čepić and Part of its Hydrological Basin (Istria Peninsula, Croatia): Report on the First Field Season. *Histria Archaeologica* 33, 265–76.

Balbo, A. L., Komšo, D. and Miracle, P. T. (in press). Prehistory of the open karst: further discoveries from the geoarchaeological survey of Polje Čepić, Croatia. *Histria archaeologica* 35/2004.

Binford, L. R. 1980. Willow smoke and dogs' tails: hunter-gatherer settlement systems and archaeological site formation. *American Antiquity* 45, 4–20.

Binford, L. R. 1983. *In pursuit of the past. Decoding the Archaeological Record.* Los Angeles, University of California Press.

Boschian, G. 2003. Environment and Hunter-Gatherer Mobility in the Northern Adriatic Region. *Preistoria Alpina* 39, 91–102.

Broglio, A. and Kozłowski, S. K. 1983. Tipologia ed evoluzione delle industrie mesolitiche in Romagnano III, *Preistoria Alpina* 19, 93–148.

Fisher, L. E. 2002a. Retooling and Raw Material Economies: Technological Change in Late Glacial and Early Postglacial Southern Germany, in L. E. Fisher and B. V. Eriksen (eds.), *Lithic Raw Material Economies in Late Glacial and Early*

Postglacial Europe, 53–78. British Archaeological Reports, International Series S1093. Oxford, Archaeopress.

Fisher, L. E. 2002b. Mobility, Search Modes, and Food-Getting Technology: From Magdalenian to Early Mesolithic in the Upper Danube Basin, in B. Fitzhugh and J. Habu (eds.), *Beyond Foraging and Collecting: Evolutionary Change in Hunter-Gatherer Settlement Systems*, 157–79. New York, Kluwer Academic/Plenum Publishers.

Habu, J. 2002. Jomon Collectors and Foragers: Regional Interactions and Long-term Changes in Settlement Systems among Prehistoric Hunter-Gatherers in Japan, in B. Fitzhugh and J. Habu (eds.), *Beyond Foraging and Collecting: Evolutionary Change in Hunter-Gatherer Settlement Systems*, 53–72. New York, Kluwer Academic/Plenum Publishers.

Komšo, D. 2003. Pećine Istre – mjesta življenja od prapovijesti do srednjega vijeka. *Histria Antiqua* 11, 41–54.

Komšo, D. 2005. Jager und Sammler: Palaolithikum und Mesolithikum, in *Histria-Istra-Istrien: Ein archaologisches Juwel in der Adria*, 21–4. Monografije i katalozi 15. Pula, Archaeological Museum of Istria.

Komšo, D. and Miracle, P. T. 2005. Test Excavations in Molinarska draga (NE Istria, Croatia). *Histria archaeologica* 34, 39–60.

Miracle, P. T. 1995. *Broad-spectrum Adaptations re-examined: Hunter-Gatherer responses to Late Glacial Environmental changes in the Eastern Adriatic*. Unpublished PhD thesis, University of Michigan.

Miracle, P. T. 1996. Diversification in Epipaleolithic subsistence strategy along the eastern Adriatic coast: a simulation approach applied to zooarcheological assemblages. *Atti della Società per la Preistoria e Protostoria della Regione Friuli- Venezia Giulia* IX, 33–62.

Miracle, P. T. 2001. Feast or famine? Epipalaeolithic subsistence in the northern Adriatic basin. *Documenta Praehistorica* 18, 177–97.

Miracle, P. T. 2005. Excavations at Pupićina Cave: Preliminary Results of the 1999, 2001 and 2002 Field Seasons. *Histria archaeologica* 34, 5–38.

Miracle, P. T. and Forenbaher S. 1998. Pupićina Cave Project: brief summary of the 1998 season. *Histria Archaeologica* 29 (2000), 27–48.

Miracle, P. T., Galanidou, N. and Forenbaher, S. 2000. Pioneers in the Hills: Early Mesolithic Foragers at Šebrn Abri (Istria, Croatia). *European Journal of Archaeology* 3, 293–329.

Turk, I. (ed.) 2004. *Viktorjev Spodmol and Mala Triglavca. Contributions to understanding the Mesolithic period in Slovenia*. Opera Instituti Archaeologici Sloveniae 9. Ljubljana, Archaeological Institute of Slovenia.

45. People and their land at the southern margins of the central Po Plain in the Early Mesolithic

Federica Fontana, Maria Giovanna Cremona, Erika Ferrari, Federico Guarisco and Davide Mengoli

Along the plain belt between Bologna and Piacenza some sites have been investigated over the last twenty years during rescue excavations. Located by the ancient river banks of some main tributaries of the Po and Reno rivers, in areas periodically covered by alluvial deposits, four of these settlements (Collecchio PR, Borgo Panigale, I.N.B.S. and Casalecchio di Reno, BO) occupy small surface areas (50 to 100m²), while another (Le Mose, PC) can be considered a unique example of an Early Holocene site-complex within the Italian record known to date. The composition of the lithic assemblages and the intra-site spatial organisation – here including the presence/absence of dwelling structures – varies from site to site, raising several questions concerning their occupation pattern and function. The relationship between these sites and the numerous settlements known in the Apennine region represents another important aspect for evaluation in terms of reconstructing the regional settlement system.

Keywords: Early Holocene, alluvial deposits, wet areas, provisioning strategies, extensive site, spatial analysis, settlement system.

Introduction

The Early Mesolithic of northern Italy is mainly known from several hundred sites discovered along the Alpine chain, mainly in mountain and valley-bottom contexts (Bagolini *et al.* 1984; Broglio 1992), as well as from numerous locations identified in the Apennines (Biagi *et al.* 1980). On the contrary, the discovery of sites in the Po Plain represents an alternate and difficult challenge resulting from the significant changes the present surface has undergone following river erosion and the thick sedimentary cover; a primary indicator of this is the burial of Early Holocene living-floors under several metres of alluvial sediments deposited by the Po and Reno rivers (and their main tributaries).

Between 1983 and 2001, construction and quarrying activities carried out along the southern edge of the Emilia Romagna Plain, close to the Apennine margin, have enabled a small group of five sites to be identified. Although their number is still limited, the characteristics of these sites appear highly varied (e.g. raw material procurement strategies, lithic technological and typological features and intra-site spatial organisation), which raises a number of interesting questions concerning their role within the regional settlement system. As investigations in most of the settlements are still in progress, the results discussed in this paper should necessarily be regarded as preliminary.

The Po Plain in the Early Holocene

The Po has the largest alluvial plain in Italy, formed by the deposits of the river and its main tributaries; the Emilia Romagna Plain represents the southern part of it. Its formation began in the Early Pleistocene, after the tectonic lifting of the area that resulted in the displacement of the coastline eastwards and the coalescence of its alluvial cones, some of which still emerge on the surface, forming a continuous belt running parallel to the Apennine edge, mostly oriented NNW–SSE.

Under the present soil the alluvial deposits that form the plain are organised in the shape of a wedge that enlarges progressively, moving from the Apennine margin northwards, reaching a maximum depth of about 600m. The basal part of the sequence is composed of alluvial cone gravel deposits transported by the watercourses rising in the Alps, on the very western side of the plain, and in the Apennines, on their central-eastern side.

During the Late Glacial/Early Holocene transition, the deposition of fine-grained sediments (clays, limes and sands) started to dominate, marking an important stratigraphic change and indicating a shift to an alluvial plain environment. Several layers of deposition of these fine-grained sediments can be readily observed, and their characteristics, particularly the sandy-clayey deposits lying

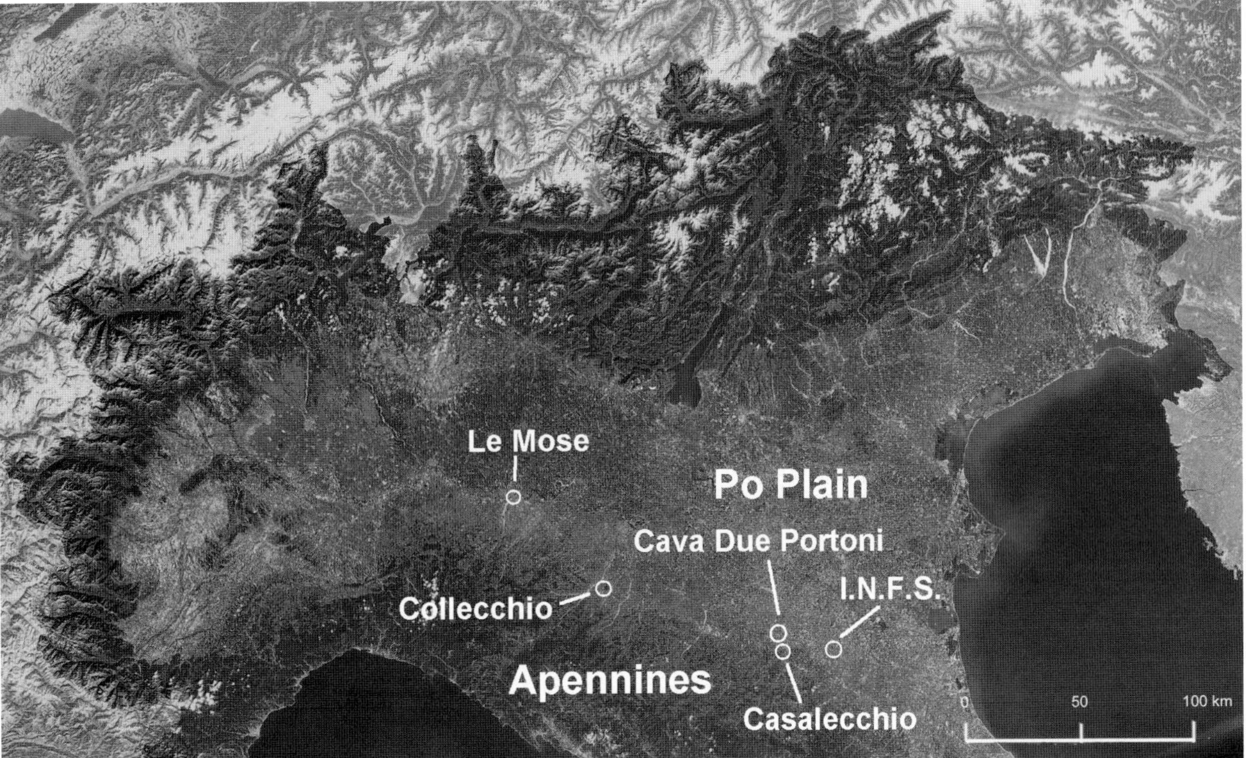

Figure 45.1. Locations of the sites of the central Po Plain mentioned in the text.

at the base, indicate the presence of repeated alternating phases characterised respectively by dry and wet conditions. The Early Holocene archaeological layers analysed in this paper lie within these soils and indicate that these areas were periodically flooded (Cremaschi 1985; Cremaschi *et al.* 1990; Cremonini 1987).

Moving from the plain to the Apennines, in the final part of the Late Glacial, the retreat of glaciers caused a reduction of erosive phenomena and brought about the progressive stability of the soils along the mountain slopes, following the expansion of arboreal vegetation. Nevertheless the study of some deposits located at high altitudes (1600–1800m asl) in the Apennine area of Reggio Emilia, shows the persistence of conditions of low vegetal cover, and of erosion phenomena, up to the beginning of the Atlantic period (Biagi *et al.* 1980).

According to a recent synthesis (Accorsi *et al.* 1999) based on the analysis of 1342 samples collected at 156 sites, the vegetal landscape of Emilia Romagna was dominated in the plain by pines (*Pinus*) – mainly Scots pine (*Pinus sylvestris*), followed by fir (*Abies*) and spruce (*Picea*), during the Preboreal. From the Boreal onwards, deciduous mixed-oak (*Quercus*) forests spread widely, often combined with lime (*Tilia*). In the Apennine area, at lower altitudes, mixed broadleaved woods always prevailed, with refuge locations for chestnut (*Castanea*) and walnut (*Juglans*) in the Preboreal and Boreal. Conifers, particularly pine (mixed with fir), was the best represented species in mountainous environments from the Preboreal to the Atlantic.

Geographic and stratigraphic position of the sites

Situated between the cities of Bologna and Piacenza, all the sites lie in similar topographic and stratigraphic positions, in areas where the Apennine rivers reach the plain, within 15km distance of the Apennine foothills (Figure 45.1).

Three sites are situated in the area of Bologna (I.N.F.S., Casalecchio di Reno and Cava Due Portoni). Another is located in the area of Parma (Collecchio), and the last one further west, in the province of Piacenza (Le Mose). Two sites were excavated in the 1980s. Cava Due Portoni was explored between 1983 and 1984 under the direction of the Soprintendenza per i Beni Archeologici of Emilia Romagna (Cremaschi *et al.* 1990), and I.N.F.S. (41m asl), between 1986 and 1987, by the University of Ferrara (Prof. A. Guerreschi) and the Museum of Prehistory Luigi Donini at San Lazzaro di Savena (Bologna) (Farabegoli *et al.* 1994).

Collecchio (situated at an altitude of 106m asl) and Le Mose were excavated (respectively from 1992 to 1995 and 2000 to 2005) by the Soprintendenza per i Beni Archeologici of Emilia Romagna, under the direction of Dr Maria Bernabò Brea. The site of Casalecchio di Reno (situated at 59m asl) was explored in 1998 and 1999 by the Soprintendenza per i Beni Archeologici of Emilia Romagna, under the direction of Dr Giuliana Steffé.

All the sites, except I.N.F.S., were investigated during rescue excavations, herefore it was only possible to record the spatial coordinates of single artefacts at I.N.F.S. At all the sites the fieldwork included water-screening the soil (mesh width 2mm) employing a fixed grid of 1/4 or 1/9m^2.

Unfortunately at Le Mose, which extended over a much wider surface area, no grid was used and most finds were collected only according to the artefact units.

The sites located in the Bologna region have surface areas that vary between approximately 30m^2 at I.N.F.S. (where the Mesolithic occupation layer was partially destroyed by the erosion activities of a palaeo-channel), and 80m^2 at Cava Due Portoni (Borgo Panigale), where it was not possible to explore the whole archaeological deposit. We may assume, therefore, that all the sites investigated extend over a greater surface area than was actually explored.

The sites lie at different depths from present-day soil levels: from about 70cm at I.N.F.S, to 6m at Cava Due Portoni. From a stratigraphical viewpoint they are all situated within Early Holocene alluvial layers, composed of thin clayey-silty and sandy deposits. These overlie the Pleistocene alluvial fan gravel sediments: the result of the activities of the River Reno and its tributaries, in the proximity of which the sites are located. During the Early Holocene, alternating erosion and sedimentation activities occurred in these areas, which were periodically flooded to a greater or lesser extent, according to the sites' distance from the main river-courses and the presence of secondary streams (Cremaschi *et al.* 1990; Farabegoli *et al.* 1994).

The site of Collecchio is situated close to the Apennine margin, directly where the River Taro reaches the Po Plain. The archaeological deposit lies within a soil that formed during a period characterised by a wet climate and a marked seasonality ('vertisol', Boreal period?), overlaying a gravely layer which documents the presence of an alluvial fan dating back to the Late Pleistocene/Early Holocene. The site extends over a surface area of approximately 50m^2 and was excavated using a grid of 1/9m^2. The finds recovered consisted almost exclusively of lithic artefacts and a less consistent collection of very fragmented ecofacts (faunal remains and charcoals).

In the archaeological area of Le Mose, covering a total extent of around 20,000m^2, several sites dating back to different periods (from the Early Holocene to Roman) were explored. The area lies about 3km from the River Nure and about 4km from the Po river-course. Although it is located at a distance of approximately 15km from the Apennine foothills, its stratigraphical position can be roughly compared to that of the other investigated sites, but with some peculiarities.

Over the whole area sedimentary alluvial deposits reach a total depth of about 150–200m. The geological units situated at the top of the series are composed of sands, clays and limestone, deposited by palaeo-channels and intercalated by Holocene soils (entisoils and inceptisoils). In the areas that are slightly in relief, the identification of coarser surface deposits (slightly stratified gravels and gravely sands with plain disposition) indicates the presence of Late Pleistocene alluvial fans which appear covered in part by successive gravely sediments. The superficial areas of the largest hills have remained substantially stable up to the present and the frequent appearance, on their summits, of horizons characterised by the presence of clasts with red patinas and of brown-red coarse sands, indicates the development of soil formation phases originating in the Atlantic period. In a lateral position to these coarse deposits is a series of large depressions, the formation of which dates back to the Pleistocene, and in which alluvial sediments are progressively replaced by marshy deposits with a lime-clayey texture that vary in peat content (Cita *et al.* 1999; Cremaschi 1987).

Figure 45.2. Pedo-stratigraphical units identified at the site of Le Mose.

Over the whole area excavations have revealed several Pleistocene gravely fans, the largest of which ran N–S and was more than 100m wide. Its presence has conditioned the hydrography and the general morphology of the area, preventing the divergence of streams lacking the power to penetrate it and forcing them to run parallel to the gravely fan or hill itself, thus bringing about the formation of large depressions. Two marshy soils were thus identified in the large depression located on the east side of this wide gravely fan or hill. The soil lying closest to the surface, at a depth of between -1.0 and -2.5m, was characterised by a slightly undulating surface. It was between 20–60cm thick and of a clayey texture (with lime and a scarce sand content), very compact, and brown-black/dark in colour (Figure 45.2). This soil, subsequently scored by river erosion and covered with channelling and deep alluvial sandy deposits, contained a rich Mesolithic record, within which at least 27 lithic artefact concentrations could be identified, varying in size from a minimum of 4m^2 to a maximum of 30m^2. Le Mose can thus be considered as the first extensive Early Mesolithic settlement or site-complex in Italy.

Two radiometric dates are available for this site, ranging between 8250±50 BP, 7460-7130 cal BC, Poz-13343 (Stratigraphic Unit 507-Locus 7) and 9220±50 BP, 8560–8300 cal BC, Poz-13344 (Stratigraphic Unit 507, Pl. 19 S), and testifying that this area was occupied over a long period of more than 1000 years, covering almost the whole Sauveterrian sequence.

No radiocarbon datings are available for the other sites, but the results – in some cases still at a preliminary stage – of techno-typological studies carried out on lithic assemblages allow them to be referred to the Sauveterrian complex (i.e. Early Mesolithic).

The lithic assemblages

Regarding the sites in the Bologna area, the lithic assemblages are composed respectively of a total of approximately 3400 lithic artefacts at I.N.F.S., about 1500 at Casalecchio and Borgo Panigale (Cava Due Portoni). At all the sites the composition of lithic raw materials appears similar and is dominated by two lithological groups. The first is represented by dull siliceous dark-coloured rocks present in large and irregular boulders (larger than 10cm), and locally known as 'ftanite'. The second consists of smaller, regular-sized marine flint pebbles. A detailed study carried out at the I.N.F.S. site indicates that ftanite was collected along the main riverbeds, whereas flint-provisioning areas can be traced within the marine deposits of Pliocene and Calabrian age, situated along the hill belt of the Bologna Apennine (Farabegoli *et al.* 1994; Fontana and Nenzioni 1995). Only at Cava Due Portoni were other groups, such as jasper, and a few artefacts obtained from non-local flints, in evidence.

In addition, the reconstruction of reduction strategies indicates that the three sites share some common features, probably also as a consequence of the use of the same raw materials. The technological study of the lithic assemblages shows that the main two raw materials – flint and ftanite – were exploited according to different reduction strategies and with different objectives. Flint pebbles were intensively knapped to produce small-sized bladelets of irregular shape, mainly for the manufacture of microliths, whereas ftanite was mostly employed for the production of large laminar flake blanks that were transformed into larger tools, especially side-scrapers and backed-knives (Figure 45.3). Nonetheless some differences between the three assemblages have also been highlighted. At I.N.F.S. the use of the microburin technique for the fragmentation of blanks is well documented, whereas microburins are totally absent at Casalecchio. The assemblage from I.N.F.S. also shows a strong specialisation in the preparation of some distinct categories of microliths (Sauveterrian points and crescents and the absence of triangles), while the composition of

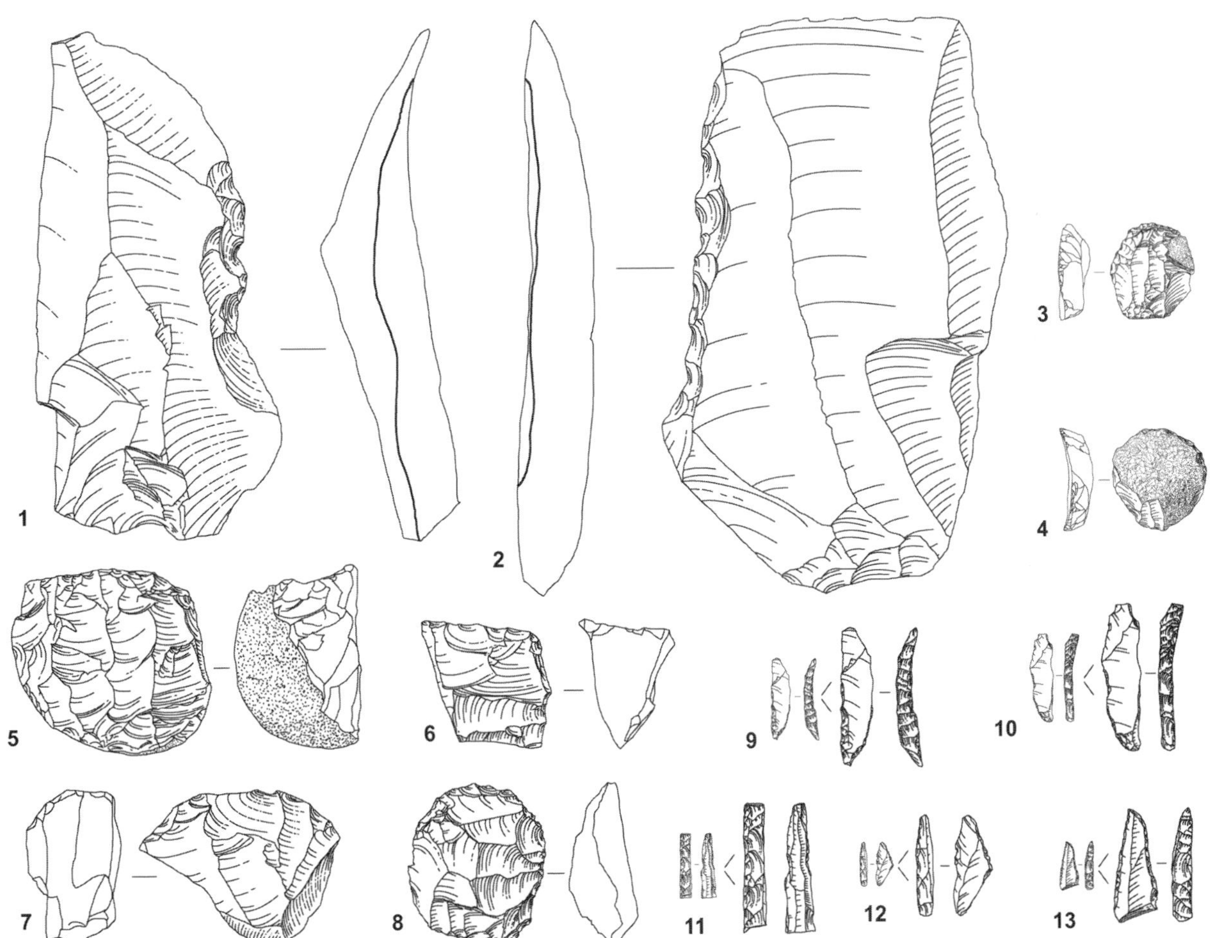

Figure 45.3. Lithic artefacts from the site of Casalecchio: 1) denticulate (ftanite); 2) scraper (ftanite); 3–4) end-scrapers (flint); 5–8) cores (flint); 9–13) microliths (flint). (Drawings: D. Mengoli).

retouched lithic artefacts at the other two sites appears more varied.

The study of the lithic assemblage from Collecchio is still in progress and no evaluation of the total range of artefacts collected is yet available. Nevertheless the first results of the study indicate that the composition of raw materials varies considerably from that of the Bologna area, showing a marked connection with the surrounding territory, as documented by the dominance of locally available rocks. Smaller flint pebbles and nodules are exploited as well as red jasper and siltstone pebbles. The high percentage of jasper is due to the presence of an important outcrop in the Parma Apennine, and this rock was probably collected in large quantities also along the Nure riverbeds. The same dichotomy in the technical system adopted at the sites around Bologna appears at Collecchio, where the role of ftanite for the production of large laminar flakes seems to be replaced by the use of siltstone river pebbles, probably collected along the watercourses running in the vicinity of the site, although this material appears to be characterised by a much lower suitability for knapping than ftanite.

Finally, at Le Mose all the excavated *loci* mainly consist of stone artefacts, ranging from 13 finds to over 1000 at the larger sites. Technological analyses carried out on a total of about 7000 finds, suggest an attribution of the whole series of identified *loci* to the Sauveterrian complex. Lithic raw materials used for artefact manufacture appear highly differentiated, including flint, jasper, ftanite and other lithological groups, among which flint always dominates. Flint-provisioning strategies vary significantly from those recorded at the sites in the areas of Bologna and Parma, because of the different geological morphology of the territory where the site is located. Preliminary observations lead us to conclude that the flint origins can be traced to the mid- and upper-Jurassic formations located in the central Trebbia valley, about 30km from the site of Le Mose, even if we cannot exclude that they could also be collected along the local riverbeds. The primary deposits contain abundant quantities of flint nodules of highly variable quality, and the presence of such flint outcrops represents a real exception within the northern Apennine geological context of Emilia. We can even suppose that the high redundancy of sites identified in this area, at least in part, might be connected to the abundance of lithic raw materials available in this territory.

Even the lithic reduction sequences recognised at Le Mose vary considerably from those documented in the other deposits, in strict relation to the morphology of the original cores used (mostly nodules of an irregular shape instead of regular flint pebbles). No reduction sequence intended for the production of large laminar flakes (as documented at the sites in the Bologna and Parma regions) has been highlighted.

Dwelling structures and spatial organisation of the sites

Data concerning the internal organisation of the sites appear severely biased, within all the deposits, by the poor state of preservation of the organic materials and dwelling structures: a direct consequence of soil acidity. At all the sites the archaeological remains are thus dominated by lithic artefacts, while organic materials are only represented by a few charcoals and some poorly-preserved bone remains, mostly attributable, at the sites where species identification was carried out, to animals adapted to wooded environments (wild boar (*Sus scofa*), roe deer (*Capreolus capreolus*)).

The only example of an evident structural feature was found at Cava Due Portoni: a shallow depression of an irregular elliptical shape, 230cm wide and 135cm long, filled in with a sandy-reddish sediment and containing charcoals. It was interpreted as the base of a hearth-pit. Several stones were also found out of context during the excavation activities and they were attributed to the possible former presence of other (destroyed) structures (Cremaschi *et al.* 1990).

At I.N.F.S. and Casalecchio, evaluation of the internal organisation of the settlements was carried out by analysing the spatial distribution of artefacts and ecofacts. At I.N.F.S. the spatial plotting of burned artefacts and carbonised organic residues has allowed the identification of a surface-hearth. Flint and ftanite artefacts are scattered liberally, showing different distribution patterns (Farabegoli *et al.* 1994). At Casalecchio two small concentrations of burned artefacts and bones, possibly corresponding to two separated surface-hearths, were recognized. Even in this deposit the spatial distributions of the flint and ftanite assemblage, and of the bone remains, seem to suggest the presence of traces of the possible functional organisation of a living-floor.

Finally, at Le Mose, over the vast area characterised by the presence of the Mesolithic occupation evidence, several features of an uncertain origin (pits, charcoal concentrations and holes) were identified, with no apparent association with the artefacts' *loci* (Bernabò Brea *et al.* 1998).

Several holes (of possible post-hole dimensions: diameter 20–30cm, depth 10–20cm) were recognised on the surface of the marshy soil. In five examples they appeared organised either in groups or along curvilinear alignments, thus suggesting the presence of former dwellings. In the same soil thirty large pits of a circular shape (diameters 50–250cm, depths 50–150cm) were also recognised. Only in five cases were single artefacts collected inside them. Even if no apparent relationship exists between these pits and the artefacts *loci*, their shape and distribution seems to suggest an anthropic origin. The hypothesis that they might be the remains of tree stumps should be excluded because of the identification of such anomalies within the same area and their different forms. To understand the meaning of these features, most have been intensively sampled for palaeo-environmental analyses but no definitive conclusions are yet available.

In addition, the first results of the spatial analyses carried out at the 27 identified *loci* show the occurrence (within most) of several burnt artefacts, indicating the presence of former fireplaces. Unfortunately no intra-site distribution sampling to identify the number and outline of these fireplaces is possible because of the lack of spatial data within the single units. High variations in artefact density and assemblage composition have also been observed. Although refittings and technological studies are still in progress, flint knapping seems to have represented a major activity in most *loci* but the assemblage typology indicates at the biggest sites a broad spectrum of activities, and at the smallest the occurrence of specialised undertakings.

Conclusions

The accidental identification of five Sauveterrian sites in the higher and middle areas of the Emilia Romagna Plain represents an exceptional event due to the thick Holocene sedimentary cover that characterizes this part of the territory. Despite the lack of ideal preservation conditions, these sites add new data to the reconstruction of the settlement pattern of this area during the ancient Holocene, which was, until a few years ago, almost exclusively represented by the sites identified along the Apennine at different altitudes – between a few hundred and 1700m asl. Some remarks can thus be drawn:

1) As previously mentioned, the sites located in the plain lie in alluvial areas that are periodically flooded and are close to marshy environments. These areas correspond to the presence of ecological niches with a high primary productivity of both vegetal resources and permanent, as well as migratory, animals (fish, molluscs, reptiles, amphibians, mammalians and birds) (Biagi *et al.* 1980; Cremaschi 1985). The alternating rhythm of wet and dry seasons that characterises these territories suggests that they were probably only occupied during some specific periods of the year, possibly between the end of the wet and the beginning of the dry season. Their richness in ecological terms is also confirmed (if not by the poorly preserved organic remains from the sites) by the almost uninterrupted repeated occupation of these areas from the Sauveterrian to the present. Moreover, in the specific case of Le Mose, it is also well documented by a real abundance of locations datable to the Early Holocene itself, a fact that appears unique in the Italian perspective of this period, making this site the first extensive Sauveterrian settlement of the whole peninsula.
2) Analyses of lithic raw materials indicates, at all sites, the use of local rocks (with a very few exceptions) that were collected both along the riverbeds of the streams running close to the sites and in the primary outcrops situated along the Apennines (with a considerable variability according to locally available resources between the areas of Bologna, Parma and Piacenza). Such behaviour seems to suggest a strong connection between the different human social groups settled in the area and the various hydrographic systems rising in the Apennines; this is further confirmed by the lithological composition of the assemblages found in the locations recognised along the Apennines, especially at high altitudes. These are mainly composed of raw materials outcropping at lower altitudes within the same river basin over which the sites are located (e.g. flint pebbles from the Pliocene and Calabrian marine deposits of the Bologna Apennine hills, at the sites of Bologna and Modena Apennine and jasper in the Parma area, etc.), as well as, when present, by locally available rocks (Ferrari *et al.* 1998; Ghiretti and Guerreschi 1988).
3) Although the plain sites are located in similar environments, an inter-site variability has been observed between them, both in terms of lithic assemblages (reduction sequences and typological composition, e.g. highly specialised sites such as I.N.F.S. and sites characterised by a wider range of tools, referring to subsistence and maintenance activities – Cava Due Portoni), and intra-site organisation (sites with the presence of '*structures évidentes*' that were probably repeatedly occupied – Cava Due Portoni – and short-term specialised locations – I.N.F.S.). A common aspect shared by most sites (except the smallest ones at Le Mose) is represented by the importance of blanks production and the organisation of subsistence and specialised activities around one or more fireplaces.

We believe that the available data does not yet allow us to propose, with sufficient certainty, a definite occupation pattern for the Sauveterrian groups that settled in the territory between the northern Apennine and the Emilia Romagna Plain, even if intra-site variability seems to suggest the presence of differentiated typologies of settlements. Yet, it seems possible to make inferences concerning group mobility strategies that appear to be strictly connected to the courses represented by the main streams rising in the Apennines, thus permitting exploitation, in the course of the year, of the natural resources offered by the different ecosystems encountered, particularly the high plain with its wet environments and the highlands, which, during the summer season, represented favourable areas both for hunting and the gathering of specific animal and vegetal species. Probably even the low altitudes must have played a considerable role not only in relation to raw material provisioning (presence of flint and jasper outcrops) but also as settlement points (stable zones, winter occupation?), and their importance is probably underestimated due to the scarcity of finds in these areas.

It is to be hoped that further contributions towards a reconstruction of the wider perspective will evolve from this present research (i.e. technological and spatial analyses in progress, identification of new sites, radiocarbon datings), as well from the application of new approaches of study (e.g. functional analyses, seasonality, etc.).

Acknowledgements

This work is part of a project on the Early Holocene occupation patterns of Emilia Romagna coordinated by Federica Fontana and Maria Giovanna Cremona. The geographic and stratigraphic framework has been developed by F. Guarisco, F. Fontana and D. Mengoli. The study of lithic assemblages has been carried out by F. Fontana, M. G. Cremona and E. Ferrari, and the intra-site spatial distribution by F. Fontana. We would like to thank Dr Maria Bernabò Brea and Dr Giuliana Steffé for granting access to materials and the necessary documentation.

References

Accorsi, C. A., Bandini Mazzanti, M., Forlani, L., Mercuri, A. M. and Trevisan Grandi, G. 1999. An overview of Holocene pollen flora/vegetation of the Emilia Romagna region – Northern Italy. *Archivio Geobotanico, University of Pavia* 5 (1–2), 3–27.

Bagolini, B., Broglio, A. and Lunz, R. 1984. Le Mésolithique des Dolomites. *Preistoria Alpina* 19, 15–36.

Bernabò Brea, M., Colombi, N., Grassi, G., Negrino, F., Ottomano, C., Strada, N. and Tramontano, A. 1998. Piacenza, loc. Le Mose, lotto IKEA. *Archeologia dell'Emilia – Romagna* II–2, 11–15.

Biagi, P., Castelletti, L., Cremaschi, M., Sala, B. and Tozzi C. 1980. Popolazione e territori nell'Appennino tosco-emiliano e nel tratto centrale del bacino del Po tra IX e V millennio. *Emilia Preromana* VIII, 14–36.

Broglio, A. 1992. Mountain sites in the context of the north-east Italian Upper Palaeolithic and Mesolithic. *Preistoria Alpina* 28 (1), 293–310.

Cita, M. B., Gelati, R. and Grignanin, A. (eds.) 1999. *Guide Geologiche Regionali: Appennino Ligure – Emiliano*. Milan, BE-MA Editrice.

Cremaschi, M. 1985. Situazione stratigrafica e paleombientale del Mesolitico nel territorio Bolognese, in F. Lenzi, G. Nenzioni and C. Peretto (eds.), *Materiali e documenti per un museo della preistoria. San Lazzaro di Savena e il suo territorio*, 195–8. San Lazzaro di Savena, Museo Archeologico Luigi Donini.

Cremaschi, M. 1987. *Paleosols and vetusols in the central Po Plain (Northern Italy). A study in quaternary geology and soil development*. Milan, Unicopli.

Cremaschi, M., Guerreschi, A. and Steffé G. 1990. Il sito mesolitico di Cava Due Portoni a Borgo Panigale (Bologna), in M. Iodice (ed.), *Borgo Panigale. Da villaggio mesolitico a quartiere cittadino*, 11–20. Bologna, Editografica Rastignano.

Cremonini, S. 1987. Alcuni problemi e idee di geologia del recente relativi all'alta pianura bolognese. La stratigrafia del tribunale nuovo di Bologna. *Studi e Documenti di Archeologia* III, 49–60.

Farabegoli, E., Fontana, F., Guerreschi, A. and Nenzioni G. 1994. Il sito mesolitico dell'I.N.F.S. di Colunga (Ozzano Emilia, Bologna). *Bullettino di Paletnologia Italiana* 85, 73–133.

Ferrari, A., Fontana, F., Pessina, A., Steffé, G. and Vicentini, P. 1998. Provenienza e circolazione delle rocce silicee scheggiate fra Mesolitico ed Età del rame in Emilia centro-orientale, Romagna e Friuli. *Archeologia dell'Emilia Romagna* II (1), 13–19.

Ghiretti, A. and Guerreschi, A. 1988. Il Mesolitico nelle valli di Taro e Ceno. *Preistoria Alpina* 24, 69–102.

46. A view from the edges: the Mesolithic settlement of the interior areas of the Iberian Peninsula reconsidered

Pablo Arias, Enrique Cerrillo-Cuenca, Esteban Álvarez-Fernández, Eloy Gómez-Pellón and Antonio González Cordero

The archaeological data that might be related to Mesolithic settlement in interior Iberia are discussed. The ethnographic evidence on empty interior areas close to coastal hunter-gatherer settlements is also considered. It is concluded that there is a reasonable probability for common Mesolithic settlement in the interior regions of the Peninsula.

Keywords: Spain, Portugal, hunter-gatherers, land resources.

Introduction

As in many other parts of Europe, Mesolithic settlement of the Iberian Peninsula is concentrated along the coastal areas. Most archaeological evidence for this period comes from central and southern Portugal, Cantabrian Spain, and some parts of the Mediterranean coastal regions (Juan and Martí 2002). However, it has not been clearly established whether this is a result of the absence of regular hunter-gatherer activity in interior areas, or rather an artefact of biases in research. This question is fairly important, and not only for a better understanding of the last societies of European hunter-gatherers, but also for its implications in the study of the transition to the Neolithic. In fact, the supposed unpopulated status of the interior areas of the Peninsula during the first half of the Holocene has been one of the main bases for the invasionist explanations of the neolithisation of interior Iberia (Estremera 2003; Kunst and Rojo 1999). Yet, some authors have considered the possibility of the existence of a Mesolithic settlement playing a relevant role in the introduction of agriculture into the Iberian interior (Delibes and Fernández Manzano 2000; Rubio and Blasco 1988–9; Rubio 2002). The aim of this paper is to discuss the archaeological data that might be related to Mesolithic settlement in interior Iberia, and to evaluate the most probable scenario with the current evidence, including not only the archaeological information, but also ethnohistorical data.

Before broaching the main issue, we should discuss a geographical question: What do we mean by 'interior'? Though this might seem an easy question, it is in no way irrelevant. We would all agree that Madrid is in the interior of the Iberian Peninsula, and that Lisbon is in a coastal region. But, where do we put the border? Moreover, for Spanish and Portuguese scholars, the issue is clearly contaminated by a subjective perception of national geography, related to political factors. Thus, frequently the archaeological discussions on the colonization of interior Iberia tend to exclude any site from contemporary political regions that do have coast, despite the evidence that some of those regions are rather large, and some parts of them are really distant from the shore. For instance, a site such as Cueva del Nacimiento, in the Andalusian province of Jaén (Figure 46.1), is not usually considered. That is probably due to the fact that the region of Andalusia (which has a surface similar to medium-sized European countries such as Austria) has a long coast. However this particular site is located more than 100km from the Mediterranean shore, in the mountains of Cazorla. In fact, the travel time from Nacimiento to the coast is probably more than double that for some sites in the northern *Meseta* that are included among the interior sites, because they are now located in the currently non-coastal region of Castile. However, it is clear that the exploitation of coastal resources was not among the usual activities of the people who were living at Cueva del Nacimiento, at least while they were occupying that particular settlement.

The criteria used in this paper has been to consider as interior sites those that are located in places which require more than twelve hours of walking to reach the coast (around 50km), that is settlements from which it would be impossible to go to the coast and return in less than two days.

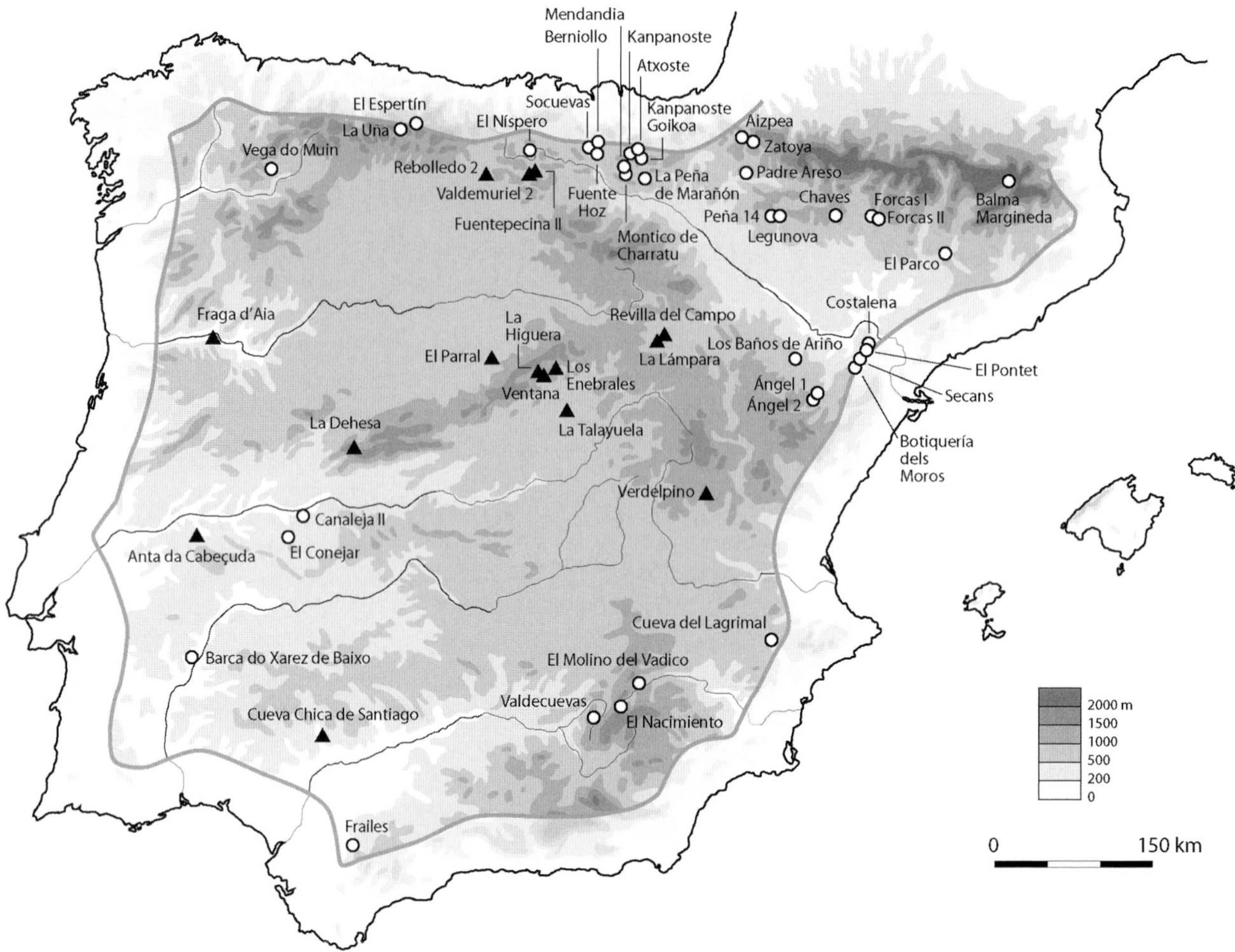

Figure 46.1. Map of interior sites where indices of Holocene hunter-gatherer activity are available. The line indicates 50km from the current coast. Triangles correspond to sites that have provided dubious or indirect evidence.

The archaeological evidence

So far, the archaeological evidence for the first half of the Holocene is very scarce. This has frequently been interpreted as evidence of the lack of human activity. However that is a dangerous inference in relation to this case. It is appropriate to remember that, from a logical point of view, the absence of evidence is not evidence of absence. Furthermore, in this case, the characteristic argument of researchers who defend the 'deserted' *Meseta* model, i.e. the negative results of exploration, is for many areas relatively weak. In most regions of interior Iberia there has never been a specific program of archaeological exploration focused specifically on the resolution of this problem (as there has been for the Upper Palaeolithic; see Cacho 1999). And when there has been, the results have often been positive. This is indeed the case of the Upper Ebro valley, in the southern part of the Basque country, where a systematic archaeological survey, including stratigraphic test pits, has resulted in the discovery of an ample number of Mesolithic sites (see below).

On the other hand, the possibilities of a casual occurrence of sites, or of finding them during general projects of archaeological survey are fairly low in this case: the interior Mesolithic has a serious problem of archaeological visibility. Lacking some kinds of evidence that are related to the seaside, such as the presence of shell middens, there are no clear criteria to assign unstratified material to this period. The most characteristic archaeological items, such as microliths, can also be attributed to other periods, such as the Neolithic. We can try to imagine, for instance, what we would know about the Cantabrian Mesolithic if there were no shell middens in that region. Equally, we could wonder what view we would have on the Upper Palaeolithic in the interior if we lacked some evident *fossil directeurs*, such as the Solutrean points, or if we did not know the open-air rock art. In fact, the history of the research in interior Iberia shows us the risks of the abuse of this kind of criteria. A little over fifteen years ago, the same arguments currently used to question the interior Mesolithic were employed to deny the existence of a Neolithic before the construction of megaliths (e.g. Kalb 1989), which is now clearly demonstrated.

In addition, although certainly scarce, there are indeed some signs that indicate the presence of hunter-gatherers in the area. Some of them may be defined as direct evidence of the activity of those societies; others just as indirect indices. The highest density of direct evidence is located in the northern third of the Peninsula, mainly on the southern slopes of the Cantabrian mountain range and the Pyrenees, and in the Ebro valley – the only areas of interior Iberia where a systematic survey has been conducted.

On the interior side of the Cantabrian mountains, recent research conducted by the University of León has included the excavation of two Mesolithic cave sites: La Uña, corresponding to the Early Mesolithic (Azilian), and El Espertín, dated to the first half of the seventh millennium cal BC (Gif-10053: 7790±120 BP; 7030–6440 cal BC) (Bernaldo de Quirós *et al.* 1997; Neira 1997). Both sites have provided strong evidence that links them with the Cantabrian Mesolithic, but they are too far away to have permitted regular contact with the coast. Moreover, the archaeological evidence from the northern slope of the same mountain range shows that it was possible for Holocene foragers of the area to live on non-coastal resources. This is what is suggested by the palaeodietary information obtained for a well-documented inland site in Asturias: Cueva de los Canes. The diet of its inhabitants appears to have come exclusively from terrestrial resources, contrasting with the stable isotope values obtained for some contemporary sites of the coastal Mesolithic (the so-called Asturian shell middens), which point to a diet in which the marine component was the dominant source of proteins (Arias 2005–6).

Moving east, to the Castilian province of Burgos, evidence of a Mesolithic occupation has been found at El Níspero, a cave site located in a rock canyon on the left bank area of the river Ebro. The site was excavated in the 1980s by S. Corchón, who identified a sequence of six layers, three of them with archaeological remains. The earliest one (layer VI) is attributed to the early Mesolithic (it is defined as 'Aziloid'), whereas layers V and IV are assigned to a 'Middle Epipalaeolithic' on both typological and palaeoecological grounds (Corchón 1988–9). The industry recovered in the latter was primarily backed bladelets, notches, denticulates and splintered pieces, including two triangles (2.89%). Faunal remains are predominantly rabbit (*Oryctolagus cuniculus*), but some remains of red deer (*Cervus elaphus*) and horse (*Equus caballus*) were also found. Palynological evidence seems to confirm the dating of layers IV and V to the Holocene. All this evidence leads Corchón (1988–9) to propose a tentative chronology in the second half of the eighth millennium cal BC (last third of the ninth millennium BP).

One of the densest concentrations of Mesolithic sites is located in Alava, the southern province of the Basque country. This has provided strong evidence of the presence of human groups from the Early (Berniollo) to the Late Mesolithic. Several rock-shelters, many of them radiocarbon dated to the seventh and sixth millennia BC, have provided assemblages comparable with the geometric Mesolithic of Mediterranean Spain: Fuente Hoz, Socuevas, Mendandia, Atxoste, La Peña de Marañón, Kanpanoste Goikoa, and Kanpanoste (Alday 2002; 2005).

The Alava concentration extends towards the southern slopes of the Pyrenees, where we can highlight some very important sequences that cover all (or at least most of) the first half of the Holocene: the cave site of Zatoya in Navarre (Barandiarán and Cava 1989a), the rock-shelters of Las Forcas I and II (Utrilla and Mazo 1997) and Peña 14 (Montes 2005) in Aragon, Balma Margineda in Andorra (Guilaine and Martzluff 1995), and El Parco in Catalonia (Mangado *et al.* 2002). Other sites contain evidence for a particular part of the Holocene: Chaves and El Parco for the early Mesolithic, Legunova for the eigth millennium, and Aizpea, El Parco, Montico de Charratu and Padre Areso for the Late Mesolithic (see Utrilla 2002 and Utrilla and Rodanés 2004 for a general view on the Mesolithic and Neolithic in the Ebro valley). Among the latter we include some sixth millennium contexts that have been usually classified as Neolithic because of the presence of pottery (Aizpea layer b, and Zatoya layer I), but which have provided no evidence of agriculture or stock herding (see Arias 2007 for further comments).

It must be stressed that many of the Alava and western Pyrenees sites have yielded Mediterranean mollusc shells (Álvarez 2003; 2006). It is much more likely that these items arrived in this area through networks of interchange amongst hunter-gatherers rather than by direct transport. Thus, this suggests that between the western Pyrenees and the Mediterranean coast there was a certain density, albeit low, of Mesolithic groups. As a matter of fact, sixteen Mesolithic sites in the Ebro valley (corresponding to all the subperiods: Microlaminar, Macrolithic and Geometric Mesolithic) have evidence of Mediterranean shells so far (Álvarez 2006).

Going south, to the other side of the Ebro, there is an important nucleus of Mesolithic settlement which is just within the limits of distance that we have proposed: the Lower Aragon rock-shelters, in the provinces of Teruel and Zaragoza, including the sites of Botiquería dels Moros (Barandiarán 1978), Costalena (Barandiarán and Cava 1989b), El Pontet (Mazo and Montes 1992) and Els Secans (Rodanés *et al.* 1996). Although some of them seem to have been occupied somewhat earlier (probably in the eighth millennium cal BC: layers d of Costalena and i and g of El Pontet), most of the evidence for this area corresponds to the late Mesolithic, characterized by geometric microliths.

Clear evidence for a Late Mesolithic settlement in a more interior location in the Ebro valley is provided by the rock-shelter sites of Los Baños (Utrilla and Rodanés 2004) and Ángel 1 and 2 (Utrilla *et al.* 2003).

Evidence of Mesolithic settlement in the central plateau of Spain (the *Meseta*) is scarce and very often problematic. Some sites which lack a precise chronology have been attributed to the Mesolithic, mainly on typological grounds, but also from stratigraphic observations (Jiménez 2008). That is the case of La Higuera cave (Barrio and Rubio 2002), where some possible evidence of an earlier occupation below Neolithic layers (providing backed bladelets and engraved schist plaques) has been tentatively attributed to the Mesolithic (Jiménez 2001, 43). More problematic are several poorly contextualized sites, generally surface surveys, such as El Parral (Jiménez 2001), Los Enebrales (Jimémez 1998), La Talayuela (Hernando 1999, 235) and some sites in the Sorbe valley (Pastor 1999). Other sites lack a precise chronology, yet many reveal lithic assemblages that may be attributed to the late Palaeolithic, although an early Mesolithic chronology (Azilian) cannot be excluded. This also occurs at such sites as La Dehesa, in Salamanca (Fabián 1997) or La Ventana, in Madrid (Jiménez and Sánchez 2004).

However, in Extremadura there are two recently studied archaeological sites that can be ascribed to Holocene hunter-gatherers without any doubt: El Conejar and Canaleja II. El Conejar, near Cáceres, is a poorly preserved site where, apart from evidence of a Neolithic settlement (Cerrillo 1999), a breccia with some Mesolithic lithics (choppers, chopping-tools, bipolar quartzite cores) has been dated to the last third of the eighth millennium cal BC (Beta-154490: 8220±40 BP; Beta-154491: 8220±40 BP; 7350–7080 cal BC) (Carbonell 2003). An engraved schist plaque with linear motives might be attributed to the Mesolithic context.

Recent research at Canaleja gorge, a valley close to the River Tagus in Cáceres province, has documented several sites in small rock-shelters, most of them corresponding to the Neolithic or later periods. However, at least one of them, Canaleja II, can be ascribed to the Mesolithic. In this site, a short-term occupation characterized by a hearth and some lithic artefacts (geometric microliths, flint cores) has been identified. A radiocarbon date obtained from charcoal from the hearth has placed this context in the second third of the eighth millennium cal BC (Beta-214600: 8740±40 BP; 7770–7580 cal BC) (unpublished information from the 2005 excavations conducted by E. Cerrillo and A. González Cordero).

There is also some indirect evidence provided by radiocarbon determinations that might be related to Holocene hunter-gatherer human activity in the *Meseta*. That is the case for the sites of La Lámpara and Revilla del Campo, where several dates from the ninth to the early the sixth millennium cal BC have been obtained for pine charcoal collected in pits together with Neolithic pottery (Rojo *et al.* 2008). As it seems unlikely that the charcoal is coeval with the Neolithic structures (well dated to the late sixth millennium by the epicardial pottery, direct evidence of human activity, such as the grave at La Lámpara, and the radiocarbon dates obtained from samples of bone or cereal), those determinations might testify to pre-Neolithic activity that was disturbed by the first farmers.

In fact, the existence of hunter-gatherers in the *Meseta* would help to explain some peculiarities of the first Neolithic in the region, such as the presence of 'mixed' traits, in a more satisfactory way than a purely colonialist model. Numerous authors have stressed that the material culture of the 'interior Neolithic' includes features which suggest contacts with the region of Valencia, while others indicate the Andalusian Neolithic or even the Portuguese (Estremera 2003). It is easier to justify such evidence via the existence of groups that became Neolithic through contacts with small groups of colonists from different sources, or through mere acculturation, than to defend the colonisation of a virgin territory by populations arriving from outside, which should result in Neolithic assemblages showing a closer resemblance to those from their region of origin.

Similar evidence has been provided by some palaeosols covered by megalithic tombs, where older lithic tools have been recovered, or charcoal has been dated to pre-Neolithic chronologies, suggesting the possibility of previous, Mesolithic, settlement in those areas. That is the case for the sites of Anta da Cabeçuda (Oliveira 1997), in Portugal, and Fuentepecina II, Valdemuriel 2 and Rebolledo 2 in Castile (Delibes and Rojo 1997).

Not far from the limits of the *Meseta*, in the upper Júcar valley, is the debated site of Verdelpino, near Cuenca, where the existence of a very old, pre-cardial Neolithic was proposed as the result of the presence of nineteen pottery sherds in a layer dated to the last third of the eighth millennium cal BC, or the first half of the seventh (CSIC-153B: 7950±150 BP; 7300–6480 cal BC) (Fernández-Miranda and Moure 1975; Moure and Fernández-Miranda 1977). Many scholars have been rather sceptical about the reliability of the data from this site, and it has been proposed that the ceramics might be an intrusion from the upper layers of the cave (Fortea and Martí 1984–5); yet, a recent revision of the site (Rasilla *et al.* 1996) shows that there is no evidence of disturbance. However, without discussing the problem (which is difficult to address with the current data) of whether the ceramics are coeval to it or not, this context, where lithics of Palaeolithic/Mesolithic tradition and only wild faunas have been found, might be evidence for the presence of Mesolithic hunter-gatherers. Certainly, the date might be the result of the average of the ages of bones of Palaeolithic and Neolithic chronology, but, as cited above, no evidence of such a severe disturbance is available, and it would have resulted in the presence of domestic faunas in layer IV, which has not been reported.

In south-eastern Spain, evidence of post-Palaeolithic hunter-gatherers has been found at El Molino de El Vadico. The preliminary reports (Córdoba and Vega 1988; Vega 1993) mention four Holocene layers that have provided industrial remains, superposed above a probably final Palaeolithic unit. Recent information (unpublished radiocarbon dates kindly communicated by G. Vega) confirms the attribution of one of these to the local early Mesolithic. Another interior site with geometric, probably late Mesolithic, lithics is the cave of El Lagrimal, in Alicante (Soler 1992).

In eastern Andalusia there are a couple of sites that have provided evidence for the presence of Holocene hunter-gatherers: the above-mentioned site of Cueva del Nacimiento, dated to the seventh millennium cal BC (Asquerino and López 1981) and Valdecuevas (with Geometric Mesolithic) (Sarrión 1980).

We may cite another Andalusian cave site that poses problems similar to those discussed for Verdelpino: Cueva Chica de Santiago, attributed to a very early, pre-cardial Neolithic (Acosta 1986) on very dubious bases. However, as with Verdelpino, there are two radiocarbon dates corresponding to the eighth to seventh millennium cal BC (7890±180 BP: 7310–6430 cal BC; 7240±230 BP: 6560–5660 cal BC) that might point to a Mesolithic settlement. Unfortunately, the information in the excavatio reportson the precise origin and the characteristics of the samples that were dated is very poor.

Finally, in a recent archaeological survey in the Guadalete valley (Cadix) an open-air site has been discovered that has provided lithic industries described as Late Mesolithic ('Tardenoid') (Giles *et al.* 1997).

In southern Portugal, the open-air site of Barca do Xarez de Baixo, in the Guadiana valley, has yielded an eighth-millennium radiocarbon date (Beta-120607: 8640±70 BP; 7850–7540 cal BC) for a context where lithic remains similar to those described for El Conejar and some other Portuguese coastal sites, and bones of horse and red deer, have been found (Almeida *et al.* 1999). Possible evidence of pre-Neolithic activity has also been recorded at the site of Xarez 12 (Gonçalves 2003).

Finally, in NW Iberia, there is some problematic evidence in the Portuguese province of Tras-os-Montes, such as the open-air settlement at Prazo (Monteiro-Rodrigues 2000), where quartz tools are associated with problematic sixth millennium cal BC dates (see Zilhão's comments in Carvalho 2003). Radiocarbon dates of the seventh millennium cal BC have been obtained for the bottom of layer 3 of Fraga d'Aia (Jorge 1991), but their significance is not yet sufficiently clear.

In the Spanish region of Galicia, the occupation of interior mountain areas during the Meolithic is attested in sites such as Pena do Pé (Criado 1991). This could also be the case for the site of Vega do Muin, in the upper Sil valley (Bernaldo de Quirós *et al.* 1997). We might add some possible indirect evidence of the activities of hunter-gatherer groups, such as changes recorded in pollen diagrams for Serra do Xistral in the second half of the seventh millennium cal BC (Ramil 1993).

The archaeological information presented above shows that there is reasonable evidence for the presence of Holocene hunter-gatherers in Iberian locations that are so far from the coast that regular visits to the seaside can be discounted (more than a 12-hour walk). It is true that for the central area (especially the *Meseta*) evidence is still very scarce and generally dubious. However we must emphasize that it is also the region where research efforts have been the lowest.

From a diachronic point of view, there happens to be an increase in the number of Late Mesolithic sites. It is not possible with the current state of research even to attempt to justify it. Amongst others, we might consider hypotheses such as the natural increase of populations, migration from the coastal areas, or a higher archaeological visibility of the Late Mesolithic geometric lithics.

The ethnographical evidence

Ethnographical and ethnohistorical evidence might be a relevant approach for this discussion. As a very general statement, we might say that real deserts are quite an unusual feature in the recent past. Hunter-gatherers tended to occupy all the available space, in part due to their adaptability, in part to the importance of maintaining low densities among band societies (Bates 1998). Really inhospitable regions such as Siberia, the Sahara (or Spanish central *Meseta* in the Late Pleniglacial) were indeed settled by human groups. It can certainly be argued that some ethnohistorical evidence would favour an opposite view. For instance, hunter-gatherer settlement in Tasmania tended to concentrate on the coastal strip (Tindale 1974). Nevertheless, we believe that this is not a good reference for the Iberian case. Tasmania is a relatively small island (68,000 km^2), and the interior resources could occasionally be exploited from a coastal network of settlements. From our point of view, a region such as Iberia, a peninsula of some 583,000km^2, is better compared to larger landmasses, such as Australia. There, the whole continent, including some of the harshest areas in the world, such as the Gibson Desert, was settled when the Europeans arrived (Gould 1969; Myers 1991; 1999). For us, it is difficult to imagine why the Iberian case should have been substantially different.

Conclusions

The information presented in this paper shows that post-Palaeolithic hunter-gatherers were present in interior areas of the Iberian Peninsula can be confirmed. Whether we are dealing with permanent settlements, or only occasional visits from the much more densely populated coastal regions, is difficult to elucidate for most sites with the currently available data. However the evidence for regions where systematic programs of archaeological survey have been developed (the Ebro valley, the southern slopes of the Cantabrian and Pyrenees ranges, the Guadiana valley) suggests that it is more likely that groups of hunter-gatherers were established in a permanent, or at least semi-permanent way in the interior areas of the Iberian Peninsula, although their densities would have been much lower than in the coastal areas. The distribution of the sites in three major sub-periods (10,000–8000, 8000–7000, and 7000–5500/5000 cal BC) also suggests a continuous presence of human groups, and possibly even a progressive increase in the density of their activity (Figure 46.2), although the low quality of the archaeological information for many sites has prevented further conclusions thus far.

Certainly, the case of central *Meseta* is still debatable, since the archaeological evidence is too scarce, and in many cases very doubtful. More research is required before claiming that this region was a desert during a large part of the Holocene, or whether we are just dealing with a problem of low archaeological visibility, or lack of an adequate survey. However, we find it very difficult to accept the existence, in middle latitudes, of empty areas in the Holocene. Even in regions apparently less suitable for hunter-gatherers than the centre of Spain (e.g. in central Europe) there are signs of the presence of these groups, and even of some type of influx in the processes of Neolithisation, as recent studies have pointed out, both from the archaeological (e g.

Chronology	10000–8000 cal BC	8000–7000 cal BC	7000–5500/5000 cal BC	Indeterminate
Direct evidence	La Uña El Níspero Berniollo Atxoste Zatoya Peña 14 Ángel 1 Forcas I Chaves El Parco Balma Margineda El Molino del Vadico	El Níspero Fuente Hoz Mendandia Atxoste Zatoya Peña 14 Legunova Angel 1 Ángel 2 Forcas II Costalena El Pontet Balma Margineda Canaleja II El Conejar Barca do Xarez de Baixo	Vega do Muin El Espertín Socuevas Fuente Hoz Mendandia Montico de Charratu Kanpanoste Goikoa Kanpanoste Atxoste La Peña de Marañón Aizpea Zatoya Padre Areso Peña 14 Forcas II El Parco Costalena El Pontet Secans Botiquería del Moros Los Baños de Ariño Ángel 1 Ángel 2 El Lagrimal El Nacimiento Valdecuevas Frailes	
Dubious or indirect evidence	La Dehesa La Ventana La Lámpara	Fraga d'Aia Fuentepecina II La Lámpara	Verdelpino Anta da Cabeçuda Rebolledo 2 Valdemuriel 2 Revilla del Campo La Lámpara Cueva Chica	El Parral La Higuera Los Enebrales La Talayuela

Figure 46.2. Table of interior sites where indices of Holocene hunter-gatherer activity have been found.

Whittle 1996; Jeuneusse 1997; Gronenborn 2004; Zvelebil 2004) and genetic points of view (Haak *et al.* 2005). The ethnographic evidence also suggests that it is not very likely that such a vast area as central Iberia would have been unpopulated during the Holocene. However, the previous information stresses that it is urgent to develop a systematic program of archaeological survey oriented towards the documentation of the extent and the significance of that elusive Mesolithic settlement that has provided so little direct information so far.

Acknowledgements

This paper is a contribution to the research project 'El origen de las sociedades campesinas en la fachada atlántica europea' (HUM2004-06418-C02-00), funded by the *Programa Nacional de Humanidades del Plan Nacional de I + D + I (2004-2007)* of the Spanish Government. All the radiocarbon dates cited in this paper have been calibrated according to the IntCal04 curve (Reimer *et al.* 2004), using the 5.0.1 revision of the CALIB program (Stuiver and Reimer 1993). The final version of the text has benefited from the most valuable comments of our colleague David Lubell.

References

Acosta, P. 1986. El Neolítico en Andalucía Occidental: estado actual, in *Homenaje a Luis Siret (1934-1984)*, 136–51. Sevilla, Consejería de Cultura de la Junta de Andalucia.

Alday, A. 2002. Las unidades industriales mesolíticas en la Alta-Media Cuenca del Ebro. *Complutum* 13, 19–50.

Alday, A. 2005. *El campamento prehistórico de Mendandia: Ocupaciones mesolíticas y neolíticas entre el 8500 y el 6400 bp.* Vitoria, Diputación Foral de Álava.

Almeida, F., Mauricio, J., Souto, P. and Valente, M. J. 1999. Novas perspectivas para o estudo do Epipaleolítico do interior alentejano: noticia preliminar sobre a descoberta do sítio arqueológico da Barca do Xerez Baixo. *Revista Portuguesa de Arqueologia* 2 (1), 25–38.

Álvarez Fernández, E. 2003. Die Reise der Schnecke *Columbella rustica* während des Mesolithikums und zu Beginn des Neolithikums in Europa. *Archäeologisches Korrespondenzblatt* 33, 157–66.

Álvarez Fernández, E. 2006. *Los objetos de adorno-colgantes del Paleolítico Superior y del Mesolítico en la Cornisa Cantábrica y en el valle del Ebro. Una visión europea.* Salamanca, Universidad de Salamanca (col. Vítor 195).

Arias Cabal, P. 2005–6. Determinaciones de isótopos estables en restos humanos de la región Cantábrica. Aportación al estudio de la dieta de las poblaciones del Mesolítico y el Neolítico. *Munibe* 57 (III), 359–74.

Arias Cabal, P. 2007. Neighbours but diverse: Social change in NW Iberia during the transition from the Mesolithic to the Neolithic (5500–4000 cal BC), in A. Whittle and V. Cummings (eds.), *Going over: the Mesolithic-Neolithic transition in North-West Europe*. Proceedings of the British Academy 144. Oxford, Oxford University Press.

Asquerino, M. D. and López, P. 1981. La cueva del Nacimiento (Pontones). Un yacimiento neolítico en la Sierra del Segura. *Trabajos de Prehistoria* 38, 107–38.

Barandiarán Maestu, I. 1978. El abrigo de la Botiquería dels Moros. Mazaleón (Teruel). Excavaciones arqueológicas de 1974. *Cuadernos de Prehistoria y Arqueología Castellonenese* 5, 49–138.

Barandiarán Maestu, I. and Cava Almuzara, A. (eds.) 1989a. *El yacimiento prehistórico de Zatoya (Navarra). Evolución ambiental y cultural a fines del Tardiglaciar y en la primera mitad del Holoceno*. Trabajos de Arqueología Navarra 8. Pamplona, Institución Príncipe de Viana.

Barandiarán Maestu, I. and Cava Almuzara, A. (eds.) 1989b. *La ocupación prehistóricas del abrigo de Costalena (Maella, Zaragoza)*. Zaragoza, Diputación General de Aragón.

Barrio, J. and Rubio, I. L. 2002. El Yacimiento Neolítico del Covacho de la Higuera (Patones, Madrid). Su valoración en el contexto de la Meseta. *Estudios de Prehistoria y Arqueología madrileñas* 12, 23–56.

Bates, D. G. 1998. *Human adaptive strategies: Ecology, culture and politics*. Boston, Allyn and Bacon.

Bernaldo de Quirós Guidotti, F., Neira Campos, A. and Fernández Rodríguez, C. 1997. Panorama del Paleolítico Superior y del Epipaleolítico en el Norte de la Cuenca del Duero, in R. de Balbín and P. Bueno (eds.), *II Congreso de Arqueología Peninsular. Tomo I-Paleolítico y Epipaleolítico*, 367–82. Zamora, Fundación Rei Afonso Henriques.

Cacho, C. 1999. El poblamiento de la Meseta durante el Paleolítico Superior, in S. Ripoll and L. Municio (eds.), *Domingo García. Arte rupestre paleolítico al aire libre en la Meseta castellana*, 237–43. Valladolid, Junta de Castilla y León.

Carbonell, E. 2003. Atapuerca: los primeros pobladores. El poblamiento antiguo de Europa y de la Península Ibérica, in *Actas IV Jornadas de Historia en Llerena*, 13–31. Llerena, Sociedad Extremeña de Historia.

Carvalho, A. F. 2003. A emergência do Neolítico no actual território português: pressupostos teóricos, modelos interpretativos e a evidência empírica. *O Arqueólogo Português* IV, 21, 65–150.

Cerrillo Cuenca, E. 1999. La cueva de El Conejar (Cáceres): avance al estudio de las primeras sociedades productoras en la penillanura cacereña. *Zephyrus* LII, 107–28.

Corchón, M. S. 1988–9. Datos sobre el Epipaleolítico en la Meseta Norte: la cueva del Níspero (Burgos: España). *Zephyrus* XLI–XLII, 83–100.

Córdoba de Oya, B. and Vega Toscano, L. G. 1988. El Paleolítico en la sierra del Segura: proyecto de investigación, in *I Congreso de Historia de Castilla-La Mancha. Tomo II: Pueblos y culturas prehistóricas y protohistóricas (1)*, 79–85. Toledo, Junta de Comunidades de Castilla-La Mancha.

Criado Boado, F. 1991. *Arqueología del paisaje. El área Bocelo-Fureles entre los tiempos paleolíticos y medievales. (Campañas de 1987, 1988 y 1989)*. Santiago de Compostela, Xunta de Galicia.

Delibes de Castro, G. and Fernández Manzano, J. 2000. La trayectoria cultural de la Prehistoria reciente (6400–2500 BP) en la SubMeseta Norte española, in P. Bueno, J. L. Cardoso, M. Díaz-Andreu, V. Hurtado, J. Oliveira, S. O. Jorge and V. O. Jorge (eds.), *Pré-história recente da Península Ibérica. 3º Congresso de Arqueologia Peninsular. Actas, vol. IV*, 95–122. Porto, Associação para o Desenvolvimento da Cooperação em Arqueologia Peninsular (ADECAP).

Delibes de Castro, G. and Rojo Guerra, M. A. 1997. ^{14}C y secuencia megalítica en la Lora burgalesa: acotaciones a la problemática de las dataciones absolutas referente a yacimientos dolménicos, in A. A. Rodríguez Casal (ed.), *O Neolítico Atlántico es as orixes do megalitismo*, 391–14. Santiago de Compostela, Universidade de Santiago de Compostela.

Estremera Portela, M. S. 2003. *Primeros agricultores y ganaderos en la Meseta Norte: el Neolítico de la Cueva de La Vaquera (Torreiglesias, Segovia)*. Valladolid, Junta de Castilla y León.

Fabián García, J. F. 1997. La difícil definición del Paleolítico Superior en la Meseta. El yacimiento de *La Dehesa* (Salamanca) como exponente de la etapa Magdaleniense Final, in R. de Balbín and P. Bueno (eds.), *II Congreso de Arqueología Peninsular* I, 219–37. Zamora, Fundación Rei Afonso Henriques.

Fernández-Miranda, M. and Moure Romanillo, A. 1975. El abrigo de Verdelpino (Cuenca). Un nuevo yacimiento neolítico en el interior de la Península Ibérica. *Noticiario Arqueológico Hispánico. Prehistoria* 3, 189–236.

Fortea Pérez, J. and Martí Oliver, B. 1984–5. Consideraciones sobre los inicios del Neolítico en el Meditérráneo español. *Zephyrus* XXXVII–XXXVIII, 167–99.

Giles, F., Gutiérrez, J. M., Santiago, A. and Mata, E. 1997. Avance al estudio sobre el poblamiento del Paleolítico Superior en la cuenca media-alta del río Guadalete (Cádiz). *Boletín del Museo de Cádiz* VII, 37–62.

Gonçalves, V. S. 2003. Comer en Reguengos, no Neolítico. As estructuras de combustão da Área 3 de Zares 12, in V. S. Gonçalves (ed.), *Muita gents, poucas antas? Origens, espaços e contextos do Megalitismo. Actas do II Colóquio Internacional sobre Megalitismo (Reguengos de Monsaraz, 3 a 7 de Maio de 2000)*, 81–99. Lisboa, Instituto Português de Arqueología.

Gould, R. A. 1969. *Yiwara: Foragers of the Australian Desert*. New York, Charles Scribner's Sons.

Gronenborn, D. 2004. Comparing contact-period archaeologies: the expansion of farming and pastoralist societies to continental temperate Europe and to southern Africa. *Before Farming* 2004 (4). Online version at www.waspress.co.uk (accessed 11/2007).

Guilaine, J. and Martzluff, M. (eds.) 1995. *Les excavacions a la balma de la Margineda (1979–1991)*. Andorra, Govern d'Andorra.

Haak, W., Forster, P., Bramanti, B., Matsumura, S., Brandt, G., Tänzer, M., Villems, R., Renfrew, C., Gronenborn, D., Alt, K. W. and Burger, J. 2005. Ancient DNA from the first European farmers in 7500-year-old Neolithic sites. *Science* 310, 1016–18.

Hernando, A. 1999. *Los primeros agricultores de la Península Ibérica*. Madrid, Síntesis.

Jeuneuse, C. 1997. *Pratiques funéraires au Néolithique ancien. Sépultures et nécropoles danubiennes 5500–4900 av. J-C*. Paris, Errance.

Jiménez Guijarro, J. 1998. La neolitización de la Cuenca Alta del Tajo. Nuevas propuestas interpretativas para el Neolítico de la Meseta. *Complutum* 9, 27–47.

Jiménez Guijarro, J. 2001. El Parral (Segovia). Caracterización del Epipaleolítico del interior peninsular. *Estudios de Prehistoria y Arqueología Madrileñas* 11, 37–44.

Jiménez Guijarro, J. 2008. *La neolitización del interior peninsular*. Unpublished PhD thesis, Universidad Complutense de Madrid.

Jiménez Guijarro, J. and Sánchez Marco, A. 2004. La Cueva de la Ventana: datos arqueológicos y faunísticos para la interpretación paleoecológica del Neolítico Interior, in *Miscelánea homenaje a Emiliano Aguirre, Volume 4: Arqueología*, 253–63. Alcalá de Henares, Comunidad de Madrid-Museo Arqueológico Regional.

Jorge, V. O. 1991. Novos datos sobre a Fraga d'Aia (Paredes da Beira-S. Joao da Pesqueira). *Trabalhos de Antropologia e Etnografia* 31, 1–4.

Juan Cabanilles, J. and Martí Oliver, B. 2002. Poblamiento y procesos culturales en la Península Ibérica del VII al V milenio A.C. (8000–5500 BP): Una cartografía de la neolitización, in E. Badal, J. Bernabeu and B. Martí (eds.), *El paisaje en el Neolítico mediterráneo*, 45–87. Saguntum extra 5. Valencia, Universitat de València.

Kalb, P. 1989. Überlegungen zu Neolithisierung und Megalithik im Western der Iberischen Halbinsel. *Madrider Mitteilungen* 30, 31–54.

Kunst, M. and Rojo Guerra, M. A. 1999. El Valle de Ambrona: un ejemplo de la primera colonización neolítica de las tierras del interior peninsular, in J. Bernabeu and T. Orozco (eds.), *Actes del II Congrés del Neolític a la Península Ibèrica*, 259–70. Saguntum extra 2. Valencia, Universitat de València.

Mangado, X., Bartrolí, R., Calvo, M., Nadal, J., Fullola, J. M. and Petit, M. A. 2002. Evolución de los sistemas de captación de recursos entre el Magdaleniense superior final y el Epipaleolítico geométrico de la Cueva del Parco (Alòs de Balaguer, La Noguera, Lleida). *Zephyrus* LV, 143–55.

Mazo Pérez, C. and Montes Ramírez, L. 1992. La transición Epipaleolítico-Neolítico antiguo en el abrigo de El Pontet (Maella, Zaragoza), in *Aragón/Litoral mediterráneo: intercambios culturales durante la Prehistoria*, 243–54. Zaragoza, Institución Fernando el Católico.

Monteiro-Rodrigues, S. 2000. A estação neolítica do Prazo (Freixo de Numão – Norte de Portugal) no contexto do Neolítico Antigo do Noroeste peninsular. Algumas considerações preliminaries, in P. Arias, P. Bueno, D. Cruz, J. Enríquez, J. de Oliveira and M. J. Sanches (eds.), *3º Congresso de Arqueologia Peninsular. Actas. Vol. 3: Neolitização e megalitismo da Península Ibérica*, 149–80. Porto, Associação para o Desenvolvimento da Cooperação em Arqueologia Peninsular (ADECAP).

Montes Ramírez, L. 2005. El Neolítico en el Alto Aragón. Últimos datos, in P. Arias, R. Ontañón and C. García-Moncó (eds.), *Actas del III Congreso del Neolítico en la Peninsula Ibérica. Santander, 5 a 8 de octubre de 2003*, 445–54. Monografías del Instituto Internacional de Investigaciones Prehistóricas de Cantabria 1. Santander, Servicio de Publicaciones de la Universidad de Cantabria.

Moure Romanillo, J. A. and Fernández-Miranda, M. 1977. El abrigo de Verdelpino (Cuenca). Noticia de los trabajos de 1976. *Trabajos de Prehistoria* 34, 31–68.

Myers, F. R. 1991. *Pintupi country. Pintupi self: Settlement, place and politics among Western Desert Aborigens*. Berkeley, University of California Press.

Myers, F. R. 1999. Pintupi-speaking aboriginal of the Western Desert, in R. Lee and R. Daly (eds.), *The Cambridge Encyclopedia of Hunters and Gatherers*, 348–52. Cambridge, Cambridge University Press.

Neira, A. 1997. Prehistoria, in *Historia de León* I, 7–155. León, La Crónica 16 de León.

Oliveira, J. 1997. Datas absolutas de monumentos megalíticos da Bacia Hidrográfica do Rio Sever, in R. de Balbín and P. Bueno (eds.), *II Congreso de Arqueología Peninsular. TomoII-Neolítico, Calcolítico y Bronce*, 229–39. Zamora, Fundación Rei Afonso Henriques.

Pastor, F. J. 1999. Ocupaciones prehistóricas en el curso final del río Sorbe, provincia de Guadalajara, (comunidad de Castilla-La Mancha). (I). *Wad-al-Hayara* 25, 7–49.

Ramil, P. 1993. Evolución climática e historia de la vegetación durante el Pleistoceno Superior y el Holoceno en las regiones montañosas del Noroeste Ibérico, in A. Pérez, L. Guitián and P. Ramil (eds.), *La evolución del paisaje en las montañas del entorno de los caminos jacobeos*, 25–60. Santiago de Compostela, Xunta de Galicia.

Rasilla, M. de la, Hoyos Gómez, M. and Cañaveras Jiménez, J. C. 1996. El abrigo de Verdelpino (Cuenca). Revisión de su evolución sedimentaria y arqueológica. *Complutum Extra* 6 (1), 75–82.

Reimer, P. J., Baillie, M. G. L., Bard, E., Bayliss, A., Beck, J. W., Bertrand, C. J. H., Blackwell, P. G., Buck, C. E., Burr, G. S., Cutler, K. B., Damon, P. E., Edwards, R. L., Fairbanks, R. G., Friedrich, M., Guilderson, T. P., Hogg, A. G., Hughen, K. A., Kromer, B., McCormac, F. G., Manning, S. W., Ramsey, C. B., Reimer, R. W., Remmele, S., Southon, J. R., Stuiver, M., Talamo, S., Taylor, F. W., van der Plicht, J. and Weyhenmeyer, C. E. 2004. IntCal04 terrestrial radiocarbon age calibration, 0-26 kyr BP. *Radiocarbon* 46/3, 1029–58.

Rodanés, J. M., Tilo, M. A. and Ramón, N. 1996. *El abrigo de Els Secans (Mazaleón, Teruel). Campañas de excavación de 1986 y 1987*. Al-Qannis 3. Alcañiz, Taller de Arqueología de Alcañiz.

Rojo Guerra, M. Á., Kunst, M., Garrido, R., García Martinez de Lagrán, Í. and Morán Dauchez, G. 2008. *Paisajes de la memoria: Asentamientos del Neolítico Antiguo en el valle de Ambrona (Soria, España)*. Valladolid, Universidad de Valladolid.

Rubio, I. 2002. Las cerámicas neolíticas de la colección Bento en el contexto de la Meseta, in C. Blasco (ed.), *La colección Bento del Museu d'Arqueologia de Catalunya. Una nueva mirada a la Prehistoria de Madrid*, 131–58. Barcelona, Museu d'Arqueologia de Catalunya.

Rubio, I. and Blasco, C. 1988–9. Análisis cerámicos de la cueva de la Vaquera (Torreiglesias, Segovia). *Zephyrus* XLI–XLII, 149–60.

Sarrión Montaña, I. 1980. Valdecuevas. Estación Meso-Neolítica en la Sierra de Cazorla (Jaen). *Saguntum* 15, 23–56.

Soler, J. M. 1992. *La cueva del Lagrimal*. Alicante, Institut Juan Gil-Albert.

Stuiver, M. and Reimer, P. J. 1993. Extended ^{14}C data-base and revised CALIB 3.0 ^{14}C age calibration program. *Radiocarbon* 35 (1), 215–30.

Tindale, N. B. 1974. *Aboriginal tribes of Australia*. Berkeley, University of California Press.

Utrilla Miranda, P. 2002. Epipaleolíticos y neolíticos del Valle del Ebro, in E. Badal, J. Bernabeu and B. Martí (eds.), *El paisaje en el Neolítico mediterráneo*, 179–208. Saguntum extra 5. Valencia, Universitat de València.

Utrilla Miranda, P., Domingo Martínez, R. and Martínez Bea, M. 2003. La campaña del año 2002 en el Arenal de Fonseca (Ladruñán, Teruel). *Saldvie* 3, 301–11.

Utrilla Miranda, P. and Mazo, C. 1997. La transición del Tardiglaciar al Holoceno en el Alto Aragón: los abrigos de Las Forcas (Graus, Huesca), in R. de Balbín and P. Bueno (eds.), *II Congreso de Arqueología Peninsular. Tomo I-Paleolítico y Epipaleolítico*, 349–65. Zamora, Fundación Rei Afonso Henriques.

Utrilla Miranda, P. and Rodanés, J. M. (eds.) 2004. *Un asentamiento epipaleolítico en el valle del río Martín*. El abrigo de los Baños (Ariño, Teruel). Zaragoza, Universidad de Zaragoza.

Vega Toscano, G. 1993. Excavaciones en el Molino del Vadico (Yeste). El final del Paleolítico e inicios del Neolítico en la sierra del Segura. *Jornadas de Arqueología Albacetense de la Universidad Autónoma e Madrid*, 3–32. Madrid, Universidad Autónoma de Madrid.

Whittle, A. 1996. *Europe in the Neolithic. The creation of new worlds*. Cambridge, Cambridge University Press.

Zvelebil, M. 2004. The many origins of the LBK, in A. Lukes and M. Zvelebil (eds.), *LBK dialogues. Studies in the formation of the Linear Pottery Culture*, 183–205. British Archaological Reports, International Series S1304. Oxford, Archaeopress.

47. Recent developments in Early Holocene hunter-gatherer subsistence and settlement: a view from south-western Iberia

Maria João Valente and António Faustino Carvalho

For the last decade new research has been carried out on several Mesolithic sites in the western Algarve, Portugal. The discovery and excavation of new sites (Barranco das Quebradas 1, 3, 4 and 5 and Rocha das Gaivotas) has provided new data on occupation patterns (geographical location, radiocarbon dates, size, archaeological context and finds) which, together with those from other known sites from south-western Iberia, allow us to construct a better framework to understand functionality and inter-site relationships, as well as subsistence, settlement and mobility. In the Algarve the sites dated from 9000 and 6700 years BP (8400 and 5600 cal BC) are mainly shell middens and were occupied by communities which came to the coast seasonally in order to collect local marine resources and, later on, flint material also available in the area. With such a varied history we are led to believe that either these occupations were made by human groups established in more northerly areas (where other sites, apparently with a more permanent settlement and wider subsistence spectrum, are already known), or the Mesolithic communities of the Algarve had high mobility indexes, with their still-to-be-identified base camps located in more interior areas.

Keywords: Mesolithic, Iberia, zooarchaeology, shell middens.

Introduction

In the south-western area of Iberia, also known as the Coast of São Vicente, several prehistoric archaeological sites dating from the Pre-Boreal to the Atlantic periods have been excavated, some of them with more or less developed shell layers. Among those, the most significant, until recently, were the shell middens of Praia do Castelejo (Silva and Soares 1997) and Armação Nova (Soares and Silva 2003).

Between 1996 and 2001, N.F. Bicho (Universidade do Algarve) implemented a project that led to the discovery of new archaeological contexts from the same period (Bicho *et al.* 2000; Bicho 2003; Stiner 2003; Stiner *et al.* 2003). After 2002 the research continued in two other projects developed by Bicho and the authors. These projects allowed not only the recognition of more contexts, but also the development of extensive excavations in two complexes of sites: Barranco das Quebradas and Rocha das Gaivotas, dated from 9200 to 6400 years BP (8250 and 5400 cal BC) (Carvalho *et al.* 2005; Carvalho and Valente 2005). (The radiocarbon dates in the text are given after applying the oceanic reservoir effect correction according to Soares 1993; for all data regarding these, see Figures 47.3 and 47.4.) New gathered data and its evaluation can now give place to interpretative considerations regarding the occupation of the territory by Mesolithic communities, and their substantial exploitation of the available aquatic resources.

Geographical context

The sites featured in this paper are located on the Algarve's western coast, near Europe's most south-westerly cape: São Vincente (Figure 47.1). The shore in this area has been exposed to deep marine erosion, together with material deposition on the lower sandy areas. The resulting irregular coast features impressive high cliffs intercalated by small sandy beaches, which lie at the base of minor ravines (Figure 47.2). The geological substrate is largely sandy or sandy-clayish, with areas of schist and limestone, sometimes including a variety of siliceous bodies, hence representing a good area to collect flint. The region itself is quite harsh, with a vegetation cover that reflects not only the dryness of the soil, but also its direct exposition to salinity and strong Atlantic winds. The plants most commonly found here include herbaceous trees and small

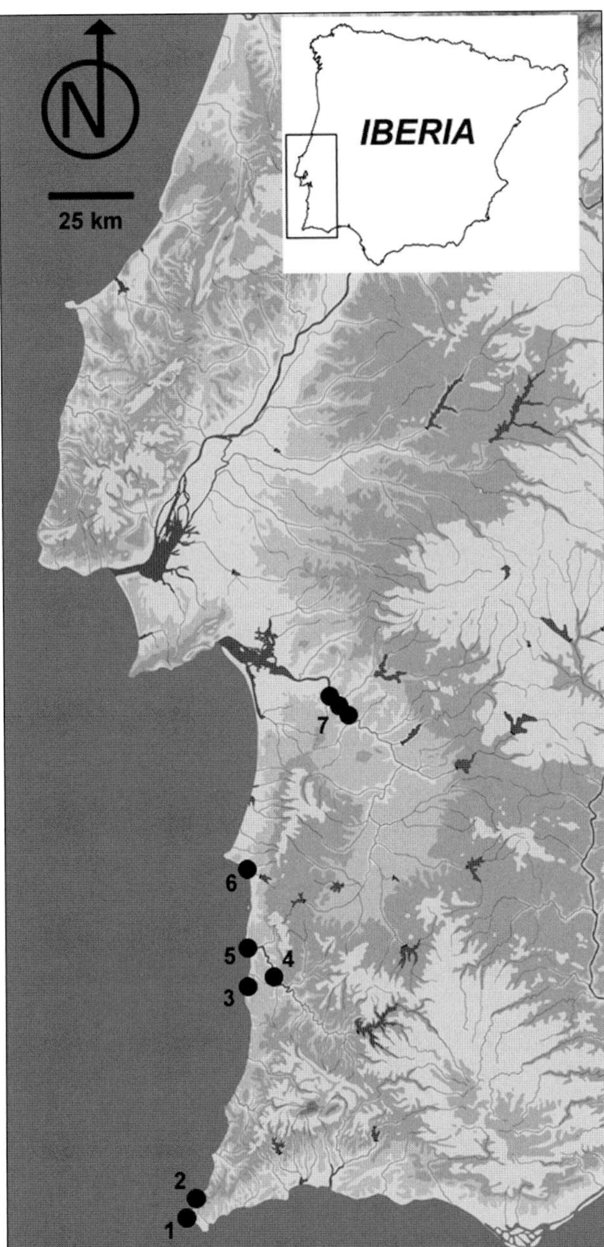

Figure 47.1. Map of south-western Iberia showing the sites mentioned in the text: (1) Barranco das Quebradas and Rocha das Gaivotas; (2) Praia do Castelejo; (3) Palheirões do Alegra; (4) Fiais; (5) Pedra do Patacho; (6) Oliveirinha; (7) Sado River Valley.

shrubs – e.g. fire tree (*Myrica faia*), service tree (*Sorbus domestica*).

Noticeably characterized by its Atlantic coast, this territory is still regarded as one of the richest areas in Portugal in terms of marine animal communities: fishes, crustaceans and especially rock-dwelling molluscs such as gooseneck barnacles (*Pollicipes pollicipes*) and limpets (*Patella* spp.).

Barranco das Quebradas

Located about 3km north of the Cape of São Vicente, Barranco das Quebradas (BQ) is a narrow, deep depression, caused by erosive draining, that runs NNE to SSW and ends directly on a sandy Atlantic beach (Praia do Telheiro), surrounded by rocky limestone cliffs (Figure 47.2).

To date, five sites have been identified along this valley, although one of them (BQ2, the only one located on the valley's left side) has been heavily damaged by erosion. The other four preserved sites are mostly characterized by abundant malacofauna, structuring small shell middens, all dated from the Early Mesolithic between 9200 to 8000 years BP (8400 to 6950 cal BC) (Pre-Boreal and Boreal. Figures 47.3 and 47.4).

The faunal material collected by the 1996–2001 works (Barranco das Quebradas 1 and 3 tests) were preliminarily analysed by M.C. Stiner (University of Arizona, Tucson, USA) and published in 2003 (Stiner; Stiner *et al.*; also Bicho *et al.* 2000 and Bicho 2003). (In publications prior to 2004, BQ1 was commonly referred to as Barranco das Quebradas I (BQI) and BQ3 was Barranco das Quebradas II (BQII).) Afterwards, the zooarchaeological analyses were pursued and revised by one of the authors (MJV) (Carvalho and Valente 2005). Associated with these faunal remains (in which vertebrates are largely absent) a few lithic materials were found, either with macrolithic or, more rarely, microlithic characteristics. A few sherds of handmade ceramics were also collected, always limited to the superficial levels of the sites.

BQ1 was tested in 1999 and more extensively excavated in 2004. It is a narrow, extended shell midden in a limestone rock shelter on the right slope of the ravine, with a stratigraphy that goes between one, to one and a half metres deep. According to the stratigraphical and zooarchaoelogical data, it is probable that this site encompasses at least two distinct periods of deposition, the younger dating from the Boreal period (8600 years BP (7600 cal BC), at the middle of the sequence), and the older dating from the Pre-Boreal (9200 years BP (8400 cal BP), at the base of the sequence), thus making this the oldest occupation of all the sites in Barraco das Quebradas. The older occupation includes mainly thick top shells (*Monodonta lineata*) and limpets, while the younger one also includes a strong percentage of rock shells (*Thais haemastoma*) and mussels (*Mytilus* spp.). Besides the general fauna composition, the lowest levels of this site have yielded some unusual materials, such as one small dolomite disc, one European cowrie (*Trivia monacha*), and one flat periwinkle (*Littorina obtusata*). In the upper levels, a unique tooth from a small ungulate was identified.

BQ2 was the only identified site on the left slope of the valley. Tests conducted in 2003 revealed a highly eroded context, with no archaeological material besides a few shell fragments of rock shells in the first 10cm of the sedimentary sequence.

BQ3, like BQ1, is a spatially limited shell midden on a limestone rock shelter on the right slope of the ravine. Well preserved, with a stratigraphy of about one metre, this site was excavated in 2002 using two areas 15 metres apart to determine the extension of occupation. The north

Figure 47.2. Coast of São Vicente with (1) Barranco das Quebradas and (2) Rocha das Gaivotas. (Photograph: F. Jorge).

Provenience (a)	Sample	Lab. Code	Date BP	Correction (b)	cal BC 1σ	cal BC 2σ
Barranco das Quebradas 1:						
(middle sequence)						
t.1, a.l. 40–50cm	*Monodonta l.*	Wk-8939	8960±70	8580±75	7680–7530	7790–7490
(lower sequence)						
t.1, a.l. 110–120cm	*Monodonta l.*	Wk-8950	9020±70	8640±75	7740–7580	7940–7540
M6, a.l. 7	*Monodonta l.*	Wk-16428	9473±54	9193±60	8470–8300	8570–8280
Barranco das Quebradas 3:						
(upper sequence)						
t.1, a.l. 0–22	*Monodonta l.*	Wk-8940	8360±80	7980±85	7050–6770	7090–6640
F21, a.l. 2	*Monodonta l.*	Wk-12133	8374±54	7994±60	7050–6820	7060–6690
(lower sequence)						
t.1, a.l. 60–70	*Monodonta l.*	Wk-8951	8780±60	8400±65	7550–7360	7590–7310
Barranco das Quebradas 4:						
L18, a.l. 2	*Monodonta l.*	Wk-12134	8873±57	8493±65	7590–7515	7610–7360
Barranco das Quebradas 5:						
M7, a.l. 15b	*Thais h.*	Wk-13693	8415±74	8035±80	7080–6810	7200–6650
N9, a.l. 4	*Patella* spp.	Wk-16427	8449±51	8069±60	7150–6830	7300–6750

Notes: (a) t = test; a.l. = artificial level; (b) marine reservoir correction of 380±30 according to Soares 1993. Calibration curve and programme used: IntCal04 Northern Hemisphere (Stuiver *et al.* 1998); OxCal Program v 3.10 (Bronk Ramsey 2005).

Figure 47.3. Radiocarbon dates for Barranco das Quebradas.

area, which was only tested, revealed much less material when compared with the south area, which was more extensively excavated. The estimated area of the site is approximately 150m^2.

The materials gathered in the south area allow the division of the unique sediment layer into at least two different settlements. The most superficial one comprises the first 20cm, and yielded some ceramics stylistically attributable to the Early Neolithic; the lower one develops between 20 and 100cm, and contained no ceramics. Since both occupations date from the Boreal (8000 years BP (7000 cal BC) for the upper levels, 8400 years BP (7500

Provenience (a)	Sample	Lab. Code	Date BP	Correction (c)	cal BC 1σ	cal BC 2σ
Early Mesolithic:						
ly. 3a	*Mytilus* spp.	Wk-16424	8420±46	8040±60	7080–6820	7170–6700
ly. 3a	*Mytilus* spp.	Wk-16426	8427±51	8044±60	7080–6820	7180–6750
ly. 3b	*Monodonta l.*	Wk-13690	8674±52	8294±60	7480–7190	7520–7170
f. 4	*Patella* spp.	Wk-13691	8965±54	8585±60	7660–7540	7740–7520
f. 5	shells (b)	Wk-16425	8673±78	8293±90	7480–7180	7530–7080
Late Mesolithic:						
f. 1	*Patella* spp.	Wk-13692	7092±48	6712±60	5710–5560	5730–5520
f. 2	*Juniperus* sp.	Wk-14797	6862±43	—	5800–5670	5850–5660
f. 2	*Patella* spp.	Wk-14793	7117±38	6737±50	5660–5630	5665–5625
ly. 2c-base	*Patella* spp.	Wk-14794	7201±39	6821±50	5740–5655	5810–5620
t. 1, a.l. 10	*Patella* spp.	Wk-6075	7270±70	6890±75	5880–5710	5980–5640
f. 3	*Pistacia* spp.	Wk-14798	6820±51	—	5740–5655	5810–5620
Early Neolithic:						
ly. 2c-top	*Pollicipes p.*	Wk-17029	6801±39	6421±50	5470–5360	5480–5310

Notes: (a) ly = layer; f = fireplace; t = test; a.l. = artificial level; (b) fragments of *Thais haemastoma*, *Patella* spp., *Siphonaria* sp., and *Mytilus* spp. (c) marine reservoir correction of 380±30 according to Soares 1993.
Calibration curve and programme used: IntCal04 Northern Hemisphere (Stuiver *et al.* 1998); OxCal Program v 3.10 (Bronk Ramsey 2005).

Figure 47.4. Radiocarbon dates for Rocha das Gaivotas.

cal BC) for the lower ones), they are not consistent with a Neolithic settlement. Therefore, it is probable that the main occupations of the site are Early Mesolithic, despite the possibility of subsequent short-term occurrences of Neolithic communities in the area – occurrences that did not result in an evident archaeological level.

The faunal assemblage shows no marked distinctions along the stratigraphical sequence. Preliminary analysis of the collection identified several marine taxa: thick top shells and rock shells are the most represented species, followed by limpets, mussels and gooseneck barnacles. Other less frequent species are dogwhelk (*Nucella lapillus*, a small gastropod), European edible abalone (*Haliotis tuberculata*), knobbed triton (*Charonia lampas*, the largest European gastropod), clam (*Venerupis decussata*) and Venus shell (*Venus verrucosa*). The relative abundance between taxa does not change significantly along the sequence.

BQ4 is an open-air shell midden on the right slope of the valley, on a platform located at the confluence of the main ravine with a subsidiary branch on its right side. The excavations done in 2002 and 2003 suggested that this site is spatially more extensive than BQ3 (200–250m^2), although with a thinner archaeological level that does not exceed 50cm in depth. Dated at 8500 years BP (7550 cal BC), this occupation was also in the Boreal period.

The fauna is similar to the one already described for BQ3; its preliminary analysis shows that thick top shells and rock shells are again the most abundant species, followed by limpets and mussels. The site also includes great scallop (*Pecten maximus*).

All three sites (BQ1, BQ3 and BQ4) are located on sandy-clayish sediments and yield some culturally uncharacteristic stone industry, mainly in greywacke (essentially macrolithics) but also in quartz, quartzite and flint (this last representing a small percentage). Several greywacke stones showed fractures caused by fire, probably a result of fireplaces used to process the molluscs as food.

BQ5 is substantially different from the other sites, both in terms of topography and sedimentary location. This site, also dated from the Boreal (around 8000 years BP) (7000 cal BC), is located in a subsidiary ravine that ends on the right side of the main valley. Unlike the other sites, where materials can be found on the soil's surface, at BQ5 the materials are only found within silts 130–140cm deep, in an archaeological sequence approximately 20–30cm thick. So far we have no data to infer the horizontal size of this shell midden.

Archaeologically the site shows several differences from the other three, starting with the distinction of multiple thin layers of overlapping shell depositions. Here, again unlike the other sites, mussels and rock shells are the most abundant taxa, while thick top shells, always so numerous in the other contexts, is rather scarce. Limpets are also frequent and some gooseneck barnacles are also present. A significant percentage of the specimens are burned, and given the occurrence of charcoal and fire-broken stones, it is reasonable to assume that some fireplaces existed even though excavation revealed none. There is also a significant presence of greywacke and quartzite macrolithic industry, with flakes, choppers and anvils. The traces on these last objects led us to surmise that they were mainly used to break rock shells, the only species visibly fractured by human action (limpets and mussels seem to have been broken by post-depositional causes).

Rocha das Gaivotas

Rocha das Gaivotas is a large shell midden located in the extensive sand dunes sited approximately one kilometre north of Cape São Vicente. It was discovered in 1998, during a systematic survey after local mollusc collectors dug an earthen track to access the nearby rocky shores.

Numerous shells and lithic artefacts became visible along the cuts of the earthen track, leading to a salvage excavation that same year, and two more field campaigns in 2003 and 2004. Some preliminary results have already been published or presented in congresses, mainly concerning its fauna (Bicho *et al.* 2000; Stiner 2003; Stiner *et al.* 2003; Carvalho *et al.* 2005; Carvalho and Valente 2005; Dean 2006; Carvalho, in press). These excavations allowed the recognition of a long sequence of settlements, which can be described as follows:

Early Mesolithic: Represented by four different levels of occupation, all preserved in layer 3 (the thickest layer, corresponding to the bottom of the dune), dated to 8600–8000 years BP (7600–7000 cal BC). Their faunal composition is characterised, from bottom to top, by limpets and mussels (level 3d); limpets, mussels and gooseneck barnacles (level 3c); thick top shells (level 3b); and mussels (level 3a), respectively. No artefacts were found. There are two fireplaces (one on level 3d, the other on level 3b) of very simple typology (burnt sand and shells only, without any kind of structuring).

Late Mesolithic: Dated to 6900–6700 years BP (5800–5600 cal BC), this is the most substantial occupation level, positioned on the lower part of layer 2. There are three fireplaces of more complex typologies, including stones of various sizes. Together with the high number of faunal (molluscs only) and lithic remains, this may represent a more stable human settlement. The most common species present are limpets, mussels, gooseneck barnacles and rock shells.

Early Neolithic: This is the reoccupation of the dune at 6400 years BP (5400 cal BC) by people carrying a distinct material culture, pottery being the most significant new artefact. Although not fully understood in its purpose, it is clear that this occupation is far less permanent than the previous one: there are no structures of any kind and the shell midden itself, on top of layer 2, is thin and stratigraphically less coherent. The gooseneck barnacle is the predominant species.

Synthesis and regional integration

Making a chronological synthesis of the sites, we have now a solid database from two different archaeological complexes: Barranco das Quebradas, with several settlements dated from the Early Mesolithic; and Rocha das Gaivotas, with a significant sequence of occupations from Early Mesolithic to Early Neolithic. These sites, together with those already known, allow us to set up a new regional framework for the Mesolithic (*lato sensu*) occupation of the most south-westerly corner of Iberia.

The dates obtained for these Mesolithic contexts go between the Pre-Boreal at 9200 years BP (8400 cal BC) (present in the lower layer of BQ1), to the Atlantic at 6700 years BP (5600 cal BC) (Rocha das Gaivotas, fireplaces 1 and 2). It is interesting to note that there seems to be a hiatus between the last Boreal occupations of about 8000 years BP (7000 cal BC) and the first Atlantic ones of 6900 years BP (5800 cal BC). However, another excavated site at nearby Rocha das Gaivotas (called Armação Nova) yielded some occupations dated within this supposed hiatus (Soares and Silva 2003). Unfortunately, to date this site has not been fully published.

The regional sites with the most ancient Mesolithic occupations (during the Pre-Boreal and Boreal) have shown us only parts of the whole picture, mostly corresponding to small sites specialised in mollusc collection, with short-term human occupations which reflect an apparent seasonal mobility to the sea shores. In fact, besides the locations presented here, only four other Early Mesolithic sites are known in south-western Iberia. Two of them, Oliveirinha and Pedra do Patacho (Soares and Silva 2004), are noticeably specialised in mollusc collection, similar to what we saw for Barranco das Quebradas and the most ancient occupations of Rocha das Gaivotas. The shell midden at nearby Praia do Castelejo is more extensive in size and contains a more diversified fauna: besides the numerous shell specimens (mainly limpets and thick top shells), some rabbit (*Oryctolagus cuniculus*) and a few fish remains were found. Although this is still not representative of broad-spectrum subsistence, such as that observed later on during the Atlantic period on the big Sado shell middens (with the association of molluscs with medium and large mammal remains), Castelejo nevertheless represents a more diversified exploration of the surrounding resources.

It should be emphasized that these sites, although similar in functions, have very different dimensions. While most Barranco das Quebradas sites seem to be small in size (notably regarding their horizontal extensions), Rocha das Gaivotas and Castelejo are much bigger, with Castelejo extending over an estimated 3000m^2 (Silva and Soares 1997). The only possible exception to this similarity of function is Palheirões do Alegra. Unfortunately, although it bears an extensive occupation of more than 8000m^2, and a rich lithic collection of more than 30,000 pieces, no organic materials were preserved, thus making it impossible to infer fully the characteristics of the occupation (Raposo 1997).

This picture changes at the beginning of the Atlantic period, when we can see the development of so-called broad-spectrum subsistence at sites such as Fiais (Odemira) and the Sado River's large shell middens. These locations imply a more organized occupation of the territory, featuring base camps – which could be utilized all year long – as well as seasonal exploitation of sites near the seashore, which specialized in the collection of local resources. However, if we narrow our focus to the Algarve, the most durable occupations are missing, even if we include the development of sites that are not only specialised in mollusc gathering but also in local flint collection and work, such as those we saw in Rocha das Gaivotas, and which can also be seen in Armação Nova (Soares and Silva 2004).

Conclusions

For both Mesolithic periods in the Algarve, we now know that the identified sites were occupied by communities which came to the coast in order to collect local marine resources and, later on, they also procured flint material that was also available in the area (Silva and Soares 1997; Bicho *et al.* 2003). Such behaviour could result in the formation of several shell deposits accumulated vertically, sometimes separated by levels of abandonment, such as those seen in Rocha das Gaivotas and Praia do Castelejo (Carvalho and Valente 2005). This pattern of occupation seems to continue during the Early Neolithic, as shown in the younger layers of Rocha das Gaivotas and in nearby Vale Santo 1. The latter is a campsite of small proportions, organized around a single fireplace, where very few ceramics were found, but which yielded a large collection of lithic industry. Probably Vale Santo 1 was a functional lithic workshop, since most of the industry was never used, or it was used expeditiously (Carvalho and Valente 2005; Gibaja and Carvalho 2004).

We have yet to establish whether these occupations were made by human groups established in more northerly areas, or whether the Mesolithic communities of the Algarve had high mobility indexes, with their still-to-be-identified base camps located in more interior areas of the Algarve. Further surveys of the area and subsequent excavations may help us respond to these issues.

Acknowledgements

We thank Nuno Bicho for inviting us to start new projects with him in the São Vicente area, and for his valuable input on the issues discussed in this paper. We also thank Carol DeLancey for editing the final version of the text. The data presented here were obtained thanks to two projects ('A Importância dos Recursos Aquáticos no Paleolítico do Algarve' and 'O Processo de Neolitização do Algarve') under Projecto SAPIENS Proj, financed by 'Plano Nacional de Trabalhos Arqueológicos' of Instituto Português de Arqueologia and by Fundação para a Ciência e a Tecnologia (Eixo 2, Medida 2.3 do POCTI do QCA-III, FEDER funding). The presentation of this paper at Meso 2005 was financed by Fundação Calouste Gulbenkian. The photograph used in Figure 47.2 is reprinted by permission of Filipe Jorge and we are grateful for his permission to reproduce it here; for the original, see Jorge 2005)

References

Bicho, N. F. 2003. A importância dos recursos aquáticos na economia dos caçadores-recolectores do Paleolítico e Epipaleolítico do Algarve, in *1º Encontro de Arqueologia do Algarve, Silves, 27-29 Setembro, 2001 (Xelb 4)*, 9–24. Silves, Câmara Municipal de Silves.

Bicho, N. F., Lindly, J., Stiner, M. C. and Ferring, C. R. 2000. O processo de neolitização na Costa Sudoeste, in *3º Congresso de Arqueologia Peninsular. Neolitização e Megalitismo da Península Ibérica* III, 11–30. Porto, Associação para o Desenvolvimento da Cooperação em Arqueologia Peninsular.

Bronk Ramsey, C. 2005. OxCal 3.10. WWW program and documentation available at http://www.rlaha.ox.ac.uk/oxcal/oxcal.htm (accessed 10/2007).

Carvalho, A. F. (in press). Le passage vers l'Atlantique. L'Algarve et le processus de néolithisation de la façade occidental de la Péninsule Ibérique, in G. Marchand (ed.), *La néolithisation de la façade atlantique de l'Europe: interactions culturelles, transferts techniques, implications des milieux naturels*. Nantes, Université de Nantes.

Carvalho, A. F., Bicho, N. F., Stiner, M. C., Gibaja, J. F., Valente, M. J. and Masucci, M. A. 2005. O projecto «o processo de neolitização no Algarve» (Portugal): âmbito e primeiros resultados, in *III Congreso del Neolítico en la Península Ibérica*, 965–74. Santander, Universidad de Cantábria.

Carvalho, A. F. and Valente, M. J. 2005. Novos contextos conquíferos pré-históricos na Costa Vicentina, in *2º Encontro de Arqueologia do Algarve (Xelb 5)*, 9–26. Silves, Câmara Municipal de Silves.

Gibaja, J. F. and Carvalho, A. F. 2004. Análisis traceológico del taller de sílex del Neolítico antiguo de Vale Santo 1 (Sagres, Vila do Bispo). *Promontoria* 2, 253–64.

Jorge, F. 2005. *Algarve Visto do Céu*, 30. Lisboa, Argumentum.

Raposo, L. 1997. O Mirense e o machados mirenses. Algumas reflexões em voz alta. *Setúbal Arqueológica* 11–12, 109–120.

Silva, C. T. and Soares, J. 1997. Economias costeiras na Pré-História do Sudoeste português. O concheiro de Montes de Baixo. *Setúbal Arqueológica* 11–12, 69–108.

Soares, A. M. M. 1993. The 14C Content of Marine Shells: Evidence for Variability in Coastal Upwelling of Portugal during the Holocene, in *Isotope Techniques in the Study of Past and Current Environmental Changes in the Hydrosphere and the Atmosphere*, 471–85. Vienna, International Atomic Energy Agency.

Soares, J. and Silva, C. T. 2003. A transição para o Neolítico na costa sudoeste portuguesa, in V. S. Gonçalves (ed.), *Muita gente, poucas antas? Origens, espaços e contextos do Megalitismo. II Colóquio Internacional sobre Megalitismo*, 45–56. Trabalhos de Arqueologia 25. Lisboa, Instituto Português de Arqueologia.

Soares, J. and Silva, C. T. 2004. Alterações ambientais e povoamento na transição Mesolítico-Neolítico na Costa Sudoeste, in A. A. Tavares, M. J. F. Tavares and J. J. Cardoso (eds.), *Evolução geohistórica do litoral português e fenómenos correlativos. Geologia, História, Arqueologia e Climatologia*, 397–424. Lisboa, Universidade Aberta.

Stiner, M. C. 2003. Zooarchaeological evidence for resource intensification in Algarve, Southern Portugal. *Promontoria* 1, 27–62.

Stiner, M. C., Bicho, N. F., Lindly, J. and Ferring, C. R. 2003. Mesolithic to Neolithic transitions: new results from shell middens in the western Algarve, Portugal. *Antiquity* 77 (295), 75–86.

Stuiver M., Reimer, P. J., Bard, E., Beck, J. W., Burr, G. S., Hughen, K. A., Kromer, B., McCormac, G., van der Plicht, J. and Spurk, M. 1998. INTCAL98 Radiocarbon Age Calibration, 24000-0 cal BP. *Radiocarbon* 40 (3), 1041–83.

48. Mesolithic people in an open Mediterranean wetland

Andrea L. Balbo, Darko Komšo and Preston T. Miracle

Open-air Mesolithic sites are extremely rare and poorly known along the eastern Adriatic coastline and in karstic environments in the wider region. The paucity of sites has led many to conclude that the region was at best thinly populated during the Mesolithic. Results from a recent archaeological survey of Polje Čepić (Istria, Croatia), are helping to fill this gap in the Mesolithic record. Polje Čepić is today an alluvial plain, located 24m asl, and about 5km from the Adriatic Sea. A shallow lake occupied the polje until its artificial drainage in 1932. In this paper we present the results from a two-year survey set around the polje, which started in 2003. Over a dozen archaeological areas, with mostly Mesolithic, but also Upper Palaeolithic to Neolithic periods represented, have been discovered in a fairly restricted region. In conjunction with geoarchaeological evidence and a 17.5m-deep sediment core, we discuss the relations those people could have had with this highly mutable and understudied wet Mediterranean environment.

Keywords: open-air, survey, karst, wetland, sediment core, flint typochronology.

The Mesolithic gap in south-eastern Europe

The lack of Mesolithic sites in south-eastern Europe has been pointed out by several authors. Among them, Inga (2003) focuses in particular on the Early Mesolithic sites at the Pleistocene-Holocene transition, while Biagi and Spataro (2001) concentrate on the beginning of the Atlantic period, with its Late Mesolithic Castelnovian assemblages.

Inga (2003, 307) characterises the scarcity of Mesolithic sites in south-eastern Europe as a 'syndrome'. Even if the Late Upper Palaeolithic, Early Neolithic, and later periods of the region are well documented, the Mesolithic is still next to invisible outside of a few hot spots like the Danube Gorges (the Iron Gates). As Miracle, Galanidou, and Forenbaher (2000, 293) observed within the northern Adriatic context, 'The Mesolithic is often lost between the Palaeolithic and the Neolithic bread'.

Another issue in the Mesolithic (actually in most of the prehistory of south-eastern Europe) is the under-representation of open-air sites compared to cave sites. In a recent review of the northern Adriatic region, Boschian (2003) notes that, although there was a sudden increase in the number of sites in the early Holocene, all but one were found in caves. This pattern is also true for the prehistory of Istria, mainly known through the study of cave sites. Since the beginning of prehistoric research in Istria, initiated by Sir R. F. Burton in the 1870s (Burton *et al.* 1878), 74 caves with archaeological remains have been registered in Istria. Out of these, 11 have given evidence of Mesolithic occupation (Komšo 2003), while Kotle (Miracle and Forenbaher 2000; Boschian 2003) and Lokve were until recently the only two known Mesolithic open-air sites. With our survey five new open-air Mesolithic sites were discovered, significantly increasing the visibility of this period in the region.

Within this paper we tackle three main issues related to the study of Polje Čepić. 1) Since when and how continuously was the polje occupied by a wet landscape? 2) Were there people living around its margins during the Mesolithic? 3) If so, why, and what kind of activities were they carrying out?

Polje Čepić as the setting for this study

The geomorphologic unit composed by Polje Čepić, with its margins and catchments, was chosen in 2003 for the setting of a systematic archaeological survey (Figure 48.1) (Balbo *et al.* 2004). Poljes are extremely common features in karstic regions; their sizes can vary from a few hundred square metres to several square kilometres. Poljes are mostly situated along tectonic faults; they often present a depression with a flat base (Gracia *et al.* 2002; Hugget 2003). The bottom of a polje is normally covered with ponors. These holes control the flow of water between the underground catchments and the surface, and consequently the water level in the basin constituted by the polje. When

Figure 48.1. Polje Čepić is situated on the eastern side of the Istrian peninsula, Croatia, and is here represented by a dark-grey spot, surrounded by its catchments. (Modified from free internet sources).

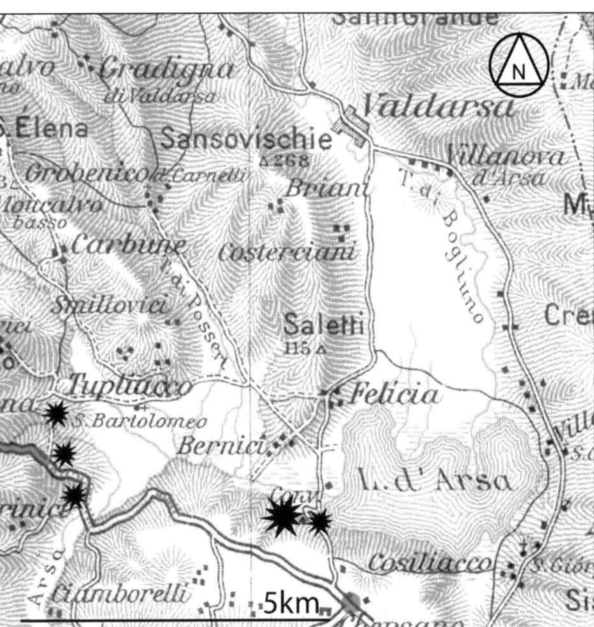

Figure 48.2. The position of the five Mesolithic scatters recently discovered around Polje Čepić is shown on one of the last topographical maps drawn before the drainage of the lake in 1932. The larger star on the southern side of the polje represents Kostadini. (Modified from TCI 1930).

ponors are filled with sediments, poljes become natural surface basins of fresh water, and eventually shallow lakes. In spite of their potential for life support in an otherwise permeable and dry surrounding (Parenzan 1928), poljes are underrepresented in prehistoric studies of karstic Mediterranean areas.

Many authors have already stressed the preference of Mesolithic people to settle near water basins, owing to their relatively high productivity and biodiversity. Because of its potential as an Early Holocene wetland, Polje Čepić was chosen as the setting for this study.

In fact, a look at any current regional map shows that the Čepić depression was potentially the only large natural basin of Istria, before its artificial drainage in 1932. Besides, the studies carried out by Miracle in the last decade demonstrate the importance of its catchments for the settlers of this region in prehistory. Indeed, a few of the main regional prehistoric cave settlements have been discovered within 10km from Polje Čepić, along its main inlet, the Boljušćica River (Miracle and Forenbaher (eds.) 2006).

The discovery and location of Mesolithic sites around the polje: Kostadini

All available technical maps were used for the planning of the survey around Polje Čepić. The topographical, hydrological, and pedological maps, in conjunction with aerial photos, were the most useful tools used during this phase. Terraces, river valleys, and springs were identified on the topographical and hydrological maps. The most stable landforms, with their mature soils, where post-glacial archaeological sites were most likely to be found, were outlined on the pedological map. The accessibility and visibility on the ground for the areas to be surveyed were assessed using aerial photographs.

The first assessment survey was carried out in the last week of July 2003, leading to the discovery of a Mesolithic scatter around Kostadini. Following those results, three extensive surveys were set in 2004 and 2005, twice in the spring, during the rainy season, and once in the summer, involving students from British and Croatian Universities. Cultivated fields, as they appear on cadastral maps, were chosen as the minimal survey unit (Qs). Out of a total of 183 surveyed fields (covering an area of 670,826m^2), 37 (119,573m^2), mainly concentrated on the southern and western sides of Polje Čepić, contained lithic scatters of prehistoric ages. The 37 positive fields were grouped in 14 wider archaeological areas, and named after the closest local name, as it appears on recent 1:5000 topographical maps. Five of these archaeological areas were classified as Mesolithic based on their lithic typology, as well as on the raw materials used for the production of stone artefacts (Figure 48.2). All of these sites are situated close to a spring, not too high above the present-day base of the polje; they are always in view of the basin, and can be seen from each other.

Between mid-July and mid-August 2005 test excavations were carried out at three of the discovered archaeological areas. Because of the high concentration of finds, the Mesolithic site found at Kostadini was chosen for the setting of a more extensive excavation. Kostadini is situated at about 500m from the bottle-neck representing the potential outlet of the lake that occupied Polje Čepić (Figure 48.4). The site is about 45m higher than the bottom of the polje, which lies at 24m asl. On the western side of the Mesolithic site, within a distance of 250m, there is an alignment composed of two dolinas and, at the lowest point, a year-round running spring. The two karstic depressions and the spring are part of the same watercourse, partially running underground. With the rise of the water table, after a rainy period, the two dolinas can fill with fresh water.

As for most open-air sites, the archaeological context at Kostadini has been disturbed by agricultural practices. The damage caused by the recent plantation of a vineyard is well illustrated by the high percentage of edge damaged lithic artefacts; about 26% of cores and tools show recent breakage. Nevertheless, the site can be considered as being in its original geomorphological position. In fact, most of the assemblage was recovered within the top 40cm of a 110cm-deep parental soil profile in the central portion of a slightly tilted limestone terrace.

The Mesolithic assemblage from Kostadini and the characterization of the site

Following the survey, the potential extension of the site was assessed excavating a total of $6.5m^2$. The bedrock was reached at a depth of 110cm, and samples were taken from the profile for the micromorphological study of this soil.

All sediments were dry-sieved in the field using a 3mm mesh. In most cases sieving was incomplete, due to the texture of the soil, and pellets were broken down to 1cm. Out of the total excavated area, four square metres were subsampled, so that about 7% of the excavated volume of soil could be wet sieved on a 1mm mesh, in order to evaluate the number of missing artefacts. The Kostadini lithic assemblage contains 423 pieces, of which 340 were recovered from the surface, and 83 from excavated trenches. We estimate that the 83 finds recovered during the excavation of four square metres with the mere support of dry sieving would have risen up to 602 pieces if wet sieving had been applied throughout the excavation. Nevertheless, most of the pieces recovered through wet sieving were very small chips with no effect on the typological study of the lithic composition.

The lithic scatter found at Kostadini seems to be quite homogeneous, and its total extension has been estimated to be more than $2000m^2$ through survey and test excavations (602/4*2000=301,000 potential artefacts).

Due to the lack of absolute-datable materials, the site was characterised by typological and raw material comparison with other locations previously studied in the region. For the purposes of this preliminary analysis, the assemblage was observed only macroscopically. Three general classes of stone artefacts were used in the analysis, namely debitage (flakes, blades, bladelets, knapping and burned debris, small debris and flakes), cores (including core fragments), and retouched pieces. We classified as retouched pieces all lithic artefacts with secondary modification (Finlayson *et al.* 2000), not including at the moment possible unretouched pieces with traces of use wear or hafting (Inizan *et al.* 1992). As for the classification of different raw materials, three groups were made, considering the distance of their source from the Mesolithic site. We considered as local all raw materials available at sources within 10km from Kostadini, while we classified as regional those found within a radius of 10 to 50km. Any raw material from sources located at more than 50km from the site was classified as exotic (Pellegatti, pers. comm.).

The lithic assemblage found at Kostadini shares many general characteristics with other Mesolithic sites in the region and contains a total of 423 pieces. Of these, 75.9% consist of unretouched specimens, 11.1% are retouched, 6.6% are cores, and 6.4% present clear indications of edge damage (also pointing to a relatively high occurrence of post depositional disturbance). Morphologically, knapping debris and flakes represent the largest categories, followed by small flakes, small debris and bladelets. Blades are almost completely absent. The assemblage shows a strong homogeneity both in terms of raw material and types of lithic artefacts. When considering raw material, we observe that 69% of tools and cores have been obtained from raw materials available within 10km from the site. About 18% of these two categories were prepared on raw materials from regional sources, located in central Istria and in the Reka Valley, in Slovenia. Only 2% of the lithic artefacts unearthed at Kostadini were made of exotic raw materials for which the source is unknown.

The assemblage produced by the people living near Kostadini is microlithic. The present analysis of the assemblage shows that the lithic production at the site was focused on the manufacturing of flakes and bladelets, while blades are almost completely absent. Armatures, mainly triangles and backed bladelets, were made with the microburin technique, of which we found one typical example (Figure 48.3: 33). All stages of the lithic reduction sequence are present, although variously represented. The high number of lithic artefacts with cortex indicates that most of the primary reductions occurred on site. The high frequency of cores, core fragments, knapping debris, and cortical flakes, suggests *in situ* production of blanks for further modification into tools.

The relatively balanced representation of triangles, backed bladelets, endscrapers, burins, pieces with lateral linear retouch, notches, piercers, and composite tools, indicates that these people were engaged in all kinds of gearing-up and transformational activities. Although the inference of activities from tool typology is highly problematic, the Kostadini assemblage appears to reflect generalized activities performed by the entire social group rather than specialized activities carried out by a sub-set of the larger group.

From both technological and typological perspectives, the lithic assemblages collected at Kostadini shares in general a number of characteristics, such as the microburin technique, clear microlithisation of backed bladelets and cores, and the consistent use of locally available raw materials, with the other lithic assemblages of Early Holocene age recovered

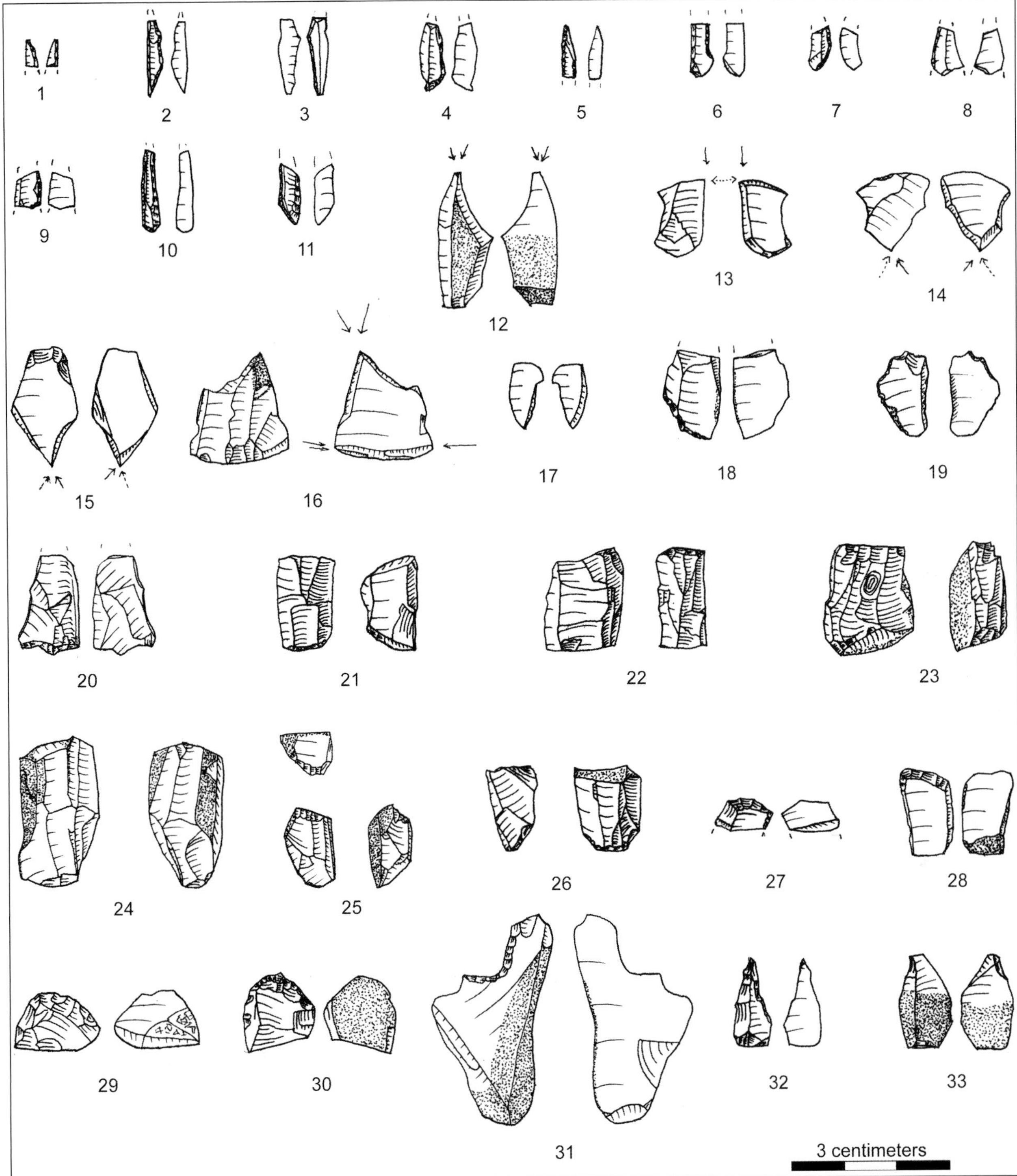

Figure 48.3. Some of the lithic artifacts unearthed during the survey and the test-excavation at Kostadini. 1, 4–5: backed points; 2–3: triangles; 6–9: unilateral backed bladelets; 10–11: bilateral backed bladelets; 12–16: burins; 17: burin spall; 18–20: truncations; 21–26: cores; 27–30: endscrapers; 31: notch; 32: piercer; 33: microburin. (Drawings: Darko Komšo).

in the northern Adriatic area. The triangles and backed bladelets, and the lack of trapezes and prismatic blades, suggest an early Mesolithic date for the site (Miracle *et al.* 2000; Komšo, this volume). Based on the existing lithic assemblage, and the density and distribution of lithic artefacts found at Kostadini, we suggest that this was a Mesolithic field camp where multifunctional activities, related to the everyday life of its inhabitants, were performed.

From geomorphology to palaeoenvironment. Mesolithic people around a Mediterranean wet place

Kostadini is situated close to a potential cross-point where a land-way and a water-way meet (Figure 48.4). In fact, the south-north direction represents a bridge for crossing Polje Čepić, when moving from the lowlands of southern

Istria to the Ćićarija Mountains in the north. Similarly, the east-west direction constitutes a potentially navigable water connection between the polje and the Adriatic Sea, through the 15km-long Raša canyon. Our study of the functioning of the polje throughout Holocene is fundamental to the understanding of the relation that Mesolithic people had with this place (Balbo *et al.* 2006).

In order to obtain information about past changes in the polje environment, in summer 2004 we extracted a 17.5m exploratory core from the sediment sequence preserved in Polje Čepić. Observations were made on the bottom 4m of the core. In contrast with the general idea of poor preservation in continental sediment archives of the northern Adriatic region (Boschian 2003), organic remains and pollen were well preserved, and in good concentration. The bottom of the sequence is constituted by a thick gravel layer representing a massive colluvium. This layer prevented our coring equipment from reaching any further depth. Just above the gravel, finer sediments testify to the passage from a detritic to a lacustrine phase with suspended sediments. The same kind of fine sediments characterise the rest of the analysed sequence. The only exception is represented by a 7cm-thick peat layer, corresponding to the only dry period so far attested. The first datings obtained from this core show a high sedimentation rate within this basin. In fact the 17m of this sedimentary sequence have accumulated in the last 7000 years.

The study of the sedimentary sequence from Polje Čepić allows us to characterise this environment as a Mediterranean karstic wetland as far back as 5000 years cal BC (Balbo *et al.* 2006). Until now the oldest proof for the existence of a shallow lake within the polje was contained in historical maps going back to the 16th century. The general morphology of the area suggests that a wet environment was predominant in the polje well before 5000 years cal BC, and most likely when people settled at Kostadini in Mesolithic times (Balbo *et al.* 2006).

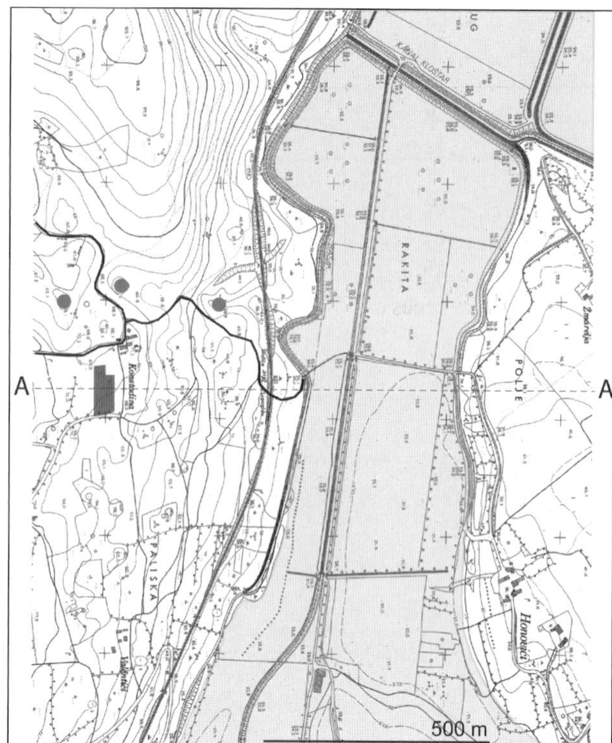

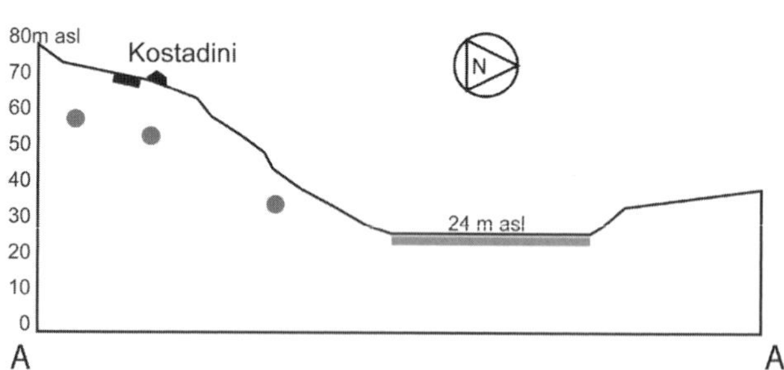

Figure 48.4. Kostadini is situated on the southern side of Polje Čepić. The A–A profile, where highs are exaggerated by about 15 times, shows the position of the site relative to the potential outlet of the polje and three nearby springs. (Modified from Croatian base map).

Conclusions: the choice of Polje Čepić by Mesolithic people

A deeper soil profile needs to be extracted from Polje Čepić in order to reach the Late Glacial and Early Holocene sediments. However, the present impression is that Polje Čepić was probably occupied by a shallow lake throughout the early phases of the Holocene.

Five open-air Mesolithic sites have been discovered on the margins of the polje. One of these, Kostadini, has been extensively explored by test-excavation, and presents the characteristics of a field camp. An outcrop of local flint has also been discovered a couple of kilometres east from the settlement, on the margins of the polje. The raw material is similar to that mainly used by the people living on the site.

For the people living in Istria during the Mesolithic, Polje Čepić could have represented the largest basin of year-round available fresh water in the region, with its varied resources. Already in the Late Palaeolithic a growth of aquatic resources like molluscs and fish in the subsistence is noted over south-eastern Europe. This trend is confirmed for Istria by Miracle's excavations at the Pupićina cave where there is a clear diversification in diet, including an increased use of freshwater fish within the Early Mesolithic levels (Miracle 1996; Miracle 2001; Miracle and Forenbaher 2000; Paine and Miracle, this volume).

The discovery of Mesolithic open-air sites such as Kostadini, and the other sites around Polje Čepić, are beginning to fill the gap in the Mesolithic of Istria and the east Adriatic. These sites are providing some guidelines on where and how to find open-air Mesolithic settlements in karstic Mediterranean regions. Their position reflects the relation that people had with their landscape. Among the reasons that brought Mesolithic people to choose Kostadini and the margins of Polje Čepić could be the vicinity to the shore of a relatively stable lake, as well as the proximity of minor watercourses and numerous springs. Furthermore,

Kostadini is situated in an ideal position for accessing both land and water passages. The presence of lithic raw material in the immediate vicinity of the site must also have played a role in the choice of this settlement.

The landscape around Polje Čepić went through the Holocene rise of the Mediterranean Sea relatively untransformed. Studying this landscape we can in part avoid the bias effect that the post-glacial increase in sea level had on the distribution pattern of archaeological sites. In addition, our chances of finding Mesolithic sites specialised in the exploitation of freshwater resources, buried under posterior alluviums, are high around poljes because of their seasonally inconsistent hydrological behaviour.

Through the study of paleolimnological record and geomorphology, as well as that of archaeological settlement pattern, this research is enhancing our knowledge of the relation that people had to their places since the Pleistocene-Holocene transgression in Istria, as well as in the wider region. In particular we are revealing the potential of an understudied Mediterranean landscape.

The on-going researches around Polje Čepić are rapidly increasing the number of open-air Mesolithic sites known in Istria. The information so far acquired from cave sites is being extended to previously unexplored environments. Our knowledge of the relations that Mesolithic people had with their places is being strengthened, so that archaeological knowledge in the region can hopefully start recovering from the Mesolithic 'syndrome'.

Acknowledgements

The authors wish to thank the Arts and Humanities Research Council (AHRC), the McDonald Institute of Archaeology, the Prehistoric Society, and the Marie Curie Training Program for their support of the present study.

References

Balbo, A. L., Andrić, M., Rubinić, J., Moscariello, A. and Miracle, P. T. 2006. Palaeoenvironmental and archaeological implications of a sediment core from Polje Čepić, Istria, Croatia. *Geologia Croatica* 59 (2), 107–22.

Balbo, A. L., Komšo, D. and Miracle, P. T. 2004. Geoarchaeological Survey of Polje Čepić and Part of its Hydrological Basin (Istria Peninsula, Croatia): Report on the First Field Season. *Histria Archaeologica* 33, 265–76.

Biagi, P. and Spataro, M. 2001. Plotting the evidence: some aspects of the radiocarbon chronology of the Mesolithic-Neolithic transition in the Mediterranean basin. *Atti del Museo Civico di Storia Naturale, Trieste* XII, 15–54.

Boschian, G. 2003. Environment and Hunters-Gatherer Mobility in the Northern Adriatic Region. *Preistoria Alpina* 39, 91–102.

Burton, F. R., Scampicchio, A. and Covaz, A. 1878. The Seabord of Istria. *Journal of the Anthropological Institute of Great Britain and Ireland* VII., 341–63.

Finlayson, B., Finlay, N. and Mithen, S. 2000. The Cataloguing and Analysis of the Lithic Assemblages, in S. Mithen (ed.), *Hunter-Gatherer Landscape Archaeology. The Southern Hebrides Mesolithic Project 1988-1998*. McDonald Institute Monographs. Cambridge, McDonald Institute for Archaeological Research.

Gracia, F. J., Gutierrez, F. and Gutierrez, M. 2002. Origin and evolution of the Gallocanta polje (Iberian Range, NE Spain). *Zeitschrift Fur Geomorphologie* 46, 245–62.

Hugget, R. J. 2003. *Fundamentals of geomorphology*. London, Routledge.

Inga, M. 2003. The Mesolithic Syndrome in Southeastern Europe. *Acta Archaeologica* 74, 307.

Inizan, M. L., Roche, H. and Tixier, J. 1992. *Technology of Knapped Stone*. Meudon, Cercle de Recherches et d'Etudes Préhistoriques (CREP).

Komšo, D. 2003. Pećine Istre – mjesta življenja od prapovijesti do srednjega vijeka. *Histria Antiqua* 11, 41–54.

Miracle, P. T. 1996. Diversification in Epipaleolithic subsistence strategy along the eastern Adriatic coast: a simulation approach applied to zooarcheological assemblages. *Atti della Società per la Preistoria e Protostoria della Regione Friuli- Venezia Giulia* IX, 33–62.

Miracle, P. T. 2001. Feast or famine? Epipalaeolithic subsistence in the northern Adriatic basin. *Documenta Praehistorica* 18, 177–97.

Miracle, P. T. and Forenbaher, S. 2000. Pupićina Cave Project: brief summary of the 1998 season. *Histria Archaeologica* 29, 27–48.

Miracle, P. T. and Forenbaher, S. (eds.) 2006. *Prehistoric Herders in Istria (Croatia): the Archaeology of Pupićina Cave*. Pula, Archaeological Museum of Istria.

Miracle, P. T., Galanidou, N. and Forenbaher S. 2000. Pioneers in the hills: early Mesolithic foragers at Šebrn Abri (Istria, Croatia). *European Journal of Archaeology* 3 (3), 293–329.

Parenzan, P. 1928. Il Lago d'Arsa. *Histria Nobilissima* 1, 47–51.

49. Occupation in a submerged Mesolithic landscape

Garry Momber, Julie Satchell and Jan Gillespie

A decade of archaeological investigations in the western Solent by the Hampshire and Wight Trust for Maritime Archaeology, utilising divers and geophysical survey data has led to the discovery of stratified Mesolithic sites within submerged prehistoric landscapes. These sites, which lie between 6.5m and 11.8m below British Ordnance Datum (BOD), and their palaeo-environmental context harbour a resource that has the potential to preserve a rich source of cultural and palaeo-environmental material. This archive can inform the archaeological record and provide index points for sea level rise during a period of rapid climate change. However, the discovery of these delicate and vulnerable features is presenting new challenges to the maritime archaeologist. First and foremost is the need to understand the geomorphological and taphonomic evolution of the deposits. Next is the ability to record, rescue and interpret the remains underwater by the development and testing of new underwater sampling, excavation and recovery techniques.

Keywords: maritime, submerged landscape, geomorphology, sea level.

Introduction

An untapped resource

As the last Ice Age drew to a close, the once habitable landmass, which stretched from the ice sheets off the north-east coast of England to the outer reaches of the Atlantic continental shelf, was engulfed by up to 120m of water. It is within these submerged lands that evidence of human activity can still be found buried beneath sediments. Recent discoveries in the Solent, England, testify the existence of well-preserved archaeological deposits off the south coast of Britain.

Ahead of the rising waters, some 8100 cal BP, the oak (*Quercus*) and hazel (*Corylus*) trees that grew on the valley floor of the western Solent, now 11 metres below Ordnance Datum, were being poisoned by the advancing sea. Salt marsh was becoming established as estuaries migrated landward. The ancient woodlands fell into coastal swamps before the valley flooded. Within a thousand years, five-metre thick sediments had encapsulated and preserved all beneath them. This was a region that had been exploited by humans whose legacy had remained safely locked within the buried landscape until recently exposed by erosion.

Sometime after 6000 cal BP the Solent waterway was formed, shifting from estuarine to fully marine conditions (Scaife 2000; Tomalin 2000a, 9). The fine-grained alluvial silts which had been deposited over the previous two millennia began to be washed away. This process of erosion continues today, steadily removing the remaining reservoirs of sediment that fringe the western Solent. These sediments represent archives of archaeological and palaeo-environmental information that can inform us about past cultures and environmental events. This has been clearly demonstrated by discoveries of artefacts interwoven within the Mesolithic terrain and preserved for over 8000 years.

Submerged Mesolithic occupation sites in north Europe

An area renowned for its wealth of submerged settlements sites is the Baltic, where over 2000 Mesolithic sites (11,500 + cal BP to 6000 cal BP) have been discovered off the Danish and German coastlines (Fischer 2003; Lübke 2002, 203). The flooded valleys and river systems which have revealed such a high density of sites would have provided a rich source of protein and were attractive places to live. Indeed, studies of north European occupation patterns during the Middle and Late Mesolithic demonstrate that activities were concentrated along the coast (Denker 1997, 91; Fischer 1997, 63; Pedersen 1975, 75; Rowley-Conwy 1983, 111; Simmons 1996).

Interest in the potential of underwater landscapes around the British Isles was stimulated in part by an audit of the English coastline in 1997, which recorded coastal prehistoric peat deposits that followed ancient river systems and extended offshore (Fulford *et al.* 1997, 217). Subsequent research has brought to light evidence of palaeo-channels and ancient land surfaces in many places around the North Sea and English Channel (BMAPA 2003; Coles 1998, 45; Flemming 2004, 11; Maarleveld and Peeters 2004, 102; Momber 2000a, 86; University of Birmingham 2005; Verhart 2004, 57).

It would appear that the more we look for these palaeo-landscapes, the more we find. Despite this, very few submerged terrestrial archaeological sites have been discovered outside the Baltic. Recent marine discoveries indicate that other areas were occupied; however the survival rates for exposed material in these more saline, exposed and tidal waters may be much shorter. A graphic example of this can be seen through the monitoring of the recession of exposed peat deposits in the Solent. Once exposed to erosion the peat becomes accessible to a range of marine boring and burrowing organisms in addition to the waves and currents of this dynamic hydrological regime (Hampshire and Wight Trust for Maritime Archaeology (HWTMA) 2000).

Archaeological implications for the origin of the Solent

The Solent is the waterway that separates the Isle of Wight from mainland Britain (Figure 49.1). The origins of the Solent can be traced back into the Pleistocene where river systems abraded a path from Dorset, running east to pass north of the Isle of Wight. Numerous academics have discussed the evolution of the 'Solent' river, interpreting the distribution of fluvial gravels recorded across the Hampshire Basin. The river emptied into the large Channel River through a deep palaeo-channel running around the east of the Isle of Wight (Fox 1862, 452; Everard 1954, 41; Allen *et al.* 1993, 503; Hodsen *et al.* 1972, 421; Dyer 1975, 239; Wenbam-Smith 2001, 57; Dix 2001, 7). However, the existence of this waterway during the last glacial has recently been challenged by Velegrakis, who detected submerged palaeo-channels flowing south through Christchurch Bay, to the west of the Isle of Wight. These channels contained infill that suggested they were active during the last glacial (Velegrakis *et al.* 1999, 73; Velegrakis 2000, 21). The passage of rivers running either side of the land that was to become the Isle of Wight implies there would have been an umbilical of higher ground connecting it to the mainland. This would have interrupted any waterway from flowing around the north of the island during and following the Devensian.

If the western Solent was not an open watercourse but a closed estuary, there could have been parallels with the sheltered embayment environments present along the drowned coastlines of the southern Baltic. As such the preservation potential of archaeological material would be greatly increased. Conversely, if open water had access through the Solent, erosion may have played a more dominant role, and the chance of preservation would be less. An understanding of the regions inundation during the Flandrian transgression is essential as a basis upon which the archaeological potential can be realised and informed, and on which predictions of future change should be founded (Tomalin 2000b, 78). To address this issue, the alluvial sediments that line the western Solent have been sampled and interrogated to provide insights into the palaeo-environment.

Interpreting the sedimentary archive

Studies of the sedimentary archive in the western Solent were conducted as part of an investigation into rates of sea level rise and cliff instability. Coastal geomorphological change formed a component of the Coastal Change, Climate and Instability, L'Instrument Financière de L'Environnement (LIFE) project orchestrated and run between 1997 and 2000 by the Isle of Wight Centre for the Coastal Environment. The site selected for analysis was an 8m-high underwater cliff about 800m offshore from Bouldnor. The cliff rises from 12m below Ordnance Datum to 4m below, and was found to hold datable material that could be used to track sea level fluctuations over the last 8000 years.

Lacustrine sediments underlying the base of the cliff supported a well-preserved matting of peat within a forest of large toppled oak trees. This was found at 11–11.5m below Ordnance Datum and dated to 8565–8345 cal BP (Beta-140104). Above this, soft alluvial silts, which contained inclusions of branches and twigs, were laid in a brackish water environment. Diatom analysis of the silts

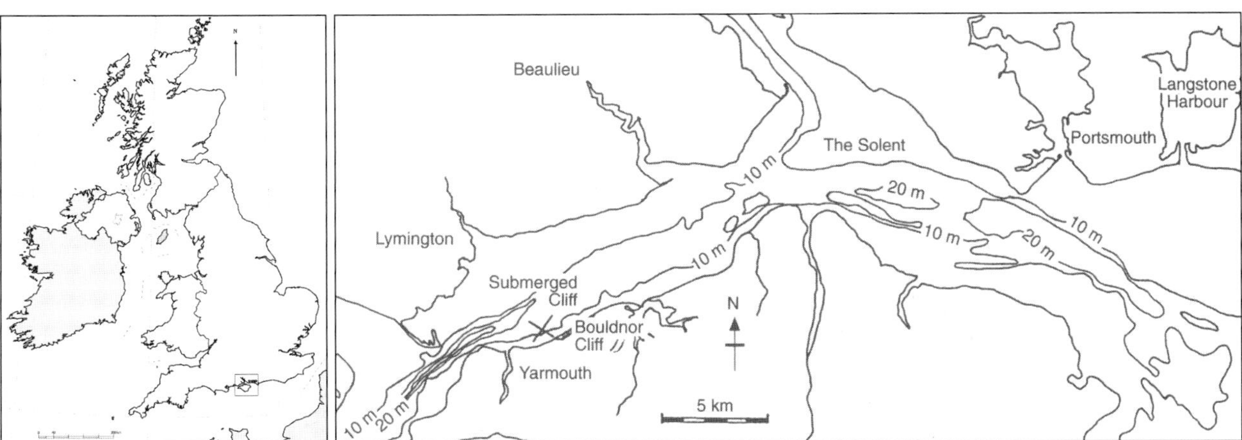

Figure 49.1. The Solent showing Bouldnor Cliff and the excavation site.

confirmed a low salinity (Scaife 2000). The alluvial/mud flat deposits were over 5m thick, above which sat another laterally consistent peat layer dated to 6870–6485 cal BP (Beta-140103). Topping this was a metre of brackish water sediment which was capped by peat at 4m below Ordnance Datum; the base of this was dated to 6475–6280 cal BP (Beta-140102). The formation of peat resulted from a stabilisation or relative drop in sea level during periods long enough to allow vegetation to colonise. Trees inlaid in the upper peat suggested the land had become well established before it was overwhelmed by the sea and again protected by silt. The silts that covered this top layer of vegetation would have had to be consolidated and thick enough to remain stable and afford the protection they did for thousands of years. Such deposits would have taken hundreds of years to accumulate.

The brackish estuarine environments that are reflected in the remaining sediments within the underwater cliff, and the magnitude of the capping peat gives credence to the hypothesis that the transition of the Solent to a fully marine environment did not begin until well after 6000 cal BP (Dix 2000; Momber 2000b; Tomalin 2000c; Long *et al.* 1995). When the sea eventually flowed over the final stretches of dry land that linked the Isle of Wight to mainland Britain, a 'proto' Solent would have been formed. As the water rose and the channel deepened, the tidal currents cut down into soft alluvial infill deposits, truncating them to leave near vertical sections. Protruding from beneath the estuarine silts, the Holocene valley floor continues to be exposed. Large tracts of these sediments may have been lost; however, remaining remnants still provide a valuable archive of palaeoenvironmental evidence (Figure 49.2).

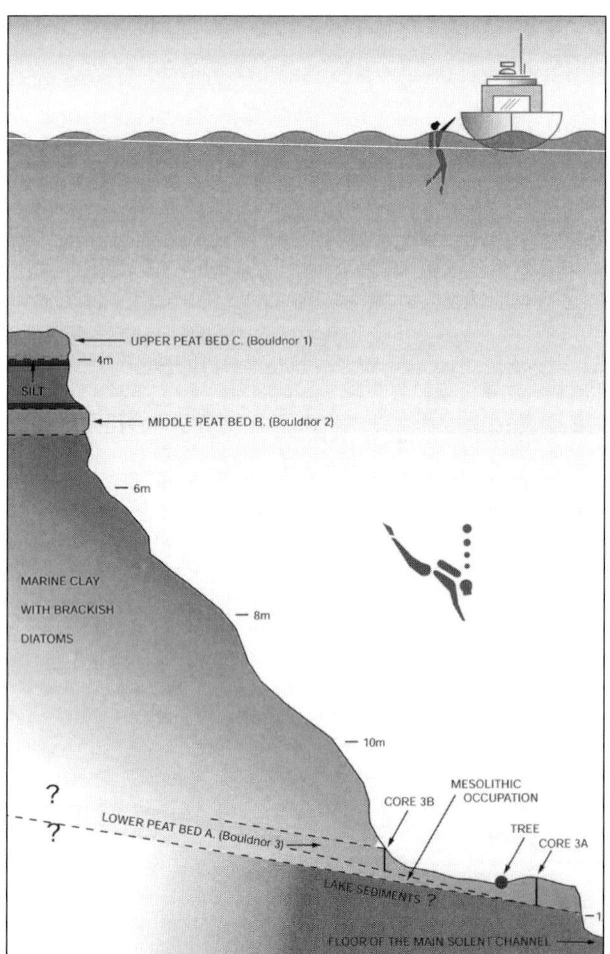

Figure 49.2. Section through deposits at Bouldnor Cliff. (Graphic courtesy R. G. McIness, Isle of Wight Centre for Coastal Environment).

Archaeological finds from the Solent

So, what of the archaeology around the Solent? Modern erosion at Wootton and Quarr beaches along the north-east shores of the Isle of Wight revealed a plethora of archaeological material ranging from the Mesolithic to the Post Medieval periods. Here, a survey was funded by English Heritage and carried out by the Isle of Wight Archaeological Unit during the 1990s (Loader *et al.* 1997; Tomalin 1993, 93). Comparable evidence was uncovered in Langstone Harbour, across the Solent on the Hampshire coast, during an archaeological research project in the 1990s. These projects have testified the geographical diversity and archaeological potential of the submerged and inter-tidal resource (Allen *et al.* 2000).

Many artefacts from the Lower Palaeolithic to the Neolithic have been found in the Solent, which have shown it to be very rich in prehistoric archaeological material. Unfortunately, most of these have been trawled up by fishermen after being washed from their original deposits and have been recovered out of context (HWTMA 2000; Sparks *et al.* 2001, 56). In an attempt to locate the source of this material, the HWTMA has been visually inspecting the floor of the Solent for over a decade. An area identified as having a high potential was the exposed peat shelf off Bouldnor cliff. In 1998 divers conducted surveys and within a week of searching the seabed, the first evidence of human activity was discovered and worked flints were recovered from the up-cast of a lobster burrow in 11m of water (Figure 49.3).

In May 2000 exploratory excavations proved beyond doubt that stratified archaeological deposits were present within the submerged cliff (Momber 2002, 633). The work also identified a complex stratigraphic sequence that held information about the geomorphological evolution of the coast as sea levels rose.

Investigating and recording a Mesolithic landscape underwater

The discovery of lithics within the seabed prompted further investigation. A key driver for research was not only to gather archaeological data that could enhance our understanding of the Mesolithic during a period when sea level was lower, but to understand the changing environment in which humans were living. Activities at the site were being played out as the sea was advancing and realigning the coast.

In 2003, English Heritage funded a project to characterise the landscape from which these archaeological artefacts were recovered. Excavation was conducted to recover archaeological material and palaeo-environment samples (Momber 2004, 39). This enabled detailed study to consider the morphological and environmental conditions, before, during and after inundation. There was concern amongst the archaeologists, however, as to how this could be done without disturbing the delicate matrix of archaeological and environmental material from a site that liquefies when in contact with water.

The principle tool employed for excavation underwater has been the air lift. This device enables the archaeologist to gently clear silts from around artefacts without causing damage. It has a place in all underwater excavations but has limitations when fine sediments have to be recovered undisturbed. Cultural deposits within ancient land surfaces need careful attention, as direct exposure to water is enough to cause important material to go into solution and be lost. This is particularly true when new areas of the deposit are laid bare in the open sea. The answer was to recover as much material as possible to the surface for detailed analysis. One method of obtaining information utilised marine grade, stainless steel monolith tins that were not too large for divers to handle but big enough to retain a cohesive sample (HWTMA 2003, 10). When the monoliths were recovered they provided a vertical sequence that could be analysed and dated to provide a calibrated sequence of change through time.

Figure 49.3. Lithics recovered from the Bouldnor Cliff site (cm grid).

Interpreting a changing cultural landscape

Initial assessment of the results suggests that a number of events and adaptations occurred within the complex stratigraphic sequence identified in the 8000-year-old landscape. The lowest exposed level contained fluvial gravel and a yellow sand. A small cluster of burnt flints was recovered from just above this horizon. This would have been the edge of a stream that attracted humans for fishing or wild fowling. Above this, a 600mm-thick band of fine grey silty sand was deposited. The silts contained freshly knapped flint blades, cores and organic inclusions throughout. These artefacts demonstrate continual use of the stream bank as the sands were laid down. A capping of gravel over the cultural deposit suggests the stream shifted direction before it ultimately disappeared, after which it was covered by vegetation and small trees.

The next stage in the evolution of the landscape was inundation by the sea. This was represented in section, first by a brown silty mudflat, or saltmarsh deposits, and then by soft grey alluvial silts laid down as the sea covered the landscape (Figures 49.4 and 49.5).

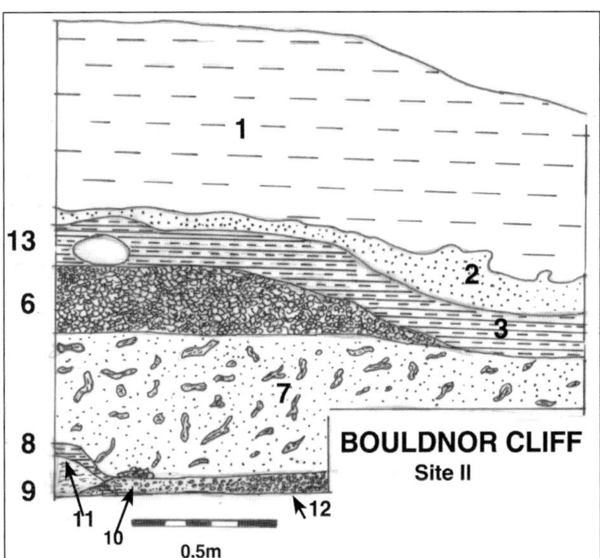

Key
1. Grey alluvium
2. Silty alluvium with dark organic staining
3. Laminated peat deposit inlaid with timber
6. Gravel with timber inclusions and rolled worked flint
7. Fine grey sandy/silt with timber inclusions and knapped flint
8. Peaty/humic deposit
9. Lower timber layer
10. Burnt flint
11. Course sand with flint and clastic material
12. Rounded gravel
13. Timber inlaid within peat

Figure 49.4. Section across horizon containing cultural material. Lithics have been recorded from within and below the peat deposit.

Full interpretation of the deposits is ongoing as part of the research project supported by English Heritage, which is currently being written up. This will present the archaeological material alongside an assessment of the changing landscape and sea level rise. What is clearly evident is that humans occupied the site and would have undoubtedly exploited resources across the landscape.

It was therefore not surprising that a further *loci* of human activity was discovered in 2004 when archaeology was recorded eroding from the edge of the submerged land surface in 11.5m of water, 300m to the west of the previous site. The discovery consisted of a hearth or oven, which looks to have been excavated into the palaeo-land surface when it was once dry land. It was filled with burnt flints and clay nodules, being uncovered as the seabed eroded. A second feature, two metres to the west, consisted of a hollow, filled with mottled grey clay. Sampling and excavation revealed that the deposit consisted of a clayey silt matrix with frequent burnt lithics and blackened organic inclusions. This was exposed in section directly below a cluster of irregular shaped timbers with flat 'plank-like' pieces sitting alongside round wood.

This anomalous timber 'feature' is roughly circular, measuring 2.1m, and forms an elevation above the surrounding present-day seabed: it is unlike any other natural wooden elements recorded in the submerged landscape to date. Archaeological material within the cultural deposit included burnt flint and a branch, or sapling, that was impaled by a worked, burnt flint tool. The whole deposit appears to be resting on a layer of twigs that have been ^{14}C dated to 8200 to 7960 cal BP (Beta-207809). This was a time when rising sea waters would not have been far away.

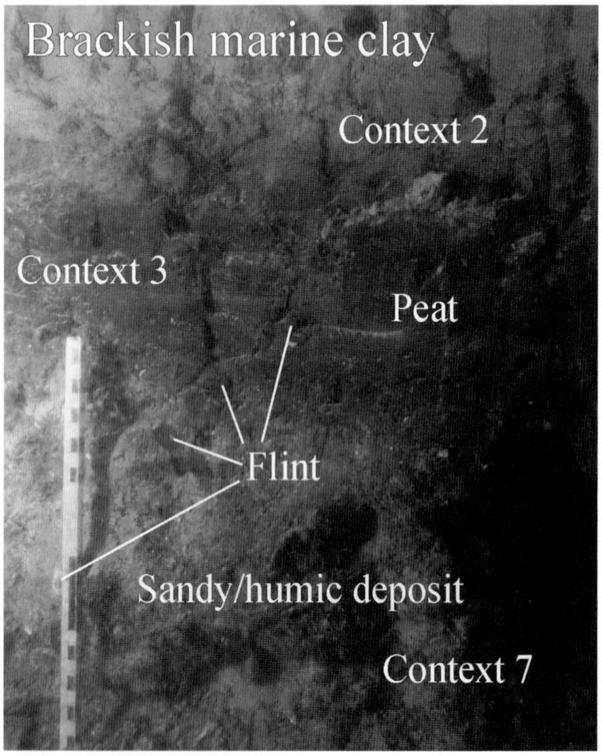

Figure 49.5. Section across peat and cultural deposit at BC II.

Spatial and temporal mapping of the sea floor

To understand the relationships of the Mesolithic sites to any submerged landscape we need to image the seabed and interpret the coastal geomorphological evolution. To do this we need to visualise its current manifestation, its internal structure, and also to understand the processes that brought about the change. Divers are invaluable when gaining detailed knowledge of sites, but they are inevitability restricted by poor visibility in silty water.

To overcome this limitation, acoustic and geophysical survey has been employed. The main tool used for characterising the seabed at Bouldnor Cliff has been swath bathymetry. This is essential for the provision of baseline data which can aid the monitoring of losses and the location of areas with high archaeological potential. As the current seabed does not represent the landscape of 8000 years earlier, we have to be cautious when reading bathymetric survey data and accept that it may not necessarily reflect the underlying landscape. These are limitations, but often the morphological or geological expressions we see today are a reflection of geomorphological adaptations and can provide clues to the processes that effected that change. When high-resolution bathymetric data is collected in tandem with sub-bottom profiling devices, traces of earlier landscapes can be revealed.

Conclusions

As the western Solent continues to evolve, submerged Holocene deposits that fringe the coastline are being exposed. Within these deposits, stratified archaeological sites have been revealed. The loss of the resource is of concern, but it has presented the opportunity for detailed research of human occupation in a changing environment over 8000 years ago.

Investigation of archaeological sites within the waterway is providing information about the habitat associated with occupation and is helping to identify the potential archaeological, palaeo-environmental and geomorphological significance of the drowned landscape. Analysis of the sediments coupled with geophysical survey of the submerged deposits is providing an insight into the terrain prior to inundation, which could help to locate areas suitable for past human occupation. This in turn will aid the management of the coastal and palaeo-environment resource below the low-water mark while informing judgements on their archaeological potential and significance.

This paper has also identified a number of challenges and opportunities for the maritime archaeologist when investigating submerged cultural landscapes. Overcoming practical obstacles to research can tell us about the pioneers who opened the way for continual occupation following the last Ice Age and provide valuable information about the rate at which changing sea level has impacted the British shoreline.

Gathering of information on submerged prehistoric landscapes is subject to a number of restraints – logistical, financial, and perceptual. While capital returns against investment may be limited and appear ethereal when looking to the past, an understanding of the physical and cultural birth of Britain is invaluable. Unfortunately, until there is a greater appetite to unlock the secrets of our prehistoric ancestry beneath the sea, we can only watch and wonder while the waters wash it away.

Acknowledgements

The research has been made possible with support from the Hampshire and Wight Trust for Maritime Archaeology, the University of York and the University of Southampton. Specific financial assistance has been provided by English Heritage, the Standing Conference On Problems Associated with the Coastline, and Valerie Fenwick. The results would not have been possible without valuable specialist contributions from Nigel Nayling, Dr David Tomalin, Dr Rob Scaife, Dr Mark Robinson, and Dr Jen Heathcote.

References

Allen, L. C. and Gibbard, P. L. 1993. Pleistocene evolution of the Solent River of Southern England. *Quaternary Science Reviews* 12, 503–28.

Allen, M. J. and Gardiner, J. P. 2000. Our Changing Landscape: an intertidal survey of Langstone Harbour. Council for British Archaeology (CBA) Research Report 124. York, Council for British Archaeology.

British Marine Aggregate Producers Association (BMAPA) and English Heritage, 2003. *Marine Aggregate Dredging and the Historic Environment: guidance note 4–5*. London, British Marine Aggregate Producers Association and English Heritage.

Coles, B. 1998. Doggerland: a speculative survey. *Proceedings of the Prehistoric Society* 64, 45–81.

Denker, J. 1997. Stone-Age settlements in the middle of Nature's Larder, in L. Pedersen, A. Fischer and B. Aaby (eds.), *The Danish Storebaelt since the Ice Age – man, sea and forest*, 87–92. Copenhagen, A/S Storebaeltsforbindelsen.

Dix, J. K. 2000. Coastal Change, Climate and Instability, in R. McIness and J. Jakeways (eds.), *Report for EU Life Environment Programme* (2). Isle of Wight Centre for the Coastal Environment. Newport, Isle of Wight Council.

Dix, J. K. 2001. The geology of the Solent River system, in F. F. Wenban-Smith and R. T. Hosfield (eds.), *Palaeolithic Archaeology of the Solent River*, 7–14. Lithic Studies Society Occasional Paper No. 7. Southampton, Lithic Studies Society.

Dyer, K. R. 1975. The buried channels of the 'Solent River', Southern England. *Proceedings of the Geologists' Association* 86, 239–46. London, the Geological Society.

Everard, C. E. 1954. The Solent River: a geomorphological study. *Transactions of the Institute of British Geographers* 20, 41–58.

Fischer, A. 1997. People and the Sea – Settlement and Fishing along the Mesolithic Coasts, in L. Pedersen, A. Fischer and B. Aaby (eds.), *The Danish Storebaelt since the Ice Age – man, sea and forest*, 63–77. Copenhagen, A/S Storebaeltsforbindelsen.

Fischer, A. 2003. Submerged Stone Age – Danish Examples and North Sea potential, in N. Flemming (ed.), *Submarine Prehistoric Archaeology of the North Sea*, 23–36. Council for British Archaeology (CBA) Research Report 141. York, Council for British Archaeology.

Flemming, N. 2004. The prehistory of the North Sea floor in the context of Continental Shelf archaeology from the Mediterranean to Nova Zemlya, in N. Flemming (ed.), *Submarine Prehistoric Archaeology of the North Sea*, 11–20. Council for British Archaeology (CBA) Research Report 141. York, Council for British Archaeology.

Fox, W. D. 1862. How and when was the Isle of Wight separated from the mainland. *The Geologist* 452.

Fulford, M., Champion, T. and Long, A. 1997. *England's Coastal Heritage: a survey for English Heritage and the RCHME*, 217. London, English Heritage/Royal Commission on Historic Monuments of England.

Hampshire and Wight Trust for Maritime Archaeology (HWTMA) 2000. *Search Annual Report 1999/2000*. Southampton, Hampshire and Wight Trust for Maritime Archaeology.

Hampshire and Wight Trust for Maritime Archaeology (HWTMA) 2000. *The Story Beneath the Solent*. Southampton, Hampshire and Wight Trust for Maritime Archaeology.

Hampshire and Wight Trust for Maritime Archaeology (HWTMA) 2003. *A Year in Depth: 2002/2003 Report*. Southampton, Hampshire and Wight Trust for Maritime Archaeology.

Hodson, F. and West, I. M. 1972. Holocene Deposits of Fawley Hampshire, and the development of Southampton, Water. *Proceedings of the Geological Association* 83–4, 421–441.

Loader, R., Westmore, I. and Tomalin, D. 1997. *Time and Tide; an archaeological survey of the Wootton-Quarr coast*. Newport, Isle of Wight Council.

Long, A. J. and Tooley, M. J. 1995. Holocene Sea-Level and Crustal Movements in Hampshire and Southeast England, United Kingdom. *Journal of Coastal Research: Special Issue No 17, Holocene Cycles: Climate, Sea-Levels, and Sedimentation*, 299–310.

Lübke, H. 2002. Submarine Stone Age settlements as indicators of sea-level changes and the coastal evolution of the Wismar Bay area, in R. Lampe (ed.), *Holocene Evolution of the South-Western Baltic Coast – Geological, Archaeological and Palaeo-environmental Aspects. Field meeting of INQUA Sub-commission V, September 2002*. Greifswalder Geographische Arbeiten 27, 203–10. Greifswald, University of Greifswald.

Maarleveld, T. and Peeters, H. 2004. Can we manage?, in N. Flemming (ed.), *Submarine Prehistoric Archaeology of the North Sea*, 102–112. Council for British Archaeology (CBA) Research Report 141. York, Council for British Archaeology.

Momber, G. 2000a. Drowned and deserted: a submerged prehistoric landscape in the Solent, England. *The International Journal of Nautical Archaeology* 29 (1), 86–99.

Momber, G. 2000b. Coastal Change, Climate and Instability, in R. McIness and J. Jakeways (eds.), *Report for EU Life Environment Programme* (2). Isle of Wight Centre for the Coastal Environment. Newport, Isle of Wight Council.

Momber, G. 2002. Instability: Archaeology in a Drowned Landscape, in R. McInnes and J. Jakeways (eds.), *Planning and management; seeking sustainable solutions to ground movement problems*, 633–40. London, Thomas Telford.

Momber, G. 2004. The inundated landscapes of the Western Solent, in N. Flemming (ed.), *Submarine Prehistoric Archaeology of the North Sea*, 37–42. Council for British Archaeology (CBA) Research Report 141. York, Council for British Archaeology.

Pederson, L. 1995. 7000 years of fishing: stationary fishing structures in the Mesolithic and afterwards, in A. Fischer (ed.), *Man and sea in the Mesolithic: coastal settlements above and below present sea level*, 75–76. Oxbow Monographs 53. Oxford, Oxford Books.

Rowley-Conway, P. 1983. Sedentary hunters: the Ertebølle example, in G. Bailey (ed.), *Hunter-Gatherer Economy in Pre-history. A European Prospective*, 111–126. Cambridge, Cambridge University Press.

Scaife, R. 2000. Coastal Change, Climate and Instability, in R. McIness and J. Jakeways (eds.), *Report for EU Life Environment Programme* (2). Isle of Wight Centre for the Coastal Environment. Newport, Isle of Wight Council.

Simmons, I. G. 1996. The Environmental Impact of Later Mesolithic Cultures. The Creation of Moorland Landscapes in England and Wales. Edinburgh, Edinburgh University Press.

Sparks, B., Momber, G. and Satchell, J. 2001. *A Decade of Diving, Delving and Dissemination*, 56–69. Southampton, Hampshire and Wight Trust for Maritime Archaeology.

The Sotton Project 2005. *The Ice Age in the Midlands and the Ancient Human Occupation of Britain*. Birmingham, University of Birmingham. http://www.arch-ant.bham.ac.uk/shottonproject/iceage.htm (accessed 10/2007).

Tomalin, D. 1993. Maritime Archaeology as a Coastal Management Issue: A Solent Case Study from the SCOPAC coast, in *The Regional Coastal Groups After the House of Commons (1992) Report: Proceedings of Seminar*, 93–112. Newport, Isle of Wight, Standing Conference on Problems Associated with the Coastline (SCOPAC).

Tomalin, D. 2000a. Geomorphological evolution of the Solent Seaway and the severance of the Wight: A review, in M. Collins and K. Ansell (eds.), *Solent Science – A Review*, 9–20. Amsterdam, Elsevier.

Tomalin, D. 2000b. Wisdom of Hindsight: Palaeo-Environmental and Archaeological Evidence of Long Term Processual Changes and Coastline Stability, in M. Collins and K. Ansell (eds.), *Solent Science – A Review*, 71–83. Proceedings in Marine Science 1. Amsterdam, Elsevier.

Tomalin, D. 2000c. Coastal Change, Climate and Instability, in R. McIness and J. Jakeways (eds.), *Report for EU Life Environment Programme* (2). Isle of Wight Centre for the Coastal Environment. Newport, Isle of Wight Council.

Velegrakis, A. F. 2000. Geology, geomorphology and sediments of the Solent system, in M. Collins and K. Ansell (eds.), *Solent Science – A Review*, 21–44. Proceedings in Marine Science 1. Amsterdam, Elsevier.

Velegrakis, A. F., Dix, J. K. and Collins, M. B. 1999. Late Quaternary evolution of the upper reaches of the Solent River, Southern England, based upon marine geophysical evidence. *Journal of the Geological Society* 156, 73–87.

Verhart, L. 2004. The implications of prehistoric finds on and off the Dutch coast, in N. Flemming (ed.), *Submarine Prehistoric Archaeology of the North Sea*, 57–64. Council for British Archaeology (CBA) Research Report 141. York, Council for British Archaeology.

Wenbam-Smith, F. F. 2001. As presented by the Solent River: handaxes from Highfield, in F. F. Wenban-Smith and R. T. Hosfield (eds.), *Palaeolithic Archaeology of the Solent River*, 57–69. Lithic Studies Society Occasional Paper 7. Southampton, School of Humanities (Archaeology), University of Southampton.

Session V

Regional Identities

50. Introduction: Regional identities

Graeme Warren

Long-standing traditions in Mesolithic research have focused on the examination of the archaeological record at a regional level and the identification of territories in the past. So dominant are these trends that it is perhaps little surprise that Eriksen, introducing the section 'Territoriality – Regionalisation' in *Mesolithic on the Move*, argues that 'most of the papers presented at the MESO 2000 conference would fit nicely within this heading' (Eriksen 2003, 281).

In part, this is due to conceptual slippage – it is not always clear what we mean by a regional study. Eriksen's definitions include those 'performed at a fairly local scale', which are argued to blur into analyses of local landscapes, as well as, and perhaps more characteristically, studies that have '...attempted a more generalised, macro-regional approach ... These endeavours have often been devoted to largely descriptive presentations' (Eriksen 2003, 281), often mapping distributions of artefacts, or raw materials, across large tracts of space and/or time. In the same section of the volume, Bergsvik argues that a basic archaeological practice from the early 20th century, mapping the distribution of archaeological 'cultures' across space, lies at the heart of such approaches to regional variation in Mesolithic archaeology (Bergsvik 2003). Importantly, Childe's original definitions of archaeological 'cultures' can be seen to have snowballed over time, accruing additional concepts such as social territories (e.g. Clark), mating networks/dialectical tribe (e.g. Price) and ultimately ethnicity (e.g. Gendel) (Bergsvik 2003, 290–1, full references in original). Much of the reaction against regional studies is critical of this jumble of accreted association.

Powerful anthropologically informed critiques of the relationship between material culture and any form of group identity have long existed, and are often trotted out to dismiss the importance of any given distribution map: on this basis, for example, Julian Thomas argues that the strong material culture differences between Ireland and Britain in the later Mesolithic do not mean that the areas were isolated (Thomas 2004). Alongside such theoretical objections to the interpretation of distribution maps, it is evident throughout the Mesolithic of Europe that the distributions of varying raw materials or artefact classes do not coincide; that some objects (and possibly people) travelled great distances; and that the period can only be understood as a complex mosaic of both movement and stability. In this situation it would be easy to dismiss painstakingly constructed distributions of artefact types, or raw material networks, as simply the legacy of outmoded archaeological practices, of little or no interest to contemporary analytical practice.

Yet, the persistent presence of regional variation in the record is a little awkward: why are things different? At times, it appears that a simplistic notion of 'tradition' is the ghost in our models: that people make things in different ways, or obtain materials from different places because that's just what they do, but really, it's not of that much analytical interest to us. This is a particularly surprising approach given the increasing centrality of notions of the everyday and routine in the wider literature (see, for example, Whittle 2003). To return to the Irish example – what does it mean that Mesolithic communities in Ireland, and on the Isle of Man, used stone tool technologies significantly different than people on the other side of the Irish Sea? Surely this cannot simply be dismissed simply as a 'tradition'; isn't it rather that this something, in some ways, relates to people and the ways in which they made sense of the world and the other things, including other peoples, which they found within it?

Alongside the nagging sense that we haven't yet come to terms with what regional variation might mean, we have often struggled to relate the varied scales, temporal and geographic, such regions presume. At different times hunter-gatherers participate in different scales of community – from the family group to the occasional aggregation of the extended kin network; and they may have moved from improvising a wooden tool to making objects reflecting thousands of years of practice. How were these wider, sometimes regional, identities and links maintained? How did Mesolithic individuals move between those different scales of life? In which ways did these traditions of practice relate to wider identities?

Furthermore, whilst ethnography does demonstrate real complexities in the ways in which material culture operates in relation to identities at different scales, it also demonstrates very real and complex patterns of regional, territorial and ethnic affiliation amongst hunter-gatherers and others – often with violent correlates (see for example Burch 2005). It is also important to recognize that concepts of self/other will be much more marked where different groups of people come into contact: contact zones, in this sense, may have been somewhat dangerous, charged spaces – so the varied boundaries on our maps may have been especially important.

The strongly regional character of some aspects of the Mesolithic of Europe has often been poorly served in general models, and, in particular, by the dominance of the Ertebølle as an archetype. In some areas, often those perceived to be at the margins, recent years have seen fresh approaches which invert notions of core/periphery and place great emphasis on the constitution of local (or regional) ways of being Mesolithic through creative use of the varying cultural resources available from different areas. Thus, for example, in Östergötland, eastern Sweden:

> '…it is the mixture which is the specific. A constant flow of cultural contacts is visible in the way people expressed themselves through their material culture. Direct and indirect contacts from several geographical quarters shaped the cultural mix that constitutes the specific character. Border zones like Östergötland reveal the possibilities that people had to accept or reject parts of a geographically extensive common Mesolithic material culture.' (Carlsson *et al.* 2005, 23)

Notwithstanding a flavour of post-modern *bricolage*, considering areas as border or contact zones provides an important corrective to the 'edges' created by many regional studies.

These sketches of interwoven concerns about how we engage with regional variation in the record, and attempt to understand the scales of human lives in the past, hopefully give some background to the definition of a MESO 2005 conference session on 'Regional Identities'. Clearly related to the long standing tradition of regional studies in Mesolithic archaeology, this session explicitly attempted to find connections between different scales, temporal and geographic; to look at links, as well as edges; and to consider how differences, as well as similarities were maintained. The results are impressive, with several key themes strongly present.

The first is, in some senses, the most basic: how are we to define or understand the scale of regions. Most contributors discuss this, but three papers focus in more detail. On the basis of detailed geological sourcing of lithic materials in the northern French Alps, Bressy shows how infrequently large-scale movement of lithic material takes place, with most procurement areas <80km in maximum dimension, noting that this cuts across long-distance networks in other materials. Bond, discussing raw materials, typology and movement, also uses lithics as the primary source for a study of varied regions in SW England. Schulting, utilising isotopic analyses of human skeletons in south Wales, and drawing parallels more widely, argues for dietary variation, presumably linked to regional structuring of activity, at a scale of 15–30km. The small scale of these regions deserves especial attention.

The second and third themes are connected; a focus on understanding regions as communities bound by common knowledge, or traditions – or, as introduced here by Hallgren, 'Communities of Practice' (Wenger 1998) – and considering the contact zones where such communities might meet. Many papers draw on these themes more or less explicitly: David's detailed reconstructions of variation in patterns of bone tool manufacture across Europe offer a clear demonstration of the existence of three broad, but related, technological traditions. The emphasis on traditions of knowledge highlights key epistemological problems, and Cobb highlights the need to develop frameworks for understanding how forms of knowledge were possible; arguing that phenomenology provides a sound basis for this task and that visual and material connections between sites provide a basis for the analysis of these topics. Solem demonstrates change over time in the characteristic views from sites in Varanger, northern Norway, arguing that these are not functional, but have clear associations with traditions of knowledge and practice. Fretheim, examining Late Mesolithic cooking-pits in south-east Norway argues for their use as feasting locations; noting that '(b)y connecting people, the feast would have spread knowledge of different local traditions'. Importantly, Fretheim reminds us that places that bring people together can also be contexts in which difference is made more visible: that regional identities must also arise through opposition and that the analyses of traditions of practice must focus on where they meet. Further examples of this are present in the exploration by Edmonds *et al.* of the place of Ynys Enlli in broader Irish Sea geographies and technical histories of stone tool production.

Several papers discuss contact zones. Holm examines one of these zones in terms of archaeological distribution, as well as exploring the impact of borders between Universities in constructing our understandings. Her conclusions about participation in different routines of association remind us of the multiple scalar dimensions of Mesolithic lives. Discussions of contact zones draw heavily on understandings of traditions of knowledge and practice. Hallgren's discussion of the adoption of pottery in the Baltic, for example, shows how the adoption of an exotic technology can be understood through the dynamism of local, and variable, communities of practice. 'None of the societies under discussion *invented* ceramic technology: they all *learned* it from neighbouring groups. This was not only a simple case of copying, but also the creation of something new, by mixing different technological recipes and designs.'

At the end of chairing the session at Belfast, I commented that the papers had provided a remarkably coherent body of work, and this is clearly demonstrated in this publication. Given the vagaries of traditional approaches to 'regions' this strength of focus is especially notable. Key problems remain, notably in resolving scalar issues and understanding the interaction between involvements in varied communities of practice. We would not pretend to have answers to the questions of regional identities yet, but a broad range of scholars from across Europe have found some interesting, and complementary, ways of exploring this question. I would like to thank all of the contributors for their input.

References

Bergsvik, K. A. 2003. Mesolithic Ethnicity – Too Hard to Handle?, in L. Larsson, H. Kindgren, K. Knutsson, D. Loeffler and A. Åkerlund (eds.), *Mesolithic on the Move: Papers presented at the Sixth International Conference on the Mesolithic in Europe, Stockholm 2000*, 290–301. Oxford, Oxbow Books.

Burch, E. S., Jr. 2005. *Alliance and Conflict: the world system of the Iñupiaq Eskimos*. London, University of Nebraska Press.

Carlsson, T., Gruber, G. and Molin, F. 2005. The Mesolithic in Östergötland: an introduction, in G. Gruber (ed.), *Identities in Transition: Mesolithic Strategies in the Swedish Province of Östergötland*, 8–23. Arkeologiska undersökningar Skrifter 46. Stockholm, Riksantikvarieämbetet.

Eriksen, B. V. 2003. Introduction, in L. Larsson, H. Kindgren, K. Knutsson, D. Loeffler and A. Åkerlund (eds.), *Mesolithic on the Move: Papers presented at the Sixth International Conference on the Mesolithic in Europe, Stockholm 2000*, 281–2. Oxford, Oxbow Books.

Thomas, J. 2004. Current Debates on the Mesolithic-Neolithic Transition in Britain and Ireland. *Documenta Praehistorica* 31, 113–30.

Wenger, E. 1998. *Communities of Practice: Learning, Meaning, and Identity*. Cambridge, Cambridge University Press.

Whittle, A. 2003. *The Archaeology of People: Dimensions of Neolithic Life*. London, Routledge.

51. Flint procurement in the French Alps during the Mesolithic: deciphering economic and cultural territories

Céline Bressy

Territorial approaches in the northern French Alps are likely to impact on lowland/upland relationships during the Mesolithic, and thus on the cyclic exploitation of different environments and resources. To deal with this issue we considered raw material procurement in terms of provenance and techno-economic patterns. The results highlight different behaviours regarding raw material use based on site status and location. They also allow us to reconstruct territorial bodies and interpret cultural identities. The part played by 'secondary' alpine valleys in the penetration of Subalpine massifs is demonstrated.

Keywords: flint, French Alps, Mesolithic, provenance, territories.

Introduction

With the new climatic and environmental era, the Mesolithic is the period that witnessed the colonization of pristine territories, including mountain environments. In the French Alps, where the occupation of uplands is evidenced to a height of 2300m (Walsh 2003), the density of sites related to this period is much higher than for earlier and later periods. The Mesolithic has been intensively investigated in northern French Alps for some thirty years (Bintz 1991; 1999a; Bintz *et al.* 1995). Models of chrono-cultural evolution have been established and compared in parallel with the environmental framework (Argant 1999; Bridault and Chaix 1999; Thiebaut 1999). The contrasted faunal and vegetation distributions in the study area, because of the altitudes involved, may have played an important part in the mobility strategies of Mesolithic groups; to obtain a diversified range of plant and animal resources, the groups were required to exploit different resources at different altitudes and travel through different altitudinal levels. Seasonal migrations have been demonstrated, with evidence of mountain-area occupation (above 1100m), from spring to autumn (Bridault and Chaix 1999). In such context, major issues revolve around upland occupation modalities, in particular the relationship between lowland and mountain environment, and territorial and cultural identities.

To apprehend territorial organization and mobility, one first has to consider site distribution and their respective statuses. However, to reconstruct a dynamic and global outline of past territories, we undertook a fruitful study focused on lithic raw material procurement and circulation. The French Alps provide a suitable context to conduct such a work as flints are widely available, and potential resources well documented.

Methods

To acquire a representative sampling of siliceous resources, the study of flint procurement in the French Alps is based on an intensive field survey (Bressy 2003) that began 30 years ago (Bintz and Grünwald 1990; Affolter and Grünwald 1999). West of the Drac and Isère Rivers stand the Subalpine limestone massifs, where flint occurs; to the east are the Crystalline massifs, where quartz is to be found. The range of geological formations providing flint in Subalpine limestone massifs of the northern French Alps spans from the Jurassic to the Upper Cretaceous. The flint potential from Quaternary formations (alluvial deposits, moraine, karstic formations) was also investigated so as to obtain a comprehensive picture of the siliceous resources of the study area. Chartreuse, Vercors and Diois are the wealthiest areas among Subalpine limestone massifs in terms of flint resources (Figure 51.1). Within these massifs, Valanginian, Barremo-Bedoulian and Senonian flints are the three geological varieties mainly exploited in prehistory. Their qualities and morphologies vary and their outcrops show specific geographical distribution (e.g. Barremo-Bedoulian flints can only be found in southern Vercors and further south). Moreover, specific deposit contexts of some varieties make their procurement easier: decarbonatation

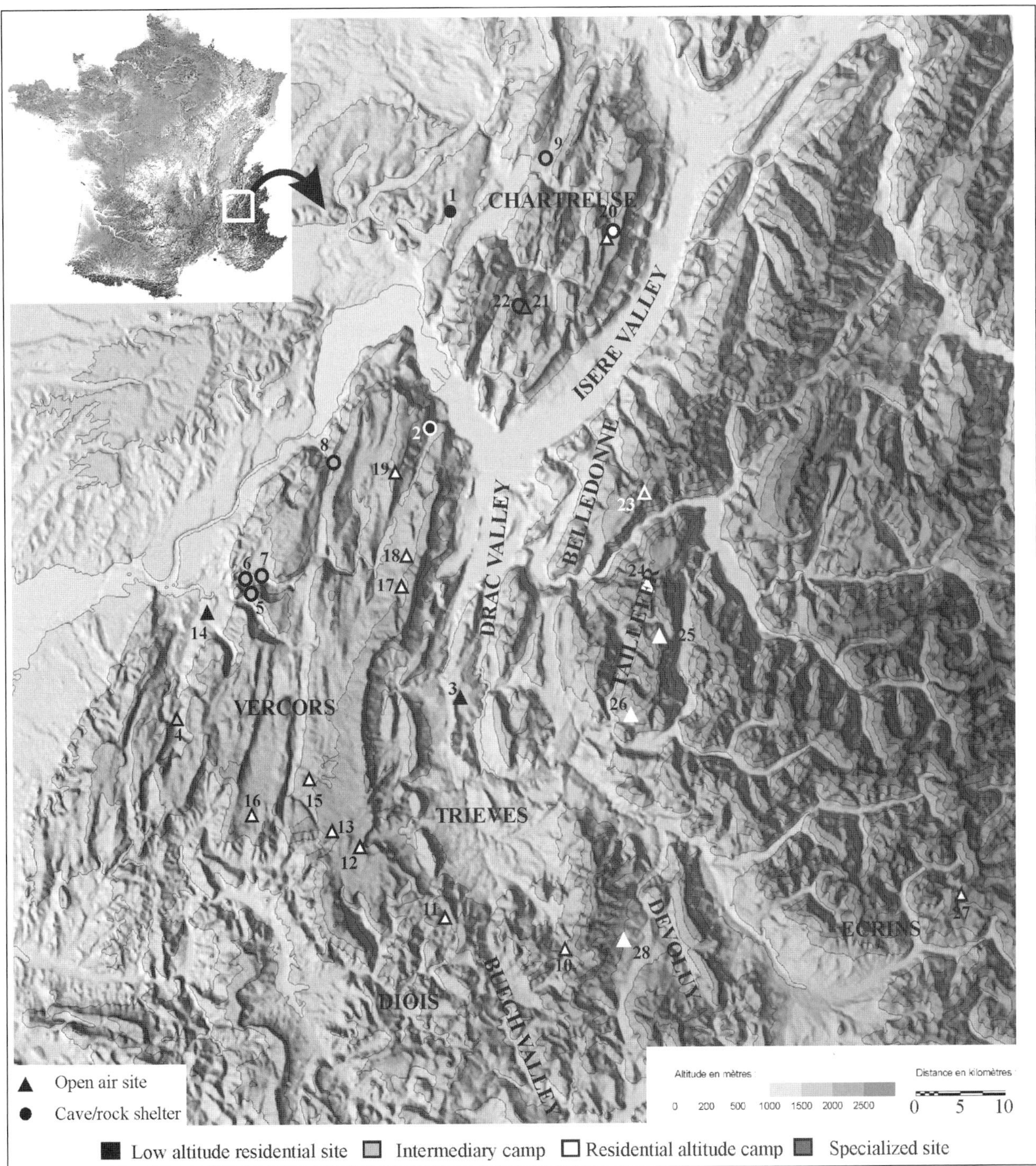

Figure 51.1. Location and status of Mesolithic sites in the French Alps. The solid white markers refer to sites of undetermined status. 1: Les Balmettes; 2: La Grande Rivoire; 3: Les Blachettes sud; 4: Bouvante; 5: Pas de la Charmatte; 6: Balme Rousse; 7: Coufins I et II; 8: Pas de l'Echelle; 9: La Fru; 10: Col de la Croix; 11: Bellemotte; 12: Pas de l'Aiguille; 13: Pré Peyret; 14: Plaine de Serres; 15: Fontaine de la Baume; 16:Vassieux-en-Vercors; 17: Roybon; 18: Machiret; 19: Les Coins; 20: Aulp du Seuil; 21: Col de Porte; 22: Canaple; 23: Lacs Robert; 24: Chalet de la Barrière; 25: Ruisseau de Vaunoire; 26: Clos de l'Alpe; 27: Faravel; 28: Les Egayères. (Background map: AVDPA, Grenoble).

clays (Barremo-Bedoulian flints), Tertiary conglomerates and sands (reworked Senonian flints).

Having established this reference point, we based our source assignments on petrographic comparison between geological and archaeological flints (Bressy 2003), using non-destructive tests under the stereomicroscope. Geochemistry was also applied to Alpine Senonian flints for methodological investigations, but, due to multiscale flint heterogeneity, the analyses only provided a fingerprint signature for one single source among the 22 analysed (Bressy 2003; Bressy *et al.* 2002; 2003).

Provenance assignments and typo-technological patterns

N° on Fig. 1	Site	Town	Location	Period	Altitude	Open air/shelter	Surface / stratigraphy	Status	Flint artefacts studied (N)
Subalpine limestone massif (rich flint environment)									
12	Le Pas de l'Aiguille (PAG II S35)	Chichilianne	Vercors	Middle Mesolithic	1650m	open air	Stratigraphy	Residential altitude camp	685
15	Fontaine de la Baume	Saint-Agnan-en-Vercors	Vercors	Late Mesolithic	1515m	open air	Stratigraphy	Residential altitude camp	564
21	Col de Porte	Sarcenas	Chartreuse	Middle Mesolithic	1320m	open air	Stratigraphy	Specialized camp	1827
22	Canaple	Sarcenas	Chartreuse	Middle Mesolithic	1580m	rock shelter	Stratigraphy	Specialized camp	613
Cristalline massifs (flint lacking environment)									
23	Lacs Robert	Chamrousse	Belledonne	Mesolithic	2000m	open air	Surface	Specialized camp	72
24	Chalet de la Barrière	Livet-Gavet	Taillefer	Mesolithic	1860m	open air	Surface	Undetermined	10
25	Ruisseau de Vaunoire	La Morte	Taillefer	Mesolithic	1500-1600m	open air	Surface	Undetermined	2
26	Clos de l'Alpe	St-Michel-en-Beaumont	Taillefer	Mesolithic	1630m	open air	Surface	Undetermined	1
27	Faravel (Fa XIII, XVIII)	Freissinières	Ecrins	Middle, final Mesolithic	2300m	open air	Surface, stratigraphy	Residential altitude camp	172

Figure 51.2. Description of the sites studied.

of each category of raw material were taken into account to characterize the procurement pattern of each site considered in the study.

Site implantation: a first insight into territorial organization

A first approach to territory is provided by site distribution. On the basis of artefact densities, site location, lithic, and eventually faunal assemblages, Pierre Bintz (1999b) proposed the following classification for the sites discovered (Figure 51.1):

- Lowland residential sites. These are fairly restricted, as their discovery is slowed down by alluvial inputs. They are located at altitudes lower than 800m and display evidence of a wide variety of activities.
- Intermediary camps, located at altitudes of *c.* 1000m. They consist of short-term camps, located on natural passes and correspond most often to rock shelters.
- Upland residential camps are numerous and often consist of an agglomeration of sites at altitudes from 1500 to 2300m (in the southern Alps). They are systematically located in the neighbourhood of different biotopes (grassland, cliffs), permitting the exploitation of several species/resources.
- A further few settlements can be related to specialized sites, mostly dedicated to siliceous raw material procurement.

Among the large corpus of Mesolithic sites in the French Alps, we studied nine settlements with varied geographical and geological locations, of different statuses and from different periods (Figure 51.2). They have unequal weight in this study, depending on the number of artefacts considered and the method of discovery (surface finds or stratigraphic site).

Flint procurement patterns

We distinguished flint procurement patterns of sites located in flint-rich environments and those areas that lacked flint.

Procurement in flint-rich environments

We focused on four sites located in the Subalpine limestone massifs (Figures 51.1 and 51.2): the Pas de l'Aiguille and Fontaine de la Baume (on the high plateaux in southern Vercors), and the Col de Porte and Canaple (in southern Chartreuse).

The Pas de l'Aiguille consists of several open-air sites, among which most are attributed to the Middle Mesolithic. They are considered as residential altitude camps, on a single access point towards Vercors, at the crossroads between the plateaux of Diois, Trièves and Vercors. Fontaine de la Baume is close to a north-south circulation axis, and both sites are close to natural springs, which remain scarce on the high plateaux.

Raw material procurement at the site of Pas de l'Aiguille is dominated by Barremo-Bedoulian flints (Figure 51.3, top), coming from a 15km range from the site. The various Barremo-Bedoulian facies correspond to both the southern Vercors and Diois source areas. The northern Vercors provenance is represented by few Senonian flint

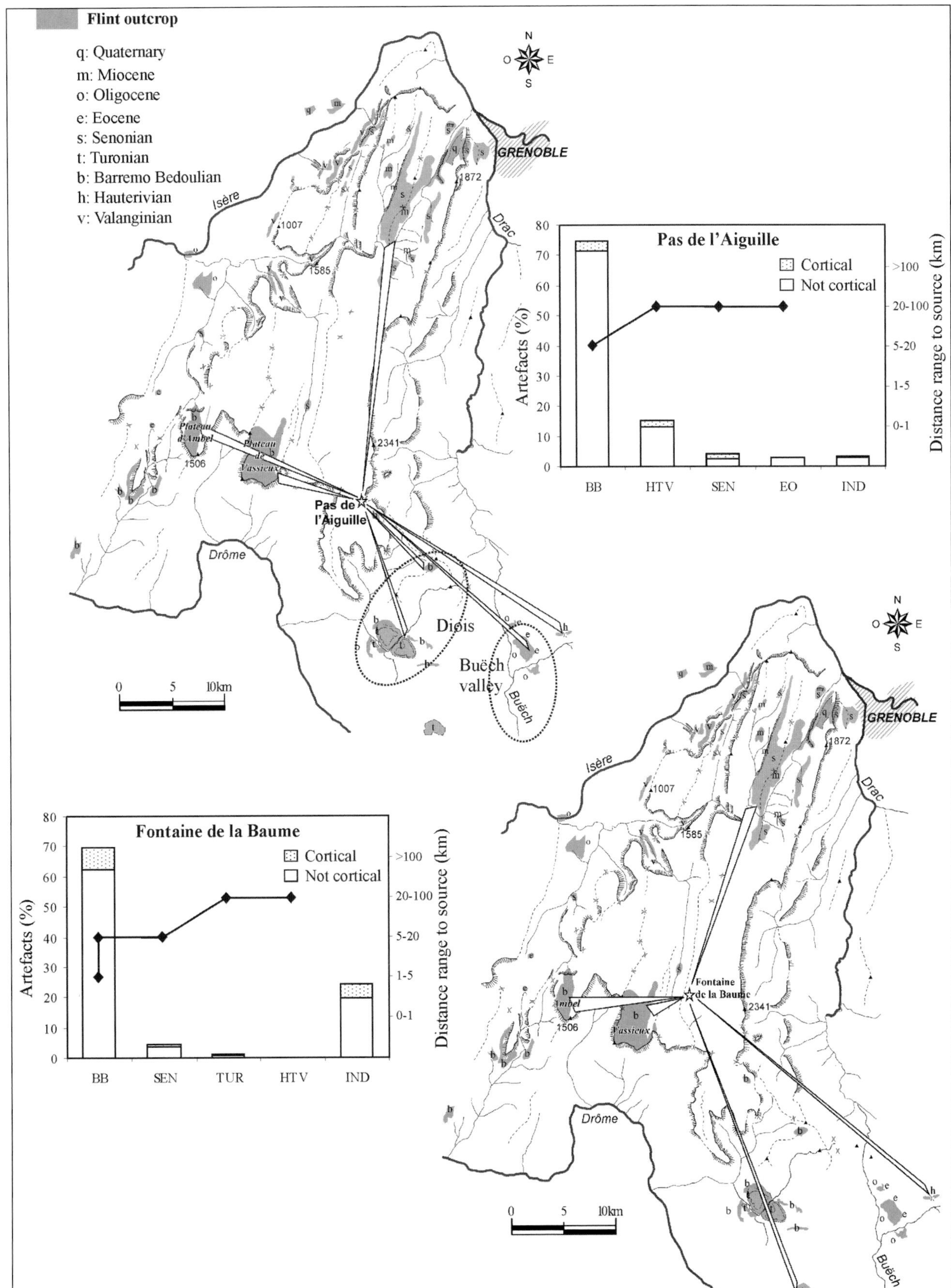

Figure 51.3. Flint procurement patterns for the Vercors sites studied. The diagram shows the proportion of raw material types (histogram), and their respective provenance distance (curve).

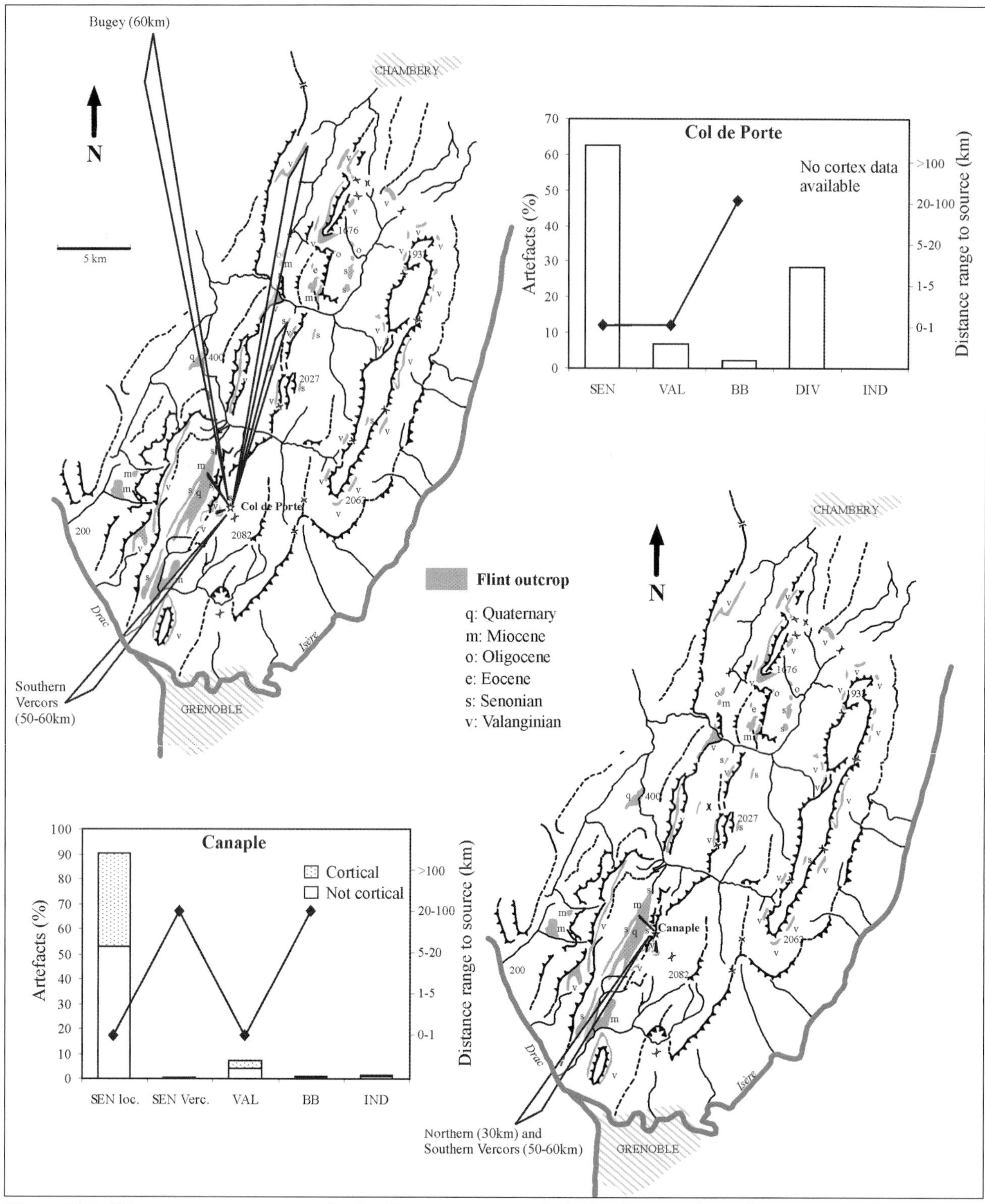

Figure 51.4. Flint procurement patterns for the Chartreuse sites studied. The diagram shows the proportion of raw material types (histogram), and their respective provenance distance (curve).

specimens. Hauterivian and Eocene flints suggest a Buëch-Valley provenance and are well represented among the assemblage: they account for more than 15%, which is a particularly high ratio given that their sources are located 25km away, to the south-east of the site. All the stages of the *chaîne opératoire* are represented in the Hauterivian flint. The material is highly represented amongst microliths and the presence of a microburin in this flint demonstrates the manufacture on-site of at least a part of the microliths. These observations suggest the transportation of a raw material supply from lower altitude areas (*c.* 1000m in the Buëch Valley) towards the high plateaux (above 1500m), either in expectation of arriving in an environment lacking flint sources, or related to exploratory raids.

At Fontaine de la Baume (Figure 51.3, lower), which is attributed to the Final Mesolithic, flint occurrences are centred on southern Vercors, with Vassieux flints well represented. As in the Pas de l'Aiguille, the northern Vercors provenance (Senonian flints) suggests movements within the whole massif of the groups occupying the high plateaux of Vercors. For both of these Vercors sites, the low occurrence of cortical artefacts, of whatever raw material, shows that the first stages of the *chaîne opératoire* were, most often, not performed on site.

In southern Chartreuse, the Col de Porte and Canaple (Figure 51.1) sites are a few hundred metres away from one another, on a natural communication route that crosses the massif in a north-south direction. The former is an open-air site, situated in a large meadow, and the latter is a rock shelter, on the watershed overlooking the Col de Porte (Malenfant *et al.* 2000): they are both attributed to the Middle Mesolithic.

Senonian and Valanginian flint outcrops are abundant, and to be found within one kilometre of the Col de Porte and Canaple sites (Figure 51.4). The preference for local Senonian flint is obvious, as it accounts for the largest proportion of raw material spectra at both sites. Senonian flint's higher knapping quality could explain this choice; the debitage is confined to bladelet production. With 2% of Barremo-Bedoulian flints present, movements from southern Vercors (i.e. at least 60km away from the site) are obvious. The link with the Vercors massif is reinforced by the presence of Senonian-Vercors flint at Canaple. At Col de Porte, one isolated raw material may originate from Bugey, a massif located in the southern Jura, some 30km from the site.

Although quantitative data are not available for Col de Porte, observations at both sites show a high rate of cortical artefacts. The technological study by D. Pelletier (Malenfant *et al.* 2000) at both locations emphasized differences in the debitage management between Valanginian and Senonian flints. Valanginian examples show expedient debitage, with end products and cores well represented. For Senonian flints, waste products are well represented, whereas cores and end products, i.e. bladelets, are missing. This suggests the departure of these products. Thus, associating raw material origins and technological data, Col de Porte and Canaple appear as sites specializing in the exploitation of local Senonian flints for the production of bladelets, and their export towards more distant sites. Moreover, the location of the sites, on a natural communication route, supports this assumption.

In flint-rich environments, procurement economy is highly based on the closest sources to the site. Even if preferences for specific raw materials can be seen in the case of Col de Porte and Canaple, due to their particular status, the high diversity of flint types within a given site suggests an opportunistic procurement and replacement of lithic equipment during trips.

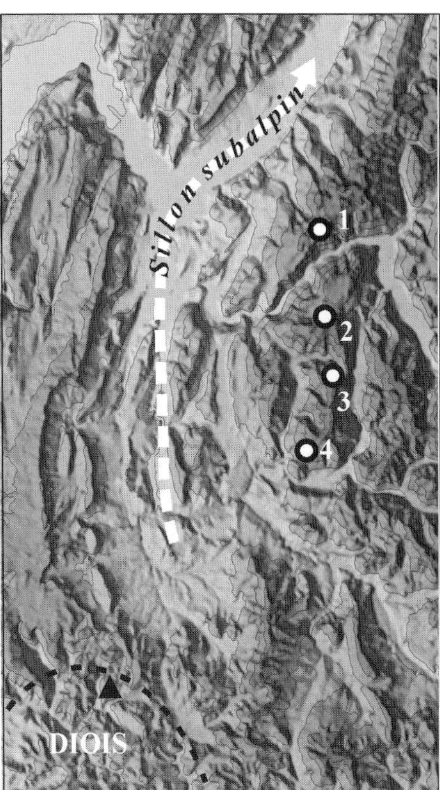

Figure 51.5. Location of flint procurement potential area and identified sources for the Lacs Robert and Taillefer sites. 1: Lacs Robert; 2: Chalet de la Barrière; 3: Ruisseau de Vaunoire; 4: Clos de l'Alpe. (Background map: AVDPA, Grenoble).

Procurement in environments lacking flint

Crystalline massifs are higher in altitude than Subalpine ones, and their geological substratum is not compatible with flint occurrence, but rather with quartz. In those areas prehistoric occupations, or clues to occupation, have only recently been discovered by chance (in Belledonne), or through archaeological field surveys (in the Taillefer, Ecrins). The oldest evidence relates to the Mesolithic period. In such environments, the provenance of flint no longer reflects the interaction between people and their local environment, but gives direct information relating to the areas in which they travelled before arriving in the mountain massifs, and from which region they might originate.

The site of Lacs Robert was discovered in 2001, in the Belledonne massif, at 2000m (Figure 51.2). The location of the site, close to a group of lakes, may be partly linked to the presence of a quartz outcrop exploited on-site, as this raw material constitutes half the assemblage. Among the 72 flint artefacts examined, only four different Barremo-Bedoulian types have been identified – coming from Diois only 40km away (Figure 51.5). The same origin is suggested for the scarce lithic remains found in three distinct locations on the Taillefer massif, which is the southerly continuation of Belledonne (Figures 51.1 and 51.2). These origins imply that the *sillon subalpin* acted as the natural communication route towards these Crystalline massifs. Regarding transport patterns, we assume from

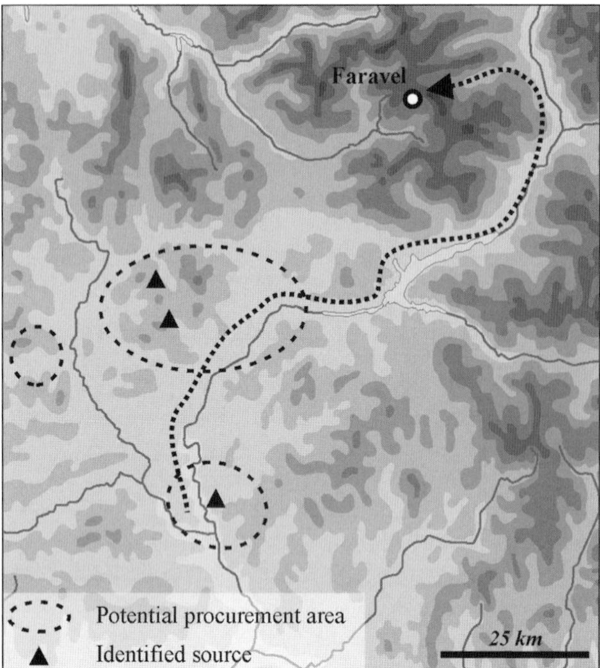

Figure 51.6. Location of flint procurement potential area and identified sources for the Faravel sites.

technological evidence, and from the near absence of cortical artefacts at the Lacs Robert site, that flint was carried into the Belledonne massif in the form of a few prepared cores, and, as no discarded cores were found, partially knapped on-site, and then transported.

In the Ecrins massif (southern Alps), surface surveys and excavations carried out by K. Walsh (2003) traced the remains of several Mesolithic occupations (at 2300m) distributed around Lake Faravel. The concomitant lithic industry is almost exclusively composed of flints, and the few quartz chips may come from the Durance alluvial deposits. The material studied derives from two areas, surveyed and partly excavated (Fa XIII and Fa XVIII), related to the Middle and Late Mesolithic. In the southern Alps, flint resources are not as well documented as in the northern ranges, in spite of specific geological surveys undertaken within the framework of the present study. Thus, we can only propose different potential areas of provenance on the basis of the geological identification of flint artefacts, and of three source assignments (Figure 51.6). All these procurement areas point to the Durance Valley as the natural route used to access the site. The distances between site and sources exceed 50km. The frequency of cortical artefacts amongst Hauterivian and Calcedonious flints helps decipher the initial morphology of the raw material, and suggests the introduction to the sites of small, un-worked, angular nodules. This pattern contrasts with that of the Lacs Robert site. These differences between the sites in terms of procurement patterns may be linked to different functions, or status, of these sites; some sites appear as being only short-term ones and not reoccupied, taking into account the low density of remains and the homogeneity of the raw materials. The different areas occupied around Lake Faravel, displaying a wide variety of flint types, may be the result of repeated residential settlements of groups coming from the same area (the Durance Valley).

Discussion

Flint procurement patterns appear to be highly variable, depending mostly on site status and on geological context: upland residential sites show the highest flint diversity.

The results show that the direct proximity of siliceous raw material sources was not a major parameter in terms of the settlement of upland residential camps. Other criteria, such as the availability of water and diversity of biotopes surrounding the site, may have played a greater part in settlement formation during the Alpine Mesolithic.

Even if movements between massifs are found, such as between Chartreuse and Vercors (Barremo-Bedoulian flint circulation), flint procurement areas appear relatively restricted, as the greatest circulation never exceeded 80km. For flint, no extra regional provenance has been evidenced, and direct procurement is thus assumed. Allochthonous flints rather suggest interactions with closer lowland areas. However, whereas flint does not feature in distant trafficking within the study area, such long distance interactions are demonstrated on the basis of other remains, such as shell ornaments from the Mediterranean and Danube regions (respectively *Columbella* and *Fagotia*), which have been discovered at several Alpine sites (Bintz 2004; Pion *et al.* 1990).

Circulation paths and mobility

Results provide interesting leads towards the reconstruction of circulation axes in terms of penetration into Alpine massifs, and within a given massif, which could not be evidenced in any other way. The groups who ventured into southern Vercors travelled through the Buëch Valley. The part played by the *sillon subalpin* in terms of movements toward Crystalline massifs was also shown. Within the southern Alps, the Durance Valley was a major communication route toward higher areas. These results, therefore, emphasize the role of secondary Alpine valleys in terms of populating the mountain areas. As a consequence, it decreases the importance of the Rhône Valley, previously considered the primary origin of Mesolithic Alpine groups.

The southern Sauveterrian, and then Castelnovian, cultural influences, perceived through lithic assemblages, are confirmed and specified through the flint provenances, which illustrate diffusion currents from the south (the Buëch Valley).

Territorial organization

From the synthesis of our results, we have attempted to outline specific territorial areas/bodies. For this purpose, the absence of some flint fingerprints is just as important as their presence with regard to the definition of connected areas and 'borders' through raw material circulation. Chartreuse and Vercors seem to form a consistent territorial body, as Barremo-Bedoulian flints from southern Vercors are found at all Mesolithic sites from Vercors to Chartreuse. This is true throughout the period – from Middle to Late Mesolithic.

The Crystalline massifs of Belledonne and Taillefer show connections with the Diois, but not with Chartreuse or Vercors, as we did not find in the Crystalline-massif sites any Senonian flint specific to the latter massifs. For the southern areas, with the example of Faravel, a limit can be outlined south to the Devoluy massif, as no Senonian flints that outcrop in Devoluy were found in Faravel. This is consistent with a link to the Durance Valley.

However, this division between Subalpine and Crystalline massifs can be questioned when considering quartz circulation (Cousseran 2002). Indeed, this raw material suggests contacts between Subalpine and Crystalline massifs, as archaeological quartz is found in the Mesolithic sites of the former area. A deeper insight would be necessary to understand the interaction between these two different geographical and geological entities: can we assume a specific collector behaviour for Crystalline-massif occupations, focused on specific resources, among which quartz is to be found? Is there a chronological pattern to the occupation of Crystalline massifs linked to the improvement of conditions of accessibility?

Conclusions

This paper has shown the significance of carrying out flint-provenance studies on a regional scale to acquire a comprehensive picture of territorial organization, occupation modalities and movement patterns linked to seasonal exploitation of altitude environments. Even if the number of sites studied, per period and per massif, remains limited, our knowledge of Alpine territories is improved, and new questions are raised.

From site distribution and raw material data, the mobility strategies recall forager behaviour, with few logistic camps in terms of the exploitation of siliceous raw material.

From the evidence of flint circulation we can define the maximum territory as extending between 60 and 80km in length. Does this correspond to the annual extent of the territory, or only to a section of it? Only considering flint may be insufficient for the apprehension of all the aspects of past economic and cultural territories. Quartz and shell ornaments provide different and supplementary informative data. Furthermore, to apprehend a global pattern of mobility and land use in mountainous environments during the Mesolithic, we will have to compare data obtained from altitude-site procurement patterns with that of sites from down in the plains.

Acknowledgements

I would like to thank Pierre Bintz, David Pelletier, and Régis Picavet for fruitful discussions. I am also grateful to Cyril Bernard and the AVDPA (association pour la valorisation et la diffusion de la préhistoire alpine, Grenoble), who provided me with maps and financial support. Progress in my research was furthered by the French 'Ministère de la Culture', the 'Conseil general de la Drôme, l'Isère, des deux Savoies' funds.

References

Affolter, J. and Grünwald, C. 1999. Approvisionnements en matières premières dans les sites mésolithiques du Vercors, in A. Thévenin and P. Bintz (eds.), *L'Europe des derniers Chasseurs. Épipaléolithique et Mésolithique. Actes du 5ième colloque international UISPP, Comission XII. Grenoble, 18-23 septembre 1995*, 603–10. Paris, Comité des travaux historiques et scientifiques (CTHS).

Argant, J. 1999. Palynologie des sites de plein air d'altitude dans les Alpes du Nord: méthodologie et premiers resultants, in A. Thévenin and P. Bintz (eds.), *L'Europe des derniers Chasseurs. Épipaléolithique et Mésolithique. Actes du 5ième colloque international UISPP, Comission XII. Grenoble, 18-23 septembre 1995*, 547–58. Paris, Comité des travaux historiques et scientifiques (CTHS).

Bintz, P. 1991. Stations mésolithiques de plein air dans les massifs subalpins du Vercors et de la Chartreuse. Attributions chronologiques et implications culturelles, in *Mésolithique et Néolithisation en France et dans les régions limitrophes, Actes du 113e Congrès national des sociétés savantes, Strasbourg, 5-9 avril 1988*, 231–43. Paris, Comité des Travaux historiques et scientifiques (CTHS).

Bintz, P. 1999a. Le Mésolithique des Alpes françaises: bilan des connaissances, in A. Beeching (ed.), *Circulations et identités culturelles alpines à la fin de la préhistoire. Matériaux pour une etude (programme collectif CIRCALP 1997/1998)*, 317–29. Travaux du Centre d'Archéologie Préhistorique de Valence, 2. Valence, Centre d'Archéologie préhistorique.

Bintz, P. 1999b. Dynamique et économie des peuplements du Paléolithique final et du Mésolithique dans les Alpes françaises, in P. Della Casa (ed.), *Prehistoric alpine environment, society, and economy, Papers of the international colloquim PAESE '97*, 11–24. Bonn, Habelt.

Bintz, P. 2004. Colombelles et Fagotia: la circulation des objets de parure au Mésolithique, in C. Jourdain-Annequin (ed.), *Atlas culturel des Alpes occidentales. De la Préhistoire à la fin du Moyen-Age*, 57. Paris, Picard.

Bintz, P. and Grünwald, C. 1990. Mésolithique et néolithisation en Chartreuse et en Vercors (Alpes du Nord): évolution culturelle et économie du silex, in P. M. Vermeersch and P. van Peer (eds.), in P. M. Vermeersch and P. van Peer (eds.), *Contributions to the Mesolithic in Europe. Papers presented at the Fourth International Symposium on the Mesolithic in Europe*, 205–8. Leuven, Leuven University Press.

Bintz, P., Picavet, R. and Evin, J. 1995. L'évolution culturelle du Mésolithique au Néolithique moyen en Vercors et dans les Alpes du Nord, in J.-L. Voruz (ed.), *Chronologies néolithiques de 6000 à 2000 avant notre ère dans le bassin rhodanien, Actes du colloque d'Ambérieu-en-Bugey, éd. Société Préhistorique Rhodanienne, 19 et 20 septembre 1992*, 41–53. Documents du Département d'Anthropologie de l'Université de Genève 20. Genève, Société préhistorique rhodanienne.

Bressy, C., Bintz, P., Poupeau, G., Keller, F. and Barrat, J. A. 2002. Flint geochemical characterization. A tool for provenance studies in French Western Alps, in L. Barba (ed.), *Proceedings of the 32nd International Symposium on Archaeometry, 15–19 May 2000, Mexico City*. Mexico, Ciudad Universitaria.

Bressy, C. 2003. *Caractérisation et gestion du silex des sites mésolithiques et néolithiques du Nord-Ouest de l'arc alpin. Une approche pétrographique et géochimique*, 295. British Archaeological Reports, International Series S1114. Oxford, Archaeopress.

Bressy, C., Poupeau, G. and Bintz, P. 2003. Contribution de la caractérisation géochimique aux questions d'origine du silex sénonien dans le Néolithique des Alpes du Nord françaises, in *Les matières premières lithiques en Préhistoire. Table Ronde d' Aurillac (20–22 juin 2002), Préhistoire du Sud-Ouest* (Supplément 5), 97–103.

Bridault, A. and Chaix, L. 1999. Contribution de l'archéozoologie à la caractérisation des modalités d'occupation des sites alpines et jurassiens, de l'Epipaléolithique au Néolithique, in A. Thévenin and P. Bintz (eds.), *L'Europe des derniers Chasseurs. Épipaléolithique et Mésolithique. Actes du 5ième colloque international UISPP, Comission XII. Grenoble, 18-23 septembre 1995*, 547–58. Paris, Comité des travaux historiques et scientifiques (CTHS).

Cousseran, S. 2002. Les inclusions fluides, un outil pour la discrimination des quartz archéologiques. Application au problème de circulation du quartz dans les Alpes occidentales et lombardes. Réalisation d'un premier référentiel de données sur les quartz alpins. *Bulletin de la Société préhistorique française* 99 (4), 833–8.

Malenfant, M., Bressy, C. and Pelletier, D. 2000. Réexamen de la série lithique du Col de Porte (Isère, Chartreuse, commune de Sarcenas): matières premières et étude technologique. Premiers résultats. *Géologie Alpine* 31 (Mémoire Hors-Série), 179–89.

Pion, G., Bintz, P., Monjuvent, G., Billard, M., Caillat, B., Cataliotti-Valdina, J., Durand, J. M. and Girard, M. 1990. L'abdri de la Fru à Saint-Christophe (Savoie). *Gallia Préhistoire* 32, 65–123.

Thiébault, S. 1999. Le milieu végétal des derniers chasseurs-cueilleurs en Vercors et Chartreuse – Nouvelles données anthracologiques et proposition d'une biozonation, in A. Thévenin and P. Bintz (eds.), *L'Europe des derniers Chasseurs. Épipaléolithique et Mésolithique. Actes du 5ième colloque international UISPP, Comission XII. Grenoble, 18-23 septembre 1995*, 589–602. Paris, Comité des travaux historiques et scientifiques (CTHS).

Walsh, K. 2003. Southern French Alps Landscape Project, 1999–2003. http://www.york.ac.uk/depts/arch/med/html/web/ (accessed 11/2007).

52. The power of place and regional identity in the British south-western Mesolithic

Clive Jonathon Bond

Cave burials and shell middens are recorded in south-west Britain. But despite this rare evidence, together with the quantity of lithics and the well-established anthropogenic impact of Mesolithic hunter-gatherers, the people remain invisible. Does this data constitute a critical mass from which we can now interpret social phenomenon? This paper will explore the implications for regional and sub-regional social identity by reviewing patterns in raw material exchange, technology and social behaviour. A case study focuses on reconsidering who the deciduous forest hunters were in the Somerset Levels and Mendip, as well as their relationship with other more distant peoples. This approach discusses the structure of daily routines, the perception of the land, its resources and places, all arguably embedded in cultural memory.

Keywords: lithic scatters, raw materials, technology, typology, seasonal movement, regional.

Introduction

This chapter will discuss the range of evidence available in south-west Britain for Mesolithic lifeways, whilst focusing geographically on central Somerset (Figure 52.1). Rather than the traditional approach listing the types of evidence, from shell middens (Palmer 1977), caves and rock shelters (Jacobi 1987; Schulting 2005), or microlith typology (Clark 1932; Norman 1975; 1982; 2003; Wainwright 1960), the starting point here is social identity. What did it mean to belong to these communities? What did it mean to live in, move across, and, in fact, most probably perceive the landscape as part of one's being (Bradley 1997; Ingold 1992)? Moreover, are there any types of evidence that can help tease out the sense of place, the social identity of these people in this topographically variable and sea-bounded region?

Three strands of evidence, or themes, are suggested to be appropriate in addressing the social identities of these regional small-scale societies:

- Raw materials
- Technology and typology
- Seasonal movements

Within south-western Britain a study area was established (Figure 52.1). This sample area has been the subject of a doctorate on the origins of prehistoric settlement (Bond 2006). The specific sample area was selected because it was topographically diverse, consisting of three regional landscape types: the Polden Hills, the Somerset Levels and the Mendip Hills. Each, it is argued, interrelated socially and economically. Lithic data was analysed across this total landscape by interrogating previously unpublished museum or private collections (see Bond, this volume). This data set, consisting of 150 lithic scatters, can be contrasted with distributions for the regional Mesolithic (Figure 52.2), and other more intensive field surveys, such as the Shapwick Project (Bond 2007). These lithic assemblages are the result of structured and repeated technical routines that discarded artefacts, representing people completing tasks at a particular point in the landscape. These discarded artefacts most likely represent an artefact residue of small groups revisiting this place over generations. This evidence for human actions, perhaps part of a cycle of seasonal visits also constitutes an attachment to a locale: a humanised place (cf. Ingold 1993). The discard of artefacts by discrete social groups at set points, also revisited as part of a seasonal itinerary, would equate to establishing a biography of that place held in the cultural memory. Here are translated the meaning and 'draw' of place, as lithic analysis records a palimpsest. It is evident that most lithic scatters (Bond 2004a; 2004b; 2006; 2007), as is also apparent with certain cave locales, such as Aveline's Hole (Schulting 2005), or Gough's Cave (Jacobi 1987, 2004), were revisited over generations.

'Power', as in the chapter title, can now be considered. The 'power' to draw people, perhaps from afar, as part of the seasonal movements of small social groups, and to engage people over millennia, is central to understanding the social identity of the people who inhabited this part of south-west Britain. The material culture reflects a social

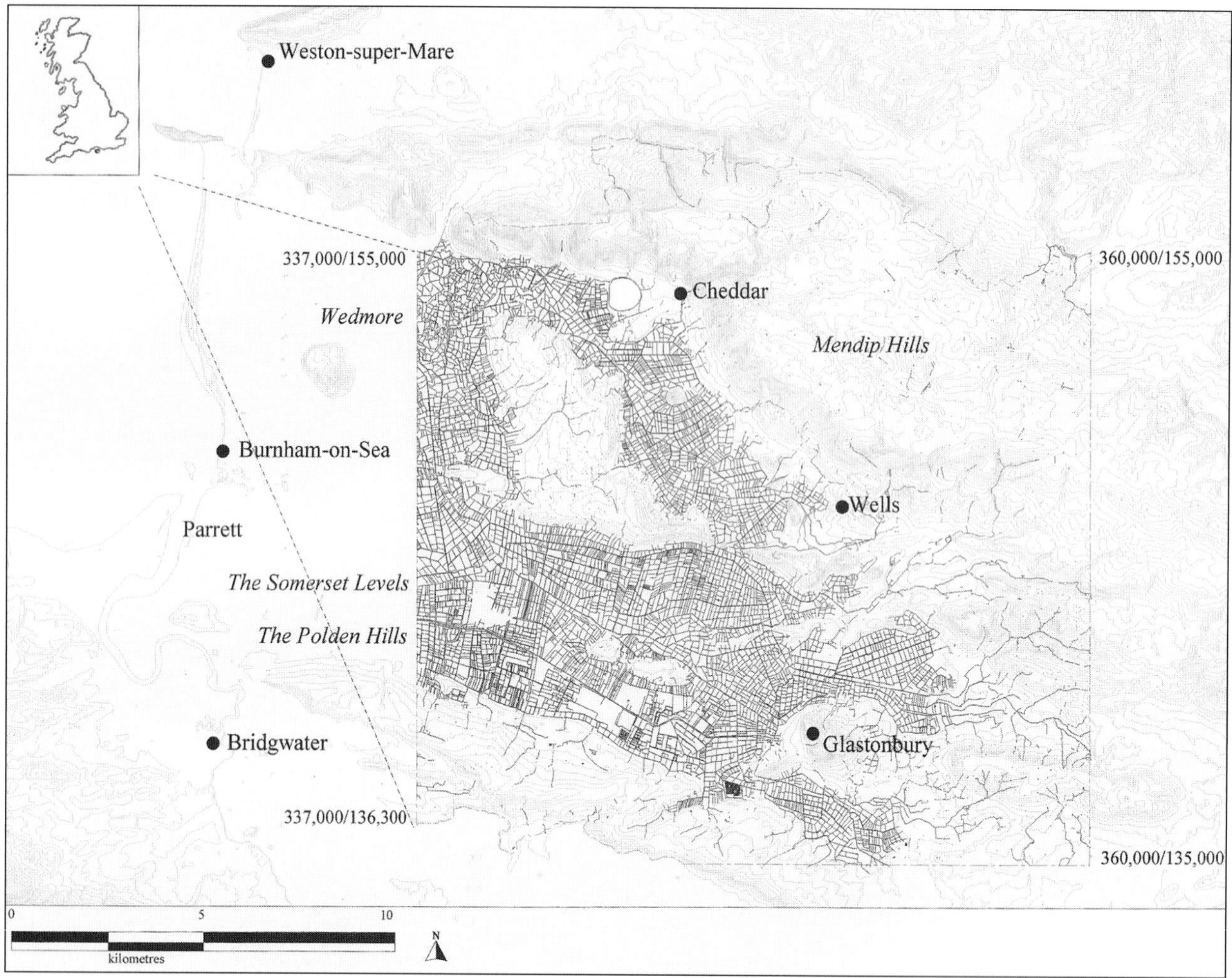

Figure 52.1. South-west Britain and the study area. Key: study area (dashed line) with national grid coordinates; towns (infilled circles); water – drains, streams and rivers (lines, black); landscape features (labelled in italics); contours at 5m O. D. intervals (lines, grey). (Map data from Ordnance Survey data, Licence Number: LA07683X).

reality: connections between groups and people, over generations, as attachments to places were maintained. This arguably is a result of many interlinked themes: one being the way people interacted across the region, their movement and negotiating of social alliances. This is important, as mobile people travelling in to, or across, the region would need to secure supplies of quality flint or chert raw materials not present there (Bond 2004a).

Raw materials, procurement and exchange

A means of assessing the economic connections that support social identity and alliances may be traced by the way lithic raw materials changed over millennia, as argued by Care (1979; 1982) and Gardiner (1990). Beyond the pragmatic utility of requiring high-quality stone for flaking, other properties may also be significant for selection, such as aesthetics and symbolic meaning (Taçon 1991). Lithic raw material could be organised logistically, as part of an embedded procurement system (Binford 1979), and/or facilitate exchange between small-scale societies as part of a mobile settlement pattern (cf. Portland-type chert in Jacobi 1981). Thus, in turn, the origin and the understanding of that origin to participating communities some distance away from territories where social groups controlled access to flint, for example, such as the chalks of Wessex, may be highly significant. Interestingly, little work has been completed on social access to lithic resources within the British Mesolithic. Indeed, access to stone may have been contingent upon seasonal movements, shifting alliances between groups, even group composition.

Within the museum collections of lithic assemblages, variation was evident in the colour and type of flint and chert. A stone tool raw material survey was completed, whereby over 80 grab samples from superficial deposits across south-western and south-eastern Britain were matched to archaeological specimens from lithic scatter assemblages within the study area (Bond 2004a; 2006). The generic distribution of raw materials in Mesolithic lithic assemblages has been commented on by Norman (1982; 2003). He has observed that Mesolithic industries west of the River Parrett appear to be centred exclusively on Greensand chert, or beach pebble flint (Norman 1975; 1982, 17). This contrasts to the picture within the study area

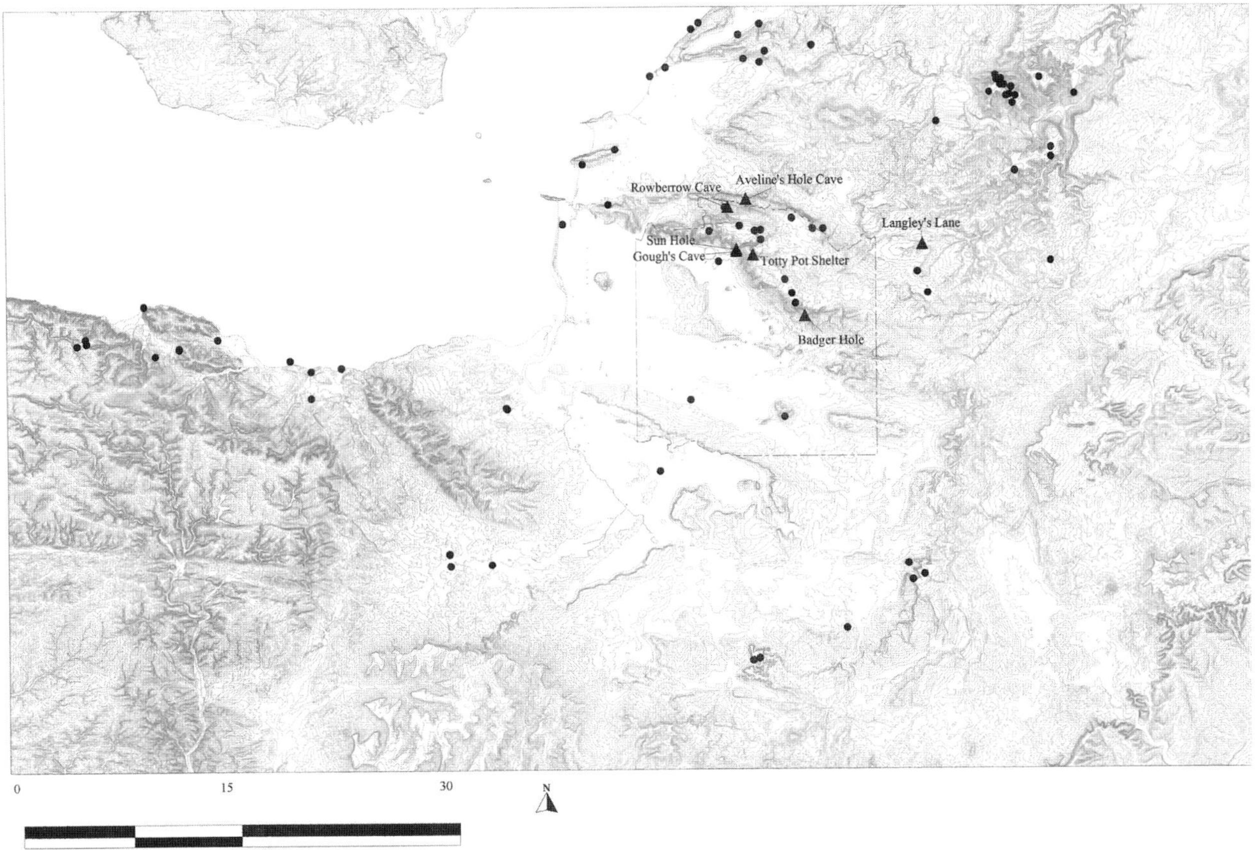

Figure 52.2. The Mesolithic regional landscape, caves and lithic scatters. Key: study area (dashed line); caves and rock shelters within the study area, the exception is Langley's Lane, Ston Easton, a tufa deposit with lithics (triangle, infilled); lithic scatters with Early and Later Mesolithic material (circles, infilled, data from Wymer 1977). NB: to aid clarity, lithic scatters analysed as part of this synthesis are not mapped within the study area. (Map data from Ordnance Survey data, Licence Number: LA07683X).

– to the north-east of the Parrett line. It has been observed in the study area that all lithic industries, including those with a significant Mesolithic component, are dominated by flint (Bond 2004a). This flint is mostly of a high-quality chalk-type, derived from Downland nodular flint (the green-black-grey flint).

The composition of flint/chert within Mesolithic assemblages can be quantitatively assessed in relation to the line of the River Parrett and the topography of the region (Figure 52.3). Here data for nine published assemblages (Berridge 1985; Norman 1975; 2003) are contrasted to the raw material composition of four lithic scatters/localities within the study area (Figure 52.2). As assemblages are recorded further north, and over the Parrett line, flint use does appear to increase, in percentage terms, per assemblage (Figure 52.3). The lithic industries in the Exe catchment, the Yarty Valley at Telegraph Cottage, Crandons Cross and Aller Farm all use Greensand chert, perhaps derived from the local Axe gravels or Black Down Hills. The flint used may be accounted for by beach pebbles, or even nodules imported from the Chard Downs (capped with Clay-with-Flints and Chert), or even imports of Beerhead flint (Tingle 1998). The Hawkcombe Head flint preference has been observed to be linked to the use of Barnstable Bay beach flint (Norman, pers. comm. 2001). Rare occurrences of Cretaceous chert probably derive from the Tone gravels, nearby Head deposits, or the Black Down Hills. Similar procurement and curation strategies may also fit the Doniford Cliff and Greenway Farm assemblages, each with a different emphasis (Norman 1975). The lithic scatters of Westleigh Farm and Fideoak Park would both be in close proximity to the chert-rich Tone gravels. However, at Parchey Sand Batch, P1, Chedzoy, just north of the Parrett, the balance between flint and chert is more equal (Figure 52.3). Further north, the four lithic scatters/localities in the Brue Valley give a preference for flint, almost to the exclusion of chert, on Mendip at Ebbor Grove Farm and Long Wood.

Although this patterning in raw material composition represents a long timeframe, within this differences can also be noted in flint/chert proportions. For example, in the Early Mesolithic, flint is more important at Shapwick Burtle than Edington Burtle (Figure 52.3). Further comments on scheduling of lithic procurement can be discussed with reference to the 150 lithic scatters analysed in the study area (Figure 52.4). Analysis here has enabled a more detailed review of this patterning, as lithic industries are grouped into four data quality and period filters (cf. Bond, this volume). The broad trends in flint and chert use in

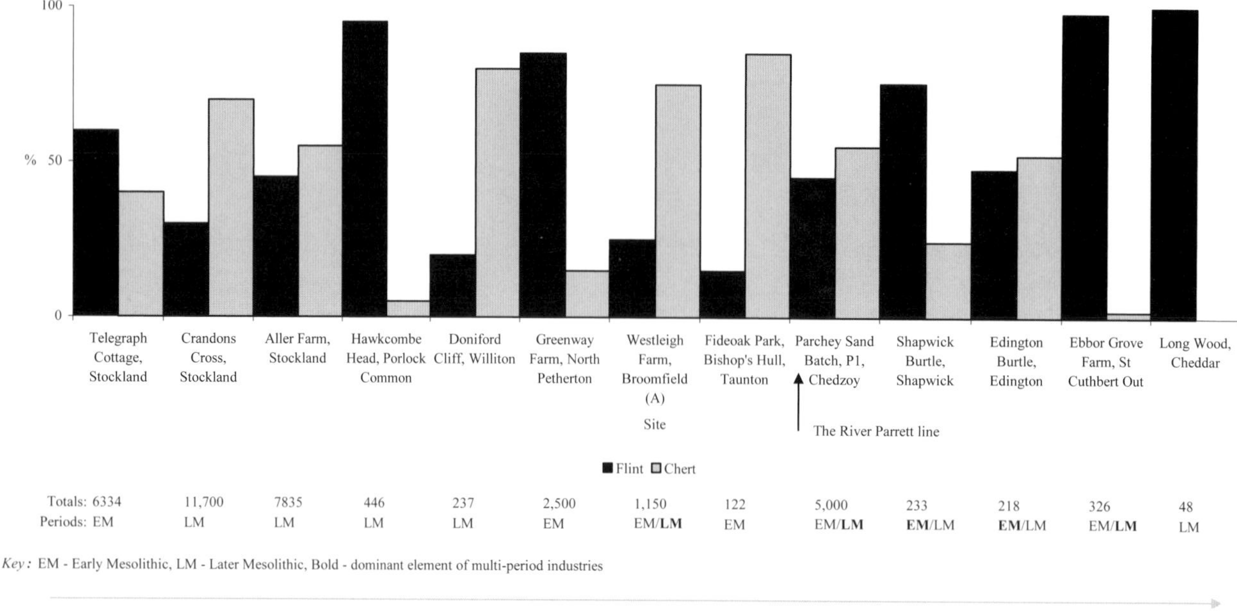

Figure 52.3. A comparison of flint and chert use in the regional Mesolithic.

Mesolithic industries are illustrated in Figure 52.4, top. Five points can be made on the trend: 1) The greatest sum of material is flint. 2) The dominant type of flint utilised is a green-black-grey chalk nodular flint derived from the east (the Wessex chalk lands, particularly those of Dorset, Hampshire and West Sussex). 3) Smaller amounts of green-black-grey flint (white inclusions) are present, especially in the Later Mesolithic and Later Mesolithic and/or Earlier Neolithic groups (from the Clay-with-Flints and Chert source on the Chard Downs). 4) Chert obtained its highest percentage in the Early Mesolithic, then declines. 5) The chert utilised in the Later Mesolithic and Later Mesolithic and/or Earlier Neolithic may be linked to the increased use of Portland-type chert (Figure 52.4, lower), part of the pan-regional network and perhaps a formal exchange system as argued by Jacobi (1981).

Further consideration of the chert composition across the data quality and period filters is instructive (Figure 52.4). Again, five points are distilled: 1) Overall, as noted above, there is a decline through time in chert consumption. 2) The blond Greensand chert, dominant early on (sourced perhaps from the Exe, Tone and Axe catchments), declines after the Later Mesolithic group. 3) The chocolate-brown, Black Down Hills derived chert peaks in the Early Mesolithic and declines thereafter. 4) The limited quantity of grey-black chert observed at the riverhead of the Brue (Blackdown facies; Edmonds *et al.* 1985, 69–70) peaks in the Later Mesolithic, but then falls. 5) As noted above, the Portland-type chert increases in the Later Mesolithic onwards. This last point is interesting, as it is also timed when other flints (miscellaneous, ungrouped) and the black (white inclusions) flint, probably sourced to Beer Head, increase in presence (Figure 52.4, top).

What do these trends mean? The variation in raw material within each assemblage, and, as here, analysed as an aggregate, may be related to changes in the directions people moved across the regional landscape, reflected in the source of stone curated (Andrefsky 1998, chapters 8 and 9; Binford 1979). Seasonal movements, territories and access to stone raw material may be implicated, as different types of stone were procured and bound up in mobile hunter-gatherer lifeways. Stone sources may trace the different social alliances and routes into the study area from the north-east or south-east, perhaps bounded by the line of the dangerous River Parrett, in accordance with Norman's comments (1982).

A chronological pattern, together with a genealogy of stone, is noted. In the Early Mesolithic chert appears to have come predominantly from the Black Down Hills or the Cretaceous lighter-coloured cherts of the Tone Vale (or the western chalk escarpment, bounded by the Cretaceous strata to the east). At this time flint was derived from nodular flints from the central southern and eastern Downs. In the Later Mesolithic, post *c.* 6700 BC–*c.* 6400 BC (Jacobi 1973, 237–8, 246; 1976, 73, 75–6, 80; 1979; Smith 1992, 5, 58, 171–2, fig. 1.1), a shift is witnessed as groups appear to abandon pathways near the Black Down Hills, and the Tone, as these cherts decrease, and overall chert falls as flint rises in consumption. In the transitional lithic grouping all chert use collapses, perhaps verging on and encompassing the onset of pottery-using peoples regionally. The diversity of flint types increases, reducing the proportions of the previously dominant green-black-grey nodular Downland flint (cf. Figure 52.4, top). This may probably mean that the established routes of communication between parts of the region were changed, as mobile groups, perhaps both

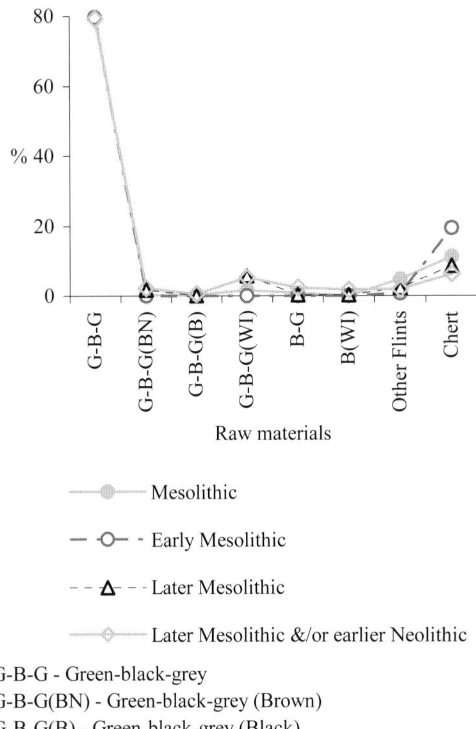

G-B-G - Green-black-grey
G-B-G(BN) - Green-black-grey (Brown)
G-B-G(B) - Green-black-grey (Black)
G-B-G(WI) - Green-black-grey (White Inclusions)
B-G - Brown-grey
B(WI) - Black (White Inclusions)

Total: 3431

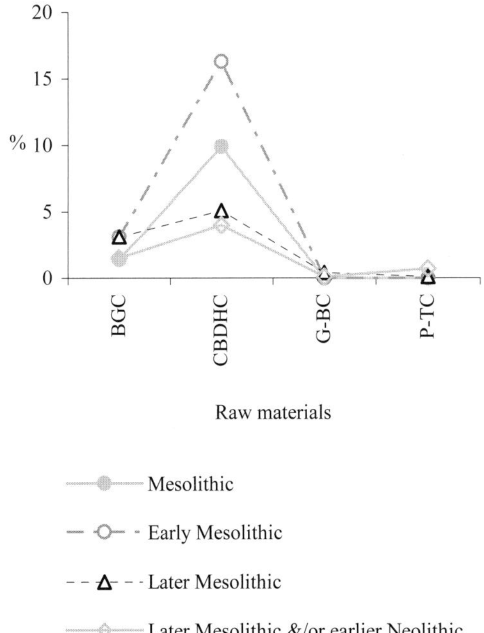

BGC - Blond Greensand Chert
CBDHC - Chocolate Black Down Hills Chert
G-BC - Grey-Black Chert
P-TC - Portland-type Chert

Total: 430

Figure 52.4. Raw material use during the Mesolithic across the study area. Data taken from the analysis of 150 lithic scatters within the study area (cf. Bond, Figure 105.4, this volume). Top: the composition of raw materials from all lithic scatters within the study area. Bottom: types of chert from lithic scatters within the study area.

the latest Mesolithic and Earlier Neolithic peoples, drew stone from a range of sources, including downs on the limestone uplands of south-west Britain (green-black-grey (white inclusions)), perhaps also the brown-grey flint and Beer Head (Tingle 1998). Competition is implied, or at least the issue of maintaining social alliances, perhaps including re-negotiation of territories and access to stone.

Technology and typology: lithics and regional small-scale societies across space and time

As commented on elsewhere (cf. Bond, this volume), the analysis of 150 lithic scatters in the study area yielded for the first time a diachronic settlement pattern, centred on different parts of this topographically varied landscape (Figure 52.1). The majority of Early Mesolithic lithics are centred in the wetlands, on the sand islands, called the Burtle Beds and Polden Hills. This settlement pattern may be contrasted to that of the later Mesolithic where most lithic industries are centred on the Mendip Hills. Only limited overlap occurs in this spatial distribution and few industries show the same density of material, or size of assemblage recovered from the same location (re-use is variable, perhaps implying different numbers or frequencies of tasks and visits, between the Early and Later Mesolithic). This spatial patterning in broad and narrow blade industries is argued (cf. Bond, this volume), as a reaction to the localised impact of the postglacial marine transgression. Other technological nuances also are noted.

Wainwright (1960) argued that there was an Early Mesolithic, his Maglemosian, comparable to that of Thatcham and other south-east lithic industries. Norman has supported this proposition (1975), but also, with Jacobi (1979), discussed the Later Mesolithic industries, typified by slender, obliquely blunted points, crescents, scalene triangles and rod forms. However, what of a third option, rather than the technological-typological divide, based on the acceptance that inversely and basal retouched points are now observed, perhaps reflecting a Horsham influence (Norman 2003, 34–5, fig. 12)? This may represent the situation that Whittle (in Smith *et al.* 1989) argued for in the Cambridgeshire Fenlands, i.e. the existence of a transitional assemblage, between the broad (and non-geometric) and narrow (and geometric) industries of the two-phase system traditionally posited (Jacobi 1973; 1976). This is what Whittle termed a 'Middle Mesolithic' industry, as recorded at Peacock Farm and Letter F Farm (in Smith *et al.* 1989, 247–8).

In Somerset there are only a few examples of these types of microlith; principally the commonest form is the hollow-based point (Norman 2003). A snapped hollow-based point is radiocarbon dated at one location, Birdcombe, Wraxall on the Failand Ridge and is argued by Gardiner to be very late in the four millennia cal BC (5050±140 BP; 4210–3540 cal BC; SRR-3200 or 6100±100 BP; 5280–4770 cal BC; IGS C14/39; Gardiner 2000, 206). Indeed, two more recent determinations, from Trench D, the location of this hollow-based point (Gardiner 2000, 201), are published,

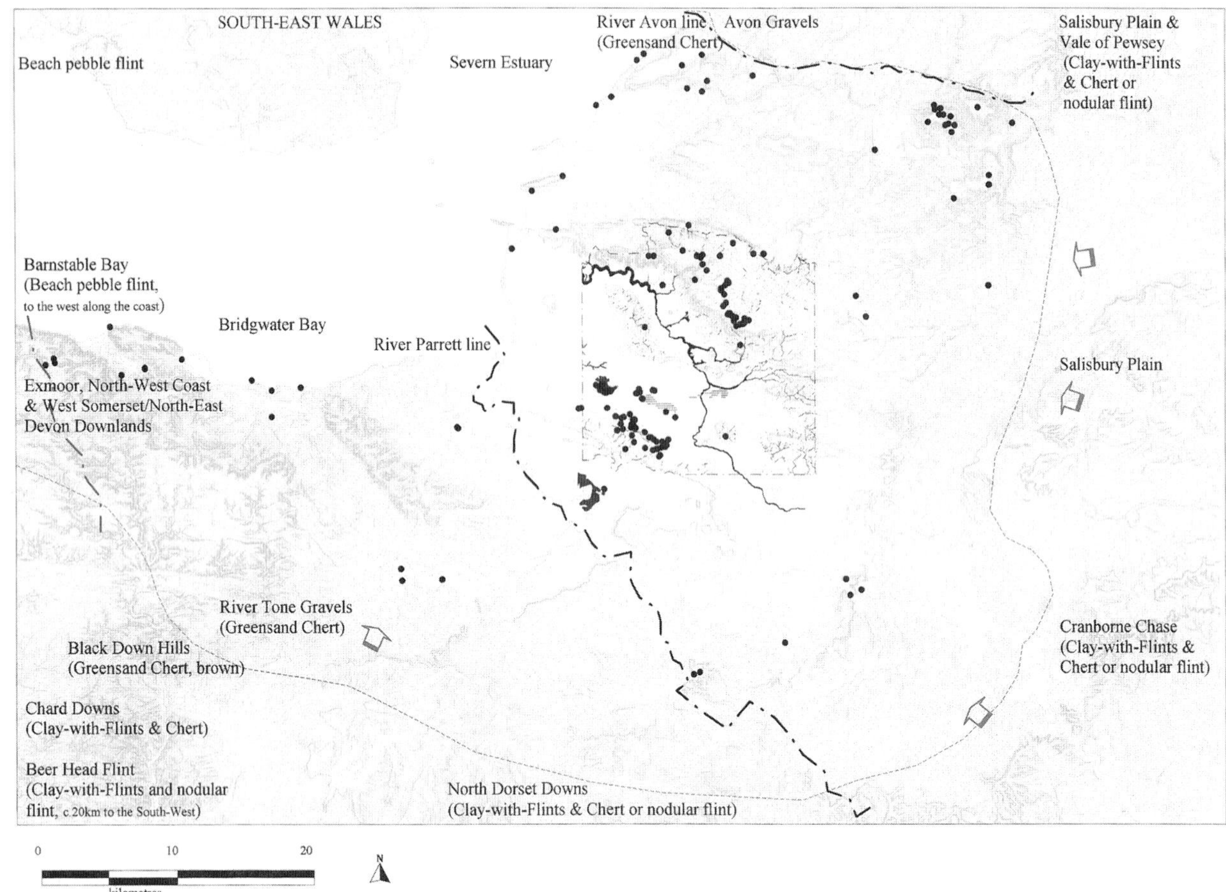

Figure 52.5. Mesolithic embedded raw material procurement strategies, the study area and regional landscape. Key: study area (dashed line, black); Early and Later Mesolithic lithic scatters (circles, closed). Data from the study area and adapted after Wymer 1977; Exmoor, raw materials of north-west coast and west Somerset/north-east Devon downland region (dashed line); River Parrett line (line, black). This hypothetical social boundary is adapted from Norman's observations on lithic raw material, chert-, contrasted to flint-dominant Mesolithic assemblages (1982, 2003); River Avon and Avon Gorge line (line); the hypothetical and topographical outline constituting the topographic crescent of historic Somerset, to the east and north skirting the Greensand Chert Escarpment and/or chalk downlands of Wessex (dashed line); arrows show direction of lithic raw material for transport into central Somerset.

both derived from oak charcoal, possibly imply a late date although the context is not clearly stated (5420±60 BP; 4370–4050 cal BC; Beta-147106, and 4700±50 BP; 3640–3360 cal BC; Beta-147105; Gardiner in Hosfield 2005, 43, table 2.4). This may be a dated case for the latest use of this technology, but Reynier has argued for this to be contemporary with Maglemosian industries, as with his Star Carr and Deepcar-type assemblages, originating well before *c.* 6500 cal BC (Reynier 1998, fig. 23.1). Importantly, there are few lithic assemblages in the central lowlands of Somerset giving the characteristic hollow-based point, perhaps only six assemblages in total. One main grouping occurs at Parchey Sand Batch, Chedzoy, also the location with an almost equal composition for flint and chert (Figure 52.3). Other assemblages often give single artefacts, such as those inversely basal retouched points from Shapwick Burtle, Brickyard Farm, and Edington Burtle (Norman 2003, 34, fig. 12), or come from the Birdcombe, the Failand Ridge (Gardiner 2000). In total, from a survey of 575 microliths known in Somerset, only 19 (3.3%) are represented by hollow-based points. In Norman's review of the Parchey assemblage, whilst commenting on this phenomenon, he suggests a broad currency for the use of this technology, *c.* 7000–*c.* 5000 cal BC (2003, 33). This would, together with the observation on the equal numbers of raw material, may well point to an Early 'Middle' Mesolithic inception in Somerset for people using this Weald-type technology (Jacobi 1978; 1981). This would accord well with Reynier's model for his Horsham-type assemblages to originate in the Early Mesolithic of the south-east (Jacobi 1978). The people using this technology may have spread west, perhaps along the chalk escarpment in a western direction via watersheds, river valleys, crossing the head waters adjacent those rivers of the central lowlands of Somerset, such as the Brue (Bond 2004a, 136–7, fig. 14.3). This would support cultural contact with the people from the Weald using Horsham technology, as asserted by Norman (2003, 35–6). The geographical/technological link may be as Norman suggested (2003, 34), Green's Hollow-based point assemblages recorded in Cranborne Chase, Dorset (2000, 21, fig. 10, type III: Stonedown). A probable eastern cultural contact between mobile groups in Somerset and the south-east was first raised by Jacobi (1979, 73). Moreover, the presence of Hollow-based points in central Somerset may also signal credence for, at least one case, of Jacobi's later 'combinations of microliths' (1979, 73). This may glimpse the diversity of later, or as suggested here, even 'middle' Mesolithic lithic assemblages. These industries still remain typologically to be identified regionally. This hypothesis may be tentatively confirmed by the use of black-grey chert, sourced to the head of the Brue, for some slender forms, including inversely basal blunted pieces from Parchey (Norman 2003; Norman, pers. comm. 2001). This may, for some, be too speculative, and it is acknowledged that further fieldwork on lithic sources and lithic analysis is required to confirm this view. However, the limited numbers of hollow-based points in the interior of the lowlands, save Parchey, a large Burtle Bed near to the Polden Hills, may be highly significant. Could the spread of hollow-based point-using peoples into these lowlands have been curtailed by the eventual localized impact of the postglacial marine transgression? Certainly, after *c.* 6500 cal BC, seasonal territories may have regularly shifted, forcing increased competition for resources, only to impact on density of activity in the wetlands and on the Polden Hills. This scenario may explain the reason why few hollow-based points are to be found on Mendip (one at King's Down, Cheddar, in Norman 2003, 34, fig. 12, no. 6), and why the slender microlith technologies, with crescents and scalene triangles are so abundant on Mendip. At present too few radiocarbon dates are available to date a framework of technological change, so this question will have to remain unanswered for the time being.

Seasonal movements: hunter-gatherers, their identity and pathways in the local and regional landscapes

Here, to return to the regional context with raw material procurement strategies and notions of seasonal movement of animals and people, the origins of social identity can be discussed. If we accept that raw material for stone was regularly imported over substantial distances (Bond 2004a; 2004b; 2007), then the hunter-gatherer's lifeway, day to day routines, world view, and their perception of self would have been bound up in journeys into and out of the study area. A community, part of a small-scale society, can travel sizable distances within a year, during the lifespan of key members (Binford 1983, chapters 6 and 7; David and Kramer 2001, chapters 8 and 9). Thus, a hunter-gatherer band resident in, for example, the summer months, within the study area, perhaps on Mendip, or winter months in the lowlands (Jacobi 1979; Norman 1982), would have the capacity to travel and maintain extensive social networks. Understanding the change in raw material consumption (Figure 52.4), and, more so, the approximate locus for these stones and thereby the links with other communities, is important (Figure 52.5). Daily routines, perceptions of the land and artefacts, including those carried, would be embedded in a long-term cultural memory. Raw materials observed within lithic scatter composition offer a means of understanding the complexities of local and regional identity. It is clear that the hunter-gatherers who occupied much of the study area, and therefore, a stretch of landscape north of the Parrett, had close ties with communities in the chalk lands of Wessex. Indeed, these connections may have existed since the Early Mesolithic, if the tentative analysis of strontium is accepted, supporting a Mendip and chalk-based territory for those buried at Aveline's Hole (Price and Schulting 2005, 225; see comments on territory in Schulting 2005, 245–6).

Conclusions

In this chapter comments have been made on raw materials, changes in technology and typology, and seasonal movements. Here the interconnections between each of these elements, and the fleshing out of the potential human events that gave meaning to the hunter's worldview, have been addressed. Concepts of local and regional identity are argued to be inter-divisible, as mobile people travelled across the total landscape. The stone procured may well have meant many things (e.g. a resource of quality flaking stone, or material that secured access to terrestrial game in other people's territories). Stone worked in the study area would have been redolent with memories of distant people and journeys lasting days, if not weeks. These stones, even perhaps the typology of certain retouched forms, as with the hollow-based point, may afford a glimpse of these social networks. These artefacts, their biographies, give access to very human stories and enable us to come closer to the corporate identity of some of those who were buried in the Mendip plateau. This social identity would have emerged over time, grounded in rites at special places, such as caves, but also in the more mundane routine forays and journeys taken by many. The social identity of the group would have been reproduced in this way over generations. Movement – kilometres of walking, and visiting places whilst working imported flint and chert cores – would cement these notions to humanized places. Therefore, it is argued here, stone, the technical routines learnt in making tools, and the journeys of people that led to the acquisition of that stone, would have lent meaning to the power of place. These journeys across regional landscapes may well provide a context for other events noted in the archaeological record outside the study area. Two 'posthole-like features' are dated to the eighth millennium cal BC, situated high on the hill, part of the chalk Downs of Hambledon Hill, Dorset (three Scots pine (*Pinus sylvestris*) charcoal fragments: 8725±55 BP; 7950–7590 cal BC; OxA-7816, 8480±55 BP; 7600–7460 cal BC; OxA-7846, 8400±60 BP; 7580–7330 cal BC; OxA-7845, in Healy 2004, table 1). Healy (2004, 16) noted this location, a hill slope faced west with views extending deep into the study area, tens of kilometres away.

This may support the existence, even at this date, of social differentiation (cf. Thorpe 2000). The probable occurrence of these wooden structures at this early date may be linked to periods of increased social differentiation (cf. Thorpe 2000). Structures such as 'totem poles', argued by Allen and Gardiner (2002), may have signalled the onset of 'between and within' group conflict, possibly preceded by increased attachment to selected locales. These places would have been part of the seasonal movements, including mobile subsistence and procurement strategies, perhaps forcing peoples to compete for access to resources or routes in the land. Episodic tensions between bands traversing the chalk and limestone landscape may be envisaged. Possibly, there was even a territorial boundary established between the Dorset Downs and those people frequenting, as part of a seasonal cycle, the Mendip Hills and the lowland in the far distance. Social identity and the 'draw' to a place is a topic worthy of comment. Central, however, are the complex social relations and cosmology (Zvelebil 2000, 2003) that may be traced beyond burials and shell middens in the south-western Mesolithic. Here a rethinking of highly mobile hunter-gatherer societies, lithics and landscape, particularly as experienced through embodied movements is addressed; places to settle, to revisit, journeys through the land. This refocuses debate on the social construction of local Mesolithic people and their changing perceptions of the landscape. Social identity, as argued in this chapter, employing lithics and raw material studies, gives a grounded sense of community that can add to discourses on a British regional Mesolithic.

Acknowledgements

Re-calibration was achieved by using atmospheric data from Reimer *et al.* (2004), OxCal version 3.10 (Bronk Ramsey 2005) and the INTERCAL04.14c calibration curve. The probability method was selected with round off by 5 years and at a single resolution.

This chapter has benefited from conversations with many people: Dr Rick Schulting (Queen's University Belfast), Dr Roger Jacobi (Natural History Museum), and Chris Norman (Somerset). Thanks go to Dr I. J. N. Thorpe for highlighting Mesolithic warfare, also my Director of Studies (The University of Winchester). Also much appreciated is the patience of the publishing committee, and particularly the support of Sinéad McCartan (Ulster Museum). Preparations for this contribution were completed during a particularly difficult time. Consequently, I would like to dedicate this chapter to the memory of Brian Large and Nancy Walters, both of whom, with my family, inspired and encouraged me with my studies.

References

Allen, M. J. and Gardiner, J. P. 2002. A sense of time – cultural markers in the Mesolithic of southern England?, in B. David and M. Wilson (eds.), *Inscribed Landscapes. Marking and Making Place*, 139–53. Honolulu, University of Hawaii Press.

Andrefsky, W. 1998. *Lithics: Macroscopic Approaches to Analysis*. Cambridge Manuals in Archaeology. Cambridge, Cambridge University Press.

Berridge, P. J. 1985. Mesolithic Sites in the Yarty Valley. *Proceedings of the Devon archaeological Society* 43, 1–21.

Binford, L. R. 1979. Organisation and formation processes: looking at curated technologies. *Journal of Anthropological Research* 35 (iii), 255–73.

Binford, L. R. 1983. *In Pursuit of the Past. Decoding the archaeological record*. London, Thames and Hudson.

Bond, C. J. 2004a. The supply of raw materials for later prehistoric stone tool assemblages and the maintenance of memorable places in central Somerset, in E. A. Walker, F. Wenban-Smith and F. M. Healy (eds.), *Lithics in Action. Papers from the Conference Lithic Studies in the Year 2000*, 124–39. Lithic Studies Society Occasional Paper 8. Oxford, Oxbow Books.

Bond, C. J. 2004b. The Sweet Track, Somerset: a place mediating culture and spirituality?, in T. Insoll (ed.), *Belief in the Past. The Proceedings of the 2002 Manchester Conference on Archaeology and Religion*, 37–50. British Archaeological Reports, International Series S1212. Oxford, Archaeopress.

Bond, C. J. 2006. *Prehistoric Settlement in Somerset. Landscapes, material culture and communities, 4300 to 700 cal BC*. Volumes I and II and DVD. Unpublished PhD thesis, the University of Winchester.

Bond, C. J. 2007. Lithics, in C. M. Gerrard and M. A. Aston (eds.), *The Shapwick Project, Somerset. A Rural Landscape Explored*, 687–728. The Society for Medieval Archaeology Monograph Series 25. Leeds, Maney Publishing.

Bradley, R. 1997. Domestication as a state of mind. *Analecta Praehistorica Leidensia* 29, 13–17.

Bronk Ramsey, C. 2005. OxCal 3.10. WWW program and documentation available at http://www.rlaha.ox.ac.uk/oxcal/oxcal.htm (accessed 10/2007).

Care, V. 1979. The production and distribution of Mesolithic axes in Southern England. *Proceedings of the Prehistoric Society* 45, 93–102.

Care, V. 1982. The collection and distribution of lithic materials during the Mesolithic and Neolithic periods in Southern England. *Oxford Journal of Archaeology* 1 (iii), 269–85.

Clark, J. G. D. 1932. *The Mesolithic Age in Britain*. Cambridge, Cambridge University Press.

David, N. and Kramer, C. 2001. *Ethnoarchaeology in Action*. Cambridge, Cambridge University Press.

Edmonds, E. A., McKeown, M. C., Williams, M. and Dewey, H. 1985. *British Regional Geology South West England* (fourth edition). Natural Environment Research Council, British Geological Survey. London, Her Majesty's Stationery Office.

Gardiner, J. P. 1990. Flint procurement and Neolithic axe production on the South Downs: a re-assessment. *Oxford Journal of Archaeology* 9 (ii), 119–40.

Gardiner, P. J. 2000. Excavations at Birdcombe, Somerset: Mesolithic settlement, subsistence and landscape use in the South-West of England, in R Young (ed.), *Mesolithic Lifeways. Current research from Britain and Ireland*, 199–208. Leicester Archaeology Monograph 7. Leicester, University of Leicester.

Green, M. 2000. *A Landscape Revealed. 10,000 Years on a Chalkland Farm*. Stroud, Tempus.

Healy, F. M. 2004. Hambledon Hill and its implications, in R. M. J. Cleal and J. Pollard (eds.), *Monuments and Material Culture. Papers in honour of an Avebury archaeologist: Isobel Smith*, 15–38. East Knoyle, Salisbury, The Hobnob Press.

Hosfield, R. (ed.) 2005. Part 2. Palaeolithic and Mesolithic, in C. J. Webster (ed.), *South West Archaeological Research Framework: Draft Resource Assessment. Version 1.0. November 2005*, 22–61. Taunton, Environment Department, Somerset County Council.

Ingold, T. 1992. Culture and the Perception of the Environment, in E. Croll and D. Parkin (eds.), *Bush Base: Forest Farm. Culture, Environment and Development*, 39–56. London, Routledge.

Ingold, T. 1993. The temporality of landscape. *World Archaeology* 25 (ii), 152–14.

Jacobi, R. M. 1973. Aspects of the 'Mesolithic' in Britain, in S. K. Kosłowski (ed.), *The Mesolithic in Europe*, 237–65. Warsaw, University of Warsaw.

Jacobi, R. M. 1976. Britain inside and outside Mesolithic Europe. *Proceedings of the Prehistoric Society* 42, 67–84.

Jacobi, R. M. 1978. The Mesolithic in Sussex, in P. L. Drewett (ed.), *The Archaeology of Sussex to 1500 AD*, 15–22. Council for British Archaeology (CBA) Research Report 29. London, Council for British Archaeology.

Jacobi, R. M. 1979. Early Flandrian hunters in the South-West, in V. A. Haxfield, *Devon Archaeological Society: Prehistoric Dartmoor in its Context*, 48–93. Devon Archaeological Society Jubilee Conference Proceedings 37. Exeter, Devon Archaeological Society.

Jacobi, R. M. 1981. The last hunters in Hampshire, in J. J. Shennan and R. T. Schadla-Hall (eds.), *The Archaeology of Hampshire*, 10–25. Hampshire Archaeology and Field Club Monograph 1. Southampton, Hampshire Field Club.

Jacobi, R. M. 1987. Misanthropic miscellany: musing on British early Flandrian archaeology and other flights of fancy, in P. Rowley-Conwy, M. Zvelebil and H. P. Blankholm (eds.), *Mesolithic Northwest Europe: Recent Trends*, 163–8. Sheffield, Department of Prehistory and Archaeology, University of Sheffield.

Jacobi, R. M. 2004. The Late Upper Palaeolithic lithic collection from Gough's Cave, Cheddar, Somerset and the human use of the cave. *Proceedings of the Prehistoric Society* 70, 1–92.

Norman, C. 1975. Four Mesolithic assemblages from West Somerset. *Proceedings of the Somerset Archaeological and Natural History Society* 119, 26–37.

Norman, C. 1982. Mesolithic hunter-gatherers 9000–4000 B.C., in M. A. Aston and I. Burrow (eds.), *The Archaeology of Somerset: a review to 1500 AD*, 14–21. Bridgwater, Somerset County Council.

Norman, C. 2003. Mesolithic to Bronze Age activity at Parchey Sand Batch, Chedzoy. *Proceedings of the Somerset Archaeological and Natural History Society* 145, 9–38.

Palmer, S. 1977. *Mesolithic Cultures of Britain*. Poole, Dolphin Press.

Price, T. D. and Schulting, R. 2005. Strontium isotopes and mobility, in R. Schulting, 'Pursuing a rabbit in Burrington Combe': New research on the early Mesolithic burial cave of Aveline's Hole. *Proceedings of the University of Bristol Spelaeological Society* 23 (iii), 224–6.

Reimer P. J., Baillie, M. G. L., Bard, E., Bayliss, A., Beck, J. W., Bertrand, C., Blackwell, P. G., Buck, C. E., Burr, G., Cutler, K. B., Damon, P. E., Edwards, R. L., Fairbanks, R. G., Friedrich, M., Guilderson, T. P., Hughen, K. A., Kromer, B., McCormac, F. G., Manning, S., Bronk Ramsey, C., Reimer, R. C., Remmele, S., Southon, J. R., Stuiver, M., Talamo, S., Taylor, F. W., van der Plicht, J., and Weyhenmeyer, C. E. 2004. IntCal04 terrestrial radiocarbon age calibration, 0-26 cal kyr BP. *Radiocarbon* 46 (3), 1029–58.

Reynier, M. J. 1998. Early Mesolithic settlement in England and Wales: some preliminary observations, in N Ashton, F. M. Healy and P. Pettitt (eds.), *Stone Age Archaeology. Essays in honour of John Wymer*, 174–84. Oxbow Monographs 102/Lithic Studies Society Occasional Paper 6. Oxford, Oxbow Books.

Schulting, R. 2005. 'Pursuing a rabbit in Burrington Combe': New research on the early Mesolithic burial cave of Aveline's Hole. *Proceedings of the University of Bristol Spelaeological Society* 23 (iii), 171–265.

Smith, A. G., Whittle, A., Cloutman, E. W. and Morgan, L. A. 1989. Mesolithic and Neolithic activity and environmental impact on the south-east Fen-edge in Cambridgeshire. *Proceedings of the Prehistoric Society* 55, 207–49.

Smith, C. 1992. *Late Stone Age Hunters of the British Isles*. London, Routledge.

Taçon, P. S. C. 1991. The power of stone: symbolic aspects of stone use and tool development in Western Arnhem Land, Australia. *Antiquity* 65, 192–207.

Tingle, M. 1998. *The Prehistory of Beer Head. Field survey and excavations at an isolated flint source on the South Devon Coast*. British Archaeological Reports, British Series 270. Oxford, Archaeopress.

Thorpe, I. J. N. 2000. Origins of violence: Mesolithic conflict in Europe. *British Archaeology* 52, 8–13.

Wainwright, G. J. 1960. Three Microlithic industries from South-West England and their affinities. *Proceedings of the Prehistoric Society* 26, 193–201.

Wymer, J. J. 1977. *Gazetteer of Mesolithic sites in England and Wales*. Council for British Archaeology (CBA) Research Report 22. London, Council for British Archaeology.

Zvelebil, M. 2000. Enculturation of Mesolithic landscapes, in L. Larsson, H. Kindgren, K. Knutsson, D. Loeffler and A. Åkerlund (eds.), *Mesolithic on the Move: Papers presented at the Sixth International Conference on the Mesolithic in Europe, Stockholm 2000*, 65–73. Oxford, Oxbow Books.

Zvelebil, M. 2003. People behind the lithics. Social life and social conditions of Mesolithic communities in temperate Europe, in L. Bevan and J. Moore (eds.), *Peopling the Mesolithic in a Northern Environment*, 1–26. British Archaeological Reports, International Series S1157. Oxford, Archaeopress.

53. Worm's Head and Caldey Island (south Wales, UK) and the question of Mesolithic territories

Rick Schulting

The Gower peninsula and Caldey Island lie some 30km apart in south Wales. Yet stable carbon and nitrogen isotope measurements on human remains directly dated to the Mesolithic show the existence and persistence over time of very different diets, with individuals from Caldey Island exhibiting a far greater emphasis on marine resources. The difference may lie partly in the earlier date of the majority of the Gower individuals, when the coast was further away, but this fails to account for later individuals exhibiting similar, predominantly terrestrial isotope values. This raises the possibility that communities with distinct subsistence practices existed within this relatively small area from early in the Holocene. Other regions of Atlantic Europe provide hints of comparable patterns, with the presence of distinct coastal and more inland communities. The distance separating groups with different diets seems to be in the order of 15–30km, with implications for the stability of Mesolithic subsistence practices, population density, and cultural identities.

Keywords: Wales, stable isotopes, territoriality, marine resources, identities.

Introduction

Over what size territories did people, and communities, habitually move in the Mesolithic? Various approaches have been taken to this question, ranging from ethnographic analogy, to stylistic differences in lithics, to the movements of raw materials. Taking another approach, this paper exploits the use of dietary differences as seen in stable isotope analysis to identify the habitually used resources of communities, and to use this in turn to infer the existence of distinct coastal and inland communities. A series of sites on the Gower peninsula and on Caldey Island in south Wales provide the initial case study, with other regions of western Europe also briefly considered.

The discussion below relies heavily on the interpretation of stable carbon ($\delta^{13}C$) and nitrogen ($\delta^{15}N$) isotope measurements on human bone collagen. It is important to keep in mind that measurements on bone collagen refer primarily to the protein component of the diet, and, in the case of humans, that measurements reflect an average of between five and ten years of an individual's diet (Ambrose and Krigbaum 2003; Ambrose and Norr 1993; Schoeninger and Moore 1992). In other words, the technique provides a medium-term (relative to a human lifespan) view of certain aspects of an individual's diet, rather than, for example, diet over a single season or year. In north-temperate Europe, the technique works best in differentiating and semi-quantifying the contribution of marine and terrestrial sources of protein (Richards and Hedges 1999), and it is this aspect that features here. The sample sizes available, especially for the Mesolithic period, are generally very small. While not ideal, this does not necessarily mean that we are limited to discussing the diets of specific individuals. Rather, for the most part (and exceptions can be acknowledged without negating the general pattern), these individuals are likely to broadly reflect the diets of their communities (cf. Lovell *et al.* 1986). The scope for exercising individual food choices greatly differing from those of the overall community would be severely limited in small-scale societies, particularly when sharing can be expected to have been a prominent feature in the distribution of food.

A tale of two caves

Worm's Head

Worm's Head Cave is located at the tip of the Gower peninsula, south Wales (Figure 53.1), and has been known since the early 20th century to contain Late Glacial and Early Holocene archaeological deposits. The site, together with other limestone caves in the region, has good bone preservation, rare for this period in Britain. Human and faunal remains have been recovered, along with a small number of Mesolithic flint tools and debitage. Excavations at the cave have been sporadic and poorly controlled, the earliest recorded being by Riches and Northwood in the

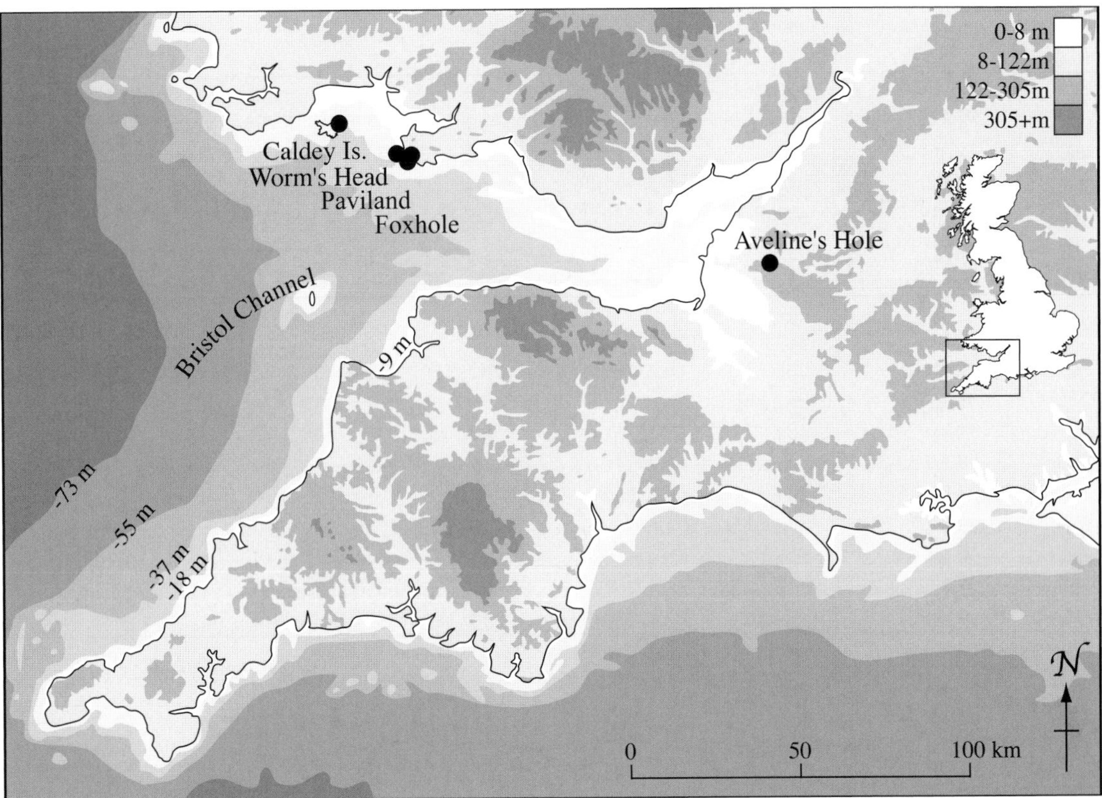

Figure 53.1. Map of south-west Britain showing key sites mentioned in the text. Sea levels after Heyworth and Kidson 1982.

early 1920s, by which time considerable deposits already appeared to have been removed (Riches 1923–24; Allen and Rutter 1948). Fragments of breccia containing human and animal bone were found fallen onto the cave floor in 1966 (Cooper 2004), while local amateur archaeologist Davies undertook some investigations in the 1980s (Davies 1986; 1989; 1993). Unrecorded visits by various individuals have undoubtedly resulted in the removal of an unknown amount of material from the cave over the years. Most recently, a small-scale excavation was carried out in 2004 with the aim of assessing the presence and nature of any surviving archaeological deposits (Schulting *et al.* 2005). Only a small amount of material was recovered, but this included additional human (minimally, an adult tibia, vertebra and molar) and faunal remains. With the exception of a sea otter (*Lutra lutra*) cranium, the faunal remains are all terrestrial. Despite wet-sieving of the clay-rich sediments, no fish bones were found. This is not necessarily surprising, as while the site is today coastal, lower sea levels in the early Holocene would place it some 20km or more inland (Figure 53.1).

An accelerator mass spectrometry (AMS) dating programme has shown that the four humans represented – each very partially – all date to the Early Mesolithic, with three grouping around 8600 cal BC, and another some centuries earlier (Figure 53.2). No later human remains have been identified from the cave. While limitations of space prevent a full discussion here of the reasoning involved, two human mandibles also dating to *c.* 8500 cal BC, ostensibly from a nearby cave site in Mewslade, may also actually derive from Worm's Head (Schulting *et al.* 2005). Taken as a group, these represent the earliest known Holocene human remains from Britain, predating the larger burial cave at Aveline's Hole, Somerset by some two centuries (Marshall and van der Plicht 2005). At least two Late Mesolithic individuals are also represented on the Gower, one from Paviland (*c.* 5800 cal BC) and another from nearby Foxhole (*c.* 5650 cal BC) (Aldhouse-Green 2000).

Most importantly from the perspective of this paper, the associated $\delta^{13}C$ and $\delta^{15}N$ values from Worm's Head and Mewslade are slightly elevated compared to an expected terrestrial signature, and so hint at a small contribution of marine resources, in the order of 5–15% of the protein consumed (Figure 53.2). There is admittedly greater than usual uncertainty over these estimates, since terrestrial end-points for carbon (i.e., the $\delta^{13}C$ value a typical terrestrial herbivore would be expected to show, *c.* -20 to -21‰) can be shown to be slightly elevated in the later Pleistocene and Early Holocene (Drucker *et al.* 2003; Iacumin *et al.* 1997; Richards and Hedges, 2003). This can be seen in stable isotope values on human bone collagen at the inland Early Mesolithic cemetery of Aveline's Hole (Schulting 2005a). If anything, this phenomenon would result in the actual contribution of marine protein at Worm's Head being slightly lower than estimated above. But the contribution of at least some marine protein here receives support from the intermediate position of the Gower sites in a plot of $\delta^{13}C$ and $\delta^{15}N$ values for Mesolithic individuals across south-west Britain (Figure 53.3). Faunal remains recovered from previous and recent excavations are currently being

Site	*sample id*	*element*	*Lab no.*	*Date BP*	±	*marine cal BC*[1]		$\delta^{13}C$	$\delta^{15}N$	*% marine*[2]
Worm's Head	2001.4H/4	L scapula	OxA-13131	9920	160	10080	8850	-19.3	10.2	3
Worm's Head[3]	WH 1	ulna	OxA-11128	9450	50	8790	8550	-18.3	10.2	16
Worm's Head	1924.6.35	femur	OxA-11083	9420	55	8800	8490	-18.8	7.2	9
Worm's Head	WH 2	cranium	OxA-11129	9360	50	8720	8350	-18.6	11.4	12
'Mewslade Bay' ?	SM 1919.41.11	mandible	OxA-11017	9385	45	8750	8490	-19.0	9.1	7
'Mewslade Bay' ?	SM 1919.41.12	mandible	OxA-11018	9235	50	8560	8300	-19.0	9.0	7
Worm's Head	WH 1	ulna	OxA-4024	8800	80	8200	7600	-18.8	-	9
Paviland	2	humerus	OxA-681	7190	80	6200	5790	-18.5	10.4	24
Foxhole Cave	FX41	tooth	OxA-8316	6785	50	5740	5570	-20.0	11.3	6
Ogof-yr-Ychen	98.2H/1	tibia	OxA-10616	8760	55	7720	7470	-14.6	15.1	69
Daylight Rock	63.336/84.1	mandible	OxA-7686	8655	60	7610	7370	-15.9	13.0	54
Potter's Cave	91.7H/308	ulna	OxA-7688	8580	60	7590	7370	-17.3	11.8	38
Ogof-yr-Ychen	98.2H/179	mandible	OxA-7741	8415	65	7450	7080	-15.9	14.3	54
Ogof-yr-Ychen	98.2H/142	innominate	OxA-7690	8280	55	7250	6820	-15.1	15.1	64
Ogof-yr-Ychen	98.2H/145	innominate	OxA-7691	8210	55	7060	6690	-14.4	14.2	71
Ogof-yr-Ychen	98.2H/54	cranium	OxA-7742	7880	55	6640	6430	-15.7	15.6	56
Potter's Cave	63.337/20	metacarpal	OxA-7687	7880	55	6650	6440	-16.1	12.5	52
Ogof-yr-Ychen	98.2H/14	mandible	OxA-2574	7020	100	5870	5490	-14.9	15.4	66

1 - calibrated with Calib 5.0.2, taking into account estimated marine reservoir correction, using regional delta R of 17±14 years (Reimer *et al*. 2004)

2 - estimated '% marine' ± 10%, using endpoints of -12 and -19.5‰ for samples pre-8000 BP, and -12 and -20.5‰ for post-8000 BP, to account for Early Holocene elevation

3 - the date reported here for Worm's Head 1 supercedes the previous determination of 8800 ± 80 BP (OxA-4024)

Figure 53.2. AMS dates and associated $\delta^{13}C$ and $\delta^{15}N$ values on Mesolithic human bone from the Gower and Caldey Island.

analysed through AMS dating and stable isotope analysis to address this issue more thoroughly, although the argument presented below is not substantially affected either way. Perhaps more surprisingly, the two Late Mesolithic individuals from the Gower also exhibit stable isotope signatures indicative of a predominantly terrestrial diet (Richards 2000).

Caldey Island

The other sites of key importance to the present discussion are Ogof-yr-Ychen, Daylight Rock, and Potter's Cave, all on Caldey Island, located some 30km west of Worm's Head (Figure 53.1). Scattered and fragmentary human remains have been recovered over an extended period from these caves and fissures, again usually under less than ideal conditions (David 1990; Davies 1989). They are here treated as a single group, and have yielded AMS determinations in the range of 7800–6400 cal BC (Schulting and Richards 2002a). In contrast to the Gower sites, the $\delta^{13}C$ and $\delta^{15}N$ measurements demonstrate a diet in which marine foods played a variable but overall important role, ranging between *c.* 35–70% of the dietary protein (Figure 53.2). There appears to be no consistent pattern of change over time, for example to increasing use of marine resources, and in fact some of the earliest individuals exhibit some of the highest values.

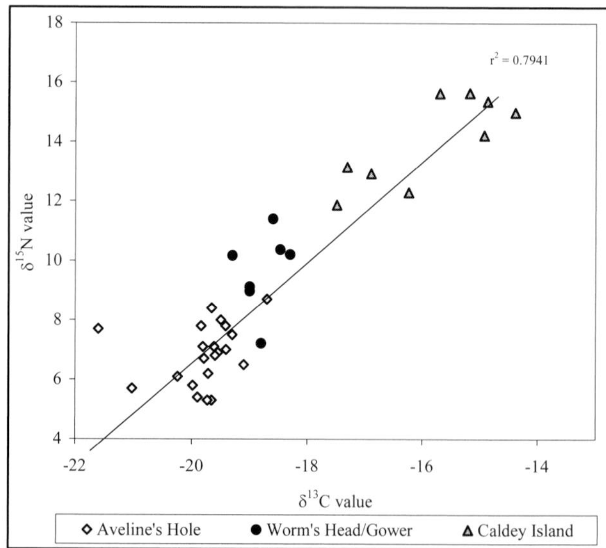

Figure 53.3. Plot of $\delta^{13}C$ and $\delta^{15}N$ values on human bone collagen from Early Mesolithic sites in south-west Britain. Their position on the regression line ($r^2 = 0.79$) suggests that there is some contribution from marine protein in the Gower group. (Sources: Schulting 2005a; Schulting and Richards 2002a; this paper).

The sites compared

There is, then, a marked difference in the isotopic signatures of the human remains from Worm's Head and the other

Gower sites, and those from the Caldey Island sites. The Caldey Island humans, while more variable, exhibit between two and seven times the contribution of marine protein compared with Worm's Head. Despite the relatively small numbers of individuals involved, there is no question of this difference being 'real', in the sense that it is highly statistically significant. It is important to emphasise that the consistent difference between Worm's Head and Caldey Island precludes any explanation invoking individual dietary idiosyncrasies, as well as community-level shifts in short- to medium-term subsistence practices, whether these might be due to fluctuations in local resource abundance, or for other reasons. On the contrary, these broad-scale differences appear to persist over the long term, given the period represented by the human remains at each site group.

How is this difference to be explained? Three possibilities are here considered. First, the human remains from Worm's Head are some centuries earlier than the earliest dated human from Caldey Island (Figure 53.2). It is conceivable, then, that marine resources were not yet exploited to a greater degree because of technological limitations, although it is difficult to imagine what these limitations might consist of. The coastlines of both the Gower and Caldey Island comprise a mixture of sandy bays and rocky cliffs and headlands, which on the face of it (and unless lower sea levels resulted in a significantly different coastline) should have provided ample opportunities for the exploitation of at least some marine species. Shellfish could have been easily collected from a range of habitats, inshore fish could have been taken with relatively simple traps or nets (that would leave no archaeological evidence), and seals (Phocidae) would have been available at certain times of the year, possibly in considerable numbers during breeding season (David 1990). All of these resources could have been exploited with relatively simple technologies. While in historic times seal colonies have tended to avoid the mainland in favour of less accessible offshore islets, this is itself probably due to human predation pressure over centuries if not millennia (e.g. Burton *et al.* 2001). The lack of sites with faunal evidence for the use of these species can be accounted for by the fact that the relevant contemporary coastlines are now submerged, affecting both the Gower and Caldey sites equally (some fish and shellfish remains are present at the latter, although their date is unknown).

A related, but perhaps more plausible explanation, lies in Worm's Head's greater distance from its Early Holocene coastline, compared to Caldey Island. It is difficult to specify precisely what this distance was, but it was likely in the order of some 20km at *c.* 8500 cal BC, compared to less than 5km at Caldey Island at *c.* 7500 cal BC. This could mean that the communities represented by the individuals at Worm's Head were focused primarily on inland resources, carrying with it the implication that other communities may have been present nearer the coast. The low use of marine resources seen isotopically could then be explained by periodic forays to the coast, and/or through exchange with these hypothetical coastal communities. The main problem with both this explanation and the one above is that the two Late Mesolithic individuals, from sites that would have been much nearer the coast, also show very limited use of marine protein. While a single exception might perhaps be viewed as a visitor to the coast originating from a more inland community, it becomes less satisfactory to try to account for two individuals in this way, although of course this remains a possibility.

The third explanation to be considered here is that the difference is primarily a 'cultural' one, involving food choices by two populations living some 30km apart, in a comparable environment that included stretches of coastline, yet choosing to focus on a very different balance of marine and terrestrial resources. Of course environmental factors may play a role in shaping human decision making, so that these explanations need not be mutually exclusive. This paper is not the place to try to resolve this question, as further research – currently underway – is needed concerning the exact position of these sites in relation to their contemporary coastlines, and the nature of those coastlines (which would greatly impact on the nature and accessibility of the available marine resources). Instead, the remainder of this paper will further explore the second and third explanations, both of which have similar implications for Mesolithic territoriality.

Mesolithic territories

Traditionally the study of Mesolithic territories has been approached through stylistic and technological analyses of lithic assemblages, and through the movement of raw materials (e.g. Gendel 1989; Jacobi 1979; Wickham-Jones 2005), or the distribution of ornaments (Newell *et al.* 1990). More recently, other stable isotopes (strontium, lead, oxygen) have been used, mainly in Neolithic contexts, to address the question of the movements of individuals over the course of their lifetimes (Montgomery *et al.* 2000). Dietary stable isotopes (carbon and nitrogen) have the advantage of providing information on the 'identity' of a population in terms of its subsistence, even though interpreting this in terms of territories (used here in the sense of an area habitually exploited for subsistence purposes) is not straightforward. Aside from the obvious problem of often limited sample sizes and biases in the location of the human skeletal remains that are available (e.g. no Mesolithic human remains are ever likely to be found in the acid soils of much of upland Wales), there is the issue of equifinality. That is, how can we distinguish the settlement pattern of a community using marine resources for half the year, and terrestrial resources *from a different location or locations*, for the remaining half of the year, from one focused on the coast year-round, but exploiting a balance of marine and terrestrial resources in a logistical fashion (*sensu* Binford 1982)? If sufficient human remains are available from both coastal and inland locations, then this problem does not arise, since a cut-off point should be evident somewhere along a coastal-inland transect, where substantially more 'terrestrial' isotopic signatures occur. If no such cut-off point can be detected, then it can be inferred that either the one and the same 'population' is exploiting both coastal and inland areas, or that change in subsistence emphasis over time was rapid and fluctuating, leaving no opportunity for a consistent (i.e. isotopically recognizable) spatial pattern to emerge.

A simpler approach, one that to some extent circumvents the problem of equifinality, is to compare human bone isotope values (preferably directly dated to address the potentially complicating factor of temporal variation) within a region. If spatially linked clustering of isotopic values can be detected and confirmed statistically, this would strongly imply the presence of distinct 'populations' (in the sense of groups of communities broadly sharing a subsistence orientation, one different from that of neighbouring groups of communities). More extreme isotopic signatures (see below) present fewer interpretive problems, as the alternative scenarios are restricted. At least in the context of north-west Europe, human isotope results exhibiting very high $\delta^{13}C$ and $\delta^{15}N$ values must indicate an economic focus on marine resources, and therefore a settlement system, or territory, also focused on the coast. Sedentism need not be a necessary correlate, although it may be suggested; other lines of evidence would then be needed to address this possibility.

The interpretation of the isotopic data from Caldey Island and Worm's Head being discussed here is that two different populations were present, each with a distinct balance of marine-terrestrial resource use. While a greater degree of isotopic variability is seen in the humans from the Caldey Island sites, there remains a complete lack of overlap with Worm's Head. What is most striking is that these practices seem to have persisted over the long term, although the problem of sample size does arise. Nevertheless, on current evidence, this persistence seems to suggest that Mesolithic populations in the two areas were 'settled in' to their landscapes, exploiting them in certain ways. Yet the two sites are only some 30km apart. What we do not know – as we lack intervening sites with human remains – is where the boundary lies between the two areas (again, assuming that the observed difference is not primarily temporal), and whether it is a distinct or a fuzzy boundary. But even without this level of detail, the picture of distinct Mesolithic groups of communities with different economic practices co-existing within 30km of one another, and persisting over the long term, is quite striking.

The wider picture

The situation described above is unique only in terms of its early date. While always dependent on the availability of human remains with well-preserved collagen, the question of coastal Mesolithic exploitation territories can, in the context of western Europe, be explored to varying degrees in west Scotland, Ireland, Denmark and north Germany, west Sweden, north-west France, north Spain and Portugal (Arias and Fano 2005; Lubell *et al.* 1994; Nordqvist 1995; Richards and Mellars 1998; Richards *et al.* 2003; Schulting and Richards 2001; Tauber 1986; Woodman 2004). The evidence is partial, with many gaps, but the potential for further investigation is clear. Human remains from the Oronsay shell middens of western Scotland (Richards and Mellars 1998) and from Dragsholm, Vænge Sø, Norsminde and Holmegaard-Jutland in Denmark (Tauber 1981; 1986) exhibit isotopic signatures so extreme (*c.* -12‰ or higher) that they must represent people – and, by extension, communities – whose subsistence and settlement was focused more or less entirely on the sea. Numerous other sites have human remains with isotopic signatures only slightly less extreme (*c.* -14‰). Examples would include Ferriter's Cove in south-west Ireland (Woodman *et al.* 1999); Hoëdic, and to a lesser extent Téviec in southern Brittany (Schulting and Richards 2001), and a host of sites in Denmark (Richards *et al.* 2003; Tauber 1981; 1986). Whether or not individuals from a series of more inland locations are present in these regions (and they rarely are), these findings are sufficient to indicate the presence of coastally oriented communities, which in turn can be used to infer the existence of distinct communities with an inland focus (since lithic remains are found well inland, often exploiting different lithic materials, e.g. Yven 2003 for Brittany).

To consider one example in greater detail, the available Mesolithic human isotopic data for Scotland all derive from scattered skeletal elements in the shell middens of Oronsay (Meiklejohn *et al.* 2005). Five samples from Cnoc Coic (although possibly representing only two individuals) exhibit extreme marine isotopic signatures, indicative of an 80–100% contribution of marine protein, while a single sample from Caisteal nan Gillean II suggests *c.* 60% marine input (Richards and Mellars 1998). Any seasonal round incorporating coastal and inland locations can be excluded for the Cnoc Coig individuals (recall that the measurements present an average diet over the last decade or so of life). Thus, these individuals, and by inference their communities, must have remained focused on the coast – although not necessarily on Oronsay itself – essentially year-round (Schulting and Richards 2002b). While we know from lithic scatters of a Mesolithic presence well inland (Edwards 1996), it is not possible at present to identify the boundary between these communities and those with a coastal orientation; it is, however, possible to postulate their existence as distinct groups following substantially different lifeways. In the absence of inland human remains, the movement of lithic materials from the coast may provide one means of addressing this further (cf. Wickham-Jones 2005).

Similarly, measurements on isolated Late Mesolithic human remains (again representing only one or two individuals) from Ferriter's Cove in south-west Ireland indicate the presence of a community focused almost exclusively on the coast for subsistence (Woodman 2004; Woodman *et al.* 1999). As with Oronsay, this then implies the existence of other groups with an inland orientation.

And, in fact, human remains from Killuragh Cave have recently been dated to the Mesolithic, with $\delta^{13}C$ values indicating terrestrial diets (Woodman 2004). This result is somewhat surprising, as the cave, while some 30km from the estuary, is close to the Shannon River, with its presumably substantial runs of salmon, which would present a strongly marine signal. Given the impoverished terrestrial fauna in Ireland (Woodman *et al.* 1997), it might be expected that this resource would feature strongly in the economies of Mesolithic groups with access to spawning rivers. Did other groups exist here nearer the coast? Further research is required, but it can at least be said that separate communities with distinct coastal and inland orientations were present in Ireland, and that the distance between the two may not have been very great.

A relatively large quantity of human remains is available from Mesolithic Denmark, making the area of great importance for isotopic studies of palaeodiet. Yet the situation here is made complex by a combination of rising sea levels and isostatic rebound, changing the Baltic from marine to lacustrine at various times in its history. Furthermore, relatively few individuals have been analysed and reported from any one site or contemporaneous locale, making it difficult to identify spatio-temporal clusters of individuals with isotopically distinct diets. There is also a bias towards coastal sites, with bone preservation from interior Jutland being very poor. Thus, while a strong maritime economic orientation can be readily identified, the degree of variability in coastal diets is unclear, as is the extent to which distinct inland orientations exist. Yet there are some hints, with Fischer (1993) and Noe-Nygaard (1988) discussing the possibility of distinct inland and coastal adaptations based on limited isotopic evidence from humans and dogs on Zealand. If the few available measurements can be accepted as indicative of a broader pattern, then the boundary between coastal and inland groups can be placed at between 15 and 35km from the coast.

Recently reported results from the Cantabrian coast of northern Spain show elevated isotopic signatures on isolated Late Mesolithic human remains from Poza l'Egua and Colomba (*c.* -16‰), while strongly terrestrial isotopic signatures (*c.* -20‰) come from burials of approximately the same date at Los Canes, only some 20km from the coast (Arias and Fano 2005). Although based on very few samples, this nevertheless suggests the existence of communities with a marked coastal orientation with a 'hinterland' extending, at least in some areas, less than 20km inland. Possibly the northern flank of the mountains facing the narrow coastal strip formed a natural territorial boundary, as Los Canes is located on the southern side of the range.

The southern Breton sites of Téviec and Hoëdic present a slightly different situation, in that it is variation between coastal diets that is seen, rather than distinct coastal-inland diets (bone preservation in the interior is so far unknown for Mesolithic sites here). Despite their being only some 30km apart, the group at Hoëdic exhibits slightly, but significantly, elevated $\delta^{13}C$ values compared with Téviec (Schulting 2005b; Schulting and Richards 2001). Again, this suggests the persistence of more or less neighbouring groups using an isotopically distinct suite of resources.

Conclusions

The results discussed here have implications for the degree to which Mesolithic communities were settled in to their landscapes from an early period, and persisted in a distinct set of economic practices seemingly over the scale of centuries if not millennia. This in turn raises questions about population densities, which have usually been seen as rather low for the Mesolithic, although local and regional variability is often acknowledged (Constandse-Westermann and Newell 1989; Smith 1992). It comes as no surprise to suggest here that coastal areas in particular may have seen higher than average populations densities and a degree of territorial packing (e.g. Vang Petersen 1984). Nevertheless, the $\delta^{13}C$ and $\delta^{15}N$ data provide a new level of detail. On the basis of isotopic values from a number of areas across Atlantic Europe, it is possible to posit the existence of distinct coastal and inland subsistence and settlement foci, seemingly separated by a remarkably consistent distance of between 15 and 30km. Much more research will be required to confirm and refine this observation, and to compare it with other lines of evidence, in particular lithic and other technologies and raw material movement.

The findings discussed here also serve to give a sense of variability in Mesolithic subsistence practices, even near the coast. While there is certainly a strong tendency for coastal Mesolithic humans in Atlantic Europe to show elevated $\delta^{13}C$ and $\delta^{15}N$ values indicating a substantial contribution of marine protein, there are exceptions, albeit, so far, these tend to be rather few in number. The main focus here has been on spatial variation; clearly diachronic change is another area to be explored. The way in which subsistence practices are embedded in wider social and cultural contexts is also an important area for further consideration, one rarely explicitly discussed for the Mesolithic. Foods and their preparation often feature in the creation and maintenance of distinct cultural identities; isotopic data should be able to contribute to this discussion.

Acknowledgements

The author would like to thank the British Academy for supporting the research on which this paper is based. Thanks also go to the Natural History Museum, London; the National Museum and Galleries Wales, Cardiff, and the Swansea Museum for permitting the sampling of remains in their care.

Note

There is a potential issue with OxA dates 11017–11128 that could make them slightly too old; these are being re-done, but should not substantially affect the arguments presented here. If anything, the dates will be brought closer in line with those from Caldey Island.

References

Aldhouse-Green, S. (ed.) 2000. *Paviland Cave and the 'Red Lady': A Definitive Report*. Bristol, Western Academic and Specialist Press.

Allen, E. E. and Rutter, J. G. 1948. *Prehistoric Gower, Part II*. Swansea, Welsh Guides.

Ambrose, S. H. and Krigbaum, J. 2003. Bone chemistry and bioarchaeology. *Journal of Anthropological Archaeology* 22, 193–9.

Ambrose, S. H. and Norr, L. 1993. Experimental evidence for the relationship of the carbon isotope ratios of whole diet and dietary protein to those of bone collagen and carbonate, in J. B. Lambert and G. Grupe (eds.), *Prehistoric Human Bone: Archaeology at the Molecular Level*, 1–37. New York, Springer-Verlag.

Arias Cabal, P. and Fano Martínez, M. A. 2005. Le rôle des ressources marines dans le Mésolithique de la région Cantabrique (Espagne): L'apport des isotopes stables, in G. Marchand and A. Tresset (eds.), *Unité et diversité des processus de néolithisation sur la façade atlantique de l'Europe (6e-4e millénaires avant J.-C. Table Ronde de Nantes 26–27 avril 2002*, 173–88. Mémoire XXXVI. Paris, Société préhistorique française.

Binford, L. R. 1982. The archaeology of place. *Journal of Anthropological Archaeology* 1, 1–31.

Burton, R. K., Snodgrass, J. J., Gifford-González, D., Guilderson, T., Brown, T. and Koch, P. L. 2001. Holocene changes in the ecology of northern fur seals: insights from stable isotopes and archaeofauna. *Oecologia* 128, 107–15.

Constandse-Westermann, T. S. and Newell, R. R. 1989. Social and biological aspects of the Western European Mesolithic population structure: a comparison with the demography of North American Indians, in C. Bonsall (ed.), *The Mesolithic in Europe*, 106–15. Edinburgh, John Donald Publishers.

Cooper, G. 2004. Worm's Head Cave: a report on the finds made in 1966. *Capra* 6. http://www.shef.ac.uk/~capra/6/wormshead.html (accessed 11/2007).

David, A. 1990. *Palaeolithic and Mesolithic Settlement in Wales with Special Reference to Dyfed*. Unpublished PhD thesis, University of Lancaster.

Davies, M. 1986. Worm's Head, Rhosili. *Archaeology in Wales* 26, 34.

Davies, M. 1989. Recent advances in cave archaeology in southwest Wales, in T. D. Ford (ed.), *Limestone and Caves of Wales*, 79–91. Cambridge, Cambridge University Press.

Davies, M. 1993. *The caves of the South Gower coast: an archaeological assessment*. Swansea (second edition), privately published by Mel Davies.

Drucker, D., Bocherens, H. and Billiou, D. 2003. Evidence for shifting environmental conditions in Southwestern France from 33,000 to 15,000 years ago derived from carbon-13 and nitrogen-15 natural abundances in collagen of large herbivores. *Earth and Planetary Science Letters* 216, 163–73.

Edwards, K. J. 1996. The contribution of Tom Affleck to the study of the Mesolithic of southwest Scotland, in T. Pollard and A. Morrison (eds.), *The Early Prehistory of Scotland*, 108–22. Edinburgh, Edinburgh University Press.

Fischer, A. 1993. Mesolithic inland settlement, in S. Hvass and B. Storgaard (eds.), *Digging into the Past. 25 Years of Archaeology in Denmark*, 58–63. Aarhus, Aarhus University Press.

Gendel, P. A. 1989. The analysis of lithic styles through distributional profiles of variation: examples from the western European Mesolithic, in C. Bonsall (ed.), *The Mesolithic in Europe*, 40–8. Edinburgh, John Donald Publishers.

Heyworth, A. and Kidson, C. 1982. Sea-level changes in south west England and Wales. *Proceedings of the Geologists' Association* 93, 91–111.

Iacumin, P., Bocherens, H., Delgado Huertas, A., Mariotti, A. and Longinelli, A. 1997. A stable isotope study of fossil mammal remains from the Paglicci cave, Southern Italy. N and C as palaeoenvironmental indicators. *Earth and Planetary Science Letters* 148, 349–57.

Jacobi, R. M. 1979. Early Flandrian hunters in the South-West, in V. A. Haxfield, *Devon Archaeological Society Prehistoric Dartmoor in its Context*, 48–93. Devon Archaeological Society Jubilee Conference Proceedings 37. Exeter, Devon Archaeological Society.

Lovell, N. C., Nelson, D. E. and Schwarcz, H. P. 1986. Carbon isotope ratios in palaeodiet: lack of age or sex effect. *Archaeometry* 28, 51–5.

Lubell, D., Jackes, M., Schwarcz, H., Knyf, M. and Meiklejohn, C. 1994. The Mesolithic-Neolithic transition in Portugal: isotopic and dental evidence of diet. *Journal of Archaeological Science* 21, 201–16.

Marshall, P. and van der Plicht, J. 2005. Dating, in '...pursuing a rabbit in Burrington Combe': new research on the Early Mesolithic burial cave of Aveline's Hole (R. Schulting). *Proceedings of the University of Bristol Spelaeological Society* 23, 226–33.

Meiklejohn, C., Merrett, D. C., Nolan, R. W., Richards, M. P. and Mellars, P. A. 2005. Spatial Relationships, Dating and Taphonomy of the Human Bone from the Mesolithic site of Cnoc Coig, Oronsay, Argyll, Scotland. *Proceedings of the Prehistoric Society* 71, 85–105.

Montgomery, J., Budd, P. and Evans, J. 2000. Reconstructing the lifetime movements of ancient people: a Neolithic case study from southern England. *European Journal of Archaeology* 3, 370–85.

Newell, R. R., Kielman, D., Constandse-Westermann, T. S., van der Sanden, W. A. B. and van Gijn, A. 1990. *An inquiry into the ethnic resolution of Mesolithic regional groups. The study of their decorative ornaments in time and space*. Leyden, E. J. Brill.

Noe-Nygaard, N. 1988. δ^{13}C values of dog bones reveal the nature of changes in man's food resources at the Mesolithic-Neolithic transition, Denmark. *Isotope Geoscience* 73, 87–96.

Nordqvist, B. 1995. The Mesolithic settlements of the Swedish west coast – with special emphasis on chronology and topography of coastal settlements, in A. Fischer, (ed.), *Man and Sea in the Mesolithic – coastal settlement above and below present sea level*, 185–96. Oxbow Monographs 53. Oxford, Oxbow Books.

Reimer, P. J., Baillie, M. G. L., Bard, E., Bayliss, A., Beck, J. W., Bertrand, C., Blackwell, P. G., Buck, C. E., Burr, G., Cutler, K. B., Damon, P. E., Edwards, R. L., Fairbanks, R. G., Friedrich, M., Guilderson, T. P., Hughen, K. A., Kromer, B., McCormac, F. G., Manning, S., Bronk Ramsey, C., Reimer, R. W., Remmele, S., Southon, J. R., Stuiver, M., Talamo, S., Taylor, F. W., van der Plicht, J. and Weyhenmeyer, C. E. 2004. IntCal04 terrestrial radiocarbon age calibration, 0-26 cal kyr BP. *Radiocarbon*, 46 (3), 1029–58.

Richards, M. P. 2000. Human and faunal stable isotope analysis from Goat's Hole and Foxhole Caves, Gower, in S. Aldhouse-Green (ed.), *Paviland Cave and the 'Red Lady': A Definitive Report*, 71–5. Bristol, Western Academic and Specialist Press.

Richards, M. P. and Hedges, R. E. M. 1999. Stable isotope evidence for similarities in the types of marine foods used by Late Mesolithic humans on the Atlantic coast of Europe. *Journal of Archaeological Science* 26, 717–22.

Richards, M. P. and Hedges, R. E. M. 2003. Bone collagen $\delta^{13}C$ and $\delta^{15}N$ values of fauna from Northwest Europe reflect palaeoclimatic variation over the last 40,000 years. *Palaeogeography, Palaeoclimatology, Palaeoecology* 193, 261–7.

Richards, M. P. and Mellars, P. 1998. Stable isotopes and the seasonality of the Oronsay middens. *Antiquity* 72, 178–84.

Richards, M. P., Price, T. D. and Koch, E. 2003. Mesolithic and Neolithic subsistence in Denmark: new stable isotope data. *Current Anthropology* 44 (2), 288–95.

Riches, W. 1923–24. Worm's Head Cave. *Annual Report of the Royal Institution of South Wales* 1923–24, 20–5.

Schoeninger, M. and Moore, K. 1992. Stable bone isotope studies in archaeology. *Journal of World Prehistory* 6, 247–96.

Schulting, R. J. 2005a. 'Pursuing a rabbit in Burrington Combe': New research on the Early Mesolithic burial cave of Aveline's Hole. *Proceedings of the University of Bristol Spelaeological Society* 23 (iii), 171–265.

Schulting, R. J. 2005b. Comme la mer qui se retire: les changements dans l'exploitation des ressources marines du Mésolithique au Néolithique en Bretagne, in G. Marchand and A. Tresset (eds.), *Unité et diversité des processus de néolithisation sur la façade atlantique de l'Europe (7–4ème millénaires avant J.-C.)*, 163–71. Memoir XXXVI. Paris, Société Préhistorique Française.

Schulting, R. J., Murray, E., Plunkett, G., Trick, S., Pilcher, J., Davison, J., Walker, E. and Macphail, R. 2005. *Excavations on the Gower peninsula, 11–25 September 2004: preliminary report*. Unpublished report prepared for the National Trust and the British Academy.

Schulting, R. J. and Richards, M. P. 2001. Dating women becoming farmers: new paleodietary and AMS dating evidence from the Breton Mesolithic cemeteries of Téviec and Hoëdic. *Journal of Anthropological Archaeology* 20, 314–44.

Schulting, R. J. and Richards, M. P. 2002a. Finding the coastal Mesolithic in southwest Britain: AMS dates and stable isotope results on human remains from Caldey Island, Pembrokeshire, South Wales. *Antiquity* 76, 1011–25.

Schulting, R. J. and Richards, M. P. 2002b. The wet, the wild and the domesticated: the Mesolithic-Neolithic transition on the west coast of Scotland. *European Journal of Archaeology* 5, 147–89.

Smith, C. 1992. The population of Late Upper Palaeolithic and Mesolithic Britain. *Proceedings of the Prehistoric Society* 58, 37–40.

Tauber, H. 1981. ^{13}C Evidence for Dietary Habits of Prehistoric Man in Denmark. *Nature* 292, 332–3.

Tauber, H. 1986. Analysis of stable isotopes in prehistoric populations. *Mitteilungen der Berliner Gesellschaft für Anthropologie, Ethnologie und Urgeschichte* 7, 31–8.

Vang Petersen, P. 1984. Chronological and Regional Variation in the Late Mesolithic of Eastern Denmark. *Journal of Danish Archaeology* 3, 7–18.

Wickham-Jones, C. 2005. Summer walkers? – Mobility and the Mesolithic, in N. Milner and P. C. Woodman (eds.), *Mesolithic Studies at the Beginning of the 21st Century*, 30–41. Oxford, Oxbow Books.

Woodman, P. C. 2004. The exploitation of Ireland's coastal resources – a marginal resource through time?, in M. R. González Morales and G. A. Clarke (eds.), *The Mesolithic of the Atlantic Façade*, 42–61. Arizona State University Anthropological Research Paper 55. Tucson, Arizona State University.

Woodman, P. C., Anderson, E. and Finlay, N. 1999. *Excavations at Ferriter's Cove, 1983-1995: last foragers, first farmers in the Dingle Peninsula*. Bray, Wordwell.

Woodman, P. C., McCarthy, M. and Monaghan, N. 1997. The Irish Quaternary Fauna Project. *Quaternary Science Reviews* 16, 129–59.

Yven, E. 2003. The deposits of raw materials and the quarry-sites during Mesolithic in the Trégor in Brittany, in L. Larsson, H. Kindgren, K. Knutsson, D. Loeffler and A. Åkerlund (eds.), *Mesolithic on the Move: Papers presented at the Sixth International Conference on the Mesolithic in Europe, Stockholm 2000*, 451–60. Oxford, Oxbow Books.

54. Show me how you make your hunting equipment and I will tell you where you come from: technical traditions, an efficient means of characterizing cultural identities

Eva David

The aim of this paper, based on the analysis of bone and antler industries from northern Europe dated around the 8th millennium cal BC, is to discuss results yielded by a technological approach, with a focus on the methodological aspects developed in order to highlight identities or 'cultures'. At that time, at least three regional entities can be distinguished on the basis of technical manufacturing traditions.

Keywords: Early Mesolithic, bone technology, technocomplex, archaeological cultures, manufacturing traditions.

Introduction

The very wide distribution of archaeological sites in northern Europe yielding similar bone barbed points – the so-called 'harpoons' (Breuil 1926, 309) – dated to the Ancylus Lake period, has led to widely diverging interpretations. Basing themselves on typological analyses, some authors have subscribed to a homogenous culture settled in the northern plains (Clark 1936, 86; Childe 1931, 327; Verhart 1990), while others have opted for differentiated cultures distinguished by the associated flint industry (Kozłowski 1973; Kozłowski and Kozłowski 1977, 224; Larsson 1990).

In this context, archaeologists have invoked the notion of 'culture' to designate the combination of remains from these occupations, because these remains yield similar data on a variety of aspects, namely settlement patterns, economic activities, and material culture. As a result, they identified in northern Europe a widespread 'Maglemose forest culture' (Childe 1931), also termed 'Maglemose civilization' (Clark 1936), literally 'civilization of the Big Bog' (*Magle Mose*).

A major issue is the extent to which technological analysis is relevant for discussing previous cultural attributions used to characterize the Early Mesolithic. The basic assumption is that the study of the technology brought into play by the last prehistoric hunters of Europe affords the possibility of discussing the various interpretations put forward, in the same way as the above-mentioned typological approach. In this respect, the contribution of bone technology is considered to be crucial: can the techniques employed for making projectile points be used as 'cultural' markers, and how can this be demonstrated? Was this equipment identically manufactured everywhere?

The database available for a technological approach comprises 23 sites, all of which, except grave 170 from Zvejnieki (Latvia), are stratified settlement sites (Figure 54.1). The remains under study come from 38 archaeological layers. Comparisons between assemblages have been made possible because of the existence of relative and/or radiocarbon dates, which range from *c.* 9000 to 7000 cal BC, i.e. from the Late Preboreal to the Atlantic/Boreal transition (David 2006). The study includes over 4500 bone and antler pieces. These are the manufactured items (weapons, tools and objects) and associated manufacture debris recovered from the eponymous Maglemosian site of Mullerup in Denmark (Sarauw *et al.* 1903) and the neighbouring and supra-regional assemblages of northern Europe. Comparisons between all these industries are successively addressed in a synchronic and diachronic perspective.

A method for detecting behaviours

In archaeology, technological approaches are at the root of the notion of 'technical system', the means by which behaviours can be studied via information collected in the field. Their purpose is to identify all the technical operations required for the manufacture of artefacts, following a

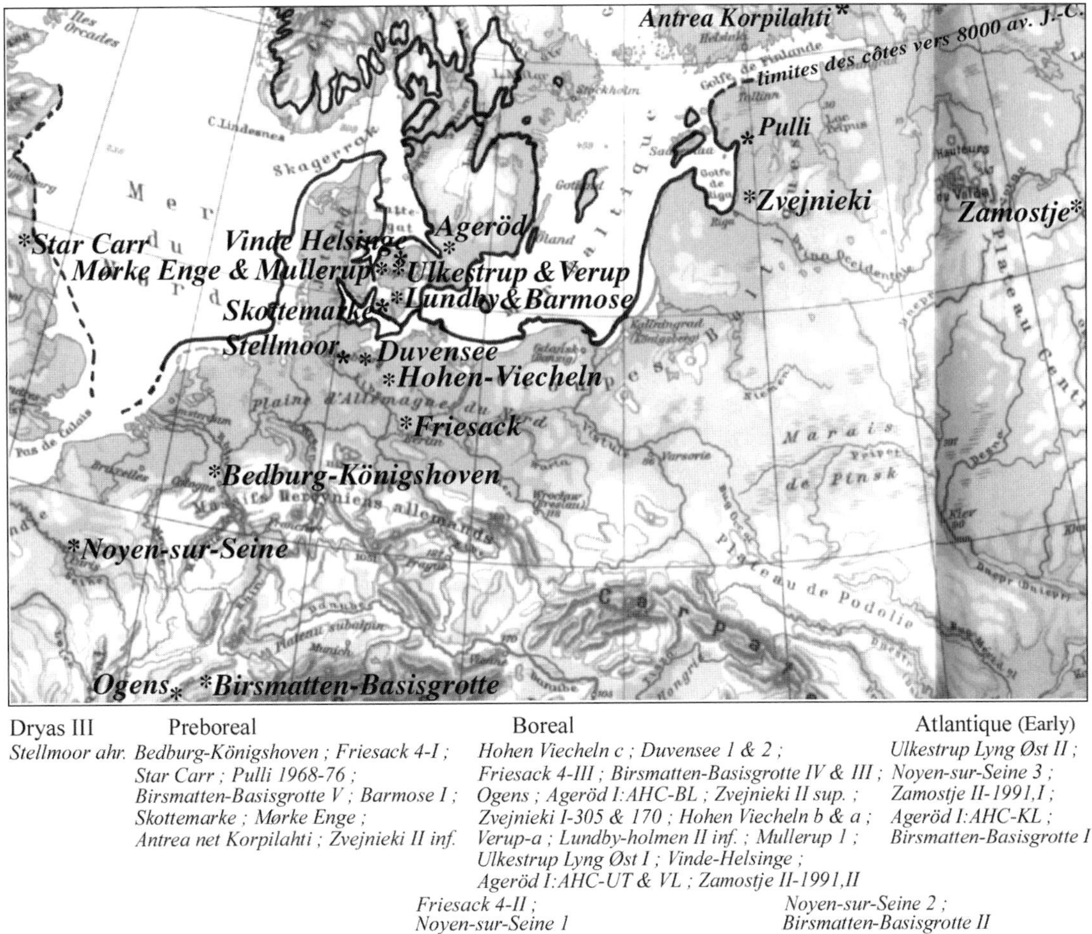

Figure 54.1. Distribution of the sites selected for study in northern Europe and mainly attributed to the Early Mesolithic. 23 settlement sites were available for study, i.e. 38 archaeological layers yielding c. 4500 bone and antler artefacts (David 2006): Ageröd I: A-H-C (Scania); Antrea Net (Korpilahti); Barmose (Zealand); Baume d'Ogens (Vaud); Birsmatten-Basisgrotte (Birstal); Bedburg-Königshoven (Rheinland); Clos-de-Poujol (Aveyron); Duvensee 1 & 2 (Schleswig-Holstein); Friesack 4, I-III (Brandenburg); Hohen Viecheln (Mecklenburg); Lundby-holmen II (Zealand); Mullerup 1, Sarauw's Island (Zealand); Mørke Enge (Zealand); Noyen-sur-Seine (Bassée); Pulli (Pärnu); Skottemarke (Lolland); Star Carr (Yorkshire); Ulkestrup Lyng Øst I & II (Zealand); Verup-a (Zealand); Vinde-Helsinge (Zealand); Warluis I/IIc (Oise); Zamostje II-1991 (Moscow); Zvejnieki (Vidzeme).

debitage and a shaping process. Debitage refers to the technical operations by which any type of blank – matrix (unmodified bone/antler), splinter (longitudinal debitage), segment (transverse debitage) or flake – is obtained from a bone in its natural original state. Shaping refers to the technical operations by which this blank is transformed into an implement (weapon, tool, object). The set of techniques involved in the making of an implement, and used, according to a logical continuum, is termed the manufacturing operational sequence (*chaîne opératoire*) (Pelegrin *et al.* 1988).

To meet the objectives of the present study, it is required that bone technology be used as a global approach, in which all the artefacts made from a whole range of organic materials (tooth, bone, antler) are taken into account. The pieces selected for study are those that display anthropogenic traces (David 2004a, 104). Analysis focuses mainly on entirely manufactured pieces, partially shaped pieces (roughouts), and also on remains shown to belong to the manufacture process (debitage waste products). On the whole, the other humanly modified artefacts tend to reflect food-processing activities. Early Mesolithic hunters seldom drew on their food-processing remains to make their tools. On the contrary, early in the butchering sequence they often set aside for this purpose specific anatomical parts, such as long limb bones providing the longest and most regular shapes. Differences in the way these parts were managed enable one to determine which bones were used, for what purpose (marrow extraction or tool manufacture), and how (manufacture waste recycled into consumables, as at Zamostje II in Russia, for instance; David 1998).

During manufacture, the hunters used techniques that enabled them to obtain from an initial volume (the bone) a blank approximating the tool in shape and size. This involves mentally visualizing the tool-to-be and assessing which are the most suitable bone parts in terms of the desired tool's volume, shape and dimensions. It also undoubtedly requires highly controlled modes of removing matter. These result in bone being detached as powder (wear technique), as shavings (nick technique), or by splitting (fracture technique). Depending on the tool he wanted, the craftsman chose one or another of these modes of removal, implementing it according to different techniques and following a variety of technical procedures (David 2004b, 122). Such manufacturing techniques are complemented by other techniques applied before or after modifying the volume (techniques pertaining to the preparation of the bone and techniques used for finishing the manufactured items).

The waste products of the debitage process thus bear traces of the operations carried out to detach the tool blanks. As a result, the manufacturing techniques can be identified through the study of such items, per type of bone (red deer (*Cervus elaphus*) tibia, for instance). This allows the tool to be situated in relation to the original anatomical part it was made from. By recording the occurrence of identical technical operations regularly applied to the same part of the same type of bone, it is possible to reconstruct the chaining of technical actions that were logically and systematically carried out in order to manufacture a particular type of tool. Each tool is characterized by the presence, the localization and the aspect of its active part(s).

At this stage and for reasons developed below, the case can already be made for the cultural value of manufacturing methods. In all likelihood, there are not several ways of producing a specific type of tool from a given anatomical part, because bones naturally show morphological and mechanical constraints, defined by the intrinsic properties of bone (internal structure). The variability in the chaining of technical actions, applied to the same type of bone, to manufacture the same type of tool is therefore indicative of the technical possibilities favoured by the hunters. The fact that some possibilities were selected over others, and applied according to a logical and systematic sequencing (like a genuine method of manufacture) has suggested for any assemblage under study that in most cases a particular method was preferentially used for making a particular type of equipment. Moreover, it has been possible to show that within a single site (Zvejnieki, Latvia) the implementation of manufacturing techniques was dependant upon the purpose of the items (tooth pendants), that is either an everyday use (in a domestic context), or conversely an exceptional use – such as in a funerary context. This reflects a deliberate choice as the techniques were probably known by all (David 2004a).

Subsequently, the contemporary and geographically close archaeological levels, whose industries display common characteristics in terms of representative types of tools and in terms of the preferentially associated method for their manufacture, have suggested the existence of homogeneous sets of assemblages, termed technocomplexes. 'A technocomplex is a group of cultures characterized by assemblages sharing a polythetic range but differing specific types of the same general families of artefact-types, shared as a widely diffused and interlinked response to common factors in environment, economy and technology.' (Clarke 1968, 357). To these shared characteristics can be added other parameters that are peculiar to each identified set. They pertain mainly to the style adopted for shaping (synchronic perspective) and to the evolutionary tendencies observed in the tool-kit (diachronic perspective). Within a technocomplex, evolutionary tendencies can be detected via the gradual rather than abrupt replacement of a least one type of tool by another belonging to the same overall category – the projectile points with an undetachable hafting system, for instance.

Thus, each technocomplex can be defined by a technical 'tradition', identified on the evidence of the chaining of technical actions bearing, for the Early Mesolithic, on the offensive equipment, on tooth pendants, and on bone and antler heavy-duty tools. (Heavy-duty tools are hafted bone and antler tools used with the mode of action termed *percussion lancée* (Leroi-Gourhan 1943). They are represented by axes, adzes and blades set in wooden sleeves, and their weight per tool (minus the wooden shaft) ranges between 40 and 400g.)

From techniques to traditions

A systematic study of the traces observed on the artefacts was conducted so as to diagnose the techniques and reconstitute the operational sequences followed during manufacture, resulting in the identification of 20 techniques related to both debitage and shaping processes. In particular, two of these techniques – *wedge-splinter* and *shaft-*

Figure 54.2. Zvejnieki (Latvia), splinter detached from an elk metapodial and showing the removal negatives resulting from the shaft-wedge-splinter technique, visible on the edges (right-hand photo, internal surface), and from the wedge-splinter technique, visible on the proximum of the bone (left-hand photo, external surface, norma verticalis). These fracture techniques have enabled the extraction of a rectilinear blank (splinter), and have ensured that the entire cortical length (that of the original medullar bone) was preserved. (After David 2004a, 115; scale subdivision: 1 cm).

wedge-splinter – are used for the debitage of metapodials. Flanked on either side by vestigial bones, the metapodial, or cannon bone, is a supporting bone of the leg in hoofed mammals, between the hock joint and the fetlock. Applied on metapodials from large ungulates (red deer, elk (*Alces alces*), aurochs (*Bos primigenius*)), these techniques enabled Mesolithic communities to obtain quite rapidly rectilinear blanks of a constant width, and therefore regularly calibrated (Figure 54.2). The metapodial is a tubular long bone, with naturally flared extremities. It is the bone most commonly used for making projectile points. The Mesolithic hunters always began by calibrating this type of bone, irrespective of the techniques they employed. This was done in order to minimize the original flare and maintain the naturally rectilinear morphology of the shaft, while preserving the cortical parts along the entire length of the medullar bone (Figure 54.3). Calibrating the bone very early in the operational sequence clearly indicates that morphological and morphometrical standards were sought, testifying to an 'industrial' productivity.

While in the Early Mesolithic the other anatomical parts generally constrained the choice of manufacturing techniques, the chaining of the ones applied to large ungulate metapodials highlights at least three ways of producing equivalent items on splinters. These are: method 'D', initially identified in Denmark, method 'Z', from Zamostje in Russia, and method 'O', from Ogens in Switzerland (Figure 54.4). The blanks obtained via these methods are equivalent (splinters), and those that were subsequently shaped into projectile points (plain points and points displaying attributes such as notches, barbs, bladelet insets, etc.) each correspond to roughly a quartered longitudinal section of the metapodial. As these projectile points are dominant in the tool-kit, their synchronic and diachronic variations are excellent markers of technical traditions.

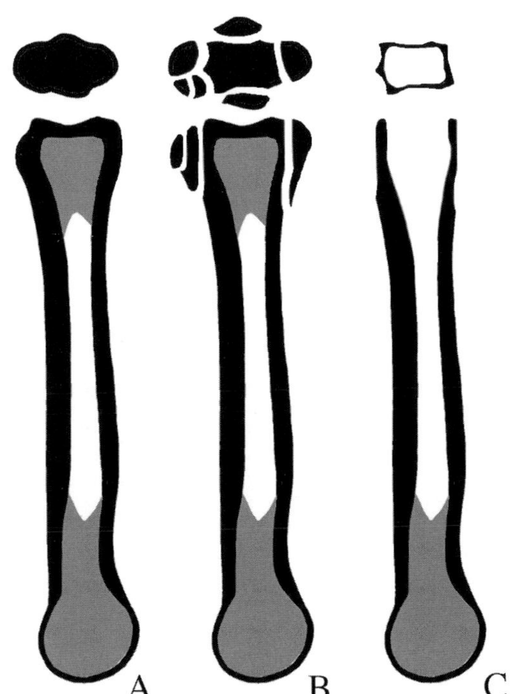

Figure 54.3. Illustration of the calibration of large ungulate metapodials in Denmark, first by wedge-splinter (B) then by dotted perforation. Calibration consisted in giving the bone a perfectly tubular shape by detaching flakes all around the proximal part (B) and then by perforating the latter (C). The naturally flared morphology of the extremity is corrected to become rectilinear, and the cortical part is preserved along the entire length. After the removal of the distal epiphysis, all that needs to be done in order to obtain splinters of a constant width and length is to split the medullar bone lengthwise according to various techniques. The shaded area emphasizes the spongy part of the bone (A – natural aspect of the bone, norma lateralis). (After David 2004b, 131).

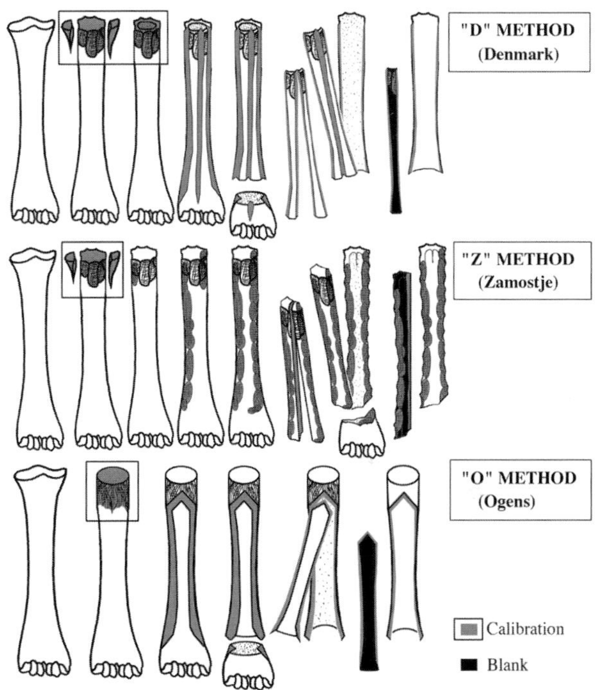

Figure 54.4. The three methods used in the Early Mesolithic of northern Europe for the manufacture of the best-represented items made from large ungulate metapodials (elk, red deer, aurochs): projectile points with an undetachable hafting system. All methods start with a calibration stage (dark grey) that consists of making the upper end of metapodials either strictly tubular (in Denmark) or cylindrical (Zamostje, Russia and Ogens, Switzerland). This indicates that standards (shape, length and width of projectile points) were sought, testifying to an 'industrial' productivity. In order to obtain equivalent blanks (roughly a quartered longitudinal section of the metapodial), method 'D' involves the following chain of techniques: wedge-splinter, dotted perforation (calibration stage) and groove and splinter; method 'Z': wedge-splinter (calibration stage) and shaft-wedge-splinter (splitting by grooving is also an option, and occurs earlier on); method 'O': scraping (calibration stage) and groove and splinter. In addition, the distal epiphyses are detached following a variety of techniques. (After David 2004c, 185, 355, 361).

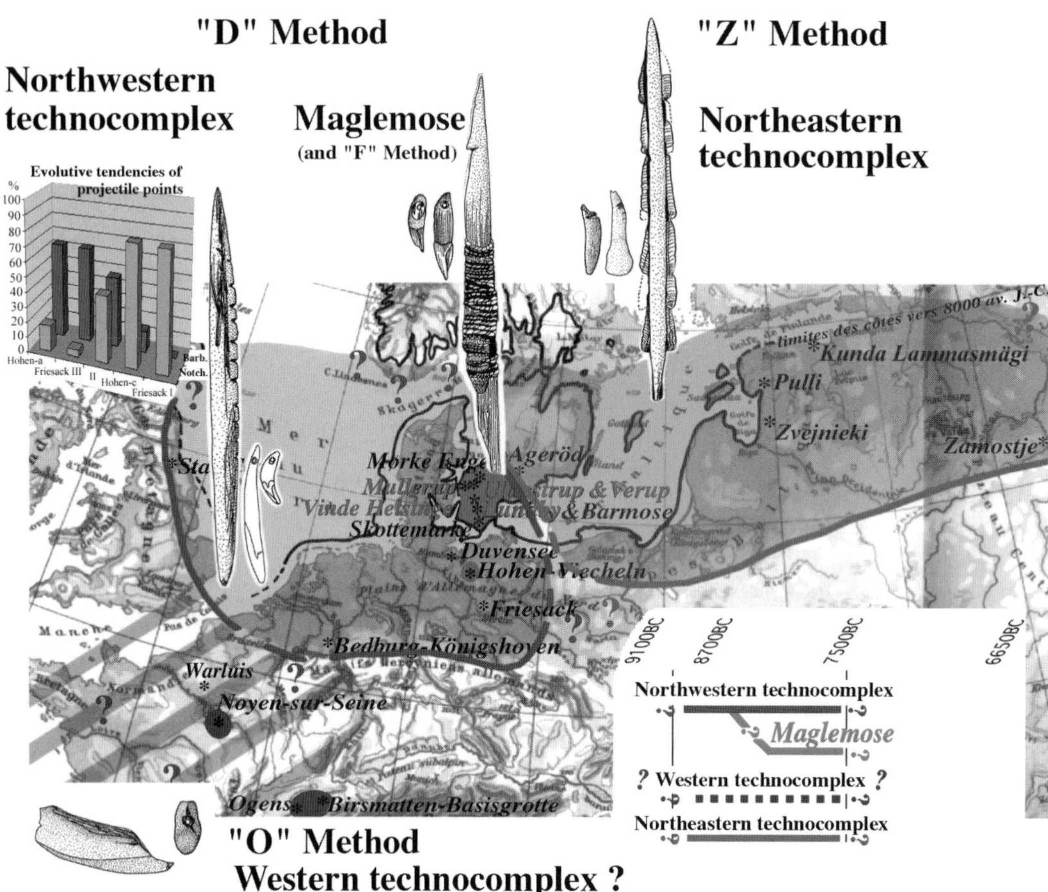

Figure 54.5. The three chrono-cultural identities recognized in the Early Mesolithic of northern Europe in the 9th and 8th millennia cal BC: the north-eastern technocomplex *around the Baltic Sea and the* northern technocomplex *around the North Sea, from which latter entity the* Maglemosian *probably diverged at the end of the Boreal period, in Zealand (Denmark). (After David 2005, 73).*

The geographical distribution of these methods in the 9th–8th millennium cal BC (Preboreal to second half of the Boreal, including the Maglemosian Stage 0, after Brinch Petersen 1973) suggests a division of northern Europe into two distinct zones (Figure 54.5). Method 'D' is associated with a northern zone that encompasses the regions around the North Sea, while method 'Z' is distributed across Baltic sites. The two zones can be told apart because the dominant elements of the offensive equipment are different: notched points in the western part, and slotted points in the eastern part of northern Europe. Working on the assumption that in both zones this equipment was intended for the same purpose (the acquisition of animal resources), it is suggested that the two geographical entities correspond to two distinct culture-areas.

On the other hand, at the end of the 8th millennium cal BC (Late Boreal, Maglemosian Stages 1 and 2, after Brinch Petersen 1973), the Zealand assemblages begin to diverge from the northern entity, as shown by the fact that the barbed points, made not only from metapodials but also from flat bones (method 'F'), are shaped by *filing*. Moreover, they are associated with a large component of heavy-duty tools. With respect to its bone industry, the Maglemosian *stricto sensu*, as it was initially defined in the classic form in which it was first discovered at the eponymous site, is therefore confined to Denmark (David 2003, 655), and this is in keeping with the Danish results of lithic studies based solely on the typological approach (Brinch Petersen 1973).

At that time, at least three entities can thus be distinguished on the basis of technical manufacturing traditions. The shaping techniques applied to pendants made from animal teeth have *a posteriori* been found to substantiate the differences between the areas located on either side of the Øresund Strait (Scandinavia), which could already be told apart by their hunting equipment and the methods implemented for their manufacture. The pendants recovered in settlement contexts are perforated in the western areas and notched in the eastern.

In addition, both synchronic and diachronic variations can be observed within each entity. Micro-regions, or even a single site, are characterized by particular styles adopted for shaping projectile points, differing in the way bases and attributes are treated (extent and number of attributes; notches, barbs, etc.). Evolutionary tendencies are well marked, illustrated in the western part of northern Europe by the progressive shift from notched points to plain and barbed points (made following method 'D'). Conversely, at the same time in the east, it seems that points with insets are gradually replaced by notched points (method 'Z').

Conclusions

The manufacture of hard, organic, animal materials is conducted according to precise conceptual schemes. The techniques implemented to meet the projects that underpin these schemes are employed in an ordered and systematic way. The operational sequences used on large ungulate metapodials are highly significant, and can henceforth be considered relevant to the identification of other technical traditions in prehistory.

Future studies by the author will incorporate data on Early Holocene sites and seek to include a larger number of assemblages to broaden the geographical and chronological range. Taking the three above-defined entities as a starting point, the issue of the adaptability of these communities will be addressed via the analysis of their material cultures. Ultimately, on the evidence of behavioural changes, the notion of 'population' will tentatively be applied to the bearers of a material culture.

Acknowledgement

I am grateful to Jehanne Féblot-Augustins for the translation of this paper.

References

Breuil, A. 1926. Un harpon maglemosien trouvé à Béthune en 1849. *L'Anthropologie* 36, 309–12.

Brinch Petersen, E. 1973. A survey of the late Palaeolithic and Mesolithic of Denmark, in S. K. Kozłowski (ed.), *The Mesolithic in Europe*, 77–127. Warsaw, Warsaw University Press.

Childe, V. G. 1931. The Forest Cultures of Northern Europe. *Journal of the Royal Anthropological Institution* 61, 325–48.

Clarke, D. L. 1968. *Analytical Archaeology*. London, Methuen.

Clark, J. G. D. 1936 (1970). *The Mesolithic Settlement of Northern Europe: a Study of the Food Gathering Peoples of Northern Europe during the Early Post-Glacial Period.* Cambridge, Cambridge University Press.

David, E. 1998. Etude technologique de l'industrie en matières dures animales du site mésolithique de Zamostje 2, fouille 1991 (Russie). *Archéo-Situla* 26 (1996), 5–62.

David, E. 2003. The contribution of a technological study of bone and antler industry for the Definition of the Early Maglemose Culture, in L. Larsson, H. Kindgren, K. Knutsson, D. Loeffler and A. Åkerlund (eds.), *Mesolithic on the Move: Papers presented at the Sixth International Conference on the Mesolithic in Europe, Stockholm 2000*, 649–57. Oxford, Oxbow Books.

David, E. 2004a. The Mesolithic Zvejnieki site (Latvia) in its European Context: Preliminary results delivered by a technological study of the bone and antler industry. *Journal of Estonian Archaeology* 2003, 7 (2), 99–122.

David, E. 2004b. Transformation des matières dures d'origine animale dans le Mésolithique de l'Europe du Nord (Fiche 9), in D. Ramseyer (ed.), *Fiches de la Commission de Nomenclature de l'Industrie Osseuse, Cahier XI Matières et Techniques. Industrie de l'Os Préhistorique*, 113–49. Paris, Éditions de la Société Préhistorique Française.

David, E. 2004c. *Technologie osseuse des derniers chasseurs préhistoriques en Europe du Nord (Xe–VIIIe millénaires avant J.-C.): Le Maglemosien et les technocomplexes du Mésolithique*, 666. Monographie de these, Available at http://web.mae.u-paris10.fr/recherche/mpEvaDavid.html (or via the author).

David, E. 2005. Preliminary results on a recent technological study of the Early Mesolithic bone and antler industry of Estonia, with special emphasis on the Pulli site, in H. Luik, A. Choyke, C. E. Battey and L. Lõugas (eds.), *'From the Hooves to Horns, from Mollusc to Mammoth, Manufacture and use of bone artefacts from prehistoric times to the present', Proceedings of the 4th Meeting of the Icaz Worked Bone Research Group, Tallinn, 26–31 August 2003*, 67–74. Muinasaja teadus 15. Tallinn, University of Tallinn.

David, E. 2006. Contribution of bone and antler industry for characterizing the Early Mesolithic in Europe, in C.-J. Kind (ed.), *After the Ice Age. Settlements, subsistence and social development in the Mesolithic of Central Europe*, 135–45. Materialhefte zur Archäologie in Baden-Württemberg 78. Stuttgart, Konrad Theiss Verlag.

Kozłowski, S. K. 1973. Introduction to the History of Europe in Early Holocene, in S. K. Kozłowski (ed.), *The Mesolithic in Europe*, 331–66. Warsaw, Warsaw University Press.

Kozłowski, J. K. and Kozłowski, S. K. 1977. Pointes, sagaies et harpons du Paléolithique et du Mésolithique en Europe du Centre-Est, in *Colloques internationaux du C.N.R.S. 568 – Méthodologie appliquée à l'industrie de l'os préhistorique*, 205–27. Paris, Centre national de la recherche scientifique (CNRS).

Larsson, L. 1990. The Mesolithic of southern Scandinavia. *Journal of World Prehistory* 4, 257–309.

Leroi-Gourhan, A. 1943. *L'homme et la matière*. Paris, Presses Universitaires de France.

Pelegrin, J., Karlin, C. and Bodu, P. 1988. 'Chaînes opératoires': un outil pour les préhistoriens, in *Technologie Préhistorique, Notes et Monographies Techniques 25*, 55–62. Paris, Centre national de la recherche scientifique (CNRS).

Sarauw, G. F. L., Jessen, K. and Winge, H. 1904. *En Stenalders Boplads, Maglemose ved Mullerup. Études sur le premier Âge de la pierre du nord de l'Europe. Aarboger for Nordisk Oldkyndighed og Historie 1903*. Copenhagen, Lynge and Son.

Verhart, L. B. M. 1990. Stone Age bone and antler points as indicators for 'social territories' in the European Mesolithic, in P. M. Vermeersch and P. van Peer (eds.), *Contributions to the Mesolithic in Europe. Papers presented at the Fourth International Symposium on the Mesolithic in Europe*, 131–51. Leuven, Leuven University Press.

55. Being-in-the-(Mesolithic) world: place, substance and person in the Mesolithic of western Scotland

Hannah L. Cobb

Current research has illustrated how theoretically untenable it is to regard aspects of the Mesolithic such as technology and subsistence as isolated from the very people who made tools and engaged in meaningful interactions between places, environments and one another. However, in reality, how can such meanings really be interpreted from Mesolithic assemblages? Through a consideration of Mesolithic materiality this paper will contribute to this critical debate by exploring the role that phenomenological perspectives may be able to play in coming to understand Mesolithic ontologies. Whilst some may find the combination of phenomenology and the Mesolithic uncomfortable, this paper will draw upon the results of current research to argue that we can both ditch the baggage that has come to link phenomenology exclusively with landscape and monumentality, and embrace the nature of the Mesolithic record as something that can be examined through phenomenological approaches in its own right.

Keywords: phenomenology, interpretive approaches, western Scotland, northern Irish Sea basin, identity, personhood.

Introduction

Interpretive archaeological theory tends to remind us, at every turn, that archaeology has 'baggage'. That is, our actions and our interpretations are imbued with modern, Western politicised meaning, and we must always be aware of that. It is no surprise then that archaeological theory itself is laden with such baggage, and depending on the theory, and the chronological period, some theories have more than others. My doctoral research addresses the Mesolithic of western Scotland and the northern Irish Sea basin, and it is this area that I would ultimately like to discuss in this paper. However before I come to discuss this, I think it is important to debunk some of this baggage. This is because my research explicitly employs an alternative theoretical and methodological approach that I am aware is heavily laden with a theoretical baggage, and so the decisions behind using this methodology and theory require a thorough discussion in relation to their application to Mesolithic studies.

My doctoral research aims explicitly to explore the Mesolithic experience of being in the world by conducting a programme of fieldwork that is firmly embedded within an interpretive and, specifically, a phenomenological perspective. At this juncture it is probably now clear why I think this requires a detailed discussion: phenomenology has accrued a lot of baggage for archaeologists recently. I believe this has led to its tenability as a philosophical stance that might inform Mesolithic research to be questioned. So I think this baggage needs to be explicitly discussed, and in many senses deconstructed, before we can even begin to talk about phenomenological approaches and how they may benefit the Mesolithic

Phenomenology in archaeology: an overview

In the last decade of the last century a number of archaeologists began to explore how phenomenological and hermeneutic philosophies could inform archaeological theory and practice. Critically such philosophical standpoints provided a means through which the dichotomous Cartesian worldview that had predominated in archaeology up to that point could be deconstructed. As a result such perspectives enriched and bolstered the growing interpretive theoretical paradigm. As such, ten years later, we are all familiar with archaeological applications of phenomenological philosophies. Chris Tilley's *Phenomenology of Landscape* (1994) is perhaps the most enduring and most well known of these, but other accounts such as Thomas' *Time, Culture and Identity* (1996), amongst others, also draw heavily upon phenomenological perspectives (see Bruck 2005 for a comprehensive review of the proponents, debates, and impacts of phenomenology on British prehistory).

There is, however, one common denominator amongst this list of proponents of phenomenological philosophies within the discipline, which for many provides a stumbling block in acknowledging the value of such perspectives in archaeology; this list comprises largely of archaeologists whose research agendas are situated specifically in the Neolithic period. Consequently, phenomenology and hermeneutics have become almost inextricably connected not only with this chronological period, but with many of the major aspects of the material record from the Neolithic, and especially monumental funerary and communal ceremonial architecture. Indeed it could be argued that this is so much so that phenomenological approaches in archaeology have become synonymous with non-domestic Neolithic contexts (Bruck 2005). As a result any suggestion of engaging with such philosophical perspectives to interpret the Mesolithic record has drawn accusations of simply and uncritically importing Neolithic approaches to the Mesolithic, and in general its value in interpreting hunter-gatherers has been questioned (e.g. Jordan 2003, 130).

This paper begins with, and stems from, an acknowledgement of this argument and an overwhelming desire to disrupt it radically. I agree that the Mesolithic and Neolithic records are significantly different. I also explicitly acknowledge that it would be ridiculous to apply approaches that work in one period uncritically onto another. Accordingly I think it is important to begin by illustrating that to explore phenomenological approaches with regards to the Mesolithic does not require the archaeologist to subscribe to such misconceptions. Rather it requires the acknowledgement that phenomenology did not just begin in 1994 with the publication of *A Phenomenology of Landscape*. Instead I contend that in order to ditch the 'baggage' of its Neolithic associations, any application of phenomenology to the Mesolithic must first begin by acknowledging that phenomenology is a concerted and varied philosophical approach whose roots lie over 100 years before its application to archaeology was ever considered.

Phenomenological roots

At its simplest, we can begin to ditch the baggage by turning to a very pared down definition of phenomenology as an approach which seeks to examine not just how things appear to people, but the conditions that make that appearance possible. Of the many phenomenological philosophers, it is Heidegger and Merleau-Ponty who have been most influential in examining how things reveal themselves, and how this contributes to the experience of being in the world. It is this influence which is visible in the work of many archaeologists, such as Tilley and Thomas. This association, in itself, is where we as Mesolithic archaeologists may switch off, reasoning that this must be the kind of perspective that can only be of use to studying monuments, structures, and funerary practices on a scale which is simply not present in the Mesolithic record. Yet this paper contends that this is not the case. Indeed a glance at the work of Ingold, someone whose work explicitly addresses hunter-gatherers, although who may not explicitly label himself as a 'phenomenologist' (Thomas 2006, 53), certainly supports this: for example see the essay *On Weaving a Basket* (Ingold 2000, 339–48).

To understand how phenomenology can be relevant to archaeologists seeking to interpret the Mesolithic, I think it is useful to consider briefly some of the influential tenets of Heidegger's and Merleau-Ponty's understandings of phenomenology. For Heidegger, the ultimate context of all action and understanding is the world in which we are always situated and always entwined in an involvement with things. Yet through that involvement, and dwelling in the world, the world itself may become so familiar that it lies unnoticed. Therefore in order for the experience of being in the world to reveal itself to us we must recognise and examine the layers of complexity that this experience is manifest within. We must explore the way in which this is constructed, through the interactions between people and things that in themselves constitute the many layers of being in the world. And in doing this we must discard definitions of being as presence and static permanence, and instead recognise that being takes place in terms of time and must be understood as such (Heidegger 1996, but also see Moran 2000 for further discussions of these issues). Clearly in a chronological period such as the Mesolithic, where studies of hunter-gatherer populations are so often abstracted and reduced to statistics of subsistence activities, accounts of technology and schemas of environmental interaction, such Heideggerian phenomenology as this – which provides a theoretical framework for returning to and considering lived human experience – cannot fail to be attractive.

But to get at the Mesolithic experience of the world it is clear that we need more than just the consideration of being that Heidegger provides, and this is where Merleau-Ponty's work on perception is useful. This is because from a Heideggerian perspective on dwelling and being in the world the role of the body within this is implicit. However Merleau-Ponty's brand of phenomenology explores this further, examining the fundamental role that the body plays as a 'mediation point between thought and the world' (Tilley 1994, 14). Consequently if we draw on Merleau-Ponty's work we can see that we should not simply regard the body as passive, but rather it is spatially and temporally active and living, interacting with, negotiating and forming the experience and perception of the world (Merleau-Ponty 1996). Furthermore, because of the centrality of the body in perception, and the nature of both the body and of perception, it is clear that perception is situated and perspectival (Moran 2000, 404). Thus the body is central in disclosing the world to us in certain ways, allowing us the possibility of experiencing objects, yet at the same time, and because of this, bodily revelations through perception are never absolute, and equally are never pure, but always meaning laden (Merleau-Ponty 1996).

To summarise, then, in essence the phenomenology of major proponents such as Heidegger and Merleau-Ponty calls upon us to think explicitly about the character of experience. Fundamentally the work of both illustrates that the Cartesian division between the mind and the body, and nature and culture, which frequently typifies Mesolithic studies, is in fact untenable, simply because of the nature of the interaction between people, things, and the world. Therefore by calling into question the way in which that experience is formed, phenomenology provides the archaeologist with the means to examine material culture from different perspectives, and through this provides an interpretation of the experience of being in the world. This is, of course, a very brief overview. Indeed the theoretical perspectives of both Heidegger and Merleau-Ponty changed significantly over time, and I acknowledge that this short paper is unable to do justice to the depth, the changes and developments of such perspectives. What I hope this short account does illustrate, though, is that phenomenology is not and should not be simply accepted as synonymous with the Neolithic and later periods, and the architectural and monumental trappings of these. It is clear that with a focus on all aspects of the world, of material culture and the situatedness of the body within these, that such perspectives are of use to us whatever the period of study, and whatever the scale of material culture. Thus it is fair to argue that a microlith played just as critical a role in revealing the world to a Mesolithic person, as a chambered tomb did to a Neolithic person, and as your experience and interaction with this book does to you.

Phenomenology and the Mesolithic

With these thoughts in mind this paper will now turn to examine how these abstract notions can be of value to studying the Mesolithic. It is probably no surprise that in using phenomenological approaches, my research involves a certain consideration of landscape. Of course I am aware that for many 'landscape' approaches to the Mesolithic are something there is a general level of dissatisfaction with (e.g. Jordan 2003; McFadyen 2006), especially because until now such approaches have been predominantly reliant upon large-scale Mesolithic sites, of which there are only shell middens (e.g. Cummings 2003, but see Cobb 2004; McFadyen 2006). The implications are thus dangerous, over emphasising the importance of the midden within the record, simply because of its preservational qualities. Similarly a focus upon visual experience alone is problematic. The notion of the importance of the gaze is one routed within modern, western, Cartesian masculist principles (Thomas 1993).

Indeed there are other fundamental reasons why it is hard within Mesolithic studies to see why undertaking a visual analysis from a site could be of any benefit to interpreting Mesolithic understandings of the world. Unlike the Neolithic monuments, where such methodologies have worked to great effect (e.g. Cummings 2001; 2003; Tilley 1994, although see Flemming 2005 for a critique of this approach), in many cases there has been much more significant environmental change. Then, there comes the critical problem of defining a Mesolithic site in the first place. *In situ* Mesolithic occupation sites and lithic scatters number far fewer than Neolithic chambered tombs, for example, and with lithic scatters it is often highly unlikely that they can be exactly provenanced, or pinned down to originating from one singular spot.

So if this kind of landscape analysis appears so flawed in the Mesolithic why do I continue with it, and why does it constitute a key methodology in my doctoral research? Firstly, because my research rests explicitly upon a very different interpretation of the notion of landscape in the Mesolithic. Critically I would like to suggest that landscape should not be understood as simply a natural environment penetrated by intermittent focal points of human activity. But rather that landscape should be understood as something that is wholly integrated with and encompassed by the action of persons, with activities dispersed across and integral to entire landscapes, akin to Ingold's discussion of taskscapes (Ingold 2000, 190). Secondly, because such a perspective emphasises landscape as a field of engagements that is so inextricably connected with actions and meanings, I believe it then becomes impossible to consider landscape without an accompanying consideration of Mesolithic materiality. What I mean by this is that, like many people before me, I am working from the effectively phenomenological perspective that all encounters between persons and material culture both constitute and are constitutive of meaningful acts of social engagement between persons and the world. Thus, while persons continuously interact with material culture in their day-to-day life, this interaction continuously allows the negotiation, creation and transformation of identities, relationships, and understandings of the world.

Furthermore, I think it is critical to recognise that such an integration of material culture and landscape stresses that meaningful relations between people and things did not just exist in a kind of bubble, or void. It may sound ridiculous to state it so bluntly, but meaningful interactions between people and things *happen in places and through places*. As the phenomenology of Merleau-Ponty has explored, experience and perception are situated within bodily practices, and thus sensual experiences, not just of materials *or* places but of materials *and* places, and the relationships between these are key to revealing the experience of the world. Thus what makes interactions between people and things meaningful is their location, their situational context, and the juxtapositions that can be created between people, things and places with that knowledge of such relationships in mind. Working on this logic, we do not need to have megalithic-style monumental Mesolithic sites, nor anything except the notion that interactions between people and things took place in a certain location, in order for a landscape analysis to function as a powerful tool when integrated with a consideration of materials at sites.

Interpreting the Mesolithic of the northern Irish Sea Basin from a phenomenological perspective

The phenomenologically influenced perspective that I have discussed here is central to my own research in western Scotland and the northern Irish Sea basin. It is my aim within this project to examine landscape and objects from such a perspective in order to start to try and explore the nature of being in the Mesolithic world. While I am only in the early stages of this project, a pilot study in western Scotland has demonstrated clear evidence that place and materiality were critically interlinked, and that the experience and interaction between specific places and specific materials both created and were created by complex understandings of the relationships between people and their wider world (Cobb 2004).

Places, for example, were often revisited and their earlier occupation incorporated, referenced or respected within the materiality of later phases. The majority of the shell middens in the area, of course, are an excellent example of this, with each attesting to the deliberate reuse of specific locales (e.g. Bonsall *et al.* 1994; Mellars 1987; Pollard *et al.* 1996; Pollard 2000). At Ulva Cave, just off Mull, for example, radiocarbon dates have demonstrated that it not only accumulated over several thousand years, but that it continued in use into the Neolithic (Ashmore 2004). Significantly, these sites were not simply reused but several demonstrate a sophisticated and deliberate accumulation of materials and substances, with an adherence to specific locales for specific activities (Meiklejohn *et al.* 2005; Mellars 1987). Crucially, however, it is also clear that such deliberate and meaningful activities were not simply confined to isolated and unrelated events at single sites. Instead there appears to have been an important and enduring trend during the Mesolithic in which visual connections between sites, topographical features and other occupation sites were established, despite a separation by the sea. On Oronsay, for example, the Priory Midden was directly aligned between the Paps of Jura and the Rhins of Islay (Cobb 2004), both topographic features that even today remain crucial navigational aids for sailors. Equally, sites often faced areas over the sea where contemporary Mesolithic sites existed. The An Corran middens on Skye, for example, have views over to the sites of Redpoint on the Torridon Peninsula and the midden of Loch a Squirr on Raasay (Hardy and Wickham-Jones 2002; 2003).

Critically, there is evidence that such visual connections did not simply exist in isolation, but reinforced and were reinforced by connecting materials or substances, and practices that involved the use and deposition of such substances at these sites. Both at Sanna Bay on the Ardnamurchan Peninsula, and at Camas Daraich, on Skye, for example, Rhum Bloodstone has been found, and both sites have clear visual links to Rhum (Cobb 2004; Lethbridge 1927; Wickham-Jones 2005). At some sites there were also patterns discernable in the treatment of substances, which indicate a clear difference in the way that animals, plants and substances from the sea were treated, to animals, plants and substances from the land. At the Oronsay middens, for example, sea animals (and this includes not only fish, but cetaceans, seal (Phocidae), and otter (*Lutra lutra*) were associated predominantly with contexts of burning and much more of their skeletal parts were found within the middens. Land animals and substances, however, were represented and treated in an entirely different manner. Not only were land animal skeletal remains less complete, they were predominantly represented by the bones of lower limbs and some tusks, and were much less clearly associated with contexts of burning (Mellars 1987). While this patterning may at once suggest that land animals were brought to the sites, already semi-butchered, for the processing and working of skins and bone tools, whereas sea animals were caught and immediately processed *in situ* for skins and fats, such a dichotomy in the record may relate to more than simply the functional explanations it has been afforded until now. Instead, recent research (e.g. Cobb 2004; Meiklejohn *et al.* 2005) is beginning to indicate that complex relationships existed between understandings of land, sea, place and personal identity in the Mesolithic of western Scotland. A re-examination of the materials from sites, combined with an examination of sites and their landscape settings, suggest that meanings were enacted and experienced at certain places and with certain substances and that this was made possible through the visual situation of these sites within a wider context (Cobb 2004). Consequently other sites considered in my own research, that were not middens, nor were necessarily situated close to the shore, critically also demonstrated the presence of similar transformative and symbolic relations (Cobb 2004; 2008).

Conclusions

By examining substances, sites and wider landscape settings, then, my research is coming to suggest that it is possible to explore Mesolithic understandings of the world, and develop new and exciting interpretations from viewing the record from alternative perspectives. Thus it is possible to suggest that substance and immediate locale forged important ideological connections, and importantly the combination of these aspects with visual relations further cemented, transformed and linked identity and the experiences of being in the world.

Where this research is continuing to draw out new connections and provide new interpretations, such as those briefly presented here, critically this is only possible through the acknowledgment that phenomenology is not just about landscape, nor is it about monumentality and structures, but rather in its essence it is about the experience of, and engagement with, materials on all levels of scale. Thus where Mesolithic studies can benefit fundamentally from phenomenological perspectives is through the simple acknowledgement that we can approach material culture with as much a phenomenological stance and perspective as we can approach landscape. Consequently, despite the difference in the record to that of other subsequent chronological periods, phenomenology has just as much value and is just as applicable to the material with which we are presented.

In conclusion, whilst this paper provides only a brief synopsis of ongoing research, and its conclusions so far, it is clear that once we have conquered all of the potentially negative associations that have accumulated with phenomenology, phenomenological perspectives can *and are* beginning to provide a valuable new way for us to begin to examine Mesolithic materiality, which will allow such examinations not simply to remain isolated from other areas, but will at once situate materiality within experience and help to reveal the many social contexts that must have existed in the period.

Acknowledgements

I would like to thank the Royal Anthropological Institute for their award of the Emslie Horniman Scholarship that has allowed me to explore in the field the ideas discussed above. I would also like to thank Julian Thomas, Chantal Conneller and Steven Price for their comments on various drafts of this paper, and Thomas Kador for having many discussions with me about phenomenology and the Mesolithic.

References

Ashmore, P. 2004. A Date List (to October 2002) for early Foragers in Scotland, in A. Saville (ed.), *Mesolithic Scotland and its Neighbours*, 95–157. Edinburgh, Society of Antiquaries of Scotland.

Bonsall, C., Sutherland, D. G., Russel, N. J., Coles, G., Paul, C. R. C., Huntley, J. P. and Lawson, T. J. 1994. Excavations in Ulva Cave, Western Scotland 1990–91: A Preliminary report. *Mesolithic Miscellany* 15 (1), 8–21.

Bruck, J. 2005. Experiencing the past? The development of a phenomenological archaeology in British prehistory. *Archaeological Dialogues* 12 (1), 45–72.

Cobb, H. L. 2004. *From Middens to Megaliths? A preliminary investigation into the possibility of using shell middens as a medium for interpreting the Mesolithic experience of the world.* Unpublished MPhil thesis, University of Manchester.

Cobb, H. L. 2008. *Media for movement and making the world: An examination of the Mesolithic experience of the world and the Mesolithic to Neolithic transition in the northern Irish Sea basin.* Unpublished PhD thesis, University of Manchester.

Cummings, V. 2001. *Landscapes in Transition? Exploring the Origins of Monumentality in South-west Wales and South-west Scotland.* Unpublished PhD Thesis, Cardiff University, The University of Wales.

Cummings, V. 2003. The Origins of Monumentality? Mesolithic World-Views of the Landscape in Western Britain, in L. Larsson, H. Kindgren, K. Knutsson, D. Loeffler and A. Åkerlund (eds.), *Mesolithic on the Move: Papers presented at the Sixth International Conference on the Mesolithic in Europe, Stockholm 2000*, 74–81. Oxford, Oxbow Books.

Flemming, A. 2005. Megaliths and post-modernism: the case of Wales. *Antiquity* 79, 921–32.

Gosden, C. 1996. Can we take the Aryan out of Heideggerian? *Archaeological Dialogues* 3, 22–5.

Hardy, K. and Wickham-Jones, C. 2002. Scotland's First Settlers: The Mesolithic Seascape of the Inner Sound, Skye and its Contribution to the Early Prehistory of Scotland. *Antiquity* 76 (293), 825–34.

Hardy, K. and Wickham-Jones, C. 2003. Scotland's First Settlers: an Investigation into Settlement, Territoriality and Mobility During the Mesolithic in the Inner Sound, Scotland, First Results, in L. Larsson, H. Kindgren, K. Knutsson, D. Loeffler and A. Åkerlund (eds.), *Mesolithic on the Move: Papers presented at the Sixth International Conference on the Mesolithic in Europe, Stockholm 2000*, 369–81. Oxford, Oxbow Books.

Heidegger, M. 1996 (1927). *Being and Time* (translated by Joan Stambaugh). Albany, State University of New York Press.

Ingold, T. 2000. *The Perception of the Environment: Essays in livelihood, dwelling and skill.* London, Routledge.

Jordan, P. 2003. Investigating postglacial hunter-gatherer landscape enculturation: ethnographic analogy and interpretive methodologies, in L. Larsson, H. Kindgren, K. Knutsson, D. Loeffler and A. Åkerlund (eds.), *Mesolithic on the Move: Papers presented at the Sixth International Conference on the Mesolithic in Europe, Stockholm 2000*, 128–38. Oxford, Oxbow Books.

Lethbridge, T. C. 1927. A settlement site of the beaker period at Sanna Bay, Ardnamurch, Argyll. *Man* 27 (September 1927), 173–4.

McFadyen, L. 2006. The Landscape, in C. J. Conneller and G. M. Warren (eds.), *Mesolithic Britain and Ireland: new approaches*. Stroud, Tempus.

Meiklejohn, C., Merrett, D. C., Nolan, R. W., Richards, M. P. and Mellars, P. A. 2005. Spatial Relationships, Dating and Taphonomy of the Human Bone from the Mesolithic sites of Cnoc Coig, Oronsay, Argyll, Scotland. *Proceedings of the Prehistoric Society* 71, 85–105.

Mellars, P. A. 1987. *Excavations on Oronsay: Prehistoric Human Ecology on a Small Island.* Edinburgh, Edinburgh University Press.

Merleau-Ponty, M. 1996 (1945). *Phenomenology of Perception* (translated by Colin Smith). London, Routledge.

Moran, D. 2000. *Introduction to Phenomenology*. London, Routledge.

Pollard, T. 2000. Risga and the Mesolithic occupation of Scottish Islands, in R. Young (ed.), *Mesolithic Lifeways: Current Research from Britain and Ireland*, 143–52. Leicester, University of Leicester.

Pollard, T., Atkinson, J. and Banks, I. 1996. It is the technical side of the work which is my stumbling block. A shell midden site on Risga reconsidered, in T. Pollard and A. Morrison (eds.), *The Early Prehistory of Scotland*, 165–82. Edinburgh, Edinburgh University Press.

Thomas, J. 1993. The politics of vision and the archaeologies of landscape, in B. Bender (ed.), *Landscape: Politics and Perspectives*, 19–48. Oxford, Berg.

Thomas, J. 1996. *Time, Culture and Identity. An Interpretative Archaeology*. London, Routledge.

Thomas, J. 2006. Phenomenology and Material Culture, in C. Tilley, W. Keane, S. Kuchler, M. Rowlands and P. Spyer (eds.), *The Handbook of Material Culture*, 43–59. London, Sage.

Tilley, C. 1994. *A Phenomenology of Landscape: Places, Paths and Monuments*. Oxford, Berg.

Wickham-Jones, C. R. 2005. Summer walkers? – Mobility and the Mesolithic, in N. Milner and P. Woodman (eds.), *Mesolithic Studies at the beginning of the 21st Century*, 30–41. Oxford, Oxbow Books.

56. Man-landscape relations in Varanger, Finnmark, northern Norway

Maria Westrum Solem

The empirical basis for this analysis is a number of Stone Age sites found by the Varangerfjord in northernmost Norway. My investigation of man-landscape relations uses visual landscape analysis based on the body as situated at points in the landscape (i.e. the sites), and the visual (i.e. bodily) experience of structures in the landscape from these points. It focuses on how one perceives the landscape from the sites. This way of systematizing Stone Age sites has high potential for revealing landscape use, and changes in use, through time.

Keywords: visual landscape analyses, landscape rooms, Varangerfjorden, man-landscape relations.

Introduction

In order to understand the past I choose to focus on the human universality of us all. By 'human universality' I mean that there are certain elements in human beings that we all have in common. Even though we are all unique individuals, bound to a culture in time and space, there is an aspect in us all that binds us together. This element transcends individuality, gender, culture, and history. Despite cultural differences there is something about us that makes us recognizable to others, and this aspect makes understanding possible. What makes us human is defined differently in different cultures and through history, and our western definition, bound up in psychology and biology, is not universal. Without going into a discussion revolving around the philosophical question concerning what it means to be a human, I will base my understanding on these three principles: that all humans have the same mental constructs, all humans have a body, and all humans live in an existing landscape/environment. I find these common human universalities a good starting point when trying to interpret man's relation to the landscape.

I believe that a focus on the visual aspects of the landscape can deepen our understanding of the past. The fact that we, today, as in the past, are all subjects in an (objective) world becomes a bonding of both the scientist and the object of his/her study. By focusing on Stone Age locations, and by actually standing on these locations, one will experience, literally, a common point of view or stand. They (the people in pre-history) stood exactly here, as physical bodies in space and time. I stand at the same point today as a physical body in space and time. Both their and my experience is personal and unique, and to a large extent influenced by cultural constraints, but we are surrounded by the same environment. How one perceives the environment is both a natural feature and a skill to be learned. To gather information about the environment surrounding us is therefore a mixture of culture, nature, and individual experiences. As humans situated in time and space (a culture), our social community becomes an important source for knowledge. Here one learns what to see and how different elements relate to each other, forming a comprehensive worldview, a cosmology. But this social community is grounded in an existing, concrete world. And this world *in itself* makes information pick-up possible. Our expectations of the world (the nature) are mental constructs, but the environment surrounding us, and the information gained from it (the nature) is not (Milton 2002, 44).

Visual landscape analyses

Man changes and forms the landscape. For a larger group of people to feel at home in a landscape, it needs to communicate with it and make it a 'home'; this includes both mental and physical changes in the environment. Physical change is delimited by the landscape's existing features, but it is also influenced by technology, ownership, boundaries, name-giving, and traditions. Social and cultural norms will therefore be a part of this process. These are cultural structures worked into the landscape, some of which will be visual, while others will be hidden and lost to the archaeologist. Archaeologists try to reconstruct past cultural structures from the material remains of that culture. An archaeological structure is the material remains of a cultural structure in the landscape. This cannot be said to be an objective process, but rather in trying to 'interpret' past cultural structures the archaeologist will have a pre-concept of the landscape. He or she will always have expectations concerning the landscape, the cultural remains, and how these remains relate to the landscape (Gansum *et al.* 1997, 15, 18–19). Thus landscape analysis deconstructs the landscape and its cultural signs, later to be reconstructed in archaeological papers.

Visual landscape analysis focuses on how the landscape is perceived, and how the people of the past chose to dwell within it (Gansum *et al.* 1997, 10). The method uses definitions from landscape architecture in order to describe topography and landscape formations. There are two central concepts:

1. Landscape must be perceived as a surface.
2. Landscape must be perceived from a human perspective; the human body is what everything is measured by/against (Gansum *et al.* 1997, 13).

Landscape architecture does not focus on the temporality of the landscape. As the landscape we study changes in time, it is a challenge for archaeologist to read the greater forms of the landscape, ignoring the transitory vegetation such as trees and bushes.

Landscape 'rooms'

A landscape room consists of a floor, walls and ceiling. Flat areas make up the floor, while hills and mountains make up the walls. The sky is the ceiling. The walls will usually delimit the room, but a break in the floor level may also delimit it. A landscape can be divided into large (superior) and small (inferior) rooms, and these will be intertwined. A large landscape room will consist of several small rooms, which can be further subdivided into even smaller rooms. Small rooms will always be part of a larger room, and together they will form an entire landscape. The terrain forms a landscape room, and how a room is perceived is dependant on where one stands (Figure 56.1). For an archaeologist it is natural to choose the cultural remains as

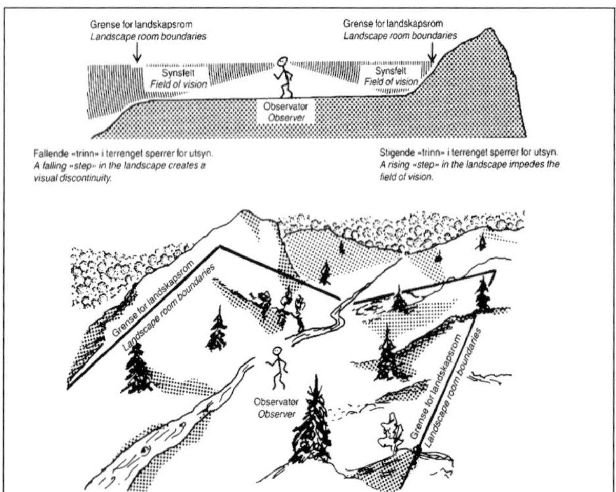

Figure 56.1. Landscape room (Gansum et al. 1997, 14).

the point of departure when identifying a room. The Stone Age sites will thus determine which landscape rooms are perceived (Gansum *et al.* 1997, 13).

The view from the location determines how the location relates to the landscape. Some locations have a good view, all the way to the horizon, while others have only a view of the close surroundings. It is often possible to identify the location's view and whether or not it focuses on a small/inferior room or a large/superior room. A site will usually relate to one landscape room, with a view toward one specific direction.

Varangerfjorden

The Varanger fjord is situated in north-eastern Norway, on the border of today's Russia and Finland. It is a long fjord, running east/west into the Barents Sea. The fjord lies at around 70º north; the area has a cold climate with long and hard winters, and short, coolish summers. During winter the sun does not rise above the horizon, nor does it set at all in summer. But despite the hard climate the area has a lot of natural resources. The fjord is the richest in Norway, with plenty of fish and sea mammals, such as whales and seals. On land, there are birds, small game, and larger animals (e.g. reindeer (*Rangifer tarandus*), elk (*Alces alces*), and bear (Ursidae). Because of the sparse vegetation and minor cultural alterations in the area, it is easy to get a clear picture of landscape formations and to survey Stone Age sites: this makes the area particularly well suited for visual landscape analysis.

I have conducted visual landscape analyses on 67 sites (both Early and Younger Stone Age) in the inner regions of Varangerfjorden. The sites are believed to have been settled along the (then) shoreline, and this, in conjunction with ^{14}C analyses and typology, makes dating possible. Because of the rise in the land after the last Ice Age, the sites are situated at different levels in the landscape. The sites from the Early Stone Age are situated high in the landscape, between 73 and 26m asl), while the sites from the Younger Stone Age are situated at lower levels, between 25 and 18m asl. But they are all situated along the same coastline and in the same environment. Even though these sites represent several thousand years, they utilized the same resources. The big divide between the Early Stone Age (the Mesolithic) and Younger Stone Age (the Neolithic) found in southern Scandinavia – where the Neolithic is characterised by farming – is not present in the Varangerfjorden. One can argue that changes in the material culture and settlement patterns mark a distinction between the Early and Younger Stone Age, but it is believed that the use of resources was the same in both periods (Grydeland 2005, 107).

The changes that appear in the archaeological material and settlement patterns cannot be explained by eco-functionalist approaches only. There is no statistical connection between climate and changes in material culture. Cold periods are not reflected in the construction of solid, warm houses, nor are the appearance of pottery and slate artefacts a result of a change in resource utilization (Grydeland 2005, 107). The change one observes in the archaeological material reflects the *choices* made by people in a given context. The changes therefore reflect the culture, not the nature.

The Early Stone Age

Finnmark was populated about 10,000 years ago, at the end of the last ice age, probably by hunter-gatherers from the continent. The Early Stone Age covers a very long period of time, from 10,000 to 5600 BP, and I will use Bjørnar Olsen's (1994) chronology and divide the era into three periods. (Unless indicated otherwise, all radiocarbon dates in the text are as cited in the publications from which they come and are expressed in uncalibrated radiocarbon years before present (^{14}C BP).)

Early Stone Age: Period One (10,000–9000 BP, 73–52m asl)

In the beginning of the Early Stone Age the sites are located on small, open places in the landscape, and they have a very good view towards a large/superior landscape room. The sites usually have a view to the horizon, often 180° or more. The sites are small, consisting of only one or two tent rings or houses. They are situated on small islands, with harbours on two sides, for use in different weather. One example from this period is Lagesiidbakhti 1 (LAG-1), dated to about 9940±101 BP (9500–9250 cal BC; Wk-11598) (Grydeland 2005, 114) (Figure 56.2). It is a small site situated on an open location about 71m asl. Two very small 'hills', made up of solid rock, facing east and west, make two very small walls that delimit the room. The location has a view towards the sea and the horizon, and it focuses on a large/superior landscape room. It is situated very openly in the landscape.

Later in the Early Stone Age, the number of sites increases dramatically. The locations become larger and have diversity in artefacts and raw materials. One example from this period is Cåkki (Cåkki-1) situated some 62m asl (Figure 56.3). This site has two tent rings, and is dated between 9780±95 BP (8480–8270 cal BC; Wk-11599) and 9170±95 BP (9350–9130 cal BC; Wk-11600) (Grydeland 2005, 116). This site also has a very good view to the horizon and it focuses on a superior landscape room. But contrary to Lagesiidbakhti, this site has very distinct walls, made of solid rock, surrounding it on three sides. This gives the site a more sheltered look, and the tent rings are situated in a small, well-defined inferior landscape room.

Early Stone Age: Period Two (9000–7500/7000 BP, 51–52m asl)

Between 40 and 35m asl (8400–8100 BP) there is a decrease in the number of sites, artefacts and raw materials. The raw material consists mainly of quartz. This unity in raw material makes it possible to ask questions such as whether there were communications between coastal (such as Varangerfjorden in Finnmark) and inland settlers (as can be found in Finland for example)? The sites appear to become more similar in shape and size, and it is no longer possible to identify special-purpose sites (Grydeland 2005, 326).

One such site from this period is Mortensnes 2 (29m asl), from the north of Varangerfjorden. It is a small site, with the remains of one small house or hut structure. This location focuses on the fjord, and the hills on the other side of the fjord can be seen quite clearly in the horizon. Even though this site focuses on a large landscape room, it is situated within a small and well-defined landscape room. There is a very big wall, in the form of a steep hill to the north of the site, which shelters the site, even from a distance. It is situated openly in the landscape.

Early Stone Age: Period Three (7500/7000–5600 BP / 6500–4500 BP, 26-22m asl)

From 29m asl there is a change in the material towards more clearly defined sites and a more diversified use of raw material (Grydeland 2005, 334–5). In addition, this last period of the Early Stone Age has sites that focus on large/ superior landscape rooms. But in this period one can also find sites that focus on a smaller room, particularly the harbour. These latter sites have a more sheltered look.

Figure 56.2. Lagesiidbakhti 1. The view towards the horizon and former sea. (All photographs: Ingrid Fuglestvedt).

Figure 56.3. Cåkki 1. The wall is to the left, the actual site in the centre. The focus is towards the horizon.

Looking at the main tendency for all the periods in the Early Stone Age, one will find that the sites are located in small landscape rooms, often with small walls on two or three sides. These walls are often so small that one can look above them and they do not provide much shelter from the wind. The sites often have a very good view, 180° or more, and most have a good view towards the horizon as well. When the sites are situated towards the fjord, the views tend towards both ends of the fjord, giving vision along the length of the fjord. The sites relate to a large/superior room: a room consisting of sea and sky. The extent of visible land included mountains on the horizon and the islets the sites were actually situated on. In the Early Stone Age the sea level was much higher than today, covering much of today's land area. During the Early Stone Age the sea level changed considerably. The land rose very fast, and the changes could be seen between one generation and the next: the landscape and the world must have been a place of constant change. The inhabitants also participated in this overall situation of change, moving from place to place and experiencing new worlds.

The Younger Stone Age

The Younger Stone Age is dated between 4500–1800 cal BC, and this period can also be divided into three different periods, following Olsen's chronology (1994). The Younger Stone Age is characterized by a new form of dwelling and the use of new raw materials. Slate and pottery are introduced, and the houses become bigger, more substantial, and more permanent; the materials found inside the houses indicate a longer and more intensive use. The labour and resources invested in the houses indicate that the houses may have had a great value in society. They may have been carriers of a cultural inheritance (Schanche 1988, 150). The houses are now located together in small 'villages', in sheltered shores and bays. The land, not the sea, takes on a more visual significance.

This change cannot be explained by eco-functionalistic approaches only. There is no evidence of changes in use of resources: fishing, hunting, and gathering are still the means of subsistence. Neither can climatic change be used to explain the changes in material culture (Figure 56.4).

Younger Stone Age: Period One (4500–3700 cal BC)

In this early phase of the Younger Stone Ages one finds the remains of pit houses in Varangerfjorden. These are quite small and have a round or oval shape. What is interesting for this period is the difference in artefacts on either side of the fjord. The locations on the north side of the fjord, like Mortensnes, have surface flakes points, pit houses, and a number of slate artefacts, but no pottery. The locations on the south side of the fjord have few slate artefacts but they do have ceramics (Olsen 1994, 53–4, 66). The material culture on the south of the fjord has great similarities with inland settlements. The difference in material culture might therefore be an indication of two cultural groups in this area: one group with seasonal movement patterns, moving from inland to the coast, and another that was more specialised to the coast. Bearing in mind that these were probably egalitarian, mobile hunter-gatherers, the pottery adds a new dimension. It might have had a socio-cultural meaning, functioning as a marker for social differentiation (Olsen 1994, 78–80).

The sites from this period are situated near the sea, often with a good view, but there was a tendency to locate the sites in more sheltered bays.

Younger Stone Age: Period Two (3700–3000 cal BC)

Around 3500 cal BC there developed a specific kind of pit house in Varangerfjorden. They are called 'Gropbakkenhus', after the site where most were found: suggestion at least 89 houses and three burial mounds. Pottery is no longer used. Despite the number of houses and their solid construction, the specialized tools indicate that this was probably a seasonal settlement. There were, in all likelihood, even more houses situated here but some have unfortunately been ruined. The houses have an inner dimension of 15–20m^2, and they are situated close together by a creek. They are situated on a plateau 22m asl, along what was the shoreline of the period. The plateau is half-moon shaped, with a large 'wall' behind the houses. This wall is 20m high, made of sand deposited from the sea, and provided excellent shelter from the elements (and making the site hard to spot).

This location has a view towards the sea, but not to the horizon. Rather it focuses on the harbour and the inner parts of the fjord. The harbour and the large wall make this site focus on a small/inferior room. It is the site itself, with the houses and nearby harbour, which is the focus of attention.

Figure 56.4. Gropbakkengen. The pit houses are situated on a plateau along the shoreline of the period. The large wall is to the left of the photograph.

Younger Stone Age: Period Three (3000–1800 cal BC)

In the last part of the Younger Stone Age the houses developed into a particular type of houses called 'Gressbakkentufter'. These are by far the biggest houses from Finnmark's prehistory, and are dated between 2200–1800 cal BC. The houses have a rectangular form, with a rectangular fireplace in the middle, divided into two parts. This has led archaeologists to believe that one or two families might have inhabited each house. The houses are built into the ground, and have an inner dimension of $4 \times 7m^2$. The houses have two to four entrances, one on either side. The square forms of both the building and fireplaces, and the special way the entrances are situated, give the impression of a structured and well-organised society. These houses are usually located together, forming small 'villages', but they can also be situated individually (Schanche 1994, 100–1). There has been a great discussion among archaeologists about the temporality of these houses, and whether or not they are contemporary. The archaeologist Kjersti Schanche has lately concluded that there is reason to believe that several of the houses were inhabited at the same time. The number of sites, and their size, has led Schanche to form the theory of separate regions, each divided into smaller groups and family units (Schanche 1994, 197–8).

Like other sites from the Younger Stone Age, Gressbakkentufter are located by the shore, with a wall behind the location (Figure 56.5). The hills that form the walls behind the settlement are earthen terraces made by sea deposits. The locations do not face the open sea but are located in creeks and bays, focusing on the inner harbour. In a very similar way to Gropbakkengen these settlements focus on small/inferior landscape rooms.

Figure 56.5. Gressbakken pit houses on Mortensnes. The focus is on the inner harbour.

	Open sites		Sheltered Sites	
	Number	%	Number	%
Elder Stone Age	108	77.1	32	22.9
Younger Stone Age	12	30	28	70

Figure 56.6. Relationship between open and sheltered locations. (After Grydeland 2005, 108, fig. 5: 7).

Conclusions

Visual landscape analysis makes it possible to systemize and compare different sites from the same reference point – the human body. Dividing the landscape into superior and inferior landscape rooms and experiencing which room the site focuses on, reveals how different cultures relate to the same landscape. The great differences found between Early and Younger Stone Age settlements patterns are strikingly clear (Figure 56.6). In the Early Stone Ages the sites are situated on open locations. The sites are small, consisting of not more than one or two houses/tents. They have very good harbours, in different directions. Each site is situated within a small/inferior landscape room, with small walls on two to three sides. The sites from the Early Stone Ages focus on a large/superior rooms, with a view all the way to the horizon.

In the Younger Stone Age the situation is quite the opposite. The houses are large and situated close together in bays and sheltered shores. To have the houses situated in near proximity to each other seems to be a choice based on social preferences rather than a need brought on by space limitations. These settlements are located on terraces in the landscape, along the shoreline of the time; they are situated within a well-defined landscape room, with a wall surrounding the settlements on three sides. The focus, therefore, is on the small/inferior landscape room consisting of the settlement itself and the harbour.

These profound changes demonstrate something more than a basic evolutionary development from simplicity to complexity. Their choices are not solely based on coincidence, nor are they only formed by the climate or restricted by natural resources: these changes reflect their way of living in the world and their relationship to the environment.

References

Gansum, T., Jerpåsen, G. and Keller, C. 1997. *Arkeologisk landskapsanalyse med visuelle metoder*. AmS-Varia 28. Stavanger, Museum of Archaeology.

Grydeland, S.-E. 2005. *Nytt lys på eldre steinalder i Finnmark. En sammenlignende studie basert på gjenstandsbruk og distribusjon av boplasser i Varanger, Alta og Nord-Finland.* Unpublished PhD thesis, University of Tromsø.

Milton, K. 2002. *Loving Nature. Towards an ecology of emotion.* London, Routledge.

Olsen, B. 1994. *Bosetning og samfunn i Finnmarks forhistorie.* Oslo, Universitetsforlaget.

Schanche, K. 1988. *Mortensnes en boplass i Varanger. En studie av samfunn og materiell kultur gjennom 10.000 år.* Magistergradsavhandling i arkeologi, Universitetet i Tromsø.

Schanche, K. 1994. *Gressbakkentuftene i Varanger. Boliger og sosial struktur rundt 2000 f. Kr.* PhD thesis, University of Tromsø.

57. Feast in the forest: creating a common cultural identity in the interior of the Scandinavian Peninsula in the Late Mesolithic

Silje Elisabeth Fretheim

On the basis of my interpretation of the function of several Late Mesolithic cooking-pits recently discovered in the interior of south-east Norway, as well as similar features known from the interior of north and central Sweden, I suggest that activities connected with the use of the cooking-pits may have played an important role in spreading the feeling of a common identity among different groups specializing in the use of the inland resources of the Scandinavian Peninsula in the Late Mesolithic (6400–4000 cal BC).

Keywords: regional identity, north and central Scandinavia, Late Mesolithic, cooking-pit feasts, house-pits/dwellings, inland vs. coast, distribution of features vs. artefacts and raw materials.

Introduction

Traditionally, distribution of certain types of artefacts or raw materials is used in defining Mesolithic cultures in Norway, as in other parts of Europe. This makes sense, since stone artefacts are often the only remains available for study on sites from this period. In relatively recent years, however, we have come to know increasingly more of certain features, such as house-structures and fireplaces, on Norwegian Mesolithic sites. A claim of this article is that a focus on the distribution of distinctive types of features is a less problematic basis for studying Mesolithic cultural entities than a focus on the distribution of artefacts and raw materials. The starting point is my interpretation of several Late Mesolithic cooking-pits discovered on sites in Gråfjell, Hedmark County, Norway. The Gråfjell cooking-pits have few parallels in Norway, whereas in north and central Sweden, similar features with Mesolithic dates seem to be more common. This, as well as a similar distribution of a certain type of Late Mesolithic/Neolithic house remains, has made me consider the possibility of a common cultural identity in the interior of the Scandinavian Peninsula, stretching from south-east Norway to north Sweden, and crossing borders that might have been drawn on the basis of artefact and raw material distribution.

Discovering 'new' Mesolithic features

Part of the increasing knowledge of features on Norwegian Mesolithic sites derives from the use of new methods of excavation, or, rather, the adaptation of methods already used on sites from other prehistoric periods. Large scale uncovering of site surfaces by machine is starting to replace the more traditional approach of excavating only where test-pitting has revealed concentrations of artefacts; a more horizontal approach to site excavations is an approach likely to focus more on features than artefacts.

Another reason for the uncovering of new types of features is the surveying in what may be called new types of landscapes. Norway is a country dominated by an extensive coastline. Mesolithic sites along the coast have been known since the beginning of last century. Inland Mesolithic sites were hardly known at all until the

Figure 57.1. Location of the Gråfjell and Rødsmoen areas.

Norwegian government allowed the damming of several high mountain river systems in the 1960s and 1970s, for the purpose of producing hydroelectric power. Certain knowledge of inland Mesolithic sites was achieved through large scale surveying projects, and through active use of the then relatively new method of radiocarbon dating (Amundsen 1999; Boaz 1997, 11–17; Fretheim 2002, 15–17; Gustafson 1988; Hagen 1979; Martens and Hagen 1961; Mikkelsen and Nybruget 1975). The interpretation of the high mountain sites was that they were the result of hunting expeditions from coastal base camps, or of seasonal movements between coastal and high mountain sites. If considered at all, the lower lying inland forests were interpreted simply as transition areas (Boaz 1997; Schaller and Skar 1981). As recently as 15 years ago, knowledge of Mesolithic inland sites unconnected to the large river systems was sparse. During the 1990s, however, two large archaeological projects resulted from the need for new military training areas in south-east Norway. Both projects involve an area that may be perceived as the western outskirts of the extensive conifer forests covering most of central and north Sweden, continuing through Finland, and far into Russia (Figure 57.1).

The Rødsmoen project was conducted by the Museum of Cultural History in Oslo, with excavations between 1994 and 1996. Among the most important results, from a Stone Age research viewpoint, was the recognition and examination of a certain type of house-pit, or sunken dwelling (Boaz 1997; 1999). These dwellings show marked similarities with house structures found in northern Sweden, the so called 'skjärvstensvallar' (Lundberg 1997), characterized by mounds containing large amounts of fire-cracked stones, burnt bones and debris from the production and use of stone tools. In Norway, similar house-pits are also found by Lake Rokosjøen in Hedmark, and near Fagernes in Oppland (Kræmer 2003). These structures all belong to the interior region of north and central Scandinavia (Figure 57.4), and are interpreted as winter dwellings (Boaz 1997, 137; 1999, 145; Kræmer 2003, 45–6; Lundberg 1997, 135–6, Mikkelsen 1989, 49–53). Most of the excavated Swedish dwellings seem to have been in use between 4600 and 2500 cal BC, making them, basically, a Neolithic phenomenon. However, at least one Swedish house-pit has an initial phase dated as far back as 5480–5144 cal BC (6345±180 BP; St-1651) (Lundberg 1997, 119–20, 189). The earliest dwelling from Rødsmoen has an initial phase with several dates around *c.* 6000 cal BC. The rest of the excavated Norwegian house-pits have provided dates overlapping the Swedish material (4900–2500 cal BC), although all of them have artefacts suggesting initial occupation in the Late Mesolithic (Boaz 1997). Another difference between the Swedish and the Norwegian house-pit sites is in the use of raw materials for stone tool production. Quartz is most common on the sites in north Sweden, while flint is the dominant raw material in the dwellings from Rødsmoen in south-east Norway. Flint is not found naturally in either area. The flint found at Rødsmoen must have been brought from the south or west coast. Even so, Joel Boaz suggests that the house-pits showing up in the interior of east Norway in the Late Mesolithic mark an end to long-distance seasonal movements between coastal and interior areas. Both coastal and inland sites show signs of a more specialised economy in this period, leading to semi-sedentary ways of life, or at least ways of life where mobility was kept within a more limited range of economic zones (Boaz 1999).

The Gråfjell project

My focus is on the second big project in the interior of south-east Norway, the Gråfjell project. The Gråfjell area is divided from Rødsmoen by the River Rena (Figure 57.2), where well over 100 Stone Age sites have been mapped in connection with both the Gråfjell and Rødsmoen projects. Although somewhat higher than the Rødsmoen area, Gråfjell is also mostly forested. The Gråfjell area covers more than 200km^2. The Norwegian Institute of Cultural Heritage Research conducted the surveying of the area (Risbøl *et al.* 2000; 2001; 2002a; 2002b). The Museum of Cultural History in Oslo has undertaken the excavations (Stene 2004; 2005; 2006).

Twenty sites containing stone implements or flakes have been uncovered in the Gråfjell area. Considering the time and effort spent test-pitting, and the abundance of sites located with the same methods along the river Rena, this number is smaller than anticipated when the survey started in 1999. However, both surveying and excavation of the area have given results that demand attention. The main reason is the finding of cooking-pits on four Stone Age sites out of six in the northern part of the area.

Cooking-pits in general

I will briefly define what type of features I refer to as cooking-pits, before I move on to parallels and interpretations of the features from Gråfjell.

A cooking-pit in a Scandinavian context is usually defined as one with a marked charcoal layer at the base, and a compact filling of fire-cracked stones in the layer above (Figure 57.3). Usually there are no finds, not even bones, in direct connection with these features. In a settlement context, however, debris is quite often deposited in/over the pits after use. In areas not disturbed by farming activity, the cooking-pits are usually visible on the surface, sometimes with a clear mound surrounding them; nevertheless, most are hardly noticeable unless you are specifically looking for them. The size of the cooking-pits varies, but the diameter is rarely more than 2.5m, and the depth usually less than 50cm. This definition excludes pits that may be interpreted simply as pit fireplaces, without a clear stratigraphy or abundance of fire-cracked stones. From my definition I also exclude those smaller pits (with a mix of charcoal, burnt bones and fire-cracked stones) that are often found in house floors of Stone Age house-pits in northern Sweden and southeast Norway.

Cooking-pits in outlying areas in Norway and Sweden

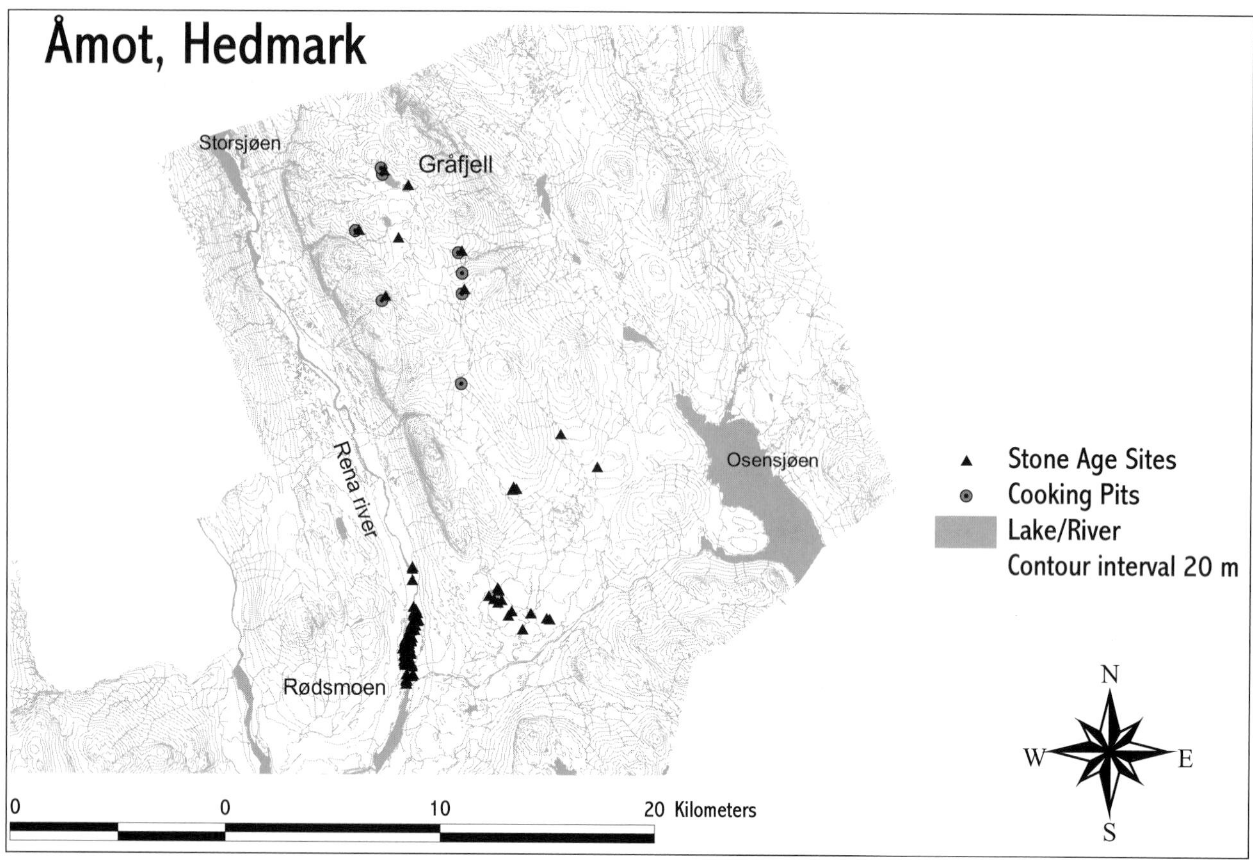

Figure 57.2. Distribution of cooking-pits and sites with Stone Age artefacts in the Gråfjell area, and along the Rena River.

Figure 57.3. Section through one of the Gråfjell cooking-pits.

are normally dated within the Late Bronze or Early Iron Ages. In farmland areas, they are among the most common types of features from these periods. Thus, it came as something of a surprise when, during the second year of surveying, charcoal from two cooking-pits in Gråfjell was dated to the Late Mesolithic (Fretheim 2003; Risbøl *et al.* 2001). Later, three more cooking-pits in Gråfjell have given similar results, with dates between 5900 and 4800 cal BC (Fretheim 2005; Stene 2006).

Mesolithic cooking-pits

In searching literature that might reveal similar features with Mesolithic dates outside Gråfjell, I initially found one other site in inland Norway and six sites in north and central Sweden, containing 10 Mesolithic cooking-pits between them. After the presentation of this paper at Belfast, I was happily informed that there were more sites containing Mesolithic cooking-pits in central Sweden. Unfortunately I have not found the time to incorporate more than two of these sites in this article. In Figure 57.4, I present a total of 17 cooking-pits, Norwegian and Swedish, with Late or Middle Mesolithic dates. The sites are widely spread within north and central Scandinavia, but I find it interesting that, except for the sites in Sjövreten, Sörmland, they are all situated in areas far from the coast.

Figure 57.4 also show sites containing groups of house-pits of the kind described earlier. Keep in mind the fact that the oldest date from a house-pit in north Sweden is roughly a thousand years younger than the cooking-pits I have marked in the area, while in south-east Norway, the situation is almost the exact opposite. The Mesolithic cooking-pits in central Sweden seem to be closer in age to the Norwegian ones. Although I know my material is still very limited, I suggest that the cooking-pit tradition within the Scandinavian Peninsula started with people using the interior of north Sweden around 7000 cal BC. This early, the interior of south-east Norway was probably utilized by people spending their winters by the coast. The interior

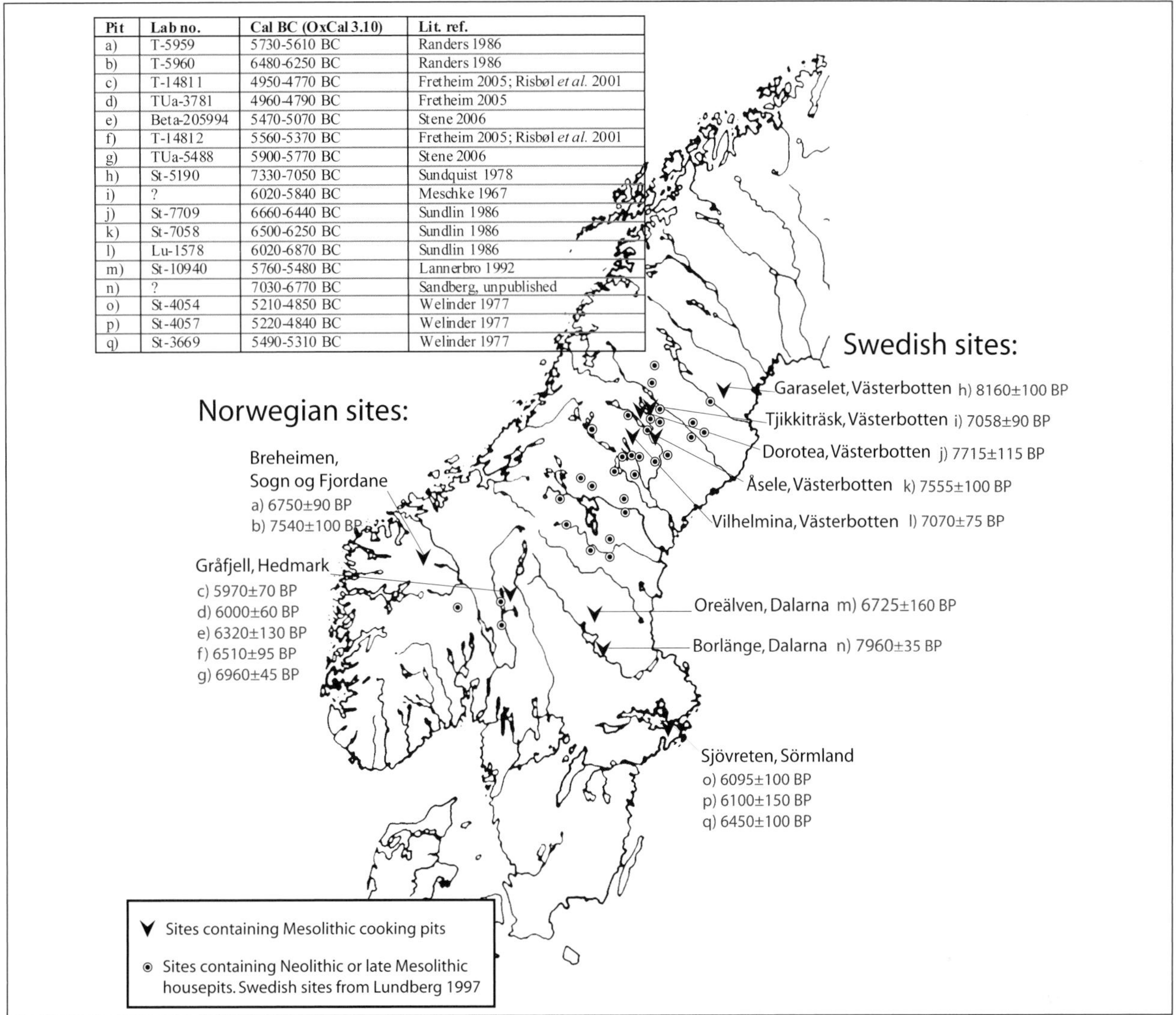

Pit	Lab no.	Cal BC (OxCal 3.10)	Lit. ref.
a)	T-5959	5730-5610 BC	Randers 1986
b)	T-5960	6480-6250 BC	Randers 1986
c)	T-14811	4950-4770 BC	Fretheim 2005; Risbøl *et al.* 2001
d)	TUa-3781	4960-4790 BC	Fretheim 2005
e)	Beta-205994	5470-5070 BC	Stene 2006
f)	T-14812	5560-5370 BC	Fretheim 2005; Risbøl *et al.* 2001
g)	TUa-5488	5900-5770 BC	Stene 2006
h)	St-5190	7330-7050 BC	Sundquist 1978
i)	?	6020-5840 BC	Meschke 1967
j)	St-7709	6660-6440 BC	Sundlin 1986
k)	St-7058	6500-6250 BC	Sundlin 1986
l)	Lu-1578	6020-6870 BC	Sundlin 1986
m)	St-10940	5760-5480 BC	Lannerbro 1992
n)	?	7030-6770 BC	Sandberg, unpublished
o)	St-4054	5210-4850 BC	Welinder 1977
p)	St-4057	5220-4840 BC	Welinder 1977
q)	St-3669	5490-5310 BC	Welinder 1977

Figure 57.4. Distribution of Mesolithic cooking-pits and Neolithic/Late Mesolithic house-pits in north and central Scandinavia. List of radiocarbon dates from the cooking-pits (OxCal 3.10; Bronk Ramsey 2005).

specialisation seems to have started a thousand years later (Boaz 1999).

Interpreting the cooking-pits

The most common interpretation of the function of Bronze and Iron Age cooking-pits is that they were used in preparing large meals: hence the term. The principle is simple, and known, with some variations, from several cultures around the world even today (Heibreen 2005). A pit is dug, and half filled with head-, to fist-sized stones, which are then heated by keeping a fire going in the pit for an hour or two. Meat, fish or vegetables, that may be wrapped in leaves (or tin foil, in a modern context), is then placed among the heated stones. The turf, and some of the earth, is replaced during the cooking, covering the pit and retaining the intense heat for several hours. (If you have never tried this method of cooking, I highly recommend it!)

There are other interpretations of the cooking-pit features, however, as well as other names (Gustafson 2005). In north Sweden, similar features have sometimes been referred to as 'drying ovens' ('torkugnar') (Melander 1986), and interpreted in connection with food conservation, for a combination of drying and smoking large quantities of meat. This method is ethnographically known from Lappland in modern times (Lundin 1992, 146). Yet another interpretation is that conservation of heat, for saunas or regular house warming, was the primary function.

For now, I simply assume that the most common interpretation, viewing the Bronze and Iron Age pits in the context of cooking, is a likely construal of the Mesolithic cooking-pits as well. I make this assumption, being fully aware that other interpretations may undermine my view of the cooking-pits' significance apart from the purely functional aspect.

Interpretations of Bronze and Iron Age cooking-pits suggest that there were other aspects to the cooking-pit meals than simply getting people fed. Concentrations of cooking-pits, limited areas containing several cooking-pits, have been viewed in connection with cultic activity, as traces of ritual meals, possibly combined with religious food sacrifice (Narmo 1996). Another suggestion is that the cooking-pit feasts had a political dimension for early Iron Age society. One Norwegian archaeologist describes the cooking-pit feast as 'a mix between a ball, a court hearing, a local council meeting and a drunken party' (Gjerpe 2001, 14: translation by present author).

I am not suggesting that cooking-pits represented the same thing for Mesolithic as for Iron Age society, but there *is* reason to believe that the Gråfjell cooking-pits had a function beyond the practical daily use. The average inner diameter of the Gråfjell cooking-pits is 1.6m. From practical tests, we know that food for 30–40 people can be made in cooking-pits with a diameter of 1m. None of the sites in Gråfjell suggests that groups this size, let alone even bigger groups, spent their time in the area on a daily basis. The sites we have found are widely spread, and contain very small amounts of artefacts (in fact, *no* certain artefacts were found in connection with two of the excavated sites). Even the abundant sites along the River Rena seem to be camps for fairly small groups of people. The cooking-pits at the sites in Gråfjell can hardly be evidence of everyday meals. If the pits were actually used for cooking, it seems more likely that small groups came together to share large common meals on special occasions.

Defining regional identities based on the archaeological record

Norwegian and Swedish archaeologists working with regions where local quartz and quartzite dominate the Stone Age assemblages, run into problems when trying to establish whether or not common regional identities were in play. The use of a common raw material is no proof of contact, unless it is hard to come by in parts of the studied area. Quartz, specifically, is difficult to classify within the well-known systems based on studies of flint and flint-like materials. This has made sites dominated by quartz finds seem strangely anonymous, compared to flint-dominated sites placed within the many named Stone Age cultures of south Scandinavia, and along large parts of the Norwegian coast (Carlsson 2003, 128–9).

In my opinion, the focus on types of features is a less problematic basis for studying cultural differences and similarities – that is, differences and similarities that were meaningful to Stone Age people – than the focus on types of artefacts and raw materials. I believe this to be the case even in areas where we find well-defined types of artefacts made from non-local raw materials. Basically, features are not physically mobile in the way that artefacts are; axes and spearheads can easily be exchanged by people with different cultural identities. The receivers of a new type of artefact may infuse it with their own cultural meaning, without changing the physical appearance of the object. Adaptations like this will necessarily complicate the relation between identifying the patterns of regional finds, and identifying actual cultural entities. It is harder to imagine types of features being exchanged between cultures in the same way. Of course, certain house building techniques or cooking methods may eventually spread from one culture to another, but I imagine this to be most likely to happen in cases where the different cultures already have some level of common identity.

I suggest that a form of common regional identity, or culture, existed in the inland forest area of central Scandinavia in the Late Mesolithic, and that the Mesolithic cooking-pits give a clue to how such a regional identity may have been maintained, or even how it came to exist.

Cooking-pit feasts and the creation of a regional identity

I envisage the cooking-pit sites as meeting places for several mobile groups using this extensive inland area, whether they were family groups or small hunting expeditions from larger base camps. Regular aggregations, involving large, common meals, may have been a factor in keeping peaceful relations between autonomous groups that might otherwise have been in conflict, as they moved around in the same landscape, and were probably dependent on the same spectrum of resources. Feasts of this type are hard to imagine unless the groups have a minimum of common cultural traits – a form of common language, similarities in material culture and behavioural codes, etc. By connecting people, the feast would have spread knowledge of different local traditions, through storytelling, through the showing off of styles in equipment and clothing, and, perhaps, through the sharing of specialities in food and drink.

Is common knowledge and cultural traits among groups within a region enough to propose a common regional identity? Studies in social anthropology suggest that this is not the case. Today, cultural identity, as well as ethnicity, is normally seen as something that rises and is maintained through contact between different people, through *opposition*, not assimilation (Barth 1969; Odner 1983; Olsen 1985). Thus, the cooking-pit feasts may initially have had the exact opposite effect of creating a common regional identity. They may have made people more aware of the many different local traditions, and thus contributed to the creation of local identities. My theory is that this initial effect changed over time. My scenario starts with an increasing number of groups specializing in the use of the interior region of the Scandinavian Peninsula somewhere between 6000 and 5000 cal BC. The cooking-pit tradition spread from the northern to the southern groups, in an active attempt by the groups themselves to interact without hostility. Possibly, the cooking-pit feasts become more ritualized as they spread towards the edges of the continuous forest region. I find it significant that while the Mesolithic cooking-pits in Sweden seem to be found on regular Stone Age sites, all the Gråfjell cooking-pits are placed in what seems close to being a 'no man's land', far from any site with material suggesting more than one single activity.

As we know that the people using the pit houses in

south-east Norway must have had regular contact with the coast, or coastal groups, to get their flint, I suggest that an idea of a common identity with other inland groups may have originated in this area (this does not mean that similar ideas may not *also* have originated with inland groups in north and central Sweden, in contact with people on the east coast). The cooking-pit feasts may gradually have come to represent traditions connecting the inland groups culturally, until, somewhere between 5000 and 4600 cal BC, the people of this vast forest region reached such a high degree of common identity that it was actually possible for the groups in northern Sweden to adopt the house building traditions of their south-eastern neighbours.

My theory involves a small material basis stretched to explain processes in a large geographical region, as well as over a long time span. I will address one of the biggest material gaps before I leave the theory to be criticised by others: why do the dates from the cooking-pits in Gråfjell and north Sweden hardly even overlap, if the cooking-pit feasts continued to contribute to a common regional identity throughout the Mesolithic? One possible explanation is that the cooking-pit feasts were moved away from the regular dwelling sites in north Sweden too. As far as I know, it applies to northern Sweden, as well as the interior of Norway, that we have little knowledge of Stone Age sites apart from the large river systems. Perhaps more survey projects in the 'no man's land' in the interior region of the Scandinavian Peninsula may provide similar results to those we find in Gråfjell?

Recent data updates

Since the writing of this article, yet another Gråfjell cooking-pit has given surprisingly old data results. Three dates from the same pit were located within the period 8170–7470 cal BC (T-18132, 8595±BP; T-18133, 8545±125 BP; Beta-216497, 8780±BP), making it about the same age as the oldest Swedish cooking pit in my Figure 57.4. Also, several of the 'stone age sites' without cooking pits in the Gråfjell area (my Figure 57.2) have been written off during closer investigation (as a result of the lack of convincing stone artefacts), making the term 'no man's land' even more appropriate (Amundsen 2007).

Acknowledgements

I wish to thank Per Falkenström for information on Mesolithic cooking-pits in central Sweden, and Thorstein Fretheim for improving my English.

References

Amundsen, H. R. 1999. Fra streiftokt til vinterbolig – Hedmarks steinalder gjennom tidene, in I. Fuglestvedt, T. Gansum and A. Opedal (eds.), *Et hus med mange rom. Vennebok til Bjørn Myhre på 60-årsdagen*, 31–42. AmS-Rapport 11A. Stavanger, Stavanger Arkeologisk museum.

Amundsen, T. (ed.) 2007. *Elgfangst og Bosetning i Gråfjellområdet. Gråfjellprosjektet Bind II*. Varia 64. Oslo, Kulturhistorisk Museum Fornminneseksjonen.

Barth, F. 1969. Introduction, in F. Barth (ed.), *Ethnic Groups and Boundaries. The Social Organization of Culture Difference*, 9–38. Oslo, Universitetsforlaget.

Boaz, J. 1997. *Steinalderundersøkelsene på Rødsmoen*. Varia 41. Oslo, Universitetets Oldsaksamling.

Boaz, J. 1999. Pioneers in the Mesolithic: The Initial Occupation of the Interior of Eastern Norway, in J. Boaz (ed.), *The Mesolithic of Central Scandinavia*, 125–52. Universitetets Oldsaksamlings Skrifter, Ny rekke 22. Oslo, Universitetets Oldsaksamling.

Bronk Ramsey, C. 2005. OxCal 3.10. WWW program and documentation available at http://www.rlaha.ox.ac.uk/oxcal/oxcal.htm (accessed 10/2007).

Carlsson, T. 2003. Mesolithic relations. Reflections on Ethnic Societies in Central Sweden during the Late Mesolithic, in J. Bergstøl (ed.), *Scandinavian archaeological practice – in theory. Proceedings from the 6th Nordic TAG, Oslo 2001*, 154–64. Oslo Archaeological Series (OAS) 1. Oslo, University of Oslo, Department of Archaeology.

Fretheim, S. E. 2002. *Steinalderminner i Alvdal Vestfjell. Utsnitt av livsmønstre gjennom 6500 år*. Unpublished Hovedfag thesis, Norwegian University of Science and Technology, Trondheim.

Fretheim, S. 2003. Ethnic Dualism in the Stone Age of Østerdalen? Possibilities in Interpreting Material from Gråfjell, Hedmark, in J. Bergstøl (ed.), *Scandinavian archaeological practice – in theory. Proceedings from the 6th Nordic TAG, Oslo 2001*, 124–36. Oslo Archaeological Series 1. Oslo, Universitetsforlaget.

Fretheim, S. E. 2005. Mesolittiske kokegroper?, in L. Gustafson, T. Heibreen and J. Martens (eds.), *De gåtefulle kokegroper*, 223–31. Varia 58. Oslo, Universitetets Oldsaksamlings/Kulturhistorisk Museum.

Gjerpe, L. E. 2001. Kult, politikk, fyll, vold og kokegropfeltet på Hov. *Primitive tider* 4, 5–17.

Gustafson, L. 1988. Fjellpionerene, in S. Indrelid, S. Kaland and B. Solberg (eds.), *Festskrift til Anders Hagen*, 50–67. Arkeologiske Skrifter 4. Bergen, Historisk museum, University of Bergen.

Gustafson, L. 2005. Om kokegrop – kokstinsgrop – kogegrube – jordugn – härdgrop – torkugn – skärvstensgrop, in L. Gustafson, T. Heibreen and J. Martens (eds.), *De gåtefulle kokegroper*, 50–67. Varia 58. Oslo, Universitetets Oldsaksamlings/Kulturhistorisk Museum.

Hagen, A. 1979. ^{14}C metoden i norsk arkeologi, in R. Nydal, S. Westin, U. Hafsten and S. Gulliksen (eds.), *Fortiden i søkelyset. ^{14}C datering gjennom 25 år*, 93–100. Trondheim, Laboratoriet for Radiologisk Datering.

Heibreen, T. 2005. Kokegroper og beslektede teknologier – noen etnografiske eksempler, in L. Gustafson, T. Heibreen and J. Martens (eds.), *De gåtefulle kokegroper* 9–21. Varia 58. Oslo, Universitetets Oldsaksamlings/Kulturhistorisk Museum.

Kræmer, M. B. 2003. Groptufter fra stenalderen på Rødsmoen, ikke i Gråfjellområdet?, in H. R. Amundsen, O. Risbøl and K. Skare (eds.), *På vandring i fortiden. Mennesker og landskap i Gråfjell gjennom 10 000 år*, 45–8. Norsk institutt for kulturminneforskning (NIKU) Tema 7. Oslo, Norsk institutt for kulturminneforskning.

Lannerbro, R. 1992. *Det södra fångstlandet. Katalog Del II, Oreälven*. Stockholm Archaeological Reports, Field Studies 3. Stockholm, University of Stockholm.

Lundberg, Å. 1997. *Vinterbyar – ett bandsamhälles territorier i Norrlands inland 4500–2500 f. Kr.* Studia Archaeologica Universitatis Umensis 8. Umeå, University of Umeå.

Lundin, K. 1992. Kokegropar i Norrbottens kustland. Et försök till tolkning av kokegroparnas funktion. *Arkeologi i Norr* 3, 139–74. Umeå, University of Umeå.

Martens, I. and Hagen, A. 1961. *Arkeologiske undersøkelser langs elv og vann.* Norske Oldfunn X. Oslo, Universitetets Oldsaksamling.

Melander, J. 1986. Torkunar, in *Studier i norrländsk forntid II*, 106–18. Acta Bothniensia occidentalis. Skrifter i västerbottnisk kulturhistoria 8. Umeå, University of Umeå.

Meschke, C. 1967: En norrländsk stenåldersboplats med skärvstensvall. *Antikvariskt arkiv* 31, 1–60.

Mikkelsen, E. 1989. En 6000 år gammel steinalderhytte i Heradsbygd. Vinerkvarter for elg og beverfangst, in *Alfarheim. Årbok for Elverum* 4, 39–54. Oslo, Elverum.

Mikkelsen, E. and Nybruget, P. O. 1975. Jakt og fiske i steinbrukende tid i Hedmark, in *Årbok for Norsk Skogbruksmuseum. Skogbruk, jakt og fiske* 7, 87–112. Oslo, Elverum.

Narmo, L. E. 1996. 'Kokekameratene på Leikvin'. Kult og kokegroper. *Viking* LIX, 79–100.

Odner, K. 1983. *Finner og Terfinner. Etniske prosesser i det nordlige Fenno-Skandinavia.* Occasional Papers in Social Anthropology 9. Oslo, University of Oslo.

Olsen, B. 1985. Arkeologi og etnisitet: et teoretisk og empirisk bidrag, in J. R. Næss (ed.), Arkeologi og etnisitet, 25–31. AmS-Varia 15. Stavanger, Museum of Archaeology.

Risbøl, O., Risan, T., Bjørnstad, R., Fretheim, S. and Rygh, B. H. E. 2002b. *Kulturminner og kulturmiljø i Gråfjell, Regionfelt Østlandet, Åmot kommune i Hedmark. Arkeologiske registreringer 2002, fase 4.* Norsk institutt for kulturminneforskning (NIKU) publikasjoner 125. Oslo, Norsk institutt for kulturminneforskning.

Risbøl, O., Risan, T., Kræmer, M. B., Paulsen, I., Sønsterud, K. E., Swensen, G. and Solem, T. 2002a. *Kulturminner og kulturmiljø i Gråfjell, Regionfelt Østlandet, Åmot kommune i Hedmark. Arkeologiske registreringer 2001, fase 3.* Norsk institutt for kulturminneforskning (NIKU) publikasjoner 116. Oslo, Norsk institutt for kulturminneforskning.

Risbøl, O., Vaage, J., Fretheim, S., Narmo, L. E., Rønne, O., Myrvoll, E. and Nesholen, B. 2001. *Kulturminner og kulturmiljø i Gråfjell, Regionfelt Østlandet, Åmot kommune i Hedmark. Arkeologiske registreringer 2000, fase 2.* Norsk institutt for kulturminneforskning (NIKU) Oppdragsmelding 102. Oslo, Norsk institutt for kulturminneforskning.

Risbøl, O, Vaage, J., Ramstad, M., Narmo, L. E., Høgseth, H. B. and Bjune, A. 2000. *Kulturminner og kulturmiljø i Gråfjell, Regionfelt Østlandet, Åmot kommune i Hedmark, Arkeologiske registreringer 1999, fase 1.* Norsk institutt for kulturminneforskning (NIKU) Oppdragsmelding 93. Oslo, Norsk institutt for kulturminneforskning.

Sandberg, F. (no date). Unpublished report (dnr. 75/98). Dalarnas museums arkiv.

Schaller, E. and Skar, B. 1981. Mesolitikum I Norge: forvaltning eller forskning? *Nicolay Arkeologisk tidsskrift* 34, 14–17.

Stene, K. (ed.) 2004. *Gråfjellprosjektet. Arkeologiske utgravninger i Gråfjellområdet, Åmot kommune, hedmark. Årsrapport 2003.* Oslo, Universitetets kulturhistoriske museer.

Stene, K. (ed.) 2005. *Gråfjellprosjektet. Arkeologiske utgravninger i Gråfjellområdet og ved Rena elv, Åmot kommune, hedmark. Årsrapport 2004.* Oslo, Universitetets kulturhistoriske museer.

Stene, K. (ed.) 2006. *Gråfjellprosjektet. Arkeologiske utgravninger i Gråfjellområdet og ved Rena elv, Åmot kommune, hedmark. Årsrapport 2005.* Oslo, Universitetets kulturhistoriske museer.

Sundlin, H. 1986. Gammal datering från Åsele. *Studier i norrländsk forntid II*, 132–36. Acta Bothniensia occidentalis. Skrifter i västerbottnisk kulturhistoria 8. Umeå, University of Umeå.

Sundquist, L. 1978. Boplatsen Garaselet i norra Västerbotten. *Studier i norrländsk forntid. Till Ernst Westerlund 9, November 1975.* Acta Bothniensia occidentalis. Skrifter i västerbottnisk kulturhistoria 1. Umeå, University of Umeå.

Welinder, S. 1977. *The Mesolithic Stone Age of Eastern Middle Sweden.* Antikvariskt arkiv 65. Stockholm, Kungliga Vitterhets Historie och Antikvitetsakademien.

58. Ynys Enlli: shifting horizons

Mark Edmonds, Robert Johnston, Emily La Trobe-Bateman, John Roberts and Graeme Warren

This paper discusses ongoing research on Ynys Enlli (Bardsey island), north-west Wales. While the island is rich in later Mesolithic material, we argue here that an understanding of its assemblages must take account of the broader currents of contact and identification in which its occupation was situated. These are difficult to address but are likely to have been bound up in traditions of procurement and stone-working at a variety of scales; from the island itself to the broader region of the Irish Sea.

Keywords: Irish Sea, stone-working, mobility, regions, contact.

Introduction

Ynys Enlli is a small island (*c.* 2.5 × 1km) 3km west of the most westerly tip of Pen Llŷn (the Lleyn Peninsula) in north-west Wales (Figure 58.1). The eastern side of the island is dominated by Mynydd Enlli, which rises to a height of 167m. The rest is low-lying and relatively flat. Ynys Enlli has a dense concentration of prehistoric archaeology, with evidence for early settlement surviving on both the mountain slopes and lower lying land (Dawson and Arnold 2002). A pollen core taken from the west of the island in the 1990s was provisionally identified as covering a continuous period from *c.* 7000 cal BC until the present day (Paterson 1994). The results of this work suggest that the low areas of the island were covered by woodland in the early Prehistoric period, with possible clearance in the second millennium cal BC.

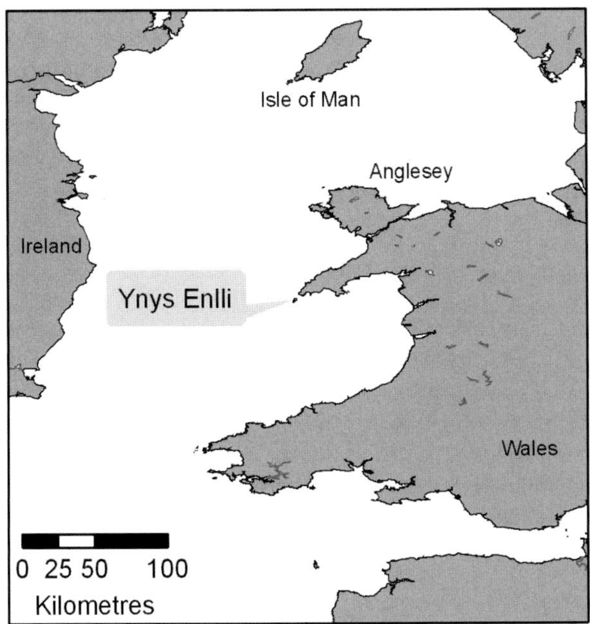

Figure 58.1. General location map showing Ynys Enlli and the Irish Sea region.

The island became an important religious centre in the early Medieval period, and is famous as the reputed burial place of '20,000 Saints'. It was an important place of pilgrimage from at least the early twelfth century. Although close to the mainland, Enlli is separated from it by the treacherous Swnt Enlli (Bardsey Sound), whose fierce tidal patterns make it one of the most difficult stretches of water in the British Isles. Some of the difficulty of the crossing (and the journey through Snowdonia) is suggested by medieval belief that three pilgrimages to Enlli were the equivalent of one to Rome. More mundanely, in three recent seasons of fieldwork, we have never been able to leave the island on the day planned. Sea levels in the Irish Sea have changed significantly, rising from approximately -37mOD at the start of the Holocene, to *c.* -25/30mOD at 8250 cal BC, and -5mOD at *c.* 4000 cal BC (Heyworth and Kidson 1982, see discussion in David and Walker 2004). Swnt Enlli is between 32m and 47m deep (Taylor 2001), and thus Enlli would have been an island from early within the Postglacial. Much of Enlli's present-day appeal to visitors lies in its relative isolation. Still used for religious retreats, the island also attracts those with an interest in ornithology and others who simply wish to 'escape' for a while. While easy to understand, these particular and often romantic *ways of seeing* the island may not be all that helpful for understanding its place in the land/seascapes of the Mesolithic.

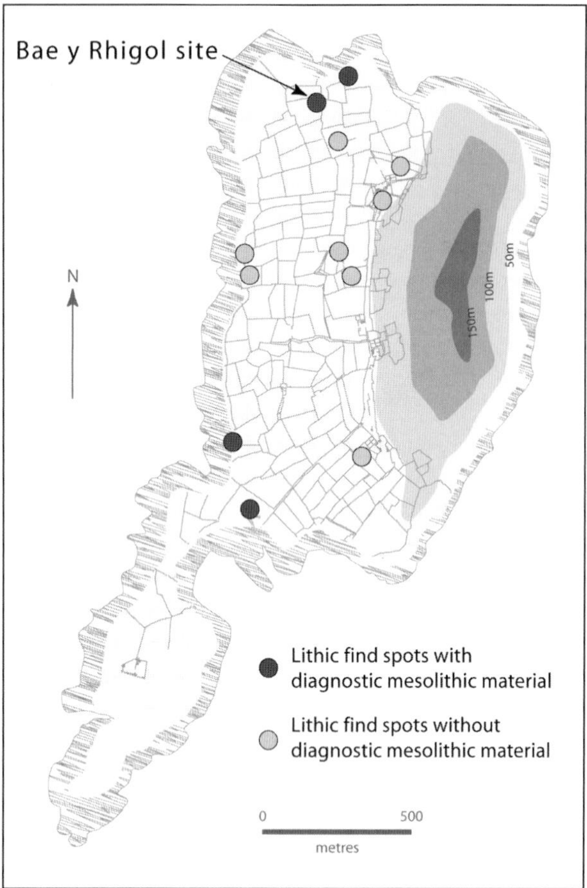

Figure 58.2. Distribution of lithic scatters on Ynys Enlli.

The Mesolithic on Ynys Enlli

Our project began in 2002, when, due to sea conditions, a group of archaeologists (including some of the authors) were stranded on Enlli, and whilst killing time, identified a dense scatter of Mesolithic artefacts in a ploughed field on a raised headland at the northern tip of the island near Bae y Rhigol (Figure 58.2, NGR 21173224). Two further seasons of fieldwork have been carried out; an extensive field survey across the island, and more intensive work, including test-pitting and trial excavation, at Bae y Rhigol. The location today is almost immediately coastal, but the lower sea levels of the Mesolithic must be noted and the contemporary shore is unknown.

With the intensive survey at Bae y Rhigol still to be completed, the full extent of the spread is yet to be established, but it extends over at least 85 × 100m and sampling has provided an assemblage of over 5000 pieces, making it the largest from north-west Wales. Detailed analysis is currently underway, but so far it suggests that the bulk of the material dates to the later Mesolithic (*c.* 8000–4000 cal BC), with a minority of pieces hinting at earlier and later phases of activity. It includes tools and tool components such as scrapers, microliths and simple blades, together with cores, bevel ended tools, hammerstones and waste; in all, a wide range of forms and an equally wide range of stone-working tasks. Diverse raw materials are represented, including till flint, pebble flint, chert, quartz, rock crystal and others. These reflect the use of a number of different sources by Mesolithic communities and at least some of the stone was most likely brought to the island. Building on earlier observations, our more extensive island survey confirmed that this assemblage is far from isolated. Other materials of varying dates, including some Mesolithic artefacts, have been found in a variety of locations across Enlli (Figure 58.2; Dawson and Arnold 2002; Reakes-Williams 1958; Wainwright 1963, 123).

With such a wealth of material and a clear potential in certain places for the survival of sub-surface features, it would be easy to take the island as frame of reference and limit for our work. However, as the presence of 'imported' materials suggests, Enlli was not entirely isolated at the time and needs to be understood in terms of its place within varied regional social geographies. Spend any time on the island and that broader world is difficult to ignore. Pen Llŷn is clearly visible, retreating or appearing close depending on the quality of the light and the wind. Beyond, the mountains of Snowdonia rise in the distance and the coast of Anglesey and much of Pembrokeshire can be picked out. Most strikingly, the setting sun sometimes picks out the very recognisable profiles of several eastern Irish landmarks: Great Sugarloaf, Bray Head, Howth, Djouce and the Wicklow Mountains. In fact, some of the nearest large present-day settlements to Enlli are in Ireland; we listen to Irish radio during our stays and local fishermen 'pop over' to Wicklow for a pint. Those connections are, of course, very much of their time. What remains to be established are the particular ways in which the island was articulated in broader networks during the Mesolithic.

Broader Worlds

Away from Enlli, a Cadw funded review of lithic finds from north-west Wales identifies 26 sites with Mesolithic stonework (Figure 58.3; Smith 2001). Of these, six have Early Mesolithic material only and one has both Early and Late components. The Enlli assemblage is already considerably larger than these documented sites. The collection from the Early Mesolithic site at Trwyn Du, Aberffraw, south Anglesey, a low coastal headland beside a river, consists of several thousand pieces, predominantly débitage but including numerous cores, obliquely blunted broad blade microliths and scrapers as well as two tranchet axes (White 1978). The most extensive later Mesolithic assemblage comes from Bryn Refail, near Abersoch on Pen Llŷn, 20km north-east of Enlli (Ridgway and Leach 1946). This consists of about 1700 pieces of flint and chert, including 11 cores and 30 tools (microliths, scrapers, denticulates and other pieces). The majority of the other assemblages are more modest in size, mostly in the 10s and 100s rather than 1000s of pieces. Many are a consequence of casual surface collection alone; only eight are derived from excavation, systematic collection or trial pitting, and only half of these are the product of work on an intensive scale. The area is predominantly pastureland and ploughing is very limited. Where surface finds have been made they

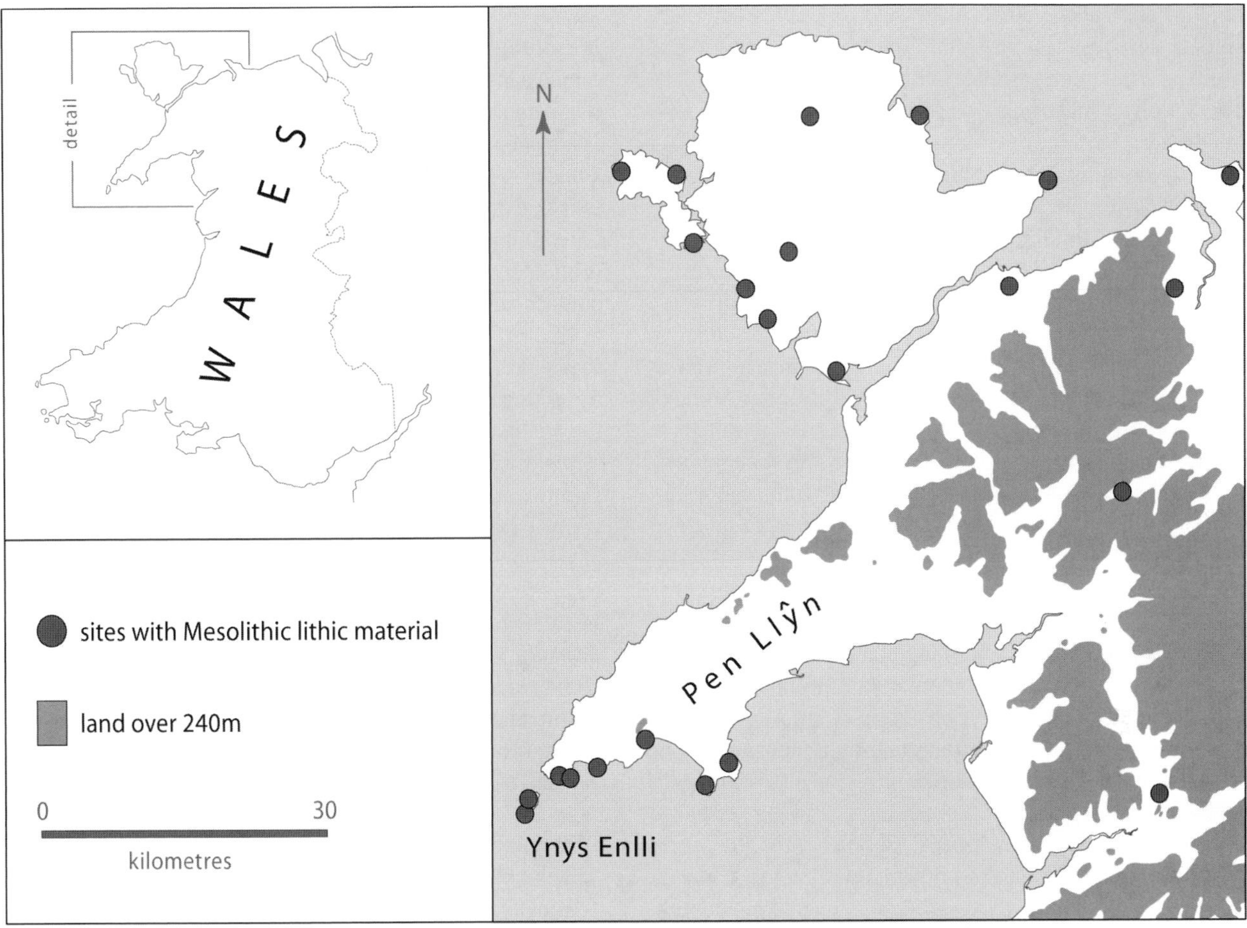

Figure 58.3. Distribution of Mesolithic lithic scatters in north-west Wales.

have usually been from eroded or poached ground or from molehills. There is a concentration of such find spots at the southern tip of Pen Llŷn, directly opposite the north end of Enlli, suggesting that more systematic recovery would probably reveal similar artefact densities to those found at Bae y Rhigol. The bulk of the Mesolithic artefacts recovered from the region are of flint (mostly pebble flint) and chert with occasional rock crystal (Smith 2001). Some assemblages include hammerstones and bevelled pebbles. A single scratch decorated pebble from Llandegai near Bangor (Lynch and Musson 2001) is comparable to six scratched pebbles from Rhuddlan, north-east Wales (Berridge 1994), with possible links to others found in Cornwall (David 2004, 314).

Known Mesolithic find locations in the region are predominantly coastal (17 of the 26 sites, including one cave site). Material is very rare from the upland interior. A group of three sites at Blaenau Dolwyddelan, a valley floor in the mountains of Snowdonia, have produced both Late and Early (small quantities) artefacts (Smith 2001). Besides this, the only other upland find consists of a single artefact from a hillside above the Conwy Valley (Gwynedd Historic Environment Record primary record number 5028). The paucity of upland material is likely to be strongly related to patterns of reconnaissance and recovery. Mesolithic material (particularly later Mesolithic) is well attested in the uplands elsewhere in Wales (e.g. Barton *et al.* 1995), including from Llŷn Aled Isaf (Brassil 1991; Jenkins 1991) and the Brenig Reservoir (Lynch 1993) just outside this area, in north-east Wales. In a broader Welsh context, the setting and character of the site/s on Enlli are not without parallel (Aldhouse-Green 2000; David and Walker 2004; Jacobi 1980). Most sites are dominated by lithics, with little structural evidence, and few faunal assemblages. Many of the larger scatters, the best known perhaps being Nab Head, evidently result from repeated episodes or phases of activity, creating large, diffuse locales which appear to us as palimpsests. Such arguments are not without their problems, not least a tendency to caricature traditions of movement and residence as a repetitive and unchanging cycle (Conneller 2005). That said, the persistent, if periodic, use of certain areas in the face of a variety of landscape changes suggests that some locations were of long-term cultural significance, places with histories that influenced the conduct of later generations (David and Walker 2004, 330).

The Bae y Rhigol 'site' appears at this stage to be very similar. Test-pitting and field-walking together hint at the existence of several concentrations within high-density 'backgrounds', a pattern entirely consistent with models proposed for Nab Head (David and Walker 2004, 330). How far this impression is borne out by further work remains to be seen. What can be said for now is that close similarities between mainland Welsh assemblages and those on Enlli demonstrate traditions of movement and the circulation of materials along the coast and, as elsewhere in southern Britain, over considerable distances. In other words, communities of the time were routinely undertaking relatively difficult sea crossings and most likely coming into contact with others across relatively broad ranges.

As a necessary part of these conditions, patterns of material procurement and stone-working itself were structured at a variety of scales. People worked the stone that they retrieved from deposits on the island, as well as materials carried in from elsewhere. On a clear day, some of the sources, or source areas, for these materials would have been clearly visible, inviting reference and the memory of more extended connections. More fundamentally, broad parallels in the form of reduction sequences in the region suggests an acknowledgement of specific traditions of stone-working – ways of reducing cores or making components – which found echoes across a wide range; preferences for single and opposed platform cores; techniques for snapping blade components and for rejuvenation. Rather than being a simple response to environmental/raw material conditions, these ways of working, however unconsidered, provided a *technology of identification* that evoked connections between scattered communities. In other words, people came to learn, recognise and make choices in stone-working in contexts that overlapped to a fair degree and over considerable distances up and down the coast. Working stone on Enlli certainly satisfied a variety of immediate needs. But it also involved working particular 'pieces of places' and the application of specific forms of *savoir faire*, each of which provided a 'way in' to recognising and thinking about the broader social landscapes of the time.

The idea that we can trace regional traditions in stone-working in the Mesolithic, however blurred, is by no means new. What matters here is that we start asking how those technical conditions were implicated in social reproduction. At this early stage in our work, it is hopefully enough that we are trying to ask the question, but even this begs others. The view from Enlli also draws the eye to the west, across a stretch of water that would have been difficult, but by no means impossible, to navigate. Where does the island sit in relation to the broader currents of the Irish Sea? In many respects, the view west looks rather different. In Ireland, later Mesolithic stone-working takes different forms, with microlithic technologies eschewed in favour of a hard-hammer industry characterised by larger flakes and blades. In a broad sense the later Mesolithic of the Isle of Man is clearly related to the Irish sequences, even if not identical (McCartan 2003). Archaeological attention has often focused on 'Bann Flakes' as a symbol of the Irish Mesolithic, frequently failing to recognise that such pieces have a tight technical definition and do not simply describe all large leaf shaped flakes (see for example, Costa *et al.* 2005; Woodman *et al.* 2006). Simplified understandings of technical differences have fostered the view that contacts across the Irish Sea were essentially rare during the later Mesolithic. In particular, recent discussions, often focused on the adoption of agriculture, have treated the question of contacts across the Irish Sea rather starkly. For example, Julian Thomas critiques arguments for lack of contact from Cooney, Sheridan and Tresset (Cooney 2000, Sheridan 2003, Tresset 2003; Thomas 2004) highlighting a range of ethnographic studies to suggest that material culture divisions are not an effective archaeological identifier of contact or absence thereof. Woodman had argued long ago (1981, 107) for low levels of contact in the context of a viable, self sustaining level of Irish population characterised by endogamous marriage networks: '... contact across the Irish sea is not be any means precluded but rather in terms of social organisation it is at too low a level to alter significantly the traditions of manufacture of stone artefacts which could in part be a product of an unconscious process of self-identification.' Such discussions suggest that a stark opposition between Ireland and Britain fails to do justice to prehistoric realities. However neither Woodman nor Thomas, who argues for substantial levels of interaction (2004), address how we might construct a more nuanced understanding of the material basis of contact over time across the Irish Sea.

Certainly, then, there are significant differences, but there are also parallels that link different regions: the use of bevel-ended tools, or the structured deposition of lithics, especially axes, in watery contexts, general similarities in site location, as well as the rare presence of human bones on shell middens (but see Meiklejohn *et al.* 2005 for arguments that this is a taphonomic phenomenon). Whilst there are clearly issues here about common cultural heritages as opposed to understandings maintained through interaction, such themes allow the possibility of more complex relationships between the peoples of the Irish Sea region. Indeed, material hints of contact remain. For example, in his discussion of a flint core tool from Wigtown, Dumfriess and Galloway, Saville (2003, 346–7) suggests that the piece is likely an Irish import, but is the exception that proves the rule. For him, the two areas should be regarded as separate in the later Mesolithic: 'a rather extraordinary regional difference of population group'. Woodman and colleagues (1997) highlight an interesting long bone from the shell midden at Sutton, Co. Dublin. Initially interpreted as cattle (*Bos taurus*) this dates to the middle of the sixth millennium cal BC. The date for the cattle fragment however is far too early, as domesticated cattle are unknown in northern Europe at this time. The possibility of misidentification is raised, before they argue that the bone 'could perhaps indicate a chance incursion of an aurochs (*Bos primigenius*) from Wales' (Woodman *et al.* 1997, 155). Again, contact is implied. Also in Ireland, the presence of domesticated cattle in a mid- fifth-millennium cal BC context at Ferriter's Cove, Co. Kerry (Woodman *et al.* 1999) is well known.

Most fundamentally, Mesolithic communities on both sides of the Irish Sea appear to have followed similar traditions of landscape occupation, in which movement and the repeated, episodic, use of locations remained important, both on land and on the water. Indeed, the use of islands is a key feature of the Mesolithic of eastern Ireland, from Rathlin to Howth, Lambay and Dalkey: involving scales of movement that encompassed the Isle of Man (McCartan 2000; 2003). Visible from Enlli, the prominent landmarks of eastern Ireland would have also been in striking distance and given this, it is difficult to believe that there was no contact at all across the water (see also Kador 2003 for a similar link between the Scottish coast and north-east Ireland). In any case, the simple fact of intervisibility makes it likely that stories and other frames of reference at the time extended to 'make sense' of these distant hills: places that certainly were no further away than other locations up and down the Welsh coast.

Of course, the simple fact of intervisibility does not itself prove a more substantive connection. The navigation of open water can present a rather different set of problems to patterns of seaborne movement that effectively hugged particular coastlines. Yet Mesolithic communities crossed the Minch to the Western Isles (Gregory *et al.* 2005), and, arguably, were present on Shetland: powerful testimony to skilled sea faring abilities (Warren 2005, 90–3). The potential for movement, however, would have also been seasonally varied, horizons drawing in and pushing out at different times of the year. But it would have been just that, a *potential*, and one that we need to bear in mind when comparing lithic assemblages.

Once again, we do not wish to question the basic idea that technical traditions followed on either side of the Irish Sea display marked differences. While overlaps and parallels can be identified, these differences are profound and, amongst other things, suggest that communities on either side of the water acquired their technical know-how in separate practical traditions: routine tasks, with all of their material requirements, bound people within certain relations to stone tool use. This in turn is highlighted by episodes of deliberate deposition of stone tools in Mesolithic Ireland, seeming to indicate that stone-working was an important facet of wider understandings of the world (Warren 2006). What matters here, however, is that any distinctions between communities within the Irish Sea region were sustained in a world where crossings and communication probably did take place from time to time. Under these circumstances such profound contrasts in the ways that people acted in relation to stone offered a metaphoric (and, on occasion perhaps, a more direct) potential for the recognition of basic differences of identity (see also Woodman 1981, 104 ff.; for one possible model, see Finlay 2003); differences in attitudes towards stone, in knowledge of sources and how to 'go on' around a task: distinctions that cut across the links made by other forms of interaction. Perhaps the key challenge posed by work on Enlli is in how to assess the ways in which routines and regions were integrated, and in understanding how presumably routine journeys in some directions might compare to other horizons that were clearly visible from the island.

Conclusions

Let us be clear (if we can!). Our work is at a very early stage and there is much about Enlli and its broader context that we have yet to explore. Our purpose here has been simply to acknowledge the different scales at which we will need to work, scales which are sensitive to the broader social geographies that people inhabited at the time. More basically, we have argued that a conception of technologies as thoroughly social may be useful for rethinking how relations were reproduced at various scales of social resolution.

Much remains to be done before those rather abstract aspirations can be met. We do not as yet know whether the material at Bae y Rhigol is simply an accumulation of small episodes or a consequence of larger cycles of aggregation. We also have more work to do to establish the broader material conditions in which the island was visited and occupied. This will mean documenting specific patterns of similarity and difference in raw material choices and in technical repertoires over a broad area.

Inevitably, this will take us to a number of places and assemblages along the Welsh coast as well as further inland. It will also mean travelling in the opposite direction. The profound differences between Mesolithic assemblages in Ireland and Wales are certainly important. Like the general absence of large mammals in Ireland at this time, such contrasts are likely to have afforded particular kinds of identification, areas of life through which specific differences could be acknowledged. This does not mean that we are dealing with 'worlds' that were entirely discrete; to assume so would be to step back to some of the cruder models of Culture History. Rather, it suggests that the region was articulated in rather more subtle and varied ways, with overlaps that did not respect a singular, sharp and unbroken line. This should not, perhaps, surprise us. Even now, the national boundaries that often 'blinker' research are far more permeable than governments would have us suppose.

These more tangled conditions are likely to have been significant for the ways that communities thought about different places, about themselves and their relations with others. Amongst other things, they may have featured in stories, in accounts of journeys made or of materials that were circulated. At least some of this was bound up with the working of the stone that we recover and in this respect, at least, there is also an overlap between present and past. While we will have to keep an eye on the task in hand, we will have the other on the horizon.

Acknowledgements

We would like to acknowledge financial support from the Research Centre Wales, the Prehistoric Society, the Cambrian Archaeological Association, and support in kind from the Bardsey Island Trust. We are also very grateful to the inhabitants of Ynys Enlli for their hospitality, especially Dave and Libby Barndon, Patrick and Gwyneth Murphy and Steven and Emma Stansfield. Tom Dawson, Amber

Godwin and Esther Roberts also took part in the fieldwork. George Smith, Gwynedd Archaeological Trust, is thanked for his interest and support. The necessary environmental permissions for the fieldwork were kindly granted by the Countryside Council for Wales. We would like to thank Peter Woodman for comments on this paper.

References

Aldhouse-Green, S. 2000. Palaeolithic and Mesolithic Wales, in F. Lynch, S. Aldhouse-Green and J. Davies (eds.), *Prehistoric Wales*, 1–41. Stroud, Tempus.

Barton, R. N. E., Berridge, P. J., Walker, M. J. C. and Bevins, R. E. 1995. Persistent Places in the Mesolithic Landscape: an example from the Black Mountain Uplands of South Wales. *Proceedings of the Prehistoric Society* 61, 81–116.

Berridge, P. J. 1994. General discussion of the Mesolithic at Rhuddlan, in H. Quinnell and M. P. Blockley with P. J. Berridge, *Excavations at Rhuddlan, Clwyd 1969–1973, Mesolithic to Medieval*, 126–31. Council for British Archaeology (CBA) Research Report 95. York, Council for British Archaeology.

Brassil, K. S. 1991. Mesolithic, in J. Manley, S. Grenter and F. Gale (eds.), *The Archaeology of Clwyd*, 47–54. Mold, Clwyd Archaeology Service.

Cooney, G. 2000. *Landscapes of Neolithic Ireland*. London, Routledge.

Conneller, C. J. 2005. Moving beyond sites: Mesolithic technology in the landscape, in N. Milner and P. C. Woodman (eds.), *Mesolithic Studies at the beginning of the 21st Century*, 42–55. Oxford, Oxbow Books.

Costa, L.-J., Sternke, F. and Woodman, P. C. 2005. Microlith to Macrolith: the reasons behind the transformation of production in the Irish Mesolithic. *Antiquity* 79 (303), 19–33.

David, A. and Walker, E. 2004. Wales During the Mesolithic Period, in A. Saville (ed.), *Mesolithic Scotland and its neighbours: the early Holocene prehistory of Scotland, its British and Irish context and some North European perspectives*, 299–337. Edinburgh, Society of Antiquaries of Scotland.

Dawson, T. and Arnold, C. 2002. *Desk-top Assessment of Ynys Enlli, Gwynedd*. Unpublished report held by the Sites and Monuments Record, Gwynedd Archaeological Trust.

Finlay, N. 2003. Cache and Carry: defining moments in the Irish Later Mesolithic, in L. Bevan and J. Moore (eds.), *Peopling the Mesolithic in a Northern Environment*, 87–94. British Archaeological Reports, International Series S1157. Oxford, Archaeopress.

Gregory, R. A, Murphy, E. M., Church, M. J., Edwards, K. J., Guttmann, E. B. and Simpson, D. A. 2005. Archaeological evidence for the first Mesolithic occupation of the Western Isles of Scotland. *The Holocene* 15, 944–50.

Heyworth, A. and Kidson, C. 1982. Sea-level changes in south west England and Wales. *Proceedings of the Geologists' Association* 93, 91–111.

Jacobi, R. M. 1980. The Early Holocene Settlements of Wales, in J. A. Taylor (ed.), *Culture and Environment in Prehistoric Wales*, 131–206. British Archaeological Reports, British Series 76. Oxford, British Archaeological Reports.

Jenkins, D. A. 1991. The environment: past and present, in J. Manley, S. Grenter and F. Gale (eds.), *The Archaeology of Clwyd*, 13–25. Mold, Clwyd Archaeology Service.

Kador, T. 2003. *Moving off the Beaten Track: mobility as a way of understanding the Mesolithic in northeast Ireland.* Unpublished MA dissertation, University College Dublin.

Lynch, F. M. 1993. *Excavations in the Brenig Valley: A Mesolithic and Bronze Age Landscape in North Wales*. Cambrian Archaeological Monographs 5. Cardiff, Cambrian Archaeological Association.

Lynch, F. M. and Musson, C. R. 2001. A prehistoric and medieval complex at Llandegai, near Bangor, North Wales. *Archaeologia Cambrensis* 150, 17–142.

McCartan, S. B. 2000. The Utilization of Island Environments in the Irish Mesolithic: agendas for Rathlin Island, in A. Desmond, G. Johnson, M. McCarthy, J. Sheehan and E. Shee Twohig (eds.), *New Agendas in Irish prehistory: papers in commemoration of Liz Andersen*, 15–30. Bray, Wordwell Books.

McCartan, S. B. 2003 Mesolithic Hunter-Gatherers in the Isle of Man: adaptations to an island environment?, in L. Larsson, H. Kindgren, K. Knutsson, D. Loeffler and A. Åkerlund (eds.), *Mesolithic on the Move: Papers presented at the Sixth International Conference on the Mesolithic in Europe, Stockholm 2000*, 331–9. Oxford, Oxbow Books.

Meiklejohn, C., Merrett, D. C., Nolan, R. W., Richards, M. P. and Mellars, P. A. 2005. Spatial Relationships, Dating and Taphonomy of the Human Bone from the Mesolithic site of Cnoc Coig, Oronsay, Argyll, Scotland. *Proceedings of the Prehistoric Society* 71, 85–105.

Paterson, D. T. 1994. *The palynology of Holocene organic deposits, Bardsey Island, North Wales*. Unpublished MSc dissertation, University of Wales, Aberystwyth.

Reakes-Williams, J. M. R. 1958. Discovery of flints on Bardsey, in *Report of the Bardsey Bird and Field Observatory* (1958) 6. Bardsey Island, The Bardsey Bird and Field Observatory.

Ridgway, M. H. and Leach, G. B. 1946. Prehistoric flint workshop site near Abersoch, Caernarvonshire. *Archaeologia Cambrensis* 99, 78–84.

Saville, A. 2003. Indications of Regionalisation in Mesolithic Scotland, in L. Larsson, H. Kindgren, K. Knutsson, D. Loeffler and A. Åkerlund (eds.), *Mesolithic on the Move: Papers presented at the Sixth International Conference on the Mesolithic in Europe, Stockholm 2000*, 340–50. Oxford, Oxbow Books.

Sheridan, A. 2003. French Connections I: spreading the marmites thinly, in I. Armit, E. Murphy, E. Nelis and D. Simpson (eds.), *Neolithic Settlement in Western Britain*, 3–17. Oxford, Oxbow Books.

Smith, G. 2001. *North West Wales Lithic Scatters Project: Evaluation of the Early Prehistoric Landscape through Lithic Finds*. Gwynedd Archaeological Trust Report 357. Unpublished report, Gwynedd Archaeological Trust.

Taylor, D. 2001. *The Lundy and Irish Sea Pilot*. Huntingdon, Imray, Laurie, Norie and Wilson.

Thomas, J. 2004. Current Debates on the Mesolithic-Neolithic transition in Britain and Ireland. *Documenta Praehistorica* 31, 113–30.

Tresset, A. 2003. French Connections II: of cows and men, in I. Armit, E. Murphy, E. Nelis and D. Simpson (eds.), *Neolithic Settlement in Western Britain*, 18–30. Oxford, Oxbow Books.

Wainwright, G. J. 1963. A Reinterpretation of the Microlithic Industries of Wales. *Proceedings of the Prehistoric Society* 29, 99–132.

Warren, G. M. 2005. *Mesolithic Lives in Scotland*. Stroud, Tempus.

Warren, G. M. 2006. Technology, in C. J. Conneller and G. M. Warren (eds.), *Mesolithic Britain and Ireland: new approaches*, 13–34. Stroud, Tempus.

White, R. B. 1978. Excavations at Trwyn Du, Anglesey, 1974. *Archaeologia Cambrensis* 127, 16–39.

Woodman, P. C. 1981. The Post-Glacial Colonization of Ireland: The Human Factors, in D. Ó Corráin (ed.), *Irish Antiquity: Essays and Studies Presented to Professor M. J. O'Kelly*, 93–110. Cork, Tower Books.

Woodman, P. C., Anderson, E. and Finlay, N. 1999. *Excavations at Ferriter's Cove 1983–1995: Last Foragers, First Farmers in the Dingle Peninsula*. Bray, Wordwell.

Woodman, P. C., Finlay, N. and Anderson, E. 2006. *The archaeology of a collection: the Keiller-Knowles collection of the National Museum of Ireland.* National Museum of Ireland Monograph Series 2. Bray, Wordwell.

Woodman, P. C., McCarthy, M. and Monaghan, N. 1997. The Irish Quaternary fauna project. *Quaternary Science Reviews* 16, 129–59.

59. In the middle, not in between: Svärdbäraren in its regional context

Jenny Holm

Mesolithic Sweden has been considered as being divided into a western district where flint was used for tool making, and a north-eastern district where people used quartz. The borderline between these two main areas, drawn between raw materials, has been looked upon as reflecting a cultural border. However if we consider other aspects of material culture during the Mesolithic period, such as the use of microblades, different geographic units will appear. Microblades and microblade cores, especially handle cores, were widely spread. They are present over the entire circumpolar area, and from northern Germany to the Arctic Ocean. Since microblades were created from several local raw materials, especially where quartz was dominant, it is possible to identify smaller areas in which a specific raw material was used. These two geographic levels may have had a practical meaning for the individuals who lived during the Mesolithic: a comprehensive level which reveals an extensive circle of contacts, making it possible for technological ideas to spread over a great distance, and a lower level which relates directly to the individuals, and recognisable through the limited spread of certain raw materials.

Keywords: regionality, ethnicity, find-spread, handle cores, raw material.

A small starting point

Some years ago, we undertook a small excavation at a Mesolithic site called Svärdbäraren, situated in the middle of Sweden. During the excavation we had no reason to believe that the site would not fit the typical archaeological models presented by current research. However, by the end we felt that the site in some respects fell outside them, positioned between different geographical units. We also felt that this 'in between' situation might have had something to do with the location – halfway between Swedish university boundaries. The Svärdbäraren site is firmly located in the middle of the Swedish landmass, at a point just between the east and west coasts. By chance, the site is also situated between, but at some distance from, the main university towns of Sweden: Umeå, Uppsala, Stockholm, Gothenburg, and Lund. Researchers connected to one or other university have, more often than not, used their own region as a starting point, and proceeding from there to the other district: central Sweden has rarely been the focus of archaeological attention (Figure 59.1). In addition, the site may also be seen as one lying between the flint-based culture groups of Hensbacka, Sandarna and Lihult, along the west coast, and the quartz-dominated culture along the Swedish east coast.

Excavations at Svärdbäraren were not extensive, with just a small percentage of the area being examined in any detail. The site, the location of several finds of round-butted axes, has been estimated to cover about 20,000m^2. Our excavations looked at only 300m^2. The finds were not extraordinary, revealing the usual flakes, quartz debris, flint, and various local rocks. Some small scrapers of quartz and some microblades of Cambrian flint were identified. There were a few pieces of burnt bone from beaver (*Castor fiber*), red deer (*Cervus elaphus*), and fish (perch (*Perca*) and pike (*Esox*)). Some of the burnt bones have been radiocarbon-dated to the Middle Mesolithic, 6440–6250 cal BC (7510±75 BP; Ua-26173).

The location now seems to be near the Mesolithic eastern coast, but at the time our site was inhabited, postglacial land elevation had shifted it far inland and it actually lay west of the watershed dividing Sweden in a north-south direction. This land area was once situated on the west coast, prior to the time of our site (Figure 59.2). Seen in a more local perspective, the site was situated midway between the Great Lake Vänern in the west and the Ancylus Lake in the east. The site was located along the north shore of a large lake, Möckeln, midway between the two rivers of Timsälven and Svartälven. The lake and the surrounding area could be easily seen from a high escarpment at the eastern end of the site. The vicinity must have been both a central and advantageous one. The River Letälven took the water from Lake Möckeln southwards to Lake Skagern, and then on to

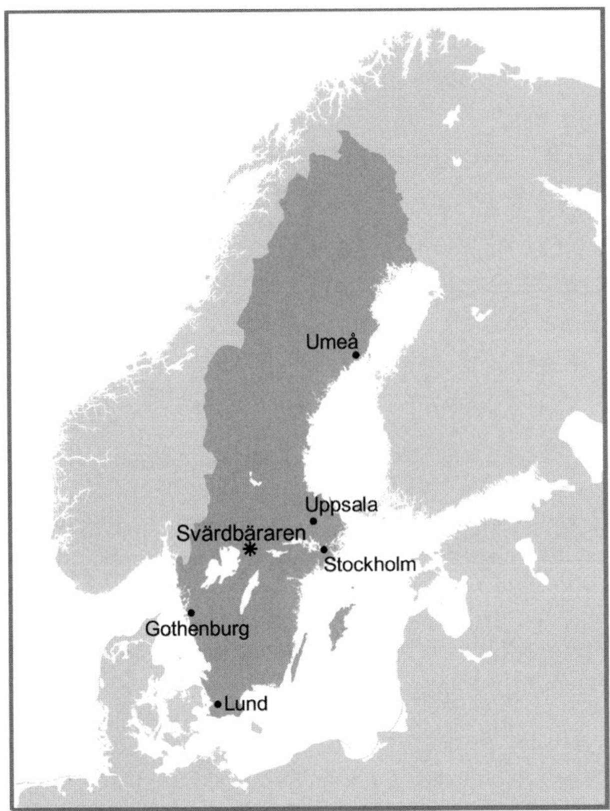

Figure 59.1. The location of the site at Svärdbäraren and the main Swedish universities.

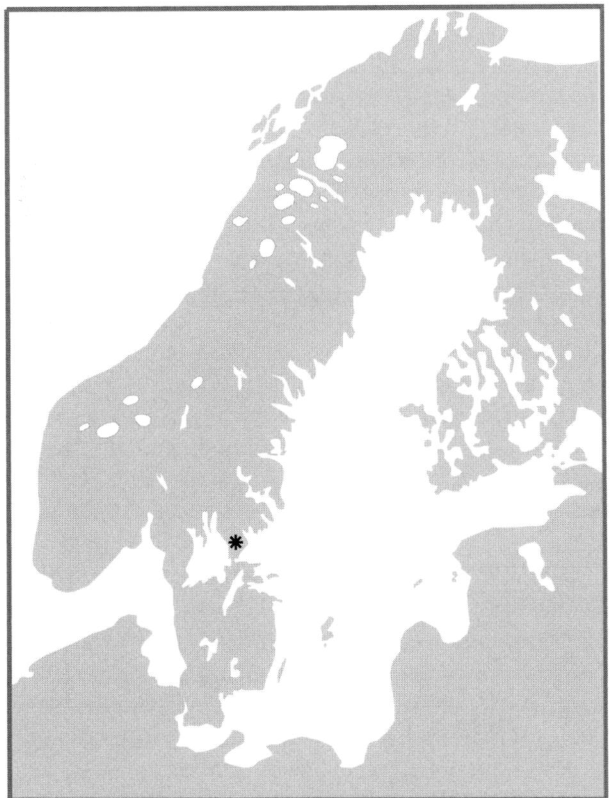

Figure 59.2. The land/water divide during the time of the Ancylus Lake, which is today converted into the Baltic Sea. The asterisk shows the location of the Svärdbäraren site.

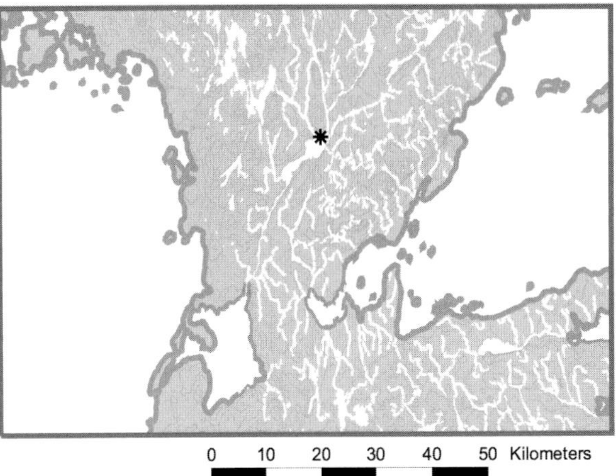

Figure 59.3. A closer view of the location of the Svärdbäraren site, situated between Lake Vänern in the west, which was then much bigger than today, and the Ancylus Lake in the east. The asterisk shows the location of the Svärdbäraren site.

Lake Vänern; en route were the rapids at Degerfors, which must have provided good fishing (Figure 59.3).

Earlier thoughts about Mesolithic regions, as seen in the material culture

In 1977, Stig Welinder attempted to classify the Mesolithic period in eastern-central Sweden. He identified two parallel groups: one that used only quartz, and another, which, besides also using quartz, made microblades from flint and flint-like materials. Welinder considered the use of microblades made of flint-like materials as representing influences from the south-west. One of the more lasting results from his study is the separation of quartz-users in the east from flint-users in the west. The same division for central and southern Sweden was made by Agneta Åkerlund in her PhD dissertation in 1996. Now, however, the picture has developed somewhat with the recognition of a small area wedged in from the north, with an unmentioned northern culture, between the world of flint and the world of quartz (Åkerlund 1996). Lars Larsson (2003) developed the same theme further still at MESO 2000 (The Sixth International Conference on The Mesolithic in Europe, Stockholm). Among other observations, he pointed out that quartz was used all the way down to Scania in the south, and that quartz did occur, more often then was earlier believed, west and south of the border that Stig Welinder introduced initially. Larsson also mentioned other remains, the distribution of which could be used in detecting regions, e.g. microliths, stone axes, and rock art (paintings). When he combined certain artefacts, which he believed had more than a functional value, he found a three-fold division (Figure 59.4).

This border between a quartz culture and a flint culture coincides with a border of sorts between the universities. The departments of archaeology at the universities of Lund and Gothenburg and the universities of Uppsala and Stockholm,

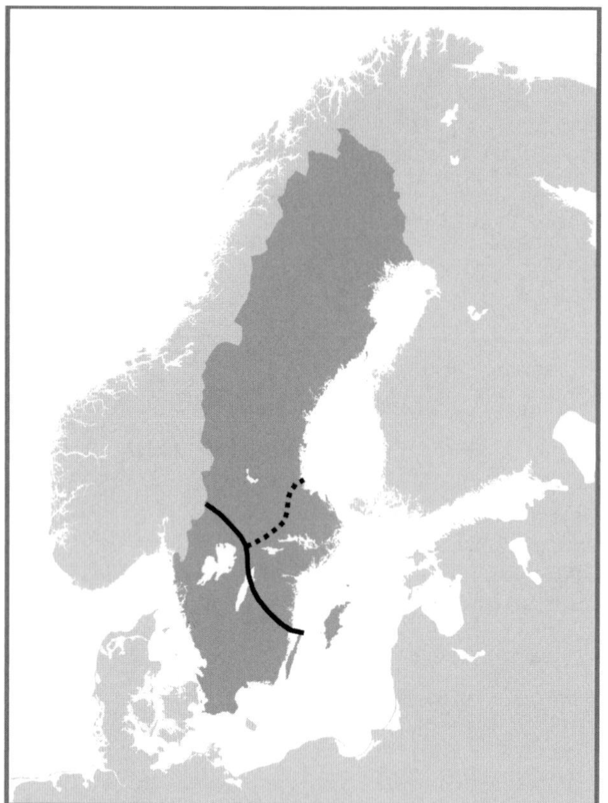

Figure 59.4. The solid line shows the border between quartz and flint, as presented by Welinder, and the border between those areas with Larsson's combinations axes – microblades – microliths in the southwest, and axes – microblades in the east. The broken line shows the border between an eastern area where Larsson's combination axes–microblade are to be found, and an area in the north where only microblades are present. The Svärdbäraren site is situated where the two lines join. (After Welinder 1977; Åkerlund 1996; Larsson 2003).

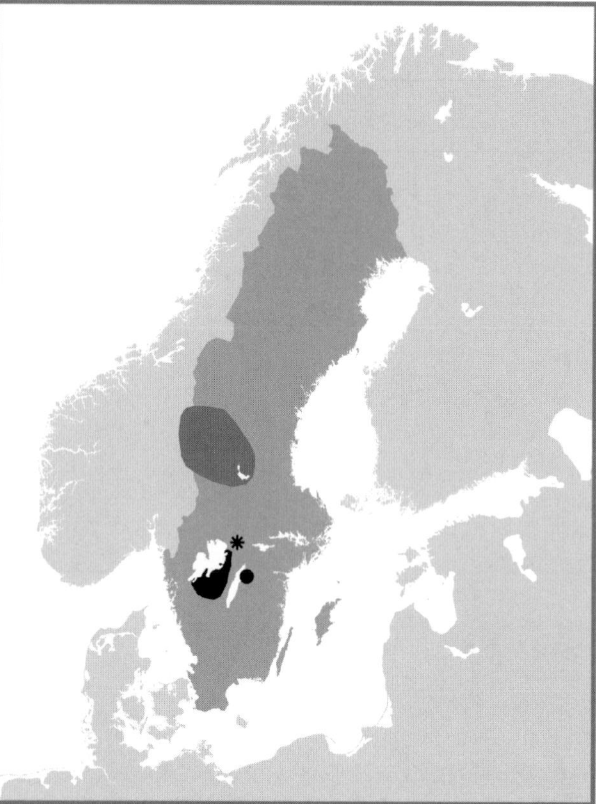

Figure 59.5. The dark grey area shows where jasper was used for making microblades, and the black area shows where Cambrian flint was used. The black dot marks the location of Motala, and the asterisk shows the location of the Svärdbäraren site. (After Sjurseike 1994; Kindgren 1991).

between themselves, have created a boundary similar to the one believed to have existed in the Mesolithic.

The microblades used by Larsson in his division of modern Sweden into Mesolithic regions may also be seen as the spread of handle cores presented by Kjel Knutsson. The entire peninsular of Scandinavia is united by microblades, and the technological unit sometimes referred to as the 'handle-core complex' (Knutsson 1993, 41). Handle cores are present all over the circumpolar area, as well as from northern Germany in the south, to the Arctic Ocean in the north (Olofsson 1995, 1). It is also possible to use handle cores to distinguish the smaller units that appear when studying the spread of certain raw materials used in making these microblades. There is, for example, an area with jasper that has been studied by Ragnhild Sjuseike (1994), and an area with Cambrian flint, studied by Hans Kindgren (1991). The areas in which these raw materials were used for microblades vary considerably in area. Jasper is found in a region of about 70,000km^2, and Cambrian flint mainly within an area of 5000km^2. But the Cambrian flint area may have been much larger, including areas to the east, towards the modern-day town of Motala, and the Mesolithic site at the rapids of Motala, where microblades of Cambrian flint were made. This area, where few finds are known, is today, to a large extent, densely forested, but there have recently been new discoveries of Cambrian flints there (Pettersson and Wikell 2006; Pettersson 2006) (Figure 59.5).

An argument used by Stig Welinder in his division of Sweden into two districts was the distribution of round-butted axes. Round-butted axes are more common in eastern-central Sweden, but their distribution may also show possible smaller regional units (Figure 59.6). Another clue for the possible detection of smaller regional units is the use of macroblade technology, as presented by Per Falkenström (2003).

Ways of understanding regional patterns through find-spread

How can those geographic regions, as seen by archaeologists in the variations of raw material and technology be understood? And where does the Svärdbäraren site fit in, sitting as it does on the borderline between different areas, as in the examples given above? The find-spread we see could be the result of two factors in particular: geographical distance, or behaviour reflecting group identity.

The geographical aspect is, of course, important: flint is more common in use along the west coast of Sweden,

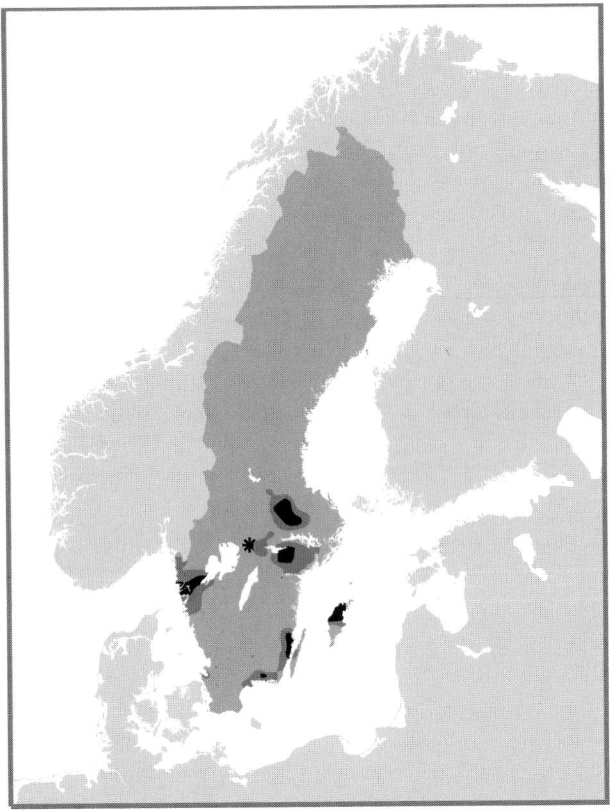

Figure 59.6. Concentrations of round-butted axes. The dark grey represents more than 20 axes per district, and the black more than 50 axes per district. The asterisk shows the location of the Svärdbäraren site. (After Forsberg and Larsson 1994, 13).

where it is found as cobbles along the shore, whereas the easily accessible quartz was used in eastern and northern Sweden. But there is no sharp boundary between these regions. It has long been recognised that flint slowly found its way into the north and east, and it has, in recent years, been evident that quartz is also to be found in areas where flint is dominant. The significance of distance may probably be more distinct when it comes to local raw materials, available in one specific place.

In those areas where it has been possible to delimit a smaller geographic unit with the help of a specific raw material, it has been clear that the source in which the rock material was found was of importance. For the jasper and Cambrian flint mentioned earlier, the source was not in the centre of the find-spread. For the jasper, the quarry was situated close to the western fringe: other factors than distance must have come into play as regards its distribution. Knowledge of the quarry was probably one of the more important factors; only those who knew where it was located could use it.

As an explanation to help delimit distribution of specific raw materials, the concept of ethnic grouping has also been used. Knut Andreas Bergsvik has claimed that a sharp break in the spread of a raw material marks a border, whereas a slow decrease in the number of artefacts found is natural because of the cost of transportation (Bergsvik 2003). It could be argued, on the other hand, that an ethnic border may be a precise one even if territorial borders were indistinct and groups overlapped. Decreasing distribution, and an overlap in the spread of artefacts in local raw materials, will show on undefined borders between territories, but group identity may still have been clear. Time also affects the definition of a border: territorial boundaries probably shifted in the way today's national borders do.

Fredrik Barth's definition (1994) of ethnicity, where common values are essential, does not help us as archaeologists to understand the distribution of artefacts. Things may be connected to ethnic identity, but they do not *have* to be. Genetic similarity does not create group identity, but group identity may create genetic similarity, i.e. through the choice of whom you marry (see Welinder 2003). Artefact distribution is, in the same way, created by choice, through common behaviour within a group. Similarity in the choice of raw materials, or the morphology of the tools, does not show group identity, but it arises as a consequence of it. A tool maker moving to a new group may impact differently on the find-spread than were a tool user to do so. A craft learned resides more in your hands than your mind (see Graner and Larsson 2004), so it may be difficult to change the way you work. The way you make your microblades will be the same wherever you end up: it is the raw material that changes. It may take time to get familiar with new rock, but any unfamiliarity may not be readily apparent among the finds.

Mobility over great distances, with many changes between the groups you inherently felt part of, ought to result in a more vague ethnic identity. Should microblades and handle cores be seen in these terms? Technologies were similar over large areas because practitioners showed great mobility during their lifetime. As outlined above, several researchers have identified specific regions where different cultures chose to meet. I would put it rather that these identifications are not special meeting places, but illustrations that the practice of travelling far and meeting others was very common and of great importance in Mesolithic society.

Conclusions

The handle-core complex reflects common values and symbols connected to microblades and their manufacture and use. These values have been the same regardless of whether flint or quartz was used for all other tools. The manufacture of microblades seems, to this author, to be the most important factor. There is a connection between microblades and handle cores occurring over such a wide area, and the restricted spread of, for example, jasper and Cambrian flint. The symbolic value of those artefacts was greater than others. It demonstrates unity through a common technology, and separation through variation in raw materials. It may be that the great difference between western Sweden, with only flint, and eastern Sweden, with quartz, was of little importance in reality. It was the overall structure, the handle-core complex, and the smaller territories that are sometimes identifiable through certain

Figure 59.7. View over Lake Möckeln from the Svärdbäraren site.

raw materials, which were meaningful to individuals living in the Mesolithic.

Our site, Svärdbäraren, has a distinct situation; it is at the same time on the fringe of Cambrian flint distribution, on the fringe of an area with meta-volcanic rocks, east of the main area for flint, on the western part of the east-central Swedish quartz area, and perhaps in the southern region of a north Swedish Stone Age wedged down into the area of this site (Figure 59.7). However, it is also certainly right in the centre of the handle-core complex. I believe that the distribution of certain artefacts and raw materials *does* signify something, and that it is possible that today's administration and university structure may have had some influence on the way we look at possible borders, as, for example, with the separation of flint-users and quartz-users, which may have been over-emphasized. Still the main question remains: did the people who lived in the Mesolithic feel that they were close to a border when they reached the point where we today recognize a border between different kinds of artefacts, or, did they feel they were in the centre of their reality?

References

Barth, F. 1969. Introduction, in F. Barth (ed.), *Ethnic Groups and Boundaries. The Social Organization of Culture Difference*, 9–38. Oslo, Universitetsforlaget.

Bergsvik, K. A. 2003. Mesolithic Ethnicity – To Hard to Handle?, in L. Larsson, H. Kindgren, K. Knutsson, D. Loeffler and A. Åkerlund (eds.), *Mesolithic on the Move: Papers presented at the Sixth International Conference on the Mesolithic in Europe, Stockholm 2000*, 290–301. Oxford, Oxbow Books.

Falkenström, P. 2003. Mesolithic territorial behaviour in Central Scandinavia and adjacent regions, in L. Larsson, H. Kindgren, K. Knutsson, D. Loeffler and A. Åkerlund (eds.), *Mesolithic on the Move: Papers presented at the Sixth International Conference on the Mesolithic in Europe, Stockholm 2000*, 316–22. Oxford, Oxbow Books.

Forsberg, L. and Larsson, L. 1994. Tidiga fångstkulturer, in K.-G. Selinge (ed.), *Kulturminnen och kulturmiljövård*, 10–15. Stockholm, Sveriges Nationalatlas.

Graner, G. and Larsson, Å. M. 2004. Tredje gruppen och andra blandformer. Keramiska traditioner och strategier vid slutet av mellanneolitikum, in J. Holm (ed.), *Neolitiska nedslag, arkeologiska uppslag*, 107–40. Arkeologiska Undersökningar, Skrifter 59. Stockholm, Riksantikvarieämbetet.

Kindgren, H. 1991. Kambrisk flinta och etniska grupper i Västergötlands mesolitikum, in H. Browall, P. Persson and K.-G. Sjögren (eds.), *Västsvenska stenåldersstudier*, 33–69. Gotarc Series C, 8. Göteborg, Göteborgs Universitet, Institutionen för arkeologi.

Knutsson, K. 1993. Garaselet–Lappviken–Rastklippan. Introduktion till en discussion om Norrlands Äldsta Bebyggelse. *Tor* 25, 5–51.

Larsson, L. 2003. The Mesolithic of Sweden in retrospective and progressive perspective, in L. Larsson, H. Kindgren, K. Knutsson, D. Loeffler and A. Åkerlund (eds.), *Mesolithic on the Move: Papers presented at the Sixth International Conference on the Mesolithic in Europe, Stockholm 2000*, xxii-xxxii. Oxford, Oxbow Books.

Olofsson, A. 1995. *Kölskrapor, mikrospånkärnor och mikrospån. En studie med utgångspunkt i nordsvensk mikrospånteknik.* Arkeologiska studier vid Umeå universitet 3. Umeå, Institutionen för arkeologi, Umeå universitet.

Pettersson, O. 2006. *Riksväg 49. Stubbetorp-Rude. Närke, Askersunds och Hammars socknar: särskild arkeologisk utredning, etapp 1 och 2.* Örebro, UV Bergslagen, Avdelningen för arkeologiska undersökningar, Riksantikvarieämbetet.

Pettersson, M. and Wikell, R. 2006. Såg någon människa Närkesundet? På spaning i Tiveden efter pionjärer för 11000 år sedan, in J. Holm (ed.), *Blick för Bergslagen*. Årsbok 2006, 39–46. Örebro, UV Bergslagen, Avdelningen för arkeologiska undersökningar, Riksantikvarieämbetet.

Sjurseike, R. 1994. *Jaspisbruddet i Flendalen. En kilde til forståelse av sosiale relationer i eldre steinalder.* Avhandling til magistergraden i nordisk arkeologi. Avdelning for nordisk arkeologi. IAKN. Universitetet i Oslo.

Welinder, S. 1977. *The Mesolithic Stone Age of Eastern Middle Sweden.* Antikvariskt arkiv 65. Stockholm, Almqvist & Wiksell International.

Welinder, S. 2003. *DNA, etnicitet, folk och folkvandringar.* Göteborg, Bricoleur Press.

Wikell, R. and Pettersson, M. (in press). Stenålder i Tiveden, in J. Holm (ed.), *Blick för Bergslagen, 2006.*

Åkerlund, A. 1996. *Human Responses to Shore Displacement. Living by the Sea in Eastern Middle Sweden during the Stone Age.* Arkeologiska Undersökningar, Skrifter 16. Stockholm, Riksantikvarieämbetet.

60. 'Foreign in origin and local in pattern': Mesolithic pottery around the Baltic Sea

Fredrik Hallgren

While the first occurrence of pottery in some parts of Europe is associated with the spread of farming, the oldest pottery along the eastern shores of the Baltic Sea appeared in hunter-gatherer contexts in the centuries before 5000 cal BC. Within a rather short time span hunter-gatherer communities in the whole region, from northern Finland and north-easternmost Norway in the north, to northern Poland and Germany in the south, adopted ceramic technology. Although foreign in origin the Mesolithic pottery of the eastern Baltic Sea region is also distinctly local in pattern, and can thus be viewed as an example of an indigenized cultural practice.

Keywords: Mesolithic pottery, ceramic technology, culture, cultural practice, communities of practice.

Introduction

The theme of this paper is Mesolithic pottery in the region around the Baltic Sea. The term 'Mesolithic' is here used in accordance with the chronological system of south and central Scandinavia, and refers to the time before the introduction of agriculture. I shall start with explaining my interest in Mesolithic pottery. My main research concerns the Early Neolithic Funnel-beaker Culture (TRB) in Mälardalen, in eastern central Sweden. In Mälardalen, ceramic technology first appeared accompanied by domestic animals and plants around 4000/3900 cal BC. As I have argued elsewhere, I see this as a case of local 'aceramic' hunter-gatherers, adopting new technologies and new ways of subsistence (Hallgren 2003). Immediately to the north of the TRB of Mälardalen, there lived hunter-gatherers of the North Scandinavian Slate Culture, who did not adopt agriculture or pottery during the Early Neolithic. In central Scandinavia, there thus formed a border between part-time farmers with pottery to the south, and hunter-gatherers without pottery to the north (Hallgren, in press).

At first glance this picture seems clear-cut, and disturbingly in accordance with stereotypes of hunter-gatherers and farmers. However, while pottery was absent in Mälardalen during the Late Mesolithic, the hunter-gatherers living immediately to the east, in the archipelago of Åland (Finland), had adopted pottery already around 5000 cal BC. During the Late Mesolithic there thus was a contrast between hunter-gatherers with pottery to the east, and hunter-gatherers without pottery to the west. This early ceramic tradition, Sperrings 1 (or Early Older Comb Ware), has been given surprisingly little attention in Sweden, or indeed anywhere outside Finland.

As will be discussed below, the Sperrings 1 pottery of Åland, is but one of several rather distinct types of pottery that appeared along the eastern shores of the Baltic Sea, and in the eastern part of the Nordkalotten, in the centuries before or around 5000 cal BC (Figure 60.1). None of the craft traditions in question represent independent invention of ceramic technology, rather they are examples of local adaptations of acquired technology, crafts that were learned from neighboring groups to the east (Nuñez 1990; Timofeev and Zaitseva 1997, 17). The Mesolithic pottery around the Baltic Sea can therefore be viewed as examples of what Marshall Sahlins has discussed as 'culture ... foreign in origin and local in pattern...' (Sahlins 2000, 515). To the extent that these traditions really differ, they do so because they were created anew in the local communities of practice where the crafts were learned, taught, modified and reproduced. I will return to this topic at the end of the paper, but first I will devote some space to the early pottery of Late Mesolithic Åland.

The Late Mesolithic pottery of Åland

The Åland archipelago of the Late Mesolithic period can be described as a scatter of small islands and skerries; the distance to the nearest islands on both the Swedish and Finnish side of the Baltic was about 100km of open – or ice covered – water (Stenbäck 2003, 85). The geographical conditions, as well as the osteological material from the early settlement sites, indicate that there was an abundance of seals in the archipelago; likely seal hunting was one of the main reasons for people to visit these offshore islands.

In my case study of Sperrings 1 pottery I have focused

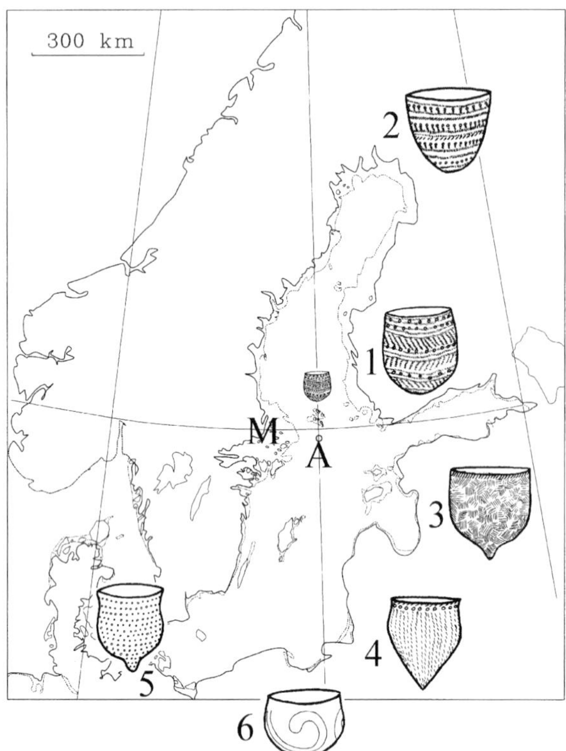

Figure 60.1. Early ceramic traditions around the Baltic Sea c. 5000 cal BC. Legend – Å: the Åland archipelago; M: Mälardalen; 1: Sperrings 1 pottery; 2: Säräisniemi 1 pottery; 3: Narva pottery; 4: Neman pottery; 5: Ertebölle pottery; 6: Linear Band pottery (not discussed in this paper). Note that Säräisniemi 1 pottery has a further distribution beyond the map in north-easternmost Norway, northernmost Finland and north-western Russia. (Shoreline map after Munthe 1940).

on the sites of Östra Jansmyra I and Vargstensslätten II, two settlements located on an island, 3km across, in the eastern part of the Late Mesolithic archipelago of Åland. The find materials on these sites is dominated by pottery sherds and knapped rhyolite, but also contain knapped quartz, stone axes, polishing stones, and bones from seal (Alhonen and Väkeväinen 1981; Andersson 1990; Dreijer 1941; Nuñez 1986; Nuñez and Storå 1992; Stenbäck 2003; Väkeväinen 1979). The Åland sites are the westernmost finds of Sperrings 1 pottery, which otherwise has a distribution that encompasses mainland Finland and parts of north-western Russia. Sperrings 1 pottery is characterised by un-profiled pots with a round or pointed base; the clay is tempered with crushed rock or sand. The vessels have surface covering decoration from rim to base; the common elements are twisted cord-stamp, drag and stab, incised lines, and different stamps (Figure 60.2). As a rule, all vessels also have pit-impressions, applied on top of other decorations. The decoration is alternately applied in horizontal, vertical, or diagonal position, forming horizontal or vertical zones around the vessel. Some of the vessels have been painted red (Alhonen and Väkeväinen 1981; Dreijer 1941; Edgren 1982; 1992; Europaeus 1927; Nuñez 1990; Väkeväinen 1979; Äyräpää 1956).

The pottery from Östra Jansmyra and Vargstensslätten was made of a clay not available in the archipelago. Thus either the ceramic vessels, or the clay for pottery manufacture, were transported from the mainland to Åland (Alhonen and Väkeväinen 1981). The fauna assemblages from the different Sperrings 1 sites on Åland are dominated by different seal species. At Östra Jansmyra only ringed seal (*Phoca hispida*) was found, whereas Vargstensslätten is dominated by bones from grey seal (*Halichoerus grypus*) (Väkeväinen 1979). The ringed seal was probably hunted on the ice during breeding in late winter, while the grey seal was perhaps hunted in open water during summer (cf. Storå 2001, 31–5, 46). Possibly different settlements were in use during different seasons, most likely by task-groups from the Finnish mainland (Welinder 1977; Alhonen and Väkeväinen 1981).

To evaluate the chronological position of the Sperrings 1 tradition on Åland, organic crust on sherds of pottery from Östra Jansmyra I and Vargstensslätten II was dated (Figure 60.2; cf. Hallgren 2004). The dates cluster around 6000 BP (uncalibrated). As the sites in question are seal hunting camps, the crusts likely contain marine products and the ^{14}C dates may therefore be affected by a reservoir effect. The reservoir effect has been estimated to be about 100 years on the coast of nearby eastern central Sweden during the saline maximum of the Subboreal (Middle Neolithic) Littorina phase of the Baltic Sea (Segerberg *et al.* 1991, 86; cf. Eriksson 2004, 151–2). During the freshwater Ancylus Lake stage of the Baltic Sea (Middle Mesolithic), the reservoir effect was considerably lower than during the succeeding Littorina phase (Lindqvist and Possnert 1997, 73; 1999, fig. 17).

Around 5000 cal BC there were rapid fluctuations in the salinity of the Baltic, ranging from fresh to brackish water; salinity during these brackish stages was lower than that of the Subboreal (Emeis *et al.* 2003). This imply that the reservoir effect in the waters around Åland may have varied from close to zero to roughly 100 years during this time. The δ^{13}C values of the dated crusts vary between -24.8 and -26.8‰, values that do not indicate a pronounced saline environment (cf. Eriksson 2004, table 3, 4; Katzenberg *et al.* 2000, 5–8; Lindqvist and Possnert 1999, 79; van Klinken *et al.* 2000, 47). Together this suggests that the ^{14}C dates are probably fairly accurate. The calibrated age of the dates from Östra Jansmyra I and Vargstensslätten II is about 5000 cal BC (Figure 60.3). The results are in accordance with ^{14}C dates from Sperrings 1 sites on mainland Finland and in Karelia and Ingermanland of western Russia (Hallgren 2004; Hallgren, in press).

Mesolithic pottery around the Baltic Sea

As mentioned above, Sperrings 1 was only one of several ceramic traditions that appeared on the eastern shores of the Baltic around or slightly before 5000 cal BC (Figure 60.1). In the following I will give a short description of each of these traditions based on information in the available literature. Associated ^{14}C dates are displayed in

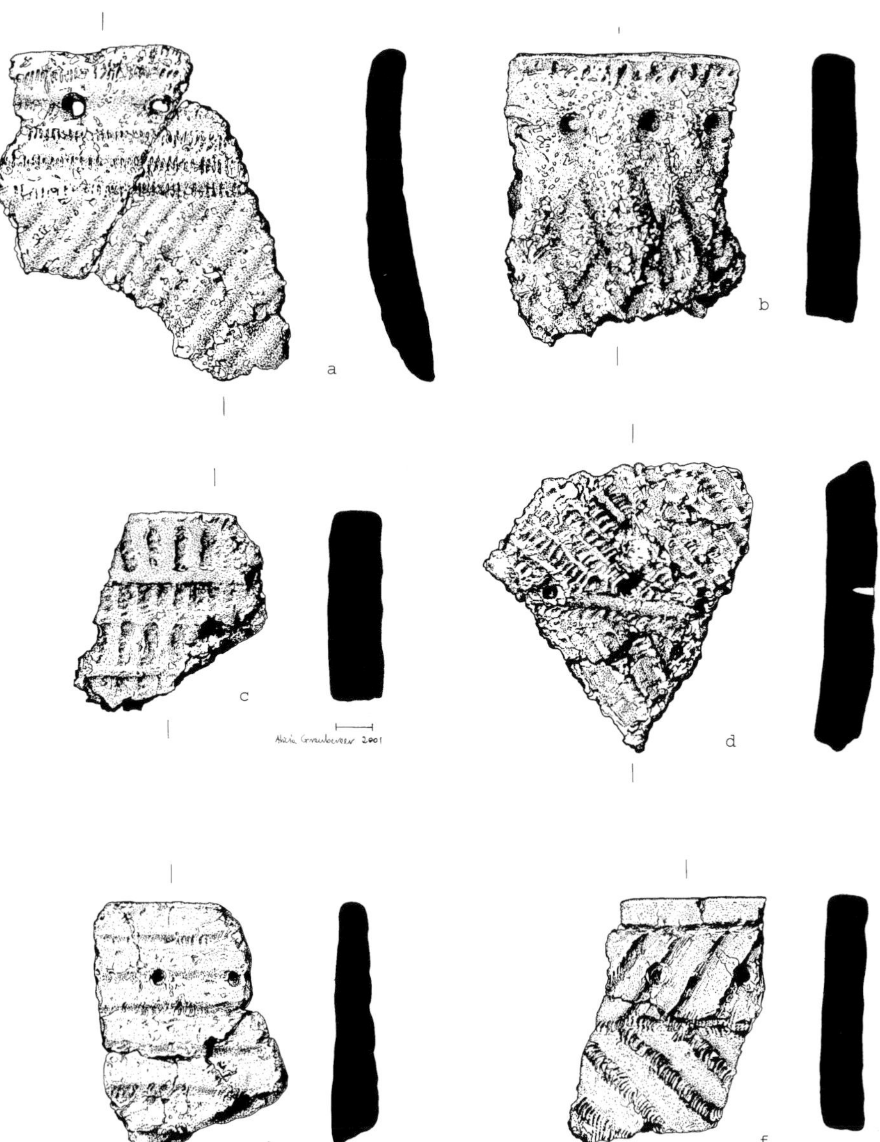

Figure 60.2. The [14]*C-dated Sperrings 1 sherds from Östra Jansmyra I* (a–c) *and Vargstensslätten II* (d–f), *Långbergsöda, Saltvik parish, Åland.* a: *Östra Jansmyra I, 6100±75 BP, Ua-17854;* b: *Östra Jansmyra I, 6065±80 BP, Ua-17855;* c: *Östra Jansmyra I, 6185±120 BP, Ua-17856;* d: *Vargstensslätten II, 5990±90 BP, Ua-17857;* e: *Vargstensslätten II, 5990±90 BP, Ua-17858;* f: *Vargstensslätten II, 6165±75 BP, Ua-17859. For the calibrated ages, see graph in Figure 60.3; Bronk Ramsey 2005; Reimer* et al. *2004. (Drawings: Alicja Grenberger: scale 1:2).*

Figure 60.3. It should be noted that some of the charcoal and wood dates in the graph may be slightly too old, due to the potential old-wood effects, and some of the organic crust dates may be affected by a reservoir effect (Hallgren 2004). Nonetheless the graph in Figure 60.3 suggests a broad contemporaneity between the oldest phase of each of these different ceramic traditions.

In the region between the northern part of the Baltic Sea and the Barents Sea further north (northern Finland, north-easternmost Norway and the Kola peninsula in north-western Russia), there occurred a style of Mesolithic pottery named Säräisniemi 1 or Early Northern Comb Ware (Carpelan 2004, 26–9; Edgren 1992; Skandfer 2005; Torvinen 2000). Säräisniemi 1 material is similar to Sperrings 1 and displays the same vessel shapes. The clay was most commonly tempered with crushed stone and sand, but the use of chamotte (grog) is also reported from a site in Norway (Skandfer 2005, 8). With some exceptions the same elements of decoration (twisted cord-stamp, cord-impression, various stamps, comb stamp and pit impressions) were also in use. Rather it is the composition of the decorative elements that differ between the Sperrings 1 and Säräisniemi 1 traditions. Within the latter, pit impressions are more actively incorporated in the decorative schemes and often form zones separating other forms of decoration. One characteristic composition is that the main decorative element (e.g. a twisted cord-stamp) is terminated by a pit impression. Red paint is common on Säräisniemi 1 pottery.

South of the Gulf of Finland, in parts of Estonia, Latvia,

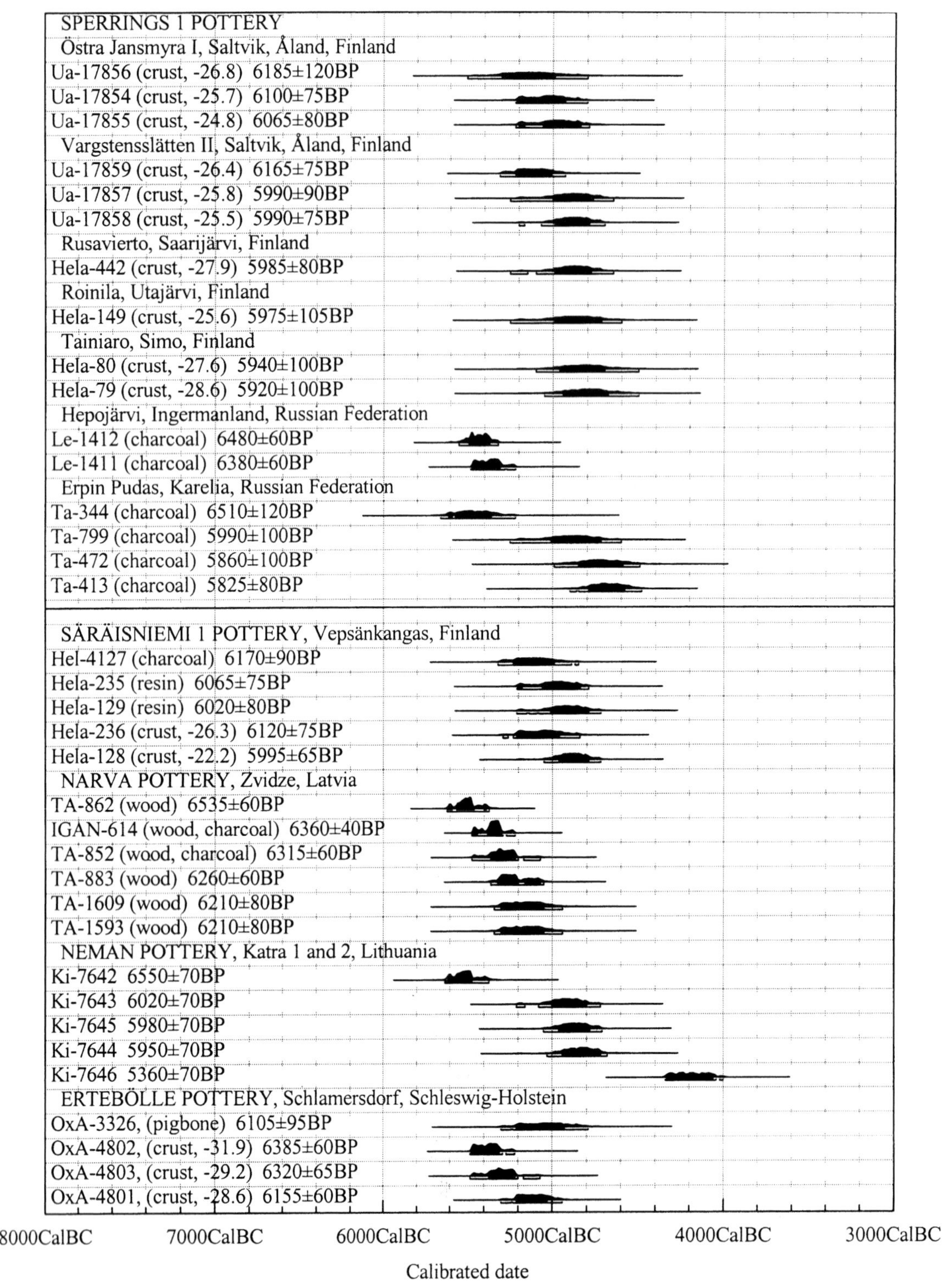

Figure 60.3. The ^{14}C dates from Östra Jansmyra I and Vargstensslätten II, Åland, compared to ^{14}C dates from different early ceramic traditions around the Baltic Sea (Dolukhanov et al. *2005; Hartz* et al. *2002; Jungner and Sonninen 2004; Leskinen 2002; Loze 1988; Persson 1999; Piličiauskas 2002; Timofeev and Zaitseva 1997; Torvinen 2000; Zhilin 2000; and Christian Carpelan, pers. comm. Note that the cultural attribution of the pottery from Schlamersdorf and the validity of the associated ^{14}C dates are debated. Tomas Terberger, pers. comm., August 2005).*

Lithuania, south-western Russia and Byelorussia, there lived hunter-gatherers with a material culture known as Narva Culture (Brazaitis 2002; Kriiska 1996; Loze 1988; Rimantienė 1992; Timofeev 1998a; 1998b). The Narva assemblages contain two main vessel types – large pots with pointed base and low plates. The clay was tempered with crushed shells and plant material, and the vessels were constructed through coiling. The decoration is dominated by shallow pits forming different patterns, but drawn lines and pit impressions also occur; vessels without decoration are frequent.

To the south of the Narva complex, in north-eastern Poland, southern Lithuania and south-western Byelorussia, there lived hunter-gatherers who made what today is known as Neman pottery (Černjawskij 1987; Kempisty 1986; Piličiauskas 2002; Rimantienė 1992; Sulgostowska 1998; Timofeev 1998a; 1998b). The ceramic vessels of the Neman Culture have a slightly profiled shape and pointed bases. During the older phase (*dubičiai*) in question here, the pottery was tempered with plant material, more seldom with crushed stone, limestone and crushed shells. The vessels were commonly constructed of clay coils joined obliquely, although some vessels may have been formed using a matrix. Decoration is often applied in horizontal zones, or as crossing net-patterns; vessels without decoration are common. One characteristic is pit-impression on the inside of the vessel wall, causing a bulge on the outer surface of the vessel.

Further south along the southern shores of the Baltic Sea, in parts of northern Poland, northern Germany, Denmark and southernmost Sweden, there is a Late Mesolithic archaeological complex known as Ertebölle Culture (Andersen 1998; Czerniak and Kabaciński 1997; Fischer 2002; Hartz *et al.* 2002; Ilkiewicz 1989; Jennbert 1984; 1998; Larsson 1990; Price 2000). The Ertebölle Culture differs from the other groups discussed above in that bones of domesticated animals occur at sites in the southern area of distribution at least from *c.* 4700 cal BC; wild resources, however, dominate all assemblages (Rowley-Conwy 1995; Terberger 2006, 162).

As was the case for the Narva Culture, both pointed-bottomed vessels and low plates (clay lamps) occur within the Ertebölle Culture. In some cases there are also similarities in the composition of decoration between Ertebölle and Narva pots (see Andersen 1991; Loze 1988). On the other hand Ertebölle ceramics differ from Narva pottery in technological details, as, for example, in the choice of temper. The Ertebölle potters used both crushed rocks and chamotte, in addition to the plant material used as temper within both traditions. Temper of crushed shells, characteristic of Narva pottery, is not known from Ertebölle contexts. The Ertebölle pots were formed by coils joined using H-, U- and N-techniques (Gebauer 1995; Gumiński and Fiedorczuk 1990, 67; Hulthén 1977; 1984; 1995; Ilkiewicz 1989; Klassen 2004, 109–19; Koch Nielsen 1987; Stilborg and Bergenstråhle 2001). There are regional differences in the type and frequency of decoration of the pots within the Ertebölle culture. In Skåne, in southernmost Sweden, the decoration often covers large areas of Ertebölle vessels. At Soldattorpet and Skateholm some 30–40% of the potsherds have decoration, often shallow, oval impressions arranged in surface-covering compositions (Jennbert 1984; 1998; Stilborg and Bergenstråhle 2001). In Denmark single rows of nail- or finger-impressions at the rim tend to dominate, although surface-covering patterns also occur (Andersen 1998, 42; Hulthén 1977, 23).

Within a rather short time-span, ceramic technology was thus adopted in a region stretching from the Barents Sea in the north, to the southern Baltic in the south. This widespread, and more or less simultaneous, spread of a new technology came to a grinding halt on the borders of the Scandinavian peninsula. In most of Sweden and Norway, pottery craft was not adopted until one or several millennia later. As I have recently discussed this rejection of pottery craft in another paper (Hallgren, in press), I will not dwell on it here. Instead I will conclude with some few words on the indigenization of culture.

Conclusions

The different traditions of pottery craft discussed above were learned and reproduced in everyday life, within local and regional social groups. A useful concept for exploring this is *communities of practice*, an approach that puts focus on the social environment of learning (Lave and Wenger 1991; Wenger 1998). This approach underscores that traditions are taught within a social context; it put emphasis on a group identity that is embedded in participation, and allows for the history of the social context to have an impact on the cultural practice of the participants.

The theory of communities of practice also emphasizes the fact that each individual has a place in a multitude of different, overlapping communities (Lave and Wenger 1991; Wenger 1998). In terms of hunter-gatherers, this could mean the family and local band from childhood, secret societies of initiates of an age-class, the, perhaps, gender specific task-groups of seal-hunting expeditions on the ice, and the new family and new local band acquired by an in-marrying spouse, following the residential move upon marriage. As discussed by Ralph Linton long ago, each of the preceding social categories, or groups, can be the locus for the reproduction of separate aspects of the culture of a society (Linton 1936, 277). Yet, while the pottery *may* have been produced by a segment of the local society, this community of practice was nonetheless part of a larger social, cultural and historical whole: '... communities of practice cannot be considered in isolation from the rest of the world, or understood independently of other practices. Their various enterprises are closely interconnected. Their members and their artefacts are not theirs alone. Their histories are not just internal; they are histories of articulation with the rest of the world.' (Wenger 1998, 103)

As mentioned in the introduction, Marshall Sahlins has stressed that culture is *always* a hybrid creation: '...all cultures are hybrid. All have more foreign than domestically invented parts.' (Sahlins 1999, 411) The early ceramic traditions of the Baltic Sea region are good examples of the inherent hybrid quality of culture: '...largely foreign in origin and distinctively local in pattern.' (Sahlins 1999, 412; cf. 2000, 515) None of the societies under discussion *invented* ceramic technology: they all *learned* it from neighbouring groups. This was not only a simple case of copying, but also the creation of something new, by mixing different technological recipes and designs. While, for example, the Ertebölle pots and lamps are very similar in shape and decoration to the slightly earlier Narva pots and lamps (Figure 60.1, 4), the two traditions diverge in choice of temper, and it has been suggested that the use of chamotte in Ertebölle pottery instead is a trait picked up from the Linear Band Pottery tradition further south (Hulthén 1977, 49; cf. Hallgren 2004, 137–9). If both these influences are acknowledged at face value, Ertebölle pottery could perhaps be characterised as a cultural hybrid, a cross between Narva and Linear Band pottery.

However, Sahlins (1999, 412) has also emphasised that: 'Hybridity is a genealogy, not a structure... It is an analytical construal of a people's history, not an ethnographic description of their way of life. In their way of life, externalities are indigenized, engaged in local configurations and become different from what they were.' The locus for this process of indigenization was the local communities of practice, where participants learned, taught, created and reproduced the craft of pottery. Surely stories about far-away places, of far-away peoples with far-out customs were discussed in those communities (Wenger 1998, 162). And through the negotiation of meaning within those communities of practice, sometimes aspects of foreign traditions were incorporated in the local cultural practice, and made their own tradition, indigenized, a hybrid no more; a material culture '*foreign in origin and distinctively local in pattern*'.

Acknowledgements

Warm thanks to Christian Carpelan, Helsinki University, who has provided extensive comments on a previous paper on the Sperrings 1 of Åland (Hallgren 2004).

References

Alhonen, P. and Väkeväinen, L. 1981. Diatom analytical studies of Early Comb Ware vessels from Åland. *Suomen Museo* 1980, 67–77.

Andersen, S. H. 1991. Norsminde. A 'Køkkenmødding' with Late Mesolithic and Early Neolithic occupation. *Journal of Danish Archaeology* 8, 13–40.

Andersen, S. H. 1998. Ringkloster. Ertebølle trappers and wild boar hunters in eastern Jutland. A Survey. *Journal of Danish Archaeology* 12, 13–59.

Andersson, J. 1990. *Undersökning av ett skadat område på stenåldersboplatsen Östra Jansmyra i Saltvik. Långbergsöda Fornlämning Saltvik 202 Långbergsöda.* Unpublished report, Mariehamn, Ålands Museum.

Brazaitis, D. 2002. Narviškos keramikos stiliai rytų Lietuvoje. *Lietuvos Archeologija* 23, 29–40.

Bronk Ramsey, C. 2005. OxCal 3.10. WWW program and documentation available at http://www.rlaha.ox.ac.uk/oxcal/oxcal.htm (accessed 10/2007).

Carpelan, C. 2004. Environment, Archaeology and Radiocarbon Dates. Notes from the Inari Region, Northern Finnish Lapland. *Iskos* 13, 17–45. Helsinki, The Finnish Antiquarian Society.

Czerniak, L. and Kabaciński, J. 1997. The Ertebölle culture in the southern Baltic coast, in D. Król (ed.), *The built environment of coast areas during the Stone Age*, 70–9. Gdańsk, Regional Centre for Studies and Preservation of The Built Environment.

Černjawskij, M. M. 1987. The Neolithic in north-western Byelorussia, in T. Wiślańskiego (ed.), *The Neolithic and Early Bronze Age in the Chelmno Land*, 429–39. Toruń, Uniwersytetu Mikołaja Kopernika w Toruniu.

Dolukhanov, P., Shukurov, P., Gronenborn, D., Sokoloff, D., Timofeev, V. and Zaitseva, G. 2005. The chronology of Neolithic Dispersal in Central and Eastern Europe. *Journal of Archaeological Science* 32, 1441–58.

Dreijer, M. 1941. Ålands äldsta bebyggelse. *Finskt Museum* 1940, 1–66.

Edgren, T. 1982. *Formgivning och funktion, en kamkeramisk studie.* Iskos 3. Helsinki, The Finnish Antiquarian Society.

Edgren, T. 1992. Den förhistoriska tiden, in T. Edgren and L. Törnblom (eds.), *Finlands Historia* 1, 9–270. Esbo, Schildts.

Emeis, K.-C., Struck, U., Blanz, T., Kohly, A. and Voss, M. 2003. Salinity changes in the central Baltic Sea (NW Europe) over the last 10,000 years. *The Holocene*, 411–21.

Eriksson, G. 2004. Part-time farmers or hard-core sealers? Västerbjers studied by means of stable isotope analysis. *Journal of Anthropological Archaeology* 23 (2), 135–62.

Europaeus, A. 1927. Stenålderskeramik från kustboplatser i Finland. *Finska Fornminnesföreningens Tidskrift* XXXVI, 45–77.

Fischer, A. 2002. Food for feasting? An evaluation of explanations of the neolithisation of Denmark and southern Sweden, in A. Fischer and K. Kristiansen (eds.), *The Neolithisation of Denmark. 150 Years of Debate*, 341–93. Sheffield Archaeological Monographs. Sheffield, J. R. Collis Publications.

Gebauer, A. B. 1995. Pottery production and the introduction of agriculture in Southern Scandinavia, in W. K. Barnett and J. W. Hoopes (eds.), *The Emergence of Pottery Technology and Innovation in Ancient Societies*, 99–112. Washington, Smithsonian Institution Press.

Gumiński, W. and Fiedorczuk, J. 1990. Dudka 1. A Stone Age peat bog site in North-eastern Poland. *Acta Archaeologica* 60, 51–70.

Hallgren, F. 2003. My place or yours?, in L. Larsson, H. Kindgren, K. Knutsson, D. Loeffler and A. Åkerlund (eds.), *Mesolithic on the Move: Papers presented at the Sixth International Conference on the Mesolithic in Europe, Stockholm 2000*, 592–9. Oxford, Oxbow Books.

Hallgren, F. 2004. The introduction of ceramic technology around the Baltic Sea in the 6th millennium, in H. Knutsson (ed.), *Coast to Coast – Arrival. Results and Reflections. Proceedings of the Final Coast to Coast Conference 1–5 October 2002 in Falköping, Sweden*, 123–42. Coast to Coast Project. Uppsala, Department of Archaeology and Ancient History, University of Uppsala.

Hallgren, F. (in press). 'Tiny islands in a far sea', in P. Jordan and M. Zvelebil (eds.), *Origins of Ceramics and Hunter Gatherers of Northern Eurasia*. London, UCL Press.

Hartz, S., Heinrich, D. and Lübke, H. 2002. Coastal farmers – the neolithisation of northernmost Germany, in A. Fischer and K. Kristiansen (eds.), *The Neolithisation of Denmark. 150 Years of Debate*, 321–40. Sheffield, J. R. Collis Publications.

Hulthén, B. 1977. *The Ceramic Technology During the Scandinavian Neolithic and Bronze Age.* Stockholm, Stockholm University.

Hulthén, B. 1984. Teknologisk undersökning av keramiska

artefakter från Löddesborg, Löddeköpinge sn, Skåne, in K. Jennbert, *Den produktiva gåvan. Tradition och innovation I Sydskandinavien för omkring 5300 år sedan*, 201–6. Acta Archaeologia Lundensia, Series in 4°, 16. Lund, University of Lund.

Hulthén, B. 1995. Ceramics artefacts – a key to ancient society, in P. Vincenzini (ed.), *The Ceramics Cultural Heritage*, 1–7. Faenza, Techna.

Ilkiewicz, J. 1989. From Studies on Cultures of the 4th Millennium B.C. in the Central Part of the Polish Coastal Area. *Przegląd Archeologiczny* 36, 17–55.

Jennbert, K. 1984. *Den produktiva gåvan. Tradition och innovation I Sydskandinavien för omkring 5300 år sedan*. Acta Archaeologia Lundensia, Series in 4°, 16. Lund, University of Lund.

Jennbert, K. 1998. From the inside: A contribution to the debate about the introduction of agriculture in southern Scandinavia, in M. Zvelebil, R. Dennell and L. Domańska (eds.), *Harvesting the Sea, Farming the Forest. The Emergence of Neolithic Societies in the Baltic Region*, 31–5. Sheffield Archaeological Monographs 10. Sheffield, Sheffield Academic Press.

Jungner, H. and Sonninen, E. 2004. *Radiocarbon Dates VI*. Helsinki, Åbo Akademis Bibliotek.

Katzenberg, M. A., Saunders, S. R. and Abonyi, S. 2000. Bone chemistry, food and history: A case study from 19th century Upper Canada, in S. H. Ambrose and M. A. Katzenberg (eds.), *Biogeochemical Approaches to Paleodietary Analysis*, 1–22. New York, Kluwer Academic/Plenum Publishers.

Kempisty, E. 1986. Neolithic cultures of the forest zone in northern Poland, in T. Malinowski (ed.), *Problems of the Stone Age in Pomerania*, 187–213. Warsaw, Warsaw University.

Klassen, L. 2004. *Jade und Kupfer. Untersuchungen zum Neolithisierungsprozess im westlichen Ostseeraum unter besonderer Berücksichtigung der Kulturentwicklung Europas 5500–3500 BC*. Jutland Archaeological Society Publications 47. Århus, Jutland Archaeological Society.

Koch Nielsen, E. 1987. Ertebølle and Funnel-beaker pots as tools. *Acta Archaeologica* 57, 107–20.

Kriiska, A. 1996. The Neolithic pottery manufacturing technique of the lower course of the Narva River, in T. Hackens, S. Hicks, V. Lang. U. Miller and L. Saarse (eds.), *Coastal Estonia: Recent advances in environmental and cultural history*, 373–84. PACT 51. Rixensart, PACT.

Larsson, L. 1990. The Mesolithic of southern Scandinavia. *Journal of World Prehistory* 4, 257–309.

Lave, J. and Wenger, E. 1991. *Situated Learning. Legitimate Peripheral Participation*. Cambridge, Cambridge University Press.

Leskinen, S. 2002. The late neolithic house at Rusavierto, in H. Ranta (ed.), *Huts and houses. Stone Age and early Metal Age buildings in Finland*, 147–69. Helsinki, National Board of Antiquities.

Lindqvist, C. and Possnert, G. 1997. Om reservoareffekt-problemet, in G. Burenhult (ed.), *Ajvide och den moderna arkeologin*, 73–4. Falköping, Natur och Kultur.

Lindqvist, C. and Possnert, G. 1999. The first seal hunter families on Gotland. On the Mesolithic occupation in the Stora Förvar cave. *Current Swedish Archaeology* 7, 65–87.

Linton, R. 1936. *The Study of Man*. New York, D. Appleton-Century Company.

Loze, I. 1988. *Poselenija kamennogo veka Lubanskoj niziny: mezolit, rannij i srednij neolit*. Riga, Riga University.

Munthe, H. 1940. *Om Nordens, främst Balticums senkvartära utveckling och stenåldersbebyggelse*. Stockholm, Kungliga Svenska Akademien.

Nuñez, M. 1986. Om bosättningen på Ålandsöarna under stenåldern. *Åländsk Odling* 1986, 13–28. Mariehamn, Ålands folkminnesförbund.

Nuñez, M. 1990. On Subneolithic pottery and it is adoption in Late Mesolithic Finland. *Fennoscandia Archaeologica* 7, 27–52.

Nuñez, M. and Storå, J. 1992. Shoreline chronology and economy in the Åland archipelago 6500–4000 BP, in T. Hackens, H. Jungner and C. Carpelan (eds.), *Time and environment*, 143–61. PACT 36. Rixensart, PACT.

Persson, P. 1999. *Neolitikums början. Undersökningar kring jordbrukets introduktion i Nordeuropa*. Göteborg, Göteborg University.

Piličiauskas, G. 2002. Dubičių tipo gyvenvietės ir Neolitinė Nemuno kultūra pietų Lietuvoje. *Lietuvos Archeologija* 23, 107–36.

Price, T. D. 2000. The introduction of farming in Northern Europe, in T. D. Price (ed.), *Europe's First Farmers*, 260–300. Cambridge, Cambridge University Press.

Reimer P. J., Baillie, M. G. L., Bard, E., Bayliss, A., Beck, J. W., Bertrand, C., Blackwell, P. G., Buck, C. E., Burr, G., Cutler, K. B., Damon, P. E., Edwards, R. L., Fairbanks, R. G., Friedrich, M., Guilderson, T. P., Hughen, K. A., Kromer, B., McCormac, F. G., Manning, S., Bronk Ramsey, C., Reimer, R. C., Remmele, S., Southon, J. R., Stuiver, M., Talamo, S., Taylor, F. W., van der Plicht, J., and Weyhenmeyer, C. E. 2004. IntCal04 terrestrial radiocarbon age calibration, 0-26 cal kyr BP. *Radiocarbon*, 46 (3), 1029–58.

Rimantienė, R. 1992. The Neolithic of Eastern Baltic. *Journal of World Prehistory* 6, 97–143.

Rowley-Conwy, P. 1995. Wild or domestic? On the evidence for the earliest domestic cattle and pigs in Southern Scandinavia and Iberia. *International Journal of Osteoarchaeology* 5, 115–26.

Sahlins, M. 1999. Two or three things I know about culture. *Journal of the Royal Anthropological Society* 5, 399–421.

Sahlins, M. 2000. What is Anthropological enlightenment? Some lessons of the twentieth century, in M. D. Sahlins (ed.), *Culture in Practice*, 501–26. New York, Zone Books.

Segerberg, A., Possnert, G., Arrhenius, B. and Lidén, K. 1991. Ceramic chronology in view of ^{14}C datings. *Laborativ Arkeologi* 5, 83–91.

Skandfer, M. 2005. Early, Northern Comb Ware in Finnmark: The concept of Säräisniemi 1 reconsidered. *Fennoscandia Archaeologica* XXII, 3–27.

Stenbäck, N. 2003. *Människorna vid havet. Platser och keramik på ålandsöarna perioden 3500-2000 f.Kr*. Stockholm, Stockholm University.

Stilborg, O. and Bergenstråhle, I. 2001. Traditions in transition. A comparative study of the patterns of Erteböll‍e lithics and pottery. Changes in the Late Mesolithic ceramic phase at Skateholm I, III, and Soldattorpet in Scania, Sweden. *Lund Archaeological Review* 6, 23–41.

Storå, J. 2001. *Reading Bones. Stone Age Hunters and Seals in the Baltic*. Stockholm, Stockholm University.

Sulgostowska, Z. 1998. Continuity, change and transition: the case of northern-eastern Poland during the Stone Age, in M. Zvelebil, R. Dennell and L. Domańska (eds.), *Harvesting the Sea, Farming the Forest. The Emergence of Neolithic Societies in the Baltic Region*, 87–94. Sheffield, Sheffield Academic Press.

Terberger, T. 2006. The Mesolithic Hunter-Fisherer-Gatherers on the Northern German Plain, in K. Moeller Hansen and K. Buck Pedersen (eds.), *Across the western Baltic. Proceedings of the Conference 'The prehistory and Early Medieval Period in the Western Baltic' in Vordingborg, March 2003*, 111–84. Sydsjællands Museums Publikationer 1. Odense, Sydsjællands Museum Publications.

Timofeev, V. I. 1998a. The east-west relations in the late Mesolithic and Neolithic in the Baltic region, in A. Kosko (ed.), *Beyond Balkanization*, 44–58. Poznan, Adam Mickiewicz University.

Timofeev, V. I. 1998b. The Beginning of the Neolithic in the Eastern Baltic, in M. Zvelebil, R. Dennell and L. Domańska (eds.), *Harvesting the Sea, Farming the Forest. The Emergence of Neolithic Societies in the Baltic Region*, 225–36. Sheffield Archaeological Monographs 10. Sheffield, Sheffield Academic Press.

Timofeev, V. I. and Zaitseva, G. I. 1997. Some aspects on the radiocarbon chronology of the Neolithic cultures in the forest zone of the European part of Russia, in E. Torsten (ed.), *Proceedings of the VII Nordic Conference on the Application of Scientific Methods in Archaeology, Savonlinna, Finland, 7-11 September 1996*, 15–22. Iskos 11. Helsinki, The Finnish Antiquarian Society.

Torvinen, M. 2000. Säräisniemi 1 Ware. *Fennoscandia Archaeologica* XVI, 3–35.

van Klinken, G. J., Richards, M. P. and Hedges, R. E. M. 2000. An overview of causes for stable isotopic variations in past European human populations: Environmental, ecophysiological, and cultural effects, in S. H. Ambrose and M. A. Katzenberg (eds.), *Biogeochemical Approaches to Paleodietary Analysis*, 39–63. New York, Kluwer Academic/Plenum Publishers.

Väkeväinen, L. 1979. Nya rön angående den äldre stenåldern på Åland. *Åländsk Odling* 1978, 49–52. Mariehamn, Ålands folkminnesförbund.

Welinder, S. 1977. Åländsk fångststenålder. *Åländsk Odling 1976*, 46–58. Mariehamn, Ålands folkminnesförbund.

Wenger, E. 1998. *Communities of Practice. Learning, Meaning, and Identity*. Cambridge, Cambridge University Press.

Zhilin, M. 2000. Chronology of the transition from the Mesolithic to the Neolithic in the forest zone of Eastern Europe. *Lietuvos Archeologija* 19, 287–97.

Äyräpää, A. 1956. Den yngre stenålderns kronologi i Finland och Sverige. *Finskt Museum* LXII, 5–52.

Session VI

Dwellings

61. Introduction: Dwellings

João Zilhão

As pointed out by Nyland and Michelsen in their contribution to this session: 'a house is not a home; the home is where the heart is'. In keeping with this familiar saying, the papers assembled here cover the entire range of possible meanings and scales of 'dwelling', from the real place of momentary activity documented by a small lithic concentration, to the categorical realm of the regional settlement system inferred from patterns of site distribution in a landscape, or the virtual sphere of extra-regional interactions as signalled by raw material proveniences. Most papers, however, deal with dwellings in a more restricted sense, focusing on the reconstruction of the nature and function of discrete places used by a person or group of persons, or on the reconstruction of the wider settlement area comprising such individual activity areas.

Åstveit reports on a 30,000m² excavation of Mesolithic deposits buried under peat in the island of Aukra, western Norway. The Early Mesolithic is characterised by clearly discernable individual residential units, whereas the Late Mesolithic is mostly represented by a dense, continuous cultural layer across the entire area, and features discrete habitation units of a more substantial nature; these differences suggest a decrease in mobility through time, reflected in a shift in emphasis, from portability to durability, in the architecture of dwellings. Ramstad's contribution reports on a project that takes this approach one step further, with the complete excavation of all sites identified in an entire island (albeit a small one, <1ha) off the coast of Finnmark, Melkøya; when seasonality data are available, these excavations should be able to highlight important aspects of Mesolithic life north of the Arctic Circle, as well as the trajectory and causes of change through to the times (Sámi Iron Age) of the latest prehistoric settlements also found on the island.

Area studies of large find concentrations also form the core of the results from the salvage operations reported by Carlsson, as well as by Casati and Sørensen. At Strandvägen (south-central Sweden), this particular framework, while setting strict limits to the size and shape of the investigated area, gave Carlsson the opportunity to study the variation in occupation features along a longitudinal transect from the river bed through the margin and into the dry land upslope; specialized activities of an extractive workshop nature were found closer to the water, and dwelling features, including a later Mesolithic 'long-house', on the higher ground. Casati and Sørensen excavated an area of 20,000m² at Ålyst, on the island of Bornholm (Denmark), a site previously known for its extensive scatters of surface finds from the Maglemose culture; despite disturbance from Bronze Age and recent ploughing, discrete concentrations could be recognized, including two oval-shaped huts whose latent outlines could be established via refitting studies, with the continuation of which the authors hope to be able to assess whether these features could have been contemporary.

In a separate paper, Larsen presents the methodology and results of a project that used 3D modelling software to test different possibilities for the reconstruction of the Ålyst features. Using more traditional techniques (plotting of refit links and mapping of isopach lines), Gelhausen *et al.* also focus on the interpretation of individual dwelling units, but with a more prosaic problem in mind: whether a number of selected find concentrations from different sites of the Upper and Final Palaeolithic of Germany (Late Magdalenian and *Federmessergruppen*) represent activity areas in the open or under shelter. Their results indicate closed space conditions, with the predominance of trapezoidal shapes suggesting cultural continuity across the Dryas-to-Allerød transition, and with the lack of evident structures pointing to an emphasis on mobility. This is in agreement with the evidence for the Early Mesolithic of Norway discussed by Åstveit and also by Nyland and Michelsen, but Molin's study of settlement and dwellings of the same period in south-central Sweden, around Linköping, adds a geographical dimension of variation; at least in this more continental setting, winter houses were quite robust and substantial buildings.

Jensen's report on the costal settlement of Nivå 10 (north-eastern Denmark) illustrates the potential of combining the large scale, area approach with detailed analysis of individual features; in Dwelling 2, for instance, the stratigraphic resolution of hut floor deposits was such that seasonal cycles of use/abandonment could be detected, whereas special finds (such as deposits of deer antlers) could be reasonably interpreted as possibly ritual, all the more so since one such find was that of a human humerus that may have been intentionally removed from a nearby grave. In the sea bed off the opposite, south-western side of island Denmark, lie the Møllegabet sites discussed by Grøn. More than the dwellings and boat burials, it is the degree of preservation of the surrounding landscapes, including the original vegetation, that is of special significance here; Grøn also reports on the successful use of seismic profile survey methods to identify accurately cultural layers buried in sea-bottom sediments, and one can hardly disagree with his conclusion that, providing the issue of costs can be solved, this is the kind of Mesolithic archaeology that holds most promise for the future in terms of the preservation of organic finds and of the spatial features of both dwellings and their wider settlement contexts.

The landscapes discussed by Wickham-Jones in Scotland and Gardiner in southern England are above the water, and reflect one of the traditional strong points of British archaeology: the emphasis on landscape and settlement archaeology rather than on sites *per se*. Wickham-Jones, in turn, points out that shell-middens are a feature of sites of diverse nature and chronology, not a specific type of site, and discusses their variability in the Scottish Mesolithic, in relation to landscape setting, season of activity, and associated remains. Gardiner's emphasis, in turn, is on special places; not from the point of view of the archaeologist but from the point of view of the Mesolithic person, for whom such places cannot have been those with good conditions for preservation and future discovery, but those playing particular roles as territorial markers, as aggregation locales, or as nodes of travel and communication networks. Among such sites, Gardiner emphasizes a shared feature of the early Mesolithic of southern England and Belgium, the repetitive burial use of caves, originating collective tombs reminiscent of those well-known in the later Neolithic of southern Europe.

From the point of view of an archaeologist of the earlier Stone Age who conducts his fieldwork in the Greater Mediterranean area, this is a wealthy collection of papers with a lot of food for thought. One must regret the geographical bias, which is certainly not due to the fact that Mesolithic dwellings were non-existent south of the 50° parallel, but at the same time find satisfaction and hope in the future of research traditions whose vitality is opening new ground (and new water!) for the study of post-glacial hunter-gatherers.

62. Is home where the heart is? Reflections around Early Mesolithic sites, exemplified with results from an excavation on coastal south-western Norway

Astrid J. Nyland

This paper is based on an excavation of an Early Mesolithic site on the south-western coast of western Norway. The material found on this site confirms our impression of a highly mobile, nomadic people that lived on the western coast of Norway in the Early Mesolithic. However, the archaeological material found does not tell us much about their dwellings. Dwelling structures from the time period are rarely found, yet the question of how to define their dwellings is not often raised. They must have lived in structures, or dwelt, in a fashion that is difficult to recognise with our current excavation methods. Perhaps we can get an insight into the Early Mesolithic sense of 'home' if we add a different perspective. With a theoretical phenomenological framework I believe we can try to leap beyond merely revisiting the old questions of where they lived, what they ate, and how their flint technology worked.

Keywords: Early Mesolithic sites, western Norway, phenomenology, places and homes.

Introduction

During the excavation of an Early Mesolithic site called Hellevik loc. 3a, a visitor came up to us and asked what we had found. The site was explained to the visitor as a campsite, but we had to admit that we had found no trace of any house structure, postholes, or the familiar stone circles used to tie down a canvas. Nor had we detected any definite fireplace. This was probably a campsite, but we could not say if, or how, the inhabitants spent the night. So the visitor asked us on what we based our interpretation of this site as a campsite. That question led to the reflections I present in this paper concerning Early Mesolithic sites. What does the archaeological material tell us when it comes to dwelling and settling in the Early Mesolithic, and what does it not tell us. I admit I have more questions than answers.

I will first give a brief introduction to the Early Mesolithic period in western Norway, the archaeological material of the period, and the landscape that the people of the western Norwegian coast inhabited; all the dates mentioned in the text are uncalibrated BP. I will then present the site that was excavated in light of recent research. This will lead me to my phenomenological perspective on dwelling in the Early Mesolithic.

The Early Mesolithic of western Norway

During the Ice Age, Norway had for several thousand years been covered by a thick ice-sheet that had prevented people from settling there. In the Early Mesolithic, between 10,000–9000 BP, the ice-sheet had melted enough to reveal the Norwegian coast as a resource-rich archipelago between the great ocean and an inland mountain area. Humans quickly migrated from the continent to the new land that appeared. Their rapid immigration northwards is traced through early ^{14}C dates and finds of homogeneous archaeological material with typological similarities along the coast. We repeatedly find small sites where the artefact assemblage is made up of tanged points, burins, microliths, unifacial cores with two opposing platforms, and flake- and core-adzes, among others. The material is made of flint, and, to a lesser degree, quartz and rock crystal. In the northern part of Norway the raw material is more local, probably due to the lack of flint found on the shores further south. The Early Mesolithic sites excavated in the lowland and coastal areas of south-western Norway are generally small. They consist of one to three flint concentrations, each of approximately 3000 artefacts, seldom more (Kutschera and Waraas 2000, 73). There are not many hearths or tent structures recognized on sites in coastal, south-western Norway, but some evidence of surface cleaning has been documented on several excavated sites (Nærøy 2000, 182).

The dates of most sites from the outer coastal zone in south-western Norway are estimated through technological and typological methods. In addition sites are dated by their height above today's sea-level in relation to the land uplift curves, which have been projected for different areas along the coast. The curves show where the seashore was at different times during prehistory. It is assumed that most Stone Age sites lay close to the shore or on the beach: a plausible assumption, as the Early Mesolithic people would have travelled by boats or kayaks, to secure mobility and access to various marine resources in the archipelago. There are however some exceptions. A few sites have been excavated in the mountainous region of Rogaland. Sites on the shores of a lake called 'Myrvatn' date to between 9600 and 9050 BP, and around lake 'Fløyrlivatn' some sites revealed charcoal dated to between 9750 and 9350 BP (Bang-Andersen 2003, 15). These sites are also rare in that they have provided preserved charcoal for ^{14}C dating, an uncommon occurrence in this region of Norway. Further north, along the western coast, more coastal sites have been dated from charcoal finds (summarized in Nærøy 2000). Overall, the ^{14}C dates have confirmed the relative dates that the Early Mesolithic archaeological material and the sites' associations with earlier shorelines have provided.

Several researchers divide the Early Mesolithic period that ranges from *c.* 10,000–8500 BP, into an Early Preboreal and Late Preboreal-Boreal period, with a shift around 9500 BP (Fuglestvedt 2001; Kutschera 1999; Waraas 2001). The shift is not as visible in their technology and tool types as it is in the site distribution pattern and site variability (Waraas 2001, 117). The rapid migration, together with the homogeneous material along the coast, make it clear that a highly-mobile, nomadic population was involved. However, it is suggested that in the Late Preboreal period the people consolidated their use of the coast and inland areas, more so than did the first pioneers (Waraas 2001): they related more to the land.

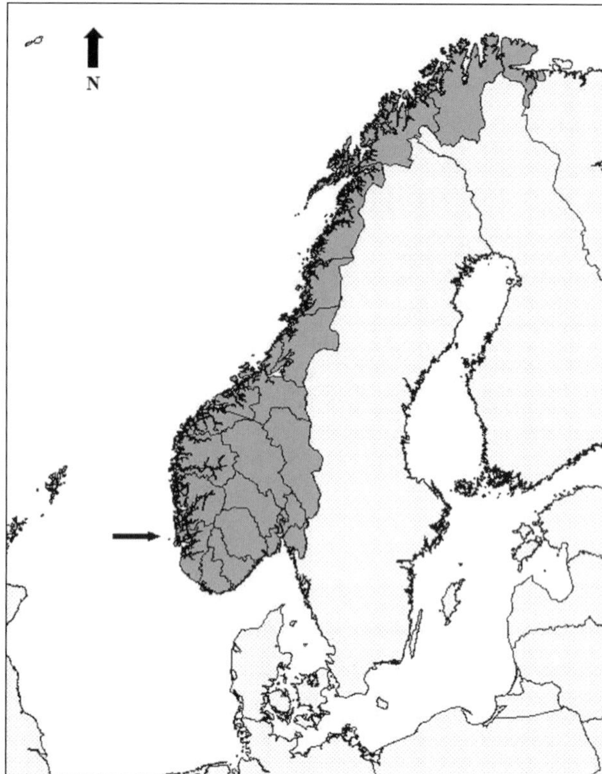

Figure 62.1. The area under discussion, in the northern part of the county of Rogaland, on the south-western coast of Norway.

Figure 62.2. The site in its landscape. The aerial photograph was taken in the 1950s (photographer unknown). It has been modified to indicate a seashore 12m higher than today's (grey shading). The site is marked 'O'.

Hellevik loc. 3a

Hellevik loc. 3a is situated in the northern part of the county of Rogaland, on the coast of south-western Norway, (Figure 62.1). It lies by a narrow stream, on one of many smaller islands sheltered from the great ocean by the larger island of Karmøy. The site is today between 12–14m asl. The main occupation area lies north of a large boulder and west of outcropping bedrock that shelters the area from the southern and eastern winds. Around 9500 years ago, it would have been nicely situated on the island with an option of two suitable places to land boats or kayaks (Figure 62.2).

The site was fully excavated and 3276 finds were recovered in an area of 12m^2. 75% of the artefacts were made of flint, 25% of quartz and rock crystal. The material was dominated by flakes and other debris but there was also a variety of tools such as two drills, a large scraper, and projectiles. Among the chronologically significant tools were microliths, some microburins, one burin, several retouched blades, and unifacial cores with two opposing platforms. We could not document a definite fireplace, but there was a slight increase in the quantity of burnt flint in one area, which might indicate a hearth (Nyland 2004). The concentration of debris was found in a 'drop zone', around a rock that would have made a good seat for the flint worker. No structures like postholes or canvas stones were identified, but an area between the knapping area and the rock was cleared from stones, and this could represent

Figure 62.3. The site after excavation of the first layers. A cleared area is visible in the centre of the photograph. The stone previously encircled by the debris can be seen in the upper left of the cleared area. (Photograph: A. Nyland).

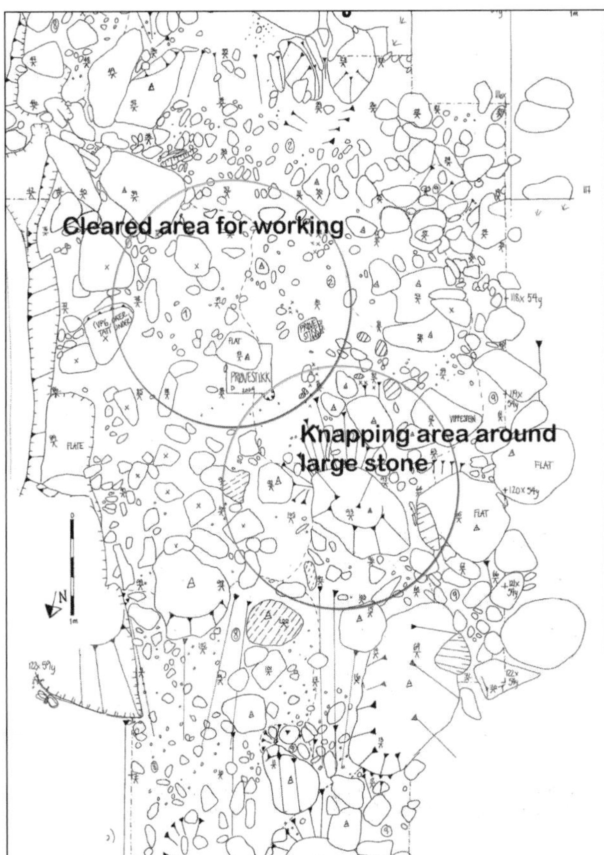

Figure 62.4. Distribution of flint superimposed on a site plan (A. Nyland; map: ArcView).

a space for sleeping, working, or playing (Figures 62.3 and 62.4).

From the distribution of the debris and tools I believe the site of Hellevik loc. 3a could have been inhabited by at least two people, perhaps sitting opposite each other. One was knapping flint, with his or her back towards the water. This worker was facing the other, who, perhaps, used the tools provided by the flint worker. The other person was presumably working with softer materials, such as wood, skins, antler or bone. One can imagine them both building a shelter close to the rocks, with the fire and working area outside, keeping the sleeping area sheltered, clean and comfortable.

Patterns in the archaeological material

At other Early Mesolithic sites on the western coast there are also records of 'empty' areas that have been cleared of stones and made suitable for other activities. Not many hearths have been recognized, and even more rare are construction elements such as stone-paved floors or circle-shaped formations of canvas stones. Other sites with such working zones are also known. At least two more sites, in the neighbouring region of Hordaland

(Knappskog 3 and Budalen 14), revealed lithic debris located around single, large stones (Nærøy 2000, 64, 96, 126). It is also suggested that on-site flint distribution, in circular or semi-circular formations, can indicate the existence of shelters, perhaps a tent, which limited the scattering of the debris. Such patterns in the material can give hints of Early Mesolithic dwelling structures (Nærøy 1995).

Ole Grøn and Oleg Kuznetsov write that several Siberian tribes claim that they never move – it is the world that moves. As long as they organize their dwellings in the same way, according to their traditions and principles, there are no new places: they are all 'the same' (Grøn and Kuznetsov 2003, 217). Analyzing and comparing site variations and similarities, such as tool distribution, artefact assemblages and on-site organisation, will give us more material to base our interpretations on. Several sites in the counties of Rogaland and Hordaland, the county immediately north of Rogaland, have been analysed and summarized by Arne Johan Nærøy (2000). His study has revealed a pattern interpreted as evidence for sites containing one or two flint workers, and also for sites where other individuals were present – not directly involved in tool production, but people who used the tools that were produced on site (2000, 126). Intra-site variability shows some sites, which, although not primarily knapping sites, were sites where people brought tools from other sites (Nærøy 2000). Accordingly, to fully excavate more small sites, and then compare them, is one way of getting to better know these people's lives. The locations give us some insights, but what do they, and the material, tell us about living in the Early Mesolithic? What do the flint-scatters represent in terms of the lives lived? How can we detect or define a dwelling if they lived in structures, or dwelt in such a way that we cannot recognise it from the material? Is it better, then, to cease interpreting the sites as camps, or settlement sites, if no concrete traces of fireplaces or tents are found? Did they not stay the night, or did they all sleep under starry skies? Perhaps not very likely, as this is the western coast of Norway, and the western coast is known for its rainy weather.

Early Mesolithic sites have been interpreted as residues of one episode, or one visit to the location. At some larger sites more flints are scattered over larger areas. Such finds have been interpreted as evidence of repeated returns to a site, or alternatively, a place where more small groups might have gathered (Kutschera and Waraas 2000, 73; Nærøy 2000, 193 ff.). That the people in the Early Mesolithic moved around a lot is well known and agreed upon. However, what can these sites tell us in terms of the lived space or the landscape experienced by the people who stayed there?

From a search for 'dwellings', to looking for Early Mesolithic 'homes'

In order to find their dwelling sites, we first have to agree on some main criteria for defining an Early Mesolithic settlement or dwelling. Did they have to stay one night, or two weeks, before it can be called a settlement site, dwelling, or campsite? How much material, how many flint flakes, or tools, are required to represent a stay longer than a few hours – 1000 items? 4000? Are amounts of processed tools, or types of tools found, the only criteria for separating locations into different sites with different functions? One could argue that since the material is scarce and fragmented, and the structures few, one cannot go beyond interpreting the Early Mesolithic sites as short-term camps, where tools for resource procurement, food or skin preparation were produced. Yet, perhaps we do not necessarily need to know how, or in what kind of structure, they spent their nights in order to discover the Early Mesolithic 'home'. A way to avoid that problem is to view the question of 'dwelling' from another angle, with a different perspective.

Ethnographic researches have written about historically known, nomadic and semi-settled tribal societies. In some societies the hearth was experienced as a human being's 'real dwelling'. The windbreak, or house, was only there to protect the hearth (Westman 1991, 18). Others regard the night-time sleeping place as the centre of their world. Some researchers note that the sleeping place and the daytime dwelling are not necessarily the same place (Westman 1991). The hearth and sleeping place were, for most people, probably the focal points of their mobile existence: moving back and forth, the same way we move between our beds, and the kitchen, to work, and home again. People did, and still do, *live* in a constant state of 'in between'. People *move* between morning and evening, between different meeting points, between different geographical areas. People are in constant movement, constantly creating narratives as they 'move on', or are 'coming back'. They move to different rhythms, the rhythm of their day, the season, and the year. 'The home might be one place, but the feeling of being home is activated by movement, to and from' (Westman 1991, 20).

The archaeological material does not really provide the answers to what defines a 'home'. As I said, hearths and house structures are rare. However, using a more landscape-archaeology-oriented perspective could be another way of developing our understanding of the Early Mesolithic sense of 'home'. One can, for example, look at site distribution in the landscape, and in a relatively restricted territory. However, one must take into account that it was not necessarily only functional qualities that made a site desirable. It is not enough just to look for patterns in functional aspects, or topographical similarities, not if one wants to understand what made that place a home.

Meaningful worlds

The knowledge of where to move next, and memories of older traditions, myths or guidelines, can be tied into practices. In this way, institutionalized practices can maintain and transfer both personal and society's memories and knowledge to other members of the group, or the next generation (Connerton 1991). In turn, practices can be attached to a place, several places, or are the actual movement between places. Knowledge of where and how to move in the landscape was part of their *habitus*, or life-world (Berger and Luckmann 2000; Bourdieu 1999). It is not easy to tie these kinds of arguments to archaeological material. Repeated patterns in distribution and site organization can be a way of identifying social groups, regional groups, or long-lasting traditions. Distribution maps of a different kind, and on different scales, may accordingly be a way of visualizing continuation or alterations of knowledge, traditions, or life-worlds.

Nevertheless, an inherent problem lies in interpreting sites over such long periods of time, with uncertain dates and scarce material. We might be drawing conclusions from sites that were perhaps in use two hundred years, or more, apart. A familiar saying runs: 'a house is not a home; the home is where the heart is…' The area could have felt like home because it was embedded in myths, stories and traditions, inherited from past generations. It follows that if a group maintains a certain way of life, old traditions are honoured and sustained; representatives could be regarded as being from the 'same' group, even though they were separated by two hundred years or more.

Be that as it may, places are more than can be determined by just their archaeological presence as plotted sequences, where we can say with certainty: they lived there in this period, and there in that. Thus, it is not necessarily the site's date of origin that is key. As John Barrett points out, just sequencing places still only gives us maps of things done to the land at different times. It does not fully acknowledge that a place may not even originally have had one single meaning, but many (1999, 27). Meaning is in the eye and the heart of the observer or participant, depending on a person's age, sex, or status, among other things. It could be the memory of a place that is the driving force for certain actions, or understanding the practices performed. Therefore, meaning is not only bestowed on a place by the tasks performed there (Evans 1985, 82). The people who used a place, travelled to a place, dwelled there and left; they did so in the light of certain knowledge they shared and acted upon. They came because of past experiences and they had expectations of what would happen next (Barrett 1999, 24). Because of this knowledge, their lives, which consisted of brief stops along the coast with occasional visits to the mountains, made sense. We, on the other hand, do not inhabit the same mental landscapes they did, and will never fully appreciate the Early Mesolithic worlds of meaning. We do, however, create a meaning out of the available material, and interpret it in ways that make sense to us.

Conclusions

Is it a question of the material, our excavating methods, or our willingness to stretch the material and also embed the people of the Early Mesolithic into social worlds? It seems that only in later periods of the Stone Age can one include social relations, agency, myths, and life-worlds in our interpretations. Ingrid Fuglestvedt's doctoral thesis is an exception in this respect, as she introduces a phenomenological perspective to research in this time period (2001). My earlier work has addressed the Neolithic. In that research area, social interpretations of the material are more commonly accepted. I have found it inspiring to try and transfer some of the concepts and theories from Neolithic research into Early Mesolithic material. To use phenomenologically, or sociologically, inspired theories, might be the key to taking us beyond merely going over the old ground of what they ate, the tools they used, their technological achievements, or sequencing their sites according to time of origin.

The people who stayed at Hellevik loc. 3a had probably lived in the region for hundreds of years. They knew the landscape, where the best fishing and hunting places were, and they knew which bays were suitable for landing their boats. The people stayed in the area, came to this island, and used this site. It was home to them, as it had been to their forefathers, whose tool traditions they had passed down from generation to generation. After 9500 BP it is suggested that people seemed to stay longer in one region. Perhaps the shape of the fjords, the islands and mountains, the changing seasons, had become incorporated into their every day life-world, myths, traditions, social and ritual practices. It felt like home, and they had no reason to move further. Other interpretations are, of course, plausible; this is only mine.

References

Barrett, J. C. 1999. Chronologies of Landscape, in P. J. Ucko and R. Layton (eds.), *The Archaeology and Anthropology of Landscape. Shaping our landscape*, 21–30. One World Archaeology 30. London, Routledge.

Bang-Andersen, S. 2003. Southwest Norway at the Pleistocene/Holocene Transition: Landscape, Development, Colonization, Site Types, Settlement Patterns, in *Norwegian Archaeological Review* 36 (1), 5–25.

Berger, P. L. and Luckmann, T. 2000 (1967). *Den samfunnsskapte virkelighet* (translated by F. Wiik). Bergen, Fagbokforlaget.

Bourdieu, P. 1999 (1972). *Outline of a Theory of Practice* (translated by Richard Nice). Cambridge, Cambridge University Press.

Connerton, P. 1991 (1989). *How societies remember*. Cambridge, Cambridge University Press.

Evans, C. 1985. Tradition and the Cultural Landscape: An archaeology of place. *Cambridge Archaeological Review* 4 (1), 80–94.

Fuglestvedt, I. 2001. *Pionerbosetningens fenomenologi. Sørvest-Norge og Nord-Europa 10200/10000–9500 BP*. Unpublished PhD thesis, Archaeological Institute, University of Bergen.

Grøn, O. and Kuznetsov, O. 2003. Ethno-archaeology among the Evenkian forest hunters. Preliminary results and a different approach to reality!, in L. Larsson, H. Kindgren, K. Knutsson, D. Loeffler and A. Åkerlund (eds.), *Mesolithic on the Move: Papers presented at the Sixth International Conference on the Mesolithic in Europe, Stockholm 2000*, 216–21. Oxford, Oxbow Books.

Kutschera, M. 1999. Vestnorsk tidligmesolitikum i et nordvest-europeisk perspektiv, in I. Fuglestvedt, T. Gansum and A. Opedal (eds.), *Et hus med mange rom. Vennebok til Bjørn Myhre på 60 års dagen*, 43–52. AmS Rapport 11A. Stavanger, Archaeological Museum of Stavanger.

Kutschera, M. and Waraas, T. A. 2000. Steinalderlokaliteten på 'Breiviksklubben'. Bratt-Helgeland i Karmøy kommune, in T. Løken (ed.), *Åsgård – Natur- og kulturhistoriske undersøkelser langs en gasserør-trasé i Karmøy og Tysvær, Rogaland*, 61–96. AmS Rapport 14. Stavanger, Archaeological Museum of Stavanger.

Nyland, A. J. 2004. *Innberetning fra for- og hovedundersøkelsen av steinalderlokaliteten Hellevik lok. 3a. Hellevik, gnr. 108, bnr. 1. Karmøy kommune*. Unpublished excavation report. Stavanger, Archaeological Museum of Stavanger. The final 'T-Forbindelsen' report will be published by Guro Skjelstad, AMS.

Nærøy, A. J. 1995. Early Mesolithic Site Structure in Western Norway – a case study. *Universitetets Oldsaksamling Årbok 1993/1994*, 59–77. Oslo.

Nærøy, A. J. 2000. *Stone Age Living Spaces in Western Norway*. British Archaeological Reports, International Series S857. Oxford, Archaeopress.

Waraas, T. A. 2000. *Vestlandet i tidleg Preboreal tid. Fosna, Ahrensburg eller vestnorsk tidlegmesolitikum?* Unpublished Master's thesis, University of Bergen.

Westman, B. 1991. What does it mean to feel at home?, in O. Grøn, E. Engelstad and I. Lindblom (eds.), *Social space. Human Spatial Behaviour in Dwellings and Settlement*, 17–20. Odense University studies in History and Social Sciences 47. Odense, Odense University Press.

63. Different ways of building, different ways of living: Mesolithic house structures in western Norway

Leif Inge Åstveit

House and tent remains from the Mesolithic have been more or less absent on the coast of southern Norway until just recently. At the Ormen Lange archaeological project, located on the western coast of Norway, large areas were exposed mechanically in an attempt to trace dwelling-remains and other kinds of structures from the Mesolithic. In a limited area, at least eight house structures dating from the Early and Late Mesolithic were found. These gave valuable construction details in structures ranging from tents to permanent dwellings. While the Early Mesolithic tent structure indicates a mobile population, the Late Mesolithic house clearly suggests a sedentary, or at least a semi-sedentary, way of life.

Keywords: Mesolithic house structures, mobility vs. sedentism, different use of landscape.

Introduction

Cultural complexity and sedentism among hunters/collectors have long been the focus of research among Norwegian archaeologists. Through the years, sophisticated models that explore and explain various movement patterns over different periods have been developed (Bergsvik 1991, 47; Bjerck 1989, 95; Olsen 1992, 255). However, to a large extent, our knowledge of key aspects of everyday life is limited. We know the location of Mesolithic settlements, we recognize their tool-types, but we know little of what their habitations looked like. Few indisputable tent-floors or house structures have been uncovered during the excavation of large settlement sites along the Norwegian west coast. Filling this particular research lacuna was one of the main goals of the *Ormen Lange Archaeological Project* carried out by the Museum of Natural History and Archaeology in Trondheim in 2003 and 2004 (Bjerck *et al.* 2008). A clear priority during the excavations was to expose as large an area as possible throughout the 15 months of continuous excavation. Several sites were covered by up to a 2m-thick layer of peat. In total, an area of some 30,000m^2 was uncovered. The thick peat layer had protected the sites, and the absence of modern disturbances meant that several houses and dwellings from the Mesolithic were preserved. Nine sites with preserved house structures were discovered, several of which were excavated in large tented halls, which allowed us to investigate extensive areas under relatively constant conditions.

The geographical and natural-historical setting

The Norwegian north-west coast comprises three main types of landscape: mountain plateaus in the interior, the inner fjord system, and the outer coastal zone where the Ormen Lange project was undertaken on the small island of Aukra (Figure 63.1). This archipelago is peppered with large and small islands. Powerful tides and exposure to the deep sea creates a rich environment. In addition, fjord arms have served as important transport routes. These outer coastal areas are optimal for populations that have their economic basis in marine resources, and, naturally enough, it is here that one encounters areas extremely rich in finds from the whole Stone Age. The shore-level displacement resulting from the isostatic land uplift after deglaciation, and the eustatic rise of the sea level, is well documented in this area (Mangerud and Svendsen 1987). The late Holocene transgression in this area has not flooded and eroded Preboreal sites, whilst most of the Boreal sites are transgressed. The stable sea level between 5500 BP and 8000 BP (uncalibrated) implies an accumulation of sites at between 12–15m asl (Figure 63.2).

Early Mesolithic Settlement

The colonization of the coastal areas of Norway is believed to have been a rapid event around 10,000–9500 BP (*c.* 9500–8800 cal BC), and equally old ^{14}C dates have been detected from almost the whole length of the coast (Bang-Andersen 1996; Bjerck 1990; this volume; Fuglestvedt 2001; Sandmo

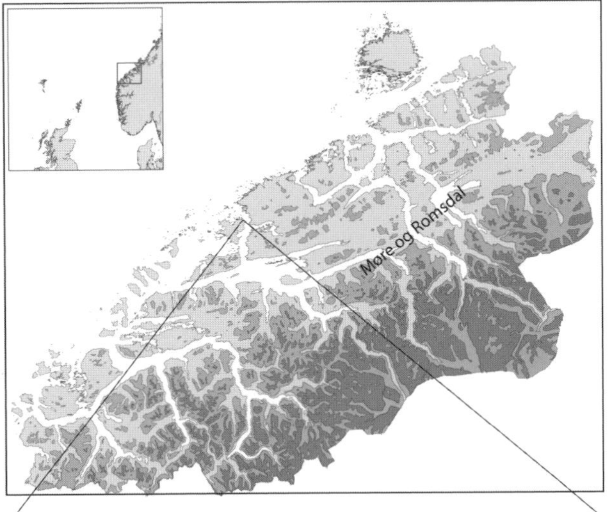

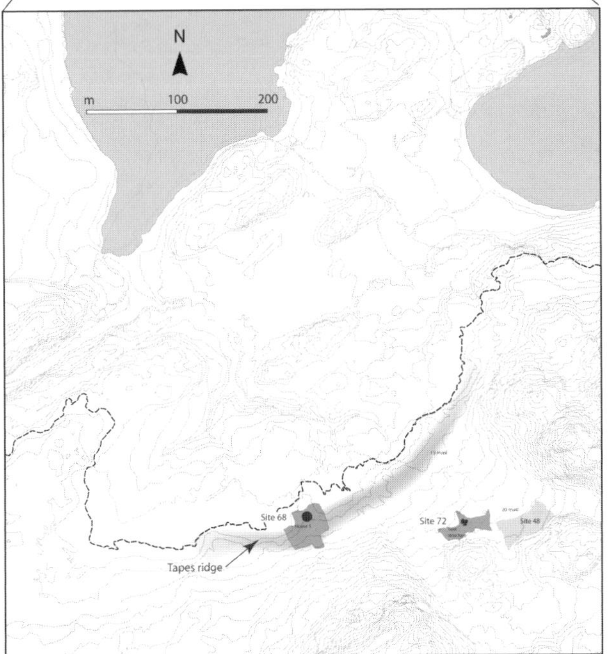

Figure 63.1. Map of the area investigated by the Ormen Lange Archaeological Project on the small island of Aukra (Møre og Romsdal County). Location of the Early Mesolithic Site 72, and the Late Mesolithic Site 68. The dotted line represents 12m asl.

1986; Schanche 1988; Skar and Coulson 1989; Waraas 2005; Åstveit 2005a; 2005b). Indisputable structures (i.e. fireplaces, tent rings, tent floors and postholes) from this period are almost entirely absent, probably because of settlement structures that are small, vague, and hard to detect. In some parts of Norway, the Late Holocene Tapes transgression has destroyed most prehistoric remains, whilst in other areas the remains are today situated well below sea level. In the last 20 years, however, one exception has emerged from the high mountains of south-western Norway. At two sites in Rogaland, Store Myrvatn and Store Fløyrlivatn, well-preserved tent rings and fireplaces dated to 9700–9400 BP (*c.* 9200–8700 cal BC) have been excavated (Bang-Andersen 2003b). For a time these structures were considered unique both in Norway and in Scandinavia, but now the Ormen Lange excavations are contributing several structures of a similar character.

The Site 72 tent remains

This site gives an interesting insight into small-scale organisation and was probably in use for a short period, in fact it could be the remains of only one occupation episode (Figure 63.3). The floor area is oval, measuring 210 × 150cm, and comprises small, hard-packed stones and gravel. The fireplace area is 110 × 90cm and has eight clear kerbstones around it. The fireplace is loosely packed and features the remains of charcoal and fire cracked stones that stand out from the surrounding hard-packed floor. Within this area, a 48 × 50cm concentration of charcoal probably represents the remains of the fire itself. In a treeless Preboreal landscape, blubber was probably an important fuel source. The floor is surrounded by a ditch 10–15cm deep, and between the ditch and the floor there is a cluster of bigger stones interpreted as tent stones. The fireplace is dated to 9485±110 BP (9220–8550 cal BC; T-17001), which corresponds with the mountain sites mentioned earlier. The lithics also clearly support this date.

Lithics

The total lithic material associated with the tent structure

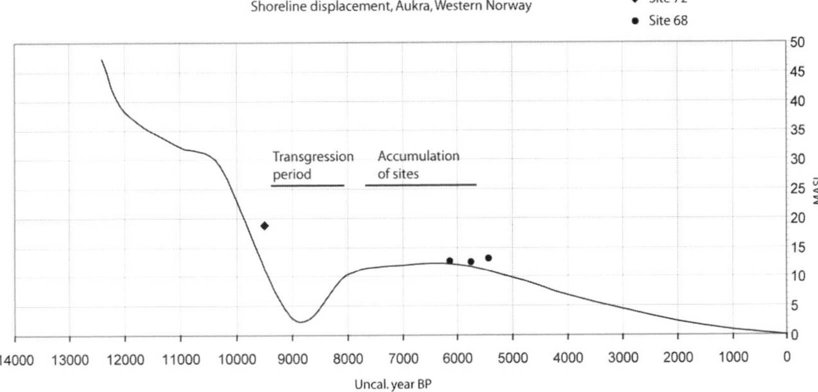

Figure 63.2. Shoreline displacement curve developed on the basis of Mangerud and Svendsen 1987. (Excel spreadsheet developed by David Simpson, University of Bergen).

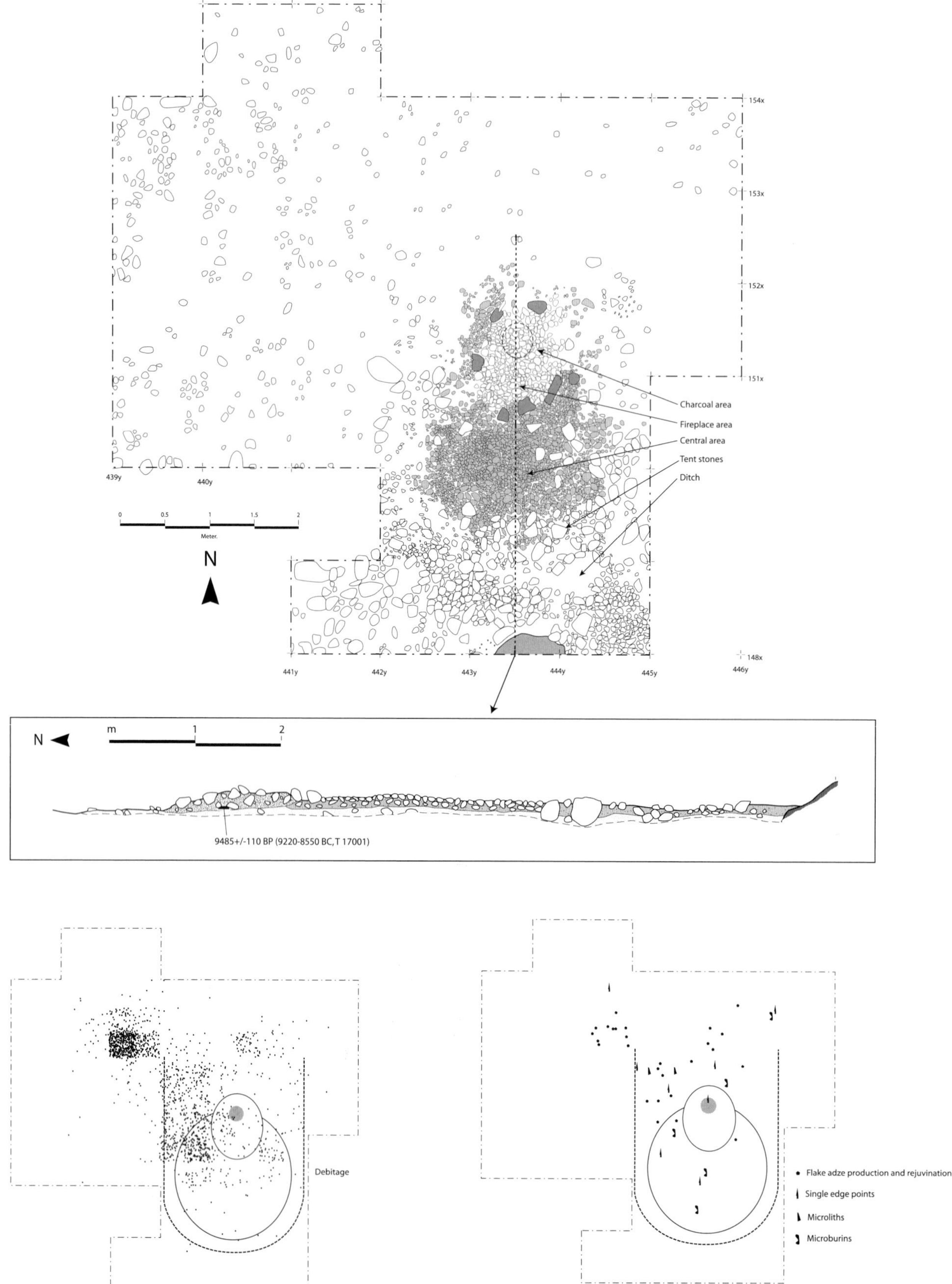

Figure 63.3. The main features of Site 72. A spreadsheet showing all debitage, the tool types, and specific debitage (microburins). Note the cluster on the outside and the wall effect on the western side of the (supposed) tent wall. (Drawing: Ørjan Engedal and Theo Gil).

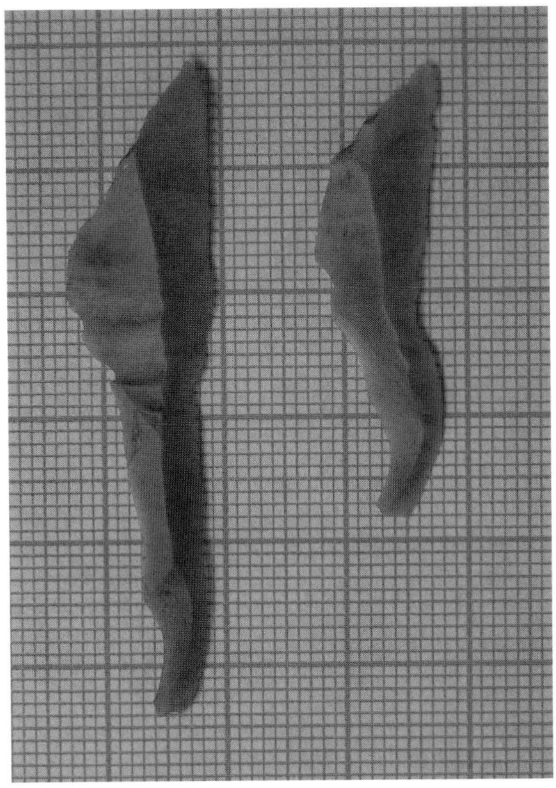

Figure 63.4. Fosna-tradition artefacts connected to Site 72. Prefabricated single-edge points and flake adze. (Photograph: Ørjan Engedal and Leif Inge Åstveit).

is comprised of 1618 individual flint finds, and in several places a clear wall-effect is visible in the find distribution. The debitage shows an obvious cluster on the outside of the tent floor/wall. 156 artefacts have traces of secondary working; of these 11 are tools, all recognised as Preboreal types associated with the Fosna tradition (Figure 63.4). To a large extend, the fireplace has been respected by the spread of artefacts and debitage, where less than 1% is burnt or fire cracked. This would again seem to confirm the impression that the open-fire itself was probably rather small. Two complete flake-adzes and 27 pieces of debitage associated with the production and rejuvenation of such axes are found. The adze-debitage has, for the most part, the same spread as the ordinary debitage, both inside and outside the supposed tent wall. Eight single-edged points are found and appear to be spread evenly across the site floor. Six of these are found within the tent walls. Two are pre-forms and together with the two microliths demonstrate the use of micro-burin technique. Single-edged points, therefore, clearly dominate the microliths on this site. The micro-burins display a somewhat different spread pattern than the other debitage, in that four of the five were found within the tent, indicating that the final stages of projectile production took place inside the tent.

The tent

There are no clear indications of postholes or other larger depressions in association with this construction. It has been proposed that Preboreal tent rings found in the mountains were remains of 'ridge-tents', such as those known as summer tents from Greenland (Bang-Andersen 2003b, 202). This type of tent will leave a subterranean 'U'-form depression, without the use of larger roof-bearing posts. The fireplace has been oriented towards the entrance; this would also be the apex of the tent. In the case of Site 72, the fireplace is situated towards the entrance, as would the apex of the tent have been. The Greenland tent size seems to fit well with the structure in question, and considering the size, the tent from Site 72 could have sheltered 2–4 people for resting/sleeping, or 1–2 people for tool production.

Comparisons with mountain sites

The excavated structures from the Ormen Lange project now

Site	Ground plan lay-out	Inner dimension (metres)	Floor area in m^2	Indoor fire	^{14}C age BP	cal BC	Artefacts
Site I, Store Myrvatnet	Oval/circular	2.8 × 3.2	7	+	9000	*c.* 8250	1400
Site D, Store Myrvatnet	Oval/rhomboid	1.8 × 2.8	5	-	9400	*c.* 8680	3900
Site K, Store Myrvatnet	Circular/oval	3.8 × 3.8	11.4	-	9500	*c.* 8800	
Site 9, Store Fløyrlivatn	Oval/circular	2.0 × 2.4	4.5	-	9600	*c.* 9000	118
Site 7, Store Fløyrlivatn	Circular	2.7 × 3.3	8	+	9400	*c.* 8680	1699
Site 6A, Store Fløyrlivatn	Circular/rhomboid	3.2 × 3.2	7.2	-	9600	*c.* 9000	2300
Site 6B, Store Fløyrlivatn	Oval/rhomboid	3.0 × 3.2	6.7	+	9400	*c.* 8680	
Site 72, Aukra	Oval/circular	2.8 × 2.3	6.4	+	9500	*c.* 8800	1618

Figure 63.5. The mountain sites compared with Aukra Site 72 Aukra. (After Bang-Andersen 2003b, 199).

make it possible to compare Preboreal tent structures from the coast with those already found in the mountains; the similarity in date, size and shape is striking (Figure 63.5).

The low volumes of finds from these sites differ somewhat from the customary picture of costal Preboreal sites, where it is common to uncover literally hundreds of thousands of artefacts (Kutschera and Waraas 2000; Høgestøl 1995). In the case of Site 72, the large neighbouring Site 48, with 15 ^{14}C dates from the Preboreal period, revealed more than 70,000 flint artefacts (Bjerck *et al.* 2008). These are found *in situ* within clusters closely associated with fireplaces, but without comparable evidence of tent structures. This should clearly be understood as representing the reuse of the same location at a time when access to ice-transported flint on the late glacial Dryas ridges was easy (flint does not exist in Norwegian geology). This is also supported by the small but distinct difference in age between the various ^{14}C samples gathered. If Site 48 had been transgressed, as is the case in other parts of Norway (Høgestøl 1995, 47), one could easily misinterpret these traces as those of a large site, while the likelihood is that they would more properly be designated aggregation sites. I find it reasonable to support Nærøy's suggestion (1998) that these huge accumulations of artefacts on coastal sites are the expression of the same adaptive and social patterns we find in the mountains. This is also well backed-up by investigations made by Nærøy further south on the western coast of Norway, where the average number of finds on single-phased Preboreal localities is around 1500 artefacts (Nærøy 1998, 62). The same point of view has been expressed by Milner and Woodman (2005, 6).

Late Mesolithic Settlement

The Late Holocene Tapes transgression ridge is clearly visible at Aukra (Figure 63.1). The sea level lay constantly between 12–14m asl for nearly 2500 years, between 5500 BP and 8000 BP (uncalibrated). This ridge appears to have been the preferred location for settlement by fisher, hunter and collector populations for the whole of this time-span, probably because of the proximity to the sea, as well as

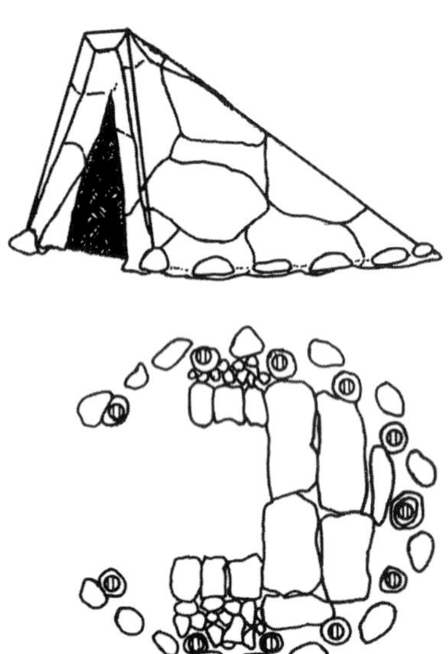

Figure 63.6. Reconstruction of a Greenland ridge-tent. The shape and size fit well with Site 72. (Lee and Reinhardt 2003, fig. 30).

Figure 63.7. Cultural deposits from the Late Mesolithic Site 68. The profile bench indicates the original thickness of the layer.

Figure 63.8. House 5 on Site 68. Note the central fireplace and the postholes, of which some are partly lined with stones.

Figure 63.9. Close up of the central fireplace from House 5, Site 68. The flagstones are heavily fire cracked. (Photograph: Torkel Johansen).

the subsoil draining effect caused by the pebbles in the ridge. Continuous settlement in a limited area for such a long period has created complex stratigraphical situations, and it is a major challenge to isolate different occupational phases within the same site. Once the thick peat layer has been removed, these Late Mesolithic sites appear as concentrated areas of artefacts. There are normally no traces of structures or even depressions to be seen on the surface. However, this changes dramatically once the site is opened up within a larger area. Millennia of settlement have deposited thick cultural layers comprising of fire-cracked stones, flint debitage, charcoal, and, in some circumstances, osteological remains.

Site 68, House 5

This was one of the most visible and least disturbed Late Mesolithic dwellings discovered during the Ormen Lange project and gave us useful insights into several construction details (Figures 63.7–10). The dwelling consisted of a sunken floor within a central depression, measuring approximately 25m² and 15–25cm deep. A total of 13 postholes were discovered, 5–15cm in diameter and approximately 15cm deep. Some were lined with stones. The divergence in size and position of the postholes indicated replacements and/or several phases. The fireplace was 50 × 60cm in diameter, and consisted of flagstones at the base; there were no kerbstones. Two channels, approximately 10–15 cm deep, ran through the wall area and into the fireplace, probably to supply oxygen to the fire. This may indicate a well-insulated construction, with massive walls and roofing, possibly of peat, where lack of oxygen may have been a problem. Similar air channels were exposed on at least three other dwelling sites. This clearly suggests that the dwellings were occupied during the late autumn and winter. It is nevertheless important to stress that on the same site, traces of lighter constructions, i.e. tents, were also found, these have much in common with the Site 72 tent but the datings are all Late Mesolithic. This may indicate that different types of structures were used according to the season. Light summer tents and more substantial winter/autumn dwellings in the same

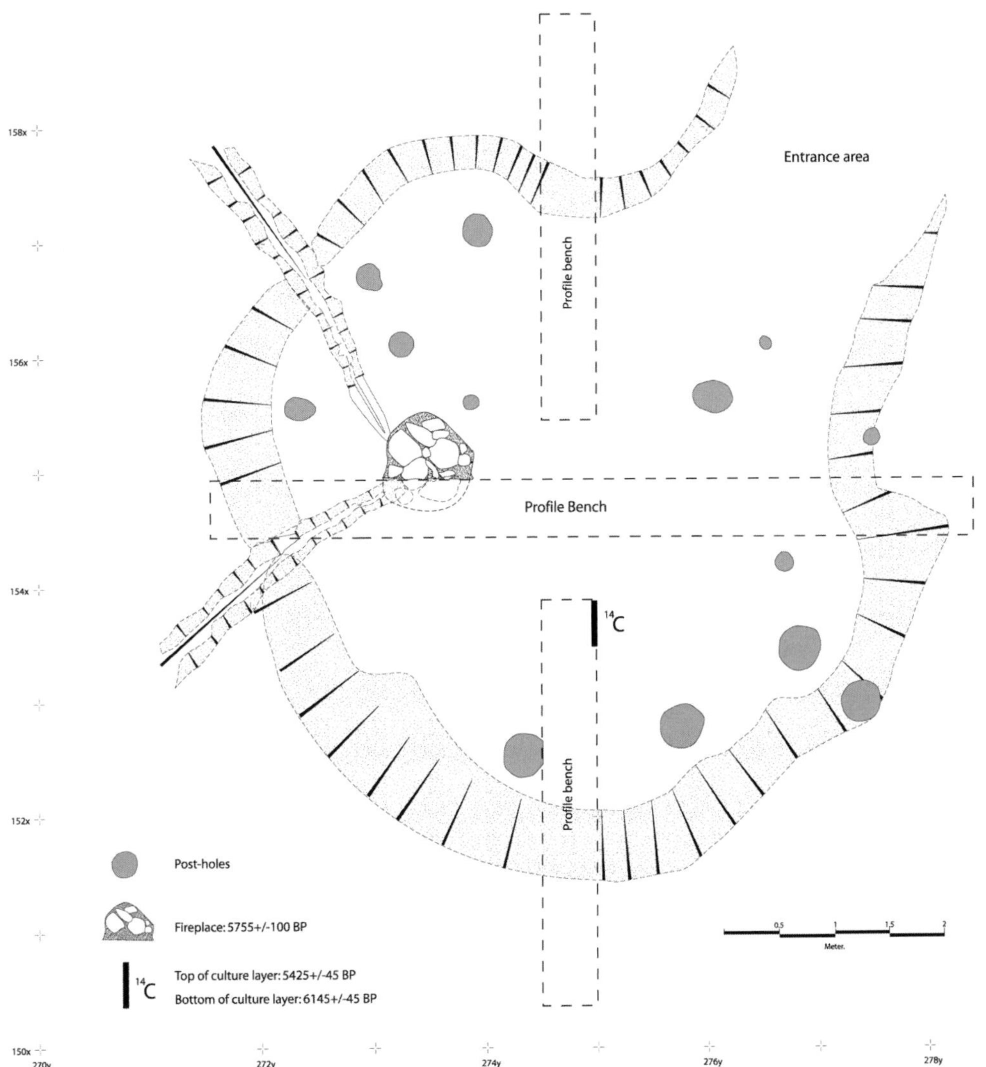

Figure 63.10. House 5, Site 68. Two air channels cut through the wall and into the fireplace. (Drawing: Torkel Johansen and Theo Gil).

area are well documented among Greenland Inuit (Lee and Reinhardt 2003, 67).

Dating

Several ^{14}C dates were obtained on charcoal from the site.

- 5425±45 BP (4355–4075 cal BC; Tua-4854), at the top of the occupation deposits
- 6145±45 BP (5215–4960 cal BC; Tua-4855), at the base of the occupation deposits
- 5755±100 BP (4830–4370 cal BC; T-17695), from the fireplace

It would appear reasonable to suppose that the fireplace represents the most reliable date associated with the dwelling.

Lithics

The lithics consist of traditional Late Mesolithic artefacts, such as flint microblades struck from conical cores, thick ground adzes of greenstone and diabase, and demonstrate a well-developed bipolar technique. Because of the continuous use and reuse, it is seldom that spread patterns of recovered lithics can give reliable results with regard to activity on the settlement floors, as was the case with the Preboreal Site 72. Nor can phosphate analyses be expected to contribute any clear information in areas that have been so massively utilised. All this seems to indicate a sedentary, or at least semi-sedentary, population in the Late Mesolithic. Unfortunately, the bone material gives no indication of the season the various sites were occupied. However, through these dwelling structures we have gained access to a new archaeological source with the potential to give us a deeper understanding of past settlement patterns. There is no doubt that these hunter, gatherer and fisher occupation sites are well suited for the analysis of social behaviour, i.e. kinship, gender, and family group relations.

Discussion: two ways of living, two ways of building

The Early Mesolithic tent structure and the Late Mesolithic house are both indicators of hunter-gatherer populations. Marine resources were probably central in both periods, but the economic adaptation was likely to been very different. The two dwellings also demonstrate two dissimilar ways of using the landscape. The Preboreal tent had *portability* as its essential feature: as critical as having a watertight top, or a large internal space, was the weight and volume of the structure itself. The main Preboreal means of transport was probably some kind of seagoing kayak, and it must have been crucial to keep the weight and volume down, thereby avoiding any compromise of the manoeuvrability of the vessel.

On the other hand, given the kind of dwelling one encounters in the Late Mesolithic, it is impossible to assume any similar emphasis on mobility. It is obvious that people invested greatly in these dwellings. With no, or very little, osteological material preserved, it is difficult to demonstrate year-round occupation, and it is possible that the main population, or smaller task groups, were away from the camp in cycles during the year. However, the main issue is that when they returned to the same area, they probably did not expect anyone else to be occupying their residential property. Given the obvious investment of considerable effort in the construction and maintenance of these structures, together with the intensive nature of their occupation, it would seem reasonable to suggest that individual groups (of whatever size and composition) were closely associated with individual structures, either as builders, users, or owners. Seen in this light, these houses could very well be indicators of the first traces of some form of 'property rights' in western Norway.

What kind of economic strategy is it possible to deduce from these structures? A common assumption is that the marine ecosystem, regardless of time period, provides a broad spectrum of resources, stimulating year-round occupation and minimizing the risks of periodic collapse. This is clearly the case in the Late Mesolithic of western Norway, but in the Early Mesolithic it is quite obvious that marine resources were not utilized in the same way. The pioneer settling of the Norwegian west coast has unquestionable links with the Ahrensburg culture of north-west continental Europe. This culture group had its economic basis in reindeer hunting. Placed deposits clearly indicate some kind of mythical orientation towards this animal (Rust 1943, 133; Fuglestvedt 2001, 225). This mono-economic orientation could have been maintained in the new geographical setting of western Norway, but with new animals now featuring as prey, e.g. seal and walrus. These mammals rest and deliver their pups in specific locations, however if they are heavily hunted they will, over time, avoid these nurseries. This is probably the main reason for the need to remain mobile in the Early Mesolithic. The Late Mesolithic demonstrates a very different picture. Populations utilized a much broader spectrum of resources, and the scarce osteological remains, together with the finds of net sinkers and fishhooks, indicate that fishing played a vital role. The houses also indicate a more sedentary population, utilizing littoral resources close to the camp, and while *resources* (the sea mammals) provided an economic basis in the Preboreal, the *area itself* seems to have been more important in the Late Mesolithic; people are connected to the landscape in a wholly different manner. This economic aspect fits well with other social, ideological, and demographic circumstances (i.e. property rights), of which the solid houses are the clearest manifestations.

Acknowledgements

I would like to thank my friends and colleagues, Hein Bjerck, Martin Callanan, Theo Gil, Jostein Gundersen, and Hanne Årskog, for fruitful discussions while working on this paper, and special thanks to Martin for his revisions to the language.

References

Bang-Andersen, S. 1996. Coast/Inland Relations in the Mesolithic of Southern Norway. *World Archaeology* 27 (3), 427–43.

Bang-Andersen, S. 2003. Southwest Norway at the Pleistocene/Holocene Transition: Landscape, Development, Colonization, Site Types, Settlement Patterns, in *Norwegian Archaeological Review* 36 (1), 5–25.

Bang-Andersen, S. 2003b. Encircling the living space of early Postglacial reindeer hunters in the interior of southern Norway, in L. Larsson, H. Kindgren, K. Knutsson, D. Loeffler and A. Åkerlund (eds.), *Mesolithic on the Move: Papers presented at the Sixth International Conference on the Mesolithic in Europe, Stockholm 2000*. Oxford, Oxbow Books.

Bergsvik, K. A. 1991. *Ervervs og bosetningsmønstre på kysten av Nordhordland i steinalder, belyst ved funn fra Fosnstraumen*. Unpublished MA thesis, University of Bergen.

Bjerck, H. B. 1989. Forskningsstyrt kulturminneforvaltning på Vega, Nordland. En studie av steinaldermenneskenes boplassmønstre og arkeologiske letemetoder. *Gunneria* 61.

Bjerck, H. B. 1990. Mesolithic site types and settlement patterns at Vega, Northern Norway. *Acta Archaeologica* 60, 1–32.

Bjerck, H. B. 1994. Nordsjøfastlandet og pionerbosetningen i Norge. *Viking* 57, 25–57.

Bjerck, H. B. (ed.), Åstveit, L. I., Meling, T., Gundersen, J., Jørgensen, G. and Normann, S. 2008. *NTNU Vitenskapsmuseets arkeologiske undersøkelser, Ormen Lange Nyhamna*. Trondheim, Tapir Akademisk Forlag.

Fuglestvedt, I. 2001. *Pionerbosetningens fenomenologi. Sørvest-Norge og Nord-Europa 10 200/10 00–9500 BP*. Unpublished PhD thesis, University of Bergen.

Høgestøl, M. 1995. *Arkeologiske undersøkelser I Rennesøy kommune, Rogaland, Sørvest-Norge bd.2*. AmS Report 23. Stavanger, Archaeological Museum of Stavanger.

Kutschera, M. and Waraas, T. A. 2000. Steinalderlokaliteten på 'Breiviksklubben'. Bratt-Helgeland i Karmøy kommune, in T. Løken (ed.), *Åsgård – Natur- og kulturhistoriske undersøkelser langs en gasserør-trasé i Karmøy og Tysvær, Rogaland*, 61–96. AmS Rapport 14. Stavanger, Archaeological Museum of Stavanger.

Lee, M. and Reinhardt, G. A. 2003. *Eskimo Architecture. Dwelling and Structure in early historic period*. Fairbanks, University of Alaska Press.

Mangerud, J. and Svendsen, J. I. 1987. Late Weichselian and Holocene sea-level history for a cross section of Western Norway. *Journal of Quartenary Science* 2 (2), 113–32.

Milner, N. and Woodman, P. (eds.) 2005. *Mesolithic studies at the beginning of the 21st century*. Oxford, Oxbow Books.

Nærøy, A. J. 1998. *Stone Age Living Spaces in Western Norway*. Vol. 1. PhD thesis, Department of Archaeology, University of Bergen.

Olsen, A. B. 1992. *Kotedalen – en boplass gjennom 5000 år. Fangsbosetning og tidlig jordbruk i vestnorsk steinalder. Nye funn og nye perspektiver. Bind 1*. Bergen, Historical Museum, University of Bergen.

Rust, A. 1943. *Die Alt- und Mittelsteinzeitlichen Funde von Stellmoor*. Neumünster, Karl Wacholz Verlag.

Sandmo, A. K. 1986. *Råstoff og Redskap- Mer enn tekniske hjelpemiddel. Om symbolfunksjonen som et aspekt ved materiell kultur. Skisse av etableringsforløpet i en nordeuropeisk kystsone 10000–9000 BP*. Magistergradsavhandling i Arkeologi, University of Tromsø.

Schanche, K. 1988. *Mortensnes – en boplass i Varanger. En studie av samfunn og materiell kultur gjennom 10.000 år*. Magistergradsavhandling i Arkeologi, University of Tromsø.

Skar, B. and Coulson, S. 1989. A case study of Rørmyr II: A Norwegian Early Mesolithic Site, in C. Bonsall (ed.), *The Mesolithic in Europe: Papers Presented at the Third International Symposium, Edinburgh 1985*, 351–61. Edinburgh, John Donald Publishers.

Waraas, T. A. 2005. Arkeologisk registrering på Baraldsneset, Haram kommune, Ormen Lange prosjektet (I), in L. I. Åstveit (ed.), *Kulturhistoriske skrifter og rapporter 1*, Molde, Møre og Romsdal Fylke, Kulturavdelinga.

Åstveit, L. I. 2005a. Arkeologisk registrering på Stavneset, Averøy kommune, Ormen Lange prosjektet (I), in L. I. Åstveit (ed.), *Kulturhistoriske skrifter og rapporter 2*, Molde, Møre og Romsdal Fylke, Kulturavdelinga.

Åstveit, L. I. 2005b. Arkeologisk registrering på Gossen/Nyhamna, Aukra kommune: Ormen Lange-prosjektet, in L. I. Åstveit (ed.), *Kulturhistoriske skrifter og rapporter 3*. Molde, Møre og Romsdal Fylke, Kulturavdelinga.

64. Island settlements and maritime hunter-fishers: spatial and temporal transformations over 11,000 years at Melkøya, northern Norway

Morten Ramstad

The Melkøya project is an interdisciplinary project based on archaeological excavations on the island of Melkøya, northern Norway. Large-scale excavations were conducted in 2001 and 2002. Chronologically the sites investigated on this small island cover the whole sequence from Early Mesolithic to the Sámi Iron Age. The main focus will be island settlements and the use of space.

Keywords: Melkøya Project, Stone Age settlements, small islands, marginal areas.

Island concepts in Norwegian Stone Age archaeology

For more than 150 years the principal concepts and crucial debates within Norwegian Stone Age research have been founded upon data that has almost exclusively been excavated from shorelines and larger islands of the Norwegian archipelago. This emphasis has, unfortunately, omitted the numerous smaller islands that dot the coastline. Either too small, or too inhospitable, or remote, compared with areas considered optimal for Stone Age settlements, small and exposed islands, such as Melkøya, have traditionally been viewed as marginal, even for Stone Age economies. This bias has probably not only reduced the amount of alternative data, but also limited our understanding of past settlements. The inclusion of these 'marginalized' areas of Norwegian Stone Age research will therefore undoubtedly enhance our understanding of island communities.

Location and landscape

Melkøya is located in the strait of Sørøysundet, at 70°, 40` N, in Finnmark, northern Norway (Figure 64.1). The island is less than 1ha, with a maximum elevation of 71m asl. The coastline consists of sheer cliffs that are open and exposed to the Barents Sea. The exception is two cobble beaches on the more sheltered south side of the island. The climate is oceanic; the sea never freezes and the annual median temperature is +2° C. The weather can be highly unpredictable, with rough seas, windy conditions and frequent storms. Because of its location, far above the Arctic Circle, the inhabitants also had to cope with dramatic environmental changes, with two summer months of constant daylight and an equally long period in winter, when the sun does not rise above the horizon. For people

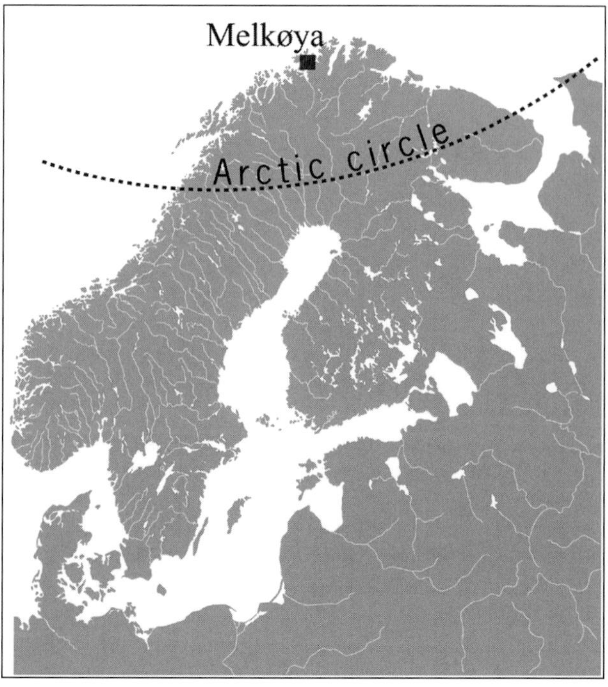

Figure 64.1. Map of northern Europe and the location of Melkøya.

living by and from the sea, such conditions clearly defined social life, as well as resource exploitation, habitation, and landscape.

Nevertheless, excavations have documented considerable amounts of settlement data from all prehistoric periods. Some of these can be explained on the basis of physical characteristics with the outer Norwegian coastal landscape. According to Hein Bjerck, this zone of islands, inlets, skerries, bays and headlands creates a situation where there is an average of 30 km of shoreline per 1 km of coastline, which makes up an abundance of sheltered seascapes and richer marine biotopes than corresponding values for continental Europe. These maritime landscapes were already present from Pre-Boreal times and would have been of great importance for Mesolithic subsistence patterns (Bjerck 2006). As well as successful cultural adaptation to these conditions, one has to take into consideration that Melkøya is located in the middle of a strong tidal current channel; such channels have a particularly high plankton production, which attracts large numbers of fish, marine birds and sea mammals, making them one of the optimal coastal biotopes for marine exploitation (Bergsvik 2001).

Deglaciation and shoreline displacements

Towards the end of the last glaciation (the Weichseian 115,000–10,000 BP) the ice disappeared rapidly from the outer coast of northern Norway. The Sørøya region was deglaciated around 13,000 BP. Significant climatic improvements around 9500 cal BC led to a rapid melting of the ice cap in the fjord areas, and somewhat later further inland, with subsequent changes in fauna and flora (Hald *et al.* 2003; Nesje *et al.* 2005). Even though the coastal areas of Norway became habitable at an early stage there seems to have been a long hiatus in human occupation before the colonisation process started around 9500 cal BC (Bjerck 1995; Bang-Andesen 2003; Blankholm 2004; Grydeland 2005). Since shorelines were approximately 20m asl around 9500 cal BC, the size and the physical characteristic of the present Melkøya would have been more or less the same from the Pre-Boreal period onwards. However, because of the relatively minor isostatic uplift the Holocene transgression would have flooded the Boreal and Atlantic shorelines.

Research strategy

The majority of Stone Age sites in Norway are defined by the presence of stone artefacts or semi-subterranean houses. Excavations have traditionally focused on the distribution of artefacts or house structures (Glørstad 2001, 20; Grøn 2000, 188–9; Ramstad 2003). Traditional hunter settlements normally take up considerably larger areas than archaeologists usually investigate (Grøn and Kuznetsov 2003, 218–19). This bias has not only reduced the amount of alternative data but also restricted our understanding of past settlements (Grøn and Kuznetsov 2003, 218–19).

One way of addressing this would be to investigate larger areas incorporating a variety of approaches in order to identify alternative sources of data. The project's main goal was to map, excavate, and identify the function of as many of the prehistoric structures and associated features on the island as possible. Mechanical surface stripping was used in order to explore as much as possible of the total extent of the past settlement areas. Due to the poor preservation of organic material, geochemical prospection comprising phosphate, magnetic susceptibility and trace element analyses were conducted in order to get more information about spatial use and organization of the settlement areas (Linderholm 2003). To get a more viable picture of the impact of hunter-fishers, as well as natural changes to the local environment at Melkøya, extensive palaeo-botanical investigations were undertaken (Jensen 2004). By giving equal attention to multiple sets of data we hoped to stimulate new and alternative perspectives on the organization and structuring of space at hunter-fisher settlements.

Results

Prior to the project no prehistoric sites were known at Melkøya. Intensive surveying and test pitting provided a more complete picture of spatial and temporal transformations in the use of the island. Sites were identified in three areas around the two more sheltered beaches on the south side of the island: Normannsvika, Kilden and Sundfjæra (Figure 64.2). In 2001 the topsoil was removed from large areas in and around the sites at Kilden and Normannsvika, while all suitable settlement areas were exposed in Sundfjæra during the 2002 season.

A large number of structures were identified ranging from semi-subterranean houses and lighter dwelling types to a variety of hearths, cooking pits, storage pits, activity areas, dumping zones, middens and grave remains (Ramstad *et al.* 2005). Kilden and Normannsvika both provided new data for the study of settlement patterns and intra-site

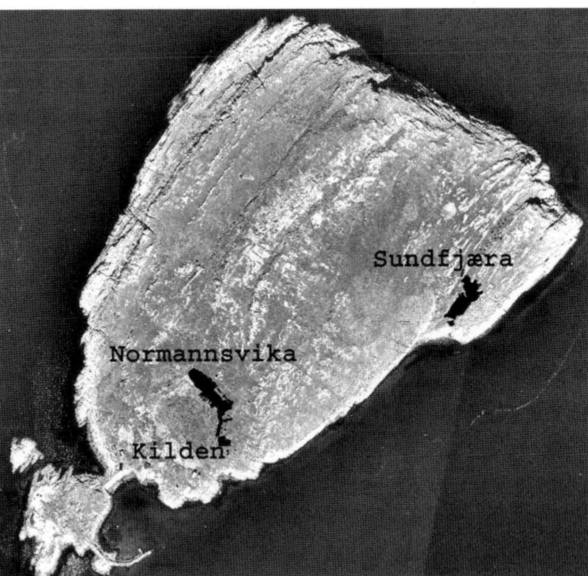

Figure 64.2. Aerial view of Melkøya and sites.

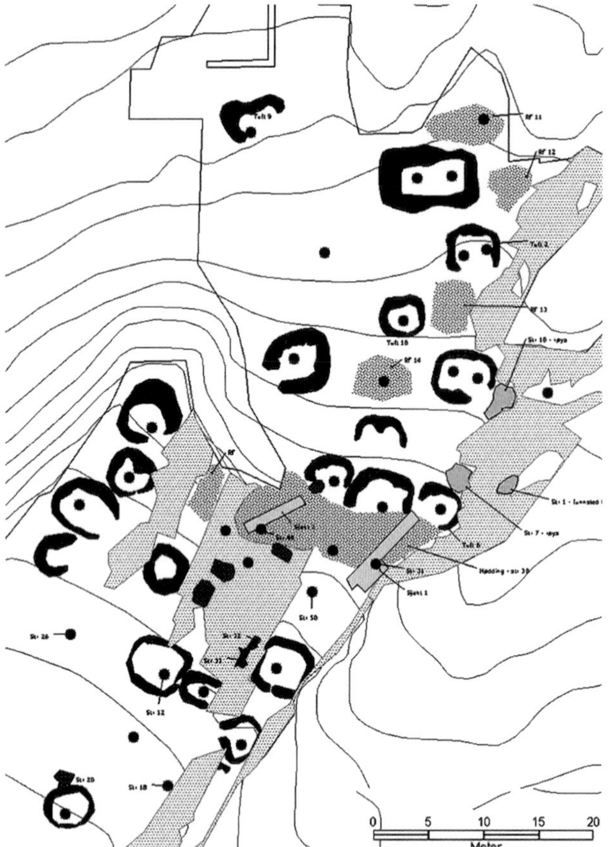

Figure 64.3. Map showing parts of Sundfjæra at Melkøya. Note the close spatial relations between landscape, topography and Late Stone Age dwellings. The size and form of individual houses vary according to features in the micro-topography. (Map: A. R. Niemi, Tromsø University Museum).

relationships during the Late Stone Age (5000–1800 cal BC) and Early Metal Age (1800 cal BC–1 AD).

Between the upper (25m asl) and lower (5m asl) sections of Sundfjæra, all prehistoric periods from the 'initial pioneer phase' of the Early Stone Age (around 9500 cal BC) to the Sámi Iron Age were documented. As a result of the Holocene transgression, shorelines between 8000–6500 cal BC were flooded and partly eroded. By penetrating the beach deposits up to 1m in depth, we were, however, able to locate and excavate partly intact phases from these periods. Treating the Sundfjæra area as a single settlement unit gave a unique diachronic picture of the way the landscape was utilized through time, thus permitting studies of stability and changes in the structuring of space over considerable time periods.

Dwelling structures

Combined with their limited size, the restricted number of settlement areas necessitated the use of landscape and micro-topography as an active component in the structuring and organisation of space at the settlement areas. Close spatial relations between landscape, topography and Late Stone Age dwellings were observed at Sundfjæra. The local micro-topography has been an integrated part of the construction in many of the houses (Figure 64.3). While access to the sea was important, no clear-cut correlations between dating of individual houses and shorelines were found. In addition, no significant relationship between chronology and house size has been observed. This contrasts with the traditionally more uniform picture of Stone Age dwelling types and typology based on sites from

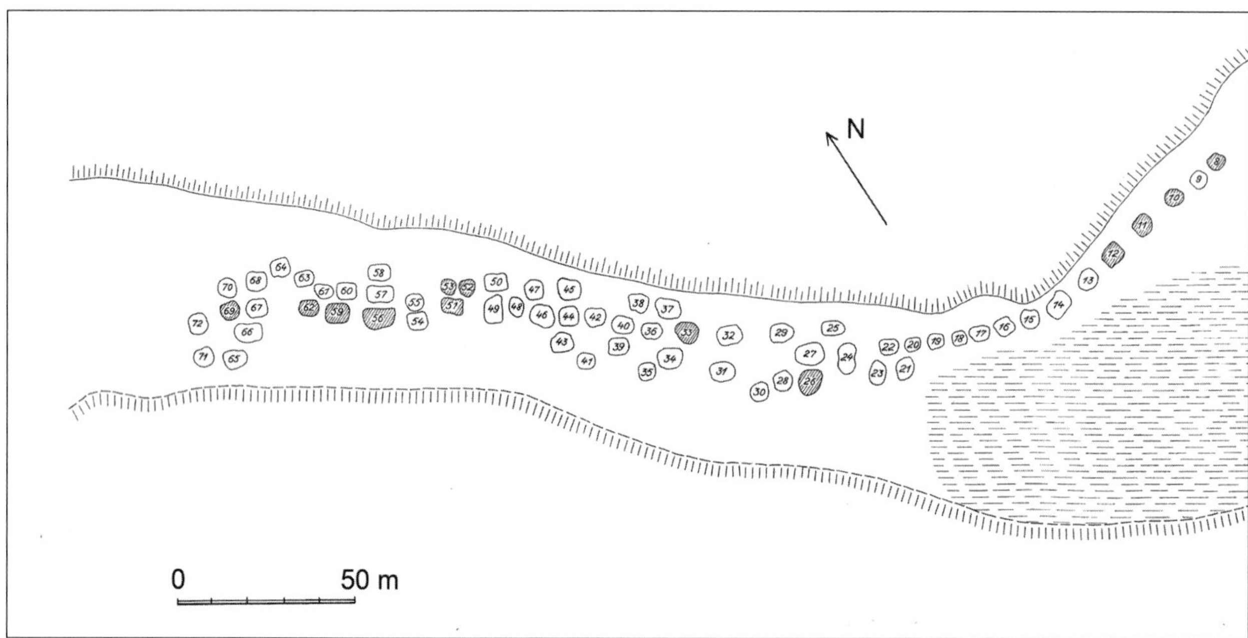

Figure 64.4. Map showing parts of the Gropbakkeengen site, Varangerfjord, northern Norway (after Simonsen 1961, fig. 35). The circles represent Late Stone Age semi-subterranean houses. The houses are arranged in rows along old shorelines, as is typical during this period. Note that there are few limitations in landscape and topography to constrain the structure and size of the dwellings.

the mainland and on larger islands. At these sites there are normally few limitations in landscape and topography that constrain the structure and size of the dwellings. The dwellings are usually arranged in rows along old shorelines (Figure 64.4). There is a strong correlation with the rise of sea level and a general increase in house size during the Late Stone Age (Simonsen 1961; Olsen 1998). The results from Melkøya clearly demonstrate that there are larger variations both in the location of individual house as well as in house typology.

New areas, new finds!

By focusing on possible settlement areas where few, if any, artefacts had been found, or no visible structures were observed, we aimed to generate new sets of data. A number of important finds were made, including possible lighter dwelling types (used during the warmer seasons?), activity areas on the cobble beaches, different types of hearth structures (some may represent production facilities for extracting oil from sea mammals), as well as small concentrations of pottery and lithics (Ramstad 2003).

We were also focusing some of these investigations on areas where topography and landscape make it unlikely that either dwellings or associated activities were present. The eastern limit of Sundfjæra consisted of a low but uneven ridge that dropped directly to the sea further east. Although there was no soil between the turf and bedrock surface, scattered lithic materials were located, as well as concentrations of charcoal from temporary fireplaces (Ramstad 2006a). However, the most surprising finds were small cairns made of beach pebbles and fire-cracked rocks. Two of these contained beads of Baltic amber, proving the existence of long-distance networks connecting Melkøya to areas over 2000 kilometres away (Figure 64.5). While no skeletal material was preserved, the amber beads and their contexts could represent Late Stone Age graves (Ramstad 2006b). This interpretation is supported by trace element and phosphate analyses (Linderholm 2006).

The diverse data documented in areas normally regarded as marginal or less important parts of the sites raises important questions regarding traditional concepts and size estimates of Stone Age settlements. These results clearly confirm that Stone Age settlements consisted of more than a central area with dwellings and concentrations of lithic material, and that they also included a larger zone where numerous daily and regular activities (including ritual ones) were carried out (Grøn and Kutnetsov 2003, 218).

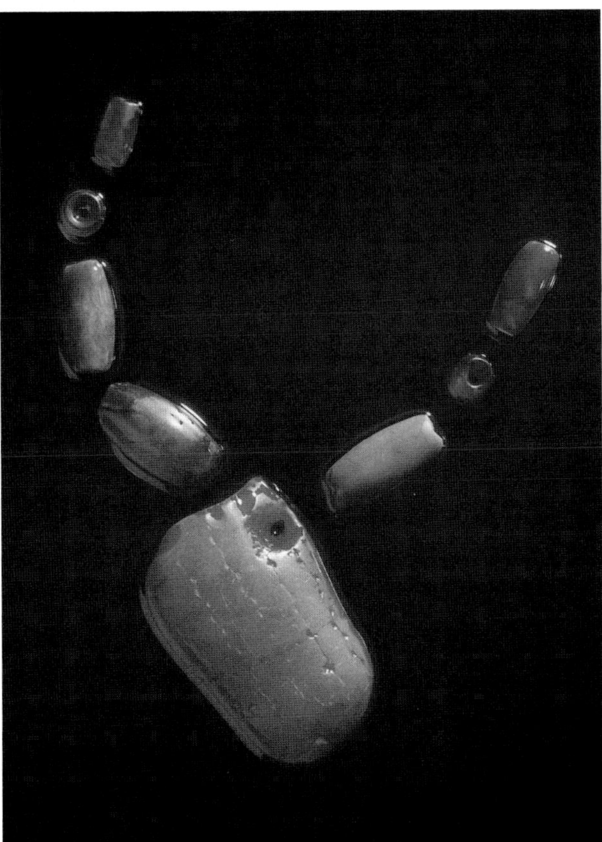

Figure 64.5. Among the finds recovered from the traditionally 'neglected' areas, eight amber beads were found under a low cairn covering a small crevice in the bedrock, some distance away from the nearest Late Stone Age house. (Photograph: A. Icagic, Tromsø University Museum).

Early Marine technology

Based on typology, the oldest site on Melkøya probably dates to the first half of the Early Mesolithic (9500–8000 cal BC. During the time of occupation it was shore bound with an excellent landing place for boats. However, compared to sites from later periods, the area is the most open and exposed of all the localities at Sundfjæra. The site is around 100m^2 and the find inventory consists of a limited number of artefacts: small tanged arrowheads and some simple lanceolate microliths being the most common tool types. Raw materials are dominated by different types of cherts, fine-grained quartzite and rock crystal. Apart from a limited number of flints, all of these raw materials were available at locations within 100km to the north-east and south-east of the island (Hood 1992). Flint nodules were deposited on beaches in coastal regions from the county of Nordland and southwards (Hood 1992, 97–100). The acquisition of these materials links the island to social networks operating over much larger parts of the northern Norwegian coastal landscape.

A large number of almost identical Pre-Boreal sites are known along the outer coast of Norway (Bjerck 2008). The location and composition of these sites clearly demonstrate the marine economic orientation and maritime knowledge possessed by these groups (Bang-Andersen 2003, 19). As evident from the location of sites such as the locality at Melkøya, marine resources (sea mammals and fish) must have been the prime nutritional source rather than reindeer and small mammals living on the ice-free strip between the coast and the inland glaciers (Bjerck 1995; 2008).

Dates from a number of sites from the south-western to the north-eastern tip of Norway (around 2500km) indicate that the colonization process took place possibly within a few generations around 9500 cal BC (Bjerck 1995; Bang-Andersen 2003; Fuglestvedt 2005; Grydeland 2005). The existence of a well-developed marine technology, including seagoing vessels would have been a prerequisite, as it would otherwise have been impossible to travel in this landscape and maintain social networks (Bjerck 2008).

Recently it has been claimed that Mesolithic marine technology in Europe was not sophisticated enough for offshore travel and deep-water fishing, and that there is no convincing evidence for seagoing vessels either of wood or skin. It is argued that it is most likely that European Mesolithic boats were wooden canoes not suitable for open sea travels (Pickard and Bonsall 2004). However, since the Pre-Boreal landscapes were treeless, apart from dwarf birches (*Betula nana*), it is reasonable to assume that skin boats rather than wooden canoes were in use from the colonization of Norway and onwards (Bjerck 2008). Indirect evidence comes from later Mesolithic vessel types and forms depicted at rock art sites, both on the mainland and islands close to Melkøya. On the larger adjacent island of Sørøya at Slettnes, skin boats are depicted on boulders buried by transgressed beach material with a *terminus ante quem* of 5500 cal BC (Hesjedal *et al.* 1996, 82). At Stone Age rock art sites in the neighbouring Alta fjord and at Forselv in Skjomen near Narvik (Figure 64.6), both skin boats, large halibut (*Hippoglossus hippoglossus*), as well as extended lines and heavy sinkers, could be taken as indirect evidence for fishing in deep seas. Similar scenes are found at several rock art sites along the Norwegian coast, stressing the level and content of marine technology, as well as its social and cultural significance (Engedal 2006, 180).

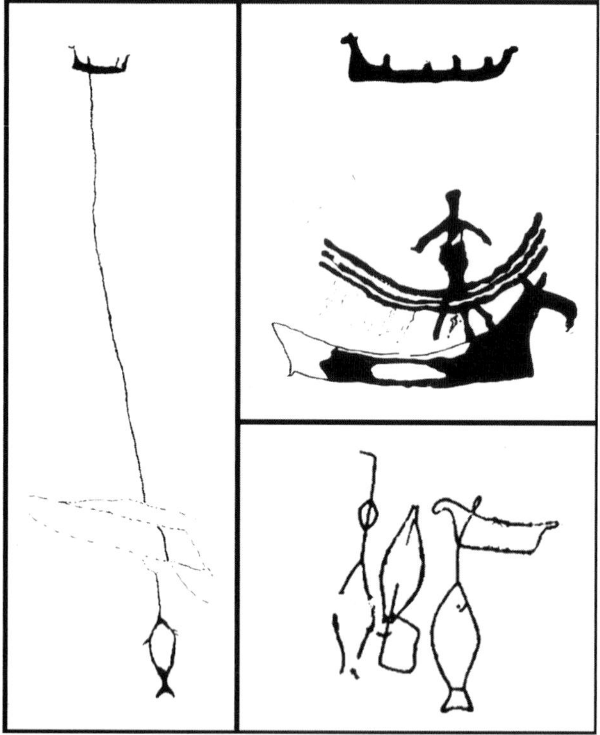

Figure 64.6. Stone Age rock art from Bergbukten, Alta (left), Slettnes (top right) and Forselv (bottom right). Similar vessels are common in the rock art of northern Norwegian hunter-fishers. Apart from halibut, fish are nearly always absent in Norwegian rock art. In this respect it is interesting to note the rich mythologies relating to halibut during historical times, when they were imbued with a variety of social and symbolic meanings. (Drawing: J. M. Gjerde, based on tracings from Gjessing 1932, Helskog 1988 and Hesjedal et al. 1993).

Pollen-botanical data and human impact during the Stone Age

A weak charcoal signal is present from the bottom of the pollen profiles on Melkøya around 8000 cal BC (Figure 64.7). There is a marked anthropogenic impact from 6500 cal BC and onwards, coinciding with the establishment of a more stable forest environment consisting of birch (*Betula pubescens)* and possibly some pine *(Pinus sylvestris).* Large scale forest clearing is traceable around 4300 cal BC, followed by periods of re-growth and clearings, with a more open vegetation consisting of birch and heath lasting until the present treeless vegetation was established around 1700 cal BC. Long periods of settlement with shorter periods of weak or no anthropogenic signals are recorded until 1100 cal BC (Jensen 2004).

Secure timber resources are crucial for wintertime occupation at arctic and sub-arctic locations. One of the most important factors regulating the seasonal use of small northern islands like Melkøya is therefore an abundant supply of firewood. Because of the island's small size, as well as the presence of only two small beaches where driftwood could accumulate, a direct correlation between the intensity and the seasonal use of Melkøya and the available amount of wood can be assumed (Ramstad 2006a).

However, the deforestation of the island around 4200 cal BC coincides with the most intensive anthropogenic impact in the pollen record on the island (Jensen 2004, 279). From the same time period and onwards several larger and more solid subterranean house structures appear, and there seems to be a general increase in the intensity and length of the occupations at the island. The fireplaces in these houses were larger and more solidly built, indicating shifts in fireplace technology (Ramstad 2006a). This is also supported by the fact that some of these fireplaces were connected to air channels in order to get a more controlled and efficient use of the fire. Outside the houses large amounts of fire-cracked rocks were deposited, making up several tons in Sundfjæra. The heating of stones in the fireplaces was used as a technology to conserve and save the energy produced by the fire. Based on the assumption that the need for heating rocks increases during winter time, and the amounts of fire-cracked rocks deposited at settlements sites are proportional with the length and intensity of occupation (Olsen 1998, 112–14), these rocks can be interpreted as indicating a shift towards an increase in the intensity and use of the island during wintertime.

Similar changes within fireplace technology are taking

place during the same time period over large areas of northern Scandinavia (Spång 1997). Deposits of fire-cracked rocks and associated fireplaces probably represent a change from a fireplace technology based on radiation to more energy-saving principles based on convective heating (Ramstad 2006a). At locations with limited amounts of wood, such as Melkøya, these changes can be interpreted as a premise for wintertime habitation (Ramstad 2006a).

Melkøya during the Early Metal Age – Sámi Iron Age

Apart from charred lenses in the peat there is little or no human impact in the pollen picture from the Late Early Metal Age (around 900 BC) onwards, probably indicating that the island was abandoned (Jensen 2004). This picture is consistent with the general trend in northern Norway where the larger coastal Late Stone Age Settlements sites disappear during the Early Metal Age. An increase in inland sites seems to reflect that terrestrial resources are becoming more important at the expense of the previous maritime orientation. Semi-subterranean houses are replaced by lighter house structures, interpreted as a shift to a more mobile settlement pattern (Olsen 1994, Hesjedal *et al.* 1996).

The charred lenses at Melkøya are found over large areas. Four of the charcoal lenses seem to be contemporaneous at different locations on the island, and are interpreted as intentional peat burning (Jensen 2004). Traditionally, burning of heath land is conducted in order to improve pastures. However, neither animal husbandry nor agriculture is documented this far north and there is a general agreement that the economy was based on hunting and fishing until medieval times (Hesjedal *et al.* 1996).

An alternative interpretation is that burning was done to stimulate growth in order to attract larger numbers of prey. The size and location of Melkøya excludes larger animals, such as reindeer (e.g. Anderson 2006, 6). However, throughout history the island has been a refuge for birds (Systad and Bustnes 1998): of these, geese – particularly the graylag (*Anser anser*) – represent the most likely candidates as they are grazing birds (Ramstad 2007). Since there were no land predators on Melkøya, the island would represent an excellent location for grazing geese during the vulnerable times of migration and moulting.

A relevant correlation between burning of heath and increased numbers of geese can be documented at the costal areas further south (from the Lofoten islands, 500km south of Melkøya, and southwards), where farmers were traditionally cultivating the coastal landscape by burning heath. Geese were considered a problem by these farmers, as they grazed on valuable pastures for the livestock. While the burning of heath further south is particularly connected to heath (*Calluna*), the Ericales heath at Melkøya is rich in crowberries (*Empetrum nigerum*) (Jensen 2004). It is therefore important to note that greylag geese, apart from grazing, are particularly fond of crowberries (Shimmings 2005, 32).

The literature dealing with Northern hunter-fisher economy has been primarily concerned with big game hunting and fishing. Little attention has been paid to fowling, although, in historical times especially, sea-fowl played an important role in the economy of coastal societies (Storå 1968). However, these were brief and seasonal activities, which were often conducted at locations far away from habitation areas. Such sites are thus probably highly underrepresented in the archaeological record dealing with hunter-fisher societies. Based on ethnographical records from northern Norway, as well as from circumpolar areas in general, mass trapping of geese was conducted during the time of moulting (Storå 1968, 319–22). These locations were avoided most of the season, as the birds tend to be very shy and nervous. Apart from eggs, meat and fat, the feathers had great economic importance (Storå 1968, 316).

If there were little or no human presence on the island during the later Early Metal Age and Early Iron Age, Melkøya would probably have attracted large numbers of birds. The numbers of geese could be further increased

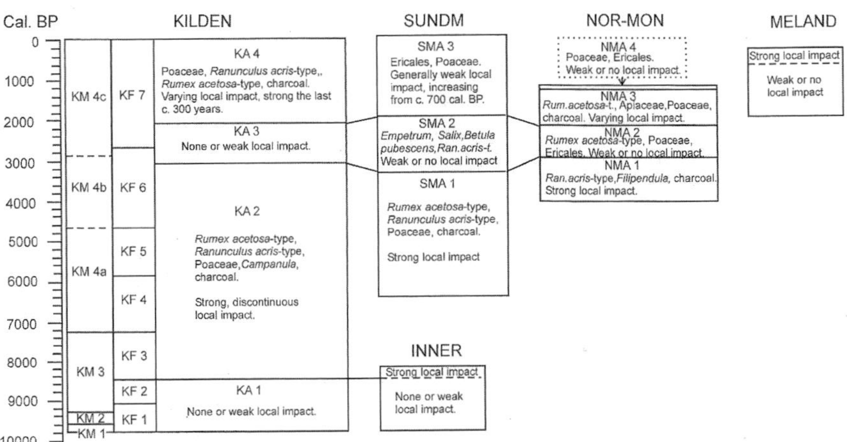

Figure 64.7. Analysis of five peat cores has created a more detailed picture of local vegetation types and anthropogenic impact extending back almost 10,000 years (after Jensen 2004, 282, fig. 12). In addition, a large number of in situ macro-fossil and pollen samples were analysed to obtain information on those plants brought into the dwellings.

by creating more optimal grazing conditions, such as by burning the vegetation on the island at certain intervals.

The birds on Melkøya could have been hunted during direct expeditions, either from inland locations, or by groups staying at other places along the coast (Ramstad 2007). The meat would probably be consumed in the local area, while feathers and other resources from the birds (such as the wings, bones and heads) were brought back to the main camp.

Conclusions

The results from the project have generated new perspectives, giving a unique and detailed picture of the use and re-use of one island over long periods of time. It has given us the ability to provide a more complete picture of spatial and temporal transformations over entire settlement sequences.

The geography and landscape of small islands such as Melkøya provide unique parameters influencing the structuring and use of space that differ from those found on larger landmasses. The work done on Melkøya thus contributes to a more balanced picture of Stone Age settlements and structure types.

The early and rapid colonization of the Norwegian outer coast has the potential to contribute further towards our understanding of early maritime adaptation not directly attainable elsewhere in Europe (Andersen 2003, 10; Bjerck 2008). Melkøya and the surrounding Barents Sea represent one of the most extreme marine areas of Europe. In order to travel and live in these environments, a highly developed maritime technology has always been a prerequisite. Small and exposed islands, where no land mammals have been present, give valuable information about the evolution and changes within Stone Age maritime societies from Early Pre-Boreal times and onwards.

Today Melkøya may seem like an inhospitable and extreme location for Stone Age settlements. However, due to its privileged location, the seasonal and spatial distribution of resources must have allowed for a variety of choices for the people living on the island. The chronological variation of settlement data collected throughout the project highlights how the available food resources structured, or constrained, past settlements on the island, but did not determine them.

Human impact on small and fragile islands is often dramatic. A combination of archaeological data and paleo-environmental studies from such locations may contribute to a deeper understanding of long-term relationships between humans and their interactions with changing environments. If burning of heath was conducted on Melkøya in order to attract larger numbers of geese, this practice also contributes important insights into hunting societies, not merely as collectors of resources but as active manipulators and producers. Even though Melkøya was apparently abandoned during the Early Metal Age this does not mean it lost its importance. The charred peat layers from Melkøya indicate that small islands were utilized in new and hitherto unknown ways providing new theories about Late Metal Age and Early Iron Age economy, habitation and landscape use.

A specialized maritime technology makes the sea an efficient highway rather than a barrier. The rich and varied material demonstrates how people on Melkøya have always been involved in networks stretching over large parts of northern Scandinavia. Small islands can thus no longer be viewed as either marginal or isolated places for Stone Age societies. This calls for a revised concept of 'marginal locations' as integrated elements of complex and far-reaching networks.

Acknowledgements

Thanks are due to Stephen Wickler for his valuable comments and corrections to the English text.

References

Anderson, D. 2006. Dwellings, Storage and Summer Site Structure among Siberian Orochen Evenkis: Hunter Gatherer Vernacular Architecture under Post Socialist Conditions. *Norwegian Archaeological Review* 39 (1), 1–26.

Bang-Andersen, S. 2003. Southwest-Norway at the Pleistocene/Holocene Transition: Landscape, Development, Colonization, Site Types, Settlement Patterns. *Norwegian Archaeological Review* 36 (1), 5–26.

Bergsvik, K. A. 2001. Sedentary and mobile hunter-fishers in Stone Age Western Norway. *Arctic Anthropology* 38 (1), 2–26.

Bjerck, H. B. 1995. The North Sea Continent and the pioneer settlement of Norway, in A. Fischer (ed.), *Man and Sea in the Mesolithic: coastal settlement above and below present sea level*, 131–44. Oxbow Monographs 53. Oxford Oxbow Books.

Bjerck, H. B. 2008. Norwegian Mesolithic Trends: a Review, in G. Baily and P. Spinkins (eds.), *Mesolithic Europe*, 60–106. Cambridge, Cambridge University Press.

Blankholm, H. P. 2004. Earliest Mesolithic Site in Northern Norway? A reassessment of Sarnes B4. *Arctic Anthropology* 41 (1), 41–57.

Engedal, Ø. 2006. På bølgje og berg – båten i røynd og ristning, in R. Barndon, S. M. Innselset, K. K. Kristoffersen and T. K. Lødøen (eds.), *Samfunn, symboler og identitet - Festskrift til Gro Mandt på 70-årsdagen*, 163–82. UBAS Nordisk 3. Bergen, Universitetet i Bergen Arkeologiske Skrifter.

Fuglestvedt, I. 2005. Contact and communication in Northern Europe 10 200 – 9000 / 8500 BP – a phenomenological approach to the connection between technology, skill and landscape, in H. Knutsson (ed.), *Pioneer settlements and colonization processes in the Barents region*, 79–96. Vuollerim Papers on Hunter-Gatherer Archaeology 1. Vuollerim, Vuollerim Museum Press.

Gjessing, G. 1932. *Arktiske helleristninger i Nord-Norge*. Serie B, Skrifter 21. Oslo, Instituttet for sammenlignende kulturforskning.

Glørstad, H. 2001. Forsøk på teoretiske og metodiske ny-orienteringer innen Svinesundprosjektet, in H. Glørstad (ed.), *Svinesundprosjektet*, Bind I, 19–24. Varia 54. Oslo, Universitetets Oldsaksamlings/Kulturhistorisk Museum.

Grydeland, S.-E. 2005. The pioneers of Finnmark – from the earliest coastal settlements to the encounter with the inland peoples of Northern Finland, in H. Knutsson (ed.), *Pioneer settlements and colonization processes in the Barents region*, 43–78. Vuollerim Papers on Hunter-gatherer Archaeology 1. Vuollerim, Vuollerim Museum Press.

Grøn, O. 2000. Etnoarkæologi, in B. V. Eriksen (ed.), *Flintstudier. En håndbog i systematiske analyser af flintinventaret*, 187–207. Aarhus, Aarhus Universitetsforlag.

Grøn, O. and Kuznetsov, O. 2003. Ethno-archaeology among Evenkian forest hunters. Preliminary results and a different approach to reality!, in L. Larsson, H. Kindgren, K. Knutsson, D. Loeffler and A. Åkerlund (eds.), *Mesolithic on the Move: Papers presented at the Sixth International Conference on the Mesolithic in Europe, Stockholm 2000*, 216–22. Oxford, Oxbow Books.

Hald, M., Husum, K., Vorren, T. O., Grøsfjeld, K., Jensen, H. B. and Sharapova, A. 2003. Holocene climate in the sub-arctic fjord Malangen, northern Norway: a multi-proxy study. *Boreas* 23, 543–59.

Helskog, E. T. 1983. *The Iversfjord locality. A study of behavioural pattering during the Late stone Age of Finnmark, North Norway*. Tromsø Museums Skrifter 19. Tromsø, University of Tromsø.

Helskog, K. 1988. *Helleristningene i Alta : spor etter ritualer og dagligliv i Finnmarks forhistorie*. Alta, Alta Museum.

Hesjedal, A., Damm, C., Olsen, B. and Storli, I., 1996. *Arkeologi på Slettnes. Dokumentasjon av 11. 000 års bosetning*. Tromsø Museums Skrifter 26, Tromsø, University of Tromsø.

Hood, B. C. 1992. *Prehistoric Foragers of the North Atlantic: Perspectives on Lithic Procurement and Social Complexity in the North Norwegian Stone Age and the Labrador Maritime Archaic*. Unpublished PhD thesis, University of Massachusetts.

Jensen, C. 2004. The vegetation history of a coastal Stone Age and Iron Age settlement at 70 N°, Norway. *Vegetation history and archaeobotany* 13, 269–84.

Linderholm, J. 2003. Miljøarkeologi i det nordligste Skandinavia. *Ottar* 248, 47–51.

Linderholm, J. 2006. *Markundersökningar innom Melkøja-prosjektet. Boplatser vid Sundfjæra och Normannsvika, Melkøja, Hammerfest, Finnmark, Norge*. Miljöarkeologiska laboratoriet. Rapport no. 2006-003. Institutionen för arkeologi och samiska studier. Umeå, Universitetet i Umeå.

Nesje, A., Jansen, E., Birks, H. J. B., Bjune, A. E., Bakke, J., Andersson, C., Dahl, S. O., Kristensen, D. K., Lauritze, S. E., Lie, Ø., Risebrobakken, B., Svendsen, J. I. 2005. Holocene Climate Variability in the North Atlantic Region: a Review of Terrestrial and Marine Evidence, in H. Drange, T. Dokken, T. Furevik, R. Gerdes and W. Berger (eds.), *The Nordic Seas – An Integrated Perspective*, 289–322. Washington, DC, American Geophysical Union (AGU).

Olsen, B. 1994. *Bosetning og samfunn i Finnmarks forhistorie*. Oslo, Universitetsforlaget.

Olsen, B. 1998. Forhistoriske hus i Nord-Norge. *Bebyggelses-historisk tidskrift* 33, 185–94.

Olsen, B. 1998b. Saqqaq housing and settlement in southern Disco Bay, West Greenland. *Acta Borealia* 15 (2), 81– 128.

Pickard, C. and Bonsall C. 2004. Deep-sea fishing in the European Mesolithic: Fact or fantasy? *European Journal of Archaeology* 7 (3), 273–90.

Ramstad, M. 2003. Som man graver finner man! *Ottar*, 248, 15–26.

Ramstad, M. 2006a. Melkøya – ild og energi gjennom 11.000 år. *Ottar* 262, 18–25.

Ramstad, M. 2006b. Perler og mennesker 4000 f.Kr. Om miljøet rundt ravfunnene fra Finnmarks steinalder, in R. Barndon, S. M. Innselset, K. K. Kristoffersen and T. K. Lødøen (eds.), *Samfunn, symboler og identitet - Festskrift til Gro Mandt på 70-årsdagen*, 129–46. UBAS Nordisk 3. Bergen, Universitetet i Bergen Arkeologiske Skrifter.

Ramstad, M. 2007. Den brente øya - nye perspektiver på den 'funntomme perioden'. *RISS* 2007 (Bergen, Department of Archaeology, University of Bergen), 28–40.

Ramstad, M., Hesjedal, A., Roth Niemi A. 2005. The Melkøya project: maritime hunter-fisher island settlements and the use of space through 11 000 years on Melkøya, Arctic Norway. *Antiquity* 79 (304), Project Gallery, http://antiquity.ac.uk/ProjGall/ramstad/index.html. (accessed 09/2007).

Shimmings, P. 2005. *Kan det gjenskapes egnede habitater for gjess i utmarksbeite? Erfaringer fra et prosjekt på Helgeland*. Tjøtta, Norsk institutt for planteforskning.

Simonsen, P. 1961. *Varanger-Funnene II. Fund og udgravninger på fjordens sydkyst*. Tromsø Museums Skrifter VII (2). Tromsø, Tromsø Museum.

Spång, L. G. 1997. *Fångstsamhälle i handelssystem : Åsele lappmark neolitikum-bronsålder*. Studia archaeologica Universitatis Umensis 9. Umeå, University of Umeå.

Storå, N. 1968. Massfångst av sjöfågel i Nordeurasien. En etnologisk undersökning av fångstmetoderna. *Acta Academiae Aboensis*, ser. A, Humaniora, Vol. 34 (2).

Systad, G. H. and Bustnes, J. O. 1998. *Ornitologiske undersøkelser på Melkøya i juni 1998. Kartlegging og konsekvensanalyse*. Norsk institutt for naturforskning (NINA) Oppdragsmelding 572. Tromsø, Norsk institutt for naturforskning.

65. Two houses and 186,000 artefacts. Spatial organization at the Late Mesolithic site of Strandvägen, Sweden

Tom Carlsson

The point of departure for this paper is the Mesolithic site of Strandvägen (Motala) in Sweden (5500–4500 cal BC). People during the Mesolithic regularly sought out places with similar locations in the landscape. Having selected a location, they arranged their hearths, storage pits and houses according to a consistent pattern. The Strandvägen site shows how the society related to natural elements – for example from wet to dry. Features and elements at the settlements were probably physical aspects of their narratives, including myths and world-views. This text focuses on two Mesolithic house remains that will be presented and discussed according to space as practised place. 'Feeling at home' was to know what to do, and where to do it.

Keywords: Late Mesolithic, Sweden, spatial organization, houses, settlement, cosmological order.

Introduction

Remains of huts, dwellings or houses, at Mesolithic settlement sites are a controversial topic in Stone Age archaeology. In cases where building remains have been interpreted as belonging to the Mesolithic, these interpretations have usually encountered severe criticism from the academic community. This source criticism has included, amongst other things, the basis for the dating, validity and representativeness of ^{14}C analyses; even the excavation methods have been questioned (Johansson 1989; Browall 1999). In Denmark, since the 1970s, there has been a fixed view of what houses (huts) of the Maglemose culture looked like, and how they were structured (Brinch Petersen 1972; Andersen *et al.* 1982). As a consequence, remains of settlement or dwellings of this period that differ in any way from the accepted picture, with differences in find distribution, have been dismissed. The narrow criteria and definitions have impeded discussions instead of taking them forward (Schilling 2001). This rigid source criticism has been criticized by Professor Lars Larsson as something he styles 'the Mesolithic house syndrome' (Larsson 1985, 101). He wonders how similar scrutiny of house remains from other archaeological periods would have affected discussions at those sites. Gaining acceptance for every new house is a struggle that continues to be waged on the academic barricades.

In the following text two Mesolithic houses from the Strandvägen site (Motala town) in Sweden will be discussed. The argument for acceptance has been conducted elsewhere (Carlsson 2005). My subject here is to present interpretations for the organization of the living space, inside the houses and around the settlement area.

Space is practised places

Understanding living space – floors, along the walls, and the space around the hearths – gives us an opportunity to look inside the actual homes of the people we study. In his famous work on the Kabyl Berber house in Algeria, the French anthropologist and philosopher Pierre Bourdieu, points to links between cosmological order and physical organization of living space (1970). Space, according to Bourdieu, is organized by representations dominated by analogies to bodies and bodily experiences. In creating the physical form of the house and the settlement, it represents and reproduces human bodies, so that space becomes deeply associated with gender. Another path to follow is offered by Julian Thomas (1993; 1996; 2004), using the concept of 'spatial story' in the archaeological context. The landscape was knit together in a web-like series of analogies, myths, and stories. Just like the rest of the landscape, the Mesolithic settlement and the house were probably equipped and used according to legends and myths. Stories were told over and over: they were well known and accepted by the inhabitants. Again referring to Bourdieu, space was lived and transformed, according to bodily experience (analogies), into the *habitus*. Even though Bourdieu's theories have been criticized, amongst other things, for translating French Berber community to society in a wider sense, and for his 'structuralist' approach (Painter 2000, 256), they afford an opportunity to understand the organization of space in ways other than just areas for flint knapping and the discarding of refuse.

Space is practised places (Crang 2000, 150). People were comfortable; they knew where to do what, and how to behave, in order to gain social acceptance. The organization of space according to a world-view is not to perceive it too strictly and statically, but to understand more the variation of themes. The context of time and place is fundamental. The concept of 'home' differs from time to time and place to place. The use of ethnographic analogies must be done very carefully, and ethnographic documents can never be translated to Mesolithic evidence: they can only make one think differently, in order to make prehistory a less unfamiliar place; e.g. what if it was like *this* instead. As Ole Grøn and Oleg Kuznetsov (2003, 217) point out in their studies of the Siberian Evenks, 'My home is where I am. They don't move – it's the world that moves'. Just as with the Kabyl Berbers in Algeria, cosmological order is always present for the Siberian Evenks.

But societies are constantly changing, even in the Mesolithic, and are always in a state of flux. At any fixed point, the way of acting (*habitus*) is a synthesis of recycling ideas from the past and translating ongoing influences, creating a new reality for the present. In other words, cosmological order was not a definite situation.

The Strandvägen site

The location of the settlement site at Strandvägen is unique in that the physical conditions, from the micro-perspective, have remained similar for at least 7000 years! The water in the river (Motala Ström) still flows at the same level it did some 7000 years ago. During the Atlantic period there was a saltwater sea only 30 kilometres away (the Litorina Sea). Motala Ström was almost certainly important for communications. Using the region's lakes (the great Lake Vättern in the west and Lake Boren in the east) was the simplest way to travel in all directions. A simplified reconstruction of the local environment during the Atlantic period describes it as place of convergence for several different ecological areas. In the south, and to the east, there were lakes, swamps, and dried eskers protruding. In the north, large forests spread over the rocky terrain (Carlsson *et al.* 2003).

The site was discovered in 1999 during construction of a new railway bridge over the river. Over the three years (2000/2003) of excavations, thick occupation layers were dug out that contained more than 186,000 finds. The investigation of the site's occupation layers (with well-preserved organic finds – bone and macrofossils) took place both on land and under water. It is worth stressing that the entire site could not be excavated – only that section directly in the area of the new railway bridge. There is a great deal to suggest that the site covered a much larger area. The main Mesolithic phase is dated 5900–4500 cal BC. A large number of features, hearths, postholes, and (presumed) storage pits, testify to intensive use of the site around 5500–5000 cal BC. According to radiocarbon dates, the site had been used in different ways later on in Mesolithic times. The ^{14}C dates (from 5000–4500 cal BC) include artefacts found underwater: leisters, worked bone, and red deer (*Cervus elaphus*) antler. Only one single feature from this period has been dated. This means that the organisation or the use of the settlement might have changed. However we still do not know how the site looked beyond the limits of the excavation area: houses, hearths, stone-knapping areas, and so on, could just have been located in different areas of the settlement in this later period.

The site was well chosen in its micro-environment: in the lee of the westerly winds on a gentle slope down towards the water, which is a calm part of Motala Ström. The whole area was covered by a Mesolithic occupation layer 20–50cm thick. This layer was thickest closest to the water, gradually thinning further up the slope. It was excavated and water-sieved, but the Mesolithic features were not discovered until the whole layer had been removed.

The Mesolithic settlement site at Strandvägen was a well-organized place for a long period. Around 5500–5000 cal BC the settlement had activity areas that were spatially well demarcated; cooking, lithic crafts, axe production were all carried out at specific places (Figure 65.1). The excavated area is a cross-section through the site from the highest point along the bank and out into the water, from the dry land down towards the water. The Mesolithic settlement site organization follows this gradual natural division. Different kinds of activities were performed in *relation* to the bank and the water. The distribution of finds reinforces this picture. Furthest from the water were the dwelling house, hearths for cooking, and separate hearths probably used for drying (or smoking) food in certain seasons. The next zone, between the dry land and the water, was used for crafts such as manufacturing, polishing, and sharpening axes. Lithic crafts, the manufacture of various tools, were also pursued here. At the wet zone, in the water, people threw their residue from tool manufacture; they also fished there. This may, of course, reflect a highly functional division of the site. No one wants to sleep in a damp house; fishing can only be done in the water; rubbish was thrown in the water to get rid of the smell, and so on. But perhaps there are other ways to explain why activities took place where they did and why things were left where they were. The river shore, with waves constantly splashing the rocks and stones, should perhaps not be regarded merely as a functional area for rubbish.

The classification of finds suggests that the relationships between objects and places had many profound meanings. Part of the top of a human skull was found at the water's edge. One interpretation is that a dead individual was buried in some way – above or under ground – and the body decomposed. When the time was propitious, part of the skull was apparently struck off. Such scenarios have been suggested for missing skeleton parts at Skateholm, Scania (Nilsson-Stutz 2003). The skull fragment was

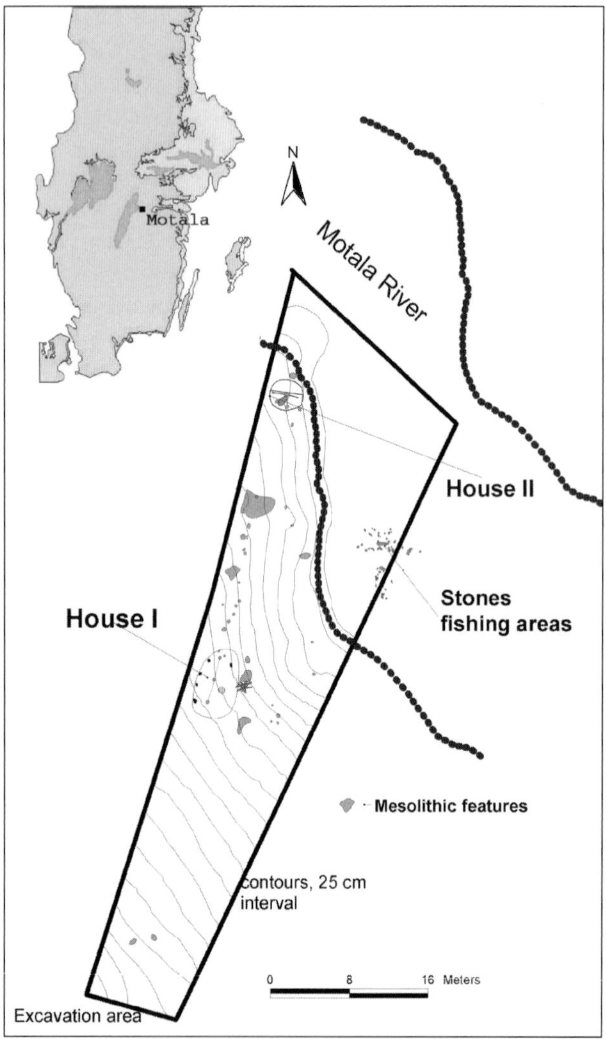

Figure 65.1. Space is practised places. Activities and activity areas at the Strandvägen site were organized according to the distance from the water.

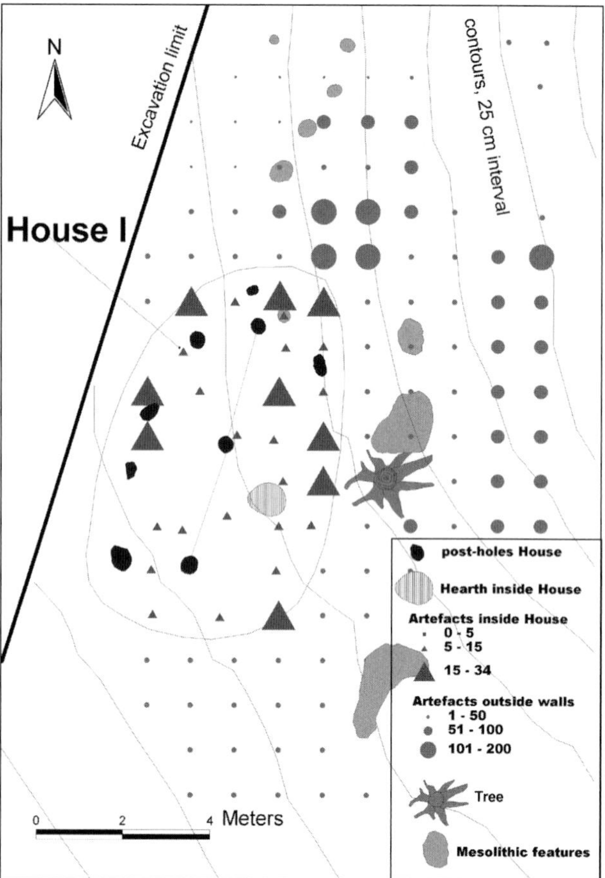

Figure 65.2. A Mesolithic living house at Strandvägen. Distribution of different artefacts (quality) and numbers of finds (quantity).

'buried/deposited/offered' in (what we call today) the refuse layer of the settlement site. Finds in the same area included a bone point with double barbs, leister points, and a decorated antler artefact (Andersson and Carlsson 2005). The same wet shoreline zone also held concentrations of handle cores. The number is disproportionately large in comparison with finds of microblades from the same zone. The fact that handle cores are found in wet environments at several places in Scandinavia has attracted attention. These too have therefore been interpreted in terms of spatial ritual organization on settlement sites (Knutsson *et al.* 2003; Karsten 2001). Farther out from the bank, marine archaeologists found on the riverbed a red deer antler, a pressure flake, and a pecked axe. The water, and the part of the site nearest the water, probably had a special meaning in the inhabitants' perceptual world. The objects could be explained as waste, but since similar finds occur in comparable settings in southern Scandinavia, they can more probably be interpreted as ritual offerings (Karsten 2001).

A Mesolithic 'longhouse'

On a slight terrace in the transitional zone, where the occupation layer ceased, a concentration of postholes was excavated and interpreted as belonging to the remains of a house (Figure 65.2). The internal structure consisted of the remains of three postholes from the roof-bearing central posts of a two-aisled house that extended north-south. In the west there were several postholes interpreted as having supported the wall of the house. There were no traces of the eastern wall, but this area had been disturbed by a number of pits containing brick and other modern material. Judging by the line of the wall and the fragmentarily preserved gables, the house was probably almost elliptical in shape. The southern gable was wider and much more rounded than the northern one, and was also placed further from the central posts. The gable in the north was interpreted as running close to the central post. In the house the excavation also uncovered a hearth with fire-cracked stone, leached soot, and charcoal. The documented postholes (and their presumed counterparts in the eastern line of the wall) form a structure, about 10 × 4m, with a rounded south gable and a slightly more pointed gable to the north. No opening/door was observed, but one interpretation suggests that it was in the east wall. This would then give the hearth a functional position just inside the door, and it would mean that the opening/door faced a given direction. (Perhaps to orientate the opening towards the rising sun; to confront new arrivals landing their canoes on the riverbank; or to overlook the many activities being undertaken immediately outside?). The western wall of the house would at that time have afforded some protection from the constant westerly winds from Lake Vättern.

When the entire occupation layer in the area had been excavated, it was also noticed that the house had stood on a levelled surface that had been partly dug out, with the postholes strikingly alike in form and appearance. Charcoals from the three roof-bearing posts and the hearth were selected for ^{14}C analyses:

- 6580±55 BP; 5630–5470 cal BC; Ua-26735. Oak (*Quercus*).
- 6440±55 BP; 5490–5310 cal BC; Ua-26737. Oak.
- 6370±55 BP; 5480–5250 cal BC; Ua-26736. Hazelnut shell (*Corylus*).

The variation of a few hundred years seems a reasonable interval, but it is also conceivable that the oak, which was used as building material or firewood, had a high initial value (core wood): in other words, that it was relatively old when felled. The hazelnut shell, on the other hand, can scarcely have had any initial value. The charcoal in the hearth could not be dated, unfortunately, since it dissolved while being prepared for the accelerator mass spectrometry (AMS) dating.

In order to analyse space and the activities carried out, we must turn to the artefacts left indoors. Inside the walls of the house there were comparatively few finds, consisting of only some 300 pieces: flakes, debris, cores, microblades, four retouched knives or scrapers, three hammerstones, and burned animal bones. Nonetheless, comparing the distribution of quantities and qualities one gets a picture of where activities were practised at home.

According to this picture, manufacturing and knapping were carried out in the northern part of the house. Cores of different raw materials (quartz, mylolithic quartz, flint) were left in the knapping area. Debris (<10mm) was constantly cleaned off the floor, but some pieces were swept to the sides and trampled down below the surface. Artefacts (ready-made knives, scrapers and so on) and larger flakes were removed, either to be used elsewhere or to keep the floor clean. Microblades made from handle cores have their own distribution pattern. Practical experiments show that they can 'flip' at least one or two metres when pressed off the core (Larsson 1983, 91). Inside the house these (mostly) microblades were found at a reasonable distance from the manufacturing (including the handle core) area. One microblade was found in the hearth. Close to the hearth, unretouched flakes dominate. Most probably these flakes were used as multi-purpose tools. Indoors, the occupation layer contained only a very few burned fragments of animal bones, scattered with no visible pattern.

Objects in larger numbers were, however, found immediately outside the wall of the house. These included flakes, debris, cores, hammerstones, grinding stones, burned animal bones, and so on. According to the quantity of objects found along the outer walls, the inside was constantly cleaned. The interpretation is that the house mainly functioned as a dwelling and that stone working mostly took place outdoors, or in other buildings (see below). Some handling of tools (resharpening? manufacture?) nevertheless resulted in the deposition of waste, chiefly along the walls. The house was in all probability cleaned, which has naturally affected our potential to reconstruct the activities performed indoors.

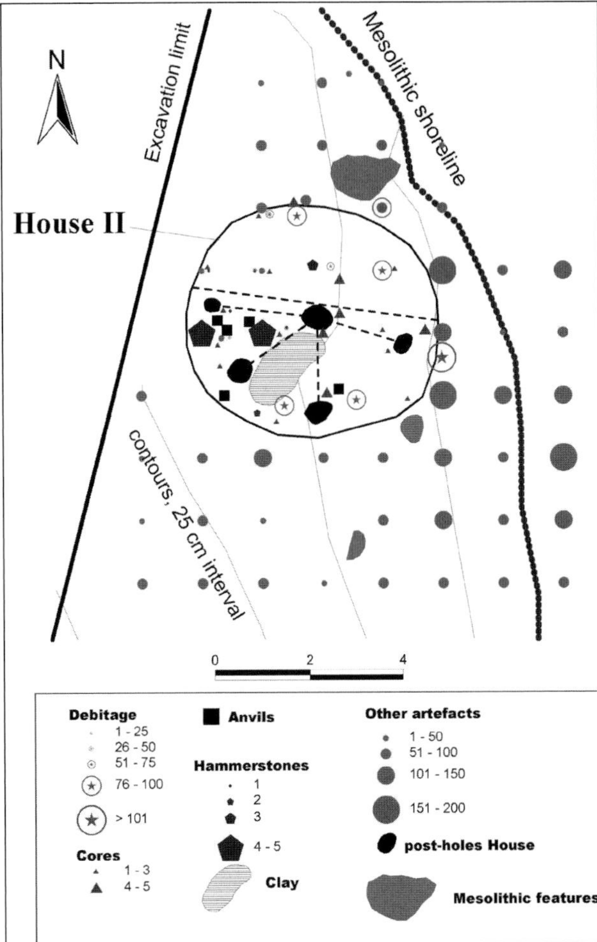

Figure 65.3. The round (or semi-circular) workshop and the distribution of artefacts.

A workshop close to the water

Yet another Mesolithic building was found, this time at the very tip of the original point, very close to the water (Figure 65.3). This house was probably round, or semicircular, and, unlike the 'longhouse', it also contained large quantities of finds. In terms of the number of items per square metre, this area has the densest quantity of finds. What remained of the house were four postholes making up a semicircle (about 5m in diameter), with the opening to the north-east. In the middle of the house there was yet another posthole. Inside the house the excavators also noted a thin layer of clay, which was probably a floor.

The ^{14}C analysis yielded the range 5470–4700 cal BC.

- 6305±55 BP; 5470–5200 cal BC; Ua-27103. Hazelnut shell.
- 6185±55 BP; 5300–4960 cal BC; Ua-27104. Hazelnut shell.
- 6040±55 BP; 5070–4770 cal BC; Ua-27105. Hazelnut shell.
- 6070±55 BP; 5210–4790 cal BC; Ua-27106. Hazelnut shell.

An important question is whether the two houses were used simultaneously, or, at least, belonged to the same settlement structure. According to the ^{14}C datings the workshop is slightly later than the larger 'longhouse'. But by comparing the dates exclusively from the hazelnut shells, the two houses might form one settlement unit (no oak was found in the postholes). The two ^{14}C dates from the oak of House I probably derive from old branch wood collected for the fires, or, alternatively, roof posts might very well have been oak. The interpretation for the two houses is that the living house and the workshop were, at least partly, used at the same time.

Conducting the same qualitative and quantitative analyses as were undertaken for the 'longhouse', a similar pattern appears. Hammerstones, anvils, cores, and debitage from tool manufacture using different kinds of stone, suggest intense activity. Cores (from different raw materials) and hammerstones are exclusively found in the central zone (close to the mid posthole), and the debitage is mainly scattered against the walls and in the open space to the north. The interior contained a smaller number of tools, or larger flakes suitable as tools. Animal bones found inside included a red deer antler. A small, decorated antler fragment, some 6cm long, was found in one of the wall-bearing postholes. The decoration in this case was very simple, consisting merely of two parallel lines that narrowed at one end to a point. The original appearance and function of the object cannot be guessed today. However, although undated, the decoration conforms well to other finds from south Scandinavia in the Late Mesolithic (Andersson and Carlsson 2005).

Along the walls and in the water just outside the house, however, there were large amounts of waste from stone working, including many different kinds of objects, debris, flakes, blades, and so on. This is most probably the result of regular house cleaning. The large number of finds, and the limited space, have led to the interpretation that this feature was a workshop for stone working, and not a dwelling.

Conclusions

The settlement site at Strandvägen was well organized. From the dry land down towards the water, cooking, lithic crafts, axe production, etc., were carried out in specific areas. Activities indoors and around the houses were organized according to the relationships of factors such as hearths, walls, knapping places, and proximity to the water. The space, inside the houses and within the settlement, was a busy complex of activities, symbols, names, and narratives, which had a deeper meaning than can be explained in mere functional terms. After all, Mesolithic men and women lived and organized their activities in ways that are beyond the modern meaning of functional: they clearly had an understanding of where to do what. Something guided and regulated the actions of people in the physical space. My suggested idea is that the spatial organization reflects a cosmological idea that activities were assigned to places within the habitation space. This organization lasted for some hundreds of years, and then the society changed and reorganized once again. Stories and myths were then told in different ways. Old habits of 'doing things' now seemed strange: *habitus* had been transformed to a new context.

The question is, finally, what picture of the Mesolithic is (re)produced by our interpretations of the settlement site. Is it familiar to us? I hope not.

References

Andersen, K., Jørgensen, S. and Richter, J. 1982. *Maglemose hytterne ved Ulkestrup Lyng*. Nordiske Fortidsminder, Series B, vol. 7. Copenhagen, Det Kongelige Nordiske Oldskriftselskab.

Andersson, H. and Carlsson, T. 2005. Ristad i rader – två dekorerade hornföremål från mesolitikum funna i Motala. *Fornvännen* 100, 5–11.

Brinch Petersen, E. 1972. A Maglemose hut from Svaerdborg Bog, Zealand, Denmark. *Acta Archaeologica* 42. 11–16.

Browall, H. 1999. Mesolitiska mellanhavanden i västra Östergötland, in A. Gustafsson and H. Karlsson (eds.), *Glyfer och arkeologiska rum – en vänbok till Jarl Nordbladh*, 289–303. Gotarc Series A, 3. Göteborg, Göteborgs Universitet, Institutionen för arkeologi.

Bourdieu, P. 1970. The Berber House or the World Reversed. *Social science information* 9, 151–70.

Carlsson, T. 2005. Home, sweet home. The spatial story of the Mesolithic settlement organisation in Östergötland, in G. Gruber (ed.), *Identities in Transition. Mesolithic strategies in the Swedish province of Östergötland*, 36–53. Arkeologiska Undersökningar, Skrifter 64. Linköping, Riksantikvarieämbetet.

Carlsson, T., Gruber, G., Molin, F. and Wikell, R. 2003. Between Quartz and Flint. Material Culture and Social Interaction, in L. Larsson, H. Kindgren, K. Knutsson, D. Loeffler and A. Åkerlund (eds.), *Mesolithic on the Move: Papers presented at the Sixth International Conference on the Mesolithic in Europe, Stockholm 2000*, 302–9. Oxford, Oxbow Books.

Crang, M. 2000. Relicts, places and unwritten geographies in the work of Michel de Certeau, in M. Crang and N. Thrift (eds.), *Thinking space*, 136–53. London, Routledge.

Grøn, O. and Kuznetsov, O. 2003. Ethno-archaeology among Evenkia forest hunters. Preliminary results and a different approach to reality, in L. Larsson, H. Kindgren, K. Knutsson, D. Loeffler and A. Åkerlund (eds.), *Mesolithic on the Move: Papers presented at the Sixth International Conference on the Mesolithic in Europe, Stockholm 2000*, 216–21. Oxford, Oxbow Books.

Johansson, L. G. 1989. Var Tingbyhuset från järnåldern? *Populär Arkeologi* 7 (2), 5–6.

Karsten P. 2001. *Dansarna från Bökeberg. Om jakt, ritualer och inlandsbosättningar vid jägarstenålderns slut.* Arkeologiska Undersökningar, Skrifter 37. Malmö, Riksantikvarieämbetet.

Knutsson, K., Falkenström, P. and Lindberg, K.-F. 2003. Appropriation of the Past. Neolithisation in the Northern Scandinavia Perspective, in L. Larsson, H. Kindgren, K. Knutsson, D. Loeffler and A. Åkerlund (eds.), *Mesolithic on the Move: Papers presented at the Sixth International Conference on the Mesolithic in Europe, Stockholm 2000*, 414–30. Oxford, Oxbow Books.

Larsson, L. 1983. *Ageröd V: an Atlantic bog site in central Scania.* Acta Archaeologica Lundensia, Series in 8°, 12. Lund, University of Lund.

Larsson L. 1985. Of House and Hearth. The Excavation, Interpretation and Reconstruction of a Late Mesolithic House, in M. Backe, C. Bergman, I. B. Hennix, L. Forsberg, L. Holm, L. Liedgren, A.-K. Lindqvist, I.-M. Mulk, M. Nejati, P. Perstrand and P. H. Ramqvist (eds.), *In Honorem Evert Baudou*, 197–209. Archaeology and Environment 4. Umeå, Department of Archaeology, University of Umeå.

Nilsson Stutz, L. 2003. Embodied rituals and ritualized bodies: tracing ritual practices in Late Mesolithic burials. *Acta archaeologica Lundensia*, Series in 8°, 46. Stockholm, Almqvist & Wiksell International.

Painter, J. 2000. Pierre Bourdieu, in M. Crang and N. Thrift (eds.), *Thinking space*, 239–59. London, Routledge.

Schilling, H. 2001. Veje til en mesolitisk multurhistorie, in O. L. Jensen, S. A. Sörensen and K. M. Hansen (eds.), *Danmarks Jaegerstenalder – Status Og Perspektiver. 2001. Beretning fra symposiet Status og perspektiver inden for dansk mesolitikum*, 201–6. Proceedings of a symposium held in Vordingborg 16–17 September 1998. Hörsholm, Hörsholm Egns Museum.

Thomas, J. 1993. The Politics of Vision and the Archaeologies of Landscape, in B. Bender (ed.), *Landscape: Politics and Perspectives*, 19–48. Oxford, Berg.

Thomas, J. 1996. *Time, Culture and Identity: An Interpretive Archaeology*. London, Routledge.

Thomas, J. 2004. *Archaeology and Modernity*. London, Routledge.

66. Ålyst: a settlement complex with hut structures from the Early Mesolithic on Bornholm, Denmark

Claudio Casati and Lasse Sørensen

The preliminary results from the excavation campaign of the Maglemose settlement complex at Ålyst, Bornholm are presented. The large-scale rescue excavation has revealed a settlement complex with at least 26 flint concentrations and at least two huts. The main lithic production in the concentrations is for blanks, in order to produce microliths. These flint concentrations have been interpreted as short-term transit, hunting and fishing camps. The remains of two huts have also been excavated on Ålyst, indicating another aspect of the internal settlement pattern of the site. Activity zones with larger pits or dumping areas have been observed around the huts. Inside the huts, the northern part is interpreted as a large activity zone with pits, hearths and a flint concentration. The southern part is void of finds and internal features. The lithic material shows a high degree of tool diversity compared to the lithic artefacts from the other flint concentrations on the site. It is argued that Ålyst must be interpreted as a complicated diachronic complex. In the present state of analysis, the settlement complex at Ålyst is best regarded as a location extensively visited during the early Mesolithic, probably by small groups of recurring hunter-gatherers.

Keywords: Early Mesolithic, Maglemose, Denmark, Bornholm, dwellings, large-scale excavation, settlement, lithic diversity, Mesolithic features.

Introduction

Since 1998, the Museum of Bornholm has been conducting large-scale salvage excavations on an Early Mesolithic site situated approximately 7km north of Rønne on the western side of the island of Bornholm, Denmark (Figure 66.1). The site will be completely destroyed in the near future as a result of gravel extraction. As excavations, as well as investigations on the already rescued material, are still in progress, the final results are not yet available. Hence, the results presented in this paper must be regarded as preliminary and subject to later modifications.

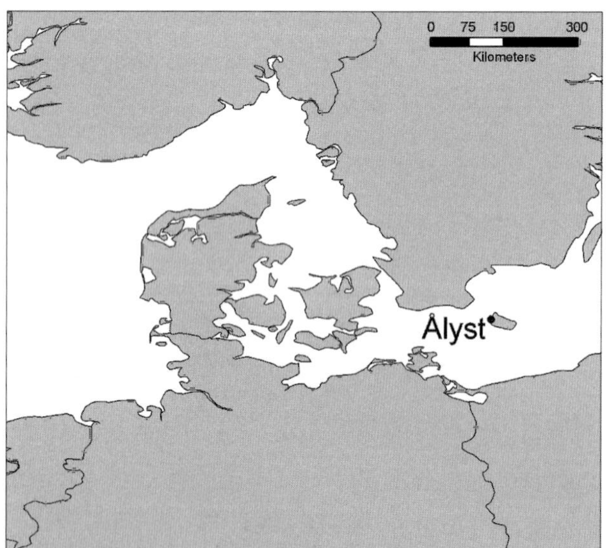

Figure 66.1. Location of Bornholm and the site of Ålyst in the Baltic Sea.

Present day Bornholm is an island in the Baltic Sea, but that has not always been the case. In Preboreal times, approximately 9500–8200 cal BC, Bornholm was a peninsula connected to Rügen in Germany, but during the transition of the Preboreal-Boreal period, about 8200 cal BC, the peninsula was transformed into an island. This situation has provided us with a unique opportunity to study the settlement pattern of a Mesolithic group (Casati and Sørensen, this volume; Sørensen 2004). This paper presents a small part of these settlement aspects.

General situation

The Mesolithic research situation on Bornholm reflects an increased focus on the investigations of Maglemose settlements, but most of these are still based on surface collections (Casati, Sørensen and Vennersdorf 2004, 113 ff.; Nielsen 2001, 85 ff.). Unfortunately, the preservation of organic material is poor on Maglemose sites as they are usually located on Late Glacial shoreline deposits, i.e. on sandy soil. Some of the settlements are placed close to the mouths of larger streams, or on sandy soil alongside streams and near a spring. The Maglemose settlement complex at Ålyst is one of these sites. It was situated on the Bagge Å (stream), at a point where the Muleby and Samsings streams join the Bagge, inland and approximately 1–3km from the present-day shoreline of the Baltic Sea.

Large-scale excavations of Late Palaeolithic/Early Mesolithic sites in central parts of western Europe previously showed tendencies indicating extensive activity areas at these settlements, as seen for example at Niederbieber (Bolus 1992), Rekem (De Bie and Caspar 2000), and Verrebroek 'Dok' (Crombré 1998, 19 ff.). The site at Ålyst was known to contain material from the Maglemose period, scattered over a widespread area, as recorded in surveys by the amateur archaeologist, Holger Kapel, conducted in the 1940s (Becker 1952, 144 ff., fig. 22, n. 9; Nielsen 2001, 85 ff.). In the light of this, it was decided to employ an excavation method at Ålyst that would enable us quickly to excavate a larger area than is usual at a Danish Mesolithic site (Casati and Sørensen 2006, 241 f.).

Excavation

The excavation began with the removal of the topsoil with a mechanical digger, down to the top of a layer deriving from the Bronze Age; this layer concealed the underlying Maglemose layer. We proceeded to a third layer that was a combination of the other two, caused by animal intrusions. In this manner, an area of about 20,000m^2 was uncovered and approximately 10,000m^2 have been excavated in full units of 1m^2 (Figure 66.2). The Bronze Age layer, the Maglemose layer, and the underlying third layer were all sieved. In this way it was possible to locate both visible and latent structures in the Maglemose layer.

So far the excavation method has provided us with a unique picture of a settlement site, with at least 26 flint concentrations and traces of two hut structures. We are well aware that the reconstruction of the internal organisation of the site can only be achieved by analysing the spatial distribution of the recovered eco- and artefacts. The information presented, relating to the spatial distribution of the finds, is solely based on field-observations and not as yet on detailed spatial studies. Likewise, the functional variability of the concentrations is still to be determined. The majority of the concentrations vary in extent from 3 × 3m to 5 × 7m. Most are discrete and only a few overlap. All of the excavated concentrations consist mainly of stone artefacts (predominantly of local, nodular flint) that were collected on the island. The main lithic products from the concentrations are blades – i.e. blanks for producing microliths. There is a distinct lack of other lithic tool types in these concentrations. The lack of tool diversity in the flint concentrations could be an indication of a short-term settlement strategy. Unfortunately, because of the poor organic preservation, it is impossible to determine whether the site was occupied within the same season throughout the whole Early Mesolithic, nor can we decide whether it always had the same function within the settlement system. The site could, for example, have been used at a given moment as a hunting camp, while at other times functioning as a base camp. There are indications that these flint concentrations are seasonal settlements, because, once a year, from October to November, trout swim upstream in

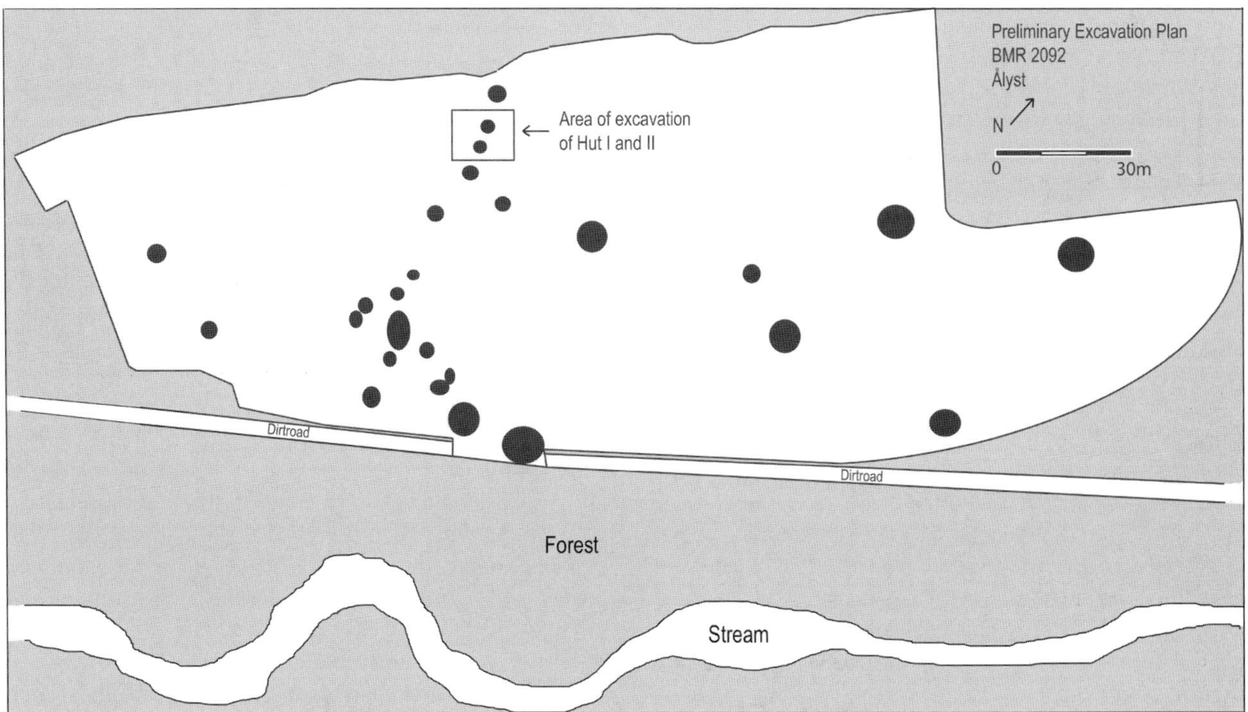

Figure 66.2. Schematic and preliminary excavation plan of the Ålyst site. Black dots indicate the concentrations.

the nearby Bagge Å to spawn. At this time local hazelnuts (*Corylus*) are also ripe and ready to be eaten. The numerous burnt hazelnut shells found in the flint concentrations add weight to the interpretation of seasonal activity in the late fall. Another motive for a returning settlement pattern at this particular spot could be the many topographical advantages for hunting; three streams run together in this region, and thus there are widespread wetlands in the area. This situation creates several forced passages, where hunting for game would be possible and favourable. All things considered, this is an ideal landscape for hunting, fishing and gathering.

On the other hand, other finds from Ålyst seem to substantiate that there was also a longer-term settlement strategy in operation. During excavations in 2002, it became clear that some of the structural evidence, in the northern part of the excavation area, represented the remains of two oval-shaped huts. These included visible features such as fireplaces, pits, postholes, and a high degree of lithic tool diversity (Figure 66.3).

Hut I

Hut I, which was partly excavated in full units of 1m², and partly in units of 0.25m², was orientated north–south and measured roughly 7 × 4m, with an interpreted entrance area towards the east. The interpretation of the place of entrance is substantiated by the lack of postholes and the fact that no lithics were found directly outside the entrance area. The 12 postholes constituting the hut's structural remains had the same morphology. They were diffuse and their colours were dark-brown, or grey, with a diameter and depth of 20–30cm. Furthermore, the postholes contained cuts for the posts and faint traces of them. Similar faint traces were observed previously at sites such as Svanemosen 28 (Grøn 1995, 75), Storlyckan (Larsson and Molin 2000, 10), and Årup (Nilsson and Hanlon 2006). Wooden poles with dimensions corresponding to these features are known from Mesolithic hut structures at Ulkestrup Lyng I and II (Andersen *et al.* 1982, 14 ff.) and Nivå 10 (Jensen 2001, 121). The backfill of the postholes at Ålyst revealed traces of human activity, providing finds such as lithic material, burnt hazelnut shells, small bits of charcoal, hammerstones, anvil stones and grinding stones; one of the features (A106) also revealed a small cache of nodular flint (Figure 66.4). This flint cache was a crucial find for the interpretation of the structure. A similar, but larger, flint cache on Bornholm was found during excavation of the Mesolithic site of Nørre Sandegård V. During its excavation, Becker noticed that the flints were located in a faint, greyish feature (Becker 1952, 111). These finds are undoubtedly Mesolithic, as the local raw material of nodular flint on Bornholm in general is ascribed to the Mesolithic. During other periods of prehistory, the population primarily made use of imported flint. The appearance of this particular feature was thus a guide to the morphology of other Mesolithic features during excavations on the site. This interpretation is supported by the first accelerator mass spectrometer (AMS) radiocarbon dates we obtained from the site. Our dating strategy is based on single-entity dating of charred hazelnut shells. A charred hazelnut shell from the feature containing the flint cache is dated to 8925±65 BP (8280–7910 cal BC; AAR-9876; Bronk Ramsey 2005).

A generally accepted method for locating the former positions of hearths on Mesolithic sites is to plot the burnt arte- and ecofacts, assuming that the squares with the highest density coincide with the centre of former hearths. There was no visible hearth in Hut I, but by plotting the burnt lithic material and charred hazelnut shells, a latent hearth appeared in the north-western part of the hut. Here we located a flint concentration (approximately 4m²) containing 2050 pieces of flint. The concentration contained debitage and different tool types, such as microliths together with knives, scrapers, burins, and greenstone axes. The larger artefacts (hammerstones, anvil stones, cores, etc.) created a wall effect, respecting the outlines of the postholes (Figure 66.4). The southern part of the hut was almost void of finds. Within the structure there were some small, light-brown, greyish-black pits, approximately 30–40cm in diameter and depth. These contained charred hazelnut shells, burnt bones and lithic artefacts, which typologically date the pits to the Maglemose culture. Outside the hut, some larger pits were excavated, approximately 1–2m wide and 40–50cm in depth (Figure 66.3). These pits are likely to have been in use at the same time as the hut. This hypothesis will be challenged by future refitting analysis of the lithic material from inside the hut and from the pits, as well as from the AMS radiocarbon dates currently being processed.

Hut II

In an area just south-east of Hut I, we excavated another hut structure (Figure 66.3). Hut II, which, for several reasons, was excavated in full 1m² units, had an oval appearance. It was orientated north-south and measured 7 × 4m, with a darker coloured area of approximately 2m² towards the east. This darker coloured area, which was slightly depressed, contained fragmented lithic material, as well as small pieces of charcoal and burnt hazelnut shells; it is interpreted as the entrance area. The 16 postholes were less distinct than those of Hut I, and all had a similar appearance. They were dark- and light-brown, with a diameter of approximately 20–30cm and with a depth of 10–30cm. The southern part of the structure was not as well preserved as the northern part. The backfill of the postholes contained the same type of material as Hut I, i.e. charcoal, burnt hazelnuts, and lithics, although some of the postholes contained larger stones, which have been interpreted as packing. Inside the hut there was a larger flint concentration (approximately 4 × 5m and with 1000 pieces of flint) with various lithic tool types, including microliths, knives, scrapers, splintered pieces, and burins. The main concentration of lithics and tools lay in the northern part of the hut, although some lithics were found outside (Figure 66.5). This distribution was influenced by a large pit and two tree falls, which were noticed when most of the Maglemose layer had been

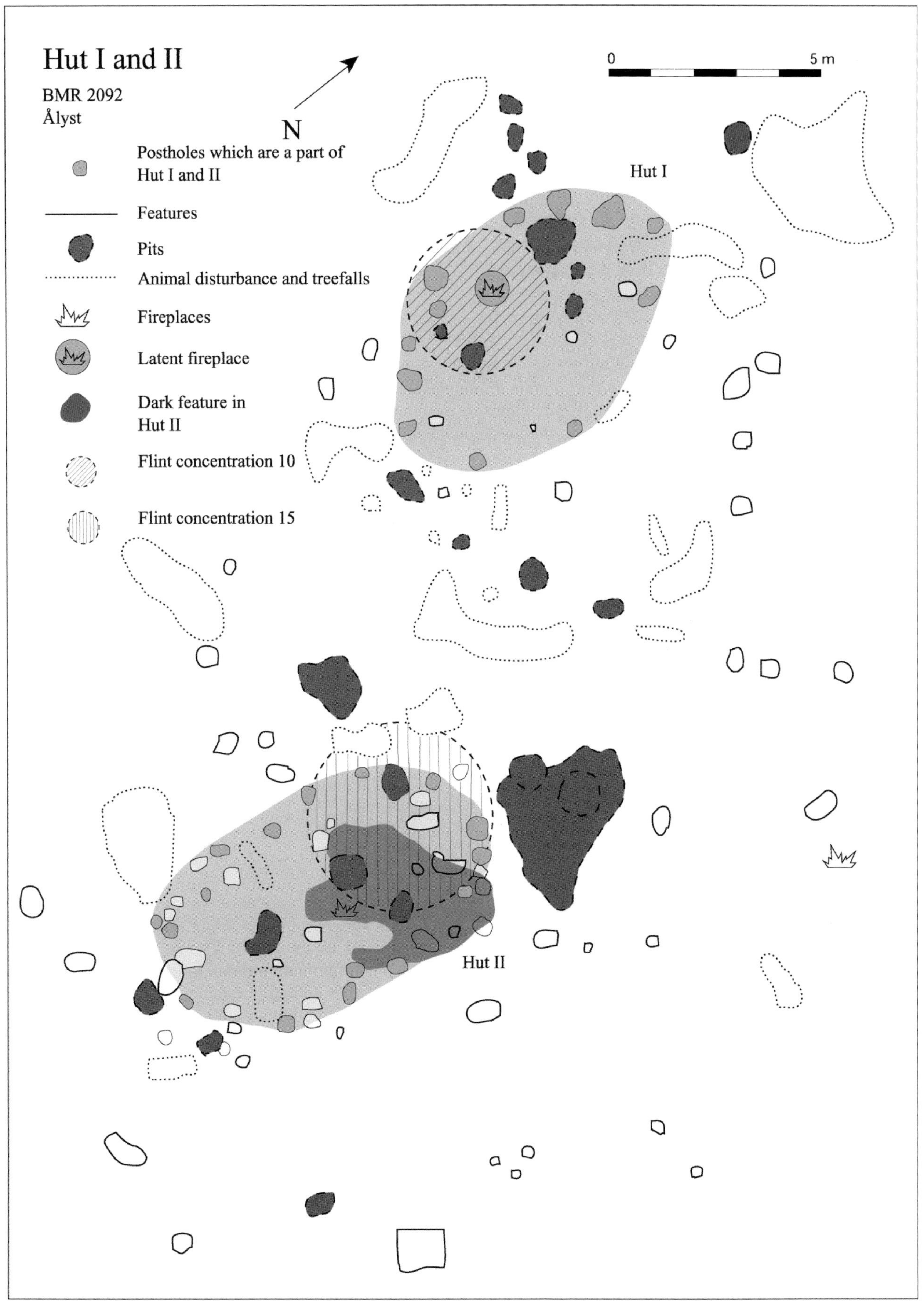

Figure 66.3. Excavation plan of Huts I and II.

excavated. These features contained a large amount of lithic material, and disrupted the real picture of the flint concentration. The southern part of the hut was almost void of finds, which, as with Hut I, could be interpreted as a cleared area where the inhabitants might have slept. The larger objects, such as hammer stones, anvil stones and flint cores, again display a wall effect, respecting the outlines of the hut created by the postholes.

A visible hearth was excavated in the centre of the hut (A270). It consisted of 20 fire-cracked stones, located in a compact stone layer. The backfill was dark brown at the centre and black and sooty at the border. In the lower level of the stone packing, a hammerstone, a lanceolate with lateral retouch, burnt flint, and charred hazelnut shells were observed. At the bottom level of the hearth, a red sandy layer was recorded: this was probably the result of the intense heat of the fire. This hearth differed from the pits and hearths of the Bronze Age layer, which were deeper, larger, and contained bigger fire-cracked stones, together with dumps of ceramics. The Bronze Age fireplaces also have a higher stratigraphic position and their fire-cracked stones are often placed in a circle. The hearth in Hut II was thus presumed to be of Maglemose date. The AMS radiocarbon sample from this hearth supports this assumption, showing 8870±65 BP, (8870±65 BP; 8240–7780 cal BC; AAR-9881; Bronk Ramsey 2005).

Inside Hut II, five small pits were found. These pits were quite homogeneous and had a dark- to light-grey fill. They could be typologically dated to the Maglemose culture by their contents, which comprised lithic material, charcoal, burnt hazelnut shells, and some fire-cracked stones. Three of the pits were located around the fireplace (A270). These pits might be indicative of food preparation around the hearth, or they might represent the remains of former fireplaces in the hut, subsequently reused as pits. Outside Hut II there were some larger pits, approximately 1–2m wide and 40–50cm deep, with a dark- to light-greyish filling (Figure 66.3). These pits could also be typologically dated, as they contained lithics from the Maglemose culture. Furthermore, we found burnt hazelnut shells, burnt bones, and fire-cracked stones in the pits. At present we are unable to determine whether these pits are synchronic with the hut; it is possible that they reflect several different habitations in the area, thus disturbing the original picture of activity zones in the hut and its dumping areas. Future AMS radiocarbon dates, as well as thorough refitting analyses of the lithic material and fire-cracked stones, should clarify the relationships between the postholes, pits, fireplaces, and presumed structures in and outside the hut.

Comparison

The two huts show remarkable similarities in orientation, size, entrance area, fireplaces and pits, as well as in the combination of lithic tool types: knives, a few scrapers, and several hammer and anvil stones are most abundant in both. However differences are seen with respect to the microliths. Lanceolates with lateral retouch and triangular microliths dominate in Hut I, while the microlith inventory from Hut II was confined to lanceolates with lateral retouch. This raises the question of the flint concentrations in the two huts: are they at all contemporary with the huts? To prove this hypothesis it is necessary to undertake extensive refitting between the flint concentrations, postholes and the pits, both inside and outside of the huts.

As the colour of the postholes in the two huts varies, we initially interpreted the huts to be diachronic, but in the light of the available radiocarbon dates we have to acknowledge the possibility that the huts were indeed synchronic – future work is required to shed light on this topic. It may also be noticed that interpretations of the fireplaces in the huts vary from a presumed fireplace (based on concentrations of burnt flint and hazelnut shells) in Hut I, to an obvious fireplace (with no concentrations of burnt flint or hazelnut shells) in Hut II. In both huts we found that the small pits inside the huts were all concentrated around the fireplace, possibly indicating a food preparation area. Both huts appear to have had a main activity zone in the northern part, whereas the southern part is void of finds: this could indicate a sleeping area for one to two families.

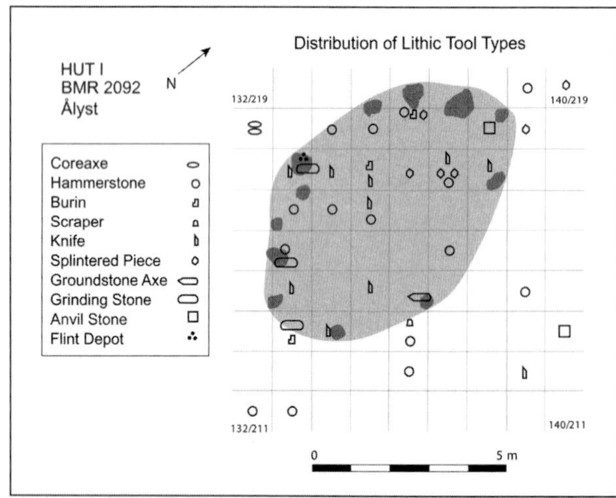

Figure 66.4. Distribution of lithic tool types in Hut I.

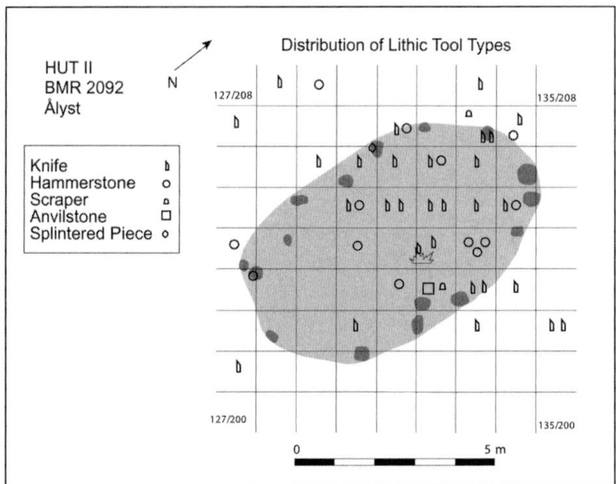

Figure 66.5. Distribution of lithic tool types in Hut II.

The artefact typology in the two huts clearly indicates that a broad spectrum of activities took place here, unlike in the other concentrations on the site, where the main products were blades for microlith manufacture. Apart from this, a most interesting observation concerning these two huts is that the southern end of the structures lacked lithic finds. Most previously published huts from the Maglemose period are based on studies of lithic material and subsequent observations of presumed structures, but they have rarely been combined with specific structures such as postholes. The excavation method applied at Ålyst, together with the state of preservation at the site, make it possible to combine postholes, flint concentrations, putative structures and pits in an interpretation which recognizes various areas of the huts, which, although they lack finds, are, nevertheless, part of the structure.

But is the picture we see at Ålyst unique and only valid for Bornholm? There are strong indications that this is not the case. At a site called Årup in eastern Scania, southern Sweden, a hut structure similar to the Ålyst huts was excavated in 2003 (Nilsson and Hanlon 2006). At the time of excavation they did not know of the structures at Ålyst. The Årup feature shows a remarkable similarity to those at Ålyst in terms of orientation, dimensions and so forth. Collaboration to conduct comparative analyses is planned for the near future.

Conclusions

Without the results of extensive refitting, microwear analysis, and AMS radiocarbon dating, a reliable interpretation of the intra-site variability and spatial patterning remains difficult. However it is beyond doubt that different factors, such as the range of activities performed, group size, duration of occupation, and frequency of reuse of the individual artefact loci, will have played a role in the formation of the site. In particular, group scale and duration of occupation have a certain effect on the size and artefact density of the units. It can be presupposed that artefact density and size will increase as the number of inhabitants and/or the length of time a place is occupied increases. However, the increase in density could be a sign of several repeated occupations on the same spot. Future refitting analyses and AMS radiocarbon dating will hopefully indicate if the concentrations are chronologically uniform, or represent different diachronic occupations.

Furthermore, we expect that the smallest artefact units excavated, i.e. small scatters of charred hazelnut shells and/or bone fragments, as well as the scattered lithics recovered in between the different concentrations, must be interpreted as the faint remains of peripheral activities.

All of this indicates that Ålyst, as a settlement, must be interpreted as a complicated diachronic complex. As well as a short-term, there was also a longer-term settlement strategy, with different needs and functions. Given the current level of our knowledge, the site at Ålyst can best be regarded as a location extensively visited during the early Mesolithic, probably by small groups of recurring hunter-gatherers.

With such a vast amount of material, more questions arise with each answer found. Future work will include further study of the finds revealed so far, and a project based on three-dimensional modelling is already in hand (Garhøj Larsen, this volume). Furthermore, AMS radiocarbon dating of the different flint concentrations, refitting analyses, and a thorough study of the flint concentrations are all planned. A detailed field survey along the nearby streams is currently underway to produce a detailed picture of the settlement pattern and raw material distribution. We also hope to make a wide-ranging study of post-excavation research and comparisons with other Maglemose sites in the Baltic region.

References

Andersen, K., Jørgensen, S. and Richter, J. 1982. *Maglemose hytterne ved Ulkestrup Lyng*. Nordiske Fortidsminder, Series B, vol. 7. København, Det Kongelige Nordiske Oldskriftselskab.

Becker, C. J. 1952. Maglemosekultur på Bornholm, in *Årbøger for Nordisk Oldkyndighed og Historie 1951*, 96–177. København, Det Kongelige Nordiske Oldskriftselskab.

Bolus, M. 1992. *Die Siedlungsbefunde des späteiszeitlichen Fundplatzes Niederbieber (Stadt Neuwied). Ausgrabungen 1981-1988*. With contributions from G. Roth, S. Stephan and R. C. Rottländer. Monographien des Römisch-Germanischen Zentralmuseums 22. Mainz, Römisch-Germanisches Zentralmuseum.

Bronk Ramsey, C. 2005. OxCal 3.10. WWW program and documentation available at http://www.rlaha.ox.ac.uk/oxcal/oxcal.htm (accessed 10/2007).

Casati, C. and Sørensen, L. 2006. Ålyst – et boplads kompleks fra Maglemosekulturen på Bornholm. Foreløbige resultater baseret på ukonventionelle udgravningsmetoder, in B. V. Eriksen (ed.), *Stenalderstudier*, 241–75. Århus, Århus University Press.

Casati, C., Sørensen, L. and Vennersdorf, M. 2004. Current research of the Early Mesolithic on Bornholm, Denmark, in T. Terberger and B. V. Eriksen (eds.), *Hunters in a changing world: Environment and Archaeology of the Pleistocene–Holocene Transition (ca 11000–9000 BC) in Northern Central Europe. Workshop of the UISPP-Commission XXXII at Greifswald in September 2002*, 113–32. Internationale Archaologie - Arbeitsgemeinschaft, Symposium, Tagung, Kongress 5. Rahden/Westphalia, Verlag Marie Leidorf.

Crombé, P. 1998. *The Mesolithic in Northwestern Belgium. Recent excavations and surveys*. British Archaeological Reports, International Series S716. Oxford, John and Erica Hedges.

De Bie, M. and Caspar, J. 2000. *Rekem. A Federmesser Camp on the Meuse River Bank*. Acta Archaeologica Lovaniensia Monographiae 10, 2 vol. Leuven, Leuven University Press.

Grøn, O. 1995. *The Maglemose Culture. The reconstruction of the social organisation of a Mesolithic culture in Northern Europe*. British Archaeological Reports, International Series S616. Oxford, Tempvs Reparatvm.

Jensen, O. L. 2001. Kongemose- og Ertebøllekultur ved den fossile Nivåfjord, in O. Lass Jensen, S. A. Sørensen and K. Møller Hansen (eds.), *Danmarks Jægerstenalder – status og perspektiver*, 115–29. Hørsholm, Hørsholm Egns Museum.

Larsson, M. and Molin, F. 2000. A New World: Cultural Links and Spatial Disposition – The Early Mesolithic Landscape in

Östergötland on the Basis of the Storlyckan Investigations. *Lund Archaeological Review* 6, 7–22.

Nielsen, F. O. S. 2001. Nyt om Maglemosekultur på Bornholm, in O. Lass Jensen, S. A. Sørensen and K. Møller Hansen (eds.), *Danmarks Jægerstenalder – status og perspektiver*, 85–99. Hørsholm, Hørsholm Egns Museum.

Nilsson, B. and Hanlon C. 2006. Life and work during 5,000 years, in P. Karsten and B. Nilsson (eds.), *In the Wake of a Woman. The Pioneering of North-eastern Scania, Sweden, 10,000–5000 BC. The Årup Settlements*, 57–178. Arkeologiska Undersökningar, Skrifter 63. Stockholm, Riksantikvarieämbetet.

Sørensen, L. 2004. Coastal Research Potential in the Early Mesolithic on Bornholm, in A. Beck, H. N. Frederiksen, L. Harvig, C. Juel, K. Langsted, T. Rasmussen and G. B. Ravnholt (eds.), *Kontaktstencil 44*, 9–26. Copenhagen, University of Copenhagen.

67. Virtual hypothesis: the Maglemosian huts at Ålyst, Bornholm. Preliminary thoughts on the morphology of dwellings on a Maglemosian site

Nicolai Garhøj Larsen

Through a series of virtual reconstructions made with the purpose of gaining insight and knowledge about the relationship between postholes and pits, it is possible to set up a string of hypothetical structures which can then be evaluated and subsequently analyzed. The virtual models produced through this method are not aesthetically pleasing, nor is it their purpose to be so. At the Maglemosian site of Ålyst on the Danish island of Bornholm, this virtual technique has been used to reconstruct a series of features interpreted as huts. Amongst other things, the virtual analysis has shown a probable form for the huts, the re-interpretation of several pits, and the re-interpretation of a latent fireplace.

Keywords: Maglemose, Bornholm, Ålyst, dwellings, virtuality, 3D modelling, visual hypothesis.

Introduction

For years the computer has been an invaluable aid to the archaeologist, be it in the form of databases, statistics, or more graphically based software – such as geographic information system (GIS) and computer-aided design (CAD) programs. In recent times hardware has become so advanced that true and photorealistic 3D modelling has become available as a tool for archaeological purposes. This so-called virtual media has seen extensive use, although it has mostly been for representation rather than as a scientific tool with its own strengths. The theme of this paper will be how to apply 3D modelling for making visual hypothesises, and 3D modelling as a tool for acquiring new knowledge about prehistoric structures. The unique feature of virtual media is that it is inherently spatial, in that elements in a 3D computer model always relate in three dimensions to other elements, unlike that of CAD or vector based drawings. Furthermore, since elements in a 3D model intrinsically possess spatial presence, it is impossible subconsciously to change their spatial relationship unless rooted in actual data. In this way 3D models abide by physical law, and not by the mind's eye as with traditional drawings. This means that reconstructions made by 3D modelling are far more useful for scientific purposes than 2D drawings, since the computer can not be deceived by visual patterns perceived by the human mind as meaningful patterns.

As a note, it should be remarked that the contents of this paper, in so far as it pertains to virtual reconstruction, originate from a thesis (Digital ReKonstruktion) submitted at the IT-University of Copenhagen (Larsen 2003).

Virtual archaeology

Over the last decade archaeologists have adopted the use of computers for a wide variety of purposes, the most prolific probably being database and GIS software. Both of these aspects of the digital revolution have more than proven their worth and are by now indispensable tools for the professional archaeologist. Conversely, there has been comparatively little emphasis on visually oriented digital tools, especially those concerned with 3D representations, linked as it is with a visual form of language. Most of the intellectual tradition of Western culture is rooted in the written word, and as such has been the chosen media for Science ever since its inception, but the notion that an illustration has less intrinsic scientific value than a written equivalent is based on cultural norms, not physiological ones (James 1999, 30). This reliance on words rather than visuals is paradoxical, since the human brain actually processes and stores purely visual information many times faster than written information. Such a notion becomes even more interesting when one realizes that traditional archaeology utilizes a wide range of visualizations in the form of graphs, which to all intents are visual representations of statistical data. In this case, visualization is barely noticed and so ingrained into the scientific norm that it can be considered a non-problematic part of scientific paradigm.

Compared with virtuality there is a marked difference in the perception of the visualized forms. Why is this so? Apart from the fact that the media is relatively new, it is really a question of complexity. The program code that generates the virtual world is far more complex than most statistical methods. This factor combined with the novel nature of the virtual media make for an exceedingly implicit tool – a phenomena which is the very antithesis of scientific thought and practice. This is where the uniqueness of the virtual media works to its disadvantage, as the advantages of inherent spatiality are only available in a digital environment. Whereas statistics originate with the world of writing and mathematics as defined hundreds of years ago, virtual spatiality originates with a media barely two decades old. As such, individuals without experience and understanding of the virtual media have basically no cognitive tools for evaluating and comprehending the implicit precepts and connotations of this particular brand of IT. It could be argued that the proposed uniqueness of virtuality is the child of the much-hyped IT revolution of the 1990s, especially since hand-drawn reconstructions have been in existence for as long as the discipline of archaeology itself. Despite the superficial similarity that both forms of visualisation are visual representations of physical objects, there is a very real difference in that the drawn version is, in essence, about fooling the human eye into believing in the illusion of space. Not so with 3D computer models. Naturally, the screen itself is two-dimensional and so are the input devices, but the virtual objects themselves exist in a true three-dimensional world. Our limited means of accessing and interacting with virtual media causes that paradox, not the media itself.

Realizing the potential of a spatially oriented media in an archaeological context should be obvious, especially for reconstruction purposes. Because of the spatial relation, objects in the virtual world relate very specifically to each other; it is impossible to make invalid assumptions about their relationship. This differs from a drawn reconstruction, which, in itself, is an illusion and ultimately a sensory deceit, where you can more or less create any kind of structure or object, as long as it does not 'look' wrong, a factor of the ability of the artist to 'trick' the human mind into believing the illusion of spatiality. Consequently the graphic display on a computer screen can very well bear more than a metaphorical relation to reality, as it is in fact far more closely related to said reality than any other media. That is the promise and the danger of virtual archaeology.

Deus ex machinae

There is a god in the machine. That god is both the giver of bountiful promises (see above), but it is also a dangerous and deceitful god. The perils of interacting with the virtual god are mainly threefold:

1. Visual information is absorbed very quickly by the human mind, bypassing our normal interpretive perceptions.
2. The current paradigm does not have a scientific language for adequately translating and evaluating visual information.
3. Modern man tends to view computers as unfathomable entities capable of providing unquestionable truths.

The first and second issues are intimately connected, since both depend on our perception of the visual. If they are to be addressed we need to explore, understand, and define the visual (virtual) media. Such a task is very much outside the scope of this paper, but rest assured that both computer scientists and computed-minded archaeologists are in the process of addressing this complicated task. For now it is sufficient to say that the best way of circumventing items 1, 2, and very much item 3 on the above list, is to be almost obsessively explicit about what choices were made during the creation of the virtual entity in question, and not least what parameters where used in that process. Seemingly in contrast with the call for explicit methods, a core concept in this context is that it is not important to list either the program codes or the mathematical considerations that form the foundation for the graphic objects manipulated in the computer interface. The reason is that the choices concerning the relations of the real-life objects mimicked by the virtual ones are not really interesting to the historian or archaeologist; it is the visual, spatial relations of these that count. After all, the persons who designed and constructed the original structure probably did not think of them as abstract mathematical entities. Even if the construction of a prehistoric object did involve mathematics, the use and everyday interaction with the said object did not entail such abstractions.

I will argue that is not the job of archaeologists to discuss the vagaries of how to represent reality through mathematical equations of x, y, and z coordinates – it is our job to research and interpret prehistoric and historic societies. Furthermore, the widespread adaptation of standardized software has alleviated the problems with consistency, since every virtual application is thus mediated through similar means, effectively eliminating discrepancies between various methodical approaches to virtuality. As a side note, the increased standardization in computer software also serves a very practical purpose, as it enables a more widespread use of virtuality. By using mainstream software, the budding virtual archaeologist not only ensures forward compatibility, but also that the largest number of people can access the product. This has been an issue with many early virtual archaeology projects, considering that many were made entirely in-house or with specialized software from a drastically different profession. Although not necessarily a wrong choice at the inception of the project, such a choice of software makes it hard, if not impossible, to share data with other researchers, yet again causing problems with the sharing of ideas and experiences that are so vital to further development and research. Also, forward compatibility is usually poor, causing such stand-alone software to become obsolete within a short span of time.

Modelling

Modelling is the term used here for the process of creating of 3D virtual objects. From an overall point of view there are three approaches to 3D graphical representations of archaeological finds and excavations: *Free-form*, *Scanning* and *Numerical Modelling*. Scanning refers to the process where real world objects are 'scanned' into digital form, a method similar to the office scanners of everyday use, but in 3 dimensions and technically much more advanced. The two main methods of 3D scanning are photometry and laser scanning. Numerical modelling is the oldest of the three approaches, based on entering numbers or measurements into a system of coordinates and thereby generating virtual objects. Both of these methods for generating and manipulating virtual objects are mechanical and not really spatial in the sense that they do not force the user to relate to a perception of correspondence between the objects. On the other hand, that is exactly what free-form modelling does. Free-form modelling is characterized by real-time interaction with shapes in a three-dimensional space, enabling the user to focus on this aspect rather than abstract mathematical relations. A real-world parallel to free-form modelling is the art of sculpting in clay, only the virtual version grants the user unlimited clay and space. This is why free-form modelling is most useful for archaeological projects concerned with re-creating ancient structures from fragmented remains. The process of reconstruction is complicated and to a large degree dependent on deductive interpretation and educated guesses, rather than hard facts, which is the reason why explicit choices are all important. This is where free-form modelling really shines, as it makes explicit the consequences of moving or reshaping individual elements of the larger structure. If a given element does not fit with another element it is immediately obvious and cannot be corrected by anything other than rethinking and reinterpreting the entire structure. In virtual space, objects are spatially inter-dependent and free-form modelling gives a 1:1 insight into such relations.

Free-form modelling is not solely a tool for making illusory, imitating shapes, as objects within the virtual environment can be given exact dimensions, be they imperial, metric, or any other standard of measurement. Not only useful for illustrating absolute size of the structure, this is essential when dealing with scientific reconstructions, since it allows the usage of excavation plans and other documentation to the correct scale. Unfortunately, the current free-form modelling software does not allow for parameters other than spatial dimensions. Parameters such as weight, durability, and gravity are outside the realm of practical use at the moment, making free-form modelling rather dependent on external sources for validation of the viability of the structure in question. However it is only a matter of time before these options become available, as simple versions are already included in the latter version of 3D modelling software. The day when virtual objects can be given the whole range of physical properties is the day virtual reconstruction will make physical reconstruction utterly obsolete for research purposes.

The Maglemosian huts at Ålyst

The Site of Ålyst

Since 1998, Ålyst, a Maglemosian site located on the Danish island of Bornholm, has been the subject of continual excavations by Lasse Sørensen and Claudio Casati of Bornholms Museum. The excavations of Ålyst have revealed the presence of at least 26 flint concentrations consisting of various lithic material, all of which is dominated by microliths. Apart from the large amount of flint, Ålyst is unusual as the site contains remains of at least two structures indicated by not only flint concentrations and various features, but also by a number of postholes. The postholes, although severely washed-out, are identifiable as Maglemosian and roughly contemporary; they measure approximately 30cm in diameter, and their depths vary from 10–30cm. The two structures, henceforth known as hut I and hut II, are located north of the Bagge Å (stream), on a sandy slope declining towards the waterline. The shore of the Baltic Sea is located approximately 1km to the west of the site.

Huts I and II are two oval areas framed by 12 and 16 postholes respectively. Both cover some $30m^2$ and are oriented with the length axis running roughly from south to north (Figure 67.1). (Please note that the Ålyst site is subject to a thorough presentation of the archaeological finds by C. Casati and L. Sørensen, this volume.)

Background

The author of this paper participated in the excavation of the Ålyst site when two dwelling structures were unearthed in 2001. By virtue of the expertise coincidently being present, it was decided to try and use virtuality as a tool for understanding the structures and how they related to each other and to various features. Thus, the purpose of the reconstruction of the superstructure of the dwelling was not to prove a definite interpretation, nor to make an aesthetically pleasing visualization, but rather to use the spatial aspect of this media to gain insight into the correspondence of the below ground features excavated. The virtual models therefore, look rather primitive and not very realistic at all to the casual viewer, but in essence that is not their purpose either. The insight to be gained lies within the process of making them, as it is then that the relation between the archaeological remains becomes apparent. Presentation of the virtual models should be considered as an illustration, or documentation of the insights gained during the reconstruction. In the case of Ålyst, a deductive and iterative methodical approach was taken, meaning that a number of different reconstruction hypothesises would be modelled, the experience and insight from each taken into account when modelling the next suggestion for a reconstruction of the huts. The hypothetical-deductive and iterative methodology was originally defined by A. Rosenberg Andersen (Andersen 2006, 77 ff.) for use in the analysis and interpretation of prehistoric ceramics. Although the methodology was intended for use with

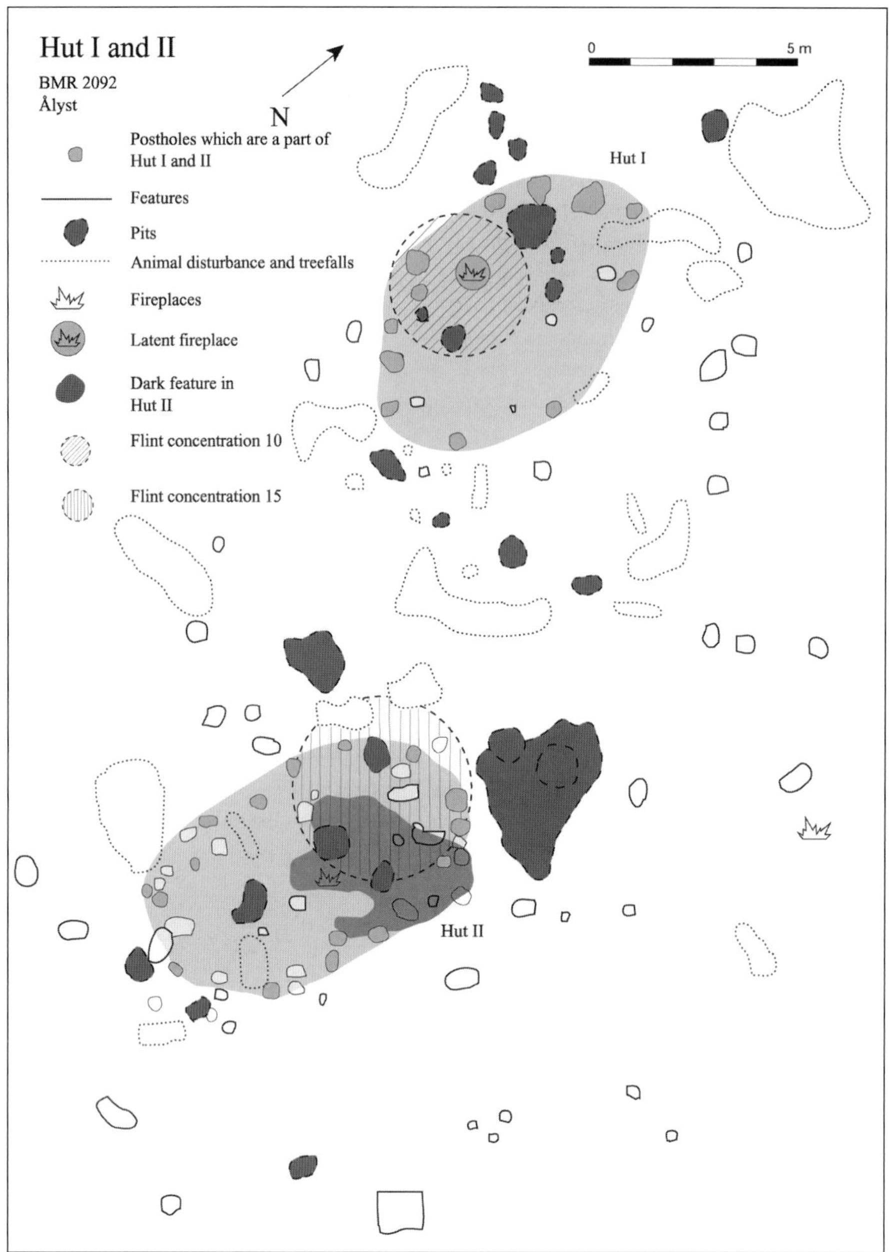

Figure 67.1. Excavation plan of the huts and their immediate surroundings. (Plan: C. Casati, C. Lindberg and S. Sørensen).

another archaeological type of material, it is very suitable for ascertaining the validity of one particular virtual hypothesis opposed to another.

In addition, time was a real issue. Since the use of the virtual tool was not part of the original schedule for the excavation, time and manpower for a separate and continual virtual project was unavailable. Given that texturing, lighting and rendering are very time consuming, these parts of the process was left out, especially since they would have nothing to do with the central purpose of the virtual reconstructions.

Method

The basis for these virtual reconstructions is a bitmap version of the excavation plan, which is then placed as a texture on a plane shape in the 3D software. The essential part of this operation is to make sure that the dimensions of the virtual plane are exactly the same as those of the original plan, and that the 3D software does not stretch or otherwise deform the original bitmap. This simple method is at the heart of the development of the reconstruction, since this creates a space exactly identical to the real world. After that it is a question of utilizing the various modelling options in the software to create the structural entities and their shape. By drawing upon inspiration from various observations by archaeologists and anthropologists, one can infer a number of probable parallels, and thus structural solutions appropriate for the site in question. Thus it was decided to attempt to reconstruct the huts in four different versions, based on the rough morphology of the archaeological remains and the observations in the field.

One version was the 'dome' type, inspired by the oval shape of the archaeological remains. Another hypothetical type was the 'Saami' type, derived from contemporary Saami dwellings. The third would be a simple tent shape, with the working name 'tepee'. The fourth original virtual hypothesis, the 'Taagerup' type was something of a long shot, since its purpose was to attempt a reconstruction that was structurally complicated and supported by central posts. The reason for the latter, and initially rather peculiar, reasoning was that the author of this paper suspected that these features, which at first were interpreted as pits, seemed uncannily central and, furthermore, were present in both huts. Therefore it was resolved that despite the status as pits, it could be interesting to try and incorporate them in the reconstruction. The appellation of the type derives from a reconstruction suggestion put forward by P. Karsten and B. Knarrström at Taagerup (Karsten and Knarrström, 156).

Problems/discussion

A main concern regarding the reconstruction of the huts is the size of the original posts in comparison to the postholes. At first glance, the size of the Ålyst postholes seems quite large (roughly 30cm in diameter), which compares to the size of Iron Age dwellings that must have been supported by posts measuring 15–20cm in diameter. Such dimensions appear overly large for what must be a temporary dwelling without the complicated roof structure of an Iron Age longhouse. Additionally, such massive posts preclude light, curved structures, since it would be impossible, or at least take considerable effort, to bend or fix posts of these dimensions. Naturally, the deterioration of the Maglemosian posts must be assumed to be considerably more advanced than 2000-year-old posts, resulting in a more widespread area of deposit around the post; that would also be consistent with the washed-out appearance of the postholes on Ålyst. Nevertheless this does not indicate now how thick the original posts were (and experimental studies in this area are conspicuously lacking). Consequently the posts of the virtual reconstructions of Ålyst have tentatively been set at an average of one third of the recorded size of the postholes, which should be compared with reconstructions of Iron Age dwellings where the same proportions are roughly 1:2. An estimate, therefore, of half that value does not seem too far-fetched, although, admittedly, it is no more than a qualified guess. Unfortunately, until further research is undertaken into this topic there is not much else that can be done.

In another vein, the result of the iterative process had already emerged by the time of the first hypothesis. The 'dome' construction could really have been erected in two ways: either by simply bending individual posts and fixing them where they converged (somewhat in the centre of the hut), or by bending them in pairs and thus creating a series of 'hoops'. Both versions of the 'dome' type were reconstructed (see below). Subsequently, and by the time of the reconstruction of hut II, the idea was raised that the construction of the hut may be a simple tent-like structure, with two larger central posts with a beam between them sustaining the smaller and irregular posts leaning on that central sustaining element. This yet again, of course, presupposed that the features in the centre are postholes rather than pits; but there was much going for this simple, yet eminently sound, suggestion (particularly the existence of several other Danish Maglemosian sites with such central posts (Grøn 1995, 37)), that this model was also tested. Conversely the Taagerup type was deemed needlessly complicated for a temporary seasonal dwelling and was abandoned after testing it with hut I. Hut II was similarly reconstructed in four versions, but with a 'Tent'- instead of 'Taagerup'-type model.

Interpretation

General characteristics of the Ålyst huts

The oval shape of the dwellings is central to the understanding of the Ålyst structures, since this indicates various defining characteristics. The first of these is the realization that an oval shape entail the existence of a length axis, implying that the use of an asymmetrical, load-bearing construction, which yet again makes a symmetrical design (such as the North American Indian tepee) unlikely. The regular oval shape also seems to preclude trapezoidal dwellings. Another defining characteristic is the asymmetrical north and south side of the dwellings, as both huts, but especially hut I, show a marked difference in the amount of postholes between the two sides. The south side, in the direction of the nearest stream, contains fewer postholes than the north side. If one assumes that the smaller number of posts indicates an entrance (which is also supported by the marked gaps between postholes), this makes sense as the huts would then face the Bagå and its rich resources, while at the same time shielding the inhabitants from the prevailing north-western wind of the Boreal climate (Grøn 1995, 10).

The lack of central postholes could indicate that the Ålyst huts are of the 'dome' type, but the virtual reconstructions clearly show that it is difficult to make such a structure. A dome with the posts put irregularly together would be difficult to construct, considering the rather large size of the posts. Posts with a diameter of 10cm could not easily be bent, and without having a central post they would also be hard to fix properly. A variant of the 'dome' could make use of a series of opposed posts (the hoops), where each pair would directly counter the pressure from the other. The problem with such an interpretation of the Ålyst huts is the asymmetry of the postholes; the virtual reconstruction indicates that it is doubtful whether such hoops could be opposed anywhere near each other in pairs, and thereby considerably lessening the supposed countering effect.

Specific observations

Hut I

Regarding the fireplaces and entrances, it is worth noting

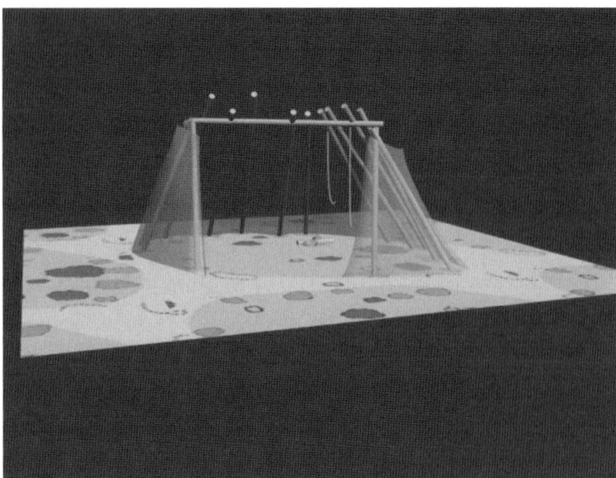

Figure 67.2. 3D model. Hut I, 'Saami' type, Viewed from the southwest.

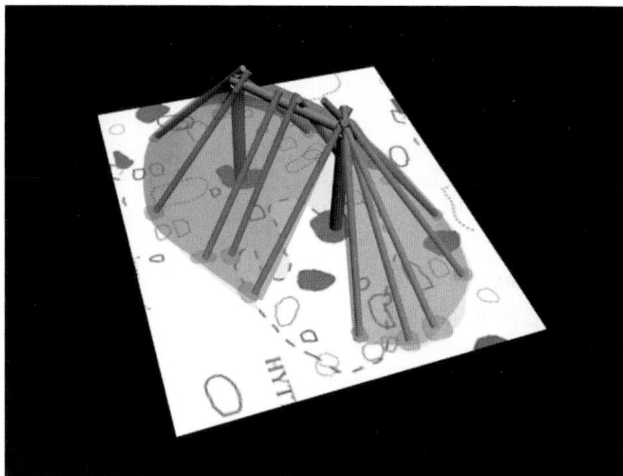

Figure 67.3. 3D model. Hut II, 'tent' type. Top view angled towards the northwest.

that the virtual reconstructions showed some problems with the latent fireplace of hut I. Reconstructions of the types 'Saami' and 'tepee' for hut I showed that the covering of such a structure would be exposed to the fire. Considering that this latent fireplace is placed spatially differently from the evident fireplace of hut II, and that the spatial social structure of the hunter-gatherers may have been quite rigid (Grøn 2000, 195), this leaves some doubt as to the accuracy of the location. But the latent fireplace in hut I exhibits an artefact density commonly regarded as a denominator for Mesolithic sites, while the evident fireplace in hut II does not exhibit similar characteristics (C. Casati and L. Sørensen, this volume). It is to be hoped that further research will shed light on this conundrum, and that by the time of the final publication on Ålyst there may be an answer to the question.

Overall, the virtual reconstructions point to the 'Saami' and the 'dome' types being the most likely (Figure 67.2). The 'tepee' type is so simple that it is always possible, but the very long posts needed (around 5m) seem unlikely given the relatively shallow postholes, and, as previously mentioned, the oval shape makes little sense if it is the remains of such a dwelling type. Also mentioned previously, the 'Taagerup' type was abandoned because of its overly complex superstructure, which made no more sense than the other types.

Hut II

Despite having a passing similarity to hut I, hut II is markedly different when actually modelled, not least because of the increased overall number of postholes. Hut II is slightly more symmetrical, which proves to be quite marked when a superstructure is added to the plan. Another difference between the two structures is that the postholes of hut II are far more irregularly aligned with each other than those of hut I. The irregular wall line which emerges from this make for an unconvincing 'Dome' type when reconstructed, and the 'Dome-with-hoop' construction seems undeniably improbable, as the hoops would vary greatly in height throughout the structure. After the good results with the reconstruction of hut I, the 'Saami' type proved almost impossible to implement with hut II. The reason is that there is no morphological indicator of a supporting lintel over the entrance of hut II, as was the case with hut I. Furthermore the depth of the southernmost postholes in hut II contradict this hypothesis, since the posts in the middle of the proposed lintel are the largest and deepest, whereas the potential load-bearing posts are set in shallow holes and not particularly thick. The simple 'tepee' type naturally fits well, but the same scepticism applies to this suggestion as it did for hut I. Conversely the new type of virtual reconstruction, the 'tent' type, proved a sensible hypothesis for hut II (Figure 67.3). Admittedly it is so simple that it could fit almost anything, and requires the reinterpretation of the central pits, but apart from these two objections there is much going for this particular solution. The 'tent' type is easy to construct; it requires no bending of wood, it is sturdy, and otherwise fits well with the archaeological remains.

Virtuality

The very process of working with the virtual reconstructions and the insight gained into the actual spatial interconnection of the Ålyst huts has provided much food for thought regarding some interpretations of the dwellings. Apart from the insight related directly to the site itself, it is remarkable that these insights seem to adhere to common sense. Now that some visually oriented spatial relations and characteristics have been revealed, they are very obvious, even to the naked eye. This aspect has, in fact, appeared with each and every virtual reconstruction that the author of this paper has been involved with. Thus, we see that 3D modelling has considerable potential in research, although perhaps not the way previously envisaged. It is the process of modelling itself which is interesting, rather than the finished 3D model. This is not really surprising since the concept of true spatial correlation is unique to 3D media, and not really something that has been available beforehand. So, to sum everything up: Virtual 3D models can be visual hypothesises rather than definitive attempts at visualizing the 'truth'.

References

Andersen, A. R. 2006. *Hvor der lighed, der maa være slægtsskab - Et speciale om de teoretiske og metodiske aspekter af kronologier baseret på keramik fra ældre jernalder.* Unpublished magister thesis at the Saxo Institute, University of Copenhagen.

Grøn, O. 1995. *The Maglemose Culture. The reconstruction of the social organization of a Mesolithic culture in Northern Europe.* British Archaeological Reports, International Series S616. Oxford, Tempvs Reparatvm.

Grøn, O. 2000. Etnoarkæologi, in B. V. Eriksen (ed.), *Flintstudier – En håndbog I systematiske analyser afflintinventarer.* Århus, Århus Universitetsforlag.

James, S. 1999. Imag(in)ing the Past: The Politics and Practicalities of Reconstructions in the Museum Gallery, in N. Merriman (ed.), *Making Early Histories in Museums.* Leicester, Leicester University Press.

Karsten, P. and Knarrström, B. 2003. *The Tågerup Excavations.* Lund, Riksantikvariäbetets förlag.

Larsen, N. G. 2003. *Digital ReKonstruktion.* Unpublished MA thesis, the IT-University of Copenhagen.

68. Find concentrations and dwelling structures. The interpretation of Final Palaeolithic find scatters

Frank Gelhausen, Jan F. Kegler and Stefan Wenzel

At the Final Palaeolithic (Federmessergruppen) sites of Niederbieber (Area IV), Andernach-Martinsberg 3 and Berlin-Tegel IX a combination of different methods of spatial analysis reveals indications of a former separation of the main accumulations of finds from the surrounding area. All three find scatters are very dense and show a marked sudden decrease at their edges. The distribution of larger objects and refitting lines between artefacts respect the edges of the find scatters. In some cases, certain finds, such as unburned larger bone fragments or larger stones, are not found within the artefact find scatter. We interpret these as indications of a formerly effective limitation of the find concentrations that show the former presence of dwelling structures.

Keywords: Allerød Interstadial, Final Palaeolithic, Federmessergruppen, settlement structures, dwellings, mapping of artefact density, density contour lines/isopachs, refitting.

Introduction

Only very few Mesolithic dwellings are preserved as evident features and even outstanding discoveries such as Ulkestrup I and Ulkestrup II (Andersen, Jørgensen and Richter 1982; Grøn 2003) have been questioned as to their character as dwellings (Bokelmann 1986, 150; Stapert 2002, 231). With regard to their size and their artefact density these settlement structures correspond to evident dwelling structures of the Magdalenian and the early phase of the Final Palaeolithic, which are characterized by floors made of slabs of schist (Bosinski 1979; Street 1995) or by stones in peripheral positions used as weights (Jöris and Terberger 2001). In this paper we will discuss the artefact distribution of three sites from the Allerød (Figure 68.1), which are noticeable by the form of their outline and by their density of finds. We would like to present considerations for the evaluation of the borders of the find concentrations and for the question of a former separation of their interiors from the areas outside. This could also be of significance for the interpretation of Mesolithic find scatters.

Fundamental considerations for the evaluation of latent settlement structures have been discussed by Leroi-Gourhan and Brézillon (1972) in the context of the analysis of the Magdalenian site of Pincevent. On the basis of mapping and the refitting of finds it was possible to reconstruct activities and work areas. Furthermore, the position of the walls of a dwelling can be detected by finds trapped within the walls (Leroi-Gourhan 1984, fig. 27). Under the influence of the work of Leroi-Gourhan, dwellings were sought in the find-poor area behind the fireplaces and their adjacent waste zones (e.g. Bolus 1992; Bokelmann 1989, 18; Vermeersch 1987). However, the evident dwelling structures mentioned above are in fact characterized by large quantities of internal finds, in particular the trapezoid tents of Etiollés W11 and of Le Closeau, *locus* 46 (Jöris and Terberger 2001).

On the basis of the criticism by Binford (1983) of Leroi-Gourhan's concepts, Stapert (1992) tried to develop a method to distinguish find concentrations derived from former dwelling locations from those concentrations which reflect open-air camp sites. Stapert's 'ring and sector method' divides the area around a central fireplace into radial sectors and circular zones. It examines the frequency of artefacts according to distance classes relative to the fireplace. If the fireplace were in a dwelling, a zone with few finds would be expected between the fireplace and the former wall. At the wall the number of artefacts would increase before reducing again in quantity outside. A bimodal distribution of the find frequencies is the result. In contrast to this, around an outdoor hearth the number of finds does not increase again beyond the waste zone around the hearth, but falls steadily towards the periphery, leading to a unimodal distribution of the find density.

In its basic principle, Stapert's method is unsuitable for demonstrating dwellings that do not have a circular ground plan, since these cannot meaningfully be analysed by circular zones. However, individual latent Allerød and Holocene dwellings were detected by the 'ring and sector' method, for example Rekem 10 (De Bie and Caspar 2000),

Andernach-Martinsberg 2 (Stapert and Street 1997), and Siebenlinden 1-I (Kind 2003).

To evaluate those find concentrations that are neither round, nor include a central fireplace, we have combined well-known methods for analysing settlement structures in the examination of three Allerød sites (Gelhausen *et al.* 2004, Figure 68.1). Our investigation is based on following considerations and observations:

1. A sudden change from high to lower find density at the edge of a find concentration points to a former delimitation. A rising number of finds directly inside the border of a concentration of artefacts, connected with a clear decrease in exterior finds, both stipulated by Stapert (1992) for proof of the barrier effect, represents only a special case as an indication of the delimitation of a settlement structure. Whether a find concentration is clearly limited can be demonstrated particularly clearly if one represents the find quantity per unit of area (here in quarters of a square metre) by isopachs (find density lines).
2. If the connecting lines of refitted artefacts often run along the border of a concentration, or terminate there, where a clear decrease in find numbers is registered, this is likewise an indication of an obstacle for human activities related to the transport of objects, preventing a diffuse distribution of the finds.
3. In evident dwelling structures retouched artefacts are essentially limited to the concentration. Cores are found more at the edge of the concentration, or beyond it. In some cases tools also group together at the edge of the find concentration.
4. Larger boulders and faunal remains lie at the edge of a concentration, or outside it, so that the area of the main find concentration is, to a large extent, void of these types of finds.

Niederbieber. Area IV

The Late Palaeolithic site of Niederbieber (Neuwied Basin, Rhineland-Palatinate, Germany) (Figure 68.1) is, with an excavated surface of more than 930m^2, one of the most intensively examined sites of the Federmessergruppen in central Europe (e.g. Bolus 1992; Baales 2001; 2002). The find concentration at Niederbieber IV is one of 17 of different shape and density (Gelhausen 2007) excavated since 1980. Niederbieber IV reveals a central hearth, rendered visible not only by burnt artefacts but also because of changes in the colour of the underlying sediment. Until recently Concentration IV was considered to have been the result of open-air activities. A significant argument for this interpretation came from Stapert's 'ring and sector' method (Stapert 1992), since the lithics displayed a unimodal distribution. In this paper, a new spatial analysis of Niederbieber IV suggests that all the recognized features, in fact, point to activities within a dwelling.

The 46m^2 surface area of Niederbieber IV was excavated between 1982 and 1984, and analysed by Winter (1986; 1987) and Bolus (1992). In Area IV, 2088 stone artefacts (>1cm) were plotted in three dimensions, and 16,827 chips were counted per 0.25m^2 and analysed using isopachs. Additionally faunal remains and larger pebbles were three-dimensionally plotted and analysed.

The distribution pattern displayed by the artefacts shows an almost square shape, measuring *c.* 4 × 4.5m, with a marked, sudden decrease at the edges (Figure 68.2a). The highest density of artefacts is directly south and north of the hearth, with 822 and 782 pieces per 0.25m^2. Most of the retouched tools lie within the surface displayed by the isopachs. Only a few pieces are scattered to the north-east and south-west. The cores tend rather towards the edges of the concentration. Pebbles (>5cm) are limited to two areas at the south-west and north-east of the excavation area. In addition, some pebbles are positioned in a way that suggests a 'ring of stones' (perhaps stone weights) around the concentration. Nine of these pebbles were classified as retouching tools with clear scar fields on their surfaces.

Faunal remains are distributed in two larger zones at the south-west and north-east of the excavation. They almost align with the distribution of the pebbles but they

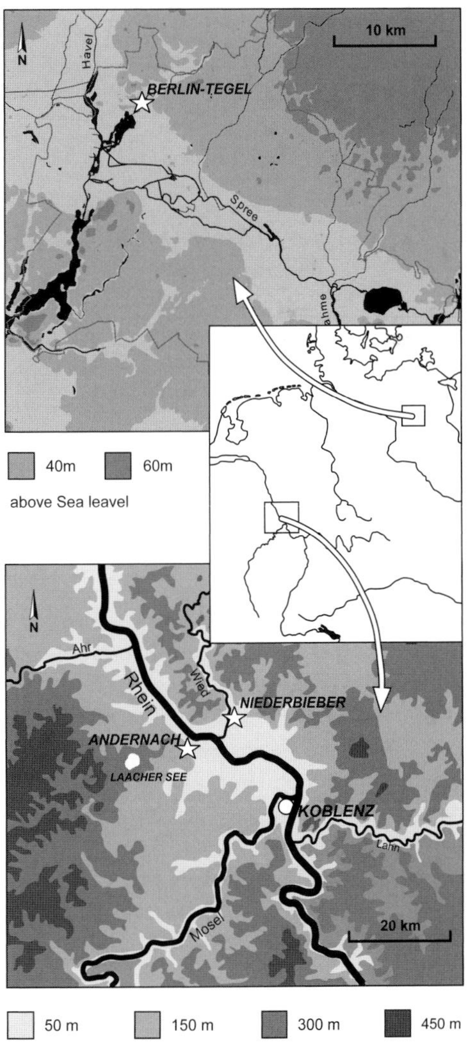

Figure 68.1. Locations of the sites at Niederbieber and Andernach (Middle Rhine Valley) and Berlin-Tegel.

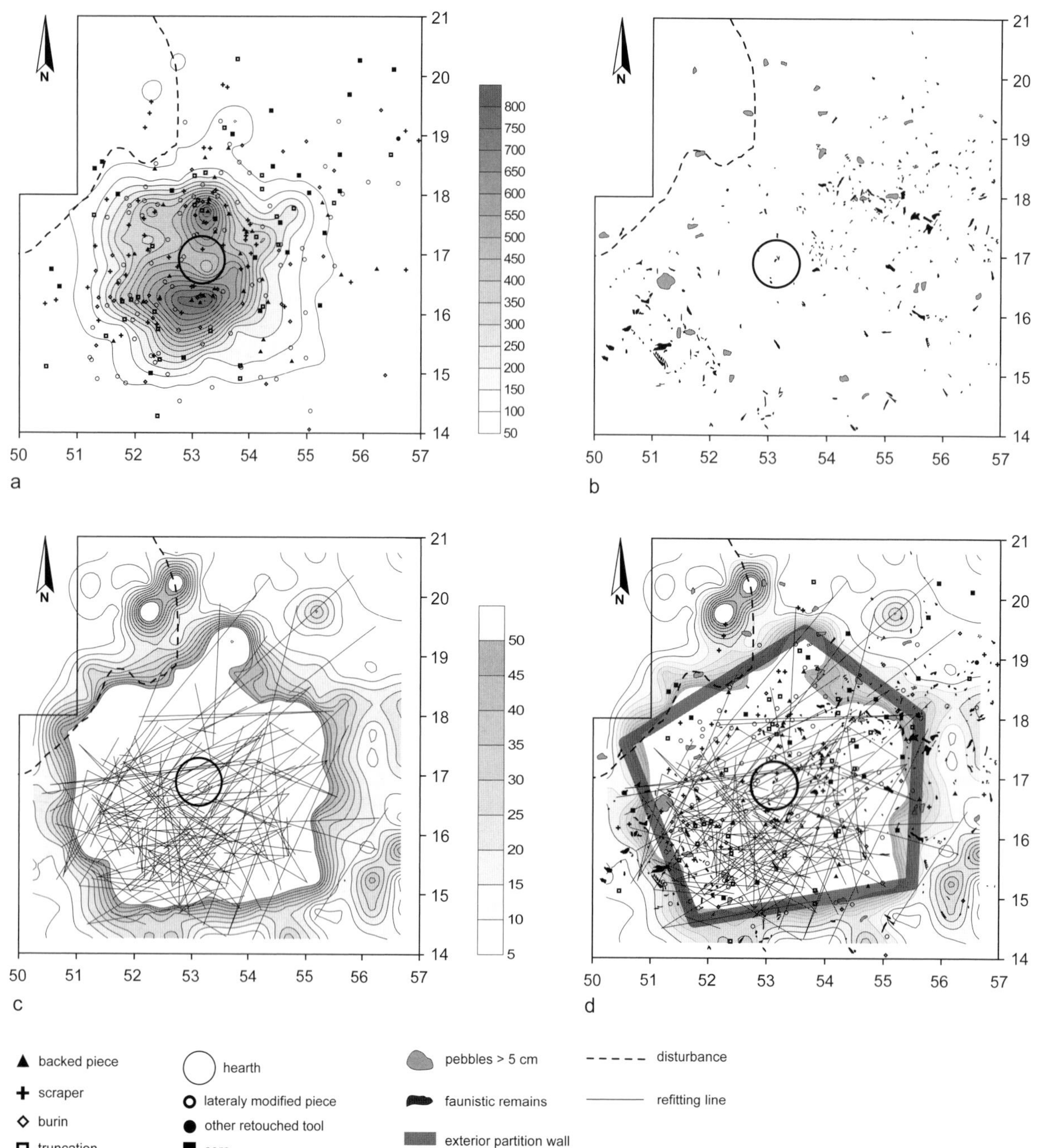

Figure 68.2. Niederbieber IV. A) Isopach distribution of the lithic finds <1cm recovered using wet sieving per 0.25m². Distribution of retouched tools and cores. B) Distribution of faunal remains and pebbles >5cm. C) Isopach distribution of lithic finds <1cm recovered using wet sieving, limited at 50 pieces per 0.25m². Conjoining lines of all included pieces. D) Suggested exterior partition wall.

are slightly more diffuse. In any event, they are distributed outside the find concentration shown by the isopachs (Figure 68.2b). Refitting lines of the lithics show that activities have obviously taken place within the find scatter. They often run along the edges of the concentration, ending there and demarcating its boundary.

The arguments specified previously permit a reconstruction of the features of Niederbieber IV as a polygonal floor plan of a former dwelling. Particularly remarkable is the relatively sudden change from high to low find density at the edges of the find scatter; the heavier objects, such as cores and pebbles, are mostly deposited here. The conjoining lines also point to a barrier at the edges of the find scatter (Figure 68.2c). It seems clear that all the activities took place within the find concentration. This interpretation is also supported by the distribution of the retouched tools, which are mainly deposited inside the concentration. Overall, the recorded artefacts show that a wall or a barrier prevented their wider distribution.

In summary, the spatial analysis of Niederbieber IV suggests a former dwelling structure with a polygonal floor plan (Figure 68.2d).

Andernach-Martinsberg 3. The upper find horizon

Between 1994 and 1996 a surface area of 113m^2 was examined on the Martinsberg, in the city of Andernach (Rhineland-Palatinate, Germany) (Figure 68.1), and a Federmessergruppen lithic concentration was documented (Kegler 2002). In this find horizon, 2417 chalcedony artefacts (>1cm) were plotted in three dimensions, and about 14,614 pieces (<1cm) were recovered by wet sieving. Additionally, 535 bone fragments (>3cm) were three-dimensionally plotted. Three basalt blocks, *c.* 25cm in diameter and found at the north-west end of the concentration, are the only larger objects; they can probably be connected with different working areas rather than the deliberations on dwelling structures presented here.

During the excavation two hearths were documented, each about 50cm in diameter: a southern fireplace within the main concentration of the chalcedony artefacts, and a further one north-west of the main concentration. A special feature is a small, circular pit *c.* 10cm in diameter in square 28/19. This probable 'posthole' has a cylindrical form and a convex base. At the bottom of this feature were found some charcoal pieces, a bone fragment, a flat plaque of quartzitic schist, as well as some lithic chips.

Mapping all the individually measured stone artefacts of the dominant raw material, chalcedony, shows a north-northwest oriented, rectangular concentration. At first view it seems to be very compact, covering *c.* 3 × 3m around the central fireplace (Figure 68.3a).

The bone fragments are concentrated directly adjacent to the fireplaces, as well as being dispersed randomly over the entire excavation area. The combination of the distribution of the bones and the stone artefacts clearly show a pattern. Between the main concentration of stone artefacts and the exterior spread of the bones is a zone with noticeably fewer finds, approximately half a metre in width. This find-poor area could have resulted from a kind of barrier between the main stone artefact concentration and the areas lying outside its western and the eastern edges (Figure 68.3b). In the south, this border cannot be traced with the same clarity, because of the use of different excavation techniques, but mapping the find densities of stone artefacts with isopachs makes very clear that their distribution was not substantially influenced in this area.

The impression of a closely defined spread of stone artefacts is confirmed by mapping all 17,031 chalcedony artefacts (single finds and finds recovered, partly, by wet sieving) by density isopachs. Their distribution corresponds to a north-north-west oriented form, as long as it is wide, with a length of *c.* 4.5m along the sides. At the edges of the feature the find distribution is remarkable: to the south, the west, and the east of the main concentration, the number of pieces decreases from more than 50 artefacts per 0.25m^2 to less than 5 pieces over a distance of only 30cm (Figure 68.3c). This reduction is clearly shown by the isopachs, the lines of which are very close to each other. In the northern area – within the area of the exterior fireplace – the isopachs enclose the working area in front of the main distribution. Here, such a clear decrease in find density cannot be observed.

The distribution of retouched stone artefacts is limited to the extent of the area shown by the density lines. Small clusters, especially of backed pieces, are adjacent to the fireplaces. In a sense, the distribution of the retouched pieces underlines the limited extent of the find concentration. The distribution of the cores does not show the suggested pattern: some cores are positioned within the main concentration while some are distributed outside. Some of the cores relate to some of the 67 refits of stone artefacts, however, these refit lines show no parallel lines, reflecting the delimitations mentioned above. Yet the refits demonstrate the close connection of activities within the main concentration and between the area containing the second fireplace in the northern part (Figure 68.3c).

For the reconstruction of a possible dwelling feature the combination of different find types, and their depiction both as single finds and by isopachs, are of substantial importance. The position of boundaries west, south, and east of the main concentration permits an interpretation that the Federmessergruppen site of Andernach 3 might be a former tent location. A boundary cannot clearly be recognized in the north-west. Only by interpreting the positioning of the possible 'posthole' can an idea of how the construction was closed off be reached. The distribution of finds does not show the clear position of a wall in this area – with the exception of the location of the bone fragments – and therefore the 'posthole' might have served only as a feature for the stability of the construction. The structure was therefore closed on three sides, and occasionally open to the north-west. Since the distribution of finds in this area extends far to the north-west, the exit of the dwelling can be postulated here. The outside hearth, together with the thin spread of finds and the scatter of retouched forms, are suggestive of an open-air zone of activities (Figure 68.3d).

Taking all the evidence into account, we regard the upper find horizon of Andernach 3 as showing a polygonal structure, oriented north-west/south-east, with a central hearth (Figure 68.3d). The approximately parallel walls at the east and the west suggest several possibilities for the form of the dwelling, including a pentagonal shape, or, taking into account the possible 'posthole', a slightly oblong, hexagonal layout. The dwelling therefore encloses a surface of *c.* 4.5 × 4.5m, with a maximum inner surface area of 14m^2.

Berlin-Tegel Concentration IX

The site of Berlin-Tegel A is situated to the north of Berlin, immediately above a small stream, the Tegeler Fließ (Figure 68.1). The site was excavated in the early 1960s under the direction of Mey and von Müller. Twenty-two concentrations of artefacts (Federmessergruppen and Ahrensburgian) were examined over a surface area of 4000m^2 (Probst 1989).

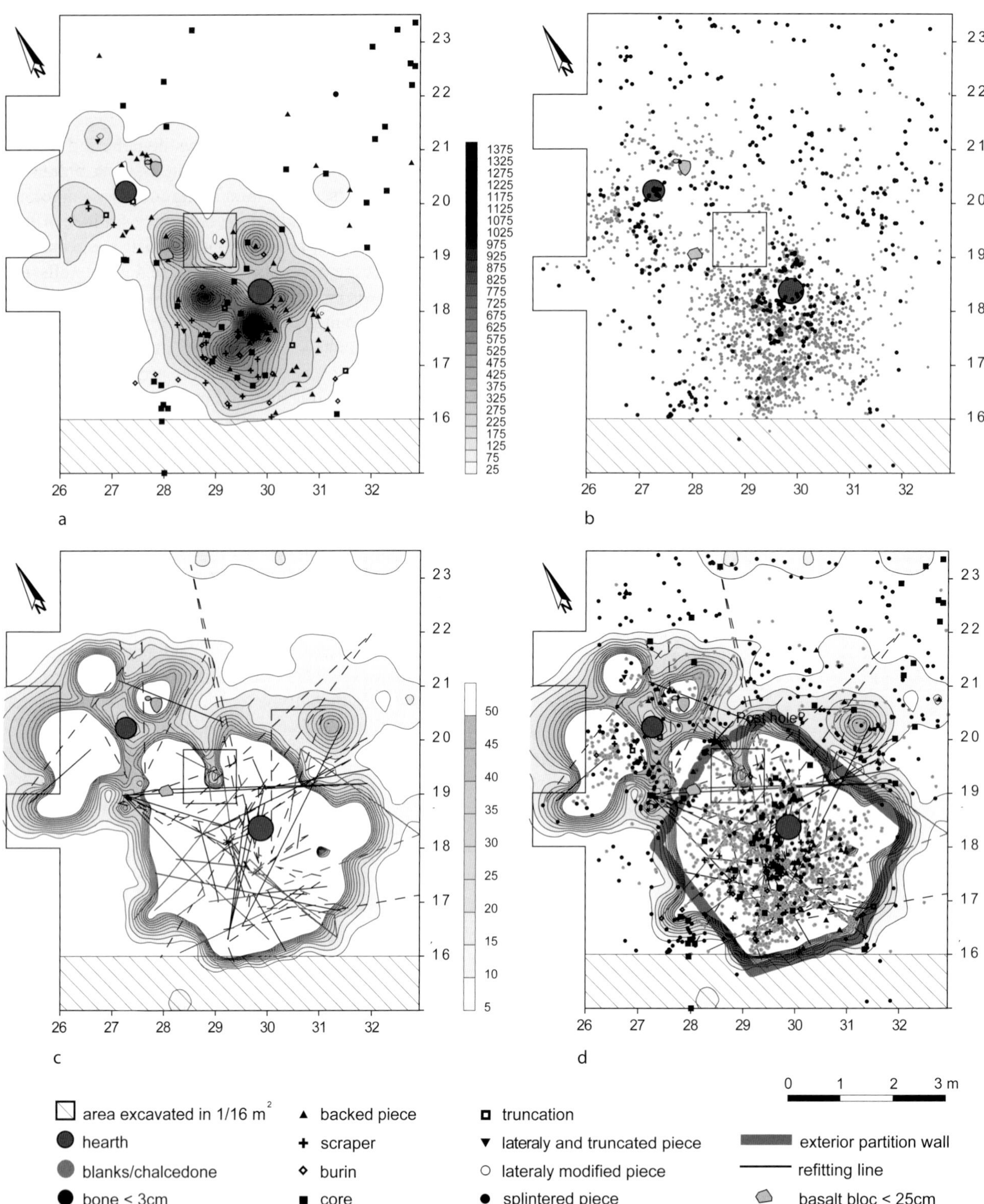

Figure 68.3. Andernach/Martinsberg 3. Upper find horizon (section of the excavated area). A) Isopach distribution of finds < 1cm recovered using wet sieving per 0.25m^2. Distribution of retouched tools and cores. B) Distribution of chalcedony blanks > 1cm and bone fragments > 3cm. C) Isopach distribution of all finds recovered using wet sieving, limited at 50 pieces per 0.25m^2. Conjoining lines of all included pieces. D) Suggested exterior partition wall.

Concentration IX has an extension of 7 × 8m (Gelhausen *et al.* 2005, fig. 7), but the find density lines show clearly the prominent western part of concentration IX, in contrast to the thin spread of artefacts in the eastern sector (Figure 68.4a). Close to the area of highest find density, a hearth was indicated by the red colouration of the sand and by burnt bones and artefacts. About 80% of the stone artefacts from the entire concentration IX are burnt. They therefore

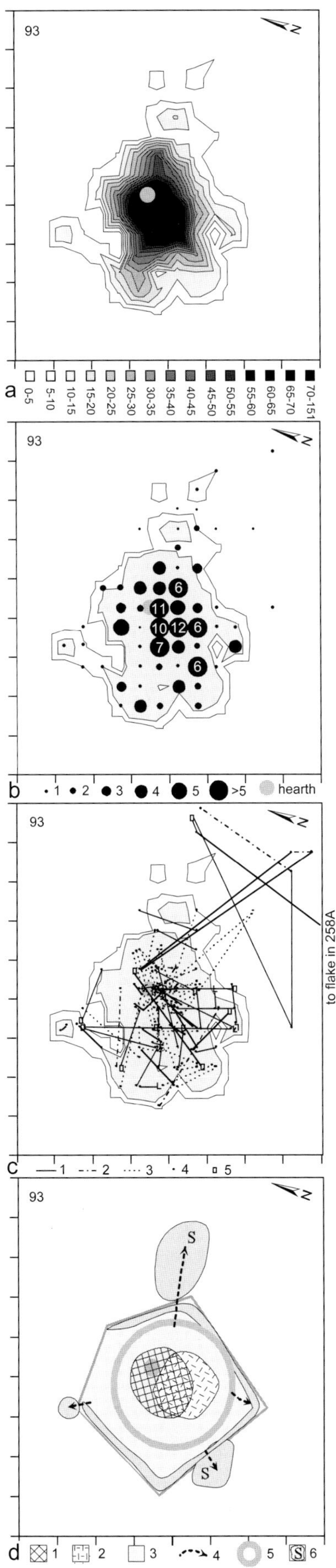

do not seem to be in primary positions but are considered as having been dispersed by settlement activities. There was an accumulation of modified tools and cores near the hearth, but considerable amounts of these artefacts were found at the edge of the actual concentration of finds (Figure 68.4b). (For the distribution of the different categories of modified tools and for the distribution of cores see Gelhausen *et al.* (2004, fig. 4c–g)). Numerous refit lines end at the border of the concentration, or run closely parallel to it (Figure 68.4c). They stress also the association of the left side of the concentration with this structure. The isopachs of find density, the distribution of larger objects at the edge of concentration IX, and the refit lines stressing this border, define a zone which was formerly limited to this space and thus suggest a dwelling. This had a trapezoidal ground plan, four metres long and no more than four metres broad, with the greatest width in its northern section (Figure 68.4d). The longitudinal axis of this structure was orientated north-north-east/south-south-west. Neither a front nor rear exit can be identified by refits of artefacts. However a small accumulation of finds located to the north-east of concentration IX might be seen as related to a tent entrance. A small cluster of artefacts (concentration X) lies on the longitudinal axis of the reconstructed dwelling and might derive from activities conducted behind the tent. This would match other better documented tent structures, which often exhibit a greater deposition of finds outside the back of the dwelling (Jöris and Terberger 2001, 168).

Results and Outlook

The three find scatters presented here show indications of the presence of former dwellings. At the edge of the artefact concentrations a clear decrease in find density can be observed almost everywhere. Due to excavation methods this is more striking at Niederbieber IV and Andernach 3 than at Berlin-Tegel IX. Numerous connections of refitted artefacts end where the find density decreases or runs parallel to these zones. Many modified artefacts are concentrated within the find concentrations and along their

Figure 68.4. (left) Berlin-Tegel A, Concentration IX. A) Isopachs of all artefacts. B) Horizontal distribution of the modified tools (scrapers, burins, retouched blades, retouched flakes, borer, splintered pieces and backed pieces). C) All refit lines (1: production sequences; 2: breaks; 3: breaks of burnt artefact fragments; 4: artefacts; 5: shatter). D) Interpretation (1: zone of activity around the fireplace; 2: backward toss zone; 3: areas of cleared out material; 4: supposed direction of clearing activities; 5: find-rich zone around the central fireplace; 6: clusters of stone artefacts). (With B–C the find density lines for 5–10 artefacts and 10–15 artefacts are displayed).

edges. At Niederbieber und Andernach the concentrations are nearly void of unburned bones. At Niederbieber, larger stones are also found at the edge or outside the find concentration. The settlement structures presented here differ among themselves with regard to small-scale artefact concentrations, which indicate working areas, and in their degree of dispersion and the intensity with which the interior area of the dwellings has been used (Gelhausen *et al.* 2005). The clarity of the distribution of larger objects at the edges of these find scatters, and the number of refit lines accentuating the borders of the find concentrations, rise with the degree of dispersion of these small clusters of tools. Even if a certain 'temporal trend' is reflected by this dispersion of finds, and by the different amounts of tool types, this does not appear to be too important: if certain types of tools are less well represented the complete 'tool set' is still always present (Kegler 2002).

The dwelling features discussed in this paper are smaller than the trapezoidal dwellings of the Magdalenian and early Federmessergruppen. We were, nevertheless, able to identify some features common to both – the trapezoidal floor plan, partitioned into sectors both rich and poor in finds, and a clearly defined area with a high density of finds around the hearth. The Mesolithic dwellings of Ulkestrup II type (Grøn 1995; Wenzel 2002) also share exactly these characteristics. The dwelling structures of the Final Palaeolithic and the Mesolithic, which hardly left any evident traces, underline, in conjunction with several other arguments (e.g. Baales 2002), the high degree of mobility of Allerød and Holocene populations, and the regularity with which they moved their dwelling sites.

Acknowledgements

The authors wish to thank Dr Olaf Jöris, Monrepos, for many references and discussions. We thank Dr Martin Street, Monrepos, for improving the English text. Stefan Wenzel thanks Mrs A. Hoffman and Prof. Dr W. Menghin for permission to work with the material from Area 6 at Berlin-Tegel, housed in the Museum für Vor- und Frühgeschichte Berlin under If 24640/1-472. He also thanks the German Research Council (DFG) for their funding of a project on Palaeolithic dwelling structures (WE2856/1-2).

References

Andersen, K., Jørgensen, S. and Richter, J. 1982. *Maglemose hytterne ved Ulkestrup Lyng*. Nordiske Fortidsminder, Series B, vol. 7. København, Det Kongelige Nordiske Oldskriftselskab.

Baales, M. 2001. Zur Fortführung der Ausgrabungen auf dem spätpaläolithischen Siedlungsareal von Niederbieber (Stadt Neuwied). Erste Ergebnisse der siedlungsarchäologischen Analyse. *Jahrbuch des Römisch-Germanischen Zentral-museums Mainz* 48, 163–98.

Baales, M. 2002. *Der spätpaläolithische Fundplatz Kettig*. Monographien des Römisch-Germanischen Zentralmuseums 51. Mainz, Römisch-Germanisches Zentralmuseum.

Binford, L. R. 1983. *In pursuit of the past. Decoding the archaeological record*. London, Thames and Hudson.

Bokelmann, K. 1986. Rast unter Bäumen. Ein ephemerer mesolithischer Lagerplatz aus dem Duvenseer Moor. *Offa* 43, 149–63.

Bokelmann, K. 1989. Eine mesolithische Kiefernrindenmatte aus dem Duvenseer Moor. *Offa* 46, 17–22.

Bolus, M. 1992. *Die Siedlungsbefunde des späteiszeitlichen Fundplatzes Niederbieber (Stadt Neuwied). Ausgrabungen 1981–1988*. With contributions from G. Roth, S. Stephan and R. C. Rottländer. Monographien des Römisch-Germanischen Zentralmuseums Mainz 22, Mainz/Bonn, Römisch-Germanisches Zentralmuseum.

Bosinski, G. 1979. *Die Ausgrabungen in Gönnerdorf 1968-1976 und die Siedlungsbefunde der Grabung 1968*. Der Magdalénien-Fundplatz Gönnersdorf 3, Wiesbaden, F. Steiner Verlag.

De Bie, M. and Caspar, J.-P. 2000. *Rekem. A Federmesser Camp on the Meuse River Bank*. Acta Archaeologica Lovaniensia Monographiae 10, 2 vol. Leuven, Leuven University Press.

Gelhausen, F. 2007. *Untersuchungen zum Siedlungsmuster der allerødzeitlichen Federmessergruppen in Niederbieber, Stadt Neuwied, Rheinland-Pfalz*. Unpublished PhD thesis, University of Cologne.

Gelhausen, F., Kegler, J. F. and Wenzel, S. 2004. Latent dwelling structures in the Final Palaeolithic: Niederbieber IV, Andernach-Martinsberg 3, Berlin-Tegel IX. *Notae Praehistoricae* 24, 69–79.

Gelhausen, F., Kegler, J. F. and Wenzel, S. 2005. Hütten oder Himmel? Latente Behausungsstrukturen im Spätpaläolithikum Mitteleuropa. *Jahrbuch des Römisch-Germanisches Zentral Museums Mainz* 51, 2004 (2005), 1–22.

Grøn, O. 1995. *The Maglemose Culture. The Reconstruction of the Social Organization of a Mesolithic Culture in Northern Europe*. British Archaeological Reports, International Series S616. Oxford, Tempvs Reperatvm.

Grøn, O. 2003. Mesolithic dwelling places in south Scandinavia: their definition and social interpretation. *Antiquity* 77 (298), 685–708.

Jöris, O. and Terberger, T. 2001. Zur Rekonstruktion eines Zeltes mit trapezförmigem Grundriß am Magdalénien-Fundplatz Gönnersdorf / Mittelrhein – eine » Quadratur des Kreises « ? *Archäologisches Korrespondenzblatt* 31, 163–72.

Kegler, J. F. 2002. Die federmesserzeitliche Fundschicht des paläolithischen Siedlungsplatzes Andernach/Martinsberg (Neuwieder Becken), Grabung 1994-1996. *Archäologisches Korrespondenzblatt* 32, 501–16.

Kind, C.-J. 2003. *Das Mesolithikum in der Talaue des Neckars. Die Fundstellen von Rottenburg Siebenlinden 1 und 3*. Forschungen und Berichte zur Vor- und Frühgeschichte in Baden Württemberg 88. Stuttgart, Theiss.

Leroi-Gourhan, A. 1984. *Pincevent. Campement magdalénien de chasseurs de rennes*. Guides archéologiques de la France 3. Paris, Imprimerie Nationale.

Leroi-Gourhan, A. and Brézillon, M. 1972. *Fouilles de Pincevent. Essai d'analyse ethnographique d'un habitat magdalénien*. VIIe supplément à Gallia Préhistoire. Paris, Centre national de la recherche scientifique (CNRS).

Probst, B. 1989. Rastplätze spätaltsteinzeitlicher Jäger von Berlin-Tegel. With a contribution from F. Schweingruber. *Ausgrabungen in Berlin* 8, 5–177.

Stapert, D. 1992. *Rings and Sectors: Intrasite Spatial Analysis of Stone Age Sites*. Unpublished PhD thesis, University of Groningen.

Stapert, D. 2002. Maglemose huts and Duvensee: Spatial analysis with 'ANALITHIC', in T. Terberger and B. V. Eriksen (eds.), *Hunters in a changing world: Environment and Archaeology of the Pleistocene–Holocene Transition (ca 11000–9000 BC) in Northern Central Europe. Workshop of the UISPP-Commission XXXII at Greifswald in September 2002*, 223–41. Internationale Archaologie – Arbeitsgemeinschaft, Symposium, Tagung, Kongress 5. Rahden/Westphalia, Verlag Marie Leidorf.

Stapert, D. and Street, M. 1997. High resolution or optimum resolution? Spatial analysis of the Federmesser site at Andernach, Germany. *World Archaeology* 29 (2), 172–94.

Street, M. 1995. Andernach-Martinsberg, in G. Bosinski, M. Street and M. Baales (eds.), *The Palaeolithic and Mesolithic of the Rhineland*, in W. Schirmer (ed.), *Quaternary field trips in Central Europe, Vol. 2. Field trips on special topics*. International Union for Quaternary Research, XIV international Congress, 3–10 August, 1994, Berlin, Germany, 910–18. München, Verlag Friedrich Pfeil.

Vermeersch, P. M., Symens, N., Vyncker, P., Gijselings, G. and Lauwers, R. 1987. Orp, site Magdalénien de plein air (comm. de Orp-Jauche). *Archaeologica Belgica* 3, 7–56.

Wenzel, S. 2002. Ein mittelsteinzeitlicher Zeltbefund von Hartmannsdorf in Brandenburg. *Archäologisches Korrespondenzblatt* 32, 1–13.

Winter, D. 1986. *Der spätpaläolithische Fundplatz Niederbieber. Fläche 50/14–56/20*. Unpublished MA thesis, University of Cologne.

Winter, D. 1987. Retuscheure des spätpaläolithischen Fundplatzes Niederbieber/Neuwieder Becken (Fläche 50/14–56/20). *Archäologisches Korrespondenzblatt* 17, 295–309.

69. Along the shores of the Ancylus Lake. Trädgårdstorp and other coastal Mesolithic settlement sites during the Late Ancylus period in western Östergötland

Fredrik Molin

The starting point of this paper is coastal Mesolithic settlement sites from the Ancylus period in the area of Linköping in the middle of Östergötland, in eastern Sweden. The background is the Mesolithic site recently excavated at Trädgårdstorp on the outskirts of the town of Linköping. The site is situated at the edge of a large ice-marginal field and along an ancient beach formation that earlier scholars have interpreted as the Ancylus limit – a shoreline formed by the Ancylus Lake. The investigations at Trädgårdstorp included the documentation of two very well preserved sets of house foundations from the Mesolithic, something which makes the site well suited for further studies of site organisation and social structures. One of the houses is dated to the oldest occupation phase on the site, between 7580–6700 cal BC, when the settlement was situated close to the seashore of that time. Preliminary results indicate that the site was occupied only during the winter season. The present text draws but a sketchy picture of the settlement remains; the focus is instead on the physical conditions during the first phase of occupation and the text emphasizes the landscape and environment, and its importance for the early coastal settlements.

Keywords: Ancylus Lake, coastal-settlement sites, shore displacement, Ancylus limit, Mesolithic houses.

Man and landscape around Linköping

Östergötland, a province in eastern central Sweden, can be divided into four physiographical parts: the southern forests, the plain, the northern forests, and the archipelago in the east. Lake Roxen is virtually at the centre of the province. On the south shore of Roxen lies Linköping, Sweden's fifth largest city. The area around Roxen and Linköping divides the large plain of Östergötland into two parts – the western and eastern Östgöta plain. During the Ancylus stage of the Baltic, 9400–8200 ^{14}C-years BP (7450–6250 uncal BC; all BP dates referred to here are in radiocarbon years BP), a large and broad bay of Lake Ancylus covered about half of this plain. In the vicinity of Linköping there are well-marked shorelines dating back to Ancylus times along the ancient coastal area. Along the edge of the plain there are a number of Mesolithic sites, of which many were established during the Ancylus Lake phase and thus constitute, so far, the oldest known settlements in the area.

The southern forest is an outlier of the southern Swedish highlands and is characterized topographically by fissure valleys running in different directions. The valleys are often elongated, containing a large number of lakes and watercourses. In the border zone between the southern forest and the plain a transition belt can be discerned, characterized by a varied landscape. This transition belt was shown to have been important as early as the Mesolithic. Several settlement sites and reflections of human activity have been documented on the edge of the southern forests since the 1990s (Molin 2000; Carlsson *et al.* 2005).

The attractiveness of this inland transitional zone may be due to an early adaptation to a broad-spectrum economy, which was a precondition for being able to spend entire seasons here. The supporting capabilities of the forest, offering big game to hunt, plants to gather, and fishing, was probably of the utmost significance. To ensure a supply of food from several different ecological niches, settlement sites were located in areas where the marginal effect could be used to the full (cf. Knarrström 2000). In recent years a pattern of early, small inland settlement sites located at water systems and small in-filling lakes has been documented at the edge of the forest and the western plains. Several large-scale excavations have been conducted that have great potential for increasing our knowledge, which, so far, is more or less at the level of basic research. The settlement sites have been interpreted as seasonal sites for small groups, places to which they returned in a repetitive, cyclic pattern at certain times during the year. In several cases the settlements were established in the Preboreal and Early Boreal periods. Recurrent visits resulted in lengthy site continuity, with the latest remains often being datable to the Atlantic period. Several of the settlement sites display clear internal structures, with hut remains and interpretable activity areas (Molin 2000; 2005; Larsson and Molin 2000).

The northern forests, including the areas around Kolmården, Tylöskogen (north of the town of Motala) and the forests north of Roxen, are limited to the south by a large fault system. This extends from the Baltic Sea with the bay of Bråviken in the east, to Lake Vättern in the western part of the province. The terrain of the northern area largely consists of fissure valleys, and, like the southern forests, has a rich water system with lakes of varying size. During the Mesolithic large parts of these areas were an archipelago with islands of different size. Several special surveys of Stone Age remains in these environments have revealed a rich Mesolithic cultural landscape with a very large number of sites of different size. The economy was based on fishing and seal hunting and the settlements were predominantly located in close connection to the shoreline, as supported by ^{14}C dates. As new islands and beaches were constantly formed, as a result of ongoing shore displacement, an almost countless number of remains were left, dominated by waste from quartz knapping. The remains reflect a mobile coastal society where the people, because of ever changing natural preconditions, were continually ready to move (Åkerlund 1996; Wikell 2005).

Linköping is situated in the transition zone between the forest and the western plains. A large number of stray finds, in the form of pecked axes, show the location of Late Mesolithic settlements in the city's vicinity, probably along the shores of the Litorina Sea. Among the finds there are also a few axes of the western-Swedish Lihult type. On the outskirts of the town there are also early-known settlement sites from the Litorina period, with worked quartz and microblades of flint (Molin 2000, 35). As a result of the city's expansion and the need for unexploited land over the last 25 years, extensive archaeological investigations have been carried out, principally managed by the National Heritage Board in Linköping. During both large-contract investigations associated with the exploitation of land, as well as a number of smaller excavations and special surveys, a large number of Mesolithic sites have been found. The bulk of these are situated at levels above the present sea, which for good reasons can be connected to the shore of the Litorina Sea. The find materials are dominated by knapped quartz, with a smaller amount of flint, quartzite and other rocks. In the quartz material, a developed microblade technology is obvious. As for the rest, diagnostic tools are predominantly scrapers and cutting pieces. The raw material is both beach nodules and chunks extracted from quartz veins. Very recently (2005), a quartz quarry with associated Mesolithic settlement remains was investigated on the outskirts of Linköping. The site has preliminary been dated to between 7000–6000 cal BC (Molin *et al.*, in press). The majority of sites from the Late Mesolithic can be connected to hills of till-like material that during this period were islands in the archipelago of the Litorina Sea.

Shore displacement in the Linköping area

The rapid course of land rise in eastern central Sweden after deglaciation created different stages in the development of the Baltic (e.g. Björck 1995). This in turn had dramatic effects on flora and fauna and on the early people who settled here in the constantly changing environment. Within a relatively short space of time conditions could be completely transformed as the landscape was reshaped; this applied in particular to the coastal zones and the extensive and ongoing displacement here of the shoreline (e.g. Åkerlund 1996; Pettersson and Wikell 2004).

The course of the shore displacement differs considerably between the regions of Scandinavia, an effect of differences in both land upheaval rates and the eustatic movements of the ocean and the lake phases of the Baltic (Björck 1995). It is necessary to have information about the regional shore displacement in order to describe the palaeogeography and to be able to understand the location in the landscape of Mesolithic sites. Often, shore displacement data are the only means to (indirectly) date coastal Mesolithic sites. This is especially true in the early phases of archaeological investigations and special surveys when no ^{14}C dates have yet been obtained (e.g. Åkerlund *et al.* 1995; Åkerlund 1996).

Thanks to certain local height and terrain conditions, the Linköping area is well suited for studies of different geographical changes since the end of the Ice Age, especially for the earliest phase of the complicated course of shore displacement. Already in the early 20th century, Henrik Munthe made a number of important observations in the area (Munthe 1922). In connection with the field survey for the quaternary map, further observations of wave washing and shorelines have been made, and therefore the conditions for the creation of a shore-displacement curve have been estimated as favourable (Fromm 1976).

During the Late Glacial, the area around Lake Roxen was depressed below the water of the Baltic and has since then been successively elevated above the surface. Therefore new areas of land have constantly been exposed to the waves of the Baltic. The shoreline has passed every level, down to the surface of the present-day Lake Roxen at 33.3m asl. Erik Fromm (1976) describes the earliest shore displacement in detail (Figure 69.1). The interpretation is based on pollen and diatom analyses, as well as on ^{14}C analyses of the ancient lake sediments in the interval between 70 and 120m asl. The isolation dates, and the height above present sea level for the isolation thresholds, have been connected to form a shore-displacement curve for the area. This shore-displacement curve covers the time

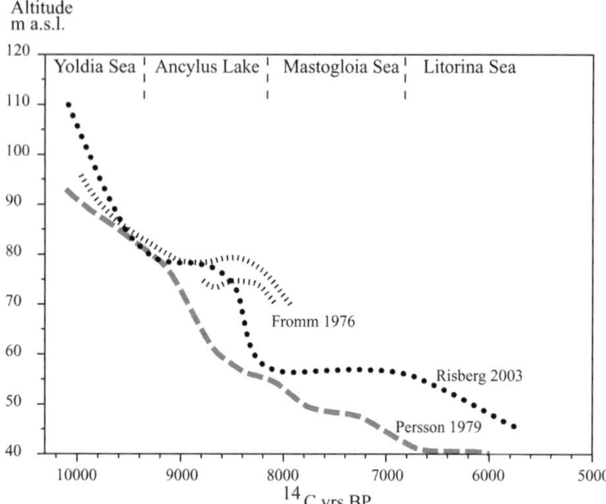

Figure 69.1. Shore-displacement curves for eastern central Sweden in relation to the province of Östergötland. Fromm 1976 show curves from both north and south of the major fault system in the Linköping area. Risberg (2003) models a curve for the central part of the Södertörn peninsula, south of Stockholm. Persson (1979) describes shore displacement in the south of Sörmland province. (Graphic: Lars Östlin, National Heritage Board).

period between *c.* 10,000 BP (8050 uncal BC) and 7900 BP (5950 uncal BC), i.e. the Baltic stages of the Yoldia Sea, Ancylus Lake, and the beginning of Mastogloia Sea.

Immediately after the withdrawal of the ice sheet, *c.* 10,500 BP (8550 uncal BC), even the highest peaks in the area were covered with the water of the Baltic Ice Lake. Glacial clay as high as 116m asl was deposited at a water depth of at least ten metres, and consequently during the Baltic Ice Lake stage. The level of this lake was, however, rapidly lowered, so that the dried-up slopes have only become wave washed to a small extent. Wave washing is generally obvious up to 125m asl, corresponding to the highest level of the Yoldia Sea in the area, and clearly demonstrates at which level the catastrophic lowering of the ice lake ended, and a more moderate shore-displacement rate started.

'The Ancylus limit'

The oldest settlement sites observed in the Linköping area date to *c.* 9000–7500 ^{14}C-years BP (*c.* 8300–6500 cal BC), that is from a phase when the ice had long since vanished. The period is characterized by the transition from the Ancylus Lake to the preliminary stage of the Litorina Sea. Initially the Ancylus Lake covered much of the province, forming a wide bay that cut in across the plains and along the edge of the fault system via Lake Roxen towards Lake Vättern (Figure 69.2). At this time the Linköping area was an open coastal zone with a relatively small inner archipelago. Thus, the area constituted an immediate interface between the mainland and the open sea (to the east, however, an extensive outer archipelago with larger and smaller islands began to form). The first outlets of the Ancylus Lake were drained *c.* 9200 BP (7250 uncal BC), which meant a land connection between southern and northern Sweden and the isolation of Lake Vänern from the sea. This also resulted in a transgressive phase in the southern Baltic basin around 9200 BP (7250 uncal BC), with gradually changing conditions for coastal settlements (Björck 1995, 31; Risberg 2003).

An especially distinctive beach formation in the Linköping area was described by Munthe (1922) as 'the Ancylus limit'. This formation is situated around 75m asl, and is most prominent as an erosion bluff (2–3m high) above the lower beach plains. The distinctiveness of this formation is due to the fact that it was formed in the easily eroded glacial gravel at the edge of a large ice-marginal field. Along a shorter section this beach formation has the form of a low sandbank. Through borings it has been proved that this bank lies on top of a thin layer of marsh peat and hence marks a transgression of the Baltic. The peat has been ^{14}C dated to 8200–7450 cal BC (8640±115 BP; St-3285). In Fromm's shore-displacement curve (Fromm 1976, 72) the height of the beach formation and the dating of transgressed peat have been taken into consideration. The date is too young to represent the Ancylus limit, but the dating is however problematic. It was made on bulk sediment, indeed after the removal of rootlets (which would make the date younger), but still the sample could contain younger ^{14}C in soluble form. We are thus left with two alternatives: either the dating of the peat is too young, which leaves the door open for the possibility that the beach formation is, after all, the Ancylus limit, or at least formed during an early phase of the Ancylus Lake, or the dating is correct, which means that the peat must have been transgressed many hundreds of years after the Ancylus event, and thus the beach formation is not the Ancylus limit but formed during a later phase of the Ancylus Lake. A new dating, on *macrofossil*, is of course desirable.

Along with the lake systems, on the edge of the northern forests, there are also places with well-formed and raised beach slopes and wave-cut terraces at levels between 75 and 80m asl. Beach formations within this altitude range can thus be assumed to belong to the Ancylus Lake in western Östergötland. In the southeastern parts of Östergötland the Ancylus Lake likewise forms distinct shorelines around 70m asl. The next major phase in the history of the Baltic starts *c.* 8200 BP (*c.* 7300 cal BC): the Litorina Sea. The initial phase is also called the Mastogloia Sea and was a brackish stage before the Litorina Sea proper with its higher salinity (e.g. Risberg 1991, 19 ff.; Donner 1995, 149). The continued displacement of the shoreline resulted in Roxen finally becoming a narrow, confined bay of the Litorina Sea, before the basin was finally isolated.

A recent study has shown that there are several Early Mesolithic coastal-settlement sites from the Ancylus period in the area around the town of Motala in western Östergötland (Molin 2005). These sites can probably be dated to between *c.* 8800–8000 BP (*c.* 8100–7000 cal BC). The background of this study is the large Stone Age

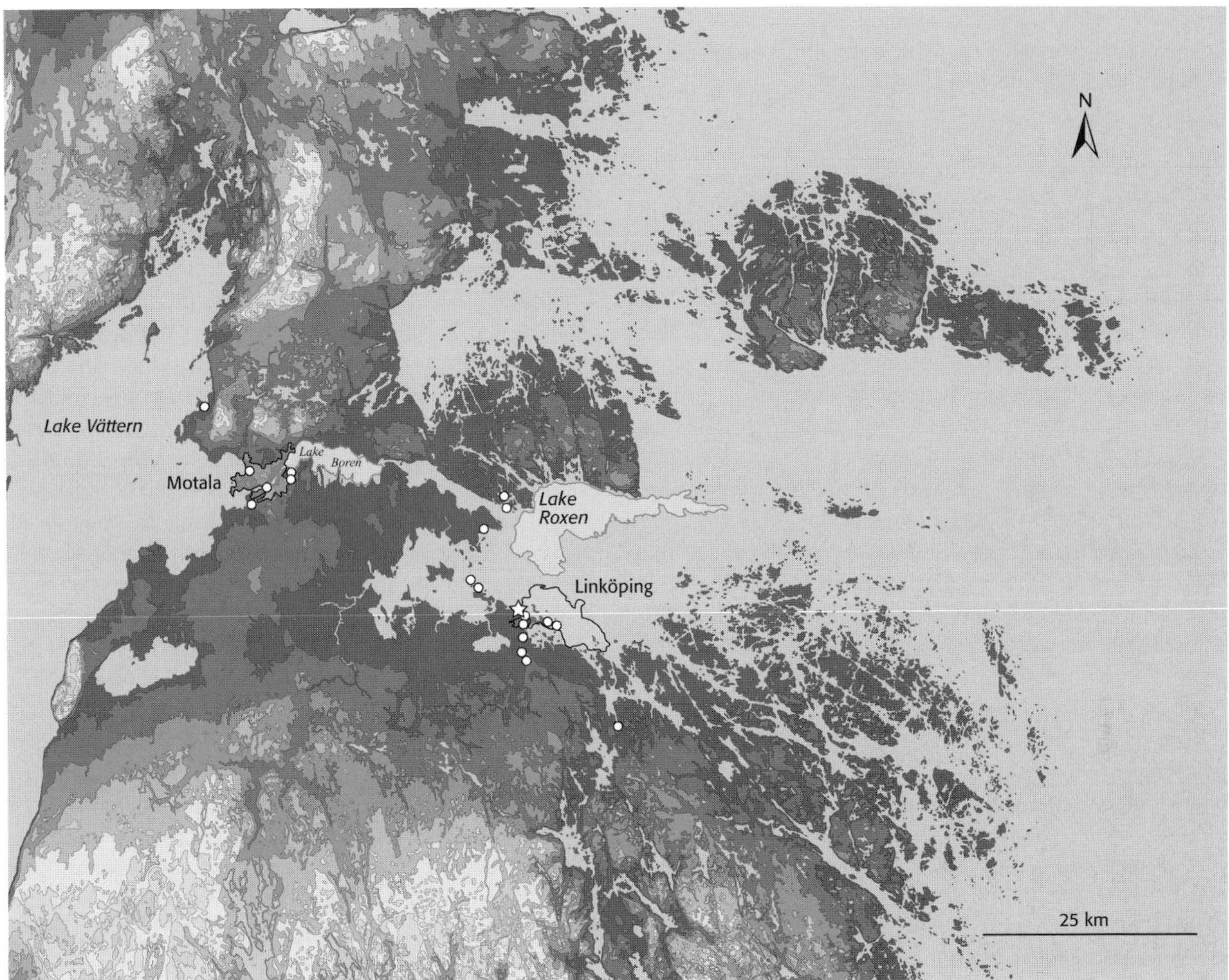

Figure 69.2. Palaeogeographical map of Östergötland showing the Ancylus Lake and the shoreline at 75m asl. Note that the shorelines in the northern and southern parts are not synchronous. The dots show Early Mesolithic sites in the western part of the province. A star marks the settlement site at Trädgårdstorp. (Map: Dag Hammar and Lars Östlin, National Heritage Board).

settlement site excavated beside the River Motala Ström, in central Motala, close to the shore of Vättern (Carlsson *et al.* 2003; Carlsson 2005). During the Early Mesolithic the water level in the northern part of ancient Vättern (Sw. *Fornvättern*) was several metres higher than it is today, and in places there are well-formed previous shorelines. Apart from the Motala site, at least three settlement sites have been observed and subjected to small-scale archaeological investigations. They all have preserved features, for example in the form of hearths, and the find material is mainly knapped quartz and flint. Lake Boren, about 3km downstream from the large site excavated in central Motala, was, at the time of occupation, the inner part of a narrow bay of the sea. Today there are clearly formed, wave-cut terraces and slopes that can be connected to the shoreline of the Ancylus Lake. A further three assemblages of early settlement site material have been found close by, beside the former Ancylus shore. These sites have been found following a specially focused survey. One of the sites shows traces of microblade manufacture from quartz, including limited finds of microblade cores and rejuvenation flakes. The finds date the remains to the Mesolithic, and the topographical location suggests that the site was on the shore of the Ancylus Lake during the Early Mesolithic. The other settlements were in a comparable position, above an erosion bluff along the former seashore (Molin 2005, 153).

This same pattern, with a number of coastal settlements along the shore of the Ancylus Lake, can be seen in the Linköping area. Along the ancient beaches are a number of Early Mesolithic sites, among them the excavated settlement at Trädgårdtorp, at around 75m asl; the 'establishment' of these sites is determined at *c.* 8400 BP (*c.* 7500 cal BC). At higher levels there are yet more Mesolithic sites, dated in their early phases as far back as *c.* 9000 BP (*c.* 8200 cal BC). A number of other places containing Mesolithic materials are known in the interval 70–80m asl, corresponding to the shoreline of the Ancylus Lake in the area. Most of these sites have been found randomly, as the result of public projects in infrastructure and house building. Only the Trädgårdstorp site has been found and excavated within a deliberate research programme aimed at investigating problems concerning Mesolithic matters in the region. So far no continuous special surveys of remains from Ancylus times have been conducted around Linköping, a factor, however, that has been brought to the fore in connection with the investigations at Trädgårdstorp.

The settlement at Trädgårstorp

The investigation at Trädgårdstorp was initiated as an ordinary, contracted archaeological project, but it gradually took the form of a research excavation. The community of Linköping planned the building of both a recycling unit and a shooting range just west of the town, and an area of *c.* 110,000m^2 was earmarked for the project. A preliminary archaeological survey established no visible ancient remains in the area, but the geological values were obvious as the diagnostic shoreline of the Ancylus Lake stretched over 500m along the entire area of investigation. Concentrations of Mesolithic remains along this shoreline were already known from adjacent areas (Molin and Molin 2004). A test-excavation during 2003 gave promising results and we found Mesolithic remains along the entire ancient shoreline. The remains were well preserved in the form of cultural layers, hearths, pits and the usual lithic material of knapped quartz and flint (Molin 2003).

The settlement zone thus stretches along and above the marked erosion bluff at *c.* 75m asl, identified by Fromm and Munthe as the Ancylus limit, on an elongated sand plateau varying between 10 and 30m in width. Behind the plateau the ground rises as a slope with a high frequency of large boulders. Below the bluff is an extensive marsh, called Kärna mosse, to which parts of the settlement area are connected. The basin in which the marsh is situated was isolated from the Ancylus Lake, but it is unclear how long a possible lake phase lasted. This is interesting because a possible lake could be one of a few circumstances that made the plateau inviting for settlement when it was no longer situated on the seashore. The marsh is therefore central to any future research, and archaeobotanical analyses, like pollen and macrofossil analysis, have been initiated to shed light upon its development.

Most of the fieldwork was conducted during 2004 and involved two areas, in sum about 2000m^2. These areas were fully excavated after the turf had first been carefully removed, providing excellent conditions for interpretations of the settlement's spatial structure. Within the areas different types of remains were investigated, the most conspicuous being the remains of two houses and a number of larger cooking pits. ^{14}C-dating shows the total time span for occupation at between 7580–6030 cal BC (*c.* 8400–7000 BP), that is from the end of the Ancylus Lake phase and into the older phase of the Litorina Sea. Therefore the settlement area was visited by Mesolithic people for a period of at least 1500 years, a not unusual fact for excavated Mesolithic sites in the province of Östergötland (Molin 2000, 37).

The archaeological interpretations of examined structures and find material, together with the ^{14}C dates, show that one of the two houses (House II), as well as a number of contemporary cooking pits, belong to the oldest phase of occupation on the site, *c.* 8400–8100 BP (7580–7350 cal BC). According to Fromm's (1976) shore-displacement curve, at least for the interval 8300–8200 ^{14}C-years BP, the shoreline would have been situated at *c.* 70m asl, in which case the house was situated only 35 to 40m from the seashore. At this time the site was on a small promontory extending into the sea. Off land there was a 500m-wide channel and, farther off still, an archipelago with a few larger and smaller islands.

House II was of a two-aisled type, with two interior roof-supporting posts and a number of wall posts, with overall dimensions of 6.7 by 4.5m (Figure 69.3). There was a sooty floor layer in which the bulk of the find material was recovered. The house also contained two deep hearth-pits. The find material was dominated by knapped quartz and flint, but some red porphyry and quartzite were also found. The spatial distribution of the lithic material inside the house exhibited a clear pattern, with diagnostic areas of activity and a spatial organization. Quartz was worked in the northern part of the house, where there were clear traces of a knapping-floor. The flint, on the other hand, was predominantly knapped in the southern part of the house. The central part of the house was distinguished by a number of flint and quartzite microblades, as well as flint and quartz flakes with traces of use-wear. The central part also contained scrapers formed of all three lithic materials. It is obvious that ready-made tools were used in the centre of the house, and, consequently, tasks associated with these. Around the hearth-pits there were hazelnut shells

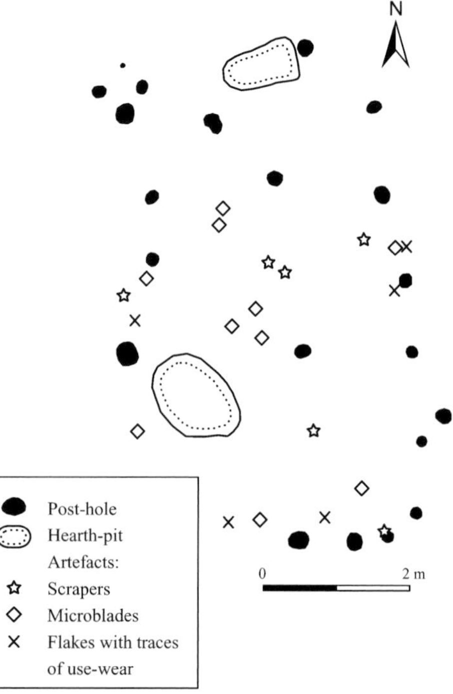

Figure 69.3. Plan of House II at Trädgårdstorp showing post-holes and hearth pits. The central part of the house contains several finds of scrapers, microblades, and flakes with signs of use-wear. (Graphic: Lars Östlin, National Heritage Board).

and fragmented, burnt bones. Part of the bone material has been identified as seal (Phocidae), but there is also game such as elk (*Alces alces*), Red deer (*Cervus elaphus*) and roe deer (*Capreolus capreolus*). Analysis of the soil chemistry shows that the houses were in all probability regularly cleaned of waste. Both phosphate analyses (P0) and analyses of magnetic susceptibility (MS) show values indicating accumulations of waste along the outside of the walls.

As a result of the ongoing shore displacement, the sea withdrew approximately 1.5km over the subsequent 1000 years. ^{14}C-dating indicates that the other investigated house (House I) belongs to the time period 7050–6340 cal BC (*c.* 7900–7300 BP), with the later half of this interval the most probable. Interestingly, this house is almost a blueprint of the first. The same find pattern and obvious spatial organization have both been observed. The environment, however, had changed since the occupation of the older house. The shoreline had been displaced from 70 to 50m asl, and *c.* 1500m horizontally. Once at the seashore, the settlement was now situated at the edge of a large wetland area. In the end, the site still remained within the coastal zone, not directly on the seashore but in a related, interior position.

Much speaks in favour of the interpretation of the site as a winter dwelling: the traces of *considerable use of fire* in the form of cooking pits, hearths, and the large quantity of fire-cracked stone; the find pattern – with *most artefacts situated inside the houses*; the soil chemical analyses; and the obviously *robust houses*. The houses are the first of their kind in eastern central Sweden; previously investigated remains of Mesolithic dwellings have revealed less robust constructions in the shape of huts or tents. An exception is a Mesolithic longhouse from the above-mentioned site at Motala (Carlsson 2005). It has been proposed that during the Middle Mesolithic there was a change towards a more sedentary settlement pattern, in the figurative sense that the people moved around within more restricted areas than before. The settlement structure would have become *semi-sedentary*, i.e. each group of people used smaller geographic areas than before: a structure with main dwelling areas ('base camps') confined to landscapes around a fjord, sound or bay, delta, archipelago, or an interior river system. This may be seen in contrast to a typical mobile pattern, in which groups cover much larger areas, perhaps hundreds of kilometres annually (cf. Fuglestvedt 1999, 28). This also implies that many dwellings were built to be used repeatedly over several seasons, which is especially possible for sites occupied during the winter season (Hernek 2005, 83, 234 ff.).

The settlement at Trädgårdstorp fits well into this proposed development and indicates that the population of eastern central Sweden during the Middle Mesolithic did not cover large areas annually. The houses from Trädgårdstorp show an extraordinarily clear connection, both chronologically and spatially, between features such as hearths, post-holes, and layers, as well as with the find material and results of conducted scientific analyses. The basis for reliable dating of the remains is thus very favourable. Forthcoming presentations and interpretations of the material could be important for future calculations of the settlement structure during the Mesolithic in the region.

Acknowledgements

I am most grateful to Mattias Pettersson for the English translation of this text.

References

Björck, S. 1995. Late Weichselian to Early Holocene Development of the Baltic Sea – with Implications for Coastal Settlements in the Southern Baltic Region, in A. Fischer (ed.), *Man and Sea in the Mesolithic: coastal Settlement above and below Present Sea Level*, 23–34. Oxbow Monographs 53. Oxford, Oxbow Books.

Carlsson, T. 2005. Home, sweet home. The spatial story of Mesolithic settlement organization in Östergötland, in G. Gruber (ed.), *Identities in Transition. Mesolithic Strategies in the Swedish Province of Östergötland*, 36–53. Arkeologiska undersökningar, Skrifter 64. Linköping, Riksantikvarieämbetet.

Carlsson, T., Gruber, G. and Molin, F. 2005. The Mesolithic in Östergötland. An introduction, in G. Gruber (ed.), *Identities in Transition. Mesolithic Strategies in the Swedish Province of Östergötland*, 8–23. Arkeologiska undersökningar, Skrifter 64. Linköping, Riksantikvarieämbetet.

Carlsson, T., Gruber, G., Molin, F. and Wikell, R. 2003. Between Quartz and Flint: Material Culture and Social Interaction, in L. Larsson, H. Kindgren, K. Knutsson, D. Loeffler and A. Åkerlund (eds.), *Mesolithic on the Move: Papers presented at the Sixth International Conference on the Mesolithic in Europe, Stockholm 2000*, 302–9. Oxford, Oxbow Books.

Donner, J. 1995. *The Quaternary History of Scandinavia*. Cambridge, Cambridge University Press.

Fromm, E. 1976. *Beskrivning till jordartskartan Linköping NO. Jordartsgeologiska kartblad skala 1:50,000*. SGU-Ae: 19. Uppsala, Sveriges geologiska undersökning (SGU).

Fuglestvedt, I. 1999. Inter-Regional Contact in the Late Mesolithic: The Productive Gift Extended, in J. Boaz (ed.), *The Mesolithic of Central Scandinavia*. Universitetets Oldsaksamlings Skrifter, ny rekke 22. Oslo, Universitetets Oldsaksamling.

Hernek, R. 2005. *Nytt ljus på Sandarnakulturen*. Gotarc Series B. Göteborg Archaeological Thesis 38. Coast to coast-books 14. Göteborg, Göteborgs Universitet, Institutionen för arkeologi.

Knarrström, B. 2000. Tidigmesolitisk bosättning i sydvästra Småland: En komparativ studie över stenteknologi och regionala bosättningsmönster med utgångspunkt i en boplats vid Hamneda, in P. Lagerås (ed.), *Arkeologi och paleoekologi i sydvästra Småland – Tio artiklar från Hamnedaprojektet*, 15–33. Arkeologiska Undersökningar, Skrifter 34. Lund, Riksantikvarieämbetet.

Larsson, M. and Molin, F. 2000. A New World: Cultural Links and Spatial Disposition – The Early Mesolithic Landscape in Östergötland on the Basis of the Storlyckan Investigations. *Lund Archaeological Review* 6, 7–22.

Molin, F. 2000. Mesolitikum i västra Östergötland – forskningsläge och aktuella problemområden, in *Vetenskaplig verksamhetsplan för UV Öst, arkeologiskt program 2000–2002*, 33–41. Avdelningen för arkeologiska undersökningar. Rapport UV Öst 2000:21. Linköping, Riksantikvarieämbetet.

Molin, F. 2003. *Tidigmesolitiska lämningar vid Trädgårdstorp. Arkeologisk utredning inför planerad återvinningscentral samt delar av ett nytt skyttecentrum*. Avdelningen för arkeologiska undersökningar. Rapport UV Öst 2003:26. Linköping, Riksantikvarieämbetet.

Molin, F. 2005. Between Ancient Vättern and the Ancylus Lake. Early Mesolithic settlement in the Motala district in western Östergötland, in G. Gruber (ed.), *Identities in Transition. Mesolithic Strategies in the Swedish Province of Östergötland*, 138–53. Arkeologiska undersökningar, Skrifter 64. Linköping, Riksantikvarieämbetet.

Molin, F. and Molin, A. 2004. *Linköpings universitet – boplatser och gravfält. Arkeologisk utredning av tre områden inom norra delen av universitetsområdet, Linköpings universitet*. Avdelningen för arkeologiska undersökningar. Rapport UV Öst 2004:11. Linköping, Riksantikvarieämbetet.

Molin, F., Rolöf, M. and Wikell, R. (in press). Mesolithic quartz quarrying in Eastern Middle Sweden. The example of Stjärneberg, in F. Sternke, L. Eigeland and L.-J. Costa (eds.), *Non-flint Raw Material Use in Prehistory: Old Prejudices and New Directions*. Proceedings of the XVth UISPP World Congress, Lisbon 2006.

Munthe, H. 1922. *Kvartärsystemet (Jordlagren m.m.). Beskrivning till kartbladet Mjölby*. SGU-Aa: 150. Uppsala, Sveriges geologiska undersökning (SGU).

Pettersson, M. and Wikell, R. 2004. The outermost shore: site-location in Mesolithic seascapes of Eastern Central Sweden. With a case-study in a burnt-off forest area in Tyresta National Park, in H. Knutsson (ed.), *Coast to Coast – Arrival. Results and Reflections*, 435–67. Coast to Coast-book 10. Uppsala, Department of Archaeology and Ancient History, Uppsala University.

Risberg, J. 1991. *Palaeoenvironment and Sea Level Changes during the Early Holocene on the Södertörn Peninsula, Södermanland, Eastern Sweden*. Kvartärgeologiska institutionen vid Stockholms universitet. Report 20. Stockholm, University of Stockholm.

Risberg, J. 2003. Landscape History of the Södertörn Peninsula, Eastern Sweden, in L. Larsson, H. Kindgren, K. Knutsson, D. Loeffler and A. Åkerlund (eds.), *Mesolithic on the Move: Papers presented at the Sixth International Conference on the Mesolithic in Europe, Stockholm 2000*, xlv–xlviii. Oxford, Oxbow Books.

Wikell, R. 2005. Many Mesolithic sites along the shores. Some results from surveys in Kolmården and Vikbolandet, Östergötland in eastern central Sweden, in G. Gruber (ed.), *Identities in Transition. Mesolithic Strategies in the Swedish Province of Östergötland*, 154–67. Arkeologiska undersökningar, Skrifter 64. Linköping, Riksantikvarieämbetet.

Åkerlund, A. 1996. *Human Responses to Shore Displacement: Living by the Sea in Eastern Middle Sweden during the Stone Age*. Arkeologiska Undersökningar, Skrifter 16. Stockholm, Riksantikvarieämbetet.

Åkerlund, A., Risberg, J., Miller, U. and Gustafsson, P. 1995. On the applicability of the 14C method to interdisciplinary studies on shore displacement and settlement location, in T. Hackens, L.-K. Königsson, and G. Possnert (eds.), *14C Methods and Applications. A Symposium Dedicated to Ingrid Olsson on the Occasion of a Birthday*, 53–84. PACT 49. Rixensart, PACT.

70. Dwellings and graves from the Late Mesolithic site of Nivå 10, eastern Denmark

Ole Lass Jensen

Excavations at a Late Mesolithic settlement on a former inlet at Nivå, north-eastern Zealand, have uncovered several graves and well-preserved sunken dwellings. So far, three of the dwellings and five of the graves have been excavated. The dwellings, dated to around 5500 and 4850 cal BC respectively, show a rather uniform spatial pattern in relation to the distribution of flints and animal bones. Furthermore, all dwellings have produced finds that may reflect ritual behaviour, i.e. deposits of antlers and – in a single case – a human bone. The latter was possibly removed from a grave found close to a dwelling. This article focuses on the dwelling and the related grave. The stratigraphic sequence in the dwelling pit and the spatial distribution of the finds are briefly presented. It is suggested that the depositions in the pit represent two or three seasonally separated 'floor levels'. The relationship between the dwelling and the grave is discussed against the background of ^{14}C dates and $\delta^{13}C$ values. Finally, it is proposed that the dwellings equate to small social units, which must either represent several contemporary households living together at one site, or reflect the presence of many small, contemporary settlement units.

Keywords: Denmark, Late Mesolithic, dwellings, refitting, graves, rituals, diet, social units.

Introduction

Recent excavations at the coastal settlement of Nivå 10 in eastern Denmark have uncovered several dwellings. As evident remains of Late Mesolithic dwellings are still rare, these finds provide new insights, not only into the dwellings themselves, but also into the spatial organization of settlements. The excavations also yielded graves, which in most cases were located close to a dwelling. This article will give an outline account of the settlement and present one of the dwellings and one of the graves, which may be linked.

The settlement

The site of Nivå 10 is one of 24 Late Mesolithic sites known from the Stone Age inlet at Nivå, on the eastern coast of northern Zealand (Figure 70.1) (Jensen 2001; Jensen 2003). In the Late Mesolithic the site was situated on a small island; today it lies in a cultivated field.

The site comprises two main periods of occupation. According to the ^{14}C dates, the first occupation phase was between *c.* 5700 and 5400 cal BC, corresponding to the Late Kongemose culture. Hereafter, the transgression of the Littorina Sea caused the island to be flooded and rendered it uninhabitable for several hundred years. The second occupation did not take place until around 4850 cal BC, i.e. the later part of the Early Ertebølle culture.

Due to the effects of ploughing it is difficult to determine the original extent of the settlement, but the primary concentration of finds and structures may not have exceeded 1500m². So far, a little more than 1000m² has been excavated during the course of eight seasons (Figure 70.2).

Primary occupation layers, consisting of up to 30cm-

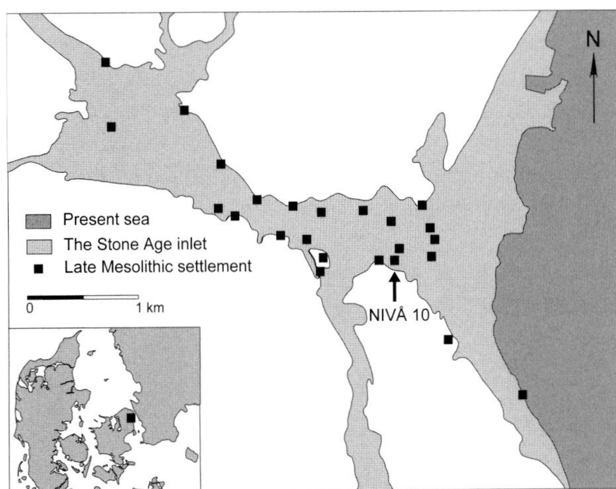

Figure 70.1. Map showing the maximum extent of the Stone Age inlet at Nivå, c. 4000 cal BC, reconstructed on the basis of the 5m contour line and the known Late Mesolithic sites. The insert locates Nivå within a map of contemporary Denmark.

Figure 70.2. Nivå 10. Site plan, excavations 1995–2005.

thick sandy layers mixed with stones, charcoal, animal bones and flint artefacts, are in general only preserved on the southern slope of the former island. These layers were deposited directly on glacial sand or clay and are covered either by marine sand or, more usually, the plough soil. To date the excavation has concentrated in this location and yielded several activity areas, refuse layers, etc. Under the occupation layers, quite a number of informative structures were located, including more than 50 pits of varying size and function, two sunken dwellings and two graves. Recently, the excavation was extended to the top of the island, where the topsoil was removed by machine, resulting in additional pits, dwellings and graves being uncovered. Some of these structures were excavated at the end of 2005, while the remainder are planned for excavation in 2006.

The dwellings

Five dwellings have been recorded at the settlement, of which three have been fully excavated. Two of the structures have so far only been registered at the surface, but there is no doubt that they also represent dwellings. All were small, sunken dwellings with an almost circular or slightly oval outline and measuring from 2.2m to 3.2m in diameter. The depth of the dwelling pits varied from 17cm to 40cm, depending on the preservation conditions, as all but one (the deepest) had been affected by ploughing. The slopes of all three excavated pits were uniform and steep, and the bases were approximately flat. The dwelling pits were filled with dark sand, coloured by finely comminuted charcoal and other organic matter, and containing varying amounts of flint waste and artefacts, animal bones, stones, etc. In all of the pits it was possible to distinguish one or more horizons with an increased number of finds and organic remains, and with clear traces of a hearth. These horizons are interpreted as activity or 'floor' levels. Along the edges, and/or inside the pits, there were distinct stake holes, probably traces of the wall and/or roof constructions.

Dwelling 1 was the first to be found at the site and has been published previously (Jensen 2001; Jensen 2003). The 3.2m-long and 2.3m-wide, oval dwelling-pit contained a single floor-layer with a distinct layout. The dwelling is dated to the Early Ertebølle culture, *c.* 4850 cal BC.

Dwelling 2 was a well-preserved dwelling with a rather complex stratigraphy, as the dwelling was occupied several times. The dwelling is dated to the Late Kongemose culture, around 5600 cal BC, and will be further discussed below.

Dwelling 3 was excavated at the end of 2005, and will

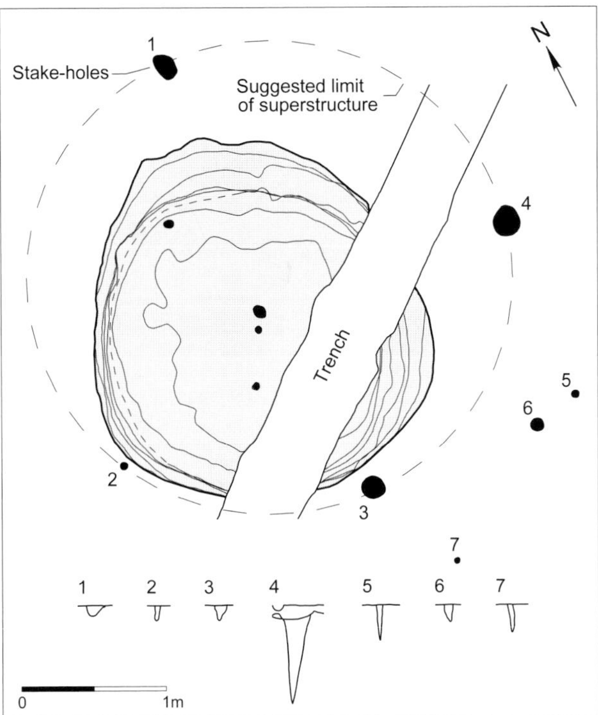

Figure 70.3. Dwelling 2. Plan of the pit and sections of the stake holes. The pit is shown with 5cm contour lines.

be subjected to further analysis in the future. The circular dwelling-pit had a diameter of 2.6m and was 27cm deep. In the upper half of the fill, a distinct floor layer with a central hearth could be distinguished. The lower half of the pit was filled with a lighter grey, sandy layer, perceived as a drainage or levelling layer. A similar basal layer was registered in dwelling 1. ^{14}C dates have not yet been obtained for the dwelling, but typologically it can be dated to the Late Kongemose culture.

Dwelling 2

In 2001 a parallel to the first dwelling found at the site (dwelling 1) was excavated. Analyses of the dwelling and the surrounding occupation layers and structures are still in progress, therefore the following is a presentation of the initial work.

The dwelling was situated on the south-western slope of the former island, probably very close to the contemporary shoreline; this lay within a distance of 5m. The structure was covered by an 'ordinary' habitation layer, and over this a *c.* 20cm-thick transgression layer of sand had been deposited. This means that the dwelling had never been affected by ploughing, and that the preservation of the find distribution, animal bones, etc. was rather good.

The pit

The dwelling-pit had an almost circular outline with a diameter of *c.* 2.4m (Figure 70.3). The pit had been dug 40cm into the subsoil, which in the western part consisted of heavy clay, and in the eastern part of gravel. The slopes of the pit were uniform and steep and the base was approximately flat. The south-eastern part of the pit had been cut by a trench, causing severe damage to the structure.

The pit was surrounded by stake-holes with diameters ranging from 4–15cm, and depths from 15–50cm. Some of the stakes had been placed a distance away from the edge of the pit, so the pit itself seemed to cover only a part of the dwelling. If the wall had had a circular outline, as suggested in Figure 70.3, the dwelling covered an area of *c.* 8m^2. At the same time, this produced an earthen platform along the edge, which was broad enough to function as, for example, sleeping quarters. In the centre of the pit there were also traces of two stakes, and stratigraphic observations revealed that one had replaced the other.

The infill and the find distribution

The infill of the pit formed a rather complex sequence (Figure 70.4). In general, it consisted of dark grey sand with stones of varying size – many of them fire-cracked – charcoal, flint artefacts and animal bones, especially fish bones in large numbers. But the finds were very unevenly distributed, both vertically and horizontally. Vertically, the finds were concentrated in three more or less distinct horizons of up to 10cm thick. In each of the find horizons the distribution of fire-cracked stones and fire-shattered flint pointed to the presence of a central hearth. This was most obvious for the two lower horizons, where concentrations of charcoal also occurred in the same areas. In general, the upper horizon seemed more disturbed, probably because of activities connected with the overlying settlement layer. Around the hearths were concentrations of animal bones and flint artefacts, indicating different activity areas. This leads to the conclusion that each find horizon corresponds to a floor level within a dwelling. The latter seems, at least, to be the case for the lower and middle horizons, whereas the interpretation of the upper horizon may be more questionable.

The floor levels

The lowermost floor level rested directly on the base of the pit and, as mentioned earlier, consisted of an up to 10cm-thick, dark sandy layer which was rather rich in finds (Figures 70.4 and 70.5). The distribution of charcoal, fire-cracked stones and fire-shattered flint documents the presence of a hearth at the centre of the floor. The majority of the animal bones, mainly comprising roe deer (*Capreolus capreolus*) and fish – flatfish (Pleuronectidae) and cod (*Gadus morhua*) – were found north-east of the hearth, whereas the flint artefacts had clearly a more central or southern distribution, lying in close proximity to the hearth. Judging from the distribution of small splinters, i.e. pieces of flint no larger than 10mm, flint knapping seems primarily to have taken place just west of the hearth. To give an impression of the amount of flint material recovered from the floor layer, the waste totals *c.* 1400 pieces, of which *c.* 500 are splinters; there

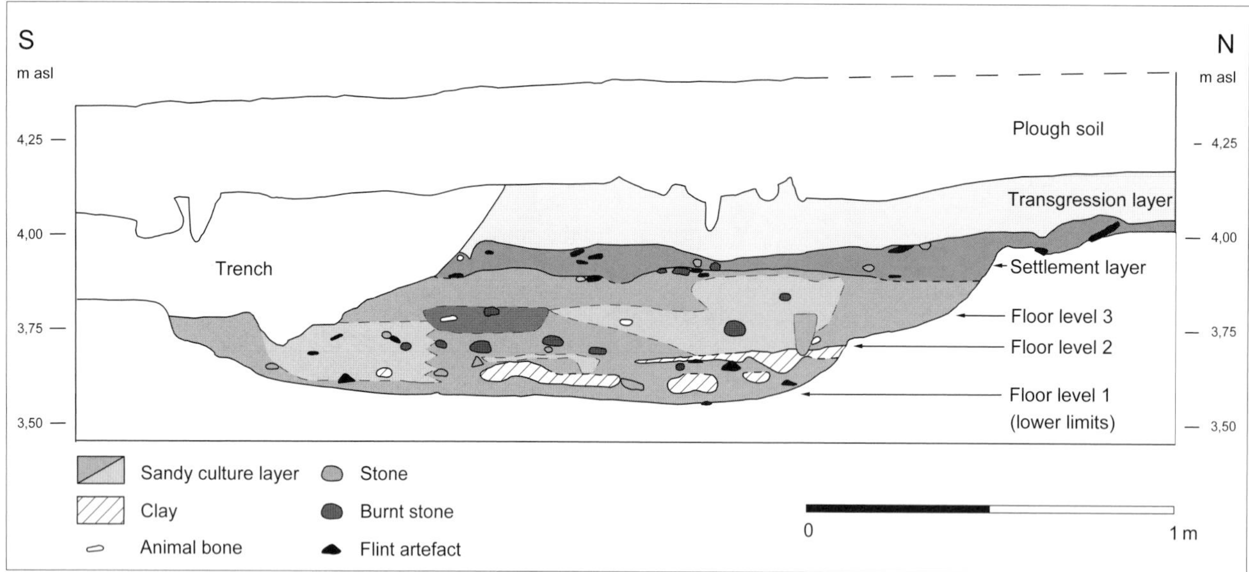

Figure 70.4. Dwelling 2. Section of the dwelling pit.

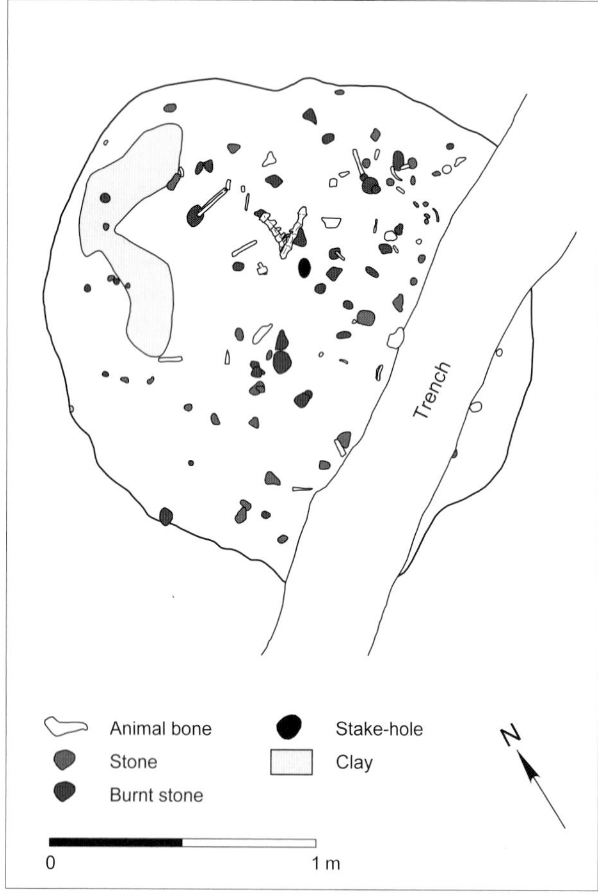

Figure 70.5. Dwelling 2. Plan of the lower floor level.

are 38 unretouched blades and 16 secondarily worked tools (six transverse arrowheads, two burins, one core axe, and seven truncated or backed pieces). Compared to the layers elsewhere at the settlement this represents a moderate quantity of flint artefacts and waste.

A considerable area of the lower floor layer was covered by an up to 10cm-thick layer of sterile clay (Figures 70.4 and 70.6). The clay may have been deliberately deposited, i.e. as a foundation for the next floor, but it is more likely that it was washed out from the edge of the pit, as it only appeared where the surrounding subsoil comprised clay and not where it consisted of gravel. If the deposition of the clay was caused by natural erosion and in-washing, then the dwelling must have been abandoned for some time before the overlying 'floor layer' was deposited.

The next floor level followed upon the clay layer and appeared as a rather thin horizon containing numerous finds (Figure 70.7). The clay marked locally a sharp distinction between this layer and the lower floor level. This second floor level showed a variety of local colouration, of which much could be related to the hearth. According to the distribution of large pieces of charcoal, fire-cracked stones and fire-shattered flint, the hearth must have been located somewhat centrally on the floor. Here there was also a shallow pit with fire-cracked stones, abundant pieces of charcoal, and a large quantity of fish bones. This feature might have been a special cooking place for fish, indicating that the hearth was not a stable 'structure', but rather a 'fire area' used in a variety of ways. There is clear evidence of cleaning-out and redeposition of material from fires, as crescent-shaped depositions of ash and charcoal were recorded around the hearth.

The floor level showed some remarkable deposits of antlers and bones. To the north-east, there was an accumulation of ribs, possibly from roe deer. South of the ribs, and just east of the hearth, a partly polished red deer (*Cervus elaphus*) antler and two unshed roe deer antlers were recovered. In the previously excavated dwelling 1, a red deer antler and an unshed roe deer antler were found in the same location relative to the hearth (Jensen 2003, 234). In a contemporary sunken dwelling from the nearby settlement of Lollikhuse, two unshed antlers from roe deer were also found (Sørensen 1995). These unshed

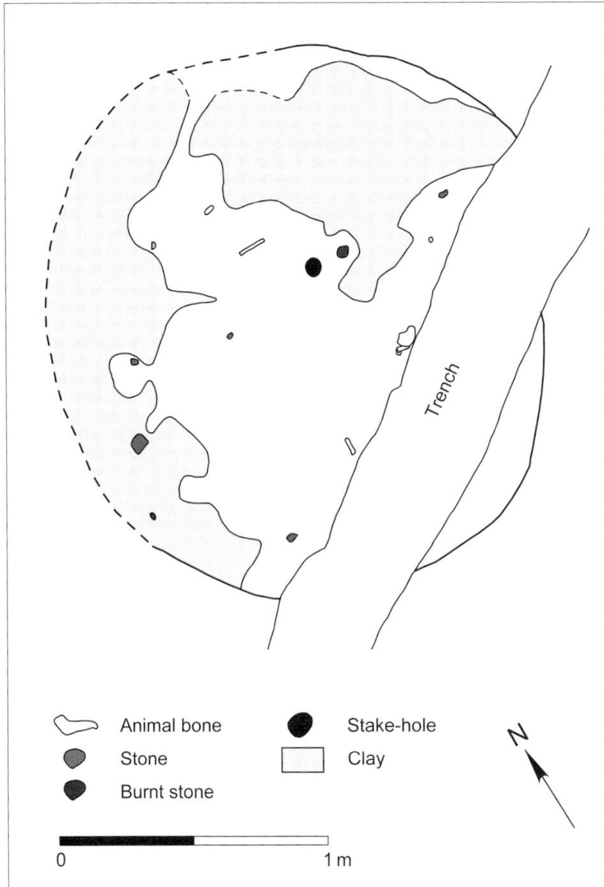

Figure 70.6. Dwelling 2. Plan of the layer of clay deposited in between the lower and the middle floor levels.

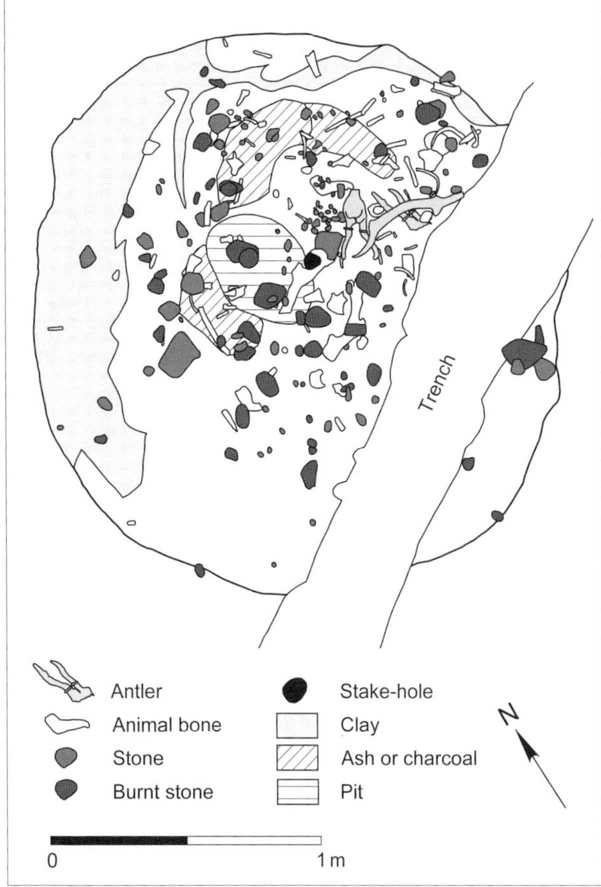

Figure 70.7. Dwelling 2. Plan of the middle floor level.

– and always un-worked – antlers could, of course, be 'ordinary' waste or they may have had a practical function; but they could equally be regarded as trophies or as ritual deposits. This latter possibility is underlined by a find from Lollikhuse, where one of the antlers was buried in a small pit. In the newly excavated dwelling 3 at Nivå, there were no such antlers, but another item of a possible ritual character was found close to the hearth, namely a partly worked, 23cm-long flint nodule, which most probably should be regarded as a symbolic phallus.

Immediately to the south-west of the antlers, two almost complete pelvic bones of a roe deer were found. A central stake had been hammered through one of the bones. The stake was probably associated with the uppermost floor level.

Apart from bones and flint waste, the finds from the middle floor level number 30 blades and blade fragments, one burin, two scrapers, three truncated pieces, two core axes, four transverse arrowheads and a single rhombic arrowhead, a bone awl, and a flint flaker made of red deer antler. The secondarily worked tools were concentrated around the hearth, whereas the distribution of the blades was more dispersed, apart from a minor concentration of blades to the northeast of the hearth, where the ribs were located. The flint waste totals *c.* 1500 pieces, of which *c.* 650 are splinters.

Over the middle floor level followed the uppermost find horizon in the dwelling pit itself (Figure 70.8). The separation between these two levels was not very distinct. However, it was noted that a thin layer with a lower find concentration was deposited in between them. The separation of the upper find horizon from the covering settlement layer was somewhat easier, as the latter had a darker colour. However, a high degree of mixing of finds at the boundaries of the layers is to be expected, resulting from both bioturbation and settlement activities. This may explain why the find distribution in the upper horizon was more diffuse. The horizon could also be infill related to later settlement activities, but the presence of a small pit in this horizon (Figures 70.4 and 70.8) points to deposition as an activity layer or a 'floor' rather than such an 'accidental' infill.

Seasonal variability?

My view, so far, is that the sequence in the pit reflects two, maybe three, seasonally separated occupations of the dwelling. This idea was tested against refitting analyses of the flint artefacts – a project carried out by Pia Mørck (2003), who has kindly permitted the main results to be referred to here. The hypothesis was: If the find horizons represent seasonally separated occupations, then no artefact

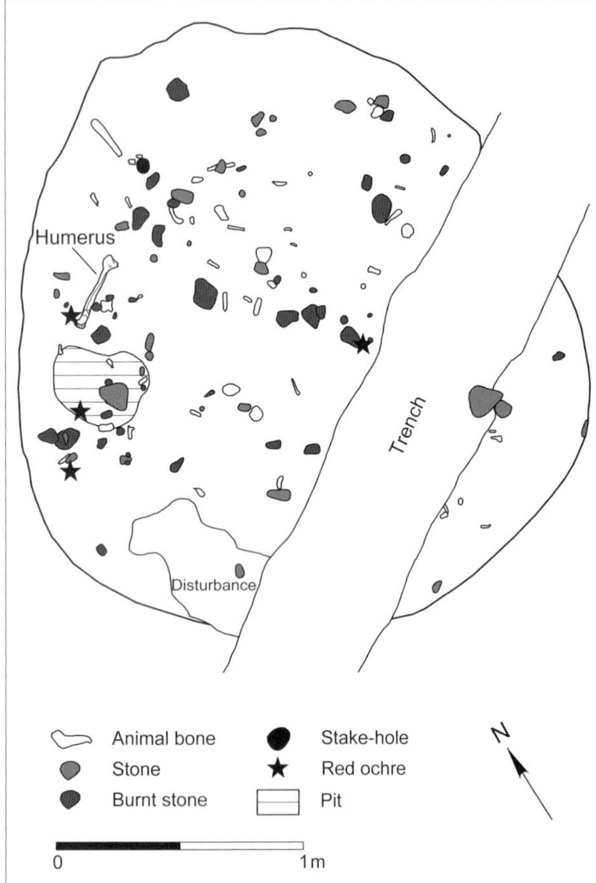

Figure 70.8. Dwelling 2. Plan of the upper find horizon with the human bone.

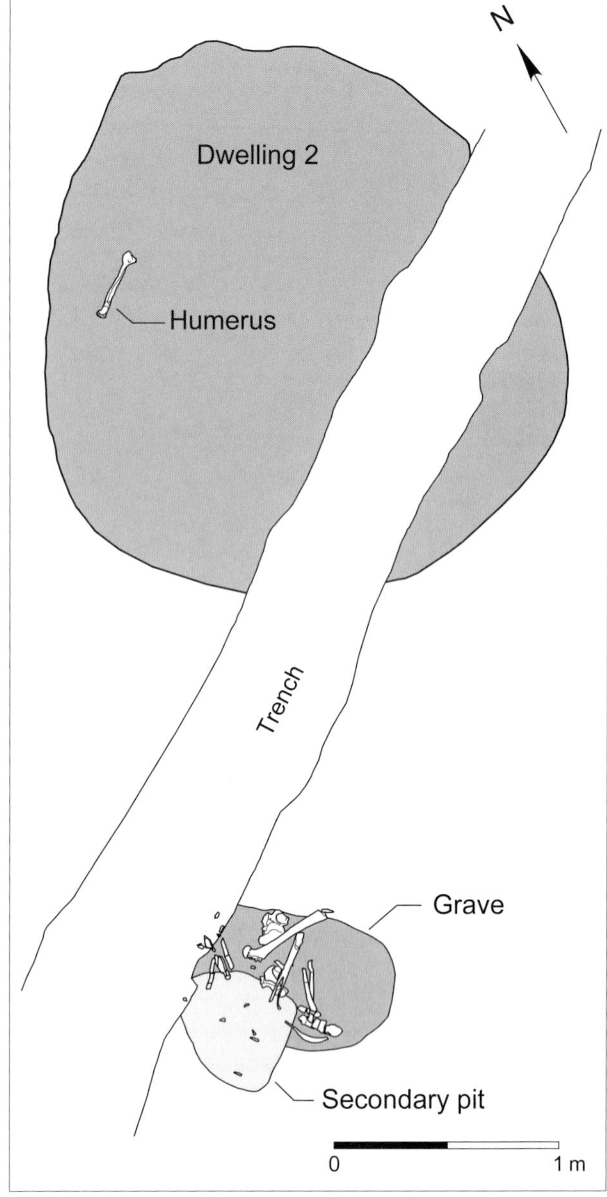

Figure 70.9. Plan of dwelling 2 and the nearby grave.

from one horizon should refit with an artefact from another horizon (or only very few, as the effects of bioturbation cannot be discounted). If the horizons, in contrast, represent a continuous deposition, then refits between the different horizons should be possible.

Only nine refits were possible out of a total assemblage of 1730 pieces (a refit rate of 1.1%). This may reflect a continuous cleaning out of waste, which was then redeposited outside the dwelling. As the settlement and refuse layers immediately outside the dwelling were virtually all removed by a later marine transgression, refitting of interior and exterior finds was only possible on a single occasion. All other refits were within one and the same horizon, apart from one (from the lower floor level to the upper floor level), which can be explained by bioturbation. Accordingly, the refitting analyses support the interpretation of the sequence as representing (seasonally) separated occupations.

Detailed zoological analyses of the bone material from the dwelling will be carried out in 2006. This work is also expected to elucidate whether the dwelling was used seasonally or all year round.

A human bone from the dwelling

A find of particular interest, arising from the base of the upper find horizon or presumed floor level of the dwelling, will be discussed in more detail. This is a human bone – a right upper arm (humerus), which, according to its size, is most probably that of a man. The bone was found close to the western edge of the dwelling pit and it had been deposited almost horizontally (Figure 70.8). Apart from minor fragmentation of the upper end, it is complete. In the area where the bone was found there were also a few small lumps of red ochre.

The bone may come from a grave situated only 1.5m to the south-west of the dwelling (Figure 70.9); this contained the bones of a man. A layer of cooking stones covered the grave and above this there was the same transgression layer that overlay the dwelling. Only the head end of the grave was preserved – a trench had disturbed the remainder. Only a part of the spine, a rib, and a pair of forearm bones were *in situ* in the grave pit. This is due to a secondary pit dug

Lab no.	Sample	^{14}C Age (BP)	Reservoir corrected ^{14}C Age (BP)	Calibrated age (2σ ranges)	δ^{13}C (‰) VPDB
AAR-7058	Human bone (femur)	6900±60	6680±60	5710–5490 BC	-16.23
AAR-10147	Human bone (humerus)	6868±46	6586±46	5620–5470 BC	-15.01

Figure 70.10. ^{14}C dates for samples of the humerus from dwelling 2 and the femur from the nearby grave. Calibrated ages in calendar years have been obtained from the calibration curves in Reimer et al. (Bronk Ramsey 2005) and terrestrial calibration curve IntCal04 (Bronk Ramsey 2001). (The world ocean marine model is not expected to represent the local Danish waters – Kattegat and the fjords – and calibrated ages are therefore obtained with the terrestrial calibration curve applied to the reservoir corrected ^{14}C age for samples from these areas.)

into the southern part of the grave. In this connection the pelvis, a thighbone and a tibia were removed and then replaced *upon* the grave. Many of the bones, which ought to be present in the preserved part of the grave, were missing, including the skull and both upper arms.

From an anthropological point of view, the upper arm found in the dwelling could belong to the skeleton in the grave. ^{14}C dates for samples from the arm bone found in the dwelling, and from the femur found in the grave, gave the results shown in Figure 70.10. As can be seen, the ^{14}C age of the two samples corresponds well, whereas the δ^{13}C values differ by 1.2‰. The difference in the δ^{13}C values leads, of course, to different reservoir corrections and thereby to different calibrated ages, although there is still an overlap between the calibrated dates. The δ^{13}C values could point to the fact that the two samples derive from two different individuals, the latter having a more terrestrial diet. However, differences within 1–2‰ for both δ^{13}C and δ^{15}N in bone samples from the same individual have been reported elsewhere, indicating a dietary transition towards either a more terrestrial or a more marine diet (e.g. Lidén *et al.* 2004, 28). Furthermore, the relatively poor preservation of the bones, especially the femur from the grave, resulted in a low recovery of both collagen and carbon and, consequently, possible uncertainty in the determination of the δ^{13}C values (Heinemeier, pers. comm.). Accordingly, the possibility cannot be excluded that the arm bone found in the dwelling originates from the man in the nearby grave. Regardless of whether this is the case, or if the arm bone came from another skeleton, it seems that we have here an example of a very direct connection between the world of the living and the world of the dead in the Late Mesolithic. This is a situation where a selected part of the dead, presumably some time after burial, was incorporated into the living society.

Dating of the dwelling

The reservoir-corrected ^{14}C age of the sample from the human bone in the dwelling has yet to be tested against dates for samples of purely terrestrial material from the same horizon. Dates will also be obtained for samples from the underlying levels. However, a calibrated age within the limits 5710–5470 cal BC (the extremes of the ranges for both dates mentioned above) corresponds to the archaeological dating of the dwelling to the Late Kongemose culture.

Other graves

Apart from two more, as yet unexcavated dwellings, the most recent excavations at the settlement have uncovered at least six, but more probably eight new graves. These numbered three cremations, three inhumations and two presumed, but still unexcavated, inhumations (Figure 70.2). A cremation containing the bones of a man of more than 30–35 years of age (Bennike 2005) was found underneath the culture layer at the southernmost part of the settlement. And 17m further to the north there was another cremation. The remainder of the graves were situated in a more restricted area on the top of the former island. Within an area of only 40m^2 there were four graves: a small cremation, heavily coloured by red ochre, and three inhumations. Of the latter, one has been excavated, while two were partly excavated and later cut out as blocks and brought back for further examination. Within the same area there are probably two further inhumations. Two of the excavated, or partly excavated inhumations, contained an adult individual, while the third grave is a double grave containing two adults. Detailed anthropological examination is still to be carried out, and so far there have been no determinations of sex and age. Just like the inhumation found outside dwelling 2, several of the newly found graves were located very close to a dwelling. As such, it may be possible to link one or more individuals to a specific dwelling.

Conclusions

The dwellings from Nivå 10 document a kind of 'type-house' that existed for at least 600 years. This may not have been the only type of dwelling in use, either within the inlet or in the region as a whole. For example, the sunken dwelling could have been restricted to a certain season (winter?) – but for further information on this we must await the detailed archaeozoological analysis.

Similar sunken dwellings from the same periods – Late Kongemose culture and Early Ertebølle culture – are known from the neighbouring site at Nivågård (Jensen 2001, 127) and from Lollikhuse (Sørensen 1995). Finds of presumed sunken dwellings from beneath Ertebølle shell middens have also been reported from western Denmark (Andersen 2000, 37; Andersen 2004, 394). Furthermore, sunken dwellings of more or less the same type have been found in southern Sweden (Larsson 1975; Larsson 1984, 32; Larsson 1985).

The area of the dwellings may vary but, like all the dwellings from Nivå, many of them were of modest size. At the same time, analyses of kitchen middens from western Denmark show that these sites comprise several very small units that may reflect individual households (Andersen 2001, 31; Andersen 2004, 405). It is difficult to imagine that just one such small unit in each of the regional inlets or fjords could maintain a viable population. Even if this were possible, then the amounts of waste and refuse layers apparent within each local area can hardly be seen as the result of the activities of just one small group, even though we are dealing with occupation extending over thousands of years. Quite simply, there must have been more people active within each local area. This means that the small units must either represent several contemporary households living together at one site, or reflect the presence of many small contemporary settlement units.

References

Andersen, S. H. 2000. Visborg. *Marinarkæologisk Nyhedsbrev fra Roskilde* 13, 36–7.

Andersen, S. H. 2001. Danske køkkenmøddinger anno 2000, in O. L. Jensen, S. A. Sørensen and K. M. Hansen (eds.), *Danmarks jægerstenalder – status og perspektiver*, 21–41. Hørsholm, Hørsholm Egns Museum.

Andersen, S. H. 2004. Danish Shell Middens Reviewed, in A. Saville (ed.), *Mesolithic Scotland and its neighbours: early Holocene prehistory of Scotland, its British and Irish context and some North European perspectives*, 393–411. Edinburgh, Society of Antiquaries of Scotland.

Bennike, P. 2005. *Antropologisk undersøgelse af brændte ben fra Nivå 10, HØM 106, A 144, AS 55/05*. Unpublished anthropological report, Panum Instituttet, København.

Bronk Ramsey, C. 2001. Development of the Radiocarbon Calibration Program OxCal. *Radiocarbon* 43 (2A), 355–63.

Bronk Ramsey, C. 2005. OxCal 3.10. WWW program and documentation available at http://www.rlaha.ox.ac.uk/oxcal/oxcal.htm (accessed 10/2007).

Jensen, O. L. 2001. Kongemose- og Ertebøllekultur ved den fossile Nivåfjord, in O. L. Jensen, S. A. Sørensen and K. M. Hansen (eds.), *Danmarks jægerstenalder – status og perspektiver*, 115–29. Hørsholm, Hørsholm Egns Museum.

Jensen, O. L. 2003. A Sunken Dwelling from the Ertebölle Site Nivå 10, Eastern Denmark, in L. Larsson, H. Kindgren, K. Knutsson, D. Loeffler and A. Åkerlund (eds.), *Mesolithic on the Move: Papers presented at the Sixth International Conference on the Mesolithic in Europe, Stockholm 2000*, 230–38. Oxford, Oxbow Books.

Larsson, L. 1975. A Contribution to the Knowledge of the Mesolithic Huts in Southern Scandinavia. *Meddelanden från Lunds universitets historiska museum*, 1973–1974, 5–28. Stockholm, Almqvist & Wiksell International.

Larsson, L. 1984. The Skateholm Project. A Late Mesolithic Settlement and Cemetery Complex at a Southern Swedish Bay. *Meddelanden från Lunds universitets historiska museum*, 1983–1984, New Series Vol. 5, 5–38. Stockholm, Almqvist & Wiksell International.

Larsson, L. 1985. Of House and Hearth. The Excavation, Interpretation and Reconstruction of a Late Mesolithic House, in M. Backe, C. Bergman, I. B. Hennix, L. Forsberg, L. Holm, L. Liedgren, A.-K. Lindqvist, I.-M. Mulk, M. Nejati, P. Perstrand and P. H. Ramqvist (eds.), *In Honorem Evert Baudou*, 197–209. Archaeology and Environment 4. Umeå, Department of Archaeology, University of Umeå.

Lidén, K., Eriksson, G., Nordqvist, B., Götherström, A. and Bendixen, E. 2004. 'The wet and the wild followed by the dry and the tame' – or did they occur at the same time? Diet in Mesolithic-Neolithic southern Sweden. *Antiquity* 78 (299), 23–33.

Mørck, P. 2003. *Hyttetomten fra Nivå 10 – resultater af flintsammensætningen fra gulvlagene*. Unpublished thesis,

Reimer P. J., Baillie, M. G. L., Bard, E., Bayliss, A., Beck, J. W., Bertrand, C., Blackwell, P. G., Buck, C. E., Burr, G., Cutler, K. B., Damon, P. E., Edwards, R. L., Fairbanks, R. G., Friedrich, M., Guilderson, T. P., Hughen, K. A., Kromer, B., McCormac, F. G., Manning, S., Bronk Ramsey, C., Reimer, R. C., Remmele, S., Southon, J. R., Stuiver, M., Talamo, S., Taylor, F. W., van der Plicht, J., and Weyhenmeyer, C. E. 2004. *Radiocarbon* 46, 1029–58.

Sørensen, S. A. 1995. Lollikhuse – a Dwelling Site under a Kitchen Midden. *Journal of Danish Archaeology* 11, 1992–1993, 19–29.

71. Dreams and Landscapes: Mesolithic archaeology under water

Ole Grøn

The paper discusses, on the basis of the investigation of an extremely well-preserved Mesolithic dwelling floor and a human burial in a dugout boat under the sea outside Ærøskøbing, Denmark, the potential of Mesolithic underwater archaeology. Not only can the preservation of the sites and entire drowned Mesolithic cultural landscapes represent an advantage, but promising results with high-resolution penetration seismics ('chirp') also indicate that submerged sites can be much easier to locate than land-based ones. The paper concludes that Mesolithic research in social organisation, exploitation strategies, settlement patterns, etc., should seriously be considered in well-preserved submerged cultural landscapes.

Keywords: Mesolithic, dwelling, boat grave, underwater archaeology, dwelling organisation, high-resolution seismics, 'chirp', preservation conditions.

Introduction

In the 1960s and 1970s Danish archaeologists who attempted to obtain detailed information about Mesolithic dwelling and settlement organization could only dream of perfectly preserved sites. The sad reality was that the famous peat bogs that earlier had delivered so many important and famous finds had dried out as a result of agricultural drainage, which was fatal to their preservation. Furthermore, they had in many cases been truncated by peat exploitation. There was no longer an obvious land-based study area that could at the same time: a) elucidate the details of the organization of the single settlements; and b) give a representative picture of the settlement pattern they represented within a confined environmental unit.

The systematic excavations of underwater Mesolithic sites, starting with the shell-midden at Møllegabet I in 1976, and at Tybrind Vig a couple of years later (Skaarup and Grøn 2004; Grøn and Skaarup 2004), demonstrated that the submerged Mesolithic sites could provide preservation conditions for organic materials similar to, or better than the land-based peat bogs. Boats, bows, stakes, axe shafts, textiles, bones, plant macrofossils, etc., were found in a surprising state of preservation.

The question was: how much more was it possible to get out of the submerged sites? Møllegabet I and Tybrind Vig provided good information about the Late Mesolithic lifestyle: what people ate, how they located their settlements to better exploit the natural resources, what their tools and ornaments looked like, and also added some new facets to our knowledge. But was that sufficient to justify the excavation expenses involved? Or was the potential under water so large that it justified significant investments, as it could add dimensions to our understanding of the Stone Age that were not possible to acquire on the basis of land-based sites alone?

A complicating factor for the ongoing discussion (and for attempts to develop landscape archaeology under water) was that of the pre-conceived ideas in the archaeological and geological environments about the extent of preservation. A widespread assumption was that the wave action of the rapid sea level rise of up to 30–40m in the southern Baltic during the Atlantic transgression (Christensen 1995) would have destroyed all sites under water. In 1996 the Danish Research Council rejected an application for an inter-disciplinary archaeological-geological project in the submerged Strynø basin with the remark: 'Since the Danish geologist Krogh in the thirties investigated a submerged peat bog it has been known what can be found in such basins.' It is interesting how such ill-founded axioms can develop and gain a life of their own as circular arguments against attempts to prove them wrong.

This paper will focus on the excavation of a Late Mesolithic (early Ertebølle) dwelling with a boat-grave beside it under water, and further discuss the submerged cultural landscapes that surround it and the research potential of submerged landscapes in general.

The Møllegabet site

Between 1990 and 1993, Langelands Museum excavated

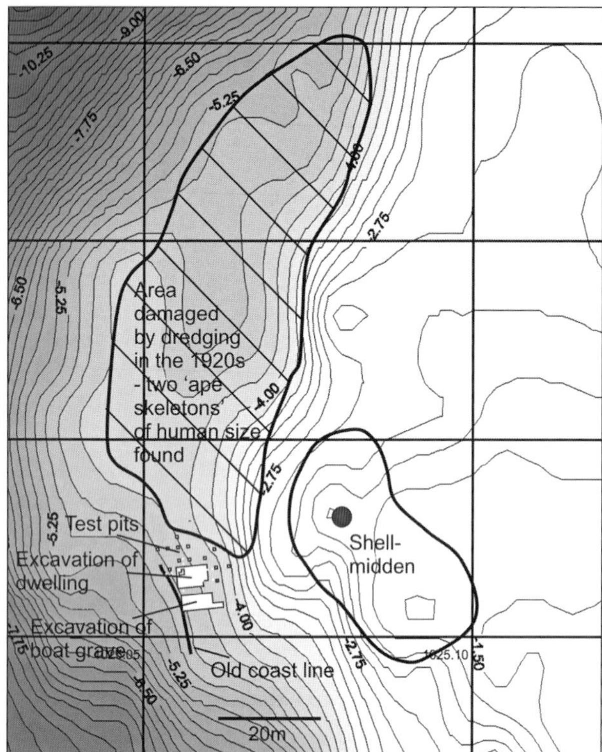

Figure 71.1. The Møllegabet site with detailed 25cm depth-contours, based on seismic recordings carried out by Grøn in 1996. Systematic excavation was started on the shell-midden in 1976 by Langelands Museum. The boat grave was excavated 1990/1991 and the dwelling 1992/1993. From the content of the test pits it is obvious that the dredging in the 1920s damaged a part of the old settlement surface. There is little doubt that the two 'ape skeletons of human size' that were observed by the dredge crew must represent two other Mesolithic graves from the site.

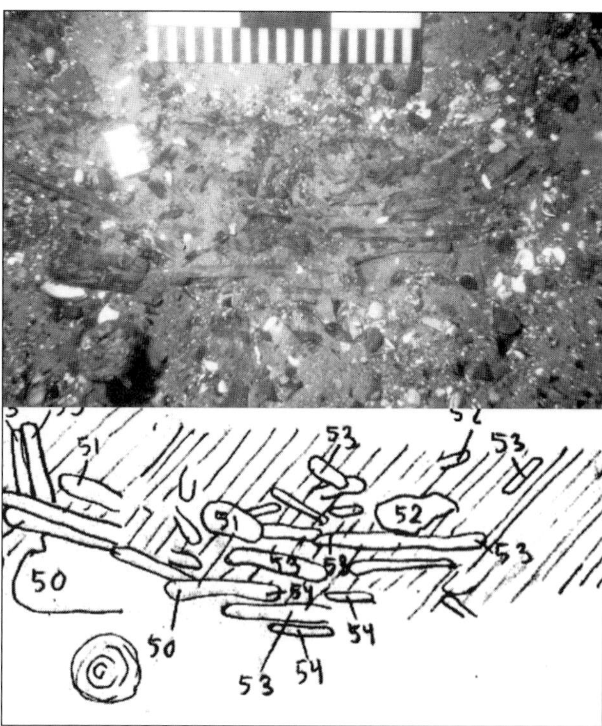

Figure 71.2. Photograph (above) and field-drawing (below) of the platform front, which seems to have been formed by cloven hazel branches that were apparently embedded in the filling of the front of the earthen platform. Even though they were fragmented they appeared to have formed a twisted band.

at Møllegabet II a submerged Mesolithic dwelling and a boat grave outside Ærøskøbing in the Archipelago of South Funen. The remains of a skeleton of a young man (5230–4960 cal BC; K-6040) lay in and around the remains of a dugout (4900–4730 cal BC; K-5640). A number of poles apparently related to the feature may originally have supported it, so that it was located above the water (Skaarup and Grøn 2004).

The dwelling (5280–5140 cal BC; K-6681 and 5280–5080 cal BC; K-6682) was located in a pit, approximately 5 × 3m wide and 20cm deep, with the lower parts of some wall stakes and two inner stakes preserved. A coherent layer of bark pieces covered the northern half of the dwelling – a feature that in section appears to be an earth-built platform. The floor and the platform were covered by twigs and bracken (*Pteridium*) leaves (Mason 2004), and the front of the platform seems to have been supported by cloven hazel (*Corylus*) branches (Figure 71.2) (Skaarup and Grøn 2004).

The two inner stakes were located adjacent to the two areas interpreted as hearths in front of the platform and the

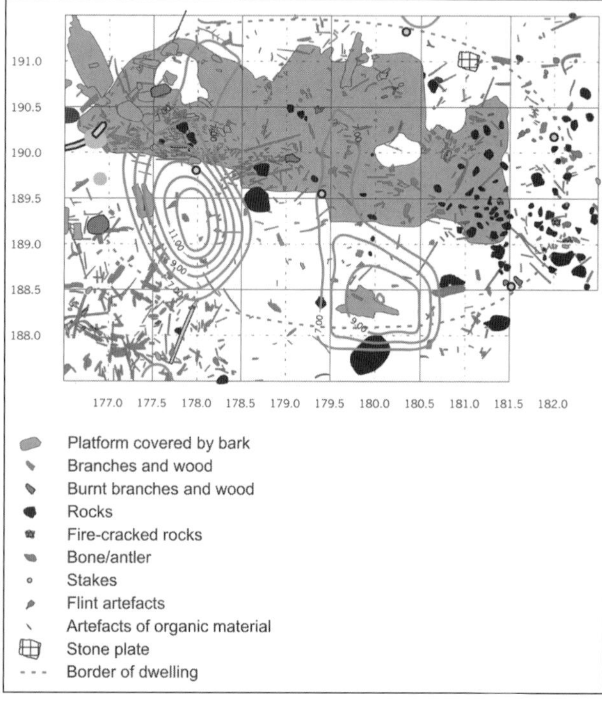

Figure 71.3. Plan of the dwelling pit with the finds it contained, apart from the lithic waste (which displayed a maximum of 3kg in a quarter of a square metre unit inside the dwelling) and most of the lithic artefacts.

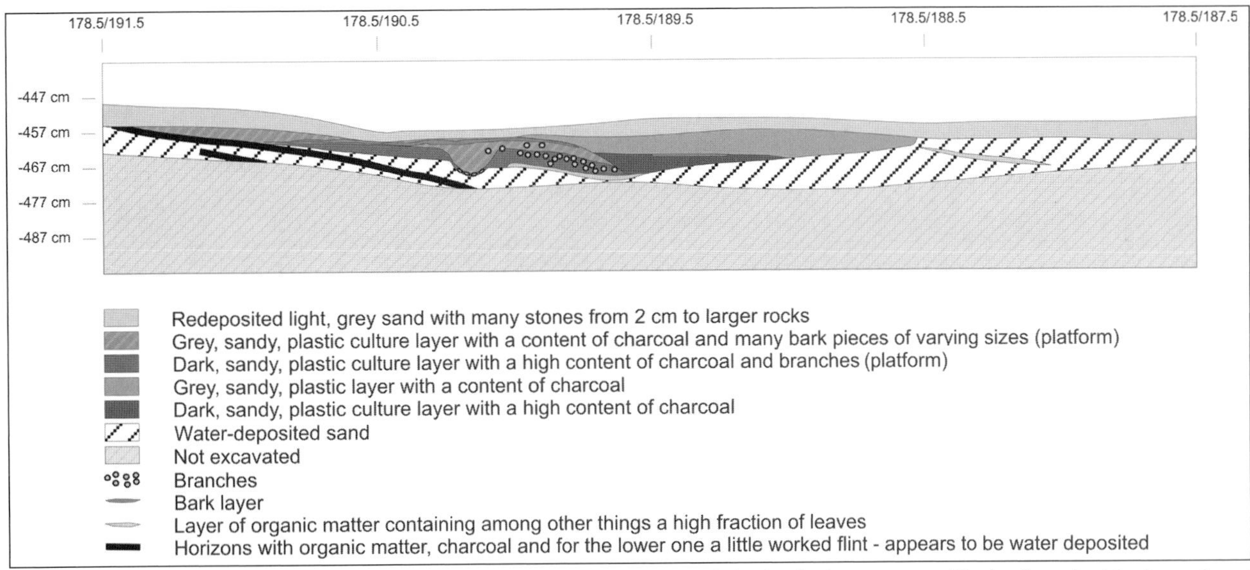

Figure 71.4. Section through the dwelling-pit. The left side has the earth-built platform, covered by bark and with cloven hazel stakes in its front.

door seems to have been in the western end, from where the sea could be observed (Skaarup and Grøn 2004).

The excavation of the site in 50 × 50cm squares and 5cm layers allowed a detailed reconstruction of the activity patterns in the dwelling. Below the platform there appear to have been two working places where flint knapping and repair of hunting weapons were carried out. Furthermore, two proposed women's seating places were distinguished on the platform. A fifth area just inside the proposed entrance seemed atypical as a regular personal seating area, but may well have been a position that was used by visitors or by inhabitants when they wanted to observe the nearby sea. On the basis of studies of dwelling organization in hunter-gatherer societies (on archaeological material and on recent hunter-gatherers in Siberia), the dwelling has been interpreted as a two-family dwelling (Grøn 2003; 1995a; Skaarup and Grøn 2004).

Apart from distributions of lithic objects, and of bones from fish, mammals and birds, food remains from plants (hawthorn (*Crataegus*) and dogwood (*Cornus*) berries, hazelnuts and acorns (*Quercus*)) could be studied *inside* the dwelling pit as reflections of the inhabitant's spatial behavioural pattern. The known sites from the peat bogs seldom show optimal preservation inside the dwelling area itself because the floor would often float as a 'floating island' with its top above the preserving water during periods of higher water level in the basins. Therefore the majority of the preserved organic remains from these finds are generally from the waste layer – apart from hazelnut shells that can in some cases form a significant part of the sediment (Bokelmann 1971).

The dwelling-find is important because it elucidates the old problem of flint knapping inside the Mesolithic dwelling. It appears that flint knapping had been carried out on the floor outside the platform, which for its part has been kept quite clean. The twig floor that seems to have covered the floor beside the platform would have absorbed flints that were not cleared out between the knapping sessions.

The Strynø Basin

On the basis of an assessment of submerged basins in the Danish part of the Southwestern Baltic, carried out by Ole Grøn and Jørgen Dencker in 1985 and 1986, it appeared that the two basins best suited for studies of the Mesolithic-Neolithic transition were the two situated north and south of the island of Strynø, between Langeland, Ærø, and Tåsinge in the archipelago of South Funen (Figure 71.5). These basins seem neither to have been exposed to heavy erosion distorting their Mesolithic-Neolithic bathymetry-topography, nor to considerable sedimentation, making finds difficult to access and investigate.

In 1990 and 1991 funding from the 'Højlunds Fond' made it possible for Langelands Museum, in collaboration with local sports-divers, the Institute of Geology, Aarhus University, and geologist Else Kolstrup, to start a systematic survey of the basin. Cores were taken over extensive areas in a 200 × 400m grid to gain information about the basic geology and formation of the basin. Five of the cores were, on a preliminary basis, used to elucidate the basin's development through analysis of pollen and diatoms. Apparently it had been a lake until flooded by the rising sea in the Sub-Boreal. This meant that the Mesolithic and Neolithic sites could be expected to be located in relation to a relatively stable water level (Grøn 1990; 1995b).

A systematic collection of fallen tree trunks for dendrochronology, and of samples from tree stumps for species analysis, was combined with conventional visual survey for new sites, as well as experimental work attempting to use a sediment echo-sounder to distinguish cultural layers embedded in the sediments.

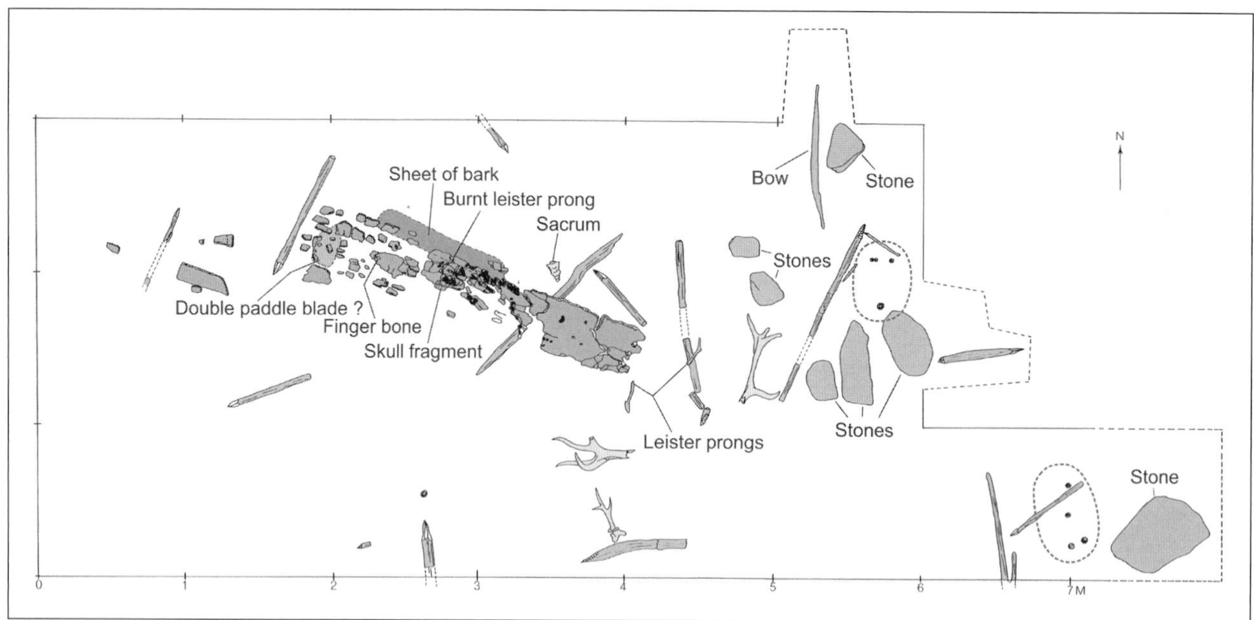

Figure 71.5. The structure interpreted as a Mesolithic burial in a dugout – probably originally placed above the ground on stakes (Grøn and Skaarup 1992).

Conclusions

It is obvious, according to experience in Denmark, that the submerged landscapes represent an important cultural resource. The registered maritime sites, which are all in the publicly accessible on-line cultural-heritage database 'Fund og Fortidsminder' (www.dkconline.dk), fully demonstrate this point; especially observations during dredging of locations where antlers, bone points, and, fairly often, human remains, in combination with large amounts of flint artifacts, underline the state of preservation of some of these sites, at times found in submerged landscapes with significant parts of the vegetation preserved.

There are a couple of practical problems that must be solved if we are to be able to manage and investigate this resource properly. Mapping is a central problem: where are the sites? A later experiment with a new generation of high-resolution sub-bottom profilers ('chirp'), on the embedded and already verified cultural layer from the submerged Kongemose site Blak from Roskilde Fjord, shows that cultural layers can be distinguished in seismic profiles. There seems to be a sound basis for further development in this direction that can lead to a much more controlled management and research situation than on land (Skaarup and Grøn 2004).

The well-preserved submerged sites produce large amounts of organic materials in comparison with land sites. The institutions involved must develop strategies for conservation and analysis of this material, as well as for processing of the data. It is furthermore important that these investigations be carried out in coordination with research and management strategies to gain an optimal outcome of the focused endeavor that the investigation of such sites represents.

There seems to be no doubt that maritime Mesolithic landscape-archaeology will be able to deliver the goods

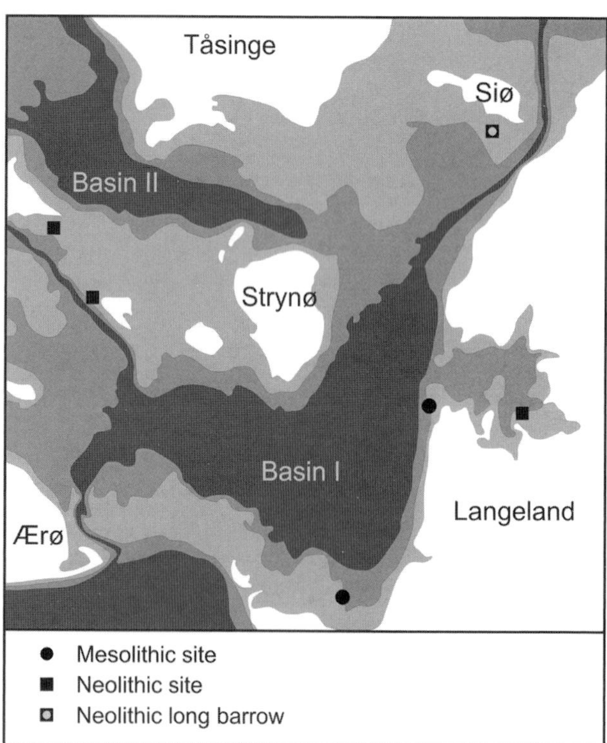

Figure 71.6. The two former freshwater lakes in the archipelago of South Funen in central Danish waters. They were submerged in the Sub-Boreal period in the 2nd millennium BC. A number of Mesolithic and Neolithic settlements with preservation of organic materials are known from these basins.

we hoped and dreamt of in the early 1980s. The central question is now to what degree one should try to solve the problems of Mesolithic and Neolithic archaeology under water. From a research point of view it seems more productive. The basic problem will be to obtain funding for such activities.

References

Andersen, K., Jørgensen, S. and Richter, J. 1982. *Maglemose hytterne ved Ulkestrup Lyng*. Nordiske Fortidsminder, Series B, vol. 7. Copenhagen, Det Kongelige Nordiske Oldskriftselskab.

Bokelmann, K. 1971. Duvensee, ein Wohnplatz des Mesolithikums in Schleswig-Holstein, und die Duvenseegruppe. *Offa* 28. 5–26.

Christensen, C. 1995. The Littorina transgressions in Denmark, in A. Fischer (ed.), *Man and Sea in the Mesolithic: coastal settlements above and below present sea level*, 15–22. Oxbow Monographs 53. Oxford, Oxbow Books.

'Fund og Fortidsminder', available at http://www.dkconline.dk/ (accessed 10/2007).

Grøn, O. 1990. Studies in Settlement Patterns and Submarine Bogs: Results and Strategy for Further Research, in P. M. Vermeersch and P. van Peer (eds.), *Contributions to the Mesolithic in Europe. Papers presented at the Fourth International Symposium on the Mesolithic in Europe*, 81–6. Leuven, Leuven University Press.

Grøn, O. 1995a. *The Maglemose Culture. The reconstruction of the social organization of a mesolithic culture in Northern Europe*. British Archaeological Reports, International Series S616. Oxford, Tempvs Reparatvm.

Grøn, O. 1995b. Research in Stone Age sites at Submerged Shore Zones. Strategies and Experiences, in A. Fischer (ed.) *Man and Sea in the Mesolithic: coastal settlements above and below present sea level*, 403–8. Oxbow Monographs 53. Oxford, Oxford Books.

Grøn, O. 2003. Mesolithic dwelling places in south Scandinavia: their definition and social interpretation. *Antiquity* 77, (298), 685–708.

Grøn, O. and Skaarup, J. 2004. Submerged Stone Age Coastal Zones in Denmark: investigation strategies and results, in N. C. Flemming (ed.), *Submarine prehistoric archaeology of the North Sea. Research priorities and collaboration with industry*, 53–6. Council for British Archaeology (CBA) Research Report 141. London, Council for British Archaeology.

Mason, S. 2004. Archaeobotanical Analysis – Møllegabet I, in J. Skaarup and O. Grøn, *Møllegabet II. A submerged Mesolithic settlement in southern Denmark*, 122–43. British Archaeological Reports, International Series S1328. Oxford, Archaeopress.

Skaarup, J. and Grøn, O. 2004. *Møllegabet II. A submerged Mesolithic settlement in southern Denmark*. British Archaeological Reports, International Series S1328. Oxford, Archaeopress.

72. Them bones: midden sites as a defining characteristic of the Scottish Mesolithic

C. R. Wickham-Jones

Midden sites are considered a defining characteristic of the Scottish Mesolithic. They are often viewed as part of a putative Mesolithic annual life-cycle. But the existing evidence is not that simple. Midden sites are rare in the Scottish Mesolithic. New Mesolithic sites occur, but few are middens. With regard to existing midden sites: there is little consistency in size and the contents vary greatly, some contain evidence for internal structures, some appear to result from specialised activities. Middens occur in a variety of locations from rockshelters and caves to open air shorelines and there is considerable chronological variation. Some go on to be used in later periods, and are often associated with Neolithic and Bronze Age burial. What do the Mesolithic midden sites of Scotland represent? Why do they occur? We may not have the answers but the evidence suggests that to interpret middens as a uniform phenomenon is wrong. The time has come to re-consider midden sites and look at the environmental and social circumstances that lead to their formation. This paper will consider evidence from both old and new sites.

Keywords: midden, coast, marine shells, microliths, preservation conditions, excavation, economy.

Them bones: midden sites as a defining characteristic of the Scottish Mesolithic

Shell middens have long occupied a central role in thinking about Mesolithic Scotland. The importance of the early midden sites in Scotland was first recognised in the late 19th century by Galloway and Grieve (Figure 72.1; Mellars 1987) but as recently as the early 1990s Mesolithic Scotland was published as a series of well-preserved midden sites, albeit not explicitly (Smith 1992). The rich organic preservation within a midden is very unusual by Scottish standards (Scottish soils tend to be acid) so that midden sites have both attracted attention and been well studied. Nevertheless, previous literature has tended to lump the remains together as if they represent a uniform phenomenon, despite the fact that in many cases all that they have in common is the presence of marine shells within a coastal location. In this paper I want to explore the variety of Mesolithic midden sites and suggest that it is time we looked for multiple interpretations.

It is interesting to note that though Scotland also has an important record of later midden sites including Neolithic sites such as Skara Brae and Knap of Howar, as well as Bronze Age material and sites that run from the Iron Age into the Viking period, such as Pool and Quoygrew, scholars of these later periods have not allowed the midden to dominate in the way that we see for the early material. Perhaps the general lack of structural remains in the Mesolithic of Scotland has biased our perception. Whatever, the dominance of the midden is such that the well-preserved Oronsay sites, although the subject of a meticulous research project in the 1970s, have only been published in part – the ecology (human and otherwise) of the sites is the subject of a well-thumbed book (Mellars 1987), while the stone tools and other artefactual material still await publication.

What fascinates me is the fact that midden sites are neither common, nor dominant, in the Scottish Mesolithic record. There are plenty of other sites, albeit sites that

Figure 72.1. Caisteal-nan-Gillean. 19th-century view of the shell midden mound on the island of Oronsay. (After S. Grieve 1882, from a photograph by W. Galloway).

Figure 72.2. Bhaile Margait, Invernaver. A typical lithic-scatter site in sand dunes on the north coast of Scotland.

Figure 72.3. Sand. The midden lies just outside a shallow rockshelter, and was not visible as an upstanding site in advance of excavation.

lack the rich remains of the midden (Figure 72.2). It is of course possible that midden sites have been systematically destroyed and Mellars has recently discussed the mining of midden material as fertiliser (2004) but I tend to feel that his view 'that the surviving sample of Mesolithic shell middens may represent no more than one or two percent of those originally present on the associated coasts' (Mellars 2004, 174) is overly pessimistic (or optimistic, I am not sure which way to look at it). Some middens have undoubtedly been lost, but perhaps not as many as that.

As a digression it is worth considering the impact on surface scatter sites if this view is true. How many are *in situ* and how many represent manuring practices using midden material? Further study of lithic scatters in the vicinity of caves and other potential midden locations is necessary.

Despite the presence of a few well-known midden sites, most Mesolithic sites in Scotland have little organic preservation. New Mesolithic sites are rarely middens: in 2004/5 six new Mesolithic sites were found in Scotland and none are midden sites. Despite the fact that visible midden material was targeted during fieldwork by the Scotland's First Settlers project over a period of five years, between 1998 and 2003, only three middens with Mesolithic material were registered, as opposed to 10 non-midden sites with Mesolithic artefacts (Hardy and Wickham-Jones, forthcoming). In my view middens are rare.

Rather than getting lost in the whys and wherefores of our past preoccupation with the midden I would like to take this opportunity to examine what we do know about them and discuss how they might fit in to current interpretations of Mesolithic Scotland. A cursory examination of known middens suggests that there is little similarity between sites, and one wonders whether the existence of (for Scotland) unusually good preservation conditions (leading to the presence of the midden material) has masked the variety of the remains.

Midden sites vary greatly in size. The large mounded middens of Oronsay are well known to all with an interest in Mesolithic Scotland, but they are, so far, almost unique. Scotland does not have great banks of middens like those in Denmark or Ireland. Scottish middens rarely occur as upstanding monuments. Only at Risga, also on the west coast, is there an upstanding midden and it is much smaller, nothing like the Oronsay middens in size. To the east a series of middens occurs along the Forth Valley, but although they also comprise visible mounds it has been hard to interpret them. There are Mesolithic dates (generally 4th millennium BC; Ashmore 2004a and b) from the lower levels of Inveravon, Mumrills and Nether Kinneil; these are backed up by the discovery of a series of Mesolithic bone and antler tools from the same area, but the sites have suffered from their location in a part of Scotland that has been subject to considerable development in the last 150 years. There has been no detailed work of the scale carried out on the west-coast sites, and the work that has taken place shows that some of these middens run into the Iron Age in date (Sloan 1984). It is thus difficult to compare them with the Oronsay sites.

Other Scottish midden sites are much smaller. That at Loch a Sguirr on Raasay – a small island off the east coast of Skye – represents the opposite end of the extreme, little more than a scraping of midden surviving inside a rockshelter (Hardy and Wickham-Jones, forthcoming). Perhaps this is closer to the norm for many Mesolithic sites, should preservation conditions have been favourable. All sites must have contained some organic material, but most of it will decompose over the millennia to leave only a black sticky deposit. Even where conditions are favourable it is the presence of shells rather than bone that gives the Mesolithic midden its characteristic form (this is a contrast to the later middens that may comprise predominantly bone material).

Between Oronsay and Loch a Sguirr there is a series of sites that completes the size range. The recently excavated midden at Sand (Figure 72.3) is not large (roughly 8 × 8m; no more than 50 cubic m), and it has been estimated that it could have built up over one or two intensive episodes of shellfish exploitation (Hardy and Wickham-Jones, forthcoming). That at An Corran, on the other side of the Inner Sound to Sand is larger, but not huge; its depth

Figure 72.4. Raschoille Cave, Oban. In common with many of the Oban Cave sites, Raschoille was subject to considerable disturbance before the archaeologists were called in.

belies the fact that, although the stratigraphy is not well documented, the upper levels seem to relate to activity in the Neolithic (Saville and Miket 1994a and b; Hardy *et al.* forthcoming). The middens of the well-known Oban Cave sites are difficult to estimate in terms of size because of the early date of their examination and the fact that they were often disturbed before archaeological work took place. This latter factor also applies to those Oban sites discovered in recent times, such as Raschoille (Figure 72.4) (Connock 1985) and Carding Mill Bay (Connock *et al.* 1992). Most of these middens were also subject to later activity, often in the Neolithic and Bronze Age periods (Pollard 1996). In the east of Scotland there are fewer surviving middens, but the best known site, at Morton, was neither upstanding nor large, although smaller upstanding middens may have existed along the mouths of the River Tay (e.g. Broughty Ferry, Lacaille 1954), and around the Moray Firth (e.g. Milltown of Culloden, Wordsworth 1992).

The above discussion makes it obvious that middens not only vary in size, they also occur in a variety of locations from rockshelters and caves to open air shorelines. The use of caves and rockshelters undoubtedly facilitated the accumulation of shells and their subsequent preservation, but it is by no means a prerequisite for midden formation. At the risk of labouring the point, this means that Mesolithic activity itself took place in a variety of locations. What a surprise! In some areas middens occur in clusters (e.g. Oronsay, Oban, the Forth Valley), while in others they appear to be more isolated (e.g. Morton, Sand, An Corran).

Comprehensively published recent studies of midden sites are few and far between and this means that it is very difficult to discuss how the behaviour that led to the formation of sites such as Morton might relate to the behaviour at sites such as Oronsay. Interpretation has tended to concentrate on economic behaviour at the expense of social studies, which do, after all, need wider information and this is a point we shall return to later.

Published accounts of midden sites may vary greatly, but it is possible to pull out some interesting information: notably, the great variety in material that makes up the bulk of the midden. With regard to the shells, some are limpet (*Patella* sp.) dominated, some cockle (Cardiidae), some oyster (*Ostrea* sp.). Recent work at Sand has highlighted the importance of crab (Milner, forthcoming) and this is supported at both Oronsay (Mellars 2004) and Morton (Coles 1971). Some sites contain deposits of fish (Parks and Barrett, forthcoming). Animal bone tends to be regarded as of less importance in the make-up of the sites, although some have significant assemblages of bird bone, most notably An Corran where puffin (*Fratercula artica*) was important (Bartosiewicz, forthcoming, for the uninitiated it is worth noting that puffin provided an important food resource for some coastal communities in historical times when the difficulties of harvesting these cliff dwelling birds meant that there was a strong element of ritual associated with their exploitation). Resources such as seaweed, samphire (*Crithmum maritimum*), birds' eggs, and sea urchins (*Paracentrotus lividus*), all of which are less likely to survive in the archaeological record, are often (but not always) overlooked by modern archaeology.

The differences in make-up are not confined to food remains. While some middens resemble straightforward (if anything in archaeology is straightforward) deposits of refuse, others contain evidence for internal structures. This is most notable at Oronsay and Morton where arcs of stake holes were recorded within and below the midden. Other sites such as Sand and An Corran had no obvious evidence of structural remains. Although it is possible that this may reflect the larger trenches at the former sites, locations such as Loch a Sguirr remind us that stake and post holes are not a pre-requisite for a midden site.

There is also variation in the artefactual component, though this is more difficult to quantify due to the differing standards of excavation (e.g. a lack of fine sieving on early sites, which may have led to an under-representation of microliths and fine lithic debris), and to the lack of publication of some more recent projects. The work at Sand has confirmed that some middens most certainly do contain microliths; while that at Oronsay confirms that others do not. In general lithic assemblages seem to lack many formal 'retouched' tool types, such as scrapers, though it should be noted that few midden excavations have put the midden into a wider local context and looked at remains running away from the midden. The recent work at Risga yielded large quantities of lithics, including knapping debris, microliths, and scrapers from an area to the side of the midden (Pollard *et al.* 1996), and these were also present at Morton (Coles 1971). Bone and antler artefacts such as bevel-ended tools are present on many sites, as is a range of cobble tools that often includes hammerstones and bevelled pebbles.

In line with the variations in make-up the midden sites have been interpreted in different ways. The obvious inference was that they represented specialised processing sites related to the use of shellfish, and this has been discussed by many, including Bonsall (1996). More recent interpretations have looked at the possibility that the shells may have enabled specialised activity without actually being the prime cause of that activity themselves, i.e. shells provided an easy and reliable source of food while you were occupied with something else. An Corran, for example, may be associated with the extraction and exploitation of local lithic material, perhaps backed up by the hunting and processing of birds. At Sand the presence of a limited range of tools of both bone and stone is one indication of specialisation, and this is supported by the ecofactual assemblage, which is strongly indicative of the working of hides. Risga has likewise been interpreted as a specialised site, and this was also originally the case at Oronsay (Mellars 1987), even though Mellars has recently argued that the Oronsay middens are more likely to represent generalised episodes of intensive occupation (2004). Morton too has been interpreted as the result of more generalised subsistence activities.

Following on from this is the question of seasonality. Hunter-gatherer-fisher behaviour in the northern hemisphere has been (and still is) strongly influenced by fluctuations in the overall climatic patterns, which work to bunch different resources at different times of the year, though this was not, of course, the only factor to influence our forebears. The development of methods to identify the seasons in which the different plant and animal resources were harvested has led to some interesting information regarding seasonal patterns of behaviour from midden sites. It is also true to say, however, that new lines of research often contradict previous wisdom, thus suggesting that our understanding of past ecological patterning and the role played by cultural and social aspects of behaviour may not be perfect.

Once again Oronsay and Morton have led the way, with the well-known interpretation, using otoliths and other evidence, that the Oronsay middens represent year-round occupation made up of different seasonal spells at the individual sites. At Morton, Deith's now famous work on shells suggested more specific seasonal exploitation (Deith 1986), and this has been picked up elsewhere. The wider ecofactual assemblages from many shell middens also lend themselves to this type of study and other putative seasonal sites include Sand (Hardy and Wickham-Jones, forthcoming), and An Corran (Hardy *et al.*, forthcoming).

The opposite end of the spectra of seasonal variation concerns the chronological variation among the sites. Until recently, midden sites tended to fall in the later part of the Mesolithic: Oronsay, Morton, and the Forth Valley sites, all tended towards dates in the fourth and fifth millennia BC (Ashmore 2004a and b). Recent work, however, has altered our perception by introducing midden sites with early dates. Sand, Druimvargie (Oban), and Ulva, among others, all have dates that relate to the sixth and seventh millennia BC (Ashmore 2004a and b). Ashmore's comprehensive list of Mesolithic dates reminds us just how few midden sites there are, but it is clear that they can occur at any point in the Mesolithic (Figure 72.5).

Combining the strands of seasonality and chronology, the sites in Oronsay have recently been interpreted as a response to economic stress in the later Mesolithic (Mellars 2004). This certainly offers an explanation that is both plausible and convenient, while at the same time matching local historical information relating to the use of shellfish as a resource in times of famine (Wickham-Jones 2003). It is interesting, therefore, that some earlier middens occur around what has come to be known as the 8.2k 'blip': a brief but significant climatic downturn that certainly affected north-west Europe (Alley *et al.* 1997). However, while it is certainly possible that some middens do reflect the use of marine resources in times of hardship, this is unlikely to explain them all. If some middens are a response to economic hardship, just how representative of Mesolithic Scotland are they? Are we suggesting that Mesolithic Scotland was a period of economic marginality that lasted for over 4000 years? Surely not (and see Edwards 2004).

It is worth noting here that midden studies have been criticised, in line with general Mesolithic work in Scotland, as emphasising the environmental influences on economic life, rather than the social, cultural and spiritual influences on society. This lack of vision relating to the people of the Scottish Mesolithic is in stark contrast to current interpretations of Neolithic Scotland that tend to concentrate on the human element at the expense of the powers of the environment in which people lived (Richards 2005). Of course, reality is likely to lie somewhere between the two, but it is worth reminding ourselves that our interpretations are just ideas: we can never be certain what took place in the past, nor why. It is also worth reminding ourselves that people are not a logical species – even today we do much that defies a simple explanation.

There have been attempts to introduce the creators of the midden sites, though they may have been overlooked in our rush to examine the economic detail. In 1971 Coles saw Morton in terms of a wider pattern of human behaviour, and both Bonsall and Pollard have more recently interpreted midden sites as resulting from the activities of women and children (Bonsall 1996; Pollard 1996). Perhaps we shall never know, even though it is important to remember that

Site (Years BC)	7500–7000	7000–6500	6500–6000	6000–5500	5500–5000	5000–4500	4500–4000	4000–3500
Druimvargie, Oban	x	x	x					
Sand		x	x		x			
An Corran		x	x		x			x
Raschoille		x	x	x	x			x
Ulva		x	x			x		x
Castle Street, Inverness		x	x	x				
Loch a Sguirr			x					
Lon Mor			x		x		x	
Morton B				x	x	x	x	x
MacArthur Cave, Oban				x				
Risga					x	x		
Caisteal nan Gillean, Oronsay					x	x	x	
Forth Valley sites					x	x	x	x
Cnoc Sligeach, Oronsay						x	x	x
Cnoc Coig, Oronsay						x	x	x
Priory Midden, Oronsay						x	x	
Muirtown, Inverness						x	x	
Carding Mill Bay							x	x
Caisteal nan Gillean 2, Oronsay							x	x

Figure 72.5. Date spans for midden sites in Scotland (information from Ashmore 2004b). Note: these dates are based on a variety of raw materials, and some were taken several years ago. The dates from Morton A have not been included because of uncertainties over the (mixed) sample.

someone was harvesting the shellfish, chucking out the bones, and lighting the fires. In this respect it is important to remember that our data are doubly incomplete until we have excavated the non-midden areas that relate to each site. At Sand, for example, large quantities of heat-fractured stone were found on the slope below the midden. In other (later) circumstances this might have been considered more akin to the remains from a Burnt Mound, but at Sand it was just regarded as evidence of the broader spectrum of activities that had taken place (Hardy and Wickham-Jones, forthcoming).

Of course the ultimate reflection of the occupants of the midden sites lies in human bone, and this is singularly lacking from most sites. Only in Oronsay was any significant quantity of Mesolithic human bone discovered: dispersed bones from hands and feet, with odd other bones and three teeth. This does not seem to have resulted from deliberate burial as we know it, though there is a general consensus that it probably does represent the material remains of purposeful behaviour (Meiklejohn and Denston 1987; Meiklejohn *et al.* 2005), perhaps the conscious burial practices in use at that time and place. If so it emphasises the difference between Oronsay and other locations, because human bone that is clearly attributable to the Mesolithic is lacking elsewhere, with the possible exception of a few isolated bones from the lower levels of the midden at Carding Mill Bay (Connock *et al.* 1992). These have been dated and are Neolithic (Schulting and Richards 2002).

In contrast to the lack of Mesolithic human bone, later human remains do occur on a number of sites and Pollard, among others, has noted that this is unlikely to be coincidence (1996). Several middens are associated with later burial practices. The Oban sites, Carding Mill Bay, Raschoille Cave, and An Corran are all associated with later burials, usually dating to the Neolithic and Bronze Age periods, and sometimes, but not always, using cists. It is interesting, however, that this is not a blanket generalisation relating to all midden sites: only certain types of midden were selected, namely locations associated with caves and rockshelters. In his discussion of this Pollard has gone on to look at potentially symbolic aspects of this behaviour which do not need to be rehearsed here, but his links between chambered tombs (which often have underlying midden deposits, as well as coastal locations) and pre-existing midden sites are interesting (Pollard 1996).

It is also worth noting that many midden sites bear traces of other later activity, but then so do non-midden Mesolithic remains. Perhaps this is just a reflection of the likelihood that human activity will return to favourable locations so that the Mesolithic material (so far the earliest indication of human settlement in Scotland) will often occur ‘at the bottom of the heap’.

To date, detailed work on the Mesolithic middens of Scotland has concentrated on economic interpretations of single sites. But people are not only driven by economics, there is always an unknown human factor to take into account. Furthermore, it is important to get to the people behind the sites. Despite the fact that our understanding of Mesolithic Scotland is based upon a foundation of human mobility, and thus of networks of sites, midden sites have rarely been looked at as part of a wider system. Only in Oronsay, where a group of sites lies in convenient and obvious proximity to one another, have the archaeologists been forced to see them as part of a wider whole. Interestingly, in this case, the sites are seen as the result of semi-permanent settlement within a very restricted land mass (Mellars 2004). Once again this interpretation would set them apart from the bulk of other midden sites in Scotland, which are still interpreted as the result of wider mobile activity patterns, although in most places we lack the information to draw such conclusions.

In order to provide social information we really need to look at more than one site. Even today the static population of 21st-century Scotland operates a system of restricted mobility within which people build up a series of different sites that relate to a complex mix of domestic, social, cultural and spiritual functions. Some sites are used repeatedly on a daily basis, while others are used occasionally at intervals that may exceed a year. As archaeologists, we need to examine the Mesolithic middens within the context of their wider system, and this has rarely been done. The lack of well-published sites undoubtedly hampers this, but the time has come to look at the middens of Mesolithic Scotland as a disparate phenomenon. They need to fit in to the wider scheme of things; middens are but a varied part of the archaeological record, although one that we need to understand better.

References

Alley, R. B., Mayeski, P. A., Sowers, T., Stuiver, M., Taylor, K. C. and Clark, P. U. 1997. Holocene climatic instability: a prominent, widespread event 8200 years ago. *Geology* 25, 483–6.

Ashmore, P. J. 2004a. Dating forager communities in Scotland, in A. Saville (ed.), *Mesolithic Scotland and its Neighbours: The Early Holocene Prehistory of Scotland, its British and Irish Context, and some Northern European Perspectives*, 83–94. Edinburgh, Society of Antiquaries of Scotland.

Ashmore, P. J. 2004b. A date list (to October 2002) for early foragers in Scotland, in A. Saville (ed.), *Mesolithic Scotland and its neighbours: early Holocene prehistory of Scotland, its British and Irish context and some North European perspectives*, 95–158. Edinburgh, Society of Antiquaries of Scotland.

Bartosiewicz, L. (forthcoming). Vertebrate remains from a shell midden at An Corran, Staffin (Isle of Skye), in K. Hardy, R. Miket and A. Saville, *An Corran, Staffin, Skye: a rockshelter with Mesolithic and later occupation*.

Bonsall, C. 1996. The 'Obanian problem': coastal adaptation in the Mesolithic of western Scotland, in T. Pollard and A. Morrison (eds.), *The Early Prehistory of Scotland*, 183–97. Edinburgh, Edinburgh University Press.

Coles, J. M. 1971. The early settlement of Scotland: excavations at Morton, Fife. *Proceedings of the Prehistoric Society* 37, 284–366.

Connock, K. 1985. *Raschoille Cave, Oban – interim report*. Oban, Lorne Archaeological and Historical Society.

Connock, K. D., Finlayson, B. and Mills, C. M. 1992. Excavation of a shell midden site at Carding Mill Bay near Oban, Scotland. *Glasgow Archaeological Journal* 17, 25–38.

Deith, M. R. 1986. Subsistence strategies at a Mesolithic campsite: evidence from stable isotope analysis of shells. *Journal of Archaeological Science* 131, 61–78.

Edwards, K. 2004. Palaeoenvironments: new work; new thoughts, in A. Saville (ed.), *Mesolithic Scotland and its neighbours: early Holocene prehistory of Scotland, its British and Irish context and some North European perspectives*, 55–72. Edinburgh, Society of Antiquaries of Scotland.

Hardy, K., Miket, R. and Saville, A. (forthcoming). *An Corran, Staffin, Skye: a rockshelter with Mesolithic and later occupation*.

Hardy, K. and Wickham-Jones, C. R. (eds.) (forthcoming). *Mesolithic and Later sites around the Inner Sound, Scotland: the work of the Scotland's First Settlers Project 1998–2004*. Scottish Archaeological Internet Reports (www.sair.org.uk).

Lacaille, A. D. 1954. *The Stone Age in Scotland*. Oxford, Oxford University Press (for the Wellcome Historical Medical Museum, London).

Meiklejohn, C. and Denston, B. 1987. The human skeletal material: inventory and initial interpretation, in P. A. Mellars, *Excavations on Oronsay. Prehistoric Human Ecology on a small island*, 290–300. Edinburgh, Edinburgh University Press.

Meiklejohn, C., Merrett, D. C., Nolan, R. W., Richards, M. P. and Mellars P. A. 2005. Spatial Relationships, Dating and Taphonomy of the human bone from the Mesolithic site of Cnoc Coig, Oronsay, Argyll, Scotland. *Proceedings of the Prehistoric Society* 71, 85–105.

Mellars, P. A. 1987. *Excavations on Oronsay. Prehistoric Human Ecology on a small island*. Edinburgh, Edinburgh University Press.

Mellars, P. A. 2004. Mesolithic Scotland, Coastal Occupation and the Role of the Oronsay Middens, in A. Saville (ed.), *Mesolithic Scotland and its Neighbours: The Early Holocene Prehistory of Scotland, its British and Irish Context, and some Northern European Perspectives*, 167–83. Edinburgh, Society of Antiquaries of Scotland.

Milner, N. (forthcoming). Mesolithic middens and marine molluscs, in K. Hardy and C. R. Wickham-Jones, *Mesolithic and Later sites around the Inner Sound, Scotland: the work of the Scotland's First Settlers Project 1998–2004*. Submitted to Scottish Archaeological Internet Reports (www.sair.org.uk).

Parks, R. L. and Barrett, J. H. (forthcoming). The Zooarchaeology of Sand, in K. Hardy and C. R. Wickham-Jones (eds.), *Mesolithic and later sites around the Inner Sound, Scotland: the work of the Scotland's First Settlers project 1998–2004*. Scottish Archaeological Internet Reports (www.sair.org.uk).

Pollard, T. 1996. Time and Tide, coastal environments, cosmology, and ritual practice in early prehistoric Scotland, in T. Pollard and A. Morrison (eds.), *The Early Prehistory of Scotland*, 198–210. Edinburgh, Edinburgh University Press.

Pollard, T., Atkinson, J. and Banks, I. 1996. It is the technical side of the work which is my stumbling block. A shell midden site on Risga reconsidered, in T. Pollard and A. Morrison A (eds.), *The Early Prehistory of Scotland*, 165–82. Edinburgh, Edinburgh University Press.

Richards, C. 2005. *Dwelling among the monuments*. Cambridge, MacDonald Institute Monograph Series.

Saville, A. (ed.) 2004. *Mesolithic Scotland and its neighbours: early Holocene prehistory of Scotland, its British and Irish context and some North European perspectives*. Edinburgh, Society of Antiquaries of Scotland.

Saville, A. and Miket, R. 1994a. An Corran rock-shelter: a major new Mesolithic site. *PAST* 18 (December 1994), 9–10.

Saville, A. and Miket, R. 1994b. An Corran, Staffin, Skye. *Discovery and Excavation in Scotland* 1994, 40–1.

Schulting, R. J. and Richards, M. P. 2002. The wet, the wild and the domesticated: the Mesolithic-Neolithic transition on the West Coast of Scotland. *European Journal of Archaeology* 5, 147–89.

Sloan, D. 1984. Shell middens and chronology in Scotland. *Scottish Archaeological Review* 3, 73–9.

Smith, C. 1992. *Late Stone Age Hunters of the British Isles*. London, Routledge.

Wickham-Jones, C. R. 2003. The tale of the limpet. *British Archaeology* 71, 23.

Wordsworth, J. 1992. Milton of Culloden. *Discovery and Excavation in Scotland* 1992, 42.

73. South-western regional identities: Birdcombe, Totty Pot and Hawkcombe Head

Paula J. Gardiner

This paper looks at the evidence for Late Mesolithic activity in Somerset, south-west England. Primary data recovered from excavation at three Late Mesolithic sites suggests that there was hunter-gatherer movement between the coastal plain and uplands for hunting and burial. Evidence from Hawkcombe Head on Exmoor suggests that activities carried out there may have been for other reasons than subsistence economy. The evidence suggests that Late Mesolithic groups made frequent visits to a site that held particular significance within the landscape. A pattern of late hunter-gatherer activity throughout south-west England has emerged, with flint often coming from a long distance, but at more specific sites like Hawkcombe Head and Birdcombe, regional identities and territorial movement can be identified.

Keywords: Mesolithic, Somerset, Hawkcombe Head, Birdcombe, Totty Pot, landscape, regional identities.

Introduction

This paper examines the primary data recovered from the excavation of three Late Mesolithic sites in Somerset: Birdcombe, Totty Pot and Hawkcombe Head, and interprets them within the context of their regional identities and hunter-gatherer activities.

The Late Mesolithic in south-west England shows a pattern of hunter-gatherer movement between coastal plain and upland locations for hunting. The evidence from sites such as Birdcombe and Hawkcombe Head in Somerset suggests that hunter-gatherer groups may be making longer visits to specific places at certain times of the year, to engage in tool production and other activities (Gardiner 2000; 2007a; 2007b). The caves and swallet-holes on the Mendip Hills are used throughout the Mesolithic for burial and the sites of Gough's Cave and Aveline's Hole verify this practice (Davies 1921; Schulting 2005; Schulting and Wysocki 2002; Stringer 1986; Tratman 1977). The lesser-known site of Totty Pot has evidence of human burial in the Late Mesolithic, and this is discussed within the context of territorial movement in north Somerset (Gardiner 2001; 2007b) (Figure 73.1).

The tool typologies of some of these late hunter-gatherer groups show certain similarities within regions and from this evidence a pattern of territorial movement can assumed to have taken place within an identifiable landscape. Within the south-west peninsula there is a diversity of upland and lowland landscapes, including the inter-tidal zone. In Cornwall there is a coastal focus of Mesolithic activity at sites such as Poldowrian (Lizard Peninsula), Trevose Head (Constantine Bay) and Gwithian (St. Ives Bay), which show evidence of microlith production from local beach pebble (Smith and Harris 1982; Johnson and David 1982; Berridge and Roberts 1986). From these areas we can assume the use of a comparatively local landscape with raw material and resources being available close by. However at Hawkcombe Head on Exmoor and at Birdcombe in north Somerset, the raw material source is not so readily available and has to be brought in from some considerable distance.

Birdcombe, Wraxall, north Somerset

Birdcombe is situated at the foot of a sheltered, south-facing slope which forms the Failand Ridge and adjacent valley eight kilometres south of Bristol (ST475718). The wooded, limestone hills of Tower House Woods rise to the north and a thick band of alluvium forms the valley bottom at 10m OD. The valley is fed by springs along its lower slopes, which are interspersed by small, spring-fed pools, two of which are adjacent to the site. The larger of these is locally called the Whirly Pool. The site was originally discovered by two amateur archaeologists; their excavations revealed evidence of extensive flint knapping and microlith production from both broad- and narrow-blade industries (Sykes and Whittle 1960) (Figure 73.2).

Excavation by the author in 1997 assessed and re-interpreted a lowland hunter-gatherer landscape and re-examined earlier interpretations. The 1997 excavation

Figure 73.1. Map showing the location of Birdcombe (Gardiner 2001, 82), Totty Pot (Gardiner 2001, 108) and Hawkcombe Head, Somerset (Gardiner 2007).

Figure 73.2. Birdcombe, Wraxall, Somerset. The Mesolithic site is located at 'X'.

revealed a sealed Mesolithic deposit containing a flint assemblage dominated by geometric microliths (Figure 73.3: 15–46). It included cores, microburins and obliquely blunted points (Figure 73.3: 1–10) (Clark 1932; 1934; Pitts and Jacobi 1979), together with three fragments of charred hazelnut (*Corylus avellana*).

Flint is not found within the natural geology of Somerset and the large quantity of debitage suggests that the raw material was brought to the site in small nodules for knapping. It was used economically and although some of the raw material derives from river gravels, much of it is high-quality flint that was probably taken directly from chalk of the Marlborough Downs, Wiltshire (Gardiner 2001).

The radiocarbon dates suggest a very late hunter-gatherer presence in the area. There was no evidence of continuity into the Neolithic and there appears to have been an abrupt abandonment of the site at the end of the Mesolithic. The deposit of approximately one metre of colluvium, which sealed the Mesolithic layers, suggests clearance at a later date, possibly in the Bronze Age. The location is sheltered and south facing and palaeo-environmental evidence suggests that there was a steeper valley slope and deeper, wetter, valley bottom in the Mesolithic (Gardiner 2001). This location would have provided essential shelter and resources in winter, with hunting in the wooded slopes behind it. It is an ideal place for a winter stop-over and the groups who visited it may have had links with other sites in the area; the River Land Yeo forms a natural route to the coast, to sites such as Blackstone Rocks (Gardiner, 2001; Sykes 1938).

Totty Pot, Cheddar, Somerset

Totty Pot is a swallet-hole that was discovered in the 1960s

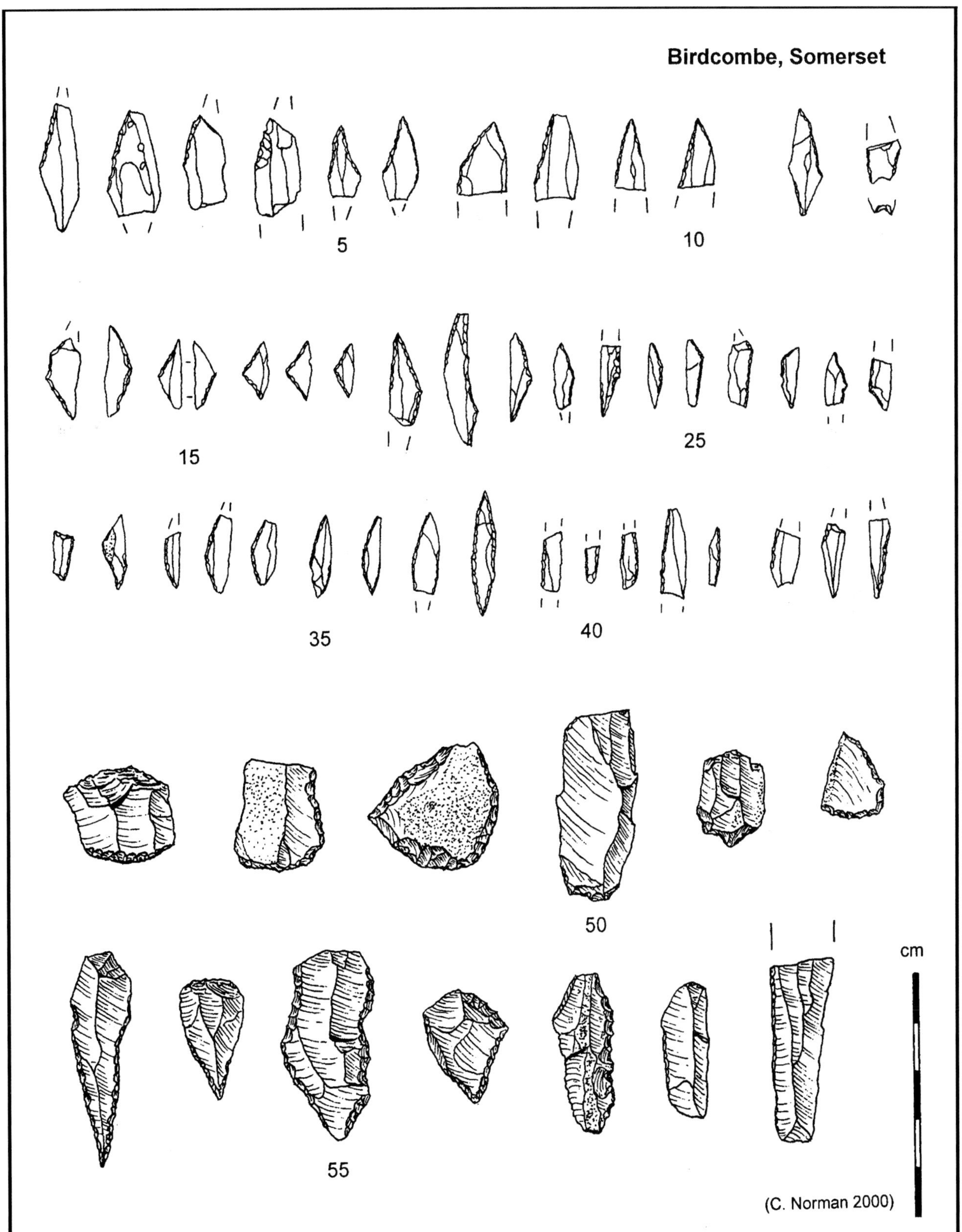

Figure 73.3. Flint from the 1997 Birdcombe collection. (Drawings: Chris Norman; Gardiner 2001).

Sample No.	*Material*	*Lab Code*	*Radiocarbon Years*	*Calibration 95%*
1	Oak charcoal	Beta-147105	4700±50	3637–3362
2	Oak charcoal	Beta-147106	5420±60	4358–4047

Figure 73.4. Radiocarbon dates from Trench D, Birdcombe, Somerset (Gardiner 2001; Stuiver et al. *1993; 1998; Bronk Ramsey 1995).*

Figure 73.5. Totty Pot swallet hole. The shaft entrance is indicated by the arrow.

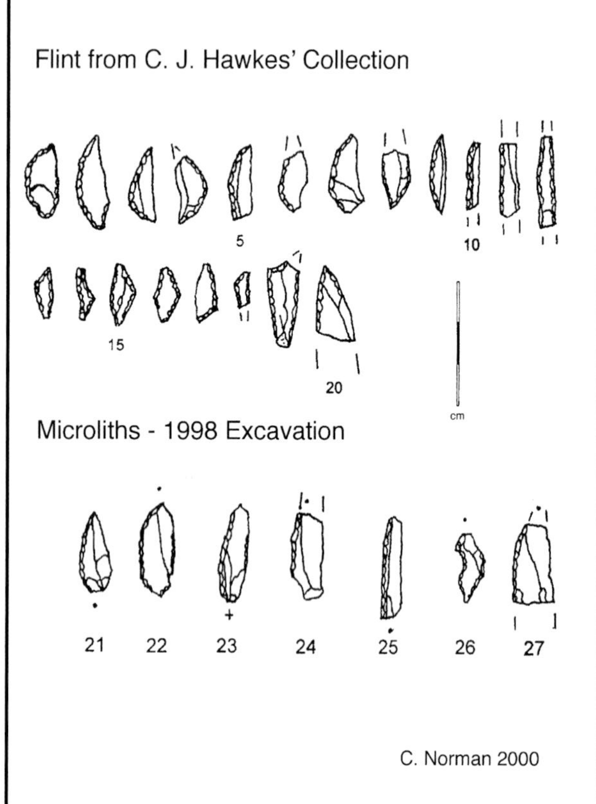

Figure 73.6. Microliths recovered from the 1960 and 1998 Totty Pot excavations. (Drawings: Chris Norman; Gardiner 2001, 111).

Site	*Lab Sample*	*Radiocarbon Years*	*Cal BC*
'Cheddar Man'	BM-525	9080±150	8700–7760
Totty Pot	BM-2973	8180±70	7450–7050
Aveline's Hole	Gr-N-5393	8100±50	7302–6864

Figure 73.7. Radiocarbon Dates from the Mendip Caves (Gardiner 2001; Stuiver et al. 1998).

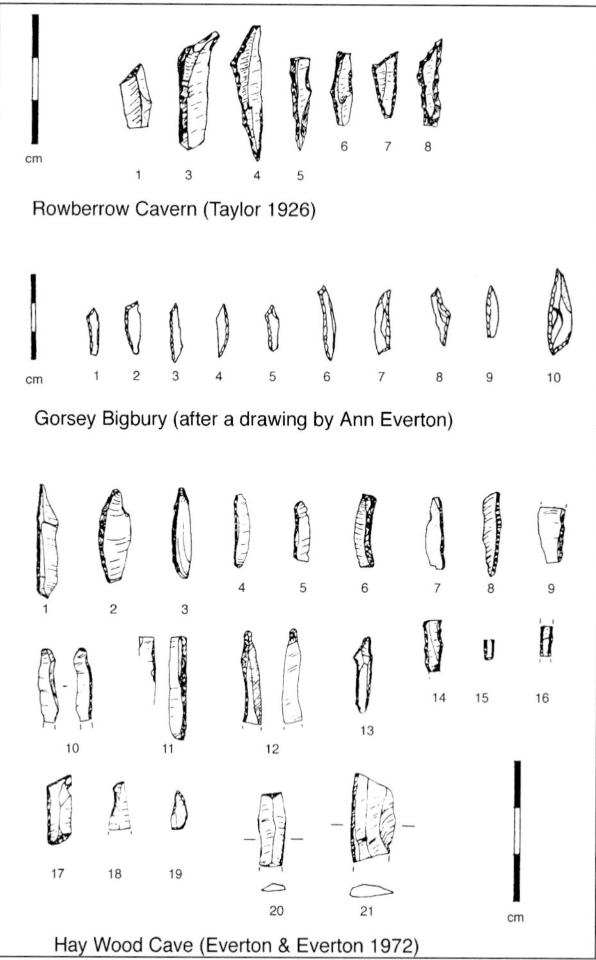

Figure 73.8. Microliths from Late Mesolithic sites on the Mendip Hills, Somerset. (Drawings: Chris Norman; Gardiner 2001, 121).

by local caver Chris Hawkes (Figure 73.5). It is situated at the top of Cheddar Gorge at 245m OD (ST482535). Its entrance is by a shaft, 4m deep and 75cm wide, which was subsequently dug out in the anticipation of locating new cave chambers. During the excavations archaeological finds were discovered, together with a large quantity of animal bone and human remains. The human remains comprised three adults and a child, but have been subsequently destroyed (Gardiner 2001). There is one radiocarbon date from a surviving humerus of 8180±70 BP (7450–7050 cal BC; BM-2973) (Schulting 2005, 231). The flint recovered from the 1960s' excavations includes 20 microliths (Figure 73.6: 1–20). None of the material is stratified and the excavation has not been published. There is a note in

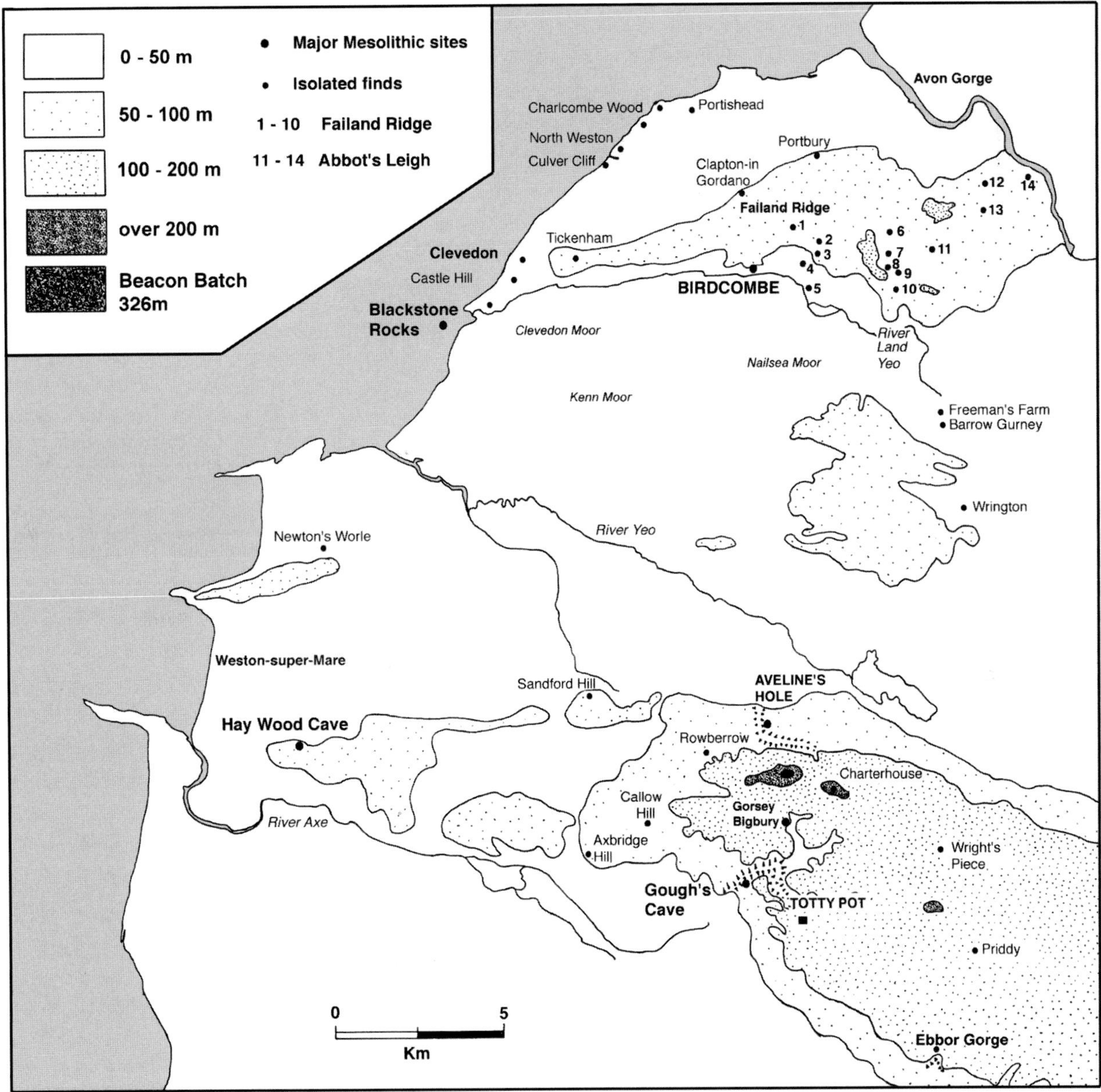

Figure 73.9. Mesolithic sites on the Failand Ridge and the Mendip Hills, Somerset (Gardiner 2001, 120).

Barrington and Stanton (1970), Smith and Drew (1975) and Norman (1982).

In 1998 the author excavated around the mouth of the swallet-hole to establish any evidence of occupation. Seven retouched tools were recovered including three lanceolates (Figure 73.6: 21, 22, 23), a backed bladelet (Figure 73.6: 25), a convex backed microlith (Figure 73.6: 26), and 18 pieces of debitage (Gardiner 2001; 2007b).

The difficult access into the cave, and the location of the human bone in the small chambers inside, suggest that the deposits had been deliberately placed there, rather than being washed in. The absence of any quantity of debitage suggests that flint knapping did not take place around the swallet-hole entrance. It is reasonable to suggest that Totty Pot was specifically used as a burial place in the Mesolithic. Two other important cave-burial sites in the area (Figure 73.9) also in use during the Mesolithic are Aveline's Hole and Gough's Cave (Davies 1921; Schulting 2005, 231; Schulting and Wysocki 2002; Tratman 1977).

Discussion

The Mendip caves provide a deliberate focus for hunter-gatherer burial in the Mesolithic and Totty Pot is no exception. There is a significant Mesolithic presence, both inside and outside Totty Pot, and the human remains suggest the site and its location held particular significance in the Mesolithic. There are other hunter-gatherer sites on the Mendip Hills which have evidence of Late Mesolithic activity: Gorsey Bigbury (Jones 1938), Rowberrow Cavern (Taylor 1926) and Hay Wood Cave, Hutton (Everton and Everton 1972) (Figure 73.9).

It is reasonable to suggest that it could be the same hunter-gatherer group moving between the coastal plain

Figure 73.10. Air photograph showing the landscape location of Hawkcombe Head, Exmoor, Somerset. (Photograph: © English Heritage (NMR 21521/32 2003)).

around Blackstone Rocks and the uplands of the Mendip Hills in summer, and occupying a lowland site such as Birdcombe in winter. The Mendip Hills are 25km from the coast, and hunter-gatherer groups could congregate at Birdcombe for shelter and safety before moving up to higher ground for summer hunting (Gardiner 2001; 2007b). This is an easily accessible territory with hunting and burial only a day's walk away.

Hawkcombe Head, Exmoor, Somerset

Hawkcombe Head (Figure 73.10) takes its name from a springhead which rises on moorland at the top of a steep combe in an area known as Porlock Common (SS844457); it is 420m OD. An extensive collection of worked flint has been recovered from surface finds (Area

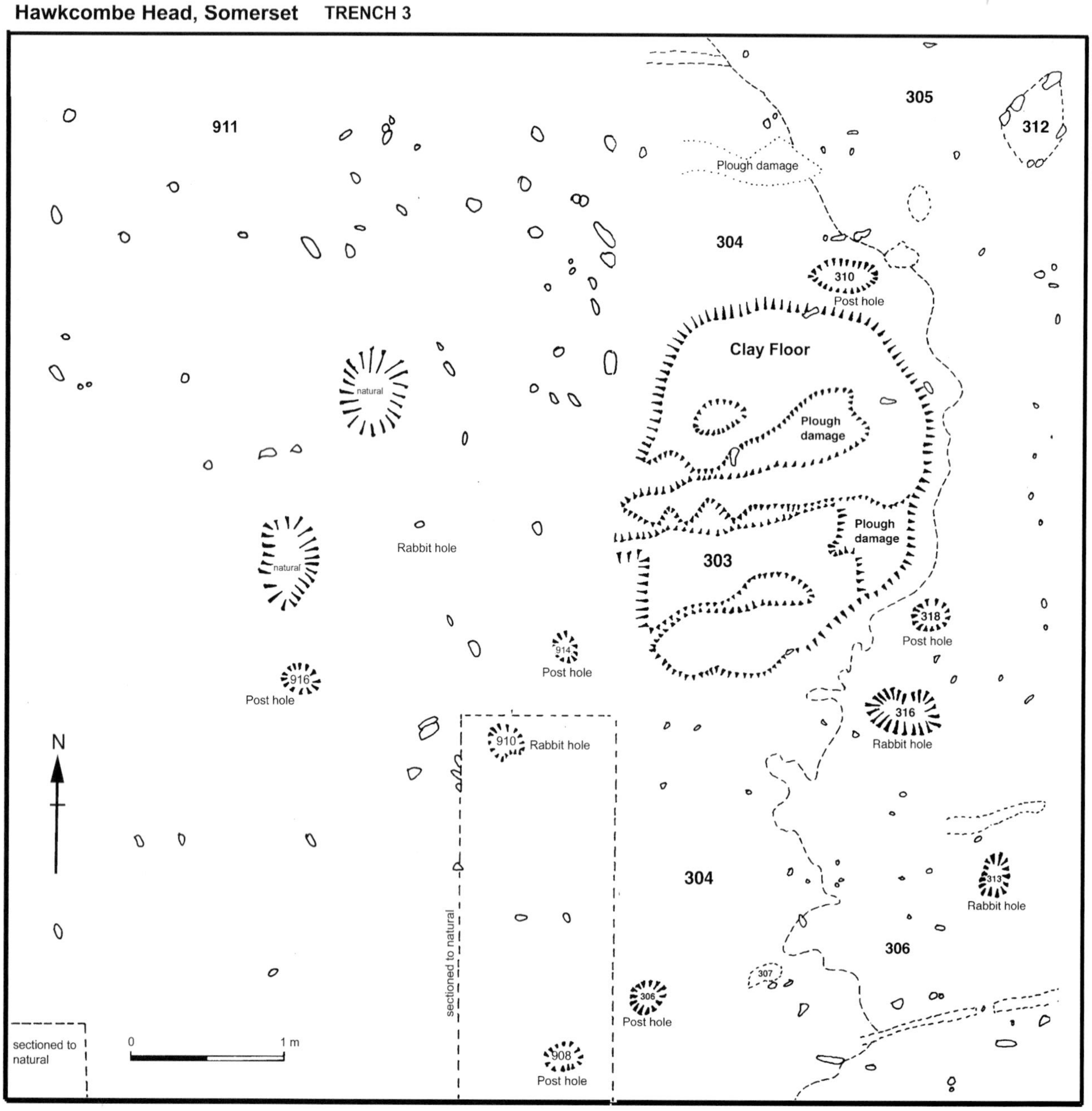

Figure 73.11. Planning drawing of Trench 3 (Area B) showing the clay floor (303) and postholes (Gardiner 2007b, 50).

Lab sample	*Context*	*Material*	*Radiocarbon age*	*Calibration 94.4%*
SUERC-2970 (GU-11979)	14-04 (Hearth)	Hazel	7420±35 BP	6390–6210 cal BC
SUERC-2968 (GU-11978)	12-08 (Posthole)	Holly	7815±40 BP	6760–6500 cal BC

Figure 73.12. Radiocarbon dates from the hearth in Trench 14 and the posthole in Trench 12 (Gardiner 2007a; Stuiver et al. 1998).

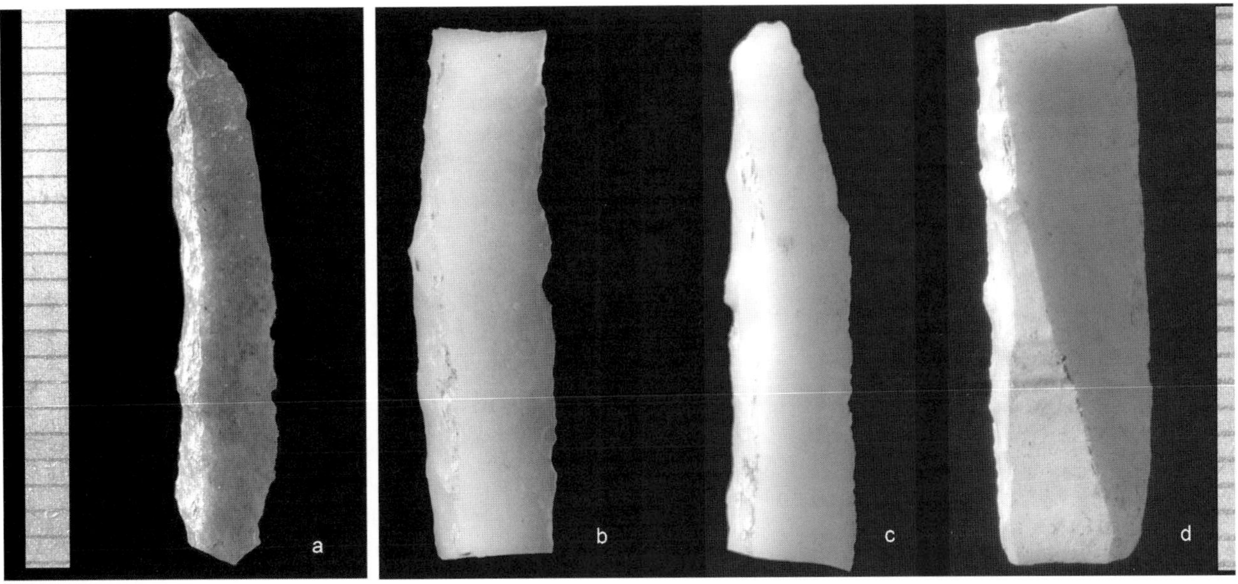

Figure 73.13. Microliths from Hawkcombe Head, Somerset: a) elongated scalene; b) backed bladelet; c) backed bladelet; d) retouched blade. (Scale: cm; photograph: Steve Knight).

A) and subsequent excavation. The flint collection contains hundreds of microliths from the later Mesolithic, together with flint debitage in excess of 8400 pieces. Three seasons of excavation (2002–4) by the author and the Exmoor National Park Authority have uncovered evidence of microlith production, temporary structures and hearths; this, together with two radiocarbon dates, has established Hawkcombe Head as the earliest hunter-gatherer site on Exmoor (Gardiner 2007a).

There is a natural route from the Hawkcombe Head springhead (Area C) down to Porlock Beach, two kilometres away. Palaeo-environmental evidence indicates that the area, which we know as a pebble beach today, was woodland in the Mesolithic, and its remains can be seen as a submerged forest at low tide (Riley and Wilson-North 2001; Wymer 1977). A second spring rises at Ven Combe (Area B), cutting another route-way down to the coast at Lynton, 13km away. Excavation close to this spring (Trench 3) revealed a small temporary structure consisting of a clay floor embedded with microliths and debitage, and three surrounding postholes (Figure 73.11) (Gardiner 2007a).

On the west side of the Ven Combe spring (Trench 14) was a hearth, encircled by stones, which contained a large quantity of oak (*Quercus*) and hazel charcoal. A radiocarbon date from the hazel charcoal confirms the feature as late Mesolithic (Figure 73.12).

Area C on the moorland adjacent to the Porlock Road (Trench 12) produced a large quantity of retouched tools, including elongated scalene triangles, backed bladelets and retouched blades. A sealed posthole containing holly (*Ilex aquifolium*) and oak charcoal has been dated to the later Mesolithic (Figure 73.12). The raw material is beach pebble flint with a small quantity of Greensand Chert. The obvious source is Porlock Beach three kilometres away, but the modern beach at Porlock consists of Devonian Sandstone and contains few nodules of pebble flint. A likely source is further west at Baggy Point or Croyde Bay (C. Norman, pers. comm.).

The microliths are dominated by elongated scalene triangles (Figure 73.13: a) and backed bladelets (Figure 73.13: b, c), with an overall presence of microburins and micro-cores. There are large numbers of modified flakes and blades (Figure 73.13: d), with either single or paired notches on the edges, including awls. Six pebble tools have been recovered, similar to those found at Poldowrian, Cornwall (Smith and Harris 1982), and they show wear marks or polishing. The elongated scalene triangles were probably used as projectile points, but the pebble tools, the awls and backed bladelets may have been used for plant processing or skin working. The radiocarbon dates confirm the tool typology as belonging to the later Mesolithic (Gardiner 2007a).

Interpretation

A variety of activities appear to have taken place at Hawkcombe Head. Within the main flint distribution areas (Areas A–C) the manufacture of microliths and other tools took place. The clay floor in Trench 3 (Area B) suggests that a temporary structure may have been erected for someone staying for a longer period, or as a protective windbreak during flint knapping. Both the areas of moorland, and the improved pasture, yield a large amount of flint, either debitage or worked tools, but further excavation is needed to define the limit of the site. It has, therefore, been difficult accurately to identify all the different temporal phases of activity or the size of the social groups involved.

There is an absence of faunal evidence that might suggest selective seasonality, but the high and exposed location of the site indicates that it would not offer very much shelter or protection from the elements in winter. It is more likely that hunter-gatherer groups would prefer to settle on lower, more sheltered slopes in winter with access to the sea. The homogeneity of the tool typology suggests that regular visits were made by small local groups throughout the later Mesolithic.

Hawkcombe Head was not a site that was chosen for its raw material source, but the evidence suggests that hunter-gatherers, moving between coastal plain and uplands, thought it important enough to bring in raw material from some distance away. The site is located on a high moorland point, where modern roads and trackways meet today. There are post-Medieval droveways still visible in the landscape that pass across the moor through the site (R. Wilson-North, pers. comm.). Hawkcombe Head's significance may have continued into later periods with the erection of monuments in the vicinity. Nearby is a monument called the Whit Stones and just under a kilometre away are stone monuments and Bronze Age hut circles (Riley and Wilson-North 2001, 47). The natural routes from the Ven Combe spring and the Hawkcombe Head spring make this site accessible and easy to find within a wooded landscape. It is a natural meeting place when climbing up on to the moor and its location may have held significance in the Mesolithic. It should be regarded as a specifically used *locale* within the Exmoor landscape, and may have formed part of an annual territorial meeting place for a particular social group during the Late Mesolithic.

Conclusions

It is clear that the Somerset evidence for the Late Mesolithic does not fit neatly into Mellars' Type A, B or C categories (1976). Hawkcombe Head rests more easily in Jacobi's general south-western grouping (1979), and the tool typologies in north Somerset suggest a persistent use of a small, local landscape. Hawkcombe Head, however, has its own unique characteristics in that the manufacture of hunting tools may not necessarily have been its prime function.

In a wider, south-western context, there appears to be small, regional, social groups who move between coastal plain and upland areas bringing in local beach pebbles for the manufacture of hunting tools (Poldowrian, Trevose Head, Gwithian in Cornwall) (Jacobi 1979). The hunter-gatherers at Hawkcombe Head conform to this pattern to some extent, but at this site a diversity of activities took place within a very specific location, which may have held significance for the groups using it in the later Mesolithic and subsequent periods (Gardiner 2007a; 2007b). Hawkcombe Head, therefore, falls into a unique category and has an identity of its own.

The hunter-gatherers in north Somerset (Birdcombe) brought in their own particular raw material from some considerable distance to a site that was frequented throughout the Mesolithic. They moved to the uplands for hunting and burial, and used the coastal plain and the Mendip Hills as their regional territory. We can, therefore, see a pattern of late hunter-gatherer activity throughout the south-west of England, with flint often coming from a long distance; but at more specific sites like Hawkcombe Head and Birdcombe, regional identities appear to remain exclusive.

Acknowledgements

English Heritage for permission to publish air photograph NMR 21521/32 2003 (Figure 73.10); microlith photographs by Steve Knight; flint illustrations by Chris Norman. My thanks to Rob Wilson-North (Exmoor National Park Authority) and George Nash (University of Bristol) for commenting on the text. The views in this paper are entirely those of the author.

References

Barrington, M. and Stanton, W. 1970. *The Complete Caves of Mendip*, 112. Cheddar, Cheddar Valley Press.

Berridge, P. J. and Roberts, A. 1986. The Mesolithic Period in Cornwall. *Cornish Archaeology* 25, 7–34.

Bronk Ramsey, C. 1995. Radiocarbon calibration and analysis of stratigraphy: The OxCal program. *Radiocarbon* 37 (2), 425–30.

Clark, J. G. D. 1932. *The Mesolithic Age in Britain*. Cambridge, Cambridge University Press.

Clark, J. G. D. 1934. The Classification of a Microlithic Culture: The Tardenoisian of Horsham, *Archaeological Journal* XC, 52–75.

Davies, J. A. 1921. Aveline's Hole, Burrington Combe. An Upper Palaeolithic station. *Proceedings of the University of Bristol Spelaeological Society* 1, 61–73.

Everton, A. and Everton, R. 1972. Hay Wood Cave Burials, Mendip Hills, Somerset, *Proceedings of the University of Bristol Spelaeological Society* 13 (1), 5–29.

Gardiner, P. J. 2000. Excavations at Birdcombe, Somerset: Mesolithic Settlement, Subsistence and Landscape Use in the South West of England, in R. Young (ed.), *Mesolithic Lifeways. Current Research from Britain and Ireland*, 119–207. Leicester Archaeology Monographs 7. Leicester, University of Leicester.

Gardiner, P. J. 2001. The Mesolithic-Neolithic Transition in South West England. Unpublished PhD thesis, University of Bristol.

Gardiner, P. J. 2007a. Mesolithic Activity at Hawkcombe Head,

Somerset. Interim Report of Excavations 2002–3, in C. Waddington and K. Pedersen (eds.), *Mesolithic Studies in the North Sea Basin and Beyond. Proceedings of a Conference held at Newcastle in 2003*, 81–95. Oxford, Oxbow Books.

Gardiner, P. J. 2007b. Chasing the tail of hunter-gatherers in south western landscapes, in M. Costen (ed.), *People and Places: Essays in Honour of Michael Aston*, 23–52. Oxford, Oxbow Book.

Jacobi, R. M. 1979. Early Flandrian Hunters in the South-West, in V. A. Haxfield, *Devon Archaeological Society Prehistoric Dartmoor in its Context*, 48–93. Devon Archaeological Society Jubilee Conference Proceedings 37. Exeter, Devon Archaeological Society.

Johnson, N. and David, A. 1982. A Mesolithic Site on Trevose Head and Contemporary Geography. *Cornish Archaeology* 21, 67–103.

Jones, S. J. 1938. The Excavation of Gorsey Bigbury. *Proceedings of the University of Bristol Spelaeological Society* 5 (i), 3–56.

Mellars, P. 1976. Settlement patterns and industrial variability in the British Mesolithic, in G. de G. Sieveking, I. H. Longworth and K. E. Wilson (eds.), *Problems in Economic and Social Archaeology*, 375–99. London, Duckworth.

Norman, C. 1982. Mesolithic Hunter-Gatherers 9000–4000 BC, in M. A. Aston and I. Burrow (eds.), *The Archaeology of Somerset: a review to 1500 AD*, 15–21. Bridgwater, Somerset County Council.

Pitts, M. W. and Jacobi, R. M. 1979. Some Aspects of Change in Flaked Stone Industries of the Mesolithic and Neolithic in Southern Britain. *Journal of Archaeological Science* 6, 163–77.

Riley, H. and Wilson-North, R. 2001. *The Field Archaeology of Exmoor*. London, English Heritage.

Schulting, R. J. 2005. 'Pursuing a Rabbit in Burrington Combe': New Research on the Early Mesolithic Burial Cave of Aveline's Hole. *Proceedings of the University of Bristol Spelaeological Society* 23 (3), 171–265.

Schulting, R. and Wysocki, M. 2002. The Mesolithic Human Skeletal Collection from Aveline's Hole: A Preliminary Note. *Proceedings of the University of Bristol Spelaeological Society* 22 (3), 255–68.

Smith, D. I. and Drew, D. P. 1975. *Limestones and Caves of the Mendip Hills*. Newton Abbott, David & Charles.

Smith, G. and Harris, D. 1982. The Excavation of Mesolithic, Neolithic and Bronze Age Settlements at Poldowrian, St. Deverne, 1980. *Cornish Archaeology* 21, 23–60.

Stringer, C. 1986. The Hominid Remains from Gough's Cave. *Proceedings of the University of Bristol Spelaeological Society* 17 (2), 145–52.

Stuiver, M. and Reimer, P. J. 1993. Extended 14C database and revised CALIB radiocarbon calibration program. *Radiocarbon* 35, 215–30.

Stuiver, M., Reimer, P. J., Bard, E., Beck, J. W., Burr, G. S., Hughen, K. A., Dromer, B., McCorman, G., van der Plicht, J. and Spurk, M. 1998. INTCAL98 Radiocarbon Age Calibration, 24000-0 cal BP. *Radiocarbon* 40 (3), 1041–83.

Sykes, C. M. 1938. Some Flint Implements from the Blackstone Rocks, Clevedon. *Proceedings of the University of Bristol Spelaeological Society* 1 (5), 75–9.

Sykes, C. M. and Whittle, S. L. 1960. The Birdcombe Mesolithic Site, Wraxall. *Proceedings of the Somerset Archaeological and Natural History Society* 104, 106–22.

Taylor, H. 1926. Fifth Report on Rowberrow Cavern. *Proceedings of the University of Bristol Spelaeological Society* 2 (3), 190–210.

Tratman, E. K. 1977. A further radiocarbon date on human bone material from Aveline's Hole, Burrington Combe, Mendip. *Proceedings of the University of Bristol Spelaeological Society* 14 (3), 261–2.

Wymer, J. J. 1977. *Gazetteer of Mesolithic sites in England and Wales*. Council for British Archaeology (CBA) Research Report 22. London, Council for British Archaeology.